THE
CAMBRIDGE
MEDIEVAL HISTORY

VOLUME VII

THE
CAMBRIDGE
MEDIEVAL HISTORY

PLANNED BY THE LATE

J. B. BURY, M.A., F.B.A.

EDITED BY

THE LATE J. R. TANNER, LITT.D.
C. W. PREVITÉ-ORTON, LITT.D., F.B.A.
Z. N. BROOKE, LITT.D.

VOLUME VII

DECLINE OF EMPIRE AND PAPACY

CAMBRIDGE
AT THE UNIVERSITY PRESS
1964

PUBLISHED BY
THE SYNDICS OF THE CAMBRIDGE UNIVERSITY PRESS

Bentley House, 200 Euston Road, London, N.W.1
American Branch: 32 East 57th Street, New York 22, N.Y.
West African Office: P.O. Box 33, Ibadan, Nigeria

First Edition 1932
Reprinted 1949
1958
1964

First printed in Great Britain at the University Press, Cambridge
Reprinted at The Whitefriars Press Ltd, Tonbridge

PREFACE.

DEATH has once again robbed the *Cambridge Medieval History* of its senior Editor. Dr J. R. Tanner devoted to it those qualities of sober judgment and organising ability which had already distinguished him in an administrative sphere; he maintained relations with the various contributors on the most friendly basis; and, besides his obvious gifts as a historian, he had a keen eye for those small corrections in style and punctuation which often add so much to the ease of the reader. His name still appears on the title page, for he had read the proofs of most of the chapters in this volume, and of some of them in their final form. In his last illness he continued to read them and to send them back with his unvarying punctuality, up to a very few days before his death. His fellow-editors mourn the loss of their distinguished colleague and close personal friend.

We have also to deplore the deaths of two of the contributors to this volume. Mr Edward Armstrong had carefully revised the manuscript of his chapters for this and the succeeding volume. Professor P. J. Blok had only completed the first part—the narrative of events—of his chapter on Germany, 1273–1313. In this he had included the Italian expedition of Henry VII, though it had already been described in Chapter I. His strong desire to retain this in his chapter, as essential to the completeness of his story, was expressed in a letter written shortly before his death and has naturally been respected by the editors. We are deeply indebted to Professor W. T. Waugh, who at short notice not only wrote the second part of Professor Blok's chapter but also compiled the bibliography.

In the maps we were fortunate in again obtaining the assistance of Mr G. R. Crone, with the exceptions of Germany and East Central Europe, for which we have to thank Professor W. T. Waugh and Professor A. Bruce Boswell. The bibliographies have once more been in the competent hands of Mr C. C. Scott, and we are greatly indebted to him for the accurate and skilful labour he has expended upon them. Finally, Miss Maris has been responsible for the index, and by her extreme care and thoroughness has supplied us with a number of important corrections.

C. W. P.-O.
Z. N. B.

January, 1932

INTRODUCTION.

THE seventh volume of the *Cambridge Medieval History* covers, roughly speaking, the fourteenth century, and this period of time forms without undue straining one of the compartments into which the Middle Ages are conveniently divided. It is a testimony to the naturalness of this division that we take up the events in France, Germany, and England at an earlier date (1270, 1273, and 1272) than the fortunes of Italy and the Papacy, for the former entered earlier on the late medieval stage of their political development than did the latter. The feudal age, we may say with some over-accentuation, has for them merged into the age of chivalry. The change marks indeed an improvement, but not improvement unalloyed. There is also a decadence, not so much retrogression, but that ossifying of regnant ideas which are slowly losing their vitality, which draw their life not from present needs and hopes but from past aspirations, whose fulfilment men no longer expect but on whose claims they are content to pay a decent percentage in the pound. A code of rules succeeds vague enchanting ideals; legal subtleties overlay the broad principles of law; the ardent enthusiasm which led the early friars to "follow naked the naked Christ," and gave birth to the ideal of Sir Galahad, has given way to a more practicable achievement. This was natural if only owing to the wide diffusion of these ideals; the many adapted the ideals of the heroic few to workaday circumstances, and while the ideals remained on the whole beneficent, their effect grew ever less and their weaker elements, one might say their narrowness and artificiality, grew ever more prominent.

Something of the same fixity of ideas under a disguise of change may be detected in the strictly political sphere. Internal peace and good and efficient government by means of strict royal supervision of the feudal fabric of society had been the aim of the political leaders of the last two centuries; to be anti-feudal was not in their thought. Their successors followed the same aim and elaborated remedies on the same principle with undefeated perseverance. In their efforts to perfect and complete they devised much that was new and that was to be fruitful in later times, but in their experiments the feudal conception was predominant. The novel ferment in these creations strained, but did not break the feudal mould which contained them.

New ferment indeed there was. The rise of the bourgeoisie in the towns, the steady increase of free peasants in the countryside, the multiplication and the grievances of the employees of the manufacturers, the

b

flagrancy of ecclesiastical and administrative abuses, the contrasts of utter poverty and extravagant splendour in the capitals and princely castles, the very growth of literacy which extended knowledge, the quickening consciousness of national divergence and antipathy, the universal disaster of the Black Death and the more local horrors of the Hundred Years' War, and finally the spectacular scandal of the Great Schism, all these could not fail of effect on men's minds. The age is one of stirring and striving: peasant and artisan beat tempestuously if in vain on that firmly-built society; kings and nobles wrestled for the control of the State; isolated thinkers discussed the theory of the Church and sowed the seeds of the future. But as yet the old foundations were too strong to be shaken. The century ends with Church and Feudalism and the accepted philosophy of life standing where they did. But they had provided no real remedies for current ills and needs; they had only baffled opposition; and the opposition they crushed or over-rode was confusedly or unconsciously germinating those new ideas which distinguish modern from medieval times.

Nowhere can the more political side of this restless fermentation be more clearly shewn than in the rival kingdoms of France and England. Their development runs parallel, alike in their broadest characteristics, contrasted in their narrower but deeper peculiarities. They were the most advanced of feudal monarchies, the countries where the feeling of nationality, in spite of provincial particularism, had most nearly coalesced with loyalty to the State. Each at the beginning of this period was a congeries of feudal jurisdictions controlled by a centralising national kingship. Against the freer feudal franchises of France may be set the greater share of the feudal class in the English royal administration. In the age of Edward I and Philip the Fair they are seen under the influence of a movement which has strong similarities in both. This is the movement to harvest the fruits of the previous unifying process, to systematise and extend the royal bureaucratic control of the State, to make the king's governance effective. Thus in both the central government is elaborated and ramified; it is a documentary age, where a host of busy clerks exercise control and harden routine by voluminous record and sedulous red-tape. Alike in both, although with a different past and divergent tendencies, these kindred bureaucracies spread their tentacles over the life of the realm. In this encroachment the ideal of better, sounder government took an active share. Edward I and Philip the Tall were reforming, legislating, codifying kings: they legislated to redress grievances, to formulate custom, to provide better method and better law. And in the endeavour to bring home their government to their subjects, they insist on personal touch and gather their people round them in national assemblies, the English Parliament and the French States General. That they thus confirmed incidentally the representative principle has perhaps more importance for the future than for their own day. What in their own time meant most was that the never complete and then declining isolation of fief and town found the main avenue of the future thus completely barred. Isolation might continue but there was contact always in one direction, that of the central power. A national or State administration had become the reigning political conception.

The second movement, earlier (as thirteenth-century history prescribed) in England, later in France, was the natural sequel. Political strife concentrates not on the endeavour to escape from the authority of the State, but on that to control it, if not completely, yet in certain wide spheres of its activity. It was the feudal nobles, the aristocracy, who took the lead in England, and their aim was, it may be said, to make the king the representative, almost the instrument of their class. The abuses of a cumbrous administration, of greedy officials, of inconsequent royal caprice gave them a perennial cause to champion. The king resisted with all his energies and worked constantly for the sole direction of the State. The vicissitudes of the conflict, which contributed to the formation of the English constitution, are told in this volume. Here it need merely be said that Edward III won a personal victory only by taking the nobles into subordinate partnership; that his French wars ended by giving them local predominance and armed forces, under the name of Livery and Maintenance, more dangerous than the obsolete feudal service, while retaining the spirit of feudalism; that the Keepers of the Peace ruled the districts in which they were country gentry. When Richard II challenged the nobles in his attempt at despotism, the system of partnership between king and lords took formal shape as the "Lancastrian experiment."

One expedient of the Edwards, which had many precedents, had been to endow their sons and increase their own hold on the nobility by raising them through marriage or grant to be the greatest nobles of the land; and this led under Richard II to the baronial instinct of control being strengthened by schemes of rival princes for the crown and complicated by endless family feuds. The same system of appanages prevailed also in France, and takes the leading place in the era of factious discontent which supervened on the death of Charles the Wise. Like Lancaster, Gloucester, and York in England, Burgundy, Anjou, and Orleans in France fought for and round the crown, and exploited justifiable discontent and strivings for reform. In France, as in England, the period of baronial control was dominated by selfish princes and feud-ridden partisans. Monarchy based on feudal ideals was breaking down, and those ideals could not bring to birth a successor to it. Feudalism itself was old.

In no feature of fourteenth-century society is the working of centralising monarchy on feudal institutions and on conditions increasingly non-feudal better seen than in the development of the assemblies known as Estates. They were strictly feudal in origin, for they took their rise in the obligations of vassalage; but they soon outgrew the merely feudal conceptions. Already in the thirteenth century, they shew a grouping of men in classes, not in the older feudal hierarchy; in the fourteenth century, the nobles, the ecclesiastics, and the bourgeois of a nation or province form in these assemblies separate "Estates," divided by their profession, their occupation, from one another. Even in the abnormal "Commons" of England, the alliance of the Knights of the Shire with the Burgesses reposes on the fact that the "Knights" represent the freeholders of the Shire bound together by their common function of raisers of crops and herds and disregarding the feudal tenure which diversified them. Thus the truly medieval society of groups received its latest and widest embodiment. The group covered the kingdom or province; it was based on the essential function of its members; but these groups were still in separate layers; they assumed a feudal class and government; and the measure of their eventual unsuccess was the measure of their mutual lack of harmony, the dissidence of the feudal and non-feudal layers. Save in England their future growth was compromised by the feudal mould in which they grew. True national solidarity and individual allegiance to the State were to find their fitter school in the absolute monarchies of a later day.

If we turn to Germany, the scene seems changed. There the centralised monarchy of the feudal type, we may say, had never arisen. On the contrary, the (to over-state a little) half pre-feudal kingship had collapsed with the Hohenstaufen, and the Golden Bull of Charles IV seems like a raft of gilded wreckage. There the particularist nobles, save in spasmodic efforts of the new College of Electors, made no attempt to control a central government which barely existed. Their efforts, like those of the Free Cities, were bent towards local predominance. But here, too, the feudal spirit shewed its inability to construct. The teeming resources of Germany were spent in insensate rivalries and the shifting pursuit of endless, incoherent petty interests. Even in the just-emerging State of Switzerland the common interest and character, which did indeed lead to its creation, are almost hid in the bewildering thicket of the broils of town and country, valley and plain, peasant and noble, burgher and artisan. Chaos indeed might be in labour, but its child, the Swiss nation, was yet unborn.

Perhaps the most striking feature of fourteenth-century Swiss history is that here the peasant class won a permanent victory over the feudal rulers, and it may be that this was because their grievances and aims were more "political" than economic or social. But all over the West the peasants and their congeners, the workmen of the towns, were seething with like tempestuous desires and struggling to divert the current of social evolution into a new channel. Much might be due to that change for the worse in the general condition of the peasant described in Chapter XXIII, much to the unprecedented phenomenon of manufacturing towns crowded with stinted workfolk. The wasteful horrors of the Hundred Years' War and the countless feuds, the misery and the opportunities of the recurrent Black Death were subordinate incitements. But something must also be allowed, sporadically if not everywhere, to the power to plan and organise given by the driblets of increasing civilisation that fell to the share of the workfolk. They had their orators, their propagandists, and statesmen even.

The Peasants' Revolt of 1381 in England was the briefest and least recurrent of these efforts; we may guess the grievances were less and already diminishing. The Jacquerie of France in the mid-century was fiercer in its rage at oppression and at the splendid incompetence of chivalry to defend the countryside from the terrible ravage of the Free Companies and the English. It ended, as it began, in despair. It is significant of the distant future that the only remedy which emerged was the national armed monarchy directed by the secret counsels of Charles the Wise. It is also significant that this wild revolt was contemporaneous, and in its immediate causes was allied with the unsuccessful attempt of the bourgeoisie, led by Étienne Marcel, to exert a degree of control over the royal government through the States General. The tide rose, in short, against feudalised, chivalric monarchy and its hide-bound bureaucratic instruments, and was repelled. Something of the same course was visible in the Cabochian movement of 1413; only here the lower bourgeoisie and the mob were predominant, and equally they failed. It was not only coherence and steady co-operation that were lacking, but the experience and daily faculty to direct great affairs.

These French movements, although they hold the centre of the stage, are yet only pale and partial reflexes of the upheaval of the industrial populations of Western Europe in the fourteenth century, to be seen from Germany to Spain. Here, however, only its manifestations in Italy and the Netherlands can be touched upon; they were the most important, and the most European; for these towns were the nerve-centres, the ganglia, of the commercial system of the West. Two fundamental facts give the basis of the history of these trading towns from 1100 to 1350 A.D.: the continuous growth of their population and the like increase of their manufactures, of which the making of the varieties of cloth always formed the staple. From these two causes arose the primitive capitalist, merchant, employer, and banker; the thronging pettier traders, retailers, provisioners, metal-workers, and the like, typical "small masters"; and last, the multitude of wage-earners in the cloth-industry. The general rise of population and the ever-widening, securer commerce of these two-and-a-half centuries, of which the towns furnish the clearest evidence, gave them their opportunity and indeed caused their existence. But the lion's share of their prosperity went to the earlier strata of the town-population, the first in the field, and already in the thirteenth century the merchant and employer class were forming in Flanders[1] (to give the most wealthy district as an instance) a narrow hereditary oligarchy, oppressive to the "small masters" and retailers, and exploiting without pity the mass of their employees, who were their subjects, their tenants, and almost help-lessly dependent on them for a livelihood. Such a state of things could not last. Defeated risings were in the early fourteenth century followed by victorious revolution, of which the "Matins of Bruges" in 1302 may stand as an example. The general result was the erection of the stormy "democratic" government of the *métiers* or gilds, in which the ancient oligarchs formed but a small opposition, while the employee cloth-workers and the "domestic" trades struggled for the mastery, and the Count of Flanders with his nobles trimmed and tacked and warred to regain their authority. The democratic forces seemed irresistible in the towns, but there were fatal weaknesses in their constitution. First, each section within them fought only for its own hand and its own supremacy: weaver hated fuller, smith, and cordwainer. Only after years of civil strife and revolutions was something like an uneasy, selfish partition of power at-tained. Secondly, these towns and gilds were at the last resort dependent on "great commerce," international exchange, which they could not control and did not understand. To their disillusion, the gildsmen derived but little economic benefit from their predominance. The Black Death and its sequels, if they put a stop to the growth of population, and raised wages temporarily, perhaps permanently, also diminished consumption in like measure. The *métiers* were incurably narrow and egoistic in external as in internal politics and economics. Their one

---

[1] See *supra*, Vol. VI, Chaps. XIV and XV. The history of the towns of the Nether-lands from 1300 onwards will be treated in Vol. VIII.

remedy for failing commerce was privilege and rigid protection; the older merchant oligarchies had aimed at freeing and easing exchange; but the *métiers* blocked it—the retailer or employee was supreme. The towns thus had one another and the countryside for their enemies; they thought only of monopolising their narrow local market. When the new large territorial power of Burgundy succeeded petty principalities, and curbed the rival German Hansa towns, and favoured the new free port of Antwerp where merchants could congregate, the older towns, with diminishing manufactures, engrossed and divided by local interests, were bound to fall into recalcitrant tutelage. The "democratic" régime had ended in failure.

The same motives as those that induced the revolutions in the Netherlands worked also in North Italy, and here the best illustration is found in the great manufacturing and exporting city of Florence, whose very peculiarities make the essential facts more clear. In the first half of the fourteenth century Florence was under the sway of the Greater Arts, *i.e.* the merchants, manufacturers, and bankers. They admitted the Lesser Arts, *i.e.* the retailers and small masters, to a subordinate partnership, and this, together with the alliance of the Papacy and the Kings of Naples, perhaps accounts for the later date of the revolutionary movement. But their exploitation of the workmen in the cloth-industry was almost ruthless, as it was in Flanders, and in the latter half of the century the bitter discontent of their victims exploded finally in the revolt of the Ciompi (1378). Brief mob-rule was succeeded by brief predominance of the Lesser Arts allied with the upper stratum of the workfolk. Yet their failure was more rapid than in Flanders. The banking centre of Europe could only be ruled and guided by a ring of the great employing merchant and banking houses, and in 1385 a narrow oligarchy once more took the reins. When their own egoistic divisions caused their fall, it was not democracy but the "Tyranny" of the greatest banking house, the Medici, with the genius to win over and to favour the lesser folk, which, under republican forms, succeeded to the rule of the State.

The control of foreign trade, in short, was the mainspring of the power both of the long-lived oligarchy of Venice, the less disciplined oligarchy of Florence, and the Medicean despotism. Elsewhere in North Italy, the solution of class-warfare and perhaps partially of the economic problem had been found in monarchy, which at least gave order and security. The Italian despots had a distant kinship to the territorial sovereigns of northern Europe; but these were firmer based on a nationalism which could unite classes and provinces in allegiance to the native prince. At the end of the Middle Ages the same sympathies and needs at length united Spain.

Two great and long-continued disasters shook both the political and the economic fabric of the fourteenth century, the Hundred Years' War and the Black Death. Neither of them created or perhaps much deflected the main movements of the time, but they hastened incipient decay and stimulated natural growth. The war found France the most prosperous and the strongest realm in Europe; it left it poor and enfeebled, if ready to revive; feudalism was therein put to the fatal proof which in the long run made absolute monarchy inevitable. That monarchy was all the more national because the long war had acted as a forcing house for the sentiment of nationality already clearly in existence. Again, the war hastened and made more complete the transference of the line of the greatest trade-route eastwards from France to Central Germany: the fairs of Champagne become negligible; Augsburg and Nuremberg, to mention no others, were now main links in the chain from the Mediterranean to the North. This factor cannot be neglected in the revivification of the intellectual life of Germany, and is one among the many causes of the later Reformation.

The effect of the Black Death on Europe was at the same time more suddenly impressive and cataclysmic and more lasting and subtly pervasive than that of the war. Its first progress was like the relentless advance of a prairie fire, destroying and inescapable. Its way had been prepared by the silent unrecorded invasion of the Black Rat, which seems to have entered Europe, perhaps in the wake of the Crusades, in the twelfth century, and if we knew the distribution of the rat in the plague years we might partially account for the "patchy" incidence of the Death. In any case the plague first fastened on the great Crimean grain port of Kaffa in 1346, and thence spread through Constantinople to Sicily, Genoa, and Provence in 1348. Before the year was out it was in England; by 1350 it had traversed Germany and Scandinavia. As was natural, it followed the trade-routes, and the rat-infested ship and barge were more deadly than the march of an army. The immediate mortality was terrible; it may have carried off one-third of the population in the three years of the first visitation. But perhaps more important for the future was its recurrence almost every ten years. Up to 1350 the population of Western Europe seems to have steadily increased. For perhaps a century afterwards a kind of stagnation seems to prevail, and the renewed upward movement hardly begins till after the close of the Middle Ages. The consequence of the first mortality was a violent, if temporary, shock to the existing economic fabric of society, but it did not initiate a new. None the less, in conjunction with its periodical recurrence, this mortality increased permanently the strain on the old order of things, while it staved off for

long the modern problem of over-population. Its effect on the mentality
of Europe seems somewhat similar. There was the usual debasement which
follows great disasters. For a while men were more reckless, less dutiful,
more callous; and if the old enthusiasms and devotion survived, we have
the impression of a certain lassitude in their pursuit. The shield and the
rosary, already too conventional, were tarnished; revival tended to be
revolutionary, and revolution to be ineffectual. It is hard to speak with
certainty on what is so intangible and obscure, but if the Black Death
hastened the decay of the old, it does not seem to have produced, even
when it promoted, the new.

Apart from the dubious repercussions of the Black Death, it is an easier
task to follow the evolution of medieval ideas in the slow transformation
of the fourteenth century, for here men formulated their thoughts in
recognisable shape. It is easiest of all when those ideas were expressed in
a living institution, the Church and its head, the Papacy. Here again we
note the symptoms of the contemporary feudal monarchy displayed. The
unity of Christendom in its hierarchical organisation remains the dominant
creed, but it seems more of a fetter than a source of energy. Over-centrali-
sation and over-elaboration of control mark the Papacy at Avignon no
less than the secular kingships. They bring more abuses than they cure.
There is a kind of restlessness in the fixity of the Church's methods, in
the rigidity of its attitude. Talents and zeal produce over-development
in government, but neither produce nor are guided by new inspiration.
Men revolve in vain in the circle of the past.

Nowhere is this clearer than in the final struggle between the Papacy
in "captivity" at Avignon and the Empire, a dull epilogue to that splendid
drama. Its material cause was the traditional dread felt by the absentee
Papacy for the revival of the corpse-like Empire in Italy; its cause in the
realm of ideas was the Popes' desire to elaborate the doctrine of their
"plenitude of power" in the secular affairs of Europe. Boniface VIII,
Clement V, and John XXII stretched the papal claims to the full. Yet
they were really defeated. Boniface VIII was ruined by Philip the Fair;
John XXII could not overthrow so mediocre an antagonist as Lewis
the Bavarian. And the claims end by being mere words; they cease to
be a practical problem.

More success attended the papal supremacy in things ecclesiastical.
The Popes' absolutism penetrated every cranny of the Church, and
John XXII, the so-called "father of annates," enlarged and enforced
the papal prerogative of provision to any benefice. Yet it was a Pyrrhic
victory. Even when unresisted, the Popes had to use their providing
power largely to gratify the national kings, and when they acted inde-

pendently they were liable to meet a steady resistance of delays, evasions, and defiance.

A large part of this resistance was due not only to the local or private rights and interests which were over-ridden by the universal Pope, but also to the national feelings and interests which resented the exploitation by a foreign monarch. The Popes and their Curia at Avignon were definitely French. Englishmen and Germans were reluctant to yield revenue and power in their own countries to a foreign and often an enemy Pope. This feeling spurred the English Parliament to pass Acts of Provisors and Praemunire, which gave a legal standing-ground to the King, comparable to the Popes' Canon Law, and it nerved the German chapters to fight a long and losing battle. The Great Schism is really its outcome. The national feeling of the Italians extorted the election of Pope Urban VI, and it was French nationalism as well as Urban's tyranny which led to the restoration of the Papacy to Avignon with Clement VII. National and State interests dictated to the kings and rulers their choice between the rival Popes, and even the Council of Constance, inspired by the ideal of the unity of Christendom, could only achieve reconciliation by dividing itself into "Nations" and not treating its members as the single body of the Church. Meantime, as had been foreshadowed by Boniface VIII's defeat by Philip the Fair, the supernatural prestige of the Papacy had severely suffered. The rival Popes had been mendicants for royal recognition; the seamless robe of Christ had been pitilessly torn in sunder; and the full demoralisation of the ecclesiastical organism had been completed and been brought to light. Yet here, too, as elsewhere, the forces of the ancient régime were still strong enough to beat back heresy, schism, and revolution, whether doctrinal or national; it was the well of life which should rejuvenate themselves that they could not find.

From the idea so strictly embodied in one institution we turn to the more pervasive ideas, spiritual and intellectual, which were woven into medieval culture. It may be maintained that the fourteenth century opened with their defeat or at least their failure, like that of Papacy and Empire. The inspiration of the Friars, along with the strange hopes of an apocalyptic millennium which we see in Dante—themselves a recognition of the hopeless odds against success—faded away and found no successors. In like manner the philosophy of St Thomas Aquinas proved no final solution of the problem of the world, while the scholastic method and the scholastic theme had hardened into an orthodoxy of field and subject, which heaped subtlety on subtlety, building up and pulling down a stereotyped pack of cards. As with the schoolman's world, so that of the knight seemed to have reached its limits and made its last discoveries. Chivalry, the sum of the knight's ideals, had become a code, a badge of good form. Much of its charm and virtue might remain, but narrowly interpreted as the freemasonry of a special class, decked in the fantastic blazonries of its coat-armour, it had become conventional and showy, a "gilded pale" to keep the vulgar out which too frequently hedged round the vulgar within. Its most religious aspect was the crusading vow, and the crusade had become an obsolescent fashion. Men took the cross as a knightly adventure due to their position, a kind of grand tour; and all the statesmanlike efforts of the Popes to organise the defence of Eastern Christendom were failures. The iniquitous suppression of the Templars, themselves completely negligent of the object of their Order, was a revelation of the veering interest of the West. The wars of the Teutonic Order were but an incident in the spread of Germany beyond the Elbe and Vistula. Yet the true spirit, however enfeebled, was not dead, as the ill-supported Hospitallers at Rhodes remained to testify.

Still more static and routine-like was the ethos of the monks and friars, the protagonists of the ascetic ideal. The ancient ardour in both had in general died away, and left respectability at best. No doubt in earlier times corruption or tepidity had always found easy entrance into the cloister, and there had been periods of marked general decadence. But these had been followed by periods of enthusiastic revival, in which a new meaning had been given to the still expanding spirit of asceticism. The last and most original of these revivals had been that of the Friars. Its aftermath had been the devoted missions among the Tartars, as far as China, and elsewhere, which had their "theorist" in Raymond Lull, and their secular counterpart in the travels of the Polos, so incredible and so true[1]. But now that creativeness seemed spent. More especially after the Black Death, which depleted the ranks of the more zealous, a lethargy settled down over convent and monastery. It was not so much corruption, although that was often flagrant and notorious, as sleepy, slack routine, the comfortable exploitation of endowments, which characterised the age. Fewer in numbers, often burdened with debt, aiming at the minimum necessary, the monks lost admiration, and even respect; the friars became self-indulgent catchpennies. No brilliant exceptions, no increase of supervision and goadings from above could excite any lasting flame from these dying embers or recapture the popular veneration of old time[2].

Yet the fourteenth century is not merely that in which the feudal age

[1] Cf. *supra*, Vol. vi, pp. 479, 753.
[2] See *supra*, Vol. v, Chap. xx, and Vol. vi, Chap. xxi.

moves slowly towards its setting; it is that in which the harbingers appear of the Renaissance and even very dimly of modern times. Sometimes they move vainly to the attack on the reigning system; much more often they undermine its embattled walls, or dig the foundations of a totally different structure, all the while believing they are loyal members of the garrison. Perhaps after all they were, and would have saved it had they been allowed. What in their diverse ways these forerunners did was in one degree or another to cultivate new intellectual territory, to change the outlook on the old, to offer a new approach to life which could replace that which had had its stimulating beauty trampled out by the thronging feet of generations. They were a product of the success of the earlier time. Comparative increase of security and opportunity, exemplified in the universities, had given men more personal freedom and wider experience. Justinian, Gratian, and Aristotle had aroused and trained the critical and observing faculties, scholasticism had refined the reasoning powers, vernacular literature and architecture had strengthened the creative imagination and applied it to the real world of mind and matter men saw before them. And the real world at this critical moment of discovery was, one might say, inevitably "nominalist." Each personality or phenomenon in it had to be noted separately. The widest classification we can adopt for the pioneers is that of individuality—not yet individualism—in themselves and in what they perceived. They dealt instinctively with each man or thing independently of their group or compartment in the frame of society or the world. It was not Dante's world-scheme, so typically medieval, but his unsubmergible personality, making him "his own party," his extraordinary power of observing and creating separate human characters and events, his eye for the particularities of Nature, each object being seen as it exactly was at some special moment, that gave him his originality and made him the founder of modern literature[1].

An analogy to this is traceable in the new attitude to ancient classic literature which begins to appear in the persons of Petrarch and Boccaccio, the founders of the Italian Renaissance. Equipped with the same social inheritance as Dante in life and in education, with his achievement too before them, they were able to appreciate the classics in a new way, to view them not only as the repositories of wise sayings but as personalities with individual traits and gifts existing in a past environment. The sense of historical perspective, so long lost, began at last to revive. Dante had studied Virgil, not only for tags and learning to be fitted into imitative

---

[1] In this evolution the English Chaucer takes a place, reminiscent of both Dante and Boccaccio.

Latin, but for the refinements of style, for reflection on human life, for insight into Nature and emotion to be emulated in the new language of Italian. So does Petrarch hold personal dialogues with Cicero and strive to realise from their works the dead authors he loved. For him and for Boccaccio was opened a new unhackneyed field of research with new treasures of thought and knowledge to be rifled, a new and sovereign clue to the study of life. Here was a world to conquer, and here the human spirit could kindle once again to a more than youthful ardour. It was no accident, but another aspect of the same revelation which made Petrarch the introspective singer of the *Sonnets*, piercing through the layers of conventional courtly love to the intricate core of his own heart; and made Boccaccio apply all the graces of his classic diction to the portrayal of men and their manners and the ironic chances of life. A veil seemed to be withdrawn; no longer hid by the doctrines of the schools, disguised by long-regnant platitudes, life spoke to them freshly; for them as for Virgil *mentem mortalia tangunt*. And this, in terms of painting, is the discovery of Dante's contemporary, Giotto.

When we look backward, Giotto does indeed begin a new age in the plastic arts, but in his own time he is only the most original and creative representative of a European development. The gradual increase of technical power over their several mediums was the common characteristic of the artists of the thirteenth and fourteenth centuries. Their art, unlike the Italians', might, as the Hundred Years' War continued, be on the way towards the exhaustion of the ideas, religious or chivalric, which were its inspiration, but its aesthetic resources were gaining still. The architect has progressed from the safe and stern solidity of latest romanesque to the daring, high-strung energy and variegated, light-filled strength of full Gothic. The sculptor, and even in some degree the painter, could make supple foliage and drapery, lissome figures, whether animal or human, and dramatic action. The faces lose their stolid glare, and become instinct with emotion; a statue can have an individual character, an instant's expression, standing out amid its rivals and separate from the world it inhabits and suggests.

It is curious to note the seamy side of this individuality in contemporary warfare. The age of systematic chivalry with its conventions and its breeding, slave of the accolade, is also the age of Free Companies and single adventurers owning no law but personal ambition and profit. Theirs was a barren freedom, but their Italian analogue, the tyrant, was more creative, for in the tyrannies there was evolved the non-class State, where men could count for their personal qualities unconditioned by their status. These premature principalities and the republics which existed beside them found a still more premature philosopher in Marsilio of Padua, in whom sceptical criticism and a direct reading from Italian life under the guidance of Aristotle produced a personal originality which anticipated the theories and methods of the nineteenth century.

The new tendencies, the new originality were also to be seen, however muffled in the frock and the gown, in the religious life of the time. It is surprising to find amid monastic lethargy and institutional petrifaction that the individual somehow shakes himself free and asserts his independence. We meet the heyday of the mystics. Whether recluse as in England, evangelistic and propagandist as in Germany, social as in Italy, the keynote of this mystical movement, alike in Eckehart, Tauler, and Groote, Juliana and Richard Rolle, and St Catherine of Siena, was the immediate search of the individual soul for God. It had its forms of aggressive heresy; but it was the obedient revolt from the stereotyped routine of passable salvation which had the greatest future significance. A crowd of deeply religious natures were patently thinking from and for themselves; they coincided with, they did not follow orthodoxy. With Wyclif this individuality entered scholasticism and the discussion of the organisation of the Church. In method and in training Wyclif was a later schoolman, treading the common round. But in his speculation and doctrine he too changed the venue. Christian doctrine had from 1100 to 1300 steadily grown legalised. The *iustitia* of St Augustine, the condition of salvation, had come to mean loyal and legal membership of the organised universal Church. Now Wyclif interpreted *iustitia* as ethical righteousness in direct relationship with the will of God; it was this alone which really counted. The singer is once more the man who can sing, not the formally appointed precentor in the legal institution. Thus it was natural that Wyclif should follow Marsilio in denying the validity of the existing government of the Church; natural, too, that he should be the father of the scheme to place the Law of God, by which ethical righteousness was determined, in the hands of the laity by the translation of the Bible into the vulgar tongue.

The individuality, which, with its corollaries of thought, appears in these scattered groups, was the beginning of the evolution towards modern times, but in 1400 it had neither developed clearly nor penetrated very far into society as a whole. The same may be said of the other portents of change, and the fact makes the fourteenth century only the commencement of a transitional age. The soil trembles under the feudal and ecclesiastical edifice; there are fissures and sudden landslides; but the old order still keeps intact and solid, as if it had been built for eternity.

CORRIGENDA.

VOL. II.

p. 304, ll. 18–19. *Delete* usually visited the Ka'ba and.
p. 306, l. 26. *For* Arabic *read* Arabic[1], *and add at foot of page* [1] *Bukhārī*, ed. Krehl, IV. 347, ll. 17 sq.
p. 312, l. 41. *For* Mus'ab *read* Muṣ'ab.
p. 313, *note* 1, l. 1. *For* al-'Abbās *read* 'Abbās.
p. 317, l. 6 from bottom. *For* and trembling violently *read* ; according to one authority he had a fainting-fit.

VOL. III.

p. 140, l. 23. *For* 960 *read* 950.

INDEX.

p. 673, col. 1. *Transfer* "143 *note*" *from* Herman I, Duke of Swabia *to* Herman II, Duke of Swabia.

VOL. IV.

p. 412, l. 22. *For* 1151 *read* 1155.
p. 637, l. 8 from bottom. *For* Pereslavl *read* Pereyaslavl.
p. 903, l. 3 from bottom. *For* 1151 *read* 1155.

INDEX.

p. 969, col. 2. *For* Pereslavl *read* Pereyaslavl.

VOL. V.

p. 22, l. 14. *For* October *read* December.

VOL. VI.

p. 457, l. 7. *For* Torun *read* Thorn.
p. 558, l. 11. *For* Nicholas III *read* Nicholas IV.
  ,,   l. 25. *For* 1225 *read* 1228.
p. 707, l. 10 from bottom. *For* Haisterbach *read* Heisterbach.
p. 716, ll. 6–7. *For* In a treatise possibly by Ivo of Chartres *read* In the *Collectio Canonum* of Anselm of Lucca, under the heading.
p. 918, l. 10 from bottom. *For* Nat. Lib., Madrid. 186 *read* Bibl. Nat., Paris. 186.

INDEX.

p. 989, col. 1. *Under* Anjou, *for* Charles, Fulk of Sicily, *read* Charles of Sicily, Fulk.
  ,,   ,,   *For* Anselm of Lucca, 578 *read* Anselm, bishop of Lucca, *Collectio Canonum* of, 578, 716.
p. 1012, col. 2. *For* Hole, bishop in Iceland, 29 *read* Hole, in Iceland, bishop of, 29.
p. 1015, col. 2. *Under* Ivo of Chartres *delete* 716.
p. 1025, col. 1. *Under* Nicholas III *delete* valuation of, 558.
  ,,   ,,   *Under* Nicholas IV *insert* valuation of, 558.
p. 1041, col. 2. *For* Thorn, 129 *read* Thorn, castle of Teutonic Knights at, 129, 457.
  ,,   ,,   *Delete entry* Torun.

TABLE OF CONTENTS.

INTRODUCTION.

CHAPTER I.

ITALY IN THE TIME OF DANTE.

By the late Edward Armstrong, M.A., F.B.A., sometime Fellow
of the Queen's College, Oxford.

CHAPTER II.

ITALY, 1313–1414.

By ROMOLO CAGGESE, Professor of Modern History in the University of Milan.

CHAPTER III.

GERMANY, 1273–1313.

(A)

By the late P. J. BLOK, sometime Professor of Dutch History in the University of Leyden.

(B)

By W. T. WAUGH, M.A., F.R.S.C., Kingsford Professor of History in McGill University, Montreal.

CHAPTER IV.

GERMANY: LEWIS THE BAVARIAN.

By Professor W. T. WAUGH, M.A.

CHAPTER V.

GERMANY: CHARLES IV.

By Professor W. T. WAUGH, M.A.

CHAPTER VI.

BOHEMIA IN THE FOURTEENTH CENTURY.

By Dr KAMIL KROFTA, Professor of Bohemian History in the University of Prague, Vice-Minister of Foreign Affairs in Czechoslovakia.

CHAPTER VII.

THE SWISS CONFEDERATION IN THE MIDDLE AGES.

By Paul E. Martin, Professor of Medieval and Modern History
in the University of Geneva.

CHAPTER VIII.

THE HANSA.

By A. Weiner, M.A., sometime Lecturer in History at
King's College, University of London.

CHAPTER IX.

THE TEUTONIC ORDER.

By ALEXANDER BRUCE BOSWELL, M.A., Bowes Professor of
Russian History, Language, and Literature in the
University of Liverpool.

CHAPTER X.

THE POPES OF AVIGNON AND THE GREAT SCHISM.

By GUILLAUME MOLLAT, Professor of Church History in the
University of Strasbourg.

CHAPTER XI.

FRANCE: THE LAST CAPETIANS.

By Hilda Johnstone, M.A., Professor of History in the
University of London.

CHAPTER XII

FRANCE: THE HUNDRED YEARS' WAR (TO 1380)

By A. Coville, Member of the Institute of France, Emeritus
Professor of History in the University of Lyons.

CHAPTER XIII.

FRANCE: ARMAGNACS AND BURGUNDIANS (1380–1422)

By Professor A. Coville.

CHAPTER XIV.

ENGLAND: EDWARD I AND EDWARD II.

By Professor Hilda Johnstone, M.A.

CHAPTER XV.

ENGLAND: EDWARD III AND RICHARD II.

By BERNARD L. MANNING, M.A., Fellow and Bursar of
Jesus College, Cambridge.

CHAPTER XVI.

WYCLIF.

By BERNARD L. MANNING, M.A.

CHAPTER XVII.

WALES, 1066 TO 1485.

By J. E. LLOYD, D.Litt., F.B.A., Emeritus Professor of History, University College of North Wales, Bangor.

CHAPTER XVIII.

IRELAND TO 1315.

By GODDARD H. ORPEN, Litt.D., Trinity College, Dublin.

CHAPTER XIX.

SCOTLAND TO 1328.

By C. SANFORD TERRY, Litt.D., Honorary Fellow of Clare College, Emeritus Professor of History in the University of Aberdeen.

CHAPTER XX.

SPAIN, 1252–1410.

By Dr Rafael Altamira, Judge in the permanent Court of
International Justice at the Hague; formerly Professor of
Jurisprudence in the University of Oviedo.

CHAPTER XXI.

RUSSIA, 1015–1462.

By Prince D. S. Mirsky.

CHAPTER XXII.

THE JEWS IN THE MIDDLE AGES.

By Cecil Roth, M.A., D.Phil., Merton College, Oxford.

CHAPTER XXIII.

MEDIEVAL ESTATES.

By C. H. McIlwain, LL.D., Eaton Professor of the Science of Government in Harvard University.

CHAPTER XXIV.

PEASANT LIFE AND RURAL CONDITIONS (*c.* 1100 TO *c.* 1500).

By Eileen E. Power, D.Lit., Professor of Economic History in the University of London.

CHAPTER XXV.

THE EARLY RENAISSANCE.

By ARTHUR A. TILLEY, M.A., Fellow of King's College, Cambridge.

CHAPTER XXVI.

MEDIEVAL MYSTICISM.

By Evelyn Underhill, Fellow of King's College, University of London.

LIST OF BIBLIOGRAPHIES.

LIST OF MAPS.

VOLUME VII

CHAPTER I

ITALY IN THE TIME OF DANTE

No higher tribute could be paid to Dante than to give his name to an age rich in famous men, the age of Boniface VIII and Henry VII, of Can Grande della Scala and Robert of Anjou. Yet it is no misnomer, for every one of them recalls a line of the *Commedia*, and, if the discredited exile had no influence upon his age in life, he has done much to keep its memory fresh in history. Dante himself would not have been content with this. He was no mere man of letters; he had plunged eagerly into politics. Yet all his efforts in public life seemed doomed to failure. His priorate of two months led to exile of over twenty years; his outspoken protest against Florentine aid for an unjust papal war was beaten; his embassy to Boniface VIII, if indeed he served on it, found no friendly hearing; he early broke from all his fellow-exiles to form a one-man party. In politics misfortune even dogged his pen. His *De Monarchia* failed of its practical purpose, and seemed to have died still-born; his letters to the Italian cardinals in conclave at Carpentras, calling for an Italian Pope with his seat at Rome, brought no response; he died in humble employment at a small Romagnol court, and that of the Guelfic party.

Dante's career then, as a man of action, which he would fain have been, was failure unrelieved. And yet no man, not even Villani, has so impressed himself upon the history of his age, and that without his writing a line of history. Consciously or unconsciously the celebrities mentioned in the *Commedia* are still classified under the categories in which he placed them. Emperors, kings, and Popes, ambitious despots and factious republicans, are all labelled for posterity. If a very small percentage is allotted seats in Paradise, the result is appropriate to an age of even peculiar violence, lust, and fraud. The mummified *De Monarchia* has become for political science the subject of constant study; the *Convivio* is ransacked for scraps of historical information; the Letters are documents of real historical interest. No reasonable man would read the story of the late thirteenth and early fourteenth centuries without his Dante within reach.

The period covered by this chapter begins approximately with the year 1289, in which the youthful Dante is said to have fought in the victory of Campaldino, and it ends within a year or so of Dante's death. Its history is confused by the number of independent States, small or large, each working out its own salvation or its ruin. A certain unity is preserved by the close relation between the Angevin house at Naples, the Papacy, and the Guelf republic at Florence. Florence, indeed, gives a centre to most of the Tuscan cities comprised in the Guelfic league, to which even Siena, her traditional Ghibelline rival, during this period belongs, but to east and west she has persistent foes in Arezzo and Pisa. Within the Papal States, Perugia, Bologna, and the lords of Ferrara have their independent story. In Lombardy, Milan and Verona seem destined to be predominant powers under their respective dynasts, though Pavia from ancient jealousy and Padua from its republicanism and wealth have to be reckoned with. Between the expansive powers Milan and Verona, with its satellite Mantua, lay a group of cities usually Guelfic but always quarrelsome. Brescia, a city of refuge for the plain, had access to Alpine pastures and northern commercial routes. Cremona controlled the northern, and Piacenza the southern, bank of the Po, with custody of the historic Emilian road. Farther south from Parma led the route across the Apennines into Liguria and Tuscany, and was of high interest in the history of despotism even to the nineteenth century. Modena and Reggio were noteworthy as bones of contention between Bologna and Ferrara, with the Ghibelline powers hungrily on the watch. The Piedmontese cities vacillate between Milan and the house of Anjou, which might have dominated western Lombardy but for its chronic preoccupation with the reconquest of Sicily. Events in Venice and Genoa might in common parlance be described as side-shows, so far as continental Italy is concerned, though each for a time became the centre of acute general conflict. Petrarch described them later as the two eyes of Italy, whose duty it was to watch her eastern and her western seas, but their invariable aim was rather to blind each other.

The Guelf and Ghibelline struggle was continuous, but in inter-State policy the cleavage was more distinct in Tuscany than in Lombardy and the adjoining papal fiefs, such as Bologna and Ferrara. Dante was nearly accurate in stating that every city had war within its walls, but strong hereditary despotism was serving as a check on internal faction. The dynast may be Guelf or Ghibelline; either of the two may rest on the people or the nobles. Dante makes the demagogue despot play the tribune Marcellus in every city; even little Assisi could claim a thorough-going tyrant. When in large cities despots do not exist, the government is compelled, as in Florence and Genoa, to submit to a foreign protectorate. Padua and Bologna struggle for so-called liberty, but the shadow of despotism is already falling. Elsewhere immunity is only due, as in Genoa, to equality in fighting force between the contending family groups. The republican polity was in process of being played out, Venice alone belying the general rule.

The advent of the Emperor Henry VII is a landmark in the confused history of the age. Here at least principles were involved. Philip IV had tested the power of national monarchy against Rome, but now the two universal sovereignties, both claiming divine origin, came into collision in the garden of the Empire, the old familiar ground. As in ancient

Athens temporary local ailments determined in the great plague, so in Italy local disorders were merged in one general conflict, which gave some unity to the history of three years.

After Henry's death the two chief Lombard dynasties again follow their respective lines of expansion, while Venice still nurses her wounds. A revival of Ghibellinism once more sets all Tuscany ablaze. The house of Anjou still casts lingering glances upon Sicily, while its princes and mercenaries are reluctantly dribbled into the Tuscan conflict. The period ends with a customary civic fight at Genoa, which becomes a focus for all contending powers, Lombard, Neapolitan, and Tuscan, the Avignon Papacy, and even the Sicilian king. The fate of Genoa was, indeed, of supreme importance to every maritime power in the western Mediterranean, and to the dominant State beyond her northern frontiers.

From the death of Charles I Naples ceased to be the focus of Italian history. On 29 May 1289, however, the kingdom of Sicily once more had a lawfully crowned head. The heir, released from captivity by Alfonso of Aragon, left three young sons as hostages, engaging to return, if within a year he had not obtained the renunciation of the Aragonese claim from Charles of Valois and peace with France and the Pope. Nicholas IV released him from his oath, and crowned him at Rieti as King of Sicily with all that his father had held. The renewal of war with James of Sicily was imperative; Loria was conquering the Calabrian coast towns, while James from his base at Ischia and Procida besieged Gaeta. Charles saved the fortress by aid of a heterogeneous crusading force, but this was his sole success; he was forced to a truce, which left James all his conquests. Alfonso had remained neutral; threatened by Castile, he made peace with France in February 1291, no mention being made of Sicily. On 18 June he suddenly died. Alfonso left Aragon and Majorca to James, who should transfer Sicily to their younger brother Frederick, so that Aragon and Sicily would remain separate. Resignation was antipathetic to James' character; he must keep both kingdoms. Leaving Frederick as governor, he sailed in July 1291 to be crowned at Saragossa. He claimed as the heir, not of Alfonso, but of his father Peter III.

Charles II on 2 April 1292 lost the papal suzerain who had crowned him. Nicholas IV was among the least distinguished Popes. Having been legate in the East, he was mainly interested in the Crusade. The Saracen capture of Acre made further operations hopeless, and Nicholas was the last genuine crusading Pope. There was often talk of renewal in papal and royal circles, but the motives were mainly financial or matrimonial. To Nicholas the Colonna owe much of their later importance, for which the Papacy paid dearly. Nicholas III had made Giacopo cardinal; his nephew Peter now became his colleague; Peter's father John, created Senator of Rome and Rector of the March, ruled Rome almost as dictator, forcing Viterbo to recognise the city's suzerainty. Napoleon Orsini, connected by marriage with the Colonna, also received the cardinal's hat, perhaps with the aim of dividing the rival family. His name was to reappear for very many years to come.

A dreary conclave, which opened at Rome in April 1292, only closed at Perugia on 5 July 1294. Charles II had intervened, only to be snubbed. The ten surviving cardinals were divided between the Orsini and Colonna factions, with Benedict Gaetani occupying an intermediate position. At length Cardinal Latino Malabranca, inspired by a dream, proposed the election of an aged hermit, who, living in a cave on Monte Murrone in the Abruzzi, had founded an Order of the Holy Ghost. Both parties acclaimed the proposal, either from a wave of repentance or from pure exhaustion. Even Gaetani, though exempt from either feeling, somewhat sarcastically adhered. The hermit was dragged unwillingly from his cave; Charles II, whose subject he was, and Charles Martel, titular King of Hungary, led his palfrey into Aquila, and hence escorted him to Naples. The new Pope took the name of Celestine; he never saw Rome. His reign was an absurdity; under the thumb of Charles he created eight French and four Italian cardinals, all of the Angevin party; a few months reduced the Curia to chaos. Celestine, conscious of incompetence, braced himself to resignation. He had learnt to rely on the advice of Gaetani, who stated that he had at first dissuaded him. It was, however, generally believed that he had intrigued for Celestine's withdrawal through the medium of a midnight voice, professedly angelic, speaking through a megaphone to Celestine in bed. The Neapolitans, furious at losing their Pope, clamoured riotously before the royal palace. But Celestine stood firm; Charles, having obtained his ends, and realising the impossibility of a pontificate based on piety alone, made no resistance. Celestine's successor thought it imprudent to leave the self-deposed Pope in his cell on Monte Murrone. Fearing arrest, the hermit attempted to escape to Dalmatia, but was captured and confined at Fumone, near Anagni, until his death in 1296. Even then it was thought safer that ten feet of soil should hide potential relics from pious exhumation. Celestine's resignation has been made famous by Dante's line on the *gran rifiuto* (*Inferno*, III, 60). There are difficulties in referring this to Celestine, but it is hardly possible to reject the tradition handed down from Dante's son. Esau is a less attractive alternative.

On 23 December 1294 Gaetani was elected at Naples by a large majority out of twenty-two cardinals; he took the name of Boniface VIII. The election was honest enough, for both Orsini and Colonna voted for him, several of the French cardinals being violently opposed. He stood head and shoulders above his colleagues in legal knowledge, diplomatic experience, and business ability. He was born at Anagni, the home of Innocent III, Gregory IX, and Alexander IV, of whom his mother was a niece. The Gaetani were a knightly family of no great importance; they were Ghibellines, and Benedict's father had served under Manfred.

Boniface's age is much disputed. Dino Compagni makes him eighty-six at death; a recent authority holds that he was not much over sixty on election. His character has been fiercely discussed between those who believed him to be the worst of all Popes and others who, regarding him as the boldest champion of papal claims, are bound to refute as libels the charges of vice and heresy laid against him by the French Court, the Colonna, and the Celestinians. The evidence seems conclusive that he was doctrinally a sceptic, but a believer in amulets and magic; in this he was but on a level with other high ecclesiastics. It is probable that for him, as later for Alexander VI, the moral code had little meaning. On the other hand, the unsavoury details of the twenty-nine articles of the French minister Plaisians, and the evidence concocted after his death by Nogaret, are suspicious commonplaces, applied to others whom the French lawyers were interested in attacking. A celebrated passage in a dispatch to James of Aragon describes him some years before his death as all eyes and tongue, with all else diseased. In 1300 in another Aragonese dispatch he is mentioned as being very well, better than three years ago, and again in 1302 as saying that he would live till all his enemies were "choked off." On exhumation his body was found in excellent preservation; such a monster of corruption could hardly have preserved all his fine teeth but two. A modern apologist admits that he kept bad company, but was not himself so bad as he has been painted.

To the historian Boniface's temperament is more important than his morals, for it explains his pretensions, his success, and his tragic fall. He was at once a law and an idol to himself. His legal learning culminated in the *ipse dixit*; he worshipped his fine person, appearing now in the full garb of Pope, now, it is said, of Emperor. He fostered this idolatry by distributing silver statuettes or larger effigies of himself. For supposed inferiors of whatever rank he had illimitable scorn; his rudeness extended from Charles II, "the miserable, whom, but for his own bounty, the earth would have swallowed up," to the kneeling Archbishop of Genoa, into whose eyes he threw the ashes expected on his head, or to a German envoy, whom he kicked in the face. Though always hated, he had the art of at once bribing and intimidating his court into submission. His chief energies were directed to the advancement of his own family at the expense of their neighbours or the Church. His views ranged from the creation of petty principalities to the claims of an old Roman Emperor, with the custody of the Keys of Heaven added. It is small wonder that Boniface incurred hatred during life and after death. If the *Commedia* is the drama of love and hate, Boniface may well stand as the villain of the play.

The Pope, in spite of his Ghibelline origin, flung himself fiercely, as was natural, into the duel between Anjou and Aragon, for he was vitally interested in the recovery of Sicily, the whole kingdom being admittedly a papal fief. James had soon found that he was in danger of falling between two thrones. The Aragonese, as distinct from the Catalans,

disliked the Sicilian connexion, in which, as an inland State, they had no
interest, and which dragged them into a drawn-out struggle with France,
the Papacy, and Castile. Patriotic Sicilians resented being an annexe of
unsympathetic Aragon. Frederick must have felt himself cheated of his
rights to the throne under Alfonso's will. Nevertheless there was no
decisive change until Boniface's election. James, now in danger of revolt,
gave in. Boniface in June 1295 arranged the terms of peace between
Anjou, Aragon, and France. James should marry the daughter of
Charles II; the French king withdrew all claims to Aragon; the surrender of Sicily was later rewarded by the promise of Sardinia and Corsica
under papal suzerainty, if James could expel the Pisans and Genoese.
Frederick was tempted with the hand of Catherine Courtenay, heiress
of the titular Emperor of the East and niece of Charles II; he resisted
so speculative an exchange, and threw in his lot with the Sicilians.

Frederick and Sicily were now left to their fate, and very terrible this
seemed. But the people and their leader never faltered. Frederick was
proclaimed king by the Parliament at Messina, and crowned at Palermo.
National support was rewarded by a liberal constitution, giving to the
three Estates the decision on peace and war, much power of legislation,
and some approach to ministerial responsibility. The king took the bold
offensive in Calabria, tempted the Neapolitans to revolt, and allied himself
with Ghibelline elements in Tuscany and Lombardy. Boniface was now
Frederick's deadliest enemy. He brought Charles II and James to Rome
early in 1297, and here John of Procida and Roger Loria, neither of
them Sicilians, threw over the cause in which they had made their reputa-
tions. Loria became Admiral of the allied fleets, which were to restore
Sicily to Anjou. Even Constance, widow of Peter, deserted her favourite
son, and left Sicily for Rome. Here too was Charles II's third son,
Robert, released from Aragon in 1295 and now his father's vicar for
Naples. Wide scandal was caused by the presumption that he was to
succeed his father. His eldest brother Charles Martel had died in 1295,
but left a son, Carobert, afterwards King of Hungary. The second son,
Louis, who had taken Orders, only renounced his rights in December 1296.
Boniface stifled opposition by recognising Robert as heir in February
1297, and in March he married Yolande, sister of James and Frederick.

At this time Boniface became involved in another war, caused almost
wholly by his nepotistic ambitions. The Colonna large estates and strong
fortresses along the hills south of the Campagna were natural objects of
papal greed, especially as they adjoined the humbler Gaetani holdings.
Cardinal Giacopo, a man of saintly character, was associated with Jacopone
da Todi and the Spiritual Franciscans; he may well have been persuaded
of the illegality of Celestine's resignation, and of Boniface's manipulation
thereof. The house moreover, being now definitely Ghibelline, was in
favour of Frederick of Sicily and opposed to any papal claims to imperial
authority in Italy. Sciarra, a violent young member of the family, provoked

attack by raiding in March 1297 a convoy of papal treasure, on the pretext that it was extorted for the purchase of estates for Boniface's nephew
Peter. Though the property was restored, a Bull was issued, depriving
the two Colonna cardinals of their benefices. The Colonna took to their
fortresses, denied the legality of Celestine's resignation, and appealed to
a council. On interdict and sentence of confiscation followed the preaching of a crusade. The Orsini, Florence, and other Guelfic, Tuscan, and
Umbrian cities sent contingents. In September 1298 the ancient walls
of Palestrina were surrendered under false promises, for which Dante
makes Guido of Montefeltro responsible. The site of the city was
ploughed up and salted. Colonna fugitives found refuge in England,
France, or Ghibelline Italian cities. A powerful State was formed for
Peter Gaetani, intended to overawe the smaller nobles and restore order
in the wide feudal lands surrounding Rome.

On this success the Jubilee of 1300 closely followed. Among all Roman
Jubilees this has been the most distinguished, celebrated by Villani's
youthful resolve to write his *History*, and by Dante's simile, describing
the dense lines of pilgrims as they crossed the Bridge of Sant' Angelo to
and from St Peter's. The touch is so intimate as to have suggested that
Dante was among their number. Amid the ceremonies, which lasted
until Christmas Eve, Boniface was at his best. His love for splendour, his
talent for organisation, his very autocracy ensured the success of this huge
European festival. His croupiers at St Peter's and St Paul's raked in the
countless pious offerings, from which he hoped to finance the conquest of
Sicily and the establishment of yet another Gaetani State, this time in
Tuscany.

Until the last month of the Jubilee papal prospects were encouraging.
The Sicilians soon felt the loss of their great admiral. Frederick, faced
by a huge fleet, which Loria had collected from the Mediterranean
powers, retired from before Naples. In July 1299 the Neapolitan and
Aragonese fleets won a decisive victory over a much inferior force off Cape
Orlando, Frederick escaping with only seventeen galleys. It was some
compensation that James sailed home in dudgeon with his allies, and,
perhaps, disgust with himself. Sicily was attacked from west and east.
Robert and his brother, Philip of Taranto, took Catania and besieged
Messina. Then fortune turned with Frederick's memorable victory of
foot over horse in the plain of Falconaria, near Trapani, in December
1300. Philip was captured, and Messina then relieved. The Sicilians
held fast in Calabria, though they had lost the islands off Naples. Charles
would gladly have made peace, but Boniface railed against the cowardly
king, called Templars and Hospitallers to join in his crusade, and dragged
Genoa reluctantly into the conflict. On 14 June 1300 Roger Loria
destroyed yet another Sicilian fleet, but on land Robert made little
progress. Naples was being starved to feed his army; news reached Rome
that he was ill-fitted to conquer Sicily, being too much under the influence

of his wife and the Catalans. The great fleet, which was to reduce western Sicily, was shattered by a tempest off Cape Passero. The aid of France seemed essential to Pope and king, and Charles of Valois was the saviour selected. Towards this incompetent personality Angevin, papal, and Florentine interests were now converging.

Side by side with his Sicilian venture Boniface had embarked upon an expensive war in southern Tuscany. Marriage was with Boniface, as with Renaissance Popes, a valuable asset for the construction of the Temporal State. His great-nephew Loffred was one of the many husbands of Margaret Aldobrandeschi, Countess Palatine of the Patrimony in Tuscany. Boniface coveted her wealthy fief and wide allodial domains, unfortunately lost to Loffred by matrimonial rupture. Boniface, elected Podestà of Orvieto, turned the city against its neighbour and ally. Margaret's relations, the six Counts of Santafiora, hitherto unfriendly, took up her cause, one of them even having courage to marry her. A severe defeat of the Sienese, old enemies of the Aldobrandeschi, forced Boniface to call in the Tuscan league against this stubbornly Ghibelline house. The war began in the first month of the Jubilee; nearly three years passed in wearing resistance down. Margaret's estates were conferred on another of Boniface's nephews, together with the Rectorate of the Patrimony. Before this happened, intervention in Florence had begun. From 1289 to 1300 she had been peculiarly free from external complications. Her close relations with Naples had been mutually profitable. She was monopolising Neapolitan commerce and finance at the expense of Italian rivals, while the Angevin kings lived upon her loans. Her bankers also dominated the papal money-market. The internal troubles which brought her into collision with Boniface must now be traced to their source.

For Tuscany the year 1289 was one of high importance. At Pisa Ugolino and his family were starved to death in the Tower of Hunger. The Ghibellines once more ruled, with Guido of Montefeltro as their captain. Arezzo had become the headquarters of east Tuscan Ghibellinism, which included the Florentine feudal families of the Upper Arno and the Apennines, the Pazzi, Ubaldini, and Ubertini, one of whom was the fighting Bishop of Arezzo. Count Guido Novello of Poppi and Buonconte, Montefeltro's son, held high command. The Aretines had heavily defeated the Sienese, while from Florence were seen the flames of her own outpost San Donato. Within her walls Ghibellines were so numerous among nobles and people that it became necessary to expel them till the sky was clearer. All depended upon immediate success. The army mobilised was unusually large, estimated at 2400 horse and 10,000 foot. Charles II had left Aimeri de Narbonne as nominal leader, with the veteran Guillaume de Durfort as guardian. Bologna and the cities of the Tuscan league sent contingents, while under the Angevin banner fought a troop of Romagnol horse under Maghinardo di Susinana, Ghibelline in Romagna and Lombardy, but Guelf in Tuscany in gratitude for the faithful guardianship of Florence.

The Aretines expected the advance by the direct road, south of the Arno, but the Florentines crossed the river, and took the Consuma pass from Pontassieve, a dangerous manœuvre had there been opposition on the rough descent. The aim was to raid the Guidi territories round Poppi, and the bishop's estates at Bibbiena. Thus the Aretines entered the Casentino from the southward, and the battle was fought in the plain of Campaldino, between Poppi and Bibbiena. The Florentines, contrary to practice, stood on the defensive. In front was a picked body of light horse consisting of Florentine gentry, among whom Vieri de' Cerchi and his sons were prominent. Their flanks were covered by cross-bowmen and lancer infantry. Behind them was ranged the main body of heavy cavalry and foot; to cover a possible retreat, a reserve of Pistoians was commanded by their Podestà, the impetuous Corso Donati, who was ordered under pain of death not to attack without express orders. The Aretines, inferior by a third in numbers, furiously attacking, pushed the light horse and main body back, but were then exposed to a flanking fire from the cross-bowmen, who stood firm. Corso, a born soldier, saw his opportunity. Crying out—"If we lose, I will die with my citizens; if we win, let who will come to Pistoia to execute my death sentence," he dashed into the Aretine flank, and turned the fortunes of the day. Guido Novello with his men rode off for safety; Buonconte and the bishop, who had respectively dissuaded and urged attack, were killed. Dante, who was now twenty-four, was probably engaged; the evidence rests on a fragmentary letter read by his later biographer, Leonardo Bruni, but now lost, which tells how Dante had much fear but the greatest delight owing to the changing fortunes of the fight.

Waste of a week or more in ravaging the Casentino spoilt any chance of capturing Arezzo, though the siege train flung donkeys crowned with episcopal mitres into the city. An attack upon Pisa by Genoese galleys and Florentine armies was thwarted by Guido of Montefeltro, wisest and wariest of generals, magnificent in defence and in surprise. Thus no very obvious military results followed on Campaldino. Yet it decided the supremacy of Florence among friends and enemies in Tuscany, until another Tuscan general, Uguccione della Faggiuola, turned the tables. All danger from Ghibellines had ceased, the split between Blacks and Whites had not begun. Trade grew apace, every one seemed rich, the gates stood open with no excise-men to rummage the sacks and baskets of country folk. Villani writes that it was the most joyous time that Florence had ever had, and, indeed, she was never to see another such, save at the height of the Medicean age. Dante enjoyed all the fun of the continuous fair; his first sonnet was addressed to Guido Cavalcanti, leader in literature, fashion, and politics, who perhaps made Dante's social fortune. It is known that the young poet dressed with care, appreciated delicate cooking and

luxurious furniture. He would not then have preferred the ladies of
Cacciaguida's day, who left their mirror without paint upon their cheeks,
and donned the products of their spindle and distaff rather than the garish
belts and low-cut silks and muslins of the fair objects of his youthful
admiration; nor would he have worn the undressed leather-suit with belt
to match and clasp of bone, as approved by his great-great-grandfather.

In spite of gaiety and prosperity all was not well with Florence. The
great gentry presumed on their new prestige to ruffle the middle and
lower classes, to add small holdings of defenceless country neighbours to
their large estates. Critics complained that the vaunted victory had no
results, that the Pisan general had even taken the offensive with success.
It was whispered that Corso Donati himself had been bought off from
pressing home an attack on Pisa. Wealthy traders, shop-keepers, and the
unrepresented classes found a spokesman in Giano della Bella, himself
noble and rich, but a reformer by instinct and principle. Hence came
about the celebrated Ordinances of Justice, initiated in 1293. Giano
himself fell before a combination of the uppermost classes with the Gild
of Butchers led by the vapouring demagogue Pecora. The populace offered
to support him; but, from a horror of civil war or fear for its issue, he
refused the offer, and left Florence for ever. His work was only half done,
but the Ordinances in their main tenor were retained, though in 1295
modifications were introduced to meet just grievances of the nobles, while
the *popolani* were reinforced by minor noble families, from whom disqualification for office was now removed; henceforth actual practice was
not essential to membership of the gilds which monopolised the
government. The Alighieri were possibly included under the former
measure, and it is practically certain that Dante benefited by the latter.
Being now thirty, he became a member of the Gild of Doctors and
Druggists, but never practised either profession.

No constitutional changes could cure the ineradicable spirit of faction
among Florentine families. This became concentrated in the feud between
groups headed respectively by the Cerchi and the Donati. The Cerchi had
migrated from the country, while the Donati were an old Florentine
family. Vieri de' Cerchi had bought and enlarged the Guidi palace, closely
adjoining that of Corso. There was no hard and fast line between noble
and bourgeois families; both Cerchi and Donati were engaged in banking,
both intermarried with the opposite class, but family pride remained.
Vieri was rich and generous, but rough in manners and clumsy in speech.
Yet he and his family were popular with middle and lower classes, with
many of the nobles and the oppressed Ghibellines. Corso headed the
extreme Guelfic families, and was the darling of the mob, who called
him *il barone*, and delighted in his martial bearing and ready wit. He
ridiculed Vieri, but his personal enemy was Guido Cavalcanti, a noble of
the first rank, poet and philosopher, high-spirited but aloof. Assaults
and charges of murder culminated in Corso's banishment in 1299 for

gross corruption of a needy Podestà in a matrimonial suit. Hitherto he had been predominant since Giano della Bella's fall; henceforth the Cerchi, in favour with the moderates, controlled the government until the coming of Charles of Valois.

By this time the two parties had become known as Blacks and Whites, nicknames borrowed from Pistoia. This city had been in uproar owing to a murderous feud between two branches of the chief family, the Cancellieri. The disorder threatened the stability of the Guelfic league with a Ghibelline revival at a dangerous strategic point. Florence intervened, took over the administration as a mediatory power, and removed the heads of both parties. The Blacks received hospitality from the Frescobaldi across the Arno, the Whites from the Cerchi. Hence the infection spread through Florence and Tuscany, even into Umbria and Lombardy. It was no longer a feud between two families and their groups, but between parties as definite as Guelfs and Ghibellines.

Present hatred and future disaster were barely concealed by the continued gaiety and prosperity. The hatred might any moment blaze up into a ruinous flame. A trifling incident, indeed, caused the outbreak. On the Calends of May 1300, two groups of young bloods, Black and White, were watching the dancing of girls on the Piazza Santa Trinità. Spurring their horses against each other, they came to blows. The only casualty was a nose sliced from a Cerchi face. But Villani justly compares this wound to the murder of Buondelmonte; as that was the beginning of Guelf and Ghibelline factions, so was this the beginning of great ruin to the Guelf party and its city of Florence.

This quarrel gave Boniface the opportunity for which he was waiting. The vacancy in the Empire had opened to him rosy prospects. After Adolf of Nassau's defeat and death in July 1298, he had refused to recognise Albert, but, alarmed by rumours of alliance with Philip IV, he changed his tactics, seeking from Albert the cession of imperial rights over Tuscany in return for recognition. This was a revival of Nicholas III's scheme for creating nepotist kingdoms in Lombardy and Tuscany. Albert was not to be tempted, whereupon Boniface strove to influence the Electors. The value of such a cession was small, unless he gained practical control over the Tuscan cities, and especially Florence. With this aim he had liberally bestowed benefices and matrimonial dispensations upon leading Florentine families. His probable attitude towards parties was displayed when, on a proposal for the recall of Giano della Bella in 1294, he threatened with excommunication any who should advocate it. Recently he had given office in the Papal States to Corso Donati when banished. Corso conspired against the White government, which in April 1300 condemned for treason three Florentines in Rome, the chief of whom was Simone Gherardi degli Spini, the papal banker. Boniface ordered the government to revoke the sentence, but it resented ecclesiastical interference with civil justice. The skirmish of 1 May stirred him to action.

Early in June he sent his chief adviser, Cardinal Acquasparta, to mediate
between Blacks and Whites. Perhaps he genuinely wished to reconcile
them, and so control both parties. If this failed, he would naturally side
with the extremist magnates against the more moderate party, which
upheld the Ordinances of Justice and favoured reconciliation with
Ghibellines. The Whites, as constitutionalists, would resist any attempt
on municipal independence; the Blacks would make any concession, if the
Pope would restore them to power.

Acquasparta on arrival repeated Boniface's order for acquittal of the
papal agents. The Priorate of 15 June, of which Dante was a member,
confirmed the sentence. Public feeling had recently been aroused by a gross
assault by turbulent magnates on the Consuls of the Gilds while carrying
gifts to the Baptistery on St John's Day. The Priors who preceded Dante
and his colleagues banished the heads of both parties. The White chiefs
were soon recalled from Sarzana on hygienic grounds, while, in spite of
promises, the Blacks were long excluded. Guido Cavalcanti, indeed, justified
the act of mercy by dying of malaria. Acquasparta published his award
for the restoration of peace, the chief obstacle to which was the corrupt
canvassing and violence which set the city in an uproar on each election
to the Priorate. He proposed that suitable names from both parties
should be placed in a ballot-box, from which those of the Priors should
be drawn by lot. The Whites, unwilling to lose their advantage, refused
the award, on which he departed in high dudgeon, pronouncing an interdict against the city.

The Pope now determined on more active measures. Corso and the
Blacks had pressed him to summon a French prince to his aid. Negotiations had long been on foot with Charles of Valois with a view to French
assistance in Sicily. During the last two months of 1300 the conditions
were settled. Charles should bring a large force for the conquest of Sicily
and the submission of Florence to the Pope's will. The White government
now strove to avoid a breach, which would bring upon the city the
suspended interdict, to the ruin of its foreign trade. Florence had sent
large contingents for the Colonna and Aldobrandeschi wars. In June
1301, however, on the demand for a further reinforcement, opposition
shewed itself, and Dante, who led this, was only beaten in the Council
of 100 by 49 votes to 32. The government had in May taken a step
which must inevitably provoke papal displeasure. In defiance of its mission
as official mediator at Pistoia, it expelled the Black population with much
cruelty. Lucca replied by similar treatment of its Whites, and this with
Boniface's warm approval. The great Tuscan Guelfic league was splitting
into fragments.

Charles joined the papal Court at Anagni on 2 September, and was
appointed Peacemaker (*paciaro*) by Boniface. The White government,
now thoroughly alarmed, sent envoys, among them Dante, as is generally
believed, to propitiate the Pope. He would only urge complete submission.

Bologna alone stood by Florence at this crisis. Charles, reaching Siena with 800 horse, reinforced by Lucchese, Perugians, Romagnols, and Sienese, sent his Chancellor to Florence to announce his mission. The Priorate, of which Dino Compagni was a member, dared not deny him entrance, for it had made no preparations for resistance. The Priors feebly tried to win the Blacks by forming an advisory committee of both parties; the Parte Guelfa rejected their advances. The Peacemaker's admission was made the subject of a referendum, a rare example, to the 72 Gilds, which included the 51 Lower Trades, usually unrepresented. The gallant Bakers alone opposed it, saying that Charles should neither be received nor honoured, for he was coming to destroy the city. All the leading citizens swore perfect peace and kissed the Gospel at the Baptistery font; tears coursed down the cheeks of those who were to be foremost in destruction. The precautions for public order were ludicrous. Abusive language was to be punished by excision of the tongue. In front of the Palazzo Pubblico, now rising from its foundations, stood the executioner with axe and block awaiting customers. Charles was warned of the imprudence of entering on All Saints' Day, when the lower classes would be full of new wine. Charles, risking the new wine, rode in by the Porta San Pier Gattolini on 1 November, unarmed "save with the lance of treachery wherewith Judas tilted, with which he was to burst asunder the bowels of Florence."[1] Of course there were omens of disaster. The comet, now known as Halley's, was in the sky. Dante in the *Convivio* describes a cross in the heavens, formed by the vapours which follow the course of Mars and portend the deaths of kings and the revolutions of States, such being the effects of his domination. At first Charles was courtesy itself, inviting the Priors to dine, with the knowledge perhaps that the law forbade them to dine out. He attended the sermon of the celebrated friar Remigio Girolami, who, like Savonarola afterwards, discoursed on the evils of tyranny. A Parliament of Peace was summoned for 5 November, and here Charles received full power to act as mediator. He swore faithfully to perform his task, but already his agents had concerted revolution with the Blacks. Only on the previous night the Medici had wounded a recent Gonfalonier of Justice; the citizens gathered round the Priorate ready to take vengeance, but the Priors refrained.

The villain of the piece now took the stage. Corso Donati, who had lurked hard by, broke into Florence by a postern, seized the nunnery of San Pier Maggiore, and fortified the campanile. Popular feeling veered with the breeze of audacity, and then arose the cry of *Viva Messer Corso il barone*. He plundered the houses of the Priors who had exiled him, and threw the prisons open. An orgy of blood, lust, and fire began; the rabble and the gaol-birds were surpassed in crimes by the noblest or wealthiest citizens, Donati, Tosinghi, Rossi, and Medici; they were

---

[1] *Purgatorio*, xx, 73.

committed against near neighbours, intimates until the recent split in the Guelfic ranks. Warehouses of merchants and tradesmen were ransacked; heiresses were married by force, and shivering fathers compelled to sign the settlements. In vain the great bell of the Priorate clanged to arms; the few faithful families found no leaders and few followers. Charles of Valois threatened to hang Corso, but never moved a finger. A gallant Pistoian, Schiatta de' Cancellieri, who commanded 300 State horse, wished to attack Corso, but Vieri de' Cerchi forbade him. No wonder that the populace was passive when the Cerchi were hiding in their palaces.

Corso put the final touch to the revolution by turning out the Podestà and Priors. The sole magistrate left was the Captain of the People. Yet even in the flush of triumph the nobles dared not touch the constitution, nor the hated Ordinances of Justice. They were content with nominating new Priors, who received absolute powers, but submitted every measure to the Black nobles before proposing it. On 1 November the new Podestà was appointed, that Cante de' Gabrielli of Gubbio to whom Dante was to owe his exile. Cardinal Acquasparta, reappearing, nominally reconciled hostile families, even the Donati and Cerchi. The futility of such friendships was proved by a fresh tragedy. Simone Donati, most brilliant of Florentine young bloods, and his father Corso's darling, saw old Niccolò de' Cerchi, his own uncle, pass through the Piazza Santa Croce towards his country house. He followed him, fell on him unawares, and murdered him. A servant, before flying, plunged his sword into Simone's side; the bloodthirsty youngster died next day.

In January, the sack now over, the trials or rather sentences began. Fifteen Gonfaloniers or Priors who had held office between December 1299 and November 1301 were condemned. Among these was Dante, whose outspoken opposition to Boniface VIII had made a verdict inevitable. Penalties varied from fine, exile, and civic disqualification to confiscation of property. If the accused failed to stand his trial, he would be burnt, beheaded, or hanged according to the Podestà's choice. There were in all 559 sentences of death. Few probably were actually executed. Citizens who fled from justice were rarely caught. A good horse or even a sturdy pair of legs would soon carry the culprit beyond Florentine jurisdiction. Fra Remigio tells a pitiful tale of houses destroyed or deserted, farms and fields lying waste, commerce ruined. The revolution had its sequel in bankruptcies among the great commercial families. Charles of Valois, on leaving Florence early in April 1302, received 24,000 gold florins for his work of peace. The Peacemaker had caused a disgraceful civil war; he went his way to Sicily to sign a degrading peace.

On arrival at Rome, Charles was appointed, in May 1302, Captain-General of the papal and Neapolitan forces. All the Tuscan Black Guelfs contributed contingents, while the Bardi and Peruzzi financed the operations. Never was fiasco more complete. The army, burning and plundering, struggled across Sicily to Sciacca, which faces Africa. Here it melted away from malaria. To avoid the chance of a resolute attack by Frederick, the Treaty of Caltabellotta was signed on 24 September 1302. With this the War of Sicilian Vespers technically ended, though in practice it proved to be little more than a truce. Frederick married in May 1303 Charles II's daughter Eleanor. Philip of Taranto was released, to prove his military incompetence on Tuscan fields thereafter. Frederick, until death, should rule a free Island of Sicily as King; after his decease it should revert to the Angevins, his heir receiving Cyprus or Sardinia in compensation. Sicilian and Neapolitan conquests were mutually restored. John of Procida was already dead; Loria retired to Spain, his brilliant reputation sadly tarnished. Boniface was, as always, furious, but Charles II for once held firm, and the Pope's quarrel with Philip IV was developing. Yet he succeeded in modifying the treaty to his own advantage. Frederick agreed to recognise papal suzerainty, to restore ecclesiastical lands, to pay substantial tribute, and provide 100 lances for papal service. He had to content himself with the title of King of Trinacria, as Boniface would not tolerate any suggestion of the divisibility of the kingdom of Sicily. The hordes of Catalans, which for years had poured into the island, formed themselves into the Grand Company, and started on their marvellous career on both sides of the Aegean, finally creating that strange soldier-State, the Duchy of Athens, which was to give a claim across the seas to the Aragonese Kings of Sicily.

Before Boniface could avail himself of his Tuscan successes, the quarrel began which culminated at Anagni; this hardly affects Italian history, except in so far as it led to the outrage. The tragedy was due to the violent, masterful characters of the two protagonists, and to Philip IV's substitution of civil lawyers for ecclesiastical councillors. The subjects under dispute were the right of the State to tax its clergy, and the subjection of criminal clerks to royal jurisdiction. Bickerings began in 1296, and an issue might have been reached much earlier, but for the necessities of both parties. To Boniface French aid was essential for the reconquest of Sicily and the coveted control over Florence, and for both Charles of Valois was the instrument. Yet the final quarrel had begun in October 1301 before Charles had entered Florence or set sail for Sicily. The celebrated Bulls, *Salvator mundi* and *Ausculta fili*, issued in December, and Boniface's wild talk which followed, might have at once caused war but for Philip's defeat at Courtrai on 11 July 1302, in which Pierre Flote, the royal minister, "the diabolical Achitophel, blind of one eye and totally blind of brain," was killed. Boniface took advantage of the disaster to issue in November the Bull *Unam sanctam*, perhaps the high-water mark of papal pretensions. Philip, still in difficulties, and under the influence of moderates, suggested arbitration. Boniface, unaware that the moderates had been replaced by Nogaret, Pierre Flote's right-hand man, who had a personal grievance against the Pope, sent on 13 April 1303 an uncompromising answer. Already on 7 March Nogaret had received instructions to proceed to Italy and bring Boniface back for trial by a

General Council. As he was leaving France, Boniface's envoy arrived, and was arrested. On 13 and 14 June Plaisians read to an Assembly of Notables the twenty-nine articles, on which the post-mortem charges against Boniface were based. Ten days later Philip sent a summons for a General Council to the European powers. The shock caused Boniface to hesitate, but his final Bull, *Super Petri solio*, which was conditionally to release Philip's subjects from allegiance, was reserved for publication on 8 September 1303.

Meanwhile Nogaret, who had enrolled adventurers in Tuscany and kindled rebellion in the late Colonna territories, moved upon Anagni, accompanied by two French subordinates, Sciarra Colonna, and Rinaldo da Supino, Captain of Ferentino. The commandant of the papal troops, the Podestà and Captain of Anagni, had been suborned; Cardinals Napoleon Orsini and Riccardo Petroni of Siena were almost certainly in the secret. The force which broke into Anagni at dawn on 7 September may have numbered 1600 horse and foot. The three French assailants hoisted the papal banner, to signify that Boniface was no Pope, but the Italians, for their security, insisted that the French flag should fly beside it. This adds significance to Dante's line on the sacrilegious outrage—"I see the fleur-de-lys enter Alagna and Christ captured in the person of his Vicar." The invaders, after hours of stubborn fighting, forced their way into the Gaetani quarter and rushed through the cathedral to the papal palace, where Sciarra found the Pope lying on his bed. To his demand that he should resign Boniface replied: "Here is my neck and here my head," but resign he would not. Nogaret then entered and stopped any attempt at violence; a dead Pope would not have served his purpose. He had planned every detail of the capture, but was baffled by the impossibility of carrying his captive through half Italy. On the third day came reaction. The people, stirred up by Cardinal Fieschi, rose against the invaders, crying no longer "Death to the Pope," but "Death to the foreigners." Sciarra and Supino fled to Ferentino, where Nogaret joined them, not without a wound; the French flag was dragged through the town and trampled under foot. Boniface, released, from the head of the staircase pronounced pardon and blessing to the citizens. On 12 September an escort, sent by the Senators, brought Boniface to Rome, where he fell from the hands of the hostile Colonna into those of his nominal friends the Orsini. The city was in such a ferment that the Senators resigned. Boniface wished to leave the Vatican for the Lateran, but the Orsini held him tight. Numerous tales, coloured by Guelf or Ghibelline taste, are told of his last days. There seems no doubt that he died in some sort of frenzy, even if he did not try to scratch the eyes of all who approached him. His natural violence had reacted against himself; he thought to be the greatest of Popes, he suffered the deepest humiliation of any. Pride was his very being, and, pride mortally wounded, he must die.

Boniface can scarcely be reckoned among the greater Popes. His was, indeed, an imposing personality, which men either hated or admired, but he had no high impersonal ideals. His reputation is due to the tragic contrast between his pretensions and his fall. The patriotic feeling of Italy was roused by the outrage inflicted on its greatest figure by an unscrupulous French king and his rascally lawyer. Benedict's reign was so short that Boniface was thought of as the last Italian Pope; the ruinous results to Rome and Italy were rightly attributed to his virtual murder. Yet he was not really a successor to Innocent III or Gregory X, but was rather the precursor of the fifteenth-century Popes, with the territorial aims of Sixtus IV and Alexander VI, and the futile ecclesiastical pretensions of Pius II's Bull *Execrabilis*. Pierre Flote had said that his master's sword was made of steel, that of the Pope of verbiage. He had no real force wherewith to face a strong national king. Florence, his best supporter, would not have raised a ducat or a man against her best customers, the French. The petty successes against Colonna and Aldobrandeschi were outbalanced by total failure in Sicily. He never had real control over the papal territories; Bologna, his chief provincial city, allied herself against him with the Florentine Whites. The absence of an Emperor seemed to give him an opportunity, but the comparative indifference of Rudolf and Albert to Italy was perhaps a disadvantage, for there was no great national cause to champion. The weakness of the Ghibellines at this time encouraged the Guelfs in each State to split into sections; Boniface had neither a nation, nor even a united party, at his back. As a battle-cry, the Church was nearly as husky as the Empire. The posthumous importance of Boniface lies not in his life but in his death, not in his triumphs but in his tragedy.

Under the shock caused by Boniface's tragic death the jarring factions in the Conclave unanimously elected an unexceptionable candidate at the first scrutiny on 22 October 1303. Niccolò Boccasini, now Benedict XI, was son of a notary at Treviso; he had pure morals, high culture, and no *nipoti*. His career had been that of peacemaker. He had negotiated between Philip IV and the Papacy, between France and England. Having promoted, when Legate to Hungary, the election of Carobert as king, he was in favour with Charles II. He restored friendly relations with Sicily, though resisting any revision of the Treaty of Caltabellotta. As General of the Dominicans, he had prevented them from joining the Spiritual Franciscans' revolt against Boniface. The Colonna cardinals were absolved, though not yet restored to their dignities. Some partial arrangement was made between the Colonna and Gaetani. The Romans elected Benedict Senator for life, yet, in spite of his popularity, the fights between leading families forced him to make Perugia his headquarters. It was impossible to fly in the face of Philip, and yet inexcusable to condone the crime of Anagni. Benedict, neglecting threats, determined to try the actual perpetrators, but acquitted the French king and nation of complicity. The compromise was rather politic than just.

Benedict's hardest problem was that of Florence. Here the expulsion of the Whites had increased external enemies, without leaving peace at home. There was hard fighting with Whites and Ghibellines, and with Arezzo, aided sometimes by Pisans and Bolognese. Corso Donati, whose policy was individualistic rather than oligarchical, expected the spoils of the Black victory. The brain, however, of the conspiracy had been Rosso della Tosa, whom not even the second place would content. Corso, playing as usual to the gallery, took up the cry that Rosso's party pocketed the profits of corn bought by the Treasury during a famine, and adulterated the supplies sold to the poor. He found an ally in the new bishop, Lottieri della Tosa, who accused them of filching episcopal estates. The rival Black sections, named *Pars populi* and *Pars episcopi*, took up arms. Corso burnt the Palace of the Podestà, but was beaten off from that of the Priors. The government invited the city of Lucca to send troops to establish order, but Corso was still unbeaten. Benedict now intervened, sending his most trusted cardinal, Nicholas of Prato, to reconcile the parties. The suspicions of the extreme Blacks were not unnatural, for the Pope had transferred his banking account from the ultra-Black Spini to the White Cerchi, and Nicholas was of Ghibelline origin. Both, however, were generally regarded as impartial. All classes below the highest longed for peace; the memory of Boniface, who had deprived them of their best customers or employers, was detested. On 17 March 1304 Nicholas was given full powers for reform, and on 26 April there followed the spectacular act of general reconciliation on the Piazza Santa Maria Novella. Florence was now *en fête*; on the Calends of May, once more fateful, crowds flocked to a well-advertised aquatic representation of Hell; the Ponte Carraia broke under the spectators' weight; hundreds were drowned, some of whom, observed the chronicler, prematurely experienced the torments which they had come to enjoy.

Nicholas passed on his path of peace to Prato and Pistoia. A web of intrigue was now spun round him. Corso having persuaded the men of Prato that the cardinal meant to restore the Ghibellines, they rose in fury. Nicholas fled for his life, pronounced an interdict, and commanded Florence to attack Prato; but the so-called crusade was a laughable fiasco, a march out and home again. Nicholas, not losing hope, brought to Florence representatives from its best White and Ghibelline families. They received an enthusiastic welcome, bystanders kissing the coat-of-arms of the Uberti as they passed. The magnates, now in great fear, were deeply divided. The Cavalcanti and other moderates supported Nicholas; the two rival extremists, Corso and Rosso, opposed him. Hostilities broke out with cries of "Death to the Magnates, Death to the People." The Ghibelline envoys escaped from Florence; and Nicholas on 9 June, when his neighbours prepared to shoot into his windows, also thought it time to leave, and joined Benedict at Perugia.

High time it was, for next day was perpetrated the worst crime that

Florence had yet witnessed. The Donati, Tosinghi, and Medici, by the aid of a disreputable priest, Neri degli Abati, threw an artificial, inextinguishable fire into their enemies' palaces, with the result that the very heart of Florence was burnt out, with some 1400 houses and warehouses. The Cavalcanti, losing heart, retired to their country estates. Thus Florence lost another of her wealthiest and most reasonable families; the Guelfic circle shrank once more. Though Corso and Rosso from illness or caution had not taken part, their nearest relatives were the criminals. The Lucchese troops had also aided the assailants. Benedict cited the communes of Florence and Lucca, with their chief magnates, to his court at Perugia. The chiefs arrived with a strong armed escort on 6 July. Next morning Benedict died of dysentery. A dish of figs, doctored as his friends believed, deprived the Papacy and Italy of a Pope who, by character and intense desire for peace, might have saved them from an infinity of woe.

While the Black leaders were still away, and the city still smouldered, the exiles attempted to surprise it. Time was precious, for Robert of Anjou's election as Captain of the Tuscan league was tightening its organisation. In Florence there was only a handful of troops; encouragement came from Whites and Ghibellines still in Florence, and from Blacks injured by the fire. Success depended upon punctually concerted action between the converging forces. A large body of exiles, Aretines, and Bolognese reached Lastra, about two miles from Florence, before the appointed day. Young Baschiera della Tosa, who commanded, was urged from within to attack quickly. Instead of waiting for night and bivouacking by the so-called Red City, the poor East-end quarter, where he would have popular sympathy and water for his horses, he made for the Porta Spada on the north-east with only a portion of his troops. 20 July was a blazing day. The exiles, crying "Peace," with olive garlands and white banners, entered by the postern with little resistance, for the prominent Guelfs were hiding in despair, and reached the Cathedral. They found, however, no aid forthcoming; men and horses were exhausted by the heat; a fire breaking out near the gate caused a panic, and every one ran. A promising enterprise was ruined. The force at Lastra broke up; the exiles from south and east, the Aretine and Bolognese reinforcements, and, above all, Tolosato degli Uberti with his fighting Pistoians, turned back without reaching the rendezvous. The last hope of the militant exiles was shattered.

War, accompanied by revolt in southern Tuscany, still continued. There could be no security for Florence while the Whites held Pistoia. In April 1305 arrived Robert as War Captain with picked Aragonese and Catalan horse, and serviceable mountaineer infantry under the Catalan condottiere Diego de Rat, who long played a leading part in Florentine battles and boudoirs. On 20 May Pistoia was surrounded by Lucchese and Florentines. After three days of grace no man or woman was allowed to pass the besiegers' lines without death, outrage, or mutilation. The siege once more brought Florence into collision with the Papacy. The Conclave of Perugia lasted till 5 June 1305. The ten Italian cardinals were still stirred by the outrage on Boniface; their six opponents were bent upon the full restoration of their Colonna colleagues, and, above all, on the favour of Philip IV, who did not spare his threats. Ultimately Napoleon Orsini by somewhat unsavoury means won the necessary majority for Bertrand de Got, Archbishop of Bordeaux, who had taken no active part against Boniface, and was technically a neutral English subject, though regarded by Philip with favour. The Gascon nobleman was crowned, by Philip's request, at Lyons, and took the name of Clement V. The procession was marred by the collapse of a wall, which killed John of Brittany, wounded Charles of Valois, and threw the Pope off his horse, causing a shock which perhaps permanently affected his health. The story of the Avignon Papacy is told elsewhere[1]; this chapter treats solely of its Italian interests. Clement had no wish to remove the Papacy from Italy, but his will was rarely compatible with his wish. He was not strong enough to break the toils of Philip, who was resolved to keep him within reach of royal pressure. Absent though he was, Clement clung closely to Italian interests. Napoleon Orsini naturally influenced his policy, and with him was soon associated Nicholas of Prato. Under their lead he continued Benedict's mediatory efforts in favour of Whites and Ghibellines, as being in Tuscany the weaker party. His envoys, on reaching Pistoia, ordered Robert to stop the intended assault; he obeyed and withdrew, but his troops remained. As no agreement was reached, his legates in November held an assembly at Siena, where they ordered the immediate raising of the siege. Siena and smaller towns withdrew their contingents, but Florence, Lucca, and Prato remained obdurate. Throughout the winter the blockade was tightened. Napoleon Orsini's appointment in February raised a flicker of hope, but only stimulated the besiegers' determination to have done with it. Florence had fostered discontent against the White government of Bologna, sympathetic with Pistoia. This culminated in a wild revolution on 1 March. Bologna joined in a treaty for the extermination of Whites and Ghibellines. Pistoia had no more hope; one day's food remained when the gallant town capitulated on 10 April. Pistoian territory was divided between Florence and Lucca with the exception of a strip a mile wide outside the walls, which were destroyed. The city was ruled by Florence and Lucca, who appointed Podestà and Captain.

The two chief Guelf republics were now at open war with the Pope, and lay under an interdict. Napoleon Orsini in May 1306 reached Bologna as Rector of Romagna. The populace turned savagely on him; he escaped with the loss of one chaplain and all his baggage to Forlì, where he organised the Romagnol Ghibellines, and then from Arezzo directed

---

[1] *Infra*, Chap. **x**.

operations against the Tuscan league. A clever flank march through the Casentino round the Florentine army in Aretine territory caused an undignified scamper home, after which Siena and smaller towns returned to papal obedience. Florence, fearing isolation, negotiated directly with Clement, who, early in 1309, relented and withdrew Orsini. A new era in papal and Florentine history was opening. The only Ghibellines who had benefited by four years of papal favour were the two Colonna cardinals, restored to their dignities, though under other titles.

During the preceding period, Florence, in spite of her conquest of Pistoia, had little stability at home. Benedict's death was a triumph for the extremist oligarchy. The nine Lesser Arts were subordinated to the twelve Greater; the twenty Companies lost their organisation; the Priors were the tools of the *Parte Guelfa*, dominated by magnates. The oligarchs, absorbed in foreign politics, class interests, and personal quarrels, had no care for ordinary justice. Financial depression became so deep that in 1307 a moratorium was granted for debts contracted since the entry of Charles of Valois. At length popular feeling asserted itself. The Companies were reconstituted as representatives, not merely of the Trades, but of all *popolani* between 15 and 70 years old; their Captains consulted with the Priors and the Council of 100 on all weighty matters. A new official, the Executor of Justice, had collateral powers with Podestà and Captain for protection against magnates, and general superintendence over all officials, especially the Podestà.

Consequent partly on this reform was the tragedy of Corso Donati. In personal prestige he stood high above his colleagues in the *Parte Guelfa*, but Rosso della Tosa, Betto Brunelleschi, Geri Spini, and Pazzino Pazzi combined to keep his adherents out of office. He had, perhaps, always aimed at monopoly of power; he made no secret of his hatred for the Ordinances of Justice. If ever he was to succeed, he must act quickly, for he was over fifty and disabled by gout. He engaged in a widespread conspiracy against the Constitution; he had promises from the old families, Buondelmonti, Bardi, and Frescobaldi, and from secondary houses such as Medici and Bordoni. Aid was expected from Arezzo and the country districts of Pistoia, Prato, and Lucca. On being sued for a debt due to Pazzino Pazzi, he fortified his quarter. The government was too quick for him; on 6 October the Companies surrounded the Donati houses; no aid came from the aristocrats across the river; he was no longer the darling of the mob. As a last hope Corso escaped from the back of his quarter; the Catalan horse soon came up with him; the Captain wished to spare his life, but he slipped from his horse, and was dragged, until he was speared. Dante has made his end famous through the ghost-lips of his brother Forese in *Purgatorio*, xxiv, 83, 84.

Corso's death was a blow to the reader of Florentine history, for he was the one picturesque figure in a somewhat drab decade. For Florence it was a blessing; there could be no peace while his restless ambition nursed discontent among the highest and lowest classes, both unrepresented in the government. He had the will and the courage to found a dynasty, but neither the character nor the clientèle. Dino Compagni, whose honourable career was wrecked by him in 1301, pays generous tribute to his capital enemy, to his knightly bearing, his personal beauty even in old age, his persuasive oratory, ceaseless political industry, and great Italian reputation. But, he concludes, Corso was unprincipled and full of wicked schemes; his life was dangerous, though the manner of his death was reprehensible.

Corso owed his death, as did Dante his exile, to the cowardice of his associates, who failed him at the crisis. Both, in their several ways, were fighting men with the courage of their convictions; but Florentine parties were riddled by personal jealousies, paralysed by physical timidity, relying on intrigue rather than on straightforward policy or arms. The best commentary on Florentine political life is given in Compagni's concluding chapters, shewing how Corso's rivals came to what are euphemistically termed middling ends. Rosso della Tosa, when out walking, made his first false step, fell over a dog, and died in convulsions under his doctor's tortures in July 1309, when over seventy-five. Betto Brunelleschi, hated for cornering corn in times of famine, was stabbed in his own house, while playing chess, by two of the Donati, and died in frenzy and unshriven, amid general rejoicing, in March 1311. Pazzino was in January 1312 murdered by a Cavalcanti, while fowling in the dry bed of the Arno. Geri Spini, more cautious and time-serving, was the sole survivor of the quartet which brought Corso to his doom. Astonishing is the contrast between these repeated scenes of bloodshed and the lofty standard of poetry and art in the Florence of Dante, Guido Cavalcanti, and Giotto, or between the horrors of Pistoia, meet den for robbers, as Dante wrote of Vanni Fucci, and the exquisite tenderness of Cino's verse.

It was nevertheless in these troublous years that the more modern Florence was coming into life, and the tragic end of the former leaders doubtless contributed to this. Davidsohn has well pointed out that, during the years of Henry VII's expedition, men of less family and personal prestige were pushing forwards, that in the Priorate names so familiar throughout the next two centuries constantly reappear, such as Acciaiuoli, Peruzzi, Ricci, Medici, Strozzi, and Soderini. The lead already lay with the bankers, who were international financiers, dealing with jewelry and commodities as much as with specie, opening commercial avenues, scrambling for concessions. Thus they had a working knowledge of foreign policy, which at Florence was mainly economic, and had the governmental experience of which the magnates had been deprived. Conscious of military weakness, they relied on skilful opportunism as to pushing or delaying, knew exactly how far bluff would carry them. These qualities in the critical years were to stand a severe test, not without success.

From the Treaty of Caltabellotta to Charles II's death on 8 May 1309, Neapolitan history is without striking incidents save for Robert's participation in the siege of Pistoia. The absence of the Gascon Pope from Rome relieved the dynasty from a potentially troublesome neighbour, though Clement's insistence on Robert's withdrawal from Pistoia proved that he was no mere cypher. The situation was difficult, because Clement was on ill terms with the Florentine government, whereas the Angevin king as traditional head of the Guelfs must support it. He must moreover propitiate both Pope and Florentines owing to huge indebtedness to both. Robert since 1306 had acted practically as his father's partner, and was thus no novice in administration when he was crowned by Clement V at Lyons. The succession came, however, at a peculiarly delicate moment, in consequence of the new election to the Empire. It seemed probable that Frederick would take advantage of this for a revision of the recent treaty. In Robert's kingdom, apart from chronic deficits and endemic disorder, there were fears of a rising against his faulty dynastic claim; Philip of Taranto was forced to suspend his eastern projects, and act as Robert's Captain-General in his absence. The Pope, moreover, dragged Robert into his Venetian quarrel, which not only seriously hampered Apulian commerce, but entailed feverish fortification of his eastern coast against possible attack from Venice. Most reluctantly also he was forced to take action against the Templars, whom his house had favoured as a valuable military asset. On the other hand, Robert was now peculiarly powerful in his county of Piedmont, and influential in Tuscany and Romagna; while in 1312 Clement made over to him the Vicariate of Ferrara. He would certainly be an all-important factor in the Emperor's Italian visit, in which for the first four years the history of his reign is merged.

The capture of William of Montferrat by the people of Alessandria had a profound effect on future Lombard history. He has been called one of the three forerunners of Lombard municipal despots, and of the three he was the most distinctive. Ezzelin and Pelavicini were rural feudal nobles, but each based his power upon a city, Verona and Cremona respectively. Montferrat was a considerable feudal State, much on a level with Savoy and Provence. William had close relations with royalty both in West and East, with England, Castile, and the Eastern Empire. His father-in-law Alfonso, when claimant for the Empire, had created him his Vicar in Italy. Dante has well portrayed him in the *Purgatorio* as seated at the feet of the great kings and looking up towards them, not quite a king himself, but worthy of their company. His power stretched from the Simplon to the Ligurian Apennines. Not only a great soldier but a subtle statesman, he confessed to buying more often than he conquered. Cities which fringed his territory, such as Vercelli and Alessandria, called him in to restore peace between factions and then converted temporary dictatorship into life or hereditary lordship. He had been chief of a Ghibelline league stretching from Turin to Verona, from Como to Genoa. The Visconti had appointed him Military Captain of Milan, but, at the time of his capture, he was an ardent supporter of the Torriani, aiming at Pavia, and drawing a ring of steel round Milan through Vercelli, Como, Lodi, and Crema. His end proved the difficulty of holding together an aggregate of Piedmontese and Lombard cities, each divided into factions. Alessandria had made him spontaneously hereditary lord, especially to protect the people from the magnates. At the instance of the wealthy city of Asti, which had long feared his predominance, the Alessandrians revolted, and on his arrival trapped and caged him in a loathsome dungeon, exhibiting him as a peep-show until his death in 1292. Doubtful whether they could have killed so great a man, they poured molten lead and lard down his throat, and drew samples of his blood to make sure that it was cold. His son John grew up into a fine fighting man, but never wielded his father's wide authority. On his death in 1305 the marquessate passed to Theodore Palaeologus, his sister's son. It is clear that William was totally distinct from the normal municipal despot. He never had an urban centre; he could not have established a highly centralised State. Municipalities welcomed the rule of a lord, far higher in rank than their own nobles, who had no prevailing interest in any single city. Yet this meant that in no single city had his power deep root; any party or popular squall could overthrow it. A feudal superiority was not in accord with the temper of the Italy of that day.

The death of the great marquess was a boon to the Visconti, and the archbishop's great-nephew Matteo was now in a position to enjoy it. For five years he had been annually elected Captain with power to alter the statutes; in 1292 he was reappointed for a term of five years. Shortly afterwards Otto made over the administration of the State, and in 1295 he died. The Visconti attributed high importance to imperial recognition. Adolf had appointed Matteo Vicar for Lombardy. After Otto's death he styled himself Vicar-General of the King of the Romans in Lombardy, Captain-General of the People of Milan. Albert of Austria confirmed his title as Vicar in 1299, while the Milanese Council extended his captaincy for another five years, empowering him to make peace and war. Matteo had taken full advantage of William's death to extend his influence westwards. He took Casale, a strong strategic point; Novara and Vercelli gave him the lordship for five years, and Alessandria the captaincy; he acted as guardian for William's heir. This was too fast to last; the young marquess, breaking from his guardian, took Casale and drove the Ghibellines from Vercelli and Novara. Pavia, now under the Count of Langosco, formed a league with Crema, Cremona, and Bergamo, backed by Azzo VIII of Ferrara. Matteo received aid from Brescia, Parma, Piacenza, and Bologna, and turned the scale by detaching Azzo.

The year 1300 was the climax. He was now among the greatest of North Italian chiefs; he married a daughter to Alboino della Scala, and gave a Court day, celebrated throughout Italy, in honour of his son Galeazzo's marriage with Beatrice d'Este, Azzo's sister, and widow of Nino Visconti, Judge of Gallura in Sardinia. Yet Matteo's position was none too secure either within or without. Among his own relatives there was discontent at his monopoly of power; some of the nobles, the chief source of his authority, were malcontent; the people groaned under the expense of wars, which they attributed to Galeazzo's pugnacity. Two late allies, Filippone Langosco of Pavia and Alberto Scotto of Piacenza, disappointed suitors for Visconti marriages, formed a fresh combination against Matteo, who found himself confronted by overwhelming odds. Scotto, professedly an arbitrator, insisted on his resignation, and the return of the Torriani as private citizens. Matteo retired to Nogarola on the Mantuan frontier; Galeazzo was reduced to living on his brother-in-law's bounty. The splendour of his marriage, followed by the suddenness of his fall, formed a literary commonplace on the instability of fortune: Dante, in the interval before the Visconti revival, might naturally write that the Viper of Milan would not make so fine a sepulchre for Beatrice d'Este as the Cock of Gallura. Ultimately Beatrice had both cock and viper sculptured on her tomb.

At Milan the populace expelled the chief Ghibelline partisans and burnt their houses; this gave the Torriani, though nominally private citizens, control over elections and foreign policy. The normal city government was ill-fitted to hold together other independent communes, whose only bond to Milan consisted in the rule of Guelfic families. Guido, now head of the house, was elected Captain for one year in 1307. At its close the Councils and the representatives of the Trades, numbering together some three thousand, unanimously elected him Captain of the People for life, with power to alter statutes. This was the *tyrannis* in form, and Guido took up his residence in the *Broletto Vecchio*, a symbol that he was the personification of the government. He was now extremely strong. Milan was protected by a ring of Guelfic cities. To the west, Novara, Vercelli, and Alessandria were under allied families, backed by the house of Anjou in Piedmont. Southwards, Pavia was ruled by Langosco, head of the noble party, always allied to the popular Guelfic party at Milan. Eastwards, Lodi, Brescia, and Cremona were friendly, though in the two latter the Guelfs were dangerously divided. The Visconti had been ruined and dispersed. In Italy, however, the individual ruler was confronted by his family, which resented a monopoly of power. Guido's cousin was elected to the archbishopric, and he, like Otto Visconti, was ambitious to revive the temporal authority of the see, and to lead the house. Other relatives concurred and were arrested. When Henry VII reached Italy, the archbishop was kept out of his see, and his brothers were imprisoned. Yet Guido, with his body-guard of 1000 and a force of 10,000 at his disposal, might well have formed a permanent dynasty. His overthrow resulted from the accidents of the imperial visit.

The power enjoyed by the Scaligeri at Verona was voluntarily conferred by the popular party, but was absolute in every department of government. Their sway had been ushered in by no display of military force; the hereditary principle was established almost as a matter of course. It was party government in the strictest sense. It was usually the aim of the tyrant to reconcile party factions, to restore exiles. The Scaligeri believed that their own power and internal peace could only be preserved by a continuous and rigorous system of party government. From the first there were stringent laws against cries for reconciliation. If a citizen cried " Peace, Peace," it was the surest sign of the wish to raise a riot. Under Can Grande such a cry was punishable by death; a gentleman was beheaded, a commoner hanged, a lady had the privilege of being burnt, for it was ungentlemanly to touch a lady. The long wars with Padua were partly a cause, and partly a result of this. The enmity dated long before the age of the Scaligeri, but henceforth it was hostility, not only of neighbourhood but of principle, for Padua represented the cause of State republicanism, Verona that of State monarchy. Alberto della Scala was only once threatened within the city. The conspiracy of 1299 was fiercely suppressed, and thenceforward there was no more trouble. It was easier to exclude opposition from the city than from Verona's crown of castles, and yet she could never be safe if exiles lodged themselves therein. From 1277 provision was made that seven of the strongest should be in the hands of Alberto himself. The municipal despot was thus reaping the succession of the feudal lords; he was developing the urban *tyrannis* into a territorial principality.

There remained the questions of external expansion and diplomatic position. For the latter the magnificent Court days, for which Verona became famous, were important, and were generally held in honour of foreign marriages. Alberto initiated such alliances in 1289 by the marriage of his daughter Costanza with Obizzo II of Ferrara, his former enemy. In 1291 his son Bartholomew married the daughter of Conrad of Antioch, grandson of the Emperor Frederick II, while her sister was later married to Can Grande. Alboino, his second son, cemented the Milanese alliance by his wedding with Catherine, daughter of Matteo Visconti. Alberto's reign was peaceful, as was that of Bartholomew, who succeeded in 1301 and reigned till March 1304. Alboino was no soldier, but was engaged in almost chronic war against Azzo VIII until his death in January 1310. His constant allies were Ghiberto da Correggio and the Bonaccolsi of Mantua, Bologna also taking part until the Guelfic revolution of 1306. Friendly treaties were made with Venice, and the Scaligeri took her side in the Ferrarese Succession War against Clement V. The closest *entente* was with the Bonaccolsi, amounting almost to a protectorate. Both Alberto and Can Grande effected changes in the dynasty on any symptom of dangerous independence. Co-operation with Mantua was essential for securing the whole course of the Mincio, and for the protection of the Po, in the contests with Padua and Ferrara. Can Grande was associated with Alboino in the government, probably in 1308. Both served Henry VII in the siege of Brescia, where Alboino caught the fever, of which he died on 29 November 1311.

Pietro Gradenigo, who was to leave his mark upon Venetian history for all time, succeeded Dandolo under gloomy auspices. After the doge's funeral on 2 November 1289, the populace, reviving a custom long abandoned, yelled for the election of Giacomo Tiepolo, nephew of one doge and grandson of another. This very hint at an hereditary principality perhaps decided the ruling aristocracy to resist popular pressure. Choice fell upon Gradenigo, who was only thirty-eight, but was already so unpopular that his election was published amid dead silence. He was soon involved in constitutional struggles and in foreign war. The storming of Acre in May 1291, followed by the fall of Tyre and Sidon, was a grievous blow to Venetian commerce in Syria and Palestine. In this year also the truce with Genoa expired. Galata, occupied by favour of the Greek Emperor, gave the Genoese a strong base for the conversion of the Black Sea into a commercial *mare clausum*. They controlled Trebizond, had a flourishing new colony at Kaffa, and from Azov commanded the trade of the Don. The war which now began extended from Kaffa to Genoa. The first great fight was at Laiazzo on the coast of Armenia (Cilicia) in the autumn of 1294. The Genoese galleys lashed and planked together formed a nautical laager in the harbour. The Venetians, scorning the use of fire-ships, bore down with wind abaft, lost their formation, and retired after their admiral was killed and 25 ships out of 68 were sunk.

Nearly four years of incessant warfare passed before another decisive battle. The Venetians stormed Kaffa, taking enormous booty; the Genoese ravaged Crete. In Constantinople itself the Genoese, abetted by Andronicus, slew the Venetians and burnt their banks. The Emperor imprisoned the survivors, even the Venetian commissioner, an outrage on diplomatic inviolability not to be overlooked. Ruggero Morosini with a strong fleet anchored off the imperial palace and, with a large indemnity and a host of Genoese prisoners, returned to Venice. In 1298 fortunes changed. A Genoese fleet of 85 galleys reached Dalmatian waters. Andrea Dandolo with 95 galleys met it off the island of Curzola, and fought the great battle of the war on 8 September. The Venetian fleet, after some success, got out of hand, and was struck in flank by the Genoese reserve squadron, which had stood out to sea and came down the wind on the unsuspecting foe. Only a few galleys escaped from the rocks or fire to tell the tale at Venice. It is said that 9000 men were killed or wounded, while 5000 were carried off to Genoa to join the Pisan captives taken at Meloria thirteen years before. The admiral, to avoid this fate, dashed his head against a mast. Misfortune seems stimulating to men of letters; but for his exile Dante would never have written the *Commedia*, while to a Genoese prison we owe the *Travels* of Marco Polo.

The Genoese fleet had been too roughly handled to sail for the lagoons. With marvellous courage Venice raised another fleet of 100 galleys, filling the gaps among her cross-bowmen with Catalan mercenaries. On either side small squadrons shewed much enterprise; a Genoese squadron caused a fright by appearing off Malamocco, and Domenico Schiavo returned the visit, and coined money, a symbol of sovereignty, in the very port of Genoa. In May 1299 Matteo Visconti negotiated a peace, and in October 1302 Andronicus was reduced to signing a truce by the sight of his subjects being flogged by the boatswains of 25 Venetian galleys under the walls of Constantinople.

In these very years, when the resources of Venice were strained to the uttermost, by the closing of her Great Council a fundamental change in her constitution, which was for centuries to be the world's admiration, was bloodlessly carried out. The Venetian sense for governance stands in marked contrast to the Genoese passion for faction, which neutralised the advantage gained by naval victories. At Venice the sea called forth from all classes the patriotism which might well have been dissipated by political quarrels. No sacrifices were grudged to retain the Queenship of the Adriatic. It was otherwise when these were demanded for territorial expansion.

Peace at sea was followed by a short war with Padua over the ever-recurring question of the neighbouring salt-pans, on which Venice was peculiarly sensitive. This was arranged, and preparations were being made for an attack on the Greek Empire in concert with Charles of Valois, when the succession to Ferrara absorbed her whole attention, involving her in a war with the Papacy, a forecast of the dangerous combination formed against her by the League of Cambrai. The death of Azzo VIII on 31 January 1308 was certain to intensify the confusion long endemic in eastern Lombardy and Romagna. His fortunes had waned with the revolt of his imperial fiefs, Modena and Reggio, in 1306, but expulsion of the Whites, his bitterest enemies, from Bologna brought relief. Aided by the victorious Blacks, the Florentines, and Naples, he was conducting a vigorous offensive when he died. He left the succession to Folco, legitimate son of his bastard Fresco, who was appointed guardian during the minority. His brothers Francesco and Aldobrandino had long claimed a share of Obizzo's inheritance; the former with Aldobrandino's sons now appealed against the will to Azzo's late enemies, but Fresco with the stronger support of Venice and Bologna assumed the government. Then in April fell the bolt from the Avignon blue. Clement declared Ferrara to be under the Pope's direct government, and exhorted her to throw off the tyrant's adulterine yoke and enjoy the blessings of papal rule. Of the Pope's suzerainty there could be no doubt, but papal charters more than once recognised the right of illegitimate succession; to cancel the authority which the Estensi had exercised for nearly a century under papal sanction was an audacity which would have startled the strongest Italian Pope. But Clement's weakness in Italy at this moment was probably the very motive for his decision; Ferrara should be the base from which to re-establish his authority. In May the papal standard was hoisted at Ravenna. Ferrarese exiles flocked to it with Francesco; the Della Torre of Milan gave ready aid, Bologna was won by the withdrawal of Napoleon Orsini's interdict. Meanwhile Gradenigo threw himself eagerly into the fray; he stood for a forward mainland policy, for the revival of former pre-eminence in Ferrara, which had left precious privileges behind it.

Fresco, now faced by popular revolt, retired to the Castle of Tedaldo, which with its bridge and fortified bridge-head commanded the town and the Po di Ferrara, which then skirted the southern walls and joined the Po di Venezia at Stellata. In October, Fresco sold his claims for a Venetian pension, and a Venetian army took over the fortress and city. The Pope would hear of no diplomatic compromise, but hostilities were not active until the end of March 1309. The peace party in Venice, headed by the Tiepoli, Badoeri, and Querini, was gaining ground, styling itself the *Pars guelfa sive ecclesiastica*. Gradenigo was empowered to send reinforcements to Ferrara, while the opposition carried the dispatch of envoys to Clement. They arrived just too late. On Good Friday, 27 March, a Bull was issued depriving Venice of all privileges of a Christian State, empowering the seizure of Venetian property and persons, the latter to be sold as slaves, the lands to be vested in the Papacy, the movables to reward the captors. To shew that he was in earnest, Clement appointed his nephew Arnaud de Pélagrue legate for North and Central Italy. Arnaud, preaching a crusade, levied troops from Guelfs and Ghibellines, bishops and cities. Appeals were made to all European powers; the Emperor supported the Pope, Philip IV preferred conciliation.

On 10 April a rising in Ferrara forced the Podestà, Giovanni Soranzo, to concentrate his forces in the castle, whence ineffectual attempts were made to seize or flood the town. Meanwhile Francesco from without was harassing the besiegers. He destroyed a relieving fleet at Francolino, where the Po di Venezia narrowed, built a bridge here and another below Ferrara. A large fleet from Venice attempted to prevent the operations at Francolino but was defeated after three days' battle. Tedaldo now was completely isolated, but Ferrara itself was in a desperate condition. The papal army was too small to storm the castle, North Italy was war-weary, Pélagrue's recruiting campaign was failing. If the Venetians could hold out till September, the autumn floods would enable their ships to operate. The legate made the desperate decision to storm Tedaldo; on 26 August the bridge and bridge-head were taken, and the fleet capitulated; on the 28th Tedaldo fell. Venice lost 200 ships and some 6000 men. Not a man was spared, save a few who were sent blinded into Venice. Abroad her commerce was destroyed, her ships taken, their crews sold for slaves, her colonies were restive or in revolt. Venice sued for peace through the mediation of Philip IV. This was granted on not ungenerous terms on 15 June 1310.

Venice had signally failed in her first attempt to annex a large mainland State. She turned her eyes away from Ferrara until 1482, when she failed again. Ferrara never became part of the Venetian State. It is strange that an alien Pope, reputed to be powerless in Italy, should be the first to make his sovereignty direct and real. His success was short, but Ferrara remained the constant aim of the Papacy until, in the last years of the sixteenth century, another Clement annexed it at the expense of yet another legitimate son of another bastard of the house of Este.

The disastrous Ferrarese war had as its sequel a conspiracy, which might have ruined Venetian stability for all time. Family feuds were, as in all cities, not unusual, but very rarely were permitted to endanger the public peace, and in this Venice stood alone. Genuine disagreement both in home and foreign policy there may well have been, but personal and family feeling caused the armed revolt of one group among the chief houses against Gradenigo and another group comprising his supporters. Parties were fiercely divided throughout the war, fighting even on the Great Council benches. It was ominous that the opposition introduced the terms Guelf and Ghibelline, which ordinarily have no meaning in Venetian history. There was, indeed, an undercurrent of popular discontent. Exclusion from the Council was a grievance with those who had intermittently attended it. The populace had howled for war and insulted papal envoys, but war had entailed heavy taxation, and, latterly, terrible sacrifice of life. After a peace, good or bad, the government which conducted the war becomes unpopular.

The chief conspirators were Bajamonte Tiepolo and Mario Querini, his father-in-law, both actuated by personal grievances. The former was a showy young noble, acclaimed by the lower classes as *il gran cavaliere*, a poor Venetian counterpart of Corso Donati, *il barone*. He had been fined for corrupt exaction in his Morean government, and had since sulked in his Villa Marocco on the mainland. Querini had been insulted by reflections on his courage in the surrender of Castel Tedaldo. A third chief, Badoero Badoer, was also a mainland proprietor. They represented the movement as purely patriotic, directed against the tyrant doge in favour of the disfranchised classes. The attack was fixed for the feast of San Vito, 15 June. Tiepolo and Querini collected their forces across the Rialto on the previous evening. Badoer with troops levied in Paduan territory was to cross from the mainland in support. During the night information of the plot reached the government. Gradenigo, aided by the Dandoli and Giustiniani, occupied the Piazza San Marco. Morning opened with a terrific gale and thunderstorm, which damped any hope of a popular rising. Badoer, unable to start, was captured with his force by the more weatherproof Podestà of Chioggia. Tiepolo, advancing by the Merceria, was held up at the church of San Giuliano. A woman threw down a mortar on the head of his standard-bearer, and the banner with its scroll of Liberty fell. The *gran cavaliere* fled back over the Rialto bridge, and barricaded his quarter. Querini fared even worse; in the Campo San Luca he was attacked and killed by men armed by the School of Charity and the Gild of Painters. Tiepolo was persuaded to capitulate on terms. The conspiracy had ignominiously failed. Badoer, taken in arms, was executed. Tiepolo and his chief associates were exiled for short terms. There was no general proscription as was usual elsewhere. Several palaces were pulled down, the first time that such a common penalty had been inflicted at Venice. Nevertheless the government had had a fright and meant to take no risks. The most stringent measures were taken to guard the canals, the doge's palace, and the piazza against further trouble.

Of all defensive measures the most important was the institution of the celebrated Ten. No one probably foresaw its unique history. It was a *balia*, an executive committee, formed at a crisis for a definite purpose, such as was often created by a score of cities. The object was to strengthen the heads of the high court, the *Quarantia*. Ten citizens were nominated by the electoral section of the Great Council and ten by the Doge, his Councillors, and the chiefs of the *Quarantia*. From these the Great Council elected ten. The office was renewed every two months until 1314, when it was established for five years, the members, however, retiring each Michaelmas and being ineligible for re-election. Gradenigo did not long survive the foundation of this memorable institution. He died on 13 August 1311. Venice, still nursing her wounds, was unable to take part in the war already raging.

The election of Henry of Luxemburg on 27 November 1308 as successor to the murdered Albert of Austria might in itself have had little influence upon Italian history. Albert had deliberately decided that his duty lay in Germany; Henry's own first acts had been to suppress disorder in western Germany, and by his son's marriage to secure a territorial power in Bohemia comparable to the eastern possessions of the Habsburgs. The Italian question was introduced by the candidature of Charles of Valois, supported by the whole weight of the French Crown. Charles had had the closest connexion with Naples and with Florence, but above all his election would rivet the chain of Philip IV upon Clement V, and through him upon papal possessions and pretensions in Italy. Charles would be the cat's-paw for further aggression upon Italy, already incurably wounded by the Pope's detention in France. Clement was determined not to strengthen French influence in Italy, and desired the creation of a counterpoise. While making vague promises to Philip, he delayed any definite steps until after the election; he probably encouraged Henry's brother, the Archbishop of Trèves, to win the other Electors for Henry. He would gladly increase Robert's power on the Franco-imperial border-land by the cession of the Arelate, which Henry might be willing to cede, as yet another counterpoise to Philip. Henry did, indeed, from the first try to win Robert by proposals for his daughter's marriage to Robert's son.

Henry was not free for an advance on Italy until the late autumn of 1310, and meanwhile his court was swarming with Ghibelline exiles and Guelf spies. His position when he crossed the Mont Cenis was none too favourable. His mission to Italy had been badly received in Florence and Bologna, though welcomed by Arezzo and the Tuscan Ghibelline gentry. Philip had refused to be bound by any definite treaty. Clement had appointed Robert Count of Romagna, which, in the event of the Angevin's hostility, would bar the southward march through the Emilia, where Henry might expect substantial support. Florence, with Robert's personal aid, was feverishly completing her third line of walls, while Bologna helped to defend the Apennine passes, especially that down the Magra valley to Sarzana. Robert had visited Siena to repress awakened Ghibel-line volitions. Nevertheless the adventure opened well. In Piedmont Amadeus V, Count of Savoy, and his nephews Louis and Philip gave him a warm welcome; he courteously refused homage from Alessandria and Asti, as they were fiefs of Robert, who promised to do fealty for them. At Turin he received the Guelf despots of Vercelli, Pavia, and Lodi, who stood next to Guido della Torre in importance. The dispossessed Ghibelline tyrant of Vercelli complained that he had suffered ruin for the Emperor's party. Henry replied that he had no party in Lombardy, that he had come for no party but for the whole. This speech pleased the Guelf leaders, who pressed him to make no changes until he reached Milan. Henry refused, and, as he proceeded, recalled exiles of either party, and established his Vicars in the cities. He meant to be ruler and shewed his meaning. At Asti arrived Matteo Visconti after an adventurous journey, mostly by night, from the Veronese frontier, and hither also came the Archbishop Cassone della Torre to beg for the release of his brothers from Guido's prison. Milan was reached without opposition on 23 December 1310.

Guido della Torre, fierce and irresolute, hysterical and sulky by turns, had not dared resist Henry as an enemy, nor was willing to welcome him as lord. Behind the crowd of citizens, ordered to meet Henry without arms, he rode with his banner flying. When this had been rolled in the mud by the German guards, he dismounted, kissed his lord's feet, and was graciously received. The first task was to reconcile Torriani with Visconti, and Guido with his cousins. This successfully performed, Henry on the Epiphany 1311 received the Iron Crown, or rather an impromptu imita-tion, Guido having privily pawned the original to a Jew. In the Council a donative to the Emperor and Empress was debated; Guido, whether or no with sinister motives, outbid Matteo. The tax of 100,000 florins was burdensome to all classes, and Henry's demand that a hundred nobles, picked equally from both parties, should accompany him to Rome dismayed the upper class. Trouble was brewing; there were suspicious meetings of Galeazzo Visconti and Franceschino della Torre, gatherings of armed men, cries of "Death to the Germans; there is peace between the lord Guido and the lord Matteo." On a search for arms Matteo was found sitting blandly innocent in his porch, and delayed the inquisitors with wine; the Della Torre palace was full of armed confusion. A skirmish between Germans and Torriani developed into hard street-fighting, in which the Visconti joined the strangers. The Torriani chiefs escaped with some difficulty; Matteo and Galeazzo were also exiled, but soon recalled. When Henry left North Italy for Rome, he created Matteo imperial Vicar for life. This was the formal beginning of Italy's greatest dynasty. Elsewhere also Henry replaced his temporary vicariates by selling the office to the ruling lords, the Scaligeri at Verona, Bonaccolsi at Mantua, Da Camino at Treviso, and Ghiberto da Correggio at Parma. By these means Henry hoped to receive reliable contingents, and, above all, to finance his campaign, for the chests of gold, upon which his officials had proudly sat during the journey, were a mere fleabite in Italy.

Meanwhile Guido della Torre and the Florentines had set revolt ablaze between the Adda and the Oglio. Lodi, indeed, gave in without a struggle. At Cremona the Guelfs, the Cappelletti of Dante's famous line, had long become divided. The head of the extremists, Cavalcabò, fled, leaving his rival Amati to make terms. These were extremely harsh, and only a petition from the Empress caused Henry to spare the great *campanile*, the Torrazzo, still the glory of Cremona. Severity was ill-timed, for it determined the desperate defence of Brescia, where on Henry's orders the Guelfs had been restored. One of these, Tebaldo Brusati, saved from ruin and knighted by Henry, headed the revolt to his own undoing, for, captured on a reconnaissance, he was sewn in the skin of an ox, dragged round the city walls, executed and quartered; his remains were exposed to intimidate the besieged. Henry's army was now large, for he had been reinforced from the Empire, while Alboino and Can Grande della Scala rendered admirable service. Brescia, however, is traditionally difficult either to storm or blockade. The siege dragged on from May to November; pestilence ravaged both besieged and besiegers; among Henry's losses was that of his gallant young brother Waleran. At length the papal envoys arranged a surrender on generous terms; Henry was free for a move on Rome.

From Brescia the imperial army marched to Genoa by Pavia. The Genoese gave Henry a warm reception, though, like Venice, they had failed to do homage; for these States, thought Nicholas of Botrinto, a papal envoy, regarded themselves as a fifth element, obeying neither God nor man, Pope nor Emperor. Here the two predominant Ghibelline families had quarrelled, and the Doria had expelled the Spinola, whom Henry now succeeded in reconciling. Nevertheless he outstayed his welcome. The expense of his court and his financial demands were onerous, while the independent, seafaring race resented his suppression of a recent popular constitution comprising both nobles and commons. Delay was largely due to the marriage negotiations with Robert, which were so far advanced that an offer from Frederick of Sicily of his son's hand for Henry's daughter was refused. Robert had begun his double game, for Henry heard that his brother, John of Gravina, reaching Rome with 400 horse, had won the Orsini and had tried to bribe the Colonna. He made the lame excuse that John was sent to represent him at the corona-tion, from which he himself would be unavoidably absent. Louis of Savoy, Vicar of Rome, was sent back thither at full speed, but failed to get general acceptance, and was barred from the Capitol. At Genoa the Empress died, an irremediable loss. Virtuous to sanctity, in Compagni's words a servant to Christ's poor, with a level head and an instinct for mercy and moderation, she was a valuable asset to the imperial cause at a time when tempers were sorely tried.

A Pisan fleet brought Henry to their city, enabling him to turn the defensive positions elaborated by Florence, Lucca, and Parma. Hence, after a stay of two months, he had a clear course to Rome. The Sienese government, endangered by a large Ghibelline populace, dared not oppose his march through the Maremma. He went to Rome with Clement's full approval, and thus it was unlikely that he would find resistance in papal cities such as Grosseto and Viterbo. Before entering Rome, however, he had to force the Ponte Molle under fire from Gravina's cross-bowmen. Henry had reached his goal, but found Rome partly occupied by a hostile Neapolitan force, while Central and Northern Italy were ablaze behind him. The focus of disturbance was still Florence, which stiffened the backbone of the faltering Tuscan league, reinforced the attacks of Bologna on the Ghibelline Romagnols, rekindled revolt at Cremona and Lodi, and worked upon the traditional republicanism of Padua, which had momentarily wavered before Henry's eloquent pro-fessions of peace and justice. Langosco, imprisoning his Ghibelline rival Beccaria, was again sole lord of Pavia. Ghiberto da Correggio betrayed his oath of fealty for Parma, and closed the Emilian Way and the Taro-Magra route into Tuscany. Henry's own Vicar, Philip of Savoy, had turned Asti and Vercelli against him. Imola, Faenza, and Forlì, long headquarters of Romagnol Ghibellinism, had fallen to Robert's Vicar, who had trapped its gallant leader, Scarpetta Ordelaffi, and thrown down the walls of Forlì, which no longer lay, as in Dante's words, under the claw of the green lion. Henry thus lost control with the Visconti and Scaligeri; Can Grande had hurried from Genoa to secure the inheritance of Alboino, who never recovered the health lost at Brescia. Werner of Homburg, one of the best imperial generals, was dispatched to counteract reverses in North Italy. In Rome Henry was only reinforced by the Colonna, the fighting nobility of Tuscany, and the small papal towns of Todi and Narni. Against him were Gravina with regular troops, the Orsini who commanded the northern approaches to Rome and half the city, while Florence poured in her Catalan mercenaries, her volunteer cavalry, and large numbers of foot; the Tuscan league followed suit to a less degree, but Perugia threw her whole considerable weight into the fray. Fighting became brisk. The imperialists recovered the Capitol, drove the Guelfs back to the west of the Corso, but were decisively beaten in attempting to force a passage across the bridge of Sant' Angelo. The coronation could not thus be held in St Peter's under the Pope's instructions to the Cardinals Nicholas of Prato, Luca Fieschi, and Arnaud Faugères. Delay might have been indefinite, had not the populace forced the legates to crown the Emperor in the Lateran. On 29 June Nicholas set the crown on Henry's head; the Emperor thrice waved his sword before placing it on his shield upon the altar, a symbol that with shield and sword he would defend the Church. But the stately open-air banquet which followed was disturbed by archers from the Aventine, and the guests were driven under cover.

Throughout the Roman struggle the determining political factors were the two least determinate of rulers, Robert of Anjou and Clement V. Since the summer of 1310 Robert had been tempted by an imperial marriage for his heir, with the Arelate as a dower, with the vicariate of Tuscany and Lombardy. On the other hand, Florence importuned him to wield the full power of the Tuscan league in opposing Henry's advance. As usual, he evaded a decision by not answering his letters. The Florentines in dismay and alarm dubbed him *Monna Berta*, old Mrs So-and-So. Negotiations for the marriage seemed nearly complete, when in March 1312 Henry sent envoys from Pisa to settle definitive terms. The reply, received at Rome, was definite to stupefaction. Robert's heir, Charles, should bear a royal title; his heirs should succeed to the kingdom of Sicily; he should be Vicar of Tuscany for life, the several cities paying a proportionate tribute to the Emperor and electing their own officials subject to confirmation by the Vicar; in Lombardy for ten years the Emperor's Vicar should be one acceptable to Robert; the contracting powers should jointly appoint an Admiral; they should reconcile Orsini and Colonna, and Henry should leave Rome four days after coronation. It is doubtful whether Robert made these proposals merely to be refused. The breach was not complete until Henry's envoy to Gravina brought the reply that he had indeed come to Rome in honour of the coronation, but had since received orders to oppose Henry's entrance to Rome, and, above all, to St Peter's. Such was the position as between Emperor and king at the time of the coronation.

Meanwhile Clement's attitude had changed. He had been whole-hearted in support of Henry's schemes for Italian peace, declaring that it would be a sin not to second them. His cardinals had promoted the treaty with

Brescia, so essential to Henry's progress; their head, Nicholas of Prato, was devoted to the imperial cause. The Council of Vienne was probably responsible for Clement's change of policy. Charles of Valois, Philip's three sons, with Plaisians and Marigny, accused him of preparing bulls commanding John of Gravina to offer no opposition to Henry's coronation; they told him that no treaty would prevent Philip from defending the French blood that flowed in Robert's veins, and demanded suppression of the bulls. Clement was suffering from internal pains and nervous exhaustion; he always disliked responsibility; he felt unequal to altercation with one who had him at his mercy. He was moreover sensitive as to papal rights in Italy; he might well fear that an attack on Naples would destroy his suzerainty, for he was probably aware of Henry's negotiations with Frederick of Sicily. Nevertheless his first overt act was a Bull of 19 June proclaiming a year's truce between Henry and Robert, and demanding an explanation of Henry's hostility.

Henry received the bull at Tivoli with high indignation; Clement had perhaps not realised that it would be so offensive. The imperial lawyers were summoned to pronounce on the question whether the Pope could impose a truce between Emperor and vassal. Henry doubtless had imperial ideals, but in practice he had been accustomed to the drastic legalism of Philip IV. The lawyers' reply was naturally in the negative. Before the delivery of the bull, the breach with Robert had become inevitable, for on 4 July the Emperor nominated Henry of Flanders as his proctor to treat of his daughter's marriage with Frederick's son, to prepare a perpetual alliance against all powers except the Pope, France, and Avignon. Robert was declared guilty of high treason, and Frederick appointed Admiral of the Holy Roman Empire. This was the long-deferred conclusion of tentative negotiations. Late in 1311 Henry had told Frederick that the Sicilian marriage was impossible, as the Pope was bent upon the Angevin match, the negotiations for which were far advanced. A general treaty was indeed signed in the spring of 1312. This had redoubled Robert's temperamental irresolution; he was pressed by Florence to attack Henry in Rome, but he feared the certainty of an attack by Frederick on Naples, and the rumours of an invasion by John of Bohemia and Carobert of Hungary. So he marched his troops out of Naples, but halted them at Aversa, to the dismay of Florence. Robert would gladly have accepted the papal truce, but was forced to insist on the inclusion of his Guelfic allies, which Clement refused. Nor probably would the Guelfic league have accepted, though two most influential Blacks, Geri Spini and Pino della Tosa, sent an emissary to Tivoli to discuss terms of peace.

On 19 August 1312 Henry left Tivoli on his march for Florence, with his army much depleted. The Tuscan Ghibellines and the levies of Spoleto, Narni, and Todi marched home; northern feudatories such as Rudolf of Bavaria and Louis of Savoy feared a Roman autumn. From Viterbo he turned aside with characteristic unwisdom to pay a grateful visit to Todi and inflict a revengeful raid upon Perugia. At Arezzo, under its bishop Guido Tarlati, he had an enthusiastic welcome and large reinforcements of Tuscan and Romagnol Ghibellines. With little resistance Incisa was reached; here all the best Florentine troops defended the walls and the bridge which spanned the Arno, there unfordable. Henry with his cavalry only, by a turning movement over country reputed impossible for horsemen, placed himself on the main road, south of the Arno, in the Florentine rear. After a sharp fight, in which Henry and his brother Baldwin of Trèves took valorous part, the Florentines fled by the secondary northern road. Henry raced them home by the southern bank, and crossing to the east of Florence established headquarters at San Salvi on 19 September. Surprise was his only chance; the siege was a hopeless effort. The garrison alone was double his own force; reinforcements and supplies could pour in from north, west, and south; his troops had burnt bare the Florentine territory behind them; autumn rains flooded the Arno and made supplies from Arezzo precarious. Henry, shattered by fever, burnt his camp, and crossed the swollen river on the night of 30–31 October. With any active courage the enemy might have destroyed him.

Henceforth, until Henry's arrival at Pisa on 10 March 1313, the campaign straggled over the valleys of the Greve and Elsa. The latter had strategic importance, for it facilitated his communications with Pisa and hampered those of Florence with Siena, Volterra, and Poggibonsi. The latter town suffered for its stalwart Guelfism by destruction and the erection of a rival, named Monte Imperiale, across the deep valley. The quarrel between Henry and Robert, and the conflict of principle between Emperor and Pope, here reached their climax. On 26 April Robert was declared guilty of high treason. Henry's edict is the highest assertion of the universality of Empire, of the divine command that every soul should be subject to the Roman Emperor; Naples was not excluded by virtue of papal suzerainty, for "Regnum Siciliae et specialiter insula Siciliae sicut et ceterae provinciae sunt de imperio, totus enim mundus imperatoris est." Clement, under pressure from Philip IV, issued the Bull of 13 June, threatening with excommunication all who should attack the kingdom of Naples. Henry's comment was: "If God is with us, neither Pope nor Church can destroy us, and God we have not injured."

The march on Rome and Naples was now decided. Baldwin went to Trèves to levy troops; pressing messages were sent to John of Bohemia, the German princes and bishops, the Lombard States, and Venice and Genoa. Homburg and Montferrat won a useful victory over Robert's seneschal near Alessandria. To break the spirit of Lucca, Henry of Flanders made a brilliant capture of Pietrasanta, in the face of Diego de Rat and all his Florentine Catalans. The Ghibelline Malaspina captured the yet more important Sarzana. The object was to clear the coast road for forces coming southward by the Magra valley; a small

Veronese and Mantuan force did indeed attempt the dangerous pass, but without success. The German reinforcements came in slowly; Baldwin, John of Bohemia, and Leopold of Austria arrived too late. Yet, when Henry started on 8 August, he had a useful mobile force of 2500 Luxemburg and German horse and 1500 Tuscan and Romagnol Ghibellines. He approached the gates of Siena in hope of a rising by gentry and populace against the bourgeois government, but the Nine were once more too strong. He was now desperately ill but would give himself no rest. Buonconvento was reached on 21 August, and there on 24 August he died. The rumours of his being poisoned in the Sacrament by his confessor Bernardino of Montepulciano caused persecution of Dominicans in Italy and Germany, but were conclusively disproved.

Such was the melancholy end of the great adventure. Failure was probably inevitable from the first. Italy had long outgrown an imperial system; its re-establishment would have endangered the interests of both parties. The aim of government, as Dante wrote, was Peace, and the path to it was Justice; but Henry was crying Peace where there was no peace, and Justice was unknown in Italy, outside Venice, for centuries to come. A permanent monarchy was a dream, yet Henry might have succeeded in his immediate objects, the recognition of his rights in Rome and the expulsion of the Angevin from Naples, where feudalism was still a living force; he had better chances than the Aragonese of the next century. The squadrons of Frederick, of Genoa and Pisa, perhaps even of Venice, would have swept Robert's galleys off the seas. Robert had long feared for his southern ports; his nobles had refused to serve outside their country, many were now on the verge of revolt; his forces were scattered in Lombardy, Piedmont, Romagna, and Tuscany; he could only cover ordinary expenses by papal and Florentine loans; he had no personal magnetism, no military skill; by long tradition the *regnicolae*, always faithless to the existing government, would welcome the first comer. Such reasons doubtless induced Villani, Guelf as he was, to testify that Henry would have driven Robert from his throne.

With Henry VII's death the Ghibelline cause, in Tuscany at least, seemed lost beyond retrieve. The only two powers of any note, Pisa to west and Arezzo to east, were separated by a wide range of hostile territory, for the old feudal families which had flocked to the imperial standard were but scattered islands in a Guelfic sea. Arezzo in its loyal grief changed the horse upon its shield from white to black. The more mercantile Pisans regretted that they had spent 2000 golden ducats on the imperial cause and had got nothing for it. In Guelfic cities exultation knew no bounds. In these the oppressed Ghibellines were forced to take a part in processions and illuminations. The imperial army broke up, the Aretines and Tuscan nobles hurrying to their homes, while Henry of Flanders with the German and Pisan contingents escorted the Emperor's remains to Pisa, where his body rests. The weak point in the Guelfic league was that, though it had baffled Henry, it had not beaten him. Diplomatic acumen and skill in organisation had been superior to military spirit. In Tuscany the complete sense of security was probably the cause of disappointment and disaster.

Pisa hoped to defend herself with the aid of Frederick of Sicily who visited the city, but his terms, the cession of Sardinia, were too high. Henry of Flanders and the Count of Savoy were approached in vain. Aid came unexpectedly from within her walls. Uguccione, Podestà of Genoa for Henry VII, accepted the office of Podestà and Captain. He was a capable condottiere from the Aretine territory, with a somewhat shady political record. Feeling that safety lay in a brisk offensive, he induced 1000 Brabançon and Flemish horse to enter Pisan service. Taking advantage of the war-weariness and internal divisions of Lucca, he sent strong raiding parties into her territory. The Florentines dispatched aid, but their retirement was followed by fresh attacks. Meanwhile King Robert was striving for a general peace, which would give him the control of Tuscany, and especially the use of the Pisan fleet against Sicily. Peace was actually signed at the end of February between Pisa, the Guelfic league, and himself. Uguccione felt his position threatened; he worked up agitation among the lower classes, rode the town, beheaded his chief opponent, and had himself declared General War Captain for ten years. Negotiations in Lucca resulted in the mutual recall of exiles, among whom were the once powerful Lucchese house of Interminelli. To this belonged the keen young soldier Castruccio Castracani, of much experience in French and Italian wars, who at once gained favour with the lower classes. Their rivals, the Obizzi, were thought to be still negotiating with Florence, whereas the Interminelli were for peace with Pisa. Castruccio conspired with Uguccione, and together they expelled the Guelfs; Uguccione established his son as Podestà and War Captain in June 1314.

The loss of Lucca was a serious blow for Florence. Her access to the sea and the road across the Apennines from Sarzana was blocked, while her hold upon Pistoia, none too secure, was endangered. The general political position was critical, for Clement V had died in April, and a fiercely disputed election was in sight. Robert was straining his resources for another attack on Sicily, but he sent his young brother Peter to Florence with 300 horse. He entered on 18 August 1314, bearing for the king the title of Imperial Vicar of Tuscany, Lombardy, Romagna, and Ferrara, and Captain-General of the Guelf party in Italy. The Ghibelline party was now tightening its consolidation. In February 1315 Pisa and Lucca made an alliance with Verona and Mantua, the Pazzi of Val d'Arno and the Ubertini; but Arezzo, feeling its isolation, had made peace with Florence. The situation in the Guelfic cities was aggravated by renewed faction and discontent with the heavy taxation, while in Siena the Tolomei and Salimbeni fought pitched battles in the streets.

In March 1315 the campaign began with an unsuccessful Pisan attack
on Montecatini, strongly garrisoned by Florentines and Lucchese exiles.
Uguccione roused the drooping spirits of the Pisans by promising a
direct attack on Florence. On an appeal by Peter of Anjou, Bologna,
always faithful to her engagements, sent troops at once, while on 6 August
Robert's brother, Philip of Taranto, arrived with Neapolitan forces and
a large Sienese contingent. Uguccione also had called on his allies, and
on 10 August again besieged Montecatini with 3000 horse and 20,000
foot, to which Matteo Visconti, the Bonaccolsi of Mantua, and the Bishop
of Arezzo, in spite of his city's treaty with Florence, contributed contingents; that of Can Grande, however, arrived too late. Philip of Taranto, reinforced by troops from Umbria and Romagna, moved to relieve
Montecatini with 3200 horse and infantry estimated at from 30,000 to
60,000. He crossed the dangerous marshes of Fucecchio, while the Lucchese
peasantry, disaffected towards their new government, cut the roads and
captured convoys in Uguccione's rear. This on 28 August decided him
to retire, but to fight, if harassed on retreat. On 29 August Philip
followed. While crossing the stream of the Vorra, his forces were attacked
by Italian mercenaries and Florentine exiles. The vanguard from Siena
and Colle fled. Uguccione's son Francesco and Giacotto Malaspina, who
bore the imperial standard of Lewis of Bavaria, pressed the attack, but
were beaten off. Here Francesco fell, perhaps in personal combat with
Philip's son Charles, for their bodies were found together; the imperial
banner went under. Uguccione then threw his 800 German horse into
the fray. The infantry protecting the left flank of the Guelfic cavalry,
being harassed by the Pisan cross-bowmen, threw their long lances into
the charging Germans, and ran for their lives. General confusion ensued,
and the Florentine rout was complete. Pursuit followed for 13 miles;
many fugitives were drowned in the marshes, prisoners were numerous,
the booty enormous. Peter of Eboli's body was lost in the marshes, and
never found. Philip of Taranto, suffering from malaria, had been carried
in a litter to the field, and managed to escape. The Catalan mercenaries
fought well, and suffered badly; Diego de Rat was a prisoner. The chief
Guelfic families lost heavily in dead, wounded, and prisoners. No such
defeat had been inflicted on Florence since Montaperti.

In view of the seething discontent within Florence and the defection
of some of her smaller South Tuscan allies, the city herself might have
fallen but for Uguccione's delay in following up his victory. A capable
soldier, he had no statesmanlike quality, no great aim beyond his immediate interest. This was now to monopolise the whole of the captured
booty. Pisa and Lucca, which under Castruccio had no small share in
the victory, were equally indignant. Jealousy of Castruccio was, indeed,
the direct cause of Uguccione's fall. The schism in the Empire was beginning to affect Italian politics. Uguccione from the first supported
Lewis; Castruccio accepted from Frederick the confirmation of his election
as Vicar by the city of Sarzana, a post of the utmost importance for

imperial communications with Lucca, Pisa, and Florence herself. Uguccione ordered his son Neri, who represented him at Lucca, to arrest
Castruccio, and if he refused to surrender his possessions, to behead him.
Realising possible danger, he rode out to support his son. The Pisans
rose against him; he turned back on the news, to find the gates bolted
and barred. Hoping to save Lucca, he hurried thither, only to fall into
the hands of Castruccio, who had already been released. The captor with
characteristic generosity sent father and son under escort to Spinetta
Malaspina in the Lunigiana, whence Uguccione made his way to Can
Grande. After a later vain attempt on Pisa he died as Podestà of Verona
in November 1319. His career illustrates the difficulty in establishing a
durable tyranny by a mere condottiere without local or dynastic ties. If
statesmanship, character, and military skill combined could accomplish
such a feat, Uguccione's successor at Lucca had a far better chance. He
was the real Tuscan hero in the drama of the Trecento. Machiavelli
had some justification in converting the hero of history into one of legend.
Castruccio's chief exploits, however, lie beyond the limits of this chapter.
After Uguccione's death Castruccio became Captain of Lucca, to be
elected in 1320 General-Captain and Lord for life. A somewhat similar
post was held by Guido della Gherardesca at Pisa. The two States continued a raiding war upon the Tuscan Guelfs, until in 1317 Robert
succeeded in promoting a general peace. This was the easier, as, in
consequence of the marriage of Frederick of Austria's daughter Catherine
to the Duke of Calabria, Naples, Florence, and Lucca recognised the same
claimant to the Empire. Within Florence, however, the incompetence
and greed of the Angevin princes led to a reaction against French influence in favour of the house of Luxemburg. Simone della Tosa headed
a party based mainly on the Gonfaloniers of the Companies and the
lower classes against the wealthy families. On 1 May 1316 dictatorial
powers were conferred on a new official, the *Bargello*, Lando Bicci, who
ruled without appeal by axe and gallows, in defiance of excommunication
by the clergy. Robert's brother-in-law, Bertrand de Baux, was powerless,
but his successor, Count Guido of Battifolle, backed by orders from
Naples and a reaction among the Companies, dismissed Bicci and broke
Simone's power. Government fell to the wealthy *popolani* for some years to
come. Abroad, military enterprise was devoted to support of the Lombard
Guelfic league against Visconti and Scaligeri, and to the relief of Genoa.
In spite of Robert's own success in this relief, the Florentines suffered
with increasing disgust the officials commissioned to represent him. This
reached its climax with the expiration of his lordship in 1322. Florence
was free for a time from a foreign protectorate, and restored to the
dubious enjoyment of her own constitution.

Clement V did not long survive the Emperor whom he had deserted,
for he died on 20 April 1314. His pontificate had rather tightened than

loosened papal hold in Italy. The impetus had been due to the genius of Arnaud de Pélagrue, but it was mainly through Robert and his Neapolitan officials that he maintained his hold upon the capital and Romagna. The conquest of Ferrara brought small satisfaction. The citizens desired either republican liberty or the recall of the legitimate Estensi. In one of the movements Francesco was murdered; Clement found himself forced late in 1312 to hand over the government to Robert, who held Ferrara with a force of Catalans. These in August 1317 were massacred by the inhabitants, who restored the sons of Francesco and Aldobrandino. Direct papal sovereignty ceased, in spite of the interdict long laid upon Ferrara by Clement's successor.

Dante has mercilessly condemned Clement to a terrible cell and unsympathetic company in Hell. His desertion of Italy, his betrayal of Henry, his unlimited simony to enrich his relatives, are sufficient reasons for his punishment. Yet it is possible to regret it. In spite of Villani's scandal, Clement lived a clean life, and was a man of simple piety, easy and pleasant in his manners, a contrast to the insufferable arrogance of Boniface VIII and the rough brutality of John XXII. Though not ascetic, he lived frugally and unostentatiously; he was always taking medicine and consulting doctors, becoming a chronic valetudinarian. This, perhaps, accounted for the weakness of will which sometimes followed tenacity of resistance, forcing him to concessions which he afterwards regretted. A see-saw between high pretensions and weak practice was a main characteristic of his career.

The disgraceful conclave of Carpentras ended on 7 August 1316 in the election of John XXII. Dante's patriotic letter to the Italian cardinals, addressed especially to Napoleon Orsini, was of no avail, and the failure to elect an Italian caused St Peter to denounce the Cahorsins and Gascons, who would drink like ravening wolves the blood of Christ's flock[1]. Napoleon himself had told Philip IV that the desertion of Rome had ruined Italy and brought danger upon France herself. During the conclave the political situation had materially changed. On 27 November 1314 Philip IV had died, while in October the elections of Frederick of Austria and Lewis of Bavaria had caused a schism in the Empire. Only five years of John's reign fall within Dante's life, but these were sufficient to cause his condemnation. He soon rivalled Boniface in the assertion of temporal claims, and outdid Clement in extortion. Having failed to close the imperial schism, he utilised it by continuing Robert's vicariate, and forbade vicars appointed by Henry VII to perform their functions. From this sprang the conflict with Visconti, elsewhere described[2].

Of all the combatants King Robert stood to gain most by Henry VII's death. He was relieved from the very real danger of a combined attack by the Emperor and Frederick of Sicily. Clement created him Imperial Vicar in Italy during the vacancy. In Rome itself he exercised senatorial

---

[1] *Paradiso*, xxvii, 58–59.   [2] *Infra*, Chap. ii.

power, through a Roman noble or through one of his own officials. If the nobles still fought without much government control, this was too normal to cause anxiety. Southwards, the reconciliation of Gaetani and Colonna made access from Naples easy. In Umbria, Perugia, the most powerful and united city, kept the Guelfic banner always flying. In Romagna and the March, Guelfs and Ghibellines under the Malatesta and Federigo of Urbino were so evenly balanced that Robert's aid was scarcely needed. As ruler of Ferrara for the Pope since 1312 he could put pressure on eastern Lombardy, while western Lombardy could be threatened from his fiefs in Piedmont, and by the Count of Savoy, now his ally. In Tuscany, Florence, Siena, and Lucca had no shame in accepting his protectorate. His undoubted wish to be king, nominal or actual, of Italy seemed to Guelfic poets well within possibility of fulfilment.

Against these advantages Robert's preoccupation with Sicily weighed heavily in the scales. During truce or peace he was always preparing for another war, and this strained his resources to the uttermost; he held that he would not really be king if he could not reunite the whole Angevin kingdom. Two actual wars took place between Henry's death and the visit of Lewis IV to Italy. For the first, Frederick was responsible by his breach of the Treaty of Caltabellotta through his alliance with Henry. He had his son Peter's claim to succession proclaimed by the assembled judges of the island, and himself reassumed the title of King of Sicily. The ensuing war was a fiasco; Frederick seized Reggio, and Robert sent a large force by sea to Trapani. Both fleets were shattered by storms before coming into action, and a truce was made until March 1316. The second war was far more serious. A large army, after pillaging the western side of Sicily, combined with the fleet in an attack upon Palermo, and, failing here, on the district of Marsala. Frederick's forces were at a low ebb when envoys arrived from John XXII and James of Aragon. Frederick assented to the surrender of the posts still held in Calabria, stipulating for a peace to last from 13 June 1317 to Christmas 1320. The negotiations at Avignon failed owing to Robert's usual delays, and the war became part of the pan-Italian struggle around Genoa. To mobilise his fleet destined for this, Frederick seized ecclesiastical property. John in January 1321 laid an interdict on Sicily, whereon Frederick completed the ruin of the treaty of Caltabellotta by having Peter crowned as his successor in April 1321. Robert's personal intervention in the siege of Genoa was the one courageous and decisive act in the first decade of his reign. The siege was compared by Villani to that of Troy for the size and wealth of the city, its long duration and violent vicissitudes. It was originally a mere incident in the everlasting struggles between the great families of Doria, Spinola, Grimaldi, and Fieschi, the former pair classed as Ghibellines, the latter as Guelfs. After Henry VII's death, renewed quarrels between Doria and Spinola led to the return and predominance of the Guelfs, stimulated by Robert's intrigues, in 1317. The Ghibelline

houses, reconciled in exile, based their attack on the malcontent cities of
Savona and Albenga, and their own far-stretching coastal fiefs. The
Guelfs, after appealing in vain to Visconti, who gave support to the
exiles, begged help of Robert. To the ruler of Naples and Marseilles
control over Genoa was all-important, for it secured the long sea passage
between these ports, opened communications through the Ligurian Alps
to his Piedmontese possessions, and provided a first-class fleet for a
Sicilian war. The exiles, in March 1318, aided by Marco Visconti with
German and Lombard troops, occupied the semicircle of hills overlooking
Genoa, the Polcevera valley immediately to the west, and the Torre del
Faro commanding the port. In July Robert with a large fleet broke the
blockade, and was recognised as lord for ten years in conjunction with
the Pope. The exiles found allies in the Lombard Ghibelline despots,
Lucca, Pisa, and the Emperor Andronicus, who could gravely hamper
Genoese commerce in the East. Robert was joined by Bolognese,
Florentines, and Romagnols, shipped from the Sienese port of Talamone.
In February Robert broke the besiegers' western lines by landing at
Sestri Levante. After this serious defeat the Lombards withdrew, and
Robert in April, leaving his fleet and a garrison, retired to join the Pope.
By August the exiles retook all their lost positions, and there was fighting
by sea from Savona to the gulf of Spezia.

The war in 1320 became truly international. A Sicilian fleet, carrying
cavalry, arrived before Genoa, while Castruccio captured Genoese towns
in the Riviera di Levante. By August the city was more closely beset
than ever. Robert then sent 82 galleys, before which the Sicilian fleet
retired, and, to draw Cardona off, ravaged Ischia. Cardona's pursuing
fleet on sighting his Neapolitan seamen's home was disabled by mutiny.
In September the Sicilian squadron, having returned to Genoa, made with
the Lombards concerted attacks, which were with great difficulty repulsed.
If only Castruccio had arrived success was certain, but the Florentines, by
attacking Lucca, called him hurriedly home. Similarly, though with less
success, the Pope sent Philip of Valois with French troops to divert the
Visconti. Winter approaching drove home the Sicilian fleet, much
damaged; the exiles retired to Savona. Though the war dragged on till
1323, the crisis was really over. Robert had saved Genoa, and recovered
the prestige lost in 1317 by his humiliating eviction from Ferrara.

If in Tuscany the Emperor's death gave apparent predominance to the
Guelfs, the position of the imperialists in Lombardy remained unshaken.
This was directly due to Henry's action in appointing as Vicars of Milan
and Verona men of real statesmanship and consistent purpose. Pecuniary
necessity may have been his immediate motive, but he could not have
made better choice than that of Matteo Visconti and Can Grande. Matteo,
indeed, like other great Visconti, had little military talent, but four warlike sons compensated for the lack. The title of Imperial Vicar gave both

rulers an unquestionable status, as is proved by the insistence of Clement V and John XXII that they should abandon it. Can Grande had a State undivided by party faction, while Matteo's justice and conciliatory spirit went far to reconcile the popular Guelf elements to his rule. The alliance between the two lords, which included Passerino Bonaccolsi of Mantua, was firmly set; there was as yet little cause for jealousy, since between the Adda and the Mincio lay a wide block containing Bergamo and Brescia, Crema and Cremona, mainly Guelf or suffering from chaotic feuds. King Robert's occupation of Ferrara was precarious, and in 1317 was to have an ignominious end. The chief danger was the brilliant, unscrupulous Ghiberto da Correggio, lord of Parma, who coveted Cremona, which, with his possession of Guastalla, would give him command of both banks of the Po. If only he could wrest Piacenza, so closely connected in history with Parma, his State would be of real importance. Westwards, Pavia was ruled by Rizzardino Langosco, son of Filippone, who was a prisoner in Milan. The Torriani had returned to Lombardy; and had influence in the eastern half of the Milanese and much sympathy in Milan. Matteo had during the first two years after Henry's death considerable trouble from such a combination supported by Bologna, Padua, and Robert. But in October 1315 Marco Visconti, after a brilliant victory on the Scrivia, took Pavia by an assault, in which Rizzardino was killed. The Ghibelline Beccaria were restored, but, to make safe, Matteo built a castle, occupied by a Milanese garrison under his son Luchino. The Visconti now ruled over Milan, Tortona, Alessandria, Pavia, Bergamo, and Piacenza, while Como was ruled by the closely allied Rusconi. Ghiberto da Correggio in 1316 induced his friend Cavalcabò, the local despot, to surrender Cremona to him. On his return to Parma, he found an organised rebellion, headed by his relatives, and probably engineered from Milan and Verona. He fled, never to return, but, by his military capacity and official command of the Guelf forces, was formidable until his death in 1323. Parma once again became stringently republican, starting a new radical club of 3000 members, who swore never to allow Parma to obey a lord or have intercourse with nobles. This strange little radical republic was in foreign politics Ghibelline, in alliance with Milan, Verona, and Mantua, receiving her Podestà from the Visconti. Cremona, after Correggio's fall, suffered horrible vicissitudes of murder and sack until her acceptance of Visconti rule in 1322.

The accession of John XXII was signalised by the Bull of 1317 excommunicating all who did not drop the title of Imperial Vicar, unless confirmed in it by himself. Can Grande took no notice of this, but Matteo abandoned the title, adopting that of General Lord of the Milanese people. His foreign policy was not affected: he sent substantial aid to the Genoese Ghibelline nobles, and with preliminary success; but the arrival of Robert with a large force turned the scale. The Milanese and Veronese gave up the contest; Genoa was not as yet within the practical programme of Visconti expansion.

In Lombardy, Matteo's success continued. Robert's Vicar, Hugh de Baux, was killed in an action with Luchino; Philip of Valois, sent by Robert to support the papal legate Bertrand du Pouget, retired rapidly before a superior Visconti force, which then occupied Vercelli. A new danger now threatened the Visconti from the east. The Pope persuaded Frederick of Austria to send his brother Henry to execute the decree of excommunication. Henry found a strong base in the zealous Guelfism of Brescia, where he received the papal banner from Pagano della Torre, Patriarch of Aquileia, in April 1322. Yet he, as Philip of Valois, disliked the look of the Visconti forces, and was bribed to retire, ending his campaign with a jovial reception from Can Grande.

The Pope's measures had failed to shake the military position of the Visconti, but they were not without effect on Milanese feeling nor on Matteo's conscience. His own envoys were persuaded by the legate to depose him, and on their return stirred up the people, who became clamorous for peace. The Council wished Matteo to resign his pretensions to the Pope. Lombard Ghibellines fiercely resented this, but Matteo's health and courage were waning; he resigned in favour of Galeazzo, and died, probably on 24 June 1322. Strangely enough, Galeazzo was unanimously acclaimed by the Grand Council as his father's successor. Thus the Visconti seemed firmly seated as the ruling house, in spite of Matteo's personal difficulties or tender conscience.

At the time of Henry VII's death Can Grande was sole ruler of Verona. He had also received the vicariate of Vicenza, which had thrown off the Paduan yoke in February 1312. Vicentine territory increased the Scala possessions by half as much again, and acted as a buffer, protecting the Veronese from the impact of the forces of Padua and Treviso. On the other hand, it was the cause of the four succeeding wars with Padua, whose resources were fully as great as those of Can Grande, and whose republican feeling was long unalterable. In his own house Can was determined to be master. He suppressed the Vicentine rural nobles, who had long been the bugbear of the city, ordering all private castles to be destroyed, an act which drove many of the owners into alliance with Padua. The defences of the State were strengthened, especially by two new forts at Marostica, the stronghold on the northern frontier. The Scala ladder incised on a bolt of one of the gates still bears witness to Can Grande's action.

Not daunted by the Emperor's death, Can Grande at once prepared an offensive movement against Padua. In 1314 he raided Paduan territory far and wide, burning Abano, to the distress of wealthy and gouty citizens whose health depended on its baths, and caused a panic in Padua itself. A counter-stroke against Vicenza had almost succeeded, when Can, riding hard from his son's marriage-feast at Verona, drove the enemy out after a hand-to-hand fight in the suburbs. A huge number of prisoners included the historian statesman, Albertino Mussato. The ensuing peace in October 1314 recognised Can Grande's rights over Vicenza. This peace enabled him, in concert with his satellite Passerino Bonaccolsi of Mantua, to uphold the Ghibelline cause in Central Lombardy. To him in great measure was due the expulsion of Ghiberto da Correggio from Parma; he had, however, no ambition for permanent expansion in this direction, and left any fruits of victory to Passerino. The recognition of Frederick of Austria as King of the Romans on 16 March 1317 has been ascribed to the influence of Uguccione, who was now his most talented general. It was, however, inevitable that Can should have direct interest in the Austrian claimant, who, through the Brenner and side passes, was in close contact with Verona and Vicenza.

While campaigning against Brescia, Can heard of a treacherous Paduan plot for the surprise of Vicenza. The attack was led by Vinciguerra, Count of Sanbonifacio, the hereditary Guelfic foe of the Ghibelline Scaligeri. He was descending from Monte Berico, which immediately overhangs Vicenza, when Can and Uguccione burst upon him. Vinciguerra was taken, and after generous treatment died, thus ridding Can of his most powerful feudal enemy. He then conquered the southern Paduan towns of Este, Monselice, and Montagnana, while the Estensi, restored to Ferrara, captured Rovigo, chief city of the fertile Polesina, lying between the Adige and the Po. The peace, which was due to Venetian mediation in February 1318, had momentous results for Padua, for Giacomo da Carrara, who had pressed for peace, was in July accepted as lord.

In December 1318 Can Grande's reputation caused him to be elected Captain-General of the Lombard League, with a handsome salary and a personal force of 1000 horse. Yet he did little service to the League's cause. His objective now was Padua's ally Treviso, now a republic, but deeply divided between the upper and lower classes. Aided by several feudal nobles and the late despot, Guecello da Camino, Uguccione besieged the city, but Henry Count of Gorizia was sent by Frederick of Austria to its relief, whereupon in July 1319 Can diverted his forces to a formal siege of Padua. Here on 1 November 1319 he lost Uguccione, who died of malaria. Padua, at the instance of Giacomo da Carrara, gave herself to Frederick, whose Vicar, Henry of Gorizia, took the besiegers completely by surprise. Utterly routed and severely wounded, Can escaped by a hair's-breadth to Monselice, losing all his military stores and gorgeous personal equipment. Fortunately the Paduans, disheartened by an attempt to take Monselice, longed for peace, which was signed on 26 October 1320. Can surrendered to Padua the strong frontier fortress of Cittadella, and by a secret arrangement gave to Henry Asolo and Montebelluna, receiving in exchange the more important Bassano, which commands the entrance to the Val Sugana. Frederick was to arbitrate on the return of exiles and the possession of Este, Monselice, and Montagnana, but his defeat at Mühldorf left them in Can Grande's hands. Shaken by the wound received at Padua and the shame of his flight, he left Padua and Treviso alone for the while; he had learned his lesson, that personal bravery does not make a general. By clever negotiations he won valuable acquisitions in Feltre and Belluno; with these added to Bassano, Roveredo, and Riva he had a fine strategic and commercial northern frontier.

At Venice the election which followed Gradenigo's death was sensational. The electors being in doubt, some of them, as is usual, looked out of the window. A retired statesman, Marino Zorzi, was passing, followed by a servant carrying a sack of bread for the prisoners. A flood of sentiment swept the charitable old gentleman to the dogeship. He was friendly to Henry VII, for deputies were sent to his coronation, and leave given to levy cross-bowmen. Having reigned but ten months, he died on 3 July 1312. Ten days later Giovanni Soranzo was elected at the age of seventy-two. No citizen had a stronger claim. With 25 galleys he had taken Kaffa from the Genoese, and then defended it against the Tartars, had fought against Padua, and was Podestà of Ferrara in the critical year 1308. Prosperity soon returned, especially in the year of double thirteens. The papal interdict was withdrawn in March 1313; the old Venetian privileges in Ferrara were restored; the fetters on foreign trade were automatically struck off. In September Zara returned to Venetian allegiance after her long revolt, and during the next decade the other Dalmatian cities surrendered their temporary independence. Soranzo's dogeship was a period of unexampled growth in wealth and population. The Genoese carried on war of a piratical character, but the most sensational incident was the appearance of the ever fortunate admiral Giustiniani before their headquarters at Galata with an irresistible demand for complete restitution. Commercial treaties were made with Sicily, Milan, Brescia, and Bologna, with Hungary and the Emperor Andronicus. The city of Trebizond granted access to trade with Persia; the King of Tunis favoured Venetian commerce. Levantine sugar was shipped to England in exchange for wool, which was worked up in Flanders for the cloth trade along the Adriatic and in the Levant. The city herself gained an impulse to silk manufacture by sheltering Lucchese refugees; three Venetian citizens introduced the art of mirror-making, which became a characteristic industry. Venice, with her arsenal enlarged, her bridges and streets improved, became worthy of a population computed at 200,000 souls. Soranzo's death did not take place until well beyond the limits of this chapter, in December 1328.

The Age of Dante closes on a future indistinct. In Lombardy, indeed, the expansive hereditary monarchies seemed likely to hold the field. Florence, uneasy within, was again endangered from without. The States of the Church, under an absentee Pope, would probably disintegrate rather than solidify. There remains King Robert. If his resources could balance his ambitions, if he could prove as effective as he was efficient, he might learn to play the spectacular part which Guelf admirers assigned to

Il buon Roberto
Rè d'un italico Regno.

CHAPTER II

ITALY, 1313–1414

In the century from the death of the Emperor Henry VII of Luxemburg (1313) to that of King Ladislas of Naples (1414) the Italian nation offers an arresting spectacle. We see, not events of universal import, but strenuous and often blood-stained local dramas, whether staged in a single town or in a province; not supermen endowed with a universal intellect, but the polished and impressionable minds of faction-leaders and of despots busied in creating and consolidating their principates on the ruins of the Commune. There are no longer great political ideals like those which lit up Christendom till the death of Frederick II (1250), and found in Dante their best interpreter, but ideals narrower and more concrete, clinging to the changing daily reality of life; no firm, implacable faiths, whether religious or secular, but constant compromises with God and with men. Few are the saints and few the heretics; more luxuriously soft and refined are the poets and artists. Commerce has become more intense and engrossing, the merchants themselves more modern. The world of business has grown wider, and with its growth the Italians have gained a new prestige. The old medieval world begins to fail, while the new humanistic consciousness dawns. But the more the memory of ancient Rome and of her ecumenic greatness is kindled, the more the life of Italy is shattered into innumerable fragments, because, in fact, the modern State can only arise in Italy by means of the formation of the local *Signorie*, and these can in no way issue from the limits of city or province. The Angevin kingdom of Naples, which occupied a third of the peninsula, is an exception indeed, but since it had never experienced the communal stage of civilisation, it could never pass through the signorial stage, which was both the epilogue of the Commune and the development of its inner tendencies.

The small State and particularism are therefore the characteristics of Italian history in the fourteenth century. But we may also say that there is a characteristic still more universal: that the age of Petrarch is the age of the Despots, the Signori. The communes are either already vanished, as in the watershed of the Po, in the Veneto, in Romagna, in Piedmont, or are hastening to disappear. Genoa is only a republic in name after the defeat of La Loiera and the surrender to the Archbishop Giovanni Visconti (1353–54), and Venice herself after the Serrata del Maggior Consiglio (1297) and the erection of the Council of Ten (1310) retains only the external features of her ancient republican institutions; in essence she is an oligarchic State near allied both in spirit and in forms to the Signoria elsewhere. The Commune flourishes still, although infected with incurable organic disease, in Tuscany, more especially in Florence and Siena, and it is slowly dying in Umbria on the confines of the Roman State. Everywhere the Signoria rises and develops owing to the same general causes, not to mention the concomitant and special causes which affect only the history of the single States. In general, we may say that, at the dawn of the fourteenth century, communal institutions no longer met the needs of the life, political, economic, and social, of the Italian cities; they no longer guaranteed the defence of the city-state against internal and external foes; they did not give to the poorer and labouring classes any share in political life; they could only oppress the countryside (where once, between the years 1000 and 1100, there had been a rich growth of free communal formations); and they were not even able to assure to the industrial and commercial classes themselves, who monopolised the local power, that security and prestige of which they stood in need. In sum, the Commune had become a hollow form, a legal survival devoid of real content, "*nome vano senza soggetto.*" The Signore, on the other hand, who was not a tool of faction or of class, who needed the concurrence and obedience of all classes both within and without the circle of the city walls, was the centre of the life of his State, its only legislator and commander of its troops. And therefore the Signoria was the logical solution of a tangle of problems which the Commune could not solve.

Among these problems that of the soldiery was peculiarly grave. In the early communal period and during almost all the thirteenth century, the city armies were composed of citizens and especially of the nobles, led by the Podestà or the Captain of the People to the frequent incursions over the lands of the *contado*; even then in the long and sanguinary contests between commune and commune these forces were always scanty and were little adapted for war. But when the communes attained a wider territorial dominion and the crisis of the subject communities, great and small, was mingled with the internal crises of the city, and when the needs of defence and of the protection of its widening commerce became more engrossing and urgent, the citizen militia became ineffective and often could not even be levied. In fact the *popolo minuto* could not be armed, for had it been it would have turned its arms against the bourgeois commune; nor could the *contadini*, for they hated the city which ruled them; the *popolani grassi* were few, and besides could not leave their manufactures and commerce to take part in war. A citizen army could not really be formed. Further, from the time of the Angevin conquest of the kingdom of Sicily, and still more after the expeditions of Henry VII and Lewis the Bavarian, and owing to the military operations on a large scale carried on in Lombardy and the Veneto by Matteo Visconti and the Scaligeri, a crowd of adventurers of every nationality wandered over Italy in search of fortune. War gave them what they sought; and so this mixed swarm (Swiss, Germans, Burgundians, Italians), led by men of courage and initiative, offered their services to any commune or insecure signore; war was their trade by which they lived. Thus, Lodrisio Visconti formed an army of 2500 men-at-arms, 800 foot, and 200 cross-bowmen, and, with the secret aid of Della Scala, who was anxious to rid himself of those fierce warriors, threw himself on Milan only to be routed at Parabiago (1337). Again, Werner, Duke of Urslingen, one of the captains in Visconti's pay, formed a new "company" of various adventurers and ravaged Romagna, Emilia, and Tuscany (1342-43), retiring beyond the Alps laden with booty amid the execration of the towns and villages they left drenched with blood. In 1354 and the following years, the territory of Siena was wasted by pitiless and starving mercenaries; and the kingdom of Naples was put to fire and sword by Conrad of Wolfort (Corrado Lupo, "Wolf"), by Conrad of Landau (the Count of Lando), and by Fra Moriale (Montréal) from Narbonne during the tragic years which followed the murder of Andrew of Hungary. The scourge became unendurable even to the employers of these bands; and hence treachery and betrayal appeared inseparable from the conduct of mercenaries. For them peace meant the end of their impunity and of the very reason of their existence.

The communal organisation could not support the weight of such armies. The Signoria was the only form of government which, disciplining each and every subject, levelling citizens and peasants, nobles and non-nobles, could form an army of its own with its own regulations and chiefs, if only because the Signore was himself almost always a soldier who knew the art of war and founded on victory the political fortunes of himself and his State.

The absence of the Papacy from Italy (1305-76) was a potent factor to exasperate the perilous and unstable situation in which Signorie and Communes were plunged. During the exile at Avignon, Rome, in truth, was only one among the Italian cities, and existed in a perpetual state of crisis, social and political, in which over-powerful houses like the Colonna, the Orsini, the Anibaldi, the Savelli, the Gaetani, fought without cessation, each in order to subject to itself the "Roman people," which, disarmed yet rebellious, was without defence and without any concrete programme whatever. Once, in 1337, the *popolo* elected the Pope himself, Benedict XII, "Senator, Captain, and Defender of the Republic for life"; and another time, during the sojourn of Urban V at Rome, the Romans (1370) gave help to the Perugians, then rebels against the Church! But doubtless the distance of the Popes from their natural seat kindled cupidities, provoked disorders, justified often the conduct of the Emperors, and weakened the moral influence of the Church. The adventure of Cola di Rienzo is thus explained, as are the pitiful events of which Rome was the scene during the strife between Lewis the Bavarian and John XXII (1327-30). Rome was ever the capital of the Catholic world, and to Rome the glances of the Emperors always turned. What wonder if the City and the Roman State were a prey to perennial anarchy, and that to the eyes of contemporaries the Church seemed to be one of the factors responsible for the unremitting tempests which beat upon Communes and Signorie.

There was indeed one element of order, one centre of activity around which the Italian nation might have been organised, the kingdom of Sicily or rather Naples, *i.e.* the continental part of the original kingdom, for the island of Sicily had been a separate realm since 1282. This was ruled by the house of Anjou. Its unitary monarchic constitution since the second half of the eleventh century, its wide extent reaching from the southern border of Latium to the Straits of Messina, the illustrious kinships which linked the Angevins to the houses of France and Aragon and to the Kings of Hungary, the very anarchy reigning in the Roman State and over the greater part of the peninsula, and the civil discords in whose fumes the surviving communes, especially in Tuscany, were choking, all these were certainly reasons for the success of the Angevin attempts to unify Italy; and the way seemed to be prepared by the frequent submissions to the Kings of Naples, to which during the reigns of Charles II (1285–1309) and Robert "the Wise" (1309–43) some communes, such as Brescia, Genoa, and Florence, brought themselves to consent. Petrarch himself believed it possible that sooner or later King Robert might succeed in uniting Italy. But it was a dream. The South of Italy, poor by nature, could not free itself from the feudal system until the dawn of the nineteenth century. It had no manufacturing or mercantile bourgeoisie, and hence no communes. Its population consisted of a minority of barons ever recalcitrant to the reign of law, and in great part poor and turbulent, and of an enormous majority of plebeian townsmen and peasants tormented by poverty and the misgovernment of rapacious officials. To complete the picture of the kingdom, let us add large townships isolated among territories stricken with malaria; little cities many miles apart; champaigns abandoned to forest or pasture as chance would have it, and totally unsafe; bishoprics and abbeys rich in lands and vassals, but poor in revenue and devoid of civilising enterprise, ever at odds as well with barons as with peasants; an amorphous court without men of real eminence or a strong king, and always poor and in debt to the merchants and bankers of the happier Italy to the north; an army and a fleet that a hostile onset or a blast of wind could soon destroy; runaway mercenaries and hired commanders (*condottieri*) always unequal to the occasion, alike without scruples and without ideals. On this base nothing could be built. Pope John XXII hoped perhaps to make of Robert of Anjou the standard-bearer of the Church and the most powerful sovereign of Europe, but before his death he had found out too surely that his hope was an illusion. Robert was merely a drab mediocrity, a narrow, parched soul, of faded energies and faded policies; and the kingdom was inferior to its king.

At Rome itself there arose an ineffectual portent of the coming

Renaissance. Cola di Rienzo, born in 1313 of very humble parentage, was an imaginative and fiery spirit. After an unhappy and meditative youth, he came suddenly to the forefront in Rome at the beginning of the pontificate of Clement VI, equipped with a considerable knowledge of the classics and longing to bring into actual politics a programme which was ill-contrived indeed but yet a grandiose conception. In substance, he wished to destroy the omnipotence of the Roman nobles by the aid of the people; and in a kind of diseased enthusiasm, recalling to life the phantoms of imperial Rome, to subject the Empire, and to make the Eternal City once more the capital of the world, now illuminated by the light of Christianity. He was sent with a few others by the Romans as ambassador to Clement VI at the close of 1342 and the beginning of 1343, and obtained from the Pope the nomination as notary of the "Camera urbana." This office he used to prepare the revolution, whose necessity seemed to his excited mind more and more compelling, even though the course it must take seemed obscure. In the spring of 1347 the propitious moment appeared to have come, and on the morning of 20 May the "Roman people," assembled on the Capitol amid pompous ceremonies in which sacred and profane rites were fused in an unprecedented symbolism, conferred on its hero the widest dictatorial powers, and received from him—as from a new Moses—new civic institutions. Soon after, on 1 August, the dictator was dubbed knight; and on 15 August, amid a crowd collected from all parts and including representatives from friendly cities, he assumed the crown of "Tribune of the People" with an evident tendency to madness or at least to baseless dreams.

The Pope, who at first watched benevolently the plebeian ennobled by his Latin learning, soon saw that his theories attacked the foundations of the Church's power, and from September 1347 began to oppose him. The Colonna revolted, but were overthrown at Porta San Lorenzo on 19 November. Yet this was an ephemeral victory. Less than a month later, while the Cardinal Legate launched a charge of heresy against the Tribune, the Colonna rose again unsubdued; the people abandoned its idol; discouraged and afraid, Cola abdicated on 15 December, and fled towards the mountains of Abruzzo.

There in a Franciscan convent he passed two years in solitary meditation; and then with no clear plan of action he set out for the court of Charles IV. At Prague he was held in honourable imprisonment for two years, but Charles did not know what to make of so abnormal a man and at last sent him to the Pope. Clement VI condemned him to death, but happily for him died before the sentence was carried out, and the new Pope Innocent VI set him free. Cola was dispatched with Cardinal Albornoz to Italy to aid in pacifying the Papal States. On 1 August 1354 he re-entered Rome with the title of Senator, and immediately after, with the troops of two brothers of Fra Moriale, attacked Palestrina, the stronghold of the Colonna, to avenge the disaster of 1347 and to begin anew his interrupted schemes. But he had lost the sense of proportion and reality; he had given way to luxury and debauchery, and the excessive cruelty of his government offended the sense of justice which is deeply rooted in popular sentiment. On 8 October 1354 an overwhelming revolt of the people took him unawares. He strove to flee, but was recognised and slaughtered at the foot of the Capitol by a multitude frantic for vengeance and blood.

Finally, the Empire contributed as it might to this age of crisis. The Germanic Emperors had never understood and could never understand that the rise of the communes, the formation of a great monarchic State in the South, and the States of the Church in the Centre, rendered the continuance of the imperial authority in Italy impossible. Henry VII had believed that he could sit as arbiter between the city factions and reduce republics then still in their prime to the level of his German towns; but he encountered insurmountable difficulties, brought war and slaughter instead of peace, and was defeated by the same townsfolk who had discomfited Barbarossa and Frederick II. Lewis the Bavarian grafted Henry's policy on the Franciscan schism, elected an anti-Pope, Nicholas V (22 May 1328), in astonished Rome, declared himself Defender of the Faith against John XXII, the legitimate Pope who was orthodox and acting in the Church's interests, threatened Robert of Naples as Henry VII had done, troubled Lombardy, Tuscany, and Emilia, but was defeated by the united forces of the Church and the Guelfs, and repassed the Alps not to return. The enterprise of Charles IV was not more fortunate; it became a shameless farce. On the other hand, by the Golden Bull the same Emperor (1346–79) snapped the bonds which had linked Papacy and Empire since the days of Charlemagne, and with them fell to the ground the motives for imperial intervention in Italy. The Empire became ever more completely a German State, with which it was profitable and prudent to keep on terms of good neighbourship; but the utopia of Dante vanished for ever, and in the Renaissance fortunately men spoke no more of a universal monarchy or a Church that crowned the Kings of the Romans. In fact Signorie and Communes had left off doing so from the death of Henry VII, being well aware that the Empire had no mission in Italy, and that its intervention invariably aroused hatreds and feuds.

At the death of Henry VII Italy seemed freed from a heavy incubus, but in fact until the close of the enterprise of Lewis the Bavarian the land found neither peace nor truce. The centres of commotion were Tuscany and Lombardy, but their repercussions were felt in every region of the peninsula. In Tuscany, first Uguccione della Faggiuola, lord of Pisa (1316–17), and then Castruccio Castracani, lord of Lucca (1318–28), continued the Ghibelline offensive of the Emperor; and the Guelfs, led by Florence and Robert of Anjou, suffered two severe defeats, at Montecatini on 29 August 1315 and at Altopascio on 23 September 1325. The Guelf arms had no better fortune immediately afterwards when

King Robert's son, Charles Duke of Calabria, was proclaimed Signore of Florence (21 December 1325) at a time when, through the defeat of the Bolognese at Zapolino (25 November 1325), it seemed that the Guelf cause was about to collapse for good throughout North and Central Italy. The Duke of Calabria was not a capable general, and the Florentine constitution did not permit an organised and effectual military effort. It was at this moment that Lewis the Bavarian descended into Italy, and everywhere the Ghibellines raised their heads. The Emperor, calculating on the incurable discord between Florence, Pisa, and Lucca, and on the traditional solidarity in policy of Florence and the Neapolitan court, aimed at striking a decisive blow at the allied republic and kingdom by means of Castruccio, whom he declared Vicar of the Empire in Tuscany; and since John XXII openly condemned his enterprise, he leant on the Franciscans against whom the Pope for some years had employed every weapon at his command, and whom he had impelled into open schism. But in 1328, within a few months, Castruccio (3 September) and the Duke of Calabria (11 November) both died prematurely. The papal legate in upper Italy, Cardinal Bertrand du Pouget, took energetic action, the anti-Pope returned penitently to the fold of the Church, and the war clouds seemed to lift for an instant from the banks of the Arno.

In Lombardy and the neighbour lands events had taken a no less momentous course. For five years (1317–22), till the day of his death, Matteo Visconti, the lord of Milan, who had been named Vicar of the Empire by Henry VII, had struggled tireless and invincible against papal excommunications and the forces of the Guelfs; but a crusade was proclaimed against his heirs and adherents, and Cardinal Bertrand began a series of *coups-de-main*, battles, and intrigues which, with alternations of defeat and victory, led him to the capture of Modena (25 June 1326), Parma (30 September 1326), Reggio (4 October 1326), and Bologna (8 February 1327). For a few years the Visconti saw their fortunes depressed, while above them rose those of Mastino della Scala of Verona. In a brief space of time he could extend his dominion over Feltre and Belluno, Brescia, Vicenza, Parma, and even Lucca (1337), founding a formidable State which reached from the eastern Alps to the River Serchio, and obstinately defending it against the fierce coalition of all whom it threatened—Guelfs and Ghibellines, lesser Signorie, and free Communes. The struggle lasted till 1341, and ended as was inevitable with the decay of a State too heterogeneous and too wide, suddenly put together and unorganised as it was, and with the victory of the hostile coalition. The Della Scala only retained Verona and Vicenza, while the Archbishop Giovanni Visconti of Milan, regarded by his contemporaries as the most powerful man in Italy, began methodically and boldly to carry out the very programme in which they had failed.

After the death of his brother Luchino Visconti, Archbishop Giovanni was freed from all trammels (January 1349). He had been appointed

CH. II.

archbishop in 1343. Handsome and generous—so the Milanese chroniclers described him—diplomatic and intensely ambitious, he was immediately invested with the Signoria by the General Council of Milan, and in order to avoid the family friction which would have been fatal to him, he summoned back his nephews Matteo, Galeazzo, and Bernabò, sons of his brother Stefano, all of whom the jealous Luchino had exiled. Lord as he was of Milan, Brescia, Bergamo, Como, Lodi, Cremona, Vercelli, Novara, Alessandria, Tortona, Alba, Asti, Bobbio, Parma, and many lesser towns, truly "regulus super Lombardis" (as the *Chronicon Placentinum* calls him), the archbishop conceived the bold design of penetrating into Romagna and thence extending his dominion into Tuscany. In this he was aided by the treaty of friendship which Luchino had concluded in 1347 with Taddeo Pepoli, despot of Bologna, and indirectly by the indiscipline of the troops of Astorge de Durfort, nephew of Pope Clement VI and his representative in Romagna. Soon the incompetent and weak sons of Taddeo sold Bologna to Giovanni (16 October 1350), and a few days after, on 23 October, Galeazzo Visconti with 1200 horse entered the city, while the troops of the Church dispersed. Ill-paid and out of hand, they were taken into Visconti's service in February 1351. The Pope protested, threatened excommunication, and deprived the archbishop of all powers, spiritual and temporal; but afterwards, following a long diplomatic struggle at Avignon in which Florence vainly attempted to deal a mortal blow to Visconti's omnipotence, Clement VI recalled the thunderbolts he had launched (27 April 1352) and made peace with his warlike foe. Bologna returned indeed to the Church, but the Church appointed Giovanni its vicar there for twelve years.

The end of the Visconti enterprise in Tuscany was not so happy. From the time of Henry VII, Florence, to defend herself and her allied or subject communes, had invoked and obtained the costly protection of the Angevins; and had shewn her internal discord and profound external weakness in the throes of the war for the subjugation of Lucca by offering the Signoria to Walter of Brienne, Count of Lecce, the husband of a niece of King Robert (1342). Now, scarcely was Robert dead (13 January 1343) when she resumed her traditional policy in Central Italy with greater liberty of movement. On her Romagnol frontier Giovanni de' Manfredi made himself master of Faenza (17 February 1350); the Malatesta enlarged their dominions towards the March of Ancona; the Ordelaffi gained possession of Cesena, Bertinoro, and other towns; and Durfort underwent irreparable reverses. The liberty of Florence was clearly exposed to the gravest danger, which came steadily nearer and grew more stifling as the Visconti's hold on Bologna grew stronger, while with regard to Pisa and Siena there reigned the old doubts and peril. The Visconti must be fought, and since Pope Clement VI's conduct could not be called the most straightforward, Florence effected an understanding with the Roman King Charles IV, forgetting her constant aversion to the

Empire and the permanent enmity of the Italian Ghibellines to herself (1351). Visconti tried to paralyse the republic in a net of enemies, rousing against her the most turbulent nobles of her *contado*; but when the moment came for a decisive stroke, neither they nor Pisa shewed the expected zeal. The fortress of Scarperia, at the entrance of one of the most vital parts of the Florentine territory, made a stout defence, and on 17 October 1351 Giovanni Oleggio, the captain of Visconti's forces, raised the siege and two days later re-entered Bologna. The state of things in Tuscany underwent a speedy transformation: the troublesome nobles were brought to account; the rival cities found themselves deserted; and the Pope himself strove to bring about a peace between Milan and Florence. The peace, in spite of the reluctance felt at first by Siena, was made on 31 March 1353 at Sarzana; but, as a treaty never by itself annuls profound divergences of interest by which wars are fed, this peace of Sarzana was but ephemeral. Soon it was seen that the archbishop, by acquiring Genoa and maintaining unchanged his formidable position in Emilia and towards Romagna, was planning a new attack; and so on 15 February 1354 Florence, together with Siena and Perugia, prepared for the inevitable fresh struggle by a new league, to which in April Venice, alarmed at Visconti's success, asked admission. Meanwhile Charles IV announced his imminent descent into Italy, feeling sure of gaining considerable advantages from the internal dissensions of Florence and Siena and the troubled and threatening aspect of Italian politics. Thus in the spring of 1354 from the Alps to the Arno and from sea to sea war was in agitation, and certainly it would have broken out had not the death of Giovanni Visconti on 5 October deferred its advent.

But the unstable equilibrium of Italy did not allow of peace. The Church wished to re-acquire the towns of the March of Ancona and of Romagna, and Pope Innocent VI felt himself in a position to embark on an organised enterprise on the great scale which was necessary. He possessed an able and obedient instrument in Egidio Albornoz, who had obtained the cardinal's hat on 17 December 1350 in reward for his excellent service in the long and bitter struggle against the Moors of Andalusia. On his nomination as papal legate in Italy on 30 June 1353, he at once perceived that it was necessary to begin his task with the States of the Church, and further with the separation at least for a time of the Visconti from the motley coalition arrayed against the Papacy. On his side, the Pope launched an excommunication against the Malatesta, who were guilty of seizing the chief towns of the March, such as Rimini, Pesaro, Fano, Fossombrone, Jesi, Osimo, Ascoli, and Recanati, and had refused to listen to the moderating counsels and commands which came from Avignon. Albornoz acted with tact and firmness, both during Charles IV's brief Italian expedition (October 1354–April 1355) and afterwards. For that matter indeed, the Emperor had been merely intent on selling as dearly as he could more or less effective privileges, and titles of Imperial Vicar which no longer increased anyone's prestige. In result, the Legate obtained in a few months the surrender of the Malatesta, the condemnation of Gentile da Mogliano, lord of Fermo, who was exiled and lost his signoria, and the submission of Ancona (24 June 1355), which was of special importance for the subjection of the March. There was the resistance of Francesco Ordelaffi, lord of Forlì and Cesena, still to be overcome, and the affairs of Bologna, then governed for the Visconti by Giovanni Oleggio, to be watched. The Legate was well aware of the support given by Bernabò Visconti to Ordelaffi, and was all the speedier in his action. Cesena, held by Ordelaffi's wife, Marzia degli Ubaldini, was forced to surrender (21 June 1357), and Forlì was besieged; but Innocent VI was persuaded by the astute policy of Visconti to negotiate over Bologna, and wished his Legate to allow for this separate programme, which could have been suitably deferred. The cardinal, however, did not believe it to be in the interest of his mission to couple things that were independent, and he continued to act as if the Pope's views were quite unknown to him. Naturally, the Pope thought of his recall and replacement by a more docile personage readier to obey than to issue commands.

Accordingly, on 28 February 1357, Innocent VI wrote to Albornoz that Androin de la Roche, Abbot of Cluny, was coming to communicate to him most important instructions. The Legate received the letter at Ancona on 17 March, but only met the abbot on 1 April at Faenza when the operations against Ordelaffi were in full swing. He at once said that to give Bologna to Bernabò would be a grave mistake, and asked to be relieved of his office. However, whether the Pope had become better informed or felt that he had gone too far, he now insisted that Albornoz should not quit his post till Ordelaffi was vanquished, and the Legate submitted for a while. Meanwhile he promulgated at Fano (29 April–1 May 1357) the famous *Egidian Constitutions*, which with but slight later modifications remained the law of the States of the Church till early in the nineteenth century. On 28 June, on his own authority, he joined the league against the Visconti made two years earlier by Mantua and Ferrara. Then on 9 September he left Cesena for Avignon. But his successor the abbot was the most unassuming of men and of no political ability, and the enemies of the Church, like Giovanni di Vico in the Campagna and Ordelaffi, quickly became formidable. The Pope saw his error in conciliating the Visconti, recalled the abbot, and sent out Cardinal Albornoz once more (18 September 1358).

The Cardinal's second period of office lasted five years. On 4 July 1359 Ordelaffi capitulated, and the Patrimony of St Peter was soon freed from disorders. Next year Albornoz snatched the opportunity provided by the attempt of Giovanni Oleggio of Bologna to make himself independent of the Visconti. He occupied Bologna, and conferred on Oleggio the office of papal Vicar of Fermo and Rector of the March of Ancona, while his own nephew Blasco Fernández was made Vicar of Bologna. Bernabò

Visconti used every means of defence; he plied the Pope with letters, and set his envoys at Avignon to work with the most ingenious diplomacy. He was not discouraged by the repulses of Innocent VI, and after continuous negotiations and warfare succeeded in the pontificate of Urban V by the aid of a strong group of cardinals in obtaining afresh the recall of Albornoz (26 November 1363) and the reappointment of the Abbot of Cluny whose first Italian mission had been so unsuccessful. With Albornoz departed it was easy for Visconti to reach the goal of his long efforts; and on 3 March 1364 there was published at Bologna the treaty of peace, by which Bernabò restored to the Church the fortresses in the Bolognese and Romagna in return for an indemnity of 500,000 florins. It was certainly a strange treaty in that it burdened the Church, whose strength in Italy had never been greater, with a charge only to be justified by defeat.

While the State of the Church was thus defended with varying success, and that of the Visconti was consolidated by the successors of Matteo, the Savoyard dynasty was developing methodically that comprehensive policy which was to lead it later to a height unguessed at in the fourteenth century. At the close of the thirteenth century, and during the expedition of Henry VII, the house of Savoy was not considered really Italian; it was occupied beyond the Alps and only in some degree within them in forming a State independent of Emperor, Pope, and King of France alike, in which aim it employed war and treaties, endless astuteness and sudden bold strokes. The very division of the house into three branches, Savoy, Vaud, and Piedmont, facilitated its variable attitude, even when it appeared and was in fact profoundly disunited by fatal jealousies. The Piedmontese branch of the Princes of Achaia (so named through the marriage of Philip of Savoy with Isabella de Villehardouin, the claimant of that Greek principality) displayed in the early fourteenth century a great activity in rivalry with the county of Savoy, but during the joint lives of Philip and Count Amadeus V their disputes were accommodated by arbitration and provisional arrangements. In the time, however, of Amadeus' sons, Odoardo and Aymon (1323–43), the conflict between Savoy and Achaia became steadily more pronounced, so that by intermarriages and alliances the two branches seemed to pursue completely different systems of policy. The Counts of Savoy seemed ever more foreign to Italy, while the Princes of Achaia—once their vanguard towards Piedmont and the valley of the Po—assumed the attitude of an Italian dynasty hostile both to the Angevins in Piedmont and to the county of Savoy.

Amadeus VI, the "Green Count" (1343–83), was the true founder of the greatness of Savoy. Well educated in a court which did not lack minstrels and poets—a characteristic of all Italian courts in that dawn of the Renaissance—he could carry to completion a unifying policy which would have been impossible half a century earlier. The marriage (1350) of his sister Bianca to Galeazzo, nephew of the Archbishop Giovanni, connected him with the Visconti; he settled the ancient controversies with

the Dauphins and the French Kings; he annexed the Valais, Geneva, and
Lausanne (1359–65); and finally he succeeded by war and diplomacy in
overcoming the resistance of his cousins of Achaia (1359–60). Yet it was
only on his return from crusade eight years later that Philip II of Achaia
was definitely beaten. Galeazzo Visconti aided his brother-in-law, while
no one moved to defend Philip, who underwent a formal trial at Avigliana
and disappeared mysteriously—perhaps he was put to death—at the end
of 1368.

Amadeus VI had gained his end, but he had for some time been aware
that the effort at unification would remain unfruitful without a solemn
recognition by the Empire, and had therefore courted Charles IV. The
Emperor was won over, and at Chambéry, as the count's guest on his way
to Avignon, he appointed his host (11 May 1365) Vicar of the Empire
in Savoy and in the dioceses of Sion, Geneva, Lausanne, Ivrea, Aosta,
Turin, Maurienne, Tarantaise, and Belley. None among the Italian
Signori now possessed more prestige than the Green Count. His unification of the Savoyard lands, his bold and generous crusade in the Levant,
his imperial vicariate, all subserved excellently his dynastic policy; and
so it was no wonder that Genoa and Venice, after a long and desperate
war, had recourse to his arbitration as the most enlightened and respected
that they could find. Genoa had been for many years torn by civil discord,
which had led to her falling under the signoria of Robert of Naples
(1318–34); and in 1339 a movement of the *popolo*, supported by the
sailors who had fought for France against England, had resulted in
breaking the power of the nobles and in proclaiming a Doge, Simone
Boccanera, nephew of that Boccanera who seventy years earlier had ruled
the republic[1]. This revolution brought a profound change over the ancient
form of government of the commune, and the dogeship it established
lasted almost without interruption till 1528. Almost immediately Genoa
resumed the policy of expansion suspended by the long internal crisis, and
took up anew the penetration of the Levant with the reconquest of Chios
and Samos and the re-establishment of her power in the village of Pera
(1344–48). Venice on the other hand had neither endured foreign rule
nor experienced the fatal civil dissensions which had everywhere rendered
the fall of communal liberty inevitable. Rather, the reform of 1297,
carried farther in the early decades of the fourteenth century, had allowed
her after the death of Doge Giovanni Soranzo in 1328 to take an active
share in the politics of the mainland from which she had long held aloof.
This meant for Venice the creation of a secure bulwark for the life in the
Lagoon and tended to make convenient and regular the natural routes of
her food-supply and of her commerce with the flourishing Lombardo-
Venetian territories and the lands beyond the Alps. Naturally, it did not
prevent Venice from continuing her preoccupation with the Levant or
from considering the safety and development of her sea-power as the

[1] See *supra*, Vol. VI, p. 181.

essential condition of her independence and her life. When therefore
Genoa renewed her Levantine advance, Venice, who had important establishments in the Black Sea, could not but be alarmed, and of these alarms
the war that broke out was the natural consequence.

From 1350 to 1355 fighting went on with various success. Genoa was
defeated on 29 August 1353 near Alghero on the shore of La Loiera in
western Sardinia, but the conspiracy of the Doge Marin Faliero against
the patricians, which was immediately discovered by the Council of Ten
and repressed with the execution of the old doge (17 April 1355), had
the effect of a defeat for Venice. And so the two parties came to a peace
on 1 June 1355 under the arbitration of the Visconti, since the Archbishop
Giovanni was then, as we have seen, Signore of Genoa. But his death
and the peace favoured the revival of the popular movement led once
more by Simone Boccanera, who held power for seven years (1356–63)
after driving out the Visconti. To him succeeded Gabriele Adorno and
Domenico Fregoso; but, as was to be expected, an alliance between
Venice and the Visconti came about, for the causes of enmity between
the two sea-powers could not be annihilated at a stroke. Their partisans
in the Levant fought without truce, and a chance occasion brought on
a new and murderous conflict. Andronicus, son of the Emperor John
Palaeologus, had been excluded from the succession to the Eastern Empire,
and was at war with his father. He was favoured by Genoa, while Venice
supported the Emperor. That was enough, but further in reward for
their assistance the two republics were each given the island of Tenedos
as an apple of discord (1376). For five years the most furious war of the
fourteenth century was waged between them. Aided by the King of
Hungary and the Da Carrara, lords of Padua, the Genoese forced their
way to Chioggia and Grado, thus threatening Venice at home; and the
Venetians in the greatest alarm, under the command of Vittor Pisani and
the Doge Andrea Cortarini, besieged the invaders at midwinter. The
Genoese captain, Pietro Doria, was slain in the fighting on 3 February
1380, and his forces were compelled to surrender with 38 galleys on
22 June of the same year.

But this did not end the war. The remaining Genoese forces kept up
the fight by land and sea, and Venice was compelled to cede Treviso to
Duke Leopold of Austria, being unable to defend it longer against
Francesco da Carrara. Capodistria, too, was burnt. It was useless to
continue the war now that both adversaries were so greatly exhausted,
and the Peace of Turin was made on 8 August 1381 under the mediation
of Amadeus VI. The losses of Venice included Dalmatia and Trieste,
while Genoa did not acquire her expected gains, and even Amadeus VI
did not achieve the greater scope of action for which he looked. In fact,
the republics came half-ruined from an adventure in which they had
squandered vast resources and had lamed without hope of speedy revival
their fleets and the very social forces which had fed the long struggle.

However, Venice could recover more quickly than Genoa, both because of her more healthy internal condition and because the sources of her prosperity had not in essentials been affected. On his side, the Green Count directly after the Peace of Turin had arranged an alliance of Venice, Genoa, and Savoy, evidently aimed against the Visconti with whom he was in seeming on the best of terms; and he was preparing to intervene as a pacificator in Genoa (whence ambassadors reached him in the first half of 1382), when the Neapolitan expedition changed the course of affairs. The ostensible object was to maintain the rights of the pretender Louis of the younger line of Anjou, the real motive to conquer by a fortunate stroke an incontestable primacy in northern Italy.

At Naples there had happened startling events, which through their political importance and their nature had aroused universal attention. King Robert had been succeeded in 1343 by his grand-daughter Joanna I, who for dynastic reasons was married to her cousin Andrew of Hungary[1]. On the night of 18 November 1345 King Andrew was cruelly murdered as a result of a conspiracy, to which public report immediately declared the youthful queen was privy; and, as was to be expected, her brother-in-law King Lewis of Hungary immediately began a ruthless war of vengeance which lasted till the end of 1350. Queen Joanna fled to the papal court at Avignon, and there begged and obtained from Clement VI both pardon and the solemnisation of her second marriage with another cousin, Louis, Prince of Taranto[2]. When a peace had been concluded with Lewis of Hungary, and she herself had been crowned, along with her new husband, at Naples in the presence of papal legates, the queen felt and acted as acquitted of all guilt and absolute ruler of her realm. She reigned for a decade in quiet with the aid of the counsel of the Florentine Niccolò Acciaiuoli, her friend and indeed her paramour, whom she made Grand Seneschal, a man with an extraordinary talent for affairs, without scruples or hesitations; he was the enemy of the insolent barons, and defended both the royal authority and the independence of the kingdom from all foreign intervention. But the death of Louis of Taranto at the age of forty-two on 26 May 1362 raised the problem of the succession to the throne. Next year Joanna married again, this time James (IV) of Aragon, the exiled and beggared heir of Majorca[3]; but, while the King of Hungary renewed his claims to the succession which he had never explicitly renounced, this marriage too was childless. The situation grew worse, for Acciaiuoli died on 9 November 1366, and King James left the kingdom, always striving and always unable to recover his paternal inheritance.

---

[1] Andrew was the younger son of Charles Robert, King of Hungary, himself the son of Robert's elder brother Charles Martel. He and his elder brother Lewis, King of Hungary, had thus claims to the kingdom of Naples as the elder branch of the family.

[2] Louis was son of Philip of Taranto, a younger brother of King Robert.

[3] See *infra*, Chap. xx, p. 589.

Joanna, however, accomplished one thing of importance: she assented to the definitive agreement (1373) with the Aragonese Frederick III, King of the island of Sicily. This treaty had been already approved and in a sense desired by Pope Gregory XI (27 August 1372); and it constituted the island a separate kingdom in legal form under the name of Trinacria and with the obligation of paying 15,000 florins yearly to Joanna and her successors.

The Great Schism, which broke out on the death of Gregory XI (27 March 1378), a year after he had brought the Papacy back to Rome, dragged the kingdom of Naples into a new series of misfortunes. The queen, after the death of her third husband, had married a fourth, Otto of Brunswick (1376), and she adhered now to Pope Clement VII against Pope Urban VI in the hope that the pontiff of Avignon would speedily extinguish the Schism. But Urban excommunicated her, calling on her cousin Charles, Duke of Durazzo[1], to combat her as a schismatic, while Joanna on her side declared her heir to be Louis (I), Duke of Anjou, the brother of King Charles V of France. War could not be avoided. Charles III, of Durazzo, was recognised as king by the Roman Pope on 1 June 1381, and immediately afterwards defeated Duke Otto at Anagni, entering Naples victoriously on 26 July. The queen held out in the fortress of Castelnuovo, but Otto's attempt to rescue her did not succeed, and she surrendered. She was imprisoned at Muro in Basilicata in March 1382, and was soon put out of the way; perhaps she was strangled. Louis of Anjou now made ready; he had succeeded to the county of Provence. After long negotiations with Amadeus VI of Savoy, a great expeditionary force, blessed by Clement VII, started from Pont Saint-Esprit and Carpentras in the spring of 1382, and having joined the Savoyard troops moved south on 8 July. It was a veteran army favoured by the Pope, the King of France, Gian Galeazzo Visconti, and some of the most powerful princes of Italy; but, whether it was due to the incompetence of Louis (I), or to Amadeus' illness at the critical moment, or to the good generalship of Charles of Durazzo and the famous *condottiere* Sir John Hawkwood, who fought in his service, the expedition attained none of the ends to which it was directed. Louis himself died at Bari on 22 September 1384. As for Amadeus VI, he had already died in the Molise, at Santo Stefano near San Giovanni-in-Galdo, on 1 March 1383 at the age of forty-nine, and his schemes vanished with him.

With Amadeus VI dead, Venice and Genoa at peace, Charles III firmly seated on the Neapolitan throne until his acquisition of Hungary (1385), the Church split by the Great Schism which was so destructive to the power of the Papacy in Italy and Europe, there appear upon the scene two personages of marked individuality, Gian Galeazzo Visconti and King Ladislas of Naples; both of them nourished vast schemes and immoderate

---

[1] Charles was the son of Louis, younger son of John of Durazzo, younger brother of King Robert.

ambition and perceived the possibility and the necessity of uniting the whole peninsula in a single State under a single master. At the same time, in Florence and the greater Tuscan communes the crisis of republican institutions clearly takes shape, and it becomes obvious that the Signoria is not far off. At Florence and Siena more especially, the insurrection of the town proletariat, led by men of the Lesser Arts hitherto excluded from power, shews that the Commune has been captured by a populace unprepared for the task of governing it, and hence that first the bourgeois reaction and then the Signoria will be able to solve a problem otherwise insoluble.

The history of republican Florence from the death of Dante to the close of the fourteenth century presents characteristic features of profound interest. As we have said, for defence against Henry VII she had given herself to the Signoria of King Robert; later for defence against the Tuscan Ghibellines to that of the Duke of Calabria; and finally, to prosecute the war against the Pisans for the acquisition of Lucca, she had created Signore Walter of Brienne, Duke of Athens and Count of Lecce, the nephew of King Robert (1342). In actual fact no political faction and no stratum of society desired the tyranny; but the magnates, always oppressed by laws of exception and restive under the rein of the Ordinances of Justice (1293), after having attempted a *coup d'état* in October 1341, hoped that the *condottiere* suddenly exalted to the Signoria would wreak revenge for them on the *popolani*, both *grassi* and *minuti*; the Priors of the republic, hesitating and surprised by events, were unable to arrest his course towards the Signoria; and the *popolani minuti*, always excluded from the government but ever more aggressive and numerous owing to the natural increase of industrial production, blindly acclaimed Walter as they had Corso Donati in open strife with the Commune forty years before. Thus on 8 September 1342, supported by his soldiers and by the enthusiasm of the *popolani minuti*, and urged on by his ambition and the incitements of the magnates, the Duke of Athens was proclaimed Signore. But he could only pursue his private interests, for he had neither statesmanship nor generosity, while those who had aided him expected something very different. The magnates saw themselves betrayed; the *popolani minuti* found that they had been cheated; and the ancient possessors of power, the *popolani grassi*, prepared for a reaction. On 26 July 1343 there broke out a general and furious insurrection, and in a few hours the duke's power was gone. On 1 August he renounced the Signoria and on the night of 5–6 August, escorted by a band of Sienese troops, he left the city for ever. The brief adventure was ended; the Commune was restored in its traditional form, and the social conflict recommenced with savage violence.

From the fall of the Duke of Athens to the outbreak of the revolt of the Ciompi the constitutional crisis grew worse and became steadily more complicated with fresh factors. The traditional classes were profoundly transformed; Guelfism and Ghibellinism lost their ancient meaning and were made the pretext for mutual accusations and reprisals. The Greater Arts, *i.e.* the industrial and mercantile associations which since the Peace of Cardinal Latino (1280) had monopolised political power, had been inwardly transmuted and refined in measure as the ever richer manufacturers and merchants entered into closer multifarious relations everywhere in Italy and abroad, adopting the life of *grands seigneurs* and shewing marked tendencies to oligarchy. Lastly, the *popolo minuto* did not participate in politics save very indirectly in the train of the Lesser Arts, themselves always in the background and always longing to regain a share of power. The question of the proletariat attained greater dimensions daily. According to Giovanni Villani the Arte della Lana alone employed 30,000 persons, and the dependants of the other arts were many in number. Certainly, the figures of the chroniclers are not to be trusted, and the most recent studies on the statistics of population have not reached concrete results; but it is clear all the same that *c.* 1350 the workmen of each Art had become exceedingly numerous, and could not but be a permanent danger to the safety of the State. They had no right of self-organisation in any way, and since the unorganised are outside the State and hence its enemies, the workmen felt no allegiance to the old republic which meant for them the most degrading of servitudes. How could they fight with legal weapons when legal weapons were not allowed to them? Only revolt remained; and in 1345, led by an ardent and genuine proletarian, Ciuto Brandini, the Florentine proletariat made its first attempt at revolution. The agitator naturally was put to death, and the crowd which eagerly sympathised with him had not the power to snatch him from the hangman. The Priors imagined that they had extinguished with one man's voice the discontent of which he was the spokesman; but the problem only became more urgent and complex.

The Black Death of 1348 strikingly diminished the city's population and did not spare the smaller neighbour towns or the countryside; but when the scourge was past the pulse of Florence soon regained the fevered beat now habitual to it. Two nuclei of forces formed in mutual opposition and prepared for civil war: the Parte Guelfa and the *popolo minuto*. The Parte Guelfa had arisen as an association of injured faction partisans when the Guelfs were for the first time driven from the city in February 1249; it had gained possession of the Ghibellines' property in consequence of the Guelf reform of 1266–67; and little by little, even when the memory of those times had faded, it had become a most powerful society, both economic and political, with rich revenues, with its own statutes and officials, often a creditor of the republic for large sums, and always the vigilant guardian of the political interests of the *popolo grasso* and of those magnates who had succeeded in entering the governing class in the first decades of the fourteenth century. After the Black Death the prepotency of the Parte Guelfa increased, and culminated with the laws of 27 August 1354 and 24 April 1358, under which on any kind of suspicion of Ghibellinism the most terrible persecutions were possible and the very lives of thousands of citizens of every rank could be and were at the mercy of the Captains of the Parte. It was in truth an intolerable situation, against which there was a reaction in Provisions (3 November, 8 December 1366, and 26 March 1367) intended to wrench the dreaded weapon of "admonition" for suspicion of Ghibellinism from the hands of the Parte Guelfa. No one could feel safe from the blows of the Parte, and many of those whose interests seemed involved in its predominance were among the authors of the Provisions which limited its omnipotence.

The *popolo minuto* on its side had been fatally favoured by the violence of the plague, since the shortage of labour had markedly increased, and wages had risen sharply; but then the rise in the cost of living had annulled this transitory advantage and had aroused in the minds of the working folk the most evil designs. In August 1368, in consequence of one of the frequent dearths which during the last forty years had afflicted not only Tuscany but a great part of Italy, the *popolani minuti* rioted furiously in the corn-market and then rushed into the Piazza dei Priori with shouts of "Viva il Popolo!" Soon after, the resistance of the employers and the demands of the workmen met at an impasse: the masters declared that they could not raise wages, and the workmen insisted on a large increase. There resulted a real strike, for the dyers refused to work in the hope of forcing from the Arte della Lana the rise in wages hitherto asked in vain. In 1371 the same thing happened at Siena, where the workmen threatened to massacre the masters, a palpable sign that the evil lay in the foundations of the economic system of the commune, and that the commune-State had not succeeded in finding a remedy. In Florence the Parte Guelfa took measures of defence by forcing through the law of 27 January 1372, which tended to make any democratic reaction extremely difficult. For six years each side strengthened itself in unconscious preparation for the explosion of 1378. The Lesser Arts won some successes, such as the entry of two of their representatives into the tribunal of the Mercanzia (1372), and in carrying about the same time a severe inquest into the finances of the commune and the conduct of their administrators. Lastly, the creation of the Ten of Liberty (1372)—composed of two magnates, two *popolani minuti*, and six *popolani grassi*—shewed that the offensive of the Parte Guelfa had encountered obstinate and unforeseen obstacles.

The "War of the Eight Saints" quieted for a time the civil strife. The relations between the Church and Florence had become very strained when Cardinal Guillaume de Nollet during the dearth of 1374–75 had impeded the exportation of food-stuffs from Romagna into Tuscany, and had become extremely bad in June 1375 when the company of Sir John Hawkwood, following the truce concluded in Bologna between the Church and Bernabò Visconti, fell upon the Florentine *contado*. It was necessary to pay the condottiere 130,000 florins to evacuate Florentine territory; and partly to prepare for the conflict which all thought imminent, partly owing to the disturbances in the States of the Church, and partly owing to the misconduct of the papal legates so vigorously condemned by St Catherine of Siena (1347–80), the Florentines created a special magistracy, the Eight of War, who were called later in mid-conflict the Eight Saints, in defiance of their excommunication by the Pope. On 4 January 1376 by order of the Florentine Priors an epistle was sent by the chancellor, Coluccio Salutati, to the Romans in order to induce them to rebel; on 19 March the Bolognese revolted and drove out the papal troops; on 31 March Pope Gregory XI launched an excommunication against Florence. He expelled ruthlessly from Avignon some 600 Florentine merchants as a reprisal, and sent a new Legate into Italy, Cardinal Robert of Geneva, at the head of 4000 horse and 6000 foot. Contemporaneously, whether for political reasons or moved by the fiery letters of St Catherine, he came himself, landing at Porto Pisano on 7 November 1376; but his presence only added to the ferment. The revolt of Cesena owing to the oppression exercised by the cardinal's soldiers, and the horrible butchery that followed (3 February 1377)—in which 2000–3000 citizens were killed—were the signal for a violent anti-papal movement in Florence and her allied towns; and since Bologna, contrary to the alliance and the demands of the Eight Saints, made a truce with the enemy, and the League threatened to dissolve, the republic resolved at all costs to detach Hawkwood from the Church; and it gained its point (April 1377). But then the Florentine captain, Rodolfo da Varano, angry at this transfer and allured by the Pope's promises of the vicariate of Tolentino and Sanginesio, abandoned the republic and in the Pope's service took command of the Company of Bretons still reeking with the blood of the Cesenese. The Eight Saints took the boldest measures: in October 1377 they violated the interdict, reopening the churches and ordering the clergy to resume their functions. The Pope replied with new severities, and the Parte Guelfa, playing their own game (which was that of a reactionary circle of magnates) against the war party, dared to domineer in the city so far as to "admonish" seventy citizens in one year. But all were weary of a war that was a stalemate, and the mediation of Bernabò Visconti was accepted by both sides; early in March 1378 a peace congress was opened at Sarzana. The negotiations, interrupted by the death of Gregory XI (27 March), were gladly resumed by the Florentines directly a new, Italian Pope was elected in Urban VI, and led to the peace of Tivoli on 28 July.

But by the time that the peace with the Church was concluded, a real revolution had for some days broken out in Florence. Already in April 1378 the Parte Guelfa had dared to touch one of the Eight Saints, Giovanni Dini, a spicer, substituting for him an extreme Guelf, Niccolò Giani; and immediately afterwards, in May and June, its opposition to

Salvestro de' Medici, the Gonfalonier of Justice[1], assumed an aspect and meaning definitely adverse both to the *popolo grasso* and to the *popolo minuto* rather than to the long war with the Church. Hence on 22–23 June both sorts of *popolani* were at one in taking the offensive against the Parte Guelfa, and many houses were burnt in a riot. On the 23rd an extraordinary Balía[2] of eighty citizens was appointed and took office, and began to draft reforms which should restrain the excesses of the Parte Guelfa and disarm the *popolani* in revolt; and when the new Priors (*Signoria* in Florentine parlance) entered office, with Luigi Guicciardini as Gonfalonier of Justice, on 1 July 1378, it seemed that tranquillity would soon return. But there followed continuous mutual accusations and suspicions. The magnate groups feared the meetings of *popolani minuti* which were being secretly held here and there; the *popolani* accused the Parte Guelfa of trampling underfoot the reforms of the Eighty; the Priors were uncertain and unready. At last it became known that the "subjects" of the Arts, that is the workmen, were gathered at Ronco outside the gate of San Pier Gattolini in contravention of the statutes and the unbroken tradition of centuries, and that they had taken dangerous resolutions. It seems that Salvestro de' Medici supported them with wise advice. In this crisis the Priors decided to act and mobilised the citizen forces, *i.e.* the few armed men at their disposal, for 20 July with the view of intimidating the *popolani* and arresting the ringleaders. But all was upset by an unforeseen revolutionary tornado, for the Ciompi, *i.e.* the populace and the poorest workmen, led by a wool-carder, Michele di Lando, attacked the Palazzo of the Commune and scoured the city burning and destroying. From 21 to 24 July the republic was in the hands of the insurgents; Michele di Lando was Gonfalonier of Justice; and the Signoria was driven from office. Between 24 July and 8 August three new Arts (the Dyers, the Jerkin-makers, and the so-called Ciompi) were officially recognised, each with their own consuls and banners, like the seven Greater and fourteen Lesser Arts; Michele seemed master of the situation. But a few days sufficed to shew the workmen and the mob that they had won a nearly barren victory; they desired absolute control of the commune, and they were not content with their chief. On 27 August they assembled in the Piazza San Marco to the number of 3000–5000 to enforce revolutionary measures on the new Signoria, which elected in a riot and by rioters was afraid of not seeming revolutionary enough; and either just before or just after, in a solemn meeting in Santa Maria Novella, they elected the "Eight of Santa Maria Novella" and swore to be "a single body and a single will"; they were famished, for the shops were closed, and there was no work to be had; and hunger inspired violence.

Thus at the end of August a new flood threatened to submerge the commune. The crowd rushed furiously to the houses of the magnates,

---

[1] *I.e.* practically the chief of the College of Priors.
[2] *I.e.* a commission with full powers to govern and reform.

to the palace of the Priors, to the shops, without definite aim or policy; and on 31 August two envoys of the Eight of Santa Maria Novella came to the Signoria to impose new conditions. The terrified Priors would perhaps have agreed to anything, but Michele di Lando, in whom a few weeks of government had developed a sense of responsibility and proportion, drove out the envoys, put himself at the head of the armed force, and immediately scattered the insurgents. The revolution was over. The two Arts of Dyers and Jerkin-makers sought their safety, the rebels were pitilessly hunted down, and, without gaining any thanks for his services either first to the *popolo minuto* or later to the State, Michele di Lando shortly afterwards vanished from Florentine history. Naturally the victory had been due to the coalition of all the threatened interests, and therefore the government which followed, and in spite of frequent difficulties ruled the destiny of the commune for three years, was a coalition government, in which the strongest element was formed by the Lesser Arts including those two new Arts which had escaped the ruin of the Ciompi. The laws of 11 and 18 September provided for the reorganisation of the State put out of gear by the revolt: the Parte Guelfa lost its ancient prestige and power, the *popolo grasso* was compelled to make the hardest terms in order not to be excluded from the new régime. This situation lasted till early in 1382, when the *popolo grasso* succeeded in recovering power, profiting by the effeteness of the democratic government and by the economic crisis which afflicted city and *contado*. Salvestro de' Medici and Michele di Lando were driven into exile; the two Arts of the *popolo minuto* were abolished; the exiles were recalled; the Priorate was made up of four members of the Greater Arts and four of the Lesser; in all offices of the commune the Greater Arts were given a majority; and the Parte Guelfa could reconquer the ground it had lost. The laws of 27 February and 15 March 1382 consolidated the new régime, and opened officially the period of about forty years which slowly rendered inevitable the Signoria of the Medici. It is the time of the oligarchy, when a few rich and aggressive families domineered over the commune. One of them, the Medici, in the person of Cosimo the elder (1389–1464), was to control completely the republic, and with that the commune of Florence really ended.

Events at Siena had the same import in that latter half of the fourteenth century which for long fixed the destiny of the provinces of Italy. There the government of the Nine had lasted from 1280 to 1354; it was a typical government of merchants, *i.e.* of a very limited group which naturally was opposed by both nobles and *popolani*. In fact, during the first half of the fourteenth century both nobles and *popolo* several times tried vainly, sometimes together and sometimes apart, to overthrow the régime of the Nine. But the Arts of Siena had always been less developed than those of Florence, and consequently there was lacking a numerous and aggressive middle class able to restrain the Nine and to balance their power. In 1355, however, nobles and *popolo* profited by the arrival of the Emperor Charles IV in the city to rise in revolt (25 March), and won the day at a moment when the commune was in extreme difficulties owing to the raids of the Free Companies. The result was the government of the Twelve. Supported by the armed citizen companies and the renewed and increased power of the Captain of the Popolo, this time not a foreigner but a citizen, it lasted till 1369, amid the opposition and risings of the nobles and the dispersed and humiliated faction of the Nine. In 1371 it was altered in a popular direction after a strike by the workmen of the Arte della Lana, and demagogues ruled until 23 March 1385, harassed indeed by the external war with the Free Companies and by the plots of those excluded from the government. On that day the nobles, scouring the city and promising peace and plenty, succeeded in overthrowing the democratic government; they acted probably in understanding with the Florentine oligarchs, and were aided by a part of the *popolo* which was most severely hit by the unceasing war and by the economic crisis which continually grew worse. Exile and persecutions diminished the citizens, and the republic lost its energy in regard to both friends and enemies. As in Florence, the fall of communal institutions was not distant.

The destiny of the Pisan republic was not different. Exhausted by the war with Genoa which was decided at Meloria (1284), constantly plotted against by Florence which needed an outlet on the sea, torn within by the implacable dissensions of classes and factions, Pisa had already fallen in the first decades of the fourteenth century into the hands of Uguccione della Faggiuola and Castruccio Castracani, remaining a republic only in name. Later, racked by the discord of the Borgolini and the Raspanti, she submitted in August 1365 to the dictatorship of Giovanni dell' Agnello; but that "Doge" was overthrown in September 1368 with the aid of the members of the Arts and many of his previous supporters. A few months after, in February 1369, there returned from exile Pietro Gambacorta, who had made his first attempt at government fifteen years earlier, and had shewn his deep knowledge of the passions of the mob and the interests of the republic. Within a year he was master of the State and felt secure in a city which the war between Florence and the Visconti had reduced to a wretched condition. The general reform of 27 October 1370 was the basis of his government and was maintained almost without change till his fall (21 October 1392). He had pursued a pro-Florentine policy which had angered all classes of citizens; and then Gian Galeazzo Visconti had skilfully undermined his power with eventual success. Pisa continued to struggle in the talons of domestic despotism and that of the Visconti for a little over ten years, and then ended under the dominion of Florence (1406).

When, therefore, Gian Galeazzo Visconti—called the Count of Virtù from the fief of Vertus in Champagne which was the dowry of his wife Isabella of France—began his brief and crowded career, the political situation of all Italy was peculiarly favourable for the boldest schemes.

He was twenty-five when he succeeded his father Galeazzo II (4 August 1378) in his share of the Visconti dominions as partner of his uncle Bernabò, who continued his cruel tyranny over Milan and his other possessions. Most accomplished in feigning and dissembling, subtle and receptive, immoderately and insatiably ambitious, he began to spread his net for his uncle and cousins, and on 6 May 1385, under pretext of greeting Bernabò during his pilgrimage to the Madonna del Monte near Varese, he succeeded in capturing him and his sons Lodovico and Rodolfo. A few months later, in December, Bernabò died, it may be by poison, in the castle of Trezzo d'Adda. Gian Galeazzo was absolute master of all the Visconti territory, and immediately gave thanks to heaven by laying the foundations, in 1386, of Milan cathedral. He quickly shewed his determination to exploit circumstances to the utmost by intervening in the war between the Scaligeri and the Da Carrara, at first as a mediator and then almost at once as an impatient and greedy enemy; and he succeeded in seizing Verona, Vicenza, and Padua (1386–88). Thence, like the Archbishop Giovanni Visconti, he aimed at the rich plain of Emilia, at Romagna and Tuscany; and seeing that Siena, after the occupation of Arezzo by Florence (20 November 1384), was in continual dread of her too-powerful rival, Gian Galeazzo fanned the flame with a view to war. And a murderous war broke out from Bologna and extended over all parts of Tuscany; but Florentine gold and Hawkwood's generalship ended in carrying hostilities into Lombardy, the Veneto, and even Piedmont, and in straining severely the resources of Visconti. So a peace was made in January 1392 which seemed to dissipate his dreams. He consoled himself by provoking the fall of Pietro Gambacorta and then that of Giacopo d'Appiano, tyrants of Pisa, and a little later, in September 1395, bought for 100,000 florins the title of Duke of Milan from Wenceslas, King of the Romans.

The duke could now aim higher, but to prevent any possible opposition from France he abandoned Genoa to her. Like Florence, Siena, and all the surviving communes, the republic of St George was racked with intestine discords and by the revolt of the poorest classes. Defence against both sorts of enemies, those within and without, was impossible; and therefore when the Duke of Orleans, called in by a group who forgot their patriotism in the violence of faction hatred, occupied Savona, promising the town very liberal municipal reforms and complete independence of Genoa, the Genoese Doge Antoniotto Adorno was caught between two fires—the French pressure and the civil war carried on with mad fury by two fallen Doges, Antonio di Montalto and Antonio di Guarco. He thought that only a foreign Signore could save the city from disaster; nobles and people ended by accepting his view, and on 25 October 1396 the republic gave itself to the King of France. Gian Galeazzo hid his wrath at so unwelcome an event, and turned towards Tuscany. He knew well that the possession of Tuscany would open his way to the States of the Church, torn by chronic anarchy and the Schism as well, and from Rome no one could hinder his march on Naples. It was a mirage; perhaps he dreamed of the crown of Italy. The "Viper" first struck at Pisa. Gherardo d'Appiano, son of Giacopo, sold him the city for 200,000 florins, and on 31 March 1399 the Pisan banners were bowed before him in the castle at Pavia. A few months after (November) civil strife and the fear of Florence gave him Siena, which he had long coveted, and the same deep-rooted general causes made Perugia follow Siena's example (January 1400). Assisi and Spoleto could not resist him, and Paolo Guinigi, Signore of Lucca, proclaimed him his protector.

Who could check the Duke of Milan on his determined road? Venice was anxious over the Levant, and loath for war in Italy; Naples was a prey to the troubles which preceded and followed the coronation of Ladislas; the Bentivoglio and the Gozzadini fought over Bologna; the Papacy was timid and decadent; the house of Savoy was hampered by the minority of Amadeus VIII and the long conflict with the princes of Achaia. Only Florence could make an effort not to lose independence and liberty, and she took for her ally Rupert, Elector Palatine, who had been elected King of the Romans on the deposition of Wenceslas (20 August 1400). Florence promised 200,000 florins down, and the same amount after Rupert had warred for four months in Visconti's dominions. The king descended into Italy, but was defeated under the walls of Brescia on 14 October 1401, and loitering by Padua and Venice (always negotiating for the balance of florins) he returned to Germany. There was still Bologna to defend; but Gian Galeazzo launched against her the veteran troops of Jacopo dal Verme and Alberico da Barbiano, and the Florentines and Bolognese suffered a bloody defeat at Casalecchio (26 June 1402). Bologna surrendered, while the Sienese Simone Serdini (called the Saviozzo da Siena) in very passable verse urged the duke to make himself master of Italy. Gian Galeazzo needed no urging. Florence seemed lost, and as was to be expected rebellion and treason muttered and ripened in the oppressed *contado*. Sir John Hawkwood was dead; the army was scattered and dispirited; the treasury exhausted. But sudden and incredible came the news that on 3 September 1402 the duke had expired at Melegnano, a few days after leaving Milan where the plague was spreading. With him vanished his "Italian" dream.

But it found a new dwelling in a bold and adventurous spirit, King Ladislas of Naples. When Charles of Durazzo was murdered in Hungary on 7 February 1386, he left behind him at Naples his widow Margaret and two young children, Joanna born in 1371 and Ladislas born in 1376. Margaret declared her son king, but the party of Louis II of Anjou, the incurable anarchy of the barons, the pro-Angevin policy of the Pope at Avignon, and the very ambitions of the Roman Pope, Urban VI, on the South caused the loss of Naples in 1387 and the flight of Margaret with her children first into Castel dell' Ovo and then to Gaeta. After Urban's death (15 October 1389), however, and the election of the Neapolitan Pietro

Tomacelli as Pope Boniface IX, the young king was solemnly crowned at Gaeta (1390) by the Pope's wish. It seemed that victory was near, but it was only obtained nine years later in consequence of one of those profound revulsions of public opinion which often take place in poor and disorganised lands. Naples was retaken, many barons abandoned Louis II, and in a few months the Angevin was compelled to return to France. The year before, Boniface IX had succeeded in subduing the republican government of Rome. Thus, when Gian Galeazzo died, Ladislas had already established his authority in his kingdom, a success all the more important because, in consequence of the duke's testament, a rapid dissolution began of the State which with such boldness and good fortune he had raised. On the other side, the Schism had thrown Western Christendom into indescribable confusion, and most of all Rome itself, where there was a veritable revolt against the new papal domination on the death of Boniface IX (1 October 1404) and the election of Innocent VII.

Ladislas saw that it was possible to intrude himself astutely into Roman affairs as arbiter between the Romans and the Pope, and that even if the immediate results of his intervention were not brilliant, it would increase his prestige, and would give him useful connexions in the pursuit of his policy. After the death of Innocent VII (6 November 1406), the rival pontiffs were Benedict XIII of Avignon and the new Roman Pope Gregory XII (the Venetian cardinal Angelo Correr); and since their mutual suspicions prevented them meeting at Savona, as was proposed, or elsewhere, Benedict sent some galleys to the mouth of the Tiber, while Gregory XII was residing at Lucca[1]. Ladislas then executed his long-planned stroke: he swiftly occupied Latium and Umbria. Since Gregory XII could not defend his State, still less reconquer it, he took the most singular resolution: to sell the States of the Church to Ladislas for 25,000 florins, and to further his designs (1409). But in these months the Council of Pisa deposed both Popes and elected a third, Alexander V (26 June 1409). The new pontiff could not but see the meaning of the king's actions, and he therefore urged a new invasion by Louis II of Anjou and followed blindly the advice of the Cardinal-legate of Bologna, the *condottiere* Baldassare Cossa. Ladislas, however, was not disturbed; he actually chose this moment to make an unsuccessful bid for the crown of Hungary, as if to shew his enemies that they could not hamper any audacity of his. *Aut Caesar aut nullus* was his motto, and arms, capacity, and boldness were its natural concomitants.

But fortune did not favour him. At first, when Genoa revolted from France (3 September 1409), it seemed as if the coalition of the Pope, the Angevin Louis II, and the Tuscan cities, aided by the forces of the most eminent *condottieri* of the day, could do nothing against him. But the treachery of Paolo Orsini at Rome, and the unwearied activity of Florence and Siena overturned his dominion in the States of the Church (October

---

[1] See *infra,* Chap. x.

1409). The death of Alexander V (3 May 1410) did not help him, for the new Pope, John XXIII, elected by the cardinals at Bologna, was his deadly enemy Cossa, who, the rumour went, had poisoned Alexander. The war blazed up again and on 9 May 1411 Louis II won a great victory at Roccasecca in the Terra di Lavoro. Ladislas escaped with difficulty, but then came better hopes: Bologna rebelled against the papal Vicar, the Prefect di Vico seized Civitavecchia, and the *condottiere* Muzio Attendolo Sforza changed over to the side of the King of Naples. John XXIII hastened to make peace with him (1412) and pretended to be engrossed in combating the heresy of Wyclif, convoking a council and hoping for the alliance of Sigismund, King of the Romans (3 March 1413). Ladislas, on his side, feigned adherence to this pacific policy; but when he thought he was ready, he began a violent offensive against the States of the Church. It was the first move to fresh conquests. Pope John was helpless: he had no troops, and was abandoned by Louis II, who, himself luckless and deserted by his friends, had returned to France. The Pope could only cling to Sigismund's alliance, and accepted his demand that Constance should be the place of assembly of the General Council. Meanwhile, Florence could give him no help, nor could the Duke of Milan. Florence was rent by discord and threatened with imminent ruin. Amid perils of every kind Filippo Maria Visconti, the younger son of Gian Galeazzo, was securing the heritage of his elder brother Giovanni Maria, who had been poniarded in the church of San Gottardo on 16 May 1412. Ladislas could therefore dream of making the possession of Rome the first step to the conquest of Italy; and in fact his treaty with Florence on 22 June 1414 seemed to protect his flank in the enterprise he had begun a few weeks before it. The little local tyrants, the republics, Pope John XXIII, King Sigismund, were all anxiously awaiting events when the news came that Ladislas, attacked by syphilis in his camp at Narni, had been carried to Naples and had there died on 6 August 1414.

The Italian powers seemed to awake from a nightmare. At Florence men felt in the felicitous words of Machiavelli that "death was the best friend of the Florentines and stronger to save them than any powers (*virtù*) of their own." Now John XXIII could more calmly await the meeting of the Council of Constance on 1 November 1414, while Naples under Joanna II fell back into the anarchy from which only a strong policy of expansion in Italy could have saved her. Amadeus VIII of Savoy was still a minor, and even later had no power to tread in the footsteps of Ladislas. The Church was only reunited, at least officially, by the election of Martin V (11 November 1417) to be followed by the recrudescence of schism when the Council of Basle deposed Eugenius IV in January 1438. Venice was preoccupied with the new Muslim peril of the Ottoman Turks in the Levant, and the Visconti could not renew the designs of Gian Galeazzo. Thus, if for a moment, a century before Machiavelli invoked a Prince to free Italy, the unification of the peninsula seemed possible, the possibility soon disappeared and for many years no one could think of it again. The fifteenth century is the time when the Signorie become ordinary principates, the time of the splendour of the Medici (not to be wholly quenched for three centuries), and the time when the geographical discoveries fatally diverted the stream of commerce from the Mediterranean and brought on Italy a long and painful economic crisis without remedy and without the possibility of compensating advantages.

In 1414 the signs of decadence were still far off. The bourgeois class was then in its highest prosperity and for that very reason tended to quit the commune for the "principate." The fourteenth century was the golden age of merchants, manufacturers, speculators, and bankers. The Arts, which in the thirteenth century had long fought to enter the government and drive thence the magnates, in the fourteenth reached the apogee of their power both economic and political. Production, which at the dawn of the commune had been circumscribed by the city walls, reaching only over an insignificant radius without, had in the fourteenth century assumed the character of "great industry," and had made an advance in technique and internal organisation only surpassed by modern times with the extensive introduction of machinery. Strictly protectionist as they were, the Arts everywhere, in Lombardy, in Tuscany, in the Veneto, and in Emilia, wherever in fact they developed freely, succeeded in producing, without set-backs and without ruinous crises; they performed miracles of ability and resource in a time of political instability and danger, and in face of endless difficulties, such as more especially the supply of food and raw material and the formation of bodies of skilled craftsmen. By controlling the quantity and the quality of the output, the cost of production and the selling price, they ended, even when breaking the immutable economic laws of production, in transforming the dead little towns of the feudal age into powerful living organisms, since their innate protectionism and particularism were natural consequences of the constitution of the commune, and were weapons of offence and defence. Round about the year 1400 the original organisation of the Arts was attacked in many vital points by germs of deadly disease, but it had been able to overcome the perils of social and political transformation, and, at least in Tuscany and the regions where the Commune was longest lived, it still shewed a surprising durability.

Commerce by land and sea had developed on parallel lines. We need only think of the radius of the influence of the Pisan, Genoese, Venetian, Florentine, Sienese, and Lombard merchants to reach unexpected conclusions. They frequented every corner of the then known world: the fairs of Champagne, the markets of the Netherlands, Germany, England, Africa, and the East knew and valued their methods, felt the influence of their law and policy, and added to their wealth. For Venice, Florence,

and Genoa commerce was an affair of State, the most delicate and fertile
affair of State, so much so that their legislation, voluminous as it was,
was inspired by mercantile interests; and these were so closely connected
with the interests of politics and manufacture that no uncertainty of
methods and aims seemed possible. For this reason Venice encountered
Genoa in the Levant, and Florence aimed at the conquest of Pisa and
the annihilation of Siena in order to open the roads to the sea and to
Rome and the South, just as the policy of the precocious communes of
the Po valley had been determined by the needs of traffic. The merchants
were the first and ablest diplomatists, the first ambassadors at Naples, at
Rome, in France, in England, in the Levant. Merchants were the founders
of the most eminent families, the favourites of Popes and kings, the
first ancestors of a new aristocracy which in the fifteenth and sixteenth
centuries was to live in splendid pomp amid the delicate refinements of
courts and academies. It was merchants who amassed that surplus
capital which fed the most varied forms of speculation at home and
abroad.

But what most captures the historian's attention is that these merchants were bound in powerful associations which were perfectly elastic
and responsive to their varying task in the world. The mercantile
societates—the "Companies" of Florence, Siena, Perugia, the Veneto, and
Lombardy—can bear comparison even with the most powerful organisations of to-day. Arising at first round the nucleus of some bold and
fortunate family, they gradually became true joint-stock companies with
directors and agents, with audited balance-sheets, with numerous share-
holders all eager for speedy and large profits. They dealt in every kind
of goods, and passed from the food supply of their city and its neighbourhood to the purchase of raw material, from ship-building to the great
commerce of all the Mediterranean lands and the northern seas. Hence they
speculated on prices of cost and of sale, on the exchange-rates of the varied
coinages, on the frequent dearths, on destructive wars and recuperative
peace, with attitudes and feelings which stood aloof from the habitual
manifestations of the little city life, with its quarrels and narrowness.
Often a wave of adversity submerged famous firms which had operated
for years in foreign lands, and then there was a crisis both for men and
property, which had its repercussions in private fortunes and the policy
of the republic. But then the rift was closed, the wounds were healed,
and the *societates* returned to the old paths or sought out new with
indefatigable energy.

Such a dizzy movement of merchandise and capital would naturally not
have been possible without adequate institutions of credit. Religious and
economic prejudices and the deplorable insecurity of political institutions
had for centuries condemned credit in its characteristic and spontaneous
forms. But the Church itself, which in the most impecunious periods of
medieval and modern history had the largest financial resources, and later

the most powerful sovereigns also were forced to recognise, in however decorous and veiled a way, that without credit commerce and production were impossible. And credit grew organised, reaching in Italy in the fourteenth century the form of the private bank, the first foundation of all State banks. Thus the traffic in money could be controlled legally and technically in so complete a way that modern times have been able to add, in substance, but few vital elements. The Bank of San Giorgio at Genoa and the Bank of San Marco at Venice have a history which has lost none of its interest. But since credit tends to become inflated, the Italian mercantile companies used and abused it till they were pledged within and without Italy for immense sums, and often could not avoid the consequence of too wide liabilities. There was the crisis and bankruptcy of the Bardi and Peruzzi in the years 1339, 1343, and 1346. They were excessively involved with Edward III of England, and with the wars in which Florence was engaged from 1332 until the *signoria* of the Duke of Athens. So the unsuccess of Edward's early French campaigns and the panic of their creditors at the first rumours of their insolvency were enough to provoke the painful crisis which Giovanni Villani endured as an investor and vividly described as a historian. These were incertitudes common to all speculations and deserve no more tears than other misfortunes. The fact remains that, wherever and however they began, institutions of credit had their greatest development in Italy, and that they meant the complete triumph of capitalistic economy over feudal, and also the social and political maturity of the early Italian bourgeoisie between the fall of Rome and the Renaissance.

CHAPTER III

GERMANY, 1273–1313

(A)

THE political condition of Germany towards the end of the Interregnum was indeed deplorable. Its kings, for more than three centuries, had ruled as Emperors over Central Europe in concert with or in opposition to the Popes. This opposition had ended about the middle of the thirteenth century to the disadvantage of the Empire in the victory of the Popes over the proud race of the Hohenstaufen. The German Kings who succeeded, albeit only nominally, had not been able to maintain their supremacy over the vassal princes, and had left the Empire in hopeless confusion. This lasted until 1273; it was in fact a period of Interregnum.

After the death of the nominal king, Richard of Cornwall (2 April 1272), there was a general desire to place at the head of the State a real king and a truly German one. The new Pope, Gregory X, elected a few days before, animated by a fervent longing to wrest the Holy Land from the Muslims, shared this desire. The question was, however, whom the German Electors were to choose as their king. They did not want a powerful German prince, neither the Wittelsbach Count Palatine Lewis nor his brother Henry Duke of Lower Bavaria, less still the brilliant Slav King Ottokar II, grandson on his mother's side of the Hohenstaufen Philip of Swabia, who ruled from Bohemia as far as the north of Italy. On the proposal of the Bavarian Duke and strongly influenced by the Count Palatine himself, they at last (1 October 1273) chose at Frankfort the Swabian Count Rudolf of Habsburg, who readily accepted the terms imposed. Rudolf, now fifty-five years of age, whose rich possessions were spread over Upper Alsace, Swabia, and the north-west of modern Switzerland— the ancestral home of the Habsburgs stands in Aargau on the Aar— entered Frankfort the next day and on 24 October was crowned with Charlemagne's crown in the ancient royal city of Aix-la-Chapelle. He was highly respected in Swabia as the descendant of an old Alsatian family from the neighbourhood of Mühlhausen, and greatly loved for his knightly talents, his solid character, and his sympathetic personality. As a partisan and connexion of the Hohenstaufen he humbly asked for the Pope's support and help, also for his "approbation" of the election and his promise to crown him Emperor in Rome. Gregory, who was at Lyons for the General Council, gave his promise in general terms (6 June 1274), although King Ottokar of Bohemia, not having been allowed to vote[1]

---

[1] From the very inception of the Electoral College a dispute had arisen about the right of the King of Bohemia to membership.

and being disappointed at the choice of the Electors, refused to acknowledge him as King of the Romans and protested to the Papal See against the violation of his own rights and those of Alfonso X of Castile, from whom he himself had nothing to fear and who during the Interregnum had been one of the nominal Kings of Germany. For that reason Gregory X did not as yet openly recognise the new King of the Romans. However, he addressed Rudolf by that title on 26 September 1274, promised him the imperial crown later on, and, ever in mind of the Holy Land, wishing to maintain peace in Europe, did his very best to effect a reconciliation between Rudolf and Ottokar as well as King Philip of France and also the king's deadly enemy, Count Amadeus V of Savoy; while Alfonso was warned to resign himself to the Electors' choice. By order of the Pope, Alfonso accordingly withdrew his claims. Rudolf's meeting with the Pope at Lausanne (October 1275), where he appeared with a splendid suite of German knights, consolidated the momentary cordiality between pontiff and king. The latter was not slow in promising to undertake the crusade so ardently desired by the Pope.

The king's conflict with Ottokar, however, was not long delayed. In the autumn of 1276 Rudolf with an imposing army laid siege to Vienna, in order to bring the disobedient prince of the Empire into subjection[1]. The proud Ottokar, excommunicated and outlawed, and forsaken by a number of vassals and subjects, was obliged to submit (25 November) and to relinquish all his states in the Empire except Bohemia and Moravia, for which he had immediately to do liege homage to the King of the Romans. The latter took temporary possession of the confiscated imperial fiefs, Austria and Styria, confirmed the Duke of Carinthia and Carniola in his fiefs, and took up his residence in Vienna, which remained the seat of his race for six and a half centuries. Thus King Rudolf became the founder of the greatness of the House of Habsburg. The proud and brave Ottokar, however, was far from feeling beaten. Taking advantage of Rudolf's quarrels with the successors of Pope Gregory, who had died in 1276, over the imperial claims to the Romagna, he allied himself with the neighbouring Polish and Silesian princes who shared with him the old hatred of the Slav tribes against everything German. In June 1278 he led his army against the King of the Romans, who on his side marched northwards with his trained Austrian and Swabian knights and supported by a large army of Hungarian horsemen under the young King of Hungary, Ladislas IV, his natural ally against the Slavs, the permanent enemies of the Hungarians. The armies met on the Marchfeld near Stillfried on the Danube in Austria (26 August 1278), and Rudolf fought with valour and success against the ineffective Slav hordes. Their brave leader was captured and forthwith murdered by a revengeful Austrian knight. On account of

---

[1] See *supra*, Vol. vi, pp. 439 sq.

his excommunication this dreaded ruler of the Czechs, the most famous of their kings, was even refused burial with the rites of the Church. His body lay in state in Vienna, was temporarily buried, and afterwards interred at Znojmo in Moravia. His young son Wenceslas II was made to marry one of Rudolf's daughters; and in payment of the expenses of the war Moravia was pledged to Rudolf for five years. Thus the mighty Slav realm fell; Bohemia alone remained in the possession of Ottokar's son, who was placed under the guardianship of the Margrave Otto of Brandenburg.

This brilliant victory tended to enhance the reputation of the King of the Romans in Germany and also to secure the co-operation of Pope Nicholas III in procuring for him the imperial crown. In order to induce the Pope to give his consent, Rudolf allowed himself (14 February 1279) to be persuaded to approve far-reaching declarations signed by the princes of the Empire concerning the subordination of the royal to the papal power. In a solemn document they likened the royal power to a smaller planet owing its light to the sun of the papal power, and recognised that the material sword was wielded at the will (*ad nutum*) of the Pope[1]. Rudolf definitively renounced all claims to imperial sovereignty over the whole Papal State including Romagna and over Southern Italy, *i.e.* Naples and Sicily, Emperor Frederick II's territory, where now ruled Charles of Anjou supported by the Pope. Charles' grandson was to become King of the feudal State of the Arelate (or Burgundy) and to marry one of Rudolf's daughters.

This self-humiliation, however, did not bring him nearer to his goal. Pope Nicholas' early death in August 1280 annulled the agreements, which appeared to have had in view the division of the German Empire into four kingdoms, and were in any case prejudicial to the interests and rights of the Empire; all this for the sake of the coveted imperial crown. Rudolf never realised his desire, although he could reckon on the co-operation of his new ally at Naples, who was now so closely connected with his house, and on that of the latter's nephew, the powerful King Philip III of France.

While the King of the Romans tried to strengthen the power of his race in the East and strove after the imperial crown with undeniable ingenuity, he allowed the numerous German princes to strengthen their power in their domains, which had greatly increased since Frederick II's time, and to settle their own feuds. The free and imperial cities were permitted to form confederations for the sake of their commercial interests. Rudolf only exercised his sovereignty by granting important favours and privileges for money, and by forming on his journeys through the Empire, whenever possible, unions for promoting peace, as had been done by Frederick II in 1235. The Hanseatic League, formed some years before between the commercial cities on the North Sea and the Baltic,

[1] MGH., *Const.* III, p. 213.

was more firmly organised under Rudolf[1]. Although the fervently desired imperial crown was not yet his, he managed at the brilliant diet held at Augsburg (27 December 1282) to obtain the consent of the leading princes of the Empire to the investment of his two remaining sons Albert and Rudolf[2] with the duchies of Austria and Styria as well as Carniola and the Wendish March as far as the Alps—formerly among the fiefs King Ottokar held of the Empire. The elder of those two sons, Albert, was to be the ruler, the younger was to be indemnified either by other territory in Swabia or in Burgundy or by a sum of money, retaining, however, his hereditary claim on the Austrian possessions. Carinthia, the duke of which had recently died, had primarily also been allotted to him but in the end (1286) was assigned to Count Meinhard of Tyrol as prince of the Empire, who also received in temporary fief Carniola and the Wendish March as a reward for his services against King Ottokar. Moreover the prospect was opened of yet more extensive territory in this "East March" of the German Empire. For his younger son Rudolf he expected soon to acquire an equally compact territory either in Swabia, by restoring the ancient duchy, or in Burgundy. Then the house of Habsburg would indisputably become the mightiest in the Empire and its way be clear to the greatest eminence in Western Christendom; it would indeed enter upon the inheritance of the Carolingian, Saxon, Salian, and Hohenstaufen imperial families.

Opposition, however, to his ambition, now becoming so apparent, was already rising in the Empire. The second marriage of the king in his sixty-seventh year with the fourteen-year-old Isabella, daughter of the late Duke of French Burgundy, in February 1284 opened to him and his family new chances of extending his possessions on the borders of the Empire, his new wife being a member of the mighty Capetian family. The institution of royal governorships in order to protect the newly established *Landfrieden* in Swabia, Bavaria, and Franconia, the annoyance of the imperial cities at the favours he bestowed on the princes of the Empire and at the monetary demands he brought forward, his manifest ambition to make his royal power superior to that of those mighty princes—all this excited anger and animosity everywhere. This animosity shewed itself especially when in 1284 a pseudo-Frederick II appeared.

For years the romantic history of the famous Emperor, whose name, together with that of his great predecessor and grandfather Barbarossa, was still held in honour among the German people, had given rise to the legend that he, like Barbarossa, was not really dead but had only been hidden by his arch-enemies, the clergy. When not actually the Emperor Frederick himself it was his grandson Conrad, who had perished in the

---

[1] See *infra,* Chap. VIII.
[2] Hartmann, the second son, had died young.

vain attempt to regain his Italian inheritance. About 1280 several pseudo-Fredericks and Conrads appeared. One of them, Dietrich Holzschuh, had a large following along the Lower Rhine and presently took up his residence at Neuss, welcomed with reverence and affection by the superstitious people from far and near, as far even as Italy and the Eastern March. In north-western Germany all those who feared and hated Rudolf gathered round him, until the king seized this dangerous impostor at Wetzlar and had him burned at the stake (7 July 1285).

This new triumph brought increased fame to the King of the Romans. His power rose even higher when his devoted friend Bishop Henry of Basle was appointed Archbishop of Mayence and primate of Germany. Already he was preparing for his journey to Rome for the imperial crown; already, encouraged by the presence of the papal legate at the German council at Würzburg, he was calling upon the German ecclesiastics for money and support; already he had announced a general German truce for three years in order to secure peace in the Empire during his stay in Italy; already he had regulated the imperial tolls, which since the confusion in the Empire had everywhere been misused or fallen into disuse; already the day for the coronation was fixed and, if that day should pass, a definite date was to be determined upon, when in April 1287 Pope Honorius IV died.

Almost a year passed before a new Pope was chosen. Moreover, since 1285 there ruled in France the powerful and ambitious Philip IV, surnamed the Fair, one of the most illustrious of French kings, whose great aim was to wrest the Arelate, the ancient kingdom of Burgundy, from the Empire, and thus to recover for France the boundaries of ancient Gaul at least along the Alpine range. King Rudolf succeeded, although with difficulty, in keeping under his control the princes of the Empire in Swabia and farther north along the Rhine. With an imposing army such as had not been seen for years, he succeeded at Besançon (July 1289) in maintaining the imperial rights over the "free county" of Burgundy (Franche Comté) against the rebel Count Palatine Otto IV and against the French intrigues.

In the spring of 1289 Rudolf made fresh arrangements for his coronation at Rome with the new Pope Nicholas IV. First, however, as he had done in the south, he had to consolidate his royal authority in northern and north-western Germany, where the ambitious Archbishop Siegfried of Cologne had repeatedly defied it. In the north-west the recognition of Rudolf's authority was still far from general. There the young and energetic Count Florence V of Holland had in a few campaigns subdued the West Frisians who had killed his father the King of the Romans William II; he had also renewed his predecessors' ancient claims on the Frisians of Westergoo. Count Florence had further invaded the bishopric of Utrecht and actually seized the western part (Nedersticht) of this important ecclesiastical domain without taking much notice of the expostulations of the Pope and the Archbishop of Cologne. Brabant and Guelders had entered upon a violent struggle over the succession to the duchy of Limburg which had become vacant, culminating in the fierce battle of Worringen (7 July 1288), in which the two parties of north-western Germany opposed one another, and the Archbishop of Cologne with his allies of Guelders, Nassau, and numerous other counts, lords, and knights were taken prisoners by the Brabantines.

The King of the Romans, certain of the friendship of the victor at Worringen, Duke John I of Brabant, did not interfere. John kept his personal enemy, Archbishop Siegfried, prisoner for a year, and only set him free on payment of a large ransom. Nor was Count Florence seriously thwarted by the King of the Romans, who saw in him a strong supporter against Philip IV of France, because he was the ally of Duke John, later on a supporter of King Edward I of England, and the hereditary enemy of Count Guy of Flanders, who sided with France. At first Rudolf saw no reason to be dissatisfied with the course of events in those parts; his authority was at least nominally recognised by the victors, although the peace of the Empire was meanwhile sadly disturbed and could only in seeming be consolidated by their victory.

In the north-east—in Saxony, Thuringia, and Brandenburg—he also met the wishes of the great princes of the Empire. Here too he consolidated the *Landfrieden* sometimes formed without his knowledge. At last, about Christmas 1289, he appeared in triumph at Erfurt; at the head of his band of knights he put down the marauders from the Thuringian woods and robbers' castles. He held another brilliant court at which he was able to point with pride to the many princes of the Empire who had come from almost every part of Germany to do him liege homage. His young son-in-law Wenceslas II of Bohemia had also appeared. For close upon a century no German King or Emperor had occupied a similar position, and he won all hearts by his innate *savoir-vivre* and by the *bonhomie* that seems hereditary in his race.

He remained at Erfurt till Easter 1290. One of the reasons for his coming, the recognition of his son as his future successor, was nearing realisation; many princes promised to recognise his second son, the young Rudolf, as King of the Romans as soon as he himself should have been crowned Emperor. To this end he granted the electoral vote to Bohemia. Before May was out, however, and shortly before the birth of his son John, who afterwards became notorious as the murderer of his uncle Albert, young Rudolf died at Prague at the early age of twenty.

The stricken king now set to work to gain the votes of the Electors and the good will of the nobles for his eldest son Albert of Austria, ever striving after increased power for his race which was to acquire the right of succession to the Hohenstaufen. However, as Albert, with the child John, was also heir to the Swabian family possessions, he was too power-

ful in the eyes of the princes, especially when in 1289 his father invested
him with the Hungarian kingdom vacant through the early death of
King Ladislas IV. Rudolf based his claim on a promise of King Béla IV
of Hungary to become a vassal of the Empire, if in return the Empire
would help him against the Mongols; and this help had not been given.
Albert's investiture bore no fruit, nor was the papal candidate, Charles
Martel of Naples, any more successful; for the Hungarians themselves
elected a member of their ancient royal house, Andrew III. On the other
hand, Rudolf invested his son-in-law Wenceslas II of Bohemia with the
vacant imperial duchies of Breslau and Silesia, and once more, this time
publicly, recognised Bohemia's right to the fifth electoral vote in the
Empire.

The king remained in Thuringia until November 1290. Thence he
went to Swabia. The old ruler, now seventy-two years of age, felt his end
drawing near and was unable to undertake the tiring and perilous
journey to Rome. He seriously contemplated abdication, but in that
case Albert's succession must first be made secure. At the end of May
1291 he therefore again convoked a diet at Frankfort-on-the-Main. He
was, however, already seriously ill and at that diet, well-attended as it
was, he was unable to fulfil his plans. Unflinchingly and resignedly he
rode, though sick to death, from the imperial city of Frankfort to the
ancient city of Spires, where so many of his royal predecessors lay buried
in the cathedral. There, he said, he wished to die, and there he breathed
his last on 15 July 1291.

He left an honoured name in the Empire. His subjects reverenced his
memory for having restored the blessings of peace in many parts of the
Empire either by force of arms or by skilful intervention and policy; they
revered him as a popular king, an exemplary knight, a capable and
intelligent ruler, under whom the Empire had enjoyed a period of peace
such as had not been known for years, freed from the rival kings who for
more than a century had fought for the mastery, of marauding knights
and ruffians who for years had infested town and country. His long
struggle for the supremacy of his house was moreover of far-reaching
future importance. The memory of his life, his rule, and his aims lived
on in the hearts of the German people, in his own and in later
generations.

Who was to succeed him as King of the Romans? Duke Albert,
recommended by his father but, from the very outset, considered un-
desirable by the Electors, especially by the three archbishops, on account
of his rough, tyrannical nature and his already considerable power, firmly
counted on being chosen; he felt certain of the support of his Bohemian
brother-in-law Wenceslas, of that of the Count Palatine Lewis, and also
of Bavaria. Towards the beginning of May, when he knew the Electors
were to assemble at Frankfort, he came to the outskirts of that city with

a large following, nearly an army. Archbishop Gerhard of Mayence, however, who did not favour Albert, had associated himself with the brave and very able, though not powerful, Count Adolf of Nassau, vassal of the Archbishop of Cologne and the Palatinate, who as head of the Walram branch of his house resided in Southern Nassau and there enjoyed a great reputation. The forty-year-old count, without wide lands, without the outstanding qualities of Rudolf of Habsburg, although a good soldier as a German king had need to be, seemed a serviceable tool in the eyes of the ecclesiastical Electors, who aspired to more power. They succeeded in obtaining the consent of the four temporal Electors, even that of King Wenceslas, Rudolf's weak and very pious son-in-law, whose still disputed electoral vote they now fully recognised. All of them exacted from Adolf exorbitant concessions in money as well as in lands, the demands of Archbishop Siegfried of Cologne being especially heavy, even shamelessly so. The ambitious count accepted his liabilities without troubling about the possibility of fulfilling his promises, surrendering to the Electors and their friends many imperial towns and rights without much resistance. As was customary, the nomination was left to the primate Archbishop Gerhard of Mayence; Archbishop Siegfried also played an important part, and Wenceslas, who had not appeared, put his vote in the hands of Gerhard. Thus the new "Pfaffenkönig" (priests' king), even less to be feared than King William II of Holland, was elected at Frankfort on 10 May and crowned at Aix-la-Chapelle on 24 June 1292.

The disappointed and embittered Duke Albert had retired to Alsace, where the hostile attitude of the neighbouring Swiss against his house caused him some anxiety. Afterwards he went to his family possessions in Austria to prepare for the struggle with his victorious rival, who had begun going round the Empire, restoring peace here and there with troops brought together with the help of the Rhenish Electors, and everywhere gaining friends and adherents by lavish granting of favours. Adolf succeeded in countering the Habsburg power in Alsace, and in the much-divided Thuringia his royal supremacy was recognised by dint of merciless pillage and robbery. His lack of regard for the immunities of churches and other ecclesiastical possessions roused the antagonism of the clergy. He, too, always kept in mind the imperial crown, which he meant to obtain as soon as circumstances in Rome and in the Empire should permit and a Pope of some personal weight should once more occupy the Holy See.

The war between England and France, which had broken out in the spring of 1294, prevented him from carrying out his plan for the present. Applied to by King Edward I of England, Adolf shewed himself quite ready to frustrate with the help of the English the designs of the French on German territory. King Edward had acquired powerful allies in north-western Germany by subsidies and clever manœuvring. Flanders, Brabant,

Holland, and Guelders had taken up his cause on receipt of considerable sums of money. On 24 August 1294 he made a close alliance with Adolf at Nuremberg, under which Adolf in his turn demanded no less than 100,000 marks for his help against Philip IV of France. Ten days later Adolf, as the King of the Romans and therefore protector of the Empire, declared war against Philip on the plea that the French king had for years violated the imperial rights on the south-western borders. The actual declaration of war, however, which bore the character of a knight's challenge, was not dispatched until the beginning of 1295. Preparations for a great campaign against France were immediately set on foot. Adolf could expect the French king to play off the opponents to his election against him. And indeed Philip immediately made sure of the support not only of Duke Albert of Austria, but also of Count Henry IV of Luxemburg, Duke Frederick of Lorraine, the Dauphin Humbert I of Dauphiné, which at that time was still a fief of the Empire, and of Otto IV, Count Palatine of Burgundy (Franche Comté), who was likewise a vassal of Adolf.

It was of great significance that the new Pope, Boniface VIII, one of the greatest pontiffs of the later Middle Ages, strongly disapproved of King Adolf's declaration of war on France. In his capacity of peace-maker in Christendom Boniface, in 1295, sent his legates from Rome to the combatants; as a Christian and Head of the Church he forbade the King of the Romans (whom he acknowledged as such) to engage in the war and told the Rhenish Electors, Adolf's powerful patrons, not to support him in a campaign against France. At first the papal interven-tion had its effect and the actual war was not entered upon by the Germans, although King Adolf declared the forfeiture of all the fiefs belonging to the Burgundian Count Palatine without, however, going so far as actually to attack him. He himself seized the lands of the disobedient Margrave of Meissen in Thuringia, and the margrave was forced to leave his country. Again his army committed ruthless pillage, especially where churches and monasteries were concerned, which vividly reminded the clergy of the Emperor Frederick II; they consequently turned against King Adolf. Meanwhile Duke Albert had again managed to draw back to his side Wenceslas of Bohemia and other princes, while Adolf saw his own patrons and adherents leave his cause one after another, deeming him not as submissive as they had expected and embittered against him because he had unwisely broken his promises. Even the Archbishop of Mayence, who had been temporarily deprived of his office by Pope Boniface, turned against him. Nothing came of the war with France; King Edward I of England was induced to open lengthy negotiations and presently saw the alliance he had bought on the Lower Rhine dissolved through the withdrawal of the "peasants' friend," Florence V of Holland. The latter's murder (June 1296) by his opponents among the nobles temporarily restored English influence in that county; King Edward, having kept as hostage the murdered count's only son John, his own son-in-law, now sent John back to Holland in order to gain that territory for England.

In 1297 Duke Albert at last considered the time ripe for attacking his opponent. An extensive plot, hatched by the clergy against the King of the Romans, was gaining more and more ground. In February 1298 a diet at Vienna was turned into a military review of the plotters, who then and there decided to depose Adolf and put Albert in his place. Archbishop Gerhard, who had hesitated a long time, was persuaded to join Albert for good and all, now that the "Pfaffenkönig" turned out to be an unwilling tool in the hands of those who had invested him with his high dignity; he had not fulfilled many of his promises, partly through inability, partly because he had no wish to keep them.

As early as February 1298 Albert left Vienna at the head of an army composed of Austrians, Bohemians, and Hungarians, and marched through Bavaria to Swabia, where many knights joined him. His semi-barbarian troops of savage Slavs and Hungarians, armed according to eastern custom with bows and battle-axes and followed by a large horde of women, were kept under control with great difficulty, and made a deep impression on the simple German townsfolk and peasants who saw them pass. Towards the middle of May, the Archbishop of Mayence summoned the King of the Romans to Frankfort, ostensibly to confer with the princes of the Empire about the means to guard the imperial interests in the midst of the increasing confusion in the Empire, but really to call him to account. Adolf did not obey the summons; he hastily collected an army, with which to keep in check his adversary who had already reached Strasbourg. At Frankfort the princes of the Empire, as of old from far and near assembled in the open, proceeded to take action. The Duke of Saxony, long ago won over by Albert, solemnly accused the King of the Romans of the spoliation of churches and the ill-treatment of priests during his devastating marches through Thuringia, of arbitrary violation of peace and law, of shameful perjury against towns and princes of the Empire, of a persecution of Church and religion in general which dangerously resembled heresy. On these grounds the princes of the Empire, finding him guilty of all these crimes, deposed King Adolf, and the Electors present immediately set about choosing a new king, who was, of course, Duke Albert. The duke, who had almost reached the royal city, received their homage in his camp.

Yet all was not lost for Adolf. Accompanied by his numerous Nassau relatives, supported by other Rhenish knights and the Bavarian dukes, he decided to take his chance against the usurper and marched north-westwards from Spires. Near Göllheim, not far from Worms, the decisive battle was fought on 2 July 1298. The valiant Nassau prince fought bravely. Fallen from his horse, he mounted another and bare-headed tried to find the hated Austrian in the throng of battle so as to settle the matter in personal combat. Albert scornfully dealt him a blow on the open face with his sword and then turned away leaving him to his friends. A moment later Adolf fell in the confused and desperate mêlée. This was the end of his dreams of royalty. His body was not buried in the venerable cathedral of Spires but in a neighbouring monastery.

King Albert lacked his father's sympathetic character and appearance. A hard and rough warrior, ambitious and intriguing, often rude and coarse, suspicious and miserly, severe and merciless in his dealings, at the same time a talented statesman, he inspired fear rather than affection in those who came into contact with him. King Philip IV congratulated him on his accession, and his coronation took place at Aix-la-Chapelle, where also the French king's partisans from the western part of the Empire paid homage to him.

One of his first acts was to take vigorous measures to suppress the scandalous persecutions of the Jews, which during the last years had again been prevalent especially in the Rhenish towns, where the ancient ridiculous accusations of ritual murders of Christians and the like were once more repeated against them. Prompted by the thought that he might reap advantage rather than by feelings of right and justice, he brought back to the Rhenish towns the Jews who had survived the massacres. This earned him the scornful nickname of "Judenkönig" in some of the monastic chronicles. He celebrated his victory over Adolf at a brilliant diet at Nuremberg and also had his consort crowned there with much pomp. There too he secured the Austrian hereditary domains for his sons, emphatically repeated King Rudolf's ordinances of peace, and confirmed the princes of the Empire in the rights they had acquired against the increasing independence of the towns; these, in their turn, had the satisfaction of seeing the imperial tolls and taxes, which had greatly increased, especially on the Rhine, since Frederick II's time, reduced to their old standards. On a long tour throughout the Empire his authority was recognised everywhere.

His relations with King Philip remained friendly: he caused the disputes in the west to be settled by arbitration, and contrived a marriage between his eldest son and successor Rudolf and Philip's sister, while a marriage between one of his daughters and one of Philip's sons was to strengthen the alliance with the French royal family still further. A solemn treaty concluded at Strasbourg (5 September 1299) was sealed in December of the same year at a meeting of the two kings at Toul. The princely splendour displayed by Albert on that occasion could not be equalled even by King Philip, although this excessive German magnificence seemed in the eyes of the French knights nothing but a coarse imitation of their own knightly customs, which had been generally adopted by the whole chivalry of Western Europe.

Very soon, however, Pope Boniface's hostile attitude caused him anxiety.

The Pope was always on bad terms with Philip the Fair; he had not yet recognised Albert as king and even blamed him severely for the violent death of King Adolf. The Electors also, fearing the rapid development of the Habsburg influence, were not long in shewing the new King of the Romans the limitations of his power.

That he himself had not much faith in this power, at least in the north-west, was clear when in August 1300 he withdrew from Nimwegen before the army with which Count John of Hainault tried to force from him recognition. John of Hainault had usurped the fiefs of Holland and Zeeland, become vacant through the death of his cousin Count John I, and had been summoned to Nimwegen to justify his acts. Menaced from the other side by the equivocal attitude of the Rhenish Electors—there was even a rumour of a plot against his life—Albert swiftly retreated, while Pope Boniface VIII reminded the Electors in a solemn bull of the supremacy of the Holy See, which might in the end recognise Albert, if he on his side fully submitted to the papal claims, especially to the demand that he should renounce the imperial rights in Tuscany and the whole of Middle Italy. Thus began the revolt of the Rhenish spiritual princes joined by the Wittelsbach Count Palatine Rudolf the Stammerer and all the branches of the offended house of Nassau, and led by Archbishop Diether of Trèves, brother of King Adolf. At the instigation and with the co-operation of the Pope, these princes formed at Heimbach on the Rhine an alliance against Albert, "who now calls himself King of the Romans" (14 October 1300). Albert, on his side, declared that he, as lawfully elected king, would withstand these disturbers of peace and order, and on 7 May 1301 he called upon the German people, in particular on the powerful Rhenish towns from Cologne to Constance, to assist him in this, promising to protect every one of them against the unlawful exactions of tolls by princes and overlords, who for more than a century had attempted to enrich themselves at the expense of the commerce on the Rhine and its tributaries down to its mouth.

The Pope's increasing enmity was a serious drawback to the king in this affair. By a bull of 13 April 1301 Boniface VIII at last openly refused to recognise him, and summoned him to defend himself within six weeks against the accusation of the murder of his predecessor King Adolf, on pain of excommunication and the annulment of the oaths taken by the princes of the Empire at the coronation at Aix-la-Chapelle. This marked the open breach between the King of the Romans and the papal authority. The whole of the Rhenish territory from Bavaria and Swabia to the Lower Rhine became involved. With skilful strategy the king, certain of the support of many lords and towns, led his troops along the Rhine for more than a year and successively conquered the Palatinate, Mayence, Cologne, and Trèves. One after another their spiritual and temporal princes were forced to submit. A subsequent campaign planned against Count John II of Holland-Hainault had, however, to be abandoned, because the great quarrel between Philip IV and Boniface had then reached a crisis.

Much more important issues than the subjection of a few recalcitrant princes of the Empire were at stake: the question whether papal authority would at last succeed in putting into practice the theory of papal sovereignty over Christendom, the great question of the later Middle Ages. This time the head of the anti-papal party was the King of France, perhaps the greatest of the French Capetians, and not, as before, the ruler of the Empire, who now only played a subsidiary part in this world-drama as an ally of France, albeit not wholly a reliable one. With talent and success Philip engaged in the struggle, which in its consequences was to bring the Papacy under French influence for almost a century and temporarily to raise France to the first place in the Christian world, while Germany's significance correspondingly dwindled. The alliance with France soon shewed to the King of the Romans its dangerous side. If he continued to follow this policy he would inevitably become involved in a violent struggle with Rome, and that might have the direst consequences for him in the Empire itself, as the fate of the Salian and Hohenstaufen Emperors had abundantly shewn in the past. The reconciliation with France had evidently only been a means to secure temporary quiet on the western frontiers of the Empire, as well as to shew the Pope that the friendship of the King of the Romans was of importance to him. Albert's policy was directed towards making both parties feel the importance of that friendship. The Jubilee of 1300 had revealed Boniface VIII in the brilliant glamour of power. His famous Bull *Unam Sanctam* (18 November 1302) once more expressed Gregory VII's great ideal, that Holy Church was one and indivisible, ruled by one worldly power, that of Christ's representative at Rome; the spiritual sword demanded the support of the temporal in upholding the supremacy of Rome in the world.

After his victories on the Rhine Albert seemed to be secure in his Empire in spite of his treaty with France. For the sake of the imperial crown he appeared willing to comply with the Pope's demands, but only conditionally. In March 1302 he sent a deputation to Rome for the purpose of justifying his conduct towards King Adolf, as the Pope had demanded, and at the same time defending his rights against the Electors who had denounced him; he also declared himself ready to recognise, or even to defend, the papal claims in general. And the Pope, needing his help against France, actually recognised him as King of the Romans on 30 April 1303. Assuming the attitude of the "Good Samaritan," he promised to crown Albert at Rome with the imperial crown, urging all his subjects to recognise Albert's sovereignty in the Empire, and released him from all the alliances and treaties, however solemn, that were inconsistent with the papal claims, consequently also from the alliance with Philip IV, against whom he hoped to use him. Albert, reminded by the fate of Adolf and the opposition of the spiritual Electors how important it was to him too to be on good terms with the mighty pontiff at Rome, sent a very humble answer to this message, promising not to appoint an imperial governor in Lombardy and Tuscany for five years, to fight the Pope's enemies, and to deal justly with the lately subdued spiritual Electors on the Rhine. At the same time he skilfully avoided too definite an expression of obedience to the heavy demands of papal supremacy; prudence as well as his own strongly developed ambition forbade him to go any further.

Thus his alliance with France threatened to be severed at one blow. The King of the Romans, whose political discernment was perhaps not inferior to that of King Philip, saw its dangers for himself and for the Empire. The papal anathema on Philip was impending and war would no doubt have broken out at once, when the French king, with the help of the Colonna, surprised the Pope in his own territory at Anagni. There followed the sudden death of the Pope at Rome on 11 October 1303 in the midst of great confusion. The victory of France was imminent.

New dangers threatened in the Empire. King Wenceslas II of Bohemia[1], elected in 1300 King of Poland also, saw, at the death of the last prince of the ancient native house of Árpád, the crown of Hungary within his reach or at least within that of his young son Wenceslas, who did in fact acquire it. King Albert fully realised the great danger in the rise of a new mighty Bohemian Empire such as Ottokar's had been in his father's time. In the autumn of 1304 he marched into Bohemia but met with violent opposition, until Wenceslas II's death from consumption (June 1305) delivered him from this adversary. The young Wenceslas III, however, was murdered soon after, and then Albert, after a second campaign, succeeded in getting his own son Rudolf elected King of Bohemia. Rudolf's reign did not last long, for he died in July 1307, and his younger brother could no more than hold his own in Moravia against the newly-chosen King of Bohemia, Duke Henry of Carinthia, Wenceslas II's son-in-law. The time for the Habsburgs had evidently not yet come in Bohemia. Elsewhere as well, in Thuringia, on the Rhine, in Swabia, in the Swiss cantons, there were disturbances. In Switzerland especially began the conflict which legend and poetry have embodied in and round the person of William Tell, the champion of freedom, and his followers. The King of the Romans saw his power menaced on all sides. He courageously set to work to compel recognition of his authority throughout the Empire. Busy with preparations for this difficult task, he was staying at Baden in Aargau (1 May 1308), when a small band of conspirators made a scheme to kill him. Among them was his eighteen-year-old nephew Duke John of Swabia, son and

[1] See *supra*, Vol. vi, pp. 440, 460.

heir of Albert's younger brother Rudolf and the proud Bohemian princess
Agnes, daughter of Ottokar, who in her inmost heart hated the Habsburgs, in particular King Albert, the merciless enemy of her race. This
hate had passed down to her son, who was discontented at what his
uncle had portioned out to him, the grandson of a King of the
Romans: he had merely the governorship and not the possession of the
Swabian domains belonging to his house and once his father's heritage.
His fellow-plotters were three Swabian-Swiss nobles, Rudolf von Wart,
young Walter von Eschenbach, and Rudolf von Balm, who had sworn to
help him in upholding his rights and claims. Counting on help from the
new Archbishop of Mayence and Count Eberhard of Wurtemberg, they
once more tried to get satisfaction for Duke John from the king; both
the princes interceded for him. The king, fearing their opposition and
the wrath of his young nephew, consented and promised to look after
the latter's interests at the end of the intended campaign. Duke John,
disappointed and discouraged at this new delay and at Albert's unreliable
promises, lent an ear to the proposals of his three friends. After the
evening meal, when the king was on his way across the Reuss to the
neighbouring little town of Brugg to meet his consort, they contrived
to be alone with him on the little ferry-boat and to ride with him to
Brugg. On the path leading to it, not far from the ancestral castle of
Habsburg, they fell upon the unarmed king, wounded him mortally, and
then escaped leaving him lying helpless. The king's attendants found
him still alive, but he died after a few minutes. The regicides, afterwards
outlawed by Albert's successor, fled into hiding. Only one of them,
Rudolf von Wart, was captured soon afterwards and delivered up to
Albert's sons; he ended his life on the spot where the crime had been
committed, by having his body broken upon the wheel. Duke John
(Johannes Parricida) lived for some years unrecognised in a monastery
at Pisa, where he still was when the new King of the Romans, Henry
VII, came there in 1312; he disclosed his identity, and was thrown into
prison as a regicide and died there soon after. Eschenbach hid in
Wurtemberg and died many years later, only disclosing his real name
on his death-bed. Balm died miserably and at a great age in his hiding-
place, a monastery at Basle. On the spot where the murder took place
Albert's widow erected the convent of Königsfeld, appointing her daughter
Agnes its first abbess. After the ancient German custom she and her
sons and daughters mercilessly took a bloody revenge on all who could
possibly be thought connected with the crime. The victim of this murder
left to posterity the memory of a strong though hard and proud
personality; he was a past-master in political cunning, always striving
after the strengthening of the royal power, in which he considered
lay the best guarantee for his own authority and for the future of his
house. His sudden death intervened to prevent the fulfilment of his
endeavour.

Philip IV immediately seized the opportunity to attempt to raise his brother Charles of Valois to the German throne, hoping thus to secure French predominance in Europe. To that end he began by bribing the Electors and other princes of the Empire and nobles with money and fair promises, and also exercised pressure on his willing tool, Pope Clement V, formerly Archbishop of Bordeaux, who owed him his high dignity, and who had taken up his residence at Avignon instead of at Rome. Though the French Pope did not venture to oppose his "patron" openly, he nevertheless feared—and with reason—too large an increase in Philip's power in the Christian world. He therefore confined himself to framing a lukewarm recommendation, in order not to prejudice the king against himself and yet to have a chance of directing the choice of a German King into another quarter.

In the Empire itself Frederick the Fair, eldest surviving son of the murdered king, naturally came forward as candidate for the throne. He immediately gave up his plans with regard to Bohemia, at least for the time being, so as not to scare the Electors by revealing too much power in the hands of the house of Habsburg. He did not, however, succeed in allaying their fears. Other princes, too, entertained expectations, such as the Electors of the Palatinate, Brandenburg, and Saxony, while the Archbishop of Cologne felt inclined towards the French proposals. Several other princes were mentioned as claimants. In the midst of all these dissensions the recently nominated young Archbishop of Trèves, Count Baldwin of Luxemburg, succeeded in drawing the attention of Archbishop Peter of Mayence, who had the first voice in the election of a king, to his distinguished elder brother Count Henry IV of Luxemburg. The latter was immediately prepared to grant to this prelate as well as to the Archbishop of Cologne, according to custom, extensive rights and advantages, should the choice fall on him.

Towards the end of October the Archbishop of Mayence called the Electors to a preliminary conference at Rense near Coblenz on the Rhine, where, after all sorts of intrigues and confused discussions, Count Henry, though not exactly elected, was designated as the most likely candidate. With the aid of yet more concessions the Archbishop of Cologne was won over for good and all; the temporal Electors were brought over in the same way, and thus the Luxemburg Count was at last (27 November 1308) unanimously elected King of the Romans by the six Electors present. The coronation took place at Aix-la-Chapelle on 6 January 1309. The new king, lord of a semi-Walloon and sparsely peopled domain, mainly situated in the ancient wild Silva Carbonaria (the Ardenne), had had a French education. He was wont to speak Walloon, the official language of Luxemburg, which, as a border-country, used both languages and was closely allied to France. He was fair and slim, had an intelligent face and pleasant manners; he was religious, kind-hearted, sensible, and temperate in all his ways; he was not yet forty years old, and therefore in the prime of life. His wife was Margaret of Brabant, the pious and amiable daughter of the chivalrous Duke John I.

Immediately after the election, Henry sent an embassy to the Pope with a letter in which he expressed his *sacramentum fidelitatis*, but in terms which were not detrimental to his royal dignity. Clement V, approving his election, answered with a somewhat equivocal friendliness, yet promised to crown him as Emperor; the date of the ceremony (2 February 1312) was mentioned in connexion with a general council to be held before that date. King Philip was far from pleased at the accommodating tone of the Curia, and accordingly gave unmistakable signs of his displeasure at Avignon. In Germany itself no demur was at first heard against the unanimous choice, although many were disappointed. Already a fine chance was opening for the new king of acquiring the Bohemian crown. Wenceslas III's enterprising younger sister Elizabeth offered herself in marriage to Henry's son; she considered herself heiress to Ottokar's family domains in opposition to the claims of her elder sister. In case the husband of this sister, Henry of Carinthia, the then King of Bohemia, could not hold his own against the Habsburgs—and that seemed probable—such a marriage would be very important.

His relations with the Habsburgs at first claimed the king's chief attention. To his great joy Duke Frederick of Austria appeared at his first court at Spires. Frederick wished King Albert's body to be interred with due ceremony in the ancient imperial cathedral, and this seemed to lead to a reconciliation between the two rivals, since Henry also demanded the interment there of King Adolf, which likewise took place. At the negotiations about their respective interests Frederick renounced the possession of Moravia, which he had held in fief, whereas he was confirmed in the investment of the imperial fiefs in Austria and Swabia, which his family had had in their possession, also in those of the absent John Parricida who had been outlawed by King Henry together with the three other murderers. Frederick promised to help the king against the ever-rebellious Landgrave of Thuringia, and also to assist him in his journey to Italy for the coronation, the ideal of King Henry's life and not in his opinion unattainable; for the much-oppressed Ghibelline party had already approached him more than once. Neither was the Pope at Avignon disinclined to fulfil his promise concerning the king's coronation at Rome, provided Henry was prepared to support the Pope against his too powerful patrons at Naples and in France. Agreements were already drawn up regarding the duties which Henry, as Emperor, was to perform for the Church and the solemn promises he was to give concerning them. A papal legate was to be sent to conduct further negotiations.

On 10 August 1310 Henry took the oath to observe his promises regarding his future relations with the Pope, declaring that he would

defend the rights and interests of the Church against the Saracens as well
as against all "heretics and schismatics"; the latter was a threat against
the French and Italian lawyers and schoolmen of anti-papal leanings
under the protection of Philip IV. He further promised to uphold the
privileges actually granted or said to have been granted to the Papal See
by his predecessors, the Emperors and kings from Constantine and
Charlemagne down to Frederick II and Rudolf. The Pope's domains,
which would include the Romagna and perhaps Tuscany, were carefully
detailed. This declaration was, of course, prefaced by the usual references to the "two swords," which the king also subscribed, though it
was not in the uncompromising terms in which Pope Boniface VIII had
formulated his demands against Albert.

Before the journey to Rome could be commenced, it was necessary to
settle affairs in Bohemia so as to consolidate and if possible strengthen
the power of the still weak Luxemburg family and its position in the
Empire. The energetic princess Elizabeth of Bohemia had contrived to
organise in her country a strong party among the nobles against her
brother-in-law the king, and this party had actually seized Prague. A
Czech deputation impeached King Henry of Bohemia before the King of
the Romans at Frankfort, and demanded sentence against him as a vassal
of the Empire. Without a proper hearing, the King of the Romans
straightway declared that Henry had forfeited his kingship, and consented
to the marriage of his own thirteen-year-old son John of Luxemburg with
the seventeen-year-old princess, who presently came to Spires with an
imposing retinue. On 30 August she married the king's son, whom his
father invested with the royal crown of Bohemia without further investigation whether Bohemia was indeed an imperial fief. The wedding
festivities at Spires lasted a week and included magnificent tournaments.
Afterwards the young couple set out for Bohemia with a considerable
German and Bohemian army. At first the enterprise was not successful,
but in the end (19 December 1310) Prague, where Henry of Carinthia
had again entrenched himself, was captured and Henry was forced to flee
to his own country of Tyrol. The young Bohemian king was crowned
at Prague; he was the first of the Luxemburg line, which was destined to
remain settled there for more than a century and to wear the German
royal and imperial crowns as well. He persuaded Duke Frederick of
Austria, who did not much appreciate the mere mortgage of semi-
barbaric Moravia, to hand this territory also over to him.

At last Henry was free to go to Italy. The wellnigh unwarrantable
way in which he had distributed the imperial rights among princes
and landowners did not add lustre to his name in the history of the
Empire. It was the imperial crown, the ideal which had also lured
his predecessors and which now seemed within his reach, that brought
him to purchase order and quiet in the Empire by giving in to the
demands from lords and towns. The situation in North and Central

Italy, the only regions where the Empire still had some power, was one of great confusion and divergent local interests. After the fall of the Hohenstaufen, imperial authority at Naples, in Sicily, and in the Papal States had disappeared altogether, at Naples to the advantage of Charles of Anjou, in Sicily to that of King Frederick of Aragon. King Rudolf had had to relinquish the Romagna, while his suzerainty over Tuscany had been seriously contested by the Pope. In the north, in Lombardy, he and his successors had kept a semblance of power, and had now and again tried to assert themselves from a distance, albeit only by feeble protests, by useless threats, or by appointments of deputies who were not obeyed. Venice had been able to keep her republican independence, which had lasted for five centuries, and was in that way more fortunate than Genoa and Pisa, who longed for the German King to restore order and imperial authority.

But no one in Italy had, after all, heeded the commands and counsels of the later kings; almost everywhere disorder and hopeless dissension reigned. Here and there a powerful noble family had succeeded in gaining the upper hand in the violent quarrels between Guelfs and Ghibellines. These names in themselves were void of significance; they had simply become party-watchwords without fundamental principles attached to them. The Guelfs no longer, as of yore, represented the papal party, nor the Ghibellines the imperial. In the ancient republics the burning question was only who should possess supreme local power and authority over the surrounding districts. Wherever the "popolo" in those numerous towns, now in fact republics, had wielded that power for a time, there prominent nobles had finally acquired an almost dictatorial control and the harassed populace in its longing for order and quiet had acquiesced. At Milan the supremacy was contested by the Visconti and the Della Torre families. The Della Scala ruled Verona; the D'Este held Ferrara and Modena. Pisa had lost her authority over Corsica and Sardinia to Genoa, and had seen her old prosperity vanishing through violent internecine quarrels. Genoa herself suffered through the eternal war with Venice and the quarrels between the Grimaldi and Fieschi, the Doria and Spinola. Florence, the magnificent and opulent Guelf city on the Arno, was likewise divided within herself. Everywhere the temporarily victorious party had killed or banished the conquered and confiscated its possessions. Every Italian city was full of ruined exiles from elsewhere. In the Papal States, where the Popes no longer resided, the same happened; the Colonna and Orsini fought for the supremacy in and about Rome. Nowhere, except in Naples under the capable King Robert of Anjou, and in Sicily under the crafty King Frederick of Aragon, was there even a semblance of well-established order. North and Central Italy seemed about to dissolve into a number of city-republics without coherence and without fixed government, where peace and order were replaced by a succession of violent revolutions.

It was a marvel that learning in cultured Padua and art in lovely Florence could develop like a flower in the midst of a desert. At Pisa and Siena the deserted buildings, monuments of still recent prosperity, already seemed only memories of a long-departed glory. In this hopeless chaos many looked towards the Emperor, who by his influence and skill might be able to restore the disturbed social order. Among them sounded the mighty voice of Dante, who, himself exiled from his native Florence, in a famous and eloquent letter called upon the "Longobardi," rulers and ruled alike, to welcome with enthusiasm the approaching Emperor, the restorer of peace and quiet. He urged them to acknowledge his authority unhesitatingly and to join the Pope, who, he reminded them, in a bull of 1 September 1310 had judged the German King worthy of the imperial crown, in promoting the welfare of the Christian world, the honour and interests of Italy, still the seat of the ideal power of the Holy Roman Empire, whose fate might be called the fate of the world. Many Ghibellines and Guelfs went with Dante to meet the Luxemburg "Arrigo," inspired with sympathy, reverence, and ardent hope.

The new German King himself, infatuated with the old ideals, yearned to fill the part allotted to him; he felt ordained by God to fill it; for was not the Pope God's representative upon earth? Educated as a knight, he had a great reverence for the ancient culture of Italy, which, in spite of everything, still exercised its fascination, a culture so immeasurably excelling that of Germany, and even of France. A king so alive to spiritual development and intellectual refinement could not be unaware that the German people had in those respects much to learn from Italy. Had not the "Minnesang," originally Provençal, been almost lost at the courts of the German princes during the confusion of the last fifty years? Did not German learning bear a narrow monastic stamp compared with that of Padua and Bologna? Was not German art paltry in comparison with what Florence and Pisa, Venice and Bologna could shew, those cities which had drunk of the eternal classical wells? Was not Italy still the country where a repeated recrudescence of classical culture occurred? Were not the German towns feeble imitations of those mighty city-republics which had defied Barbarossa and Frederick II? What was German commerce, even that of the rising "Hanse," of Hamburg, Bremen, Lübeck, Augsburg, Ulm, Nuremberg, the Rhenish towns, compared with that of Venice, Genoa, Milan, and Florence? Was not Italy, were not Tuscany and Lombardy, the centres of banking and finance, which dominated commerce more and more? Italy was still the Promised Land in the eyes of the German, who, however, was there looked upon as a semi-barbarian. In his heart he himself, the German from a Walloon country, felt barbaric.

With these expectations and in this frame of mind Henry left Alsace at the beginning of October 1310 on his long journey southward to Rome. He reached Lausanne via Berne; from there through Geneva and

Savoy he crossed the Alps, climbing the Mont Cenis, which was already thickly covered with snow. This route through the domain of Count Amadeus of Savoy, his brother-in-law, was the proper one to take, since the easier Brenner Pass was closed to him on account of its being within reach of his bitter enemy Duke Henry of Carinthia, whom he had driven out of Bohemia. When he reached Susa only a small escort of 3000 men, mainly consisting of Walloon knights and their followers, accompanied him, a heavily armed band renowned for their savage prowess. During the summer he had sent envoys to all the towns in Lombardy and also to Venice to herald the peace he came to bring. On his arrival in Italy he repeated that message in a solemn manifesto. As the king of peace he was welcomed by everyone. From all sides armed partisans flocked towards him, Guelfs as well as Ghibellines, for the new ruler—he had loudly proclaimed it—did not wish to be a party-leader, nor an upholder of "imperial" principles against the "papal," which in fact seemed by now to have fallen into oblivion in Italy. Delegations from the principal Lombard and Tuscan towns came to greet him respectfully, and blessed him as the long-expected rescuer of country and people from dire distress, who was to make his powerful manifesto of peace heard by all without consideration of parties or persons. A papal legate also came to welcome him and Henry begged that the coronation at Rome by Clement V, who was expected from Avignon for the purpose, should take place at Whitsuntide.

With an ever-increasing army he reached Milan in December via Turin, Asti, and Novara. On his way he restored order everywhere, reconciled combating factions, appointed governors over States and towns. At Milan even the mighty and proud Guido della Torre, who had at first been unwilling and uncertain, actually greeted him with at least simulated humility. There too the archbishop crowned him King of Lombardy with the Lombard crown (6 January 1311), although this time it was not the iron crown of his predecessors, which had temporarily disappeared and only turned up again long after. Here too, however, he experienced his first—and decisive—disappointment. Matteo Visconti cunningly induced the Della Torre to join in a revolt, and then deserted them. The Della Torre, considered untrustworthy from the very beginning as ancient enemies of imperial power, were attacked without warning by the king's followers, and the latter, supported by the Visconti, burnt down Guido's palace, plundered, robbed, and killed his adherents in large numbers, and drove the remainder out of the city. Guido saved himself by flight. Contrary as this was to Henry's peaceable plans, so loudly proclaimed beforehand, he deplored the course of events, which had cost many lives and had reduced a considerable portion of Milan to ashes. In future, however, he was forced to stand by the Visconti, who had remained faithful, and to keep aloof from the not altogether trusted Della Torre, in other words to support the ancient Ghibellines against the ancient Guelfs.

Milan's fate roused everywhere in Italy the bitterest animosity at the conduct of the royal troops, against the German barbarians who, according to the general complaint, had been let loose on Italy—those Germans, despised and hated from time immemorial, beside whom the Italians still felt themselves the proud heirs of classical civilisation. In Lombardy too these feelings spread, and one town after another, indignant at what they called the king's treachery, drove out the royal governors. Cremona received Guido della Torre, and from all sides the Guelfs enthusiastically rallied under him. King Henry, embittered at the course of affairs and now firmly resolved to reach his goal by force, immediately placed rebellious Cremona under the ban of the Empire; his clergy also excommunicated her. Passionately angry at the disappointment, he marched his army up to the city, refused her humble submission, and mercilessly punished her by putting to death the principal instigators of the revolt, banishing hundreds of others, destroying her walls and gates, and pulling down the houses of the culprits. Brescia, however, whose turn came next, had to be regularly besieged. She bravely held out from May till the end of September 1311. Now adversity commenced in earnest. A violent plague swept away thousands in the royal army, among them Guy, the chivalrous son of the Count of Flanders, and many other famous generals. Only when famine and pestilence had broken the courage of the inhabitants did the town surrender, and, like Cremona, it was severely punished for its mutiny. One of the king's most distinguished followers, the famous Count Werner of Homburg, greatly feared for his ruthlessness, was appointed royal captain-general of Lombardy.

All this delayed Henry a long time in North Italy. Besides, the Guelf cities, Florence and Bologna, now prevented him from taking the land-route to Rome, so that he would be obliged to travel by sea via the seaports Genoa and Pisa, which were on his side. Genoa, hoping for future advantages in the Levant over her rival Venice, was perfectly willing to oblige him, nay put herself unconditionally at his service, even acknowledging him as sovereign lord of the republic and accepting his governor. During his stay at Genoa he sustained a great loss through the death of his noble consort, the universally beloved Queen Margaret, who had up to then shared all his anxieties. These anxieties increased more and more. Philip IV of France desired, in return for his acquiescence in the Italian situation, that his son and namesake should become Count of the imperial fief of Burgundy. King Robert of Naples stated his claims and meanwhile seized Rome, or rather the Leonine city on the opposite bank of the Tiber with the strong castle of Sant'Angelo. The Pope was in no hurry over the preparations for the promised coronation. At length, in the spring of 1312, Henry decided to leave Genoa to go by sea to faithful Pisa. There he made a triumphal entry on 6 March, welcomed on all sides by the Ghibellines, while the other Tuscan cities adhered to the Guelfs and accordingly were put under the ban of the Empire.

At last the king marched to Rome straight through Tuscany with a
retinue of 2000 heavily armed knights. On 7 May he entered the Eternal
City near the Porta del Popolo and took up his abode in the Lateran,
appointing Louis of Savoy commander-in-chief of the half-conquered
city, whilst John of Gravina was still holding Trastevere with the
Vatican and St Peter's, the Capitol, the Campo dei Fiori, and the
Piazza Navona for his brother King Robert of Naples. Henry VII failed
in his attempts to persuade the Neapolitans to surrender by agreement,
or at least to give up St Peter's, where the imperial coronation always
took place; the rebellious Roman nobles and the cardinals were only
compelled by force or strategy to side with Henry. Thereupon the
struggle began; barricades in the streets, fortified palaces, and strongholds of hostile nobles had to be attacked and captured before the
Germans could venture an advance in the direction of St Peter's (26 May).
This attack, however, failed and the fighting in the city continued for
weeks without advantage to either party. A large portion of the Eternal
City was destroyed by burning and plundering, and the inhabitants
were massacred.

The Pope having refused to leave Avignon, Henry had for a long time
been urging the cardinals to crown him in the Lateran, the papal
residence next in importance to the Vatican. At first they refused,
because the Pope had explicitly designated St Peter's for the ceremony;
at Henry's insistence, supported by the threatening attitude of the
Roman populace, they at last consented. The coronation took place on
29 June 1312 at St John Lateran and was performed with the usual
ceremonies by Cardinal Nicholas of Ostia assisted by two other papal
legates. Henry proudly accepted the golden crown, imperial globe, sword,
and sceptre. The sublime goal of his arduous journey was reached, and the
acclamations of the Ghibellines, in which the Guelfs only sporadically and
reluctantly joined, resounded throughout the whole of Italy.

The new Emperor was, however, far from able to enjoy his triumphs in
peace, for Rome itself was for the most part still in the hands of the
Neapolitans, and his greatly diminished German troops wanted to go
home. And this they did in spite of his protests; only 900 German and
Walloon knights remained with him. With this handful of followers he
did not venture farther than Tivoli, to seek respite from the hot summer
for himself and his men; and even there he was scarcely safe from his
enemies in the neighbourhood.

The Pope, highly incensed at the fighting in Rome between Henry
and the Neapolitans and incited by Philip IV, now joined Henry's Guelf
adversaries. He demanded, on pain of excommunication, an armistice
until the quarrel should be settled by his arbitration, the Emperor's
promise not to return to the papal capital without papal permission, the
release of all prisoners, and the return to the nobles of all the city
strongholds. King Henry protested against the hostile attitude of the

Pope and maintained that he and no one else was the head of the Empire, just as the Pope was of the Church; he protested at being virtually placed on a level with King Robert, his vassal and the Pope's, with regard to papal commands. As Emperor, he claimed the right to enter Rome without the Pope's permission; on the other hand, he consented to the release of the prisoners and the restitution of the Roman towers and castles. Eventually he did leave Rome on 20 August in order to bring the Tuscan Guelfs to reason, and he promised to withdraw the small garrison he had left in the Eternal City. As Emperor, however, he called King Robert to account before the imperial tribunal.

After having subdued Perugia and other Tuscan towns he besieged Florence, but did not succeed in taking this powerful city. Moreover, he had to contend with lack of provisions and severe outbreaks of fever, from which he himself did not escape. He then convened a diet at Pisa, where he again took up residence in March 1313. King Robert, who had not obeyed the imperial summons, was declared an enemy of the Empire and the Emperor decided to attack him in his own kingdom. While at Pisa he tried to reinforce his army, which had suffered greatly through illness, casualties in fighting, the return home of many lords and knights, and the defection of the Guelfs, by calling up new troops from Germany and Italy in preparation for a campaign against Naples. The sentence pronounced on King Robert at Pisa (26 April 1313) declared him a rebel, deserving of death and the ban of the Empire with confiscation of all his fiefs and rights. Robert called on the assistance of Philip IV, violently protested against the Emperor's attitude, and found a ready supporter in the Pope, who, in a solemn bull, with dire threats forbade the war against Naples in the interest of Christianity. The Emperor replied with counter-demands, including the immediate deposition of Robert. A considerable period was spent in these reciprocal complaints, demands, and reproaches; meanwhile John of Bohemia prepared to come to his imperial father's help with a large army of Germans and Czechs. Henry had long ago allied himself with Frederick of Sicily (Trinacria), and in September Naples was to be attacked from the land as well as from the sea, while King John's army was to subdue Lombardy and Tuscany, where the Guelfs had risen once more. Indeed the whole of Italy dreaded the Emperor's revenge, remembering the fate which had already befallen many of his adversaries. An unexpected event caused the failure of all the Emperor's plans. Henry, who had left Pisa on 8 August with a considerable army of knights in order to recommence the siege of Rome, had for a long time been suffering from malaria. His doctors had advised him to put off his departure until he had quite recovered, but he refused to wait and hurriedly marched up to Siena, which, however, he failed to take. He then hastened southwards. At Buonconvento on the Ombrone he collapsed and died suddenly of an attack of fever (24 August 1313). In popular belief his death was of course ascribed to the effect of poison, said to have been administered to him by a Dominican priest in the Sacrament. His body was taken to Pisa and interred with great pomp in the cathedral. The news of his death was received with joy by the Guelfs, with consternation by the Ghibellines, who had fixed all their hopes on him. His faithful followers returned to their country; his son had only reached Swabia and now disbanded his army.

In Germany his death was no less deeply lamented than in Italy; fervent partisans deplored the loss of a second Charlemagne. Dante bemoaned his death and wrote beautiful lines in his honour in the *Divina Commedia*. Villani described in admiring terms what the insignificant German King had wrought and had wanted to achieve. Henry VII was the last of the really medieval Emperors; he passed away at the very moment when he was triumphantly grasping the supremacy in Italy and when he was on the point of renewing the old struggle against papal authority. In Germany he was universally acknowledged to have been the restorer of imperial sovereignty, which since Barbarossa's death had been impotent against the rising power of the German princes. Dante's *De Monarchia*, written after Henry's death, evinces not only deep gratitude for all he had accomplished but also great disappointment at the sudden frustration of so many hopeful expectations.

(B)

Although the forty years between 1273 and 1313 are among the most bewildering and dreary in her history, they were more fateful for Germany than many a period crowded with heroic figures and thrilling events. In the first place, they started her on a political path which she was to follow until the nineteenth century. One must, it is true, beware of the misleading implications of the term Interregnum. Throughout its length—save for the interval, not abnormally long, after the death of William of Holland—there had always been one claimant to the imperial title and generally two. Still, over the greater part of Germany no one had paid any serious attention to either Richard of Cornwall or Alfonso of Castile; and in 1272 there was a real possibility that the very name of Holy Roman Emperor might disappear. Yet more likely was it that the title would become merely honorary, attached to anyone whom the Pope wished to compliment or entrust with the leadership of a crusade; in that case there would be no more reason for bestowing it on a German than on any other Catholic Christian. Now the forty years after 1273 decided that the Holy Roman Empire was to survive, that it was to be more than a name, and that it was still to be peculiarly associated with the German nation. Rudolf's election alone would have settled none of these things. But after he had been succeeded by Adolf of Nassau, after the title of King of the Romans had been considered worth fighting for at much risk, after Albert I had maintained his claim to it in the teeth of rebellious Electors and an unfriendly Pope, after Henry VII had received the imperial crown at Rome and, despite his reverses, inspired the Italians with a just respect for his vigour and an exaggerated fear of his might, there could be no doubt that the Empire was to live for a long time yet and that it was still a force in the life of Europe. And that the *imperium* was to be wielded by Germans, as in the past, was equally assured. Successive Popes, by actions and words, had countenanced the time-honoured connexion; it was largely due to Gregory X that the claims of Alfonso had been finally set aside and that Rudolf of Habsburg had been chosen; and in 1308 Clement V, Frenchman though he was, had failed to give effective support to the candidature of Charles of Valois. In this relation, the theory of the "translation of the Empire" had its value from the German point of view. Much was heard of it in these years; it was generally accepted by imperialists as well as papalists, and the Kings of the Romans have been much denounced by modern historians for countenancing it; but one should remember that while it was by the Pope that the Empire was supposed to have been transferred, it was to the Germans that he was supposed to have transferred it. The *imperium* had gone abroad during the Interregnum; there were not wanting foreigners, especially Frenchmen like Pierre Dubois, who argued that it should be "translated" again; even patriotic Germans were sometimes perplexed that their country should have received it rather than France, which had equally belonged to the Empire of Charles the Great. Hence the usefulness of a theory, first enunciated by the Papacy, which expressly sanctioned Germany's imperial rights.

The Empire, then, was to continue to mean something. But these forty years decided that it was not to mean much. Of the four kings with whom we are concerned, only one went to Italy for the imperial crown. His expedition was encouraged and supported by the Pope; his arrival was hailed with delight by a very great number of the Italian people. But his experiences shew plainly—though it is true that contemporaries did not realise their full significance—that Italy, while willing to applaud imperial ideals, would not brook imperial rule. There was no attempt to enforce royal authority in the kingdom of Arles. It was not indeed forgotten; one of Rudolf's most spectacular and successful undertakings was his expedition in 1289 against the Count Palatine of Burgundy (Franche Comté); and the rights of the Empire in the kingdom proved useful more than once in bargaining with the royal houses of France and Naples. But if the great feudatories of the Arelate did homage to the King of the Romans, it was as much as he could expect; and after Albert I's treaty with Philip the Fair it looked as if Franche Comté, now in the hands of the French king, would soon be severed from the Empire, both in fact and in law. Needless to say, there was no extension of imperial power to regions where even the greatest of the Emperors had never made it effective. The rulers of Poland during the years under review sometimes paid allegiance to the Empire, sometimes not; while the independence of Hungary was now beyond serious question, notwithstanding Rudolf's pretence of treating it as an escheated fief.

It has commonly been assumed in modern times that for Germany the continuance of the Empire after 1273 was a calamity. As before, it is asserted, the claims inherent in the imperial title diverted the German kings from their proper task, the government of Germany. On the other hand, one may well doubt whether, but for its association with the Empire, the German Crown would have survived at all. And, in reality, the glitter of imperial pretensions had little effect on the actions of three out of the four kings of these forty years, nor, for that matter, did it often have much influence on the policy of their successors. The rights of the Empire might be cited to lend colour to some project that had really been suggested by other considerations; it was seldom that they furnished a motive for any important undertaking. Rudolf, Adolf, and Albert (though none of them despised the imperial dignity) busied themselves almost exclusively with German affairs. The Empire, it is true, proved a fatal lure to Henry VII; it was the cause of much trouble to Lewis the Bavarian; and in the fifteenth century it enticed Sigismund into ambitious undertakings which, in the interests of Germany, had been better left alone. The connexion with the Empire, moreover, brought the German King into a peculiar and embarrassing relationship with the Pope. But there was no need of an imperial crown to tempt the kings of that time into foolish foreign adventure; and in the later Middle Ages the Holy Roman Emperors were no more likely to fall out with the Papacy than were the Kings of France or England. In the past, no doubt, the Empire had done great mischief to the German monarchy, but it did little more, partly because that monarchy was so weak that there was not much left for it to lose.

For the years we are surveying revealed plainly the plight of the German Crown. The kings of the time were all capable and vigorous men; but none had the least chance of doing what Henry the Fowler had done 350 years before. Feudal disintegration had gone too far; and for another thing, there was lacking the public spirit that in 918 had led the magnates of Germany to choose as their king the strongest man in the country. Three times did the Electors deliberately bestow the crown on men of small account, and when, to gratify their hatred of Adolf, they were constrained to elect the powerful Albert, they soon tried to get rid of him. It was vain for any king at this time to try to secure the succession for his son.

After the Interregnum the German Crown was of necessity weak. Frederick II had dissipated its resources and impaired its authority by his policy towards the princes; and, in the confused years after his "deposition," royal lands had been seized, royal rights usurped. Rudolf, to do him justice, really tried to get back what had been lost; and his prospects seemed fairly good when in 1274 the Diet authorised him to take into his hand all royal domain held by Frederick II at the date of his "deposition." The measure afforded a legal pretext for Rudolf's proceedings against Ottokar, whose principal acquisitions were alleged to be usurpations of imperial fiefs or domain. Rudolf also recovered a good deal of royal domain in small fragments scattered here and there, and several imperial cities were rescued from princely rule or control. His systematic use of *Landvögte* in the administration of the domain shewed, moreover, that he recognised the value of a local organisation such as had enabled the kings of France to keep vast territories under their direct rule. But the need of conciliating the princes drove him, notably before his campaigns against Ottokar, to exempt many of them from the effect of the Diet's decree; and where he sought to enforce it he often met stubborn resistance, which he sometimes failed to overcome. In the last quarter of the thirteenth century even a poor knight might have a stronghold far more formidable than those "adulterine" castles which Henry Plantagenet, little more than a hundred years before, had destroyed so easily. The remaining resources of the Crown, in short, were inadequate for the recovery of what had been lost, and the hereditary Habsburg possessions were not sufficient to supply the deficiency, even if Rudolf had been willing to risk them in such a cause. Perhaps, indeed, he foresaw that what little he laboriously achieved would be in great part undone by his successors when bargaining for election. Though Adolf and Albert were not indifferent to the duty of restoring to the Crown lost lands and rights, it is not astonishing that their efforts to that end were less resolute than those of Rudolf.

Perhaps the most valuable asset of the Crown was its right to dispose of vacant fiefs that lacked heirs. Unfortunately, it was now established custom that escheated or confiscated fiefs must not be kept in the king's hand, but must be granted to a new lord[1]. The recipient might be a member of the king's family, even his son, so that Rudolf's treatment of the forfeited possessions of Ottokar was constitutionally correct. Had the crown been hereditary, the rule would scarcely have harmed its power. As things were, it made the crown a prize worth seeking, but encouraged a king to exploit his prerogative in the interests of his family rather than of the nation.

As the revenue from the royal domain was insignificant, as the imperial cities paid their dues reluctantly, resenting and resisting all extraordinary demands, and as all the kings save Albert were poor when elected, they could rarely afford big enterprises. Feudal military service was no longer exacted from the princes, and when waging war the king had to rely on

[1] Cf. Henry VI's failure in 1191 to retain Thuringia in his own hands on the death of the Landgrave without heir, *supra*, Vol. v, p. 462, n. 1.

his personal resources or bargain with over-mighty subjects for their support. At this very time Edward I of England was converting the English feudal host into a paid volunteer army, to his own great advantage and the vast increase of English power. But the King of the Romans lacked an Exchequer like Edward's, and when Adolf went to war with France, it was as the subsidised ally of the English King.

Thus the German monarchy, though its life had been saved, was not restored to health. It was not negligible. It still had prestige; its prerogatives were still worth something. Possessing the crown, the Habsburgs and the Luxemburgs quickly sprang into the front rank of German princes. Even poor Adolf, once he was king, became formidable. But the crown was an investment, to be bought in the hope that it would eventually yield a little profit to the purchaser.

It was the Electors who drew most benefit from the continued existence of the crown. The years under review consolidated their position and powers. There was now no doubt that there were seven Electors, though it was not quite certain who the seven should be. One debatable point, however, was settled by Rudolf's formal recognition of the electoral right of the King of Bohemia. Some writers have argued that the Electors at this time regarded themselves as a standing Council of the Empire, whose duty it was to deliberate together in times of crisis and if occasion arose to constrain the king to good behaviour. But there is no real evidence that the Electors thought thus of themselves; between elections they acted as seven individuals, and it was only when the throne was vacant that they worked together. The status and prospects of the Electors were to be much affected by the reign of Lewis the Bavarian and still more by that of Charles IV; and further consideration of the subject may be deferred until it becomes necessary to examine the effect of the Golden Bull.

Considering the weakness of the central government, it is surprising that Rudolf and his successors, when dealing with other potentates, upheld the rights and dignity of Germany as well as they did. All of them, of course, had much to do with the Papacy. The relations between the *regnum* and the *sacerdotium* were not as simple as they had formerly been. The kings after 1273, not caring very much about imperial authority and often needing papal support for their domestic ambitions, were disposed to be conciliatory towards the Church and to accept contentions and theories which their predecessors had denied. Thus it was seldom disputed that the relation of the sun to the moon was an analogue of the relation of the Papacy to the Empire, and, as we have seen, the doctrine of the Translation of the Empire was regarded with equanimity. Nevertheless, it is fair to add, papal claims which were new, or believed to be so, were never expressly conceded. As for the Popes of this period, they rarely wanted to destroy the Empire or even to weaken it. They needed it as a counterpoise to France—a consideration which greatly influenced the most Francophil of all, Clement V. Consequently, even when they voiced the most extreme pretensions, they did not press them persistently.

The main source of disagreement between the two powers was the papal "approbation" of a newly-elected king. During these forty years every king as a matter of course wrote to the Pope, asking for favour and support, and expressing the hope that in due time he might receive from the Vicar of Christ the imperial crown. Each king was "approved," though only after he had taken a *sacramentum fidelitatis*, while Rudolf's approval was preceded by elaborate negotiations and the grant of important concessions by the king, especially in Italy, and in the case of Albert some years passed before Boniface VIII would recognise him. What was the significance of this "approval" and this oath? The Papacy maintained that the election of a King of the Romans had no legal effect until the Holy See had approved it, and that in the meantime the king-elect had no right to exercise royal authority. On the other hand, the kings and Electors of the time, almost without exception[1], held that election followed by coronation at Aix-la-Chapelle warranted the exercise not only of royal but also of imperial power, and that nothing was sought of the Pope but his friendly countenance and support, the refusal of which, however regrettable, would in no wise impair the king's rights. Usually both sides used ambiguous language when touching upon this question, neither wishing to force a quarrel or to give anything away. But Boniface VIII, and also Clement V after his breach with the Emperor, stated the papal view in uncompromising terms; while after Henry's death Clement tried to act upon the contention that, when the Empire was vacant, its administration belonged to the Papacy—a claim which was to have practical results of great moment in the reign of Lewis the Bavarian. With respect to the *sacramentum fidelitatis*, the question was whether it was an oath of fealty, such as a vassal took to his lord, or merely a promise of loyal support such as any Christian might fittingly make to the head of the Church. Canonists had long maintained that it was feudal in character, like the oath which the King of Naples took to the Papacy; the Popes of this time accepted this interpretation as a matter of course, and when Clement V urged it strongly in his quarrel with Henry VII, he was putting forward nothing new. There is no doubt that the customary oath was virtually identical with the one sworn by Otto I to Pope John XII[2], and was not feudal at all. Albert I, it is true, took an oath couched in more submissive terms, and, though it is not necessarily feudal in character, there is no doubt that Boniface VIII

---

[1] In 1303 Albert I, to gain over Boniface VIII, recognised that it is from the Holy See that *reges et imperatores, qui fuerunt et erunt pro tempore, recipiunt temporalis gladii potestatem ad vindictam malefactorum, laudem vero bonorum* (MGH., *Const.* IV, i. 155).

[2] Gratian, *Decr.*, Dist. lxiii, c. 33; cf. MGH., *Const.* I, p. 29.

construed it as such and that Albert expected him to do so[1]. Imperial compliance with papal pretensions never went farther. But Albert's oath was not repeated by Henry VII, and although before setting out for Italy Henry swore to protect and defend the Holy See, recognising the superiority of the *sacerdotium* to the *imperium*, his undertakings fell short of an oath of fealty.

In general, it must be recognised that the kings of this period were too ready to shelter behind ambiguities and to accept theories which, if harmless in themselves, might be used as bases for claims very damaging to the Empire. The doctrine of the "Translation" was dangerous; it was imprudent to concede that the Empire was the "lesser light" in the firmament, even though Dante for a while was willing to do so; but it was suicidal to admit, as Rudolf and Albert did, that the Electors owed their existence and rights to the Papacy, a belief which, under Rudolf, was actually countenanced by the Electors themselves. It can hardly be disputed that in the verbal skirmishes of these forty years the Papacy had on the whole the better of it.

There were, nevertheless, several able publicists who at this time vigorously defended the authority and rights of the Empire against the Papacy. The most famous was of course Dante, whose *De Monarchia* was probably, to the medieval mind, the most cogent vindication of the Empire ever written. And just at the end of the reign of Henry VII the imperialists opened a counter-attack, with ammunition mainly supplied by the civil lawyers of Italy. In a circular announcing his coronation in Rome—a verbose and pompous document—Henry used phrases which might be construed as a claim to the lordship of the whole world, including the Church. Later, while not going so far, Henry, in reply to the Pope's claim of feudal overlordship, urged that all temporal authority belonged to the Emperor and that he received it direct from God. It was the beginning of a great imperial offensive, which under Lewis the Bavarian was to assume a practical importance far greater than it possessed in the reign of Henry.

Of more serious consequence than all this talk were the relations between the Empire and France. It was under Philip the Fair that France embarked on the policy of fomenting dissension in Germany and taking advantage of the consequent confusion to nibble at her territory. The German kings of the time have been bitterly denounced for failing to frustrate and chastise the national enemy. They were aware of the danger and sometimes tried to check it, Adolf's alliance with Edward of England being the most ambitious step towards this end. Albert of Austria, however, was ready to ally with the King of France against his own sovereign, and when he himself sat on the throne, he maintained his friendly relations with Philip for several years. Henry VII's Italian enterprise of course

---

[1] For Albert's oath, see MGH., *Const.* iv, i. 155. It closely resembled that taken by bishops. Cf. R. Moeller, *Ludwig der Bayer und die Kurie im Kampf um das Reich*, p. 171.

prevented him from doing much to protect the western border against France, even if he seriously wished to do so. It should be understood, however, that Philip the Fair did little actual harm to Germany itself. Lyons and Viviers were definitely annexed by France, and it looked as though Franche Comté had fallen under the lordship of the French king; but these encroachments were at the expense of the kingdom of Arles, not of Germany, and in Arles imperial authority had for generations been little more than nominal. It was indeed a loss to Germany when the Count of Bar did homage to Philip for his lands west of the Meuse, and when the city of Toul placed itself under Philip's protection; and it was a blow to the German Crown when several princes of the west allied with him against Adolf and declared themselves vassals of France. But these traitors were simply seeking a momentary advantage, and few princes can have wished to subject themselves to the hard yoke of Philip the Fair in preference to the negligible overlordship of a King of the Romans. The sequel shewed that it was only a very favourable conjunction of circumstances that enabled Philip to gain so much; his successors, troubled by domestic discord or foreign invasion, could not follow up his successes or even retain all that he had won; and it was not until the reign of Louis XI that France again became a serious menace to the territorial integrity of Germany. It is probable, too, that if French encroachments had become more serious, German resentment, which shewed itself more than once, would have stimulated a national resistance. Far more perilous than Philip's intrigues, from the German standpoint, was the advance of French culture within the German kingdom. Brabant, Hainault, Luxemburg, Lorraine were becoming more French than German in language, customs, and institutions. Henry VII spoke French as his native tongue. At the marriage of his son John and the Bohemian princess Elizabeth it was remarked that much French, some Czech, and little German could be heard, and from what was said and done it seemed as if those taking part in the ceremonies were all foreigners. It was, in the main, a French-speaking army which Henry led to Italy. This Gallicisation of western Germany was of course nothing new, and no political force could have stopped it.

What German culture was losing in the west it was gaining in the east. French encroachment at the expense of Germans was more than balanced by German conquest and colonisation at the expense of Slavs. The greatest days of the medieval *Drang nach Osten* were indeed just over; but the movement was still strong, and it was during these forty years that the Teutonic Knights completed the conquest of East Prussia, acquired the lordship of East Pomerania, and began the erection of Marienburg. It was not merely that Germans were occupying new territory; Germany's political centre of gravity was moving eastward. Henceforth it was on their possessions in the east that the leading German dynasties were to base their power. Gone was the greatness of Swabia; but eastward of it the

CH. III.

Wittelsbachs remained strong, and there was still a formidable duchy of Bavaria. The Habsburgs, hitherto petty counts of the south-west, were now mighty potentates on the eastern frontier. Throughout the four reigns that we have been surveying there was intrigue and dispute concerning the succession to Bohemia, the final victor being the House of Luxemburg, which was thus enabled, after Henry VII's death, to retain its place in the front rank of German families. The old duchies of Saxony and Franconia were now shattered; but the Ascanians and the Wettins, in virtue of the Marks over which they ruled, were as powerful as any prince of the centre or west. Nor should it be overlooked that several Slavonic princes of much influence, just within or just without the bounds of the kingdom, were becoming Germanised. But for the great Rhenish archbishoprics, the west of Germany would have carried little weight in the politics of the country.

It is a commonplace that it has seldom been safe to draw inferences about the state of the German people from the state of their central government. For the Crown, times were bad in the forty years that followed the succession of Rudolf of Habsburg, but to the ordinary German they seemed much better than they had been for a long while. There was still, nevertheless, a great deal of violent disorder, and in trying to check it the kings relied mainly upon *Landfrieden*, a poor substitute for strong-handed retribution. The term *Landfriede* was used in more than one sense. It might mean simply a royal ordinance embodying regulations for the establishment and maintenance of public order[1]. The term, however, was increasingly used to denote a league for preserving peace, whether founded at the instance of a great potentate or not[2]. Such an organisation commonly consisted of the temporal and spiritual magnates, knights and cities of a specified area, each member undertaking (usually for a specified time) not to wage war on any other, to observe certain rules in the interest of public order, and to assist, whether by money or by men, in chastising disloyal members or troublesome outsiders. Scores of these *Landfrieden* were organised in Germany during the two centuries following the Interregnum. Their very number indicates that they were usually ineffective, but many did useful work and lasted a long time, though all broke down sooner or later.

The spirit of self-help which gave rise to many of these *Landfrieden* produced other associations destined to greater success and renown, though just as humble in their origin. It was the reign of Adolf that witnessed

---

[1] When such a measure applied to the whole realm, it was properly called a *Reichsfriede*, but when, as was more common, it referred merely to a particular locality, it was correctly styled a *Landfriede*. But the distinction between the two terms was not strictly observed by contemporaries.

[2] *Landfrieden* were used not only by kings but also by the greater princes, as, for instance, by the archbishops of Cologne in their attempt to make their dukedom of Westphalia a reality outside the "domain" lands. See Bock, *Zeitschrift d. Savignystiftung, Germanist. Abt.* xlviii.

the lowly beginnings of the Swiss Confederation. This, indeed, was something out of the common, for united action on the part of peasants was
difficult. The growth of the Hansa, at the other end of Germany, was
less astonishing, for it was in the cities that co-operative enterprise found
the most congenial atmosphere. The kings of this period, while not
deliberately hostile to the burghers, were as a rule inclined to take the
side of the princes against them; but the cities shewed that they were
quite capable of protecting their own interests, though it must be admitted that they frequently displayed a selfish indifference towards the
welfare of Germany as a whole. The best days of the German cities, it
is true, were yet to come, and the favours bestowed on them by Lewis
the Bavarian were to modify their attitude towards the Crown. Already,
however, the best and most scientific government in Northern Europe was
to be found among them. What they had most to fear was internal
dissension, and at the end of the thirteenth century many of them, both
imperial and princely, were torn by feuds between the merchant aristocracy
and the craft gilds, a conflict which sometimes ended in the introduction of a democratic element into the civic constitution, but often in the
defeat of the artisans. But, whatever their troubles and defects, the German
cities were already proving that the weakness of the central government
was not incompatible with the economic progress of the German people.

While the cities are the most attractive feature of the Germany of
late medieval times, it would be unjust to dismiss the princes as so many
self-seeking ruffians. It is doubtless true that high ability and lofty
motives were not common among them. The best of them, however,
brought to their lands a measure of order and prosperity. Albert of
Austria made his eastern territories more peaceful than they had ever
been. Brandenburg became very powerful and wealthy under the last
Ascanians, who inherited the administrative capacity of the earlier margraves of the line, and strove, notwithstanding the growing power of the
feudal nobility, to continue their paternal rule. Where the princes were
less capable, their subjects often profited by securing political concessions.
Many a *Landstadt* enjoyed privileges which left it no reason to envy
imperial cities; and it was in the years immediately after the Interregnum
than *Landtage* first acquired real importance, the Estates of Bavaria being
conspicuously influential. The *Landtage*, indeed, were soon to be of more
practical consequence than the *Reichstag*.

The period under review was a time of much outward splendour. For
a love of extravagant pageantry it would be hard to excel the German
kings and princes of these years. Usually their means did not justify their
ostentation. Nevertheless, the country at large was not unprosperous.
Nearly all the cultivable land of Germany was being exploited. There
were more villages in Germany then than now, and in certain regions,
notably in the west, there was some congestion of population. On the
whole, the peasants were well off. The number of free cultivators was

increasing, and even the unfree, their obligations fixed by custom, were profiting by the general rise in prices.

At the opening of the fourteenth century the Germans themselves were certainly not pessimistic. To the average man the Empire had seldom been more than a resounding name, and he did not understand that it had lost whatever grandeur it had possessed. The king was to him a great personage; he did not share the modern historian's knowledge of the weakness of the Crown; on the contrary, he knew that it had recently been revived, and that the condition of Germany, however disorderly, was better than it had been during the Interregnum. The Germans of the time had a very good conceit of themselves, which appeared in the oft-proclaimed opinion that they surpassed all other peoples in military prowess, a belief which seldom had less warrant than at this moment. At all events, the disunion of Germany had caused among the Germans no such demoralisation as afflicted the French a century later during the feud between the Burgundians and the Armagnacs. Throughout the last centuries of the Middle Ages, the morale of the German people, though it naturally suffered, remained astonishingly high.

CHAPTER IV

GERMANY: LEWIS THE BAVARIAN

THE death of the Emperor Henry VII took Germany by surprise. There would inevitably have been some delay in choosing a new king, and the interregnum was prolonged by the desire of Archbishop Peter of Mayence, the convener of the Electors, to secure the crown for John of Bohemia, who at his father's death was a minor and so ineligible, but would be eighteen in the following year and therefore of age in the opinion of most German princes. The interval was marked by the customary intrigues between the Electors and aspirants to the crown and also, as it happened, by events which altered the whole outlook of German politics.

Despite the favour shewn towards John of Bohemia by the influential Archbishop Peter, it at first seemed likely that the choice of the majority of the Electors would fall on Frederick the Handsome, Duke of Austria, head of the house of Habsburg. He was young, brave, and honourable; and his family was no longer hated and feared as it had been in the days of King Albert. Frederick, however, was of an unstable temperament, readily discouraged by difficulties, and his self-confidence and ambition had continually to be stimulated by his younger brother Leopold, a man equally famous for knightly accomplishments and superior in energy and resolution. Unfortunately for the Habsburgs, the internal troubles of Lower Bavaria had just involved them in war with the Wittelsbachs. An invasion of the Wittelsbach lands by Frederick and Leopold was foiled by Lewis, Duke of Upper Bavaria, who in November 1313 gained a brilliant victory at Gammelsdorf, in which he performed feats of arms which made him the talk of Germany.

Lewis of Wittelsbach, thus thrust into prominence, attracted the interest of the Electors. Preliminary conferences between them had given little hope of agreement. Peter of Mayence and Baldwin of Trèves, the supporters of John of Bohemia, began to doubt the possibility of his election. At the same time Peter was implacably opposed to the choice of a Habsburg. He and Baldwin therefore transferred their support to Lewis of Bavaria, who had not even put himself forward as a candidate. John of Bohemia, Baldwin's nephew, would vote as his uncle bade him. The Brandenburg vote and the good will of one of the claimants to the Saxon vote were also secured. Lewis was admired but not feared, and the Wittelsbachs, never having possessed the crown, seemed less dangerous than either the Habsburgs or the Luxemburgs.

Frederick the Handsome, however, retained the support of the Archbishop of Cologne and had purchased that of Rudolf of the Palatinate, elder brother of Lewis, with whom he was almost always on bad terms. He could also count on Duke Rudolf of Saxe-Wittenberg, who had the better claim to the Saxon vote, and on Duke Henry of Carinthia, who still asserted his right to Bohemia.

In October 1314, towards the day appointed for the election, the rivals, attended by the Electors favourable to them, led armed forces to Frankfort and camped on opposite sides of the Main, the city, in fear of violence, having closed its gates to both. On 19 October Frederick was hastily elected by his supporters, next day Lewis more ceremoniously by his. Five votes, three of undisputed validity, were cast for Lewis; four, two of which were unchallenged, for Frederick[1].

There followed attempts by the would-be kings to secure formal investiture and perform the traditional ceremonies. Lewis was admitted to Frankfort after his election, and was solemnly placed on the altar of St Bartholomew's church according to ancient custom. On 25 November, moreover, he was crowned at Aix-la-Chapelle. Frederick, on the other hand, though his coronation, which took place on the same day, was performed at Bonn, could boast that he had been crowned, if not at the proper place, at least by the proper person—the Archbishop of Cologne; and it was to his advantage that he had possession of the imperial insignia. In popular estimation there was little to choose between the claims of the rivals to recognition. It is unlikely that foreign influences had much to do with the policy of the Electors on this occasion. Clement V had exhorted them to choose no one likely to persecute the Church, but he died during the interregnum, and the Holy See was vacant when the election took place. Philip the Fair is known to have been keenly interested and to have entered into negotiations with some of the Electors, but it cannot be shewn that his wishes carried much weight.

The disputed election of 1314 was followed by an eight years' war. Neither protagonist was unworthy of devotion. Lewis was about thirty and, like Frederick, was a fine-looking man, tall and muscular, with a good-natured countenance and lively brown eyes. He was temperate and clean-living, liked good company, and had a passion for hunting. He was pious in a conventional way, and had had the usual education of a man of his rank, which had apparently not given birth to any intellectual interests except a fondness for German poetry. His military skill was highly estimated, his courage unquestioned. But—and here too he resembled his rival—he was of a wayward disposition, easily excited and easily cast down, with an ever-growing tendency to hypochondria. Nevertheless he greatly exceeded Frederick in ambition and determination; and, when all is taken into account, there were few abler men among the German princes.

Despite the personal attractiveness of both Lewis and Frederick, the

---

[1] The Archbishop of Cologne, though not present, had empowered Rudolf of the Palatinate to vote and act on his behalf.

struggle between them was singularly uninspiring. A great part of
Germany, including nearly the whole of the north, took no part in the
fighting. Even in the west and the south, where the lands of the rivals
lay, little enthusiasm was shewn; and such support as either received had
usually to be paid for at a high price. Though he was inferior in territorial resources, Lewis' adherents in Germany at large outnumbered those
of Frederick. Actuated by enmity to Frederick's chief supporter, the
Archbishop of Cologne, a number of important princes of the Lower
Rhineland espoused the Bavarian cause; while most of the imperial cities
of the west and south were on the same side, won over or confirmed in
their loyalty by the privileges and concessions which Lewis lavished on
them. The Electors generally shewed little disposition to risk anything in
promoting the success of their respective nominees, though Lewis received
valuable military assistance from John of Bohemia.

As in most of the German wars of the later Middle Ages, there was
not much bloodshed. Numerous castles and a few towns were besieged, as
a rule in vain. The open country traversed by an army was mercilessly
ravaged. But a knight or man-at-arms of the fourteenth century was too
costly to be lightly hazarded by a German prince; and though every now
and then one side would invite the other to a pitched battle, the challenger
was generally found to have previously occupied so advantageous a position
that it would have been folly for his enemies to fight. In 1315 it seemed
likely that a decisive battle would be waged near Spires, but Lewis, disappointed of expected reinforcements, evaded an engagement. Next year,
it is true, an attempt by Lewis to relieve Esslingen, besieged by Frederick,
led, against the will of both commanders, to a confused and bloody fight,
but this had no decisive consequences. For some time, however, the cause
of Lewis was in the ascendant. The power of the Habsburgs was gravely
impaired by the defeat inflicted on Leopold at Morgarten by the infant
Swiss Confederation; in 1317 Lewis forced his brother Rudolf to sign a
treaty favourable to himself; and in the next year the Archbishop of
Cologne virtually withdrew from the conflict.

Suddenly, however, the tide turned. Troubles with his Bohemian
subjects prevented King John from continuing his military aid to Lewis.
The Habsburgs rallied their forces, ravaged the Wittelsbach territories,
and easily defeated an attempted counter-invasion. In 1320 Lewis lost a
valuable friend by the death of Archbishop Peter of Mayence, a very
sagacious politician, to whom Henry VII and John of Bohemia, besides
Lewis himself, owed their crowns. Lewis fell into despair and talked of
abandoning the struggle. The Habsburgs, however, neglected to press
home their advantage till the autumn of 1322. Then Leopold invaded
Bavaria from the west while Frederick came up the Danube with a large
and motley force, which included pagan Hungarians who ate cats and dogs.
Lewis, who again enjoyed the assistance of John of Bohemia, shewed
unexpected enterprise, and got into touch with Frederick at Mühldorf on

the Inn before Leopold could join him. John kept Lewis' sagging resolution to the sticking-point, and a challenge to battle was accepted by Frederick, who in reply to the remonstrances of his captains declared that he had made too many widows and orphans and wanted the issue settled. In the battle Frederick fought brilliantly, while Lewis kept aloof amid a body-guard of knights dressed exactly like himself. The Habsburg horse, at first irresistible, were checked by the Bavarian footmen, and the knights and men-at-arms of the Wittelsbach army, having rallied after their discomfiture, dismounted and reinforced the infantry. The issue was determined, however, by a timely charge of fresh cavalry under Frederick of Hohenzollern, Burgrave of Nuremberg, before which the Habsburg troops broke and fled. The battle was one of the greatest in Germany during the later Middle Ages. The victors took 1400 prisoners, among them being Frederick and his brother Henry. At a stroke all the advantages previously gained by the Habsburgs were nullified. Most of Frederick's supporters speedily abandoned his cause, the collapse of which was accelerated by the wise clemency of Lewis towards the vanquished.

Lewis was now secure. He did not long leave in doubt the policy he meant to pursue. He was to use the German crown as a means of promoting the interests of his family, regardless of the effect of his plans on royal authority and German unity, regardless too of the claims of others on his gratitude. In his eyes, what the Wittelsbachs needed most was more territory, and, as his family increased, the desire to add to its landed possessions outweighed all other considerations. It cannot be denied that in the pursuit of his end Lewis displayed remarkable pertinacity, ingenuity, and acumen.

The victory of Lewis over the Habsburgs had been due in great measure to the steadfast loyalty of John of Bohemia. John was one of the most interesting men of the time. Since he was King of Bohemia and Count of Luxemburg, his possessions lay at the opposite ends of the Empire, but to one of his temperament that mattered little. He lived in a hurry. The speed of his movements was the wonder of his contemporaries; he was known to travel from Prague to Frankfort-on-Main in four days. He would rush light-heartedly from Poland to France, from the Netherlands to Italy, in furtherance of some plan of the moment. His ubiquity corresponded to the range of his interests. There was no political quarrel or intrigue in Western or Central Europe but he had a finger in it. His fertility and resource were inexhaustible. The moment one scheme failed—often indeed before that happened—he was eagerly prosecuting another. While his knightly prowess was admired by all, there were some who thought him a little mad; but there was generally more than a grain of sense in his projects, and that his career, despite many reverses, was on the whole successful was due as much to his energy and ability as to the luck for which he was famous.

John, like his father, was at heart a Frenchman. Bohemia he hated, and the Bohemians reciprocated the dislike. They regarded him as an intruder, dreaded his visits with their invariable accompaniment of oppressive exactions, and were shocked by his disreputable tastes and habits. In 1318 a rising of the nobles nearly dethroned him, and it was only at the cost of great concessions that an agreement was reached. Then the long-growing estrangement of John and his queen widened into an irreparable breach. He left Bohemia and for some years had hardly anything to do with it.

Gratitude and policy alike counselled Lewis to maintain his friendship with John. By lending his countenance to some of John's designs outside Germany, he might have secured his continued loyalty to the German Crown. Instead, caring only for the aggrandisement of the Wittelsbachs, he pressed forward a scheme which conflicted with John's ambitions at more than one point. After the battle of Mühldorf had decided the civil war, the burning question in German politics was the future of the Mark of Brandenburg. The Brandenburg line of the house of Ascania had of late dwindled rapidly away, and with the death of Margrave Henry II in 1320 became extinct. Henry's predecessor Waldemar had shed a gleam of splendour over the last days of the family; but while holding all the territories of the elder branch of the Ascanians, he had squandered his resources on fantastic schemes and ostentatious display. Feared even more than he was admired by his neighbours, he was in 1316 defeated by a combination of princes headed by the King of Denmark and had to acquiesce in the loss of territory. Three years afterwards, before he could recover from the disaster, he died. When his cousin and heir followed him a few months later, Lewis of Wittelsbach claimed that the Mark was at his disposal as an escheated imperial fief. This, however, was disputed by the Archbishop of Magdeburg, and while his claims to the overlordship of Brandenburg had but flimsy foundations, there was real doubt as to the feudal status of some of the other Ascanian lands. John of Bohemia claimed Lusatia, and Lewis bestowed on him the district of Bautzen and other estates in this region. For some years, however, he made no announcement about Brandenburg itself, though it was widely believed that he had given John to understand that it would be granted to him.

Later in his reign Lewis was repeatedly charged with raising hopes which he did not mean to fulfil. Whatever may have happened in this case, Lewis no sooner felt secure on the German throne than he bestowed the Mark, with several adjacent fiefs, on his son Lewis, a boy of eight, John's services at Mühldorf being rewarded by a few gifts and concessions of no great consequence in the estimation of the recipient. About the same time, Lewis, anxious that the new margrave should have at least one friendly neighbour, induced Frederick the Quarrelsome, Margrave of Meissen and Landgrave of Thuringia, to break off a match which had been arranged between his heir and one of John's daughters and to substitute for the latter a daughter of his own. Fortunately for Lewis, John's hands were very full at the moment, and before he could attempt reprisals, in fact before the grant of Brandenburg to young Lewis had been formally proclaimed, the attention of Germany was diverted to a very different problem, and Lewis found himself compelled to play his part as a German king.

Since 1316 the Holy See had been occupied by John XXII. His favour had been sought by both Lewis and Frederick, especially the latter, on whose behalf his father-in-law, James of Aragon, had vigorously exerted himself. But the Pope had remained inflexibly neutral, usually addressing each claimant as "king-elect of the Romans." The reason for John's attitude is to be found in his resolve to re-assert papal authority in Italy. As long as Lewis and Frederick were fighting, neither was likely to interfere seriously with his projects. Moreover, to justify some of his doings beyond the Alps, John appealed to the doctrine, lately upheld by Clement V, that when the Empire was vacant its authority in Italy devolved on the Papacy. He therefore wished to avoid recognising anyone as King of the Romans, and perhaps, under Neapolitan influence, had thoughts of ending the Empire altogether.

The nature and consequences of John's policy in Italy are treated at length in another chapter. Both Lewis and Frederick appointed vicars-general for Italy, but for some years these had scarcely any influence. The participation of the Habsburgs in the crusade against the Visconti in 1322 caused bad blood between them and the overbearing Pope, who had treated them as servants rather than allies; but John nevertheless remained true to his neutrality as between them and Lewis. Even the news of Mühldorf did not alter his attitude. But the victor was now able to listen to appeals for help from the Ghibellines of North Italy. An imperial vicar, Berthold of Neiffen, appeared in Lombardy, and in defiance of the protests and threats of the papal legate, saved Can Grande of Verona from overthrow and relieved Milan when it was about to surrender to the besieging Guelfs.

The Pope was alarmed and furious. He was old and irascible, and his Italian plans lay very near his heart. But even the doings of Berthold seem hardly sufficient to account for the ferocity of the onslaught which he suddenly launched against Lewis, who, apart from his intervention in Italy, had done nothing to kindle the Pope's anger. On 8 October 1323 John XXII promulgated a bull in which he asserted that, while it belonged to the Holy See to judge of the validity of imperial elections, Lewis, without receiving papal recognition of his disputed title, had presumed to exercise the powers appertaining to both *regnum* and *imperium*, though the latter in time of vacancy ought lawfully to be administered by the Church, and that he had furthermore lent aid to condemned heretics in the persons of Galeazzo Visconti and his associates. Lewis was therefore summoned, on pain of excommunication, to lay down his authority within three months and to annul all acts performed by him as king. His subjects were to withdraw their obedience from him within the same term, or suffer both excommunication and forfeiture of their ecclesiastical and imperial fiefs. Lewis, who was completely taken aback by this assault, asked for a prolongation of the three months in order that he might have time to prepare his defence. John granted an extension of two months, a concession of small value, seeing that when it was made the original three had almost elapsed. Lewis therefore resolved to await events. He had already, on 5 January 1324, at Frankfort, published an elaborate vindication of his rights and conduct, which, though no further use seems to have been made of it, shews that he was already disposed to offer uncompromising resistance.

On 23 March 1324 the Pope excommunicated Lewis, and again called upon him to comply with the demands made in the previous October. Failure to do so within three months would involve him in the loss of any rights which he might conceivably have derived from his election. He was, further, to appear at Avignon, in person or by deputy, to receive final sentence. All clergy who should still recognise him were to be suspended, and if obstinate, to be excommunicated and deprived. Princes and cities who had disregarded the Pope's orders were graciously reprieved for the present, but if they persisted in their contumacy, they were to undergo the punishments named in the previous bull and their lands were to be placed under interdict.

The bull, though arrogant in tone, betrays certain weaknesses in the Pope's position. He had made the tactical mistake of using too many weapons in his first attack and now he had few terrors in reserve. Perhaps somewhat perplexed by the refusal of Lewis to shew his hand, he went so far as to hint that formal surrender might be rewarded by confirmation of his election as king. And John was plainly disconcerted at the general indifference of the Germans to his threats against those who obeyed Lewis. On 26 May, indeed, he wrote to the Electors disclaiming any intention of infringing on their rights. The same hesitation to exacerbate the German princes appears in another bull which the Pope issued in July. It declared that Lewis had now been deprived by God of any right to the German crown which he might previously have possessed; failing his submission by 1 October he was to suffer further penalties, including the loss of Bavaria and all his imperial fiefs. His subjects were again forbidden to obey him, but only the clergy and the cities were to incur immediate punishment for recalcitrance.

The reserve at first shewn by Lewis was perhaps due in part to his relations with the Habsburgs. Leopold, the younger brother of Frederick the Handsome, had refused to accept the verdict of Mühldorf. Lack of support in Germany had frustrated his military plans, and he had reluctantly entered into negotiations with Lewis. These, however, had been fruitless, owing, if Leopold is to be believed, to Lewis' double-dealing. When John XXII issued his first bull against Lewis, Leopold naturally regarded him as a welcome ally; but the Pope, though friendly, was determined to uphold his contention that the German throne had been vacant since 1313, and still refused to recognise Frederick. Leopold, more eager for revenge on Lewis than for the victory or release of his brother, then entered upon an intrigue with Charles IV of France. It is an obscure episode; but it seems certain that in July 1324 Charles and Leopold, then at Bar-sur-Aube, signed a treaty in which the latter recognised that the German throne was vacant and undertook to work for the election of the French King, while Charles promised to finance the Habsburgs in their war against Lewis. The treaty led to nothing, for Leopold's younger brothers did not approve of his sacrifice of Frederick's rights.

Lewis must have had some notion of what was happening, and for some time he probably thought that Leopold's dealings with France had been instigated by John XXII. Late in the spring, indeed, he had become convinced that the Pope was bent on his ruin, and that nothing was to be gained by submission or quiescence. On 22 May, therefore, he accepted the Pope's challenge by publishing the celebrated Appeal of Sachsenhausen. This manifesto is a long, verbose, and ill-compacted document. John XXII is denounced as a man of blood, a friend of injustice, and an enemy of the Holy Roman Empire, to which the Church owes her temporal power and possessions. He is striving to ruin the Electors and princes—nay, he has openly sworn to trample down the Empire. His claim to confirm imperial elections is hardly worthy of notice. Lewis' election and coronation were regular, and thus in themselves entitled him to exercise authority as King of the Romans. If there is a disputed election, ancient usage refers the issue to the arbitrament of war; and in the present instance God has given the victory to Lewis. When the Empire is vacant, the Count Palatine is lawful regent. Lewis holds the Catholic faith, but will not suffer his loyal subjects to be falsely styled heretics. Nay, John is a heretic himself, as is shewn by his denial of the absolute poverty of Christ (a subject which is treated at length). Finally, Lewis appeals to a General Council, at which he is willing to confront the Pope and make good his accusations. In the theological part of the Appeal, the influence of the Spiritual party of the Franciscans is evident. Much of it indeed is drawn from a writing of Petrus Johannis Olivi. It was probably through Emicho, Bishop of Spires, who became one of his most faithful adherents, that Lewis was brought into touch with the party, with whom he had no natural affinity.

It has been argued that the imperialists were unwise to confuse the issue between Lewis and John XXII by dragging theological questions into the dispute[1]. The object was doubtless to give churchmen, many of whom,

---

[1] It is doubtful whether Lewis approved or even knew of the inclusion of the long treatise on poverty in the Appeal. See K. Zeumer, *Zur Kritik der Appellationen Ludwigs des Baiern* (*Neues Archiv*, xxxvii, 1912, pp. 221 sqq.).

especially in Germany, were sympathetic with Lewis, a pretext for openly espousing his cause. This policy certainly gained him the support of a powerful party in the Church, and it cannot be shewn that it did his cause any practical harm. The truth is that the denunciations and arguments flung backwards and forwards did not mean much to either Lewis or John. The conflict was essentially political. The Pope wanted a free hand in Italy. He might have secured himself from interference on the part of Lewis by offering recognition of his royal title; but believing that he could hector Lewis into unconditional surrender, he gave the impression that he was bent on depriving him of his hard-earned crown, on the retention of which depended all his hopes of increasing the territories of the Wittelsbach family. Lewis had no wish to be a Barbarossa, and as soon as he realised that the Pope could not do him serious injury in Germany, he betrayed his eagerness to have done with the controversy, even at high cost to the Empire. By that time, however, Avignon realised that, if the Pope could not do much harm to Lewis, neither could Lewis do much harm to the Pope; so the papal terms of peace were kept high, and the barren dispute dragged on to its uninspiring end.

For a few years indeed the conflict appeared to be of vital significance to European religion and thought, for it looked as if John XXII was to be ignominiously worsted. It was at this time that Lewis appeared at his best. He recognised that he must give his full attention to the struggle with the Papacy. The key to the Pope's position, as Lewis saw, was Italy. There he could strike blows which the Pope would really feel; there, too, he could add to his prestige by securing the imperial crown. So for the two years following the publication of the Sachsenhausen Appeal his aim was to dispose German affairs in such a way that it would be safe for him to leave the country. In pursuit of this object he shewed a most acute judgment of the persons and conditions that had to be taken into account.

Recognising that Leopold of Habsburg was implacable, Lewis resolved to attempt a reconciliation with his prisoner Frederick, who, a victim of nervous depression, cared no more for the crown but only desired freedom. He was soon induced to sign a treaty, dated 13 March 1325, whereby, in return for his release and perhaps a promise of lands and dignities, he renounced all claim to the throne. He persuaded all his kinsmen save Leopold to recognise Lewis, but failing to secure the accomplishment of some of his undertakings, he returned to captivity. Lewis rewarded such conduct as it deserved; the two former rivals became fast friends; and in September Lewis, apparently carrying out a proposal already discussed in the negotiations of the previous spring, made Frederick joint-king. He and Lewis were to rule as though they were one person, the regulations for the exercise of their authority being drawn up in great detail. If either went abroad, he was to act with full power there, the other at home.

Lewis evidently felt sure of his personal ascendancy over Frederick.

CH. IV.

Leopold, however, did not approve of the arrangement, nor did the Electors, whose consent was necessary for its execution. Lewis resolved to go farther, and his next move was as daring as it was clever. At the beginning of 1326 he announced that he would be willing to abdicate provided that Frederick were recognised as king by the Pope before 25 July. In return, Frederick promised that, if the condition were fulfilled, he would confirm Lewis' son in the possession of Brandenburg and would give Lewis his general support. This agreement actually placated Leopold, though his death immediately afterwards robbed this result of its significance. The rest of the Habsburgs were for the time fully reconciled to Lewis, while the Pope was forced to reveal clearly to the German people his determination to accept no one as their king. For, as Lewis had doubtless foreseen, the agreement proved abortive; John XXII, when the Habsburgs applied for his recognition of Frederick, first put them off politely, and soon afterwards, under pressure from France, broke off negotiations altogether.

With the Habsburgs friendly to him and estranged from the Pope, Lewis was in a strong position. So far, indeed, the Pope had small ground for satisfaction at the effect which his denunciations and threats had produced on Germany. The interdict was seldom enforced in the Wittelsbach territories, and elsewhere only when the ordinary of the place was an exceptionally fiery partisan of the Papacy. It is true, however, that many old supporters of Frederick the Handsome welcomed a pretext for withholding obedience from Lewis. In the south, under the influence of the Archbishop of Salzburg, John's "processes" were published in most dioceses. The ecclesiastical Electors wavered for some time, but all in the end complied outwardly with the Pope's commands, though Baldwin of Trèves long afterwards remained on friendly terms with Lewis. Of the other prelates few shewed much zeal for the Pope. In many cathedral churches the dispute between king and Pope simply added fresh bitterness to an existing feud between the chapter and a papal provisor. Some bishops indeed, such as those of Spires, Freising, and Augsburg, were openly on the side of the king. Among the regulars, the Cistercian monks and the Dominican friars were mostly hostile to Lewis. The Spiritual Franciscans and for some time many of the main body of the Order were opposed to the Pope rather than friendly to the king, but their influence worked in Lewis' favour; while the Carmelite and Austin friars, and the Premonstratensian Canons, were for the most part on his side. Of the Military Orders, the Hospitallers, while providing Lewis with many trusted supporters, were divided in sympathy; but the Teutonic Knights were whole-heartedly for him, and from their ranks came some of his most valued counsellors. As for the parish clergy, their attitude depended on that of the authority, ecclesiastical or secular, which could most readily be brought to bear upon them.

To judge by the writings of the chroniclers, the dispute was regarded very coolly by the majority of Germans. It occasioned little bloodshed or violence. Few laymen paid any heed to John's fulminations. The cities were for the most part devoted to Lewis, though Mayence and Cologne, strange to say, were more papalist than their archbishops. In the Lower Rhineland one or two princes, such as the Counts of Jülich and Cleves, professed zeal for the Pope; but the only part of Germany which gave Lewis ground for serious concern was the north-east. Brandenburg, it is true, was generally loyal to him, and the people of Berlin killed an envoy sent by Rudolf, Duke of Saxe-Wittenberg, to seduce them from their allegiance. The Archbishop of Magdeburg, too, a very bitter foe of the Wittelsbachs, was opportunely murdered by the municipal authorities of his own cathedral city, with whom he had long been at strife. But the Pope succeeded in stirring up the King of Poland and the nobles of Silesia, Pomerania, and Mecklenburg, to invade the Mark; and in 1326 an army of Poles and Lithuanians, many of whom were heathen, ravaged a great part of the land and massacred many of the inhabitants.

Nevertheless, towards the end of the same year, Lewis felt able to press forward preparations for an expedition to Italy. In January 1327 he went to Trent to confer with some of the Ghibelline leaders. He intended to return to Bavaria after a few days, but they urged so strongly the advisability of immediate action that he summoned troops from beyond the Alps, and in March moved southwards. He had with him, besides a number of Franciscan scholars, Marsilio of Padua and John of Jandun, who had fled from Paris to his court in the previous spring. Marsilio, there is no doubt, had much influence on Lewis' conduct during his sojourn in Italy, and was often employed to vindicate in public the policy of his royal patron.

The events of Lewis' Italian expedition are narrated elsewhere[1], and we are here concerned with it merely as an episode in his conflict with the Papacy. In April, while Lewis was advancing towards Milan, John XXII issued bulls depriving him of his imperial fiefs, declaring him a public maintainer of heretics, ordering him to leave Italy within two months and appear at Avignon on 1 October to receive sentence, summoning his son to surrender Brandenburg, and excommunicating a number of his companions, including Marsilio and John of Jandun. Much of this was vain repetition, and no effect seems to have been produced. Lewis received the iron crown at Milan in May. There now reached him an invitation to Rome, purporting to come from the Roman people, and he solemnly called upon the Pope to return to his see.

In the autumn, John, who was demanding from the German clergy funds for organising resistance to Lewis, formally condemned him as a heretic and declared him deprived of all his goods and dignities. Nevertheless, it was amid popular rejoicing that, on 7 January 1328, this spiritual outcast entered the Pope's own city. His army consisted mainly

[1] *Supra*, Chap. II.

of Italians. Very few German magnates were with him, the most notable being his nephew Rudolf of Bavaria, Elector Palatine, and Frederick, Burgrave of Nuremberg. Not a single German bishop was present. If there was little enthusiasm for the Pope's cause in Germany, there was not much more for the king's.

While it is true that Lewis did his utmost to conciliate the people of Rome, treating them as rulers of the city, and that at his coronation as Emperor the crown was placed on his head by the four Syndics of the People, from whom he also received the rest of the imperial insignia, he was careful to avoid any express recognition of Marsilio's theory that his imperial authority was derived from his choice by the Romans. It was essential to him to stand by the view that his rights were grounded on the vote of the German Electors, and that while coronation at Rome gave him the right to style himself Emperor, it added nothing to his legal powers. It must be admitted, however, that Lewis never contradicted Marsilio's theory in public during his stay in Rome, and probably tried to give the people the impression that he accepted it. There is no need to emphasise the fact that, on whatever theory they were based, the proceedings at Lewis' coronation involved a denial of the Pope's right to any share in the appointment or investiture of an Emperor.

A few days after the coronation, and before he could have heard of it, John XXII played his last card by proclaiming a crusade against Lewis. The Emperor replied by declaring that the Pope, as a heretic and traitor, had been deposed by Christ. In support of the charge of heresy were adduced John's inciting of infidels to attack Brandenburg, his arrogation to himself of the authority of the divinely-instituted Empire, and his encroachment on the rights of cathedral chapters, as well as his opinions on the poverty of Christ. He was sentenced to the total loss of his clerical orders and subjected to the secular power for punishment. The formal proceedings which led up to this pronouncement took place before great assemblies of the people in front of St Peter's. The populace, however, were mere spectators; it was solely in his capacity of Emperor that Lewis condemned the Pope.

It is true that Peter of Corvara, the Pope chosen in place of John by a committee of Roman clergy and laity, was accepted by another popular assembly. It does not appear, however, that the people's acclamations were regarded by either Lewis or Peter as adding to his authority. At all events, it was the Emperor who invested him with the ring and fisherman's cloak and subsequently placed the papal crown on his head. The Florentine Villani asserts that after his own coronation the new Pope, Nicholas V, crowned Lewis. It is hard to believe this, even if the statement be interpreted as referring to a piece of pure ceremony, devoid of legal significance. For anything that suggested the dependence of the Emperor's authority on papal consent or countenance cut away the ground from Lewis' feet and made ridiculous everything he had done since his arrival in Rome. A possible explanation is that Lewis hoped to recover some of his popularity with the Romans, who were growing tired of him, by submitting to a sham coronation at the hands of a Pope whom they regarded as having been chosen by themselves. But either Villani's report is wholly false, or Lewis, whatever his motives, was guilty of gross folly.

It is evident, at any rate, that Lewis' situation at Rome grew rapidly worse. On 4 August 1328 he and his Pope left the city. No success attended his efforts to retain some of the advantages which he had gained in northern Italy. The death of John of Jandun, it is true, was counterbalanced by the arrival at his court, while he was staying at Pisa, of Michael of Cesena and William of Ockham, an event which raised hopes of the adhesion of the whole Franciscan Order to the imperial cause, and encouraged Lewis to lay new charges of heresy at the door of Pope John and to revive his proposal of a General Council. But Italian politics took an unfavourable turn, and at the beginning of 1330 Lewis returned to Bavaria. Nicholas V, left without support, soon submitted to John XXII. The Emperor's great stroke had failed.

In Germany, however, Lewis was still powerful. While in Italy, he had composed a family quarrel by making the Rhenish Palatinate independent of Bavaria, and surrendering to its rulers a piece of Bavarian territory henceforth known as the Upper Palatinate. John XXII's intrigues among the Electors during his absence had borne no fruit. On the other hand, Baldwin, Archbishop of Trèves, was incensed with the Pope for refusing to confirm his election to the see of Mayence when it fell vacant in 1328, and was now waging war against the Pope's nominee. The younger Habsburgs, indeed, were disposed to use any opportunity of revenge on Lewis, but the death of Frederick the Handsome just before his return deprived them of their most dangerous weapon. Among the people at large Lewis' prestige seems to have been somewhat increased by his expedition; but how little his controversy with the Pope meant to most Germans is shewn by the fact that, while he was commonly regarded as lawful Emperor, John was commonly regarded as lawful Pope.

The conflict, in fact, was now one between the elephant and the whale. The Pope might renew his excommunications and interdicts: they had no more effect than before. Lewis had struck at his enemy's one vulnerable point, but had done him no serious hurt; and while he talked of returning to Italy, he can hardly have expected a second expedition to yield more decisive results than the first. At all events he henceforth gave the greater part of his mind to his schemes of family aggrandisement. At the same time, recognising that papal hostility was a nuisance, if not quite a danger, he shewed himself anxious to end the quarrel and willing to make notable concessions and even to undergo personal humiliation in pursuit of his object. Nevertheless, while admitting that he had sometimes encroached on ground that was lawfully the Pope's, he always resisted ecclesiastical interference in matters which he regarded as secular.

CH. IV.

The seven years after Lewis' return from Italy are among the most dreary in German history. Those who still cherish the old delusion that diplomacy was invented by the Italians of the fifteenth century could not do better than study the relations of the German princes during the latter years of Lewis the Bavarian. Entente, alliance, betrothal, and betrayal, with a score of States—independent for all practical purposes—taking a hand in the game, follow in bewildering succession. Of good faith and self-respect there is small trace. There is some skill and no lack of subtlety, but, except with Lewis, little fixity of purpose. In the background there is the dispute between Empire and Papacy, several princes making vain attempts to mediate, followed by equally vain negotiations between the principals.

The hinge on which German politics turned for several years after 1330 was the question of the Carinthian succession. Duke Henry, ruler of Carinthia and Tyrol, was an elderly man with two young daughters, one of whom was betrothed to John Henry, son of John of Bohemia. Lewis had promised the old duke that, if he left no male issue, a daughter or a son-in-law should succeed to his lands. In September 1330 John Henry was married to the second daughter, Margaret, commonly nicknamed Maultasch; and King John, confident that his son's succession to Carinthia and Tyrol would be accepted by the Emperor, set off light-heartedly on an expedition to Italy. Although, as we have seen, Lewis treated him shabbily after the battle of Mühldorf, John at first lacked time to undertake serious reprisals and of late had needed the Emperor's friendship for the accomplishment of his Carinthian ambitions. Lewis, on his part, had planned a joint expedition to Italy with John, whom he had led to believe that he had no objection to John Henry's succession to Carinthia and Tyrol. Nevertheless, as soon as it was known that John was about to go to Italy, Lewis made an agreement with the Habsburgs whereby on Duke Henry's death he would enfeoff them with Carinthia, while they would help him to secure Tyrol for the Wittelsbachs. Even if Lewis had not expressly committed himself to the support of John of Bohemia's plans, his dealings with the Habsburgs were in violation of his promises to Duke Henry.

Lewis was in a strong position. Both the Habsburgs and King John coveted Carinthia and could not hope to secure it without his consent. Neither party wished to see the Emperor under the influence of the other; thus, a few months earlier, John, fearful lest Lewis might be defeated, had intervened to avert the outbreak of war between him and the Habsburgs. The Emperor was thus well placed to play off the two rivals against each other, and he made the most of his opportunity. For the next few years, however, he was generally inclined to favour the Habsburgs, for John's initial success in Italy had seemed to presage a dangerous increase of his power. Still, he avoided an open breach with John, who seems not to have known the terms of his agreement with the Habsburgs, and after prolonged negotiations at Ratisbon in 1331 the Bohemian King went away with the belief that his son would be allowed to succeed to both Carinthia and Tyrol if he would undertake to exchange them for Brandenburg, a condition to which he was apparently willing to agree.

Nevertheless John gradually came to the conclusion that Lewis was against him, and sought to obtain by pressure what he could not get by friendship. Attempts were being made to effect a reconciliation between Lewis and the Pope. In 1330 John of Bohemia himself, his uncle the Archbishop of Trèves, and Duke Otto of Habsburg had suggested at Avignon, apparently with Lewis' approval, that if he would withdraw his appeal to a General Council, abandon his anti-Pope, revoke everything he had done against John XXII's lawful authority, acknowledge the validity of his excommunication, and seek the Pope's pardon, he might be permitted to retain the royal and imperial titles and be restored to the Church. The acceptance of these terms would have been an admission of defeat on the part of the Papacy, and John XXII decisively rejected them. Direct negotiations between Lewis and the Pope in 1331 were also abortive. John XXII seemed slightly less implacable in 1332, when the Count of Holland joined Baldwin and the Habsburgs in an effort to make peace; but nothing came of their mediation, perhaps because John of Bohemia was now looking to the Papacy for aid against Lewis.

In 1333 and 1334 there occurred obscure negotiations with the object of securing the succession to the German throne for Duke Henry of Lower Bavaria, Lewis' cousin. The motive of the Emperor in countenancing the plan was probably a desire to conciliate the King of Bohemia, who was Henry's father-in-law. While Lewis seems merely to have agreed to the election of Henry as prospective king, John and Henry himself had hopes that Lewis would abdicate in his cousin's favour. The Pope was naturally favourable to this scheme, and John and Henry gained the acquiescence of the King of France by lavish promises, which included the transference to Philip of imperial rights over the kingdom of Burgundy and the bishopric of Cambrai in guarantee of the payment of a large sum of money. But the project collapsed when, in the summer of 1334, the Emperor emphatically announced that he had no thought of abdicating[1].

About this time events took a turn in favour of Lewis. First, the Italian party among the cardinals, using as a pretext the suspicion of heresy under which John XXII had fallen for his views on the Beatific Vision, intrigued with the Emperor against him; it was largely due to their encouragement

---

[1] Duke Henry and King John were certainly guilty of hard lying, and perhaps of forgery, in this affair; cf. R. Moeller, *Ludwig der Bayer und die Kurie im Kampf um das Reich*, pp. 206 sqq. But that there were genuine negotiations on foot is shewn in *Nova Alamanniae*, ed. E. Stengel, nos. 338, 339, 342-6.

that Lewis threw over the scheme for the election of Duke Henry. Then, in December, came John's unexpected death. His successor, Benedict XII, appeared to be inclined towards a settlement with the Emperor.

From the point of view of Lewis, the death of Duke Henry of Carinthia, which occurred on 2 April 1335, could not have come at a better moment. A month later he bestowed on the Habsburgs Carinthia and the southern part of Tyrol, the northern part being granted to his own sons. Luck was still with him, for John of Bohemia was lying sick at Paris, having been grievously wounded in a tournament. The triumph of the Emperor's policy was indeed somewhat spoiled by the Tyrolese, who obstinately upheld the rights of Margaret Maultasch. Faced with the certainty of war as soon as King John should recover, Lewis now made a desperate attempt to reconcile himself with the Papacy. The Emperor soon found, however, that the new Pope, for all his pacific professions, was in reality no more conciliatory than John XXII. Lewis went to great lengths in his desire to placate him. He was willing to admit that he had sinned against Pope John, to abandon the title of Emperor, to revoke all imperial acts of himself and Henry VII, to promise never to visit Rome save with the Pope's permission and in order to receive the imperial crown, and then to enter and leave the city within one day. He offered to go on crusade over-seas, to found churches and monasteries, and to perform pilgrimages, as the Pope might order. If he had fallen into heresy, he had done so unintentionally. The responsibility for the Sachsenhausen Appeal and other obnoxious documents he shabbily tried to throw onto the Franciscans or Marsilio, whom he undertook to cast off if they would not follow him in returning to the grace of the Holy See. But on one point, and that a crucial one, he stood firm. He would admit no invalidity in his title as king, for which he sought papal approval only as his predecessors had done. It must not be forgotten that the basis of John XXII's first attack on Lewis was the contention that without papal recognition he was no true king at all. If Lewis could make peace without accepting this doctrine, he might claim to have been victorious on the main issue.

The offers summarised above were not made by Lewis all at once. During this phase of his relations with the Pope he sent several separate embassies to Avignon. The first, dispatched in March 1335, lacked sufficient power to deal with the Pope's demands. The second reached Avignon in September of the same year. The consequent negotiations lasted a long time; but the Kings of France and Bohemia threw their weight against peace and ruined whatever small chance of agreement there might otherwise have been. Another abortive embassy was commissioned early in 1336. In that year things went badly for Lewis in Germany. He failed to get possession of Tyrol. The Habsburgs and the Wittelsbachs accused each other of failing to give proper support to the common cause; and when John of Bohemia opened war and ravaged Austria, the Habsburgs made peace, keeping Carinthia and consenting to leave Margaret Maultasch in possession of Tyrol. It was after this that Lewis sent Margrave William of Jülich, who was married to a sister of his wife, to negotiate a marriage alliance with Philip of Valois and to offer to Benedict XII the most humiliating of the concessions mentioned above. The negotiations occupied the early months of 1337. They were impeded by the French, but broken off finally owing to the hectoring tone of the Pope, who in Consistory likened Lewis to the dragon of the Apocalypse and asserted that the insincerity of his repentance was proved by his refusal to abandon the title of king.

Lewis' policy since his return from Italy, despite the shrewdness and resource which he had shewn, had led to failure. Nothing had been added to the possessions of his family. He had alienated both the Luxemburgs and the Habsburgs. In his dealings with the Pope he had abased himself to no purpose. Yet in a few months he was more formidable to his enemies and more respected by his subjects than he had ever been before. He owed this sudden change of fortune, however, to a happy conjunction of circumstances rather than to any skill or insight of his own.

War between England and France was on the point of breaking out. Edward III was seeking allies, and the Pope had warned Philip that by repelling Lewis' attempt to conciliate France and the Papacy he risked driving him into alliance with the English. Philip took no notice of the advice, but Benedict was right. Lewis knew that war with France would not be disliked by the Electors, who regarded the chief protector of the Pope as an enemy of their rights, and he thought that Philip might be constrained by fear to change his attitude towards the dispute between the Empire and the Papacy. A number of Lewis' vassals in the Netherlands and the Rhineland were already allied to Edward, and in July 1337 the Emperor followed their example, undertaking to supply 2000 men for service against France in consideration of a large sum of money.

John of Bohemia had promised aid to France against both Edward and Lewis; Henry of Lower Bavaria took the same side; the Habsburgs, reluctant to offend the Pope, remained friendly with the French, though at first they gave no military support to either cause. But there is no doubt that most Germans, while not disposed to take any active share in the war, approved of the Emperor's policy and liked to see him playing a part in international politics instead of intriguing with his own subjects in order to gain a few square miles of territory for his family. This feeling merged itself with a growing indignation excited by the Pope's refusal to consider any terms offered by Lewis short of unconditional surrender. It was some of the clergy who first gave public expression of the general sentiment. The Pope's nominee to the archbishopric of Mayence was now in undisputed possession of the see, having come to an understanding with Baldwin of Trèves. He was on good terms with Lewis, and at his instance his suffragans and a number of other clergy, meeting at Spires, begged the Emperor to make peace with the Pope, and when Lewis offered to commit his cause to the German bishops concerned, they sent a mission to ask Benedict to shew him favour. About the same time, the Archbishop of Cologne dispatched envoys on a like errand; and a little later, at Lewis' request, a number of cathedral chapters and imperial cities wrote to Benedict setting forth their view of the true relation between the Papacy and the Empire.

To the messengers from Spires the Pope returned a curt and insulting answer. He suggested, indeed, that the Electors should mediate; but it was probably at the instance of Lewis himself, acting through the Archbishop of Mayence[1], that they resolved to intervene. The Pope's conduct pointed to the conclusion that it was the settled policy of the Holy See to destroy the Empire and subject the German monarchy to itself, thus abrogating the rights of the Electors. On 15 July 1338 a conference was held at Lahnstein, and was attended by the three ecclesiastical Electors, the Emperor's son Lewis of Brandenburg, four other Wittelsbach princes (representing the vote attached to that family), and Rudolf of Saxe-Wittenberg. The Bohemian electorate was the only one not represented. It was unanimously resolved to uphold the German kingdom and the rights of the Electors against all persons whatsoever.

Next day, at a meeting at Rense on the opposite bank of the Rhine, the resolution was published in expanded form. The oath taken by those who subscribed to it was declared to be binding on their successors and to pledge their own loyalty to Lewis. It was proclaimed in uncompromising terms that whoso was elected King of the Romans by the Electors or a majority of them had no need of the approbation or confirmation of the Apostolic See before entering upon the administration of the Empire or assuming the title of king, nor was he under any obligation to seek recognition by the Pope. It belonged to the Pope to crown the Emperor-elect and so give him the right to bear the imperial title. But his coronation as Emperor in no way increased the authority which he possessed in virtue of his election.

Early in August a Diet met at Frankfort. Its main business was to ratify the declaration made at Rense. Lewis recounted in public the efforts he had made for peace with the Pope, and recited the Lord's Prayer, the *Ave*, and the Apostles' Creed in proof of his orthodoxy. The Diet gave its approval to two imperial ordinances. One, drafted by the Franciscan canonist Bonagratia, gives a long demonstration of the illegality of the Pope's pretensions regarding the Empire, forbids Lewis' subjects to take any notice of excommunications or interdicts announced by the Pope in support of such pretensions, and threatens with forfeiture of their imperial fiefs all who disregard this decree. The second measure was the celebrated ordinance *Licet iuris*. Although it is manifest from both Civil and Canon Law that in ancient times imperial power proceeded directly from the Son

[1] For this view, see R. Moeller, *op. cit.* pp. 114 sqq., and G. Uhl, *Untersuchungen über die Politik Erzbischofs Heinrichs III von Mainz* (*Arch. Hess. Gesch.* xv, 1).

of God, and the Emperor is made true Emperor by the election of those
to whom the choice pertains and does not need the confirmation of anyone
else, nevertheless some, blinded by avarice, ambition, and ignorance, assert
that the imperial power and dignity come from the Pope and that no one
is truly Emperor or king unless he has been approved and crowned by
him. Wherefore, to avert the discord occasioned by such pestiferous
doctrines, the Emperor, with the consent of the Electors and other princes,
declares that, according to ancient right and custom, after anyone is
chosen as Emperor or king by the Electors or a majority of them, he is
to be deemed and styled true King and Emperor of the Romans, and ought
to be obeyed by all subjects of the Empire as possessing and lawfully
exercising imperial jurisdiction and the plenitude of imperial power.
All those who deny anything in this ordinance shall *ipso facto* incur
forfeiture of all their imperial fiefs and the privileges granted to them by
Lewis or previous Emperors and shall be held guilty of high treason.

The ordinance claims that the choice of the Electors is sufficient authority
for the assumption of the imperial title. In this it goes beyond the
declaration of Rense, and it has been argued that the Diet can only have
meant that after election the king was to be treated as if he were Emperor.
But the wording of the ordinance is perfectly clear[1] and leaves no room
for reasonable doubt that the princes deliberately treated the royal and
the imperial power, the *regnum* and the *imperium*, as one and the same
thing, and denied to the Pope any share in the conferring of either[2]. In
accordance with the ordinances, Lewis now commanded all clergy to
perform the regular services of the Church on pain of outlawry—a measure
which was widely enforced. He also forbade the reception and execution
of papal letters except with the permission of the bishop of the diocese
concerned.

Hard upon the Diet at Frankfort came the famous meeting of Lewis
and Edward III at Coblenz, when, with all the wealth of pomp and
symbolism that marked the formal transaction of imperial business, Lewis
appointed the English King imperial vicar, promulgated the laws enacted
at Frankfort, and announced various measures for the promotion of the
war against France. The occasion was graced by the presence of a multitude of princes and lords, who seem, at least for a time, to have felt
something of the loyalty which they displayed. It was a brilliant climax
to the astonishing events of the past few months.

Many German writers of modern times have regarded the declaration
of Rense, the ordinances of Frankfort, and the ceremonies at Coblenz as
evidence of a strong national feeling. The war with France, it is said,
appealed to the animosity which most Germans felt towards that country,

---

[1] "Ex sola electione est verus rex et imperator Romanorum censendus et
nominandus."

[2] For arguments in favour of the other interpretation, which is preferred by
several eminent scholars, see R. Moeller, *op. cit.* pp. 144 sqq.

though some of the princes naturally fall under the suspicion of having been influenced by "English gold." There is, however, no good reason to believe that there was any widespread hatred of France, except perhaps in the extreme west, where some of the princes were justifiably apprehensive about the designs of their restless neighbour. At all events, the proceedings at Rense and Frankfort referred exclusively to the relation of the Empire to the Papacy. As the sequel shewed, if patriotic fervour influenced their course, it did not go very deep. The Electors, we may believe without injustice, were actuated mainly by concern for their threatened rights. The other princes, too, had no wish to admit the overlordship of so great a potentate as the Pope. As for the clergy who had pleaded for Lewis, they were in a most perplexing position owing to the dispute between their spiritual and secular lords, and naturally were eager for an agreement, while recognising that Lewis had gone as far to meet the Pope as could reasonably be expected. Had Lewis been a man of imaginative ambition and forceful personality, he might indeed have turned the situation to the advantage of the German monarchy and people. But he was not equal to the opportunity. He was interested in the recent stirring events only in so far as they affected his chances of retaining Brandenburg and getting Tyrol or anything else that offered itself. Thus the rumblings of Rense and Frankfort produced nothing but smoke.

At first, it is true, there seemed a prospect of important results. Lewis withdrew or modified nearly all the concessions he had offered to the Papacy, and Benedict, while outwardly unyielding, actually sent an agent to the Emperor to discover his real intentions. In Germany, the Habsburgs allied with Edward III, and in 1339, after the death of Duke Otto, his brother Albert, sole survivor of the sons of King Albert I, joined Lewis in an attempt to coerce Henry of Lower Bavaria, who forthwith made peace. John of Bohemia, abandoned by his allies and estranged from his son Charles (who was ruling Bohemia), reconciled himself with Lewis and for the first time acknowledged him as overlord, having hitherto treated him merely as an ally. He would not abandon his alliance with France, but went so far as to promise to stand by the Empire if it were attacked by the Pope.

Lewis was thus most favourably situated for vigorous action whether against France or against the Pope. Unluckily for Germany his attention was diverted from large issues by the death of his cousin Henry of Lower Bavaria and his assumption, as next of kin, of the wardship of Henry's infant son. In the autumn of 1339, indeed, Lewis of Brandenburg and Frederick of Meissen commanded an imperial contingent in Edward III's futile invasion of the Cambrésis; but this was the full extent of the Emperor's participation in the war. Next year the battle of Sluys made Philip of Valois anxious for peace: he asked the Emperor to mediate; and Lewis, jumping at the opportunity, concluded a treaty with France in March 1341. Each party was confirmed in the enjoyment of his actual possessions, the French being thus left in occupation of some pieces of territory which till lately had been German. Edward was deprived of his vicariate, and Philip undertook to mediate between Lewis and the Pope.

The English King took his dismissal with nonchalance. The Pope refused to listen to Philip's representations on the Emperor's behalf. In Germany Lewis' behaviour was angrily condemned, and he was widely accused of cowardice. All hope of a national stand against the Papacy disappeared. The Electors felt that the Emperor had betrayed them, and the Archbishops of Mayence and Trèves hastened to conciliate Benedict. Lewis was growing old and had perhaps lost some of his mental alertness. However that may be, his abandonment of the English alliance was undoubtedly one of the gravest mistakes he ever made.

It was probably the fatal Tyrolese question that determined the Emperor's policy at this time. He wished to be free to take advantage of an opportunity to retrieve his former failure. Margaret Maultasch, a high-spirited and sensual woman, had for some time been on the worst of terms with her impotent husband, John Henry of Luxemburg, while the Tyrolese nobles resented the strong rule which had been imposed on the country by his elder brother Charles. A conspiracy was formed to drive out John Henry, call in Lewis of Brandenburg, and marry him to Margaret. The plot succeeded, and early in 1342 the Emperor and his son visited Tyrol. Marsilio of Padua contended that Lewis' imperial authority empowered him to dissolve the marriage between Margaret and John Henry, but Lewis acted on the more moderate opinion of William of Ockham that the marriage, never having been consummated, was void. Even so, Margaret and the younger Lewis were within the prohibited degrees; but no regard was paid to the lack of a papal dispensation which would not have been granted, the marriage was celebrated, and the Emperor enfeoffed his son, not merely with Tyrol, but also with Carinthia.

These doings outraged German opinion, but reprisals on the part of the Luxemburg family were delayed by the death in April of Pope Benedict XII. The new Pope, Clement VI, was already known as an enemy of Lewis, and John of Bohemia soon gained his ear. It behoved Clement, however, to walk warily, lest he should exasperate the Electors, and when, in April 1343, he instituted new proceedings against Lewis, he carefully limited himself to misdeeds committed since the beginning of the dispute in 1323 and laid special emphasis on the marriage of Lewis of Brandenburg and Margaret Maultasch. In face of the new attack, Lewis repeated the offers which he had made in 1337, but still refused to admit that the votes of the Electors required to be supplemented by papal recognition. Clement, who seems to have set his mind on the complete overthrow of Lewis, declared the terms inadequate.

The Emperor unwisely reported the recent negotiations to the Electors.

Some were probably genuinely concerned at the extent of the proffered concessions. To others, notably Baldwin of Trèves, now hand-in-glove with his kinsmen, they were a useful instrument for compassing the Emperor's downfall. A Diet declared itself ready to support the Electors in any measures which they might adopt to maintain the rights of the Empire. It was generally known that the deposition of Lewis was contemplated, for in the opinion of the more public-spirited Electors it was desirable to have a king who was under less temptation to barter away the rights of his subjects.

Lewis was still formidable; his diplomacy surrounded Bohemia with a ring of enemies, and Philip of France feared a renewal of his alliance with England. Once again, however, his incorrigible lust for territory caused him to throw away his advantages. After the death of his childless brother-in-law, William Count of Holland, which occurred in September 1345, Lewis, not content with his wife's inheritance of Hainault, bestowed on her Holland, Zeeland, and Friesland, shewing no regard for the interests of her sisters, married respectively to Edward III and the Margrave of Jülich. His action was not illegal and does not seem to have been resented by the inhabitants of the regions concerned. But it freed Philip from the dread of a new league between the Empire and England, and it exacerbated the Luxemburg princes, who saw in it a threat to their western possessions. The Pope, himself concerned at reports of an impending invasion of Italy by Lewis and the King of Hungary, was easily persuaded to attempt a decisive blow. The Archbishop of Mayence, who refused to consent to the deposition of the Emperor, was himself deposed from his see, and the dean, Gerlach of Nassau, whom the Pope could trust, appointed in his stead. Immediately afterwards, in April 1346, the Pope published a tremendous bull reciting the recent misdeeds of the Emperor, repeating the sentence of forfeiture of all his goods, pronouncing his sons and grandsons ineligible for any ecclesiastical or secular office, involving him in a comprehensive curse which covered both time and eternity, and calling upon the Electors to choose a ruler for the long-vacant Empire.

Clement recognised that the Electors would not agree to the claims put forward by John XXII and still cherished by himself. He must therefore consent to the choice of a king who would give him what he wanted behind their backs. He had found his man in Charles of Bohemia, who, thanks to the assiduous intrigues of his father and himself, could count on a majority of the Electors. In April 1346 Charles went to Avignon and signed the documents purchasing Clement's consent to his election. He conceded practically everything which Lewis had offered in his most conciliatory mood, approved of his condemnation as a heretic and schismatic, guaranteed the Papacy in its temporal possessions, and promised to submit to papal arbitration all disputes between the Empire and France. On the crucial question of the confirmation of the election by the Pope,

Charles was willing to establish a precedent without admitting a principle. He promised in writing to seek papal recognition before he exercised any authority in Italy, and he agreed verbally to await it before being crowned King of the Romans or acting in that capacity.

Charles' conduct at this juncture has had its apologists even among patriotic German historians, though they can say little in his defence except that he did not agree to everything the Pope demanded. What he had done was not known, and it mattered little what was suspected. The Archbishop of Mayence was the Pope's creature. The other ecclesiastical Electors and Duke Rudolf of Saxe-Wittenberg had been well paid. These three received without apparent resentment the Pope's order to obey the summons of the Archbishop of Mayence, and, together with John of Bohemia, assembled at Rense—a cynical choice of place—at the beginning of July. The two Wittelsbach Electors did not appear, and Charles was chosen unanimously.

Very soon afterwards the new king and his father hastened to France in response to a call for help from Philip VI, and a few weeks later John was slain at Crécy. Though blind for several years, he had to the end displayed his marvellous activity, both mental and physical, and if it is true that his achievements were hardly proportionate to the energy expended in accomplishing them, it is also true that at his death his house was stronger than at his accession, secure in Bohemia (thanks, it must be admitted, to his son), with its overlordship recognised almost everywhere in Silesia, and with the prospect of still greater power in future.

Charles' situation, however, was not cheering. He swore to the promises made at Avignon, and having received Clement's recognition as king was crowned at Bonn by the Archbishop of Cologne, both Aix-la-Chapelle and Cologne standing by Lewis. The Electors did nothing to help him. The Pope's exhortations to the princes were ignored. He was popularly derided as a *Pfaffenkönig*. He crept home to Prague, which he reached in January 1347.

Lewis had viewed the plots against him with apparent indifference; but when the election of Charles had actually taken place, he suddenly displayed the energy and ability of his best days. Nearly all the imperial cities were on the side of their constant patron; so were many of the princes; and the Habsburgs promised neutrality. An attempt by Charles to conquer Tyrol was defeated, and in South Germany and the Rhineland Lewis' party gained some notable military successes. But in October the old Emperor died suddenly while hunting.

Though Lewis cared little for the Empire or the German monarchy and missed an opportunity of adding to the power and prestige of both, he can hardly be said to have weakened either. Indeed, his quarrel with the Pope and his expedition to Italy gave the idea of the Holy Roman Empire a prominence in men's thoughts which it had not enjoyed for a long time. The most lasting result of his rule in Germany is to be seen in the increased power and independence of the cities. In Bavaria he shewed himself a competent but hardly a distinguished administrator. There can be no doubt, however, that he would have accounted himself a successful man. During his reign Brandenburg, Tyrol, and four Netherandish provinces had been added to the resources of the house of Wittelsbach. It was not his fault that the family proved unworthy of the great inheritance he left them.

CHAPTER V

GERMANY: CHARLES IV

WHEN he heard of the death of Lewis, Charles was on the point of invading Bavaria with a large army. The loss of the Emperor was fatal to the Wittelsbach cause. Charles ravaged Bavaria, traversed Swabia, and passed down the Rhine to Mayence, returning to Bohemia at the beginning of 1348. The Wittelsbach princes held out, and a few cities remained faithful to them. But nearly all the princes of South and Central Germany, and most of the cities, had recognised Charles, and the north, which cared little who was king, acquiesced in his rule. His success, however, cost him heavily in gifts and concessions of all kinds.

Charles, now thirty-one years old, was not such a poor creature as the circumstances of his election might lead one to suppose. His boyhood had been mainly passed at the French court. As a youth he had for a time represented his father in Italy. Thence he had gone to Bohemia, where he became very popular and ruled with conspicuous wisdom and success. He had already, as the previous chapter shewed, taken a prominent part in the politics of Germany. He could speak and write Latin, French, German, Czech, and Italian with equal facility. He was thoroughly well versed in the arts of international diplomacy and the conditions under which it must be carried on. Few princes of that age had strong national prejudices, but Charles was conspicuously free from them.

Charles was not handsome. He had proved his courage and prowess in both real and mimic warfare, but his health was poor and he did not share his father's love of fighting. He was simple in his tastes, and after a precocious scattering of wild oats, was austere in his private life. For a medieval king he was well educated, with a special interest in theology and jurisprudence. He wrote an autobiography of his early life, a treatise on Christian ethics, and a life of St Wenceslas, and his letters were much admired by learned contemporaries[1].

Charles was a careful administrator, a great advocate of order and system, and under him the chanceries of the Empire and the various parts of his territories were conducted with great efficiency, and many improvements in their organisation and routine introduced. Finance claimed much of his attention, and he gained a reputation for avarice. But if he was somewhat greedy after money, he was willing to spend it lavishly in pursuit of his political ends.

[1] It is likely that he also wrote a *Mirror for Princes*—a handbook of political maxims; but the authorship of this work is disputed. In any case, it shews small originality.

According to the standard of his age, Charles was a very religious man. He was devoted to the Church and punctilious in attendance at her services. His piety indeed merged into childish credulity and morbid superstition. He was an indefatigable and guileless collector of relics, of which he possessed an amazing variety. Future events, he believed, were frequently revealed to him in dreams.

Charles left behind him a high reputation as a diplomatist, and at various critical junctures he certainly shewed much political judgment and address. Too often, however, he got out of a difficulty by buying off opposition without trying to overcome it, and in his eyes the authority and resources of the Empire were merely useful to bargain with. The tendency of modern historians has been to whitewash Charles; but when vindications of his treatment of Germany are scrutinised, they seldom amount to more than a demonstration that he might have done more harm than he did. Maximilian I described him as the most pestilent pest that ever afflicted Germany, and if this is an exaggeration, there is much truth in the famous epigram in which the same Emperor called Charles "arch-father of Bohemia, arch-stepfather of the Empire."

Like Lewis, Charles regarded the advancement of the interests of his house as his main object, and, like Lewis, he had to begin his reign by quelling those who denied his title to the crown. He had, however, to encounter less powerful opposition than had confronted his predecessor. Still, even had the Wittelsbach princes been wholly without allies, their extensive lands would have made them formidable enemies. Lewis left six sons, three of whom were of mature age—Lewis of Brandenburg, Stephen, and a second Lewis, commonly called the Roman, apparently because he was born soon after his father's return from Italy. Had they known their own minds, they might have given Charles much trouble. They could count on the support of the Wittelsbachs of the Palatinate, the Duke of Saxe-Lauenburg (who claimed the electoral vote of Saxony), and Henry, the deposed Archbishop of Mayence, who still held the temporalities of the see. But instead of promptly electing a German prince in opposition to Charles, they delayed till January 1348, and then offered the crown to Edward III of England. Charles, however, promised to allow his subjects to enlist in Edward's service against France, and his envoy had little difficulty in persuading the English king to decline the invitation. Then the Wittelsbach brothers turned to their brother-in-law Frederick of Meissen, but Charles bought him off without much trouble.

Meanwhile luck had offered Charles an opportunity for embarrassing the Wittelsbachs without involving himself in costly and hazardous military undertakings. In 1348 there appeared an old man who claimed to be the Ascanian Margrave Waldemar of Brandenburg, supposed to have been in his grave for nearly thirty years. His story was that, being troubled in conscience because he and his wife were within the prohibited degrees, he had put about reports of his death, procured a corpse which was passed off as his own, and retired to the Holy Land, where he had since led an obscure existence. He was doubtless an impostor, but he had been well drilled in his part—by whom has never been discovered—and was evidently a plausible fellow. Many people sincerely believed in him; he was recognised by Waldemar's kinsmen, the ruling family of Anhalt; and all enemies of the Margrave Lewis lent a credulous ear to his tale. On entering Brandenburg he was welcomed almost everywhere. Charles, having instituted an official enquiry by Rudolf of Saxe-Wittenberg and others who had known Waldemar personally, professed himself convinced by their verdict, and bestowed the Mark on the old man, who in his gratitude agreed that Charles might take possession of Lower Lusatia, a strong indication that he was not the real Waldemar.

The Wittelsbachs, now in dire straits, still lacked a candidate for the crown, and in their desperation the Electors of the party on 30 January 1349 chose Günther of Schwarzburg, a brave but impecunious Thuringian count, who received acknowledgment only at Frankfort and in its immediate neighbourhood. Charles went with an army to the Rhine, bought a number of princes and cities, detached the Count Palatine from his kinsmen by proposing to marry his daughter, and after a little trivial fighting forced Günther and his friends to accept the treaties of Eltville, which virtually ended the conflict for the crown. Charles treated his enemies with singular forbearance. Henry of Mayence, in defiance of the Pope, was allowed to retain his temporalities. The Wittelsbach family were confirmed in the possession of all their lands and rights, and the elder Lewis was expressly recognised as lord not only of Tyrol but also of Carinthia. Charles further promised to give no more aid to the alleged Waldemar, and to use his good offices with the Pope to obtain the removal of the excommunication under which the Wittelsbachs still lay. Günther was consoled with cities and revenues in pledge, but died very soon afterwards. On the conclusion of the treaties, Henry of Mayence, the Count Palatine, and Lewis of Brandenburg announced that they now gave their votes to Charles, who, to render his title unassailable, had himself ceremonially placed on the altar of St Bartholomew's at Frankfort, and was crowned at Aix-la-Chapelle by the Archbishop of Trèves.

Lewis of Brandenburg, allying himself with Denmark, next began a vigorous attack on the pseudo-Waldemar. The princes who had previously recognised him now discovered timely reasons for doubt, and when he failed to answer a summons to prove his case before an assembly of princes and lords at Nuremberg, judgment was given against him. Charles renounced Lower Lusatia, and formally bestowed on the three Wittelsbach brothers Brandenburg, Lusatia, and the right to the electoral vote. It was several years before the opposition in the Mark was finally broken down, but in 1355 the Ascanian Counts of Anhalt, the most obstinate foes of the Wittelsbachs, made peace in consideration of an indemnity. They continued to hold the *soi-disant* Waldemar in honour, and when he died buried him among their ancestors at Dessau.

Meanwhile, from 1348 to 1351, Germany had shared with most other parts of Europe the calamities which attended the Black Death. Its approach from the east had occasioned a great persecution of the Jews, instigated in part by the Flagellants, a characteristic product of the fear which the impending catastrophe excited. The experiences of Germany under the pestilence did not differ in any notable particular from those of other countries, but it is worthy of remark that one or two regions, such as Bohemia and Eastern Franconia, enjoyed almost complete immunity.

After the peace of Eltville, Charles set his mind on going to Italy to receive the imperial crown. He soon found that there were serious obstacles in the way. Clement VI was annoyed because Charles, though always deferential to the Holy See and devoted to the Church, had shewn an independent disposition in politics, having indeed encouraged the rebellious Henry of Mayence and made peace with the contumacious Wittelsbachs. Consequently, when Charles raised the question of a visit to Rome, Clement refused his consent, and it was not until he was succeeded by Innocent VI that cordial relations between Charles and the Papacy were restored. It was also necessary to compose discord in Germany before Charles could safely leave the country. Despite the treaty of Eltville, the sons of Lewis the Bavarian still nourished a grudge against him, and only the intervention of Albert of Habsburg prevented a renewal of civil war when in 1354 Charles pronounced that the electoral vote hitherto shared by Bavaria and the Rhenish Palatinate was in future to be exercised by the Palatinate only. In return, Charles tried to avert strife between Albert and the growing Swiss Confederation, and, when war nevertheless broke out, lent him military aid in his attack on Zurich. In 1353 he had begun a long progress through Germany with the object of establishing universal peace before his departure for Italy. Wherever he went he established *landfrieden*. He placated the Swabian cities, which eyed him with special suspicion, by giving them permission to defend themselves unitedly if their rights were attacked. He went as far as Metz, where no German king had been since the days of the Hohenstaufen, and, having handed over Luxemburg to his younger brother Wenceslas, evidently felt that Germany might be safely left. The course of his journey was marked by a trail of gifts, franchises, and royal prerogatives, which he had scattered abroad to purchase a period of quiet.

If Charles cared little for Germany, he set even less store on Italy. He had shewn small interest when Rienzo went to Prague for the express purpose of persuading him to go to Rome; indeed he had imprisoned the demagogue and handed him over to the Pope. A letter from Petrarch with a similar invitation met with more politeness but no practical response. To Charles Italy was probably not worth the quarrel with the Pope that would certainly follow any attempt to assert his authority there.

Still, there was some revenue to be got out of the cities of Lombardy and Tuscany, and the title of Emperor carried with it a certain prestige.

In September 1354 Charles left Nuremberg with a small escort, and, riding quickly through Salzburg to Udine, achieved his object of arriving on Italian soil unexpectedly. The details of his doings in Italy do not concern us here. He scrupulously observed the promises regarding Italy which he made at Avignon before his election as king. He was crowned Emperor at Rome by Cardinal Peter of Ostia, papal legate, on Easter Sunday 1355, entering and leaving the city that same day. Then he hurried back to Germany, towards the end of the journey riding even at night. He had raised considerable sums of money from the Italian cities, but had made himself a laughing-stock to the people. Lewis the Bavarian had stirred up indignation and hostility but never ridicule.

On his return, Charles resumed his efforts to establish peace in Germany. Neither the German kingdom nor the Holy Roman Empire possessed what can properly be termed a constitution. There were traditions, there were also imperial laws on miscellaneous subjects. These, however, were little known, for the royal and imperial records were not only imperfectly preserved but were scattered in various places, while the imperial enactments cited in the writings of jurists were so overlaid with glosses that it was hard to tell what was law and what was comment. Advocates of the Empire's rights cited natural law, Aristotle, Scripture, the Fathers, the Civil Law, the facts of Roman History, or, like Marsilio, founded their case on some general political principle, but rarely appealed to any legislation or precedents subsequent to the time of Charles the Great. Their arguments and theories consequently were of little practical value to fourteenth-century Germany, a collection of virtually independent principalities and city-states. There was, it was true, no desire among Germans to abolish the office of king or of Emperor, for on one or other were based the powers and privileges enjoyed by the princes and the cities. But the Crown was fast becoming a legal fiction. Its authority, still theoretically great despite the lavish alienation of royal and imperial prerogatives by recent Emperors, was in practice commonly ignored. The German king was invested with supreme legislative authority over all his subjects; but the laws which he promulgated, with or without the concurrence of the Diet, were not much more than pious exhortations, for he had no means of enforcing them. The same might be said of judicial sentences of the royal court, to which appeals were still sometimes brought and disputes between princes submitted; the execution of the sentence, indeed, was generally left to the successful party. This lack of administrative power was mainly due to lack of money. The royal domains, which had belonged to the Crown whoever might wear it, had been lost during the reign of Frederick II and the Great Interregnum, and notwithstanding the efforts of later kings few had been recovered. The revenues still at the disposal of the Crown were scanty and uncertain.

The dues of the imperial cities made up a large part of the royal income, but were hard to collect without the good will of the contributors—a consideration which explains the remarkable favour displayed towards them by Lewis the Bavarian and other kings of the later Middle Ages. A certain amount was yielded by tolls, mines, the royal mint, and the Jews; but the kings can hardly be blamed for frequently succumbing to the temptation to gain some political end by the alienation or pawning of such insubstantial and unreliable resources. It is the poverty of the Crown which offers the best justification for the neglect by Lewis and Charles of their royal rights and for their absorption in the concerns of their families.

Charles IV had an orderly mind. For the Empire, as we have seen, he cared little, and indeed openly stated his opinion that it was an anachronism. The German crown, however, was an asset of some value, particularly because it carried with it the right to dispose of vacant fiefs. But facts must be recognised: it was idle to suppose that the Crown could aspire to attain in Germany the position it held in France. After all, the situation of the Luxemburg family was pleasant enough. Charles possessed in Bohemia a prosperous and compact realm of his own, and, having as yet no son, he had not the same motive as his predecessor to plot and scheme for the increase of his family's possessions. Could not existing conditions be stabilised? Could not further disintegration be prevented, and occasions for civil strife diminished? Was it possible to find a powerful body or class of Germans who were satisfied or might easily be made satisfied with things as they were, and who would be interested to prevent change and disorder? Nothing could be hoped for from the Diet. Once it assembled, indeed, the king had great influence upon it, but the nobles attended reluctantly and irregularly, and at best it was a body of very divergent interests. On the other hand, the Electors had of late manifested a growing corporate spirit. They were a small manageable body and shared in common certain dominating ideas and ambitions. Everything pointed to them as the natural upholders of peace and order in Germany. Their number, functions, and duties must be defined; the powers they enjoyed in practice must be granted full recognition in law. Thus they might be ranged on the side of conservatism.

Of the existing Electors none was likely to raise factious opposition to Charles' plans. Henry of Mayence was dead; Gerlach, now in unchallenged enjoyment of the see, was not a man of strong character. In 1354 Baldwin of Trèves, who had held the archbishopric for forty-seven years, also died; his successor, Bohemund of Saarbrücken, was an elderly man of no great account and on good terms with the Emperor. William of Gennep, Archbishop of Cologne, a prelate of ability, was likewise well disposed towards Charles, and so was Rupert, Count Palatine of the Rhine. The chief causes of anxiety were the sons of Lewis the Bavarian and the rival claimants to the Saxon vote. It was essential to define precisely to whom the electoral vote belonged. In the days of Lewis, it had been agreed among the Wittelsbachs that their right should be exercised alternately by the Palatinate branch and the Bavarian branch. This arrangement did not commend itself to the Emperor, partly because it was generally taken for granted that the number of Electors must be strictly limited to the mystic seven, and partly because if the scheme was followed, the Bavarian Wittelsbachs, being in possession of Brandenburg, would have two votes at the next election. Charles therefore, as has been mentioned, declared that the Count Palatine had the exclusive right to the original Wittelsbach vote. Luckily, Lewis the Roman and his brother Otto, joint-rulers of Brandenburg, were at this moment friendly to the Emperor, and though other members of the family protested, they were at variance among themselves and could be safely disregarded.

The Ascanian ducal house of Saxony had for long been split into the two hostile lines of Wittenberg and Lauenburg. The latter sprang from an elder brother, but was inferior to the former in territory, and its lands, moreover, had undergone subdivision. The Wittenberg line had consistently exercised its vote since the reign of Rudolf of Habsburg, and its head, Duke Rudolf, had voted for Charles in 1346. After weighing these considerations Charles gave his decision in favour of Saxe-Wittenberg, Duke Rudolf in return and for other compensation renouncing a troublesome claim to Brandenburg which might at any moment have caused war between him and the house of Wittelsbach.

Charles was thus fairly sure of his ground when in the winter of 1355–56 he met at Nuremberg a Diet, to which he had summoned an unusually large number of princes. His decisions on the doubtful points just mentioned were approved by the undisputed Electors. He announced his intention of creating a new and good currency, of reducing tolls and providing for the maintenance of peace on rivers and highways, and of introducing new regulations for the conduct of royal elections, with a view to reducing occasions of strife. He promulgated laws on the first two topics, but they were not of special account. The measure about elections, however, was of the highest moment. It was supplemented by several clauses published at a Diet held at Metz in December 1356, and the whole document is commonly known as the Golden Bull. This title was popularly given to it at an early date—why, is not clear, for the golden capsule impressed with the imperial seal was no peculiarity of the document but would be appended to any other emanating from the imperial chancery if the recipient was willing to pay for it.

The Golden Bull opens with a verbose and pompous preamble on the evils of discord, the purpose of the law being described as the cherishing of unity among the Electors, the securing of unanimous elections, and the avoidance of strife in general.

Much space is then devoted to the preliminaries of an election. All subjects of the Empire are to facilitate the passage of Electors to the place of meeting, and to each Elector are allotted certain princes, lords, and cities who shall be bound, if required, to furnish him with an adequate escort while he is passing through their territories. To avoid long vacancies of the throne, it is laid down that within one month after the death of an Emperor has been made known, the Archbishop of Mayence shall communicate the news to his fellow-Electors and summon them to choose a successor within three months, the election to be held at Frankfort-on-Main. Precautions against violence at elections are prescribed. No Elector may bring with him more than 200 mounted followers, of whom only fifty are to be armed men. Those who absent themselves and omit to send proxies shall forfeit their votes for the election concerned. The citizens of Frankfort, while the election is in progress, shall admit to the city no one except Electors and their attendants.

The clauses dealing with the election itself are less elaborate. On the day after the Electors have assembled, they shall hear a mass of the Holy Ghost in St Bartholomew's Church, and each shall then swear that he will direct his full discretion and wisdom to the choice of one suitable to be King of the Romans and future Emperor, and that he will give his vote without any payment or reward or promise of such. The Electors shall not disperse until they have chosen someone, and if they fail to do so within thirty days they shall thenceforward be fed on bread and water. A majority vote shall constitute a valid election, which shall be deemed unanimous[1]. The king-elect shall immediately confirm all the rights and dignities of the Electors.

A number of clauses deal with questions of the precedence to be enjoyed by the Electors in relation to one another and to other princes, and to the duties which each has to perform on formal or ceremonial occasions. An important clause lays down that during an interregnum the Empire shall be administered, under certain limitations, by the Count Palatine of the Rhine, save that, where Saxon law is followed, this function shall be performed by the Duke of Saxony. In the case of lay Electors, it is declared, the right to vote shall descend according to the rules of primogeniture and shall be heritable only by and through males. The principalities to which an electoral vote is attached are declared to be indivisible, and the vote to be inseparable from them. An electoral principality falling vacant shall be disposed of by the Emperor according to established custom, saving to the people of Bohemia the right to elect their king. The Electors shall have full right to all mines of metals or salt in their lands, and to the taxes payable by Jews for protection. They may coin and circulate gold and silver money. No subject of an Elector may sue or be sued, on appeal or

---

[1] The object of this stipulation was to preclude the recurrence of those disputes over the crown which had wrought such mischief in Germany. Though the opposition of Günther had soon been overcome, men still remembered the much more serious conflict between Lewis the Bavarian and Frederick the Handsome.

otherwise, in any court outside his territories. Conspiracy against the life of an Elector is proclaimed high treason, and the children and accomplices of the plotters are to be visited with total or partial disinheritance. It is asserted to be desirable that the Electors should meet together more frequently than has been customary, in order to treat of the affairs of the Empire and the world. It is therefore ordained, on their advice, that they shall assemble four weeks after every Easter in some city of the Empire; this arrangement is to last, however, only as long as both Emperor and Electors approve. It is highly characteristic of Charles that he inserted an injunction that the sons of Electors should be taught Italian and Czech.

The Bull, furthermore, forbids the formation of conspiracies or leagues between the cities or subjects of the Empire, except such as have been established for the maintenance of public peace. Cities are not to receive *Pfahlbürger*, and civic privileges are to be enjoyed by none but *bona fide* residents. On the whole the document is dignified and impressive in tone, but there is one pitiable clause which lays down that challenges to private war shall not be valid unless notice be given three days before the opening of hostilities, while all "unjust" war, rapine, and robbery are sternly prohibited.

The Golden Bull was a measure of immense importance, which in the sixteenth century became recognised as a fundamental law of the Empire. To say with Bryce that Charles "legalised anarchy and called it a constitution" is brilliant but not history. There was no more anarchy in Germany after the Golden Bull than before, and if the Golden Bull did recognise the legality of private war within certain limits, it was the limits and not the legality that would seem remarkable to contemporaries. What Charles did was to acknowledge publicly the futility of pretending to revive the Roman Empire or even to maintain a strong centralised monarchy. The Golden Bull was an essay in *Realpolitik*. It was based on the assumption that Germany had ceased to be a unitary State, and it sought to make of the Electors a kind of Concert of Germany, whose business and interest it would be to preserve the *status quo* and compose the quarrels of other princes. Of this body the Emperor was to be the president and mouthpiece; but so great was the independence ascribed to the Electors in the Golden Bull that they were now in law as in fact rather his allies than his subjects. The plan of holding annual conferences, however, at once broke down, and it soon became evident that the Electors were still as restless and rebellious as other princes. One principal merit of the Bull was that it retarded the disintegration of the German principalities, which had been proceeding at a bewildering rate. It was not merely that electoral principalities were henceforth indivisible, but other princes gradually saw that, unless the subdivision of their estates was checked, their families would soon be of no account in comparison with the Electors. The Bull has earned much praise because from beginning to end there is no mention of the Pope. But though the need of papal confirmation of an elected king is nowhere admitted, it is nowhere repudiated, and there is nothing in the document which precludes it. The claim of the Papacy to the administration of the Empire during a vacancy is indeed implicitly rejected, but on the rights of the King of the Romans the Golden Bull is far less definite than the Declaration of Rense and the ordinance *Licet iuris*[1].

The Diet of Metz, at which the Golden Bull was published in its complete form, was a brilliant assembly. John of France had lately begged Charles for help against the English, and the Emperor had demanded the restoration of Verdun, Cambrai, and Vienne, and called upon John's eldest son, who had inherited Dauphiné in 1349, to do homage for this fief of the Empire. Before the Diet took place, the battle of Poitiers had been fought; King John was a prisoner, and the dauphin came to implore aid. The Pope had sent Cardinal Talleyrand de Périgord and the Abbot of Cluny to justify his recent demand of three tenths from the German clergy—an imposition which had aroused a storm of protest. The French prince having done homage, Charles formally enfeoffed him with the Dauphinate, and appointed him imperial vicar within its bounds, receiving in return rich presents and the promise of much money. For the relief of France, however, he did nothing, merely renewing an existing treaty with that country which contained only vague promises of mutual support. As for the Pope, Charles, after consulting the German bishops, offered him a sum much smaller than the yield of the taxes he had wished to levy, and with this Innocent was fain to be content. The Diet of Metz, which was accompanied by magnificent festivities, made a great impression on contemporaries, and certainly Charles appeared to better advantage on this occasion than he usually did when acting in his imperial capacity.

Charles, however, was soon enmeshed once more in the petty politics of Germany. It was in his favour that the Wittelsbach brothers were losing ground through their incompetence, while in Holland the differences between Lewis the Bavarian's widow and her son William had expanded into a war out of which was to grow the desolating feud of the "Hoeks" and the "Kabbeljaws." But a new danger to the Emperor appeared from among the Habsburgs. In 1358 occurred the death of Duke Albert of Austria, who, though a cripple for many years, had directed the affairs of his house with great skill, shewing a moderate and statesmanlike temper. But his son and heir, Rudolf—a handsome and conceited young man, nineteen years old, and married to one of Charles' daughters—had extravagant ambitions for the aggrandisement of Austria. It galled him that the Habsburgs did not belong to the sacrosanct aristocracy created

---

[1] There has been much controversy among modern scholars as to the text, origin, meaning, and purpose of the Golden Bull. See Zeumer, *Die goldene Bulle Kaiser Karls IV.*

by the Golden Bull, and he resolved to assert for his family a position to which not even an Elector could lay claim. He accordingly caused to be forged five documents purporting to emanate from earlier Emperors, one being ostensibly a confirmation by Henry IV of edicts issued in favour of Austria by Julius Caesar and Nero. The object was to prove that Austria was independent of the Empire and that the Habsburg lands were indivisible. The fraud was not badly executed, but Charles' suspicions were apparently aroused by Julius Caesar and Nero, and he referred the documents to his friend Petrarch, who decisively condemned them. Rudolf, however, was but little abashed; and though when laid before the Diet his claims were rejected out of hand, he assumed a number of high-sounding titles on the strength of them, sought allies, and repulsed Charles' characteristic efforts to placate him. The Emperor in fact had reluctantly to make war on the Count of Wurtemberg, who took up arms for Rudolf. On the defeat of his supporter, however, Rudolf gave in and received Charles' pardon.

Soon afterwards the political outlook of Germany underwent a sudden change. In 1361 Charles' third wife bore him a son, the future King Wenceslas. This disappointed the hope cherished by Rudolf that on the death of his father-in-law he would succeed to the Luxemburg lands and the German crown. His hostility to the Emperor consequently revived. Charles, on his part, had now a new incentive for increasing his power, and from this time his policy in Germany was less conciliatory and conservative than it had hitherto been.

In the same year died Lewis, the eldest of the Wittelsbach brothers, to be followed sixteen months later by his son and heir Meinhard, who had married a sister of Rudolf of Habsburg. Meinhard's mother, Margaret Maultasch, handed over Tyrol to Rudolf, and retired to Vienna, where she died some years later. She left an unsavoury reputation for profligacy and ferocity. Both her husband and her son were believed to have been poisoned by her, but the unexpected deaths of prominent people were always ascribed to poison in the fourteenth century, and there seems to be no specific evidence of Margaret's guilt or indeed any reason why she should have murdered either Lewis or Meinhard.

The surviving Wittelsbachs protested against Margaret's action in surrendering Tyrol, but their mutual jealousies were fatal to the family fortunes. In 1363 Stephen, breaking an agreement, laid hands on Upper Bavaria, whereupon, to spite him, Lewis the Roman and Otto, the joint-rulers of Brandenburg and Lusatia, announced that, should they both die without male issue, these lands were to fall to the house of Luxemburg. Both princes were young, and it seemed unlikely that the condition would be fulfilled; but Charles took their offer seriously, entered Brandenburg with an army, and by cajolery and threats induced the Estates to do him homage.

Charles might have secured Tyrol for his house as well, but Stephen of

Wittelsbach was trying to win it by force, and the Emperor apparently did not think it worth fighting for. Instead, he used it to buy the friendship of Rudolf, who had lately formed a threatening alliance with Hungary and Poland. The bargain pleased Rudolf, and in February 1364 peace between the Luxemburgs, the Habsburgs, and Hungary was concluded at Brünn. The terms were of great moment for the future of Germany and indeed of Europe. It was agreed that on the failure of heirs, male and female, of Charles and his brother Wenceslas, all their lands should pass to the Habsburgs; while should descendants of Rudolf, his brothers and sister, and the royal house of Hungary be lacking, the Habsburg lands should go to the house of Luxemburg. Tyrol was formally granted to the Habsburgs, who held it, save for one brief interval, till 1918. After some years the Wittelsbachs renounced their pretensions to it for an indemnity and some territorial compensation. Rudolf did not enjoy his acquisition long, for in 1365 he died. He represents a type which appeared from time to time in the Habsburg family; but the resemblance often traced between him and the Emperor Joseph II is fanciful. He was succeeded by two brothers, both under age, and the Habsburgs were consequently dependent on Charles for the rest of his reign.

For some years after the treaty of Brünn Charles' attention was largely given to ecclesiastical affairs. He had usually been on good terms with the German clergy, and had issued decrees safeguarding their privileges against encroachments by secular authorities. With Innocent VI, however, his relations had not always been happy. He had, as we have seen, given a passive support to the German clergy in their resistance to the Pope's exorbitant demands for money, and he had urged on Innocent the need for reform in the German Church, hinting broadly that unless abuses were checked the secular princes would seize the Church's temporalities. His reforming zeal, however, was not very deep, and when the Pope abandoned his opposition to the Golden Bull and shewed a conciliatory spirit on other questions at issue, Charles at once became ready to meet his wishes half way.

On Innocent's death in 1362 he was succeeded by Urban V, who was eager to organise a crusade against the Turks, and for that reason and for fear of the Free Companies could not afford to quarrel with the Emperor. For his part, Charles was uneasy about Italy. Lewis of Hungary, whose interests clashed with his own at many points in Central Europe, was trying to make good a claim to Naples, and if he should succeed would become a very grave danger to the house of Luxemburg. Charles was therefore anxious to visit Italy and to persuade the Pope to return thither. Once the Emperor ceased to value his Italian crown, it was to his interest that the Pope should reside in Rome, removed from French domination, and in a position to frustrate the designs of princes whose establishment in Italy might result in trouble for the Emperor elsewhere. Urban himself was not ill-disposed to Charles' suggestions; opposition to them came chiefly from the cardinals, though their affection for Avignon had been considerably cooled by the Free Companies.

In 1365 the Emperor visited Avignon, where his enthusiastic and ostentatious devotion to the Church caused some amusement. He promised to promote a crusade in which the Free Companies were to be employed, and agreed to let them pass through Germany. The first consequence was that a united force of the companies broke into Alsace, murdering and ravishing up to the gates of Strasbourg. Charles, who was believed to have invited them, had to assemble a great army, which indeed forced them to withdraw, but inflicted on the Alsatians nearly as much harm as they. Fortunately for Germany, the Black Prince's expedition to Spain tempted the mercenaries to other fields, and enabled Charles to evade his obligations to the Pope. As for the return of the Papacy to Rome, Urban shewed himself favourable to the project, and in fact proved better than his promises.

During his visit to the Pope, Charles tried to restore the almost vanished prestige of the Empire in the kingdom of Burgundy by having himself crowned at Arles. No one had received the Burgundian crown since Frederick Barbarossa; no one was to receive it after Charles. The coronation had only a ceremonial interest, though some modern German historians have written as if it indicated a real revival of imperial authority in the old Burgundian kingdom. As a matter of fact, French influence remained in the ascendant from one end of it to the other. To do him justice, Charles seems to have had no illusions about Burgundy, and after he had by diplomatic means tried to uphold a precarious influence there, he apparently lost heart, and one of his last acts was to bestow on the dauphin for life the imperial vicariate for the whole kingdom except the Savoyard lands.

Charles was now anxious to lead an expedition to Italy to prepare the way for the Pope. The princes, who had no intention of taking part in such an enterprise, were ready enough to approve; but the clergy, on whom Charles relied for money, and the cities, to whom he looked for men, responded to his demands reluctantly and sometimes flatly refused them. Times were bad in Germany, and a return of the Black Death, together with pestilence among cattle and disease among crops, made 1367 a year long remembered with horror. Thus, though Charles managed in the end to raise a sufficient force, he could not set out until Urban was already in Rome. His expedition did no good to his power or repute. His military operations against the Visconti failed; his subservience to the Pope while in Rome made him foolish in the eyes of the Romans; Urban, annoyed at not receiving more help from him, turned to his arch-enemy the King of Hungary; and though certain Italian cities paid him large sums of money in return for privileges or in hope of his speedy departure, this was but poor compensation for the general ill-success of the undertaking. Charles returned to Germany in 1369, Urban to Avignon in 1370. It was lucky for the Emperor that the Pope died immediately afterwards, for his successor Gregory XI was already a firm friend of Charles.

Had Charles also died on his return from Italy, he would have gone down to history as one of the most unsuccessful rulers that Germany ever had. For the rest of his life, however, luck was on his side, and everything he took in hand prospered. He had three sons, Wenceslas, Sigismund, and John, and it behoved him to make provision for them, if possible without dividing his existing territories. In 1369, indeed, his prospects were gloomy. Suspicion of his designs for increasing the Luxemburg possessions had turned many princes against him. The Wittelsbachs had suddenly become formidable again, for the grandsons of Lewis the Bavarian were coming to the front. Two of them, Stephen and Frederick, sons of Duke Stephen of Upper Bavaria, had already made a reputation for bravery and resolution, while Frederick, who was a shrewd and ambitious politician, had associated himself with a powerful alliance hostile to the Emperor, to which belonged the Elector Palatine and the Archbishop of Mayence, whom Charles had offended, besides the Kings of Poland and Hungary. Further, Charles' interests had suffered a blow in Brandenburg. After the death of Lewis the Roman in 1365, the feeble and impecunious Otto handed over to Charles the government of the Mark for six years; but during his absence in Italy the Brandenburg nobles, under the leadership of Klaus von Bismarck, had expelled the council which he had left in charge of the administration. On his return from Italy Charles demanded from Otto the renewal of the treaty of 1363, but at the instigation of his nephew Frederick he refused. The Emperor had resort to his usual diplomatic methods in order to divide the combination against him. In his difficulties he transgressed the Golden Bull by allying with certain Swabian cities; but his cause benefited more by the opportune deaths of the King of Poland and the Archbishop of Mayence than by any measures of his own. Meanwhile, Otto declared Frederick his heir, and prepared armed resistance with the aid of Hungary, whose king attacked Moravia. Charles accepted the challenge and invaded Brandenburg. But neither there nor on his eastern frontier was there fighting on a large scale. Taking advantage of a truce, Charles detached the King of Hungary from the alliance by suggesting a match between his son Sigismund and Lewis' daughter Mary, and when the Emperor renewed the attack on the Mark, the two Wittelsbach princes had to struggle unaided not only against Charles but also against several neighbouring princes whom he had gained to his cause. They soon lost heart, and in August 1373 the treaty of Fürstenwalde gave Brandenburg to the house of Luxemburg. Charles as usual shewed moderation in victory. Otto was allowed to retain for life the title and rights of an Elector, though these had been declared inseparable from possession of the Mark by the Golden Bull. Several cities and castles were handed over to him for the rest of his life, and he and his nephew received a vast sum of money, much of which was extorted from the cities of South Germany on the pretext that they had not furnished the Emperor with the aid due from them for the Brandenburg war. Otto went on pilgrimage to the Holy Land, and died in 1379.

Thus, of the lands which Lewis the Bavarian, at the cost of so much scheming and sacrifice, had acquired for his family, only the Netherland provinces remained in Wittelsbach hands, and these, ruled now and for long afterwards by Albert, Lewis' fifth son, were detached from the main currents of German life and politics and added little to the influence of the Bavarian branch of the family, which now fell into the second rank of German princely houses.

Inspired by good fortune, Charles next embarked on a scheme which he might well have rejected as impossible—the election of his son Wenceslas as King of the Romans during his lifetime. The melancholy experiences of the Wittelsbachs shewed how desirable it was, in the interests of the Luxemburg family, that Wenceslas should succeed to the German throne; but it was most improbable that the Electors, whatever promises they might give while Charles was alive, would elect his son after he was dead. The Golden Bull had nothing to say about the election of a successor to a living Emperor, but the whole tenor of the document suggests that, to those who framed it, such a proceeding would have seemed highly irregular, if not positively illegal. At first sight, too, it looked as if the Electors were unpromising material for Charles' machinations. Otto of Brandenburg, it is true, was at Charles' mercy and the Elector of Saxony under his influence. The see of Mayence was again a prey to strife, but the archbishop recognised by the Pope and Charles belonged to the family of Wettin and was naturally disinclined to contribute to an increase of the already great power of the house of Luxemburg. The archbishopric of Trèves was ruled by Kuno von Falkenstein, an energetic and warlike prelate, who, putting the temporal interests of his see above everything else, was opposed to the exaltation of any princely family. He would doubtless determine the attitude of the Archbishop of Cologne, his nephew. As for the Elector Palatine, though he had done nothing to save his Wittelsbach kinsmen in the recent war, he had been the chief promoter of the league against the Emperor, and he and Charles had not been reconciled. Furthermore, the Pope was to be considered, and, friendly as he was to Charles, he was not likely to welcome the plan.

Nevertheless every Elector had his price, and Charles was prepared to pay it. Money changed hands, cities were pledged, imperial and royal rights were dissipated. There must have been much perjury when the Electors took the oath before the next election. Similar means were used to win over certain important princes outside the circle of Electors, whose good will it was important to gain.

Avignon, as was to be expected, proved hostile, but was outwitted by Charles. On being informed of Charles' project, the cardinals counselled

Gregory XI that he should not lose so good an opportunity of strength-ening papal control over the Empire. The Pope therefore replied that everything done in the matter must be subject to papal approval, which could not be looked for unless Charles and Wenceslas repeated the promises made by the former in 1346. Charles led the Pope to believe that he would comply, but gave no formal undertaking. There the matter was left for about a year. Suddenly, in the spring of 1376, Gregory learned from the Emperor that the election of Wenceslas would take place in two months and would straightway be followed by his coronation. Charles had chosen his time well, for Italian affairs were going badly for the Papacy. The Curia could only threaten, and demand that the coronation of Wenceslas should not take place until his election had been confirmed by Gregory. Charles took care that the Pope's messenger was present when he laid this request before the Electors, and warned him that the anger they displayed would be generally felt by the German magnates. Out of empty politeness to the Holy See, it was agreed to postpone the election for ten days, but on 10 June Wenceslas was elected at Frankfort. The Electors reported to Gregory what they had done, asked his favour for Wenceslas, and requested that he might in due course receive the imperial crown. Before an answer could come, he had been crowned at Aix-la-Chapelle.

In view of the circumstances which attended it, the election of Wenceslas has been often celebrated as a great victory of the Empire over the Papacy. It appears, however, that the skill and resolution which Charles had undoubtedly shewn were due mainly to a fear lest concessions to the Papacy should alienate the dearly-purchased Electors. As soon as these had done their part, he threw away many of the fruits of victory, for Wenceslas agreed to confirm the oath taken by his father in 1346, and Charles consented to draw up a document, dated as written on the day of the election, in which he asked the Pope to approve of his son's election during his own lifetime. To this Gregory returned a gracious reply, though it was his successor who pronounced the papal approbation.

Charles' family policy had achieved an astonishing triumph, but the methods he had employed gave rise to unexpected trouble for himself and his successor. The cities of Germany had on the whole prospered since the beginning of the fourteenth century, and the Hanseatic League in the north was now a great political force and paid little regard to the Emperor. But the imperial cities of the south viewed Charles with much suspicion. He had supplanted their benefactor Lewis; he had lavished favours on princes, but to cities he had shewn himself niggardly; clauses in his Golden Bull were specially directed against those leagues of cities for common defence which Lewis had actively encouraged; while Charles' demands on the cities for men and money had been heavy, especially at the time of his second Italian expedition. In 1372 war broke out between the cities of a Swabian *Landfriede*, organised by the Emperor himself, and the knights of that region, who were aided by Eberhard, Count of Wurtemberg. The war went against the cities, but as Charles happened to visit the disturbed area while it was in progress, the issue was referred to his judgment. His verdict was on the whole favourable to the cities, yet he demanded from them large sums in expiation of alleged breaches of the terms of their agreement with him and for the promotion of the war in Brandenburg. Later, as was mentioned above, they were further mulcted to pay the indemnity which Charles gave to the Wittelsbachs.

The news of the Emperor's negotiations with a view to the election of Wenceslas filled the cities with alarm. They expected, and rightly, that many of them would be given to princes as security for the payment of large sums of money—a fate which often meant the permanent loss of direct relationship with the Emperor and subjection to a lord who could make his authority effective. Soon after Wenceslas' election. therefore. fourteen Swabian cities formed a league for mutual defence against anyone who should threaten them with fresh taxation, grant them in pledge, or otherwise derogate from their status. They demanded a guarantee of inviolability from the Emperor, but Charles. with unwonted truculence, laid them under the imperial ban, and, supported by a number of princes, attacked Ulm with a strong force. After being ignominiously repulsed, he abandoned the conduct of the war to the princes of South Germany; but these fared no better, and in 1377 Ulrich, son of the Count of Wurtemberg, was defeated by the league at the famous battle of Reutlingen. Wenceslas, appointed imperial vicegerent, then made peace at Rotenburg on behalf of his father, the cities receiving guarantees against being given in pledge, and permission, notwithstanding the Golden Bull, to unite for defence. Next year the war between the league and Wurtemberg was ended by Charles to the advantage of the cities. These successes naturally gained for the league much prestige and many new members, but its later history belongs to the reign of Wenceslas.

Charles' lack of vigour in the war was perhaps due to the exceptionally bad health from which he was suffering. After a visit to Paris in the hope of arranging a marriage between Sigismund and the heiress to the county of Burgundy, he turned his mind to the disposal of the family possessions. For his third son John he created the duchy of Görlitz in Lusatia and allotted to him also the Neumark, an appendage of Brandenburg. The last he bequeathed to Sigismund, regardless of a promise to the Estates of the Mark that it should be for ever united to Bohemia. The rest of the lands over which he had ruled went to Wenceslas. Charles has been blamed for making this division, but it is to be remembered that, except for the small duchy of Görlitz, the lands given to his younger sons had been acquired by himself, and that his efforts to secure them had probably been dictated by a desire to provide for his children without destroying the territorial importance of his house.

Charles died at Prague on 29 November 1378. His character and policy have been the theme of controversy from his own time to now, and may best be considered in connexion with a survey of his rule in Bohemia. That he did grave harm to the Empire and the German Crown can hardly be disputed, and if the Golden Bull in the long run proved beneficial to Germany, the credit which Charles deserves as its author is gravely impaired by the offences against its provisions which he himself committed.

CHAPTER VI

BOHEMIA IN THE FOURTEENTH CENTURY

WITH the violent death of the youthful King Wenceslas III on 4 August 1306, the ancient dynastic line of the Přemyslids became extinct; and the kingdom of Bohemia, which had flourished so splendidly under the last kings of the Přemyslid line, was subjected to a severe test. From the foundation of the Bohemian State the Bohemians had chosen their ruler only from the Přemyslid family, and from the end of the twelfth century there was no further need for such elections, because the throne came to be occupied always by the eldest, and as a rule the only, son of the previous ruler. Now there was no male Přemyslid but only a few princesses of the Přemyslid line. These laid claim to a privilege alleged to have been granted by a German king, who was said to have recognised the right of the female descendants of the family of Přemysl to the Bohemian throne, but this charter was not regarded as valid. On the other hand, it was certain that, according to the Golden Bull of the Emperor Frederick II (1212), the Bohemians had the right to elect their king freely and that the function of the Emperor was merely to ratify the election by conferring the insignia of royal power. By making use of this right, the Bohemians could call to the throne at least the husband or the betrothed of one of the Přemyslid princesses. As a matter of fact the majority of the Bohemian nobility was in favour of Henry of Carinthia, the husband of the eldest daughter of King Wenceslas II.

But by means of the proclamation that Bohemia was a vacant fief of the Empire, and with the help of gifts and promises, entreaties and threats, the German King Albert of Habsburg succeeded at last in causing the majority of the Bohemian nobles, in October 1306, to elect as their king his eldest son Rudolf. Thus the Bohemian throne was occupied for the first time by a member of the family whose lasting rule in Bohemia was not established until 200 years later. And perhaps the Habsburg dynasty might have been established in Bohemia even then on a permanent basis, if it had not been for the sudden death of the young king, who died on an expedition against some of the nobles in opposition to him, in July 1307, not quite nine months after his election.

According to the agreement made by King Albert with the Bohemian nobles, Rudolf's successor in Bohemia was to have been his younger brother, Frederick the Handsome. But only part of the nobility were willing to accept him. The majority elected as king Duke Henry of Carinthia (1307–10). The King of the Romans, Albert, indeed did not recognise him, for he insisted on the right of his own sons to the throne of Bohemia, but when in the spring of the year 1308 he was murdered, his son Frederick the Handsome, by friendly agreement with Henry of Carinthia, renounced in return for a large sum of money all his rights to the Bohemian crown. Henry, however, did not prove a success in Bohemia and soon lost the favour of the Bohemians. The serious increase in disorder and the conflicts between the Bohemian nobles and the wealthy German burghers undermined all his prestige. Thus there arose in Bohemia the idea of getting rid of Henry of Carinthia with the help of the new King of the Romans, Henry VII, and of inviting to the Bohemian throne a member of his family if the latter took as his wife Elizabeth, the only unmarried daughter of King Wenceslas II. After some hesitation King Henry VII accepted this plan and agreed that his son John, at that time a boy of scarcely fourteen years of age, should become the husband of Elizabeth and ascend the throne of Bohemia. In August 1310 John was married to Princess Elizabeth, and his father granted him the kingdom of Bohemia in fief. Then, driving out Henry of Carinthia from Bohemia with armed force, John seized possession of the government before the end of the year 1310, and his power was soon recognised throughout the country.

The accession of John of Luxemburg (1310–46) meant that the Bohemian throne was now occupied by a new royal dynasty, in whose hands the Bohemian crown remained for more than a century. The election of Henry, John's father, as King of the Romans had added considerable power and prestige to the Luxemburg family, and it was to be expected that the kingdom of Bohemia also would derive advantage from this fact. But Henry VII died in the summer of the year 1313 in Italy, where he was seeking to enforce his imperial rights, and thus the young King of Bohemia was suddenly deprived of the powerful support provided by his father's personality and particularly by his rank as Emperor. He attempted, indeed, after his father's death, to gain the German crown, but when the attempt failed, mainly on account of the influence of the Habsburgs, he satisfied himself with supporting the efforts of Lewis of Bavaria to secure the crown against the Habsburg candidate, Frederick the Handsome.

In Bohemia the young and inexperienced King John met with great difficulties from the beginning. When accepting John as king, the Bohemian nobility extracted from him some very onerous promises. It obtained substantial privileges and concessions as to military service and the payment of taxes, and also a considerable restriction of the royal power in the conferring of territorial administrative functions, which in the future were to be given only to men born within the country. Nevertheless, after his arrival in Bohemia, King John was surrounded by the German advisers of his father, and in the government he leaned chiefly on them, to the great dissatisfaction of the Bohemian nobility. But at last, in 1315, King John was obliged to dismiss all the foreign nobles from his court and to replace them by Bohemian lords. Of the latter, Henry of Lipa, to whom the king entrusted the administration of the royal revenue, in particular gained great power. Owing to the activities of his opponents, among whom was Queen Elizabeth herself, he was for a time deprived of this power and even thrown into prison by order of the king. When he was released from his imprisonment, the hostility between his supporters and those of Queen Elizabeth continued, and culminated in armed encounters and mutual pillaging. Placing himself on the side of Queen Elizabeth, King John made use, in the autumn of 1317, of troops sent to his assistance by the German King Lewis. But he met with the concerted resistance of the entire nobility and was compelled to give way. In the spring of 1318 peace was restored between the king and the Bohemian nobility. The nobles returned to their allegiance when the king promised them that he would send the German mercenaries out of the country, that he would never confer on foreigners any official positions in the country, and that he would govern only with the assistance of a council composed of men born within the country. Through this settlement the Bohemian throne was preserved for the Luxemburg family, which the Bohemian nobility was already beginning to oppose by seeking an alliance with the Habsburgs; at the same time the administration of the country was put entirely into the hands of the Bohemian lords. The deciding power in the kingdom was again acquired by Henry of Lipa, under whose influence the king himself fell so completely that he believed his assertions that Queen Elizabeth was endeavouring to deprive him of the throne and to seize possession of the government as the guardian of their three-year-old son Wenceslas, who later became Charles IV. At the beginning of the year 1319 he separated, by violent means, the mother from the child, and ordered her to be guarded as a prisoner for a few weeks in the fortress of Loket (Elbogen).

But towards the end of that year he decided to leave the country, where his inconstant character, delighting in deeds of knightly prowess, did not find sufficient satisfaction. Entrusting the administration of the country to Henry of Lipa, who in the meantime had been raised to the rank of senior marshal, he crossed the frontier, never again to return to his own kingdom except for short visits. His subsequent restless and mostly magnificent activity is only to a small extent connected with the internal history of Bohemia. Leaving his kingdom entirely in the hands of the Bohemian nobles, with whom up to the year 1320 he had struggled to maintain his rights as monarch, he henceforth regarded it mainly as an important source of revenue. In this way peace returned to the country. The conflicts between the king and the nobility ceased, and the attempts to bring about a change of ruler came to an end. In time the Bohemian nobility even came to feel pride in the knightly fame of John and did not hesitate to take part in his adventurous expeditions. But this reconciliation was effected only because John relinquished the actual government in favour of a few noble families. These, of course, profited by this circumstance to consolidate their class privileges and to enrich themselves at the expense of the power, rights, and property of the king. Thus John's reign was a period of great decline of the royal power within the country, and also a period of the stabilisation and increase of the class privileges of the Bohemian nobility.

To the political disputes were added, in the very first years of John's reign, conflicts in the sphere of Church affairs. About the year 1310 there began in the neighbouring duchy of Austria a great persecution of Waldensian heretics, and soon afterwards it was ascertained that there were heretics also in Bohemia. In the year 1315 fourteen heretics, mostly Waldensians, were burnt in Prague. But certainly there were many more heretics in Bohemia. It was asserted that there were hundreds of them and that they had an archbishop and seven bishops. It is thought that among them there was a physician named Richard (an Englishman?) who wrote a special tractate in defence of their errors. The correctness of all these assertions is rather doubtful. It is certain, however, that John of Dražice (1301–43), Bishop of Prague, who belonged to an old Bohemian family and was a man of education, a lover of art, and an ardent patriot, was more tolerant towards the heretics than was pleasing to certain zealots amongst the Bohemian clergy. For this and other reasons, therefore, he was denounced by them before Pope John XXII, who temporarily deprived him of his office and summoned him before the papal court at Avignon. In 1318 Bishop John departed for Avignon to attend the court, and although he was declared innocent, he was unable to return to his native land for eleven years.

From Avignon Bishop John brought back to Bohemia many important ideas on art and other matters. In the episcopal town of Roudnice he founded a monastery of Augustinian Canons, building for it a magnificent structure with a church. Undoubtedly the builders were French architects called to Bohemia by the bishop. They also constructed a large stone bridge at the bishop's request across the Elbe at Roudnice. Further, the bishop's castle in that town was rebuilt in the time of John of Dražice in a manner revealing French influence, particularly that of Avignon. From France Bishop John also brought to Bohemia many rare manuscripts decorated with artistic miniatures, which became the models for the manuscripts illuminated in Bohemia and had a great influence on the development of Bohemian painting.

All this took place without the least assistance on the part of King John, who paid very little attention to the internal affairs of his kingdom. On the other hand, by reason of his knightly deeds and military enterprises he spread the fame of the Bohemian name throughout the whole of Europe, and zealously and very successfully fought for the territorial expansion of Bohemia. In 1314 the German King, Lewis of Bavaria, assigned to him as an imperial pledge the town and territory of Cheb

(Eger), which under Přemysl Ottokar II and Wenceslas II had been joined for a considerable period to Bohemia. After the battle of Mühldorf, in which King Lewis won in 1322, mainly owing to John's assistance, a decisive victory over Frederick of Austria, John took charge of the government of the district of Cheb, which never again was to be separated from the Bohemian State and in the later centuries was completely incorporated in the kingdom of Bohemia.

John also added Upper Lusatia to the Bohemian Crown. After the year 1158, when the Emperor Frederick Barbarossa granted this territory as a fief to the Bohemian King Vladislav, it was united to Bohemia for nearly a hundred years. In the middle of the thirteenth century King Přemysl Ottokar II pledged Upper Lusatia to his brother-in-law Otto, Margrave of Brandenburg, whose two sons later divided it between them so that it was split up into the Bautzen and Görlitz sections. After the extinction of both branches of the Margrave of Brandenburg's family (1317 and 1319), the whole of Upper Lusatia should have reverted to the Bohemian Crown. John succeeded in occupying first the district of Bautzen (1320), and later the town of Görlitz and its surrounding territory (1329). He secured a hereditary claim also on the remainder of the district of Görlitz, which had been seized by Henry of Jauer, Duke of Silesia, so that after the death of the childless Henry of Jauer the remainder of the district of Görlitz was joined to the kingdom of Bohemia (1346). After that period the whole of Upper Lusatia was joined to Bohemia for nearly three hundred years.

King John increased the territories of the Bohemian State much more considerably when he obtained the sovereignty over a large part of the Silesian principalities. Already in the reign of King Wenceslas II four princes of Upper Silesia had accepted the overlordship of the King of Bohemia, who thus became the overlord of the whole of Upper Silesia. Afterwards, however, the feudal bond between Upper Silesia and the Bohemian Crown disappeared, while the disintegration of Upper Silesia into small principalities continued. Separating themselves more and more from Poland to which they originally belonged, these principalities again began to gravitate towards Bohemia. In 1327 Prince Henry of Breslau concluded with King John a treaty of inheritance, according to which the principality of Breslau was, after his death, to belong to Bohemia, and when in the same year King John undertook an expedition to Poland to urge the validity of old Bohemian claims to Poland, a number of other Silesian princes submitted themselves to his overlordship. During the succeeding years further Silesian principalities became fiefs of the Bohemian Crown, so that at the end of John's reign only two of them, the principalities of Schweidnitz and Jauer, were not under Bohemian suzerainty. In 1335 King Casimir of Poland recognised the overlordship of Bohemia over Silesia in return for the renunciation by King John of the title of King of Poland and of the rights annexed thereto.

The extension and consolidation of John's rule over Silesia were greatly furthered by the important and successful military expedition which in the winter of 1328–29 he undertook to Lithuania in order to assist the Order of Teutonic Knights against the pagan Prussians and Lithuanians: for during this expedition he was presented with the opportunity of intervening effectively against certain Polish and Silesian princes. In later years he undertook two further similar expeditions against Lithuania (1337 and 1345), but neither of these expeditions, in which his son Charles also took part, met with success.

Soon after his first expedition to Lithuania, his love of fighting took him southwards as far as Italy, where for a time he gained considerable power. He was led to this by his stay in southern Tyrol, where in 1330 he conducted negotiations with Henry, Duke of Carinthia and Count of Tyrol. King John had previously made his peace with this former Bohemian King and one-time rival by marrying his second son John to Henry's younger daughter Margaret, who was to inherit all her father's possessions. When in the autumn of 1330, after concluding the treaty of inheritance with Henry of Carinthia, he was staying with his son in the Trentino, he received a deputation from the Lombard city of Brescia which requested his assistance against the powerful lord of Verona, Mastino della Scala. King John set out once more in the winter with an army of mercenaries on an expedition to Italy, where not only Brescia but also many other Lombard cities, including Milan, and various magnates placed themselves under his protection. Thus in the course of the year 1331 the Bohemian king was master of the whole of central Lombardy and of the territories of the later principalities of Parma, Modena, and Lucca. This sudden and dazzling growth of power aroused against John all his powerful neighbours, whose hostility compelled him to accept his Italian territories from the Emperor as vicar of the Holy Roman Empire and after a time to depart from Italy altogether.

When he was not occupied with diplomatic negotiations and military expeditions, King John lived either in Luxemburg or at the court of the French King Charles IV, who had married his sister Mary. There he took part in knightly tournaments and magnificent festivities, and the fame of his bravery, generosity, and chivalrous manners spread throughout the whole of Europe. He came to Bohemia only rarely, generally to obtain money for the purpose of maintaining his luxurious standard of living and of equipping his military expeditions. His attitude towards Queen Elizabeth was always cool right up to her death (1330), and at times his relations with her were very strained. Fearing lest his eldest son Wenceslas might be proclaimed king, he took him away at the age of seven, in 1323, to be educated at the French court. At his confirmation, which took place there, Wenceslas received the name of Charles, which he kept for the rest of his life. In 1331 John called his son, aged fifteen, to Italy and made him governor of his Italian dominions. After the collapse of his rule in

Italy, John sent Charles back to Bohemia, gave him the title of Margrave of Moravia, and entrusted him with the administration of Bohemia and Moravia (1333), which he conducted with great success. In 1336 King John sent Prince Charles to Tyrol to the assistance of his brother John Henry, who after the death of his father-in-law Henry of Carinthia fought for his inheritance against the Dukes of Austria and the Emperor Lewis. In the same year John ended this struggle by a treaty with the Dukes of Austria; Carinthia was ceded to them, so that Henry and his wife retained only Tyrol. Five years later, however, when Margaret divorced her husband and married the Emperor's son Lewis, Margrave of Brandenburg, the rule of the Luxemburgs in Tyrol came to an end for ever. Before then, however, Charles had already in 1338 left Tyrol for Bohemia and had resumed the administration of the country. In 1341 King John also arrived in Bohemia; from an illness which he had contracted during his second expedition against Lithuania in 1337, he had become blind at first in one eye and then in both. At Domažlice the general Diet of all the countries under the Bohemian Crown recognised Margrave Charles as his successor on the Bohemian throne, and at the same time recognised the hereditary right of all the direct male descendants of Charles to the throne.

Five years later, when his father was still alive, Charles was elected King of the Romans in place of the Emperor Lewis. The friendship of King John for this Emperor, whom at the beginning he had helped with such self-sacrifice, had grown cool in the course of time. In the great conflicts of the Emperor with the papal Curia, King John sided more and more with the Popes, who at that time resided in Avignon and were in very close relations with the French Court, with which he was on such friendly terms. The consolidation of these friendly relations between the Bohemian King and his son on the one hand and the Papacy on the other was increased later when Clement VI, the former tutor and special supporter of Charles, was made Pope in 1342. Acceding to the desire of Charles, who accompanied by his father paid him a visit at Avignon, Pope Clement VI raised the Prague bishopric in 1344 to an archbishopric and subordinated to it the bishoprics of Olomouc (Olmütz) and Litomyšl, the latter being newly established. At the same time he began to exert his influence in favour of the election of Charles to the throne in place of the Emperor Lewis, who had been repudiated by the Curia. At a further meeting of King John and his son with Pope Clement VI at Avignon in the spring of 1346, a complete agreement was reached in regard to this question, and on 11 July 1349 five Electors of the Holy Roman Empire elected Charles King of the Romans at Rense.

Precisely at that period France was attacked by the army of Edward III of England. King John of Bohemia and his son Charles at once hastened to the assistance of the French King. Both of them took part in the decisive battle of Crécy on 26 August 1346, where the blind King John together with many Bohemian nobles died an heroic death; his valour could not turn the scales in favour of the French. It is said that, approaching the dead body of the Bohemian King, the victorious English King took from his helmet three ostrich feathers with the motto "Ich dien" (I serve), and gave them to his son the Black Prince who adopted them on his coat-of-arms. This may be a legend only, but it is certain that by his heroic death the blind King John contributed to the glory of the Bohemian State, the territory of which he considerably extended, although he remained foreign to the life of the State to the day of his death.

Charles IV (1346–78) was one of the most remarkable rulers that Bohemia ever had. A later age called him "the Father of his Country," and this title well describes his self-sacrificing and fruitful love for Bohemia, his wisdom and unwearying energy, and his truly paternal solicitude for the welfare of the people. Apart from his rare qualities of statesmanship as head of the Holy Roman Empire, he had also unusual opportunities to further the interests of his Bohemian fatherland, and he made very effective use of those opportunities. He was the first King of Bohemia to wear the German and then the imperial crown, and thereby Bohemia rose to the forefront of the political and cultural life of the Empire and of the whole of Central Europe.

At his father's death Charles was thirty years of age, but he had already lived through a life packed with stirring events and distinguished activity. He had taken an important share in directing the fortunes of Bohemia even during his father's lifetime. As representative of his father in the administration of the State, he had introduced good order, restored the declining power of the Crown, and had laboured also in other directions for the improvement of the condition of the country. The raising of the bishopric of Prague to an archbishopric in 1344, whereby the Bohemian State was emancipated from the tutelage of Germany in Church affairs, was due above all to him, although it took place while his father was still alive.

Ascending the throne after his father's death, he utilised his position in the Empire above all to effect a far-reaching improvement in the constitutional conditions of the Bohemian State. At the general assembly of the Estates of the Bohemian Crown held at Prague in the spring of 1348 in the presence of some of the Electors and other magnates of the Empire, Charles issued, after careful deliberations, several important charters (7 April 1348). He confirmed separately the former privileges granted by the German kings and Emperors to Bohemia, especially the privileges granted in the years 1158, 1212, 1289, and 1290. Then in two charters he regulated the relations of Moravia, and also of Silesia and Upper Lusatia, to the Bohemian State. Moravia, including the bishopric of Olomouc and the duchy of Opava, Silesia, and Upper Lusatia were definitely joined to Bohemia, thus enlarging the Bohemian State to a broader constitutional structure, the size of which was now first stabilised. The individual parts of the extended Bohemian State, the individual components of the Bohemian Crown, could no longer be separated from this larger unit in accordance with the will of the German kings; they could not be assigned as a direct imperial fief to anyone else than the King of Bohemia. Yet the King of Bohemia could assign them as a fief of the Bohemian Crown. They remained in the German Empire only as a part of the territories of the Bohemian Crown.

At the spring assembly of 1348 Charles IV also made an important decision regarding the order of succession in Bohemia. Having confirmed in his capacity as German king the charter of the Emperor Frederick II (1212) on the election of the Kings of Bohemia, he appended to it the explanation that the right to elect the king resided in the Estates of the kingdom of Bohemia and of the territories belonging to it, but only when there was no legal male or female heir of the Bohemian royal family. Thus it was now expressly and clearly laid down that the female descendants of the Bohemian royal family also had the right of inheritance to the Bohemian throne. The term Bohemian royal family was clearly understood to mean only the direct descendants of Charles and not a lateral branch of the Luxemburg family. But soon afterwards Charles endeavoured to extend the right of inheritance to the Bohemian throne to his brother John Henry and to the latter's male descendants. In accordance with the last will and testament of his father, Charles assigned the margravate of Moravia in 1349 to his brother as a fief of the Bohemian Crown, a fief which could be inherited only by male descendants. By a special charter he fixed, in agreement with the Bohemian Estates, the mutual hereditary precedence of the Bohemian and Moravian branches of the Luxemburg dynasty, so that after the extinction of the Bohemian branch the Kingdom of Bohemia and all the lands belonging to it would pass to the Moravian branch, whilst Moravia would pass to the Bohemian branch after the extinction of the Moravian branch. This provision was confirmed by Charles IV as Emperor at the general Diet of the Bohemian kingdom in September 1355, together with the charters of the year 1348 which regulated the constitutional conditions of the Bohemian Crown.

The relations of the Bohemian kingdom to the German Empire were regulated by the Emperor in the imperial law of 1356 which is known as the Golden Bull of Charles IV. Here the Bohemian king was solemnly proclaimed one of the seven Electors whose duty it was to elect the German king. In addition to the rights which the Golden Bull gave to all the Electors, the kings of Bohemia were granted certain important special rights. The Bohemian king was given the first place amongst the four temporal Electors, and it was laid down that at the meetings of the Diets and on other ceremonial occasions in the German

Empire the King of Bohemia should enjoy the position of priority, even if any other king were present. The Golden Bull gave the Bohemian kingdom important privileges before the other electorates in the order of succession. Whereas after the extinction of the direct line of the ruling house other electorates were, as vacant fiefs, at the Emperor's disposal, the kingdom of Bohemia retained its old rights and privileges, according to which the right to elect the king appertained in such a case to the Bohemian Estates. Thus it was again solemnly proclaimed that the Bohemian kingdom could never fall into the possession of the Empire like any other imperial land, that the Bohemian Crown was not transferable at the will of the German kings, because the Bohemian kings ascended the throne either by hereditary right or on the basis of election by the Estates. Of course even the Golden Bull declared that the Bohemian king, on being elected, acquired his full royal authority only when confirmed in his position by the Emperor. The Golden Bull ratified the special position of the kingdom of Bohemia also in the sphere of jurisdiction. Laying down that the inhabitants of any electorate were not to be brought before any foreign law-courts, and that they could appeal to the imperial law-court only if justice had been denied them, the Golden Bull declared that no inhabitant of the kingdom of Bohemia and of the territories belonging to it could be forced to appear before any law-court outside the frontiers of his State, and that no appeal whatever could be made from the Bohemian courts to foreign courts. According to the Golden Bull, the Bohemian kingdom differed from other electorates also in the fact that it lay outside the jurisdiction of the Emperor's lieutenants or administrators, who exercised the rights of the Emperor if the imperial throne was unoccupied.

The Golden Bull, then, did not slacken the old connexion between Bohemia and the German Empire, but recognised to Bohemia the premier position in the Empire before all the other electorates and therefore also before all the imperial principalities. Likewise it recognised and solemnly confirmed the internal independence of the Bohemian State, which in preceding periods certain of the German kings had endeavoured to curtail.

Having ensured by the laws of 1348 and 1355 the unity and integrity of the possessions of the Bohemian Crown, Charles IV did not cease to busy himself with the task of enlarging its territories. Gradually gaining various rights to the possession of Lower Lusatia, he annexed this territory in 1369 to the Bohemian Crown, and a year later he proclaimed its permanent incorporation with the kingdom of Bohemia after the manner of Silesia and Upper Lusatia. At the same time as the incorporation of Lower Lusatia, the Bohemian Crown acquired the two Silesian principalities of Schweidnitz and Jauer which in the reign of King John had not submitted themselves to Bohemian suzerainty. Charles prepared the way to the acquisition of these two territories by marrying in 1353, after the death of his second wife Anna, the fourteen-year-old daughter of the last Prince of Jauer, who was also the niece of the last Prince of Schweidnitz. After the incorporation of the principalities of Schweidnitz and Jauer, the Bohemian Crown was in possession of the whole of Silesia. Through the simultaneous acquisition of these two principalities and of Lower Lusatia, the Bohemian State attained the area which it held until the Thirty Years' War.

Five years before his death, Charles IV added to this State the Mark of Brandenburg also. In 1363 the Emperor Charles concluded with the two Margraves of Brandenburg, Lewis the Roman and Otto, sons of the deceased Emperor Lewis, a treaty of inheritance, according to which the Mark of Brandenburg was to pass, if they died childless, into the possession of the Bohemian royal family. When subsequently Otto, who after the death of his brother became the sole ruler of Brandenburg, endeavoured in disregard of the treaty of 1363 to transfer Brandenburg to his nephew Frederick of Bavaria, Charles invaded Brandenburg in 1373 with a considerable army and compelled Margrave Otto and his nephew, in their own name and in that of the entire Bavarian dynasty, to renounce the Marks of Brandenburg and to cede them to the sons of the Emperor. The Emperor immediately took over the administration of the Mark of Brandenburg on behalf of his sons, who in 1374, at the request of the Brandenburg Estates, laid down by charter that the Mark of Brandenburg was never to be separated from the Bohemian Crown, even if the Bohemian kings of the Luxemburg family were to die without legal issue. Charles immediately ratified this charter in his capacity as Emperor.

The future enlargement of the Bohemian State was furthered also by the treaty of inheritance concluded in 1364 between the Luxemburg royal family and the Habsburg ducal line, which in the preceding years had added Carinthia and Tyrol to its original Austro-Styrian possessions. The former hostility between the two families had been fed partly by their opposition to each other in the struggles for the throne of Germany in the reign of King John, and partly by the contest for Carinthia and Tyrol after the death of the former Bohemian King, Henry of Carinthia. This hostility afterwards gave place to friendly relations, which were shewn by the fact that Charles' daughter Catherine became in 1357 the wife of the Austrian Duke Rudolf IV. By the treaty of 1364 which was concluded at Brno (Brünn), with the written consent of the leading Bohemian nobles and of Charles, on behalf of his infant son Wenceslas, it was laid down that, after the extinction of the male and female lines of the Emperor Charles IV and of his brother the Moravian Margrave John Henry, the lands of the Bohemian Crown were to pass into the possession of the Austrian dukes; and conversely, the Bohemian king was to inherit the Austrian lands after the extinction of the male and female lines of the Austrian ducal family and of the Hungarian royal family, with which the Austrian dukes two years previously had concluded a similar treaty of inheritance. Soon afterwards, at the instigation of Charles, this Austro-Hungarian treaty of inheritance was denounced by both parties, and the Austro-Bohemian treaty of 1364 was renewed in 1366 with the full consent of the Estates of both countries, and with the omission of the provision relating to the hereditary claims of the Hungarian royal family to the Austrian territories. Owing to the fact that the Luxemburg family was extinct before the Austrian dynasty, all the gains were forfeited which could and, according to the intention of Charles, undoubtedly would have accrued to his family and to the Bohemian Crown from the treaty of inheritance with the Habsburg family. On the contrary, this treaty later became one of the factors that helped the Habsburg family to obtain possession of the Bohemian throne.

His unwearying zeal in the territorial enlargement and external improvement of the Bohemian State did not in any degree prevent Charles from paying fatherly attention to the betterment of its conditions. Indeed, his work in this direction was particularly great and enduring. Even in the period when he acted as his father's representative, Charles accomplished much for the restoration of order in the country and for the exaltation of the royal power. On becoming king, he made great efforts to rid the country of robbers and violent men who harassed the defenceless common people and attacked and plundered wealthy persons. According to the words of a contemporary chronicler, he introduced into the land "such peace as had not been in the memory of man nor had even been read of in the chronicles." Crushing violence in general, Charles strove to prevent the violent tactics adopted by the authorities towards the common people. At the Diet of 1356 a special law guaranteed to the latter the right to prosecute their lords before the territorial law-court, a procedure which the nobility of the time opposed. It is said that the Emperor himself was frequently present in person at the sessions of the territorial court in order to see that the lordly assessors did not side with the lords against the common people.

Connected with the endeavour of Charles to put down all violence and to protect the weak from oppression, was the attention which he paid to the improvement of the administration of justice in Bohemia. In the very first years of his government he prohibited, in concert with Ernest, Archbishop of Prague, the superstitious ordeal by hot iron. Again, soon after his accession to the throne, he gave orders for the compilation of the code of laws known as *Maiestas Carolina*, the purpose of which was to give a firm foundation for the activities of the territorial law-courts. The opposition of the Bohemian Estates, however, frustrated the issue of this code, just as it had frustrated the similar attempts of the earlier kings, Přemysl Ottokar II and Wenceslas II. This code contained old and new decrees in the field of public, civil, and criminal law, regulations relating to the system of judicature, and various police regulations. It reflected the endeavour to strengthen and raise the royal power, an endeavour which in places manifested itself also by statements derived from Roman jurisprudence as to the sovereignty of the monarch. This tendency explains why Charles' proposed code of laws met with such determined opposition on the part of the Bohemian Estates, who were proud of the fact that in the territorial law-courts they did not come within the scope of the written law, and who resisted every attempt to lay down fixed juridical rules in a written code. Yielding to the opposition of the Bohemian Estates, Charles withdrew the proposed code and declared at the same time that its ratification and the bringing of it into operation depended on the good will of the Bohemian princes and lords.

Great attention was paid by Charles to the economic development of his hereditary lands. By a law of the year 1358 he ordered vineyards to be established on the bare heights and slopes around Prague and elsewhere in Bohemia. Further, he ordered excellent vines to be brought from Austria and perhaps also from Burgundy, so that in a short time Prague was provided with a wide belt of vineyards, while elsewhere, particularly in the neighbourhood of Mělník, there was an increase in the cultivation of the vine, and in some places the vineyards have been maintained up to this day. Another novelty was also introduced by Charles into Bohemia when he established large fish-ponds in various places, and by his example he stimulated other landowners to increase the productivity of their estates.

It is to the undying credit of Charles that he greatly furthered the development of intellectual and cultural progress in his State, and especially among the Bohemian people, by the foundation of Prague University. For this purpose he secured in advance the consent of the papal Curia, which was given by the bull of Pope Clement VI in January 1347. In his capacity as King of Bohemia he issued in April 1348 the Prague University foundation charter, which he confirmed in January 1349 in his capacity as King of Germany. By this charter Charles granted to the new university all the liberties enjoyed by the two famous Universities of Paris and Bologna. Immediately afterwards Charles appointed the first professors, who consisted both of men born in Bohemia and of foreigners specially invited for this purpose, so that teaching was commenced at Prague University in the course of the year 1348. The final organisation of the university was perhaps not stabilised until after many conflicts between the members of the young institution. In 1372 the law-students seceded and established a new university which was connected with the remaining three faculties only by the common Chancellor, who was the Archbishop of Prague. Each of the two universities was divided from the outset into four "nations," Bohemian, Polish, Bavarian, and Saxon. The Bohemian "nation" included also Hungarians and South Slavs; in addition to Poles, the Polish "nation" included Silesians, Lithuanians, and Russians; the Bavarian "nation" included Austrians, Swabians, Franconians, and Rhinelanders; and the Saxon "nation" included students from Meissen, Thuringians, Danes, and Swedes. This distribution was of great importance, particularly on such occasions as the election of the Rector and the appointment of other university officers and officials. In spite of its international character and the great prevalence of foreigners, particularly Germans, both among the professors and the students, the University of Prague soon attained a position of considerable importance for the intellectual life of the Bohemian nation, which after a time took a leading and decisive part in its activities. From the outset the university added brilliance to the life of the Bohemian capital by filling it with crowds of foreigners, who came there in order to study or at least to enjoy the legal privileges of student life.

The external appearance of Prague and Bohemia was considerably improved by the numerous great buildings erected by Charles. During the first period of his rule (1333–35) he began to build at the Castle of Prague on the ruins of the royal palace, which had been burnt down, a new palace on the model of the French royal seat at the Louvre; this building was greatly praised by contemporaries, but has been completely overshadowed by later reconstructions. It was undoubtedly owing to the initiative of Charles that in the lifetime of his father, and in connexion with the establishment of the archbishopric of Prague, the foundation stone was laid of the magnificent structure of St Vitus' Cathedral in the Castle of Prague. The building operations were directed first by the French architect Matthew of Arras whom Charles brought from France, and after his death in 1352 by the German Peter Parler of Gmünd who worked for over forty years on the building. Although the building operations continued throughout the entire period of Charles' reign, only part of the new cathedral, namely the magnificent chapel of St Wenceslas, was completed in his lifetime. In addition to this, several other large churches were erected in Prague in the reign of Charles IV. Prague was not big enough for the influx of foreigners, and in order to enlarge the city Charles founded the New Town in 1348. The new stone bridge across the Vltava at Prague was also constructed by Charles' orders under the direction of the above-mentioned Peter Parler. Further, Charles built in the lands belonging to the Bohemian State several castles, monasteries, and churches. The most celebrated of these buildings is the castle of Karlštejn, which was founded in 1348 and possesses splendid internal decorations. It was here that Charles deposited the State jewels of the kingdom of Bohemia, which he had had made during the lifetime of his father in place of the old jewels which were lost in the reign of King John (the new crown dedicated to St Wenceslas was afterwards known as the Crown of St Wenceslas), all the important State documents of Bohemia, the imperial jewels and German sacred insignia, and many relics of the saints.

The numerous large buildings erected by Charles led to a golden age in the history of decorative art in Bohemia. Architecture, sculpture, and painting flourished. The mural paintings and pictures executed for the decoration of the chapels and churches attained a high artistic level and had a character of their own, so that we may rightly speak of a special Bohemian school of painting in that period. Great progress was also made in the painting of miniatures and in small artistic objects.

Charles' endeavours in the direction of the territorial enlargement of the Bohemian State and his internal activities as a founder of institutions necessarily involved a large expenditure. Hence, although he was very economical and a model organiser, he was very often obliged to make extraordinary financial demands on the population of the State and to impose heavy taxes. In addition to this, the financial obligations undertaken by King John and also by Charles himself made it necessary on each occasion to seek the approval of the Estates. Thus whenever Charles wished to impose a tax, he was obliged to enter into negotiations beforehand with the Estates. In this way the Estates acquired a regular and constantly increasing influence on public affairs. All the decrees of Charles regarding the Bohemian throne, all his laws regulating the external and internal conditions of the Bohemian State, were issued with the participation and consent of the Bohemian Estates. And Charles' great legislative work, the *Maiestas Carolina*, did not acquire validity, because the Estates did not agree to it. The Estates shewed their agreement or disagreement with the intentions and actions of the king both through their representatives in the highest departments of the State administration and in the territorial law-courts, and also in the general diets which gradually became regular institutions. In addition to the diets of the separate countries, Charles used to summon, when it was a question of matters affecting the interests of the State as a whole, common or general diets of all the lands of the Bohemian Crown. Thus, although he had a great opinion of his royal rights and used to declare his adherence to Roman juridical views of the sovereignty of the monarch, Charles lent his support to the development which tended towards the stabilisation and deepening of the conception that the king was not the sole and unrestricted holder of the supreme power of the State, but shared it with the representatives of the free classes of the nation, *i.e.* with the Estates. The Bohemian Crown, the Bohemian State, was no longer represented by the king alone, but also by "all the community of the Bohemian Kingdom," *i.e.* by the Estates. Both together, the king and the Estates, formed a higher State unit, the symbol of which was the crown of St Wenceslas; supplied in the year 1346 by Charles IV, it rested on the head of the saint in St Vitus' Cathedral, and only at coronations and on other ceremonial occasions was it worn by the Bohemian kings.

The period of Charles' reign was one of splendid development for the Church and its institutions. Through the raising of the bishopric of Prague to an archbishopric, effected with the help of Charles in 1344, all Bohemia and Moravia were freed, in regard to ecclesiastical affairs, from dependence on the archbishop of Mayence, who up till then had been the metropolitan of the Bohemian Church. To the archbishop of Prague was transferred the existing right of the archbishop of Mayence to crown the Bohemian king. Bishop Ernest of Pardubice, a truly eminent man and one of the greatest ornaments of the Bohemian Church, became the first Archbishop of Prague. Like John of Dražice, his predecessor on the episcopal throne in Prague, Ernest sprang from a Czech noble family. He studied for fourteen years at the celebrated Italian universities of Bologna and Padua, and acquired not only a thorough knowledge of theology and Church law but also a classical education which was unusual for that period. By this, and also by the rare delicacy of his moral conscience, he aroused the admiration of Petrarch himself. Ernest of Pardubice combined a genuine love for the arts and sciences with deep piety, moral earnestness, and zeal in the fulfilment of the great duties of his office. It was only under him that the victory of Church principles was completed in Bohemia in the relations between the spiritual and temporal authorities; it was not until then that all the rights were entirely realised which Přemysl Ottokar I had granted in principle to the Bohemian Church after the great struggle with Bishop Andrew.

In addition to great rights the Church at that time possessed enormous wealth; one-half of all the land in Bohemia belonged partly to the secular clergy and partly to the monasteries. This wealth, however, was divided very unequally; there were prebends with immense incomes and also benefices which were quite poor. In that period the proportion of clergy to population in Bohemia was much greater than it is to-day. It is calculated that in Prague alone, which at that time had less than 40,000 inhabitants, there were at least 1200 clergy and monks. Being almost entirely freed from the jurisdiction of the temporal authorities, they were subordinated only to the ecclesiastical authorities, and thus they had a privileged position as compared with the rest of the population. Combined with the great wealth of the Church, this had a very unfavourable effect on the morals of the clergy; their conduct was generally on a rather low level. The unhealthy development of Church life in Bohemia was furthered by the Curia itself owing to its excessive and unfortunate intervention in the internal affairs of the Bohemian Church. Having the chief voice in the bestowal of Church benefices in Bohemia and in the appointment of the higher dignitaries, the Curia derived financial profit therefrom and contributed in the highest degree to the accumulation of benefices and other abuses.

These evils were opposed by the Emperor Charles as well as by Archbishop Ernest. In 1352 it was laid down by law in Bohemia that no one could give or bequeath his property to Church dignitaries or institutions without the special permission of the king. The reforming mind and endeavours of Archbishop Ernest are shewn particularly in the statutes which he gave to the clergy in 1349 and later supplemented in the different synods; by these regulations all the evil habits and immoral proceedings of the clergy of that time were prohibited and severely punished.

The Emperor Charles and Archbishop Ernest shewed their favour towards the efforts of reform in the Church most clearly by the support which they extended to two eminent preachers. In 1363 Charles called to Prague an Augustinian canon, Conrad Waldhauser (of Waldhaus in Upper Austria), who for many years had been court-preacher to the Dukes of Austria and had gained a great reputation by reason of his moral earnestness. Being a German with no knowledge of Czech, Waldhauser preached in Prague chiefly to the German inhabitants who, owing to their wealth, were particularly addicted to lives of pleasure. The success of Waldhauser's sermons was very great. Germans and Czechs thronged to hear him, and under the influence of his words many of them turned away from sinful living. Soon, however, the preaching activities of Waldhauser aroused the hostility of the mendicant friars, who were jealous of his success and disturbed by his attacks on the abuses which were prevalent among them. They laid complaints against the bold preacher before the archbishop, and spread rumours that he dealt in heresies. Refusing to desist from his preaching, Waldhauser defended himself, and after a time, in concert with the other Prague priests, he charged all mendicant Orders before the Pope with conducting interments in their convents contrary to Canon Law. For this purpose he travelled to Rome, but returning before the conclusion of the conflict he died in Prague towards the end of 1369.

Almost at the same time as Waldhauser, a native-born preacher began to preach in Prague, whose fame soon outshone that of the Austrian Augustinian and who far surpasses him in the historical significance of his work. This was the Moravian, John Milíč of Kroměříž, who after giving up his Church dignities began to preach in Prague about the autumn of 1364. His sermons soon became unusually popular and attracted large congregations, particularly of the Czech population. Surpassing Waldhauser by his fiery eloquence and soaring enthusiasm, Milíč acted even more powerfully than he on the minds of the common people. The effect of his words was enhanced by the splendid example which he gave in his own life. He lived in absolute poverty and exercised the strictest bodily asceticism. He never allowed himself any rest, but devoted himself constantly to prayer, study, and a severely ascetic mode of life; he despised all bodily comfort and fasted often.

This mode of life and the disturbed conditions of contemporary Christendom stimulated in Milíč a natural tendency towards mysticism He formed the conviction that in the years 1365–67 Antichrist was to appear in the world in accordance with the prophecy of Daniel. In 1366, while delivering a sermon on Antichrist, he pointed with his finger directly at the Emperor Charles who was present and declared him to be the great Antichrist spoken of in the Scriptures. On account of this statement, Archbishop John Očko, the successor of Ernest, had Milíč put in prison and the monks of Prague laid an accusation against him, but he was not sentenced to any punishment. A year later he departed to Rome, where Pope Urban V was expected to arrive shortly from Avignon. When, however, in May 1367, he announced in Rome a public sermon on Antichrist with the declaration that Antichrist had already come to the world, Milíč was imprisoned by order of the Inquisitors and brought before the Court of the Inquisition. In prison he wrote for an inquisitor his "Tractate on Antichrist," in which he recommended the summoning of an ecumenical council as the only means of removing the evils in the corrupted Church. The same counsel was contained also in a letter which he wrote to Pope Urban V in about the year 1368. After the arrival of the Pope in Rome, Milíč was released from prison and returned to Prague. In 1369 he set out on a second journey to Rome, but on receiving news of the death of Waldhauser he quickly returned.

In order to fill the gap left by Waldhauser's decease, Milíč now also began to preach regularly in German; his preaching activities were considerably increased, for he used to deliver four or five sermons daily in different languages and before different congregations, becoming at the same time more and more strict in his asceticism. The glamour of his words manifested itself particularly in the year 1372, when under the influence of his preaching a large number of Prague prostitutes abandoned their immoral mode of life and resolved to serve God. Milíč established for them a special institution, where they were taught to pray and to work and were prepared for a return to normal life. Having obtained from the Emperor the once famous house of sin called Benátky (Venice) and having secured by purchase and in the form of gifts the neighbouring houses, Milíč built there a chapel and homes to house the women, who sometimes numbered over 80. The new institution was named Jerusalem, and as it was freed from duties to the neighbouring parishes, it became practically an independent parish community. This aroused the resentment of the parish-priests of Prague, who joined the monks, the former opponents of Milíč, and laid a charge against him, accusing him of heresy. When their attempt failed in Prague, the parish-priests charged Milíč with heresy directly before the papal Court, which in the meantime had again moved to Avignon. They found fault with Milíč for introducing in Jerusalem the daily receiving of the sacrament, for condemning all trade, for proclaiming that the clergy ought to live in poverty, and for denouncing the study of the liberal arts. As a result of these complaints, Pope Gregory XI instructed the Archbishop of Prague and the other Bohemian bishops to make a strict investigation and to punish Milíč as a warning to others of like mind. Milíč now set out once more on a journey to the papal Court at Avignon, where he was well received and given permission to deliver ceremonial sermons before the cardinals. But before the suit was concluded, he died in Avignon in August 1374. His influence in his native country, however, did not cease with his death, but became one of the main sources of the great movement which later led to the burning of Hus at the stake and to the revolt of the Czech nation from the Roman Church.

Just as the reign of Charles manifested clearly the beginnings of the later severe religious struggles in Bohemia, so also it prepared and proclaimed the struggle between the Czech and German nationalities, a struggle which developed in connexion with the religious conflicts and for the most part was combined with them. The gradually increasing influence of the Czech element at the University of Prague, which originally was almost entirely in the hands of German foreigners, prepared the way for the later victory of the Czechs in this foremost educational institution of the Bohemian State. In the towns also the Czech element grew stronger, almost entirely unnoticed and by a natural process, through the influx of peasants from the surrounding country districts; for the towns had been founded and at the beginning completely dominated by immigrant families of German burghers. In Prague Charles contributed to this development by establishing the New Town, not exclusively for Germans as had been the custom on previous occasions when towns were founded in the Bohemian lands, but for everyone who wished to settle there. So it came about that from the very outset New Town was overwhelmingly Czech, and thus had an indirect influence on the development of a Czech character in other parts of Prague. Although he liked the German culture and the German language, the Emperor gave many proofs of his genuine love for the Czech nation and the Czech language which was his mother tongue.

The religious and national factors in the history of the period announced the great movement which soon afterwards burst into flame. As a harbinger of the more distant future, we may consider the beginnings of the humanistic predilections and endeavours which we find in the environment of Charles. Their actual seeding-place was his chancery, at the head of which, during a considerable part of his reign, stood Bishop John of Středa (von Neumarkt, de Novoforo), who was an eminent humanist, an enthusiastic collector of classical manuscripts, and a friend of Petrarch. The predilection for humanism spread from Charles' chancery to the highest levels of Bohemian society. The Emperor himself was strongly influenced by this current of humanism, and had confidential meetings both with the native exponents of humanism and also with the most important foreign humanists. In 1356 Petrarch, with whom the Emperor was in correspondence, paid him a visit in Prague; the Court overwhelmed the distinguished visitor with enthusiastic praise. Six years before that, Prague received a visit from the Roman tribune, Cola di Rienzo, who wished to induce the Emperor to take up his residence in Rome as the sole and absolute monarch of a united Italy and of the whole Christian world. Considering the views of the visionary Roman on Church matters to be obnoxious, the cautious Emperor handed him over to the Archbishop of Prague for instruction and improvement. Thus Cola spent some time in imprisonment in the archbishop's castle at Roudnice, and afterwards was sent to the papal court in Avignon.

At the end of his life the Emperor concerned himself with the question of the distribution of his hereditary lands among the members of his family. The eldest son Wenceslas, who in 1363 had been crowned King of Bohemia and in 1376 had been elected King of the Romans, was to rule in Bohemia and Silesia, over parts of Upper and Lower Lusatia, and over scattered fiefs of Bohemia in Bavaria and Saxony. The second son Sigismund obtained the district of Brandenburg, while for the third son John a special duchy of Görlitz was formed from parts of Upper and Lower Lusatia. Jošt, the first-born son of Charles' brother the Margrave John Henry, ruled in Moravia after his father's death in 1376, while his younger brothers John Soběslav, later Patriarch of Aquileia, and Prokop received from him subordinate fiefs. Of the Emperor's daughters, Anne, a child by his last wife Elizabeth of Pomerania, became in 1382, three years after her father's death, the wife of the English King Richard II, and gained in England the very honourable name of "Good Queen Anne."

Having lived to see the beginning of the Great Schism in the Western Church, the Emperor Charles IV died on 29 November 1378 in his sixty-third year.

Wenceslas IV (1378–1419) was not yet quite eighteen when by his father's death he was called to rule over the territories of the Bohemian Crown and over the German Empire. For the fulfilment of the heavy duties which now fell to his share he possessed not only natural gifts and a considerable degree of education, but also a practical knowledge of State affairs which he had acquired owing to the fact that his father had from his childhood associated him with himself on important occasions in Bohemia and in foreign countries. He certainly had much good will, but he lacked judgment and perseverance. From the outset his passion for hunting prevented him from carrying out his duties as a monarch. In addition, he had a decided tendency towards immoderate drinking, and as the years passed the habit grew on him to such an extent that at times he lost command of his reason, for by nature he was irritable and violent. Thus it happened on more than one occasion that Wenceslas allowed himself, in an excess of rage, to act in a hasty, harsh, and even cruel manner. His actions on these occasions only increased the strife of which the period of his rule was full, and stained his memory in after times.

Not all of the great extent of territory under the rule of the Emperor Charles IV passed into the hands of Wenceslas. According to the dispositions of his father, the second son Sigismund obtained the district of

Brandenburg, the third son John received the district of Görlitz, while
Moravia remained under the rule of Charles' nephew, Margrave Jošt.
This wealthy and learned man obtained also, in 1388, the county of
Luxemburg from King Wenceslas, who had inherited it in 1382 from
Wenceslas, his father's second brother. In addition, Jošt received the
district of Brandenburg from Sigismund, who in 1385 had become King
of Hungary. Later, in 1401, King Wenceslas, who by the death of his
brother John had obtained the district of Görlitz, ceded to him Upper
and Lower Lusatia. After the death of Jošt (1411) the two Lusatias
returned into the possession of Wenceslas and the district of Brandenburg
was restored to Sigismund. The latter, however, immediately pledged
the Mark of Brandenburg to Frederick of Hohenzollern, the Burgrave of
Nuremberg, in whose family it now remained permanently.

Wenceslas' rule in the German Empire was by no means of a happy
character, for his heavy task was rendered still more difficult both by the
schism in the Church and by the internal dissensions of the Estates in
the Empire. Although he strove hard to obtain the recognition of the
Pope in the Empire and in his own lands, and constantly prepared to set
out on an expedition to Rome in order to obtain the imperial crown, he
did not succeed either in contributing towards the removal of papal
dualism or in realising the plan of a Roman expedition. And although
his intervention in the disputes between the Estates of the Empire was
often timely and justified, it produced for him in the Empire many
enemies who in 1384 began to intrigue for his deposition. This took
place in 1400, when King Wenceslas was deprived of the German throne
by the Electors, who chose Rupert of the Rhine as king.

This inglorious end of Wenceslas' reign in the German Empire was
prepared in no small measure by the unfavourable development of
internal conditions in Bohemia. For some time, indeed, Wenceslas' reign
appeared to be a worthy continuation of the excellent reign of his father,
but later serious unrest arose from the conflicts of the king both with
the Bohemian lords and also with the dignitaries and officials of the
Church.

While King Wenceslas was popular among the common people on
account of his good nature and because he did not exact such heavy taxes
as his father, he soon incurred the displeasure of the higher nobility by
choosing for his advisers mainly members of the lower nobility and
burghers, and by staffing the public offices with persons devoted to himself and belonging to these classes. After a while the dissatisfied nobles
formed against the king a conspiracy which was joined even by the king's
cousin Jošt, Margrave of Moravia. In the spring of the year 1394, Jošt
entered quite formally into a union with the leading Bohemian nobles,
the aim of which was declared to be the removal of various defects in the
territorial administration and in the law-courts. With a large number of
armed men they took the king by surprise at his country-seat near Prague,

cast him into prison in the Castle of Prague, and after a time even removed him to a castle in Austria. About three months later the king's brother John of Görlitz compelled the rebellious nobles by armed force to release the king from imprisonment, on the promise that a decision would be made with reference to their complaints. New conflicts, however, soon arose between the king and the nobles, who towards the end of 1394 organised a new coalition against him. In addition to Margrave Jošt, the conspiracy was joined by the Dukes of Austria. The complaints and demands which the rebellious nobles submitted to the king involved an unheard-of limitation of his power. When the king hesitated to comply with these demands and the nobles began to wage open war against him, he requested his brother Sigismund, the Hungarian King, to undertake, after the death of John of Görlitz, the office of mediator between the parties. Sigismund induced the parties to entrust the decision regarding their complaints and demands to him and to Margrave Jošt. Their award, made in the spring of the year 1396, signified a great success for the nobles. Almost all the highest offices of the land were adjudicated to them, and at the side of the king was established a council composed of the Bohemian and Moravian nobles and bishops. Without this council the king was not to undertake any action in internal affairs.

Owing to the fact that King Wenceslas submitted only with unwillingness to this award and that the nobles did not cease to strive to obtain a further restriction of the king's power, new disputes arose between the king and the nobles in the course of time and became exceedingly embittered. In 1397 certain of the nobles who were members of the king's council murdered four of the leading advisers of King Wenceslas at Karlštejn. All attempts at a reconciliation were in vain, and in the winter of 1400 the Bohemian nobles headed by Margrave Jošt formed an alliance with King Rupert and his German adherents. In the spring of 1401 King Wenceslas was besieged in Prague for more than eight weeks by the armed forces of the native and German members of this association. In the summer the king and the Bohemian nobles concluded a treaty, whereby King Wenceslas agreed to accept a standing council consisting of four nobles and enjoying great powers. Thus was established a permanent committee of nobles whose task was to govern in common with the king; they had a deciding voice also in the administration of the royal estates and revenues which up to that time had been under the control of the Bohemian kings alone. At the beginning of 1402, however, the power of this council was transferred to King Sigismund of Hungary, whom King Wenceslas appointed administrator of the kingdom of Bohemia while he himself was preparing to go on another expedition to Rome, which once more did not take effect. Soon conflicts again arose between the royal brothers, and Sigismund, whom Wenceslas had a short time before generously assisted to gain his release from imprisonment in Hungary, gave orders for his brother to be arrested in the spring of 1402 and to be imprisoned in

Prague Castle, where he had been incarcerated eight years previously. After a time, however, on leaving the country, he brought King Wenceslas with him, and finally, in August 1402, took him to Vienna, where he was kept under the protection of the Dukes of Austria. Only in the autumn of 1403 did King Wenceslas succeed in escaping from his imprisonment at Vienna and returning to Bohemia. In the meantime the party which supported him had grown in strength, so that he was received practically as a deliverer, even by many of his former opponents. Wenceslas made use of this favourable state of things to abolish the new regulations by which his royal power had not long before been limited, and to restore the former method of government.

In the last years of Wenceslas' reign the conflict over the boundaries of the royal power and that of the Estates was replaced by great disputes in the field of ecclesiastical affairs. These disputes were preceded by numerous and mostly very serious conflicts between King Wenceslas and the Church authorities. The first collision was that between the king and the cathedral chapter in Breslau, the capital of Silesia. When King Wenceslas visited the town in the summer of 1381, it had just been placed under an interdict by the cathedral chapter (the bishopric being then vacant), because at Christmas 1380 some barrels of foreign beer had been confiscated which had been ordered for the canons in defiance of the general regulations of the municipal authorities. When the chapter refused to comply with the king's request that the interdict should be removed at least for a time, he felt that his royal authority was flouted and caused the chapter's estates in the vicinity of Breslau to be occupied and pillaged. At the request of the king the interdict was removed shortly afterwards by order of the Pope, and the dispute with the Breslau chapter was settled in the spring of 1382, so that the power of the Bohemian Crown over the bishopric of Breslau was considerably strengthened.

More serious and more fateful were the disputes between the king and John of Jenštejn, the Archbishop of Prague. Conspicuously gifted and possessed of an extensive education which he had acquired through his studies at several Italian and French universities, particularly at Paris, this young man (he was scarcely twenty years old when in 1379 he took over the administration of the archbishopric of Prague) lived at first in an effeminate and worldly manner. But his severe illness and the terrible death of the Archbishop of Magdeburg at a dancing entertainment brought about a change in his mind and manner of living. He turned away from the world and lived like a penitent, devoting himself to fasting and bodily mortification, prayer, religious meditation, and the writing of religious treatises of a mystical tendency. At the same time, however, he had an excessively high opinion of his ecclesiastical authority and did not cease to surround himself with splendour, being convinced that this was required for the maintenance of his dignity. He was very sensitive about the rights of his office, and thus found himself engaged in numerous conflicts with the higher clergy of his diocese as well as with several laymen and with the temporal authorities. In 1384 he had a very sharp dispute with King Wenceslas himself over a dam on the River Elbe, and thus incurred his displeasure. This fact was exploited by some of the favourite officials and advisers of the king, who began to interfere more boldly with matters belonging to the sphere of the ecclesiastical authorities and did not always respect the rights which had previously been granted to the Church in Bohemia. Thus in 1392–93, on the order of one of these officials, two priests were executed in Prague for various base crimes; and in other directions also the temporal authorities disregarded the liberties which were claimed at that time by the Church. In view of these circumstances the archbishop presented a complaint to the king in 1393, and also summoned before the archiepiscopal court the royal official who had ordered the execution of the two priests. This action greatly enraged the proud and irascible king against the archbishop and his officials. The king, however, lost his self-control completely over another event which happened soon afterwards.

Intending to establish a new bishopric in western Bohemia and to endow it with the estates of the Benedictine monastery at Kladruby, Wenceslas desired that after the death of the abbot his position should remain vacant. But when the abbot died, the monks at Kladruby elected a successor and Archbishop John, although he knew of the king's intention, gave instructions for the election to be confirmed by his vicar-general, John of Pomuk. The news of this enraged the king to such an extent that during the negotiations regarding the archbishop's complaints he ordered the arrest of the archbishop and his three advisers, including the vicar-general John of Pomuk. The archbishop was released, but his advisers remained in the power of the king, who cross-examined them and then ordered them to be tortured; in particular John of Pomuk was burnt with torches and lighted candles so that he almost lost consciousness. Finally, the king ordered them all to be drowned, but on reflection promised to grant them their lives on condition that they undertook on oath to tell no one that they had been imprisoned and tortured. The others did so, but John of Pomuk, exhausted by his tortures, was unable to sign the document presented to him. The king then ordered him to be taken away to his death. John of Pomuk was dragged away to the stone bridge built by the Emperor Charles IV, and bound hand and foot was thrown into the Vltava on 20 March 1393.

When his rage had passed, the king tried to make amends. Making use of the advantages of the quinquagenary year which was just then proclaimed in Prague by permission of the Pope, he obtained absolution from the Church by carrying out the prescribed acts of penitence. He also invited the archbishop to enter into negotiations with a view to a reconciliation. The archbishop accepted the invitation, but when the negotiations fell through, he began to entertain fears as to his safety; he fled from Prague and went to Rome. There he presented to the papal Court a lengthy report containing all his complaints against King Wenceslas, and requested the Pope to appoint judges to try the king and his assistants and to inflict ecclesiastical penalties on them as sacrilegious persons and murderers. However, he achieved no success at the papal court; none of his complaints, not even the report on the cruel death of the vicar-general John of Pomuk, induced Pope Boniface IX to take action against King Wenceslas in defence of the rights of the Church. At that time the Pope was expecting the king to arrive in Italy and to help him to gain a final victory over his enemies there and over the Pope at Avignon. Hence the Curia turned a favourable ear towards the king's request that Archbishop John should be removed from his position. In these circumstances Archbishop John considered it advisable to give up his office of his own free will towards the end of the year 1395; he remained in Rome, where five years later he died. Thus if the Curia abandoned without hesitation such a distinguished prelate as Archbishop John of Jenštejn in his struggle against the king for the liberty and rights of the Church, it is little wonder that it passed over in silence the martyrdom of his vicar-general, John of Pomuk, a man otherwise of small importance, who was given a martyr's halo only on account of the religious struggles of a later date, and was raised to the position of a great national saint under the name of John of Nepomuk (for in the meantime the name of his birth-place had been changed from Pomuk to Nepomuk) by the victorious Counter-Reformation. The attitude of the Pope towards the king changed when the latter endeavoured to bring about the end of the papal schism by the resignation of both Popes. Then Pope Boniface IX took the side of Wenceslas' opponents in the German Empire and contributed considerably towards his deposition.

In all these conflicts with the dignitaries and officials of the Church, King Wenceslas appears to us as determined an upholder of royal rights as he was an opponent of Church principles and claims that affected the power of the king. It might be thought that a king who so energetically defended his rights against priests and Church institutions at home would also have resisted no less resolutely the excessive interference of the Curia with the ecclesiastical administration in his lands, and have stopped the abuses which arose therefrom in the Church of his time. Wenceslas, however, not only did not do this; he tolerated and even supported the growth of the Pope's influence on the ecclesiastical administration in Bohemia and willingly reconciled himself to the harmful sides of the papal administrative system; it was precisely at this period that this harmfulness reached its zenith, and the king did not hesitate to draw benefit for himself from the fact. Perhaps the greatest culprit in respect of accumulation of benefices in territories governed by Wenceslas was one of his foremost advisers and favourites, Wenceslas Králík, who probably obtained all his benefices by the Pope's favour. The Pope's tithe was exacted year by year in the early part of Wenceslas' reign, and the collection of the plenary indulgences, authorised at the occasion of the quinquagenary year of grace given to Wenceslas' territories in 1393, was likewise permitted and supported by the king, who did not fail, of course, to secure a share for himself. Thus while the Bohemian clergy and ecclesiastical institutions were engaged in disputes with the temporal authorities, there existed between King Wenceslas and the Curia a full agreement, which both parties bought, of course, by making mutual political but morally very doubtful concessions.

There is no wonder that in such circumstances as these the moral deficiencies and abuses, the beginnings of which may be observed in the reign of Charles IV, greatly gained ground in the Church of Bohemia. But the resistance to them also increased, for it was strengthened by the genuinely moral movement which was stimulated in the reign of Charles IV by the activities of the famous preachers Waldhauser and Milíč, and grew wider and deeper during the reign of Wenceslas IV. Milíč was succeeded in his labours by Thomas of Štítný and Matthias of Janov, two distinguished Czech thinkers of the first period of Wenceslas' reign. Thomas of Štítný (*ob. c.* 1401), a devout and educated landowner, wrote in Czech, and mostly following foreign models, a number of works of a moralising and religious character; they clearly demonstrate the influence of Milíč's thought and spirit. Some of the masters of arts of the university found fault with him for writing on difficult religious and philosophical questions in the language of the common people, but Štítný paid no heed to such reproaches. Genuinely devoted to the Church, he avoided all dogmatic deviations from Church doctrine and disagreements with the Church authorities. Matthias of Janov (*ob.* 1394) obtained the degree of master of arts at the University of Paris and studied theology there. As a preacher and writer in the spirit of Milíč, he followed his example by recommending frequent attendance at the sacrament of the Holy Eucharist, but he also condemned an excessive worship of the saints, relics, pictures, and miracles, and opposed in general external and ostentatious manifestations of piety. His views aroused the anger of the Church authorities. At the Prague synod in 1388 it was strictly forbidden to give the Holy Eucharist to the laity more frequently than once a month. A year later Matthias of Janov, together with two priests of the same way of thinking, was compelled at the synod to recant in public his views concerning the worship of the saints, their relics and pictures, and the frequent receiving of the Holy Eucharist. He recanted, of course, unwillingly, nor did he give up his views afterwards. But he soon died, leaving a great Latin work entitled *De regulis veteris et novi testamenti*. This work makes a comparison between true and false Christianity and contains a severe criticism of the Church and its abuses at that time; later, in the time of John Hus, by reason of its explanation of the need for frequent Communion, it provided the impulse for the introduction of the habit of receiving the Eucharist in both kinds.

The movement of reform aroused by the work of Milíč continued to live amongst the common people even after his death. The proof of this may be seen in the predilection of the people of Prague for sermons dealing with the need for moral improvement. It was for this reason that the Bethlehem Chapel was founded in the year 1391. Its founders, a knight and a burgher, imposed on the administrators of this chapel the duty of preaching in Czech twice on every feast day, and it was certainly their intention that the preaching should be in the spirit of Milíč. This, however, was only completely fulfilled a few years later when in 1402 the Bethlehem Chapel was placed under the charge of John Hus.

This moral and intellectual movement arose and developed outside the Prague University, which was the highest cultural institution of the Bohemian State. The international character and special purpose of the university did not allow it to influence directly the moral and spiritual life of the country. Nevertheless, the university could not remain entirely shut off from the questions and problems of the day in Bohemia. Several of the foreigners who taught at the University of Prague were famous as writers and preachers of a reforming tendency. The celebrated Heidelberg professor, Nicholaus Magni de Javor, a Silesian, who was in Prague during the years 1378–1402, not only wrote there religious works of a reforming character, but was also the German preacher in the church where Waldhauser used to preach. In the years 1365–90 there lived in Prague the celebrated Matthias of Cracow, who is generally recognised as the author of two famous works, *Speculum aureum de titulis beneficiorum* and *De squaloribus curiae Romanae*, in which he criticises with extraordinary sharpness the system of Church administration adopted by the Curia. Albert Engelschalk of Straubing, who is considered by some to be the author of the first of these works, lectured at the University of Prague in the years 1373–1402. The two works in question were only finished after the departure of these two scholars from Bohemia, but it seems that their origin was in Prague.

Although it is difficult to imagine that the activities of these men produced no effect upon their environment in Prague, it is impossible to ascertain their direct connexion with the Bohemian religious movement. A direct connexion between this movement and the University of Prague was only formed when the foreign and mainly German element at that institution (at the beginning the foreigners formed the absolute majority) began to give way before the Czech element. This was brought about partly by the gradual departure of the foreign professors and students to other universities which were established in Central Europe during the years following the foundation of Prague University (the Universities of Cracow, Vienna, Heidelberg, Cologne, and Erfurt), and partly by the natural development of learning in the Czech nation. From the steady

strengthening of the Czech element at the university, and from its growing national consciousness, there naturally arose the endeavour to provide
the Czech masters of arts with a greater degree of influence over the
administration of the university and with a larger share of its income than
they had received at its foundation. Hence arose the conflicts between the
Bohemian "nation" and the other three "nations" at the university. For
example, a dispute arose in the year 1384 over the places in the university
colleges of the Emperor Charles IV and King Wenceslas IV. In order
to settle the dispute, it was decided to grant the Czech masters of arts
five places out of six in each of the two colleges, the sixth being reserved
for the foreign masters of arts. In the succeeding years the Czech influence at the university became still stronger. There was an increase in the
number of Czech professors, and their influence over the administration of the
university grew in consequence of the fact that more and more of the higher
offices within it were given to Czechs. At the beginning of the fifteenth
century the number of Czech masters of arts at the University of Prague
was only a little lower than that of the foreign masters, while in the most
important Faculty, Theology, the Czech masters were now beginning to
form the majority.

It was just at this time that a confidential relationship developed
between the university and the Bohemian movement of reform. The
connecting link in this relationship was John Hus. A special chapter
will be devoted to this great figure of Bohemian history in the next
volume of this work. There, in due connexion with historical events in
Bohemia, a detailed account will be given of his great conflict with the
Church of Rome, a conflict which brought him in 1415 to a martyr's
death at the stake at Constance. Here it is sufficient to say that King
Wenceslas, who survived Hus by four years, lived to see the beginnings of the
great struggle which the Czech nation was preparing to wage in memory
of Hus against almost the whole of Christendom. The king's death was
accelerated by the first revolutionary outbursts that accompanied this
decision by the Czech people. Excited by the news of the violent treatment meted out by the riotous crowd to the Prague councillors who
opposed the ideas of Hus, the king had an apoplectic seizure to which he
succumbed on 16 August 1419.

CHAPTER VII

THE SWISS CONFEDERATION IN THE MIDDLE AGES

THE Swiss Confederation was the product of that tendency towards co-operation which, with varying success, inspired the medieval communes of all lands. The league formed by the co-operation of several small districts succeeded in preserving local autonomy from the destruction which else-where followed the establishment of a central and unified power in the heart of a great nation; while, at the same time, it awakened in the members of the league a new sentiment of solidarity capable of giving birth to a real State. This principle of union in diversity, of cohesion in independence, has become the modern idea of "federalism"; thanks to the common interest which united them, populations of varying origin and different tongues became members of a single nation.

The history of the territory which now composes Switzerland can be traced back to a very ancient civilisation; vestiges of human habitations dating from the Stone Age have been found, and the palafittes prove that there were extensive lacustrine settlements. The Roman conquest assimilated the natives, whether of Celtic or Ligurian origin, on both slopes of the Alps: the Helvetii who, driven southwards by the Germans, crossed the Rhine and reached the plateau and the valleys between the Alps and the Jura, but were stopped by the Rhone, where Geneva, the chief city of the Allobroges, commanded the way across the river; the Rhaeti, who occupied the upper valley of the Rhine and the mountains of the Grisons; and, finally, on the southern slope of the Alps, the Lepontii of the Ticino valley. The subjugation of the Helvetii, which was begun in 58 B.C. by Caesar's first expedition into Gaul, was accomplished before the Christian era, and Roman civilisation advanced, under the protection of the *limes*, eastward into Rhaetia, westward as far as the Valais, and even into the heart of the country, in the mountainous region of Lake Lucerne, as also along the routes of the Oberalp and the Furka Pass.

In the third century this country, intersected by fine Roman roads, became a frontier land shielding Italy from the German barbarians; the fortifications on the Rhine prevented invasions, but when they were no longer defended by Roman garrisons, the Germans in their turn oc-cupied the Alpine provinces, and either shared the land with the former Helvetio-Roman proprietors or else colonised districts hitherto sparsely populated.

The Burgundians, the first of whom had arrived from the south, by way of Sapaudia (Savoy), in 452, had by the end of the century advanced to the Valais, to Avenches, and even to the river Reuss and the neighbourhood of Basle. The Alemanni had often crossed the river in their marauding expeditions; early in the sixth century they checked the advance of the Burgundians and drove them back to the Aar; with a steady pressure they pushed up the valleys to the snow-covered Alps; they advanced into Rhaetia and left to the Roman population only a constantly diminishing territory. Finally, in 569, the Lombards made their appearance on the southern slope of the Alps.

This expansion of the Alemanni from the Rhine to the summit of the Alps, on the Swiss plateau, was the work of centuries. But by the end of the sixth century, the territory formerly held by the Helvetii and the Rhaeti had become divided into regions of varying culture, according to the degree in which Roman civilisation had survived or succumbed to the new settlement.

In the Burgundian sphere, the German colonists adopted the language of the Roman provincials and their institutions respected Latin civilisation. Burgundian Switzerland became Romance Switzerland. The Alemanni, more barbarous and still pagans, effaced all traces of the Roman conquest in country districts; in a few urban centres only, the old Christian communities still survived; and even when Alemannic Switzerland had been converted to Christianity, the impress of the recent conquerors remained apparent; it became German Switzerland.

To the east, Chur-Rhaetia, which was in contact with Lombard Italy, preserved her Roman institutions and language; although she was encroached on in the north by the advance of the Alemanni, her ancient traditions were saved from destruction by the protection of her lofty mountains and the convolutions of her high valleys.

The domination of the Merovingian and Carolingian Frankish kings hardly modified the state of affairs caused by the Germanic invasions. Although the name of the Burgundians, or Burgundy, was revived in a new independent kingdom between 888 and 1033, it was no solid and homogeneous State which established itself astride the Jura from Provence to the Rhine. The duchy of Alemannia, which had been destroyed about 748, re-appeared in the tenth century and, under the name of the duchy of Swabia, included the Alemanni on both banks of the Rhine. In 1033 the new Germanic Empire included all the region of the Alps, Transjurane Burgundy, the Valais, Alemannia, Rhaetia, and the Lepontine valleys of Italy; the linguistic frontiers still remained, but the Empire brought fresh bonds to unite regions of diverse civilisation; thus, under the Salic Emperors, the temporary institution of a Rectorate of Burgundy established direct contact between the duchy of Swabia and the kingdom of Burgundy.

It was on the frontiers of Alemannia and Burgundy, where the two languages met, that the first consolidation of seignories and feudal powers was attempted by the house of Zähringen in the twelfth century. Having inherited large estates between the Rhine and the Lake of Geneva, the Zähringen endeavoured to transform their rectorate into a permanent power; westward they encountered the growing influence of the Counts of Savoy, and, to counteract the hostility of secular and ecclesiastical lords, they founded towns, Fribourg and Berne. But in 1218 their line died out, the rectorate of Burgundy reverted to the Empire, and no new power again intervened between the Emperor and the cities or dynasts who were his immediate subjects.

The progress of feudalism occasioned an ever more marked subdivision of authority as well as the gradual disappearance of the class of freemen. The Kiburgs, heirs to the Zähringen, engaged in struggles with the urban communities of Berne and Morat, as well as with Peter II of Savoy. The Savoyard power penetrated as far as Alemannia; it was, however, checked at the Aar, and did not succeed in emulating the example of the Zähringen between the Alps and the Rhine. That achievement was reserved for the Habsburgs, heirs to the Lenzburgs, counts of Zurichgau and landgraves in Thurgau; in the days of Count Rudolf III, they seized the land of the Kiburgs and contested with Savoy the possession of the territories and ecclesiastical advocacies on the left bank of the Aar.

After the death of Peter II of Savoy in 1268, Rudolf of Habsburg obtained Fribourg, and forced Berne to perform its duties to the Empire. In 1278 he secured for his sons wide lands to the east: Austria, Styria, and, temporarily, Carinthia and Carniola. In central and north-eastern Switzerland from the Üchtland to Thurgau, from the Rhine to the shores of Lake Lucerne and as far as Urseren, he took possession of fiefs and advocacies, rights and jurisdictions, on a thousand different pretexts; when he was elected king in 1273, he established throughout his domains a uniform administration and a burdensome system of taxation. When he died at Spires on 15 July 1291, everything seemed to point to the definite consolidation of the feudal rights of the Habsburgs into a strong territorial power on the northern slope of the Alps, reaching beyond the Jura in the west, and beyond the Sarine on the borders of the Savoyard lands to the south-east.

Resistance to the establishment of this monarchical and centralised State did not originate among the rich burgesses or urban centres of Zurich, Basle, or St Gall. It was peasant communities who first united in defence of the local liberties threatened by the Habsburgs. Here, as elsewhere in the Empire in the thirteenth century, the class of small free land-holders had become much impoverished and had dwindled in number; it had nevertheless survived in various proportions on the soil of the Waldstaetten, or Forest Cantons washed by the Lake of Lucerne. The freemen subject to the count's jurisdiction followed him to war; they assembled, as in the *centena* or hundred-court, to exercise petty justice. Beside them were other classes of the population, of various conditions: nobles, "*ministeriales*" (ennobled by their office) who were often recruited from the ranks of the serfs, the tenants on monastic domains whose personal rights lessened their original serfdom, and men who were protected by some ecclesiastical or secular lord.

The three Forest Cantons differed not only in their geographical position, but also in the distribution of social conditions and feudal tenures.

Uri consisted of the valley of the Reuss, from the end of Lake Lucerne to the foot of the St Gothard. The upper valley of Urseren formed no part of it, but belonged to the Rhaetian abbey of Disentis. Even in the days of the Romans, Urseren was in communication with Valais by the Furka Pass, and with Chur-Rhaetia by the Oberalp; the road to Ticino was open; but throughout long centuries Urseren and Uri were sundered by the impenetrable gorges of Schollenen; the road to the St Gothard was not open in this direction until a bridge had been constructed along the face of the rock, and this was not done until a comparatively late period, although, according to recent researches, it took place before 1140. The district of Uri, which led to the St Gothard, thus became a place of much resort, and a strategic point on one of the best roads between Italy and Germany; and the Emperors attached great importance to its possession. In 835 the valley belonged to the abbey of Fraumünster in Zurich; the Counts of Rapperswil, the barons of Attinghausen, and the monastery of Wettingen participated in the seignorial rights; but the freemen formed an economic association, the "Markgenossenschaft," for the exploitation of the common pastures, or "Allmende"; and their neighbours, the men of Fraumünster, had almost attained personal liberty.

The policy of the Emperors, even in the thirteenth century, displayed a tendency to conciliate Uri; on 26 May 1231 King Henry of Germany, who was administering the country beyond the Alps in the absence of his father Frederick II, emancipated the people of Uri from the authority of the Count of Habsburg; he promised that they should never be alienated from the Empire, and took them under his protection. The whole valley was thus constituted imperial territory. The "Markgenossenschaft" corresponded to a single legal and administrative division, and prepared the way for the political transformation of the country. The *ammann*, or "free judge," became the *landamann*, the leader of the community, whose members met in a *landsgemeinde*.

Originally the district of Schwyz only extended from the foot of the Mythen, or Rigi, to the valley of the Muota. The Habsburgs as heirs of the Lenzburgs exercised the higher justice; the monasteries of Einsiedeln, Cappel, Muri, Schännis, and Engelberg, shared the land with them; but the characteristic feature of Schwyz was the preponderance of freemen, who formed two-thirds of the population, and the association of freemen and serfs in a single "Markgenossenschaft." The natives of Schwyz were hemmed in by their lofty mountains; in the twelfth century they cleared the northern slopes of the Mythen and thus came into violent conflict with the abbey of Einsiedeln. In the thirteenth century, the abolition of serfdom by the Habsburgs encouraged the fusion of social classes; and the agricultural association betrayed an increasing tendency towards the formation of an established political assembly.

At Unterwalden (*Inter Silvas*) the freemen had originally a single tribunal, one centre of jurisdiction for the whole district, but they were in a minority of perhaps a third of the population; local interests predominated, and the two valleys Ob and Unter dem Kernwald (Obwald with Sarnen, Nidwald with Stanz) no longer maintained their former cohesion. The feudal rights and landed properties were in the hands of petty local nobles, and especially in those of the monasteries of Engelberg, Muri, Murbach, Lucerne, and Beromünster; the freemen were subject to the courts of the Habsburgs, who were moreover the advocates of the various monasteries, except Engelberg. In Unterwalden there are no traces of a "Markgenossenschaft."

In 1231 the opening of the road across the St Gothard had brought about the recognition of Uri as territory under the direct control of the Empire. The Hohenstaufen strove everywhere to command the passes across the Alps; when the Emperor Frederick II was excommunicated in 1239 he was unable to control as he wished the Guelf bishoprics of Chur and the Valais; the St Gothard remained his only way to Italy; he retained Leventina for the Empire and converted Urseren into an imperial *vogtland*; in 1231 he became master of Uri. Schwyz and Unterwalden mark farther stages on the same road. Thus the three Forest Cantons assumed a place in the foreground of imperial policy; and the struggle with the Papacy conferred on them an equally great strategic importance. Meanwhile the road across the St Gothard brought them into contact with the outer world by the continual succession of merchants and knights, convoys and soldiers, who passed to and fro.

This outer world was agitated by the new ideas resulting from the revolution of the communes; to the north in France, in Flanders, and on the Rhine, and to the south in Italy, the towns were fighting for the maintenance of their privileges. On the southern slope of the Alps communal emancipation had reached the country districts; the "communes" in the valleys and villages of the Ticino were resisting feudal rights; they were shaking off serfdom, they administered freely the "Allmende" and seized on the lower jurisdiction. There, as among the Forest Cantons. the original organisation was that of the "Markgenossenschaft"; in the thirteenth century it became a political autonomy and gave birth to a peasant commune. This gradual emancipation, legal and economic, of the Milanese valleys of the Ticino, their struggles against feudalism with the help of men from the northern side of the Alps—all this contest, alike local and heroic, was not without influence on the thoughts and actions of the men of the Forest Cantons.

Finally, the sense of political union between the three valleys received great encouragement from the very formula which first expressed it—the legal act of an oath. The coalition so common in the Middle Ages in Italy, in France, and in Flanders, under the form of the *conspiratio*, or *coniuratio*, united, at first personally, by a common act, the inhabitants of the Forest Cantons; then, under the stress of the conflict, this oath became an alliance of communes, and, later, a real Confederation, the "Eidgenossenschaft."

At first the Forest Cantons relied on the Empire to support them in their resistance to the claims of the Habsburgs. Rudolf of Habsburg, nicknamed the Silent, had sided with the Holy See, whereupon the natives of Schwyz addressed their petitions to the Emperor Frederick II; on 20 December 1240 they obtained from him in his camp outside Faenza a charter guaranteeing their position as freemen directly subject to the Empire. From documents we surmise that in the years 1239 and 1240 there was armed resistance by Schwyz and Unterwalden to the agents of the Habsburgs; the Ghibelline League spread to the Romance districts, Estavayer and Fribourg, and to Berne and Morat. In the Forest Cantons the pact of 1291 refers to an *antiqua confederatio*, which was an alliance of a personal character under the form of an oath; for the maintenance of public peace the men of Schwyz, Unterwalden, and Uri undertook to supply each other with mutual help, and also jointly admitted the elements of a common local law. This alliance, of which the probable date is 1240[1] or thereabouts, also included Lucerne.

In 1252 the Habsburgs were again masters of Schwyz and Unterwalden; Rudolf the Silent was reconciled with the Emperor, and Lucerne had already submitted in 1244. In 1249 Como was gained by the papal party, and, when Frederick II died in 1250, the St Gothard was lost to the Empire. The accession of Rudolf of Habsburg, of the elder branch, to the imperial throne on 24 October 1273 reversed the situation; the immediate dependency of Uri on the Empire was not contested, but in 1274 the court at Nuremberg revoked the charter enfranchising Schwyz. In 1283 Rudolf, having acquired the possessions of the Kiburgs and Laufenburgs and the city of Lucerne, bestowed on his sons the imperial advocacy of Urseren. Thus Schwyz and Uri could no longer oppose the advocacy of the Empire to the rights of the count. Under Rudolf they indeed enjoyed a position similar to that which they had acquired by immediate dependence on the Empire, and the fiscal policy of the Habsburgs encouraged the union of their subjects of every category; but the incorporation of the three valleys into a solid State, though still under the Austrian government and administration, was inevitably in process of development, in spite of the military assistance lent by the men of Schwyz to Rudolf at the siege of Besançon in 1289, in return for which he guaranteed to them anew that they should remain independent of any outside tribunal.

[1] Recently Professor K. Meyer has placed this alliance in 1288.

It is therefore not surprising that when Rudolf died at Spires on 15 July 1291 a movement of resistance began among the inhabitants of the Forest Cantons. Possibly the conspirators planned their action against the house of Habsburg in secret conferences which took place on the shores of the Lake of Lucerne, especially in the meadow of Grütli; in any case, the decisive step was taken at the beginning of August: Uri, Schwyz, and Nidwald revived the former *Confederatio* in a new alliance.

The federal pact of 1291 is the historical foundation of the Confederation. It constituted an alliance for the maintenance of public peace solemnly consecrated by the oath of the contracting parties; although it had originally been purely personal, in 1291 this oath tended to include the whole of the three cantons, just as the agricultural and legal associations were approximating to real political organisms. The three cantons guaranteed mutual help and succour against any aggressor from without or any fomenter of trouble from within; difficulties which might arise between the contracting parties were to be settled by arbitration; seignorial courts of justice were recognised, but no judge was to be accepted who had bought his office with gold, or who was not a native of the valley; and detailed regulations provided for the apprehension and punishment of any criminals amongst the Confederates, and for the execution of sentences. The prohibition of outside judges seems to have been aimed at the appointment of Austrian officials; furthermore, resistance to Austria is proved by the conclusion on 16 October 1291 of an offensive and defensive alliance which for three years bound Uri and Schwyz to Zurich. Zurich, an imperial town, combined with Constance, Lucerne, and the Swabian and Burgundian princes in the movement which opposed the claims of Albert of Habsburg, Rudolf's son, over the territory between the Alps and the Jura; while the Forest Cantons supported the revolt of the men of Leventina against Milan, and thus sought to regain free passage across the Alps.

In 1292 Albert defeated the coalition, but vainly laid siege to Zurich; and Lucerne, having fallen into Austrian hands, closed her markets to the Forest Cantons. But the three valleys were not discouraged: the liberty of Schwyz was re-affirmed by the *Landrecht* of 1294, while about the same time Obwald and Nidwald amalgamated, thus restoring their former community of origin. In 1297 the new German King, Adolf of Nassau, renewed to Uri and Schwyz the exemption granted to Schwyz by Frederick II; but when he died at Göllheim on 2 July 1298, the Empire passed to his rival, Albert of Austria, son of Rudolf of Habsburg.

During the reign of Albert of Austria, Rudolf's strict methods of government were revived in the Forest Cantons, which were restored to order in 1299; the imperial privileges were not confirmed, but there is no proof that the Austrian bailiffs were as tyrannical as has been depicted in legend. Albert endeavoured to encourage traffic by the St Gothard and levied heavy taxes on the country. But matters were abruptly altered when he was murdered by his nephew, John of Swabia, on 1 May 1308. The new Emperor, Henry VII of Luxemburg, had no objection to the renewal of the immediate dependency of Uri on the Empire (3 June 1309), as also of the charters of Frederick II and Adolf of Nassau in favour of Schwyz; he went even farther, confirming Unterwalden in liberties which had never yet rested on any written charter. The three cantons were freed from all external jurisdiction except the imperial courts of law, and were converted into an independent bailiwick; the office of imperial advocate of the bailiwick was entrusted to Count Werner of Homburg, and was shortly extended to Leventina. The St Gothard still remained the centre of this administrative and political district. But the Austrian Dukes did not acknowledge their defeat; and in 1311 they obtained the promise of an impartial enquiry into their claims.

The interregnum which followed Henry VII's death in 1313 was skilfully employed by the Forest Cantons. The violent measures to which they resorted can hardly be justified as a mere defence of their rights: on the night of 6 January 1314 the men of Schwyz pillaged the monastery of Einsiedeln, with which they had an old quarrel about Alpine pastures; elsewhere, the Confederates constructed entrenchments of stone and earth, called *letzi*, at vulnerable points on their frontiers; and they supported Lewis of Bavaria in his struggle for the imperial crown with Frederick the Handsome, Duke of Austria and son of Albert. Ere long Austria subjugated all the region round Zurich, Berne, Glarus, the Bernese Oberland, and Lucerne, which closed its markets to the Forest Cantons. Frederick's brother, Duke Leopold of Austria, considered this a favourable opportunity for conquering these rebellious peasants; having assembled a mighty army of knights and footmen at Zug, he attempted the invasion of the country by the pass of Morgarten, beside the Lake of Egeri, while Count Otto of Strassberg invaded Obwald by the Brünig Pass, and the men of Lucerne landed in Nidwald. On 15 November 1315 the brilliant Austrian column was held up in the narrow pass of Morgarten, on the frontier of Schwyz; attacked on flank and front by the men of Schwyz and Uri, the Austrian knights were put to flight, the footmen driven back or cast into the lake. Duke Leopold hastily fled, leaving on the field of battle between 1500 and 2000 men, the flower of his nobility; the very tidings of his defeat caused the Count of Strassberg to retire, and delivered Unterwalden from all fear of invasion.

This overwhelming victory of the Forest Cantons proved the superiority of the Swiss infantry armed with halberds over the heavy feudal cavalry; but its immediate result was the confirmation of the alliance between the three cantons. On 9 December 1315 the new pact of Brunnen accentuated the transformation of a sworn union between private individuals into a union of States, as also its federal character; it was aimed at Austria, as it provided for a refusal of obedience to any lord who might attack any one of the three contracting parties, and it also prohibited any foreign alliance without the permission of the confederates.

The fact that King Lewis of Bavaria in 1316 transferred to the Empire the rights and subjects of Austria in the Forest Cantons, and confirmed the liberties of Uri and Unterwalden on the same footing as those of Schwyz, accentuates the legal emancipation of the three valleys after the victory. And when, on 1 March 1317, a native of Uri was appointed imperial bailiff of Leventina and Urseren, King Lewis rendered Uri secure in the possession of the St Gothard; the pass was open, and the blockade which threatened the victors of Morgarten became impossible. Duke Leopold, prevented from organising a punitive expedition by reasons resulting from the policy pursued elsewhere by the house of Austria, was obliged to conclude a truce with the Forest Cantons on 19 July 1318: the frontiers were thrown open to trade; the Austrian Dukes recovered only the feudal rights which they had enjoyed in the days of the Emperor Henry; in fact the Confederates now formed independent circumscriptions within the Empire.

The alliance of the Forest Cantons soon distinguished itself from the other coalitions of the German Empire by its capacity for gaining new adherents. After the death of Frederick the Handsome in 1330, Lewis of Bavaria became reconciled with the Habsburgs, and prepared to restore their comital rights in the three valleys and to annul the privileges granted to their detriment. The Forest Cantons realised their danger; they therefore sought new allies. Their natural market, easily accessible by the lake, was the town of Lucerne, which also desired to protect itself from Austrian despotism. The town, which had been ceded to King Rudolf of Habsburg by the abbey of Murbach, formed a sworn community, constantly in conflict with the Austrian bailiff at Rotenburg. On 7 November 1332 the burgomaster, the council, and the burgesses of Lucerne concluded a perpetual alliance with the peasants of Uri, Schwyz, and Unterwalden; the rights of the overlord were reserved, but the contracting parties promised mutual assistance in case of danger and resort to arbitration in the settlement of differences, and prohibited the formation of alliances without each other's knowledge. This first treaty involved the men of Lucerne in hostilities which did not always result in their favour; an arbitrator's award on 18 June 1336 annulled the alliances concluded by the burgesses, but could not definitely put an end to the union of 1332. Tradition has preserved the memory of an Austrian plot which was discovered and suppressed in 1343; this at least proves the victorious progress of the federal policy.

During the course of the thirteenth century the town of Zurich had reached a high pitch of development and prosperity. As the metropolis of the silk industry, and a town alike commercial and intellectual, it enjoyed an advanced state of self-government with regard to the imperial advocate, the chapter of canons of Grossmünster, and the nunnery of Fraumünster; but after a temporary alliance with the Forest Cantons in 1291, it had been forced to submit owing to defeat at Winterthur, and to remain faithful to Austria. It was an internal revolution which drove it to join the Confederates.

A knight, Rudolf Brun, having overthrown the old council, on 16 July 1336 promulgated a sworn declaration which, after the model of that of Strasbourg, gave the artisans a share in the government; having been proclaimed burgomaster for life, he sought to obtain support for his policy from the Forest Cantons. On 1 May 1351 Zurich concluded a perpetual alliance with Lucerne, Uri, Schwyz, and Unterwalden: the town was to remain free to contract other engagements of the same sort, but the new alliance was to have preference over all others; public peace was to be assured throughout a wide region, from the course of the Aar to that of the Thur, from the Rhine to the Alps, so that the trade routes remained free; and the assistance promised mutually by the allies referred not only to defensive but to offensive measures. The devastation of the March by Brun's troops and the encroachments of the Confederates on the rights of Austria determined Duke Albert to settle accounts with his old adversaries. The first siege of Zurich in 1351 led to the opening of peace negotiations, but the duke having been summoned to Vienna by his wife's death, the Confederates took the offensive, after having refused to submit to the arbitration of Queen Agnes of Hungary.

The district of Glarus, with the upper valley of the Linth, belonged to the nunnery of Säckingen; about 1264 Rudolf of Habsburg inherited its advocacy, and King Albert united Glarus in a single bailiwick with the districts of Gaster and Wesen. In 1351 the men of Zurich and their allies occupied the valley, whose inhabitants appeared favourable to the Confederates; on 2 February 1352 the men of Glarus repulsed an Austrian army at Näfels, and on 4 June they concluded a perpetual alliance with Zurich and the three Forest Cantons. In this new pact, Glarus was placed in a slightly inferior position, inasmuch as it was bound to assist the Confederates in all their wars, and was not allowed to conclude any alliance without the assent of Zurich and the Forest Cantons; while, on the other hand, the latter were only bound to assist it under certain conditions.

On 27 June 1352, Zurich, Lucerne, and the three Forest Cantons contracted an alliance similar to the pact of Zurich with the council and burgesses of Zug and the people of that bailiwick. On 23 June they had taken the town after a fortnight's siege. The territory of Zug possessed, for them, great importance, as it established a link between the Forest Cantons and Zurich; Austrian rights were reserved in the alliance, but even so the position of Zug appeared superior to that of Glarus. The large army assembled by Duke Albert of Austria in the same year

(1352) was not homogeneous enough to storm Zurich; and, by the mediation of the Margrave Lewis of Brandenburg, peace with Austria was concluded on 14 September 1352. Austria retained numerous advantages: Lucerne promised her obedience; Schwyz and Unterwalden renounced their attempts to hinder the exercise of feudal rights within their territory; Lucerne and Zurich surrendered the Austrian subjects who had been made burgesses without domicile. Zurich became reconciled with the nobles of her district; but while Glarus and Zug were excluded from the alliance of the Confederates, the alliance with Lucerne was recognised.

After the extinction of her founders, the Zähringen, Berne had become a free imperial city, and, during the fourteenth century, had acquired very appreciable autonomous and territorial powers; by means of agreements and conquests, she had established herself at Laupen, Gümmenen, in the Häsli, and in the upper valley of the Aar, which formed an independent rural community contiguous with Unterwalden. The whole basin of the Aar up to the Alps had thus become dependent on Berne, and the local nobility was perturbed at the surprising growth of its power. Resistance was soon offered by Fribourg, Berne's rival, and involved the nobles of the Swiss plateau, from Gruyères to Neuchâtel, from the Kiburgs to the Bishop of Basle. This coalition collected a formidable army which laid siege to the stronghold of Laupen. But on 21 June 1339 the Bernese troops, reinforced by men from the Forest Cantons, Häsli, and Simmenthal, won an overwhelming victory near Laupen itself. Mistress of her fate, Berne obliged Fribourg again to recognise her alliance and renewed that which had bound Solothurn; in 1342 she came to terms with Austria, but retained her freedom to remain at peace with the enemies of the Habsburgs.

The earliest alliances of Berne with the Forest Cantons date from 1323 and 1341. Fearing the too democratic influence of Unterwalden on her territory of Häsli, after the victory of Laupen the city decided to conclude a pact of eternal alliance with Uri, Schwyz, and Unterwalden at Lucerne, on 6 March 1353. Its alliance with Austria prevented Berne from treating with Zurich or Lucerne, and from promising military aid to the Forest Cantons against the Habsburgs; a call for help was not to take effect until after the decisions of a Diet to be assembled at Kienholz near the Lake of Brienz; but the Confederates were bound to answer this appeal against any who might injure or attack, not only the Bernese themselves, but also their subjects or vassals.

The future of Zurich was not so quickly decided. In 1354, to escape the assault of an army which included contingents from the Emperor Charles IV as well as those of the Habsburgs, the town hoisted the imperial standard, intending thus to shew its direct dependence on the Empire. The peace of Ratisbon in 1355 gave, as a whole, satisfaction to Austrian demands. Zurich had to relinquish its conquests; the federal alliances were only maintained when they did not interfere with the

fulfilment of the engagements made by the city. The death of the
burgomaster, Rudolf Brun, in 1360, at the moment when he had succumbed to Austrian influence, brought about a change of attitude on the
part of Zurich which coincided with a state of tension between the Empire
and the house of Austria; on 31 March 1361 the Emperor Charles IV
confirmed to Schwyz, Uri, and Unterwalden all their new privileges,
especially those which concerned the lake. In 1365, 1367, and 1368, the
town refused to take the oath of fidelity to Austria which had been agreed
on in the renewed peace of Ratisbon. Then in 1364 or 1365 Uri, Schwyz,
and Unterwalden conquered the town and suburbs of Zug; they
governed this little district while agreeing to pay Austria her dues; and
in 1368 a general war was only averted by the truce of the knight
Peter of Torberg on 7 March, by which Austria relinquished Zug to the
Confederates.

These incessant struggles had tested the pacts of alliance between the
Confederates; their union emerged therefrom strengthened. In itself this
unequal league of country districts and towns did not differ essentially
from the associations which had elsewhere been called into being by the
insecurity of the Empire; each member of the league retained its liberty
of action, and the Austrian party possessed powerful adherents, especially
in Zurich. But the three Forest Cantons, since they were the only
participants in the Confederation who were allied to all its members,
represented a principle of unity, a power of co-ordination which may
vainly be sought for among other organisms of the same kind; Uri, Schwyz,
and Unterwalden were resolute adversaries of Austria, they possessed a
formidable warlike force, and, from the middle of the fourteenth century,
the name of Schwyz began to be applied to the whole Confederation.

In 1370 a concordat of great importance united the six cantons, with
the exception of Berne; this was the *Pfaffenbrief*, or Priests' Charter,
which was drawn up on 7 October 1370 as a result of the violent measures
taken by the clergy in opposition to the advocate of Lucerne. The *Pfaffenbrief* may be regarded as establishing a common public law among the
members of what it definitely styles "our Confederation": it imposed
various punishments on priests who dared to cite the Confederates before
foreign courts of law; above all, it obliged anyone inhabiting the territory
of the Confederates to work for the advantage of the allies, even though
he remained an Austrian subject. Moreover the Confederates undertook
to protect all the roads from the "stibende Brug" of the St Gothard as
far as Zurich.

The truce of Torberg remained precarious. In 1375, however, Duke
Leopold III of Austria was himself obliged to seek assistance from the
Confederates in repelling the incursions of French and English freebooters
known by the name of *Gugler*, whom Enguerrand de Coucy had launched
against the Austrian states in support of his claims to the inheritance
of his grandfather, Duke Leopold I of Austria. Only Berne and Zurich

consented on 13 October to the conclusion of a defensive alliance with Leopold. De Coucy's bands having advanced as far as Lower Aargau, the men of that district took up arms and expelled the pillagers by a series of victorious engagements at Büttisholz, at Ins, and, finally, during the night of 26 December, at Fraubrünnen, where the Bernese behaved gallantly. In the spring of 1376 Enguerrand de Coucy retreated by way of the Jura, but the duke's inaction before this danger and the systematic devastation of Aargau caused profound resentment against the Habsburgs throughout the countryside; nevertheless, on 28 March 1376, the truce of Torberg was prolonged until 23 April 1387.

It was about this time that the decline of the house of Kiburg caused an increase in the power of Berne. On the night of 10 November 1382, to rid himself of his numerous law-suits, Count Rudolf of Kiburg attempted a surprise attack on Solothurn; the Bernese, who were Solothurn's allies, called for help from the Forest Cantons under the terms of the treaty of 6 March 1353; thanks to their intervention, the Kiburgs were forced to surrender Burgdorf and Thun to Berne. Their house became extinct in 1417; but this final conflict damaged the cause of Austria, inasmuch as it strengthened the union between Berne and the Forest Cantons.

The Habsburgs had not been able to intervene in the quarrel between Berne and the Kiburgs; but the ambition of the young Duke Leopold III soon led to a new war. When, in 1379, Albert III received as his share Austria proper, Leopold inherited Styria, Carinthia, and Carniola, as far as the Italian frontier, from his brother Rudolf IV; he very soon also asserted his authority over Rhaetia, and even beyond, by the acquisition of the county of Feldkirch, the domains of Nidau, Büren, and Little Basle, and the advocateship of Upper and Lower Swabia. The first resistance came from a union of Swabian and Rhenish towns, which was joined on 21 February 1385 at Constance by Berne, Zurich, Zug, and Solothurn. But the final rupture was caused by the action of Lucerne, which continued to admit numerous burgesses who were Austrian subjects. On 28 December the men of Lucerne seized the Austrian stronghold of Rotenburg; then, in the spring of 1386, with the help of the Forest Cantons, they destroyed the castle of Peter of Torberg at Wolhusen, and freed the whole of Entlebuch up to Escholzmatt from the Austrian domination. The Confederates did not follow the Swabian towns in concluding a truce with Austria on 17 July 1386; they seceded from the Swabian league, trusting to their own powers to defend the interests of their cause.

Berne was exhausted by the war with the Kiburgs, and did not seem anxious to fulfil the obligations undertaken in the alliance of 1353. But the men of Zurich, Glarus, and Schwyz deliberately started the campaign. The duke assembled a formidable army of mercenaries and knights at Brugg in Aargau; at the end of June 1386 he took and burnt Willisau, and on 9 July his army, under the command of John of Ochsenstein,

advanced on Sempach, a little town recently allied with Lucerne. At
Meierholz, north-eastward from Sempach, it encountered the fifteen
hundred men assembled under the banners of Lucerne, Uri, Schwyz, and
Unterwalden; some of the knights having dismounted, the Confederates
succeeded, after many efforts, in battering their way through the lances
by the blows of their halberds, thus spreading panic throughout the
Austrian army; the duke was slain during a charge, and the dismounted
knights were cut to pieces by the peasants. In the north, the men of
Zurich and Glarus took the offensive, seized Wesen, and on 11 August
the Bernese declared war on Fribourg. The imperial towns of Germany
succeeded in restoring peace, which was concluded on 12 October, and
renewed till 2 February 1388, with the adhesion of Berne and Solothurn.

Hostilities nevertheless continued in the district of Glarus, which had
recently revived the old alliance, and was freeing itself from its feudal
overlord, the monastery of Säckingen. After surprising Wesen, the army
of Duke Albert III, Duke Leopold's brother, on 9 April 1388 stormed
the entrenchments barricading the valley. The mountaineers, reinforced
by a contingent from Schwyz, stood firm on the heights to the south-west
of Näfels; then, falling on the enemy, they drove them back to the bridge
over the Maag, inflicting sanguinary losses. The victory of Näfels was
the signal for a fresh campaign by the Confederates, at Rapperswil in
Aargau, at Büren, and at Nidau, until by the mediation of the Swabian
towns the treaty of Zurich was initiated (1 April 1389), and ratified by
Duke Albert under the form of a truce which lasted until 23 April 1396.
The Confederates retained the castles and lands they had taken from
Austrian nobles, and the federal alliances were maintained.

The Confederates realised the necessity of strengthening their union
in view of the dangers which might recur at any moment; therefore on
10 July 1393 all the members of the league, with the addition of Solothurn, concluded the Covenant of Sempach. The *Sempacherbrief* settled
the military measures which were to be shared by the Confederates: it
established a strict discipline of the contingents, apportioned the booty,
and suppressed pillage; no military action was to be taken save in
defence of a just cause.

Even though all the Confederates had agreed to this new pact, all
hostile efforts could not at once be overcome, and the alliance was still
precarious. When, between 1393 and 1395, the two Dukes, Albert and
Leopold IV, united in a new series of treaties all the bishops, princes,
and cities of South Germany, the Austrian party, which was in a majority
in the council at Zurich, involved the city in this union, and on 4 July 1393
undertook that for twenty years Zurich should remain neutral in case of
a war with the Confederates. Envoys from Lucerne and Schwyz thereupon incited the burgesses to rise against the Austrian faction; Rudolf
Schorro, the burgomaster, was forced to leave the city; and a third sworn
declaration placed the supreme authority of the State in the hands of the

Grand Council, or Council of the Two Hundred, in which the gilds were dominant. This abortive attempt led to a fresh demonstration of union in the renewal of the alliances on 10 August 1393, and the attitude of the Confederates convinced the Austrian Dukes that it would be advisable to make peace with them. On 16 July 1394 a twenty years' peace was concluded: Glarus was recognised as an autonomous member of the Confederation; Zug was to pay only a modest tribute to her former overlord; Schwyz retained possession of the Upper March and the advocacy of Einsiedeln; Berne retained Unterseen, Nidau, and Büren; Lucerne was freed from its vassalage and secured Entlebuch, Sempach, and the bailiwick of Rotenburg; freedom of trade and arbitration were re-established; while the Confederates promised no longer to harbour burgesses not domiciled among them, and undertook not to molest the possessions of the house of Austria.

About the same time the league of the Rhine towns was dissolved; the Counts of Wurtemberg checked the development of the league between the towns on Lake Constance; north of the Rhine, the power of the princes triumphed. South of the river, on the contrary, country districts and towns retained their traditional rights, their local governments, and their democratic institutions; having consolidated their union, they were organising their forces to defend the liberties they had acquired in common, respecting only the suzerainty of the Empire.

Peace with Austria having been assured, the Confederates took advantage of their security to consolidate their territory and extend the system of their alliances. By gradual purchase Berne had extended her possessions on the right bank of the Bielersee, in the valleys of the Kander and the Simme, the districts of Signau, Wangen, and Aarwangen. Lucerne, a fortified town, established itself securely in Entlebuch, and also at Weggis and Gersau. Glarus repurchased the feudal rights of the monastery of Säckingen. New bonds of friendship sought to guarantee the maintenance of peace and the security of the trade routes. Alliances and treaties of *combourgeoisie* united Berne and Solothurn with the Margrave of Hochberg and the city of Basle; and Berne alone with the Counts of Aarberg-Valangin, the Counts of Gruyères, and the town of Fribourg.

Eastward, Zurich admitted the Count of Toggenburg as one of her burgesses. In Rhaetia, a land of lofty mountains, the league of Caddée (Maison-Dieu) in 1367 brought together the burgesses of Chur and the ecclesiastical subjects of Bregaglia, Oberhalbstein, the Engadine, and Domleschg. On 24 May 1400 the people of Glarus concluded their first alliance with the other Rhaetian league—the "Upper" or "Grey" League —which included the popular communities and nobles of the Upper Rhine valley, and also with the Abbot of Disentis, the barons of Raezuns and Sax, and their people.

On the southern slope of the lofty Bernese Alps, in the Valais, the Bishop of Sion, invested with the rights of count, had been obliged to yield the low country as far as the Morge to the Counts of Savoy. Many feudal landholders were hesitating between the two powers; in the fourteenth century the burgesses of Sion and the rural communes, or "dizains," elected a general council for the whole of the Valais; on 3 June 1403 Bishop William V de Rarogne and the peasants of the Valais, who had recently rebelled against the La Tour family but had been weakened in 1392 by a burdensome peace imposed by Savoy, concluded a *combourgeoisie* and perpetual alliance with Uri, Unterwalden, and Lucerne.

About this time there began the transalpine conquests of the Forest Cantons, notably those of Uri, which even before 1331 exercised the advocacy of Urseren. In 1403, as a result of certain incidents at the fair of Varese, a band of men from Uri and Unterwalden descended into the Leventina and forced the subjects of the Duke of Milan to swear obedience; the inhabitants of the Leventina entrusted themselves to the protection of the two cantons, who established a joint administration on the other side of the St Gothard. On 12 June 1410 the natives of Urseren were admitted as burgesses of Uri.

To the north-east, the city of St Gall had, by the middle of the fourteenth century, attained great material prosperity based on the textile industry and the cloth trade. It had been granted the rank of an imperial town, and the Council gradually emancipated itself from the tutelage of the abbey, which was falling into decadence; the trade-gilds were becoming political associations and shared in the government.

Not far from St Gall, the district of Appenzell, which derived its name from its largest commune, consisted of legal and political communities of a markedly democratic character, which in 1345 were placed under the imperial advocacy of the Abbot of St Gall. On 17 January 1401 the conflict with their advocate and overlord induced eight communities of Appenzell to enter into an alliance of seven years with the burgesses of St Gall. The mountaineers destroyed the abbatial fortress of the Clanx, then, abandoned by St Gall, they had recourse to the Forest Cantons; Schwyz admitted them to her citizenship early in 1403, and sent them a *landamann*. Relying on this support, the men of Appenzell, on 15 May 1403, repelled contingents from the towns of the Empire who opposed them at the defile of the Speicher. In 1405, with the help of the Count of Werdenberg-Heiligenberg, they defeated the troops of Duke Frederick IV of Austria, who had espoused the cause of the Abbot of St Gall; after victories near St Gall and at the Stoss, they instituted a campaign of singular violence against the feudal lords. The League of "Above the Lake" was joined by the burgesses of St Gall, Feldkirch, and Bludenz, and the peasants of Rheinthal, Walgau, and modern Lichtenstein; the expeditions of the mountaineers advanced as far as Thurgau, and beyond the Arlberg; Duke Frederick of Austria was obliged to come to terms with the League, and the Abbot of St Gall placed himself under its protection.

The dissolution of this ephemeral coalition was brought about by the failure of the siege of Bregenz and the resistance of Constance with the help of the Knights of the Cross. When King Rupert condemned them to return to the suzerainty of the Abbot of St Gall, the men of Appenzell, on 24 November 1411, obtained the *combourgeoisie* of the seven cantons of Zurich, Lucerne, Uri, Schwyz, Unterwalden, Zug, and Glarus. This first alliance did not ensure them complete equality of treatment; expeditions in their aid were carried out at their expense, and the consent of the cantons had to be obtained for the execution of any military operation. On 7 December 1412 the city of St Gall in its turn concluded a treaty of *combourgeoisie* for ten years with the seven easterly cantons, but without securing the armed support of the Confederates.

On the other side of the Alps the increasing strength of the Confederates continued to carry all before it. In 1407 Uri and Unterwalden obtained from the barons of Sax-Misox free admission to the fortresses of Bellinzona and exemption from customs for their goods; in 1410 a quarrel about Alpine pastures caused the occupation of the valley of Ossola, between the Ticino and Valais; but in 1414 Count Amadeus VIII of Savoy succeeded in wresting their latest conquest from the Confederates. It was King Sigismund who deterred the men of Uri from their intention of avenging this reverse; he had summoned to Constance for Christmas 1414 a great Council intended to restore peace to the Church and to end the Schism. At this time the Confederates were on more peaceful terms with Austria; but on 20 March 1415 Pope John XXIII abruptly retired from the Council and went to Schaffhausen to join Duke Frederick of Austria, who had espoused his cause. Sigismund promptly put the duke under the ban of the Empire on 30 March, and handed over his states to his vassals and enemies. In the course of a few weeks the duke lost his possessions from Alsace to the boundaries of Tyrol. Sigismund declared to the Swiss that they ought to obey the Emperor, in spite of the peace which bound them to Austria; he abolished the seignorial rights still possessed by the Habsburgs in the cantons, and confirmed the latter in their privileges.

Thus relieved from their just scruples, in April 1415 the Confederates proceeded to conquer Aargau, a district of pastures, full of castles and large market-towns. The Bernese, reinforced by men from Biel and Solothurn, advanced from the west; from the south and east came the men of Lucerne and Zurich, and strongholds and little towns quickly fell into their hands. Then the united Confederates laid siege to Baden; the Austrian bailiff resisted in the castle of Stein for a week after the surrender of the town; on 20 May the fortress was burnt. Meanwhile Frederick of Austria had made his peace with Sigismund, and the king summoned the Confederates to cease their operations and to restore Aargau. But they insisted on the assurances they had received, and, in spite of the slender justice of their claims, Sigismund had to accede to their wishes; he mortgaged some of the conquered territory to Berne, and yielded the rest to the men of Zurich in return for an indemnity. The final division did not take place until ten years later: Zurich retained the Freiamt to the east of the Reuss as her share; Lucerne obtained Sursee, Münster, and St Urban. The county of Baden and the rest of the Freiamt became a bailiwick under the joint jurisdiction of all the Confederates. Berne, however, had no share in the Freiamt, and Uri kept aloof from the conquered territory and insisted that it should be surrendered to the king. Thus the country which separated Zurich from Berne was now in the hands of the Confederates; instead of admitting the inhabitants of Aargau to their *combourgeoisie*, they treated them as subjects and governed them by means of bailiffs. And while the conquest of Aargau averted the Austrian danger from the cantons, it likewise accentuated their emancipation from the Empire itself; thanks to the privileges so lavishly bestowed by Sigismund, the cantons shewed an increasing tendency to become a State, the *Landleute und Städte in der Schweiz*.

So far Berne had been only indirectly allied with Lucerne and Zurich; this peculiar position ended when, on 1 March 1421 and 22 January 1423, all details of the military support and economic relations between Berne and each of the other two cities were fully settled by treaties of agreement and friendship. In consequence of this, Berne and Zurich assumed particular importance in federal policy. This was very soon proved by the Italian expeditions, which in September 1416 were resumed by way of the Upper Valais. Ossola, Val Verzasca, and Val Maggia were quickly occupied and administered jointly by the Confederates, with the exception of Schwyz and Berne. On 1 September 1419 Uri and Obwald purchased the town and feudal domain of Bellinzona from the lords of Sax, in order to have free scope in Leventina. On 4 April 1422 Filippo Maria Visconti, Duke of Milan, retaliated by abruptly seizing the place. Uri and Obwald did not succeed in obtaining the unconditional support of their allies, and the Duke of Milan recaptured all the valley of the Ticino as far as the St Gothard. In view of the danger, most of the cantons determined to take the field; the first contingent, consisting of men from Unterwalden, Uri, Lucerne, and Zug, reached Bellinzona, but on 30 June 1422 they were overcome by the Milanese troops at Arbedo. Val d'Ossola was lost, and the Milanese obtained a firm hold in Leventina and the valleys of Maggia and Verzasca. The defeat was caused by a lack of co-operation between the Confederates, and by the fact that the pact of alliance with Zurich limited its assistance within a definite zone. After various attempts at reprisal, the struggle was ended, in July 1426, by the two treaties of Bellinzona, which did not safeguard any ancient privileges, except that for ten years there were to be no tolls on the roads to Milan and Varese.

The difficulties experienced by the Confederates in their association appeared even more clearly in the opposition between Schwyz and Zurich. During the fifteenth century Zurich acquired from various nobles vast feudal domains, which gave it a very important territorial position.

Schwyz, which was a rural community, pursued a forward, and a much more democratic policy. In 1408 Zurich formed a separate alliance with Glarus on the basis of perfect equality of rights, with the intention of arresting the influence of Schwyz; soon the two tendencies clashed in a grave difference caused by the inheritance of the last Count of Toggenburg, who died in 1436. Relying on promises made by the count, the men of Schwyz occupied a large part of his territory, formed *combourgeoisies* with his subjects, and barred the road to Zurich, which was intent on rounding off its bailiwicks near the Upper Lake. A conference of the cantons, on 9 March 1437, decided the matter in favour of Schwyz, which retained the Upper March, and—jointly with Glarus—obtained on mortgage Uznach, Windegg, Gaster, Amden, Wesen, Walenstadt, and the bailiwick of Schännis. Zurich, which had to remain satisfied with a *combourgeoisie* with Sargans, closed its markets to Schwyz and Glarus, and, abandoning legal methods, rejected all arbitration. Ital Reding, *landamann* of Schwyz, replied to this obstinacy by joining with Glarus in the occupation of Sargans and Lachen; on 2 November 1440 he declared war on Zurich; contingents from Uri and Unterwalden arrived at the Etzel and supported Schwyz, so that Rudolf Stüssi, burgomaster of Zurich, was obliged to withdraw his army to the town. Thus humiliated, Zurich had no alternative but to submit to the decisions of the Diet.

After the death of Sigismund of Luxemburg, the imperial crown reverted in 1438 to the house of Austria. The Confederates had good reason to fear that the imperial power might further the dynastic interests of their old adversaries. And indeed, King Frederick III, who wished to recover the hereditary lands of his family in Switzerland, made skilful use of the resentment felt by Zurich against her Confederates; on 17 June 1442 the city yielded the county of Kiburg to Frederick, in his capacity as Austrian prince, and also recognised his right to recover Aargau. In return, the king undertook to reconquer Toggenburg and Uznach for Zurich, which, in alliance with Austria while still retaining its alliances with the Confederates, was to become the leader of a new Confederation extending from the Black Forest to Tyrol. The king's attitude was rewarded by an oath of fidelity from the inhabitants of the city, which led to a rupture with the Confederates, with whom Solothurn was associated. On 20 May 1443 Schwyz and Glarus declared war against Zurich and Austria, and the other cantons joined in this decision.

From the start of operations, contingents from the Forest Cantons and Glarus laid waste the territory round Zurich and threatened the town; on 22 July 1443, at St Jakob on the Sihl, the forces of Zurich were put to flight and the burgomaster Stüssi killed. Rapperswil was successful in defending itself; then, as a result of mediation by Constance and by a great Diet summoned at Baden, Zurich agreed to abandon all alliance with Austria and to submit to arbitration. But the Austrian faction caused the rejection of all conciliatory proposals, and executed those members of the Council who were likely to agree to them; the cantons resumed the campaign, with the assistance of Solothurn and Appenzell; the stronghold of Greifensee was carried on 27 May 1444, the garrison being put to the sword, and on 21 June the city of Zurich was besieged by an army of 20,000 Confederates.

In these circumstances Frederick III appealed to a new ally, the King of France. Charles VII was only too pleased to dispatch to the Rhine the troops whose task in France had been ended by the truce with England, and who bore the significant names of *Écorcheurs* or *Armagnacs*; while he cherished the hope of profiting by the weakness of Germany to seize Basle, a rich commercial city which excited the envy of the nobles possessing land in her vicinity. The Dauphin of France, Louis, himself took command in Champagne of 40,000 men, horse and foot, armed with cannon and provided with siege-material. At this time 15,000 men from Berne and Solothurn were investing the fortress of Farnsburg. The nobles of southern Alsace, the Sundgau, facilitated the advance of the French army, whose vanguard on 23 August penetrated beyond Basle to Pratteln and Arlesheim; on the opposite bank of the Rhine the Austrian troops advanced to Säckingen. When the arrival of the Armagnacs was announced, the Swiss reinforcements on the way to Farnsburg marched straight on the enemy; 1300 men from the seven cantons, Solothurn, and Neuchâtel, and two hundred armed peasants from Liestal reached Pratteln on 26 August, and put the French cavalry to flight; crossing the Birs, they opposed great masses of cavalry under Jean de Bueil near Basle; then, exhausted by the struggle and their retreat cut off, they entrenched themselves in the Leper's Hospital of St Jakob on the Birs, where they died gloriously, after refusing to surrender.

The fine resistance offered by this little body of Confederate troops made a great impression on contemporaries. The sieges of Farnsburg and Zurich were immediately raised, but garrisons remained in Aargau and outside Rapperswil. The dauphin was unsuccessful in his attempt to occupy Basle, which was protected by its alliance with the Confederates; and on 21 October 1444 the French plenipotentiaries concluded a final peace at Zofingen with the seven cantons, Basle, and Solothurn, which was signed by Louis at Ensisheim on 28 October. By this first peace between the throne of France and the Leagues, the dauphin guaranteed security to the persons and property of the Confederates, the people of Basle, and members of the Council; he undertook not to invade the territory of the Confederates; on both sides, trade was to remain free. Frederick III, thus abandoned by his ally, experienced great difficulty in clearing his territory of the French freebooters; but the war was prolonged in Switzerland with much tenacity.

At last the wearied belligerents agreed to have the points at issue settled by arbitration at the peace of Constance on 12 June 1446. Subsequently the court of arbitration intervened between the Confederates, and after fresh conferences at Einsiedeln, both parties abandoned their claims to indemnities and agreed to restore Zurich's conquered possessions; and on 13 July 1450 the chief arbitrator, Henry von Bubenberg, decided that the alliance between Zurich and Austria was inadmissible. As regards Austria, negotiations ended on 24 June 1450, in the conclusion of a formal alliance of three years with the young Duke Sigismund: the former treaties were recognised; Sigismund undertook not to wage war against the Confederates in future, and tacitly abandoned Austria's claims to Aargau. At Breisach, on 14 May 1449, peace was assured to Basle, by which the autonomy of the city was guaranteed. Finally, Fribourg also was lost to Austria; when that city attacked Savoy in 1447, Berne supported the duke and imposed on her ancient rival the peace of Morat on 16 July 1448. Fribourg was condemned to pay an indemnity of 40,000 florins to the Duke of Savoy, and to cede Grasburg to Berne. After this defeat, which involved a financial and social crisis, the Savoyard party took the upper hand; on 10 June 1452 the assembly of burgesses proclaimed the abolition of Austria's suzerainty, and accepted Louis of Savoy as their overlord, while retaining the rights and liberties of the city. Thus, by the application of the judicial regulations of confederate law, was ended an extremely dangerous crisis in the history of the Confederation. Zurich was delivered from a policy which tended to separate her from her allies; in 1450, in concert with the three cantons, she renewed her alliance with Glarus, and owing to her influence the people of Glarus became members of the League almost on the same conditions as the other Confederates.

The insecurity of the times and the long wars coincided with a great economic change in the allied districts, which became obvious at the middle of the fifteenth century. Switzerland never produced enough to support her inhabitants; in the very early days martial expeditions became necessary to secure the means of livelihood. In the Forest Cantons industry had not yet assumed any importance. In Appenzell and St Gall, as also in Berne, economic activity was increasing; but at Zurich the silk industry was in jeopardy; trade had been affected by the intestine quarrels, and transit dues brought in more to the public revenue than indigenous trade. The constant disturbances, caused by war, and the shipwreck of fortunes encouraged adventurous expeditions and mercenary service; the pursuit of indemnities and of booty replaced normal labour; by their military renown the Confederates spread terror around them; organised campaigns were undertaken on very slight pretexts; confederate free-lances entered the service of the highest bidder; lack of work favoured this martial trade of mercenary service; and very soon the consequences of this moral and economic transformation became evident in all parts.

The first years of peace were, however, marked by an immense movement of expansion. The Abbot of St Gall sought protection from the Confederates in his difficult position; on 17 August 1451 he concluded a perpetual treaty of *combourgeoisie* with the four cantons of Zurich, Lucerne, Schwyz, and Glarus. On 15 November 1452 the seven easterly cantons granted a more favourable charter of alliance to Appenzell. On 13 June 1454 Zurich, Berne, Lucerne, Schwyz, Zug, and Glarus recognised the burgesses of St Gall as confederates in perpetuity, and placed them on the same footing as the men of Appenzell. On 1 June 1454 Schaff-hausen, which had resumed its immediate dependency on the Empire in 1415, obtained an alliance on terms of complete equality with Zurich, Berne, Lucerne, Schwyz, Zug, and Glarus. In 1459 Stein-am-Rhein followed this example, allying herself with Zurich and Schaffhausen. Finally, on 18 June 1463 the imperial town of Rottweil on the Neckar associated herself with the eight cantons by a provisional alliance of fifteen years. In 1440 the men of Uri again took possession of Leventina. The new dynasty of the Dukes of Milan, the Sforza, left them un-disturbed, and granted exemption from the customs at Bellinzona to Berne, Lucerne, Uri, Schwyz, and Unterwalden; in 1467 the importation of goods as far as the moats of Milan was guaranteed to the seven easterly cantons.

As regarded Austria, all causes of difference had not yet been removed. In 1452 Zurich succeeded in regaining the county of Kiburg by means of a mortgage. In September 1458 an expedition against Constance was undertaken in consequence of a quarrel at a shooting-match; a few thousand Confederates got no farther than Weinfelden, but on their return they seized Rapperswil. Duke Sigismund demanded that the peace of fifty years should be respected, but was obliged to conclude a truce on 9 June 1459.

The war of aggression was presently revived by Pope Pius II (Aeneas Sylvius), who invited the Confederates to intervene in his quarrel with Austria; in the course of a few days Swiss contingents, from which the Bernese were absent, seized Thurgau and Frauenfeld and crossed the Rhine (October 1460); the siege of Winterthur was interrupted by a truce, and, despite the Pope's displeasure, on 1 June 1461 a fifteen years' peace was signed at Constance. Thurgau was to be retained by the Confederates, and became a subject district; the advocacy, *i.e.* the suze-rainty, was retained by the duke, and the higher jurisdiction devolved on the city of Constance. This new possession brought the frontier of the Confederate States right up to the Rhine; in 1460 Appenzell had purchased the Rheinthal, and in 1467 Sigismund ceded Winterthur to Zurich in exchange for a sum of money; on the left bank of the Rhine there now only remained in Austrian hands Rheinfelden and Laufenburg with their dependencies.

The peace of Constance did not at once end all antagonism between Austria and the Confederates, especially between the Austrian and Swabian nobles and the towns and communities of the Leagues. In 1467 a Confederate garrison went to protect Schaffhausen from the local nobles.

On 17 June 1466 Mühlhausen formed an offensive and defensive alliance with Berne and Solothurn; an act of violence on the part of the burgesses led to the investment of the city by the Austrian bailiff, Türing von Hallwil the Younger, whereupon the Confederates on 25 June 1468 invaded Sundgau in force and drove back the nobles. Berne wished to proceed to an occupation of the Black Forest, but the other Confederates would not consent to this plan, and peace was signed at Waldshut on 27 August 1468. The duke promised the Swiss an indemnity of 10,000 florins, in guarantee whereof he pledged the homage of the people of Waldshut and the Black Forest if the said sum were not paid by 24 June 1469.

To escape from these financial embarrassments, Duke Sigismund now had recourse to the Duke of Burgundy, Charles the Bold, son of Philip the Good, who, although a vassal of the King of France and of the Empire, reigned over an autonomous State consisting of Burgundy, Franche Comté, the Netherlands, and Flanders. By the treaty of St Omer on 9 May 1469 Sigismund mortgaged to Charles the territory he had pledged to the Confederates, in addition to the towns of Laufenburg, Rheinfelden, Säckingen, and Breisach, the landgravate of Upper Alsace, and the county of Ferette, in exchange for 50,000 florins and his protection against all enemies, especially against the Confederates. By means of this alliance Sigismund hoped to deprive the Swiss of their pledge. Charles, for his part, was impelled by his ambition and his political designs; he was ex-tending his possessions beyond the Vosges, and preparing the marriage of his daughter Mary to Maximilian, son of the Emperor Frederick. In 1469 the Burgundian administration took possession of the territory on the Upper Rhine; but the harsh measures of the bailiff, Peter von Hagenbach, provoked so much discontent among the towns and nobles that, in October 1473, the towns of Basle, Colmar, Célestat, and Stras-bourg formed the association called the "Basse Ligue" in defence of their liberties. This League at once entered into relations with the Confederates, who considered the alliance between Charles and Sigismund as an in-fraction of a treaty concluded with them by the Duke of Burgundy when he was Count of Charolais; they regarded as provocative the threats aimed at Mühlhausen and the violence done to Swiss merchants.

Louis XI, having emerged victorious over the League of the Public Weal, was delighted to secure Swiss support against his implacable enemy the Duke of Burgundy, who personified the resistance of feudal power to the monarchy. Foreseeing an attack, he concluded a treaty of neutrality with the Confederates in 1470; in 1471 he presented each canton with a sum of 3000 livres, subsequently encouraging them to make peace with Sigismund and to attack Charles the Bold. At first negotiations hung fire, but in 1473 the Emperor took the part of the King of France against the Burgundian. In Switzerland, Nicholas von Diesbach and Jost von Silenen, provost of Beromünster, actively espoused the cause of Louis XI;

the Diets of January and February 1474 consented to make peace with Austria subject to the condition that the districts pledged should be redeemed, and negotiations began at Constance. On 30 March a project of Perpetual Peace was agreed on: it secured the contracting parties in the possession of their present territories, and provided for the settlement of disputes by arbitration; the Confederates undertook not to conclude fresh *combourgeoisies* with Austrian subjects; they promised armed assistance to the Duke of Austria, and all old disputes were settled. On 31 March, still at Constance, a defensive alliance for ten years was signed between the Confederates and the Bishops of Strasbourg and Basle, and the four towns of Strasbourg, Colmar, Célestat, and Basle; finally, on 4 April Duke Sigismund joined the Basse Ligue with the aforesaid bishops and cities, and on 6 April he denounced the treaty of St Omer. Louis XI sanctioned the "recess" of Constance, and decided that the duke ought likewise to support the Swiss, and that his heirs should be bound by the treaty as well as himself. The actual confirmation of the agreement between the King of France, Duke Sigismund, and the Eight Cantons was signed at Sens on 11 June 1474.

The tidings of the Perpetual Peace was hailed with joy in Switzerland; with the help of French diplomacy, the prevailing insecurity was to come to an end. The Confederation was recognised as independent by its hereditary enemy, and it was guaranteed in the full possession of its conquests.

The treaties of Constance necessarily involved war with Burgundy. The revolt of the Alsatian towns started hostilities; Peter von Hagenbach was seized at Breisach by the enraged burgesses, and was beheaded on 9 May 1474. Sigismund again took possession of Alsace, which was then laid waste by Charles the Bold.

Louis XI saw that this was a favourable opportunity for exerting all his diplomatic efforts to win the Swiss over to his plans; he worked mainly by means of Nicholas von Diesbach, promising his aid and substantial subsidies to the cantons and to Fribourg and Solothurn, in return for a contingent of hired troops. Following Berne's example, all the cantons on 21 and 26 October accepted the clauses of a treaty signed at Feldkirch; at the same time Sigismund ratified the Perpetual Peace. In a secret declaration of 2 October, Berne had agreed that the king's help should only be summoned in case of dire necessity; on the other hand, the cantons undertook to supply a fixed number of 6000 mercenaries. The first petition for their aid came from the Emperor Frederick, whom Charles the Bold attacked at Neuss; this was followed by appeals from Duke Sigismund and the members of the Basse Ligue, and the Confederates declared war on the Duke of Burgundy on 25 October.

They won their first success at Héricourt on the Lisaine, where, on 13 November, 8000 Swiss put to flight the relieving army of Henry de

Neufchâtel, lord of Blamont, and likewise captured the town. In 1475 Nicholas von Diesbach carried on the campaign; at the head of an army of free-lances, he seized Pontarlier, Grandson, Orbe, Jougne, and Échallens. In July 1475 15,000 men from Berne, Fribourg, Solothurn, and Lucerne, together with contingents from the Basse Ligue, captured Isle on the Doubs, and Blamont.

After the death of Nicholas von Diesbach, which occurred at Porrentruy during the siege of Blamont, the *Vogt* Nicholas von Scharnachtal continued to prosecute Berne's warlike policy in the same direction. Duchess Yolande of Savoy and her brothers-in-law, John-Louis, Bishop of Geneva, and James, Count of Romont and Baron of Vaud, were bound to the party of the duke by an understanding with Galeazzo Maria Sforza, Duke of Milan; on 14 October 1475 the Bernese declared war on the Count of Romont and summoned aid from Fribourg and Solothurn. In less than three weeks the district of Vaud was conquered, after the surrender of Avenches, Cudrefin, Payerne, Estavayer (the population of which was massacred), Moudon, La Sarraz, and Les Clées. Geneva herself was threatened by the Confederates, reinforced by men from Zurich and the Forest Cantons, and only saved herself by paying a ransom of 26,000 *écus de Savoie*; on 13 November the men from Upper Valais, supported by troops from Gessenay, repulsed the attack of the Savoyards near Sion and occupied all the country up to Martigny.

Meanwhile a reconciliation had taken place between the Emperor and the Duke of Burgundy, and on 13 September Louis XI concluded a truce with Charles the Bold, abandoning the Swiss to his tender mercy. Charles began by putting out of action the Duke of Lorraine, whose capital, Nancy, he occupied; then, at the head of an army of 20,000 men he laid siege to Grandson, the only place in Vaud still garrisoned by the Swiss; on 28 February 1476 he took the castle and hanged the garrison. In these straits Berne called for the assistance of her allies; on 1 March contingents of Confederates assembled round Neuchâtel, over 18,000 men commanded by the Bernese leaders, Nicholas von Scharnachtal and Hans von Hallwil. On 2 March the vanguard came into contact at Vaumarcus with a Burgundian outpost. The whole Burgundian army thereupon left the camp at Grandson and marched to meet the Swiss, who advanced in two successive columns and quickly spread panic throughout the duke's troops; the whole force fell back in disorder to Grandson, their camp was taken with enormous booty, and only darkness and the lack of cavalry checked the pursuit. The Swiss infantry had overcome the cavalry and artillery of Charles the Bold, and the moral effect of this success was considerable; but the Confederates were not anxious to carry on the war and to maintain Bernese interests; they retired, after placing garrisons in Morat and Fribourg.

Charles the Bold retired to Lausanne to prepare his revenge, and with surprising energy assembled a new army. On 10 June the town of Morat was invested by numerous contingents, amounting to over 23,000 men. Adrian von Bubenberg, who was in command of the Bernese garrison, repulsed all assaults, and patiently waited for reinforcements. Fresh appeals by the Bernese caused the Confederates to assemble their forces, first near Berne, later at Gümmenen and Ormey; with the Confederates were associated 1800 mounted men of the Basse Ligue and the garrison of Fribourg under the command of Hans Waldmann of Zurich. On 22 June 1476 an attack was delivered on the centre of the Burgundian lines; it was at first checked by artillery fire, but later broke all resistance by the effect of its compact masses, and the whole Burgundian army was caught in a trap. The army corps of the Count of Romont to the northeast of Morat made its escape; elsewhere the Swiss slaughtered without mercy; between eight and ten thousand of the duke's army were left on the field of battle. Charles hastily fled through Morges to Gex; with some hesitation the Confederates pursued him as far as Lausanne, where the intervention of Louis XI arranged a preliminary truce with Savoy on 29 June. The Congress of Fribourg, which sat from 25 July to 16 August, did not achieve the results anticipated by Berne and Louis XI. The Confederates only retained a provisional jurisdiction over Vaud in pledge for an indemnity of 50,000 florins; Berne only the Savoyard seignories of Grandson, Orbe, and Échallens; pending a final decision, the men of Upper Valais were allowed to establish themselves beyond St Maurice.

In the same year Charles the Bold resumed hostilities against René of Lorraine; on 22 October he laid siege to Nancy. The Swiss mercenaries, numbering over 8000, under Hans Waldmann, encouraged the Lorrainers and Alsatians to advance towards Lunéville. The Duke of Burgundy was defeated at Jarville by these forces, which were superior to his own; and he was found dead on the battle-field, where, for the last time, he had valiantly and tenaciously opposed adverse fate. Louis XI, delivered from his old enemy, took possession of the duchy, and announced his intention of requiring homage from Franche Comté. Berne wished to occupy this territory, but the other cantons were opposed to any fresh conquest. Finally, they agreed to the proposals of the Emperor, whose son Maximilian had married Mary of Burgundy, daughter of Charles the Bold; a definitive peace was signed at the Congress of Zurich on 24 January 1478. Thereby the Confederates renounced all right to Franche Comté; Maximilian, as lord of the Burgundian lands, undertook to pay an indemnity of 150,000 florins to the contracting parties, the Confederates, the Basse Ligue, Austria, and Lorraine.

The Burgundian wars did not change the territorial or political situation of the Confederation; they secured for the Confederates great consideration and caused their alliance to be much sought after. Berne did not abandon its policy towards Savoy. It obtained from Duchess Yolande the release of Fribourg from the suzerainty of Savoy (23 August and 10 September 1477). The town thus remained directly subject to the Empire. On

14 November 1477 Berne and Fribourg concluded a treaty of *combourgeoisie* with John-Louis of Savoy, Bishop of Geneva, and with the town of Geneva, but only for the duration of the bishop's life; in the Valais, the bishop and the *dizains,* as a result of a truce in 1478, retained the Lower Valais as far as St Maurice and the valleys of Bagnes and Entremont.

As regards France, the treaty, which specifically promised armed assistance, was annulled when the king died on 30 August 1483. The peace of Arras between France and Austria bestowed Franche Comté as dowry on Maximilian's daughter, who was betrothed to the French dauphin; and the treaty of Senlis, in which the Confederates acted as mediators, on 23 May 1493 secured the return of this province to the house of Habsburg.

In Italy, the Duke of Milan, Galeazzo Maria Sforza, the ally of Charles the Bold, having been killed on 26 December 1476, his widow, Duchess Bona, renewed the old capitulations with the Confederates on 10 July 1477. Encouraged by Pope Sixtus IV, and by local conflicts in Leventina, the men of Uri decided to intervene in Italy. In November 1478 they crossed the St Gothard and summoned to their aid an army of 10,000 Confederates, in which Hans Waldmann commanded the men of Zurich and Adrian von Bubenberg those of Berne; an attack on Bellinzona, badly led, failed; and a retreat was undertaken in the very heart of December. But the ducal troops found out their mistake when they attempted to profit by this event; they were abruptly stopped at Giornico by a rear-guard of Confederates supported by the inhabitants of the country. The peace agreed on in September 1479 and ratified in March 1480 assured Uri in the possession of Leventina. The lack of union between the Confederates caused the loss of Biasca and the valley of Blenio, which commanded the passage across the Lukmanier Pass.

Henceforward the Confederates displayed a tendency to avoid intervention in foreign affairs. It was this prudent reserve which enabled them to reconcile the frequently contradictory clauses of the treaties to which they agreed, and which, in particular, assured their friendship and the recruitment of mercenaries to Duke Sigismund of Austria (13 October 1477), to the King of Hungary, Matthias Corvinus (26 March and 18 October 1479), and to Pope Sixtus IV (18 October 1479).

In the midst of these successes, the Confederation passed through an acute crisis. The thirst for gold aroused by the fabulous booty taken from Burgundy had excited violent passions in the populace; the measures adopted by the cantons to combat the system of foreign subsidies were everywhere nugatory; and venality shewed itself to be the predominant vice of the period. Moreover, in spite of the regulations forbidding private expeditions, mercenary service was becoming the national industry.

The lawlessness of the mercenary bands was most scandalously exhibited in the expedition called *la Folle Vie*, which launched two thousand adventurers from Schwyz, Uri, Unterwalden, Zug, Lucerne, and Fribourg on Savoy; Geneva was threatened, and had to pay down the sum of 8000 florins and to hand over hostages in order to secure the withdrawal of these free-lances. The cantons which possessed urban centres, such as Berne, Zurich, and Lucerne, were dismayed at the revolutionary exuberance of the country districts. Against their advice, the five cantons of Uri, Zug, Schwyz, Unterwalden, and Glarus had, on 12 January 1477, concluded a *combourgeoisie* with the Bishop of Constance; on this occasion the towns determined to act; and at St Urban, on 23 May 1477, they signed an offensive and defensive alliance, which included Zurich, Berne, Lucerne, Fribourg, and Solothurn.

The antagonism thus declared degenerated into a serious conflict, which a diet assembled at Stanz between 22 and 30 November 1481 attempted to avert. The suggested arrangement was that both parties should renounce their private alliances and that Fribourg and Solothurn should be admitted into the pact; but all hopes of conciliation gradually vanished, and on 22 December a rupture seemed imminent, when the parish priest of Stanz, Henry am Grund, repaired to Ranft to take counsel with the hermit of Obwald, Nicholas von Flüe, who enjoyed a reputation of miracle-working sanctity among all the Confederates, and who was greatly respected for his judicious advice. The intervention of Nicholas von Flüe secured an immediate reconciliation, and the agreement resulted in a perpetual alliance of the eight cantons with Fribourg and Solothurn, and the compromise which takes its name from Stanz (22 December 1481). The two cities became members of the Confederation; they were bound to send assistance wherever it might be required, and were forbidden to conclude other alliances without the consent of a majority of the eight cantons. On the other hand, the Covenant of Stanz confirmed the Charter of the Priests (1370) and that of Sempach (1393), and strengthened the common alliance for the maintenance of public peace, while providing various measures for the repression of sedition and for the division of booty and of conquered territory. The Federal bond was renewed more firmly than ever by this happy ending of a crisis which had for a time seemed mortal and irremediable.

Within the cantons, equally grave conflicts aroused the violent passions of the period and proved the necessity of a more stable government and administration. At Berne a democratic movement triumphed in 1471 over the *Twingherren*, the feudal lords and possessors of ancient rights; an agreement henceforward regulated the exercise of justice in opposition to the feudal system.

At Zurich, the burgomaster, Hans Waldmann, autocratically inclined the policy of the government in the direction of reforms imposed by coercion on the nobles, clergy, and peasants. He was violently attacked by his political opponents on account of the ostentatious luxury of his private life and his arbitrary tendencies, and allowed himself to be bribed into an Austrian alliance. On 14 September 1487 Maximilian concluded a closer alliance with seven cantons, among which were Berne and Zurich. Lucerne, Schwyz, and Glarus, who were in favour of a French alliance, were much incensed. Waldmann was accused of treachery and was held responsible for a defeat sustained at Ossola by volunteers from Lucerne; in retaliation the burgomaster, on 20 September 1487, seized and executed his chief accuser, Frischhans Teiling, at Zurich. But the country districts round Zurich rebelled against Waldmann's edicts against dogs; the insurrection spread to the city; and Waldmann was in his turn imprisoned, sentenced, and executed on 6 April 1489. Peace was restored to Zurich by the mediation of the federal deputies; the fourth charter on 14 January 1498 modified the constitution while retaining certain regulations which had been introduced by Waldmann.

The fall of the powerful burgomaster led to certain consequences in the Confederation. In Lucerne the populace obtained some changes in the law of the State. In the north-east, the men of Appenzell, in conjunction with those of St Gall and Rheinthal, destroyed the preparations made by Abbot Ulrich Rosch for the transference of his monastery to Rorschach; relying on the support of Uri, Zug, and Unterwalden, the townsfolk of St Gall, those of Appenzell, and the subjects of the former ecclesiastical principality united in the alliance of Waldkirch, on 27 October 1479. The cantons which had undertaken to protect the abbot—Zurich, Lucerne, Schwyz, and Glarus—were obliged to intervene; the town of St Gall surrendered on 15 February 1480; the alliance of Waldkirch was dissolved, and the abbot regained his authority over his subjects and lands. Nevertheless, he abandoned his intention of transferring the abbey to Rorschach, and in fact recognised the protection and intervention of the Confederates in his affairs.

After the Burgundian wars, the Confederates had achieved an almost complete emancipation from the German Empire, which no longer retained either their respect or their confidence. In 1487 and 1488 Frederick III combined the states, princes, knights, and urban communities of Swabia in a league to preserve public peace, which was designed not only to strengthen imperial power, but also to support the house of Habsburg against that of Wittelsbach. The Diet of the cantons refused to join the league; in 1491 eight cantons concluded a treaty of neutrality with the Dukes of Bavaria; in 1495 a majority of the cantons accepted a renewal of alliance with Charles VIII, King of France.

Maximilian I, who succeeded his father Frederick III in 1493, attempted a widespread reform of the Empire based on the power of the house of Austria; at Worms, in 1495, he instituted an Imperial Chamber and a general system of taxation. The Confederates refused to carry out the decisions of Worms, and did not send delegates to the imperial assemblies.

When the three leagues of the Grisons were threatened by Austria, they approached the Confederation; on 21 June 1497 the seven easterly cantons signed a treaty with the Grey League, and on 13 December 1498 with the League of the Maison-Dieu and the town of Chur. At the beginning of 1499 contingents from Uri and other federal cantons supplied help to the Grisons, who had been attacked by the Tyrolese with the encouragement of the Swabian league; on 11–12 February 1499 the Grisons and the Swiss took the offensive against Vaduz and Walgau, and the League of the Ten Jurisdictions in the Grisons made common cause with the other two.

War thereupon broke out with terrible violence from Rhaetia to Sundgau; for the Swiss it was the war of the Swabians, for the Swabians the war of the Swiss. After the first campaign in Hegau, all the cantons and allied districts gradually engaged in the struggle, except Basle and Rottweil. Louis XII, King of France, promised help or monetary support to the Confederates, and the German armies were successively defeated, in March at Bruderholz near Basle, in April at Schwaderloo near Constance and at Frastenz in Walgau. Maximilian then formally placed all the Confederates under the ban of the Empire; on 22 May his attack on Rhaetia failed at Calven, but the Austrian troops laid waste the Engadine. In western Switzerland, Count Henry of Fürstenberg laid siege to the fortress of Dorneck on the Birs, which commanded the territory of Solothurn; contingents from Berne, Zurich, and Solothurn assembled at Liestal, and, with the help of reinforcements from Zug and Lucerne, surprised the German army, and on 22 July inflicted on it a sanguinary defeat. Maximilian prepared to embark on fresh attempts, but the Empire and the League were at the end of their resources; Lodovico il Moro of Milan took the first steps towards mediation, and difficult negotiations terminated in the peace of Basle on 22 September 1499. Galeazzo Visconti played the part of intermediary between Maximilian and the Swiss, and the treaty rendered the latter entirely independent of the imperial courts of law; on other matters, the preliminaries arranged on 25 August formed the basis of the agreement; the alliance between the Rhaetian Leagues and the Confederation was recognised, and means of arbitration were provided to ensure the settlement of difficulties between the Swabian League and the Confederation; on both sides conquests, law-suits, and indemnities were relinquished. The treaty did not formally declare the separation of the Confederates from the Empire, or their reconciliation with the Emperor, but the latter virtually renounced his rights of suzerainty, and the Swiss thenceforward remained independent of the imperial power.

Another result of the Swabian war was the admission of Basle and Schaffhausen into the Confederation. Basle had been a free city since 1386 and had become enriched by her trade and industry; although allied with Berne and Solothurn since 1400, she had remained neutral during the Swabian war. On being attacked by the Austrian nobles of her vicinity, she returned a favourable reply to the advances of the Confederates, and a formal alliance was signed at Basle on 13 July 1501. Its clauses forbade the city to declare war or conclude an alliance without the preliminary consent of the Confederates; but at the same time she was appointed to act as arbitrator in case of disagreement among the Confederates. At Schaffhausen the treaty of 1 June 1454, which had rendered the city an allied district, was converted into a perpetual alliance on 10 August 1501; like Basle, Schaffhausen was to exercise mediation in cases of dispute between members of the League. In spite of a revival of distrust between the Forest Cantons and Fribourg, Solothurn, and Schaffhausen, these three new cantons were placed on the same footing as the others in 1502. Finally, on 17 December 1513 Appenzell's persistent efforts were crowned with success; it was granted the position of thirteenth canton, with the same rights as the three preceding ones.

At the beginning of the sixteenth century the "Great League of High Germany" was an aggregate of districts differing widely in their political conditions. The thirteen cantons, or *Orte*—Uri, Schwyz, Unterwalden, Zurich, Lucerne, Glarus, Zug, Berne, Fribourg, Solothurn, Basle, Schaffhausen, and Appenzell—were the Confederates; they sat in the Diet, had full right to vote, took possession of conquered territory, and acted externally as Sovereign States of the League.

The allied districts, or *Zugewandte*, enjoyed the protection of the Confederates and owed them military support; they were linked by treaties or *combourgeoisies* to one or more of the cantons. The Valais and the Grisons were themselves, like the Confederation, federal groups; to a certain extent they acted externally as autonomous. The towns of Biel, St Gall, Rottweil, and Mühlhausen, the abbey of St Gall, and the county of Neuchâtel, temporarily administered by the cantons, were also allied districts. There may also be included in this category the abbey of Engelberg, the republic of Gersau, the county of Toggenburg—*combourgeois* of Schwyz and Glarus—the subjects of the Count of Gruyères who were allies of Berne and Fribourg, and Rapperswil which was under the protection of the Forest Cantons and Glarus.

Moreover the thirteen cantons had actual subjects. Schwarzenburg, Morat, Grandson, Orbe, and Échallens were owned jointly by Berne and Fribourg; Uznach and Gaster by Schwyz and Glarus. The county of Baden, the Freiamt, Thurgau, Rheinthal, and Sargans were subject to seven or eight cantons; the county of Bellinzona was dependent on Uri, Schwyz, and Nidwald, and Leventina on Uri; the other bailiwicks beyond the mountains from Val Maggia to Mendrisio were subject to twelve cantons. In conformity with contemporary ideas, the Confederates did not dream of putting these possessions on the same footing as their own territories; they respected local privileges, especially in the towns, but regarded themselves as legitimate successors of the former lords.

From the internal point of view, the members of the League were bound by no written constitution; in 1515 it was proposed that a minority should yield to the decisions of a majority of the cantons in matters affecting the weal of the Confederation and not interfering with alliances, but this plan was not adopted. Various pacts and agreements laid down rules for the maintenance of peace and the prosecution of war, such as the Charter of the Priests (1370), the Charter of Sempach (1393), and the Covenant of Stanz (1481). The only federal authority was the Diet, an assembly of delegates or envoys from the sovereign cantons who tended to become actual representatives of the various members of the League; the deputies were provided with instructions, and the execution of the decisions arrived at and expressed in the official reports (*abschied* or *recess*) depended on the good will of the States. Although the legal capacity of the Diet was never defined, this institution actually acquired the position of the directing power of the Confederation, and foreign countries regarded it as such.

Notwithstanding such slight legal bonds, the Confederates were inspired with a common sentiment of cohesion and solidarity which was developed during the course of their wars. Their military organisation, which became remarkable in the fourteenth century, rested on compulsory service from the age of sixteen to that of nearly sixty, on the training of the young men, and on pike-drill; periodical inspections ensured the use and upkeep of weapons; marksmanship began to be greatly esteemed, but artillery was still much neglected in the fifteenth century. The Diet and the government of cantons acted as a General Staff at the beginning of a campaign; by an elaborate system of signals and intelligence the army, when required, could be rapidly mobilised; in the latter half of the fifteenth century the Diet could call up between 50,000 and 60,000 men, though in practice never more than half of these were summoned. Discipline was not always perfect, but their warlike spirit and the sense of danger generally saved the situation and averted the gravest catastrophes. The military preparedness of the Confederation was the chief reason of its power; its infantry easily overcame the foot-soldiers of other European countries.

Even after Marignano (1515) the conquests of the Confederates had not attained what they regarded as their natural frontiers: on the left bank of the Rhine Austria still retained Frickthal; she commanded the river at Kaiserstuhl and Laufenburg, and held certain important parts of the Grisons. Constance still held aloof from the League. Southward and westward Ossola had been lost, Geneva was not yet attained, and the house of Savoy was in occupation of Vaud; in this direction Berne had not yet relinquished all hopes of extension. The perpetual alliance of 1516 put an end to the position of the Confederation as a great military power; whenever permitted to do so by the French alliance, henceforward in the conflicts of her neighbours Switzerland adopted and cherished a policy of neutrality which suited her political situation.

Popular sentiment increasingly tended to encourage the Confederates in keeping out of great international politics and in restricting themselves to their own affairs. Moreover a violent reaction shewed itself against the evils which had unquestionably enfeebled this strange little body politic, namely venality, incapacity for reform, military agreements, and discord between towns and country districts. Her security being now attained, Switzerland was faced with the task of arriving at a national conception of her political and social life, so as to become an actual State.

CHAPTER VIII

THE HANSA

THE gradual expansion of the German people eastwards, following upon the conquest and Christianisation of the numerous Slav tribes beyond the Elbe, together with the foundation of towns in the conquered area, were the two conditions that rendered the rise and development of the Hansa possible. Initiated by the Saxon Emperors, the building of towns was continued by their successors and other territorial lords, so that by the twelfth century many of the later Hansa towns already existed. Among them, Hamburg and Lübeck, prominent in subsequent history, had arisen upon the site of older settlements several times destroyed. Both owed their importance to their situation near the sea and upon rivers that then afforded the easiest and safest roads to the interior. Henry the Lion must have realised the unique advantages possessed by Lübeck, when he conferred upon it extensive privileges of local self-government and invited foreign merchants to trade there *absque theloneo et absque hansa*, "without tax or toll."[1] This grant, confirmed, amplified, and extended by Frederick Barbarossa and his successors, made Lübeck an imperial city, free from the cramping influences of local feudal potentates, enabling her subsequently to play that decisive rôle which earned her the title of "Queen of the Hansa."

By the end of the twelfth century medieval Germany had begun to assume its familiar features. The imperial power, everywhere declining, was already almost a negligible factor in the north. Of greater importance was the rapidly rising commerce along the Baltic shore, Germanised and colonised by the joint efforts of the Church and the military Orders of the Brethren of the Sword and the Teutonic Knights. The towns that arose in these regions gave the Germans the control of the great river mouths, so that commerce, and not conquest or colonisation, became their goal, until merchant and townsman became synonymous. Nature had herself marked the course which the fearless energies of the Germans, when directed to foreign trade, were to take. The rivers, flowing from the south-east to north-west, from the central European uplands to the North and Baltic Seas, were the first highways of medieval commerce; and the lands they drained produced the materials and afforded the markets

[1] The term Hansa is derived in *New Eng. Dict.* from Old Fr. hanse, and Med. Latin hansa; O.H.G. and Gothic hansa, equivalent to O.E. hos, a military troop, band, or company; M.H.G. hanse, fellowship, association, merchants' gild. It is there defined as a company or gild of merchants in former times; an association of merchants trading in foreign parts; the merchants' gild of a town; also the privileges and monopolies possessed by it: sometimes the Gildhall or house. Cf. Gross, *Gild Merchant*, ii, pp. 194-8, and *Economica*, No. 5, p. 145.

exploited by the adventurous trader in search of profit. The first mention of such traders occurs about the year 1000 A.D. when the "men of the Empire," who probably came from Cologne, are deemed "worthy of the good laws of England." About the same time German merchants had already created a settlement in the island of Gotland, almost ideally situated for easy access to Sweden, Finland, and Russia. Quite early, the island had become a mart for the "peoples of many tongues," and an interchange of privileges had taken place between its inhabitants and the Germans. By c. 1163 the latter were sufficiently numerous to enjoy the then coveted right of being judged by their own officers, administering their own laws. This points to a permanent settlement of traders, obliged under the conditions then prevailing to spend a considerable part of the year abroad. The need for companionship in a strange land, the desire to take part in religious exercises in the mother tongue and after their own practices, the occasional necessity for performing the last rites for a colleague, the collection of debts, securing and safeguarding freedom of trade, were the centripetal forces impelling the Germans in Gotland to form an association for mutual assistance and protection. Nor was this an isolated instance of combination for common ends. Almost at the same time (1157), the "men of Cologne," and some Westphalian towns associated with the Rhine city, obtained from Henry II of England protection for themselves and their *hansa* in London. From Gotland the Germans had, before the end of the twelfth century, established a factory, or "Kontor," at Novgorod, on Lake Ilmen in Russia, whence later they reached out to Pskov, Polotsk, Vitebsk, and Smolensk, where subsidiary factories were afterwards founded. The Russian settlement, from its earliest days, epitomises both the difficulties of medieval trade and the methods employed by the German associations and their successor, the Hansa, to overcome them. To the heavy duties and other obstacles interposed by the local officials the foreigners replied by a suspension of trade, lasting a whole decade (1189–99), until the town authorities yielded. In 1199 it concluded a treaty "with all the German sons, with the Goths and the whole Latin tongue," which redressed most of the grievances that had arisen, arranged for uninterrupted trade, regulated the punishments for offences, and determined the conditions that should govern the arrest of the goods and persons of the foreigners[1].

The close association among German traders which this implied is equally well illustrated by events in England. Here Lübeck, Hamburg, and Wisby, the capital of Gotland, obtained various grants from Henry III that placed them on an equality with Cologne. By 1282 all of them are definitely amalgamated into one body, described in a document of that year as "the merchants of Almain trading in England who have their house in London, usually called the Gildhalla Theutonicorum,"

[1] The treaty, translated from an old Russian original, is printed in *Hansisches Urkundenbuch* (H.U.B.), I, no. 50.

responsible, in return for the freedom of trade conferred upon them, for the watch and repair of the Bishop's Gate. About the same time the subsidiary "hansas" at Boston and King's Lynn are first mentioned. But both London and Novgorod were soon out-distanced as centres of German trade by Bruges, already by 1200 the greatest international emporium of Northern Europe. Conditions of commercial intercourse in Flanders were at first as uncertain as in Russia, but they improved rapidly when Hamburg and Lübeck appeared on the scene in 1252 to negotiate on behalf of themselves and their associates. Describing themselves as "nuncii speciales mercatorum imperii habentes plenam potestatem per quarundam civitatum ipsius imperii patentes litteras super hoc," the envoys obtained a charter containing extensive trading privileges. A permanent settlement followed, and Bruges was made the staple for the furs, wax, copper, herrings, and other commodities imported from the north-east and exchanged for Flemish cloth and manufactured articles of the west. German trade in Flanders was thus centralised, and the weapon already effectively employed against Novgorod, the commercial blockade, was employed with equal force and success against Bruges whenever the chartered privileges were infringed. First resorted to in 1307, it extorted from Bruges freedom from the control of the town brokers and the authority to settle all legal disputes according to their own customs.

The circle of foreign depots was completed by the creation of the settlement at Bergen. Though Norway owing to its economic backwardness had at first failed to attract the Germans, the grants of freedom to trade made by Hakon IV (1217–63) to Lübeck, Hamburg, and other towns, soon induced them to enter into commercial relations with the northern kingdom[1]. The privileges obtained formed the foundation for the superstructure of commercial supremacy which the Hansa subsequently erected upon them. Thus by the end of the thirteenth century north German, *i.e.* Hansa, commerce had staked out its claims, with London, Bruges, Bergen, and Novgorod as the chief foreign centres in Northern Europe, the nodal points of the vast region whose trade they were to dominate for so long.

Simultaneously with the formation of these foreign settlements, the towns themselves were beginning to enter into close alliances, impelled by common interests, such as the protection of trade routes or the adoption of a common legal system or common currency. The former was the motive for the treaty of 1241 between Hamburg and Lübeck, which older writers regarded as the foundation of the Hansa; while by the end of the thirteenth century some nineteen towns had adopted "das lübische Recht" as their system of local self-government, and a number of them, "in subsidium omnium mercatorum qui iure Lubicensi gaudent et reguntur," jointly devised measures for suppressing piracy. Similar common action

---

[1] "Ad instanciam ac petitionem prudentum consulum et communitatum multarum civitatum maritimarum Theutonie."

deprived Wisby of her leadership in Novgorod, transferred appeals from the settlement to Lübeck, and decreed that no seal of the "common merchant" should any longer be kept in Gotland. Even more important was the alliance of the so-called Wend towns under the leadership of Lübeck, for it was this group that shaped and directed Hansa policy during its effective existence[1]. The maintenance of peace, indispensable to trade and industry, became a primary object of the Wend towns, and to further it they allied themselves with a number of local potentates in the *Landfrieden* of 1283.

The strength of these alliances was soon tested by the ambitions of Denmark. The early attempts of Waldemar II to obtain control of the southern Baltic shore had been crushed by the battle of Bornhövede (1227), but they were revived towards the end of the century by Eric VI Menved (1286–1319), who compelled all the Wend towns, except Stralsund, to accept his overlordship. His timely death, however, saved the nascent Hanseatic League from being strangled at its birth. Not until it recovered from the disintegrating anarchy into which it fell was Denmark again a menace to the Hansa, but by that time it was powerful enough to affront and defeat its aggressive power. Almost at the same time these towns successfully blockaded Norway, whose King, Eric II Priesthater (1280–99), and his officials had infringed the trading privileges granted to them. So effective did this method prove that the king agreed to submit the dispute to the arbitration of the King of Sweden (31 October 1285), whose decision was wholly in favour of the towns, though it was not finally settled until 1294 when the Treaty of Tönsberg was concluded with Norway. Though containing no new principles, this treaty formed the basis of all future commercial intercourse between the Hansa and Norway. On this occasion, too, the towns for the first time resorted to the expulsion of a member (later called *Verhansung*) for refusing to act jointly with its colleagues. For more than half a century Bremen remained outside the growing organisation. Despite the Treaty of Tönsberg, relations with Norway, dependent largely upon the relations between Norway and Denmark, always caused the towns great anxiety. The Hansa now played off the one against the other, but not until the weak reign of Magnus Smek (1319–55) was it in a position fully to exploit the privileges it had acquired, create the famous centre, the "deutsche Brücke" at Bergen, expel its English and Scottish competitors, and almost entirely monopolise Norwegian trade with the rest of Europe.

These events reacted upon the movement towards unity among the towns. Terms like the "ghemeene Koepman," "universitas omnium mercatorum," or "merchants of the German Hansa," now occur with increasing frequency in the documents, especially those relating to Norway. The older privileges, obtained by single towns, were transformed into

---

[1] The group consisted of Lübeck, Stralsund, Wismar, Rostock, and Greifswald. The last fell out later, and Lüneburg seems to have taken its place.

Hansa privileges, and those not entitled to them were rigidly excluded. At the same time the foreign associations were being more closely organised; thus the *Kontor* in Bruges received new statutes (1347). Though its members still styled themselves "de ghemeenen Koeplude uten Roomischen rike van Almanien," the term "dudeschen hanse" soon replaced it. In Bruges too we find the division into "Thirds" which sometimes figures in Hansa history. These were: a Wend-Saxon group under the leadership of Lübeck, a Westphalian-Prussian under Cologne, and a Gotho-Swedish-Livonian under Wisby. Six aldermen, two from each group, administered the affairs of the Kontor[1]. The difficulties encountered by the Bruges settlement, partly due to the economic crisis produced by the Anglo-French war, led to the final step in the formation of the Hanseatic League. Infringements of the German privileges by the town authorities, as well as disputes among the Thirds, caused the allied German towns to intervene. Their representatives, who in 1356 visited Bruges, compelled the Kontor to accept the towns as the superior authority, directing the foreign policy, protecting the merchants who ventured abroad and safeguarding their privileges. The greater solidarity thus obtained was at once utilised against the town. The staple was transferred to Dordrecht in Holland and trade with Flanders suspended. This step was the work of the "stede van der dudeschen hense,"[2] the term by which the League was henceforth known. The evolution of the Hansa had been slow and halting, but it had at last emerged as a union of towns organised in the pursuit of trade by land and sea and prepared to spare no efforts in the attainment of that end. As such, it soon became a power to be reckoned with in its use of political means for commercial objects. Bruges was the first to realise the strength of the new power. It felt the absence of the German merchants most keenly. By 1360 the town and its overlords yielded to the pressure, and confirmed and extended the older privileges, with the additional one of exemption from the town brokers and brokerage. The settlement was made none too soon, for the Hansa was on the eve of a greater conflict, fraught with far-reaching and enduring consequences to itself and the whole of Scandinavia.

After twenty years of successful labour in restoring the royal authority, Waldemar IV of Denmark felt powerful enough to resume the ambitious schemes of his predecessors. He began by arranging a marriage between his daughter Margaret and Hakon, heir to the thrones of Norway and Sweden, and then wresting the province of Scania from the latter. This immediately aroused the anxiety of the Hansa, for the herring-fishery of Scania was the corner-stone of Hansa prosperity. During the fishing season this remote region of Europe, with its villages of Skanör and Falsterbo, became an international mart of the highest importance.

---

[1] Shortly after this Bremen, at its own request, was readmitted into the Hansa, on condition that it observed the ordinances of the common merchant.

[2] Cf. *Hanserecesse* (H.R.), I, 212, § 10.

On account of the rights the Hansa had secured from Sweden, the trade
in herrings and the subsidiary industries associated with it were almost
entirely under Hansa control. At each change of sovereign the Hansa
had been most careful to obtain the confirmation of its extensive privileges.
Waldemar, however, could only be induced to do so after prolonged
negotiations and the payment of a substantial sum of money by the
Wend towns, the most directly interested in the herring trade. The king's
next act was an even more direct challenge to the Hansa. He attacked
Gotland and sacked Wisby. Though the town was no longer the chief
foreign centre of the League, it was still a staple of the Baltic trade, in
which a considerable amount of German capital was invested, the head
of one of the "Thirds" at Bruges, and it shared with Lübeck the supervision of the settlement at Novgorod. Though Waldemar restored its
former rights, Wisby never recovered from the blow inflicted upon it.
The Hansa reply to the king's high-handed act was the immediate
suspension of all trade with Denmark and the building up of a great
coalition against the aggressor. Within six weeks of the attack on Wisby,
an alliance was concluded between the Hansa, Norway, Sweden, and the
Teutonic Order (31 August 1360), which Holstein joined later. Preparations for war were made and a poundage upon all exports imposed to
meet its expenses. The Kings of Norway and Sweden agreed to hand
over four castles of Scania to the League until it had reimbursed itself
for its outlay, and confirmed all its privileges in the province when it
should be reconquered. In the first stages of the war, however, the Hansa
received but little assistance from its allies. But the League realised the
grave import of the struggle for its future, "quod nunquam tam necesse
fuit omnibus mercatoribus et mare visitantibus in resistendo, sicut nunc
est." Nevertheless it was severely defeated at Helsingborg (1362) by
Waldemar, who then detached the Kings of Norway and Sweden from his
enemies by concluding the marriage previously arranged between Margaret
and Hakon. The Hansa was glad to accept a truce, followed by a
definite peace (22 November 1365) that left many important questions un-
settled, more especially the considerably enhanced dues imposed upon
its traders in Scania and elsewhere. The defeat had broken up the
formidable coalition and caused many towns to waver in their allegiance
to the common cause. Waldemar, continuing to exploit the weakness of
his enemy, disturbed Hansa trade in Scania and upon the sea. Urged by
its Dutch and Prussian members, to whom the freedom of the Sound was
indispensable, the Hansa met at Cologne to consider the situation. The
meeting, out of which the famous "Cologne Confederation" emerged (1367),
was fully representative, the envoys describing themselves as "plenipotentes
legati suarum et aliarum quarundam civitatum." Vigorous prosecution of
war was decided upon and preparations made accordingly. Once more a
number of princes joined the coalition, including the Duke of Mecklenburg
whose son sat uneasily upon the throne of Sweden. War was declared in

1368, trade suspended, and the German merchants recalled from Bergen. But, prior to the outbreak of hostilities, Waldemar had left Denmark in search of allies in Germany. Before he could accomplish his aims, the League had won a signal victory over his forces (1369) and seized Scania. Master of the Sound, the League was content with its achievement, and readily entered into negotiations with the Danish Council. Preliminaries, signed at Stralsund (30 November 1369), were converted into a definitive peace on 24 May of the next year and accepted by the envoys of all the Thirds present[1].

The Treaty of Stralsund is epoch-making for Hanseatic and Scandinavian history[2]. On the economic side the Hansa obtained complete freedom of trade throughout Denmark, exemption from the laws of wreck, authority to appoint its own officers at the fishing centres and in all German settlements in Scania, while matters of currency, retail trade, customs and other dues were also regulated. As political guarantees for the security of these invaluable concessions, the Hansa was to hold four of the most important castles in Scania and receive two-thirds of the revenue of the province for fifteen years. Furthermore, no successor should ascend the Danish throne without the consent of the Hansa and without confirming its privileges. This sweeping agreement required the king's ratification. Waldemar delayed giving this until, by skilful diplomacy, he had somewhat softened the drastic character of this remarkable treaty. The victory over Denmark made the League the dominant power in Scandinavian politics, a power it utilised for building up its commercial supremacy in the north.

Waldemar, fortunately for himself, did not long survive his humiliation. By his death, in 1375, he made room for his celebrated daughter Margaret. As regent for her young son Olaf in Denmark, and from 1380 also in Norway, she now began to play a decisive and lasting rôle in northern affairs. Olaf had a rival in Albert of Mecklenburg, King of Sweden, also a grandson of Waldemar. Both claimants competed for the support of the Hansa, but Margaret outwitted the League by securing the election of her son, so that the Hansa had reluctantly to acquiesce in a *fait accompli*. On the other hand, it obtained favourable terms from Hakon of Norway in the Treaty of Kallundborg (14 August 1376) which terminated the war with that country. Margaret now followed her husband's example and confirmed the Hansa privileges, together with the Treaty of Stralsund and all that that instrument implied, except that the League abandoned its claim to interfere in Danish royal elections[3]. Peace at last reigned in the north, though it still rested on insecure bases.

[1] Wismar and Rostock of the Wend group were absent. They belonged to the Duke of Mecklenburg, who was continuing the war on behalf of his son, King Albert of Sweden.

[2] The text of the treaty and subsidiary documents are in H.R. i, 523–30.

[3] H.R. ii, 134–6. In No. 135 the exception is set out: "uttgenommen doch allene den Artikel des Köres den König to Denemerken."

The position so hardly won required constant vigilance on the part of the Hansa to maintain. The rivalry between Margaret and Albert of Sweden soon developed into a war in which the latter, supported by his father the Duke of Mecklenburg, created a monster—piracy on the grand scale and under the cloak of legitimate warfare—that became a curse to all peaceful commerce and in particular to that of the Hansa. Under the pretext of provisioning Stockholm, long besieged by the Danes, the pirates formed an organisation, notorious for the next half-century as the Vitalian Brethren, and played an important and sometimes even decisive rôle in the events of that period[1]. Hansa trade suffered enormously from the depredations of the pirates, and the League had at last to equip patrol ships, so-called "Friedenschiffe," to protect its trade. The task was made more difficult by the protection that two of the Wend towns, Rostock and Wismar, which were subject to Mecklenburg, openly afforded the sea-robbers. The situation was further complicated by the efforts of Margaret to obtain the release of the Scanian castles, pledged to the Hansa for fifteen years by the Treaty of Stralsund, and by the friendliness of the Prussian members of the League and their overlord, the Grand Master of the Teutonic Order, to Mecklenburg-Sweden. The conflicting interests of all the parties were most difficult to reconcile, despite the seemingly endless negotiations and frequent truces that were arranged, to which the pirates were sometimes a party. Margaret's tortuous but skilful diplomacy at last succeeded in retrieving the Scanian castles, since the Prussian and Dutch sections of the League which had hitherto opposed their surrender were now threatened by other dangers: Prussia by the Jagiello succession in Poland, and the Dutch by the rising power of Burgundy. Piracy was also for a time scotched by the extraordinary procedure of farming out the task of suppressing it to a private citizen of Stralsund. He was of the real *condottiere* type, having no motive but financial gain; and he achieved a certain measure of success.

But peace was once more disturbed by a change in the political situation. Olaf died in 1387 and Margaret, now Queen of Denmark and Norway, also laid claim to Sweden. Unexampled success crowned her arms. At the battle of Aasle (near Falköping) on 24 February 1389 she defeated and captured King Albert, his son, and a number of their leading supporters. This merely led to more embittered warfare, in which the Hansa, pre-occupied by strained relations with England and Flanders, and weakened by the rise of a democratic revolt against the patrician government in some of the towns themselves, notably in Lübeck, was obliged to remain neutral. Only when, in the piracy that inevitably revived with the prolongation of war, the pirates attacked, burnt, and plundered Bergen did the Hansa abandon its neutrality. Employing

---

[1] For an account of the rise of the Vitalian Brethren cf. K. Koppmann's introduction to vol. IV of the H.R.

every possible weapon, diplomacy, commercial blockade, reprisals, and "Friedenschiffe," the Hansa at last induced all parties to agree (Lindholm, 17 June 1395) to a peace. King Albert and his son were to be released for three years, and then they could purchase their freedom for 60,000 silver marks[1] or return to captivity. Stockholm, at last freed from its long siege, was to be handed over to the Hansa as guarantor of the peace. Trade was to be everywhere freely carried on according to the local laws, and the pirates recalled. Hansa energy had secured a respite for three years, but the changing politics had prepared the road for the Kalmar Union, consummated by Margaret two years later (1397). For the time being piracy was the chief menace to commercial enterprise. Some of the Vitalian Brethren, driven from the Baltic, transferred their nefarious activities to the North Sea, while others, aided by Mecklenburg, captured Gotland and converted it into a veritable pirates' nest. A joint Hansa-Prussian force re-captured the island from them, but Margaret, as regent of Sweden, claimed it in the name of the first Union king, Eric of Pomerania, her kinsman. She likewise demanded the surrender of Stockholm, and with this the Hansa readily complied in return for the confirmation of their privileges in all three kingdoms. Margaret, now the undisputed mistress of the north, further strengthened her position by a permanent peace with the Grand Master and Mecklenburg (1404). For a time real peace existed around the Baltic, but the politic Lübeck, looking ahead, constructed the Trave-Elbe canal, which was to render her trade less dependent upon the Sound and those who controlled it. For, despite the almost ceaseless disturbances that had plagued this region since Waldemar IV's attack on Wisby, the Hansa had tightened its hold upon the trade of the whole north. In Scania the Wend group, ably led by Lübeck, was supreme in the herring trade; in Bergen the same section had ousted all rivals, while the Livonian group dominated the Slav lands and Lithuania.

Not only in the north-east but likewise in the west, Hansa trade was expanding in every direction. In England its progress in the thirteenth century had been slow but secure. It had obtained trading rights and a domicile in London and elsewhere, and when Edward I issued his well-known *Carta Mercatoria* (1303) in favour of foreign merchants, the Hansa by its closer organisation was able almost to transform this general charter to a particular one in its own favour. Nevertheless, the German merchants in London had constantly to contend with their native competitors in the capital, supported by the city authorities. The strength of the opposition varied with the nature of the government. Under Edward I it had little force, but under Edward II the anti-alien agitation assumed serious proportions. This, however, was mainly directed against the Italians; the Hansa owed its comparative immunity from

[1] According to Koppmann (*op. cit.* p. xvi) this sum was equal to over 2,525,000 pre-war German marks—an enormous sum.

attack to its relative obscurity[1]. In fact, in return for some financial aid, Edward II, before the tragic end of his inglorious reign, granted a number of Hansa merchants letters of denization that enabled them to trade unmolested. The position so far won the Hansa was able to develop, since Edward III's war with France made him even more dependent upon foreign financiers and merchants. Upon these he showered constantly increasing favours and the Hansa naturally shared in them. Their export of English wool increased rapidly, and a *consortium* of more wealthy German merchants entered upon the less onerous and more lucrative business of advancing money to the king. By 1340 he was already considerably indebted to this group, most of whom came from Dortmund, at this time head of the Westphalian Third at Bruges. For a time they held the customs in pledge, which enabled them to export their wool free of all dues until they had reimbursed themselves for their advances.

Although these financial transactions never attained the scale of the Italian bankers, yet the Hansa group rendered Edward valuable services, especially in redeeming his crown and other jewels from that astute money-lender, the Archbishop of Trèves, and some Cologne merchants. The Black Prince also resorted to the Germans and pledged his Cornish tin mines with them for three years. In return for their complaisance, the Hansa merchants reaped a rich reward in the facilities which Edward granted them for their trade. They enjoyed immunities denied their competitors, including exemption from the increased dues imposed in 1347 on cloth and worsteds. England derived substantial benefit from the Hansa privileges. The market for English wool was widely extended; valuable commodities, such as furs, potash, pitch, tar, wax, turpentine, iron ores, copper, timber, wood and wood products including yew bow-staves, cereals, flour, flax, yarn, linen, boots, brass, copper and silver ware, silk, woad, madder, drugs, etc. were imported by them in exchange for our raw materials. The trade in herrings and dried cod, indispensable for the numerous fast-days, was almost entirely in the hands of the Hansa. These commodities were imported from the Norwegian and Scanian fisheries. The Hansa zealously excluded all intruders, and even Edward III's intercession on his subjects' behalf failed to gain them a footing in it. Nevertheless English traders began to penetrate the Baltic lands. From the sixties of the fourteenth century they traded directly with Prussia, claiming privileges in its towns similar to those held by the Hansa in England, a claim that was to prove an almost ceaseless source of friction between the League, the Teutonic Order, and England[2]. The friendly

[1] While London was opposing the Hansa, King's Lynn and Kingston-upon-Hull were granting them additional trading facilities. Cf. Lappenberg, *Urkundliche Geschichte des Hansischen Stahlhofes zu London*, II, 35, 205, H.U.B. II, 170, 189; and *Lübisches Urkundenbuch* (L.U.B.), II, 268.

[2] Cf. Sattler, *Handelsrechnungen des deutschen Ordens*, pp. 165 sqq. The merchants were mainly from London and the East Coast.

relations between Edward III and the Hansa changed towards the end of
the reign with the ever-increasing demands of the king for subsidies and
other contributions, as for example in 1371, when tonnage and poundage
were raised to 4*s*. and 9*d*. respectively. The Hansa resisted these new
rates as contrary to its privileges, and when its letters failed to attain
the desired end, it sent an embassy to England for the first time (in 1375)
to negotiate on the question. But the envoys were presented with a long
list of counter-complaints about the treatment of the English merchants
in the Hansa towns and in territories under its control. These the envoys
merely referred to the next meeting of the League. As for their own
grievances they received but little satisfaction.

The struggle between the English merchants and the Hansa persisted
with varying fortunes throughout the reign of Richard II. A breach of
commercial intercourse might have actually occurred in 1378 but for the
divergent interests of the League and its ally, the Teutonic Order. The
English traders, led by London, presented four demands to the Hansa:
(i) freedom of trade for all Englishmen throughout the Hansa lands, including Prussia; (ii) the removal of all restrictions upon trade with Scania;
(iii) freedom from arrest for debts for which a merchant was not personally
responsible; (iv) the names of all the Hansa towns. These demands were
summarily rejected by a well-attended representative meeting of the
Hansa at Lübeck (24 June 1379), but a fresh embassy was sent to
London. Here an additional demand was made of them, that Englishmen
should be admitted to the Hansa. The Hansa diplomats resisted the
Englishmen's claims so stubbornly that they were tacitly dropped, but on
accepting the insertion of a clause in the agreement, in vague and uncertain language, assuring English merchants of fair treatment, they
obtained the unconditional confirmation of their privileges—an undoubted
triumph for Hansa diplomacy. Complaints on both sides, however, did
not cease with this settlement, but the Hansa, owing to its peculiarly
loose organisation, was always able to evade responsibility. Thus there
was continual tension between England and the League, frequently
aggravated by attacks upon each other's shipping, with the consequential
reprisals. These measures led to a suspension of trade in 1386, followed
by an English embassy to the Grand Master. A treaty was arranged in
August 1388, which enabled the Englishmen to return to Danzig and
other Prussian towns, where they were hospitably received, and to enter
into closer commercial relations with the Order itself, which was now a
great independent trading concern as well as a territorial sovereignty.
The Englishmen, with the approval of their king, now tried to imitate
the Hansa, and formed an association in Danzig similar to the Steelyard
in London, but as they failed to obtain the consent of the Grand Master,
this body had only a brief, unofficial, precarious existence. The rival claims
of the Hansa, especially of its Prussian group, and the English merchants
were irreconcilable, and before the end of the century the treaty of 1388

was suspended. Even Richard II's exemption of the Hansa from the payment of tenths and fifteenths failed to induce the Prussian towns to remove their restrictions upon English residents in their midst or their dealings in cloth. So matters stood when the Lancastrian revolution ushered in a new era and new policies in England. The Hansa too was busy with Flemish and Scandinavian affairs, and postponed the English question, declaring that it should be "adjourned with good patience."

Within the Hansa itself there was no harmony. The accession of Jagiello, Grand Duke of Lithuania, to the Polish throne, brought his duchy into the ranks of commercial peoples, and the Germans were not slow to take advantage of the new situation. At Kovno a settlement was established, chiefly under the aegis of Danzig. Riga, which had for two hundred years monopolised the Lithuanian trade via the river Dvina, resented this intrusion of a rival. Stettin at the mouth of the Oder also acquired additional importance. All three towns were pursuing a selfish, monopolistic policy that brought Lübeck, that stout champion of Hansa rights, upon the scene. It had itself possessed chartered rights in Riga since 1231 and in Danzig since 1298. A lively dispute ensued, which, however, was soon settled, in order not to endanger the valuable trade with Novgorod. The Russian city ranked next to Bruges in its importance for Hansa trade, and its settlement was under the control of two aldermen, one from Lübeck and one from Wisby. The decline of the latter encouraged Riga to obtain equality with the leader of the League, an end she ultimately attained in administrative and trading questions. The Novgorod trade was always liable to disturbances on account of the low commercial morality of the backward Russians and the peculiar political relations between the semi-independent town and its princes. Throughout the sixties and seventies of the fourteenth century there were frequent disputes—embassies, treaties, and agreements notwithstanding. Finally the Hansa, in 1388, resorted to its familiar weapon, the commercial blockade, until Novgorod was almost completely cut off from the rest of Europe. This had the desired effect. Novgorod yielded and agreed to restore all the old treaties regulating its trade with the Hansa (1392)[1], and the treaty now concluded remained as the foundation of all future intercourse until Novgorod's independence was destroyed by the Grand Duke of Muscovy.

About the same time, Hansa trade with Flanders was also encountering fresh difficulties. It had suffered enormously during the first stages of the Hundred Years' War, but revived rapidly and attained unparalleled prosperity after the Peace of Brétigny. Only the democratic movement of the Flemish towns under Philip van Artevelde set limits to its profitable

[1] The Russians named this treaty the "Cross-kissing of John Niebur" after the leader of the Hansa embassy, as the signature of treaties was, with them, always accompanied by a solemn kissing of the cross.

development. Furthermore, the revival of Anglo-French hostility again endangered the safety of persons and property, for the Norman privateers that infested the Channel preyed upon neutral as well as enemy commerce. The Hansa seemed helpless, especially when its embassies to Flanders returned empty-handed. The feeling of insecurity reacted upon individual towns of the Hansa in opposite directions. At first it brought them into closer union, but when the steps taken failed to achieve their object, fissiparous tendencies at once appeared. On this account it was found impossible to break off relations with Flanders in 1379, since the Prussian group made terms with the count independently of the rest[1]. Matters became worse when Philip of Burgundy became Count of Flanders. Only a rigid commercial blockade with the transfer of the Hansa staple to Dordrecht in 1388 made the Flemings yield. Relations were resumed in 1392 upon the old bases, and new regulations added that strengthened the authority of the Kontor. Despite this apparent harmony, the rise of the House of Burgundy and its extension of the ducal power over the Flemish towns altered the conditions of Hansa trade materially, as the events of the next century were to prove.

The dominating commercial and political situation acquired by the Hansa since the Treaty of Stralsund was to be severely tested in the fifteenth century. Its monopolising aims naturally found no favour in other countries, while the vigorous competition between town and town or group and group always tended to weaken the bond of unity. Only when a grave danger threatened, as in 1367, was general assent for common action attainable. Divergence of view was not always due to divergent interests. Not all the towns were free imperial cities like Lübeck, and those that were not, like Wismar and Rostock or the Prussian towns, had always to trim their Hansa policy to that of their feudal overlords. And now a new factor arose that considerably influenced Hansa history. Democratic movements against the patrician oligarchical rule in the towns began to manifest themselves. At first the Hansa was strong enough to repress them, as for instance at Brunswick in 1374, but in 1407 Rostock and Wismar were obliged to admit representatives of the re-bellious gilds into the charmed circle of the town council. More serious still was the uprising in Lübeck. For a whole decade (1408–18) the brilliant leader of the League was crippled by its internal dissensions and the League itself almost dissolved[2]. Not until these democratic movements had been suppressed could the League revive, but meanwhile fluid fact had outrun the rigid theory of Hansa policy. In the fifteenth century the League began to find that its old weapons were blunted, that new commodities, new trade routes, new political powers were steadily undermining its position throughout the vast area of its activities. Of

[1] Bremen attended this *Hansetag* for the first time since its expulsion in 1284.

[2] For a summary of these democratic uprisings cf. Miss M. V. Clarke, *The Medieval City State*, pp. 87–98.

the political changes that affected the Hansa adversely, the most important were the renewal of the Anglo-French war with its concomitant privateering and piracy, in which the Scots also took a hand, and the defeat of the Teutonic Order by Poland. Although this meant the crippling of a commercial rival, it also weakened a valuable ally. The Grand Master was treated as an equal by the European sovereigns; his support was invaluable for Hanseatic diplomacy[1]. Moreover the fall of the Order occurred at the height of the constitutional struggle in Lübeck, and the attempts made to maintain the authority of the League by transferring the leadership to Lüneburg failed. Even important members refused obedience to its decrees, notwithstanding the persistent reminders by the Bruges staple of the damage suffered by the trade of the Hansa through the continued disturbances.

The end of the constitutional struggle in Lübeck witnessed the revival of the League. An unusually large number of towns—35—representative of every group attended the summer meeting of 1418. Its main purpose was naturally to recover the lost ground. In fact the statute of 24 June of that year was the first really united legislative act of the Hansa, binding upon and applicable to all members. Regulations were also framed to support the established government in the towns, to guide the conduct of merchant and shippers towards competitors so as to restore the old-time monopoly. Finally, a close alliance for twelve years was concluded for mutual defence and safeguarding of the land and sea routes; Lübeck was formally invested with the leadership, assisted by the other Wend towns as a kind of executive committee. Recent events had therefore resulted in closer union, with an embryonic constitution capable of further development to replace the inchoate organisation. Nevertheless the revived League was not strong enough to regain its former position abroad. Meanwhile the Scots, the Vitalian Brethren, and a new enemy, Spain, preyed upon its commerce[2]. Its weakness for the first time led the League to seek the aid of the Emperor, but Sigismund's intervention on its behalf in England, Friesland, and elsewhere merely brought disappointment. It was the attempt of the Kalmar Union king, Eric, to conquer Schleswig-Holstein that compelled the League once more to enter the field of international politics and postpone the solution of many pressing problems in the east and west.

The Holstein war was accompanied by a recrudescence of piracy by the Vitalian Brethren. Their depredations inflicted enormous damage upon Hansa trade, and no sea, from the Gulf of Finland to the North

---

[1] The general aristocratic opinion of the time is well expressed by the English Council in 1386 when it declared that belief should be given more readily to knights and squires than to lesser folk, mariners and such like. Cf. H.R. I, iii, 198, § 10, and v, 390 (p. 289).

[2] In 1419 the Spaniards captured a Hansa fleet of 40 ships *en route* from Bruges to La Rochelle.

Sea, was safe from them. All efforts to induce Eric to come to terms with his adversary proved fruitless. He continued to seize strategic points and to prey upon all commercial shipping within his reach. He even introduced a debased coinage into Denmark, which reduced all legitimate trading to a gamble. After many efforts to bring about peace, the League was obliged to equip a fleet in defence of its interests. This made the obstinate king somewhat more pliable. He agreed to settle all outstanding questions in return for an alliance with the Wend towns. But as the Prussian and Livonian towns opposed this policy and the Grand Master allied himself to Eric, the unity of purpose necessary for successful action was absent. A temporary cessation of hostilities was, however, provided by Eric's pilgrimage to Jerusalem, only to be renewed with greater ferocity in 1427 after his return. The naval war developed on a large scale, and both sides recruited ships and men in England[1]. In 1427 the Hansa suffered several defeats and enormous losses. On one occasion a whole fleet laden with Bay salt was captured by the Danes. The sea-going trade of the north was almost brought to a standstill, and old and neglected land routes were revived. Only by sailing in fleets and under convoy, and then only with great difficulty, could Hansa ships pass through the Sound. Even neutrals, like the English and Dutch, suffered from the belligerents as well as from the pirates. The commercial supremacy of the Hansa was seriously threatened; it became war-weary. Many towns even discussed the advisability of continuing their membership. Rostock and Stralsund, two of the Wend towns, actually made separate terms with Eric. At last the Grand Master's mediation was so far successful as to induce Eric to conclude a truce for five years (22 August 1432). This made the resumption of trade possible and the Hansa returned to Bergen, where the monopoly of the Wends was re-established. The pirate evil however was not laid; as in 1390 so in the Holstein war, it was easier to raise the monster than to destroy it.

Permanent peace was still far off when a rebellion broke out in Sweden, where the Kalmar Union had never been popular. This uprising at last induced Eric to make peace. After the usual preliminaries, a treaty was signed at Vordingborg on 17 July 1435. The conditions were brief and simple. Trade was to be resumed upon the pre-war conditions, while disputes that might arise were to be settled by an annual meeting of representatives of both parties at Copenhagen just before the commencement of the Scanian herring-fishing season. Apart from preparing the way for the break-up of the Kalmar Union, the war had produced great dearth of certain commodities in the north. Salt reached famine prices, since none could be imported from the Bay. On the other hand, the Lüneburg salines, under the direct control of Lübeck, revived. The Prusso-Livonian towns found no direct outlet by sea for their furs, wax,

[1] Eric's queen, Philippa, was a daughter of Henry IV of England. Cf. H.U.B. vi, 661, 694, H.R. i, viii, 336 and *Proceedings of the Privy Council*, iii, p. 271.

and timber products, and prices fell considerably. Merchants of the Wend towns bought them up, transported them westward overland, and reaped huge profits that enabled them to bear the strain of the war and recover from its ravages.

A more serious and permanent result was the impetus the war gave to Dutch competition. Hitherto Holland had only served the Hansa as a stepping-stone to England or a convenient centre for the Bruges staple when trade with Flanders was suspended. But the Dutch towns made a great leap forward when Philip of Burgundy became the ruler of Holland (1433). Their prosperity, like that of the Hansa itself, was largely founded upon the humble herring. Curing was introduced in 1400, with the result that Brill became a serious rival to Scania. Before long the North Sea herring drove the Scanian from the Rhineland markets, and even began to penetrate the Baltic lands. Dutch progress was materially assisted by the frequent failure of the Baltic fisheries, in part due to the migration of the herring[1]. Up to the end of the fourteenth century the Hansa had ignored these new rivals. The Prussians and Livonians, however, welcomed them as importers of Bay salt and freighters. Moreover the Dutch harbours were more suitable for their own larger ships than the shallower ones of the Zuyder Zee and Flanders, especially when the Zwin, the port of Bruges, was silting up, despite the strenuous efforts of the Flemings to keep it clear. When at last the Hansa realised the menace to its supremacy and wished to take measures to cope with it, a variety of causes led the League to hold its hand. Apart from the war with Eric, there was the threatened break-up of the Kalmar Union, the tension with England, the Anglo-Burgundian alliance, and above all the refusal of the Grand Master and of Cologne to co-operate in a commercial war with Holland, while Hamburg preferred privateering to a blockade. The war between the Hansa and the Dutch, conducted mainly by piratical methods with fluctuating fortunes and interrupted by frequent truces, seemed endless, when a new turn of the political wheel created a new situation. In the west, the League sharpened the commercial blockade of Holland, made peace with England (1437), and broke off relations with Burgundy, now, after the Congress of Arras, the ally of France. In the north, Eric had been driven from the throne and betaken himself to Gotland, which he converted into a pirates' stronghold and whence he preyed upon all commerce indiscriminately. His activities, together with the Dutch war, had, by 1439, almost destroyed the profitable and indispensable trade in Bay salt. The losses incurred by the League, more especially by the leading Wend group, and the difficulty of reconciling the divergent sectional interests induced the Hansa, after a meeting at Lübeck (12 March 1441), to accept the offer of mediation made by Christopher of Bavaria, who had not only replaced Eric on the throne of Denmark, but had temporarily restored the Kalmar Union.

[1] For the development of Holland cf. Blok, *History of the People of Holland* (Eng. trans.), ii, c. 12.

CH. VIII.

The negotiations ended in a ten years' truce with the Dutch, the removal
of all restrictions upon their trade, and the reference of all outstanding
questions to arbitration. The Dutch had vindicated their claims to a share
in the commerce of Europe, making a wide breach in the wall of monopoly
erected by the Hansa. But the trade in Bay salt fell ever more into Lübeck's
hands. The seemingly invincible strength of the Hansa attracted new
members to the League, while others who had withdrawn from it began to
seek re-admission. Common hostility led the Dutch and King Christopher
to make common cause against the Hansa. The king was determined
to diminish the hold the League had in his realms, but he had to
bide his time on account of the rising tide of nationalist sentiment in
Norway and Sweden, always hostile to Denmark. Accordingly, after many
delays the king, in 1445, confirmed the Hansa privileges in Scandinavia
and granted it exemption from Sound dues for two years. But the Norwegian officials, especially those of Bergen, still strove to curtail Hansa
activities in the country. Christopher, pursuing two irreconcilable policies,
maintaining the Hansa privileges and securing the rights of his own subjects,
ultimately alienated both parties. His officials failed in their aims. The
Hansa tightened its grip upon Bergen. Lübeck and her neighbours had
complete control of its chief article of export, dried cod, which they exchanged for corn and manufactured goods. To retain this trade in their
own hands they decreed that cod could only be shipped to their own
harbours, on pain of expulsion from the Hansa[1]. The peace so painfully
reached in the north was again disturbed by the death of Christopher (1448)
and the succession of Christian of Oldenburg in Denmark, and the election
of a native noble, Charles Knutson, to the throne of Sweden, while Eric, from
his stronghold in Gotland, continued to prey upon the commerce of his
former subjects and the Hansa. A clash seemed inevitable, but was staved
off by a temporary arrangement between Christian, Charles, and the League
(1450). Yet Christian still withheld his confirmation of the general privileges of the Hansa and only confirmed those of the Bergen settlement for
one year, at the same time encouraging the German artisans in the town
to resist the authority of the Hansa aldermen. For the time the League
had to acquiesce in this unfriendly attitude, as the West again claimed its
attention.

The return of the Kontor to Bruges in 1392 had been followed by a
period of peaceful prosperity, which the Hansa exploited for its own ends.
After decreeing that Hansa commodities, except herring, wine, and beer,
should, in Bruges, be sold to its own members, it forbade partnerships
between members and non-members and sought to remedy abuses in the
cloth trade. But in face of the development of cloth manufacture in
England and in parts of the Netherlands outside Flanders, the cloth trade

---

[1] Wend shippers gave preferential rates for freights to their fellow-townsmen in
order to exclude the Prussians and others. Cf. Daenell, *Die Blütezeit der deutschen
Hanse*, I, p. 335 and H.R. II, 35, 397.

in Bruges was declining. This made the town complaisant towards the
Hansa and eager to improve its communications with the sea, in order to
keep the Hansa staple within its walls. But once more external events
proved serious disturbing factors. Of these the worst were the war between
Holland and Friesland at the end of the fourteenth century, the renewal
of Anglo-French hostilities after the Lancastrian succession, and, above
all, the revived activity of the Vitalian Brethren in the North Sea, which
not even the severe defeat inflicted upon them by the Hansa could entirely
suppress. Moreover the League was crippled by the democratic revolution
in Lübeck. The Hansa, though neutral in the Anglo-French war, was
attacked by French privateers and their Scotch allies. Its embargo upon
trade with Scotland had to be withdrawn because the Grand Master and
some important Hansa towns refused to enforce it.

An even more truculent enemy now appeared on the scene, namely
Spain. The Spaniards resented Hansa competition west of Flanders and
with the aid of their allies, the Bretons, began to attack Hansa shipping,
so that many of the Hansa traders sailed under the Flemish flag. In
Flanders itself complaints of the Hansa were not so readily listened to.
The province was now under Burgundian rule, and the duke could not be
coerced to accept the Hansa view in disputed matters. Nor did the frequent
embassies bring any satisfaction. On the contrary, the expenses entailed
by these missions had compelled the League to impose a levy upon its
merchants in Flanders. Many of them, however, refused payment, and the
opposition at one time threatened the very existence of the Bruges Kontor
itself. Matters grew even worse when the whole of the Netherlands became
Burgundian territory (after 1433), and the duke, on breaking off his alliance
with England in 1435, expelled the Merchant Adventurers, thereby dealing
a severe blow at the Hansa trade in cloth. Protests against the duke's financial
policy met with the reply that he could not brook any interference with
his sovereign authority; and now the Hansa could no longer exploit the
jealousies and rivalries of a number of local potentates to its own advantage.
In fact the Hansa was failing to realise that the old system was passing,
that medieval methods and ideas were giving way before new strongly-
centralised and nationalist States with little respect for obsolete chartered
privileges that hampered their own development. But the League was
still strong enough to struggle against its many enemies, though its western
problems had to wait until it had made peace with King Eric, and
Hamburg had finally destroyed the pirates' nest in Friesland. The strained
relations with Burgundy were further aggravated by an anti-German riot
at Sluys in which nearly a hundred Germans were killed (1436). Trade
with the Netherlands was forthwith suspended and the staple removed to
Antwerp, despite the opposition of the Grand Master and the Prussian
towns. This was a most severe blow at Bruges, for the failure of the
harvest in Western Europe had sent the price of foodstuffs up to famine
rates, which the importation of corn from the Baltic lands might have

alleviated. By 1438 the resistance of Bruges was broken. It conceded all the German demands, including compensation for damages; and there was great joy when the importation of corn was resumed. The duke remained obdurate, though, after he had made peace with England and the wild naval war ended, matters improved. Nevertheless the star of Bruges was setting.

Antwerp and the Dutch were soon to prove most formidable rivals. Trade between the Hansa and Antwerp rested upon privileges granted the League by the Duke of Brabant early in the fourteenth century. It grew steadily as Antwerp, by encouraging foreign merchants, developed into an international centre of considerable importance. In 1431 Antwerp granted the Hansa specially wide privileges with low tolls and customs dues. Sluys also sought to attract Hansa trade to itself, and succeeded in doing so after it had settled the disputes that had arisen from the riot previously mentioned (1443). In the same year an amicable settlement was likewise concluded with Spain. The Duke of Burgundy was now the only outstanding enemy. In order to negotiate with him, the Hansa first held a meeting at Lübeck in 1447. It was largely attended and included representatives of all sections, as well as of the Grand Master, and the Kontors of London, Bruges, and Bergen. After once more fixing Bruges as the staple, an embassy was sent to the duke, but although it remained in Flanders six months, it returned almost empty-handed. The League did not relax its efforts; a second embassy found the duke more pliable, and he promised to redress the Hansa grievances. His promises, however, proved illusory, and the Hansa once more, and for the last time in its history, removed the staple—this time to Deventer and Kampen, both outside Burgundian territory. This action was opposed by the Grand Master, Cologne, and other western members of the League, the former on account of the unsuitability of the new centres for his trade, the latter on account of Lübeck's anti-English policy at this time. Consequently Cologne threatened to split the League and withdrew its representative from the meeting of 1452 (2 February). Timely concessions to the Prussians prevented the rift developing. A new regulation divided the articles of commerce into staple and so-called Vente commodities. The former, the costly articles such as wax, furs, metals, and skins, might still only be dealt with in the staple; the latter, mainly Prussian commodities, such as pitch, tar, corn, flax, hemp, etc. might be sold anywhere[1].

Although these regulations found general acceptance, Cologne refused compliance, as its chief trade was in wine; and as it had too many competitors outside the Hansa, it ran the risk of losing its trade with Flanders as long as the blockade remained. Bruges was helpless, but Ghent, in open revolt against the Duke of Burgundy, loudly disapproved of his policy. The Hansa was also not happy at Deventer; its harbour was too

[1] For an explanation and discussion of Vente goods, cf. Rogge, *Der Stapelzwang des hansischen Kontors zu Brügge im 15 Jahrhundert* (Inaug. Diss., Kiel, 1903).

shallow for the large ships used by the Prussians and Livonians, and the staple was removed to Utrecht with no better results, despite the extensive privileges granted by the bishop. Attempts to reach an understanding several times repeated, failed partly because the Grand Master was at war with Poland and could not exert his power in favour of peace. Moreover, trade was not entirely at a standstill; it was still carried on illicitly and by devious routes through neutral countries. Only when the duke had succeeded in placing his illegitimate son upon the episcopal throne of Utrecht did the Hansa yield. A Burgundo-Flemish embassy attended the League meeting at Lübeck and concluded peace (1457). Reciprocal concessions were made. The Hansa agreed to accept the jurisdiction of the duke's officers instead of those of the Flemish towns, while the duke promised to set up a permanent commission to deal with future disagreements; the Hansa also renounced its claim to the free import and export of the precious metals, and the duke confirmed all privileges granted by him and his predecessors. The settlement was joyfully acclaimed by Bruges, where special taxes were readily shouldered to pay the compensation allotted to the Hansa. This last use of the commercial blockade against Flanders was only a partial success. The western members of the League had resented it, and so it tended to weaken the organisation. The Hansa itself had learnt the strength of the Duke of Burgundy, and realised that its policy afforded a valuable opportunity to its rivals. Against the most formidable of these rivals, the Dutch, the League, after 1441, renewed the old restrictions upon their trade, to the entire satisfaction of its Prusso-Livonian and Zuyder Zee members. But the Dutch were not so readily repressed. Utilising their ten years' truce with the Wend towns and the blockade of Flanders, they began to push their trade with energy in all directions. In Christian I of Denmark they found a friend anxious to help them, as a set-off to the Hansa[1]. The privileges he granted them enabled them to use a land route between the Baltic and the North Seas that rendered them independent of the Hansa. But the Hansa was at this time too exhausted for further hostilities and was glad to prolong the truce to 1461. If the Hansa seemed to be losing ground in the north, it had, since the middle of the fourteenth century, developed the trade in what was then a new commodity of international commerce, the so-called "Bay" salt[2]. So great was the demand for salt in Scania during the herring-packing season that the old salines of Lüneburg were no longer able to satisfy it. This supply was, in the fifteenth century, under the complete control of Lübeck; hence the Prusso-Livonians became keenly interested in the Bay salt trade. The Dutch, too, frequented

---

[1] Christian I (1448–81) became King of Sweden in 1457 and in 1460 acquired Schleswig-Holstein.

[2] This name was given to the product of the salines south of the Loire estuary, in Brittany. The headquarters of the trade was the small town of Bourgneuf on the bay of that name, in the modern department of La Vendée. Cf. H.U.B. viii, 29 and A. Agats, *Der Hansische Baiensalzhandel,* Heidelberg (Inaug. Diss. 1904).

Bourgneuf, either as dealers or freighters. By the middle of the fifteenth century this branch of commerce had assumed such proportions that fleets of a hundred ships or more frequently passed through the Sound *en route* for various Baltic destinations. To render it secure, the Hansa entered into relations with Brittany, obtaining the necessary privileges from 1430 onwards. Search for salt also induced the Hansa to open up trade with Spain and Portugal. Russia provided a ready market for it, and Riga was the intermediary. But as Castile was the ally of France and Henry V of England had Hansa ships in his service, the Spaniards, who resented the intrusion of the Hansa into their trade, had a ready excuse for attacking their shipping in the Atlantic. By the efforts of Bruges, the Grand Master, and other interested parties, a truce was arranged in 1443 and frequently prolonged. Conditions became more favourable to trade when the English were finally expelled from France, and when the mean but far-seeing Louis XI ascended the French throne.

With England relations were strained from the commencement of the fifteenth century, despite the fact that Henry IV confirmed the Hansa privileges on his accession. English attacks on Prussian shipping impelled the Grand Master to suspend trade and expel the English traders from his dominions. The Hansa followed suit. Owing to the demand for English cloth on the continent, the blockade was not rigidly observed, and the Grand Master was himself the first to lift it partially and to enter into negotiations with Henry. After many delays and postponements an agreement was at last reached in October 1407 with the Prusso-Livonian groups, followed by another with the Hansa[1]. Two years later the latter obtained further compensation and the renewal of their privileges, thanks to the famine which visited Europe in that year and made England dependent upon imported corn. On account of the Grand Master's selfishness and the skill of the English envoys, the Hansa had almost split during these prolonged negotiations, weakened as it already was by the internal disorder in Lübeck and the defeat of the Teutonic Order by Poland. This encouraged Henry to disregard the settlement of 1407 and his subjects to continue their attacks upon Hansa shipping. Hansa reprisals were rendered nugatory by the policy of the Grand Master[2]. More than ever Prussia needed the English trade; even Danzig became more tolerant towards English merchants and allowed them to form an association of their own with their own alderman. But this no longer satisfied them. English opinion, as reflected in *The Libel of English Policy*, demanded rights in Prussia equal to those enjoyed by the Hansa in England. As in the time of Richard II, London again took the lead in this anti-alien agitation, so that when the Germans refused

[1] Cf. K. Kunze, *Hanseakten aus England* (H.A.E.), nos. 304–64, pp. 205–327, where the negotiations with claims and counter-claims are set out in detail.

[2] In 1417 the English captured ten Hansa ships laden with Bay salt.

to pay a subsidy in 1423 the Steelyard was closed and its members imprisoned. Still the Hansa insisted upon its privileges, and gradually prevailed upon Parliament to induce the city authorities to be more conciliatory. Fresh fuel was added to the rising flames of passion when the Hansa, at war with Eric of Denmark, tried in 1427 to exclude neutrals from the Sound, and when four years later the English government increased the rates of tonnage and poundage and altered the bases of assessment. The energetic protests of the Hansa were so far successful that the new rates were suspended and the old method of assessment revived. After a meeting of the Hansa an attempt at a settlement was made in 1431. But the negotiations dragged on until they were outstripped by the Congress of Arras, which transformed the whole political situation. Burgundy, now hostile to England, strove to prevent an understanding, but, thanks to Cardinal Beaufort, a treaty was concluded in 1437. This was a triumph for Hansa persistence. Not only were its privileges again confirmed, but it was freed from all dues not mentioned in the *Carta Mercatoria*. The only concession obtained by the English was a vague assurance that they could trade in all Hansa towns according to the old customs. Even these modest claims aroused hostility in Prussia, and the Grand Master refused to ratify the treaty. Henry VI was being urged to withdraw the Hansa privileges, and after many delays promised to do so if the Grand Master persisted in his attitude. But neither side was anxious to drive matters to extremes, since the renewal of the Anglo-French war had closed the Flemish harbours to the English. Henry VI therefore sent envoys to Lübeck to negotiate with Denmark, the Hansa, and the Grand Master and, after an adjournment, a truce was concluded at Deventer (June 1451) which once more opened the Sound to English shipping. Prospects of permanent peace were disturbed by the seizure by the English of a German and Dutch Bay salt fleet of 110 ships. The Dutch ships were liberated, while those of the Hansa, mainly belonging to Lübeck and Danzig, were confiscated and their cargoes sold. Reprisals by the Hansa naturally followed, but more extreme measures were ruled out by the opposition of Cologne and her western colleagues, who had no interest in the salt trade. Henry VI, faced by the growing discontent with his government that burst into Cade's rebellion, was ready to settle with Prussia and Lübeck, but the latter demanded compensation for losses and seized an English ship that was carrying English envoys to the Grand Master[1]. Lübeck in fact was prepared to force a breach with England, but receded from her intransigent position and concluded a truce for eight years (March 1456).

The dynastic struggle which threw England into disorder reacted upon Hansa trade with England. The redoubtable Warwick, now governor of Calais, against whom Henry VI was powerless, preyed upon Hansa

---

[1] The Germans alleged that among the grievances of Cade's rebellion was the suspension of trade with the Hansa. Cf. H.R. ii, 3, nos. 638, 647, 669, and 670.

shipping[1], with the inevitable reprisals by the Hansa and its ally
Christian I of Denmark, who closed the Sound to English vessels. Before
the questions raised by this piratical act could be settled, Warwick's
protégé, Edward Earl of March, had ascended the English throne. But
the League, doubting the permanency of his success, did not at first
apply for the confirmation of their privileges. Edward, on his part,
could not afford to alienate the capital, whose merchants and civic
authorities were pressing for the suspension of the Hansa privileges until
Englishmen had obtained similar ones in the Baltic lands. He did, however, grant the League a temporary confirmation, pending a full investigation of the whole subject. As the king's position was still difficult, he
was anxious for peace and even sent envoys to Hamburg to bring it about.
The Hansa might now have achieved a real diplomatic success, but it
was hampered by its own want of unity. Cologne and its associates were
pursuing an independent policy, which ultimately led to the withdrawal
of the Rhine city from the League for a whole decade. Meanwhile
Edward prolonged his temporary grant to the Hansa from 1462 to 1468,
on condition that a final settlement of outstanding questions was reached.
But when he had made peace with Burgundy and Anglo-Flemish trade
was resumed, he refused to send further embassies to meet the Hansa
negotiators. The latter had for once shewn lack of wisdom and missed a
great opportunity. It had now again to face English hostility and even to
bear the blame for Christian I's seizure of English ships in the Sound.
The resentment felt in London resulted in an attack upon the Steelyard,
which was partially destroyed, and Germans in England were arrested
and imprisoned. This further encouraged Cologne to pursue its particularist policy. It separated itself from the League and formed an association of its own such as it had had in the time of Henry II.

On the other hand, Edward had alienated Warwick and so yielded to the
pressure of the cloth-makers of the western counties, who felt the loss
of the Hansa trade severely, and of his ally, the Duke of Burgundy[2]. On
the duke's mediation Edward liberated the arrested Germans for 4000
nobles and agreed to resume negotiations with the Hansa. But before
these could be undertaken, Edward was a fugitive, and Henry VI was
again seated on his unstable throne with Warwick in possession of all
real power. The Hansa seemed master of the situation. Its alliance was
courted by both the English parties and their respective allies, Charles
the Bold and Louis XI. After an unusually well-attended meeting of the
League in September 1470, trade with England was suspended and
an energetic privateering war initiated. Edward himself promised full
confirmation of the Hansa privileges in return for assistance to regain his

[1] In July 1458 Warwick captured a Lübeck fleet of 18 ships, whose cargo was
valued at 168,000 Rhine gulden.

[2] Among those who wrote to Edward on behalf of the imprisoned Germans was
Caxton, at that time Governor of the Merchant Adventurers in Antwerp.

throne. The League as a whole hesitated, but Danzig accepted, and its fleet formed a considerable part of the armada that brought him home. But Edward IV failed to keep his promise and the war was resumed. All Hansa harbours, as well as those of Denmark and Poland, were closed to English trade. Danzig naturally resented the royal ingratitude and exerted itself to the utmost in the naval war that now developed on a large scale. Edward therefore secretly approached the Bruges Kontor, and this culminated in the negotiations at Utrecht in 1473. These almost assumed the nature of a European congress. Not only the League, but its staples at London, Bruges, and Bergen were present as well as Kampen, Cologne, and some individual Flemish towns. England, Burgundy, Brittany, and some minor potentates were the other principals to the transactions. The discussions lasted nearly a whole year. Point by point the Hansa diplomats forced the Englishmen to yield, despite the efforts of Cologne to wreck the proceedings. Finally a series of treaties were arranged and signed (February 1474). The Hansa privileges were restored and later received the approval of Parliament; it obtained the ownership of the Steelyard as well as its warehouses in Boston and King's Lynn, and London again agreed to allow it the partial control of the Bishop's Gate. The English claim to equality in Hansa towns failed entirely. Though the League had scored an undoubted victory, Danzig and some other towns still hesitated to ratify the treaties, so that the League only entered into the possession of its establishments in London and the eastern ports in the spring of 1475. The treaty with England was followed by similar agreements with Burgundy and the Dutch provinces and towns. With Brittany a final settlement was postponed, but the duke extended his protection to the Hansa until a treaty could be concluded.

Although the treaties of Utrecht brought commercial peace in the West, the arrangements could not last in the face of the rapid dissolution of medieval institutions now going on. The trade with England was, however, still a factor in Hansa policy, but it never attained the importance of Bruges except for the Prusso-Livonian groups. Bruges (though never so closely organised as the other foreign settlements) was the guardian of Hansa interests in the West, and not infrequently it inspired its policy and guided its action. It was dominated by Lübeck, since 1418 the official head, and long before then the directing brain of the League. But the Bruges Kontor, like the parent organisation, did not always command the obedience of all sections. The self-seeking policy of the Westphalian group has already been mentioned. Under Cologne's leadership they had built up a prosperous trade in wine with England, Holland, and Flanders that reached its apogee in the last quarter of the fourteenth century. Decline then set in, so that Cologne felt impelled to oppose the Hansa whenever its action disturbed the peaceful trade between its members and the best markets of the Rhineland towns. At the same time Bruges itself was losing its dominant position as an international market, causing many

German merchants to seek trading outlets elsewhere. To arrest the threatening disintegration the Kontor made efforts to obtain privileges in other Flemish towns, in Holland, and elsewhere, and to unify its control by amalgamating the separate funds of each Third into a common fund under the control of one alderman. But, thanks to the prolonged resistance of Cologne, it was only in 1447 that this programme was partially carried out; the funds were amalgamated but the management was not unified. The Kontor was likewise invested with authority over all German merchants trading throughout the Netherlands, and permitted to tax them to defray the costs of embassies and of keeping the seas clear of pirates. This provided a fresh spur to the opposition of Cologne, whose example was imitated by other towns as well as by individual merchants. Serious results followed. Already Bruges was declining, partly on account of the competition of rivals, the gradual silting up of the Zwin, the rise of the English and Dutch cloth manufacture, and the frequent commercial wars of the Hansa, including the ten years' blockade of Flanders itself (1448–58). Prior to this, the Hansa had, in 1442 and in 1447, issued stringent ordinances that aimed at compelling its members to purchase cloth only in Bruges and a limited number of "free" markets in Flanders and Brabant, while the peace of 1458 included a promise of the League to re-establish the staple at Bruges in all its former strength. The efforts to do so, as well as to levy the contributions previously mentioned, proved an endless source of friction. Cologne even went so far as to invoke the aid of the Duke of Burgundy against the Kontor, an act that broke one of the strongest bonds of the Hansa, since it had always resisted the interference of outside authorities in its internal affairs. Despite all difficulties, the Kontor did not relax its efforts on behalf of the common good. Thus in 1463 and 1464 it obtained special privileges from Louis XI, in 1460 it prolonged the truce with Spain, in 1461 with the Dutch, and it continued to enjoy the protection of the Duke of Brittany. Naturally the Kontor was supported by the League. An ordinance issued in 1465 that all Hansa merchants were to resort to Bruges proved ineffective. Cologne definitely withdrew and submitted its case to the Duke of Burgundy, who, however, failed to give a clear decision on the points at issue between the protagonists. Breslau likewise threatened withdrawal, while the Duke of Burgundy, and Antwerp also, resented the action of the League. Antwerp, therefore, concluded a treaty with the Hansa in 1468 on such favourable terms to the latter that Bruges was severely hit by it.

If the ground seemed to be slipping from under the Hansa in the west, in the north it still continued its monopoly, thanks to the assistance of Christian I of Denmark. Once more he forbade the Dutch to transport Bay salt through Danish waters and restricted English trade in Norway. This encouraged the Hansa to persist in its old methods. The meeting of 1470 renewed all the old regulations relating to the staples, and threatened Cologne with expulsion if it did not submit to the traditional arrangements. As it had incurred the hostility of the Duke of Burgundy and the Treaty of Utrecht threatened its privileged position in England, Cologne was reconciled to the League in 1476 upon terms dictated by the latter. This, together with further extensions of the truces with Holland and Spain for twenty-four years and a grant of freedom of trade by the Duke of Brittany for seven years, shewed that the Hansa was still a power in the commerce of Europe. These gains must, however, be set against other losses. The rapid decline of the Teutonic Order after 1410 deprived the League of a valuable ally. Many Prussian towns suffered impoverishment and practically withdrew from the Hansa. Danzig was the only exception. Lübeck also profited by it, since it annexed the amber trade, formerly a monopoly of the Order, which had exported it to Bruges to be manufactured into rosaries and thence exported to all parts of Europe. Prussia's losses were Poland's gains, despite the attempts to destroy its competition. Only one branch of Prussian trade still flourished— the trade in salt with Lithuania. But this too was mainly in the hands of Danzig, from the middle of the fifteenth century almost the sole centre of Prussian overseas trade and shipbuilding. Danzig had established a depot at Kovno with a branch at Vilna. The attempt of the Order to revive its waning fortunes was frustrated by a fierce civil war. Its rebellious towns allied themselves with Poland, receiving valuable privileges in return. Those granted to Danzig were almost sovereign rights that wellnigh made her an independent State. These advantages reacted in favour of the Hansa at a time when they were most useful, when the imbroglio with England and the war between Denmark and Sweden seriously threatened its commerce.

In other directions the middle of the fifteenth century was also a testing time for the Hansa. Christian I was none too friendly until Sweden rebelled against him. He then (May 1455) made peace with the League and added a new clause which annulled any grants of his predecessors that conflicted with the privileges of the Hansa. This, however, found no favour in Norway and could not be exploited in Bergen in face of the hostility of its governor. The Dano-Swedish war again jeopardised the trade of the Baltic, especially as Danzig, which had given shelter to the fugitive King Charles Knutson, was waging a fierce piratical campaign against Denmark. By Lübeck's insistence, a brief truce between the warring parties was arranged, so that the disputed questions might be submitted to arbitration. Although this failed and old causes of strife were revived, the ceaseless efforts of the Hansa, which armed its ships trading with Riga and Novgorod, and the defeat of the Order in the civil war, brought about a general peace. By the Treaty of Thorn the Order lost all its territory except East Prussia, and accepted the suzerainty of Poland. Trade was able once more to resume its interrupted course, but not along its old lines. Important developments had occurred in the meantime. Thorn lost its pre-eminence as a regional staple, and Stettin replaced it as the mart for trade in Scania herrings; Danzig lost its hold over the Lithuanian trade, since Kovno now had a rival in Vilna; the

German merchants withdrew from the interior, preferring to have their merchandise transported for them to the maritime towns. They had followed a narrow restrictive policy which could no longer be maintained. Only Danzig grew in strength as its rivals declined. Denmark, too, required the constant vigilance of the Hansa. Christian I had, on the whole, been friendly, but the Hansa became apprehensive after he had acquired Schleswig-Holstein (1460). Hamburg and Lübeck renewed their old close alliance, since Christian, desirous of developing his new territories, had granted Amsterdam a favourable tariff, as well as the use of a land route that threatened the supremacy of the old one between Hamburg and Lübeck. The king's hostile attitude even led him to interfere in the internal affairs of the towns, so the League had to exercise its power to prevent him from excluding Wismar from the Scanian fisheries, and brought about a peace between him and Bremen. Christian could not shake himself free from the Hansa. Financial stringency, partly due to the fall in the value of money, and partly to the decreasing revenue from the herring-fisheries when the herring began to exchange the Baltic for the North Sea, had compelled him to impose higher tolls upon Hansa shipping. But he had to yield to the protests of the League and withdraw them.

The Baltic herring trade, though still considerable, was declining rapidly and the great international fair in Scania during the fishing season had ceased; new packing centres outside the Hansa influences arose. Danish towns began to compete with those of the League. These now initiated an anti-foreign policy, and though Christian maintained the Hansa privileges as long as he needed its political support, he was obliged also to encourage his own subjects. The new developments reacted upon the towns in various ways. Stettin had its depot at Malmö and enjoyed the special protection of the king, while Rostock retained its supremacy at Oslo and other Norwegian towns. On the other hand, the Wends were still pre-eminent in the Bergen trade, with Lübeck taking the lion's share. Political considerations still compelled Christian to acquiesce in this situation, though he resented his dependence upon the League. Peace with Sweden was still far off, so that when the Swedes raised Sten Sture the elder to the throne, Christian had again to purchase the aid of the League. At its instigation he again restricted non-Hansa trade in Bergen and forbade the transport of Bay salt through Danish waters by the Dutch. Meantime the Swedes had inflicted a crushing defeat on the Danes at Brunkeberg (10 October 1471). They initiated a strictly nationalist policy that ultimately liberated them from German influence. The Germans lost their secular right to half the membership of the Stockholm town council, and the Swedes opened their harbours to the Dutch[1]. A durable peace between Denmark and Sweden followed, which

[1] Intellectual independence was likewise obtained by the foundation of the University of Upsala (1477); Denmark followed this example by establishing the University of Copenhagen in 1479.

brought definite advantages to the Hansa and in particular to its leader Lübeck with its Wend associates. In return for a loan, Christian pledged a number of towns to Lübeck which gave it the control of the harbours of Holstein. The king's efforts to free himself from the incubus of the Wend towns were frustrated by the peace which for a time succeeded the stormy period through which Europe had passed even after the conclusion of the Hundred Years' War. Thus the commercial domination of the North by the Hansa remained substantially unimpaired, though Christian's bitterness against the League was displayed in a series of decrees designed to diminish its power. But they remained a dead letter. In Bergen the Hansa was stronger than ever. The English had ceased to frequent it; the Dutch were kept within strictly narrow limits. Only in the trade with Iceland did the Hansa feel the competition of the English, since Christian readily sold permits to them. Nevertheless the close of the fifteenth century saw the rise of new forces that ultimately deprived the Hansa and its leaders, the Wend towns, of the political and economic influence they had so long exercised in the three northern kingdoms.

But political and military events were not the only disturbances affecting the smooth course of trade. Fluctuation of prices, the varying yield of the herring-fisheries, disputes between different groups of the Hansa itself, as for example between the Livonian towns and Novgorod, Cologne, and Lübeck, difficulties that arose from abuses in trade itself, all contributed to create unstable conditions. Hansa merchants frequently complained of the quality of the furs and wax delivered to them by Russians and Lithuanians; the latter retorted in kind and pointed to the falsifications in quality and quantity of the cloth and other commodities sold them by the Hansa. Nevertheless the Hansa managed to retain its hold on the Russian trade by its customary measures to exclude all competitors. It even forbade the Dutch, whose shipping was indispensable to the Livonians, to learn Russian or to trade directly with Russians visiting the Livonian towns. Here Riga took the lead in carrying out the Hansa policy, for the town aimed at attaining a position within its sphere of influence such as Danzig had reached in Prussia. A conflict with Lübeck, representing the common interest of the whole League, was inevitable, especially as Riga's action again disturbed relations with Novgorod. Peace between the latter and the Hansa had been concluded in 1392 (*Niebur's Cross-kissing*), but Novgorod began to demand better treatment for its own traders in Livonia and at sea, just as the English had demanded of Prussia. Though relations were not broken off, thanks to the mediation of Dorpat (Yuriev), yet the Russians and Lithuanians began to press their claims with greater insistence, especially after the fall of the Teutonic Order had lowered German prestige throughout the Baltic region. Consequently suspensions of trade and reprisals were frequent, especially as the Hansa was unable to put forward its whole strength on account of its endless entanglements in the north and west, and earlier in the century on account of the democratic revolt in Lübeck. This enabled Riga to obtain an equal share with Lübeck in the administration of the Novgorod Kontor, since the latter had become ever more dependent upon its Russian and Livonian trade during the prolonged disputes and wars with other parts of Europe. By 1459 Riga, thanks to the rapid decline of Novgorod, was able to prohibit strangers visiting it from trading with one another; even members of the Hansa were no longer allowed to trade directly with the Russians. The constant quarrels between Novgorod, the Livonian towns, and the Livonian Order reacted in favour of Polotsk, though its trade never reached the proportions of that of the older city. But Novgorod's days were numbered. The rising power of the Grand Dukes of Muscovy was jealous of its independence. In 1471 Ivan III subjected it to his authority, and as he confirmed all the old privileges and customs of the Hansa it seemed to promise a period of peaceful, prosperous trade. Ivan was, however, still hostile to Novgorod. After sacking the town in 1478, he deprived it of its independence, and the proud old city republic sank to the level of an ordinary Russian town. In 1494 the German settlement disappeared for ever before the strong centralised State that had emerged. The history of the Hansa in Novgorod thus bears a close analogy to that in Bruges.

This unexpected development induced the Livonian towns to resume closer relations with the Hansa and to cling more tenaciously to the trade with Polotsk. But in the new world that was arising there was no room for independent or even semi-independent towns. Against the new monarchies that ruthlessly destroyed all those who had formerly withstood the authority of the feudal overlord, the Hansa failed to hold its own. Medieval systems were disappearing, and with them the old Hanseatic monopoly of Russian trade with the west was lost for ever. To this result the Hansa had itself, in a considerable measure, contributed by its selfish and narrow policy. Its frequent blockades and restrictions upon freedom of commercial intercourse not only led to evasions of its decrees, but also to the rise and development of new routes. While the Hansa dominated the Baltic and certain land routes in North Germany, traders who felt the severity of its control created new routes that circumvented those which the Hansa had made its own. These were mainly the work of the South German cities that now became serious competitors to the Hansa as intermediaries between the north and south, and the east and west, of Europe, and in the next century Nuremberg, Prague, Frankfort on the Main, and others outstripped the towns of the League. Naturally the Hansa endeavoured to erect barriers in the way of their development. But the old weapons were becoming blunt and rusty. Artificial limitation and restrictive legislation were giving way to greater freedom and enterprise in all directions. Even Lübeck itself, the tireless protagonist of Hansa monopoly, could no longer dispense with the Frankfort market when its famous fair began to acquire international importance. These South German rivals also profited by the progress of the Turks in South-eastern

Europe. The capture of Constantinople closed the market in Venice to the Slav lands and they had to seek new outlets and new routes for their products, and these the south afforded them. That the League did not immediately succumb to the blows it received on all sides is indisputable evidence of its inherent strength and of the political far-sightedness of its leader, Lübeck. Nevertheless the changing conditions were not without their effect. Inland towns gave up direct overseas trading, purchasing foreign commodities from the maritime towns. No longer needing the Hansa, they gradually withdrew from participation in its affairs. Such towns consequently suffered loss of population and of revenue and gradual impoverishment. The fifteenth century was for the Hansa a period of depression, but old systems may long survive unless destroyed by some cataclysmic upheaval. This the Hansa was spared, and so it lingered on as an effective organisation for yet another century. But at the close of the Middle Ages its position had developed somewhat differently from what its earlier days promised. It had drawn to itself the trade of the northern half of the continent, and later stretched its tentacles towards Spain and Portugal. It had created a monopoly in the north, banished the English from the Norwegian trade, and rigidly circumscribed the activities of the Dutch. Only in Venice did it fail to secure that exclusive position which it attained in Bergen, Bruges, Novgorod, or London. Until the accession of the Tudors, it is true, its position in England was strengthened by the Treaty of Utrecht. Even the rise of Burgundy did not entirely destroy the trade through Bruges. A more severe blow, however, was the decentralisation of trade in the Netherlands. This proved fatal to the authority of the Bruges Kontor and the League whose spokesman it was. Even the Baltic, at one time almost a Hansa lake, could no longer be maintained as its special preserve.

The Hansa had developed out of associations of Germans trading abroad. Membership depended upon the right of the citizens of given towns to enjoy the privileges acquired. These were the special functions of the early associations, and all Germans were allowed to participate in them without too close an investigation of their claims. Later, these unions of individuals influenced the home towns, which began to form close alliances for furthering common interests. With its growing strength membership became more valuable and was limited to citizens of Hansa towns. As the prestige of the League increased, membership was eagerly sought; expulsion, or "Verhansung" as it was called, became a severe punishment[1]. But centrifugal forces were not always under control. Many towns formally withdrew, or allowed their membership to lapse by abstention from the deliberations of the League. An important city like Cologne was, however, compelled, against its will, to remain within the fold. Yet so vague and uncertain were the conditions of membership that

---

[1] The League often called the entry of new members " re-admission," in order to impose upon foreign countries.

no accurate list is extant, nor can such a list be confidently compiled from the existing records, though it has been generally assumed to range about the seventies[1]. Around the larger centres were often grouped smaller towns and even districts that frequently held local assemblies for common action. Such was the case with the Livonian group that held its first meeting in 1358 and then annually. In Prussia only the six largest towns were members, and after the civil war only Danzig retained any interest in the foreign affairs of the League. It is doubtful whether the Hansa itself ever knew exactly who were members and who were not; and if it did know it kept it a close secret, steadfastly refusing all information on the subject. On several occasions, notably in 1449, 1462, and 1473, the English demanded the names of the members but were categorically refused, either because the envoys of the League did not know or because they would not disclose them. Similarly the League refused to regard itself as a corporation acting through a common head and possessing a common fund or seal. It claimed to be no more than an association of towns for safeguarding trading privileges acquired abroad[2].

Quite early in its history the League divided itself into territorial groups—the well-known "Thirds," each later subdivided into two Sixths, but this had little significance outside Bruges and Flanders where it originated. Such importance as it had was due entirely to the supremacy of Flanders in Hansa commerce. In the Middle Ages no other division applicable to the whole organisation existed. Leadership was early assumed by the Wend group, and among them Lübeck was pre-eminent and generally acknowledged as head long before it was officially recognised in 1418 and again in 1447. The Wends formed the nucleus, Lübeck the nerve-centre of the whole system. Yet Lübeck cannot be said to have been the "head" of the League. The highest authority for all purposes was the meeting of representatives, or *Hansetage*, though only such meetings can be regarded as full *Hansetage* at which all the Thirds were present. Such complete assemblies were never very frequent; from the fifteenth century onwards they were only held at long intervals of 20 to 30 years. At this time the subjects dealt with mainly concerned commercial and political relations with the north, the monopoly of the Wends.

[1] Prof. Walther Stein in H.G.B. pp. 223 sqq. has investigated the question with the aid of all the documentary material available, and enumerates some 200 towns, villages, and districts that somehow, at some time, were associated with the Hansa.

[2] The English definition of the Hansa in the negotiations of 1469 (H.U.B. 9, 570, § 1) as "Quaedam societas, collegium, universitas, seu unum corpus vulgariter nuncupatum Hanza Theutonica" the Hansa envoys repudiated. In 1473, at Utrecht, when the Burgundian emissaries repeated the English view, the Hansa representatives replied: "dat de stede von der hense eyn corpus weren in eren privilegien, de se in itliken rüken, landen und herschoppen hadden und wanen ere privilegien werden ingebroken, so plegen se darumme to vorgadderende und darup to radslagendeunde denne sampliken statute unde ordinancie to makende uppe solke gudere der lande dar en ere privilegien wurden ingebroken de in der gemenen stede der hanse nicht to lidende." Again, in the same discussion they reiterated "dat se nicht eyn corpus weren, noch geweset hadden, wolden ok noch eyn corpus wesen."

Very few other towns attended. The direction of Russian affairs passed into the hands of the Livonians. Lübeck was by far the most frequent meeting-place.

The number of towns attending was small, rarely exceeding thirty. The smaller towns usually entrusted their representation to the larger ones and furnished them with plenary powers. Some towns, such as Cologne, advanced claims to precedence, but it had to yield to Lübeck and content itself with second place; Hamburg and Bremen contended for the third place. Similar orders of precedence were evolved among the groups and the officers in charge of the packing-centres in Scania. Long notice of meetings had to be given, not only on account of distances and slow travelling, but also because local groups often met beforehand to discuss the agenda, decide upon their policy, and draw up instructions for their envoys. On account of the cost many towns evaded attendance. After 1430 the League imposed a fine upon absentees, and threatened arrest of goods and persons as well as "Verhansung" unless a sufficient excuse, on oath, was furnished; these drastic measures were, however, not enforced. Fines were also imposed upon late arrivals or early departures unless the grounds alleged were satisfactory. Decisions were by majority. Not infrequently members repudiated them; many towns often purposely withheld full powers from their representatives so as to refuse acquiescence in resolutions which they did not approve. The decisions of the *Hansetage* were embodied in a protocol known as a "Recess" and sealed with the seal of the town where the meeting had been held, since the League had no common seal. Abroad, Lübeck's seal was so regarded, as all correspondence was carried on from there. The Hansa had no permanent diplomatic service, but the foreign settlements or Kontors, where such existed, fulfilled admirably the duties of an ambassador. For special purposes embassies *ad hoc* were sent, usually consisting of councillors from the leading towns. Just as it had no common seal, so the League had no common purse. Its nearest approach to one was the poundage levied in 1361, and subsequently for the war against Denmark or for freeing the seas from pirates. This was often collected with great difficulty and under the stress of threats of exclusion from privileges abroad and cessation of commercial intercourse at home.

Though it continued far into the seventeenth century, the Hansa had outlived its great days. It was a purely medieval creation destined to disappear in the modern world. It could not be transformed into a single State nor amalgamate with a territorial sovereignty. The geographical discoveries shifted the centre of gravity of the world's trade from the inland seas to the great oceans. These the Hansa could not control as it had once controlled the Baltic and North Seas. With the change, its disappearance as a world power was inevitable. Its life in the sixteenth century was but the reflex action, the dying struggles of a once powerful giant.

CH. VIII.

CHAPTER IX

THE TEUTONIC ORDER

THE lands that surround the inland sea of Northern Europe were till the twelfth century quite unknown. The ancients knew of them only as a source of amber and as a region, like Arabia and Central Asia, which sent forth periodically hordes of warriors. Even the Viking age threw little light for civilised Europe on the homeland of these redoubtable invaders. The Ostsee of the Germans, the Varyag sea of the Russians, remained a region of darkness and legend; and to Adam of Bremen, the first writer to use the name "Baltic," the land directly east of the Elbe was "Slavia," while the vague territories beyond were still known as "Scythia." Apart from the Scandinavians, the inhabitants of the Baltic region fell into three linguistic groups: the Slavs, the Balts, and the Finns. Of the *Slavs* east of the Elbe, the Obotrites and Lyutitzi had long been known to the Germans. The Pomeranians, "dwellers by the sea," who occupied the seaboard between the Oder and the Vistula, were less known. Farther east, the Poles and Russians were cut off from the sea by the Baltic and Finnish tribes. The *Balts* or *Letto-Lithuanians* are quite distinct from the Slavs. The group originally consisted of (i) the Prussians[1], who occupied the seaboard from the Vistula to the Niemen; (ii) the Jadżwings, who dwelt on the upper Narew; (iii) the Lietuva or Lithuanians, comprising the Aukstote, *i.e.* "uplanders," on the upper Niemen and its tributaries and the Zhemoyt (Samogitians or Zhmudz), *i.e.* "lowlanders," on the lower Niemen; (iv) the Latuva or Letts, consisting of the Letgals north of the Dvina, the Sels or Selones between the Dvina and Lithuania, the Zemgals north-east of the Zhemoyt, and the Lettish tribes in Kurland who were just absorbing the Finnish Kurs and taking their name. The *Finns* inhabited an enormous area on the Volga and in North Russia. The Finns on the Baltic comprised (i) the Kurs stretching from the Kurisches Haff to the Gulf of Riga; (ii) the Livs[2] who dwelt between the Dvina and the Salis; (iii) the Ests who dwelt in the islands and formed a compact mass between the Salis, the sea, and Lake Peipus; (iv) the tribes between the Narva and the Neva; (v) the

---

[1] The name "Prussia" is derived from the native word Prusiskai (*Lithuanian*, Prusas), the meaning of which is not known. The ingenious theories based on the form Borussia, which was first used in the sixteenth century, are absurd.

[2] From the Livs the colony was called Livland or Livonia (*Polish*, Inflanty), although the Letts, who were conquered later, were more numerous than the Livs. To-day the Livs are practically extinct; their land is a province of Latvia and is inhabited solely by Letts. The Livs (Livones) and Letts (Letti or Letgalli) must not be confused with the Lithuanians, whom some chroniclers call Lettones.

tribes north of the Gulf of Finland and round the Gulf of Bothnia. These tribes, who were called Finns by the Germans and Chudes by the Russians, had no common name for themselves.

All these peoples dwelt in scattered tribal groups near the sandy coasts, the remote swamps and lakes, and in the wooded plains of the Baltic region. The Lithuanians alone were plunged in the more remote primeval forest. All were pagans, with little civilisation and no political cohesion. Only slowly did any idea of racial unity grow up among them, owing to the pressure of the more advanced peoples on their borders. The Scandinavians were the first to penetrate these remote lands. The Swedes had sailed up the Dvina and Neva and played a great part in the history of Russia. The Danes had early relations with the Ests and the Prussians, and by the thirteenth century were a great power in Pomerania and Mecklenburg. The Russians had penetrated to the coast at an early date. Novgorod had conquered the Vods and Ingrians between the Narva and the Neva, and from time to time took tribute from some of the Esthonian tribes, among whom Yaroslav founded the city of Yuriev (*Est*, Tartu). The Letts of Tolova on the Aa paid tribute to Pskov; and Polotsk founded principalities for its junior princes at Gersike and Kokeynos on the Dvina to rule the riverine Letts and Livs and to safeguard the trade route to Gotland. The Poles made several attempts, notably under Boleslav I, to conquer the Prussians, but all these expeditions, like the missionary efforts of SS. Adalbert and Bruno, failed to impress the stubborn pagans. Boleslav III, with the aid of Otto of Bamberg, successfully converted the Pomeranians, whose land came into the Polish political orbit. But the most effective penetration of the Baltic lands was made by Germans. The work of Henry the Lion and Albert the Bear established strong German outposts in Mecklenburg and Brandenburg, and, by the foundation of Lübeck in 1143, brought Germany into the Baltic as a commercial power; and soon the German trader sailed eastwards to the unknown lands. The missionary followed; and in the century 1184–1284 almost all the pagan lands were won for Christianity and civilisation.

The Danes first sent missionaries to Esthonia, and soon began to settle on the north coast, where they founded the city of Reval (*Est*, Tallinn). It was the old Varangian trade route up the Dvina that attracted the traders of Bremen; and in 1184 an Augustinian canon, Meinhard of Holstein, set out to convert the heathen. Asking permission of Vladímir of Polotsk to preach the gospel to the Livs, he settled some way up the Dvina at the village of Ykeskola (*German*, Uexküll) where he built a church. His colleague Theodoric converted the Livs of the neighbouring province of Toreida on the Aa, and Meinhard was made Bishop of Uexküll under Hartwig, the ambitious Archbishop of Bremen. He died in 1195, and his successor Berthold, who believed in more militant methods, perished in battle. An abler man was needed to direct the infant colony, and in Albert, a nephew of the archbishop, a real statesman was found, whose foresight, ability, and ambition transformed a small missionary enterprise into one of the greatest colonial achievements of the Middle Ages. Albert soon made use of the opportunities that fortune offered him. The decline of German monarchy made many knights and burghers disposed to adventure and settlement over the sea. The golden days of the Crusades were over, but it was easy to win men for a crusading effort in a less remote country, where the risks were less and the opportunities greater than in Palestine, especially when indulgences were granted by Innocent III, who saw in Albert a kindred spirit and gave him every support. Besides recruiting crusaders and preachers from North Germany, Albert solicited help from Canute VI, the greatest ruler in the Baltic, from the Swedes of Gotland and the merchants of Bremen and Lübeck. In 1201 he set sail from Lübeck with his great fleet carrying warriors, priests, traders, and artisans, especially stonemasons—for the building art was to play a great part in the success of the new colony. On a small tributary on the right bank of the Dvina he founded his new capital Riga, where he persuaded a number of German burghers to settle with full municipal liberties. Finding that his casual enlistment of crusaders was inadequate for the defence and expansion of the colony, he founded a crusading Order, the *Fratres militiae Christi*, popularly known as the Sword Brothers. The Order, which adopted the rule of the Templars, received a charter from the Pope in 1204. Supported by a sufficient military force, the bishop proceeded to strengthen his spiritual resources by the foundation at Dünamünde of a Cistercian monastery. With occasional setbacks, the work of conquest and conversion proceeded apace, and by 1206 the Livs of the lower Dvina, of Toreida, Idumea[1], and Metsepole were members of the Christian colony, so that Albert had fresh fighting material and a little time to consider his future plans. The situation of the colony was not secure. To the east, it is true, lay a large Lettish population, which had suffered from the raids of the war-like Livs and Ests and was not likely to be an obstacle to German expansion. But they fell within the sphere of Novgorod and Polotsk, which deeply resented the spread of German influence. South of the Dvina were the warlike Zemgals and Kurs. North of Livonia were the aggressive Ests. Moreover the bishop had to keep his Livs fast in the faith, to check the growing pretensions of his Knights, and to emancipate his episcopate from the metropolitan claims of the Archbishops of Bremen and Lund. He attached Kaupo and other Livonian chiefs to him by the impressions they gained during visits to Germany and Rome. With the help of the Order and fresh crusaders he succeeded in driving the Russians out of their Dvina principalities, where he built the castle of

[1] This was not a scriptural name, but represents the Liv words *Idu maa* meaning "north-eastern land." Metsepole means "along the forest."

Kokenhausen, and conquered the Sels south of the river and the tribe of Vends[1], among whom the Knights built the castle of Wenden (*Lettish*, Kes).

As the result of these successes, Albert won the support of the Lettish chiefs of the interior, who solicited his help against the Ests. This marks the second stage in the expansion of the colony. Esthonia consisted of three distinct regions: the two great provinces of Saccala and Ugenois (of which the latter was tributary to Novgorod) in the south; the provinces of Jarwe, Viro, and Harju (where the Danes were founding a rival colony) in the north; the maritime provinces and the islands of Oesel and Dago in the west, the inhabitants of which were hardened pirates, the most pagan and warlike of all the Baltic tribes. With an army of 8000 men, half of whom were Livs and Letts, the bishop and the Master invaded Esthonia. Their first occupation of the southern provinces was followed by a great effort on the part of the natives, aided by their Russian allies. It was not till the stubborn battle of Fellin (*Est*, Wiljandi) in 1217, in which the gallant Kaupo on the German side and the Est leader Lambito were killed, that Saccala was won. The Russians and Ests held out obstinately in Yuriev, and it was not till its capitulation in 1224 that Ugenois was conquered. A last advance culminated in the overthrow of the Osilians in 1227, when Oesel was conquered and the cult of the local god Tarapilla brought to an end. Conversion followed conquest, but conflicts continued unceasingly with the Russians and with the Danes, to whom the Germans were forced to yield the northern provinces of Viro and Harju, which they held till 1346. Any attempts to conquer the south were foiled by the growing power of the Lithuanians, who were gaining influence over the Russians of Polotsk and helping the Letts of Semigallia and Kurland to resist Christianity and the German sword.

The colony of Livonia was organised administratively during the actual campaigns. To Albert's bishopric, which embraced the whole of the south, *i.e.* Livonia proper, were added two new dioceses for Esthonia: that of Ugenois or Dorpat[2] (first held by Albert's brother Herman) for Saccala and Ugenois, and that of Leal or Oesel for the maritime provinces and the islands. The bishopric of Reval in Danish Esthonia was under the Archbishop of Lund, but Albert, who now called himself Bishop of Riga, was freed from the metropolitan control of Bremen. Albert had now to reckon with the claims of the Order, which had played so gallant a part in the work of conquest. Happily for the peace of the colony, the Pope sent as legate William, Bishop of Modena, whose religious fervour completed the conversion of the natives, while his tact and statesmanship effected a peaceful partition of the land between the

---

[1] The Vends or Vendi had no connexion with the Slavonic Wends of the Elbe. They were a tribe of unknown race which had recently been driven by the Kurs from the river Venta or Windau.

[2] The name given by the Germans to Tartu-Yuriev.

ambitious prelate and the truculent Knights of the Order, whose two Masters Wenno (1204–23) and Volquin (1223–36) were determined to hold the lands they had won by the sword. The conquered territories were divided between the bishops and the Order in the proportion of two-thirds to one-third, each bishop still to retain spiritual control over, and exact tithes from, the whole of his diocese. The bulk of the Liv country west of the Aa and on the Dvina fell to the Bishop of Riga, the Order receiving the lands of the Vends and Letts east of the Aa. Farther east, the southern Lett country fell to the bishop, the north to the Order. In Esthonia, all Ugenois and some lands north of the Embach were awarded to the Bishop of Dorpat, Saccala and Jarwe to the Order. The islands and most of the coast fell to the Bishop of Oesel. The lands of the Order were divided into administrative units, each under a Komtur or a Vogt. Such were Ascheraden, Segewold, Wenden, Fellin, Weissenstein, and Pernau. The headquarters of the Master were at the Jürgenhof in Riga, but Wenden and Fellin always remained the chief castles of the Order. If we consider that the monastery of Dünamünde owned the land along the Dvina estuary, that the cities like Riga, Dorpat, and Pernau became prosperous communes owning considerable estates, it can be realised that the colony was not a unitary State but suffered from all the disruptive elements of feudalism. Both the Order and the bishops gave large estates in fee to their vassals, some of them natives like Kaupo, the ancestor of the Lieven family, but mostly immigrant nobles from Westphalia like the Meyendorffs, Tiesenhausens, and Rosens. No German peasants settled in Livonia. The native population soon lost its liberties, but retained its various languages.

The great bishop died in 1229, having seen the completion of his main task, but leaving many difficult problems for the future. The relations of the Order and the bishops, the conquest of the Zemgals and Kurs, and the danger from external enemies offered possibilities of trouble. But the most urgent question was the drying up of the sources of military power. The depression of the natives and the scarcity of crusaders were as serious a problem as the depletion of the Order by their losses in war. The burghers were hastening to exploit the lucrative trade with Russia; the vassals were settling down to enjoy their new lands. The heroic age of the colony was nearly over. An attempt to conquer the Kurs and Zemgals ended disastrously on the Saule, where Volquin was killed with the majority of his Knights. The Order was forced to seek outside support, and approached the Teutonic Order which had just begun its triumphant career in Prussia.

While the Germans were thus successful against Dane and Slav in the north, they were engaged in a similar rivalry with Dane and Slav in Mecklenburg and Pomerania. The Pomeranians never became a united people, but they displayed some tenacity in resisting German and even Polish pressure, though they welcomed the civilisation that was diffused

from such monasteries as Kolbatz and Oliwa. German influence was
strong in Western Pomerania, but Eastern Pomerania was part of the
diocese of Kujawia and still considered as within the Polish sphere,
though a native dynasty had supplanted the Polish princes in the twelfth
century. Prussia was quite outside the German sphere of influence. It
was the ambition of the Poles to convert these formidable neighbours to
Christianity, as they had converted the Pomeranians a century before.
Godfrey, Abbot of the Cistercian monastery of Lekno in Great Poland,
revived the missionary effort in Prussia; and so successful was his enterprise that his colleague Christian was made Bishop of Prussia by the
Pope, and was granted considerable lands by his Prussian converts in the
border region of Lubawa (*German*, Löbau). Unfortunately, the Prussians
at this time (like the Lithuanians a century later) underwent a transformation which made them a menace to their neighbours. Kujawia and
Mazovia suffered terribly from their raids. At this time Poland was
divided into several principalities which had little connexion with each
other. The Prince of Mazovia, Conrad, was able to defend his possessions
during the lifetime of his brilliant general Krystyn. But the frontier was
constantly over-run, and the border district of Chelmno became almost
a desert. The bishop and the prince persuaded the Pope to preach a
crusade which attracted a number of Poles and a few Germans. Chelmno was
won and again lost. The disputes of the Polish princes convinced Conrad that
a permanent military force was indispensable, and he was advised to open
negotiations with the Teutonic Order. In 1225 he approached the Grand
Master and built a castle for the Order near Torun. Meanwhile the
Bishops of Kujawia and Plock had organised a new Order, on the model
of the Livonian Knights, which took its name from the district of
Dobrzyn granted to it. This donation to a rival stirred the Teutonic
Order to activity. This famous Order—*Ordo militum hospitalis S. Mariae
Teutonicorum Hierosolimitani*—was an association formed during the
Third Crusade, on the model of the older Orders, to support the German
hospital and to organise Germans to fight against the infidel. It owed
its importance to the influence and statesmanship of Herman of Salza,
Grand Master for nearly thirty years (1210–39), under whom it had
acquired wide possessions in Palestine, Armenia, Achaia, Sicily, and
Germany. But its career in Transylvania (1211–24) had shewn Europe
how far more usefully and successfully a crusading Order could be employed nearer home. The King of Hungary, however, alarmed at the
growth of a German power on his borders, revoked his concessions just
about the time that Conrad's suggestion was offered. The prospect of a
crusade in a land suitable for German settlement, where the conversion
of the heathen could be accompanied by the accumulation of wealth and
power, was irresistible. Herman accepted Conrad's offers (in 1228 and
1230) of Nieszawa, the land of Chelmno, and the possession of all lands to
be conquered in Prussia, and he also negotiated with Bishop Christian

for the lands of his diocese. It is probable that Conrad, who was a poor diplomat, did not intend to confer in perpetuity the complete ownership of Chelmno, and that he hoped to share in the future conquests. But Herman outwitted him by obtaining the right to both Chelmno ("terra Colmensis"; *German*, Kulm) and all conquests in Prussia from both the Emperor and the Pope. On this firm legal basis he sent Herman Balke with a body of Knights to occupy Nieszawa and begin the campaign in Kulm.

The conquest of Prussia was completed in fifty years. What the Poles had failed to do by hard fighting and religious fervour was accomplished by building, sea-power, method, and discipline. The Order had a great advantage over the Poles in that it was a corporation with a consistent policy, with a large experience of warfare, with diplomatic and legal skill, and with all the prestige and resources of the Empire and the Holy See behind it. On the site of Torun and Chelmno strong castles called Thorn (1231) and Kulm (1232) were built. The Prussians who had occupied the land were dislodged by astute diplomacy; German settlers were brought in, while many Poles and Pomeranians returned to their former estates. The recovery of the province with scarcely any fighting was followed by an expedition down the Vistula which resulted in the foundation of Marienwerder in 1233. All was favourable for a campaign against the Pomezanians, the Western Prussian tribe beyond the Ossa. A crusade was preached, and a large army consisting mainly of Poles and Pomeranians descended the Vistula, and, through the strategy of Sventopelk of Pomerania, won a decisive victory on the Sirgune (1233). In three years, with the help of the Margrave of Meissen, all Pomezania was occupied. The crusaders sailed along the Frisches Haff against the Varmians and Natangians, built the castles of Elbing (1237) and Balga (1239), and soon the coastal strip as far as the Pregel was occupied. Otto of Brunswick helped the Knights to complete the conquest of these tribes and to build castles at Kreuzburg, Bartenstein, and Rössel in the territory of the Bartonians (1241).

The conquest was followed by the wholesale conversion of the natives. So high did the credit of the Order stand that the Livonian Order requested to be united to the Teutonic Order, an offer which was accepted and confirmed by a papal bull in 1237. Herman Balke, who had shewn moderation and ability in his treatment of the Prussians, was sent to Livonia as Landmeister with sixty Knights to restore the situation there. At first he was successful. The jealousy of the local Germans was gradually overcome; the Danish question was settled; and the situation was restored south of the Dvina. An aggressive policy was inaugurated against the Russians. Crossing the Narva, the Germans occupied the country of the Vods, built a fort at Koporie, and projected a Catholic diocese there. Izborsk and then Pskov, the great bulwark of north-western Russia, were captured, and a plan for the conversion of Orthodox

Russia to Catholicism was concerted by the Order and the Pope—a mirage that has often deluded Western Europe. But a great man was found to save Russia in the person of Alexander Nevsky, the Prince of Novgorod, who had recently defeated the Lithuanians and driven the Swedes from the Neva. He quickly recovered Koporie and Pskov and in 1242, on the ice of Peipus, he utterly routed the Order in one of the most decisive battles in Baltic history.

In Prussia also dark clouds were gathering. A quarrel had broken out with the bishop, who resented the high-handed treatment he met with from the Order, which regarded him as a subject rather than an equal— a very different position to that in the northern colony where the bishop was the predominant partner. But a more serious enemy arose in Sventopelk of Pomerania with whom a dispute was inevitable, since his position on the Vistula was always a threat to the vital communications of the Order, while he resented the claims of the newcomers to the Vistula delta, and viewed with surprise and misgiving the rise of a new State and its alliance with the Poles, who claimed suzerainty over his country. He found fruitful soil for intrigue among the Prussians. Only superficially Christians, mindful of their past liberty and resentful at the forced labour imposed on them by the preparations for a Mongol invasion, the Prussian leaders were ready for mischief. The departure of Balke left native affairs in the hands of less sympathetic Knights, while the prestige of the Order was lessened after its defeat at Liegnitz by the Mongols. Sventopelk attacked Prussia, murdered all the Germans he could reach, and raised revolt all over Prussia. Only the Pomezanians remained loyal. All the other tribes rose and massacred the Germans. In Kulmerland 40,000 Christians are said to have perished. Only Thorn, Kulm, and Reden held out. In the north Varmians, Natangians, and Bartonians drove out the Germans everywhere except from Elbing and Balga. Particularly formidable were the unconquered Pogezanians of the interior. Luckily for the Order, they were loyally supported by the Polish princes. The castles were relieved and recovered, and the rebels forced to surrender. The Pomeranian prince made peace in 1243 and 1248, but war again broke out and ended finally in 1253. The Order did not really extricate itself from its dangerous position till the arrival of large crusading forces. In 1254 the Czech King Ottokar, Rudolf of Habsburg, and Otto of Brandenburg with over 60,000 men assembled at Elbing, marched to Balga, and not only recovered Varmia, Bartonia, and Natangia, but embarked on a campaign against the Sambians of the peninsula, the most important of all the Prussian tribes, strong in their military resources and their geographical isolation, wealthy with their amber and their horses. The peninsula was conquered, and a city was built called Königsberg in honour of the King of Bohemia. The conversion of the Sambians was a great blow to the pagan tribes—the Nadrovians on the Pregel, the Skalovians on the Niemen, and the Sudavians of the lake district—who continued to raid Sambia and incite the natives to revolt.

Meanwhile events were happening in the north which vitally affected East Prussia. The submission of the Kurs had been effected in 1245–50 by the Landmeister Grüningen, and his successor Stuckland, although he had to face the hostility of the Zemgals and Lithuanians, was equally successful. The Zemgals were forced to pay tribute; Kurland became a tranquil province, and a new diocese was established there. The prince of Lithuania, Mindovg[1], failing to hold the Kurs and Zemgals by force, resorted to a new device. He feigned to become a convert to Christianity, was crowned king by the Bishop of Kulm, renounced all pretensions to Kurland, and endowed the Order with extensive territories in Samogitia. The simultaneous successes in Kurland and Sambia and the conversion of Mindovg led the Order to conceive the great project of uniting their territories by the annexation of Lithuania—a plan which had the hearty support of the Papal See. Stuckland in 1252 built a new town, Memel, on the Tange to prevent the import of arms to the Kurs, and to check the mutual help given to each other by the Kurs and Sambians. Communication with Memel was established by the foundation of Labiau on the Deime, and a fort called Georgenburg was boldly set up on the Niemen; so that, on the legal basis of Mindovg's concessions, it was hoped to occupy Samogitia and effect a junction with Kurland at Amboten. But the Zhemoyt invested Georgenburg, and Lithuanians attacked the Livonian army at Durben in 1260 where, through the treachery of the Kurs, the Order suffered one of the greatest disasters in its history, the Landmeister, the Marshal of Prussia, and 150 Knights being left on the field. The results of this defeat were appalling. The Kurs revolted. Mindovg apostatised and over-ran Livonia. The Russians ravaged Ugenois and besieged Dorpat and Wenden; the Lithuanians swept over Livonia as far as Pernau; and the Osilians rose in Esthonia. The repercussion of these events was felt in Prussia, where the natives headed by the Sambians apostatised and threw off the German yoke. In the north the situation was restored by valour and by good fortune. The Est revolt was quelled by the Danes; the Kurs were gradually crushed; the Lithuanians were defeated at Dünamünde; and a Russo-Lithuanian force failed before Wenden. The death of Alexander Nevsky in 1263 was followed by the death of Tevtivill, the able Lithuanian ruler of Polotsk, and of Mindovg himself. Russia was weakened, and Lithuania relapsed into anarchy. The Order was able to subdue not only the Kurs, but also the stubborn Zemgals, in whose territory they built Mitau. Livonia was saved.

In Prussia, the rebellion lasted over thirteen years. The Order owed its salvation to its strong position in Kulm and Pomezania, where the population was mainly German and Polish, to the quiescence of Pomerania,

[1] His Lithuanian name was Mindaugas: the Germans called him Mindowe.

to its command of sea communications, and to the assistance given it by the numerous crusaders who flocked to defend threatened Christianity. It had to deal now not with mere barbarians, but with able national leaders who had lived in Germany, had mastered the art of war, could take fortresses and work in concert. The mild attitude towards the natives was abandoned, and a policy of extermination was the German answer to the atrocities of the Prussian rebels. It is owing to the ruthlessness displayed in this war that Prussia is to-day German rather than Lithuanian. Some cities held out in the darkest hour, especially Königsberg, which was relieved by the ingenuity of a Lübeck sailor. The Knights made their greatest effort in Sambia, to which they had access by sea, and which they reduced to such a desert that forests grew where once a numerous people had dwelt. By 1263 the Sambians were practically exterminated, and in 1266 Otto of Brandenburg built a castle called after his own country. The rebels, aided by the independent Sudavians, not only held their own, but continually raided Kulmerland and Pomezania. In 1272 with the help of the Margrave of Meissen the Knights obtained some successes, but it was the death of leaders like Charles Glappon and Henry Monte which disheartened the natives, and in 1273 the Varmians and Natangians made peace. The Bartonians followed suit, and from 1274 to 1283 the Knights took the offensive against the independent tribes. Despite a fresh rising in 1277 among the obstinate Pogezanians, who were exterminated, the Nadrovians, Skalovians, and Sudavians were reduced to obedience. A great many of the Sudavians were settled in desolate Sambia, where they retained their language for four centuries. The irreconcilables under Skurdo left Prussia for ever, and were given lands by the Lithuanians, whom they inspired with an undying hatred of the Germans. By 1283 the war was over, and Prussia was completely in the possession of the Order.

Successful in its Prussian mission, the Order turned its attention to Lithuania. For the Order as a religious body the conversion of the pagan Lithuanians was as natural a task as the occupation of Samogitia was essential to its political security. For the next hundred years, while the acquisition of Pomerania and its relations with Poland bring the Order most prominently before Europe, its main tasks were the colonisation of the interior and the Lithuanian Wars. The two are inseparably connected, because hostile raids were the chief obstacle to settlement, while systematic colonisation was the best basis for the penetration of Lithuania. The German colony of Prussia was quite small and was separated from Lithuania by an enormous area called the Wilderness. The Galindians and Sudavians of the lake district and the Jadźwings farther east had disappeared. Lithuania was practically bounded by the Niemen, so that the wide stretch of country in between, separating Prussia from Mazovia and Lithuania, was mainly forest, marsh, and lake, inhabited by a few pioneers (Prussians, Mazovians, and German adventurers). This gave the

war certain peculiar features. Colonisation by means of fortified towns
was the best method of defence, so we see a great development of peasant
and burgher settlement. Strassburg (1285) and Neumark (1325) defended
Kulmerland on the Drewenz. In the Komturei of Christburg grew up
Saalfeld (1315), Liebemühl and Deutsch Eylau (1335), Osterode and
Gilgenburg (1336). From Elbing there were founded Preussisch Holland
(1290) and Möhrungen (1327); in the diocese of Varmia, Guttstadt (1325),
Rössel (1337), Seeburg (1338), and Allenstein (1348); in the Balga
Komturei, Bartenstein and Lunenburg (1326), Preussisch Eylau and
Landsberg (1335), Rastenburg (1344), and in the heart of the Wilderness
Johannisburg (1345); in the Komturei of Brandenburg, Barten and Lötzen
(1285). From Königsberg were founded Gerdauen (1325), Wehlau (1335),
and in 1289–93 Ragnit and Tilsit, which formed a separate Komturei.
It will be noticed that each Komturei occupied a zone in the Wilderness.
Another characteristic feature of the period was the development of
guerrilla warfare. Already during the rebellion a band of Germans and
Prussians under Martin von Golin used to make its way into hostile
country, cut off supplies, kill small bodies of the enemy, and even surprise
towns. Later on, they made their way through the marshes and surprised
a Lithuanian ship which they successfully piloted some 250 miles down
the rivers to Thorn. Another guerrilla leader Mucko is mentioned as
operating in Varmia. These people were called "struter" by the Germans,
"latrunculi" in the Chronicles. Even Knights of the Order did not
disdain this mode of warfare, and in 1376 the Chronicler mentions them
as organising an expedition *pedestres more latrunculorum*. Probably
Skumand the Sudavian and other loyal Prussians taught the Germans
this craft and shewed them the paths through the lake district. There
were two main routes for the invasion of Lithuania—the route through
the Wilderness to the upper Niemen, and the water route to Samogitia.
The former had the merit of surprise, since no one could tell what force
might emerge from those vast solitudes. On one occasion the movement
of an aurochs might disclose a whole army. On another the Lithuanian
prince might be captured by a small band. But the distances were great:
Balga to Grodno 170 miles, Brandenburg to Merecz nearly as much.
Provisions for several months had to be carried; armour could not be
donned till the Niemen was near; starvation, flood, and surprise by the
foe were the normal conditions of warfare. The second route was easier.
Across the river from Ragnit was Samogitia, and 75 miles up the river
was Kovno, from which the enemy's capitals were quite accessible[1].
Consequently the main German attacks were made by this route, and
the prosperous city of Memel and the Komturei of Ragnit were its bases,
connected by sea with Kurland and by water through Labiau with
Königsberg. The activities of the brothers Liebenzell led to the occupation of Karsovia, the western part of Samogitia, and to the establishment

[1] Kernov and Troki were 110 miles from Ragnit, Vilna 130 miles.

of a new base at Christmemel in 1315. The fate of Lithuania depended on the strip of river between Ragnit and Kovno; yet it took the Order a hundred years to occupy it. Seldom has a war been waged so stubbornly and with such ferocity. It was not uncommon for captured Knights to be burned alive in their armour and for Lithuanian raids to devastate whole areas, even in Kulmerland. The Knights used to ravage systematically and massacre all the inhabitants. The Chronicler records that the Livonian Master in 1378 *per ix dies et noctes occidit, cremavit, vastavit et destruxit omnia.* On the lower Niemen castle after castle was set up by the Germans, Christmemel, Baierburg, Gotteswerder, Marienwerder, Ritterswerder, only to be captured by the enemy, whose more primitive forts, Bissene, Kolayn, Junigeda, Valevona, and Kovno, always rose again after each defeat. At least two raids were made annually into Samogitia, sometimes supported by raids from Livonia, though these were generally directed towards Upita, Vilkomir, and Vilna.

The explanation of the obstinate resistance of Lithuania is to be found in her rapid expansion under Gedymin[1]. While Keystut (1342–82) at Kovno fought the Order, his brother Olgierd (1345–77) at Vilna was ruler of all Western Russia. The mobility of their armies was amazing. One year raiding Esthonia, another year invading the Crimea, Olgierd would leave the siege of distant Moscow and appear suddenly on the Drewenz to threaten Thorn. Lithuania's successes were facilitated by the growing hostility to the Order in Poland and by the feud in Livonia between the Order and the archbishop. A further calamity for the Order was the Esthonian revolt of 1343 and the ravages of the Black Death. But the campaigns against the pagans continued to attract crusaders, and the house of Luxemburg were specially fervent supporters of the Order. John of Bohemia made three great expeditions to Lithuania, while Lewis of Hungary, Albert of Austria, Lewis of Brandenburg, Charles of Lorraine, William of Holland, Henry of Derby, and many others[2] made the Crusade there. In 1348 a great victory was won on the Strawa over Keystut and Olgierd by Winrich von Kniprode, whose tenure of the Grand Mastership (1351–82) was the golden age of the Order. He died the same year as Keystut and Lewis of Hungary and Poland; and the next year saw a political revolution of sinister import for the Order. By the Treaty of Volkovysk the Poles effected by diplomacy what the Germans had failed to do in a century of warfare—the conversion of the Lithuanians to Christianity. Olgierd's son Jagiello was to marry Jadwiga Queen of Poland. The conversion of Lithuania changed the whole situation for the Order, and marks the end of the Baltic Crusades.

The dynastic union of Poland and Lithuania was the direct result of the aggressive policy of the Order. Although the Poles had supported the

---

[1] See *infra*, Vol. VIII.

[2] One expedition was interrupted in the depths of Lithuania by a fight between English and Scottish crusaders.

Knights against Sventopelk, they came to see that the Pomeranian prince had been right, that the Order did not intend to share its conquests with any ally, and that it was becoming a far more formidable neighbour than the barbarian Prussians. Moreover the national feeling, just then reviving in Poland, was conscious of the dangerous German element with which it was confronted. The external aggrandisement of Brandenburg, the German colonisation of West Pomerania and Lower Silesia, were no less a menace than the widespread settlement of Germans inside Poland, especially in the towns. The settlement of German peasants and burghers in Prussia was a further economic and political blow. The loss of Kulm seemed permanent, and the Order was casting covetous eyes on Dobrzyn, Micha-low, and the Mazovian borderlands. It was the Pomeranian question which brought matters to a crisis. The adroit diplomacy by which the Order was wont to extract profit from its disasters was never better displayed than in their occupation of strategic points on the Vistula during the war with Sventopelk. They received further accessions of territory on the death of his son. But it was when Pomerania passed by inheritance to a Polish prince that an opportunity for interference really presented itself. By unscrupulous tactics and by violence culminating in the notorious massacre at Danzig, they gained possession of all Eastern Pomerania. This high-handed action first revealed to Europe how far the Order had abandoned its Christian ideal, and earned for it the undying hatred of the Poles. Securely established in the Vistula delta, the Order decided to make Prussia the centre of its possessions. The Grand Master, who had moved from Acre to Venice in 1291, took up his residence in 1309 in the magnificent castle recently built at Marienburg. The reasons for this step were the failure of the Crusades in Palestine and the need for justifying the existence of the Order. It was scarcely a coincidence that the transference took place during the trial of the Templars in France. The change also marks the formal appearance of the Order as a territorial power in Europe, and was a recognition of the vitality with which German life was pulsating in outlying colonies when the Empire was declining. The Order's relations with Henry VII reveal it as a German colony, not an international crusade. Once the spoilt child of the Papal See, the Order had found Boniface VIII supporting its enemy Poland, and its policy was to ignore his weaker successors and seek support among the German princes. In the long process of the Poles against the Order—one of the most elaborate lawsuits of the time—and in the wars and diplomatic struggles that ensued, the Order was consistently supported by the Bohemian kings, while Poland sought aid from the Angevins of Hungary. The first wars of Poland against the Order (1326–33) were purely defensive and confined to the maintenance of integral parts of Poland like Kujawia, Mazovia, and Dobrzyn rather than to the recovery of Pomerania. Such, at any rate, was the policy of that stern realist Casimir the Great who by the Peace of Kalisz in 1343, definitely shelved the Pomeranian question and left the Order for over sixty years in undisturbed possession of its gains.

Between the Peace of Kalisz and the "Great War" the Order attained its greatest power and influence, and amazed Europe by its military strength, its wealth and prosperity. Apart from its estates in Germany and Italy, the Order was now the supreme power in Esthonia—Danish Esthonia had been annexed in 1346—Livonia, Kurland, Prussia, and East Pomerania. By the purchase of the Neumark in 1402 its position in West Pomerania was strengthened, and the occupation of Samogitia gave it an unbroken territory from the Narva to the Oder. All these lands were ruled by the Grand Master (*Magister generalis, Hochmeister*) from his capital at Marienburg. The Grand Master was elected for life by all the Knights at a general Chapter. The Order was nominally subject to the Pope and the Emperor; but in practice these feudal relationships were manipulated with great dexterity. While the Papacy was strong, the Order was its most devoted servant. When it was weak, the Order ignored its exhortations on behalf of Poland or the Archbishop of Riga. The bond with the Empire was regarded as a means of support rather than as involving any responsibility. In practice, then, the sovereignty of the lands of the Order, with certain qualifications, rested in the Grand Master and his Council, which consisted of the five chief officials—the Grosskomtur, the Ordensmarschall, the Spittler, the Trapier, and the Tressler. The administration was subject to the criticism of the Grand Chapter of the Knights, which met annually in September. Under the Grand Master were the Deutschmeister and a few lesser officials in charge of the scattered Balleien of the Order, the Landmeister of Prussia, and the Landmeister of Livonia. But even in Prussia the Order had to share its possessions with the ecclesiastical bodies—the four bishops and the four cathedral chapters; these received definite parts of their dioceses in which they were absolute landowners with their own jurisdictions and administrative officials; so that Prussia really consisted of eight distinct States besides the Order. The partition of the land was carried out during the conquest by William of Modena on the principle that two-thirds of each area was awarded to the Order and one-third to the bishop, of whose share one-third went to the chapter. In the diocese of Kulm, owing to the dispute with its first bishop, the apostle Christian, the episcopal estate was less than a third and was mainly in Löbau, with smaller tracts of land at Kulmsee where the cathedral was situated. The Bishop of Pomezania was granted actually a third of his diocese—a compact estate between the Vistula, the Ossa, and the lakes, with a cathedral at Marienwerder. The Bishop of Sambia, too, received a third of Sambia proper, but a very small addition (near Insterburg) from the later extension of his diocese between the Pregel and the Niemen. The largest diocese was that of Varmia, embracing the whole centre of Prussia from the Komturei of Elbing to the Pregel. The bishop received as his property the central portion with a cathedral at Frauenburg. These large ecclesiastical domains were administered by the bishops and chapters quite independently of the Order. But in practice, in lands that were surrounded by the territories of the Order, they found it expedient to conform to the administrative system and customs of the Order. The Grand Master had control of foreign affairs, war, and peace, and the ecclesiastical troops served under him in the field. Moreover, three of the chapters were persuaded to accept the Rule of the Order, so that the difference between the Priest Brothers and the canons disappeared except in the diocese of Varmia, where the bishops, who were great colonisers and soldiers, were more independent, like the Livonian bishops. In these ecclesiastical domains there were landowners—vassals of the bishops, towns, monasteries, and peasants, to whom they granted privileges. All four bishops were subordinate to the Archbishop of Riga.

The rest of Prussia was administered by the Landmeister. The unit of organisation was the "House," a group of twelve or more Knight Brothers with Priest Brothers and Serving Brothers, who led a communal life in a castle under a Komtur (Commendator) or a Pfleger, and occupied a definite area called a Komturei. All the Knights took the oath of chastity, obedience, and poverty, *i.e.* they could not own land or marry, and their life was one of equality, stern discipline, and war against the heathen. With the growing prosperity of the Order these ideals ceased to influence the Knights. From such small "Houses" grew the great Komtureien into which Prussia was divided. They were ten in number. Kulm, from its special position as a semi-Polish region, had a special Landkomtur with subordinate Komturs at Thorn, Graudenz, Golub, Strassburg, Kulmsee, and Birgelau. It comprised such parts of Kulmerland and Löbau as were not under the bishop. The small region of Marienburg was under the Grosskomtur. The great part of Pomezania became the Komturei of Christburg and extended south into the Wilderness at Osterode, which in 1341 became a separate Komturei with new castles at Soldau (1349), Hohenstein (1359), and Neidenburg (1376) in Galindia. The Komturei of Elbing comprised the Pogezanian land and possessed an isolated portion of the Wilderness with castles at Ortelsburg and Passenheim. East of the bishopric of Varmia were the two Komtureien of Balga and Brandenburg, originally small coast districts but gradually extending in thin strips to occupy all the Sudavian lake region. Farther east was the great Komturei of Königsberg, usually held by the Ordensmarschall, originally comprising Sambia only, but later occupying the vast land of the Nadrovians on the Pregel and Angerapp. In the far north the Komturei of Ragnit was an important military area, and the small Komturei of Memel was annexed to Prussia in 1328, but remained part of the diocese of Kurland.

In the wide territories of the Order sweeping changes had taken place through the conquest. From the first, the Order shewed that it intended to base its power in the new colony on German elements, and it took advantage of conditions in Germany to attract nobles, burghers, and peasants to Prussia. In the lands of the Order, as well as in the ecclesiastical domains, there grew up a large class of vassals who held land on feudal tenure and formed an important part of the military forces. Beginning with a charter to Dietrich von Tiefenau in 1236, a great number of nobles, at first from Westphalia and later from Thuringia and Franconia, received privileges. Polish knights also settled down as vassals and formed an important part of the nobility of Kulmerland. Even some of the Prussian nobles retained their lands, but they gradually became Germanised. The wide liberties granted to urban and rural communities, under the Kulmische Handfeste (1233)[1] and similar charters, attracted large numbers of German settlers to Prussia. The foundation of a castle on the site of an old town like Thorn or Kulm, or in a new strategic position like Christburg or Balga, soon led to the growth of a town. The Prussian towns, with full autonomy, were allowed to group themselves together as members of the Hansa League, and played a separate, but very prosperous part in the history of the colony. The peasants were partly Prussians, especially in Sambia, partly Polish (in Kulmerland) and Pomeranian (in Pomezania). The natives were at first well treated by Balke, but after the revolts those who survived had their liberties curtailed and soon sank to serfdom. The position of the German peasants is of special interest. Even if we admit that the life of the medieval peasants was far more fluid than used to be supposed, that by negotiation, revolt, or desertion they could better their position, the German peasants had special opportunities for migration into the east. In Prussia, as in Poland, there was a vast field for settlement under conditions far better than in the homeland. Their migration took place in groups under a *locator* who usually settled down with land of his own as Schultheiss or head of the village, which became a corporate community with its own privileges and law based on the Kulmische Handfeste. The peasants in Prussia had as their main obligation the payment of rent and feudal dues to the Order, bishop, or vassal on whose land they settled. But they possessed their own land and were not burdened at first by "forced labour," since their landlords were soldiers rather than agriculturists. They had to perform certain labour for the army, in which the Schultheiss was forced to serve. During the early period, then, the German peasants were not badly off, because it was in the interests of the Order to attract colonists to fill the empty spaces of Prussia and to supply labour for military purposes.

The colonisation of Prussia was successful because it was near to Germany and because Germany had the men to send. It was only 260 miles from Meissen, itself about 100 miles from Weimar, to

[1] Most of the privileges conferred were modelled on Magdeburg law, but certain cities, like Elbing, took Lübeck as their model.

Thorn through Kottbus, Zbandzin, and Poznań (Posen). Along this road
in the thirteenth century marched crusaders, adventurous younger sons,
monks, burghers, and peasants to the new colony. Even by sea it was
only half as far from Lübeck to Königsberg as to Dünamünde. Thus, while
Livonia, with its numerous peasant serfs, attracted the nobility of Westphalia and the traders of Bremen and Lübeck, Germans of every class
and from a wide area flocked to Prussia. The first settlements at Kulm
were among a Polish population, but German colonisation established
itself firmly in Pomezania, along the coast, and in Sambia. These early
settlements clung to the waterways, and all advanced posts inland disappeared in the great revolt. The first capital, Kulm, gave place to Elbing
and then to Marienburg. Elbing became a prosperous port which, like
Danzig and Riga, possessed considerable territory and was the seat of a
Komtur. Balga, Brandenburg, and Königsberg, at first mere outposts,
became great centres of military movements and of colonisation. The
second wave of colonisation after the Prussian war, in the years 1285–
1350, has been mentioned. The third advance in the days of Kniprode
is marked by the activity of the Komturs in the Wilderness, especially
at Osterode (1341), Ortelsburg (1360), Rhein (1377), Seesten (1374), and
round advanced posts like Angerburg, Insterburg, Lyck, and Johannisburg. During this period the central inland part of Prussia really became
a German colony, but it was not till the cessation of Lithuanian raids that
permanent settlement took place in the Wilderness. Pomerania, which
had been divided into six Komtureien at Danzig, Dirschau, Mewe,
Schwetz, Tuchol, and Schlockau, also received German colonists in the
towns, but the country remained Slav.

Livonia, a far larger country than Prussia[1], always retained important
features of its own. In relation to the Grand Master the Livonian Landmeister was far more independent than the Prussian Landmeister. But his
power over the colony was far less, because in Livonia the bishop had been
the chief founder of the colony. The ecclesiastical territories were larger
than the lands of the Order, though the Order had received the lion's share
of the more recent conquests in Kurland and Semigallia, where new Komtureien were established at Goldingen, Amboten, Mitau, Frauenburg,
Neuenburg, Doblen, and finally at Dünaburg in 1275. With the annexation
of Danish Esthonia in 1346 the Order's lands were ruled by about 20 Komturs and 13 Vogts. The Lithuanian wars enhanced the prestige of the
Knights, and its position in relation to the Church was strengthened by
the depression of the natives to serfdom and the immigration of nobles.
The depression of the peasants was a natural phenomenon. They were all
natives who spoke no German, they were mostly captured in war and on
many occasions revolted, particularly in Esthonia where the "jacquerie"
of 1343–45 was one of the most serious peasant outbreaks in the Middle
Ages. Only a few groups of natives, like the so-called Kur "kings,"

[1] Livonia and Esthonia without Kurland were twice as large as Prussia.

retained their liberties. The nobles, while they obtained relatively small estates in the lands of the Order, grew very powerful in the ecclesiastical domains and in Danish Esthonia. They began to combine as in the Dorpat League of 1304, and from the Landtag of Pernau in 1315 an active constitutional life began, such as did not exist in Prussia till the middle of the fifteenth century. The strong position of their vassals—the Uexkülls, Tiesenhausens, Rosens, Ungern-Sternbergs, and others—weakened the position of the bishops; and from the time of Albert Suerbeer, a German from Cologne who had been Primate of Ireland and became in 1253 Archbishop of Esthonia, Livonia, Kurland, and Prussia, a long struggle for predominance began. The purchase of Dünamünde by the Order and the capture of Riga in 1330 were the first events in a struggle in which one side called in the pagan Lithuanians, the other the Russians —a feud which only ended with the Reformation, and which raised the nobility to unexampled power. The history of the towns belongs more properly to the history of the Hansa League, and rivalled the prosperous development of Danzig and Elbing. Above all Riga, situated on two great trade routes, was the seat of the archbishop and the capital of the Landmeister. Apart from internal differences Livonia was sharply divided from Prussia by its interest in Russia and its complete detachment from the Polish question, which became the main preoccupation of the Prussian Knights.

The dynastic union of Poland and Lithuania made war with the Order inevitable. One of the terms of the treaty had been that Jagiello should recover the lost lands of the Polish crown, but any hope of recovering Pomerania seems to have died down in Poland, while the reoccupation of Kulmerland was not even thought of. In 1404 Poland solemnly reiterated her renunciation of all claims to Pomerania. The direct causes of the "Great War" were the occupation of Samogitia by the Knights and the frontier questions involved in the purchase of the Neumark by the Order in 1402. Brandenburg had once been a great danger to Poland, but had declined with the rise of the Order. The possibility of a union between the two—as history shewed later—would be fatal to her existence as a State. The war was delayed by the tortuous developments of Lithuanian policy under Vitold, which were due to the presence in Lithuania, alongside the Catholic, philo-Polish party, of a pagan element in Samogitia which followed the traditions of Keystut, and of a great Orthodox population in the Russian provinces which drew Vitold into Muscovite and Tartar questions away from Poland and Prussia. Swayed by the ambition to create a great Russian Empire and drive the Tartars over the Volga, Vitold was for a time indifferent to the fate of Samogitia. After the disaster of the Vorskla in 1399 he pursued a more purely Lithuanian policy, which gave a possible basis for co-operation with Jagiello; and when the crisis became acute in 1409 he joined Poland in the war against the Order. The first year of the war was indecisive, but the second year saw the complete overthrow of the military power of the Order at the battle which the Germans call Tannenberg, the Poles Grunwald[1]. The Order survived this disaster through the support of Hungary, the arrival of help from Livonia and the Neumark, the withdrawal of Vitold, and the exhaustion of Poland. The land was all occupied by the Poles except a few castles, but by the peace that followed only Samogitia was given up. But the Order was doomed. Mercenaries took the place of the old levies and crusaders, and a second war (1414–22) ended indecisively. A third war, due to the rise of the Russian party under Swidrygiello, culminated in the decisive victory of Zygmunt, Jagiello's cousin, at Vilkomir in 1435. Jagiello had won over his Russian subjects by the concession of political rights, and his successors now took advantage of the situation in Prussia, where the colony was in revolt against the Order, to hold out the lure of Polish constitutional liberties to the nobles and cities. The first appearance of constitutional life in Prussia was the Prussian League (1240), initiated by the Polish nobles of Kulmerland and directed against the oppressive rule of the Order. In the last war (1454–66) the Knights of the Order with their castles and mercenaries had to fight against their own vassals and cities as well as against the Poles. Danzig, in particular, threw all her wealth and men into the struggle against the Order. The ferocity and greed of the mercenaries on both sides made the war a tedious succession of sieges and devastations, in the course of which it is calculated that the Order, the Prussians, and Poland each lost 100,000 men. At one time Poland possessed nearly the whole of Prussia, but the victory at Konitz (Chojnice) enabled the Order to recover, and in the end the Poles, who shewed great diplomatic ability in dealing with the European powers, consented to a partition of Prussia. The Peace of Thorn was concluded in 1466 on the following terms: (1) The annexation to Poland of Kulmerland, Pomerania, Marienburg, Elbing, and the diocese of Varmia. (2) The Order to retain the Komtureien of Christburg, Elbing (without its capital city), Osterode, Balga, Brandenburg, Königsberg, Ragnit, and Memel. (3) The Grand Master to do homage to the Polish king for these lands. (4) The Order to be open to Poles.

Prussia was henceforth divided into the lands of the Order with Königsberg as capital and Royal Prussia, which was divided into three Wojewodztwa and became an integral part of Poland. It was granted a very extensive autonomy including a Senate and House of Deputies presided over by the Bishop of Varmia, who had made a special treaty by which his vast possessions became a principality and his diocese was held directly from the Pope. The line of Prince-Bishops contained many eminent Polish scholars from Kromer the historian to Krasicki the satirist; but Varmia's chief title to fame is the tomb of Copernicus in the magnificent cathedral at Frauenburg, where the great astronomer

[1] See infra, Vol. VIII.

lived and worked. The struggle of the Order against Poland became an internal one, and the Grand Masters constantly refused to do homage to the kings. But the most important development in the fifteenth century was the colonisation of the Wilderness. It had been the deliberate policy of the Order, for military reasons, to keep Galindia and Sudavia a desert and concentrate their energies on the northern frontier, so that only a scattered population fished and hunted in the lake district—nomad outposts who may be compared with the early Cossacks in the Russian borderlands, save that they lacked the stimulus of religious and national fervour which led the latter to combine in free communities. With the cessation of the great Lithuanian raids this region became open for settlement. The Bishops of Varmia were the first to plant settlers in the southern part of their lands. The "progress" of Kniprode through the Wilderness in 1377 was symptomatic of the growing importance of the south. The hostile raids gave place to regular warfare on the lower Niemen and the Vistula, which did not affect the colonisation but rather brought fresh human material. The Prussian natives were few in number, but the wars brought in refugees from the devastated areas of Prussia and Poland and Lithuanian converts. Above all, Mazovia, the most densely populated part of Poland, sent so many emigrants over the border that Galindia and Sudavia are now known as the Mazurian lake district. When the Order lost its best provinces it was natural that an intensive colonisation of the south should take place. New Komtureien appeared at Rhein and Insterburg, but generally settlement proceeded through smaller units under a Pfleger. Round Rastenburg, Rhein, Angerburg, Lyck, Johannisburg, and Ortelsburg appeared numerous settlements which received privileges under feudal law, canon law, local custom, and burgher law, especially Kulm law. German nobles and burghers and Mazovian peasants formed the majority. The rent registers of Elbing, Balga, and Brandenburg shew the phenomenal growth of settlement, and when Prussian settlers reached the borders of Mazovia and met Lithuanian settlers in the new Wojewodztwo of Troki, the Wilderness disappeared.

Meanwhile the Grand Masters realised the artificial position of a crusading Order in the fifteenth century, and saw in the lax morality of the Knights and their privileges over the other classes the need for drastic reform. They sought for help in Germany, and it was no accident that a Hohenzollern was chosen as head of the Order. Albert, the last of the religious Grand Masters, took advantage of the Reformation to break off from the Order and transform its Prussian territory in 1525 into an hereditary, secular duchy under the suzerainty of the King of Poland. With the extinction of his line in 1611, the Brandenburg branch of the family succeeded to the duchy and availed themselves of the embarrassments of Poland to throw off the suzerainty of the king. Royal Prussia remained part of Poland till the Partitions; and Chelmno and East Pomerania were reunited to the other Polish lands in 1919. Livonia recovered from the disaster of 1435, but was faced with the rise of a dangerous neighbour in Moscow, which threw off the Tartar yoke and annexed Novgorod. The danger was averted by the statesmanship of a great soldier and diplomat, Walter von Plettenberg (1494–1535), but the weakness of the Order excited the cupidity of Sweden and Denmark. The last Master, Gotthard Kettler, solicited the support of Poland and, following the example of Albert, formed a secular duchy of Kurland and Semigallia for his own family under Polish and Lithuanian suzerainty. Ivan IV failed to make any permanent gains, and after the great Northern War Poland obtained the south-east of Livonia with Marienhausen and Dünaburg, the rest falling to Sweden. The Swedish part was conquered by Russia in 1721, the Polish part fell to Russia at the Second Partition. After the Russian Revolution of 1917 the whole region was divided between the new republics of Esthonia and Latvia.

The great services rendered to civilisation by the achievements of the two Orders were the conversion of the pagan tribes and the colonisation of the waste spaces of Northern Europe. This was carried out partly by the ideals of the Orders and the zeal of the preachers and monks who accompanied them, and partly by a wonderful military organisation, made possible by the permanence and concentration of energy of a corporation which was in itself a standing army and united its vassals, its native subjects, its allies, and large forces of crusaders under a common banner. A direct result of these efforts was a great development of municipal life, trade, and commerce which did for the Baltic Sea what had been done by the Italians in the Mediterranean. If the rise of the Hansa League was due largely to the independent enterprise of German cities, it was the Order which built, developed, and administered, and gave it security in the lands where its trade thrived most. And in these lands art and learning flourished, particularly in the construction of magnificent castles and cathedrals and in the account of human events recorded by the accurate rhymed Chronicles and in the fine history of such an annalist as Henry the Lett. Generally speaking, the history of the Teutonic Order is one of the most glorious achievements of the Middle Ages, and, in a narrower sense, it is the greatest triumph of medieval German civilisation. The work of the Swedes in Finland was on a smaller scale, the brilliant expansion of civilisation by the Poles and Russians was less complete.

The darker side of the picture shews the extermination or reduction to serfdom of almost all the natives of the new colonies, the decadence of morals among the Knights and the continuance of strife and intrigue when the work of conversion was accomplished, the retention of privileges by the Knights over the subjects of the Order which led inevitably to revolt, and the aggrandisement of Prussia at the expense of its Christian neighbours which led ultimately to defeat. A religious Order of soldiers had become an anachronism in the fifteenth century if it failed —as the Teutonic Order failed—to turn its arms against the infidel. The

Order was not dissolved, as is sometimes stated, since it retained its possessions in Germany and Italy, and as late as 1784 the first History of the Order is dedicated to its contemporary Grand Master, Maximilian of Austria. But in Prussia and in Livonia it suffered defeat, and then simply disappeared beneath the rising tide of Protestantism. When Albert secularised his lands, all but five of the Knights had abandoned the Rule of the Order.

The rise and decay of an institution is a natural phenomenon, but certain later developments can be traced back to the activities of the Order. The establishment of a German colony in East Prussia and of German upper and middle classes in Livonia was permanent, and the unfortunate fact that these colonies cut two great Slav races off from the sea and planted Germans amid a Slav population in Prussia and among the Letts and Ests of the Baltic, left to posterity an ethnological puzzle in Livonia and a national feud and complex political problem between Germans and Poles. The aggression of the Order led to the Union of Poland with Lithuania and the rise of a new great Power with parliamentary institutions. The long Prussian wars enabled the Polish gentry to extract from their kings, in return for financial support, wide constitutional liberties, which enabled the kingdom of Prussia, later on, to hinder reform and bring about the partition of Poland. The German nobles in the Baltic Provinces, after contributing to the rise of Sweden, were utilised by Peter the Great, after 1721, to mould his administrative machine, and played an important part in the maintenance of the autocratic principle in Russia. If the civilisation of the Baltic had been achieved by international co-operation rather than by a German association, it might have been slower and less methodical, but it would not have left so unfortunate a legacy to later history.

CHAPTER X

THE POPES OF AVIGNON AND THE GREAT SCHISM

THE seven Popes from 1305 to 1378 resided, more or less continuously, at Avignon. This prolonged absence from Italy constitutes a fact of the first importance and quite unprecedented in the history of the Church. The explanation of it lies in a combination of events and circumstances most complex in character.

When Bertrand de Got, Archbishop of Bordeaux, became Pope under the name of Clement V (1305–14), the situation in Italy was extremely critical. The cardinals who notified to him his election depicted the country as plunged in anarchy, and the States of the Church as ruined by war. Nevertheless, the new Pope on several occasions manifested his firm intention of going to Italy, so soon as peace should be concluded between England and France and the crusade organised. He fixed on Vienne, in Dauphiné, for his coronation, in the hope that the Kings of England and France would consent to come there and to discuss the terms of a settlement, without which an expedition to the Holy Land was impossible. Though the meeting he planned did not take place, negotiations were set on foot and soon resulted in a reconciliation. But even so, the Pope was not able to depart for Rome. In July and August 1305 Philip the Fair reminded him of the prosecution instituted against the late Pope Boniface VIII, which had not been terminated. Clement, wishing to avoid its resumption, made a concession pregnant with results: he went to Lyons, where his coronation took place on 14 November 1305, and there negotiations were begun. It was agreed to defer the question of Boniface's trial to a later interview, and so the Pope had to put off his departure for Italy. At this point he fell ill and all but died. The interview eventually took place at Poitiers in April 1307, but the parties separated without arriving at a decision. On 13 October 1307 came the dramatic stroke—the wholesale arrest of the Templars. This necessitated a further meeting with Philip the Fair, but at Poitiers (May to July 1308) the French King shewed himself so exacting that Clement determined to escape from his clutches. To go to Rome was not to be thought of. It would have been madness to leave Philip master of the situation on the eve of the assembling of the Council of Vienne, where most important issues for the Church were to be decided, and above all the scandalous trial of the Templars was to be debated. The papal court was removed to Avignon.

The town of Avignon, indeed, provided advantages of many kinds. It assured speedy communication with Italy. It was close to, but not dependent upon France. Its overlords were vassals of the Church, and there was nothing to fear from them. Finally, it formed an enclave within the county of Venaissin, which was itself a possession of the Holy See. No other town could offer the Pope such strong guarantees of security and independence.

After the close of the Council of Vienne, which lasted from 16 October 1311 to 6 May 1312, the Pope's health, always feeble, took a serious turn for the worse, and he finally succumbed on 14 April 1314.

Yet, even if the Pope had enjoyed better health, he would hardly have braved the danger of crossing the Alps in the years 1312 and 1313. The coming of Henry VII, King of the Romans, into Italy had thrown the whole country into confusion. The city of Rome, from 7 May 1312 onwards, was little more than a battle-field for the sanguinary strife of Guelfs and Ghibellines. Henry VII treated the Pope as an enemy, and proclaimed his complete independence of the spiritual power. In concert with Frederick, King of Trinacria (Sicily), he collected a large fleet against the Pope's vassal, King Robert of Naples. In these circumstances, Clement V judged it prudent to remain in the Venaissin, and his successors followed his example.

In fact, during the whole of John XXII's pontificate (1316–34), Italy continued to be devastated by war. In 1332, however, the victories won by the Cardinal-legate Bertrand du Pouget over the Ghibellines made possible the crossing of the Alps. John XXII planned to bring about the pacification of Lombardy and Tuscany, and to take up his residence at Bologna. But the distraction of a crusade, the pressure of the King of France, and, above all, the rebellion of the Bolognese put a speedy end to his designs.

At the beginning of Benedict XII's pontificate (1334–42), it was decided at a consistory held in July 1335 that the papal court should start about 1 October and should establish itself provisionally at Bologna. At a second consistory the cardinals changed their minds, and postponed the departure to a later date. There were various urgent matters, including the projects for a crusade, that impelled them to this course. But also alarming news had arrived from Bologna. The town seemed to be in too disturbed a condition to furnish a secure home for the Holy See.

The forebodings of the cardinals were soon justified. Bologna revolted; the local lords in Romagna and the Marches planned to make themselves independent; even in Rome revolt broke out, and lasted from 1347 to 1356. War became inevitable under Clement VI (1342–52), and continued to rage fiercely under Innocent VI (1352–62). It only came to an end when Cardinal Albornoz had reduced to impotence the various nobles who troubled the peace of the peninsula. Urban V (1362–70) thought the time had come to re-establish the Papacy at Rome. The Romans, who had so often clamoured for his return, now devised schemes for his expulsion. They allied against him with Perugia, which was already in revolt, and the Perugians were emboldened to hire the condottiere John

Hawkwood and his bands, and to launch an attack on Viterbo, where the Pope was residing. They were forced to submit, but the situation was little improved thereby, for the free-lances in the pay of Bernabò Visconti were overrunning Tuscany and threatening to invade the Patrimony. In alarm for his safety and naturally distrustful of his subjects after their recent behaviour, Urban V was also anxious to intervene to check the hostilities which had broken out again between France and England. On 27 September 1370 he returned to Avignon.

To come back to Italy was the uppermost thought in the mind of Urban's successor, Gregory XI (1370–78), but for some years circumstances thwarted his good intentions. At last on 17 January 1377 he landed at the port of Rome[1]. The re-establishment of the Papacy in the Eternal City might have provoked the Romans to gratitude. Far from it, however: once more the faction-fights broke out. And, if credit can be given to the testimony of a contemporary, a Roman cardinal even plotted against the life of the sovereign Pontiff. So, if the Popes deserted Italy for about seventy years, Italy was to blame in giving them regularly so inhospitable a reception.

The lack of security afforded by Italy in the fourteenth century is not the only explanation of the sojourn of the Holy See on the banks of the Rhone. The dominant idea with the Avignonese Papacy was a crusade, and the achievement of this splendid task could only be realised if the disastrous war between France and England was brought to an end by a definitive peace. The Curia displayed extraordinary zeal in attempting to reconcile the hostile nations, as is attested in its voluminous diplomatic correspondence. It is at least open to doubt whether it could have pursued this laudable endeavour with as much vigour, had it been far removed from Avignon.

Besides this, the Holy See had a vital interest in preserving the good-will of the kings of France, who aimed at keeping the Papacy within the sphere of their influence, and who were also its most reliable allies in its bitter struggle with Lewis of Bavaria from 1317 to 1347[2]. As soon as it was freed of all anxiety from the Empire, the Papacy worked unceasingly for the pacification of Italy, in order to make its own residence there possible. When it had achieved this object, the urgent entreaties of Charles V did not prevail to keep it at Avignon.

Although endowed with very diverse qualities and with temperaments often conflicting, the Avignonese Popes had the same ends in view, and

---

[1] It has hitherto been the fashion to attribute the return of the Papacy to Rome to the efforts of St Catherine of Siena. This view has already been challenged by L. Mirot. Now R. Fawtier has reduced the political influence of St Catherine to its proper proportions (*Sainte Catherine de Sienne. Essai de critique des sources: sources hagiographiques.* Paris, 1922).

[2] See *supra*, Chap. IV.

in matters ecclesiastical pursued the same policy. Their work, coherent
and characteristic, consisted in organising the administration of the Roman
Church on a new basis and in centralising it under their authority, in
restoring the papal finances, combating heresy, reforming abuses, preaching and directing the crusading movement, and spreading abroad overseas
the knowledge of the Gospel.

Under the Avignonese Papacy the central administration of the Roman
Church was distributed among four main departments: the *camera apostolica*, the chancery, the judicial administration, and the penitentiary.

The *camera apostolica* was the name given to the aggregation of offices
in which the financial business of the Holy See was transacted. At the
head were two high officials—the chamberlain and the treasurer. The
chamberlain was a real finance minister. Appointed by the Pope and
holding episcopal rank, his chief function was to supervise the collectors
of papal taxes throughout Christendom in the performance of their duties,
and to check the receipts and expenditure of the various departments in
the papal court. Having as his prime duty the safeguarding of the rights
of the Roman Church, the chamberlain became the most weighty and
intimate councillor of the Pope, who consulted him on all political issues.
He was a sort of Secretary of State, who drew up the instructions addressed
to nuncios, and communicated directly to kings the views of his master.
He had under him scribes, known after 1341 as *secretarii*, who wrote the
political correspondence and the confidential letters of the Pope. The
chamberlain was, therefore, the most important personage in the papal
court, and most of the functionaries of the palace were under his orders.
The treasurer and the financial advisers (clerks of the chamber) assisted
him in the performance of his duties. The auditor, vice-auditor, and
procurator-fiscal dealt with contentious business. From the tribunal of the
auditor an appeal lay to that of the chamberlain, whose sentence, whether
pronounced by himself or by deputy, was final. Lastly, the coinage was
also under the chamberlain's control. The Mint was situated first at
Sorgues, and then from 1354 onwards at Avignon. The management of
it lay in the hands of a master of the Mint, a keeper, a provost, an en-
graver, and an assayer, with a number of workmen under them.

The term chancery was applied to a group of departments occupied,
each with its own particular share, in the business of preparing the papal
letters relating to the administration of the Church. These departments
were seven in number, and were concerned respectively with petitions
(*supplicationes*), with the examination (*examen*) of candidates for benefices,
with preparing the draft (*minuta, nota*) of the letter, with writing it out
in full (*grossa*) on parchment, with inspecting it with a view to correction
(*correctoria*), with affixing the seal (*bulla*), and finally with entering a copy
in the register (*registrum*). The head of all this complicated organisation
was the vice-chancellor, but he had not the same liberty of action as the
chamberlain. He could only act on the Pope's mandate.

In the region of judicial administration, the number of cases which came to the Holy See, whether of first instance or of appeal, had grown by the fourteenth century to such proportions that a subdivision of judicial powers became necessary. Up till then judges-delegate had only acted as examining magistrates; at any rate the sovereign Pontiff had, with very few exceptions, reserved to himself the right of pronouncing sentence. From the time of Clement V regular courts of justice were established, and against the decisions of some of these there was no appeal. They were the Consistory, the tribunals of the cardinals, the *audientia sacri palatii*, and the *audientia litterarum contradictarum*.

The Consistory, the assembly of Pope and cardinals, heard complaints, informations, accusations, and pleas of all kinds. It was in fact a court of appeal. The business that came before it was either referred to local judges who were appointed delegates to investigate or decide cases, or after enquiry to the Consistory itself when the parties concerned agreed to a compromise, or to one of the two following tribunals. The tribunals of the cardinals were only occasional tribunals. Before the cardinals heard a case, it had to be specially referred to them by the Pope, who notified to them in detail their exact powers. As a rule they did not give final judgments. For the most part they drew up a précis of the facts of the case[1], and then reported on it to the Pope, who passed sentence. Usually they handed over their duties to a deputy, known as *auditor*, who listened to the pleadings and to the parties concerned. Notaries, or clerks of the court, an usher, and a keeper of the seal, completed the personnel of the court. The *audientia sacri palatii* became known after 1336 as the tribunal of the *Rota*[2]. The constitution *Ratio iuris* (16 November 1331) defined its functions. The *auditores*, whose exact number is unknown, gave final judgments. They were distinguished jurisconsults, graduates, and were classed in three ranks according to seniority. However, this classification, adopted in 1331 by John XXII, fell rapidly into disuse; by about 1341 it was no longer current. When the *auditores* who were trying a case had concluded the hearing, they were obliged to communicate their conclusions to their colleagues of the same rank in 1331, or after 1341

---

[1] P. Fournier (*Les officialités au Moyen Âge. Étude sur l'organisation, la compétence et la procédure des tribunaux ecclésiastiques ordinaires en France, de* 1180 *à* 1328, pp. 170–74, Paris, 1880) has given a careful account of the procedure in such cases.

[2] Historians have differed widely as to the origin of this name. According to Cardinal Ehrle (*Historia bibliothecae romanorum pontificum*, p. 696, n. 652, Rome, 1890), the tribunal of the *Rota* was so called because of the presence in the council-chamber of a lectern with law books on it. F. E. Schneider (*Die Römische Rota*, p. 89, Paderborn, 1914) thinks that the name came from the circular arrangement of the seats of the auditors, when they were sitting in council. On the other hand, Dr Colombe (*Au palais des papes d'Avignon*, p. 14, Paris, 1921 believes that it arose from the circular building in which the auditors sat. The question, it seems to me, is not decided. I myself prefer the view of Cardinal Ehrle.

of the same group. When they were in possession of the views of their colleagues, they pronounced judgment, which, if there was a difference of opinion, had to express the views of the majority. Their competence extended to all cases referred to them by the Pope or the vice-chancellor. Their usual business was to decide actions to which the collation of benefices, resulting from papal reservations, gave rise. Litigants employed all sorts of expedients to delay the normal procedure. It was the *audientia litterarum contradictarum* that decided all pleas in bar of action. This court also heard the arguments upon the documentary evidence, investigated the documents, arranged for copies to be made, and decided on their validity. It also heard the various legal points arising out of the execution of sentences.

The duties of the Apostolic Penitentiary were to put an end to the effects of an ecclesiastical censure (excommunication, suspension, or interdict), to remove an irregularity, that is to say a canonical bar to the exercise of ecclesiastical functions, to grant dispensations for marriage, to give absolution in reserved cases. The head of this administration, to which Benedict XII on 8 April 1338 gave an important body of rules, was the Grand Penitentiary, a cardinal-bishop or cardinal-priest in every case. A numerous personnel assisted him in his work. From twelve to eighteen *penitentiarii minores* heard the confessions of the faithful, between the hours of prime and tierce, in the cathedral or principal church of the town where the Pope had his residence. In cases easy to decide, they granted absolutions or dispensations; other cases were referred to the Pope himself or to the Grand Penitentiary.

It is true that most of the institutions, the working of which has been briefly indicated, existed before the fourteenth century. But the Popes of Avignon put upon them a special imprint; they developed them systematically. They laid down the rights and duties of the officials so meticulously, and with such care to avoid fraud and to prevent abuses, that some of their regulations were to remain in force for several generations, while others were to serve as the basis for improvements in detail which Popes of later ages adjudged necessary. Their work, in short, was a lasting one.

The Avignonese Popes were not content with reorganising the administration of the Church. They accelerated the movement of centralisation which had been developing since the eleventh century. It can even be said that in the fourteenth century this movement in some respects attained its apogee. Appeals to the court at Avignon became very numerous. The Curia directly conferred university degrees, to an unusual extent. It intervened more frequently in the affairs of the religious Orders, suppressing some, such as the Templars, reforming others against their will, such as the Order of Grandmont and the Knights of the Hospital of St John of Jerusalem, appointing in others the head and subordinate

officials. From 1305 to 1378 only one Ecumenical Council was celebrated, at Vienne (1311–12). There Clement V peremptorily affirmed his
sovereign authority. To those fathers of the Council who would not
assent to his project of uniting the possessions of the Templars with
those of the Hospitallers, he replied: "If you agree to the conferring of
these possessions on the Hospital, I will gladly pronounce my assent; if
not, I will do it all the same, whether you like it or no."[1] As this did
not silence the opposition, Clement overruled it. Contemporaries had no
doubt as to the real implications of the attitude taken by the Pope. An
English chronicler affirmed, with a little exaggeration, that the Council
of Vienne "did not deserve to be called a council, because the lord Pope
did everything on his own (*ex capite proprio*)."[2]

There is nothing that manifests so clearly the progress of centralisation
in the Church as the way in which the Popes assumed an ever increasing
share in the collation to benefices. They made use of the right of reser-
vation, by which the Pope took upon himself, in virtue of his primacy of
jurisdiction, to confer benefices, whether for an actual or a future vacancy,
to the exclusion of all those, ecclesiastics or laymen, who had the right
of election, nomination, or presentation thereto. Previous Popes, indeed,
had set the example. The Popes of Avignon did not make an innovation;
they were content to multiply reservations and to extend them more and
more widely. The final stage was reached under Urban V, when the
elective principle was in the last phase of decline, and the collation to
benefices not subject to election had almost everywhere passed out of the
hands of the ordinary collators. In no period of history did the Holy
See exercise its powers of jurisdiction in so extreme a form.

It can be easily realised that a policy so destructive of private liberties
and privileges aroused violent opposition. Discontent was rife throughout
Europe. Everywhere there were bitter criticisms of "the unbridled
multitude of provisions apostolic" in favour of clergy who were strangers
to the dioceses in which the benefices lay, and especially of cardinals.
From all sides came the same story of the disastrous consequences resulting
from the direct nomination to benefices by the Holy See: the absence
from their benefices of those who "have never seen the crucifix of the
churches of which they eat the bread of sorrow," the exodus of capital
from the national territories, the decay of piety among the people, the
decrease of divine worship, the wretched state of the sacred edifices which
were falling into ruins for lack of repair, the neglect of almsgiving, the
cessation of hospitality to the needy, the manifest breach of the express
intentions of pious founders, the collapse of discipline in the monasteries,

---

[1] H. Finke, *Papsttum und Untergang des Templerordens*, Vol. ii, p. 299, Münster,
1907. (The quotation is from a dispatch of the Aragonese envoy.)

[2] Walter of Hemingburgh, ed. Hamilton (English Historical Society), Vol. ii,
p. 293, London, 1849.

the accumulation of benefices[1]. The chroniclers echo the complaints continually uttered by the cathedral chapters who were deprived of their right of election. They claim that the apostolic provisions are tainted with simony[2]. Their grievances are to be found in the writings of bishops[3], and even of a cardinal. According to Cardinal Napoleon Orsini, almost all the episcopal sees and even the smallest prebends in Italy were the object of barter and family intrigues during the pontificate of Clement V[4].

The denunciation pronounced everywhere against the papal policy with regard to benefices was nowhere more bitter than in England. Edward III was bold enough to remind Clement VI that "the successor of the Apostles was commissioned to lead the Lord's sheep to the pasture, not to fleece them."[5] The numerous Parliaments in the fourteenth century, from that of Carlisle in January 1307 to that in 1376, did not cease from breaking out into invective against the actions of the Holy See. The continual complaints of the representatives of the English nation penetrated in time down to the mass of the people, and there engendered a very dangerous opposition to the Papacy. Men's minds were attuned to listen with sympathy to the violent attacks of John Wyclif on the constitution of the Roman Church.

From words they passed to deeds. In England, the *Statute of Provisors* (9 February 1351) did away in theory with the practice of the Holy See in the matter of benefices, and the *Statute of Praemunire* (23 September 1353) with the right to appeal on these questions to the Roman courts. In the Empire, the position was still worse. The cathedral chapters jealously, and often successfully, defended their privileges against the encroachments of the Avignonese Popes; they persisted too in granting canonries and prebends to the younger sons of noble families, in defiance sometimes of the canonical penalties pronounced by papal officials. At Würzburg, three clerks, who had come to read an apostolic mandate

---

[1] These grievances were uttered especially in England, at the Carlisle Parliament in January 1307; cf. *Rotuli parliamentorum*, Vol. I, pp. 217–23. Succeeding Parliaments only repeated the same complaints. In France they are specified in almost the same terms in the writings of Bishops Guillaume Durant and Guillaume Le Maire; cf. C. Port, *Le livre de Guillaume le Maire* in *Mélanges historiques*, new series, II, pp. 477–82 (*Collections des Documents inédits*), Paris, 1877, and the *De modo concilii generalis celebrandi*, Lyons, 1531.

[2] *Flores historiarum*, ed. Luard, Rolls Series, Vol. III, pp. 182, 192, London, 1890; Adam Murimuth, *Continuatio chronicarum regum Angliae*, ed. Thompson, pp. 174–5, London, 1889.

[3] Guillaume Durant, *De modo*, fol. 24ᵛ.

[4] Baluzius, *Vitae paparum Avenionensium*, ed. G. Mollat, Vol. III, p. 238, Paris, 1921.

[5] Rymer, *Foedera*, Vol. II, pt. II, p. 1233, London, 1830. I have made a lengthy study of the reception given to papal provisions in England in *La collation des bénéfices ecclésiastiques sous les papes d'Avignon* (1305–1378), pp. 227–69, Paris, 1921. Cf. also, Miss A. Deeley, *Papal provision and royal rights of patronage in the early fourteenth century* (EHR. XLIII, pp. 497 sqq.).

conferring the archdeaconry of Künzelsan, a canonry, and a prebend in the cathedral church on a Frenchman, John Guilabert, were seized upon, bound hand and foot, and thrown into the Main. The conflict which broke out between the Church and Lewis of Bavaria gave an opportunity to the cathedral chapters to inflict a series of humilating rebuffs on the Papacy in the matter of episcopal appointments. In vain the Holy See annulled elections made in defiance of apostolic reservations, nominated fresh candidates of its own, pronounced excommunication on the bishops elected and severe penalties on the electors; its nominees could rarely get their authority recognised in the dioceses entrusted to their charge, and had to be transferred to other sees. The bishoprics of Würzburg, Freising, Augsburg, Mayence, Hildesheim, were all occupied by "intruders."

The accession of Charles of Bohemia to the imperial throne did not materially alter the religious situation in the Empire. He had indeed promised Clement VI to drive the "intruders" from their sees and to support the candidature of prelates nominated by the papal Court. But even if he had the intention of keeping his oath, he did not possess sufficient authority to do so. He avoided the use of force and preferred to make terms with the supporters of the house of Wittelsbach. Henceforth elections in chapters or abbeys took place in spite of apostolic reservations and in defiance of them. In order to safeguard their authority, the Popes had no other resource than to appoint as abbots or bishops those very persons whose election they had previously quashed.

Tenacious and widespread though it was, the resistance to papal provisions from 1305 to 1378 failed in the long run to be effective, even in the Empire; the final victory lay with the Holy See. Success was often achieved only by means of a fiction; but that was sufficient to determine the defeat of the chapters and the ordinary collators, and to assure the triumph of papal omnipotence. For, while papal provision was disadvantageous to some people, on the other hand it entailed real benefit to others as well as to the Church itself. It brought to an end the prolonged vacancies of episcopal sees, so damaging to the welfare of souls and to the good management of episcopal revenues; it remedied the negligence of the ordinary collators in providing incumbents for vacant benefices, and the illegalities they committed in their choice of candidates; it put an end to the intrigues which broke out within the chapters at the time of an election, the violent competitions, the settlements in which simony played a part, the long and disastrous schisms when the electors could not agree. Finally, it was attractive to the public authorities and to some of the ordinary collators as well. For between them and the Holy See grew up a tacit concordat, advantageous to both of the contracting parties. Instead of imposing their candidates on the chapters by methods that were hardly canonical, the kings preferred to request the Pope to reserve such and such a church for his own disposal, at the same time recommending their candidate to him. Ordinary collators or patrons did the same; they addressed petitions to the Roman court in favour of the clerk of their choice. The Pope, for his part, by means of the mandates he issued for provisions, furnished himself with important financial resources. He made the bishops and abbots, who received their appointments from him, pay to the chancery the regular and the petty dues. As for the smaller beneficiaries, they had to pay annates. And not only were taxes imposed on bishops and abbots; they also had to take an oath of fealty to St Peter, to the Roman Church, and to the Roman pontiff. Thus was accomplished the centralisation of power in the hands of the sovereign Pope.

But merely to retain the nomination to benefices was not enough for the Popes who had their seat at Avignon. In the fourteenth century, it was impossible for a power even of an essentially spiritual character to dominate the world unless wealth supplied the driving force for its activities. This the Popes of Avignon acquired by creating or developing a vast fiscal system, designed to secure to them considerable pecuniary resources. Two kinds of taxes were levied on ecclesiastical benefices: the one paid directly to the Curia by those liable, the other levied locally by collectors.

The taxes paid at the Roman court were numerous. The ordinary dues (*servitia communia*) consisted of fees payable by bishops or abbots when appointed to their offices by the Holy See, and amounted to one-third of a year's income. The petty dues (*servitia minuta*), the *sacra*, the *subdiaconorum*, were gratuities paid to the personnel of the papal court and of the cardinals' households. Abbots and bishops also had to pay high chancery dues, quittance fees, charges levied on the occasion of their visits *ad limina*, and fees on receiving the *pallium*. More important still were the taxes levied locally by the agents of the papal treasury: the *decimae*, or one-tenth of the net income of a benefice; the *annatae* (*annalia, annualia, fructus primi anni*), the revenue of a benefice in the year following the institution of a new incumbent; and *subsidia caritativa*, which were extraordinary contributions. Further, on the death of any beneficiaries, clergy or bishops, the Popes exercised right of *spolia* and took possession of their effects; and during the whole vacancy of a benefice to which they collated, they received the revenues, *fructus vacantes* as they were called. Finally, they deprived the bishops and other prelates of the profits arising from *procurationes*, the pecuniary dues payable on the occasion of the canonical visitations they all were in duty bound to make.

While the number and the variety of the papal taxes constituted a heavy burden for the clergy, the nature and methods of their collection made them still more odious. No limitation of time could wipe out the debts of the taxpayers. Whether due from personal or from real property, they remained a charge on the benefice, however old they might be. Every holder of a benefice was made liable for the debts of his predecessors.

Certainly he could take action against them or their heirs; but this was a doubtful advantage and often too expensive. The methods employed in exerting pressure so as to hasten the payment of taxes and overcome resistance combined to make the papal treasury universally execrated. In the fourteenth century, outside the Church as well as within it, harsh measures were the general rule. The collectors smote the recalcitrants with ecclesiastical censures, excommunication, the *aggravatio*, the *re-aggravatio*. It can be imagined what a deplorable impression it must have made on Christian people, when, during the holy offices, they heard the thunders of the Church hurled, with all the formalities, against their own pastors; and what a scandal it was for the people of Mondonnedo to see the mortal remains of their bishop deprived of Christian burial until his heirs made themselves responsible for his debts.

The accounts of contemporaries leave us in no doubt as to the general feeling. The fiscal measures of the Popes of Avignon, though there was a reason for them—and the maintenance of the papal court, the preparation for a crusade, the Italian wars, the transference of the Holy See to Rome, give ample explanation—excited the most lively discontent throughout Christendom. Not to mention the statements of chroniclers, we get from documents in archives and from the very account-books of the collectors themselves a rough idea of the state of mind of the clergy. In England, Parliaments expressed themselves with great bitterness against the papal exactions. In France, the resistance of the incumbents took the form of embarrassing the papal agents in the performance of their duties. In the Empire, the collectors were hunted down, thrown into noisome prisons, mutilated, and even strangled. The excitement among the clergy in the dioceses of Cologne, Bonn, Xanten, Soest, and Mayence reached such a pitch that in 1372 they bound themselves by oath not to pay the tenth demanded by Gregory XI, and to support in their resistance all against whom action was taken; any incumbent who betrayed his pledge was to be deprived of his benefice and declared ineligible to possess one again in the future.

The grievances of the clergy were well-founded. The reasons they alleged against the paying of taxes—the evils of the time, the disasters of war, the high cost of food, the scarcity of money, famine, and, lastly, plague—were certainly just. In France, above all, most benefices were ruined or destroyed by the Grand Companies. As a result the papal taxes inevitably reduced the incumbents to penury; and it cannot be wondered that these wretched people deserted their parishes. On the other hand, the withdrawal from those who had enjoyed it hitherto of the right of *procuratio* (provision of entertainment during a visitation) resulted in the cessation of canonical visitations, the relaxation of discipline, the abandonment of divine worship, and the non-residence of the clergy. A contemporary gives a slightly exaggerated account of this: "The people saw themselves everywhere deprived of the Word of God, and in several places of participation in the sacraments, because there remained no means of subsistence for their pastors to whose care they had been entrusted; churches and other buildings were almost everywhere in ruins, there being no possibility of keeping them in repair; while the poor died of penury, deprived both of consolation and of succour."[1]

The Popes of Avignon were not ignorant of the abuses that arose from their fiscal policy. In claiming the taxes they were in fact simply exercising the right of ownership over the property of the universal Church; this had been timidly asserted in the thirteenth century, and now in the fourteenth was often proclaimed aloud. Their pecuniary needs forced them to this regrettable extremity. When John XXII became Pope, he had in his chest only 70,000 gold florins. The papal treasure had been exhausted by the excessive legacies of Clement V; and the new Pope created taxes to meet his difficulties. The receipts amounted to a high figure, about 4,100,000 florins for the whole duration of his papacy. But the expenses, in great part owing to the Italian wars, came to 4,191,466 florins. The *camera apostolica* would have been driven to bankruptcy, had not John XXII paid in 440,000 florins out of his private exchequer and also extracted 150,000 more from the estate of Clement V. He left Benedict XII in a sufficiently favourable financial position to save him from having to exact some of the taxes. In 1342 the sums in the papal treasury amounted to 1,117,000 florins.

The brightness of the financial situation was abruptly dimmed after the accession of Clement VI. Accustomed to the life of a great nobleman, Clement scattered money far and wide. The balance of the papal treasury had sunk at his death to 311,115 florins; and even this was a fictitious balance, for it had only been created by borrowing. Innocent VI had an annual revenue of 253,000 florins, but the Italian wars swallowed up more than the taxes brought in. Henceforward the deficit was an ever yawning gulf. Innocent found himself obliged to sacrifice a great part of his silver plate, and a large number of jewels and precious ornaments. He was reduced to extreme penury; even works of art were sold for their weight in gold and silver, regardless of their artistic value. Urban V, at the end of his resources, had to borrow 30,000 florins from his cardinals, and Gregory XI was in debt to Louis of Anjou to the extent of 120,000 gold francs. Perforce they had to load taxes upon the holders of benefices.

The Italian wars were not the only interest of the Popes. They reckoned that, in view of the general increase in wealth, they would sink in the esteem of their contemporaries if they did not display themselves as the centre of social pomp. In consequence they lived like temporal princes and supported a gorgeous retinue. Their court shone with a display of

[1] Bourgeois du Chastenet, *Nouvelle histoire du concile de Constance*, p. 7, Paris, 1718.

CH. X.

luxury, though relatively to their other expenditure it was not excessive[1]. The first place in the entourage of the sovereign pontiff was taken by his relatives, male and female, who attired themselves in precious stuffs and costly furs; then came knights, squires, serjeants-at-arms, chaplains, ushers, chamberlains, chefs, and so on. In sum, the private court of the reigning Pope was composed of three or four hundred persons or even more; and they were all supplied with clothing, food, lodging, and wages. Avignon under Clement VI became the rallying-place of the finest spirits of the age. In it could be met Italian and German painters, French sculptors and architects, musicians, poets, men of letters, lawyers, philosophers, astronomers, doctors; it was the scene of balls, tournaments, fêtes, wedding banquets. An Italian eyewitness has left us an account of a magnificent reception given by Cardinal Annibale da Ceccano to Clement VI in 1343[2]. Further, the Head of the Church needed a residence both secure and stately. Benedict XII and Clement VI built on the Roches des Doms the gigantic towers which still strike the visitor with astonishment, and connected them with imposing walls. Inside their palace, which was like an impregnable fortress, the Popes could defy the troops of free-lances who held France and Provence to ransom. This was not sufficient, however. The invasion of the Grand Companies into the county of Venaissin forced them to enclose both the old town and the new with a common girdle of walls, having magnificent ramparts, crowned with battlements, pierced with posterns, and defended by moats[3]. Luxury was displayed especially in the internal decoration of the papal palace. Carpets adorned the various apartments and state chambers. Rich stuffs hid the none too gorgeous furniture. On the walls, if they were not decorated with frescoes, hung tapestries of high warp, the products of Spanish and Flemish workshops, silken hangings, taffetas, green and red serge. The tables were loaded with vessels of gold and silver.

The cardinals, like the Pope, led a life of pomp and magnificence. In 1351 Bernard of Garves rented fifty-one houses or parts of houses in order to lodge all his retainers. Peter of Banhac needed ten stables for his horses, and five of them could alone take thirty-nine horses.

So in the fourteenth century a new state of affairs had come into being. The Papacy set itself to extract all that heaped-up wealth could supply

---

[1] K. H. Schaefer (*Die Ausgaben der apostolischen Kammer unter Johann XXII*, p. 36*, Paderborn, 1911) has worked out exactly the percentage of each item in the expenditure of John XXII, the chief of them being: war, 63·7; upkeep and entertainment of the personnel of the court, 12·7; alms, 7·16; dress, 3·35; buildings, 2·9; kitchen and cellar, 2·5; purchase of land, ·4; stables, ·33; works of art and Church ornaments, ·17; library, ·16.

[2] E. Casanova, *Visita di un papa avignonese* (*Archivio della società romana di storia patria*, Vol. XXII, pp. 371–81, Rome, 1899). On the luxury of the court at Avignon see E. Müntz, *L'argent et le luxe à la cour pontificale d'Avignon* (*Revue des questions historiques*, Vol. LXVI, pp. 5–44, 378–406, Paris, 1899).

[3] R. André-Michel, *Avignon. Les fresques du palais des papes.* Paris, 1920.

of worldly renown and human delights. In this it imitated the temporal powers, who in the same period were increasing their pomp. The papal court underwent a transformation similar to that of the royal courts of France and Aragon. It extended too the cult of arts and letters inaugurated by Boniface VIII. In sum, the period of the Avignonese Popes was marked by a profound transformation. The Papacy had rapidly recovered the moral prestige which it had lost at the time of the contest between Philip the Fair and Boniface VIII. It aimed at creating a strong temporal power by continually rounding off its lands that lay in imperial territory, and by reducing to obedience those Italian States which, to a greater or lesser extent, recognised its authority. The Pope declared himself as king, and as such surrounded himself with a magnificent court, in which the cardinals played the part of princes of the blood.

Undoubtedly, to make the Church rich and powerful, they ran the risk of introducing into it the spirit of the world and the desire for its gains. Would not the care of souls be thereby neglected? In truth, the Pope's example became contagious. The clergy dressed in sumptuous garments, made of fine material patterned in squares like a chess-board; they had on their feet pointed shoes of the latest fashion; and, contrary to the canonical regulations, they wore their hair long. A canon of Liège, Jean Le Bel, came to divine service every day accompanied by a guard of honour composed of some sixteen to twenty persons. There were numerous exceptions, but far too many bishops, as the Cistercian James of Thérines remarks, "were principally occupied with increasing their power and worldly goods." They practised luxury and ostentation. Provincial councils ordered them to reduce their establishments, and forbade them to keep jesters, dogs, and falcons; but without success.

This new orientation given to the Church was to some minds a grave scandal. The loudest in their censures were the Franciscans in Provence, who were partisans of absolute poverty. Known as Beguins or Spirituals, they drifted into strange errors. According to them, the era of the Holy Spirit had arrived; the Church, given up to avarice, pride, and the pleasures of the flesh, had finished its course; the Pope was Anti-Christ; the official priesthood was to be succeeded by monachism. These revolutionary views aroused the attention of John XXII, who excommunicated all Fraticelli, Béguins, Béguines, Bizochi, and Brethren of the Poor Life, and ordered them to dissolve the associations which, under cover of privileges from Celestine V, they had tried to form in Italy and the south of France (1317–18). A much more serious issue brought the Holy See into conflict, no longer with a small body of fanatics, but with almost the whole Order of Franciscans. It arose on a theological question: did Christ and the apostles practise poverty to the extent of having no possessions either in common or individually? The constitution *Cum inter nonnullos* (12 November 1323) taxed with heresy those who maintained the affirmative on this point, and an important section of the Friars Minor revolted.

CH. X.

Both against the Spirituals and other more or less kindred sects, and against the supporters of absolute poverty, the tribunal of the Inquisition took action. It had just been reorganised by the Council of Vienne. The friar-inquisitor, whether Franciscan or Dominican, who up to then had been in sole charge, had henceforward to collaborate with the bishop to whom the accused was subject. The presence of the ordinary was necessary for the use of torture, for the custody of those under arrest or condemned, for the management of the prisons, and for the publication of sentences. The errors professed by the Spirituals and by the Franciscans in revolt against the Holy See were energetically suppressed. Recalcitrants perished at the stake or languished in prison. By the end of the century their numbers were very small.

Other heretics, the Vaudois (Waldenses), who had taken refuge in the deep valleys of Dauphiné, were zealously tracked down. Their theological beliefs can be practically summed up as the direct negation of the authority of the Roman Church. The priests, they declared, soiled by the thirst for lucre and the love of riches, had lost all right to lead Christians in the path of salvation. Their own *barbas* (guides), men of upright and intelligent minds who observed evangelical poverty, alone were qualified to absolve sins. Expeditions were equipped by the orders of Gregory XII and were completely successful; the prisons became too small to hold those whom the sword and the stake had spared. The Great Schism gave the Vaudois the opportunity to raise their heads again; and their numbers grew to such a point that in 1488 an army was dispatched to massacre them to the very summits of the Alps.

In spite of the impulse given to it by the Popes of Avignon, the Inquisition was becoming moribund. The public authorities were jealous and suspicious of it, and refused it their support. The ill-feeling against the Church went on increasing; and heresy, though persecuted, left its traces everywhere. In the last half of the fourteenth century, Wyclif succeeded in stirring Europe by the trenchancy of his writings and the thunders of his preaching, while the Bohemian priests Conrad Waldhauser, Milíč of Kroměříž, and Matthias of Janov lashed the disorders of the clergy unsparingly. The spirit of insubordination with which these innovators inspired the masses made ravages throughout Christendom; their gravity was to be realised in the period of the Great Schism.

If abuses existed under the Popes of Avignon, it was not because they were tolerated. On the contrary, the different Popes who resided on the banks of the Rhone strove to suppress them. Clement V added to the *Decretales* a sixth book, the *Clementines*, full of wise rules on discipline. John XXII published a series of constitutions, later to form an addition to the *Corpus iuris canonici* under the name of *Extravagantes*. He also created new dioceses in South France, Aragon, and Italy, thinking by extraordinary measures to provide for the salvation of souls. New bishops, he believed, could more easily feed less numerous flocks. Benedict XII,

Innocent VI, Urban V, and Gregory XI enforced residence on incumbents, drove the parasites from the court, favoured study, and combated the abuses whose existence they were the first to note.

With the reform of the religious Orders these Popes were equally concerned. While the Franciscans were suffering from dangerous dissensions within the Order, the Dominicans, the Knights of St John of Jerusalem, the Order of Grandmont, the Cistercians, the Benedictines, the Canons Regular living under the rule of St Augustine, had all considerably abated their pristine fervour. The Popes, especially John XXII, Benedict XII, and Innocent VI, tried to restore the monastic life in its integrity. They imposed new constitutions, they appointed to the headship men more likely to combat abuses, after having deposed those who were unworthy of their high office, and they restored in the cloisters the practice of poverty, work, and study. One of the great evils in the Church in the fourteenth century arose from the crowd of vagabond monks (*gyrovagi*), who had been expelled from their convents or had left them without the permission of their superiors, and who roamed the world in quest of adventures and lived a hand-to-mouth existence dependent on the charity of the public. Benedict XII and his successors were at pains to enforce the return of these vagabonds to their own monasteries, or, if that created difficulties, to others of the same Order. They also endeavoured to check the practice among members of the Mendicant Orders of transferring to the Benedictines and Cistercians, thus becoming eligible for benefices. Some of their regulations remained in force until the Council of Trent; others, which they had propounded but not put into force, were promulgated by that Council.

The reforms inspired by the Popes of Avignon might have produced more effective and lasting results, had it not been for the counteracting influence of events of a disastrous nature and beyond papal control. The Black Death of 1348–49 depopulated the convents and profoundly disturbed monastic life; the wars which raged almost throughout Europe, and particularly in France, led to the most terrible disorders. The freebooting bands that devastated the country brought ruin to monasteries and priories; they laid waste the fields, pillaged the granaries and warehouses, burnt the dwellings, violated the nuns. This accumulation of evils, detailed by chroniclers and documents alike, resulted in the absence of discipline and the neglect of the essential principles of monastic life. The number of wandering monks increased, and many of them went to swell the ranks of the Flagellants, those fanatics who began by scourging the body until blood flowed as a means of appeasing the wrath of God, but who ended by becoming a public danger. Their blind zeal drove them to persecute the Jews, to threaten ecclesiastical property, to emancipate themselves from the authority of the Church, to scorn the ordinary means of salvation, and to create a definitely revolutionary movement, against which prison and the stake were the only methods that succeeded.

The Popes of Avignon were obsessed with the idea of a crusade. They preached it with a praiseworthy devotion that deserved to earn success. At their appeals, the princes solemnly took the cross; but the enthusiasm, which was possibly quite sincere, died as rapidly as it had come into being. The warfare which raged unceasingly in Europe prevented the kings from undertaking the pious journey overseas; and finally the fall of Acre in 1291 had numbed the energy of the West. The era of general crusades was over for good. Henceforward there were only to be limited expeditions, brilliant indeed, but barren in their effects, because of the small numbers of soldiers or sailors that took part in them; thus there might have been great results from the capture of Rhodes on 13 August 1310, and the naval victory of Negropont during John XXII's pontificate. However, the papacy of Clement VI was marked by important achievements. Judging that an appeal to arms addressed to the kings would receive an inevitable rebuff, he took on himself to plan a crusade. His idea was to form a naval league between the Latins of the East and the Venetians against the Turkish corsairs who infested the Archipelago; then to profit by the weakness of the Greek and Armenian schismatics to make them solicit the alliance of the Latin league and abandon their schism.

The first part of this ingenious plan was put into execution. After laborious negotiations, in which Clement VI displayed both patience and ingenuity, a league was formed between the Papacy, the Venetians, the King of Cyprus, and the Hospitallers. In the spring of 1344 a flotilla of twenty-four vessels assembled at Negropont, and, under the direction of the Patriarch Henry of Asti, surprised Smyrna, which for long had been the head-quarters of the Turkish corsairs, on 28 October 1344. Emboldened by their victory, the Latins, after some further successes, wrested from the emir Omar Beg the command of the sea. On land the Christian arms were less fortunate. The Turks could not be dislodged from the citadel which dominated the town of Smyrna; and even, following on a sortie of the Christians, killed all their leaders (January 1345). However, the early victories had roused the West from its apathy; an army of about 15,000 crusaders came to Smyrna in 1346 to act under the command of Humbert, the heir to Dauphiné. Unluckily Humbert was irresolute and incapable of initiative. His indecision paralysed his troops, who had not the spirit to make a move against the enemy. Soon sickness and dissensions among the allies discouraged the unstable commander of the crusade; he obtained his recall to Europe and retired into a Dominican convent. In spite of this, the fleet won a striking success at Imbros, and destroyed more than a hundred Turkish vessels. But, left without a leader, the league gradually disintegrated; the Venetians had in view only the extension of their influence at the expense of the Genoese and the Hospitallers of Cyprus. There was nothing to be done but to sign a truce which should assure to the Christians the advantages won at Smyrna (1350–51).

The formation of the Latin league brought about a rapprochement between the Holy See and Constantinople. The death of Andronicus Palaeologus had aroused disturbances in the Eastern Empire, where the leading minister, John Cantacuzene, disputed the throne with Andronicus' heir. The Empress-regent in alarm sought the help of the Holy See, and addressed to it written promises of submission to the Roman Church. Clement VI replied that if the Greeks gave serious pledges of their sincerity, he would give them his assistance. But for the Byzantine Court to treat of reunion at a time of civil war was to run the risk of alienating a people strongly attached to its traditions; so it took no action on the papal terms. It meditated an alliance with Omar Beg, the powerful emir of Smyrna; but the capture of that town by the Latins compelled the Greeks to change their policy and to veer round once more to Clement VI. In the same way Cantacuzene had intrigued with Omar Beg and now felt his position prejudiced thereby. He shared the throne with John Palaeologus, and paid court to the Holy See, in order to prevent the Empress and her party from allying with the Latins, and also to fetter the actions of the Genoese and Venetians who were advantaging themselves at his expense. Clement VI at first rejected the advances of Cantacuzene and then gave heed to them; but he made his alliance conditional, especially on the union of the Churches and the recognition of papal supremacy. When the break-up of the Latin league took place, the scheme of reunion, which for Cantacuzene had really only been a diplomatic counter, entirely collapsed.

While preaching and organising the crusade and working for the union of the Churches, the Popes of Avignon kept in the forefront an object which they had much at heart—the expansion of Catholicism in Asia. They did their best to get into relations with the rulers of the Far East who seemed well-disposed to Christianity, to the prejudice of the doctrines of Islām; secondly, they took in hand the conquest of paganism. In place of temporary missions with no fixed centre they substituted permanent missions which gave birth to new Churches. In 1312 the episcopate included an archbishop and ten suffragans in China; by 1314 there were almost fifty Franciscan convents. On 1 April 1318 John XXII created ten suffragans for the metropolitan of Sultānīyah. And in the Persian provinces twenty churches could now be counted. One measure adopted by John XXII in 1324 greatly assisted the expansion of the missions. The *Societas Peregrinantium propter Christum*, founded by Innocent IV, received new statutes, and was placed under the direction of a vicar-general. His duties consisted in the sending of missionaries, Franciscan or Dominican, to the infidels wherever the needs of the moment required. A few years later, about 1330, the Basilian monks in Armenia abjured the schism, adopted the Dominican rule and habit, and under the name of United Brethren (later Uniats) swelled the missionary ranks. The Franciscans established themselves once more in the Holy Land, and

CH. X.

built convents at Jerusalem and Bethlehem. In Tartary, Turkestan, India, at Tabrīz and elsewhere, Christianity was preached. Political events, however, in the second half of the fourteenth century put a sudden check to the advance of the faith. The overthrow in 1368 of the Mongol dynasty in China and the accession of Tamerlane (Tīmūr) to the throne of Transoxiana resulted in the expansion of Islām in Asia. Tamerlane undertook a holy war and set himself to get possession of the Caliphate. The Muslims quickly regained the ground lost by them at the beginning of the century; they subjugated Kipchak in 1389 and India in 1398. Soon there was nothing left in Persia but the bishopric of Sultānīyah, and on this its prelates had but a precarious hold.

The prolonged stay of the Papacy at Avignon had the effect of withholding from the Italians the considerable advantages which they reaped from its presence among them. Rome became a city of the dead. Instead of being the capital of Christendom, it was reduced to the level of a provincial town torn by faction-strife. Petrarch echoed the Italian grievances. With inimitable vigour of expression he denounced the pontiffs who had deserted Italy. Avignon is hateful in his eyes. "How shameful," he writes, "to see it become suddenly the capital of the world, in which it ought only to take the lowest place." He even calls it "the impious Babylon, the hell on earth, the sink of vice, the sewer of the world. There is in it neither faith, nor charity, nor religion, nor the fear of God, nor shame, nothing that is true, nothing that is holy...." The matchless poet is not content with abuse of Avignon. He makes his talents subserve his hatred, and paints the papal court in the blackest colours, as given up to the worst debaucheries. For long the impassioned invective of Petrarch has been taken as truthful and repeated complacently. But recent historians have recognised its real value, in refusing to it any semblance of truth. One of them speaks of Petrarch as "the implacable detractor of the Popes of Avignon," and this is the phrase that exactly describes him.

However, there is one point on which the poet has not exaggerated. He is for us a standing witness of the state of exasperation to which Italian opinion had come. The Romans, especially, wished to end what was meaning ruin to them, the absence of the Papacy. In Gregory XI's time, their ambassadors summoned the Pope to return within their city's walls. They averred, according to Nicholas Eymerich, inquisitor in Aragon, "in the name of those that sent them, that if he did not transfer the papal court to Rome, the Romans would create a Pope who would pledge himself to fix his dwelling and his residence among them." According to the warden of the Castle of Sant' Angelo, the Abbot of Monte Cassino was ready to play the thankless part of anti-Pope. Further, several Romans plotted to massacre the foreigners of whom the Curia was composed, and especially the cardinals, in order to force the Pope to fix his residence for ever in the Eternal City. If, as he declared his intention of doing, Gregory XI had quitted Rome again, in all probability the schism would have broken out. In his lifetime the crisis would have been easier to settle. Unfortunately he died too soon, with the gloomy presentiment of the dissensions which were to rend the Sacred College. However, before he died, in order to dispel the danger, he thought it sufficient to allow the cardinals to carry out his successor's election under irregular conditions. He authorised them not to preserve the interval prescribed by custom, not to stay in Rome, and not to shut themselves up in conclave (19 March 1378).

The forebodings of Gregory XI were speedily realised. The day after his death, which occurred on 27 March 1378, the Romans began to bring pressure to bear on the Sacred College. Steps were taken collectively by the municipal officials and separately by individuals, all directed to prove to the cardinals the necessity they were under of electing a Roman, or at least an Italian, as Pope. These different demonstrations of the popular will were accompanied too by threats. One man apostrophised Jean de Cros in the following terms: "Give us an Italian or a Roman Pope; otherwise, all the ultramontane cardinals will be knifed."

The attitude of the Romans became still more dangerous. Getting possession of the guard of the conclave and of the Borgo San Pietro, they evicted the papal functionaries and drove the nobles out of the town. As they were afraid that the members of the Sacred College might think of escaping by water, they confiscated the oars and rudders of all the vessels anchored in the Tiber. Moreover, from the Campagna and the neighbouring hills armed bands poured into Rome, who did not scruple to molest the followers of the cardinals. Panic spread on all sides, and there was fear of pillage. The far-sighted put their possessions in safe custody. Peter of Luna dictated his will, while Robert of Geneva donned a coat of mail before adventuring into the street. And yet the cardinals do not seem to have fully appreciated the danger. They did not think of hiring mercenaries in the service of the Church or of shutting themselves up in the Castle of Sant' Angelo. They relied on the promises of the Romans to respect their freedom of voting.

On Wednesday, 7 April 1378, the entry into conclave took place, accompanied by the clamour of the populace demanding a Roman or an Italian Pope. The municipal officials, faithfully interpreting the popular will, took an attitude which was to bear important results: "Name a Roman or an Italian Pope," they said to the assembled cardinals; "otherwise your lives and ours are in danger, so determined are the people to obtain what they want." A disturbed night followed. About day-break the alarm sounded. Soon the crowd, massed near the Vatican, became tumultuous; its shouts grew more menacing. The three priors of the Sacred College felt obliged to hold a parley with the demonstrators; but the guard of the conclave represented the peril that threatened them: "You run the risk of being torn in pieces, if you do not hasten to elect an Italian or a Roman. We are outside, and can judge of the danger better than you can." This language had the effect of persuading the cardinals. The scrutiny was taken, and the Archbishop of Bari, Bartolomeo Prignano, received the unanimous vote of all the cardinals except Orsini, who refused to participate in an election conducted in such circumstances. His colleagues also seemed to have the feeling that they were acting without due consideration. Some of them voted in these terms: "I *freely* name Bari"; "I name the Archbishop of Bari with the intention that he shall be *veritably* Pope." The expressions they employed shewed that they were conscious of having committed some irregularity in the election. By using them, they wished apparently to give a belated legality to their actions and to ease their consciences. But doubt was uppermost; one of them, at the meal following the election, proposed that it should be held again.

While a deputation was on its way to make sure of Prignano's consent, the Romans, in ignorance of the result of the scrutiny, were getting impatient. They broke through the conclave enclosure and invaded the Vatican. There was a general rush for safety. The cardinals scattered and took refuge where they could; the cardinal of Brittany climbed to the roof of his house and hid behind a chimney. Those most in danger shut themselves up in the Castle of Sant' Angelo or escaped from Rome. On 9 April twelve out of the sixteen cardinals enthroned Prignano. No one thought of denouncing the invalidity of the election of 8 April or of proposing the holding of a new conclave. They even, individually or as a body, announced to the Christian rulers the accession of Urban VI to the papal throne.

The Pope in a very short while revealed himself in an unfavourable light: he was capricious, passionate, and extremely violent. The cardinals repented of their choice, and one after the other they left Rome and assembled at Fondi. There, thirteen in all, they elaborated a sort of encyclical, in which they declared Prignano's election invalid and pronounced anathema on his person (9 August 1378). On 20 September the foreign cardinals gave their votes to Robert of Geneva (Clement VII); their Italian colleagues gave a tacit consent to the election by their presence in the conclave. So began the period which bears the distinctive title of the Great Schism of the West, partly because of its exceptional duration (it lasted from 1378 to 1417), partly because of the gravity of the crisis, which almost brought the Church to ruin and at any rate afflicted it with the direst consequences.

Opinion in modern times is much divided on the subject of the legitimacy of Urban VI and of his rival Clement VII. The problem amounts to this. There are certain points that are beyond dispute: the election of Prignano was preceded and accompanied by popular disturbance, which brought a certain pressure to bear on the electors; it took place under the sway of a definite fear, but not entirely as the result of that fear; it was carried out with undeniable precipitancy; its validity appeared doubtful from the first to a number of the electors. Were these different circumstances sufficient to deprive the cardinals of the freedom they ought to enjoy in the choice of a Pope, and therefore to vitiate the election of 8 April 1378? This is the crucial question, and in order to settle it we need not turn to the legal texts that define wherein freedom in the election of a Pope consists. We have to deal, on the contrary, only with the evidence of persons interested in legalising their own conduct. The difficulty is not one peculiar to modern times; contemporaries felt incapable of coming to a decision. The Council of Constance, which met to end the crisis, Martin V and his successors, the Church in fact—all have avoided pronouncing a verdict. "The solution of the great problem posed in the fourteenth century escapes the judgment of history"—such is the wise conclusion of Noël Valois, and to this we must subscribe[1].

Since the Church had two heads, it was only to be expected that each would excommunicate the other or at least the opponents of his cause; also that each would nominate to benefices, and that in consequence the partisans of Clement VII and the partisans of Urban VI would be at daggers drawn in every diocese. Religious warfare threatened the peace of every State, and the governments found that they had either to give their adherence to one of the rival Popes or to remain neutral. It has long been the custom to explain the composition of the rival obediences solely by political expediency. To France is attributed the design of having sought for its own advantage to re-establish an Avignonese Pope and to associate its allies with its own aims; opposed to it were England and the Empire, anxious, in concert with other smaller States, to free themselves from French influence. The facts, however, are somewhat different. Undoubtedly policy played a part, but conscience played its part as well. At first, Charles V shewed no hostility towards Urban VI in spite of the unfavourable reports that reached him from Rome. Ignorant where the truth lay, he adopted an official neutrality (11 September 1378). It was only after having consulted the clergy of the realm assembled at Vincennes on 16 November 1378, and after having examined the documents dispatched by the cardinals from Fondi and from Avignon, that he gave a tardy decision in favour of Clement VII.

[1] Diverse historians have maintained the contrary view and pronounced for the validity of Urban's election; *e.g.* L. Salembier, *Le Grand Schisme d'Occident* (*Revue pratique d'apologétique*, Vol. IV, pp. 467–72, 579–94, Paris, 1907); *ib. Le Grand Schisme d'Occident*, pp. 45–51, 5th ed., Paris, 1921; Mgr A. Baudrillart in *Bulletin Critique*, p. 148, Paris, 1896; E. Chénon in Lavisse et Rambaud, *Histoire Générale*, Vol. III, p. 319, Paris, 1922; L. Pastor, *Geschichte der Päpste*, Vol. I, Freiburg-im-Breisgau, 1907. But the weakness of their arguments has been exposed by H. Hemmer, *Le Grand Schisme d'Occident* (*Revue du clergé français*, Vol. XXXVII, pp. 603–21, Paris, 1904).

Castile, although the ally of France, preserved for some time a strict neutrality. At last King John I determined to abandon this equivocal attitude. In May 1380 an embassy was sent to Avignon, Rome, and Naples; it heard evidence from eye-witnesses of the election of Urban VI and from the surviving cardinals. The enquiry was strictly conducted and its results communicated on 23 November 1380 to the clergy assembled at Medina del Campo; on 19 May 1381 adhesion to Clement VII was proclaimed.

The Kings of Aragon took the same attitude as their neighbours of Castile; after having instituted two enquiries, in 1380 and 1386, they adopted the cause of Clement VII. On 6 February 1390 Charles III, King of Navarre, followed their example. The King of Portugal had already, at the end of 1379, declared against Urban VI; it was only the intervention of England that caused him to retract (29 August 1381). In fact, it was England that in every way opposed Clement VII. It saw in him an ally of its enemy, France; and it tried to checkmate him in Flanders, Italy, Tuscany, Umbria, Provence, and Guienne. Hardly at all did religious motives inspire its conduct. The contest with Clement VII was for the Plantagenets only a particular phase of the struggle in which they had been engaged for many years with the Valois. They declared in favour of Urban VI without having seriously examined the validity of his election; their information as to what took place at the conclave seems to have been scanty and often erroneous. They carried their intolerance so far as to refuse to receive the delegates of the cardinals. Policy equally dictated the attitude taken by Scotland towards the rival claimants to the papal tiara; as an ally of France it adopted the cause of the French Pope.

That the Emperor declared for Urban VI was decided as much on political as on conscientious grounds. His choice was defended by strong arguments derived from the inconsistency of the cardinals' actions: first the enthronement and recognition of Urban, then the election at Fondi. His manner of judging the events did not equally impress all the princes of the Empire; some of them were for Urban, others for Clement. Some went through strange alternations: after recognising Clement VII as the true Pope, they abandoned his cause under pressure of circumstances, in spite of their French sympathies. Hungary, on the other hand, never hesitated; from June 1379 onwards it adhered to Urban VI.

The situation in Italy was very complex and variable. In Sicily the Duke of Montblanch[1] and his son Martin I corresponded both with the Pope of Rome and with the Pope of Avignon. Their desire was to range themselves within the Avignonese obedience, but the opposition of the nobles and people prevented them from ever realising their aim. At Naples, during the reign of Joanna I, there was considerable excitement.

[1] Martin II of Sicily (and I of Aragon). He actually succeeded his son on the Sicilian throne.

The people were on the side of Urban VI, while the queen at one time proclaimed him as Roman pontiff, at another as usurper. The accession of Charles of Durazzo to the throne on 2 June 1381 ought to have strengthened the position of Urban; for was it not to him that Charles owed his crown? But the violence and extravagant conduct of the Pope of Rome turned the mind of Charles against him. Urban VI seemed, in fact, to have been seized with madness. He stirred his own partisans into revolt against him; he set himself to empty his own court. He put to the torture several cardinals who disapproved of his strange conduct; five others were moved by his barbarous proceedings to issue a sort of encyclical branding the character and actions of him who had raised them to the purple. Pileo da Prata and Galeazzo Tarlati di Pietramala left Italy and went to Avignon to make submission to Clement VII, who hastened to add them to his own Sacred College (13 June 1387). The fantastic character of Urban frightened the towns of Umbria and Tuscany, and they concluded a treaty of defensive alliance against him. Gian Galeazzo Visconti, Florence, Bologna, and many other towns entered into relations with Clement, and though not actually recognising him received his ambassadors. Even at Rome riots broke out, and Urban, feeling his position to be unsafe, left the city. So an examination of the map of Europe some ten years after the double election of 1378 forces the conclusion that the area of the two obediences is practically equal, but that on the whole the balance is on the side of the Pope of Avignon. This is of little consequence, however, beside the melancholy fact that the West was rent asunder into two factions, each of which hurled its anathemas against the other.

This abnormal state of affairs could not last, Had not then the Church the power within herself to heal her wounds? Had she not in the past had recourse to a remedy of which she had proved the healing effects— the assembling of a General Council? But the application of such a measure necessitated the assent and the co-operation of both the heads of Catholicism. Neither Urban VI nor Clement VII would consent, nor would their cardinals either. Theologians pointed out that a council had no authority over the person of a Pope. Who would convoke it? The two rivals in concert? They could not be counted upon to take a step which put their rights on an equality. One of them by himself? The partisans of the rival obedience would not listen to a summons issuing from one whom they regarded as a usurper. The cardinals, or the prelates? The Emperor? The kings acting in harmony? All these solutions went right against tradition. A council assembled under such abnormal conditions would be devoid of authority. From it, men thought, the schism would only emerge the more vigorous.

To this almost official doctrine certain writers gave formal contradiction. Henry of Langenstein in the *Epistola Pacis* (1379), Conrad of Gelnhausen in the *Epistola Concordiae* (1380), an anonymous writer—possibly Pierre d'Ailly—in the *Epistola Leviathan* (1381), pleaded the cause of the council. In 1381 Henry of Langenstein wrote a treatise even more unorthodox. His *Concilium Pacis* suppressed all the embarrassing questions as to the summoning of the council, the person of its president, its legitimacy. It expounded the views that the council is superior to the Pope, that infallibility resides in the congregation of the faithful or their pastors, that the council can assemble at the summons of the kings, can listen to the statements of Clement VII and Urban VI, and can give a decision, whether in favour of one of them or for the holding of a new election by the college of cardinals.

The subversive theories enunciated by Henry of Langenstein were not new. They practically reproduced the revolutionary propositions put forward by William of Ockham, Marsilio of Padua, and John of Jandun at the height of the struggle between Lewis of Bavaria and John XXII. William of Ockham, some fifty years before, had attacked the ancient prerogatives of papal power. In 1324, in the *Defensor Pacis*, which was condemned by John XXII shortly afterwards (23 October 1327), Marsilio of Padua and John of Jandun had maintained "the supremacy of the Empire, its independence of the Holy See, and the invalidity of the powers *usurped* by the sovereign pontiffs." They had taught that the Papacy was of human institution and only obtained its pre-eminence by a long series of usurpations. The supreme authority in the Church belonged to the general council, the summons to which devolved on the *humanus legislator fidelis*, "which has no power above it," or its representative, "the *princeps*." From council and "legislator" the Pope derived his powers. By them he could be punished, suspended, or deposed. In short, Marsilio of Padua and John of Jandun preached the subjection of the Church to the State; they overturned the ecclesiastical hierarchy, despoiled the clergy of their privileges, and degraded the sovereign pontiff to the position of president of a sort of Christian republic governing itself, or rather putting itself under the government of Caesar[1].

The writings of Henry of Langenstein were too bold to win at once the assent of the mass of the clergy and of the governments; they needed time to accomplish their work. The ideas that the German doctor enunciated penetrated at last into university circles and ended by being put into practice, when all other means of ending the schism had been exhausted; especially when the cardinals of both obediences seemed to shew their desire to perpetuate the schism by electing successors to Urban VI and Clement VII, to the former Boniface IX on 2 November 1389, and to the latter Benedict XIII on 28 September 1394.

The French government was the first to take the way of innovation. Charles VI, interfering in spiritual affairs, assembled at Paris a national council, which sat from 2 to 18 February 1395 and numbered as many as

---

[1] See the excellent study on John of Jandun and Marsilio of Padua by N. Valois in the *Histoire littéraire de la France*, Vol. XXXII, pp. 568-87, Paris, 1906.

109 members. This imposing assembly voted, by a majority of about three-quarters, the adoption of the method of cession (the joint resignation of both Popes). The Dukes of Berry, Orleans, and Burgundy went to Avignon to communicate, in the name of the king, the decision to Benedict XIII. They received a point-blank refusal. But their journey had the result of linking up the Sacred College with France; the cardinals met at Villeneuve-lès-Avignon on 1 June 1395, and adopted, with only one dissentient voice, the French plan. More than a year passed in fruitless negotiations; the sovereigns of Europe disliked the method of cession. At last England and Castile changed their minds. Their ambassadors joined with those of France, in the summer of 1397, in begging Benedict XIII and Boniface IX to renounce the tiara simultaneously and to submit to the decision of a council. Both Popes refused to listen to them and put forward proposals to create delay.

In despair of obtaining the end of the schism, the French clergy met at Paris from 14 May to 8 August 1398 and adopted an extremely serious resolution. They decided that the best way of bringing the Papacy to their view was to deprive it of all the sources of influence of which it disposed—the receipts from the heavy taxation, which supplied it with abundant resources, and the collation to benefices. By a process of self-deception they were ingenuously persuaded that such a resolution did not amount to an act of disobedience; they adopted as a pretext the fallacy that, in prolonging the schism by his refusal to abdicate, Benedict XIII was guilty of heresy and therefore deprived of all right to govern the Church. This revolutionary doctrine, borrowed from Ockham, Marsilio, John of Jandun, and Henry of Langenstein, overturned the constitution of the Church. It suppressed papal independence, and handed over the Holy See to the mercy of the princes and the lower clergy. It assured the triumph of disorder and the introduction of anarchy into the government of the Church. In spite of all these consequences, the total withdrawal of obedience from Benedict XIII was published on 27 July 1398. The king announced it by ordinance; like the clergy, he thus attributed to himself the right of dominating the Papacy. So, in a moment, the edifice cleverly and patiently built up by Clement V and his successors toppled to the ground. The collation to benefices that had taken so much trouble to acquire passed back into the hands of the ordinary collators. The fiscal régime, imposed on ecclesiastics in spite of their resistance, came to an end; but the bishops and the king clearly meant to maintain it for their own advantage.

The withdrawal of obedience necessitated the solution of certain problems, which were decided by the clergy in August 1398. It was decreed that those elected to the headship of monasteries, whether exempt or not, should receive confirmation from the bishop of the diocese; that bishops should submit their elections to the metropolitans; that elections, postulations, and provisions should be made free of charge. The reversions to benefices granted by Benedict XIII lapsed, unless the recipients had already acquired a *ius in re*. In cases reserved for the Holy See, absolution was given by the bishops, failing the papal penitentiaries, who kept their powers provided they abandoned the cause of Benedict; even so the penitents had to apply to the next Pope recognised. Dispensations for marriage in urgent cases were also a matter for bishops and cardinals. Appeals were conducted in three stages: bishop, archbishop, and provincial council.

The publication of the royal ordinance of 27 July 1398 at Avignon on 1 September produced a panic within the Curia. Almost everyone decamped, for fear of losing their benefices. Five cardinals alone remained faithful to Benedict XIII; the remaining eighteen crossed the Rhone and took up their quarters at Villeneuve. Though separating themselves from the Pope they yet claimed to be maintaining the government of Christendom. They confiscated the papal seal, and named one of their number captain of Avignon. Fighting soon broke out in the town; the inhabitants began the siege of the papal palace in which Benedict remained enclosed.

The King of France and the Sacred College had thought to prevail over the Pope; they underestimated his obstinacy and his endurance. The aged Pope did not give way; on the contrary, it was he that imposed his will on his adversaries. He actually eluded the vigilance of the besiegers and escaped on 11 March 1403. Once in his native Provence he was in safety. His escape had an immediate effect. The cardinals on 28 March, the people of Avignon on 31 March, France (28–30 May) returned to the obedience of Benedict XIII. Apostolic reservations appeared again as in the past, and elections and collations made contrary to them were declared null. The payment of annates was claimed from all who had entered upon their benefices since 1 August 1398. The papal collectors exacted even the payment of arrears of taxes, however far back they went. The policy of violence adopted by the King of France had ended in a complete check.

The experiment of a self-governing Church had satisfied nobody; the mirage of liberty had rapidly vanished. The principle of free elections had been outrageously violated; and the chapters had had to obey nobles, princes, kings, and to do violence to their own wishes. Hardest of all was the lot of the ordinary collators and patrons; the clergy of their choice were evicted in favour of university nominees and the candidates of the king or the princes. Their last illusions were swept away by royal letters dated 20 March 1400: collators received the injunction to provide alternately, according to the vacancies, for protégés of the king, the queen, the dauphin, the king's brother, or his uncles, and for nominees of the University of Paris. The Archbishop of Rouen was made to suffer for refusing a benefice to the confessor of the Duke of Orleans: his temporalities were seized by the royal officials. Also, during this period, the royal power, which had approved, if not provoked, the suppression of papal taxes, quickly re-established them for its own profit in the form of aids, extraordinary subsidies, and tenths. Needless to say, the king's agents shewed no moderation in collecting the contributions. The monk of Saint Denis, who witnessed their brutality, states bitterly that "the first fruit of the withdrawal of obedience was to expose the Church to the persecution of the secular arm." Thus had another chronicler written long before of Pope and king: "While the one shears Holy Church, the other flays it."

The withdrawal of obedience might perhaps have produced lasting results, if it had had the assent of all the clergy. But some of the bishops, the universities of Toulouse, Angers, and Orleans, and a large number of clergy and laymen, felt invincible repugnance at breaking with a Pope regarded by them all as legitimate; their consciences prompted them to obedience. These scrupulous souls made up a minority working in favour of Benedict XIII, and they finally brought about the reopening of negotiations with him. Outside France, in spite of an active propaganda, only the Queen of Sicily (Naples)[1], the King of Castile, the Bishops of Metz and Verdun, the Dukes of Bar and Lorraine, the Archbishop of Besançon, the Count of Namur, the Duchess of Brabant, and the towns of Cambrai and Liège, joined in the withdrawal of obedience; while in 1401 Provence, a dependency of the Queen of Sicily, submitted of its own accord to Benedict XIII, and in February 1402 Henry III of Castile, responding to the almost unanimous wish of his people, did the same. The French policy, therefore, met with a humiliating rebuff.

Benedict XIII, who had taken refuge at St Victor's in Marseilles, thought he ought to give a proof of his good intentions for unity by entering into negotiations with Boniface IX in September 1404. His ambassadors proposed a meeting, or at any rate that discussions should be entered into by arbitrators appointed by both parties. But Boniface IX refused, and treated his adversary as an obdurate heretic. In this he was consistent with his previous attitude; for on 1 March 1391 he had declared it to be a sin for anyone to maintain the view that a General Council was capable of ending the schism. At bottom, Boniface IX had never doubted the justice of his cause; he could only see one solution for the crisis from which the Church was suffering—the submission of the usurper, as he regarded him. So naturally he repelled with indignation a project which implied his recognition that the rights of his rival were on an equality with his own. His cardinals were of the same mind. When Boniface IX died on 1 October 1404, they had the opportunity of displaying their altruism by suspending the election of a successor and coming to terms with the delegates of Benedict XIII, who were in Rome at the time. On the contrary, they demanded the abdication of the Pope, "hoping to remain in sole possession of the field." In their defence, it

---

[1] Mary of Brittany, mother of Louis II, who was actually only pretender to the throne of Naples. She was administering Provence during her son's absence in Italy.

must be acknowledged that the representatives of Benedict refrained from enquiring about the guarantees that might be forthcoming if their master should consent to surrender power. To the demands of the Roman cardinals they replied with a direct refusal, and then took their leave and departed.

The Roman cardinals then met in conclave. After having all bound themselves to work for unity and to abdicate if they obtained the tiara, they elected as Pope Cosmo Migliorato, better known as Innocent VII, on 17 October 1404. The new Pope seemed to intend to keep his promise. He invited the ambassadors of Benedict XIII to return to Rome and renew the conversations that had just been broken off. But he changed his mind and decided otherwise. When the ambassadors proposed a conference with their master to debate the question, Innocent would no longer receive them. Benedict XIII resolved to profit by the advantage which his rival's refusal gave him. On 16 May 1405 he landed at Genoa, and renewed to the Roman Court his proposal of a conference. As he expected, he met with a fresh refusal. A cleverly-worded bull, of 27 June 1405, pointed out that the wrong did not lie on his side. The princes were invited to overcome the obstinacy of Innocent VII by force; but they remained deaf to this appeal to arms.

On 6 November 1406 the Roman Pope died after a short illness. Gregory XII was elected as his successor on 30 November, and on 11 December he published a bull expressing his determination to renounce the tiara, provided that the Avignonese cardinals would consent to unite in conclave with their Roman colleagues. While making it clear that his own preference was to act by way of conference, Benedict XIII in somewhat ambiguous terms accepted the proposal. In short, it was agreed that a meeting should take place at Savona from 29 September to 1 November 1407. When the time came to carry out the agreement, Gregory XII repented of his proposal of joint abdication. He did not conceal his dislike of entering a port which was under the French King's authority, and he merely announced that he would approach as near as was possible to Benedict XIII. This was a vague and not very helpful assurance. It delighted Benedict, for it gave him an excellent part to play; he did not fail to reach Savona by the appointed date. The festival of All Saints arrived with Gregory at Siena, and refusing to go any farther. There were various reasons for his not keeping his word: the fear of losing in his absence the Papal States, which were threatened by the King of Naples, Ladislas of Durazzo; the advice of his supporters among the lay rulers, who dissuaded him from going to Savona; his mistrust of the King of France; and possibly too, the control that his nephews and courtiers exercised over him. When Benedict, to maintain his advantage, came to Porto Venere, Gregory brought himself to leave Siena and go to Lucca, on 28 January 1408.

A comparatively short distance now separated the two Popes.

Gregory XII invented countless excuses to avoid crossing the gap, and proposed various meeting-places, such as Pisa, Avenza, and Leghorn. Then came the capture of Rome by Ladislas of Durazzo on 25 April 1408, and this gave him the opportunity to break off negotiations. The cause of unity seemed for ever ruined. The Roman cardinals felt that they had been tricked; in May, nine of them abandoned Gregory XII and went to Pisa; from there they sent envoys to Benedict XIII, and discussions were begun at Leghorn. Four cardinals represented Benedict, and they readily conferred with those from Rome. Without the knowledge of their masters and in direct revolt against them, the cardinals of the two obediences quickly came to terms. It seemed to them that as the Popes lacked the courage to heal the schism, the duty devolved upon them. They announced to the Christian world that a General Council would meet at Pisa on 25 March 1409.

For the Council to have a definite result it was necessary that the whole of Christendom should be represented in it; this implied the withdrawal of obedience by all countries from the reigning Popes. Now, in spite of the efforts of the cardinals and of France, Europe was divided into two parties. On one side were England, Lorraine, Holland, the Bishop of Liège, the Electors of Cologne and Mayence and some other German princes, the King of Bohemia (Wenceslas, King of the Romans), Poland, Austria, Lombardy, Tuscany, the Romagna, France, Navarre, Portugal, the King of Cyprus, and Louis of Anjou, Ladislas' rival for Sicily; on the other, the rest of the Empire including Rupert, King of the Romans, the Scandinavian countries, Hungary, Venice, the March of Ancona, a portion of the Romagna, Rome, Ladislas, King of Sicily (Naples), Castile, Aragon, and Scotland. Policy, indeed, inspired the conduct of more than one government; but the opponents of the Council were on strong ground in contesting the right of the cardinals of the two obediences to convoke the Council while Gregory XII and Benedict XIII were still regnant.

On the day fixed, 25 March 1409, the Council met at Pisa; it numbered some 500 members. Its first care was to institute proceedings against Benedict and Gregory. On 5 June sentence was pronounced: the two Popes were deprived of the tiara as heretics. It remained to choose a successor. To the cardinals present at Pisa was given the commission of proceeding to the election of a Pope; twenty-four in number they entered into conclave, and on 26 June 1409 elected Peter Philarges, cardinal of Milan, who took the name of Alexander V. The new Pope did not occupy the chair of St Peter for long; he died suddenly during the night of 3–4 May 1410. The Sacred College fixed its choice on Baldassare Cossa, Pope John XXIII, on 17 May 1410. The fathers of Pisa had thought to relieve the conscience of Christendom. By their precipitancy in electing a Pope they had only aggravated the evil which they fondly imagined they were curing. In place of two obediences there were henceforward three.

Fearing for his personal safety, Benedict XIII had taken ship on 16 June 1408; on 1 July he landed at Port Vendres and made his way to Perpignan. There he took up his residence, and summoned a council, which opened on 21 November. It was, all things considered, an imposing assembly; it comprised about 300 members, including eight archbishops and thirty-three bishops. But of the cardinals who had formerly composed his court, only three were present. The fathers of the council came from Castile, Aragon, Navarre, Provence, Savoy, France, and Lorraine. The other States were not represented, so that the council had not the necessary qualification of universality. The question of unity figured on the programme; but Benedict's actual purpose was, by equipping himself with resolutions of the council, to combat those who had deserted his cause. Contrary to his expectations, he found himself obliged to give his promise to abdicate; but his abdication was to take effect from the day on which Gregory XII was deposed, both *de facto* and *de iure*. This condition relieved him of apprehension for the future, for Gregory had no intention of abdicating. Far from it; he had taken refuge in the territory of Friuli, and held a council there at Cividale from June to August 1409. One decree was published, citing Benedict XIII and Alexander V to appear before him, and affirming that he alone was the rightful successor of St Peter. If he made mention of abdication, he was careful to hedge his promise round with conditions which made it nugatory. To avoid the danger of compulsion being brought to bear upon him, he put himself under the protection of Ladislas of Durazzo; it was to Ladislas' interest to undertake his defence and to ensure its efficacy. So neither Benedict XIII nor Gregory XII would bring themselves to surrender their office. Their partisans, undoubtedly, were only thinly scattered throughout Christendom, but there was always the chance that reasons of State or weariness of the strife might cause a revulsion of feeling, and that the government of the Catholic world would thus be restored to them.

In fact, the countries which had decided for the obedience of the Popes of Pisa were not long in realising that the expectations they had based on them were being sadly deceived. The Council had demanded from Alexander V the establishment of reforms which would restrict the rights of the Holy See to an alarming degree. They amounted to this: restitution to the bishops of the rights of procuration, suppression of annates, *servitia*, tenths, and other taxes, re-establishment of canonical elections and of collation to benefices by the ordinary collators. The Pope resisted demands so contrary to the practice hitherto observed in the Church. He consented to certain limited concessions: for example, that the ordinary collators should have the power of appointing to one out of every four of the benefices within their gift; and that arrears of taxes due under previous Popes should not be exacted. But these concessions vanished into thin air. The old taxes reappeared. Freedom of elections, especially from papal provisions, was not restored, with the connivance certainly of the lay rulers. The general discontent increased when John XXIII imposed on Christendom a collection of crushing fiscal measures. In short, the reforms promised at Pisa miscarried; they were betrayed by those who had shouldered the responsibility for seeing them carried into effect.

John XXIII had to pay a heavy reckoning. The Council of Constance deposed him on 29 May 1415, and he himself ratified the sentence. Gregory XII adopted a more dignified attitude: after having issued his summons to the Council, he abdicated on 4 July. As for Benedict XIII, the Emperor Sigismund made a special journey to Perpignan, and tried to obtain from him the abdication he had promised so often, notably at the council in Perpignan itself. The old Pope obstinately refused to abdicate. He believed in the legitimacy of his rights and in the loyalty of his supporters, who still numbered about one-fifth of the Catholic world. Here his calculations went astray. On 13 December 1415 at Narbonne, the representatives of the Kings of Aragon, Castile, Navarre, and the Count of Foix signed an instrument by which they bound themselves to leave the Council of Constance to proceed against Benedict, provided, as his legitimacy was not contested by them, that he did not voluntarily abdicate. On 26 July 1417 Benedict XIII was deposed. On 11 November 1417 Cardinal Odo Colonna was elected unopposed as Pope Martin V.

This election did not immediately end the schism. Benedict, enclosed in the castle of Peniscola, persisted in resistance until his death on 29 November 1422. Before he died, he reconstituted his court by the creation of four cardinals. The intrigues of King Alfonso V of Aragon, who was interested in prolonging the schism, caused this college of cardinals to elect Gil Sanchez Muñoz, provost of Valencia, on 10 June 1423 as Pope Clement VIII. He held office for six years, and abdicated on 26 July 1429. He even experienced a schism within his party. John Carrier, one of Benedict XIII's creations, who had not been summoned to the conclave of 1423, set up a rival Pope, Benedict XIV; of him no single act is recorded. The Aragonese schism ended thus in farce.

The crisis through which the Church had passed had been in the highest degree detrimental; its constitution was wellnigh overturned. For the great achievement of the Popes of Avignon had been to increase the papal sovereignty over Christendom by encroaching gradually upon episcopal rights, and to develop a system of centralisation, complete in all its details, by absorbing little by little every individual activity in the Church. The withdrawal of obedience adopted in 1398 by France, Castile, and other countries dealt a grave blow to tradition. In spite of the inconveniences it created and the discontent to which it gave rise, it taught the clergy to organise, and to govern without the Pope. The attempt made, fruitless as it was, acted as a spur some ten years later, when the neutrality voted at the fifth council of Paris in 1408 was received with enthusiasm. The general discontent degenerated into revolt against the Papacy. Profiting by the lessons of the past, the council organised on systematic lines the autonomy of the French Church. For the papal power were substituted two main organs of government—provincial councils and primacies.

The provincial councils were held each year, and lasted for at least a month. They gave dispensations for marriage, heard appeals, exercised jurisdiction over all the clergy including the bishops and the metropolitan, and examined and confirmed the elections of the primates. The primates confirmed the archbishops in office, consecrated them, and heard appeals from their courts. In case of death or other impediment, their powers were exercised by their suffragans and the provincial council. In the religious Orders the central authority was in the hands of the general chapters; a permanent committee, composed of four members and having its seat at Paris, heard cases from exempt monasteries. Minute regulations were laid down about benefices; especially they aimed at preventing the secular authorities from exercising pressure over elections by the chapters. The disputes to which the collation to smaller benefices gave rise were dealt with by a committee of five members who, in the event of absolute disagreement between collators and privileged clergy (_i.e._ royal and university nominees), themselves appointed to the benefices, though only alternately with the ordinary collators. Papal taxation was entirely suppressed.

As we have seen, the violent attacks made by Henry of Langenstein in the _Squalores curiae romanae_ and Dietrich of Niem in the _Speculum aureum de titulis beneficiorum_ had passed in time from the realm of theory to that of practice. Their revolutionary phrases reappeared on the lips of the various orators who prepared with skill and virulence the charges against the Papacy in the Paris councils—Pierre Leroy, Gilles Deschamps, Jean Jouvenel, Jean Petit, Gerson, Pierre d'Ailly, Jean Cortecuisse. Moreover, from 1408 onwards, national Churches with their own liberties and customs were being formed outside France also, in the various kingdoms that adopted neutrality both towards Benedict XIII and Gregory XII. These Churches, however, had no vitality apart from what they obtained from the royal power. In spite of their desire for independence, they were obedient to the rulers. They were essentially State Churches, and in a few years they were to acquire so much power that Martin V had to negotiate and make concordats with them. The constitution of the Roman Church was thus profoundly modified. The Holy See could no longer communicate directly with the episcopate; it must henceforward beat against the royal will which barred its way. The ideals of the Middle Ages faded away in the troubles that resulted from the Great Schism. Even the power of the Pope was to be limited in a dangerous fashion.

Faced with the evils that grew out of the schism of the West, controversialist writers and speakers of the late fourteenth and early fifteenth centuries transferred to the days of uncontested Popes the grievances which could justly be formulated against the Popes of the three obediences. In domineering tones they demanded the reform of the Church in head and members; some of them aimed at more radical measures. One verse-writer, a member undoubtedly of the University of Paris, compares the Church abandoned to schism to a woman with two husbands, and made a Greek address it, or, to be more precise, counsel it, thus:

L'Eglise ha pour espous Jhesu, vray Dieu et home[1].

John Wyclif went so far as to refer to the Papacy in the following terms: "To get rid of such a demon would not harm the Church, but would be useful to it; in working for his destruction, the Church would be working solicitously for the cause of God."[2] However, though these daring propositions found some echo among contemporaries, most people were not so extreme as this. They confined themselves to proclaiming the need for reforms and the superiority of the Council over the Pope, as the only practical way of bringing the schism to an end; and their theories were to triumph, at long last, at Pisa and Constance. The prestige of the Papacy was, therefore, profoundly affected; its absolute power seemed to have been taken from it, or at least to have been considerably limited in scope.

Grave as was the crisis through which the Church had passed, it is advisable to avoid exaggeration about it. Historians who base their views on the violent charges made in the controversial literature of the time, above all in the celebrated work of Nicholas of Clamanges, the *De corrupto Ecclesiae statu*, have depicted the moral condition of religious society in the fourteenth century in the blackest colours. Going back to the period before the Great Schism, they have drawn plentifully from the writings of Dante, Petrarch, the chroniclers, and even of convinced champions of papal omnipotence, such as Alvaro Pelayo, St Catherine of Siena, and St Bridget of Sweden. Their enquiries all end in the same conclusions. But the documents published out of the Vatican Archives have caused other historians to revise the charges by which the memory of the Popes of Avignon has been assailed, at least to a certain extent. While condemning what was deserving of condemnation, these recent writers have clearly distinguished Clement VII and Benedict XIII from their predecessors. Though in every pontificate there were abuses, it is necessary to take note of the sum of Christian endeavour, and of the manifestations of popular piety. The evils of the time drove the faithful to the exercise of severe penances.

There were saints in all ranks of society and in every country. Raymond Lull (1256–1315) and Pierre Thomas (1305–66) died as martyrs for the

---

[1] N. Valois, *La France et le Grand Schisme d'Occident*, Vol. i, p. 390, Paris, 1896.

[2] *De discussione paparum* in *John Wiclif's polemical works in Latin*, ed. Rudolf Buddensieg, Vol. ii, p. 573, London, 1883.

faith, the one at Bougie, the other at Famagusta. Bertrand of Saint-Geniès, Patriarch of Aquileia, fell a victim in 1350 to his zeal for recovering the property and privileges of which his Church had been unjustly deprived by predatory vassals. The Blessed Venturino da Bergamo (1304–46) excited the crowds by his ringing eloquence, and at his voice they forgot their feuds, practised charity, gave themselves up to exercises of penance. On 1 February 1335 he left Bergamo, and drew after him to Rome a mass of pilgrims who numbered up to 20,000 or 30,000 persons, all of whom devoted themselves ardently to prayer and the strictest asceticism. In 1343 his enthusiastic sermons excited the populace in Lombardy to take the cross, and when they embarked for the Holy Land he followed them, to meet his death at Smyrna. The Blessed Giovanni Colombini (1304–67) also traversed Italy, not to preach the crusade, but to announce and prepare the kingdom of God. "Praised be Jesus Christ" was his motto and device. As his Divine Master had set the example of charity, so he continually preached peace. His disciples took the name of Gesuati in 1364, and gave themselves up to the care of the poor and the sick. The Sienese Giovanni Tolomei, St Bridget of Sweden, St Catherine of Siena, St Colette, the Blessed John Discalceatus, Peter Ferdinand Pecha, Gerard Groote of Deventer, James of Bourbon, the Blessed Peter of Luxemburg, and others, were all famed for terrible austerities. These pious souls were not isolated cases. Besides the Gesuati, other new religious congregations were founded such as the Olivetans, the Hieronymites, the Brethren of the Common Life, and the Brigittines. Mystic Christianity, preaching the renunciation of the things of this world and the abandonment of the soul to God, had in the fourteenth century its most illustrious representatives—Master Eckehart, Margaret Ebner, Johann Tauler, Heinrich Suso, Jan Ruysbroeck, Jean Gerson, and above all Thomas à Kempis, the author of that admirable treatise of perfection, the *Imitatio Christi*. Around these diverse persons were gathered lay folk, themselves in love with mysticism and the spirit of penance. The fourteenth century counted an indefatigable apostle in Vincent Ferrer, who evangelised in turn Aragon, Castile, Languedoc, Auvergne, Touraine, Brittany, Burgundy, the Lyonnais, Dauphiné, and Flanders, and everywhere won the multitudes by his eloquence. Finally, at the summit of the ecclesiastical hierarchy, the Blessed Urban V, with his gentle mien, illumined the whole Church.

So there existed in the fourteenth century a remarkable contrast of good and evil, and, in spite of the deep wounds from which the Church was suffering, she gave proof of an intense vitality. One most anxious question, however, still demanded an answer. Could the Church herself heal her own wounds?

CHAPTER XI

FRANCE: THE LAST CAPETIANS

PHILIP III's reign is by no means such a colourless interlude between the two great reigns of Louis IX and Philip IV as it has sometimes been represented. Its purely military aspects, it is true, are lamentable. One great army in 1276, on its way to invade Castile, came marching tamely home again without crossing the frontier. Another, in the Aragon "crusade" of 1285, endured many sufferings in a hopeless and uninspiring cause, to which the king's own life was sacrificed. These Spanish expeditions, however, were merely the premature outcome of the growing importance, confidence, and ambition of the Capetian monarchy. The process by which the king's power was exalted and the royal domain extended is the capital interest of French history in the thirteenth and early fourteenth centuries, and to that process Philip III's reign made a real contribution, overt or concealed. The failure of designs of foreign conquest must not be allowed to blind us to the significance of this fact, or cause us to turn from the reign with a shrug, like the contemporary poet who sang:

> De celui roi ne soi que dire
> N'ai pas este a son concire
> Ne ne sais rien de son afaire
> Nostre Sire li donst bien faire.

Whether Philip himself pursued a consciously formulated policy is another question. It is hard to say how he earned that title of *Audax* which is traditionally his. Contemporary writers praise him as a mighty hunter and a good churchman, but blame him for illiteracy and over-absorption in secular affairs. Even Guillaume de Nangis, in anxious quest of polite metaphor, could do no better than to call his king "the carbuncle sprung from that most precious gem of Christ," St Louis. At any rate, Philip held that father's memory dear, and accepted the consequences of his father's actions. He kept in office the household clerks who had learnt their business in St Louis' service, men of sagacity and experience, wonderfully patient in turning the wheel of routine, if ever expectant of reward. Pierre de la Broce, who retained under Philip the post of chamberlain to which he had already risen during St Louis' lifetime, was an exemplar of the strength and weakness of this class. After eight years, court jealousy achieved his undoing, and he was hanged (1278). His disappearance cleared the way for his chief enemies, the great feudalists, notable for courage, pride, limitation of vision, and impulsive response to stirring appeals. Head and shoulders above the rest towered the king's uncle Charles, Count of Anjou and Provence and King of Sicily, whose pressure had already been felt by Louis IX and who from 1274 onwards

had a friend at court in Philip's second wife, Mary of Brabant, a lady as
pretty and affectionate as she was consequential and intriguing. The
Queen-mother, however, Margaret of Provence, hated Charles because in
right of his marriage with her sister Beatrice he had acquired the whole
county of Provence when his father-in-law died, denying any share in it
either to herself or to the third sister, Eleanor, mother of Edward I of
England. Concerted schemes of the anti-Angevins on both sides of the
Channel were constant, but none bore permanent fruit.

In his general treatment of the great feudal magnates Philip shewed
a becoming dignity and self-respect. At the very outset, the royal domain
received a magnificent addition in the escheated lands of Philip's uncle,
Alphonse, Count of Poitou and Toulouse, who died on his way home
from the crusade in 1271, leaving no heirs. Though Charles of Anjou
and his cousin, Philippa of Lomagne, both laid claim to a share in this
inheritance, it passed to the Crown undivided, with the exception of the
Comtat Venaissin, east of the Rhone, which was presented to the Papacy,
and the district of the Agenais on the middle Garonne, which was in
1279, by the Treaty of Amiens, handed over to Edward I, King of
England and Duke of Aquitaine. At the same time Philip promised to
begin an enquiry as to English rights in Quercy, and recognised Edward's
queen Eleanor as countess of the little northern fief of Ponthieu, which
she had just inherited from her mother. Philip did well to acquiesce in
this way in new conditions, and to fulfil promises, contingent on the
death of Alphonse, which had been made as long before as the Treaty of
Paris of 1259, for a quarrel with his neighbour the English duke would
have made the absorption of his new southern dominions very difficult.
As it was, he was able to carry out the *saisamentum comitatus Tolose* on the
whole with surprising ease, though he could not entirely avoid complications inevitable for the northern lord of southern fiefs, watched across the
frontier by Castile, Aragon, and Navarre. Roger Bernard III, Count of
Foix, and Gerald V, Count of Armagnac, shewed in a local quarrel such
insolent indifference to the symbols of royal power used in protection of
their enemy, that Philip was compelled to a military demonstration,
followed by the imprisonment of the Count of Foix for a year. Meanwhile James I, King of Aragon, put forward claims which took years to
settle concerning his rights over parts of the county.

Another substantial addition to the lands of the Crown was quite
unexpected. Henry I, King of Navarre and Count of Champagne, died
in 1274, leaving as his heiress Jeanne, a three-year-old child, already
betrothed to whichever son of Edward I of England should survive to
marriageable age. However, the widow, Blanche of Artois, whose brother
Robert was one of Philip's greatest subjects, took refuge at the court of
France, and soon Philip secured the betrothal of Jeanne to his own second
son, his namesake and future successor. French armies took possession of
Navarre, and French officials proceeded to introduce innovations bitterly

resented by its inhabitants. The county of Champagne, however, was administered till Jeanne's marriage in 1284 by an Englishman whom her mother now took as her second husband, Edmund, Earl of Lancaster, brother of Edward I.

Other acquisitions, individually small but cumulatively important, were gained by purchase or exchange. Moreover, the local representatives of the Crown, *baillis* and *sénéchaux*, everywhere pressed forward royal influence and rights, sometimes even more vigorously than the Crown itself thought prudent. Before the reign ended, the seneschal of Beaucaire had coerced the Bishop of Viviers into recognising the royal rights over his subjects; the *bailli* of Mâcon had by constant interference with the suzerainty of the Archbishop of Lyons paved the way for the official union of Lyons with France under Philip IV; and James II of Majorca had been forced to admit the authority of the Crown in Montpellier. In several quarters the Crown had acted as mediator: in the quarrels between Guy of Dampierre, Count of Flanders, and the great Flemish towns; in the "war of the three Roberts," where Philip's brother-in-law, Robert II, Duke of Burgundy, was beset by rival claimants in the persons of his nephews Robert, Count of Nevers, and Robert, Count of Clermont; and in disputes in the county of Brittany. In all sorts of ways the feudalists were being taught that, while on the one hand the way of the transgressor was hard, on the other there were advantages in securing the friendship and support of the Crown. In some respects they found Philip more congenial than his saintly father, for he tolerated the judicial combat, enjoyed tournaments in spite of their political undesirability, and was, in fact, a human and conventional person of like parts and passions with themselves. Had he lived longer, indeed, he might have done something to ease the difficulties due to the double position of the king as feudalist and sovereign.

In ecclesiastical policy Philip III's reign was not marked by any crisis or the settlement of any outstanding problem. The king met his personal religious obligations with decency and even zeal; secured preferment for his protégés when possible; tried to keep some hold through his officials on the hosts of clerks in minor orders whose unruliness so often endangered public peace; avoided as far as he could taking sides in the quarrel between the Mendicant Orders and the secular clergy, in the University of Paris and elsewhere; and was, on the whole, no more and no less criticised in clerical circles than was usual. The papal throne was vacant when he became king, but in 1271 was filled by that admirable and energetic Pope, Gregory X, who aimed at orderliness, reconciliation, and the sinking of political quarrels in common efforts towards spiritual ends. Though Gregory turned a deaf ear to suggestions that Philip III should be chosen as Emperor, his relations with the King of France were kindly throughout his pontificate (1271–76). There followed in rapid succession four Popes of whom nothing need here be said, until in 1281

Charles of Anjou's personal friend, Cardinal Simon of Brie, ascended the papal throne as Martin IV.

Now at last Charles had the leverage for which he had been waiting so long. The character and career of the great Angevin, his masterful personality, his successes, and the fantastic dreams with which his successes inspired him, have been described elsewhere[1]. The wine long mixed seemed ready at last for pouring, when suddenly, in 1282, the cup was dashed from his lips, for his Sicilian subjects threw off his rule in the "Sicilian Vespers," and the rest of his life was spent in vain efforts to retrieve his shattered fortunes. Martin IV did all he could to help. When the Sicilians offered their throne to Peter III, King of Aragon, husband of Constance the heiress of the Hohenstaufen, the Pope not only excommunicated him for accepting, but also declared that he had forfeited the throne of Aragon. Now came the critical moment for France, for the Pope offered the vacated throne to Philip for one of his sons.

From some points of view the offer was tempting. Navarre, the western of the two Spanish kingdoms which marched with French soil, was already secured for Philip's eldest surviving son; it would be well if Aragon, its eastern neighbour, could be in a similar position. And Philip had some stinging memories with regard to Spain, which he would be glad to salve if possible. In 1275, on the death of Philip's brother-in-law, Ferdinand de la Cerda, heir to the throne of Castile, King Alfonso X had entirely ignored the right of the dead man's two little sons to step into their father's place, and had proclaimed as his heir their uncle Sancho. The widow, Blanche of France, left, as Guillaume de Nangis says, "destitute of almost all human comfort, in desolation with her children amid the rude manners of the Spaniards and their horrible appearance," had appealed to Philip for help, and he had not only sent protesting embassies but had set off with a huge army of invasion. However, the army had got no farther than Sauveterre, near Pau, and most of its members had never had a chance of fighting, though some, it is true, went on to punish a revolt in Navarre, and did dreadful work there. The whole business was ineffective, and as by 1283 Alfonso was engaged in a fierce struggle with his former protégé Sancho, Philip need not fear interference from Castile if he chose to blot out its humiliation by new ventures in Aragon. If to these considerations we add the feudal love of war for its own sake, and further the fact that the Aragonese expedition was to involve all the spiritual and temporal privileges of a crusade, it is not surprising that the Pope's offer was accepted, after discussion in two assemblies of magnates, one at Bourges in November 1283, the other at Paris in February 1284. Enthusiasm ignored the difficulty of war in an unknown region, the strength of local feeling in Aragon, and the misery of acting as cat's paw in another man's quarrel. There may well have been moments later, however, when this last thought came home with bitterness; for

[1] *Supra,* Vol. vi, Chap. vi.

Charles of Anjou died in January 1285, and Martin IV in the following March, so that Philip was left alone to face the consequences of other people's actions.

The story of the ill-starred crusade is short. Philip set out in March 1285, accompanied by his two sons and by the papal legate. His army was huge but cumbrous, fiery but undisciplined, and as it advanced from Narbonne across Roussillon horrible atrocities occurred, especially at Elna (25 May). Aragon was entered in June, after a painful crossing of the Pyrenees, and on 27 June Philip settled down to a ten weeks' siege of Gerona. What with shortage of supplies, which had to be brought at irregular intervals from the supporting fleet off Rosas, until this was defeated in August at the battle of the Islas Hormigas; what with disease, due to the heat, the flies, and the deadly stenches of warfare; what with the disheartening effect of long periods of inactivity, only now and then broken by trifling skirmishes; the army which at last, on 7 September, marched into ruined Gerona, was hardly victorious in anything but name. In any case that victory, such as it was, represented the extreme of possible success, and within a week the invaders were in retreat towards France. At Perpignan, on 5 October, Philip III died, while his rival, Peter of Aragon, lived scarcely another month. The reign ended, as it had begun, in an atmosphere of general mourning.

With the accession of Philip IV there opened a period full of great happenings in French history. How far was this due to the king himself? M. Langlois' weighty support is given to the view that we shall never know. "This little problem is insoluble." A German biographer[1], on the other hand, argues that a careful reconsideration of contemporary evidence suggests that Philip had real driving force. As the pupil of William of Ercuis, and the recipient of many learned works, he had had frequent opportunities of acquiring wisdom, and although contemporaries were unanimous in ascribing the responsibility for Philip's actions to others, in each case it is easy to see why they should wish to do so. The monks of Saint-Denis did not want to criticise a patron; Villani, a partner in the firm of the Peruzzi, must not blame a valued client; Dubois thought it tactful to speak freely of past royal mistakes as due to bad advice; Nogaret dared not alienate opinion from his master by revealing to the outside world that *Drang nach Herrschaft* by which he knew him to be possessed. And finally, Philip himself on his death-bed assumed responsibility in striking words which were recorded by an impartial witness in a letter written only eight days afterwards. "He said...that in many ways he had done wrong and offended God, led by evil counsel, and that he himself was the cause of that evil counsel (*quod ipsemet erat causa mali consilii sui*)." All this, however, is slender evidence from which to deduce

[1] K. Wenck, *Philipp der Schöne von Frankreich*. Marburg, 1905.

personality, and the self-accusation of a dying man in his remorse is not enough to counterbalance the silence of a lifetime.

The few definite remarks made by contemporaries about Philip do not help us much. The French called him the Fair and the Flemings the Fat. That indiscreet and hot-headed southerner, Bernard Saisset, was in the midst of the irritations of his own trial when he declared: "The king is like the eagle owl, the finest of birds, and yet worth nothing at all. He is the handsomest man in the world, yet all he can do is to stare at people without saying a word." Yves of Saint-Denis, on the other hand, coming from an abbey closely linked with the destinies of the monarchy, found as he stood by Philip's death-bed exactly those qualities that he would wish to find in a son of St Louis, and phrased his admiration in terms suitable to any pious end. Official documents conceal the individual by their formulae. And even the achievements of the reign are no testimony of royal skill, for historical experience proves that royal indifference was, in administrative connexions at any rate, sometimes more beneficial than royal interference. On the whole we must leave Philip's personality where we found it, a riddle without an answer.

Next to the king, the greatest position in France belonged to Charles of Valois, who had been compensated for losing his promised kingdom of Aragon by marriage with Margaret, the daughter of Charles II, King of Naples, who brought to him the counties of Anjou and Maine. However, Charles had little time to spare for his brother's affairs, for he married three times and had to provide for the futures of fourteen sons and daughters; he acquired with his second wife, Catherine Courtenay, who was the granddaughter of Baldwin II, claims on the Latin Empire of the East; and in 1308 he became an unsuccessful candidate for election as Emperor in the West. Philip's chief instruments—or leaders, if we adopt the idea of his personal insignificance—were chosen from among those professional administrators whose activities are so characteristic of the age, and who had learnt their business in the personal service of the king or his family. The researches made of late years into administrative history have shewn us how united, to the thirteenth-century mind, were public and private, State and domestic, and how experience gained in one field was utilised in another. Pierre Flote, to whom, as his enemies put it in bitter mockery, Philip said, "Thou art Peter, and upon this rock I will build my council," had started his career as head of the pantry in the queen's household. Men of this sort, Guillaume de Nogaret, Enguerrand de Marigny, and others, counted enormously with Philip. Vigorous, impudent, and ingenious, they encouraged him in certain bold departures from the policy of his father and grandfather. Foreign policy deserted the Spanish peninsula for efforts in new fields, and the relations of the Crown with Church and Pope put on startling and scandalous colours. Three huge upheavals mark the reign—the bitter quarrel with Boniface VIII, the establishment of the Avignon Papacy, and the suppression of the Order of the Knights Templars.

It was in 1294 that Cardinal Benedict Gaetani ascended the papal throne as Pope Boniface VIII. He was already known, and disliked, in France. In 1263 he had accompanied Cardinal Simon of Brie when he came to preach an anti-Ghibelline crusade in the interests of Charles of Anjou. So recently as 1290 he had again visited France, this time as legate, and although his instructions were to make peace and assuage the griefs of the clergy, his bitter tongue put such an edge on the policy of Nicholas IV, whom he represented, that he brought not peace but a sword. And as Benedict had begun, Boniface was to continue, robbing his real qualities of courage and energy of some of their value by a contemptuous disregard of other men's prejudices or principles. In Philip IV, however, or in those who dictated Philip's attitude, Boniface soon found a pride and an impatience to match his own. Even in the days of Nicholas IV, who had done his best to veil in elaborate courtesy any difference of opinion between himself and Philip, there had been signs of French resentment. "It is delightful for us," wrote Philip sarcastically in 1289, "to find that when we are in question, he [the Pope] shews far more alacrity in attending to our correction, on bare suspicion, than to that of other kings." Under Boniface VIII this soreness was rubbed into an open wound.

The first friction occurred in 1296. Philip had in 1295 made his final peace with Aragon, but twelve months before had become embroiled with Edward I of England, who in turn set up alliances with Philip's troublesome northern vassal, Guy of Dampierre, Count of Flanders. Both the English and French Kings demanded for their war expenses clerical subsidies, Philip having fresh in his memory that "crusading" tenth which by papal permission had financed the campaign against Aragon. From both countries, however, clerical protests reached Rome, and in February 1296 Boniface asserted himself by the issue of the bull *Clericis laicos*. Though this bull was addressed in a general way to all secular rulers, the circumstances made it clear that it was aimed especially at England and France, and though the doctrine it contained was not novel, both monarchs felt resentful at its being emphasised at this particular moment. The bull began by a provocative quotation from Gratian's *Decretum*—"Antiquity reports that laymen are exceedingly troublesome to clerks," and went on to insist that before kings exacted or clergy paid any *collectae* or *talliae* papal authorisation must always be sought, on pain of excommunication.

Philip shewed extreme irritation at this, and the French clergy trembled lest his wrath should recoil on them in worse than words. The bull was discussed in an assembly of prelates, envoys were sent to Rome, and in August Philip forbade the exportation of gold or silver from France. This may have been a mere war-time precaution, but Boniface took it as a personal affront, and commented on it indignantly in September in the bull *Ineffabilis amor*, by which he disclaimed any intention of preventing the clergy from contributing when required for the defence of the realm, but still insisted that they must never do so without papal permission. After an interval of spluttering wrath and windy threats at both the French and the Roman courts, Boniface came to terms in a series of graduated withdrawals. In February 1297 he authorised the king to accept voluntary contributions from ecclesiastics, in pressing necessity, without consulting the Pope. In July he committed to the king the decision as to whether in any given case the necessity was pressing or not, and on the last day of the same month, by the bull *Etsi de statu*, he formally renounced the claims made in *Clericis laicos*. During August Boniface made several friendly gestures, including the canonisation of Louis IX. This outward good will was maintained for another four years and more, but as both Boniface and Philip matured their policy it became certain that a new clash of pretensions would occur, especially as the celebration of the papal Jubilee in 1300 surrounded the Pope with compliments and deference which left him less than ever disposed to endure criticism.

The second quarrel, in which the questions at issue were wider, the conflict longer, the defeat of the Pope more complete, and the historical results more lasting, began at the end of 1301. Philip had asked the Pope, in a tone rather of command than of request, to degrade from his orders Bernard Saisset, Bishop of Pamiers, who was accused of trying to rouse Languedoc against French rule, speaking treasonably of the king, his councillors, and his policy, preaching heretical doctrines, and blaspheming against God and the Pope. These charges, first made in the early summer of 1301 after a local enquiry, had been confirmed and extended in October, when Bernard was arraigned before the king and the magnates in assembly at Senlis. The bishop was then placed in the custody of the Archbishop of Narbonne, and was regarded by the Crown as a culprit whose guilt was proven, but whose punishment would be deferred, out of respect for the Church, until he had been deprived formally of his clerical status. "The king is only waiting for this before making to God the agreeable sacrifice of a traitor whose reformation is no longer possible."

Now it is unlikely that in the first attack on Saisset Philip had in mind ecclesiastical considerations. He was, for political reasons, curbing an unruly subject in a part of his dominions where local independence and loose attachment made unruliness particularly dangerous. Yet Saisset was a bishop, and Philip shewed either an incredible naïveté or a deliberate blindness when he assumed that the Pope would ruin an ecclesiastic upon secular judgment alone, even after Philip had fed his indignation with tales of Bernard's spiritual shortcomings and impertinences in speaking of the Pope himself. To any Pope such a course would have been a sacrifice of dignity; to Boniface, especially with pride newly inflated by the Jubilee, it was unthinkable. Besides, Bernard was his protégé, occupant of a new bishopric carved out for his benefit from the see of Toulouse. It is not surprising that Boniface refused Philip's request.

Letters of 5 December 1301 ordered the king to release Bernard's temporalities and set him free to go to be judged at Rome, and though on 13 January 1302 this order was countermanded, Boniface still insisted that the bishop must be tried in the court of his superior, the Archbishop of Narbonne.

This check to Philip's wishes might in itself have been enough to cause a quarrel, which became certain when Boniface surrounded the immediate decision with a pomp and circumstance that almost concealed it from sight, reasserting papal claims in terms intolerably harsh and pretentious. By the bull *Salvator mundi* he revoked the concessions made in 1297, and once again forbade French prelates to make grants to the Crown without papal permission. In the bull *Ausculta fili* he took the tone of a pedagogue to an unruly pupil, rebuking Philip for seizure of ecclesiastical goods, debasement of the coinage, and other offences, and announcing that in November 1302 representatives of the Gallican Church would be required to come to Rome to a synod at which Philip himself might be present if he chose, but which in any case would proceed to take measures for the reform of his realm. Letters of summons addressed to the French prelates, chapters, and masters of theology, plainly named "the correction of the king" as among the business to be dealt with. What was Philip to do?

For nearly eighteen months it seemed as if victory was this time to go to Boniface. For one thing, Philip seemed so absorbed in the wider conflict that he ceased to trouble about Saisset, who remained in obscurity for some years, but in the end was restored to his see. The bull *Ausculta fili* was burnt, by accident or design, and trouble was taken to circulate an inaccurate and mocking summary of its contents, possibly with a pretended reply in which Philip offered to "Boniface who calls himself Pope little or no greeting." For the first time in his reign, Philip summoned clergy, nobles, and townsfolk of his realm to meet together at Paris in April, and there "begged most earnestly, as a lord commanding and as a friend asking and urging with entreaties," for their support. He was so far successful that each order did address a letter to Rome, rejecting any idea that the realm which the French kings held "from God alone" could possibly be in temporal subjection to the Pope. So scant was the civility of the laymen's letters that the cardinals solemnly protested. "It was indecent...not to name the Most Holy Father in your letters as supreme pontiff....Laying aside all filial and customary deference, you referred to him by some roundabout phrase of newly-invented words." And yet, when the threatened synod actually met, thirty-nine abbots and bishops from France were present in person, while others were represented by proxies. This was encouraging for Boniface, and so was the news that in July the Flemings had inflicted a crushing defeat upon the French. He accordingly published the bull *Unam Sanctam*, "the most absolute proclamation of theocratic doctrine ever formulated in the Middle Ages." Reiterating well-worn metaphors such as that of the two swords, firmly emphasising the inferiority of the temporal to the spiritual, the bull closed with a striking pronouncement. "Further we declare, say, define, and pronounce that it is a necessity of salvation for every human creature to be subject to the Roman pontiff."

There was not a word in this bull, however, directly naming France; nor did the synod, for all the talk beforehand, proceed to the chastisement of Philip. However, after the meeting, Cardinal Jean Lemoine was sent as legate with a sort of ultimatum. He was to ascertain Philip's views on various points—the withdrawal of hindrances, direct or indirect, to French prelates wishing to visit Rome, especially those who had attended the council just ended; recognition of the Pope's rights in the collation of benefices, the dispatch of legates whenever and wherever he chose, and the disposal of ecclesiastical revenues; and royal respect for Church property and for the goods of bishoprics during vacancies. Philip, much shaken by his ill luck in Flanders and by the loss of Pierre Flote, replied with surprising patience. Boniface, misjudging his man and the moment, then tried him too far. In April 1303 he rejected Philip's answers, and bade the legate threaten him with excommunication unless he would make entire submission. That was the end of the upward trend of the Pope's fortunes. Philip pulled himself together, and lent a willing ear to Flote's bold successor, Guillaume de Nogaret, who since February had been increasingly in his confidence. By the end of the year the tables had been completely turned.

Nogaret's advice, in a nutshell, was to forsake the defensive for the offensive. Layman and lawyer though he was, many a polemical sermon-writer might have envied the skill with which he turned Scripture to his own uses in the "requisition" which he laid before the king and magnates in March 1303. Was it not St Peter himself, he said, who wrote, "There were false prophets also among the people, even as there shall be false teachers among you"? The present occupant of St Peter's throne was the embodiment of that fulfilled prophecy, and guilty of enormous crimes. The King of France must flash the light of his drawn sword before the Pope's eyes, like the angel before Balaam. In other words, he must secure the summons of a General Council to judge and condemn Boniface, and in the meanwhile make the Pope a prisoner and set up, with the help of the cardinals, a vicar to rule the Church until a new Pope could be elected. This was all pleasant hearing for the anti-papalists, but although Philip had already given Nogaret and three colleagues vaguely-worded credentials to go "to certain places upon certain business," he does not seem to have decided to proceed from words to deeds till he found that Boniface had rejected his overtures to Cardinal Lemoine, while that rejection itself shews that Boniface was as yet unaware of the seriousness of the danger. It was not till April 1303, then, that there opened the final conflict which was to reach its climax in September.

Both sides were henceforth uncompromising. Boniface, giving solemn audience on 30 April to the proctors of his former enemy, the King of the Romans, Albert of Austria, with a view to his "edification and confirmation," said many things which were meant to reach a wider circle than those who listened to him in the Lateran. God made literally, he said, both sun and moon, but also the metaphorical sun of the ecclesiastical power and the metaphorical moon of the secular power. "And as the moon has no light save that which it received from the sun, so too no earthly power has anything save that which it received from the ecclesiastical power....Some princes are making their confederations, but we say boldly that if all the princes of the earth were leagued against us and against the Church, so long as we had the truth and were standing by truth, we value them not a straw....Let the king know therefore that if he defends himself well and recovers his rights and the rights of his realm and Empire, we say boldly that we will defend his rights even more than our own, and this against the King of France or anybody else....We with him and he with us will put the pride of the French to confusion." In September, Boniface issued the bull *Super Petri solio*, reciting the history of the quarrel, exhorting Philip to repentance, releasing his subjects from allegiance to him, and declaring null any alliance he might make, but not actually pronouncing him deposed.

Meanwhile, in June 1303, before an assembly of magnates in the Louvre, accusations of the most precise, varied, and startling kind were set forth, and even the bishops and abbots present agreed that a General Council ought to meet, "thinking it useful and very necessary that the innocence of Boniface should shine forth clearly," but refusing to commit themselves to any party. Royal commissioners were then sent round the country to relate what had happened and canvass general support. If some stalwarts, such as the Dominicans of Montpellier, would have nothing to do with the project, and were accordingly ordered out of the country, a certain number of new adhesions were secured. Meanwhile letters were addressed to the cardinals, the Italian republics, Castile, Portugal, and Navarre. Nogaret himself had gone to Italy to supervise the arrest of the Pope, and from headquarters at Staggia, near Siena, organised an armed band inspired by personal hatred of the Gaetani, greed of money, or general rowdiness, quite as much as by loftier motives. This force, led by Nogaret, Sciarra Colonna, and Rinaldo da Supino, burst into Anagni on 7 September 1303, and after sack, fire, and violence, secured the person of the Pope himself. This was the supreme moment. The French, indeed, failed to carry Boniface away, for many of their loudest advocates fell silent when they actually saw, as Dante said, "Christ made captive in the person of his Vicar." A revulsion of feeling drove the invaders out of the town, while a band of Roman knights led Boniface back to Rome. Yet the audacity of the attack had been in itself impressive, and became more so when a month later Boniface, by this time a very old man, succumbed to the shock he had undergone. Philip was left in possession of the field, and it would be a bold man who would dare to pick up the sword that had fallen from the hand of the dead Pope.

The definite results of the conflict remained uncertain for about two years longer. Benedict XI, who succeeded Boniface within eleven days of his death, but whose pontificate lasted less than nine months, tried to hunt with the hounds by releasing Philip from all sentences pronounced against him by Boniface, yet to protect the hare by demanding that Nogaret should be punished for the scandal at Anagni. Death relieved him of this awkward task, and after a vacancy of nearly two years, French influence secured, in the person of Bertrand de Got, Archbishop of Bordeaux, a Pope congenial to Philip in birth, career, and personality. Clement V (1305–14), patron of art and learning, arbitrator in many European quarrels, begetter of a large addition to the Canon Law, was no *pape fainéant*; but he was a French subject, he and his family owed much to court favour, and he was temperamentally, or perhaps physically (since he was in the throes of an illness which modern science suspects to have been cancer), incapable of resisting Philip's coercion. This became gradually evident. Out of 28 cardinals created in 1305, 1310, and 1312, 25 were French. Clement did not venture to return to Rome, but was consecrated at Lyons, and after 1308 set up a court at Avignon, which was geographically situated in France, but was on the way to Italy, and in the midst of the papal Comtat Venaissin. Politically, it was under the control of that younger branch of the Capetian house which ruled Naples and Provence. Thus began the "Babylonish Captivity," though so little idea had Clement himself that it was destined to continue, that he did not even send to Italy for all his treasures and archives, much less set about building himself a palace. Meanwhile he had to respect French wishes, and in 1311 at last gave up the effort to shelter his predecessor. He congratulated Philip on the zeal which had led him to attack Boniface, and ordered the erasure from the papal records of all matter in a contrary sense. In 1312 he made a further surrender, by yielding at last to that demand for the destruction of the great Order of the Temple which Philip had been pressing upon him for the last six years.

However mixed may have been Philip's motives in this attack, there were plenty of reputable reasons to put forward. As the crusading movement declined during the thirteenth century, the fortunes of the Military Orders had begun to tremble in the balance, and even St Louis himself and his friend Pope Gregory IX had wondered if it might not be advantageous to combine them all into a single organisation. Nothing had been done, however, by the time that the Holy Land had to be abandoned after the fall of Acre in 1291. The Templars could no longer ply their trade of fighting, and the by-product of their activities, finance, was not, like the nursing of the Hospitallers, an argument for continued existence, but on the contrary a temptation to themselves and an invitation to their enemies. The Popes now revived the project of fusion, and Clement V himself, very early in his pontificate, consulted Jacques de Molay, Grand Master of the Temple, as to its advisability. Unluckily, the Grand Master held as a general principle the view that, in his own words, "rarely if ever does an innovation bring anything but danger." He argued soundly enough that competition in well-doing had its uses, and that the forcible absorption into one Order of men who had taken their vows in another was an obvious injustice. He shewed less wisdom, however, when he professed himself at a loss to know how the two Orders would ever be able to do as much almsgiving jointly as they had done separately, or to provide a safe escort for pilgrims unless the vanguard was composed of one Order and the rearguard of the other, as had been customary hitherto! The plan of union thus came to nothing, and the Templars soon found that the alternative, in the eyes of their enemies, was their disappearance.

The last chapter of the Templars' existence opened in 1307 and closed in 1312, though almost to the end it was uncertain what would be the final sentence written. Accusations of heresy and immorality were brought forward, and the Pope in August 1307 ordered an enquiry. In September Philip, calling to his assistance Nogaret to be keeper of the seals, proceeded to an attack far swifter than anything the Pope had contemplated. "Placed by God on the eminence of royalty for the defence of the liberty of the faith," as he said, he ordered the arrest of every Templar in France, caused an inventory of their property to be made, and examined the prisoners before royal commissioners, who were to hand on their victims for a second questioning, with torture if required, before the representatives of the Inquisitor. Numbers of bewildered Templars soon made confessions which, by a suspicious coincidence, corresponded almost verbally with the accusations set forth in the commissioners' instructions. Nor was this surprising. "You shall go on making enquiry by general words till you drag the truth out of them and they persevere in the truth." Not much imagination is needed to fill up the gaps in the process thus indicated. Trembling old men, who might well have forgotten the details of professions made as much as forty years before, produced particulars of offensive ceremonial of the sort the commissioners expected, offering their evidence with piteous little excuses and reservations. The aged Grand Master was sure he had been told to deny Christ and spit on the crucifix, but spat but once, unwillingly, and that upon the ground. Hugues de Pairaud, visitor of the Order, admitted that he had given very questionable instructions to those he was receiving, but had always done so "not from the heart, but only from the mouth." Occasionally the commissioners could not extort what they wanted, as in the case of that knight of thirty years of age whose profession must have been quite recent, and who swore that "after he had made many promises as to keeping the good statutes and observances of the Order, the mantle was placed on his neck, and the brother receiving him let him kiss him on the mouth, and all the other brothers present also. Nothing else was enjoined upon or commanded to him." Firmness of this sort, however, was unusual, and by the end of the year Philip was able to confront the Pope with so nauseating a list of horrors that Clement ordered all Christian rulers to arrest the Templars in their dominions. In December the French prisoners were handed over to the custody of two papal envoys.

The tale was not yet told, however. Once out of Philip's grip, many of the prisoners took back their confessions, and in January 1308 the Pope decided to begin an investigation on his own account, suspending, with rebukes, the powers of the French inquisitors. For more than six months progress was checked, while Philip took every possible means to coerce the Pope into fresh action. Harangues and anonymous writings inflamed French opinion not only against the Templars but against Clement himself. The States-General were called together at Tours by a summons representing Philip as the avenger of the Crucified against the enormities of the Templars. "Laws, arms, beasts, the four elements themselves, should rise against a crime so impious." Thus instructed, the deputies (among whom, representing Coutances, was Pierre Dubois himself, *advocatus regalium causarum* in far more than the merely technical sense) were of the dutiful opinion that no punishment could be too severe for criminals so odious, and Philip was able to go on encouraged to negotiate personally with Clement at Poitiers. In public and in private, every resource of ingenuity was used. In particular, stress was laid upon that unfortunate secrecy which was a feature of the Templars' rule, and which was now said to be cover for the evil deeds which love darkness rather than light. Finally, in July, Pope and king came to terms. The examination of individual Templars (except the great dignitaries, who were now reserved for judgment by the Holy See itself) was to begin again, under the guidance of the bishops, helped by secular and Mendicant colleagues, and by inquisitors if required. A further enquiry, into the guilt or innocence of the Order as a whole, was entrusted to papal commissioners, who were to report to a General Council, summoned to Vienne. The two enquiries were to proceed simultaneously, and it need hardly be pointed out how easily persons on their trial as individuals in one process could be intimidated as witnesses on the general question under judgment in the other. How many more witnesses were there like Aimery de Villiers-le-Duc in 1310? Pale and terrified, alternately beating his breast in penitence or stretching out his hands to the altar in passionate asseveration, he swore that all he confessed to the discredit of the Order was untrue. But he had seen fifty-four brothers being taken in carts on their way to be burnt alive, "and because he was afraid that if he himself were to be burnt he would not be able to shew good endurance," he had confessed that the errors imputed to the Order were true. "And he would have confessed that he had slain God Himself, if they had asked him that." "All the brethren are so struck with terror," wrote some defenders of the Order, "that there is no reason to be surprised at those who tell lies, but rather at those who stand by the truth." Moreover, many of the rank and file of the Templars were, as their Grand Master acknowledged himself to be, "poor and unlettered," floundered just as helplessly as he did when confronted with swift and subtle arguments, and were fain, like him, to fall back upon the thought that "when the soul is separated from the body, then it will appear who was good and who was bad, and everyone will know the truth."

The Council of Vienne, often postponed, met at last in October 1311, and in April 1312 the Pope was forced into his last surrender. The bull *Vox in excelso* admitted that the evidence produced was insufficient to warrant the canonical condemnation of the Order, but as a measure of expediency, without sentence, brought it to an end. "Thus perished the Order of the Temple, suppressed not condemned, butchered unresisting." Its belongings were transferred to the Hospitallers, and in 1314 its last remaining dignitaries were condemned to perpetual imprisonment. Two of them, the aged Grand Master and the Preceptor of Normandy, now summoned strength for a final protest, declared the charges false and the suppression unjust, and were rewarded by execution. The affair was at an end, but not before it had demonstrated for all Europe the impotence of the Papacy in the hands of the King of France.

Nothing in the internal relations of Philip IV with the Church in France was nearly so striking as these external conflicts with the Apostolic See. He continued, like his predecessors, to enjoy and protect royal rights, such as the authorisation of elections to bishoprics and abbacies, the custody of their temporalities during vacancy, the special guardianship, with special privileges, of churches or abbeys which placed themselves under royal protection, and the right of *amortissement*, or levy of a sum due for permission given to the Church to acquire fresh lands. He exchanged with the bishops the usual mutual reminders of the limits of ecclesiastical and secular jurisdiction, with protests in particular instances, but he took no drastic measures in defence of the secular courts of the kind recommended to him by the ingenious Pierre Dubois in his *Brevis Doctrina*. He had no desire, indeed, to quarrel with the bishops, many of whom owed their position to his influence while others were among his administrative officials, so long as they would reward his complaisance by financial and other support. On the whole, his relations were much easier with the secular clergy than with the regular, who were less identified with French interests as such. His new responsibilities in Languedoc brought vividly to his notice the sufferings of the inhabitants of those parts through the Dominican inquisition into heresy. Horrified in 1301 at the stories he heard from Bernard Délicieux, a brother in the Franciscan convent at Carcassonne, confirmed by the reports of two royal envoys freshly returned

CH. XI.

from a commission of enquiry, he secured the removal of the Dominican Inquisitor of Toulouse, fined his chief supporter, the Bishop of Albi, and issued an ordinance directing the Dominicans to admit episcopal, and even sometimes Franciscan, supervision in their dealings with heresy. So indecent, however, was the window-smashing, rioting enthusiasm of the southerners in their victory, so complete the absence of the peace and good will which were expected after righted wrongs, so vigorous the action of the Dominicans themselves both in France and at Rome, that even after a personal visit to the south, in 1302, Philip was disinclined to go farther along the path he had entered. Délicieux's impatience over this delay led to an abortive plot with the Aragonese heir to the throne of Majorca against the northerners, which alienated Philip's sympathy completely. He made no further attempt to help the southerners.

Before examining Philip's relations with other groups of his subjects, it will be well to consider his foreign and military ambitions. Here Philip broke with recent tradition. He gave up all idea of active enterprise south of the Pyrenees, while on the other hand he embarked upon aggressions bolder than Philip III had ever attempted, in trying to bring under the direct rule of the Crown the two great independent fiefs of Gascony and Flanders. Mutual danger made the two ally, and in neither quarter did Philip achieve permanent success.

For ten years after the death of Philip III the diplomatists were kept busy over the question of the rival claims to Aragon and Sicily. Philip IV, himself the son of an Aragonese mother, had no intention of going to war, in the interests of his younger brother Charles of Valois, against his cousin Alfonso of Aragon. A settlement was almost reached in 1291 when at Tarascon the rights of James of Aragon, King of Sicily, were thrown over in an agreement among the other powers concerned, by which Charles of Valois renounced his claim to Aragon, Charles of Naples, heir of Charles of Anjou, was to have Sicily, and in return Charles of Valois was to receive Anjou and Maine with the hand of Charles of Naples' daughter. Immediately afterwards, however, Alfonso III's death without sons made James of Sicily King of Aragon also, and hot in his own defence. Finally, in 1295, by the Peace of Anagni, he agreed to give up Sicily. The last trace of the crusade was effaced seventeen years later, when the Spaniards recovered the Val d'Aran, occupied by the French during the campaign of 1285. Philip forbore officially to take advantage of the fact that the Sicilians declined the settlement of 1295 and chose James of Aragon's younger brother, Frederick, as their king. In 1301, indeed, Charles of Valois, who regarded Italy as a half-way house to his designs on the Eastern Empire, was allowed to take an expedition to the help of Boniface VIII and the Guelfs, but Charles was unsuccessful and Philip tepid, and the troops were recalled to France in 1302. Philip was equally apathetic about the cause of Blanche of France and the Infantes de la

Cerda with regard to Castile. Though he offered a refuge to such Castilians as chose to flee to France, he avoided any quarrel with the supplanter Sancho IV. That was bare prudence. If there was to be war in the south over the English possessions, an essential preliminary was to secure the good will of the adjacent Spanish kingdoms.

War between France and England, indeed, was becoming increasingly probable, and the partisanship which would seek to deny in the one side or ascribe to the other the first motion towards it is really debating an unimportant question. In Philip IV's own lifetime, an anonymous French chronicler declared that Edward's behaviour was that of one "who for long enough had been making ready to fight the king," while on the English side Edward was represented as peace-loving, law-abiding, and forced to defiance in the end by French treachery. The truth was that neither king could fail to have felt the irritations created by the treaty made at Paris in 1259. "The essential article of that treaty," says M. Bémont, "is that by which the King of England, Duke of Guienne, declared that he became the liege man of the King of France. From the feudal point of view, this dependence was in no way humiliating; but it created a legal situation difficult for a king to endure." Either side might at any moment find pretext for quarrel, and, as it happened, Philip was ready to strike first. Bickerings between French and English seamen reaching unusual heights of violence caused him to call his vassal Edward to account before the Parlement of Paris in 1294. Edward, though he did not respond in person, sent his brother Edmund in his place, and it was amicably agreed that the chief strongholds in Gascony should be put as a matter of form into French hands for forty days while enquiry was made into disputed questions. Such an arrangement was by no means uncommon, and Edmund shewed no unusual stupidity in accepting it. Its sequel also was not unparalleled. The castles were not returned when the stipulated period had elapsed. All Edward could do was to make public protest, renounce his homage, and prepare to fight for the recovery of his duchy.

The war which thus began in 1294 did not come to a final and legal end till the Peace of Paris of 1303, but all the campaigning was done in the first four years. Edward, detained by trouble in England, was not once able to go in person to lead his forces in Gascony, and those who represented him were defeated year after year by the French armies, led in 1294 by Raoul de Nesle, Constable of France, in 1295 by Charles of Valois, and in 1296 by Robert of Artois. Edward was pinning his main hopes on a counter-offensive, to be undertaken with a series of allies made by expensive diplomacy all along the northern and eastern borders of France. Guy of Dampierre, Count of Flanders, was the weightiest of these, and it was to join him that Edward at last in 1297 crossed the Channel in person. Little came of their efforts. The Flemish towns were divided in their sympathies, and when Robert of Artois arrived, fresh from the memory of his Gascon successes, he was victorious in a battle at Furnes.

Lille was taken, Bruges opened its gates, and Guy and Edward were bottled up in Ghent. In October a truce was proclaimed at Vyve-Saint-Bavon, while in June 1298, as a move towards peace, marriages were arranged between Edward, now a widower, and Philip IV's sister Margaret, and also between Edward, his young heir, and Philip's daughter Isabella. Five years passed by before in 1303 a final peace was made at Paris, but the delay was to England's advantage, because French fortunes took a turn for the worse in the interim. Consequently peace left both sides much as they were, and the balance established was not disturbed while Philip IV lived.

Flanders, meanwhile, could not keep up the struggle without English help, and Guy went with two of his sons to submit himself to his overlord, only to find himself made prisoner. Philip came to make a triumphal progress through the confiscated fief, and seemed well received. When he had gone, however, leaving James of Châtillon to rule as his representative, French popularity soon waned, and after one or two minor incidents came the startling "Matins of Bruges" on 18 May 1302, when in the grey of dawn the burghers fell upon the half-wakened and unsuspecting French lodged within the town, and massacred all who could not pronounce a phrase in Flemish previously agreed on as a shibboleth. All west Flanders flamed into emulation, and on 11 July 1302, the blackest of days in French annals, a punitive force rich in great names was miserably defeated by the rebels at the battle of Courtrai. A chronicler writing at Tournai describes how from the church-towers the roads and the paths and the fields were seen black with fugitives, glad in a day or two to give their very armour to anyone who would let them have bread in exchange. "The pick of the French," wrote a Paris chronicler in amazement and disgust, "were disgracefully defeated by a handful of rustics, unarmed as compared with themselves." In August Philip himself arrived to the rescue, but neither then nor next year could make headway, and even when, in September 1303, a truce was made and Count Guy was released from prison in order that he might persuade his subjects into submission, he failed to cool the ardour of the "Flandrenses Flamingantes." It was not till a French success in August 1304, at Mons-en-Pévèle, an isolated hill between Lille and Douai, had done something to diminish the confidence of one side and restore the self-respect of the other, that negotiation became hopeful, and a year later, in June 1305, a treaty was concluded at Athis-sur-Orge.

The French in seeming came well out of their adventures, for the terms they gave were hard. Though, on Guy's death in 1305, his son Robert was to recover the county, he was to pay a large war-indemnity, compensate any of his subjects who had suffered through helping the French, and leave in Philip's hands for the time being the castellanies of Lille, Douai, Béthune, and Courtrai, while 3000 men of Bruges were to go on pilgrimage to expiate the Matins, and in five towns the walls were to be pulled down.

Much of this remained empty words. The Flemish towns would not ratify the treaty till 1309, and then only with modifications. The indemnity was hard to collect. Philip blamed Robert, Robert blamed the Italians who had the collection in hand, and the Flemings blamed a count who could allow himself to make this financial apology for a war they had gloried in waging. After some threats of fresh confiscation, Robert in 1312 saved himself by agreeing to the permanent transference to France of the castellanies of Lille, Douai, and Béthune, with their appurtenances. In 1314 cumulative friction actually provoked war again for a few months, but again the campaigning was indecisive, and in September the previous terms of peace were confirmed again.

The only solid result, then, of all Philip's activities with regard to Flanders had been the addition to the royal domain of some Walloon lands. Frontier readjustments of this sort, however, made by treaty or by peaceful penetration, constitute in modern eyes Philip's chief claim to success in external policy, and can be traced from north to south, all along the imperial frontier. Valenciennes, in Ostrevent, that province of Hainault which marched with the Scheldt and Flanders, made good with French help its claim to be and "to have been from very ancient times of the realm of France," and the Count of Hainault, after resistance, was forced to do homage to Philip for Ostrevent. In 1300 the town of Toul offered itself to France. In 1301 Henry III, Count of Bar, whose wife Eleanor was a daughter of Edward I of England, and who had been much tangled in anti-French alliances, came to terms with Philip IV, promising to do homage to the French King for his lands on the left bank of the Meuse. A very formidable encroachment on imperial ground was made when Otto IV, Count of Burgundy, agreed that his daughter should marry Philip IV's son, the future Philip V, and by the Convention of Vincennes (1295) transferred Franche Comté to France. In the Rhone valley, Lyons, after a renewal of old disputes between the French Crown and its archbishop, was detached from the Empire and united to France, while French suzerainty was finally established over the fiefs of the Bishop of Viviers. The sum total of this long line of encroachment is impressive, especially when there is added to it the constant extension of French influence in border regions which were not actually annexed.

Contemporaries, or some of them, aiming at a million, missed the unit, and would have had Philip embark upon foreign schemes far more showy and far less practical. A man like Pierre Dubois, pouring out treatises in which world-reforms were to be achieved by the means of that King of the French "who knows no superior on earth," may have been regarded as a visionary even by men of his own age. But still, minds much more sober saw no reason why Philip should not achieve in the sphere of secular politics something comparable with his triumph over the Papacy, and Philip let himself to some extent be tempted by their suggestion. In December 1299 he conferred at Quatrevaux, between Vaucouleurs and Tours, with

King Albert I, and contemporary observers believed that matters far more momentous were discussed than the marriage alliance between Philip's sister and Albert's son which was the public outcome of the interview. Subsequently, Philip's thoughts turned to securing the imperial crown for some member of his family. In the elections after the deaths of Albert I in 1308 and Henry VII in 1313, he advanced as successive candidates his brother Charles of Valois and his son Philip of Poitiers. In neither case was he successful, and had he secured his end his problems would have been increased rather than diminished. France had nothing to regret in his failure.

Three successive wars—against Aragon under Philip III, against England and Flanders under Philip IV—had put the French monarchy to huge expense. Constant diplomatic activity also, notwithstanding the incessant complaints of the medieval envoy that he was not adequately provided with funds either for his own maintenance or for the persuasion of others, involved lavish outlay. Regular expenses of many other kinds were increasing with the increasing obligations of the Crown. It is clear, therefore, that a most complex financial problem confronted Philip IV. His vigorous and even violent efforts to cope with it make his reign stand out as critical in the financial history of the Capetian kings, and had political, social, and economic consequences of the first importance.

The nucleus of Philip's revenue was, of course, that derived from his domain and feudal rights; but neither additions to the former nor rigorous exaction and extension of the latter could suffice to meet his needs. The novelty of his policy lies in his treatment of his extraordinary revenue. He carried taxation to a height hitherto unknown, organised its collection, and turned into regular and permanent sources of income some contributions which hitherto had been regarded as exceptional and occasional. We have already seen how Philip asserted successfully against Boniface VIII the right to demand ecclesiastical tenths when he judged it necessary; such tenths became normal and frequent. On several occasions the king demanded *annates*, or the first-fruits of benefices. Clergy and laymen alike were taught to attach precise significance to that *auxilium* which with *consilium* made up the feudal duty of vassal to lord. A few specimens of the taxes levied will shew their variety, and their intimate connexion with successive political crises. The failure of the war with Aragon led to money exactions from those southern towns which had not responded to the call to arms. The Flemish wars brought burden upon burden. In 1302 any noble who had forty *livres* revenue, or any non-noble with three hundred *livres*, might ransom himself from personal service by a payment in which the minimum fixed was one-fiftieth, but the maximum might be whatever the collectors could extort. In 1303 whoever had a hundred *livres* in land must pay one-fifth, and those with five hundred *livres* in movables one-twentieth. For the great campaign of 1304, each prelate and noble was required to equip one man-at-arms for every 500 *livres* of revenue, and to maintain him for four months. The renewal of war in 1313 at once brought fresh demands. Besides *aides de l'ost*, there were aids to be given on other occasions, such as the marriage of Philip's daughter Isabella in 1308, or the knighting of three of Philip's sons in 1313. In 1292 for the first time, but thereafter repeatedly, there was levied *denarius alias vocatus mala tolta*, which began as a payment shared between vendor and buyer on every commercial transaction and became a tax levied on such essential things as wheat, wine, and salt, whether sold or owned. "King Philip," wrote John of Saint-Victor, "vexed and troubled the people of his realm in every way with new exactions, such as hundredths and fiftieths, setting a yoke of novel servitude upon the neck of a once free people." And, after all, the sum total obtained was insufficient, so that Philip was obliged also to borrow money, from Italian financiers, the towns, and individuals, on an enormous scale.

It was financial need, also, which led Philip into that debasement of the coinage which was the chief crime imputed to him by contemporaries. M. Borrelli de Serres has proved[1] that the chroniclers and time between them have made legend rather than history concerning this, and that the fluctuations were less frequent and less extensive than has often been supposed. Yet the fact remains that from 1295 onwards the currency was steadily debased, and that two sudden attempts to return to a sounder basis, in 1306 and 1313, were almost equally injurious. Trade was dislocated, public feeling incensed. Even Pierre Dubois had to utter a lament. "I, the writer of these presents, know...that since they began the change of the money, I have lost through it at least five hundred *livres tournois*. And I believe, taking all things into consideration, that the king has lost and will lose by this far more than he has gained."

It is not easy to summarise with brevity the many-sided effects of Philip's financial methods. He was compelled, as we shall see, to extend or invent elaborate administrative machinery for financial purposes. He was led into jealousy and suspicion of other financial organisations. The Jews were driven out in 1306, the hurrying on of the attack on the Templars in 1307 was due to financial as well as other motives, and in 1311 Philip expelled the Lombards, those Italian experts who had made him large loans and had acted as his agents in all sorts of business. In each case, of course, the Crown seized the property belonging to its victims, and assiduously collected outstanding debts due to the disgraced creditors. In some directions Philip's policy was modified or liberalised by his financial needs. Thus, when he wished to collect taxes in the lands of the great feudalists, he had to propitiate them with a share of the receipts or by

---

[1] In highly technical form in his *Les variations monétaires sous Philippe le Bel* (*Gazette numismatique*, 1902–3), and in summary in his *Recherches sur divers services publics*, ii, pp. 503–54.

granting them privileges. Moreover, since a tax imposed by consent was easier to collect than one forced in the teeth of public opinion, he was driven into consulting both individuals and groups more frequently than might otherwise have seemed necessary. Sometimes this consultation was local, and royal envoys either negotiated separately with magnates and town officials or explained matters to them collectively in an assembly representing a given area. Sometimes, again, it was central, and a tax would be blessed by the approval of such prelates and magnates as the king could easily gather about him. Finally, but not until the very last year of the reign, it occurred to Philip to take the problem of finance, as he had already taken problems of other sorts, to a central assembly of the kind which later would have been called a meeting of States General.

Students of the origins of the States General have been wont to go to Philip IV's reign in much the same way that students of the origins of Parliament have sought out Edward I's. And it is true that repeated experiments in this direction were made at Philip's instigation. In February 1302 the seneschals and *baillis* were ordered to cause the towns in their area to choose each two or three of their "more substantial and experienced" men to represent them at an assembly to be held at Paris, where the king wished "to treat and deliberate concerning several difficult matters…with the prelates, barons, and other lieges and subjects of his realm." On 10 April, accordingly, a numerous company assembled in the cathedral of Notre Dame, heard Pierre Flote, in the king's presence, denounce Boniface, and then dissolved into its three component parts, each of which finally addressed a letter to Rome. On this occasion, therefore, Philip's hands seemed to have been strengthened just in the way he had wished. Yet in the still more embittered dispute which followed next year, after the issue of *Unam Sanctam,* he did not adopt exactly the same plan, but instead had at Paris a solemn assembly of bishops and barons with proctors for chapters and towns, and in the summer sent round commissioners to address local assemblies. In 1308, however, the Templar dispute drew him back to his earlier practice, and he summoned the magnates to Tours together with two men "strong in the fervour of the faith" from every *locus insignis,* a term which was applied in the most liberal spirit to market towns and even villages as well as the great cities. The elections were made in various ways—sometimes in two degrees, by electors chosen by the common consent; sometimes by the whole body of burgesses; sometimes by that *sanior pars* to which medieval custom was fond of trusting in many connexions. To the chronicler John of Saint-Victor the assembly appeared as "a parliament of nobles and non-nobles from every village and city of the realm." He put its summons down to the fact that "the king wished to act wisely, and therefore he wished to have the judgment or consent of men of every sort." Those summoned, however, knew well enough that no alternative was offered to unquestioning, premeditated obedience, as is clearly shewn both by the formulae used in the towns' instructions to their deputies and in the procurations given to representatives by nobles and prelates unable to attend in person.

The last assembly of this kind was provoked by the need for financial support when war against Flanders was renewed. It met on 1 August 1314, in the palace of the Cité at Paris. One chronicler gives a detailed description of what took place. First, Enguerrand de Marigny preached on the iniquities of the Flemings; next he appealed to the representatives of the towns to say whether they would not give an aid. The implied alternative was quite unreal, as the hearers knew well. They had been summoned *ad obediendum*, and, one by one, the representative of Paris speaking first, they made the required promise. Only in the most artificial sense could it be said that the king had asked for popular consent to taxation.

What, then, had Philip done, and how far may his reign be said to mark a step forward in the consultation of the nation by the Crown? There was nothing new in having a popular element present, and it is quite possible that even in detail precedents for the method of summons existed as far back even as the twelfth century. But Philip had made more frequent use of the expedient than any king before him. Three times within six years, and that at the most critical moments, with matters at issue of importance not only for all France but for all Europe, Philip had summoned nobles, prelates, and townsfolk to his support; in 1314 he had used the same machinery when in terrible financial straits; and on other occasions he had made other experiments of which we have less full particulars. The fact was that he was being driven, by impulses and needs not confined in that age to France or himself, to a policy which other kings also adopted—an ostentatious appeal for general support. We need not take the view that he sought a model in England, for we know on the one hand that English practice in this respect was still variable, and on the other that for precedents he need only go to his own forbears. Yet we must be equally cautious about over-accentuating the contrast between institutions on the two sides of the Channel. The French States General and the English Parliament sprang from origins very similar, just as the French administrative system suggests at every turn analogies with Angevin England. It was not some fatal flaw of construction in the French assembly, or some masterpiece of engineering in the English, which made the subsequent history of the two so different. If Parliament became the tutor of royalty and the States General, except on rare occasions, its instrument, that was mainly due to reasons which came into play later, and especially to the acuteness of the English opposition in putting to its own uses what was primarily a royal invention, whereas in France critics hurled themselves blindly into rebellion.

The term "States General," used here for convenience, was not as yet in being, and historians who occupy themselves in discussion as to which of Philip IV's assemblies were, and which were not, States General, are disquieting themselves in vain. One contrast may be noted between Philip's assemblies and their descendants. The later States General were summoned only at the rarest intervals; these, on the contrary, and their successors under Philip V, met surprisingly often. Had that practice been continued, their dumb docility might soon have been exchanged for critical discussion and gradual acquisition of new powers. Even as it was, they played their part in political education, for no doubt the tongues of the deputies wagged freely enough after they had returned to their homes.

If exceptional crises thus forced Philip to use exceptional means of consulting his subjects, he had also, of course, to obtain advice for the ordinary and daily purposes of government. He might seek this when he liked and from whom he chose, but, by the beginning of the fourteenth century, contemporary usage, hesitatingly and without consistency, had begun to refer to two sorts of council to which the king would normally turn. The one, a large assembly of important persons, meeting at intervals when summoned, they called the *grant conseil* or *plein conseil*; the other, a group of advisers attached to the royal household and moving about with the king, so that he always had at hand at any rate some of its members, was the *étroit conseil* or *conseil secret*. Letters patent of 1310, quoted by Boutaric, shew Philip definitely appointing a man to membership of this body. "We retain him in our council and our household as our councillor and household clerk, wishing to add him to the company (*consortium*) of our other councillors and household clerks." Such officials took a special oath[1]. It is clear, then, that organisation was on the way, though it was to be a long time still before the fluid stage was to end and the *conseil du roi* take final shape.

Administration, as the royal authority and responsibilities widened, became a matter of increasingly serious concern. By Philip's time, processes of administrative improvement which had had a start in the days of Philip Augustus and St Louis, and which in Philip III's time were in good working order, had resulted in making the chief administrative organs so prominent that the mistake has often been made of thinking that they first came into being at the command of Philip IV. The fact was that he simply continued the double process which explains medieval administrative development—the drawing of a distinction between what was private and what was public work, and the specialisation of functions within what was once a universally responsible *curia regis*. The idea came gradually that to supply the king's domestic needs was a function too humble to be performed by the same persons who aided the king to govern. Great men who still held such a title as that of Butler no longer performed any of the duties it would suggest; and even the deputies who

---

[1] Boutaric printed by mistake as the councillors' oath a form which was not theirs (*Philippe le Bel*, p. 165). The actual formula can be seen in M. Langlois' *Textes relatifs à l'histoire du Parlement*, p. 127.

had replaced them when first they abandoned these functions were by this
time themselves no longer busied with domestic tasks, which were left to
the domestic offices of the household (*ministeria*). Further, whereas the
household must always move from place to place with the king, it had
by this time been found convenient to cause certain persons who in the
old days would also have travelled with him to remain stationary in a
specified place to deal with indispensable public business. Thus specialisation of functions began. It must always be remembered, however, that
such powers were simply delegated from the Crown, and might at any
moment be recalled or redistributed. The same men did different work
at different times, and the same work was not always sent to the same
place to be done. In short, the complications of Philip's medieval system
must not be unduly simplified by the modern mind, nor must categories
and water-tight compartments be substituted for the vagueness of termi-
nology which was inevitable in an age when institutions were slowly
shaping themselves to meet needs which were also in process of development.

Foremost among early administrative improvements were those connected with the keeping of the king's revenue and the supervision of those
who had to spend it. Although France was slower than England in making
a clear distinction between financial bodies inside and outside the household, by Philip IV's time the line had been drawn, both as to the keeping
of the royal treasure and the supervision of its spending. The domestic
treasury was in charge of a staff of household clerks known as the *Chambre
aux Deniers*, while with regard to more public funds the king at first
relied on the banking and storage facilities of the Templars. The Treasurer of the Temple at Paris in consequence had so much business to do for
his royal client that he received a payment from the Crown that might
almost be called a salary. Even before the destruction of the Order, however, Philip had discarded this plan, and from 1295 onwards set up treasurers
of his own at the Louvre. Thus began a new office which gradually got
its own staff, its own traditions, its own methods. As to supervision,
various experiments were tried. At first, delegates from the court used
to sit for three short sessions each year to examine the accounts of all
who were financially responsible to the Crown. It soon became clear,
however, that the task was much too big to be disposed of in sessions
lasting only two or three weeks, and a permanent sub-commission was
kept hard at work between whiles, completing what was left unfinished
at the last meeting and preparing for the next. These officials at first
worked with the *Chambre aux Deniers*, but soon became a separate body;
in an ordinance of 1309 they are called the *Chambre des Comptes*, and were
henceforth so known. They had really superseded the more magnificent
but less expert group of whom at first they had been the servants. Already
in 1300 they had complained that the *grands seigneurs* hindered their
work, and a royal ordinance had bidden the ushers to shut the doors all

morning against "prelates, barons, and others of our council who come into the chamber to talk and importune you about matters other than those with which you are busied." Even uninterrupted, the department found its work sufficiently harassing, and was often behindhand with the mass of supervision entrusted to it. When Philip IV rebuilt the palace of the Cité, it secured good quarters there, with ample storage room, under the same roof with the Parlement.

Of parallel importance with all this financial business was the secretarial work of government—drafting, copying, registering, and sealing correspondence and documents of the most varied kind. These duties were performed on the domestic side by yet another body called a Chamber, this time without any additional explanatory phrase, and on the national side by the Chancery. Again, the power of the Crown in France made the line between the two less clear-cut than in England. But though there was a Chancery, and an official at its head in charge of the great seal, there was not, at this date, a Chancellor. The strengthening Capetian monarchy, jealous of over-mighty subjects, had suppressed that title in 1185, and though it reappeared under Louis VIII and in the early years of Louis IX, it then vanished again for nearly ninety years. Documents issued from the Chancery of Philip III and Philip IV were subscribed "data vacante cancellaria," while the head of the department was called "custos sigilli" or "qui defert sigillum." That change of title was meant to reflect a real change of position, emphasising the fact that the holder's main duties were administrative, not political, and that he might be a very great man indeed in his own office without counting very much anywhere else. Even so the post was desirable, for it carried a salary, larger or smaller according as its holder was or was not being boarded at the royal expense, a percentage of the fees, and a share in the common purse of the Chancery, as well as such privileges as a seat in the court of peers and the right of prise when travelling. What a man of strong personality could do when holding it, even under these limitations, was plainly seen in the case of Pierre Flote and Guillaume de Nogaret. After the death of Philip IV, the suppression of the title ended, and in 1315 Étienne de Mornay was appointed Chancellor[1].

The domestic secretariat, or Chamber, was a group gradually specialised for this purpose out of the household staff. Its head, the Chamberlain, was in particularly intimate relation with the king, and by 1312 certainly, and perhaps earlier, was in charge of the king's personal, "secret" seal.

There remains for examination the Parlement, that delegation from the *Curia regis* which came to act on behalf of the king as the supreme judicial tribunal. The steps towards this consummation were slow, and Philip IV did much to complete what Louis IX had begun. Normally

[1] The problems with regard to the Chancery in this period have recently been illuminated by M. Lucien Perrichet's *La Grande Chancellerie de France des origines à 1328*. Paris, 1912.

once a year, occasionally twice, and normally at Paris, occasionally elsewhere, there met for a session lasting three or four months a body mainly
composed of professional members nominated by the king, but reinforced
as required by other officials, nobles, and prelates. At the end of each
session the date of the next was announced, and to each administrative
area a certain number of days was allotted. By Philip IV's time three
chambers are discernible. The *Chambre des Plaids* or *Grand' Chambre*,
now and then supplemented by an *Auditoire du Droit Écrit* for cases
coming from the Midi, was Parlement in its most solemn aspect, where
the pleadings took place, and where alone until the days of Charles VI
sentence could be pronounced. The *Chambre des Requêtes* dealt with
petitions for the gracious jurisdiction of the Crown, and the *Chambre des
Enquêtes* with judicial enquiries. The whole organisation, with its impressive archives, its orderly procedure, its staff of lawyers, clerks, notaries,
and servants, and the spacious halls assigned to it when the palace of the
Cité was rebuilt, was a magnificent advertisement for royal justice.

If the central organisation of government had thus by Philip IV's time
become elaborate, and within its limitations and difficulties efficient, there
remained a very hard problem to be faced in the shape of local government.
The whole of the royal domain was divided into administrative areas which
were known in the north as *bailliages,* but in the south as *sénéchaussées,*
headed by an official known as the *bailli* or *sénéchal.* Under whichever
name, he was a hard-worked and much-abused person. "His competence,"
says M. Langlois, "may be defined in one word. It was universal." He
was the channel through which all royal orders and announcements reached
his district, and the instrument of their execution. He was responsible to
the central government for the collection and expending of the royal
revenue. He had at all times to keep his district in as good order as he
could, and, when required, to prepare it for defence or aggression. Sitting
in his court as representative of royal justice, he had to deal with feudal
disputes, punish breaches of the peace, and lend as discriminating an ear
as possible to endless appeals against the decisions of his subordinates or
of the local magnates. And beyond such duties, capable of definition, he
had others which were undefined and indefinable, involved in his position
as the representative for all purposes of a distant, unseen majesty. As
subordinates he had *prévôts* in the north or *bailes* in the south, whose
functions were as varied as his own, and who as a rule had bought their
office for a price and were in consequence bent upon recouping themselves.
Below these again came a crowd of minor officials, called by different titles
in different parts, and rarely so disinterested or intelligent as was desirable. Thus even the best-intentioned *bailli*, by the multiplicity of his
duties and the shortcomings of those through whom, in part at any rate,
he must perform them, was handicapped severely, while the brutal, stupid,
or greedy had golden opportunities for doing mischief. The records of the
time brim over with accounts of the iniquities of such men. They must

be read, however, with a lively sense of the difficulties of such posts and with a discount for the ingenuity of the injured parties.

None of the many devices used to keep the local administration up to the mark were entirely satisfactory. Sometimes the local men were called to the centre to render account and receive instructions. Sometimes they were inspected on the spot. In Normandy and Champagne assemblies known as the *Échiquiers* and the *Grands Jours*, survivals of the days of independence, were kept alive as royal instruments to hear local accounts and examine local causes. At Toulouse, intermittently, the experiment was tried of dealing with cases for the whole of Languedoc, except the English lands, in a local parlement composed of delegates from the Parlement of Paris. Commissioners arrived from time to time in the local areas to advertise the royal needs or the royal policy. *Enquêteurs-réformateurs*, whose very name testifies to the admirable intentions of their original founder St Louis, were by this time very doubtful blessings. It was said that they set the existing officials by the ears, used their powers to extort money or to satisfy private grudges, and so often left things worse than they found them.

What are we to think of the success or failure of Philip's internal policy, considered as a whole? Though developed from that of earlier kings, it had reached lengths and made impressions far more notable, partly because of the cumulative effect of repeated experiments, partly because Philip's violences, assertions, and quarrels had made him the cynosure of all eyes. It is clear that in the last years of his reign public opinion was setting against him. When, in August 1314, he went to war again with Flanders after a nine years' interval, he did indeed get lip-service from an assembly summoned to Paris to grant an aid, but in the subsequent campaign little enthusiasm was shewn, and still less about continuing to pay the tax after peace had been made in September. On 6 October, the twenty-ninth anniversary of Philip's accession, he shewed that he was nervous of giving his subjects a chance to meet in arms by issuing another ordinance against tournaments. Finally, in November and December, angry feeling culminated in the formation of leagues of protest and mutual support, in Burgundy, Champagne, Vermandois, and elsewhere. Their instigators were not, for the most part, the greatest of the French feudalists but the smaller men, and the latest historian of the movement[1] is sure that they do not represent a feudal reaction. Great magnates such as the Count of Valois, the Countess of Artois, and the Duke of Burgundy, not only stood aside but were themselves attacked, while the towns and the clergy in some parts associated themselves with the protest. Philip thought so seriously of the situation that he at once yielded what he conceived to be the main point at issue by proclaiming the cessation of the Flemish levy on 28 November. Two days later he

---

[1] A. Artonne, *Le Mouvement de* 1314 *et les Chartes Provinciales de* 1315. Paris, 1912. For a different view see Lehugeur, *Hist. de Philippe le Long*, pp. 1-9.

died. Had he lived, he would have found that his concession had not
been effective. Nor did his dying regrets for the more violent of his actions
appease his critics.

> Croiserie ne penitence,
> Aumosne, oroison, ne jeusne,
> Ne te vaudra ja une prune,

wrote the author of the chronicle attributed to Geoffrey of Paris. As to the
Leaguers, they continued to excogitate their grievances during the winter,
and were ready in the spring with a list of demands from the new king.

Louis X's short reign, which lasted for less than two years (November
1314—June 1316), has sometimes been represented as a reaction against
that of his father. That view exaggerates the significance of certain
changes which now came about, either as natural consequences of Philip
IV's own actions or to meet the wishes of advisers who saw their opportunity of securing things they had long desired. To the first class belong
the charters of 1315; to the second, the restoration of the office of
Chancellor and the fall of Enguerrand de Marigny, both largely due to
Charles of Valois. Louis himself, a very ordinary young knight, dying
prematurely *sicut puer* because he could not resist a cold drink in a cold
cavern after exercise, was the last man in the world to speculate about
constitutional problems. His chief guide, his uncle Charles of Valois, had
no wish to associate with the rebellious or revolutionary. He did, however, secure the fall of one old enemy in the person of Enguerrand de
Marigny[1]. "The man who knows all the king's secrets" had been climbing the ladder of advancement ever since 1295, but it was not till 1313
that, by royal ordinance, without any change of office or title, he was
placed in a position of autocracy in financial matters, accountable to nobody but the king himself. There is no evidence that Enguerrand abused
this trust. A first enquiry was interrupted by the death of Philip IV; a
second, in January 1315, acquitted him. Yet on 11 March 1315 he was
arrested, tried on forty-one counts, including intercourse with a familiar
spirit, and on 30 April was hanged. His real crime was that he was too
inventive, too ambitious, too well rewarded, and his downfall was a personal matter unconnected with the Leaguers and their protests.

A contemporary chronicler assures us that Louis X earned his nickname
of "le Hutin" (the stubborn) "because he always desired with his whole
heart to go to war against the Flemings." As Count Robert did not obey the
order to do homage, the court of peers sentenced him to deprivation of
his fiefs, and a French army went out in the rain in 1315 to stick in the
autumn mud in Flanders and return with little accomplished. Experiences
of that sort were becoming commonplaces of Franco-Flemish campaigning.
On this occasion, however, a special importance attached to it, because

[1] See Borrelli de Serres, *Recherches sur divers services publics*, III, pp. 49–75.

Louis had paved the way by going as far as dignity permitted toward meeting the demands of the Leaguers. The various groups presented in the spring the *cahiers* they had prepared in the winter, and received in answer a whole series of royal charters, beginning, curiously enough, with a charter to Normandy, which had taken no share in the original outbreak. But neither the sort of thing for which the Leaguers asked, nor the sort of thing that Louis gave, was to remain outstanding in French history. Most of them wanted, in a vague way, a return to undefined halcyon days of the past—the laws of good King Louis. They wanted respect for noble privilege, the right to fight and tourney at their will, the right to hold their own against the meddlesomeness of royal officials, and to have the full feudal courtesies respected however much time or money was lost thereby. "Their programme," says M. Langlois, "was neither new, nor bold, nor of a sort to command sympathy. There is a striking difference between their attitude and that of the English barons under John Lackland, Henry III, and Edward I." "For want of unity," says M. Artonne, "they did not, like their neighbours in England, obtain a Great Charter applicable throughout the realm, but a number of local charters, often confused, almost always filled with unimportant details, with concessions annulled almost at once, which could not form a basis for public law." On this side of the Channel, perhaps, we may think that our own baronial opposition was quite as old-fashioned and self-centred, especially if we use the strictly contemporaneous comparison with the magnate quarrels under Edward II. At any rate, in neither country, at this moment, did the party of protest shew any such constructive ingenuity as could turn the tables permanently on the Crown. Yet just as in England, in the Middle Ages as well as later, Magna Carta was used, without too specific reference to its details, as a sort of symbolic embodiment of liberty, so in France the charters won in 1315 took somewhat the same position. The charter to Normandy, for example, was again and again presented for confirmation in the fourteenth and fifteenth centuries. In so far, the League movement did warn the monarchy that public opinion was not ripe for over-rapid centralisation; but the vague, polite, and cautious terms of the replies given shew how little definite practical change resulted.

Louis X's death on 5 June 1316 left, for the first time in Capetian history, a vacant throne without an heir. Louis' second wife, Clementina of Hungary, was expecting the birth of a child in the coming autumn; meanwhile, there was only the four-year-old Jeanne, daughter by his first wife, and niece of Odo (Eudes) IV, Duke of Burgundy. For the time being, the dead king's brother Philip, Count of Poitiers, acted as regent without much opposition from possible rivals; but when in November the queen's son was born, only to die a few days later, a final settlement had to be made. Philip now claimed to succeed his brother, and was duly crowned on 9 January 1317. Charles of Valois, though displeased, as is shewn in a series of bulls issued by John XXII, countenanced this step by his presence. He and Mahaut, Countess of Artois, however, were the only lay magnates present. The Burgundian party, represented by the Duke Odo IV and his mother Agnes, appealed to the court of peers on behalf of the rights of little Jeanne, and whipped up support from their Burgundian subjects and from the Leaguers in Flanders, Artois, and elsewhere. Nevertheless, an assembly of prelates, magnates, citizens of Paris, and doctors of the university, held at Paris in February 1317, approved Philip's claim and went on to enunciate the general principle that "a woman does not succeed to the throne of France." Similar circumstances in 1322 and 1328 were met by similar expedients, and soon legal ingenuity sought analogies in the laws of the Salian Franks, while verbal ingenuities deemed it natural that the lilies of France should not be borne by a labourer or a woman, for "they toil not, neither do they spin." In Philip V's case, all danger of civil war was over by 1318, and the Burgundians came to terms. Duke Odo married Philip's daughter, another Jeanne, while his niece was compensated for losing a throne by a revenue of 15,000 pounds *tournois*, the promise of Champagne should Philip V die without male heirs, and the hand of her father's cousin Philip, Count of Évreux. From the practical point of view this solution was certainly the best. France was in no state to face the dangers of a minority.

Philip V, moreover, was an excellent king—prudent, intelligent, active. "When we received from God the government of our realms, the greatest desire which we had, and still have, was and is to keep and maintain justice and righteousness.... And to this end we began straightway to ponder, consider, and search for in every possible way the means by which we could arrive at this." These words are put into Philip's mouth in July 1318, as preamble to one of his letters, by the clerks who drafted it. They need not be discounted as conventional formulae, for they are borne out by his whole policy. Ordinance after ordinance, generally issued after consultation with some assembly of his subjects, revived wholesome legislation of St Louis or Philip IV, swept away the *desordenement* which had arisen since the time of "le roy monsieur St Loys," or found new remedies for new troubles. Notable among the last was the establishment, in March 1317, of a system by which in each town or castellany the inhabitants were to provide themselves with such weapons as after enquiry were found suitable to their rank, and be placed under the command, for military purposes only, of a *capitaine bon et souffisanz*, whom they should swear to "obey and aid," while he in return swore to guard them. These captains themselves were to be grouped under a captain-general for each large district. Because "the poor being necessitous may sell or pawn their weapons," they were to surrender them for common storage after each man had marked his own. The Crown by these means secured a force which when need arose could rapidly be put on a war footing, under commanders to whom it was accustomed and who were entirely identified with the royal interests. Philip thus carried to completion much the same sort of idea that had inspired the Assize of Arms under Henry II or the Statute of Winchester under Edward I. Less novel, but equally important, were the measures by which Philip renewed or developed the efforts of Louis IX and Philip IV for the improvement of the governmental machine. There were arrears to make up. The Chambre des Comptes, for example, as an ordinance of 1320 shews, had to enlarge its staff to four *maîtres clercs* and eleven subordinates, to cope with its "great multitude of accounts". The clerks were to arrive in good time each morning, and work till noon without leaving the room or wasting time upon any business of their own or their friends. Even after the mid-day bell had rung, they must stay to deal with any letters urgently requiring answers. Similar minute instructions were issued with regard to Parlement. Immediately after the first Mass had been said in the royal chapel, the officials must go to their duties, and apply themselves till noon, forfeiting a day's wages if they so much as left their seats without permission. The Chambre des Requêtes kept the same hours, but the Chambre des Enquêtes, from Easter to Michaelmas, sat in the afternoon. Every month a certain number of the members of the Great Council, named by the king (*Conseil du Mois*), were to meet and deal, among other business, with reports on the state of the households of the king, the queen, and other members of the royal family. Twice a year the Treasurer and household staff were to account. As to local officials, the *baillis* and others were warned to appear at the accustomed times, to reside in their bailiwicks, to carry out their duties without oppression, to send up their moneys secretly and safely, and to see that these were paid directly into the treasury.

There was still, of course, no idea of transferring, but only of delegating, the Crown's responsibility for government, and Philip took a real and personal share. Though he consulted both councils and wider assemblies of the States General type, he did so of choice rather than of necessity, and selected his advisers much as he pleased. The ordinance of 1318 which set up the *Conseil du Mois* left its composition to the king's nomination each month; its sessions cannot be traced after November 1320; and even while they lasted Philip could issue acts "*non contrestant le conseil du mois*." Even a cursory survey of the ordinances gives the impression that Philip was genuinely anxious to secure peace and order, and that largely with an eye to economic advantage. Brigandage, private war, and tournaments were put down. Officials were to be moderate about prises and other exactions, and in commandeering horses or carts. An effort was made to set up a uniform coinage and standard weights and measures, though this met with so much opposition that it could not be carried through. "All those who work," in fact, as M. Lehugeur puts it, whether on the land or at trades or handicrafts, had reason to be grateful to Philip. To the Church, too, he took and enforced in others a tone of great respect, and though by ordinance he forbade prelates to sit in the Parlement, this was only, as he explained, because his desire was that those in Parlement should give their whole time to their duties there, whereas prelates would necessarily be called away, or ought to be, to govern their dioceses and exercise their spiritual functions.

It is in internal affairs, then, that Philip V's reign is memorable. He had little fighting to do. He intervened in Artois to protect the Countess Mahaut against her nephew Robert of Artois, and completed successfully the work there begun by Louis X. He carried on with Flanders the usual alternate warfare and diplomatic negotiation, and in 1320 persuaded Count Robert to do homage and agree that his heir should marry Philip's daughter Margaret; but the good feeling was as short-lived as usual, and in 1321 Philip was complaining that Robert had kept none of his promises. War with England seemed likely for a time, but it is to Philip's credit that without pressing matters to this extreme he induced Edward II, who had never done homage to Louis X at all, to carry out this obligation by proxy in 1319, and in 1320 to perform it in person in the cathedral at Amiens. A similar prudence caused Philip to refuse Pope John XXII's invitation to come forward as the champion of the Guelf party in Italy against the Ghibellines. He was, in fact, exactly the sort of king to win the admiration of the modern historian of administrative and constitutional development, while to the warlike feudalist of his own day, or to the conventionally-minded contemporary chronicler bent on praising the conventionally correct, he was a disappointing figure. John of Saint-Victor, for example, wrote of Philip with an obvious sense of something being wrong, though in a king so "gentle, easy to get on with (*tractabilis*), and kindly," he found it hard to say exactly what was the matter. When an illness, beginning in August 1321, resulted in Philip's death in January 1322, some at any rate of his subjects felt actual relief. "He was mourned bye veryone," wrote one anonymous chronicler, but John of Saint-Victor, though cautiously, took another view. Interference with the coinage and the weights and measures, he said, would have meant heavy expense in compensation to those deprived of privileges, and possibly rebellion on the part of the injured. "Wherefore perchance it seemed to some that it was expedient that one man should die for the people, rather than that so great a people should be exposed to so great a danger." It was a more grudging epitaph than Philip's merits deserved.

For the second time, a Capetian king had died without leaving a son to succeed him; for the second time, to the exclusion of the dead man's daughters, a brother was crowned. In this case a real change of policy resulted, for Charles IV, who as Count of La Marche during Philip's lifetime had been anything but contented and loyal, had friends very different from those of the late king. His godparents were Mahaut, Countess of Artois, who held his foot at his baptism, and Charles, Count of Valois,

who had lifted him from the font. This spiritual relationship not only
secured their influence over him, but also, many years later, came in a
curious way to his relief when he wished to get rid of his first wife, Blanche,
daughter of the Countess Mahaut. The Church, which did not recognise
as sufficient ground for release the adultery for which Blanche was imprisoned in 1314, permitted Charles to repudiate her in 1322 as being,
as the child of his godmother, within the prohibited degrees. He was
thus enabled, in August 1322, to marry Mary of Luxemburg, daughter
of the late Emperor Henry VII and sister to John, King of Bohemia.
Such a connexion inevitably enmeshed him in imperial politics. The year
of his accession was that of the battle of Mühldorf, in which Lewis of
Bavaria finally triumphed over Frederick of Habsburg, who had been
his rival for the imperial crown ever since the votes of the Electors
had been divided between them in 1314. John of Bohemia, who had been
passed over on that occasion, was full of schemes for at any rate diminishing the importance of a suzerain whom he could not dislodge. In one
of these, for the revival of the kingdom of Arles, he tried to interest
France by offering its throne to Charles of Valois. Nothing came of this.
A still more tempting offer was made to Charles IV himself in 1324, when
Pope John XXII, who had quarrelled with and excommunicated Lewis IV,
suggested that for a substantial consideration it might be possible to
secure the election of Charles to the dignity thus theoretically vacant.
Charles certainly nibbled at this bait, but matters went no farther.

Opportunities less grandiose but less visionary were meanwhile presenting themselves nearer home. In September 1322 Louis of Nevers succeeded
Robert of Béthune as Count of Flanders and was led by the need of support
against a rival to a rapprochement with France. The *leliaert* party raised
its head again, and when the populace of Bruges and the coastal district
rose in revolt in 1323, Charles IV proposed to go to the rescue of Louis
and the pro-French party. In 1326 a peace at Arques reiterated the usual
promises of submission and amends, but the rebels remained sulky, and
were still unsubdued when Charles IV died. He had not, after all, got
any farther than his predecessors towards subjecting Flanders. There
remained the parallel question of tightening the grasp of the Crown upon
Gascony and its English duke. Here the weakness of Edward II combined
with Charles' personal inclinations and the desires of his uncle Charles
of Valois to achieve something tangible. The tale is told in another
chapter[1] of the relations between Charles and Edward, the affair of Saint-
Sardos and the war to which it led, the prospects of peace in 1325 and
their ruin in 1326. The revolution which cost Edward II his throne left
his supplanters, Isabella and Mortimer, with their young charge Edward
III, in too weak a position to prolong war or even to extort a favourable
peace, so that when, on 31 March 1327, yet another Treaty of Paris was
made, it was much more to French than English advantage. France

[1] See *infra*, pp. 428 sqq.

restored to England Ponthieu and a much diminished Gascony, but retained Agen and the Agenais, Bazas and the Bazadais. Nothing was said about the points in dispute as to Saint-Sardos and Montpezat. The English had to pay a war indemnity of 50,000 marks sterling, and the only concession made with regard to eight great Gascon loyalists who had stood by England was that their sentence of death was commuted to banishment. The moral effect of all this, of course, was enormous, and Charles could congratulate himself upon a real shock given to the prestige of a vassal who, in name at any rate, had always hitherto remained formidable. This triumph is the capital incident of Charles IV's reign.

In February 1328 Charles died. Though he had married three times, no son was left to follow him. His one boy, the child of Mary of Luxemburg, was dead, and his third wife, Jeanne of Évreux, bore him daughters only, including a baby yet unborn at the time of its father's death. Following and developing the precedents set in 1316 and 1322, not only women but also male heirs descended through heiresses were now excluded, so that the crown passed to Charles IV's cousin, Philip of Valois. The direct line of Hugh Capet was now at an end.

CHAPTER XII

FRANCE: THE HUNDRED YEARS' WAR (to 1380)

From 1337 to 1453 a fresh conflict, severe and prolonged, was waged between England and France. It was wellnigh continuous, interrupted only for about ten years (1360–69) by a definite peace, and again for about twenty years (1388–1406) by truces of almost equal efficacy. It is owing to this continuity and this duration that it has been called The Hundred Years' War. It had, as will be seen, a profound repercussion upon the history of England. But as its normal, almost exclusive, theatre was the soil of France, as its object was the ruin of the Capetians of the house of Valois or at any rate the dismemberment of their kingdom, as the military, political, and economic effects weighed upon the whole country and even extended in some measure to neighbouring countries, it is in France and on the continent that its development has principally to be viewed.

In considering the origin of the Hundred Years' War, we find at its opening interests of all kinds involved: territorial disputes, economic rivalries, political coalitions, and a dynastic rivalry. But these were only the inevitable consequences from the past history. Even the characters of the kings, the conscious part they played in its inception, and their resultant responsibility, deeply as they influenced the nature and progress of the war, seem at the commencement to have been of secondary importance; Edward III was a mere youth, Philip VI a mediocrity. Actually the war represents the laborious liquidation of a heritage from the past that was no longer endurable. The danger to the kingdom of France arising out of the conquest of England by the Duke of Normandy had been removed by Philip Augustus; it remained to remove by degrees the further danger arising out of the Aquitaine marriage of Henry II; and so the initial importance of Guienne and Gascony has very rightly been thrown into relief. The continued efforts of the kings of France in this direction since the Treaty of Paris, whether by way of military conquest or legal expropriation, inevitably aroused the definite hostility of the English king; they stirred him to dynastic claims, caused him to seek in every quarter for profitable diversions, as in Flanders and Brittany, and at last led him to adopt the offensive and to invade France.

When the conflict broke out, the kingdom of France had just passed through what may be termed a genealogical crisis. By a singular fatality the three sons of Philip the Fair had died without male issue. The last, Charles IV, left a widow with child. Twice already, on the deaths of Louis X and Philip V, had the king's daughters been set aside in favour of the next male heir, in each case the king's brother. But Charles IV had only cousins; and of these cousins, the King of England, Edward III, the son of a daughter of Philip the Fair, held the first place. If it was admitted that his mother could transmit to him a right she could not have enjoyed herself, he was the next male heir; he could assume the regency, and as a result, in a certain contingency, the crown. But if the Capetian succession could only be transmitted through the male line, it must revert to Philip of Valois, the nephew of Philip the Fair. There was no formal law of the State that was precise on this point, and at the assembly of barons held after Charles IV's death Edward III upheld his rights. Probably this claim of a foreign king worked powerfully on a lurking national sentiment and caused the victory in a more precise form of a principle that had been invoked and applied already in 1316 and 1322.

So Philip of Valois was recognised first as regent, and, after Charles IV's widow had given birth to a daughter, as king. This event was to have serious repercussions. Meanwhile, however, it appeared to be readily accepted. In order to meet the claims of the heiress with the best title in the female line, Jeanne of Évreux daughter of Louis X, the new king admitted her right to the kingdom of Navarre; a fact to be borne in mind, for her son, the future Charles the Bad, was to go back on the agreement which Jeanne had accepted. As for Edward III, after hesitations and a threat of the confiscation of Guienne, he decided to come to do homage in June 1329 at Amiens for all his actual possessions. But first there had to be negotiations and discussions to decide whether this was to be simple or liege homage, and it was only by letters patent of 30 March 1331 that the King of England recognised himself as the liegeman of the King of France.

The new King of France, Philip VI, had not been fashioned to reign. Hot-headed, undecided, somewhat simple-minded, he readily allowed himself to be controlled. His policy was usually inspired either by the Pope or by his wife, the "masculine queen" Jeanne of Burgundy. He was above all a knight, with all the prejudices of the chivalry of his day. With the same knightly tastes as Edward III, the same love of holding festival, he was politically very much his inferior.

Such was the king who found himself the mighty ruler of a kingdom larger than England, but less coherent and less adaptable. His domain, comprising nearly half the kingdom, provided a strong basis for his power. But the survival in the four corners of France of great independent fiefs—Flanders, Burgundy, Brittany, and Guienne—weakened the authority within and the defence from without. The royal institutions, already highly centralised and encumbered with officials, were developed without any counterpoise from, or direct collaboration with, the governed. Above all, the King of France lacked regular and adequate financial resources established on a solid footing. What he derived from the exploitation of the domain, and from a few limited taxes, sufficed only, and even then with frequent deficits, for the daily life of the court and for the royal administration. There was no provision for extraordinary needs apart from feudal aids, which were themselves limited to definite and exceptional circumstances. There was no war-chest. If a great crisis occurred, such as a long and difficult war, it would be necessary for the king to draw on the pockets of his subjects by means of subsidies, direct or indirect, by debasing the coinage, by subventions from the clergy or the Pope, by confiscations and other expedients. Even the right of the king to levy subsidies without the assent of his vassals and subjects was uncertain. The Crown was obliged to take account of the ideas of the time and the example of England, and, in order to make its position secure, it had adopted the method of asking for money from its subjects in each town separately, or in provincial assemblies and the States General of Langue d'oïl and Languedoc. Moreover, by this time war could no longer be waged without plenty of money. The military services due to the king from the nobles, or from townsmen and country-folk, were varied in character and limited in extent; usually they had been replaced by money-payments or had fallen into disuse. By these means it was impossible to get together an army. An army, in fact, could only be raised by special musters, with promises of high pay and large rewards to nobles, both knights and squires, and to Genoese or German adventurers. The assembling, equipping, provisioning of this mixed horde gave rise to abuses and to trickery. Further, the equipment of the nobility was both clumsy and ridiculous; their offensive weapons were very awkward to handle, their defensive armour was cumbersome. The whole science and tactics of chivalry consisted in dismounting one's opponent and holding him to ransom, or in butchering the common folk, and it required all the verve and imagination of a Froissart to instil any charm into the story of their "apertises."

What made an effective resistance possible for the kingdom of France was the fact that its prosperity and its resources were then so great. For long no invasion had touched it. The exactions of previous kings had removed more grievances than they had created. Never in the Middle Ages was the population so numerous; it certainly amounted to some twenty millions. Encouraged by the regulation or the redemption of feudal burdens and by the progress made by the royal peace, this population was spread over the open country rather than concentrated in the towns. Cattle were abundant. The holdings were sown with a variation of crops, and in spite of the system of fallow they yielded a good return in the fertile regions; the vines prospered in the South. In the towns, commerce and industry were organised. Paris, with its university, its Lombard banks, its great Company of the *Marchands de l'eau*, its markets, its great trades, its artisan gilds, was already the most important intellectual and economic centre of the West, and had more than 200,000 inhabitants.

The power of the king and the resources of the kingdom gave scope for great enterprises. A fact, too, of contemporary history increased the confidence of Philip VI. Pope John XXII, a native of Cahors, who had been Bishop of Avignon, had decided to establish in that town the papal court and had begun upon the Palace of the Popes. The new Rome was within the ancient Gaul, on the frontiers of France, at the mercy of the Capetian kings. Close relations were henceforth maintained. The king relied on the Pope in finance and in diplomacy; the Pope relied on the king in the endless contest he maintained with the Empire, both in Italy and in Germany.

In the first years of Philip VI's reign, thanks to these favourable conditions, it was clear that the royal policy was considerably widening its range. As Philip the Fair had done, the new king intervened at once in Flanders. At the call of Bruges and Ypres, the western part of the land had revolted against the nobility in the country and the patriciate in the towns. The King of France had barely been crowned when he came with a large army at the appeal of the Count of Flanders, and at Cassel on 23 August 1328 his knights crushed the people of Flanders, who were butchered in thousands. The county was harshly punished, and the king and count were enriched by confiscations. Within the Empire, the King of France had made firm alliances. Continuing in the family tradition, he made closer still the link with the house of Luxemburg, which had held the imperial throne and was still ruling in Luxemburg and in Bohemia. John of Bohemia, prince of adventurers, loyal knight, lavish and fantastic, was ever the faithful friend of Philip VI. A Capetian, uncle to the King of France, Robert of Anjou, ruled in Provence and Naples. Philip VI, who had fought in Italy before his accession, was in close relations with the Lombard towns, and the Pope had accorded to him the right of occupying Modena and Reggio, while John of Bohemia sold him Lucca. But this was not enough; the King of France revived the splendid dream of a crusade, strongly incited thereto by John XXII. Preparations began in 1330; the king took the cross on 22 July 1332, and sought to draw in with him the whole of the West.

The crusade was to remain a dream, for between France and England the storm was gathering. Edward I, and quite recently Edward III too, had shewn considerable solicitude for their possessions in Guienne, while at the same time they had firmly established their authority in it. They had associated the inhabitants with the administration, granted privileges to the towns, assured a sound coinage, and encouraged the trade of the merchants of Bordeaux, Libourne, and Bayonne. Under Charles IV a part of Guienne had been occupied by the French king's vassals. Restitution had been promised in 1327, but it had clearly not been made. Interviews, negotiations, agreements could not avail to settle the legal issues of the past. The French encroachments went on, and this invasion of the duchy by process of law was openly pursued; even the question of confiscation was raised. For Edward III the choice lay between surrender and taking the offensive.

Elsewhere, too, the situation was hardly less difficult. The kings of England made continuous and energetic efforts to dominate Scotland. Now the alliance between France and Scotland was becoming a tradition of Capetian policy; the first agreements dated from 1295. When Edward III imposed on the Scots his creature Edward Balliol as king, it was in France that the dispossessed king, young David Bruce, took refuge, and he found there an asylum "moult débonnaire." Philip VI at first attempted to get his mediation accepted. But, from the end of 1335 onwards, he directly lent his aid to the Scots, and an expedition was prepared for the spring of 1336. For Edward III this constituted a serious grievance.

In Flanders, the victory of Cassel had imposed the penalty of French influence; the count was wholly bound to the King of France. And yet, for their industry, the Flemings had need of England. To restore the balance, Edward III cleverly exploited the fact that the Flemish clothiers could not do without English wool; on 12 August 1336 he boldly prohibited the export of wool to Flanders. Reprisals followed: English merchants were arrested in Flanders, Flemish merchants in England. The Flemings thus found themselves in a dilemma between their economic interests and their duty of fealty to the count and the King of France. Relations between France and England became still more critical.

Another incident added to the hostility. Robert of Artois, the brother-in-law of Philip VI, considered himself to have been defrauded of the county of Artois. To provide more evidence of his rights and to oblige the king to do him justice, he let himself be guided by a band of intriguers who fabricated forged documents. Through a maze of complicated proceedings, with enquiries, oaths, imprisonments, executions, Robert of Artois maintained his rights against all comers. He was banished and deprived of his possessions; consumed with shame and hatred, he finally took refuge in England, where he received a noble welcome from the king and queen; there he never ceased to incite Edward III against France and the King of France.

Finally, a coalition was formed in the north against Philip VI. Edward III skilfully made use of family connexions and the greed of the princes of the Empire. A very successful diplomatic campaign, starting at the end of 1335, was conducted by the Bishop of Lincoln in the Low Countries and western Germany. He held great state and purchased allies, from the Duke of Brabant to the Margrave of Brandenburg. But his finest achievement was the alliance with the Emperor, who promised on 15 July 1337 to supply 2000 men-at-arms in return for 300,000 florins.

At the same time Edward III was making his military preparations. For long the English kings had imposed on their subjects the obligation of arming themselves according to their means. This had recently been regulated in detail by an ordinance of 1334. Firstly, the barons and knights had to respond to the summons of the king, who took them into his pay or allowed them to buy themselves off; secondly, the king made a levy among the freemen with arms, "the strongest, most adept, most skilful in shooting with the bow or handling the lance, most inured to fatigue." Thus was created a redoubtable body of infantry, armed with light bows made of yew and rapidly discharged, or with long pointed knives. A regular military education was envisaged. The knightly sports, so different from real warfare, were forbidden, and were replaced by contests with bows and arrows. The making of bows even became a privileged trade. Finally, all Englishmen were encouraged to have their children taught the French language, "which would make them more apt and useful in the wars."

In face of these menaces and preparations, Philip VI was slow to determine his attitude. Up to 1336 he seems to have been entirely occupied with the crusade. But his policy was dependent on that of Benedict XII, who was little interested in the crusade but wished above all to settle to his own advantage the conflict between the Papacy and the Emperor Lewis of Bavaria. On the other side, the royal administration pursued its work in Guienne with a stolid tenacity, refusing to make any concession and at the same time making no stay of legal process. French sailors came to blows with English sailors, and preparations to help the Scots were continued. The embassies which passed between London, Paris, and Avignon seemed but an idle game. Benedict XII, though successful in imposing his mediation between England and Scotland, failed between France and England; facts were too strong for him. At the end of Lent 1336, full of uneasiness and distrust, he suspended the crusade, to the great disappointment of the King of France. At the Parliament at Nottingham in September 1336, Edward III spoke of the safety of his kingdom, and affirmed his rights to the crown of France. Then at last Philip VI began to rouse himself, and on 24 May 1337 the forfeiture of Guienne was proclaimed. The alliance of Edward III with the Emperor disturbed the Pope's zeal for peace and further precipitated events. On 27 October 1337 Edward III in a letter to Benedict XII described Philip VI as "soi-disant" King of France. On All Saints' Day the Bishop of Lincoln brought to Paris a formal letter of defiance, and a few days later the English devastated the island of Cadzand off the coast of Flanders. The Hundred Years' War had begun.

The opening stages were at once complicated by a local crisis. Edward had indirectly dealt a decided blow at French influence in Flanders by stopping the Anglo-Flemish trade and prohibiting the export of English wool to Flanders. The Flemish cloth-trade, thus deprived of its raw material, was brought to a standstill, especially in the important town of Ghent, the chief centre of the trade; unemployment and distress were rife there, and sullen passions were rising against the count and the King of France, stirred by the rigorous treatment meted out to anyone suspected of English sympathies. The hostility of the commonalty to the rich burgesses yielded to the graver issues, and it was a rich clothier, James van Artevelde, a man in the prime of life, circumspect, eloquent, influential, who was invoked by the common people as their saviour. He counselled the people of Ghent to have no fear of France, but to come to terms at once with the King of England for a resumption of the wool-trade, and to organise a kind of economic defence of the Flemish towns. They put their trust in him; all factions ceased. As captain-general of the city he was able to frighten or to persuade the other great towns into the coalition. The Count of Flanders, Louis of Nevers, was helpless, and took refuge at the French court. The negotiations of Ghent with Edward III were immediately successful: English wool reappeared in Flanders, and a commercial treaty was concluded.

In the summer of 1338 Edward III appeared himself in the Low Countries. At Antwerp he lavishly distributed the money he had borrowed; at Coblenz, in a picturesque and symbolic ceremony, the Emperor made him imperial vicar. But it was not until 1339 that the King of England was able to assemble his allies, who were more prompt to receive money than to come into action. Philip VI also arrived with all his force; at the end of October the two armies were at Buironfosse in Picardy half a league apart, but they did not come into touch with each other. As some consolation for this check, Edward III obtained the effective alliance of the Flemings. To overcome their repugnance to disown their lawful lord, the King of France, he took at the Parliament of Ghent in January 1340 the title, the arms, and the seal of the King of France. All kinds of commercial advantages were granted to King Edward's new subjects; at the same time the union of Flanders, Brabant, and Hainault was effected.

The campaign of 1340 was hardly more fruitful than the preceding one, in spite of the fact that it opened with a great victory by sea. Edward III on his return to England had collected an imposing fleet. Philip VI, for his part, tried to organise a royal fleet, which was increased by vessels requisitioned in the Channel ports and by Genoese galleys. The Normans even had the design of a descent upon England and a second Conquest. On the French admirals was imposed the duty, under pain of death, of preventing the English from crossing and landing in France. The fleets met off Sluys. The French, hampered by their method of recruitment and with all the worst of the position, were decisively defeated after a battle lasting nine hours. But the actual campaign, in spite of the assistance of 60,000 Flemings, was limited to the useless siege of Tournai. As Edward III was in debt, and affairs in Scotland and Guienne were going unfavourably for him, the first "grand truce" of the war was signed on 25 September 1340.

Following on Flanders, came the partial defection of Brittany and its influence on the Hundred Years' War. On the death of Duke John III without issue, his brother John of Montfort and his niece's husband Charles of Blois disputed the duchy. The rights of both were open to question, but both of them, without admitting any doubt, requested the King of France to receive their homage. The court at Paris after long discussions gave the verdict to the king's nephew, Charles of Blois, who based his rights on grounds analogous to those of Edward III to the crown of France. Before sentence was given, however, preparations for a struggle had already been made. Brittany was by nature set apart, a land of heath and furze bushes, firmly attached to its traditions, inhabited by a pious and stubborn people, and divided up among a numerous squire-archy little better than peasants, with a few great barons. On the other hand, it was cut in two by difference of language: to the East, the French half, the *Gallot*, more fertile, and exposed towards Anjou and France; to the West, the *Bretonnante*, with the old Breton language and the moor-lands. French Brittany was for Charles of Blois, the Bretonnante for Montfort. The two adversaries provided a similar contrast: Montfort was daring and intriguing; Charles was pious and learned as a clerk, scrupulous and merciful.

Montfort at once sought to lay hands on the duchy and to occupy the principal posts. To make himself more secure, he journeyed to Windsor to meet Edward III, and obtained his ready co-operation; the English could have no better means of entry into the kingdom of France. Charles of Blois could not hesitate any longer. Philip VI provided him with an army, commanded by his son John, who besieged Montfort at Nantes and forced him to surrender. But Charles, though the great Breton lords were all on his side, had still two-thirds of his duchy to conquer. So began the fierce Breton war which lasted more than twenty years, an obstinate and complicated struggle, which gave employment and entertainment to the men-at-arms, while the two leaders, Montfort and Blois, made prisoners in turn, were as often as not absent. The first campaign alone had some unity of plan; it was conducted at first with heroic energy by Jeanne of Montfort, a woman "with the heart of a man and a lion," who defended Hennebont in a siege which has become legendary. Later, English assistance arrived, and in the autumn Edward III himself appeared. As in Flanders, Philip VI brought a strong army. Both sides, however, were anxious to avoid battle on the approach of winter, and two cardinals intervened to bring about a truce at Malestroit in January 1343. But the English maintained their footing in Brittany.

When war broke out again, Edward III, with fewer cards in his hand, was singularly more fortunate. The situation had been modified: in the spring of 1341 the Emperor had abandoned the English alliance and revoked the imperial vicariate of Edward III; many German princes imitated his withdrawal. Secondly, Artevelde had disappeared from the scene. Faction had appeared again in Flanders, and the mass of the artisans had risen against Artevelde, suspecting both his financial administration and his dealings with England. The Captain of Ghent was basely murdered by those who had raised him up. However, Philip VI, "bien hâtif homme" and entirely under the influence of his queen, Jeanne of Burgundy, was not able to profit by these circumstances. In Brittany war broke out again as the result of the mysterious and impolitic executions of Breton nobles. A great Norman baron, Godfrey of Harcourt, a feudal noble through and through, was prosecuted by the king's justice and took refuge in England, where he did homage to Edward III. Treason surrounded Philip VI and embittered his temper. Then, Edward III made a new effort, this time in Guienne, where the King of France was continually encroaching by legal process or direct attack. The King of England had done everything to earn the gratitude of his subjects in Aquitaine, and, thanks to them, in the summer of 1345 the Earl of Derby was able to make a preliminary expedition, which drove back the French and took from them nearly fifty strong posts. The great effort made the next year by Duke John of Normandy with a splendid army against Aiguillon failed miserably, and in a second expedition the Earl of Derby pushed as far as Poitiers and Saint-Maixent, driving all before him.

Encouraged by these initial successes of Derby and by the promises of Godfrey of Harcourt, Edward III decided in July 1346 to land in Normandy near Saint-Vaast de la Hougue. With a small but dependable army of 20,000 men he penetrated, without striking a blow, as far as Caen, under the guidance of Godfrey of Harcourt, took the town after a courageous defence by the inhabitants, and, after profitable raids in all directions, pushed forward to the Seine, which he wished to cross in order to join hands with the Flemings. Philip VI, "dolent et angoisseux," fearing fresh treasons, bustled about uselessly; he was unable to prevent the crossing of the Seine by the English at Poissy. Then at last he decided to initiate an active pursuit of them; he hoped to entrap them in the triangle between the Channel and the estuary of the Somme. But on 23 August Edward III managed to force the passage of the Somme at a ford below Abbeville, and on 25 August entrenched himself strongly on the plateau of Crécy. There, on the following day, took place the first great battle of the Hundred Years' War. The reckless charges of the French chivalry broke before the strong position of the English, the volleys of the archers, and the knives of the foot-soldiers who penetrated into their ranks. The day ended in a headlong rout; the King of France was in flight; his army was broken and left some 4000 men on the field. King John of Bohemia was among the dead.

From Crécy Edward advanced to lay siege to Calais, which was to be the prize of victory. The town was a vigorous one, inhabited by good seamen, well fortified, two sea-leagues distant from Dover. The siege lasted for almost a year. To ensure the blockade, the English erected a new town, Villeneuve-la-Hardie. Jean de Vienne, a Burgundian, defended the town with a fierce energy, but the English could not be induced to loosen their grip by any diversion. Moreover, the Scots were beaten at Neville's Cross in October 1346, and Charles of Blois was defeated and taken prisoner before La Roche-Derrien in Brittany on 20 June 1347. The King of France made a tardy effort to relieve the loyal town, but retired without fighting. Calais was reduced to extremity; they ate "toutes ordures par droite famine." The defenders resolved "to die honourably in their places rather than to eat one another." However, they discussed capitulation; but the conditions were very harsh. Edward III at first wanted to put to death all who remained within the walls; he contented himself with insisting that six burgesses should be sent to his camp with the keys of the city to suffer for the rest. Eustace of Saint-Pierre and five other burgesses volunteered; when they came before him stripped to their shirts with halters round their necks, he ordered them to be led to execution; and it was only the queen that was able to melt his wrath. The inhabitants had to migrate, and they found a hospitable refuge in France. Englishmen came to people the city anew; Calais was to remain English for two centuries. After the fall of Calais, two cardinals arranged a general truce which lasted till after the death of Philip VI. Moreover, peace was made in Flanders, where the new count, Louis de Maële, came to terms with the towns; but he was to prove a very lukewarm vassal for the King of France.

Philip VI was to end his days amid gloom and mourning. Yet, in spite of his mediocrity and his misfortunes, his reign was not without distinction and usefulness. He was devoted to the chase, living as a rule close to the great forests in the neighbourhood of Paris, holding high state; it was only war that forced him to rigid economy. Numerous important ordinances regulated in detail the Parlement, the treasury, the king's justice, the river and the forest laws. The royal administration held in check the ecclesiastical jurisdiction, of which the very principles were freely discussed at an assembly of bishops and barons held at Vincennes at the end of 1329. By skilful policy, for which the royal officials were mainly responsible, Philip VI was assured of the definitive possession of the great southern town of Montpellier and the acquisition of the Dauphiné for the endowment of his grandson Charles; thus was France happily rounded off in the south and east. But, more important still, war obliged the king to develop and organise his finances. On several occasions he had to have recourse to the States General, to listen to their grievances and even their reproaches, especially after Crécy. To the provincial assemblies of Normandy and Vermandois he made important concessions on the administration of subsidies. Improved and detailed regulations were laid down for the various kinds of royal taxes, whether direct taxation, in the form of the hearth-tax (*fouage*), or indirect, such as charges on the sale

of merchandise, the salt-tax (*gabelle*), the tenths permitted by the Pope
from the clergy, loans, and changes in the currency which were often made
secretly and caused great disturbance to trade. The financial stress
arising from defeat in war was not the only trial to which the kingdom
was exposed at the end of the reign. On top of this came the Black Death
in 1347, with a frightful mortality among the king's subjects. Finally,
Philip VI experienced the loss of most of those dearest to him; he himself
died on 22 August 1350.

Under John II, the war was to take a still more unhappy course for
France. John was a little over thirty years of age; his father had made
him Duke of Normandy, but he had failed to learn in his duchy the
profession of king. As general in Brittany and Languedoc he had shewn
himself greedy for money but of poor judgment and extremely self-willed,
"slowly making up his mind and difficult to move from his opinion." He
was subject to impulses and terrible rages. Otherwise, in spite of his
unpleasing countenance and stolid expression, he was in many ways quite
attractive; he could inspire affection by his generosity and spirit; he was
known as John the Good[1]. Unfortunately he was the victim of bad advice;
not that his counsellors, for instance, Simon of Bucy, Robert of Lorris,
Nicholas Braque, were knaves and rogues, but they were unscrupulous,
intriguing, and greedy men.

While King John was ordering the execution of his Constable, Raoul
de Brienne, to make way for his favourite, Charles of Spain, and while he
was founding, with much pomp and circumstance, the Order of the Star,
a new danger was arising for the kingdom. Charles, King of Navarre,
born in 1332, was the nearest in descent from Philip the Fair, and
through his mother, the daughter of Louis X, the prince most adjacent
to the throne. In spite of his short stature, this young man of eighteen
gave promise of the happiest gifts: he was affable, eloquent, and winning;
but he was also full of ambition and covetousness, a hypocrite and mischief-
maker. John married him to his daughter, a child of eight. Unfortunately
misunderstandings soon arose between him and his son-in-law. Out of
revenge and spite, the King of Navarre caused the new Constable to be
stabbed, boasted of the murder, and at once entered into negotiations with
the English. As he possessed extensive domains in Normandy, his alliance
might be of priceless value to Edward III; so the King of France preferred
to make a humiliating peace, in betrayal of his own interests, and increased
the Norman domains of Charles. But the execution of the treaty gave
occasion for a fresh conflict. Charles, who from that time earned his
surname of "the Bad," fled to Avignon and secretly proposed to the King
of England to partition the kingdom of France. Under the threat of an
invasion, King John capitulated a second time.

This unexpected alliance decided Edward III to an active renewal of

[1] "Jean le Bon"; "genial" would be a better English equivalent.

the war in 1355; in spite of the efforts of the Pope, successive truces had not been converted into a regular treaty of peace. An attempted invasion of Artois by Edward III himself yielded no result. But the eldest of his sons, the Prince of Wales, the Black Prince, haughty and magnificent in bearing, an intrepid and successful warrior, had arrived at Bordeaux. In the autumn, during a sudden expedition lasting two months, he ravaged Languedoc up to Narbonne, and returned unmolested to Bordeaux; never had been seen such destruction.

The year 1356 was to be full of remarkable happenings. In November 1355 John assembled the States General of Langue d'oïl to demand supplies for the approaching campaign, and though they granted the subsidy they shewed themselves very distrustful and exacting, wishing to keep in their own hands the administration and the disposal of the taxes which they had voted. At this meeting the lead was taken by the Provost of the Merchants of Paris, Étienne Marcel, a rich clothier like Artevelde, and like him daring and ambitious. Then in April 1356 a dramatic event happened at Rouen. The King of Navarre, continually bent on intrigue, sought to draw into a mysterious conspiracy the dauphin Charles, King John's eldest son; a disturbing movement was revealed in Normandy. John's wrath was roused, and in the middle of the festivities to celebrate the accession of the dauphin to the duchy of Normandy, to which he had just been appointed, the king suddenly appeared, and ordered the arrest of the King of Navarre and the execution of several nobles of Normandy and Navarre. At the same time, the possessions of the King of Navarre and of the Harcourt family in Lower Normandy were seized; the princes of Navarre and the Harcourts appealed for help to Edward III. Actually the Duke of Lancaster arrived soon afterwards, and advanced to Verneuil; and he only retired before a large army led by the king himself.

These events took place in the month of July. At the same time, the Prince of Wales, leaving Bordeaux with a small but very reliable army, penetrated as far as Touraine; on 7 September he was at Amboise on the Loire, with the obvious intention of uniting with the rebels in Normandy. But John concentrated all his forces against this redoubtable adversary. The English retired; it was a contest of speed almost to the gates of Poitiers. They had been pressed by the French, and on the morning of 17 September near Maupertuis they were preparing to continue their retreat when they were attacked by a large mounted advance-guard. They halted. The French dispositions for the attack were badly conceived; the advance-guard was repulsed and driven back in disorder. In succession the "battles" of the King of France, who fought on foot contrary to his custom, were routed: the first was broken by the volleys of the English archers; the second was overcome by panic; the last, led by the king, hoped to save the honour of the day, but John himself was taken prisoner. 7,000 English had cut in pieces 15,000 French; in three hours all was over. The Prince of Wales treated his royal prisoner with all chivalrous courtesy; but he hastened to take him to safe custody at Bordeaux. In the early spring of 1357, after accepting a truce for two years, he conducted him to England, where all London thronged to see the King of France enter the city. The unfortunate John waited there for his release for more than three years, engaged in hunting and jousting, keeping great state and receiving every consideration. His subjects sent him money and good wines. It was only in the last year, 1359, that a stricter régime was enforced.

In France the grief and the distress were extreme. In the South, the States of Languedoc passed an ordinance forbidding the wearing of "cointises" of any kind and imposing silence on the minstrels. There were mutterings of sullen anger against the nobles, who had failed to defend the king and the kingdom. Some ambitious and discontented spirits started an intrigue against the Valois in favour of the descendant in the direct line from the Capetian kings, Charles of Navarre. As ruler there was the eldest son of the king, the dauphin Charles, a young man of nineteen, who had hitherto kept silently in the background; he had at an early stage abandoned the field of battle at Poitiers. He was only the king's lieutenant and so had but a limited and uncertain authority. He had immediately to face the States General summoned for October. There the strength of the bourgeoisie of Paris was displayed in all its might, led by Étienne Marcel, who undoubtedly was inspired by an ideal of reform and government, and by Robert le Coq, Bishop of Laon, an ardent partisan of the King of Navarre. They had the whole populace of Paris behind them, for they spoke readily and well, and they had just grievances in their attack on the dishonest administration of King John's officials. "Now is the time to speak," said Le Coq. "Shame to him who speaks not well, for never was the time so good as now."[1] The States strove to impose detailed restrictions on the royal prerogative, to get rid of the bad officials, to release the King of Navarre, and above all to organise round the dauphin a new form of government which would narrowly confine the young prince under the tutelage of the States. But skilfully, without any display, and without any sign of weakness, the dauphin managed to prorogue the States for a time while he went to Metz, under the pretext of seeking the alliance, useless though it was, of the Emperor Charles IV.

On his return, he found Paris much excited by the debasing of the coinage which he had ordered as a means of raising money. Since Marcel had made himself all-powerful, he had for the moment to yield to the storm. The leading officials of King John were imprisoned or in flight, and the States General had to be reassembled in February 1357. Less rash than their predecessors, they extorted a great ordinance which aimed at restoring order to the royal administration without going so far as to

---

[1] *Acte d'accusation contre Robert Le Coq* in *Bibl. de l'école des chartes*, Vol. II, p. 350, Paris, 1840.

put the dauphin under tutelage, as designed by the previous States. But the times were too troubled for this wise reform to be permanent, or for a reasonable control by the States to be organised. Besides, no new right had been created; no proper charter had been presented and accepted; reforms and control alike were, as before, closely linked together and depended upon internal dues and the raising of temporary subsidies. Moreover, above the dauphin, his lieutenant, was the king, who had relinquished none of his power; he forbade the payment of the subsidy granted by the States and any further meetings of the States. So everywhere there was a certain number of refusals to pay, and the later meetings of the States, to which the dauphin was compelled to submit, soon came to be but the shadows of assemblies. A decided check had been given to the doubtful experiment of the States General.

Meanwhile the dauphin was too short of money to be able easily to shake off the yoke of Marcel, Le Coq, and their party. Moreover, the King of Navarre had reappeared on the scene; his release had on several occasions been demanded by the States. While a session was in progress in November 1357, Charles the Bad escaped from the castle of Arleux, thanks to the intrigues of Marcel and Le Coq. The Provost of the Merchants reckoned on finding in him the necessary support so as to dominate the dauphin more securely. Charles the Bad hoped to profit by the circumstances to obtain money and lands himself, and perhaps to arrive even at the throne. Henceforward he turned to his own advantage the movement of reform. In fact, as soon as he was released, he displayed himself and made speeches to the people of Amiens, Rouen, and Paris; he demanded reparation; he thrust himself upon the dauphin; he was all-powerful in council.

At the end of a month, however, the dauphin had exhausted "the virtue of patience which God had given him." He took the offensive. Like Marcel and the King of Navarre, he made speeches himself, and had them made by others, to the people of Paris. It was Marcel and his friends, he gave out, on whom fell the responsibility for the revolutionary government to which he had been obliged to submit. All was now going from bad to worse: no serious reforms had been made; the subsidies brought in a poor return; the enemy, English and Navarrese, were everywhere; communications and provisioning had become difficult. Who was to blame but those who controlled and paralysed the royal authority? So it was the dauphin who now criticised the government imposed upon him, and denounced the new officials and their evil administration of the finances; he had received nothing from the subsidies. His masters replied, but the harm was done. King John, moreover, had arranged in London a satisfactory treaty of peace.

To meet the threatened transformation, Marcel and the King of Navarre thought to find two remedies. Firstly, in order to terrorise the dauphin by deeds of bloodshed, the two marshals of Normandy and Champagne were murdered at the prince's own table. Secondly, they made the young prince regent, believing him to be entirely in their power for the future and hoping thus to profit by a complete authority equal to that of the king. But the dauphin was too subtle: a month later he found a clever pretext for leaving Paris, to which he was only to return as master. Once free, he applied himself to using his full power as regent against those who had put it in his hands. In fact, he now became confident and daring: he assembled at Compiègne a meeting of States entirely devoted to his cause; he collected soldiers; he occupied important positions around Paris; and he replied firmly and haughtily to the demands that he should return to the city. Marcel was uneasy: he wrote letters reproaching and threatening the prince; he organised the resistance of Paris, sought to raise money, put the walls in a state of defence, and assembled the artillery.

A tragic episode complicated the situation still further. The English had advanced up to the region around Paris; to them were added the officers of the King of Navarre; finally, the dauphin had collected his soldiers also. English, Navarrese, Bretons, and Gascons lived on the open country. The country people were the chief victims; continually they had to take refuge in towns, castles, churches, woods, or marshes. So their anger increased against the nobles: the nobles who had been defeated at Crécy and Poitiers, and now could not even defend their own people, but remained under arms, living on pillage and exactions, pretending to assist the dauphin and fight the English. In 1358 exasperation reached its height; and a spark started the conflagration. On 28 May, in the south of the Beauvaisis, the first *effroi* took place; several of the gentry were murdered. Immediately there were bands of peasants roaming the countryside, especially in Picardy and north of the Île de France. They were known as the Jacques, from the garment of that name worn by peasants. These bands set themselves to hunt the gentry down, and to sack and burn the castles; besides the peasants, there were also craftsmen from the towns, and clerks. The Jacques tried to create an organisation and took as their leader one Guillaume Cale. A few towns—Beauvais, Senlis, Clermont—were on their side. The terror of the nobles and burgesses finds an echo, rising to legendary heights, in the chroniclers. But, perhaps because the nobles fled before them, the Jacques seem to have indulged in pillage rather than bloodshed.

Marcel, without making an open alliance, acted in concert with them, and organised a kind of Jacquerie around Paris. The chief exploit was the attack by a troop of Parisians and peasants on the market-town of Meaux, on an island of the Marne, where the dauphiness and a part of the court had taken refuge. The ladies would have been captured and come to grave harm but for the unexpected arrival of Gaston de Foix, who was returning from Prussia. The assailants were routed and slaughtered wholesale. At the same time, Charles the Bad, in whom the common folk had placed so much hope, was himself conducting reprisals on the peasant bands to the north of Paris. He it was who got possession, by treachery, of the person of Guillaume Cale and had him put to death; the Jacques were now a body without a head and were cut in pieces. The nobles were pitiless. Before 24 June, 20,000 persons had been put to death. The Jacquerie was drowned in blood, and the villages were reduced to destitution by crushing fines.

At Paris, this marked the end of the power of Marcel and Charles the Bad; they were becoming unpopular, for the only object they had in view was to make war on the dauphin and to serve the interests of the King of Navarre. Besides, the dauphin was in front of Paris with an army and was attempting a kind of siege. Conferences failed to re-establish an accord that had become impossible. In vain Marcel called to his help the Flemings; they would not move. To protect himself, he was reduced to admitting the English into the city, to the great wrath of the Parisians. For his part, Charles the Bad was in negotiation with Edward III for a partition of the French kingdom. The common people, however, wished to fight the king's enemies, who were pillaging the suburbs; they made a sortie, but fell into an ambush and many Parisians perished. The provost was hooted in the streets. The King of Navarre, who had prudently established himself at Saint-Denis, entered into pourparlers with the English and the dauphin in turn, but made no progress. Possibly at the end of his tether, he was about to return to Paris and proclaim himself as king, when on 31 July some resolute spirits roused the populace against Marcel as he was going the round of the defences, and killed him without anyone interposing on his behalf. His chief accomplices were immediately seized, and put to death or banished, and their goods confiscated. On 2 August the dauphin entered Paris, which gave him a great welcome. He sensibly granted a pardon to the Parisians at once; those who had remained faithful to him were rewarded out of confiscations, and the deposed officials were reinstated; the royal prestige and authority were restored. Thus ended in failure a premature attempt to limit and control the royal government. Of Marcel little was known; he was too exclusively Parisian, and his purpose was not understood by the rest of the country. Finally, the King of Navarre came and upset everything by his foolish ambition, and completed the ruin of the party of reform.

The dauphin had still to bring to an end two wars, the English and the Navarrese. The defeat of Poitiers had disorganised the defence of the kingdom. Around Paris, the towns of Poissy, Creil, Melun, Lagny, and Meulan had fallen, and remained in enemy hands. Brie and Champagne were overrun by English and Germans, Normandy and Picardy by the Navarrese. The valley of the Seine was pierced at several points, and from the Loire to the Garonne bands or companies occupied numerous castles. At the head of these Companies were enterprising leaders, whom Froissart has celebrated, such as Robert Knolles, Eustace of Auberchicourt, James

Pipe, Bertucat d'Albret. The dauphin lacked money to resist them: the subsidies, both general and local, were poorly paid, owing to the universal distress; the debasement of the coinage brought in less and less profit because of the increased value of the silver mark. However, an energetic local defence was concerted with the inhabitants of every district. These were only "petites besognes," but they were pursued harmoniously and tenaciously, and had happy results. Lieutenants and captains nominated by the dauphin were in charge of these local defences; among them appeared Bertrand du Guesclin. The burghers of Rouen, the communes of the district of Caux, the inhabitants of Caen, the burghers of Rheims and Châlons, among others, united in this way with men-at-arms and recovered a large number of fortresses from the leaders of the bands. The sentiments of sober folk were demonstrated in a striking fashion when King John, in March 1359, sacrificing his kingdom for his freedom, accepted in London the draft of a treaty which reconstituted in its entirety the domain of the Plantagenets prior to Philip Augustus, abandoned to Edward III all the west of the kingdom from Guienne to Calais, including Normandy, and imposed a ransom of four million gold crowns. The States General, diplomatically consulted by the dauphin in May, declared without hesitation that the treaty was "neither tolerable nor feasible," and that they must "make goodly war upon the English." By means of the subsidy voted, the dauphin was able to attack the King of Navarre. Siege was laid to Melun; it was distinguished by the prowess of du Guesclin in the royal army. But Charles the Bad had grievances against Edward III, and the dauphin was afraid of an English invasion. So they made peace at the end of July 1359: Charles recovered his lands and received money and fresh territory, but ceded Melun; at an interview the two princes were reconciled. The King of Navarre came back to Paris, where he received a poor reception from the people, who cherished rancour against him. The reconciliation, indeed, was only a verbal one; he remained an enemy.

The truce made at Bordeaux after the battle of Poitiers had expired; as peace had not been concluded, the English invasion recommenced. Edward III only appeared in Picardy in the autumn of 1359. His army was an imposing one and well provided; it was like a festal progress, for Edward III wished to be crowned at Rheims. But, on the French side, orders had been issued to everyone to take refuge in fortresses, and to the men-at-arms to refrain from battle. Edward III arrived before Rheims without encountering an enemy or capturing a stronghold; nor could he take the town. At the end of a month the English went into winter quarters in Upper Burgundy. In the spring of 1360, while a humiliating treaty freed the rest of Burgundy from invasion, Edward III appeared before Paris. The gates were firmly closed; for twelve days not a move was made. The English were at a loss what to do; the Scots were stirring, and Picard seamen had ravaged the English coast. A terrible storm in the plains of Beauce did grave damage to the English baggage train; and famine was threatening. At last Edward III decided to listen to the papal legate, who "every day held parley with him for the making of peace."

On 1 May 1360 conferences were opened at Brétigny near Chartres. In a week's time the draft of a peace had been accepted and signed by the dauphin and the Prince of Wales. The King of England recovered the Agenais, Périgord, Quercy, Rouergue, the county of Bigorre, the Limousin, Saintonge, Angoumois, Poitou, the counties of Montreuil, Ponthieu, and Guines, and he retained Calais. The King of France was to abandon all jurisdiction over these territories. He bound himself to pay a ransom of three million gold crowns, the first payment, of 600,000 crowns, to be made at Calais within four months, the other payments to be guaranteed mainly by the surrender of numerous hostages. The English restored the fortresses of which they were in possession. Throughout the kingdom the relief was immense, though to some the terms of peace seemed too onerous. John left England in great pomp on 1 July. At Calais he waited until the hostages were ready and the money had been collected for the first payment of his ransom. When Edward III came to join John at Calais, only 400,000 crowns had been collected; but this satisfied the English king. In the midst of great festivities, a definitive form was given to the conventions of Brétigny; the charters were dated 24 October 1360. Very cleverly, the French negotiators caused the renunciation of sovereignty over the ceded territory by the King of France to be separated from the treaty proper. This renunciation, together with Edward III's of the title of King of France, was subjected to various delays and conditions, and so it was much more easy to postpone and even to evade it altogether.

Once back in France, John had to carry out the treaty. It was a hard task: the handing over of territory was a slow process, performed with a bad grace and delayed by the reluctance of common people and nobles alike; it was not complete until 1363, when the Prince of Wales came to govern the English domains. The collection of the ransom was more laborious still. It was only in February 1361 that John completed the payment of the first instalment. An aid was established on the sale of merchandise, under a special administration, to last for the whole period in which the ransom was being paid. The burden fell mainly on the Île de France, Champagne, Normandy, and Languedoc. From 1360 to 1364 there were bad harvests, disastrous frosts, and a return of the plague. Finally, a part of the money collected was employed for the various needs of the kingdom; in 1364 King John was a million in arrears.

The kingdom at that time was the prey of armed bands or Companies. Disbanded at the peace, the Companies, whose trade was war, did not disarm; and they kept the strongholds they should have surrendered. The men in these Companies, Englishmen, Germans, and Spaniards, dreamed of nothing but surprises, pillagings, and above all ransoms; when they

could not hope for good ransoms they were deliberately cruel. Each
Company was organised like a small army, and was accompanied by various
craftsmen, by clerks to draw up the "pàtis" (ransoms of villages) and
safe-conducts, by dealers, mistresses, and pages. Sometimes they spread
over a whole district, sometimes they joined up together; they were
extremely mobile. They preferred the pasture-lands and wine-growing
districts of Normandy, Burgundy, and Languedoc. In Normandy they were
hunted by du Guesclin, appointed captain of the open country, and with
remarkable success. Around Paris the Companies were more difficult to
uproot. Meanwhile a number of these bands united together in
Champagne and spread into Burgundy; they were known as the Grand
Company. Their plan was to lay violent hands on the convoys of money
coming from Languedoc for the king's ransom. Geguin of Badefol, "the
king of the Companies," and other leaders surprised Pont Saint-Esprit
near Avignon. There was great panic, and the Pope excommunicated the
Companies. From there the bands penetrated into Italy; others established themselves in Languedoc; others again poured back northwards
into the Lyonnais. A small royal army opposed their passage; it was cut
to pieces at Brignais on 6 April 1362. The Companies, incapable of
turning their victory to account, dispersed in different directions. In order
to deliver the kingdom from them, King John revived the crusading
project of Philip VI, and came to Avignon to interview the Pope. But
it never amounted to more than a dream.

At the end of 1363 the king's attention was occupied with the question
of the succession to Burgundy. Philip of Rouvres, ruler of both the duchy
and the free county of Burgundy, and also of Artois, Auvergne, the
county of Boulogne, and other territory, died without immediate heirs,
leaving a widow herself heiress to the county of Flanders. The King of
France at once united the duchy of Burgundy to the Crown, as next of
kin; the counties of Artois, Boulogne, and Auvergne were given to col-
laterals of the late duke. But the King of Navarre, who considered
himself to have claims, received nothing. The entry into possession of
the duchy was speedily effected. King John came himself to Dijon,
and appointed his son Philip first as his lieutenant, then as Duke of
Burgundy, and obtained from the Emperor the formal investiture with the
county of Burgundy as well. Thus was founded the second Burgundian
house, which was to become so powerful and so formidable. A few months
later the King of Navarre made his protest; without replying to the
Pope's offer of mediation he prepared for war, and entered into correspondence with the English and with the leaders of the Companies.

But at this moment John disappeared from the scene. While he was
negotiating, at the price of dangerous concessions, for the release of the
princes of the blood who were hostages in England, one of them, his
second son, the Duke of Anjou, broke his parole and escaped. John
honourably decided to return to England in order to guarantee by his

presence the execution of the treaty and to be able to negotiate. The dauphin was made regent. John was received with great pomp at London; after a winter spent in entertainments, he died there on 8 April 1364.

The work of Charles V was to repair the harm done by King John. The new king was twenty-six years of age. Physically he resembled his father, except that he was sickly and awkward in manner; he had a thin and angular figure, a pale, grave countenance, and an intent gaze. The last eight years had endowed him with experience and patience; so he had renounced the glamour and the bustle of war for tactics that brought no glory and also no risk. He had, besides, acquired great self-control and the power of hiding his feelings, which he considered necessary in a king. Above all things he liked order and moderation. No king had higher ideas of the royal dignity; he honoured his ancestor St Louis with a deep reverence. His devotion and zeal for all that had to do with religion were remarkable, and yet he could be tolerant. He was bountiful and spent money readily, and liked to surround himself with a truly royal luxury, to heap up precious objects among his treasures. He built the Hôtel Saint-Paul, a vast residence, full of variety and richly decorated; he transformed and embellished the Louvre; he completed the castle of Vincennes. A lover of deep designs, astrology fascinated him. He enjoyed speculative ideas, liking to delve into causes and principles, and he was keenly interested in all that made up the science of his day. He collected a splendid library, which was housed in the Louvre; in particular he enriched it with translations of ancient works, specially made for him. There is, however, a darker side to this portrait: his magnificence did not permit of economy, and he loaded his subjects with taxes; and his thoughtful and acute mind often led him to prefer cleverness to straightforwardness, legal finesse to equity in judgment. His subtle sophistry and the secrecy of his ways made him more to be feared than did his actual power.

Charles V knew how to surround himself with men of high worth: speculative thinkers like Raoul de Presles, translator of the Bible and of St Augustine; Philippe de Mezières, who inspired the *Songe du Verger*; Nicholas Oresme, translator of Aristotle, a great opponent of astrology; above all, with men of affairs, like his chancellors the two brothers de Dormans and Pierre d'Orgemont, his companion and closest friend Bureau de la Rivière the provost of Paris, the redoubtable justiciar Hugues Aubriot, and the skilful financier Jean le Mercier. But the most illustrious of all was Bertrand du Guesclin, who has already been mentioned more than once. Born in 1320, between Rennes and Dinan, after a rough and stormy childhood he had revealed his strength at jousts and tournaments, had fought for Charles of Blois in Brittany, and then for the king in Lower Normandy. When Charles V came to the throne, he was already famous for his marvellous exploits. He was a rough and stubborn soldier, without any of the prejudices of chivalry, fond of exposing his own person but very careful of his men; further, he was upright, dependable, and straightforward.

Charles' first task was to settle up the legacy from the past: war with Navarre was beginning again, war in Brittany was still going on, and the Companies were spread over and terrorising the kingdom. It was the succession to Burgundy that had provoked Charles the Bad to fresh hostilities. The dauphin, as regent for his father on the latter's return to England, wished to bring this new war to a quick end; by skilful surprises du Guesclin got possession of Mantes and Meulan just at the moment of King John's death. This freed the valley of the Seine. A Navarrese army, derived mainly from the Companies and commanded by a famous Gascon adventurer, the Captal de Buch, arrived with all speed. Halted near Cocherel on the Eure, it was cut in pieces by du Guesclin, and the Captal was taken prisoner. The king learnt the news on the eve of his coronation at Rheims. The war, indeed, dragged on in Normandy, and not very satisfactorily, until the end of 1364. The Pope and the Captal, who was tired of captivity, persuaded the King of Navarre to treat for peace; he once again recovered his domains, but he exchanged Mantes and Meulan for the distant and strategically valueless Montpellier. Troublesome as ever, he would not seal the treaty with his great seal, and the Captal had to guarantee his master's signature. It was, indeed, a "paix renard."

In Brittany the situation had become lamentable. To avoid the expenses of war, Edward III had "farmed out" various parts of the duchy among his captains, who in their turn sub-let the government and possession of castles to adventurers who made the best offers. The peace of Calais had not put a stop to this intolerable state of affairs. Meanwhile, Edward III, in the capacity of guardian or practically of gaoler, had since 1343 been keeping John, the Montfort heir, by his side. In 1362 he released him to go to Brittany, after having tied his hands by rigorous conditions. In order to escape from them, John wished to come to terms with Charles of Blois. But Jeanne of Penthièvre, from whom her husband Charles of Blois derived all his rights, would not consent; hostilities were resumed, and the issue appeared as the judgment of God against her. In front of Auray, in spite of the support of du Guesclin, the army of Charles of Blois was overthrown in September 1364; Charles was killed and du Guesclin taken prisoner. It was useless to prolong the struggle. Charles V caused peace to be signed at Guérande a few months later: John of Montfort was recognised as Duke of Brittany; in default of male heirs the duchy was to revert to the children of Charles of Blois. John did homage to Charles V but remained English at heart.

After this peace the Companies, thrown out of employment, were more than ever a public danger. As it was impossible to destroy them or to drive them out, the Pope and the King of France sought to dispatch them on distant expeditions; the first objective was Hungary, to make war on the Turks. But Hungary was far off; the bands got no farther than Alsace and poured back into France. The next idea was Spain. The ruler of Castile was Don Peter the Cruel; by his justice and his rapacity he had aroused great hatred. Moreover he had deserted, and either allowed or caused the death of his wife, who was Charles V's sister-in-law. Finally, he had pursued with success a policy of hostility to Peter the Ceremonious, King of Aragon, a ruler of vain and restless temperament. One of the illegitimate brothers of the King of Castile, Don Henry, endeavoured to profit by these circumstances to organise a coalition with the Kings of France and Aragon against Don Peter. With Charles V's help, Don Henry and du Guesclin collected a large number of the Companies; at Avignon they compelled the Pope to absolve them and to pay them large sums. On the other side of the Pyrenees they conquered Castile for Don Henry within two months. But the expedition had had too speedy a success, and most of the Companies poured back again into France. Meanwhile, Don Peter had come to Bordeaux to entreat the Prince of Wales to undertake his defence and help him to reconquer his kingdom. The prince was tempted by this expedition, which revived in Spain the struggle of French and English. He came himself, with an army of Gascons and various Companies; the King of Navarre, without declaring openly for him, delivered to him the passes over the mountains. At Navarete (Nájera), in April 1367, the English defeated Don Henry and du Guesclin, who was again taken prisoner. But the Black Prince was ill, his army was decimated by dysentery, and he had rapidly to return to Bordeaux. Du Guesclin, after the payment of an enormous ransom, immediately brought fresh bands into Castile; Don Peter, abandoned to himself, was defeated at Montiel and killed by his brother's hand in March 1369. Don Henry was now definitely King of Castile, thanks to the support of Charles V and the tenacity of du Guesclin. As for the Companies, they had been exhausted by these successive campaigns. Throughout the kingdom defensive and repressive measures were taken against them, and the last bands were reduced to great distress. It was just at this time that the great war was about to recommence.

It seems certain that up to 1378 the government and policy of Charles V were dominated by a single idea, the reversal of the Treaty of Calais and the desire for revenge. Undoubtedly, in his love of order and authority, which was known in his entourage as the "bonne policie," he maintained and affirmed his rights against all men without hesitation; he watched over the constant increase and the proper administration of his domain and of his justice; he firmly and prudently applied himself to the preservation of the public peace. But his chief care was to make preparation and provision for a new war. The reforms in the domain, even with the complete reorganisation of its administration, could not suffice for that. The taxes on sales of merchandise and on liquors, instituted to pay the ransom of King John, were gradually diverted from their object. At the beginning of 1363, and especially in 1369, with the more or less direct concurrence of the States, the necessary revenue was made up by a direct tax, the hearth-tax. The new taxes were in course of time made permanent, and a timely revision of their administration assured their proper collection and employment. To these were added special subsidies from Languedoc, the salt-tax, local taxes raised to meet special requirements, and loans. A reform of the currency, which was firmly adhered to, relieved the royal finances as well as commercial transactions from fluctuations that were usually disastrous. In spite of malversations, exemptions, reductions granted to towns, and gifts to princes of the blood, Charles V had in this way the means to renew and to maintain the struggle.

He was, in fact, able to reorganise the army. The nobles of the kingdom, from princes of the blood to the humblest squire, were enlisted in the king's service, paraded for review by his marshals, grouped in companies under his captains, and led to battle by his lieutenants or his Constable. The pay was carefully fixed and regularly paid by the war treasurers. Besides the nobles there were the cross-bowmen of the towns and some auxiliary corps of foreigners. Shooting with bow and cross-bow was, as in England, to replace all other sports, and meetings were to be held for the purpose. An already powerful artillery, which could discharge projectiles of more than 100 pounds, was an effective contribution for siege-warfare. The fortresses were regularly inspected, and were put in order at the expense of the lords, or destroyed if they were in bad repair and unfit for defence. Paris was surrounded with a new circuit of walls, and the neighbouring citadel of Vincennes was completed. Lastly, Charles V created a regular royal navy, the organisation of which was carried out by the admiral, Jean de Vienne. The arsenal was Clos des Galées at Rouen, on the Seine. Royal fleets could thus take part in great military operations.

Armies and fleets were not enough; Charles V was no less active in diplomacy. At the beginning of the conflict, great danger was to be feared from the direction of Flanders, which, from the time of Artevelde, lay open to English influence. The count, Louis de Maële, was much less reliable than his father. His only heir to his counties of Flanders, Artois, Burgundy, and Nevers was his daughter Margaret, widow of the late Duke of Burgundy. He would have liked to marry this great heiress to one of Edward III's sons, but the Pope and the King of France put obstacles in his way; and in return for the cession of four towns which Flanders had lost in the time of Philip the Fair, he had to accept Charles V's brother Philip, who was already Duke of Burgundy, as his son-in-law and heir. This marriage, the important political consequences of which will appear later, brought Flanders again, for a time at any rate, under French influence. An equally valuable alliance was that with

Castile, to which Don Henry steadfastly adhered, and which was further supplemented by an alliance with Portugal; the imprudent designs of the Duke of Lancaster against Castile helped to strengthen the tie. Lastly, Charles V ensured the good will, if not the actual support, of the Emperor. The diplomatic work of Edward III at the beginning of the war had been almost completely undone; Charles V had managed to reconstruct it to his own advantage.

It soon became evident how insecure the peace of Calais was. The handing over of territory to the English was done slowly and with a bad grace. Edward III had been suspected of encouraging the Companies and giving his support to John of Montfort, and the Prince of Wales had fought against the French in Castile; on the other side, King John's ransom had not regularly been paid, and intrigues had been conducted by the French in the ceded districts. From 1368 onwards the tension grew, until it reached a crisis. The Prince of Wales held great state at Bordeaux; his government was hard, his demands high. He surrounded himself with Englishmen, and cultivated the friendship of a few of the larger towns, granting them privileges and exemptions. This disquieted the great local nobles; led by the families of Armagnac and Albret, they turned to Charles V. Moreover, by the Treaty of Calais, the King of France had only suspended his jurisdiction and sovereignty over the ceded districts. The renunciations agreed to at Brétigny, but skilfully excluded from the Treaty of Calais to be made into separate acts, had not been handed in by the appointed date. Charles V had discovered a legal way, a lawyer's dodge the Duke of Lancaster called it, of escaping from the most serious of the concessions promised. After the campaign in Castile, the Prince of Wales was obliged to demand heavy subsidies from his subjects. John of Armagnac, Count of Rouergue, made a vigorous protest, which was not heeded, and then went off to the King of France; at the same time the Sire d'Albret married Charles V's sister-in-law. An agreement was quickly concluded between the King of France and the great Gascon lords, and the appeal which they addressed to the Parlement against the Prince of Wales was entertained. The proceedings were conducted coolly and carefully. In January 1369 the Prince of Wales was cited to Paris. At the same time French sympathies were manifested in most of the districts ceded by the Treaty of Calais; the towns of Rodez and Cahors set the example, and by March more than 800 localities had rallied to the cause of French sovereignty. The Prince of Wales, a sick man, sent for the most famous of the English captains, Chandos, to conduct the war in his place; and hostilities were begun in Rouergue. In the north, Ponthieu was similarly won over. At the beginning of May, in an important assembly at Paris, the States General approved the actions of Charles V. An ultimatum was sent to Edward III, who immediately resumed the title of King of France.

The war was conducted with method on the French side and had re-

CH. XII.

conquest for its object; in a few months, the whole of Rouergue, Agen, Tarbes, with most of the Agenais and the county of Bigorre, had been recovered, and Poitou was invested. The English, true to the memories of Crécy and Poitiers, recommenced their invasions; but the French tactics, tested already in 1359, of creating a void in front of the enemy, reduced to impotence the expeditions of Lancaster in Picardy and Normandy, and of Robert Knolles from Calais to Burgundy. After an unsuccessful demonstration in front of Paris, Knolles disappeared into the west; then du Guesclin arrived, summoned in all haste from the Limousin by the king. On 2 October 1370, at a solemn assembly, Charles V made him Constable and promised him his full confidence. In December, as the sequel to a daring raid near Pontvallain, du Guesclin surprised a part of Knolles' army, overwhelmed it, and drove the remnant by the valley of the Loire into Brittany. In the south, the English had lost the town of Limoges. This new disaster enraged the Prince of Wales and brought him into action again; he made a furious assault on the town and handed it over to his troops to pillage. Shortly afterwards, his illness obtained the upper hand, and he retired to England to die a lingering death.

The most decisive achievement was the conquest of Poitou, which was accomplished in three years by the Dukes of Burgundy and Berry, mainly owing to du Guesclin and his Bretons, with the aid of Castilian ships and of the adventurer Owain of Wales[1], who claimed to be descended from the ancient princes of Wales dispossessed by the kings of England. An English fleet was burned by the Castilians in the bay of La Rochelle. The captures of Chauvigny, Sainte-Sévère, and Soubise were occasions of Homeric exploits; in front of Soubise the Captal de Buch was taken prisoner a second time. Poitiers opened its gates with enthusiasm. La Rochelle, though thoroughly French at heart, was jealous of its privileges; it refused to be intimidated by the rough threats of du Guesclin, and did not open its gates until it had obtained from the royal princes the full extent of its demands. Every attempt made by Edward III to bring help to his captains ended in failure. After the capture of Surgères, in which the Poitevin nobles who had remained faithful to the English cause had taken refuge, and the defeat of a small enemy force by du Guesclin outside Chizé, the last English posts surrendered. Poitou, Aunis, Saintonge were, and remained for ever, restored to the French kingdom.

Charles V could well expect to win a similar success in Brittany. The Duke, John of Montfort, brought up in England and bound by personal ties to Edward III, gave a great welcome to Englishmen: Knolles, Chandos, and many others held castles and lands in his duchy. It was a source of considerable embarrassment to him when war broke out afresh between France and England; in the summer of 1372 he decided on alliance with England. But, in spite of the men-at-arms and the captains sent him by

[1] See *infra*, Chap. XVII, p. 522.

Edward III, he was deserted by the leading nobles and towns in Brittany, who since the Breton war of succession had hated the English. After having renounced his homage and set Charles V at defiance, John IV fled to England. Du Guesclin occupied the principal positions in the duchy, and by the end of 1373 only four Breton fortresses remained in English hands.

To make up for all these disasters, Edward III attempted a fresh invasion. He was too old to lead it himself, and the Dukes of Lancaster and Brittany could not break the spell of bad fortune; they followed the road that had been trodden three times already, from Calais to Burgundy. At a great council held at Paris, du Guesclin and Clisson, a leading Breton noble who had recently come over to the king, advised that now above all the policy of creating a void in front of the English should be adhered to. Lancaster's army was sorely tried: after having crossed the Loire, it could only capture Tulle and Brive; and out of 30,000 horses only 6000 reached Bordeaux at the end of a campaign of five months. Once this expedition was over, the Duke of Anjou and du Guesclin pushed forward to La Réole. At the same time, Jean de Vienne, after a siege memorable for the part played in it by artillery, captured Saint-Sauveur-le-Vicomte, a town in Normandy, one of Chandos' fiefs. The English had failed to maintain a defence, and Charles V had attained his end. So both adversaries listened to the efforts of the Pope on behalf of peace; on 27 June 1375 a truce was concluded at Bruges, but, as the English adhered to the Treaty of Calais, a peace was impossible. It was during this truce that two of the principal actors vanished from the scene: the Prince of Wales in June 1376, and in June 1377, abandoned by victory and deserted by his friends, the aged Edward III.

Left by himself, Charles V experienced vicissitudes of fortune. Jean de Vienne with the French and Castilian fleets ravaged the English coast, but was unable to recover Calais; and the Duke of Burgundy was no more fortunate on land. On the other hand, Bergerac fell into the hands of the Duke of Anjou, and Bordeaux was threatened. But the grave anxieties of the worst days were revived when the king learnt through the capture of some agents of the King of Navarre that Charles the Bad had not ceased to play the traitor, and that in 1370, 1372, and again in 1378, he had negotiated with the English for the dismemberment of the French kingdom. All sorts of crimes were imputed to him, the last being a cunningly-laid plot to poison Charles V. The king shewed no hesitation: he forced Charles the Bad's son to disavow his father; and du Guesclin and the Duke of Burgundy were sent to Normandy to occupy the domains of the King of Navarre. Cherbourg alone held out, because Charles the Bad had handed it over to the English; but a diversion of the Duke of Lancaster against Saint-Malo failed miserably. At the same time, Don Henry of Castile attacked Navarre. English succour came from Bordeaux, but could not save the king; his principal castles were seized.

Charles the Bad was ruined; he was despoiled of his domains in France, even of Montpellier, and dragged out the rest of his life in hopeless destitution.

After the King of Navarre, the Duke of Brittany. At the end of 1378 Charles V commenced a rigorous process against him in the Parlement. By a judgment of 18 December, he was declared felon and his possessions were attached to the royal domain. The solution was too abrupt and hasty; this annexation to the domain did violence to Breton sentiment, which adhered above all to its ultimate independence. The oaths which the king exacted from the great Breton lords, du Guesclin, Clisson, Rohan, did nothing to lessen the popular indignation; and even Jeanne of Penthièvre took the side of the native Bretons against the King of France. John IV was recalled, and appeared at Dinard on 3 August 1379; the French were helpless against him. Du Guesclin, divided between his Breton and his French sympathies, spent his time in insignificant operations. Some of his enemies, accordingly, sought to destroy Charles V's confidence in his Constable. They failed in this, but du Guesclin, in order to remove all suspicion, went off to fight the Companies, which had appeared again in the centre of France. Before Châteauneuf de Randon the Constable fell ill; the keys of the town were handed to him when he was on the point of death. His body was brought back to Paris and buried at Saint-Denis next to the tomb prepared for the king. In him were personified the stubbornness, heroism, and subtlety of the tactics that effaced the consequences of the great defeats.

From this time hostilities began gradually to die out. The new King of England, Richard II, was only ten years old at the death of his grandfather Edward III; and symptoms of trouble were beginning to appear in England. Charles V, who had attained his end, had turned aside from the war to other objectives. At the end of 1377 he received the Emperor Charles IV at Paris with majestic pomp; receptions, solemn councils, secret conferences followed one another in turn. Charles V held the Dauphiné in the name of his son; his brother Philip was heir to the county of Burgundy; another brother, the Duke of Anjou, had tried to establish himself in Provence; and all of these were imperial territory. There was also mutual business to be discussed and difficulties to be provided for. The Emperor gave the King of France the imperial vicariate in the ancient kingdom of Arles; and alliances were concluded between Charles V and several princes in the Rhine valley. After this came the question of the Schism, the return of Gregory XI to Rome, the election at Rome of the Italian Urban VI, and at Fondi of the Frenchman Robert of Geneva, Clement VII. As Clement could not establish himself at Rome he returned to Avignon, and the royal diplomacy was henceforward entirely engrossed in obtaining his recognition in France and in Europe. So with regard to England the only idea was peace. Conference followed conference. Charles shewed himself conciliatory, and offered to give back

Quercy, Périgord, Rouergue, and Saintonge as far as the Charente, with a large indemnity, and also to give his daughter in marriage to the young King of England. A fresh English expedition, led by the Earl of Buckingham, through Picardy and Champagne and as far as Brittany, yielded no result; while the attacks of the French fleet at the mouth of the Thames caused more fear than harm. Further, the King of France also tried to come to terms with the Duke of Brittany. From all this a genuine peace might have resulted, when suddenly Charles V was stricken with a mortal illness. Gregory XI, Don Henry of Castile, his queen Jeanne of Bourbon, a daughter, and finally du Guesclin, had all predeceased him. Now he himself passed away, fully conscious to the end, grave and devout, on 16 September 1380.

With Edward III and his son, and with Charles V, the first part of the Hundred Years' War came to an end. Long and bitter though it was, and interspersed with disasters and terrible crises for France and unheard-of successes for England, outwardly it made no change at all. Of their ephemeral conquests the English only kept Calais, Cherbourg, and Brest, and their possessions in Aquitaine were hardly more extensive than in 1336; England was no stronger, no more prosperous because of it. France was certainly covered with ruins and was still infested by armed bands. But the Valois had triumphed over rivals and over traitors: Charles V was more firmly established on his throne than any of his predecessors; the monarchical government was more strongly organised; Brittany had not been separated from France; and a Valois was Duke and Count of Burgundy, and was soon to become Count of Flanders. And, in particular, there was one consequence, not yet visible but of capital importance; for in the struggle national sentiment in the two kingdoms had already become definitely self-conscious.

CHAPTER XIII

FRANCE: ARMAGNACS AND BURGUNDIANS (1380–1422)

THE last twenty years of the fourteenth century and the opening years of the fifteenth provided for France, if not a rest, at least a respite between the two great crises of the Hundred Years' War. But if this period was one of inaction as far as the English war was concerned, it was full of incident for France: popular disturbances, political strife and adventure, the dissipation and luxury of the court life and the king losing his reason therein, the strife of the princes resulting in the gradual disruption of the kingdom. And finally, from 1415 onwards, civil war brought back foreign war again, and with it the direst disasters. Such was, from its opening to its close, the long reign of Charles VI.

Charles was a boy of twelve, of amiable disposition and gracious bearing, but unstable and weak-willed; and anyhow, by reason of his age alone, incapable of governing by himself. Around him there was no lack of princes ready to monopolise power: his four uncles—the Dukes of Anjou, Berry, Burgundy, his father's brothers, and the Duke of Bourbon, his mother's brother. Charles V with his usual foresight had ingeniously provided for the division between them of the government and the guardianship in case of regency, but his dispositions were not respected. There arose at once in the minds of the princes the desire, almost openly avowed, to do away with everything that might recall or continue the previous régime. The Provost of Paris, Hugues Aubriot, was sacrificed to the hatred of the University and was thrown into prison; the chancellor, Pierre d'Orgemont, had to go into retirement. It was at once decided that Charles VI should reign without a regency, and should be crowned as soon as possible. It was only until the day of his coronation that the Duke of Anjou held the title of regent, but this sufficed for him to appropriate a large part of the treasure left by Charles V. The coronation took place at Rheims on 4 November 1380, and at it were revealed in full the jealousies of the princes. On returning to Paris, the administration of Languedoc was entrusted to the Duke of Berry; thus South France was handed over to a pleasure-loving spendthrift. Olivier de Clisson, a great Breton noble, was made Constable. As Charles VI was in fact incapable of directing the affairs of the kingdom, the chief power was put into the hands of a Council of Twelve, presided over by the Duke of Anjou; but in less than a year he had gone off to seek adventure in Italy, and it was the Duke of Burgundy whose influence dominated in the Council.

This government of the princes had a critical situation to face. The people were everywhere in a state of unrest; they refused to bear any longer the burden of the taxes laid upon them to support the war and the pomp of king and princes. Formerly the taxes had been temporary; now they had been continuously imposed for more than ten years. Since 1378 disturbances had begun in Languedoc, where the Duke of Anjou, as royal governor, had shewn himself both harsh and rapacious. The distress was so great that Charles V, not satisfied merely with multiplying exemptions and remissions, had for the time at any rate abolished the hearth-tax. This act of mercy was to create nothing but difficulties; for what the people wanted was, not merely the abolition of the hearth-tax, but of all the taxes. In October and November 1380 there were outbreaks of violence at Compiègne, Saint-Quentin, and Paris. The States General had been summoned to provide a substitute for the hearth-tax, and assembled on 14 November. Alarmed by fresh popular demonstrations at Paris, the royal Council suppressed everything—hearth-tax, aids, salt-tax. The people of Paris in their joy rushed to pillage the shops of the Jews, with shouts of "Noël, Noël!" The royal government, however, was at its wits' end, and proceeded at once to summon numerous local and general assemblies in order to raise money; it was only able to obtain the grant of a meagre subsidy, and this was definitely allocated to the provision of the army and was administered by the States.

The agitation was not confined to France. Since 1379 it had been manifest in Flanders also, where the count was always in need of money. In consequence of a new tax, Ghent revolted; Bruges, on the other hand, remained faithful. Once more appeared the "white hood" of the days of Artevelde. Gradually the revolt spread, and became at last a kind of civil war. But it was in England that the gravest happenings took place. The Peasants' Revolt had economic and social causes behind it, which will be described elsewhere. The immediate cause was the levy of a new poll-tax; within a few days, at the beginning of June 1381, a formidable insurrection broke out, starting in Kent and Essex, and the rebels got possession of London, which was the scene of pillage and massacre.

Examples like this only added fuel to the agitation at Paris and in France generally. In February 1382, on the occasion of a repetition of the aid granted in the previous year, a rising, "La Harelle," broke out in Rouen and lasted for three days. There were disturbances also at Amiens, Saint-Quentin, Rheims, and Laon. A new tax was also the cause of the outbreak of insurrection at Paris which started on 1 March, when the people armed themselves with the leaden mallets stored in the town-hall by Hugues Aubriot, and were known in consequence as *Maillotins*. Jews and tax-farmers were hunted down; houses were pillaged. The king was at Saint-Denis, and the princes attempted negotiations; but the people continued their violence and opened the prisons of the Châtelet. Meanwhile the wealthy and more moderate party among the citizens intervened, with Jean des Marès at their head, an aged and popular attorney who could recall the days of Étienne Marcel; and the University followed suit. The taxes were again abolished; but the ringleaders were arrested and for the most part put to death, amid the angry mutterings of the populace, who had expected a pardon. Executions also took place at Rouen, and the king went there in person to abolish the commune; yet another riot broke out in the town because of a tax granted by the States of Normandy. The king then returned to Paris, on 1 June 1382; he had obtained a considerable sum of money, but dared not re-impose the aids. At the same time there were similar disturbances in the South, where the arrival of the Duke of Berry provoked a riot at Béziers. A new hearth-tax caused a storm of protest, and Carcassonne, which had shut its gates against the duke, had its territory ravaged. Elsewhere the poor in the towns and in the open country united in bands and devastated the countryside; these "Tuchins," as they were called, had systematically to be hunted down.

The solution of this state of disorder was to be found in Flanders. Ghent maintained an obstinate resistance to the count, who had his headquarters at Bruges. The distress at Ghent was great, and the people, worked upon by skilful suggestion, turned to James van Artevelde's son Philip, who accepted the post of captain-general. Philip was harsh and autocratic like his father. He instituted a régime of terror, putting to death all who resisted or opposed him, demanding money from the rich, keeping the town under severe and gloomy restraint; everyone had to resume work. Negotiations with the count having failed, Artevelde, faced by the alternatives of victory or death, led an expedition against Bruges. An attack by the count in the open country was repulsed, and Bruges was taken, the count making his escape with great difficulty. All Flanders joined in the revolt, which spread as far as Liège.

The Count of Flanders had a natural resource in his son-in-law and heir, Philip the Bold, Duke of Burgundy, who induced Charles VI, in spite of opposition in the Council, to intervene. The proposal was a tempting one for a young man who delighted in action. Besides, the Flemings were wholly on the side of the Pope of Rome, and so, from the royal point of view, schismatics; and again, a blow aimed at them would indirectly strike all the malcontents in the kingdom. Not until 18 November 1382 was the royal army, 40,000 strong, ready to start; and already the weather conditions had become atrocious. The crossing of the Lys was effected by surprise. Artevelde entrenched himself on a small hill at Roosebeke. On 27 November the Flemings in close formation attacked "like a maddened wild boar." But the French knights, closing in upon them on both sides, smothered and overpowered them, with no more pity "than if they had been dogs."[1] 25,000 Flemings perished, and Artevelde was among the dead. Bruges at once submitted to the count, the king, and the Pope of Avignon. Charles VI did not make an entry into the town, nor did he attack Ghent. The count was not anxious for the French to remain longer in Flanders, and it was the depth of winter. So the royal army returned to France.

[1] Froissart, *Chroniques*, ed. Reynaud, xi, p. 55.

The king came back with the prestige of victory, and his government could without fear proceed to punishment. Further, Paris had been on the point of revolt during the campaign; Charles' return was like the entry of a conqueror. Several hundred citizens, those who had interposed as mediators as well as those who had taken part in the riots, were arrested. All intervention was fruitless: every day "they cut off heads, three or four at a time"[1]; thus died, with a proud courage, Jean des Marès. All the aids were re-established and with no limit of time. The gates of the town were thrown down. The office of Provost of the Merchants was abolished, and its jurisdiction given to the royal provost. There was to be no more organisation by wards, no more masters elected by the mysteries, no more assemblies of crafts or confraternities; even the University had to bend the knee. At Rouen, fresh penalties were imposed. Everywhere enormous fines aggravated the loss of privileges and threw commerce into confusion. Languedoc had to pay 800,000 francs, and this completed its ruin. In England, the Peasants' Revolt had been more quickly repressed; but it had been done by process of law and with the exercise of moderation.

Peace came about at last in Flanders, where Artevelde, like his father, had turned to England. But the moment was unfavourable, and it was not until 1383, after the Flemish defeat and Artevelde's death, that English intervention arrived, and then in peculiar circumstances. It took the form of a crusade, led by the Bishop of Norwich, in the name and at the expense of the Roman Pope, Urban VI. The most curious fact was that this Urbanist crusade operated from Dunkirk to Ypres in a country firmly Urbanist. It came to a halt in front of Ypres, on the approach of a French army led by the king himself. Both camps were full of priests and monks. The bishop prudently beat a retreat and went back to England. The French also retired, and a truce was signed between France and England. For the attention of the Duke of Burgundy was absorbed by a matter of grave moment, since the Count of Flanders died at the beginning of 1384. Philip the Bold, who through his wife was the count's heir, displayed himself from town to town and entered into possession of the county; he refrained, moreover, from handing over the three towns of Lille, Douai, and Orchies, whose restitution had been promised to Charles V at the time of the Burgundian-Flemish match. There remained Ghent, which had received a tardy succour from the English. Thanks to this reinforcement, the Captain of Ghent, Ackerman, was able to seize Damme, the port and mart of Bruges. At this moment great preparations were being made in France for a descent upon England. They were all diverted to Damme, which the king himself came to capture. But the ravages of the French led to a general desire for peace. Ghent could no longer hold out against its new master, and Philip for his part realised that these expeditions were ruining his fair county and were likely to alienate it from him. So peace was concluded at Tournai at the end of

[1] *Le ménagier de Paris,* i, p. 138.

1385. It was not made burdensome on anyone; everything was done to wipe out former hatreds and to further the restoration of industry and commerce. But it was too late, and indeed the government of the Dukes of Burgundy was to put an end to the municipal constitutions. Flanders never completely recovered from a generation of disturbance and political anarchy.

For nearly twenty years, from 1385 to 1404, the history of the kingdom of France loses its unity of sequence and coherence and becomes fragmentary. Until 1388 the Duke of Burgundy was the real head of the royal government, and, setting the example of selfish policy to be regularly pursued by the house of Burgundy, he primarily directed it to serve his own interests. But in 1388 Charles VI, at a solemn council at Rheims after his return from an expedition to Germany, influenced undoubtedly by his young brother Louis, Duke of Touraine, after expressing his thanks to his uncles announced his intention of governing henceforward by himself. Actually it was the old counsellors of Charles V—Bureau de la Rivière, Jean le Mercier, Jean de Montagu (the "Marmousets," as they were called)—backed by the Constable Clisson and above all by the king's young brother, Louis of Touraine, who held all the power in their hands. A general reform was ordered; the Parlement, the Chambre des Comptes, the Council were all purged. Excellent ordinances, inspired by those of Charles V, effected the reorganisation of the administration. The members of the Parlement and the judicial officials were henceforward to be chosen in the Council or the Parlement itself. The office of Provost of the Merchants was detached from that of the royal provost and was put in the charge of an advocate of sound sense and upright character, Jean Jouvenel. Further, the king went himself to Languedoc to reform the abuses and extortion of the Duke of Berry's administration; the principal financial agent of the duke, Bétizac, was condemned and executed under the curious pretext of heresy.

This painstaking government of the "Marmousets" was brought to sudden disaster by a catastrophe that occurred in 1392. The king had run through a surfeit of pleasures and excesses of every kind. In the spring he was seized with "a fever and a burning sickness." At this juncture, an old quarrel between the Duke of Brittany and the Constable Clisson flared up again; for, in spite of the concord established between them from time to time, there had been no change of heart. In June, Duke John IV tried to get Clisson assassinated by a knight of high birth but blemished reputation, Pierre de Craon. Though Clisson was only slightly wounded, the king, who was devoted to his Constable, swore to avenge him. The Duke of Brittany refused to surrender the assassin, and an expedition, led by the king himself, set out in August. On a boiling day, the king was riding through the forest of Le Mans, oppressed with the weight of his velvet doublet; suddenly a man threw himself at his horse's head, striving to turn him back. This shock was followed by another when, a few minutes later, a lance accidentally fell and clashed upon a steel helmet close to the king. Charles went at once into a fit of raging madness; only with difficulty could he be controlled. Everything was done to cure him, but in fact his case was incurable; doctors, devotions, pilgrimages, sorceries were of no avail. The madness was intermittent; but the lucid intervals each year became shorter and shorter.

The madness of the king brought about great changes in the government. At Le Mans, the evening after the king's collapse, the Dukes of Berry and Burgundy dismissed all the royal counsellors. Public opinion, scandalised by the riches lavished on these men by the two kings, was definitely hostile to them, and was further alienated by their aloofness and pride. Clisson fled; the Sire de la Rivière and Jean le Mercier were thrown into prison. In time, however, they were all released and pardoned. But most of them retired into obscurity; only Clisson recovered his place at court. The government was again in the hands of the princes; and Philip the Bold, in accord with Duke John of Berry, became all-powerful once more. The king's brother Louis, recently created Duke of Orleans, laid claim to the leading place in the Council, and this gave rise to stormy scenes. At first he could not make headway against his two powerful uncles; but by degrees, as time went on, he grew bolder and assumed more importance at court, and his resources were augmented by royal grants. He gradually adopted a more aggressive policy. When the king recovered his sanity, or when the Duke of Burgundy was in his own domains, the Duke of Orleans, with the king's partiality and affection to support him, appeared as master, and the finances and the disposal of favours were at his command. So there was constant vicissitude in the government of the kingdom.

At any rate, there was a lull in the war with England. There had, indeed, been great schemes on foot in 1386 and 1387. On the morrow of the Peasants' Revolt, England was in a disturbed condition: the absolutist tendencies of Richard II brought him into conflict with Parliament; the war with Scotland dragged on; the Duke of Lancaster used the royal resources in vain in his endeavour to conquer Castile. The Duke of Burgundy thought it a favourable moment to attempt a descent upon England, which would at once enhance his own glory and put a stop for the future to English intervention in Flanders. Enormous preparations were made on the Flemish coast in the accumulation of ships, men, and provisions, and in the actual building of a wooden town to serve as an entrenched base. But it was all to no purpose. In 1386 the Duke of Berry delayed his arrival until it was too late; the days were already "short and dull" when he reached Sluys at last in October. In 1387 the Duke of Brittany brought everything to an end by causing Clisson to be seized and imprisoned just as the Constable was about to bring the Breton fleet to join the rest of the expedition. Some fighting went on still at sea, and spread as far as Spain, where French detachments came to the support of Don Henry against the Duke of Lancaster. But, from August 1388 onwards, the practice of long truces became the rule.

These truces developed into a kind of peace. Active negotiations began in 1391, and the question of an interview between Charles VI and Richard II was mooted. The project failed in 1392, and at the conference held at Amiens the Dukes of Lancaster and York were the English representatives. But it was resumed again in a more definite form after the king's outbreak of insanity. Since his military schemes had failed, the Duke of Burgundy now wanted peace, which was necessary for the prosperity of his Flemish domain. And there were some altruistic minds who believed that peace would make possible the unity of Christendom against the infidel—against the Turks, in fact, who were conquering the Eastern Empire. Official pourparlers were opened in July 1395 for a definitive settlement and to arrange the marriage of Richard II with Charles VI's daughter Isabella, who was then a mere child. The betrothals were celebrated at Paris on 12 March 1396, and at the same time the truce was prolonged for twenty-eight years. On 27 October the two kings met between Ardres and Calais; their interview was characterised by lavish display and formal ceremony. Two months later a settlement of the question of Brittany was similarly arranged by means of a marriage of another daughter of Charles VI with the heir to the duchy; and Brest, the last English stronghold in Brittany, was restored to the King of France. It seemed that the old legacy of war had in this way been almost definitely liquidated.

The conclusion of this last peace was the occasion of an outburst of feasting and luxurious display. Before his collapse, Charles VI had been a passionate devotee of violent exercise, jousting, feats of horsemanship, dances, and all-night revels. Reckless and gay, unable to curb his desires, he set his court the example, which was eagerly followed, of frivolous and fantastic conduct. In April 1385 he went to Cambrai to attend the double wedding of the son and daughter of the Duke of Burgundy, and the festivities lasted for five days. The king and the princes lent jewels, tapestries, and plate; the dresses of the ladies were such as to bring a blush to the cheeks of ecclesiastics; Charles himself rode nine courses in the lists. There too was arranged his own marriage with Isabella of Bavaria; this was celebrated quite simply at Amiens, for the king displayed the impatience of a spoilt child. As soon as he took over the government, there was a dizzy round of pleasure. In May 1389, on the occasion of the knighting of the sons of the Duke of Anjou, four days and four nights were spent in jousting and revelry at Saint-Denis. A few days later came the marriage of the Duke of Orleans at Melun, and in August the solemn entry of the young queen into Paris, which in costumes, spectacles, jousts, banquets, and stately ceremony outdid everything that had gone before; the rejoicings lasted for five days. During the following winter, the journey of the king to Languedoc was one continuous festival, at Lyons, Avignon, Montpellier, Toulouse; solemn entries, processions, banquets, concerts, masquerades followed one another almost every day. The return journey, from Bar-sur-Seine to Paris, took the form of a wild race all the way between the king and the Duke of Orleans. In the succeeding years there was a constant succession of jousts, tournaments, dances, and nightly festivals. Even after the king's madness, this frenzied round of pleasure went on at court and among the princes. One episode in the early days of 1393 has remained famous. Some young lords organised a masquerade dressed as savages, in which the king was to take part. While this was in progress, the Duke of Orleans arrived, preceded by torch-bearers. He seized a torch so as to look closely at the savages; one of the costumes, which were made of tow and pitch, caught fire, and five lords were burned to death. The king was only saved by the presence of mind of the Duchess of Berry.

The ladies ruled the court. The queen, Isabella of Bavaria, a dark lively little woman, displayed a great zeal for pleasure and extravagance. More beautiful and more cultured was the Duchess of Orleans, Valentine Visconti, who rivalled the queen in luxury and in the pursuit of novel fashions. The head-dresses were extravagantly devised, of complicated pattern and ridiculous height and size. " The ladies, young and old," said Jouvenel des Ursins[1], "kept great and excessive state; their horns were marvellously tall and wide." The dresses were made of costly stuffs, streaked with varied colours, tricked out fantastically, and covered with gilt and jewelry and devices. As always where luxury and pleasure are the rule, morals were lax; moreover, the king and his brother had hardly any sense of decorum. Hence there were frequent intrigues and scandals, and disturbing crises at court. So it was that one day, in 1390, Valentine Visconti fell a victim to the jealousy of the queen and the calumnies that were disseminated against her, and was exiled to Blois. The natural brutality of the time was, withal, masked under a veneer of elegance and poetry. Princes and lords were as fond of witty phrases and sentimental subtleties as of boisterous pleasures; many of them practised impromptu versification and exchanged affected and intricate ballades. At the court itself was organised a *Court of Love*, where everything was debated and regulated in ballades and rondeaux. Equally did they delight in the mystery-spectacles, in minstrels' songs, jugglers' tricks, and tableaux vivants, which were given as interludes between the courses of a long banquet. And yet this society, enervated with pleasure and enjoyment, was very changeable and impressionable, hopelessly credulous and superstitious, always ready to listen to impostors and magicians, incapable of generous ideas or sturdy virtues.

Pleasant as it was, this life was not by itself sufficient to satisfy the

[1] *Histoire de Charles VI.*

princes and nobles; nor did the war with England any longer provide them with occupation. Through ambition, through desire for adventure, and in order to please the ladies, they went off continually on distant expeditions, of war or pilgrimage. Some, like the Duke of Bourbon, went to Spain to give assistance in their wars to the Kings of Castile, the allies of France. The Scots, also allies of the French King, were waging war continually with England; and to their succour went Jean de Vienne, Jacques de Heilly, and others, at the head of small bands of French knights, who found the country most uncomfortable and whose conquering airs were little to the liking of the austere Scots. Italy was full of attraction for French adventurers, Gascon and Breton, and Popes and Italian princes had always need of their services; so to Italy went Bernardon of Sens, Olivier du Guesclin, Raymond of Turenne, John III of Armagnac, Enguerrand de Coucy. But what tempted them most, and gave them most prestige in the eyes of the fair sex, was the war against the infidel. A large number of nobles were drawn to make the journey to Prussia against the still pagan Lithuanians. To the East departed regular armies of knights: in 1390 the Duke of Bourbon led 1500 knights to Barbary (Tunisia). There was a fresh crusade in 1396 led by John, son of the Duke of Burgundy, through Hungary, which ended in disaster at Nicopolis. Shortly afterwards, Boucicault, the model of a knight-adventurer, went to the help of the Eastern Emperor, ravaged the coast of Syria, and attempted a descent upon Alexandria. Others, too, went to the aid of the relics of the Latin settlements in Achaia and Cyprus, or made as simple pilgrims the dangerous journey to the Holy Places; while Jacques de Heilly even fought on the side of the Turks against the Egyptians, and Jean de Fay won distinction in the army of Tamerlane. Lastly, two French knights achieved the conquest of the Canary Islands.

It was all to the advantage of this state of affairs that the princes who usually governed on behalf of Charles VI, especially the Dukes of Anjou and Burgundy, and later the Duke of Orleans, were able to lay hands on the finances of the kingdom and to pursue a policy in their own interests; and as they had little opportunity of increasing their territorial power within the kingdom, it was to the service of their external ambitions that they applied the resources and the prestige of royal authority. In the case of the Duke of Anjou, this was of short duration. The French Pope, Clement VII, in order to obtain an ally who could restore him to Rome by force of arms ("the way of deeds," as they called it), promised him a kingdom to be carved out of Central Italy and further assured him of the succession to the old Queen Joanna, ruler of Naples and Provence. Urban VI, for his part, supported another competitor for the throne of Naples. After Joanna had been strangled in 1382, the Duke of Anjou came himself to conquer the kingdom of Naples, with the aid of the money he had extracted from the royal treasury of France. But he died, in September 1384, while still engaged in the work of conquest.

After the departure of the Duke of Anjou, Philip the Bold of Burgundy was in command. Full of energy and busy schemes, fond too of display, he had the air of a sovereign. When he was unsuccessful in his plans for a descent upon England, he did not persist in a policy that could yield no results. Henceforward, Germany attracted his attention, and at first he pursued a policy of marriage alliances. A neighbour in Alsace of the house of Austria, and in the Low Countries of a branch of the house of Bavaria, he married one of his daughters to Leopold of Austria, another to William of Bavaria, heir to Hainault, Holland, and Zeeland; and, further to consolidate this last very important marriage, his eldest son John, the heir to his domains, was wedded to the sister of William of Bavaria. Finally, he put the crown on his work by effecting the marriage of Charles VI to another princess of the house of Bavaria, Isabella, daughter of Stephen III the Fop. Nor was he content with peaceful measures alone. His aunt, the Duchess of Brabant, was at war with the Duke of Guelders. In spite of the accord between this prince and the King of France, Philip the Bold in 1388 drew Charles VI into an expedition against the duke, in defiance of the real interests of the kingdom. The expedition, which took place in the autumn, came to a halt at Gödersheim, and they had to be satisfied with a pretended submission. It was after this expedition that the king took over the power from his uncles.

When, from 1388 to 1392, the administration was in the hands of the "Marmousets," the general policy of the kingdom was inspired by the king's young brother Louis, Duke of Touraine and afterwards of Orleans. Endowed with only a meagre appanage, he too had soaring ambitions, and these Philip the Bold had allowed to have free course in Italy. In 1387 the Duke of Touraine had married Valentine, daughter of Gian Galeazzo Visconti, Duke of Milan. He thus acquired the county of Asti and an eventual claim on the duchy of Milan. But therein lay a grave danger, for Queen Isabella was the grand-daughter of Bernabò Visconti, who had been dispossessed of Milan by his nephew Gian Galeazzo; so there was a cause of permanent ill-feeling, which was soon to create hostility between the queen and the Duchess of Orleans, and to provide a centre for intrigue. In consequence of his marriage, the king's brother worked with all his might to give an objective to the energy of Charles VI by directing it towards Italy. Florence, Gian Galeazzo, and Clement VII each in turn made most tempting propositions. Clement, in particular, offered to enfeoff Louis of Touraine with a portion of the States of the Church, to be known as the kingdom of Adria. At the same time, he gave his support to Louis II of Anjou, who, renewing his father's attempt, sent Otto of Brunswick to occupy Naples, and himself entered the town in August 1390. Then a great scheme was set on foot: Charles VI was to come down into Italy, to make good the establishment of his brother in the kingdom of Adria and of Louis of Anjou in the kingdom of Naples, and finally to instal Clement VII at Rome. But the intrigues of the Dukes of Burgundy and Brittany, and pressing negotiations for peace with England, interrupted the whole design. And then came the king's first attack of insanity.

The Duke of Orleans, however, did not abandon his efforts. Clement VII seemed to have lost faith, but Gian Galeazzo partly resumed the papal project. One circumstance was in their favour. Genoa was seeking for a protector, in order to escape from the anarchy of popular government; and some of the Genoese nobles applied to the King of France. The Duke of Orleans seized the opportunity; he sent the Sire de Coucy to introduce a garrison and to fly his banner in Savona, a neighbouring town to Genoa. But the queen, the Duke of Burgundy, and Florence, the enemy of the Visconti, united in a coalition to wreck the ambition of the Duke of Orleans; and the doge himself offered the overlordship of Genoa to the King of France. Charles, under the influence of his wife and uncle, accepted. In November 1396 a French governor came to take possession of the great city; while the Duke of Orleans had to renounce his dreams and abandon Savona. The French domination of Genoa lasted until 1409.

Throughout all this political activity, among all these ambitions, these schemes, and these undertakings, were to be seen the first symptoms of a troublesome rivalry between the Duke of Burgundy and the Duke of Orleans. Louis of Orleans had too much ambition to be satisfied with an intermittent authority, liable to suffer eclipse in the presence of the Duke of Burgundy, and especially during the king's frequent fits of madness. By dint of persistence and patience he had greatly increased his domains and resources; to the duchy of Orleans had been added by royal bounty, by inheritance, or by purchase Périgord, the counties of Valois, Dreux, Blois, and Angoulême, and several places elsewhere. It must be borne in mind, however, that the most important of these territories were scattered about in the heart of the kingdom; they might be useful as a rallying-point for resistance, but not as a base for operations abroad. When in charge of the government, the king's brother employed to his own advantage a large part of the revenue derived from aids and taxes. Louis was a gracious prince, eloquent and witty; frivolous and pleasure-loving, while at the same time very devout; a lover of sports, festivals, and hunting, a connoisseur of jewelry and of sumptuous and strange attire. People criticised him for his luxury and his continual need of money; his irony intimidated them; and, finally, they watched with anxious eyes his attitude towards the situation in the Church, in Italy, and in Germany, where, in close touch with the house of Luxemburg, his policy pursued an unsteady and at times a risky course.

While Louis of Orleans at the beginning of the fifteenth century was only twenty-eight years of age, the Duke of Burgundy had almost reached his sixtieth year. To the authority of age he added that of experience, of coolness of judgment, and of semi-regal dignity. Above all, his power was to be feared: master of the two Burgundies, of the counties of Charolais and Nevers, of domains in Champagne, of Artois and the county of Rethel, and finally of Flanders, he was the greatest noble in the kingdom and a prince of the Empire. Brabant, Limburg, Hainault, and Holland were later to revert to his house. His resources were enormous, and yet for his splendour and his aims they were insufficient. He was in direct relations, dynastic, political, or economic, with England, the Bavarian houses, Lorraine, Austria, Savoy, numerous German princes, the Swiss, Florence, and other powers. He spent vast sums on pensions and gifts, on embassies and dispatch services. He could not, any more than the Duke of Orleans, dispense with the royal revenues, and he used his authority to draw huge sums from the receipt of aids. The necessity for both princes to draw from the same source was still further to heighten their rivalry.

While Philip the Bold was alive, this rivalry did not degenerate into violence or civil war. But all the circumstances of the time made it manifest and aggravated it. First of all came the question of the Great Schism. Christendom was divided between the Pope of Rome and the Pope of Avignon. Both of them, and especially the violent and obstinate Benedict XIII, the Avignon Pope, refused all means of reconciliation or of ending the schism, in spite of the passionate endeavours of the University of Paris supported by the Duke of Burgundy. Exasperated by the resistance it encountered, the University, at a great assembly held at Paris in May 1398, achieved with some difficulty the proclamation of the withdrawal of obedience from both Popes. This, they said, was the restoration of the old liberties of the Church, which was now freed from the control and exactions of the Pope and recovered its right to dispose of benefices. The only result was profoundly to disturb religious life, the more so because even in France there had not been unanimity for withdrawal. The Duke of Orleans, in particular, was unfavourable to this radical solution of the University and the Burgundian party. He did not appear at the assembly at which it was proclaimed, and only gave his adhesion to it with reluctance. As the withdrawal, far from healing the evil, only made it worse, Benedict XIII would not give way and suffered siege at Avignon. Soon a strong opposition was revealed, against the withdrawal and in favour of Benedict. The Duke of Orleans put himself at the head of it; he made himself the champion of the persecuted Pope, helped in his rescue, visited him at Avignon, obtained the most splendid promises from him, and finally, in May 1403, effected the restoration to him of the obedience of the Church of France. Benedict XIII, however, kept none of his promises.

In England and Germany there were violent changes of government, the effect of which was felt even in France. Richard II had become quite unpopular at his court and with the people at large, and in the course of a few weeks (July–September 1399) he was dethroned by his cousin Henry of Lancaster and then mysteriously disappeared. Henry IV, in order to make good the succession, at once encouraged the anti-French sentiments which were then widespread in England. At the same time, there was a profound feeling of indignation at the French court; Louis of Orleans, who had given a warm welcome to the Duke of Lancaster during his exile in France, was now one of the most bitter against him. No open change took place in the relations between the two kingdoms so long as negotiations were in progress for the return of the little queen, Isabella of France. But after she had been handed over to the Duke of Burgundy, the situation became strained and war threatened once more. The Duke of Burgundy pursued a peaceful policy: he caused the twenty-eight years' truce to be renewed, cleverly got into his hands the guardian-ship of the children of the late Duke of Brittany, in order to prevent fresh English attempts in that quarter, and by special conventions safe-guarded Flanders in the event of a renewal of hostilities. But the Duke of Orleans adopted a provocative attitude: he posed as the avenger of Richard II, offered to Henry IV practically to fight a duel, and sent him a formal challenge in 1403.

Germany was no less disturbed at the beginning of the century; the house of Luxemburg, which held the imperial throne, was in a dangerous position. Wenceslas, aloof in his Bohemian forests and addicted solely to hunting and drinking, had endangered, and even himself directly dimi-nished, imperial rights in Italy and on the French frontier. He was closely associated with the Duke of Orleans, whose ambition gave rise to alarm; and he was suspected in Germany of wishing to support the French Pope. The threat of deposition did not move him. Then, in August 1400, the Diet declared him deposed, and Rupert of Bavaria, Elector Palatine, was elected King of the Romans. Wenceslas did not yield to this decision; there were accordingly two Emperors in the Empire, as there were two Popes in the Church. Both turned their eyes to France: Rupert counted on the queen and the Duke of Burgundy, Wenceslas on the Duke of Orleans. This troubled situation and the difficulties of the house of Luxemburg provided scope for the new ambitions of the king's brother. As he had been obliged to give up Italy, he turned his energies towards Germany: he acquired at an enormous price the domains of the heiress of the Sires de Coucy; he bought the homage of the Duke of Guelders; he got Wenceslas to recognise him as governor of the duchy of Luxemburg. By virtue of La Fère, Chauny, and the county of Porcien, which he already possessed, and of his new acquisitions of Coucy and Luxemburg, his possessions were now thrust in as a wedge between the two great groups of Burgundian territories and into the Empire itself. It was said that Louis had visions of the imperial dignity. Burgundian policy sought to rouse Germany against him, and at the end of 1402 the Diet took steps to check this invasion.

To these conflicts of policy was added domestic strife. In the spring of 1401 there was a regular plot hatched at court by the queen and the Dukes of Berry and Burgundy against the Duke of Orleans. Towards the end of the year warlike preparations were being made by both sides. In April 1402, during the absence of Philip the Bold, the Duke of Orleans got himself made controller of the aids and gave orders for the raising of a heavy tax. The Duke of Burgundy returned and protested at once against this levy, declaring that he had refused 100,000 crowns offered to him as the price of his assent to it, and thus won great popularity for himself. The king, for the sake of peace, made them joint controllers of the aids, but was soon obliged owing to their maladministration to revoke the appointment. Such were the circumstances, with crisis looming on every side, when Philip the Bold, the founder of Burgundian greatness, died in April 1404. He was buried with great pomp at the Chartreuse at Dijon, where, to perpetuate his glory, Claux Sluter was already at work upon his tomb.

When John the Fearless succeeded Philip the Bold, the situation developed into tragedy. The new duke, Louis' senior by a bare year, was small in stature, with no grace or majesty, and deficient in eloquence. He possessed both intelligence and curiosity, and could be brave when need be; but he had a restless ambition, a distrustful and cunning nature, and little continuity of purpose. In 1396, to make him known to Christendom and especially in the Empire, his father had him put at the head of a crusade against the Turks. John was not able to avoid the fearful disaster of Nicopolis, and for several months was a prisoner among the Turks.

While the new Duke of Burgundy was entering into possession of his states, the Duke of Orleans was supreme in the government. The queen had now come over to his side, Valentine Visconti still remaining in exile. The intimacy of the queen with the king's brother, their zest for pleasure, the luxury and licence which they paraded at court, all tended to alienate opinion from them. The finances were in disorder; the coinage was debased; and a new tallage was ordered. Then the Duke of Burgundy appeared; he had given out that the new aid would not hold good in his territories, and he arrived in arms. The queen and Orleans took to flight. John at once became master of Paris; he denounced the bad government and talked of reforms. At the end of two months, however, there was a hollow reconciliation between the two princes. Actually at this time hostilities had recommenced between France and England; piracy at sea had already begun, and French knights had gone to join the Welsh. The Duke of Orleans, full of self-confidence, wished to make his mark in the war, and John the Fearless would not play second fiddle. In the autumn of 1406 Louis was conducting a regular campaign in Guienne, and John threatened Calais, at a respectful distance; each accused the other of having spoiled his undertaking. Certainly the hatred between them was growing at a great rate, in spite of touching scenes of reconciliation.

CH. XIII.

In the evening of 23 November 1407, the Duke of Orleans was returning from a visit to the queen. As he was riding along on his mule in the rue Barbette humming a tune, he was attacked by a band of armed men, who disappeared leaving him dead upon the ground. He was given a solemn funeral, at which all the princes were in tears. The investigations of the provost of Paris soon arrived at the truth. John the Fearless, feeling that discovery was near, confessed to the Duke of Berry and the King of Naples (the Duke of Anjou) that "through suggestion of the devil" he had caused this deed to be done. The princes requested him not to appear again in the Council, and he took horse and galloped off to Artois. This assassination not only removed from the scene a prince who, in spite of his youthful levity and the somewhat vain character of his ambition, might with his mental qualities have rendered great services to the kingdom in times of crisis, for he was a true Frenchman; it also created mortal hatreds, and for more than thirty years it delivered up France to civil war at the very time that war with the foreigner was starting afresh.

For three years there were remarkable fluctuations before the struggle properly broke out. Charles, the new Duke of Orleans, was only fourteen years of age. His mother, Valentine Visconti, in vain laboured for the punishment of the murder; the king and the princes were profuse in promises to her, but the Duke of Burgundy was too formidable. He reappeared in Paris at the end of February 1408, and was greeted quite courteously by the princes. Already, at Amiens, they had come to terms with him, and on 8 March he was able at a solemn sitting to have a justification of his crime pronounced by the Norman theologian, Jean Petit, who developed at length and in scholastic terms the most specious arguments for the duke and the most odious charges against his victim; no one spoke in opposition. Six months later, when John the Fearless had been recalled to the north by a revolt at Liège, Valentine Visconti reappeared at Paris, and, at an assembly no less solemn and before the same princes, an eloquent reply to Jean Petit was delivered by the Abbot of Cérisy. But, though severe measures were announced and a great deal of noise was made, nothing was done; the disconsolate widow died in disillusionment at the very time that John the Fearless, victorious at Liège, was returning to Paris, to be received as before with honour. The Orleans party twice had to agree to reconciliations of a rather humiliating nature, at Chartres in March 1409 and Bicêtre in November 1410.

From that time the kingdom seemed torn between the Burgundians and the supporters of Orleans, or Armagnacs as they were called. As his second wife the Duke of Orleans married the daughter of Bernard VII, Count of Armagnac, who brought to his son-in-law the formidable Gascon contingents; hence the name Armagnacs. The Duke of Orleans soon had on his side the princes, Berry, Bourbon, and Brittany; his chief support came from the west and centre of the kingdom, from a part of Languedoc, and from Gascony. John the Fearless was supported by his brothers, the Duke of Brabant and the Count of Nevers, by the leading nobles of Artois and Picardy, by the Flemings, and by German princes and nobles; he could count too on the people of Paris and the chief towns of the north, and on the University of Paris. In spite of these popular sympathies, it could not be said that the Burgundian party was the more democratic and the Armagnac the more aristocratic; the popular sympathies of John the Fearless were only a matter of policy. But the Armagnac party had fewer foreign elements in it and was less swayed by foreign interests. Between the contending parties the enmity was from the beginning profound. On all sides bands of armed men made their appearance. At Paris, the excommunications hurled by Urban VI against the Grand Companies were published from the pulpits against the Armagnacs. Mansions and castles were pillaged, and murders were of frequent occurrence; "they had no more pity in killing men than if they were dogs."[1] In other towns most violent measures were adopted. Both parties had their badges, and the very statues in the churches were decorated with them. But, what was much more serious, each party called in the English to its aid: first of all John made mysterious proposals and in 1411 actually received English reinforcements in Paris; then it was the turn of the Armagnac princes, who in 1412 promised Henry IV the whole of the ancient Aquitaine and arranged a meeting with an English army at Blois.

Civil war began in earnest in 1411. In July the Duke of Orleans sent an insulting challenge to the Duke of Burgundy; the battle took place in the autumn outside Paris, and the Armagnacs were with difficulty repulsed by the Burgundians and English. In May 1412 the Duke of Burgundy took the king and the dauphin with the Oriflamme to besiege the Duke of Berry at Bourges. After a fruitless siege and an informal congress of princes at Auxerre, a peace of a kind was patched up; while the Duke of Orleans had to pay the English, though they arrived too late, a high price to depart. All these troubles had brought great disorder into the machinery of government, especially finance and justice. The princes, to satisfy their personal ambitions and quarrels, had laid hands on the resources of the kingdom and had multiplied the taxes. The leading officials, who in most cases were their retainers, had no security of tenure, and so built up as quickly as possible fortunes that were a scandal; the staff of the Chambre des Comptes and the finance ministers set the example. In the Parlement all the old traditions were forgotten, and a few families divided a large number of posts among themselves. The court was still as frivolous and extravagant as ever, and the queen had constant need of money for her luxury and her pleasures, and in order to enrich her household. The poor sick king was usually neglected, and was left in a pitiful condition by his greedy and indifferent attendants. The people became restless and agitated in this state of disorder. Especially

[1] *Journal d'un bourgeois de Paris* (ed. Tuetey), p. 10.

at Paris, the populace was liable to rapid change of mood; it was at the same time both suspicious and childishly credulous. There was much murmuring, and, after 1407, the town was in a condition of unrest and disturbance. This was especially the case with the butchers of Sainte-Geneviève and the Markets, who were joined by the tripe-dealers, the skinners, and the tanners. They took command of the streets, which they were able to barricade with strong chains. Everybody went about armed. The office of Provost of the Merchants and the *échevins* were revived again in their old form, and the wards regained their individual organisation. Finally, the Duke of Burgundy took this discontented and turbulent element under his protection; he had a regular following of citizens, butchers, and skinners. He gave them presents and salaries, and above all left them a free hand. A powerful Burgundian coalition was soon in command of Paris.

Attention had already been called to the danger. The Augustinian Jacques Legrand, in a vehement address to the court, and Jean Gerson, in moving sermons, had in the presence of the princes denounced the disorders of the court and the distress of the realm, and had demanded a reform of government and morals. In 1409 there was an attempt in that direction; but it only resulted in the execution of one of the richest royal officials, Jean de Montagu, and the spoils fell to the princes. At the end of 1412 a more favourable opportunity presented itself. With the prospect of an English invasion, as the royal treasury was empty, it was found necessary to assemble the States General; it would have been too dangerous to impose new aids and taxes without their concurrence, as had been done for the past thirty years. The meeting was not numerously attended, but it spoke its mind clearly. A Burgundian abbot, in the name of the ecclesiastical province of Lyons, delivered a violent diatribe against the royal officials, denouncing them and demanding their punishment. After a colourless speech on their behalf, the University and the town of Paris presented a long list of grievances, in which all the abuses were stated and the culprits mentioned by name; they demanded the reduction of the number of offices, the deposition of the existing officials and the confiscation of their property, and a general reform of the administration of the kingdom; in this way the necessary money could be found. Most of the officials of justice and finance were in fact suspended, and a great commission of reform was immediately set to work.

As the task was a long one and no result seemed forthcoming, rioting broke out in Paris. All sorts of reasons were adduced: the gifts to Lewis of Bavaria, the queen's brother, the fêtes given by the dauphin, the return of suspended officials who were feared and detested by the people of Paris. The first rioting started on 27 April 1413; its leader was the skinner Caboche, who has given his name to this period of disorder. The crowd besieged the Bastille, which capitulated the next day. Then the dauphin's residence was invaded, and a hunt was set on foot against the nobles and officials who were the objects of popular distrust; they were caught and shut up in the Châtelet and the Louvre. The Duke of Burgundy, adopting a non-committal attitude, took no steps to prevent all this. The rioting was renewed on the following days. On 22 May it was the royal palace that was invaded; the king had recovered his sanity, and the people wished to explain to him what had happened. Then the crowd again proceeded to hunt down suspects and to get hold of them; among its hostages were fifteen ladies of the court. The tardy and embarrassed intervention of John the Fearless was quite ineffective.

It was then decided to publish the work of the commission of reform. The so-called "Ordonnance Cabochienne" was read solemnly before the king in the Parlement on 26 and 27 May; the reading lasted for three lengthy sittings. It was in fact a long and detailed reform in 258 articles of the whole of the royal administration, a vast compilation from previous ordinances. But the whole was elaborately framed and provided with safeguards. The political administration was to be directed by the Council, the judicial by the Parlement, the financial by the Chambre des Comptes; in them everything was to be deliberated, decided, and controlled. And even in the local administration the most important business was to be deliberated by councils of officials and notables. All offices were to be conferred as the result of election in the Council, the Parlement, or the Chambre des Comptes; so too the local officials were to be elected by the local councils, which were to comprise the seneschals and bailiffs. The conception, remarkable at a time of rioting and civil strife, was of a monarchy tempered by royal officials and by a species of local self-government.

But the moment was not suitable for reform of this kind. On the day after the promulgation of the "Ordonnance Cabochienne," rioting began again. The butchers had got out of control, and nothing could stop them; there were more imprisonments and executions, and scenes of brutality even in the dauphin's mansion. The princes of the Armagnac party, gathered round the Dukes of Orleans and Berry at a distance from Paris, had collected their forces and were returning full of threats. Conferences were held at Vernon between the princes of both parties, and an agreement was arrived at: there was to be a general amnesty, the disbanding of troops, and the suppression of the revolutionary government which had dominated the court. The leading citizens of Paris, led by Jean Jouvenel, put themselves at the head of the movement of reaction, and made themselves responsible for the enforcement of the peace which was concluded at Pontoise on 28 July. The people were weary of disturbances which had lasted for over three months; on 2 and 4 August they ranged themselves definitely on the side of the moderates, and the dauphin, escorted by the populace, went to release the prisoners. The Cabochien leaders fled in all directions. Soon, however, the movement passed from reaction to violence. The frightened Parisians seemed all to have become Armagnacs, and the party badge was openly displayed. The Duke of Orleans and the Armagnac princes made a solemn re-entry into Paris; the official personnel was restored; and on 8 September, at a solemn bed of justice at the Parlement, the "Ordonnance Cabochienne" was torn up. Prosecutions, imprisonments, banishments, and executions became the order of the day.

The Duke of Burgundy had been speedily left in the lurch by this swift and general reaction. Abandoning his partisans, he had first tried to carry off the king, and then had suddenly departed to Lille. In February 1414 he reappeared before Paris, accompanied by a strong escort of armed men; the town made no move, and he had to retire. The Armagnac princes caused him to be banned and declared a rebel, and a great expedition with the Oriflamme was organised against him. This meant the open renewal of civil war. But the campaign, directed against Compiègne, was of no importance; negotiations were opened, and peace was concluded at Arras in February 1415. There were a few upheavals at Paris; and then all disturbance seemed to die away.

Just at the time that these troubles began in Paris, the King of England, Henry IV, was dying. His chief anxiety had been to make good his dynasty on the throne; he suffered besides from ill-health, and so he had shewn no enthusiasm for war with France. His son Henry V, now twenty-seven years of age, was austere, self-important, and of unlimited ambition. He wished for his own advantage to bring to life again the claims of Edward III to the crown of France, to renew the victories of the previous century, and, if God would grant his aid, to revive the crusade. Circumstances were in his favour, for no agreements could definitely extinguish the embers of civil war in France. Since the end of 1413 it was easy for Henry to obtain the alliance of the Duke of Burgundy; and this was actually done in May and again in August, by the conventions of Leicester and Ypres. Henry and John were to be associated in war against the Armagnacs; as regards the king and the dauphin, the Duke of Burgundy was to maintain neutrality, but he was to receive his share of the royal domain and, in the event of the English King achieving the conquest, to do liege homage to him. At the same time he assured Charles VI that he was under no engagement to the English. Henry was very much emboldened by this pact; in August 1414 he claimed the kingdom of France from Charles VI and demanded the hand of Catherine of France. A great French embassy, composed of 600 persons, actually came to Henry V at Winchester and solemnly offered him the king's daughter in marriage together with a large dowry and some land in Aquitaine. But the King of England shewed himself entirely unreasonable in his demands; sharp words were exchanged which made a breach inevitable; and Henry told the ambassadors to go, and that he would soon be after them.

These negotiations were in fact a sham, for the invasion of France had been in course of preparation for several months. A fleet, an army, and full provisionment were all ready. On 13 August 1415 Henry cast anchor near the mouth of the Seine, at Cap de la Hève, and his army, his artillery, and his siege-engines were drawn up on the plateau of Sainte-Adresse. Harfleur was immediately besieged; there were no ships in the harbour and only a few hundred soldiers in the town. No help could be brought, and Harfleur had to capitulate on 22 September. The King of England made his entry with many signs of pious devotion; a careful inventory was made of the booty; and the English took in hand the permanent occupation of the town, to be a second Calais for them. Henry proclaimed that he had come "into his own land, his own country, his own kingdom." Then as winter was approaching, he departed for Calais, crossing the Somme at Nesle; and it was only on his arrival in the plains of Picardy that he at last found himself face to face with a French army.

Henry V had appeared in France in the middle of August, but it was not until October that the French army assembled at Rouen. It was mainly composed of nobles and knights, who would not associate with townsfolk and seemed to have learnt nothing since Crécy and Poitiers. As for John the Fearless, he was treacherously negotiating with both kings. In pompous language he offered his services to the government of Charles VI; they thought that he was aiming at getting the chief power into his hands, and declined his offer. He immediately ordered the nobles on his territories in Picardy and Artois to hold aloof. In spite of this defection, an army of 50,000 faced Henry's 13,000 English on 24 October 1415 at Agincourt. The Duke of Berry in vain counselled against fighting. The French position was a bad one; it had rained all night, and the men-at-arms had remained on horseback in the ploughed fields until daybreak. In order to fight they had to dismount, and the weight of their armour was enormous. They were drawn up in three battles, huddled together in ranks thirty or forty deep in the slippery mud. The English had passed the night in silence and prayer; they formed up in a long line of little depth. The action commenced, at the late hour of eleven, with heavy and well-directed volleys from the English archers. Shaken already by these volleys, the serried mass of French knights were anxious to attack, but only the front ranks could do any fighting. The English then attacked this helpless human wedge with cold steel, "and it seemed as though they were striking blows upon an anvil." It was merely massacre and rout, and all was over by four o'clock. The English were encumbered with prisoners, and put many of them to death. On the French side, 7000 men-at-arms were killed or mortally wounded, among them the Duke of Brabant and the Count of Nevers, who had not been willing to follow the example of their brother, the Duke of Burgundy; and the Duke of Orleans was taken prisoner. The English lost only 500 men. Henry V, who believed himself to be chosen of God, went at once to Calais, and from there to England.

The kingdom's worst days now began. The king was in a wretched state, almost continuously insane; the queen, obese and gouty, was as frivolous as ever, and she was exiled to Tours as the result of scandalous happenings in her palace. Two dauphins died, the first in December 1415, the second in April 1417; Charles, the next in succession, was only thirteen years of age. The actual master of the king's government was the Duke of Orleans' father-in-law, the Constable Bernard of Armagnac, a fearless and stubborn Gascon, who surrounded himself with bands of Gascons. By them the suburbs of Paris were ravaged, and within the city there was a virtual reign of terror. All the prisons were full of suspects; in three weeks, during the summer of 1417, 800 persons were banished; and a period of famine set in. No serious military operations were attempted against the English; negotiations were undertaken, but with no success. In May 1416 the Emperor Sigismund came to Paris on the question of the Schism. He proved to be exceedingly parsimonious, and boorish in manner; but, as he was going on to England, he was counted on for his mediation. Sigismund was won over by the magnificent reception accorded him by Henry V, and was dominated by the conqueror's personality. Henry proposed a truce for three years only; he refused to give up Harfleur; and he claimed the restoration of the territories ceded by the Treaty of Calais. Finally, the Emperor made an alliance with Henry, saying: "My relatives are in France, but my friends in England." On the top of this, John the Fearless, who had approached Paris during the winter of 1415–16 to make good his position there but had gained nothing in spite of promises and threats, came to a closer understanding with Henry V: the Burgundian domains benefited by a special truce, and the duke's subjects were forbidden to take up arms on behalf of the King of France. During a whole week, in October 1416, the King of England and the Duke of Burgundy were in conference at Calais. It is possible that John made more serious engagements still, and that he promised Henry V to recognise him as King of France and to recommence hostilities in concert with him. Anyhow, in August 1417 Henry landed with an army at Trouville, and John the Fearless marched on Paris.

Henry's intention was to make a systematic conquest, and he commenced with Lower Normandy. He kept his troops under strict discipline, shewing particular respect for the personnel and property of the Church; as a result, the great abbeys of Caen opened their gates to the English. The town of Caen attempted resistance, but in vain. Henry started there the introduction of an English administration, after 25,000 persons had been forced to migrate. Bayeux, Argentan, Alençon, and Falaise capitulated. Everywhere an English government was introduced with rigid particularity. All who would not submit were banished in set form; but, since security had taken the place of disorder, submission was the general practice. The neighbouring princes, the Duke of Brittany and the Duchess of Anjou, sought special truces for themselves. By the spring of 1418 the conquest of Lower Normandy had been achieved; the English were established at Évreux and Avranches, and only Cherbourg and Mont Saint-Michel still held out. In June Henry advanced into Upper Normandy, and on 29 July 1418 he encamped in front of Rouen with 45,000 men.

Meanwhile, the Duke of Burgundy had been equally fortunate. He came with his army in the guise of a liberator, promising the suppression of all the taxes. Arrived in front of Paris, he fetched the queen from her exile at Tours and established her, in the capacity of regent, at Troyes. The moment was a propitious one: at Paris people had grown weary of the tyranny of the Armagnacs, and refused to continue the payment of taxes. There was a dearth of everything, and the wildest stories were abroad. Negotiations undertaken by two cardinals in May 1418 gave rise to hopes; it was thought that peace was certain, but the Constable of Armagnac dashed all these hopes to the ground. Then, during the night of 20–21 May, an ironmonger, Perrinet Leclerc, opened the Saint-Germain gate to a Burgundian captain, the Sire de l'Isle Adam, and 800 men-at-arms. At once the old sympathies awoke. Everyone wore the Burgundian cross and shouted "Peace! peace! Burgundy!" The crowd went to fetch the king and brought him on horseback through the streets. The Duke of Burgundy should have intervened to maintain order, but he had gone off to hunt in his duchy; so Paris was delivered over to extreme disorder. On 12 June bands of wild men, led once more by butchers and especially by the hangman Capeluche, went to seek out the prisoners and put them to death with every refinement of cruelty; there were 1600 victims, and even women were murdered without pity. At last the Duke of Burgundy decided to put in an appearance. He arrived with the queen on 14 July 1418, and compelled a reorganisation of the government including a complete change of personnel, both in finance and justice. But John the Fearless was no longer master of Paris. On 20 and 21 August rioting began again, more violent and more savage than before; there were fresh massacres, as horrible as the preceding ones. This brought things to a head. As soon as the disturbances had quietened down somewhat, Capeluche was made prisoner and executed forthwith, and several other leaders of bands suffered the same fate; all violence was forbidden. In addition to all this, Paris was decimated by a severe epidemic. Many other towns gave in their submission, and the greater part of the South adhered to the Burgundian cause. In return, on 1 October the aids were abolished.

While Paris was opening its gates to the Burgundians, Rouen was resisting the English with all its might. In its industry and commerce this town was almost the equal of Paris, and, now that refugees had flocked into it from the whole of Normandy, its population had risen to more than 300,000. It was defended by a circuit of substantial walls; the captain, a Burgundian, had 5500 soldiers under him; and, thanks to the strenuous activity of Alain Blanchart and to assistance from refugees and from Paris, the town could put into the field a militia amounting to nearly 20,000 men; finally, the walls were furnished with a powerful artillery of about a hundred cannon. Sorties from the town were frequent. Accordingly the English completely invested it; English ships were posted on the Seine both above and below the town, and the river was barred with iron chains. From the beginning of August to the end of December the Norman capital held out. During this time it might have received assistance, but the Duke of Burgundy, "slower than ever at his business," did not budge. An old priest was sent from Rouen and in the king's presence he "raised the great *haro* of the Normans"; but nothing was done in response to this call for help except to hold useless negotiations through the medium of a cardinal. In November, John the Fearless did make a start, bringing with him the king preceded by the Oriflamme, but he got no farther than Pontoise and Beauvais. At Rouen the misery and famine became extreme. Henry V refused to allow 12,000 women, children, and old men to pass through the lines, and they had to live during the month of December in the ditches on refuse and grass. Every attempt at a sally came to nothing, and a last appeal to the Duke of Burgundy elicited the reply that " they should treat for the best terms they could get." Negotiations for surrender were difficult; the people of Rouen were too haughty in their language and would not surrender at discretion. At last Henry V, whose interest it was to conquer without destroying, gave way on 13 January 1419: the town had to pay a ransom of 300,000 crowns, hand over nine hostages, and recognise itself as subject to the King of England. On 20 January Henry made his solemn entry, and went to the cathedral to give thanks to God. One man was made the scapegoat, Alain Blanchart; he was hanged. The town was not, however, at an end of its sufferings: a severe epidemic broke out; and the payment of the ransom was only completed in 1430. English government was organised there at once. At last the conquest of the whole of Normandy was achieved, though it was not until the end of 1419 that Château Gaillard capitulated; after that Mont Saint-Michel alone remained French.

Meanwhile, one centre of resistance was being formed within the kingdom. After the entry of the Burgundians into Paris, a Breton noble, Tanguy Duchastel, had carried off the Dauphin Charles and made his escape with him. The dauphin, then sixteen years of age, became the real head of the Armagnac party. Further, in 1417, the king had appointed him lieutenant-governor of the kingdom with full powers. The authority of the dauphin was recognised between the Loire and the central plateau, as far as Lyons and the Dauphiné; besides this, the Armagnacs held numerous points north of the Loire and even north of Paris. In virtue of his powers, the dauphin organised a regular government, with a Council, though not a very adequate one, attached to his person, a Parlement at Poitiers, and a Chambre des Comptes at Bourges; local governors and lieutenants administered the districts that remained loyal, and provincial estates voted him subsidies. Finally, in October 1418, he proclaimed himself regent.

But neither the dauphin nor the Duke of Burgundy was disposed to fight. Hence incessant negotiations, which seemed as if they must have a result, but which were always brought to nought at the last moment by John's lack of decision or by his excessive demands. Peace was almost concluded between the dauphin and the Duke of Burgundy in September 1418 at Saint-Maur. Then John turned again to the English, without, however, breaking off negotiations with the dauphin. To Henry V he offered the fulfilment of the Treaty of Calais, the acquisition of Normandy, and the hand of Catherine of France; these were terms that could not be refused, but an interview between the queen, the Duke of Burgundy, and the King of England near Mantes had no result except to leave everything in suspense. This failure brought John back to the dauphin again. On two occasions in July 1419 the two princes met, first at Pouilly, then at Corbeil. At the second interview they swore friendship, exchanged the kiss of peace, and bound themselves to unite for the expulsion of the English; peace seemed to be well and truly made. At this point the English captured Mantes, Meulan, Pontoise, and threatened Paris. The Duke of Burgundy with his troops turned tail, and removed the king to Troyes. Meanwhile, it had been settled that he should hold a third interview with the dauphin at Montereau to complete their accord. Still he hesitated, and adopted all manner of subterfuges; the dauphin's party began to be suspicious of him. The appointed day passed by; at last, on 10 September, at five o'clock in the evening, they met on the bridge at Montereau each accompanied by a few followers. The conversation, however, became bitter, and violent words were exchanged. Then the dauphin retired; but some of his companions threw themselves upon John the Fearless and pierced him through several times with their swords. This murder, which was certainly unpremeditated, upset everything and revived all the old hatreds. In the light of the circumstances, it appears more excusable than that of the Duke of Orleans; but it was to have still more melancholy results.

There was an immediate outburst of anger from the Burgundians, the people of Paris, and the University. The only talk was of vengeance, and the English were declared to be preferable to the Armagnacs. The new duke, Philip, in spite of his youth—he was only twenty-three—was of a discreet nature though proud. After assembling his family and his chief partisans, he decided to make "treaty and alliance" with the King of England, and to pursue vengeance with all his might. Negotiations began at once, and at Christmas the alliance with England against the dauphin was concluded. Then a treaty was prepared at Troyes between the King of England and the King of France. Henry V himself arrived there in May 1420. His marriage with Catherine of France was at once settled and arranged, and on 21 May the Treaty of Troyes was signed. Charles VI declared that Henry V had become his son; he and the queen disowned their son Charles, "the so-called dauphin." The King of England was recognised as heir to the King of France; and even in Charles VI's lifetime he was to retain Normandy and the rest of his conquests, and to share the government with the Duke of Burgundy. This meant the annexation of France by England. Moreover, to speak ill of the treaty was forbidden and was made an act of treason.

On 2 June Henry V married Catherine, and the next day was off on campaign once more. Sens, Montereau, and Melun (which held out for four months) were captured. Before that, he had been careful to garrison Vincennes, the Bastille, and the Louvre with his own men. On 1 December he made his entry into Paris with Charles VI, and received a magnificent reception from clergy and people, in spite of the famine which was still very severe. The States General and the University swore to observe the treaty. Henry held great state at the Louvre, while Charles VI lived wretchedly at Saint-Paul; Paris had become "a second London." Soon afterwards, the King of England returned to his own country.

All, however, was not settled by the Treaty of Troyes. There was always the dauphin to be considered, and he seemed to be making sensible progress. He had traversed Languedoc, which had abandoned the Burgundian cause to rally round him, and in May 1421 his troops won a real success at Beaugé; the Duke of Brittany also came over to his side; and he himself went to besiege Chartres. Immediately, in June 1421, Henry reappeared; in two campaigns he made a complete sweep of the neighbourhood of Paris, and recaptured several places. The dauphin beat a retreat, and seemed to have abandoned the cause. But, at the end of the spring of 1422, Henry fell dangerously ill. He returned to Vincennes, and had just time to give his last instructions: he impressed on his brother and his uncle the importance of the alliance with Burgundy; he begged them never to make peace without at least ensuring the retention of Normandy; above all he was concerned to arrange the regency for his son, who was only ten months old. Then he rendered up his soul to God most devoutly on 31 August. He was a great king, for he had a strong will and was a relentless administrator of justice. At the same time Charles VI lay dying too. His end, which came on 21 October, was a pitiful one; around him he had only a few officials and servants of the palace. One prince alone accompanied his body to Saint-Denis, the Duke of Bedford, brother of Henry V and regent for Henry VI. Under the vaulted roof of the old French abbey rang the cry of the King-of-Arms: "God grant long life to Henry, by the grace of God King of France and England, our sovereign lord."

Such was the result of forty years of fruitless changes and disorder in the government, of rival ambitions and royal insanity, of princely intrigues and mortal hatreds. But this result was too unnatural, too violent a break with the past, too contrary to the feelings to which the war itself had given rise. It could not endure.

CHAPTER XIV

ENGLAND: EDWARD I AND EDWARD II

"The tomb had not even been closed when we all who were there present, with a multitude of your lieges, took an oath of fealty to yourself as lord and king, and did all that was fitting for your lordship and honour, as far as was possible in your absence."

When Edward, son of Henry III, read these words in the letter, sealed by sixteen of the greatest English magnates, which brought to him at Trapani in Sicily the news of his father's death, they must have surprised and gratified him. This was the first time that full legal recognition had been given to an heir before coronation, and Edward may have seen in the confidence thus displayed the reward for those long, patient, difficult years of youth and manhood in which he had done his full duty as a son to a father whose defects in some directions were as conspicuous as his merits in others, and yet had shewn a spirit of reasonableness, an appreciation of other people's position, a readiness to profit by experience, which had won him golden opinions. It was not all loss that Edward had had to live through a civil war, had added to the normal round of a king's son experiences so unusual as confinement as a hostage and appointment as a sheriff, and had watched men and theories at a time when feeling and expression were at their most intense. He himself had for years been facing problems of his own, for from early youth he had been ruler of wide lands, not in England only, but in the Channel Islands, Ireland, and Wales, and above all in Gascony, where conditions were peculiarly difficult. His latest adventure had been on traditional lines, for the call to kingship reached him when on his way home from crusade. The double note, of conservatism and experiment, which was to sound throughout his reign, seemed already struck before he began it.

It was not till 19 August 1274 that Edward was crowned, and various matters, notably the need to do homage to Philip of France for his lands overseas and to establish order within them, kept him abroad till a few weeks before that date. When he did return, he was given a great welcome. The populace liked his kingly looks, his straight back and tall stature; the ring of great magnates, lay and clerical, found him congenial and sufficiently conventional; while those who had had business to do with him knew that he had qualities rarer among monarchs of his age, a power of application and an appreciation of the expert.

For the first twenty years of his reign Edward was in the main occupied with works of peace, with the exception of the war in Wales. He had not been in England more than three months, and his friend Robert Burnell had been chancellor for only three weeks, when an important step was taken. Commissioners armed with a list of some forty questions sought from juries in every county answers which filled the bulky documents which came to be called the Hundred Rolls. Many of these questions aimed at an exact definition of royal possessions—the number of the king's domain manors, the value of the farms of hundreds and cities, and so on. Others concerned encroachments on royal rights. What lands and tenements have been given or sold to religious or others, to the king's prejudice? What liberties "hinder common justice and subvert the royal power"? Others, again, searched into the carelessness or cheating of officials, "even servants of the king himself"—sheriffs who "for prayer, price, or favour" concealed felonies or neglected their duties, escheators too harsh or too complacent in consideration of a bribe, jacks-in-office of all sorts who made themselves a nuisance to others or put public money to private uses.

Now such questions were not very novel. Some of them had been gradually accumulating, from Henry II's time on, in the lists which itinerant justices took with them when they went on a general eyre. Others had precedents in special inquests or reforming legislation such as that due to the crises of Henry III's reign. What was unprecedented was the persistence which Edward shewed in attacking these problems, and the lasting body of law he built up in his effort to find remedies. Masterful but not tyrannical, his general policy was to respect all rights and overthrow all usurpations.

A long list of great statutes[1] stands to Edward's credit. From his first parliament, in April 1275, there emerged the First Statute of Westminster. Many of its chapters dealt with the administrative abuses revealed by the recent commission, which had completed its work about a month before parliament met. Edward's mistrust of the "franchises" which formed exceptions to administrative uniformity was shewn in the ninth chapter, which threatened the lords of these with confiscation if they or their bailiffs were negligent in the pursuit of offenders against the king's peace. In 1278 the Statute of Gloucester went farther, ordering that the justices when next on eyre should enquire by writs of *quo warranto*, a process already in use in Henry III's time, into the grounds upon which the magnates claimed such franchises. "We must find out what is ours, and is due to us, and others what is theirs, and due to them." Edward's aim, it is clear, was from the first not abolition but definition. Chartered

---

[1] This term, familiar from long usage, may be used for convenience, but it must be remembered that Edward's laws bore no title at the time, that their diplomatic form was very varied, and that contemporary literary custom applied the term statute to all sorts of public instruments, including papal bulls. Contemporary lawyers often spoke of each chapter within the document as itself a statute, as does the unknown author of "Rishanger's" chronicle from 1272 onwards, who wrote at some date after 1327: "statuta quae Westmonasterii secunda dicuntur," etc.

privileges remained untouched, prescriptive right was accepted as warranty if it ran far enough back, the date being fixed in 1190 at the coronation of Richard I, and even unwarranted liberties were generally restored and secured by charter if an adequate fine was offered[1]. The main usefulness of the enquiry was to remind the great feudalist that he had duties as well as rights, the more so if the possession of a franchise transferred to his agents work which would normally have been done by royal officers. In 1285 the Statute of Winchester attacked local disorder. "Robberies, homicides, and murders grow daily more numerous than they used to be," said its preamble, and therefore stringent penalties were laid down for any persons concealing felons, the towns were ordered to shut their gates at night and keep watch on strangers, while every man, armed in proportion to his means, was to be ready to help when needed in pursuing offenders. In the same year was issued the Second Statute of Westminster, usually known as *De Donis Conditionalibus*. This was intended to protect the donors of "tenements which are often given away on some condition," and did so by restraining the right of the donee to alienate. The interpretation of the statute at first was difficult, but by Edward II's reign it was already considered that the donee's heirs, as well as himself, were bound. Fees tail, or strictly limited estates, became common, and every capital lord, especially the king as the greatest of such, had something to gain from the increased chances of reversion opened by the limitation imposed. Another measure to the common interest of all landowners was the Third Statute of Westminster, or *Quia Emptores*, issued in 1290. This dealt with land held not upon condition but in fee simple, and while it preserved the right of alienation for all who held such estates, it stipulated that in future the buyer must hold his purchase from the lord of the seller by the same services and customs as were attached to it before the sale. It thus prevented "prejudice to magnates and others" caused by changes in the services due from their vassals, but was most of all to the king's advantage because it increased the number of tenants who held in chief direct from himself, and by stereotyping feudal relations robbed them of some of their vitality.

Enacted law of the sort just analysed was only one of many means used by Edward in the pursuit of his ideal of efficiency. Side by side with it must be put his personal contact with his subjects by that incessant travelling for which he was praised in the *Commendatio Lamentabilis*; his encouragement of groups outside the central feudal ring, such as the burghers of towns which he founded or favoured, and the lesser magnates of the type who had helped him to secure the Provisions of Westminster; and above all his reliance upon expert professional help instead of upon the amateurish assistance of great feudalists staggering under the weight

[1] Recent work among the eyre rolls and other legal records has much modified the views of historians on this question. For a summary see Miss H. M. Cam's revision in *History*, xi, pp. 143–8.

of their own dignity. By Edward's time, the days were coming to an end when a member of the king's court, in close attendance on the king's person, could be a governmental man-of-all-work. Three great engines of administration were in action. One was the Exchequer, the board of finance which stored in its treasury revenue received, and, more important still, checked and superintended the accounts of the official world. This board had "gone out of court" into offices of its own at Westminster as early as the reign of Henry II, when master and disciple held the famous Dialogue concerning the Exchequer in "an oriel window close to the river Thames." Less separate as yet, but no longer always in the king's company, was the Chancery, a general secretariat which wrote and drafted innumerable royal charters, writs, and letters, authenticated them by the king's great seal, and kept in a series of rolls registers of their contents. Finally, there was the Wardrobe, the staff of clerks attached to the ever-moving royal household, who combined financial and secretarial functions, and might include in their purview anything and everything from a pennyworth of pepper bought by the king's cook up to a continental war.

Now during Edward's reign there was little friction between these departments, and few signs that outside critics thought any one of them less suitable than any other for dealing with matters of public importance. "The whole state and realm of England were the appurtenances of the king's household," and as the king was neither weak nor wicked no harm came of that. Experience gained in one office qualified for promotion in another. A typical civil servant of the time was Edward's first chancellor, Robert Burnell, Bishop of Bath and Wells—a man of easy morals, careless of his episcopal duties, but an industrious chief minister for eighteen years (1274–92). An Exchequer official, Walter Langton the treasurer (1295–1307), succeeded to the first place in Edward's confidence, and resembled Burnell both in his preparation for office by long service in the royal household and in his view of his bishopric rather as a reward for his administrative skill than as an ecclesiastical obligation. The Wardrobe trained many capable men, among them the clerk John of Benstead, who became the keeper of Edward's personal or privy seal.

Edward's standard of efficiency, however, was too high for some of his servants, and when in 1289 he returned from a stay of three years abroad, he found that there had been a breakdown in every rank of official life, from the pettiest bailiffs up to great justices and heads of departments. Instantly he proceeded to enquiry and punishment. An anonymous contemporary satirist was able to make a good mock Scriptural story of the scandal.[1] "The king...said to his servants, 'Go through the land and walk round about it, and hear the voice of my people which is in Egypt. For the comfortless troubles' sake of the needy, and because of the deep sighing of the poor, I will up, I will render vengeance to mine enemies,

[1] *The Passion of the Judges*, printed by T. F. Tout and the present writer as an appendix to *State Trials in the Reign of Edward I* (Royal Historical Society), 1906.

and will reward them that hate me.'" Some guilty consciences had already
taken alarm. "The king...entered into a ship, and passed over, and came
into his own land. Now the children of Israel were walking on dry land
by the sea; and some of them adored with gifts, but some doubted."
Thomas of Weyland, chief justice of common pleas, a "Didymus who
was not with them when the lord came," fled "to the fount of Babylon,
and was there in garments of sheepskin for fear of the judges." In other
words, he took refuge in Babwell, a house of friars minor, called to mind
that long ago, before he was married, he had been a subdeacon, and put
on the friars' habit, only to be starved out ignominiously. The peccant
Exchequer official, Adam of Stratton, once before disgraced, now met a
second retribution. "The king...entered his paradise that he might seek
the man he had created, and said, 'Adam, Adam, where art thou?...Render
an account of thy stewardship.' Adam answered, 'I cannot dig, to beg I
am ashamed.' And when he was accused of many things he answered not
a word. But at length came two false witnesses and said, 'This fellow
said, "I am able to destroy your house in three days, and never to build
it up again." He spake and it was done, he commanded and it was undone.' Then said the ruler unto him, 'Hearest thou not how many things
they witness against thee?' And he answered him never a word, but went
out and wept bitterly." The satirist represents it as Edward's chief
anxiety to "gather up the fragments that remain, that nothing be lost,"
and it is true that, since the supply of trained lawyers and men of business
was not unlimited, Edward was content in many cases with the exaction
of enormous fines, reinstating the culprit not very long afterwards. The
lesson, perhaps, would none the less linger in their memories with salutary
effects.

Secular matters were far from being Edward's only preoccupation during
these first twenty years. He had to make up his mind about his relation
to the Church, a problem which confronted every king of the ages of faith,
but which was acute for him because his father had allowed the Church
to assume undue political influence. Edward, with a livelier sense than
Henry of what was due to Caesar, was equally anxious to pay his dues to
God. Circumstances, however, forced him on more than one occasion into
an attitude of protest.

One almost inevitable source of friction was the question of the appointment of bishops. Ecclesiastical preferment was so natural a reward
for good service, and a great bishop so important a factor in politics,
that even the most high-minded of kings and Popes were tempted to
ignore the injunction of the canons that a bishop should be elected by
the free choice of his cathedral chapter, to bring influence to bear on
the electors, to utilise every chance of interference given by their disagreements or mistakes, and sometimes to over-ride their choice. During
these years several elections were annulled to make room for papal nominees, while twice in succession Popes rejected the choice made by the

chapter of Canterbury, and gave England two Mendicant Archbishops of their own nomination—Robert Kilwardby the Dominican (1272–78) and John Pecham the Franciscan (1278–92). Edward accepted both with what Pecham himself called "benignity," and forbore in Pecham's case to take advantage of the fact that the clerk who wrote to announce the appointment had forgotten to ask him to restore the temporalities of the see. He protested, however, against this "assumption of the power of providing" to Canterbury. "It seems to the king and his council that in this respect there may be prejudice to himself and to the Church of which he is the patron and defender, especially if the example is followed with regard to other churches in England." His disapproval was sharpened by personal disappointment, since the Canterbury chapter in 1278 had selected his minister Robert Burnell, whom neither persuasion nor threats could induce them to choose at the previous vacancy. In 1282 the Winchester chapter was similarly obliging, but again in vain.

No bold advance of ecclesiastical claims seems to have been made during Kilwardby's primacy, and it may have been for that reason that in 1278 he was removed by the most courteous method possible, being promoted to a cardinalate and thus recalled to Rome. His successor Pecham, however, netted himself round with activities of every possible kind, made many enemies, and left written records of his work so abundant that they have not yet been fully explored. When they are fully examined, it is likely that we shall have to revise our traditional conception of Pecham as the fussy prelate without a sense of proportion, and do more justice to the courage, high principle, and zeal with which he pursued his ends.

Pecham's first provincial council was held at Reading within six weeks of his arrival in England (July 1279), and from it issued a large body of constitutions. The archbishop was mainly concerned with purely spiritual matters, though the abuse which angered him most, pluralities, touched politics closely, since kings were accustomed to use benefices, in such numbers as might be convenient, to supplement the salaries due to their servants. Edward, however, seems to have made no protest over this, but took alarm at a section entitled "Concerning the public announcement of sentences of excommunication," which distinguished eleven categories of persons liable to such sentences. The first group comprised all who "maliciously deprived the Church of her right" by getting royal writs of prohibition to stop cases in progress in ecclesiastical courts, while the last included all who violated Magna Carta. "We order," said Pecham, "that a copy of the charter of the lord king with regard to the liberties of the Church and kingdom granted by him, well and clearly written, shall be publicly posted in every cathedral and collegiate church, in a place where it can be seen by all who enter, and that at the end of a year, on the vigil of Easter or Pentecost, it shall be renewed, the old one being removed and replaced by another, well and freshly written." To this Edward objected strongly, and when parliament met in the autumn,

Pecham had to appear in person, declare "annulled and as though never issued" the clause about writs of prohibition, withdraw three other articles, and remove the copies of the charter from the churches. The king supplemented this protest by a counter-offensive in the shape of the Statute of Mortmain. Twenty years before, one of the Provisions of Westminster had forbidden religious persons, in the technical sense of those who had taken monastic vows, to acquire fiefs without the licence of the chief lord. This, said the new statute, had been disregarded. In future, every buyer and seller of land, whether a religious or not, must have licence before alienating it in such a way that it would fall "into mortmain," that is to say, into the dead hand of a corporation whose grip would not be relaxed by the changes and chances of this mortal life. The clergy declared indignantly that this violated the opening promise of Magna Carta that "the English Church shall be free, and have her rights entire and her liberties uninjured." The king's answer was that all the statute had done was to compel men to seek a licence, which would not be withheld unreasonably. A glance through the Chancery enrolments of the next few years, indeed, shews plainly how little the pious founder was hampered by the new law.

Archbishop Pecham had swallowed, but not digested, the rebuke of 1279, and when in 1281 he summoned another provincial council, this time to Lambeth, Edward suspected that there would be fresh trouble. Accordingly, before the council met, he issued writs to all its members, forbidding them " to hold counsel concerning matters which appertain to our crown or touch our person, our state, or the state of our council," reminding them that they were bound by oath to defend the rights of king and kingdom, and warning them to do nothing to the prejudice of either on pain of losing their temporalities. It has been generally assumed, as the contemporary historian Thomas Wykes assumed, though he ought to have known better, that hereupon " the archbishop in terror entirely withdrew from his presumption." Quite the contrary. Pecham reinserted, in the legislation at Lambeth, almost verbatim, the eleven articles of Reading; prefaced them with an even more explicit assertion of ecclesiastical liberty; and ended, though without renewing the order for the publication of the charter, with instructions to the archdeacons to see that their clergy kept their flocks well informed as to the significance of the eleven clauses, including, of course, the article directed against violators of the charter.

A month later, Pecham followed this up by a remarkable letter to the king. "By no human constitution," he wrote, "not even by an oath, can we be bound to ignore laws which rest undoubtedly on divine authority." He went on to trace the "bitter dissension" which had often prevailed between clerics and kings, quoted Constantine, Canute, Edward the Confessor, and William I as examples of good conduct, and ascribed the beginning of oppression to Henry I and Henry II. "We are driven by conscience to write these things to you, most excellent lord, as we wish to answer at the dreadful day of judgment. We humbly pray you, incline your ear to our exhortations, for you are bound by oath to root out all evil customs from your realm." "A fine letter," commented an admiring clerk when he copied it out into Pecham's register. Taken in conjunction with the Council of Lambeth's defiance, however, it might well have provoked a crisis comparable in magnitude with the Becket controversy. Actually, Edward seems to have quietly accepted or ignored the *fait accompli*. Royal writs of prohibition, however, continued to be freely issued, the sheriff's officers kept a jealous eye upon the proceedings in Church courts, and many of the provisions of the Second Statute of Westminster (1285) provoked loud criticism in clerical circles. In 1286 Edward went some distance in concession, for the writ *Circumspecte agatis* issued in that year[1] to itinerant justices in Norfolk, where protest had been particularly vehement, recognised as within the purview of the ecclesiastical courts not only cases concerned with wills and marriages, but also cases of defamation, of spiritual correction, of violence done to clerks, and of disputes about certain tithes. Yet this was the grant of only part of the Church's whole demand, and the dispute outlived both Pecham and Edward.

Very soon Edward's attention was distracted from internal affairs to other matters. The Welsh war and its results occupied him from 1282 to 1285; delicate points about the Scottish succession were under discussion long before Alexander III's death in 1286, and no long pause was possible in their consideration till John Balliol had been chosen king in 1292; and continental problems became so pressing that in 1286 Edward went abroad and did not come back to England for three years. Wales and Scotland are dealt with elsewhere in this volume, but foreign policy must now be considered.

When Edward I became King of England, the throne of France was occupied by his cousin Philip III (1270-85) and the official relations of the two countries rested on the Treaty of Paris of 1259, which had been intended to put an end to the uncertainties due to King John's losses in northern France, but which in fact inaugurated a new set of problems. The situation as Edward confronted it on his accession was this. As "a peer of France with the title of Duke of Aquitaine," he owed liege homage to each successive French king. He was in possession already of the main block of southern lands to which the treaty entitled him, namely "Bordeaux, Bayonne, Gascony, and the islands," but he had not secured the promised cession of the French king's rights in the three dioceses of Limoges, Cahors, and Périgueux, nor had the "privileged" vassals in those districts been bribed or persuaded to transfer their

---

[1] Not in 1285, as traditionally stated. In 1928 Mr E. B. Graves in an important article on the date and contents of this writ (EHR. XLIII, pp. 1-20) solved conclusively several problems which had long puzzled historians.

allegiance from France to England. Further, though in 1271 Alphonse of Poitiers' lands had escheated to the French Crown on his death without heirs, Philip had not handed over those portions, notably the Agenais and Saintonge south of the Charente, which were in such an event to go to England because Alphonse had acquired them through his wife Joan, a great-grand-daughter of Henry II of England. Edward's double duty, then, was to fulfil his obligations and exact his rights, and he expressed this neatly in the formula he used when he duly did homage at Paris in 1273: "My lord king, I do you homage for all the lands that I ought to hold of you." Though some chroniclers thought at the time that this referred to the lost northern lands, expansions of the same phrase used later seem definitely to connect it with the treaty. "I become your man for the lands which I hold of you on this side of the sea," said Edward to Philip IV in 1286, "according to the form of the peace which was made between our ancestors." A formula proposed for the homage that was never done by Edward II to Louis X combined this with the earlier wording: "I become your man for the lands which I hold and ought to hold on this side of the sea according to the form of the peace made between our ancestors."[1]

For some time relations remained amicable. In 1279, by the Treaty of Amiens, Philip agreed to hand over the Agenais, and did so, while making promises, which, however, remained unfulfilled, to enquire as to certain other English claims. On the same day he also recognised the succession of Edward's queen, Eleanor of Castile, who had inherited from her mother the county of Ponthieu, a little fief all sand, salt-marsh, and forest, round the estuary of the Somme. Again in the same year, Edward was chosen to mediate, in a conference to be held at Bayonne, between the Kings of Castile and France. This friendly attitude might well have continued had not French politics become entangled in the struggle between the Papacy and the Hohenstaufen. Philip III's uncle Charles, Count of Anjou and now, thanks to the Pope, established on the dismembered Hohenstaufen lands as King of Sicily, began to gain increasing ascendancy over his nephew, with the result that a breach gradually widened between France and England. Charles won the alliance of the King of the Romans, Rudolf of Habsburg, who thereupon threw over a project, much cherished by the English King, of a marriage between his son and Edward's daughter. Little spurts of temper revealed Philip's waning cordiality. He objected to Gascon charters being dated "regnante Edwardo rege Anglie," instead of "regnante Philippo rege Francie," though he consented as a compromise to the cumbrous formula "regnante Philippo rege Francie, Edwardo rege Anglie tenente ducatum Aquitanie." Cumulative friction might even have brought about war, had not French attention been diverted when in 1282 the Sicilians suddenly drove out the Angevins and offered their throne to Peter III, King of Aragon. Pope Martin IV then declared Peter's

---

[1] *Ancient Correspondence*, xxxvii, p. 74.

own throne forfeit, and offered it to Philip's second son Charles, afterwards Count of Valois. In the struggle which followed to recover Sicily and conquer Aragon Philip fought, lost, and died alone, for both Charles of Anjou and the Pope predeceased him.

By 1285, therefore, the outlook for England seemed brighter. It was a great thing to have the influence of Charles of Anjou removed, and the new French King, Philip IV, seemed ready to be friendly. Edward did homage to him in June 1286, and in August concluded a treaty at Paris, by which France at last resigned Saintonge south of the Charente. Also, Philip welcomed Edward's efforts, not very successful, to bring the Anjou-Aragon contest to a peaceful end. It was therefore without much fear of French interference that Edward now applied himself to the internal problems of his duchy of Aquitaine, which occupied him till 1289.

Neither Ponthieu, with its strong French traditions, nor Guienne, with the proverbial Gascon pride, fed, as a seventeenth-century author would have it, by their diet of "garlic, onions, radishes, and the headiest of wines," were easy lands to rule. In the South, great nobles, fortifying themselves in their castles, terrorised the countryside, defied royal orders, plunged light-heartedly into anybody's quarrel. The king-duke's natural allies against such touchy lordlings would be found in the towns, whether the great ports of Bordeaux and Bayonne or the little walled settlements up the river-valleys. Most of these lived by the wine trade, most had therefore reason to value the English market, and all had an interest in maintaining peace as against war. Edward tried to encourage urban life both by a conciliatory policy to existing, and often exacting, towns, and by foundations of those artificial, privileged towns which in the South were known as *bastides*. All up and down the lands once English, there sleep in the sun to this day quiet villages, with their gates and walls, their arcaded central square, their straight streets, which are the remnants of such *bastides*. One, which Edward founded in the outskirts of Bordeaux during his long stay, was to keep green by its name of Bath the memory of his friend Burnell and Burnell's English see. Edward carried to Gascony, too, his love of orderliness, trying to stimulate his officials as well as to insist on the obedience of his subjects. When domestic affairs recalled him to England, he had done much, but not enough to secure a peaceful future. By 1292 France felt that the time was ripe for fresh measures against a king-duke whose very presence within her borders, quite apart from his personal merits or defects, offended her pride.

New perplexities, therefore, opened with Edward's twenty-first regnal year, and in meeting them he could no longer shew his former resilience and vitality. "Never was that king sad at heart," wrote a contemporary, "save on the death of those dear to him." But by this time Edward had often had cause for such sorrow. Three little sons had died, though in a fourth, his namesake, he now had a sturdy heir. The wife, whose gracious comradeship had meant so much to him, lay in Westminster Abbey, and not twelve months after her death Edward lost his mother also. Burnell died in October 1292, while two months later the death of Pecham removed an equally familiar, if less congenial, figure. This series of losses combined with external circumstances to make the years 1290 to 1292 a real dividing point in the reign. Alone, Edward had to turn to breast a sea of troubles.

Mutual irritation between France and England was now rapidly increasing. However little the details of the tale-telling on both sides can be trusted, there was certainly abundant excuse at any moment for either country to take offence. Disputes at sea or in the ports often developed *de verbis ad verbera*, and while peace still nominally reigned, in 1293 a great fight took place off Saint-Mahé (Saint-Matthieu) near Brest, between Norman and Gascon sailors and their respective supporters. In the autumn Philip summoned Edward to appear in January 1294, to answer before the Parlement of Paris for his subjects' misdeeds. Edward did not go in person, but tried to arrive at an understanding through his brother Edmund, Earl of Lancaster, who was thought likely to be congenial because he was the step-father of the French queen and had for years shared with her mother the rule of the county of Champagne. The subsequent negotiations delayed but did not avert the outbreak of war, for though the English agreed to make a formal temporary surrender of six Gascon castles, in recognition of Philip's rights as overlord, the Parlement of Paris declared Edward contumacious and his duchy forfeit. Whether Philip had or had not intended this from the first, at any rate he now approached the execution of the court's sentence with the advantage that he was already in possession of the strongest places in Gascony.

The war which now began lasted in theory till 1303, but there was no fighting after October 1297, and even before that date there were lengthy intervals of truce or inactivity. Edward himself was long detained in England, and derived little good from expeditions dispatched to Gascony. For five years the French could not be dislodged from Bordeaux, and English occupations of towns higher up the Garonne, such as Rions (1294), Langon and Saint-Macaire (1297), proved to be only temporary. Bayonne opened its gates in the very first campaign, but little progress was made from this base, and in 1297 the English suffered a considerable defeat not far away, near Bonnegarde. Systematic efforts were made to organise English shipping, yet the French were active in the Channel and once raided Dover. In 1297 Edward, who had allied himself with the Count of Flanders and some of his neighbours, went over in person to lead an attack on France from the north, but found his allies quarrelsome and the enemy strong, and was glad to make a truce within two months. Philip, however, was busied with troubles of his own, and could not press his advantage. Successive truces culminated in the Treaty of Montreuil (1299), by which Edward was to marry Margaret, Philip's sister, while his heir Edward was to be betrothed to Isabella, Philip's daughter. These marriage connexions, intended to increase cordiality, were practically the only satisfaction Edward got out of the war, which ended officially in 1303, when another Treaty of Paris restored the *status quo ante*. On domestic affairs the effect of the war was all to the bad, for it was an irritant, an expense, and a distraction, and it was used by English malcontents as a weapon of offence.

Edward had begun by explaining the whole ground of quarrel to a parliament of magnates at London in June 1294. "He sought their advice and their help," says the chronicler Hemingburgh, "and he swore that, had he no better following than one boy and one horse, he would pursue his right even to death and avenge his injuries; but they all with one accord answered him and said that they would follow him to life or death." Liberal aids were promised, the feudal army was to meet at Portsmouth on 1 September, available ships were organised into three groups under three leaders, envoys were sent abroad to make alliances with Adolf of Nassau, King of the Romans, and others, and criminals were offered pardons if they would serve in Gascony. But the war fever began to cool as the seriousness of the task in hand became clearer. Officials went round to take inventories of the treasures and coin of the religious houses, commandeering what they found for the use of the king whenever he should signify his need of it. The sheriffs were ordered to seize all wool, wool-fells, and leather—England's great exports—even within liberties, and to permit merchants to regain their property only upon the payment of a customs duty of 40s. on the sack instead of the half mark (6s. 8d.) which had been granted by Edward's first parliament in 1275. Indignant public opinion, which at the time had recognised a novelty in the custom of 1275, now began to label it, in contrast, the "ancient" custom, while the fresh demand was a "maletolt" hard to endure. In September came the turn of the clergy, who were ordered to contribute one-half of their revenues. "This they granted liberally and graciously," say the royal letters patent, but as a matter of fact the demand excited great indignation, and the dean of St Paul's, trying to voice his colleagues' protests in the king's own terrifying presence, fell down in a fit and died. In November, with the consent of a parliament to which county members were summoned as well as the magnates, and after consultation of the towns by royal officials, a tax was granted on the personal property of all persons whose moveables amounted in value to ten shillings or over, at the rate of one-tenth in the counties and one-sixth in the cities and boroughs. This grant was the fourth and highest of its sort made during the reign. As the collection of the taxes proceeded, feeling became sourer, and was further embittered as bad news came from abroad, French invasion seemed likely, and alarmist rumour mingled with disloyal talk.

One hindrance after another came in Edward's way. At Michaelmas 1294 he was called away from Portsmouth, with the bulk of the forces assembled there, to put down revolts in Wales. When these were suppressed, by July 1295, he returned to find that Scotland had made an alliance with France, cemented by the betrothal of Edward Balliol, heir to the throne, to the daughter of that Charles of Valois whose invasion of Gascony in the spring had been so disastrous for the English. Edward took this as a disloyal action, and summoned King John to account for his conduct at Berwick in 1296. On his refusal to appear, war began, and though in five months' campaigning Edward reduced Scotland, deposed John, and annexed his kingdom, the position could not be maintained, and for the rest of the reign war with Scotland was generally either smouldering or flaring.

The year 1295 was thus one of anxiety in several directions, and Edward determined to explain his difficulties to an assembly summoned to Westminster for 13 November. His desire to make a telling and extensive appeal is shewn not only by the fact that in the writs to the prelates his Chancery clerks felt that this was an appropriate occasion on which to quote the tag from the Codex of Justinian, "What touches all should be approved by all," while the archbishops and bishops were told to secure the presence of their archdeacons, the prior of each cathedral chapter, one proctor of that chapter and two of the diocesan clergy; not only by the stress laid in the writs to the lay magnates upon the "dangers which at this time threaten the whole of our realm"; but also by the instructions given to the sheriffs to cause two knights from each county, with two citizens or burgesses from each city or borough within it, to be elected and empowered to act on behalf of those they represented at the same assembly. What Edward could never have foreseen was that after many centuries had gone their way, and England had developed a constitution in which a representative parliament with wide powers was a central feature, historians and politicians would go back to this assembly of November 1295 and see in it, as Stubbs saw, "a pattern to all future assemblies of the nation." That idea, the use of the term "the Model Parliament," and concentration upon the presence of representatives as the outstanding interest, has taken a surprisingly firm hold upon historical teaching and writing, so that even scholars who rightly challenge much that used to be said about Edward I's parliaments themselves unconsciously take a tone which implies that, even to the thirteenth century, "parliamentary origins" were of vital interest. It seems desirable, therefore, to pause at this date, and to set forth three considerations which seem worth attention.

The first concerns the actual word "parliament." This, like many other hard-worked medieval words, served a variety of uses, linked together by a common idea, which in this case was that of a parley, a conversation. Such a *parliamentum* might take place between envoys of different countries, or the clergy in convocation, or the king's councillors met in smaller or greater numbers, or monks whom their superiors thought too

talkative[1]. Gradually, however, and quite naturally, the *parliamentum*
which took place in a solemn court or assembly became more conspicuous
and oftener on men's lips than the others, and the term was transferred
from the talk itself to the assembly in which the talk occurred. Plenty of
instances occur in chroniclers of the thirteenth century. Official documents
were slower about adopting the usage, and the phrase most common in
Chancery writs summoning men to what we and the chroniclers should
call a parliament is *colloquium et tractatus.* In judicial connexions, however, by 1290 at any rate, the law had come to recognise a special peace
which protected men *durante parliamento.* Mr H. G. Richardson, to
whose work, alone or in collaboration with Mr G. Sayles, on parliamentary
antiquities medievalists owe much[2], infers from this that the judicial
aspect of parliament's activities outweighed all others. "We would,
however, assert that parliaments are of one kind only and that, when we
have stripped every non-essential away, the essence of them is the
dispensing of justice by the king, or by someone who in a very special
sense represents the king."

Is it necessary, however, to draw this inference? Fads of office custom
are often quite enough to account for the difference of phraseology used
by clerks drawing up different records, and the lawyers would naturally
stress that aspect of parliamentary activity which specially concerned
them. From what can be seen of the working of the medieval mind in
other fields, it seems exceedingly unlikely that in this one the thirteenth
century had already worked out a water-tight division of functions. This
modern criticism, however, has been of great value in warning us that
it is misleading and dangerous to limit our definition of Edwardian
parliaments by so naming them only when some great piece of legislation
is in the wind, or taxation in progress. Still less, of course, should we
nowadays be prepared to confine the term to assemblies in which a
representative element was included. We shall think most sanely and
most historically about Edward's parliaments if we so name an assembly
whether it is legislating, advising, granting taxes, or dealing with judicial
business, and whether it does or does not contain representatives. There
is no advantage, but rather actual danger, in seeking to introduce precise
definition into an age that had not yet defined.

In the second place, however, we must admit that even if the thirteenth
century itself did not feel that there was anything epoch-making about
the addition to parliament of something besides the old magnate element,
that addition undoubtedly has an interest for later ages in view of subsequent developments. Even granting that, we must remove the parliament
of 1295 from its pedestal. The fortunate discovery in our own time of

---

[1] Parliamenta vestra de truphis in exitu capitulorum inhonesta (*Registrum Rad.
Baldock*, p. 28, C. and Y. Soc.).
[2] Cf. *Trans. Royal Hist. Soc.*, 4th ser., XI, pp. 137–83, and *Bulletin Inst. of Hist.
Research*, V, pp. 129–54 and VI, pp. 71–88 and 129–55.

original writs addressed to four sheriffs, as well as fragments of returns from several counties, placed beyond doubt the fact that at the first parliament Edward ever met, in April 1275, there were arrangements for representation not unlike, though not identical with, those made in 1295. If Edward made a model at all, then, he made it twenty years earlier. But in fact there was no model. To Edward's second parliament, in the autumn of 1275, he invited knights but no burgesses. Later on, sometimes representatives were summoned, sometimes they were not, and whether they were or were not present, chroniclers at any rate, if not officials, were ready to call the assembly a parliament. The inclusion of clerical representatives did not persist. All that can be said with certainty is that by the end of Edward I's reign the custom of afforcing the magnate nucleus with representatives was less of a novelty than it had been in his father's time. It is dangerous to try to reduce thirteenth-century doings to too rigid a system; to look for theoretical or deliberate constitutional ideas; to feel it necessary to explain action as due to imitation of similar action in other countries. Opportunism and the king's initiative decided who should be summoned to any given parliament. And incidentally a warning may be added that the "model" is almost as unreal when applied to the magnate element as to the representative. Edward summoned his officials and his great men; he would have been surprised if anyone had told him that in so doing he was initiating anything like that "hereditary peerage" which later on served the aristocratic opposition so well as a weapon against royal aggression[1].

The third and last point worthy of notice is that one contemporary, at any rate, when enumerating Edward's merits as king, drew attention to his parliamentary policy. This was John of London, author of the *Commendatio Lamentabilis*, who placed the allusion in the mouth of Edward's widow Margaret. "Call on the Lord," she cries to Mary and Martha, "if perchance He may rouse him from sleep. For had He been here, he had not died, my lord and my king, yea, a king terrible to all the sons of pride, but gentle to the meek of the earth. To the peace of the flock committed to his charge he gave every thought, every word, every deed. Well know we that for the peace of his people he *assembled parliaments*, made treaties, allied himself with strangers, threatened battle, struck terror into the hearts of princes." The exact significance of such praise is hard to gauge. Possibly the writer had in mind Edward's effort, frustrated by circumstance in the later part of his reign, to hold two parliaments a year with regularity, a practice which would have obvious advantages from the point of view of suitors and petitioners. Perhaps, on the other hand, the allusion has no legal flavour whatever, and merely approves Edward's willingness to explain to his assembled subjects what he was about when demanding their help. At any rate, it is interesting to find that parliament was thought worthy of mention.

[1] Cf. Tout, *Chapters in Medieval Administrative History*, III, pp. 136-9.

CH. XIV.

We must return, however, to the main thread of our story. Edward found his parliament of November 1295 very unresponsive. The laymen reluctantly granted a tax on personal property at the rate of one-seventh in the cities and boroughs and one-eleventh elsewhere, while the clergy were even slower about agreeing to pay a tenth for one year, or for a second if the war should last so long. Their reluctance was shared and supported by the new primate, Robert of Winchelsea, whose consecration had been delayed by a vacancy in the Papacy till September 1294, though he had been elected two years earlier. Scrupulous and obstinate, Winchelsea found his position very difficult, and doubly so when in February 1296 Pope Boniface VIII by the bull *Clericis laicos* forbade rulers to exact, or clerics to pay, extraordinary taxes without papal authorisation. When in the autumn of 1296 parliament met at Bury St Edmunds, Winchelsea pointed out to the clergy that their promise of a subsidy clashed with this prohibition, and after considerable delay they decided in Convocation (January 1297) that they were "unable to discover for the present any sure way of giving help by means of a contribution or tax."

There followed the worst dispute the reign had yet seen. The king outlawed the clergy and declared their lay fiefs forfeit; the archbishop and his agents retaliated by repeated publication of the excommunication of any who should disobey the papal decree. However, both sides gradually cooled. Before Easter 1297, Winchelsea agreed not to penalise any clergy whose consciences would allow them to ransom their possessions by a contribution of one-fifth, and in July he himself was publicly reconciled with Edward. Meanwhile the Pope had receded step by step, till in July, by the bull *Etsi de statu*, he surrendered completely. This news, with a victory of William Wallace followed by a raid so thorough that "the praise of God ceased in every church and monastery from Newcastle-on-Tyne to Carlisle," brought the clergy to a more accommodating attitude, and in October they granted one-tenth in the southern province and one-fifth in the northern. In the meantime, however, opposition had arisen in a new quarter. In February 1297 Edward proposed to the earls and barons assembled at Salisbury that some of them should go to Gascony, while he himself was campaigning in Flanders. "Everybody began to make excuses." Humphrey de Bohun, Earl of Hereford, the constable, and Roger Bigod, Earl of Norfolk, the marshal, declared that their hereditary functions could only be exercised in the king's company. After sulking apart through the spring, they came with the rest when the army assembled at London in July, only to put their protest in a fresh form, which the king himself made public in letters patent issued before he sailed. The two officials, he said, refused to perform their duties on the pretext that to do so would be to admit an obligation, whereas they had come at request only (*par vostre priere*). When he appointed substitutes they withdrew in anger, refused repeated overtures, and spread a report to the effect that the king had refused to consider "certain articles for the common profit of the realm," whereas they had never placed any such before him. "Among the said articles, so it is said, there is mention of oppressive action which the king has taken in his realm, as well he knows, such as the aids which he has often demanded from his people; but to this he was forced by reason of the wars which broke out in Gascony, Wales, Scotland, and elsewhere.... It vexes him greatly that he has aggrieved and troubled his people so much, and he begs them to hold him excused, as one who did not do these things in order to buy land, or tenements, or goods, or towns, but to defend himself and themselves, and on behalf of the whole nation."

The fact was that Edward's views were longer than those of most of his subjects, and that until now he had shewn little patience in explaining them. To carry out ends which roused no lasting general enthusiasm, he was using means which excited general alarm. Measures which to himself appeared regrettable but temporary expedients seemed to others to be dangerous precedents which might harden into custom. It was now three years since the first French expedition had been summoned, the first war subsidy imposed, the first maletolt exacted. Yet military demands were as insistent as ever, subsidies constantly required, and the maletolt had just been taken again at the same rate as in 1294. Recent assurances that the extraordinary taxes should not be made precedents, the offer of pay to those who would serve in Flanders as a matter of grace instead of obligation, satisfaction made in tallies to all whose wool was seized, and proclamations in mildly apologetic tone like the one quoted above came too late. The leaders of public opinion proceeded, as soon as Edward had left the country, to a decisive protest.

It had become the habit of the thirteenth century to put such protests into the shape of a demand for the confirmation of those two charters, the charter of liberties and the charter of the forest, which were the final version of the charter extorted from John. The magnates now made the usual request, and also drafted six additional articles. No tallage or aid was to be imposed in future except with the consent of spiritual and temporal magnates, knights, burgesses, and other freemen; corn, wool, and the like must not be seized against the will of their owners; clergy and laity of the realm must recover their ancient liberties; the two earls and any who agreed with them must suffer no penalty for their refusal to go to Gascony; the prelates must read aloud the present charter in their cathedrals, and cause to be proclaimed in every parish church, twice a year, the excommunication of all who should neglect it. Armed with this ultimatum, and in more than metaphorical readiness for battle, the magnates arrived in London for parliament, at which the absent king was represented by his heir Edward of Carnarvon, a boy of thirteen. The result was inevitable. On 10 October, under the great seal which remained in England, the charters were confirmed, and on 5 November, at Ghent, under the privy seal, the king ratified this confirmation, together with additional articles. The document he thus issued, written in French, summarised the demands which the magnates had drafted in Latin, but did not adopt the same order or translate the exact words, and added clauses which reserved to the Crown "the ancient aids and prises due and customary" and "the custom on wool, skins, and leather already granted by the commonalty of the realm."[1]

Both Edward and his subjects attached enormous importance to this concession, and for four years longer the king was suspected, probably with justice, of trying to withdraw, if not from his obligations, at any rate from these definite pledges. He failed to do so. The magnates lost no chance of giving publicity to his promises before assembled parliaments or armies, and pressed him steadily towards their execution. In 1298 a bishop and three earls had to swear on his behalf that he would give further security as soon as opportunity served; in 1299 a clause "saving the rights of our crown," appended in Lent to a further confirmation, had to be withdrawn at Easter; in 1300 twenty *Articuli super Cartas* were issued; and on 14 February 1301 the king was driven at last, by the arguments and menaces of a parliament at Lincoln, to grant a new confirmation of charters and articles, thus giving solemn and final shape to the concession first made on foreign soil. Rather more than five years later Pope Clement V absolved the king from his oath to the charters and annulled the additional articles, but the only advantage Edward took of his release was to revoke certain disafforestments which had been made.

It was a curious fate which thus extorted from the well-intentioned Edward I constitutional securities comparable in solemnity with that first great charter wrung from King John, and it was the more exasperating to the king because his critics had applied logically principles he himself had commended to their notice. "It is abundantly clear," Edward had said before the parliament of 1295, "that common dangers should be met by remedies devised in common." In his own headlong pursuit of his military ambitions, flinging aside conventions, precedents, and safeguards, the magnates had discerned just such a common danger, and in the remedy devised for it they had defined explicitly common action as the consent "of archbishops, bishops, and other prelates, earls, barons, knights, burgesses, and other free men." Further, they had clung to their demands so perseveringly for years after the first outbreak, that Edward could not sweep them away as war clamour to be forgotten when better times came.

---

[1] The Latin articles are given in Hemingburgh's chronicle under the title *Articuli inserti in Magna Carta*. Stubbs thought that they might either be Hemingburgh's own abstract or the barons' original draft; Bémont and most modern historians accept the latter view, which receives some support from the fact that Archbishop Winchelsea's register contains letters of 10 October, issued by the young Edward, reproducing in French almost the exact words of the fifth of the Latin articles. "Tallage," mentioned in the first of the Latin articles, was not named in the French version, and Edward continued to take tallages without requesting consent. Yet in the seventeenth century, in the preamble to the Petition of Right, reference was made to this article as the *Statutum de tallagio non concedendo*.

So the Crown was once again committed solemnly and publicly to the principles of Magna Carta, viewed from a standpoint more than narrowly feudal. The concession was all the more valuable because remedies of actual recent abuses had been added to the nucleus consisting of the original charters. This was a real constitutional triumph.

In the last years of his life Edward became a lonely and wrathful old man. He had had much to disappoint him. His French efforts led only to an unremunerative peace; the Scottish war was a Penelope's web where, as one chronicler said, every winter undid every summer's work; there were terrible bills to pay, and the charter struggle had left a sting behind it. A new generation stood about the old king, and there were few magnates of age and dignity sufficient to oppose or adequately to advise him. Queen Margaret was young enough to be his daughter, and was sometimes, indeed, ally and spokeswoman of her step-children in their quarrels with their father. His heir Edward, created Earl of Chester and Prince of Wales in 1301, knighted and made Duke of Aquitaine in 1306, fell in 1305 into complete disgrace for months on account of his impudence to his father's chief minister, Walter Langton. The earldom of Cornwall escheated to the Crown in 1300, and that of Norfolk in 1306, at a convenient time for its lands to be used to make provision for the king's little sons by his second marriage, Thomas of Brotherton and Edmund of Woodstock. Twice Edward quarrelled with Anthony Bek, Bishop of Durham, and in revenge annexed the temporalities of that great see.

Windfalls of this kind, combined with the utmost ingenuity in securing all ordinary sources of revenue, and a great deal of borrowing besides, were insufficient to meet Edward's increasing financial needs in these closing years. The political effect was bad, for Edward was sometimes led by a money lure into compromising with his usual desire for thoroughness, and at other times into pushing his legal rights in a way that was resented. In 1303 he made a bargain with the foreign merchants in the *Carta mercatoria*, which granted alien traders wide privileges in England in return for their promise to pay, on all goods exported or imported, additional duties beyond "the ancient customs due and accustomed." This was much disliked, and English merchants firmly refused to follow suit. It is to Edward's credit that in the spring parliament of 1305, when he imagined that his Scottish campaigns were over, he undertook work of his old kind for the improvement of public order by starting an enquiry into the misdeeds of "trailbastons," or clubmen, who were terrorising the countryside. As war was renewed in 1306, however, there was little hope of further action of the same sort.

With the Church, Edward's relations varied in these later years. Boniface VIII regarded him, at any rate in the language of written compliment, as an obedient son of the Holy See, and bent his energies, not as Pope but as a private person, to the settlement of the French quarrel. On the other hand, in 1299 he claimed Scotland as a papal fief, and assured Edward that "it was not, and is not, a feudal possession of either your ancestors or yourself." In 1301, after consultation with his magnates at the parliament of Lincoln, Edward replied that a contrary belief had been inscribed upon the tablets of his memory by the pen of the Most High. After the fall of Boniface in 1303, and the short pontificate of Benedict XI, the election of a Gascon archbishop as Clement V gave Edward a friend in the papal chair, who not only released him from his oath to the charters, but also, out of respect for his accusations, suspended Archbishop Winchelsea and called him to account in the Curia. Winchelsea had continued to side with the opposition after the reconciliation of 1297, and had offended Edward further by a personal attack on his treasurer Langton. He remained in exile for the rest of the reign, while the temporalities of his see were administered by the papal agent, William de Testa.

Testa's name is memorable because it was the centre of a protest made against papal oppression by "earls, barons, magnates, and commonalty" assembled at Carlisle in January 1307. The points brought forward were just such as those which were the basis of anti-Roman legislation half a century later—the preferment of foreigners by papal provision, the exaction of firstfruits, the introduction of innovations in the collection of Peter's Pence, and so on. It was alleged that papal business was growing so much that the Pope intended in future to keep four agents in England instead of one. Little came of the protest except that the matter was taken up with Cardinal Peter of Spain, the papal legate who now arrived to proclaim the peace with France and to make final arrangements for the marriage of Isabella with Edward, Prince of Wales.

All the king's thoughts were now bent upon the invasion and subjugation of Scotland. He had replied to Robert Bruce's defiance in 1306 with terrible threats, and had sworn before the crowds in Westminster Abbey on the day on which his son was knighted that, "dead or alive, he would march into Scotland to avenge the injury of Holy Church and the death of John Comyn and the perjured faith of the Scots." A man of sixty-eight has no time to spare, and Edward was impatient for his opportunity. Even as it was, he was too late. He was still south of Solway, on the marshes of Burgh-by-Sands, when he died on 7 July 1307.

Edward I's death may not have seemed to contemporaries an unmixed evil. It led to a welcome pause in campaigning, and brought home some exiled victims of the old king's wrath, such as Archbishop Winchelsea, Bishop Bek, and above all Peter of Gavaston. The son of a Gascon gentleman who had served Edward I well, Peter had been brought up with the heir to the throne, but had developed into such an empty-headed, extravagant, dragon-fly of a man that the old king had come to dread his influence, and in 1307 had banished him. He could not prevent his son from establishing the exile in idle comfort at Crécy, in his own county of Ponthieu, and now the new king at once recalled Peter, gave him the great earldom of Cornwall, and married him to Margaret, niece of the king and sister to the Earl of Gloucester.

Among the great families the king had many relatives and some staunch friends. The aged Earl of Lincoln, and the rising baron Hugh Despenser the elder, had both interceded for him when estranged from his father. The warmest partisan of all, his sister Joan, was now dead, but her son Gilbert, Earl of Gloucester, kept up his mother's tradition. Aymer de Valence, Earl of Pembroke, had royal blood in his veins, and it was to Aymer's sister Agnes that Edward in his youth had written, "You are and wish to be our good mother....Command us as your son." John of Brittany, Earl of Richmond, had been brought up with Edward's elder brothers; Humphrey, Earl of Hereford, had married his sister Elizabeth; Thomas, Earl of Lancaster, Leicester, and Derby, was his first cousin.

In personality, Edward had much to commend him to his subjects. Though of a delicate family, he was unusually strong, a fine, upstanding young man. He was generous if prodigal, frank if indiscreet. He liked display and fine clothes, and found amusement in gambling, in practical jokes, and in the shows of actors[1] and buffoons. Contemporaries thought it rather shocking that he was fond of bathing and swimming, and of the company of people who taught him to ditch and drive and thatch and work at a blacksmith's forge. Probably they were not equally scandalised at his scanty education and inability to read Latin, for in 1312 the greatest of the magnates chose on one occasion to boast rather than confess that they "had no knowledge of letters, but were learned in knighthood and the use of arms." In religion, Edward added to the conventional devotions and benefactions demanded by his position some personal tastes, especially a great affection for the Dominicans. Within four months of becoming king he gave a site in the park at King's Langley in Hertfordshire, the home of his youth, for the erection of a Dominican priory.

Public opinion noted with rising disapproval Edward's entire absorption in his friend Earl Peter. When he went over to France to be married in January 1308, he left Peter as *custos* of the realm during his absence. When he was crowned, in February, the order of the procession made his preferences scandalously plain. If to the Earls of Hereford, Lincoln, and Warwick, to the Marshal, Chancellor, and Treasurer, there were allotted honourable places and significant emblems; if Thomas, Earl of Lancaster, bore that sword *Curtana* which Matthew Paris had declared to be symbolic of the right of its bearer to coerce even a king; it was Peter who, flaunting in purple and pearls instead of the conventional cloth of gold, immediately

---

[1] In 1303 buckram and similar things were sent to South Warnborough *pro quibusdam interludis factis ibidem per principem* (Exch. Accts. 363/18, m. 8). This is better evidence of his theatrical tastes than the much-quoted sneers of the chroniclers.

preceded the king himself, bearing the most sacred of all the regalia, St Edward's crown. The indignation excited by this and similar marks of special favour grew hotter when it was found that anyone who ventured a remonstrance became the butt of venomous witticisms on the part of Peter, received by Edward with delighted appreciation.

The situation soon became intolerable. In May 1308 Edward had to agree to Gavaston being exiled for a second time, though he gilded the pill by appointing him his lieutenant in Ireland, and within a year wheedled the magnates into permitting his return. However, Peter soon gave offence again, and when in 1310 a committee of magnates, who came to be called the Lords Ordainers from the work they had to do, drew up Ordinances for the reform of the realm, they were agreed that the condition precedent of such reform was to get rid of Peter. Accordingly, the twentieth Ordinance was devoted to his sins and their penalties, and he was sentenced to be for ever exiled not only from England, but from Ireland, Wales, Scotland, and the king's lands on both sides of the sea. Edward and his protégé were quite blind to the seriousness and finality of this pronouncement. After a few weeks' absence Peter again returned, and at York Edward reversed the magnates' decision. The Chancery clerks were ordered to affix the great seal to letters they found already drafted for them on their arrival, announcing that Peter's exile was "contrary to law and custom," and that he had returned at the king's bidding. Edward superintended the clerks in person, and "as soon as the writs had been sealed in his presence, took them in his hand and put them on his bed." Two days later, writs for the restoration of Peter's lands were "made in the king's presence, by his order, under threat of grievous forfeiture."

The magnates' reply was to take up arms, and Edward and Peter found themselves hurrying from one place to another to avoid a rigorous pursuit. At Newcastle they were so nearly caught that they had to leave their arms, horses, and treasure behind them to fall into the hands of the Earl of Lancaster. Finally, Gavaston shut himself up in Scarborough Castle. That huge pile, strong as its position and defences were, needed more men and victuals than he could get, and after three weeks he surrendered on condition that his life should be safe, and that if negotiations between the Ordainers and himself came to nothing he should be replaced in the castle to begin the struggle afresh. Such terms sound strange to modern ears, and although the besiegers had confirmed them in all honesty with a solemn oath, angry human nature was too much for them. The Earl of Pembroke escorted Peter safely as far south as Deddington in Oxfordshire, but there, during his temporary absence, Guy of Beauchamp, Earl of Warwick, succeeded in seizing his captive, and, on 19 June 1312, Peter was executed on Blacklow Hill near Warwick.

This lynch law, in disregard of a solemn safe-conduct, was as outrageous as anything of which Edward or Gavaston themselves had been guilty. The four earls chiefly responsible, Lancaster, Warwick, Hereford, and

Arundel, found themselves criticised even by their own circle, and Pembroke and Warenne broke off relations with those who had forced them into the betrayal of their oath. The king alternated between heart-broken lamentations over his friend's brutal end and violent threats of vengeance against those responsible for it. For six months at least it seemed as though the outcome would be actual civil war, both sides opposing obstinacy and abuse to the efforts of would-be mediators. By the end of December 1312, however, the adversaries came stiffly and unwillingly to an agreement, in which the king promised to take no action against those concerned in Gavaston's death, while the magnates agreed to support the king's demand for an aid to be used for a war with Scotland, to give up their recent habit of appearing at parliament in arms, and to make a solemn profession of loyalty in the great hall of Westminster. Deprived of the satisfaction of honouring Gavaston's memory by revenge, Edward fell back upon the consolation of surrounding it with reverence and splendour. The body, which had been carried to Oxford after the execution, was in January 1315 transferred for burial to the new church of the Dominican priory at King's Langley, close to the manor-house where Edward and his "dear Perot" had been boys together. Since the first grant of a site in 1307, Edward had three times increased the endowment of the community, which by this time numbered no less than a hundred friars, and as long as he lived he continued his favours. He never forgot Gavaston. As late as 1326, when in pursuance of a grant of his father he gave an advowson to Leeds priory for the maintenance of four canons and a clerk to say mass daily in the chapel in Leeds Castle for the soul of Queen Eleanor, he added a proviso that a fifth canon should celebrate in memory of Peter. The friendship, mixed up with all kinds of youthful memories, was probably much more innocent than scandalous tongues of the time alleged, and its cruel end remained for Edward one of the most vivid and outstanding things in his life.

To the magnates, on the other hand, Peter's fate, though gratifying, was only part of a wider movement, which took written shape in three documents—the Articles of Stamford of 1309; the Ordinances, accepted in August, published in September 1311; and the second Ordinances, which Professor Tout recently assigned from internal evidence to a date between 25 and 30 November 1311.

The Articles of Stamford represent the bargain struck between the king and the magnates in order to secure Gavaston's return from his second exile. The remedies sought in them were for time-honoured grievances, such as the encroaching jurisdiction of the royal household, or the collection of extra customs from foreign merchants. When next the magnates voiced their views, however, in the parliament of 1310, which met after Gavaston's return and renewed offences, they spoke less generally. Edward, they said, had been reduced to disgrace and poverty by the advice of evil counsellors, had dismembered the inheritance received intact from his father, and had wasted the grants made for war with Scotland. On 16 March 1310 the king agreed that the magnates should choose a committee to sit till Michaelmas 1312, "to ordain and establish the state of our realm and our household." So came into being the Lords Ordainers. They included seven bishops, with the Archbishop of Canterbury at their head, eight earls—Gloucester, Lancaster, Lincoln, Pembroke, Hereford, Warwick, Richmond, and Arundel—and six barons. They produced six preliminary Ordinances at once, and announced that while doing their further work they would sit in London so as to have records and legal advice close at hand. And there, indeed, most of them remained busy for many months, though Gloucester went off to the Scottish war in the autumn, and Lincoln died early in 1311. By August 1311 they had their draft ready to submit to king and parliament, "since," as they remarked with an echo that may have been irritating, "what touches all should be approved by all." Under coercion, and unwillingly, Edward confirmed their work. On 27 September some forty Ordinances, including the six of 1310, were published in London, and as quickly as possible copies under the great seal were sent out all over England.

The contents of the Ordinances were comprehensive and well-intentioned. The old formulae were repeated. Holy Church must have her liberties, the king's peace must be kept, the Great Charter must be observed. Some clauses had a rather old-fashioned flavour, and suggested that complex problems created by new conditions could be solved by simple means based upon a return to past custom. Take, for example, the undoubted fact of the inadequacy of the royal revenue to royal needs. If no grants of offices or other profits were made till the king's debts had been paid (Ordinance 7); if natives instead of aliens managed the customs, and saw to it that all issues went direct to the Exchequer (4 and 8); if foreign merchants who had been battening on the revenues were arrested and forced to account (5); then surely the king would once more be able to "live of his own" without making novel and excessive exactions. Or consider the follies and extravagances of the king, his advisers, and the executive which carried out their will. Was not the obvious remedy to restore the baronage to their place as the native and natural counsellors of the king? Let him never leave his country, or go to war, until the baronage, "and that in parliament," had consented, and had arranged for the custody of the realm during his absence (9). Let all bad counsellors be removed, and better ones be substituted (13). Let all the great offices of State, not in England only, but also in Gascony, Ireland, and Scotland, as well as all posts of authority in the ports and on the sea-coast, be filled by the advice of the baronage in parliament, or, in emergency, at least by the help of the "good council" present with the king (14, 15, 16). Let sheriffs be substantial men, appointed by the Chancellor, Treasurer, and others of the king's council (17). Many of the remaining ordinances reiterated prohibitions against encroaching jurisdictions, abuses in local government, and other evils of a kind repeatedly execrated, and never cured, in earlier times. One new safeguard, indeed, was provided. In future parliaments a bishop, two earls, and two barons were to hear complaints against delinquent officials (40). Moreover, while adopting the common device of exacting an oath to the scheme of reform from all the chief royal officials, the Ordainers struck a new note by including in that category the two leading domestic officials, namely the steward of the king's household and the keeper of his wardrobe.

The king disliked this programme, and was disloyal to it from the first. Within two months of the expiration of their commission, the Ordainers found it needful to issue the so-called Second Ordinances, which are little more than a recital of the various points, numbering more than thirty in all, in which the stipulations made in the first Ordinances had not been fulfilled. In particular, enormous numbers of proscribed persons, varying in importance from Gavaston's relatives down to the humblest of carters and porters, had not been ejected. The dissatisfaction felt over this naturally redoubled when Gavaston himself returned, and the personal fight which ended in his death was thus a fight not only for revenge but for the maintenance of the scheme of reform.

It might therefore be expected that the years immediately following the reconciliation of 1312 would be marked by a vigorous enforcement of the Ordinances, with a corresponding improvement in the general well-being. Not at all. It is true that in 1313 there was issued the famous "Ordinance of the Staple," which for the first time made it compulsory for all merchants, whether native or alien, to export their wool to a single foreign port, St Omer being chosen as the site of this "fixed staple." As "the merchants of this realm" had the task of enforcing and executing the Ordinance, it worked to their advantage rather than to that of the foreigners, and was meant also to lead to greater efficiency and better organisation. However, the innovation was by no means universally popular, either abroad or at home, and in any case could not bring in its results all at once. Meanwhile other circumstances persisted which were far from beneficial to trade. Bruce steadily extended his power in Scotland, while his brother Edward between 1315 and 1318 nearly succeeded in making himself king of Ireland. Not the northern counties only, but even far distant shires to which the huge death-roll of Bannockburn brought home the fact of the Scottish peril, began to live in a state of perpetual expectant depression. There was a general infection of misery, a general loosening of discipline. Conspicuous among many similar examples was the case of Bristol, where, not for two years only, as the chroniclers say, but for nearly four, as the records shew, trade, law, and order were paralysed while the townsfolk set at defiance both the king's constable and their own governing oligarchy. It happened, too, that six successive bad seasons diminished supplies, spread disease among men and beasts, and caused general despondency. Parliament in 1315 tried to mend matters by fixing statutory prices for essential food-stuffs, but sellers thereupon ceased to bring their wares to market, and in 1316 the legislation was repealed. Vague popular thinking blamed the powers that were, not only for their mistakes and hesitations, but also for troubles for which no human agency could justly be held responsible.

Circumstances forced the Ordainers to choose as their leader a man calculated to do their cause more harm than good. After the death of Henry Lacy, Earl of Lincoln and Salisbury, in 1311, his two earldoms passed to his son-in-law Thomas of Lancaster, already lord of three, and made him, so far as landed power went, incomparably the greatest of the king's subjects. When to this is added the fact of his royal blood, it is hard to see how, at this stage, his claims to leadership could have been disregarded. Earl Thomas' personality, however, by no means corresponded with his dignities. He was both touchy and sulky—a deadly combination; he was unforgiving and revengeful; and he was as unwilling as the king himself to make the sacrifices demanded by a position of responsibility. After the defeat at Bannockburn had put the king at the Ordainers' mercy, and Lancaster's advice was required at every turn, he could rarely be induced to give it in person, but expected business to wait till there had been time for a deputy to report to him, or for letters to be exchanged.

Meanwhile, the king for his part was being as irritating as he dared. His response to the demand for dismissals in his household and elsewhere was partial, grudging, and temporary. In 1313 he said that he could not attend parliament because he was ill, an excuse which no one would accept from a monarch whose rude health was proverbial. In April of the same year he went off to France, ignoring Ordinance 9, which required him to ask the permission of parliament before leaving the country, and to seek the common consent to the appointment of a *custos* in his absence. He did not return at the date at which he was expected, and the magnates, after waiting for him a fortnight, went away indignant. He deeply resented the prominence of Lancaster, and by 1317 the *domestici* of earl and king were at each other's throats, while Edward was trying, but failing, to get the Pope to release him from his oath to the Ordinances, and Lancaster was protesting that it was as much as his life was worth to come near the king. Edward gave some colour to this assertion when in October, travelling south from York, he put his train into battle array as soon as he drew near Lancaster's castle at Pontefract. It seemed as if civil war alone could decide between the rivals.

That this disaster was avoided was due to the efforts of a new "middle party" which had been built up during 1317, largely by the efforts of Aymer de Valence, Earl of Pembroke, out of courtiers and moderates united by a common dislike of Lancaster. Its leaders actually succeeded, in August 1318, at Leake near Loughborough, in getting Lancaster to set his seal to one half of an indenture of agreement, to the other half of which were affixed the seals of two archbishops, eight bishops, eight earls, and twelve barons. Soon afterwards the king and the earl exchanged a kiss of reconciliation at Hathern, and writs were issued for a parliament to confirm and complete the settlement.

This parliament of York, which met on 20 October 1318, was in some ways the most notable of the whole reign, though there hangs about it the tragedy of work accomplished only to be undone. It remained in session for seven weeks, and addressed itself to its task in a spirit of greater energy and hopefulness than had been known for years. As had now become usual on solemn occasions, representatives were summoned, though by no means all of them attended, and those present played quite a subordinate part as compared with the prelates, earls, and barons, who, indeed, were definitely instructed to "treat apart" on various important matters.

Parliament's first care was to fulfil the promises made at Leake. The indenture was read aloud and confirmed, and the king was induced to accept as permanent the arrangement which had been in provisional use since August, by which, "in all weighty matters...which can or ought to be transacted without parliament," he was to be advised by a standing council of two bishops, an earl, a baron, and a baron or banneret from the household of the Earl of Lancaster. To ease the burden to the magnate back, each group was to act for three months at a time only, and nine more names were added to the existing panel to make the turns come round at wider intervals. Charters of pardon were issued to Lancaster and his adherents, and the king made public announcement of his loyalty to the Ordinances. The whole matter was solemnly enrolled in the records of the Chancery, the Exchequer, the two Benches, and Parliament.

As a preliminary to the next business, both Magna Carta and the Ordinances were read aloud to the assembled company, and real vigour was shewn in following the example thus suggested. Household reform was entrusted to a committee of five, conferring with three prelates named by the king, and a few days before parliament dispersed the results of their work were embodied in the Household Ordinance of York. A revising survey of the king's grants was undertaken, resulting in some cases in considerable reductions. Enquiry was made into the competence of every Crown official, high or low, central or local. Some were retained, some were dismissed, some were promoted. When, on the steward of the household being made seneschal of Gascony, Bartholomew of Badlesmere was appointed in his stead, Lancaster set up a very characteristic protest, losing sight of any question of general benefit in the alleged injury to his own right, as Steward of England, to appoint the steward of the household. His claim was treated courteously, but nothing was done to meet it, either then or when in 1319 he renewed it. Parliament attacked the old trouble of abuses in local government and delays in legal procedure, and issued the Statute of York, which contained many wise provisions, such as that which forbade any official in charge of the assize of wine to sell wine himself, or that which directed the bailiff of a franchise to return a writ to the sheriff in indenture form, so as to minimise the risk of falsification. Important debates were held with regard to the advisability of fixing staples in England instead of abroad, though in the midst of parliament's great press of business no actual economic legislation resulted from the discussion. A vast number of petitions were dealt with, some of them of general interest. It was decided to summon the army to make a fresh effort against Scotland in June 1319, and to hold another parliament at York or Lincoln within a month of Easter (8 April).

Parliament's activity, and the reconciliation of Leake, made the year 1318 a real turning-point. All the forces dangerous to moderation had been silenced. Future prospects seemed bright, and there must have been many other contemporaries who, like the author of the *Vita Edwardi*, believed that the king's twelfth regnal year was to herald a period of peace and success.

From the summer of 1318 to the winter of 1320 the trend of events did undoubtedly, on the whole, bear out the prophets of good fortune. The famine ended, and wheat came down from 3s. 4d. to 6d. the bushel. Although no successes were won by the Scottish campaign, at any rate in December 1319 a truce was secured, and for two years England was able to draw breath. Advantage was taken of this to tackle the question of Anglo-French relations, which for some years had been menacing. Philip IV had died in 1314, and, during the reign of his successor Louis X (1314–16), Edward had never found time or opportunity to go to do the homage incumbent upon him, as Duke of Aquitaine and Count of Ponthieu, whenever a new king came to rule in France. After the accession of Philip V, Edward continued to postpone this duty, and intrigued against the French King as much as he dared. Philip had retaliated in kind, much acrimonious correspondence had been exchanged, and, without formal warfare, there had been constant friction on the narrow seas and wherever English lands touched French. Meanwhile, neither in Ponthieu nor in Gascony was English administration any more efficient than usual, and Philip as overlord lent a ready ear to complaints. France seized Ponthieu in 1317 or 1318; the Pope rebuked Edward for leaving Gascony *sine lege et sine rege*; and finally, when Bayonne broke a treaty arranged between its own sailors and those of Normandy, the Parlement of Paris sentenced Edward, as duke, to a fine. In this connexion, therefore, the pacification of England in 1318, followed by the truce with Scotland in 1319, gave a welcome opportunity for readjustment. Edward did homage to Philip by proxy in June 1319, and in June 1320 performed the same ceremony in person at Amiens. Though his stay in France was only for about six weeks, the good will established lasted for the rest of Philip's reign. Ponthieu was restored to English rule, by no means to its entire satisfaction. Gascon troubles had meanwhile received attention, when in February a new seneschal was appointed and Hugh Despenser the elder and Bartholomew of Badlesmere were commissioned to enquire into the state of the duchy and the conduct of its officials. Their report led to the issue in August of a drastic ordinance for reform, which, for a time at any rate, acted as a deterrent and made many a petty tyrant conscious of observation. Abroad as at home, therefore, the period 1318–20 was marked by pacification and improved administration.

How was it that the hopes raised by this situation were so quickly disappointed? Before Christmas 1320 there were clear signs of coming trouble; in 1321 the middle party was broken up by armed conflict between the extremists on both sides; and a brief Lancastrian triumph in that year was succeeded in the following spring by a royalist victory, which found symbolic expression in the repeal of the Ordinances in May 1322. Thenceforward, till his deposition in 1327, Edward II remained master of his own actions.

The responsibility for the breakdown in 1320 must be divided. Something no doubt was due to the instability of Edward, something to the indecision of Pembroke, something to the jealousy among the magnates which prevented lengthy co-operation. The chief onus, however, must lie upon the man who gradually succeeded Gavaston in the king's affections. This was Hugh Despenser, husband of Eleanor de Clare, one of the three heiresses among whom, in 1317, were divided the estates of Gilbert, Earl of Gloucester, slain at Bannockburn. That inheritance, the first spur to Hugh's ambitions, provoked him to a policy which in the end ruined both himself and the king.

Hugh Despenser the younger, as he was often called to distinguish him from his father and namesake, was a man of much more weight than Gavaston, both by birth and in personality. His family had been pushing its fortunes ever since Henry III's day, when his grandfather was one of the baronial nominees on the committee which drew up the Provisions of Oxford, and afterwards twice acted as justiciar. His father, Hugh the elder, had thrown in his lot with the revived fortunes of the monarchy under Edward I, and under Edward II had been marked down for censure by the Ordainers and Lancaster. The younger Hugh's intimacy with the king dated at least from the time when Edward was Prince of Wales. He had been knighted on the same day with him, and at the date we have reached held in the royal household the office of chamberlain, which ranked third in the domestic hierarchy and involved a specially close relation with the household's head. Yet Hugh's attitude, court official though he might be, had been hitherto one of such cool detachment that nobody feared his influence or his ambition. In 1318 the York parliament prayed the king to continue him in office, and confirmed, though with some redistribution, the grant to him of lands of the value of 600 marks yearly to meet the expenses of his residence at court. He was regarded as a safe man, treading his prudent course midway between extremes, whether of royalism or reform.

Once more, however, as so often in medieval England, central politics were deflected by causes originating in the March of Wales. When in 1317 an agreement was arrived at for the division of the great Clare inheritance between three co-heiresses, Despenser, as the husband of one, secured the marcher lordship of Glamorgan, prized not only for its size, but for its tradition of unusual dignity and independence. Lords of Glamorgan had had their own sheriff, denied any right of appeal from their court to the king of England, and welcomed such kings when they visited South Wales rather as fellow potentates than as superiors. Hugh felt that the cream of the inheritance had fallen to his lot, so that by an energetic use of his opportunities he might become the greatest of the magnates and secure an earl's title. Even before the partition, he had tried to seize the great Clare castle of Tonbridge in Kent; after it, he sought to undermine the position of his brother-in-law Hugh of Audley, to whose share Newport had fallen. In both attempts, and in breaches of the peace along the borders of Glamorgan and Gower, he found himself checked by royal orders. He became convinced that his ambitions could be realised only by close co-operation with the king, and by 1320 he was leading Edward "like a cat after a straw," as one annalist said, in pursuit of his own ambitions. There was something more revolting in calculating self-interest of this sort than in the haphazard irresponsibility of a Gavaston. To contemporaries, Hugh was a rival and a renegade. At the bar of history, he must stand convicted of upsetting for personal reasons a political equilibrium hardly won and much to the public advantage.

The course of events can here be traced only in the barest outline. The storm centre was the peninsula of Gower, coveted by Despenser because it lay between his Glamorgan lands and Cantref Mawr in Carmarthen, which had been granted to him for life. The lord of Gower, William de Braiose, having no son to succeed him, had been offering his lands for sale to various marcher neighbours, including the Mortimers, the Earl of Hereford, and his own son-in-law John of Mowbray. After William's death in 1320, Mowbray entered into possession, but Despenser egged on the king to take Gower into his own hands, on the ground that since Braiose was a tenant-in-chief, he had no right to give his land, or Mowbray to take it, without the licence of his lord the king. It was typical of Despenser's cleverness that he chose an argument apparently so much in keeping with the laudable efforts of Edward I himself to establish uniform authority inside as well as outside privileged areas. Every marcher lord, however, resented the claim as a breach of "the custom of the March," and the sub-escheator sent to take possession of Gower found himself prevented by armed force. Commissions of enquiry, written expostulations, and a personal visit made by the king to the Welsh border in March 1321, could not quench the flame thus lighted. During May a league of marchers overran Hugh's manors in South Wales, burnt his muniments, damaged what they could not carry away, and slew or put to ransom the few subjects who remained faithful to him. The infection of disorder spread far beyond Wales, and gave Lancaster his first chance since 1318. On 24 May all the chief magnates of the north met at his invitation in the chapter-house of Pontefract priory to make a league of mutual defence. A month later he brought together in the parish church of Sherburn-in-Elmet a much bigger assembly, which included not only lay magnates both from south and north, but abbots, priors, bishops, and the Archbishop of York himself, to consider a long list of grievances drawn up at Lancaster's direction. Public opinion having thus been well drilled beforehand, it is not surprising that when, in July 1321, the king met a general parliament, including representatives of the counties, towns, and lower clergy, he found it set upon ruining the Despensers. Both father and son must be dismissed as "false and most evil counsellors, disinheritors of the crown and destroyers of the people." In vain the Despensers challenged technical errors in the charges made, appealed to Magna Carta and the Ordinances, and offered to meet complaints in a legal way. Resistance and quibbles were bludgeoned down by the magnates' determination, backed by the sight of the large armed forces they had brought to London. The Despensers left the country, the Chancery clerks were set to work on the drafting of innumerable pardons to those who for a great right had done a little wrong, and the magnates dispersed well satisfied.

As a matter of fact, they had done more harm than good. The temporary unity was broken up; the king was again enraged; the old devices of private warfare and armed parliaments had restored the old atmosphere of disorder and suspicion; and even the alliance of northern and marcher lords did not long outlive their victory. Pembroke could not hope to rebuild his middle party until both sides had forgotten renewed grievances, and before that could happen the king seized a chance to revive hostilities.

His perfectly respectable pretext was an insult offered to his queen. Isabella, travelling through Kent about Michaelmas 1321, was refused admission for the night to Leeds Castle by the wife of Bartholomew de Badlesmere. Now Badlesmere, still in name steward of the king's household, had not actually visited it since the middle of June, though he had received a pardon in August like others who had joined the league against the Despensers. Edward was delighted to make the wife's offence a pretext for summoning an army to punish the husband's "disobedience and contempt." To many correct feudal minds her breach of feudal etiquette seemed so gross that they willingly responded, while Badlesmere, on the other hand, found that he could secure little help. Lancaster hated him as the living evidence of the defeat of his own claim to appoint the steward of the household, and made no effort to rouse the northern baronage. Some of the Welsh marchers, indeed, hurried to the rescue, but when they got as far as Kingston-on-Thames they heard so much of the king's strength that they dared advance no farther, and left Leeds Castle to its

fate. By the end of October it was in the king's hands, and its occupants
were sentenced to death or imprisonment.

The matter was not to rest there. Badlesmere himself was still at large,
and Edward was in a mood of concentrated obstinacy not uncommon in
a weak man enraged. He followed the retreating marchers westward,
recalled the Despensers under safe-conduct in December, kept Christmas
on the Welsh border, and prepared to advance early in 1322. So firm
was his attitude that before January was ended the Mortimers and many
of the other marchers had submitted without striking a blow. A few
stalwarts, however, notably those whose interests in South Wales clashed
with Despenser ambitions, such as Humphrey, Earl of Hereford, Roger of
Amory, and John of Mowbray, made good their escape to the north, and
convinced Lancaster that the time had come to speak or for ever hold his
peace. In February and March, accordingly, the quarrel put on wider
aspects. It became a duel to the death between the royal cousins, and a
conflict of principle between monarchy under control and monarchy free
and independent.

The question was soon settled. Step by step the "contrariants" retired
as Edward advanced. They abandoned the siege of Tickhill; they failed
to hold the passage of the Trent at Burton; they moved north again after
a temporary stand at Pontefract; and on 16 March 1322, at Boroughbridge
on the Ure, finding their way barred by forces brought down from the
border under Andrew Harclay, they fought to a finish and lost. By Lady
Day the more notable rebels had already paid the penalty. The Earl of
Hereford had died fighting at Boroughbridge. Lancaster was beheaded
on 22 March within sight of his own castle of Pontefract, though the
more degrading accompaniments of a sentence for treason were remitted
in deference to his royal birth. Many others had to drink the cup to the
very dregs, and all over England there were hangings, drawings, and
quarterings. Badlesmere himself was hanged at Canterbury. In some other
cases, such as that of the Mortimers, sentence of death was commuted to
lifelong imprisonment because they had surrendered early. It remained
for the victors to distribute the spoils of conquest, and provide, if they
would or could, for a better future. With 1322, therefore, there opens
the last well-marked period of the reign. Lancaster was dead, Pembroke
died in 1324, the Despensers, though authoritative, had not the same
overwhelming influence which Gavaston had exerted. It followed that
onlookers identified the policy of these years with the king in person,
and that when in 1327 revolution overturned his ministers, he shared
their fate.

On 14 March, two days before Boroughbridge, while the issue was still
in suspense, writs had been issued for a full parliament, which in due
course met, on 2 May, at York. Prelates and religious attended in their
usual numbers, but the ranks of the lay magnates were thinned by recent
events. The commons, on the other hand, were more numerous than usual,

for besides proctors of the beneficed clergy, borough members, and knights from the counties, there were also present, for the first time in history, forty-eight representatives of Wales. The commons continued to be invited regularly to parliament as long as the Despensers held power, though as the expense of paid members soon mounted up, it was never thought desirable to keep them long in session. On this occasion, as we know from an interesting memorandum recently discovered and printed[1], the king asked his council to discuss and formulate proposed legislation beforehand, "in order that the people who come to parliament may be the sooner set free." Presumably they managed well, for the commons went home after eighteen days, though the magnates continued in session for another nine weeks.

"Let the council bear in mind the following things: first, the statute on the repeal of the Ordinances; second, the putting of the good points of the Ordinances into a statute." These words, which opened the above memorandum, suggest one marked feature of the victorious party's policy. It combined the assertion of liberty of royal action with the offer of orderly government. Such an aim could have been stated theoretically in terms which would have beseemed Edward I at his best. Its failure in practice must be explained, not by insincerity, only partly by incompetence, mainly by the facts that Edward II had not his father's power either of terrifying enemies or attracting friends, that the Despensers were even more isolated and unpopular than he was, and that circumstances had changed so much that even an Edward I would have found himself hard put to it.

The form of the statute which repealed the Ordinances, and which was probably drafted by the council, shewed at once the trend of the new policy. A clause declaring void any ordinances or provisions made against the estate of the king or his crown was followed by a more famous reminder that "matters which are to be established for the estate of our lord the king and of his heirs, and for the estate of the realm and of the people, shall be treated, accorded, and established, in parliaments, by our lord the king, and by the assent of the prelates, earls, barons, and commonalty of the realm." Mr Lapsley has suggested, and Prof. Tout has accepted, the view that this principle was to apply not to any and all legislation, but only to fundamental constitutional change. Dr Conway Davies would have it, on the contrary, that the statute drew a careful distinction between matters concerning the estate of the crown and the royal power, which are indeed questions of fundamental law, as against general legislation and administration, with which parliament, both magnates and commons, might rightly concern themselves. It is just possible that both interpretations are a little too subtle, and that all that the Despensers meant to do was to follow up a clause in which they asserted the royal

---

[1] By Conway Davies, *Baronial Opposition to Edw. II*, Appendix, pp. 582-3.

right with another in which they gave assurance that the Crown intended to act in consultation with parliament.

To destruction succeeded construction. A statute embodying remedies for many standing grievances utilised for this purpose parts of the *Articuli super Cartas* of 1300 and the Ordinance concerning the forests of 1306; revived the Statute of Lincoln of 1316 with regard to the appointment of sheriffs, which was itself the amended form of Ordinance 17; and incorporated the very words of Ordinances 33, 35, and 36, which dealt with complaints against the Statute of Merchants, the grievances of persons outlawed through malicious appeals of felony in counties where they had no land, and the encouragement of robbery and murder by the too easy abatement of appeals in the king's court. All this shews that the desire of those now come to power was rather to remould than to destroy what they had shattered.

Enunciation of sound doctrine was to be backed if possible by efficiency in the routine of government. Processes of administrative reform, some of which had by fits and starts already begun, went on more rapidly during these years, partly by the efforts of officials in their departments, partly by the help of ordinances issued by the king and his council. The changes were particularly striking in the Exchequer. Three ordinances (1323, 1324, 1326) were directed to the clarifying of its records, the improvement of its accounting system, and the organisation of its staff. Already, as early as 1317, its central record, the Great Annual or Pipe Roll, had begun to shew signs of efforts to investigate and diminish the bad debts which had accumulated; now the process went forward steadily, and by the end of the reign a substantial clearance had been made. Such reforms came from men of varied political views. Two of the Exchequer ordinances were issued during the second treasurership (1322–25) of Walter of Stapledon, a moderate politician of the Pembroke type; the third belonged to the treasurership (1325–26) of William of Melton, a courtier all his life. Another curialist, Robert of Baldock, became Chancellor (1323–26) under the new government. Previously, combining the post of Keeper of the Privy Seal with that of Controller of the Wardrobe, he had been a living contradiction of the Ordainers' principle that the Privy Seal office should be emancipated from the Wardrobe and be subjected to public control. Now, however, by sending three Chancery clerks in succession to act as Keepers, he tried to subordinate that office to his own after a fashion quite in tune with the Ordainers' wishes.

One of the most remarkable and personal expressions of the Despenser triumph is to be found in the prominence and widening activities of the Chamber, of which the younger Hugh as Chamberlain was official head. The quiet rebuilding of that fortress, concealed from view by the commanding structures of the Wardrobe and Exchequer, had indeed begun earlier in the reign; and it is also true that in the early summer of 1322 the king gave up, very likely under pressure from Stapledon, a grandiose scheme by which so magnificent a bulk of "contrariants'" lands were to be assigned to the Chamber that it would have become a state within the State, practically exempt from the ordinary national administrative and judicial system. Nevertheless, it is in these last years of Edward II's reign that the power of the Chamber is openly displayed, and that by a deliberate policy, personal to Despenser and the king[1].

The weakness of Edward's general position, politically, was shewn by his relations with the Papacy. The Popes were not hostile to England, but their increasing demands, coupled with a gradual change for the worse in Anglo–French relations, soon created a very serious situation. Two notable events during the pontificate of Clement V affected England —the suppression of the Order of the Temple (1312), and the imposition (1306) of annates, *i.e.* of payments equivalent to a year's revenue of a bishopric or benefice due to the Pope from each fresh holder. The former brought some gain to the king and to many private persons, besides the Hospitallers who were officially the Templars' heirs. The latter, though described in the Statute of Carlisle (1307) as taxation of a kind "hitherto unheard-of," became gradually an accustomed and therefore not an unbearable burden. On the whole Clement V and Edward got on very well, despite the intermittent exchanges of complaints and the laments of chroniclers which give a contrary impression. At Stamford in 1309 the forty-seven lay magnates addressed to the Pope an almost hysterical appeal for that "widowed lady," the English Church, destroyed by papal exactions and provisions; yet four out of the six episcopal vacancies which occurred between the king's accession and Clement's death were filled by the canonical choice of the electors, and only two by papal provision. Clement himself in 1310 made counter-complaints that payments due were in arrears, clerks and religious injured by laymen, and encroachments made on ecclesiastical jurisdiction. Yet in some ways Clement shewed himself very friendly. If he would not release Edward from his oath to the Ordinances, he was always ready in his official capacity to rebuke his enemies, and in a private capacity lent him £25,000. Meanwhile the see of Canterbury was occupied first by Winchelsea, returned older and wiser from exile, and next by Walter Reynolds, who had been for many years a trusted official in Edward's household.

With the accession of Pope John XXII, however, the situation changed, and appointment by papal provision, hitherto exceptional, became almost invariable. Edward acquiesced as long as a reasonable proportion of the appointments made coincided with his wishes, but found the Pope as time went on less and less ready to humour him. So far as merits or learning went, there was rarely much to choose between royal and papal nominees. When Edward secured the promotion of Louis de Beaumont to the see of Durham (1317), the bull of provision described him as not

---

[1] The subject deserves more extensive treatment than space here permits. Cf. Tout, *Chapters*, II, pp. 338–60.

only of royal stock and suitable age, but also as skilled in letters, commendable in conduct, wise in spiritual matters, circumspect in temporal. Perhaps the cardinals present at his consecration stopped their ears while this lettered prelate fought and lost his fight with the word "metropolitice." "Take it as said," was his counsel of despair. In 1321 Edward pressed the Pope to make an English cardinal, but without success. Sometimes he had to swallow very nauseous doses, as in 1317, when he told the Pope that his honour could not endure that Adam of Orleton should be made Bishop of Hereford—and had to accept him within two months. How meaningless were the praises bestowed by the jobber on the jobbed is illustrated by the case of Badlesmere's nephew, Henry Burghersh. In 1319 Edward belauded him as a candidate for the see of Winchester, and in 1320 secured Lincoln for him. A year later, after the Badlesmere outbreak, Edward informed the Pope that his conscience was troubling him because of Henry's "manifold unsuitability," and begged that he might be rooted out. All this bargaining, which affected every sort of preferment, must have disgusted zealots, while it raised up many enemies among disappointed rivals, angry patrons, and offended chapters.

No triumph of Edward over his private enemies was notable enough to enable him to rally the country to a firm stand against Scotland. In March 1323 Andrew Harclay, who had been rewarded for his services at Boroughbridge with the title of Earl of Carlisle, was executed as a traitor for going to Bruce to suggest a peace on the basis of England's recognition of "King Robert." In June the government itself made a thirteen years' truce, which could not become a peace because touchy stupidity forbade it to recognise accomplished facts by admitting the royal title. Still, so long a pause was welcome indeed, and it may well have been that some of Edward's advisers felt in the summer of 1323 that the time had come for reconstruction undisturbed by storm abroad or at home. They were sadly deceived. In that very year there arose a little cloud like a man's hand, which was destined before long to blacken all the heavens, and finally to sweep away the king and his friends in a great rain of revolution.

In January 1322 Philip V of France had been succeeded by Charles IV, who forbore for many months to trouble his English brother-in-law to do homage, in view of the "grantz empeschementz" which detained him in England. The truce with Scotland, however, seemed to remove the last reasonable excuse, and Charles accordingly required Edward to come to do homage at Amiens by 1 July 1324. Edward, while replying politely, began at once those delays which were the stock device for such occasions. Like a tenant who tries to get repairs out of his landlord before he renews a lease, so the Gascon Duke made his renewal of homage an opportunity for protest on all the time-worn grievances—the French officials who "put their reaping-hooks into our harvest," the encouragement of appeals to the suzerain over the head of the duke, the vexations inflicted upon French subjects over-loyal to England. This time, however, the ordinary diplomatic game could not be played with the usual calm, for there had already occurred that "affair of Saint-Sardos" which was to embitter the relations between the two countries to a point that could only end in war.

Saint-Sardos stands on the top of a little hill in the Agenais, in the pleasant rolling country immediately east of the confluence of the Lot and the Garonne. To this day a Romanesque doorway and some splendid fragments of early capitals in its little church recall the twelfth century, when the land already belonged to the abbey of Sarlat in Périgord. Now the abbey of Sarlat was one of those "privileged" tenants in the three dioceses of Limoges, Cahors, and Périgueux whom Louis IX had excepted, when by the Treaty of Paris of 1259 he surrendered royal rights in those dioceses. In 1279, by the Treaty of Amiens, Philip had handed over the Agenais, and Edward I had agreed that no further effort should be made to induce privileged tenants in the three dioceses to transfer their allegiance from France to England. Did this, however, apply to lands which the privileged held elsewhere? "Certainly," said the French. "Not at all," said the English; and when in 1289 the Abbot of Sarlat effected a *pariage* of his land at Saint-Sardos with the King of France, who proposed to construct a *bastide* there, Edward's view was that a subject in his land of the Agenais was acting with undue independence. He had obvious reasons for disliking the idea of a centre of French influence established in the heart of a district so recently ceded to England. Again and again he appealed on the legal point to the Parlement of Paris. One decision was given in his favour, but this was soon challenged and reversed, and in 1323 French officials entered Saint-Sardos to begin building. Before fresh diplomatic protests had had time to take their course, a host of English sympathisers, led by Ralph Basset, seneschal of Gascony, swept down upon the little place, murdered, burnt, and ravaged, hanged the French official to the post on which he had displayed the royal arms, and made off to the neighbouring castle of Montpezat, whose lord, Raymond Bertrand[1], had been prominent in the attack. The French King cited the culprits before the Parlement of Toulouse. Some forty submitted, the rest shut themselves up in their strongholds, and were condemned in absence to banishment and the confiscation of their possessions. When, in execution of this decree, a French representative arrived to seize Montpezat, he was captured and put to ransom. Outraged at this second

---

[1] The continuator of Guillaume de Nangis, the Chronicles of St Denis, and other French chronicles based on these (see *Hist. de la France*, Vols. xx and xxi), state that Raymond Bertrand himself had set up a *bastide* at Saint-Sardos; but I can find no evidence of this, and they may have been as wrong about it as they were about most other points in the story. Henry of Blaneford, a monk of St Albans but possibly a native of Blanquefort near Bordeaux, gets very near the facts when he says that the French King was trying to attract settlers to "a broad and pleasant site" at Saint-Sardos, which he had got by exchange with "a certain religious" (*Chron. Hen. de Blaneford*, Rolls Series, p. 144).

CH. XIV.

insult to authority, Charles prepared to send armed forces to avenge it
and to enforce the sentence. During the first six months of 1324, though
Edward disavowed the action of his officials to an extent for which he
almost apologised to them in subsequent letters, and though embassy
after embassy exhausted all the resources of diplomacy in efforts to stave
off reprisals, Charles quietly continued to make ready to defend his
dignity. The last of the English envoys, making for the coast with all
speed in July lest they should get caught in the campaigning, wrote to
Edward that they heard it commonly said that Charles was tired of
"words and parchment." Meanwhile 1 July, the date fixed for the
reception of Edward's homage, had passed by without any attempt on
his part to appear, and so sure had Charles made of his default that even
before that date, so said the envoys, he had declared Gascony and Ponthieu
forfeit.

In the actual fighting which followed in August and September 1324,
the French had much the best of it. Here and there, at Penne, at Saint-
Sever, at Puymirol, strongholds resisted, but when Charles of Valois invaded
the Agenais, Agen soon surrendered, and though the king's brother
Edmund, Earl of Kent, with such loyalists as could reach him, stood a
five weeks' siege behind the walls of La Réole, on 22 September they gave
in, and made a truce to last till April 1325. Meanwhile in England
Edward had been fuming ineffectively, and with gross misjudgment had
included among his war-time precautions the seizure of the lands of Queen
Isabella. She put down the measure to Despenser spite, and bided her
time. By and by papal envoys, seeking a bridge between French and
English demands, suggested that the queen might be sent over to France
to intercede with her brother. She reached Poissy on 21 March, secured
a new truce to last till June (later prolonged to July), and obtained the
consent of both kings to a treaty by which Charles was to take formal
possession of Gascony, but, as soon as Edward had done homage, surrender
all except his recent conquests, as to which there was to be a judicial
enquiry. Even when, in August, Edward once more failed to keep his
appointment, on the ground or the pretext of illness, Charles was still
sufficiently complacent to agree that if his young son Edward were invested
with Ponthieu and Guienne he might act in his father's stead. On
14 September, accordingly, the boy performed this duty, and by November
the French were ready to hand over everything except their recent conquests. But quite suddenly, Edward flared up at the idea of this retention,
committed to it though he was by treaty. The war cloud gathered
again.

As so often in this reign, a personal reason was directing political
action. Scandalous stories reached Edward concerning his wife and Roger
Mortimer, who had been in France since he escaped from the Tower in
1323. The king's one idea was to undo all that Isabella had done, recall
her, and remove her son from her influence. The queen, however, ignored

all orders to return, and Edward struggled in vain. He resumed responsibility for the overseas lands by taking the title of "governor and administrator" for the young duke. He set a watch on the coasts, and sent Mortimer's mother to a nunnery for addressing meetings of disaffected persons. In May he made a bid for the support of the merchants by the Ordinance of Kenilworth, which abolished the foreign staple and set up eight places in England, three in Ireland, and three in Wales, as staples for wool, wool-fells, and leather. Isabella was now in open defiance, and had been dismissed from her brother's court. She found a new refuge in Hainault, betrothed her son to the daughter of its count, used the marriage-portion to equip troops, and invaded England in September. General hatred of the Despensers, and pleasure at her declaration of affection for the Ordinances, brought her many adherents, including her brother-in-law Thomas, Earl of Norfolk, and Henry, Earl of Leicester, to whom had been granted many of his brother Lancaster's forfeited lands. With her had come Roger Mortimer, Edmund, Earl of Kent, the Bishops of Winchester and Norwich, who had been envoys to Paris, and many others.

The modern historian will not want to linger over the grim details of the final conflict, dear as they were to the contemporary chroniclers. The most brutal concerned the murder of Edward's loyal treasurer, Bishop Stapledon, outside St Paul's. Other scenes took place in Wales or the March. The elder Despenser was hanged at Gloucester in October. Edward himself, and the younger Hugh and Baldock the chancellor, were captured as they tried to make their way in a great storm of rain and wind from Neath Abbey to Llantrissant Castle. Hugh was hanged at Hereford, while Edward was put into the care of his cousin Henry of Leicester at Kenilworth.

Careful of appearances, the victors called a full parliament to seal their triumph. It met at Westminster on 7 January 1327, and contained representatives of the commons of England and Wales as well as the magnates. The magnates present swore to uphold the queen and her son, and Orleton, Bishop of Hereford, after haranguing the assembly on the queen's wrongs, gave it a day to consider whether Edward or his son should reign in future. William of Melton, Archbishop of York, with four other prelates, protested on Edward's behalf, but the rest, and all the laymen, accepted the substitution of son for father. Six crimes were laid to the disgraced king's charge. He had followed evil counsellors, despising the advice of the great and wise; he had neglected public business for his own amusements; he had lost Scotland, Ireland, and Gascony by bad government; he had injured the Church; he had put many great men to death; he had broken his coronation oath. On 20 January 1327, at Kenilworth, Edward accepted his own fate and his son's elevation. For a little longer he lived in captivity, and even for a brief space was rescued from it by old friends, whose sympathy became doubly eager when in April he was transferred from the care of Henry of Leicester to harsher custody in Berkeley Castle. He was recaptured, and in September 1327 either died a natural death, as the government took pains to make all men believe, or, more probably, was murdered to save them the anxiety of the plots which would continue as long as he was known to be alive. A persistent tradition asserted that the body buried was not that of Edward at all, and that the king made good his escape to Ireland, France, and finally Italy, where he lived out his days in seclusion. The chief documentary evidence for such a belief is a strange letter written to Edward III by a Genoese priest, who said that his information came from what he had heard in confession. A man might have many motives, however, for telling such a story to the late king's supplanter, and on the whole it is probable that the crowds who flocked on pilgrimage to the tomb of the "martyred" king in St Peter's Abbey at Gloucester were right in believing that it contained the bones of Edward II[1].

Modern research, which has been very busy of recent years with the period reviewed in this chapter, has not so far altered traditional values as to make Edward I a small man or Edward II a great one. It has, however, demonstrated unmistakably that the two reigns are far more closely connected than used to be supposed. Contemporaries, many of whom had a tale to adorn or a moral to point, exaggerated surface contrasts, and moralisers of later generations found the opportunities opened by such treatment too tempting to be abandoned; as late as 1640 a pamphleteer of the Fronde was using Gavaston's fate as an awful warning to Mazarin. Yet the records and literature of the period, when studied impartially, make it clear that Edward I could on occasion be as violent, as overbearing, as unscrupulous as his son; that before he died he was already faced with a growing opposition which made the execution of his policy increasingly difficult; and that this, combined with the general drift of historical development and the huge expenses entailed by his manifold activities, created problems which had to be met by Edward II.

With the exception of the conquest of Wales, every great problem of the period is common to both reigns. The independence of Scotland was already foreshadowed when Edward I died, and it is unlikely that the prolongation of his own life, or a more desperate energy on the part of his son, could long have delayed its establishment. The miserable treaty which, shortly after Edward II's deposition, reduced the English lands in France to a mere shadow of their former greatness, was the outcome of a situation which dated from the Treaty of Paris of 1259, which amid a rising sense of nationality became increasingly impossible, and which could only temporarily be readjusted even by such later victories as those of the more glorious periods of the Hundred Years' War. Turning from political to constitutional matters, it is clear that both reigns were marked by experi-

[1] For a survey of all the evidence, see Tout, *The Captivity and Death of Edward of Carnarvon*, 1920.

ment, friction, and misunderstandings, while to both Edward I's enthusiasms and Edward II's follies the baronial party opposed suspicion and narrowness as well as legitimate criticism. As to the widening of the parliamentary circle, begun by Edward I's experiments and continued as a growing habit in his son's time, it was due to Edward I's needs rather than to his ideals, and its full consequences were not to be felt till long afterwards. Meanwhile, in the daily routine of government it might almost be said that Edward II's indifference proved more beneficial than Edward I's energy, for whereas the father found great difficulty in securing trustworthy and efficient helpers, under his son the efforts of inventive and intelligent officials made the reign a great turning-point in administrative history. In general social conditions there is little to choose between the two reigns; while in economic matters, whereas for the expelled Jews Edward I had substituted the Italians, Edward II's reign saw the ruin of the Frescobaldi, competition between other Italian firms and a rising class of English capitalists, considerable municipal growth, and a start made with some devices which were to be fully developed under Edward III. As to ecclesiastical affairs, though it is true that in the later years of Edward II England became more and more a vineyard with a broken hedge, whose grapes could be plucked by every passer-by, her exploitation was not due to the king, but to general conditions in the Church after the establishment of the Avignon Papacy. On the whole, therefore, a prudent historian will refuse to stress the personal aspects of the two reigns, or to exaggerate the contrast between them, and will prefer to treat the two together as a single episode in the story of the medieval world during one of the most vital periods of its development.

CHAPTER XV

ENGLAND: EDWARD III AND RICHARD II

On 24 January 1327 the son of Edward II, a boy not yet fourteen years old, was proclaimed king, in accordance with the decision of the Parliament which had met at Westminster on 7 January. His reign as Edward III was reckoned to begin on 25 January, but the real power lay in the hands of his mother Isabella and Mortimer her paramour, and so remained for nearly four years. The first period of the reign turns, therefore, on Mortimer, though he had no place in the Council of Regency.

The revolution had been easy because almost every influential person promptly deserted Edward II. Mortimer and Isabella, with their personal following and their mercenaries from Hainault, had taken the initiative, but the whole baronage gave its support. Only five prelates, including the Archbishop of York, had remained faithful to the king, and only two prominent officials, the chancellor and the controller of the wardrobe and the chamber. The constitution of the Council of Regency reflected this state of public opinion; it cannot be considered as packed with Mortimer's creatures. Consisting of four prelates, four earls, and six barons, it was presided over by Lancaster, and contained the young king's uncles, Norfolk and Kent, and the two archbishops. Orleton, Bishop of Hereford, and John Stratford, Bishop of Winchester, were the other episcopal members, and in Orleton at least Mortimer had a representative of his interests. The proceedings of the Parliament were open to little criticism. It secured, as a natural result of the revolution, a reversal of the proceedings against Thomas of Lancaster and his party, with restitution; it also asked for a confirmation of the proceedings against the Despensers, and for steps to procure the canonisation of Earl Thomas and Archbishop Winchelsea. The long list of grievances concerning abuses in the late king's dealings with the Church, and his feudal, military, and judicial rights, was answered in detail; the Charters were confirmed; and most, but not all, of the requests received favourable replies. The lavish provision for Isabella, said by the chroniclers to leave the king hardly one-third of his revenue, betrayed the triumph of a faction, whilst generous charters rewarded the Londoners for their support in the crisis of the preceding autumn.

Two urgent problems called for the attention of the new government. It was only by their handling of these that Mortimer and Isabella did anything to redeem the shameful behaviour by which they had attained power. The uncertainty of their position in England, Edward II being still alive, helped them to recognise the actual situation in France and Scotland, and without delay they proceeded to seek a peaceful settlement in France based on the *status quo*. The *status quo* was extremely un-

favourable to English claims. The treaty, signed 31 March 1327, provided
for a war indemnity payable by England, left Charles IV in possession of
what he had occupied in 1324, and reduced the English possessions to a
strip of coastland with Bordeaux as its centre and some disconnected
fragments insecurely held in Gascony. When a year later, on 31 January
1328, Charles IV died leaving his widow pregnant, Edward III claimed
the regency of France as heir presumptive, maintaining that his mother
could transmit a claim which she could not herself use. The claimant by the
male line, Philip of Valois, was, however, made first regent and then, when
Charles IV's child proved to be a girl, king. To Philip, on 6 June 1329,
after some show of reluctance by Isabella, Edward did homage; but
whether the homage was liege homage or not, and whether it was for the
lands claimed by Edward or only for those actually held, were questions
in dispute between the parties.

By a similar recognition of humiliating facts, Mortimer and Isabella
secured peace with Scotland, but not until the way of war had been tried.
The Scots were not unwilling to fight, and the English were not yet
prepared to allow Bruce the title of king. A scrambling summer campaign
in 1327, on the English side of the border, failed to produce a pitched
battle where the English superiority in numbers might have told; it
merely exposed the northern counties to ravaging. With tears of boyish
disappointment over the failure of his first campaign Edward had to return.
The continuance of the raids convinced the government that they could
no longer hold out against Scottish desires, and they made the "shameful
treaty" named from Northampton, where it was ratified in Parliament in
May 1328. England recognised Bruce as king of a completely independent
Scotland, and the restoration of lands in each country to subjects of the
other who had been wrongfully dispossessed was promised in vague terms
productive of future troubles. The betrothal of Bruce's son David, aged
four, to Joan, Edward's sister, aged seven, sealed the alliance of the two
States. Edward himself appears to have shared the popular feeling of
dislike for this unpalatable, but useful settlement. Bruce died on 7 June
in the following year, and the boy David began his uneasy reign.

Not merely the unpopularity of its concessions in foreign policy, but
also internal divisions were weakening the government. The coalition
which had overthrown Edward II was breaking up. Though the Lancastrian party had reaped some profit in lands and offices, they found themselves gradually ousted from influence. Lancaster, though nominally head
of the Regency Council, was not allowed personal dealing with the king;
Stratford was kept out of office; the old cleavage between the baronial
party and the party in power at court began to reappear. From the
autumn of 1328 Mortimer had to meet recurring challenges to his
authority. Meanwhile he was making his personal position more commanding. He had an enormous patrimony, and had made such additions
to it that he came near to complete supremacy in Wales and the March.

He was justice of Wales for life. He had large interests in Ireland and the Midlands. By the marriage of his daughters he made more alliances. In October 1328 at the Parliament of Salisbury his unique power was recognised: he received the new title of Earl of the March of Wales, the like of which, complained the chronicler, had not been heard in England before. But at this same Parliament appeared also signs of serious opposition to Mortimer. Lancaster would not attend it; the archbishops and Stratford left it; and there was sympathy for them among the barons.

Mortimer had failed to keep a party together. There was constant change in the offices of State. Orleton had left the Treasury in pursuit of personal advancement at Avignon, and on the death of Reynolds efforts to get the see of Canterbury for Burghersh, Orleton's successor at the Treasury, met with no success. Meopham, who was not a partisan of Mortimer, became archbishop. On 2 January 1329 a meeting summoned by Lancaster in London and representative of the opposition to Mortimer called for the assertion of the authority of the Council of Regency and for the end of Mortimer's control of the king.

Mortimer accepted the challenge, and won the first round. He ravaged Lancaster's Leicester estates; and Lancaster, deserted by Norfolk and Kent, made his peace by submitting to a fine of half his estate. Mortimer pressed his advantage with vigour. Blindness made Lancaster a less dangerous enemy, and Kent he destroyed by a stratagem. Kent was an unstable man. He had put some faith in the rumours that Edward II was still living, and had (it seems) played with designs which brought him under suspicion of treason. Maltravers, who had the most shameful reason for knowing that Edward II was dead, was used as a decoy, and after confession Kent was executed on 19 March 1330.

It was the king himself who was to play the decisive part. He was now approaching the age of eighteen. Two years before, on 24 January 1328, he had married Philippa, daughter of the Count of Hainault who had assisted Isabella in 1326. On 15 June 1330 was born Edward of Woodstock, his heir. The indignity of submitting to Mortimer's yoke became more apparent as that yoke grew more hateful. Edward had already gathered a few personal adherents in an inner circle, and had opened private negotiations with Pope John XXII. A plot, to which the king was privy, took effect at Nottingham on 19 October 1330 as a Great Council was being held. A party of young nobles, led by Edward's confidant William Montague, broke into the royal apartments by stratagem at midnight. Mortimer was arrested, and Edward announced his intention of ruling for himself. Isabella could not save her lover. At a Parliament in Westminster a month later the lords condemned Mortimer without a hearing, and he suffered ignominious execution. He was charged with compassing the deaths of Edward II and Kent, estranging Edward II and Isabella, appropriating royal power and property, and injuring Lancaster. Condemnation was also pronounced against the principal agents in the late

king's murder, but only one was brought to justice. Isabella was made to
live on her original dower, but she retained her freedom and did not die
till 1358.

For the first ten years of his personal rule Edward's main concern was
with Scotland. Difficulties arising from the land settlement promised in 1328
gave an occasion, and perhaps a reason, for disturbing the unpopular Treaty
of Northampton. The story will be told elsewhere[1]. Here it is sufficient
to notice that, despite the crushing defeats of the Scottish nationalists by
the young Balliol at Dupplin Moor (12 August 1332) and by Edward at
Halidon Hill (19 July 1333), Edward's hold on Scotland was even more
insecure than his grandfather's had been. The Scottish campaigns had
great importance as a school for future warfare. It has often been pointed
out that the tactics of Dupplin Moor and Halidon Hill—the use of
archers in open order on the wings—prepared the way for English
victories by similar tactics on the continent in the later part of the reign.
The great size of the armies used in Scotland has attracted less attention.
In 1336, the year in which he penetrated as far north as Forres and
Kinloss, Edward had in Scotland an army which surpassed in size any
continental expeditionary force, except that which made the Crécy-Calais
campaign. A great part of these armies was raised by a few magnates and
was composed of their knights and followers organised independently of the
king's forces. Similar procedure was followed in raising and organising the
armies for the French war. Convenient as the method was at the moment
for Edward, the armed factions of Richard's reign and the Wars of the
Roses revealed how perilous a legacy he had bequeathed to his successors.

The relations of England and Scotland after the outbreak of the
Hundred Years' War form a commentary on the misfortunes brought
on Scotland by the alliance with France. The capture of the Scottish
king, David, at Neville's Cross a few months after the battle of Crécy
provided Edward with large sums by way of ransom. The childless David
was personally disposed to favour an agreement with England, but plans
for the union of the two crowns in the English line after his death came
to nothing. Alike in pitched battles and in victorious raids, Edward had
proved that he could defeat the Scots with ease, but a series of worthless
treaties promising homage stood as witness that he could not conquer
Scotland. He was to go on to prove that the same was true of France.

The reign of Edward III is sometimes said to have less importance in
constitutional history than its length would make us expect. Certainly it
was less crowded with constitutional crises than the reigns of his father
and his grandson, and it has not taken the same place as Edward I's in
the classical statement of constitutional development. This absence of
dramatic incident is due mainly to the personal character and behaviour
of Edward III himself. He has indeed his place in that line of English
medieval kings which has been described (perhaps with a touch of harshness)

[1] *Infra,* Vol. VIII, Chap. xv.

as "an almost uninterrupted succession of champions of personal power, passionate and lustful men, who loved domination, strife, war, and the chase."[1] But though Edward loved his own way and had an exalted notion of what was due to him as king, though we may acquit him of any conscious "acceptance of the theory of parliamentary institutions," he was fonder of the chase and war than of political domination; and his reign shews a long-drawn tendency to sacrifice the one for the other. In some ways Edward, who began to reign as a boy, never grew up. To the very end of his life he retained that boyish charm and graciousness of manner which enabled him in a personal interview to reconcile, at least for the moment, almost any adversaries and to persuade those who came to criticise his doings that in fact all was well. But he retained more than this: he retained too a certain youthful petulance and shortsightedness, a readiness to sacrifice the future for the present, to give almost any price for what at the moment he passionately desired. He was able, agile, strong-willed; on occasion he was violent and overbearing and unjust; he had no scruple about going back on his word, if he had promised for his own advantage what it was inconvenient to perform; but he was not of the stuff that tyrants are made of. He did not care enough about politics for that. The immense prestige of his victories in France, and genuine admiration for a king who so nearly fulfilled their own ideal of what a knightly gentleman should be, made it difficult for a baronage that shared his tastes and views to oppose him. The chase, the tournament, the display of the court, the pomp of war, the pride of life—these were the things that he valued most. In order to get these he would say and do almost anything, and would leave the future to take care of itself. It is this attitude to the business of a fourteenth-century king which explains the long years of smooth working with his ministers and his Parliaments, the occasional constitutional crises, and the very different place that the commons held at the end of his reign from that which they had held at the beginning.

Although, therefore, it is true that in the fifty years of his reign Edward had for the most part his own way and neither baronage nor Parliament gave him much trouble, it is also true that his reign did not permanently strengthen the monarchy as an institution in its relation to its old rival the baronage. On the contrary the baronage had made the beginnings of a working alliance with the social classes that had been lately called to the Great Council of the nation and that were increasing in political as they increased in economic importance. Such success as Edward had was due to personal agility and prestige, to transient rather than to lasting causes. He had not erected a strong household service which could carry on the government independent of the baronage. He had allowed the growth of new Parliamentary procedure which, though

[1] Petit-Dutaillis, *Studies and Notes Supplementary to Stubbs' Constitutional History*, III, p. 310.

it caused him no embarrassment, might be in future a useful instrument in the hands of the opponents of the Crown. With these general considerations in mind we may examine the course of domestic politics in the several sections of his reign.

The first period begins with Edward's assumption of power, and ends with the outbreak of serious hostilities with France in 1338. Edward had not freed himself from Mortimer and his mother to put himself under another yoke. He plainly wished to rule for himself, through ministers responsible to himself and chosen by himself, as his successful predecessors had ruled; and for him, as for them, the principal obstacle to this programme was the opinion of the barons that they were the natural advisers of the king, and that he was doing wrong when he did not follow their advice.

In this period the Stratford brothers were the ministers on whom Edward chiefly relied: John, who followed Meopham as Archbishop of Canterbury in 1333, and Robert, Bishop of Chichester. They were at once representatives of the Lancastrian interest and examples of the official clerical class who rose from moderate circumstances by efficient service. Edward worked tactfully. He did not offend the great barons who had been pleased by the fall of Mortimer, but as time passed he strengthened the element of the *familiares* in the administration. Towards the end of this period there were signs that the household administration was regaining some of the importance which it had not had since the days of Edward II. The rise of Kilsby, an uncompromising supporter of the policy of government by the king's servants, to the office of Keeper of the Privy Seal in 1338 was evidence of the direction of Edward's intentions.

In these years Parliament[1] met frequently, more often twice than once a year. Its main public business was to grant money. It did this readily. The country was prospering, and the Scottish war had general support. These Parliaments were not always, nor indeed usually, held at Westminster. The conduct of the war carried the court and central government to York for a great part of the years 1332–38. It was the Hundred Years' War which made Westminster the administrative capital of England. From 1337 to 1377 Parliament met steadily at Westminster.

The opening of the Hundred Years' War affected domestic politics in several ways. In the first place it took the king out of England. This not only removed his personal influence, which always made for smooth working, but, still more important, it made necessary a second centre of administration, one which could follow the king abroad. Hence came the difficult problem of relating the government outside England with the government at Westminster. In the second place the war called for a vastly augmented revenue, especially in the early years when Edward was negotiating in the Netherlands and Germany an expensive series of

---

[1] For the distinction between Parliament and the Great Council in Edward III's reign see H. G. Richardson and G. Sayles, *The Parliaments of Edward III*, in *Bulletin of the Institute of Historical Research*, Vol. VIII, No. 23 (Nov. 1930).

alliances. In the king's opinion the chief business of the home government was to provide funds which would be at the disposal of the administration accompanying him. The policy of the king and the permanent officials found expression in the Ordinances made at Walton in Suffolk on 12 July 1338, four days before Edward sailed for the Netherlands. The more public departments, the Treasury and the Chancery, were subordinated to the household authorities. That personal rule towards which for some years Edward had been working seemed now at hand. It was the triumph of the views of "the high curialist party" over those of the Lancastrian baronage at a moment when national politics made reasonable an over-hauling of the governmental machine. Kilsby was in charge of both the Great and the Privy Seal out of England.

Had Edward been of a different temperament or cared less about the immediate prosecution of the war, a dangerous situation might have followed his unsuccessful attempt to carry out the Walton Ordinances. As it was, the failure of the home administration to send adequate supplies (its authority being in leading-strings and its desire to make the scheme work perhaps not very great) led Edward to modify the arrangements made at Walton and to restore real power to Stratford and the public departments. But when Stratford met Parliament in October 1339 to seek supplies, it shewed for the first time in the reign a disposition to make conditions first. Again in January 1340 it persisted in the same mood. Edward, after his unsuccessful Thiérache campaign, left sureties with his foreign creditors, and returned to deal with Parliament for himself. In March 1340 he won success by his usual method: he accepted the conditions made by Parliament and secured an enlarged grant. The conditions were embodied in the four Statutes of 1340[1]. The episode marked the triumph of the baronage, lay and clerical, over the policy of the household. But Archbishop Stratford, unwilling to work in the new circumstances despite recent events, resigned the Great Seal, and his brother, the Bishop of Chichester, succeeded him. Despite the victory at Sluys, which Edward won on his way back to the Netherlands on 24 June

---

[1] The four Statutes. (1) covers a variety of abuses and defects in the course of justice and administration, and abolishes the customary aids for knighting the king's eldest son or marrying his eldest daughter, and grants that the maletolt, or extra duty on wool, shall not be taken from Englishmen; (2) provides that no charge or aid shall be made but by the common assent of the prelates, earls, barons, and other great men, and the commons, and that in parliament. By this, "the real act *de tallagio non concedendo*" (Stubbs), Edward gave up that right of tallaging the demesne which he had hitherto maintained despite protests; (3) protects Englishmen from any claims by Edward or his successors as kings of France; (4) provides against particular grievances of the clergy: concerning purveyance, delay in exercising royal rights of patronage, and administration of temporalities of vacant sees.

The financial effect of the statutes was to take away from the king most of the independent powers of raising extraordinary revenue which had been left by the Confirmation of the Charters in 1297; the manner in which the "common consent of the realm" was to be given was now much more closely defined.

1340, his campaign on land was not a success, and he had again anticipated his revenue. He arranged an unsatisfactory truce, and suddenly returned to England on 30 November 1340 to put an end to the government which had forced him to modify the Walton Ordinances and to accept the four Statutes, and yet failed to give him adequate financial support. Against the archbishop he shewed vindictive bitterness: "I believe he wished me to be betrayed and killed," he complained in a characteristically petulant letter to the Pope.

The great officers and judges were dismissed. Many were arrested, but most were reinstated later. The chancellor, Robert Stratford, and the treasurer, Northburgh, escaped because of their clerical status. Edward, vowing that he would now have ministers amenable to his own courts, appointed laymen in their places: Sir Robert Bourchier on 14 December became the first lay chancellor, and Sir Robert Parving, chief justice of the King's Bench, treasurer. Too much can be made of this change as an anti-clerical movement; Kilsby, himself a clerk, was one of Edward's advisers; but the king, who on other occasions shewed himself glad to have a blow at the clergy, seems to have used lay jealousy in his attempt to humble the archbishop and his circle.

The archbishop had fled to Canterbury on the king's return, and was modelling himself on Becket. In this there was a certain appropriateness, for Stratford's early career was at least as full of selfish ambition as Becket's. A violent campaign to win public opinion followed. The archbishop delivered sermons, and excommunicated breakers of the Great Charter; Edward addressed to the bishops and chapters of the Canterbury province the *Libellus Famosus*, an unworthy tirade mixing mere abuse of the archbishop with more serious charges of failure in public duty. Stratford refused to go to Flanders as security for the king's debts, and claimed that only in full Parliament he should be called on to meet any charges. Edward had appointed a commission to investigate the minister's conduct. On 23 April 1341 Parliament met. The lords spiritual and temporal took the view that none of their number should be tried or bound to answer except in full Parliament and before their peers. This view was embodied in a statute. Stratford's personal career in politics was ended, but it is noticeable that the king comes to rely more and more on the hereditary counsellors of the Crown, who seem to be forming a definite body, the peerage.

Nor was this the only episode of constitutional importance. The audit of accounts and the nomination of the chief ministers in Parliament were demanded as a condition of a grant. The importance of these demands was shewn by Edward's reluctance and delay in conceding them[1], and by

---

[1] Edward did not agree to accept the nomination of ministers in set phrase, but conceded that he would appoint certain specified officers with the advice of the magnates and councillors near at hand. These should be sworn in the next Parliament and in each Parliament should answer all complaints. Tout, *Chapters*, III, p. 133.

the fact that he was not content merely to disregard them in practice as he usually did when he had promised what he did not like; he definitely revoked the "pretended statute" of the last Parliament by letters close on 1 October 1341, and even had it repealed by the next Parliament in April 1343.

The period of stress now ended, and there was no repetition of it while Edward personally had control of the government. He did not attempt to revive the household system independent of the great magnates, but turned again to episcopal ministers of the type that he had used in the first part of his reign. "The anti-clerical movement, artificially fomented by ambitious ecclesiastics for their own purposes, died a natural death."[1] Kilsby disappeared from home politics.

The chief offices of State returned to clerical holders in 1345. In the Chancery Offord, Dean of Lincoln (1345–49), Thoresby (1349–56), and Edington (1356–63), and in the Treasury Edington (1345–56) and Sheppey (1356–60) maintained a steady tradition. Bishops of this type, who had the wider interests of their sees as well as their court duties, did not alienate the secular lords. There was no repetition of the disharmony between the government at home and the king's officers abroad, and if Parliament shewed signs of a desire for peace in the 'fifties, it found the cost of the war less than in 1338 or 1345. Edington, who was in office high and low from 1335 to 1363 almost without a break, has been called by Dr Tout the typical minister of this period whose special merit it was to reconcile the royal and the public interest. To him England owed much for his helping to make the tradition of a civil service which would obey indifferently whatever faction was in power at the time.

The Treaty of Brétigny, the high-water mark of Edward's success, ended a distinct period of the reign. It was a period filled by active, and on the whole successful, war with France. The first visitation of the Black Death divided it sharply into two parts, holding up the war, Parliaments, and much other public and private activity for the greater part of three years.

The Black Death was a variety of the contagious bubonic plague which has visited Europe with severity on several occasions. In the fourteenth century it was believed to have come from the East, and to have been carried by ship from the Crimea. It reached England probably in August 1348. From Weymouth, where it was first reported, it spread through the southern and western counties. It appeared in London in the late autumn and was at its height there till Whitsuntide 1349. In the course of 1349 it covered all the central counties of England, and raged in Wales. It reached Scotland in 1350, when it was already dying down in England. Ireland suffered in 1349 and 1350. The most familiar sign of the disease was the appearance of hard, dry swellings that might be as large as a hen's egg, especially under the arm, in the groin, or on the neck.

[1] Tout, *Chapters*, III, p. 160.

Smaller pustules sometimes appeared all over the body; and in the most deadly form of the disease livid patches marked the back and chest, and there was vomiting of blood. Death usually occurred within three days, and might come much earlier. If the swellings broke there was a chance of recovery. The first visitation of the Black Death carried off especially the young and those in middle life. As was to be expected from sanitary conditions, the magnates suffered less than the poor. Among the secular and the regular clergy the death rate seems to have been extremely high. Safe generalisation about the numbers or the proportion of the population destroyed is impossible until local records have been more thoroughly examined, but even when allowance has been made for panic exaggeration and for the looseness of fourteenth-century statistics, an estimate near one-third of the population of England has commended itself to many whose opinion deserves respect. It is needless to picture, and it would be difficult to exaggerate, the immediate devastation of the plague. Its more remote and permanent results will be best considered in connexion with the Peasants' Revolt of 1381. When the plague died down in England at the end of 1349 it did not completely disappear, but broke out at intervals with various degrees of violence. There were three or four such revivals before the end of the fourteenth century.

In this central period of the reign Parliament was used less frequently than in the earlier period. It met on an average less than once a year. For this the Black Death was partly responsible, but a process of differentiation was going on. Parliament was not now merely a reinforced sitting of the Great Council, meeting as often, or almost as often, as the Great Council. It was beginning to be something distinct. The one was summoned by the Great Seal, the other by the Privy Seal; and the king was calling the Great Council more often without the commons. As the bodies were beginning to be more distinguishable, so were their labours. From about the middle of the reign it may be said that statutes, the work of Parliament and more permanent in character, were felt by contemporaries to be different from ordinances, the more temporary work of the Council. There was as yet, however, no clearly defined difference.

That process of differentiation which separated statute and ordinance can be traced too in the more precise definition going on in the middle of the fourteenth century in the courts. The older courts were losing their administrative functions and settling down to the more regularised decision of cases according to the rules of common law. The Exchequer, which had lost some of its political importance as it became more differentiated from the Council, received a sort of compensation in 1357 by the creation of a statutory Court of Exchequer Chamber to which appeals of error should go. The King's Bench was becoming, as the Court of Common Pleas had become before it, a court of common law, losing the power which it had carried over from the Council of inventing new procedures. The Chancery too, as it lost its general oversight through the development of separate organisations for the other courts and through the tendency of the household to supplement it politically, developed a jurisdiction of its own under Edward III. In 1349 the king definitely announced his intention of referring to it questions which he had formerly decided in person. Common law and equity themselves were being distinguished, though the same court might administer each.

The years in which these distinctions of function were becoming clearer were not unnaturally years productive of some very important legislation. The nation was more and more conscious that it had common problems calling for a common treatment. Beside the Statutes of Provisors and Praemunire[1], dating from this period, were the Statutes of Labourers[2] and Treasons, and some of the most famous of the many statutes of the staple. The object of the Statute of Treasons[3] was partly to protect the financial interests of the magnates against the king; for the lands of traitors, of whomsoever held, became the king's in perpetuity, whereas the lands of felons returned in due time to the lord. It was also perhaps partly due to a desire to prevent the growth in England of the Civil Law doctrine of *lèse-majesté*. Edward in 1352 consented to embody in this statute requests which he had refused previously; but, although it provided that doubtful cases should come before Parliament, the statute did not put an end to the definition of treason by common law.

The multifarious regulations of the staple illustrate the manner in which the central government was coming to control and direct more and more of the activities of the king's subjects. In the fourteenth century the export of English wool was at the height of its importance, though the development of the native cloth industry which was to reduce its importance was also a feature of the period. Attempts have been made to see a fully developed economic policy behind the shifting devices and tortuous courses of the king. A policy of "plenty," in the interests of the consumer, has been attributed to Edward III and contrasted with the beginnings of a mercantilist policy of "power" under Richard II. Justification for such opinions is hard to find. The actions of Edward with regard to commerce seem to have been opportunist in detail, though dominated by simple motives. For Edward the export wool trade had unique importance in two ways: diplomatically, it was a lever by which to force Flanders into co-operation with him against France; financially, a tax on the export of wool was a mainstay of his revenue. The rapidly changing treatment of the trade revealed, therefore, the diplomatic situation or the financial needs of the moment, and in these an explanation of it is to be sought. According as Edward had more or less to hope at

---

[1] See *infra*, pp. 450–51.   [2] See *infra*, pp. 463–64.

[3] The Statute defined treason as compassing the death, or violating the persons, of certain members of the royal house; slaying certain ministers when officially engaged; counterfeiting the Great Seal or the king's money; levying war against the king within the realm or adhering to his enemies.

any particular juncture from Flemish politicians, a little group of English capitalists, the small merchants, or the general trading community, he prohibited the export of wool, or he established a monoply and a staple at Antwerp or Bruges or Calais, or he established staples in England and forbade English merchants to export staple produce.

In the earlier years of the French war there was a possibility that by forcing the export trade into a particular channel, securing a whole, or a partial, royal monopoly, and bargaining about the control of it with groups of merchants in merchant assemblies, the king might establish a method of taxing wool independently of Parliament. From this danger England escaped partly because of the king's continuous breaches of faith with the merchants, but still more because of the growing realisation of a divergence of interest between the little group of capitalists and the mass of the smaller traders. The former were in a sufficiently large way of business to benefit by the manipulation of rigid staple rules; they had, moreover, sufficient capital to make it worth the king's while to barter with them; they could offer substantial cash advances in return for commercial privileges. The smaller men could take no part in bargains on so large a scale; they had more to gain from less restricted trade. Their interest drove them against the great merchants to make common cause with the general mass of wool-growers and the public represented by the commons. The "free trade" settlement of 1351 represented, therefore, not a royal policy of plenty, but the desire of the commons to prevent the king from repeating his manipulation of the trade to the advantage of himself and a group of merchants who could pay him for their privileges. The abandonment of the Bruges staple and the establishment in 1353 of staples in England shewed that, since the Bruges staple was losing its political significance, the king thought it well to conciliate general English opinion rather than the group of great English exporters on whose resources and trustfulness he had drawn very heavily. From this time the division in the merchant interest put an end to any danger that a strong estate of merchants might challenge the commons for the control of commercial revenue. The king, however, did not cease to balance one set of interests against another, and the commons did not make it worth his while to bargain with them alone. In 1363 he renewed the staple that had been established temporarily at Calais in 1348, and at Calais it remained with certain interruptions till the end of the century and beyond, which is evidence of its suitability for traders. The rival advantages of staples at Middelburg and in England were much canvassed and sometimes tried in the reign of Richard II; but Richard's policy vacillated greatly too.

The decade which followed the Treaty of Brétigny has likewise some marked characteristics. It began with the second visitation of the Black Death and closed with the third, which carried off Queen Philippa in 1369. Edward was still under her beneficent influence, and comparatively active in State affairs. There was peace with France till 1369, though the war between the rival claimants in Brittany provided employment for the soldiers of England and France. In internal politics, too, the peace continued under a series of clerical ministers similar to those who had immediately preceded them. Langham was treasurer from 1360 to 1363, Barnet 1363–69, Brantingham 1369–71. Langham followed Edington at the Chancery from 1363 to 1367, and Wykeham from 1367 to 1371. In one sense the career of Wykeham was a triumph for the household system. He was of low, if not servile, origin; he had neither academic nor ecclesiastical backing; but he rose by diligence in the king's private service, especially as an organiser and financier for building, to be Keeper of the Privy Seal in 1363 and in effect prime minister. Besides attaining the highest influence in the State, he amassed benefices to an extent remarkable even for that age, and followed Edington as Bishop of Winchester. To churchman and noble he appeared as a thrusting, ill-qualified creature of the Crown; but the development in his character reveals part of the secret by which Edward maintained harmony between the official and the baronial party. As he achieved promotion, Wykeham adapted his views to his circumstances. His liberal foundations of Winchester College and New College, Oxford, indicate the inherent or acquired princeliness of his mind, and at the end of his life this self-made man stood as the chosen representative of the temporal and spiritual aristocracy in opposition to the new court party supported by the king's son, John of Gaunt.

The first years of peace saw a serious attempt to carry out administrative reforms and perhaps to produce a national balance-sheet. Despite the cessation of the war the king was far from being able to live of his own. Parliament continued to meet almost once a year, and grants, though not excessive, were regular. The sums received as ransoms were considerable. About one-third of the three million gold crowns due for King John of France had been paid when he died. But the ministers were administrators rather than statesmen, and when French use of the disaffection in Aquitaine produced a situation in France demanding active policy they proved unequal to their task. The problem would indeed have taxed the resources of minds greater than Wykeham's, and the last crisis of the reign, in many ways reminiscent of that of 1341, followed.

These years, 1360–69, produced further notable legislation. In 1361 came more labour regulations. In 1362 Parliament was opened for the first time by a speech in English; the use of English instead of French was ordered in law-courts because French was "too little known in the realm," and the king had observed elsewhere the advantages of administering law in the vulgar tongue. This statute remained an aspiration for some time. In the same year a limitation of the commission of purveyors was ordered, and a scale of charges for spiritual services was authorised to prevent undue charges on account of the scarcity of clergy since the plague. In 1363 among many attempts to regulate prices an attempt (repealed two years later) was made to control the dress of persons with income under £1000 per annum. In 1365, as noted elsewhere[1], the Statutes of Provisors and Praemunire were confirmed and enlarged.

In this decade much progress was made with what has sometimes been regarded as an original scheme of Edward III for amassing English estates and dignities in the royal family by discreet marriages. It may be doubted if it was either original or a scheme. Other English kings had acted similarly; Edward had a large family; and he pursued his usual opportunist policy probably without much thought of the wisdom or unwisdom of his action. The dying out of many of the great baronial families led to the accumulation of great estates in comparatively few houses, and gave to Edward's action a sinister importance. Edward, Duke of Cornwall, Prince of Wales, and Earl of Chester, married in 1361 his cousin Joan of Kent, daughter and heiress of the murdered earl. In the next year Edward III created the principality of Aquitaine and conferred it on his eldest son, at once providing for him and giving a show of independence to the Gascons. The king's second son died as a child. Lionel, the third, in 1342 married Elizabeth de Burgh, only daughter and heiress of one of the chief Anglo-Norman houses in Ireland and heiress also of part of the Gloucester estates. In 1362 he was created Duke of Clarence. When his wife died he returned from Ireland in 1368 to marry into the wealthy Visconti family just before his own death. His only child, Philippa, married the Earl of March, great-grandson of the traitor, and so to the March inheritance was added not only that of Clarence but an interest in the succession to the Crown; for after the Black Prince and his son came Philippa. John of Gaunt in 1359 married Blanche, who inherited the duchy of Lancaster, and in 1362 the title Duke of Lancaster was revived for him. His son Henry, the future Henry IV, about 1380 married one of the Bohun heiresses, and in 1376 Edward III's youngest son, Thomas of Woodstock, married the other Bohun heiress. By these marriages the earldoms of Hereford, Essex, and Northampton came into the royal family. Edmund of Langley, the only other surviving son of Edward III, married Isabella, younger sister of Gaunt's second wife, Constance of Castile; he became Duke of York, and the union of his descendants with those of Lionel gave the house of York wider estates and an augmented claim on the Crown. The houses of Lancaster and Mortimer, which had ruined Edward II, were in new forms finally to ruin the English medieval monarchy; but it would be fantastic to lay the responsibility for these later developments on Edward III.

Edward's reign covers a critical period in the history of the local machinery by which peace was maintained and justice administered. The practice of specially commissioning magnates and gentry with responsibility for their own counties was continued. The classes which had operated the local machinery of feudalism were now enlisted to operate the newer local machinery of the central government. Many experiments were

[1] See *infra*, p. 451.

made, but in the course of the reign what had been originally the police functions of the *custodes pacis* developed into the judicial functions of the justices of the peace. From the beginning to the end of Edward III's reign the commissions of the peace varied considerably from time to time, sometimes giving power to hear and determine felonies and trespasses, sometimes withholding it. The commons appear to have been on the whole more anxious to see the powers included in the commissions extended than the Crown was to extend them; they failed, however, to secure the nomination of the justices in Parliament. The various statutes which have been represented as decisive in creating or modifying the office did little but sanction what experiment had already proved useful; but the commissions which followed the parliamentary resolutions of 1380 gathered up results of half a century of experiment and served as a standard for the future.

Edward's reign, if it produced in proportion to its length few constitutional crises, was equally barren of dramatic ecclesiastical events. To this several factors contributed. During most of the reign the Papacy was at Avignon, and at a time when English relations with France were almost continuously unfriendly this circumstance made England peculiarly jealous of papal influence. Edward's personal inclinations accorded well with the state of the public mind. Never particularly devout, he seems to have welcomed limitations on papal or clerical influence. His policy, unlike that of some of his predecessors and successors, was not dictated or coloured by undue consideration of ecclesiastical interests. He is indeed rather remarkable for shewing practically no conscious desire to co-operate with papal policy. Most of his ministers were churchmen, but this had no particular significance at a time when, though there was an increasing number of qualified laymen in the routine offices of administration, clerks still greatly outnumbered the laymen fit for the highest State responsibilities. What was of some significance was that at two periods Edward broke away, apparently with no reluctance, from the tradition of employing clerical ministers in the highest places. He was acutely aware, and he shewed that he was aware, that, efficient as clerical ministers might be in ordinary circumstances, they were always liable to be influenced in a crisis by their second allegiance and by loyalty to the interests of their order. To speak of anti-clericalism in Edward's mind or policy would be anachronistic, but to emphasise the predominantly "lay" temper of the king is justifiable. This appears whether his relations with the Papacy or with the Church in England are considered.

When in 1330 Edward assumed control of English policy he found Pope John XXII engaged in his conflict with the Emperor Lewis, and until Lewis' death in 1347 the hope of obtaining French help against him and the fear that a disagreement between the French and English kings might be serviceable to Lewis had a not insignificant part in framing papal policy. Immediate interest, as well as higher motives, therefore led the Popes, both before and during the war, to intervene frequently for the sake of friendly relations between England and France. After Edward had admitted in 1331 that his homage to Philip was liege homage, while as yet his thought was on the conquest of Scotland, he played with the notion of an alliance with France, to be sealed by the marriage of his son and Philip's daughter, and to be consecrated by co-operation in a crusade. But insoluble difficulties in Gascony and Edward's irritation over Philip's intervention in Scotland nullified Philip's crusading idealism and papal policy alike. As England and France drifted into war, Edward, as a natural result, turned to Lewis, who had married his wife's sister. The alliance of Edward with Lewis and Lewis' Low German vassals in 1337, and the appearance of Edward and Lewis together at Coblenz in 1338, threatened what the Papacy had most feared. Edward received vigorous warnings against the danger of alliance with a deposed and schismatic prince; but, though Edward got little help from Lewis against France and Lewis got none from Edward against the Papacy, the incident provided a dramatic example of the cavalier manner in which Edward treated papal attempts to intervene in his affairs. In 1345 he behaved to the cardinals sent by Clement VI to discuss peace with a scant courtesy that savoured of contempt; and ten years later the Black Prince was only imitating his father in his contemptuous attitude to Innocent VI's peace proposals.

Appointments in the Church in England presented many opportunities for negotiation between the Popes and the king. The chapters, the Pope, and the king continued to compete or co-operate in appointments, and the chances of each party's victory in cases of disagreement continued to depend on the personalities concerned and the actual circumstances of the king and the Pope at the time of each election. That the king could by no means always get his way a number of appointments shewed. The weakness of Edward II at the end of his reign had been indicated by the promotion of Orleton to Hereford. His further promotion to Worcester in 1328 and the failure of Burghersh in the same year to secure the archbishopric of Canterbury illustrated the limitations of the influence of the English government. The most remarkable example of a defiance of the king's wishes was provided in 1340, when Edward's confidence in the rule of Stratford was ending. On the death of Melton, Edward struggled hard to get his favourite confidential clerk, Kilsby, made Archbishop of York and as a preliminary appointed him to a prebend. But the chapter elected de la Zouche, the dean, who had been Stratford's colleague as treasurer. Though Edward wrote to Avignon and every effort was made to keep out de la Zouche, yet after two years' agitation the new Pope Clement VI induced Edward to receive de la Zouche in 1342.

Such opposition by the papal Court was not usual. Clement's own reign indeed corresponded with part of that central period of Edward's when it was the king's definite policy to secure high ecclesiastical promotion for his ministers. From 1345 to 1355 each keeper of the Privy Seal became an archbishop or bishop of an eminent see. The intervention of the papal Court in English promotions was by no means wholly deplorable, though it was so steadily denounced in Parliament. Innocent VI and Urban V, perhaps less complaisant than Clement VI, tried to put occasional obstacles in the way of ignorant business men whom Edward nominated for episcopal office. The cases of Stretton and the diocese of Lichfield in 1360, and Buckingham and Lincoln in 1363, shewed how ineffective the papal protest was likely to be. The legislation about Provisors in the later part of Edward's reign had the practical effect of putting the king in an improved position for arguing such matters with the Pope.

As a natural result of his policy and predilections Edward's reign was not remarkable for eminent churchmen—saints, scholars, or ecclesiastical statesmen—in the highest offices of the Church. The Archbishops of Canterbury made a commonplace series, certainly not distinguished by zeal for the spiritual duties of their office and, except for Stratford, not notable as servants of the State. The one great name is Bradwardine; but he was not the first choice of the king, and the Black Death carried him off before he had time to shew his quality as primate. The see of York had fewer, but better, occupants in Edward's reign: Melton (1317–40), who dared to speak against the deposition of Edward II, and was treasurer after Mortimer's fall; de la Zouche (1342–52), who shared command at Neville's Cross; and Thoresby (1352–73), whose long, vigorous, and devoted rule was one of the brightest parts of the Church history of the century. Though the primacy and many other bishoprics went to members of the official class of royal servants, representatives of the great noble families filled other sees. The magnates as well as the *familiares* had their hold on the Church, and some prelates represented both.

Edward's legislation on Provisions is famous, but was not unprepared for. In 1343 the commons protested against the increasing use of English patronage by the Pope, a custom which among its other evil results sent money to the king's enemies. The "Statute of Carlisle" of 1307 was read, and at the king's suggestion a petition was sent to Clement VI. This asked for an end of reservations, provisions, and collations by which strangers unable to minister to the people drew rich revenues from England. No answer was made, and the practice continued. So did the complaints: Edward wrote to the Pope, and from time to time ordered bulls to be seized at the ports before they were put into operation. The commons still pressed for attention to the evil and for the making of a permanent statute to effect what the temporary ordinances sometimes prescribed. In 1351 the desire took definite form in the first Statute of Provisors. This ordered the observance of the rights of canonical electors and of patrons; all persons using papal provisions were to be imprisoned and the provisions declared null; to the king was made over the patronage of the canonical electors affected. The object was to prevent the Pope from usurping the rights of spiritual patrons who would not avail themselves of the protection for patronage rights offered by the king's courts. Nominally affording protection to canonical electors, it had in fact no such effect. By increasing the legal powers of the king it put him in a more favourable position for bargaining about appointments with the Pope; and a common history of appointments was that the king nominated and the Pope provided the same person, the chapter duly electing him. This strengthening of the king's position was one of the many ways in which the ecclesiastical events of this reign foreshadowed Tudor policy.

Two years later, in 1353, another subject of constant complaint was dealt with by the so-called first Statute of Praemunire. In 1344 and 1347 the commons had petitioned about the matter. This ordinance of 1353 was not at first enrolled as a statute, probably because the body which decreed it was not a full Parliament as a full Parliament was now understood[1]. Outlawry and forfeiture were threatened against all who should have recourse to foreign courts for matters cognisable in the king's courts. The papal court, though not named, was aimed at. In 1365 these two laws concerning benefices and legal actions were reasserted by another Statute of Praemunire. Lay patrons were now included and the court of Rome was mentioned explicitly. The prelates assented, "saving the rights of their order."

In the later part of the reign interest passed mainly to the financial side of the relationship with the Papacy. From the time of John's submission a thousand marks a year had been due from England and Ireland. Payment had been irregular. In 1365 Urban pointed out in very moderate terms that since 1333 Edward had paid nothing; the Popes had not pressed him in the time of his wars, but he had now come to peace and the Church had need of defence of its Italian estates. Urban therefore asked for payment. There was no threat. Edward consulted Parliament. The lords spiritual and temporal agreed that "neither John nor any other person could place the realm under such subjection without their consent"; the commons concurred; and the whole Parliament declared that John had broken his coronation oath. The lay estates said that they would resist any attempt of the Pope to make good his claim. This answer was sent to Avignon, but it neither set the question at rest for ever nor introduced Wyclif into politics, as has sometimes been supposed.

Gregory XI was elected in 1370, and in the early part of his reign the struggle reopened. A papal collector, Garnier, arrived in England in October 1371, and it was significant that he was made in February to swear that he would not act against the interests of the realm nor export

---

[1] It consisted of the lay and spiritual magnates with one knight from each shire and two burgesses from thirty-eight towns, and its main business was to change the policy about staples.

money. In the next year Parliament renewed its complaints about provisions, which nothing had been able to stop. Edward had sent a deputation to Avignon to discuss this and other matters, but it returned with no definite answer. Gregory was in particular need of money for his Italian wars, especially against the Visconti of Milan, and on 2 February 1373 demanded 100,000 florins from the English clergy. The difficulty was that the king was also in great need, and the urgency of finding a *modus vivendi* brought this perennial discussion to a more definite issue than usual. Both king and Pope were active, but the clergy jibbed at voting the royal tax unless the king would help to protect them from papal demands. Courtenay, Bishop of Hereford, was particularly loud in his complaints. On 11 March 1374 Edward asked for a conference with papal representatives at Bruges or Calais to deal with all matters in dispute; until it had been held no proceedings should be taken against his subjects. On 6 March he had ordered a return to be made before 16 April of all benefices held by aliens with a statement whether they were resident or not. The returns, said to have filled "several sheets of paper," were at least a useful weapon in controversy. It was in these circumstances that Gregory, not unnaturally, renewed the demand for tribute.

On 21 May 1374 a Great Council of prelates and barons met at Westminster to consider the Pope's claim to tallage the English clergy on the ground that, as vicar of Christ and lord spiritual, he was also "general lord of all temporals"[1] and in particular was lord of England on account of John's action. A Durham monk who had been on the Avignon deputation put the papal case. Mardisley, a Franciscan who became Provincial Minister, backed by an Augustinian, presented on the other side the full Franciscan argument that our Lord had no temporal dominion and gave His apostles none; the claims of Boniface VIII had done harm to the Church. The archbishops and clergy were in a difficult position, but finally agreed that they would be well pleased not to see the Pope such lord in England. The barons, it appears, returned answer to the claim on John's action similar to that made in 1366. We may have an echo of the debate in the statements which Wyclif put into the mouths of seven lords (especially the seventh lord) in his *Determinatio de Dominio*.

As the place for conference Gregory XI had named Bruges. The Bishop of London had made a vain journey thither in the winter of 1373–74, and Langham, now a cardinal, had headed an embassy to England. On 26 July 1374 the famous commission headed by Gilbert, Bishop of Bangor, and containing Wyclif, was appointed. This commission has been regarded too often as an isolated negotiation. Like others it effected little. By September it had returned and broken up. Edward levied a tenth on the English benefices held by cardinals in April 1375; and in August a second commission went out to carry on the discussions which had never been definitely abandoned. On 1 September 1375 Gregory, in six bulls addressed

---

[1] See reference to Aegidius Romanus, *infra*, p. 499 note.

to Edward, outlined the proposed concordat. It amounted to an abandonment of papal claims so far as these would disturb the *status quo* in the English Church, but it secured nothing for England for the future. Nothing was done to ensure the freedom of the chapters, because neither party sincerely wished it. Even so the concordat was not settled in 1375. The old system in fact continued. Papal aggression, foreign clergy, and the corruptions of the sinful city of Avignon were to appear among the complaints of the Good Parliament in 1376. It was not until his jubilee that, on 15 February 1377, Edward published verbal promises from the Pope. Gregory promised to allow free elections, to abstain from reservations and demands for first fruits, and to be moderate in granting provisions and expectations and in giving preferment to foreigners. Meanwhile he obtained a subsidy of 60,000 florins, with a promise of 40,000 more if peace should be made between England and France. No real change had been made except perhaps in public opinion about the Papacy. John of Gaunt, too, who was now definitely in control, had added nothing to his reputation, and had no claim on the gratitude of the English clergy.

The outbreak of war with France raised the problem of dealing with the "alien" priories dependent on foreign superiors and making payments to mother houses abroad. Edward III followed the plan used by his grandfather. The monks in such priories were not disturbed, but the Crown took over their revenues and paid them a maintenance allowance. In 1337 bishops were required to make returns of "alien" priories in their dioceses, and the long continuance of the war had the effect of ultimately breaking most of the connexions between the houses in England and the parent houses in France.

A stormy period, which closed the long reign, began in 1371. Personal changes prepared the way for the end of the political peace which had endured at home since 1343. Edward himself came to count for less and less. The death of Philippa in 1369 left him a prey to his lust. He fell under the influence of one of the queen's maids, Alice Perrers, who at the end of his life is said to have interfered shamelessly in the conduct of business and the administration of justice. The Black Prince returned in 1371 from his inglorious rule in Aquitaine a sick man, though only just turned forty. His younger brother Gaunt, therefore, became the most prominent public figure and acquired great influence over the king.

Though the commons had sometimes, as in 1354, shewn a desire for a peaceful settlement with France, Parliament had not been unwilling to see the war renewed in 1369, and had voted supplies. But failure to renew the successes of the past and a fear of invasion shook the hold of the ministers. In 1371, when Wykeham asked for financial support, a storm broke which has been compared with that of 1341. The lay estates petitioned that, inasmuch as churchmen could not be brought to account for their actions—language like Edward's own in 1341—laymen should replace them in the offices of chancellor, treasurer, barons of the exchequer, clerk of the Privy Seal, and other great positions. Edward agreed: Wykeham and Brantingham resigned; laymen replaced them. Sir Robert Thorpe, chief justice of the court of Common Pleas, became chancellor, and Sir Richard le Scrope treasurer. A subsidy was then voted. To represent this as anti-clericalism may well be an exaggeration. The desire for vigour in the conduct of the war was at least as prominent as distrust of the episcopal ministers, and there were cross-currents in clerical opinion itself. The articles urging increased taxation of prelates and the endowed Orders submitted by friars to this Parliament indicate that. Nevertheless, it is clear that the Parliament of 1371 definitely wished to end the rule of clerical ministers of the sort who had held office for many years and that the king at least acquiesced in this wish. Lay control, too, was more complete and lasted longer than in 1341. This change was unlike the earlier in being due to public opinion in Parliament, not to the petulance of the king. At a time when the bias of papal policy was believed to have been French, lay ministers, who were less likely to take any account of papal desires, had an obvious advantage over clerics. Feeling certainly ran high in these years between laymen and clerics; the difficulty of raising money for the war led to increasingly serious discussions about the possibility of heavier taxation of ecclesiastical property. The interest taken by politicians in the academic teaching of Wyclif concerning property is in itself evidence of the direction of government opinion; here was a schoolman who might justify theoretically what was desired for practical reasons. It is important not to antedate here the clash between Wykeham and Gaunt. Sir John Hastings is represented as the leader of the attack on the ministry; Gaunt was in Aquitaine. Moreover, in 1371, though dismissed, Wykeham was not disgraced. Nor is it necessary to assume that the miscalculation of the number of parishes in connexion with the raising of the grant was due directly to lay incompetence. It is, however, of interest to find the next Parliament attacking the lawyers and by statute forbidding them to act as knights of the shires. Lawyers, it was thought, used their position in Parliament to press for private petitions affecting their individual clients rather than for public petitions in the interest of the common good. Lawyers were the only alternatives to clerical ministers, and public opinion appeared to be hostile to both official classes.

The new lay ministry could contrive no more success than Wykeham's. In 1372 Pembroke failed at Rochelle; the king's projected expedition came to nothing; Poitou was falling away. In 1373 Gaunt, with the best equipped force sent to France since the war began, could only march uselessly from Calais to Bordeaux. In November 1373, Parliament voted money only after a committee of lords had conferred with the commons, a device for common action which became a regular part of parliamentary procedure. This was the last Parliament till 1376; the intervening years were filled by fruitless negotiations at Bruges for peace and for a settlement of outstanding questions with the Papacy. Gaunt was now in charge, and the last years of Edward were not merely inglorious, but full of scandals. Perrers, the king's mistress, Lord Latimer, the chamberlain, and Lord Neville, the steward of the household, working corruptly with financiers like Richard Lyons, brought discredit on the new household administration, and roused a new opposition among the magnates. Wykeham and Courtenay led this opposition. The Black Prince and the Earl of March, who began to figure as the regular opponent of Gaunt, were said to sympathise with it.

The "Good Parliament," the longest and best reported Parliament hitherto held, met on 28 April 1376. The magnates, lay and clerical, attacked the court administration in the familiar manner, but the attack was remarkable because the commons were now active and prominent in supporting, and almost acting for, the lords. A committee of lords consulted with the commons, who had chosen Sir Peter de la Mare, the steward of the Earl of March, to speak for them officially when the whole Parliament sat together. Through him the commons denounced Latimer, Lyons, and others of the courtier officials. When it became clear that nothing else would content Parliament, they were removed from court and condemned to imprisonment. Perrers too was banished from the king. The traditional remedy for bad government, additions to the ordinary council of the king, to "afforce" it, was pressed for, and by the advice of Parliament Edward chose nine lords to be a permanent part of the council. Six or four of them were to be present for all business. March, Wykeham, and Courtenay were among the nine, but not Gaunt, who grew steadily more opposed to the critics of the ministers. By providing that the chancellor, the treasurer, and the keeper of the Privy Seal should not be prevented from carrying out the duties of their offices the king partly nullified the concession. The death of the Black Prince on 8 June gave another occasion for an exhibition of distrust in Gaunt; his suggestion that the question of the succession should be considered was countered by the demand of the Parliament to see Richard. That he was the heir there was no doubt, but whether the two-year-old son of the Earl of March stood next after him was an open question.

The Good Parliament, though most of its work was undone, had permanent importance. The commons had taken a prominent part in a well-considered attack on the administration; their accredited spokesman had emerged as one of the most prominent men in the Parliament; and in denouncing offenders to the lords they had set precedents of importance in the history of the process of impeachment.

The immediately important fact was that the administration had not been changed. The great ministers remained in office, and Gaunt, definitely alienated from the magnates' opposition party, had no rival in personal influence at court. He must indeed be regarded as the ruler of England. The courtiers who had suffered, including Perrers, returned. The triumph was driven home by the imprisonment of de la Mare, the banishing of

Wykeham from court, and the seizure of his temporalities on charges relating to the period before 1371. March was forced out of the office of marshal, and was succeeded by Henry Percy, who left the opposition forthwith.

The next Parliament met in January 1377. Just before its meeting the lay ministers gave way for two bishops: Houghton, of St David's, became chancellor and Wakefield, of Worcester, treasurer. Whether or no Gaunt influenced the election of the commons, their temper was different from that of their predecessors. Instead of March's steward, they elected Hungerford, the steward of Gaunt's lands in Wales and the South. But although the commons gave little trouble, the magnates were less obliging. Convocation, led by Courtenay, would grant no aid till Wykeham, despite his banishment, had taken his place with the king's acquiescence. Courtenay also attacked Gaunt through Wyclif, and the rioters in London on 20 February 1377 by attacking Gaunt's and Percy's residences shewed the government's unpopularity. Gaunt, however, kept the reins until Edward died on 21 June; and though Wykeham recovered his temporalities three days before the king's death he had to conciliate Perrers, it is said, in order to do so.

The reign of Richard II was held to begin on the very day when Edward III died; in this way was sounded that note of an inherent royal right which was to be heard often through the reign. In many respects the new reign did not open a new epoch. The change from the senility of Edward to the minority of Richard made no change in the main matter: no controlling personality was on the throne. The more general conditions abroad and at home which had governed the last years of Edward also continued. Abroad, the war with France, unsatisfactorily renewed in 1369, dragged on unsatisfactorily with temporary interruptions and truces till 18 June 1389. In that year a three years' truce heralded continuous peace. At home Gaunt continued after the deaths of his brother and his father, as he had done during their illnesses, to be the dominating personality. For some years indeed the political problem may be stated in the terms of his varying control of the government. The main influence competing with his for control was that of the Black Prince's household now headed by the Princess of Wales, Joan. Her position of vantage, as permanently in touch with the young king, was partly neutralised by her not very strong character. There is a danger throughout the reign of representing the transitions as too sharply marked. Gaunt had not had such complete control before Edward's death as has sometimes been made out, nor was he eclipsed totally by his nephew's accession or by the Peasants' Revolt. The departure of Gaunt for the "voyage of Spain" in July 1386, when Richard was approaching the age of twenty, rather than the Peasants' Revolt, is therefore a convenient point at which to end a first division of the reign.

Some general observations may be made before examining this period. Richard, beginning to reign when he was ten, was four years younger than his grandfather had been when he came to the throne. In other ways also Richard was placed more unhappily. He found the country in a false position with respect to the war. Public opinion had not yet learned to distinguish between winning battles and conquering a State; it insisted on the continuance of campaigns from which no government could win credit, but which served only to make taxation necessary and to keep England in frequent fear and in occasional danger of the horrors of a French invasion. The government was, then, during the whole of this first period faced by an insoluble problem, and when Richard came to rule for himself he had to make the unpopular peace. He could not, like his grandfather, benefit by a peace that others had made whilst he won popularity by ending their power. To complicate the traditional opposition between the court party and the magnates there was an incalculable factor in Gaunt's immense influence. The king's other uncles, Edmund of Langley, later Duke of York, and Thomas of Woodstock, later Duke of Gloucester, were as yet of less account. York indeed was almost wholly given up to the passion for field sports so characteristic of the royal house, and was always a feeble figure in politics. Thomas of Woodstock came to prominence as leader of the magnates only after Gaunt had left for Spain.

But Richard's worst handicap was his own temperament. Of ability, of moral worth, and of attractive qualities he was by no means destitute. He proved able to carry out political schemes, to strike hard and effectively, and to shew little cruelty or malice in his triumph; but though sometimes capable of self-control, he was at other times incapable of it, and he had the harsh, pedantic manner of the doctrinaire who neither knows nor cares to know the wisdom of the man of the world, who is not concerned to conciliate general opinion but only to cherish friends and to crush foes, who is not content to get his own way unless he also appears to have got it. Richard seems to have seen life too sharply coloured and to have taken too little account of the indifference and lazy good humour of most men. The result was that, whereas Edward ruled a kingdom as if he were in charge of a hunting party, Richard too often postured as if he were the tragic hero of a melodrama. But this was not all. The king and his circle had imbibed high notions of indefeasible royal authority. Similar notions were held also by Charles V of France, and the source of them was probably among the students of Roman Law who had advised Philip the Fair. Formulated in the early part of the century by anti-papal controversialists, these doctrines had become by Richard's time the familiar mental environment of royal officials. Talk of prerogative and *regalie* was then not accidental or a mere flourish. It was the appropriate language of a country and a generation which was producing *De Officio Regis*. Richard's rather beautiful, delicate features, with a hint of both weakness and violence, are a not unfaithful index of some sides of his character. He had, like two other unfortunate English kings, Henry III and Charles I, a love of beautiful things and something of the artistic temperament. Like theirs, his career illustrated the inadequacy of cultured taste and private virtue as an equipment for public duty. Nevertheless his love of books, his connexion with Gower, Chaucer, and Froissart, and his rebuilding of Westminster Hall do not deserve to be entirely forgotten.

Something must be said of Gaunt, a man of only thirty-seven when his nephew became king. Gaunt appears to have been a rather ordinary man, made important by his wealth and position. He had not his elder brother's military ability, but it must be remembered that he entered the war after the French had learnt not to present to the English the chance of such victories as Poitiers. He was not, however, as negligible a figure as York nor was he as unpleasant as Gloucester. His morality, his religion, his romantic pursuit of his Spanish claims, and his final abandonment of them in consideration of a marriage for his daughter and cash payments for himself shew him to have been a typical man of his age. Too much has been made of his connexion with Wyclif. His sympathy with Wyclif's teaching about State rights over ecclesiastical property was not peculiar to himself nor incompatible with orthodoxy. The court party and the Princess of Wales took an attitude not very different. Too much may be made also of his interest in the succession to the crown. For a great part of the central period of his life, at a time when the rules of succession were debatable, he stood with only delicate boys between him and the throne. His raising of the question on the death of the Black Prince was not necessarily sinister; and when Richard later was believed to have intended Mortimer to be his heir Gaunt accepted the situation. In an atmosphere of intrigue and suspicion, and in a position which made him inevitably a target for rumours, Gaunt bore himself on the whole with credit and restraint. At the end of his life, when the factiousness of the opposition of Gloucester had declared itself, he supported the king loyally and effectively. He had no reason to imagine that the king would behave as outrageously as he did to Hereford; he was no longer irritated by the obstacles in the way of getting national support for his Spanish adventure; and it is likely that he deserves no little credit for the quiet of the years that followed his return from Spain.

The machinery of government set up on Richard's accession was in accordance with precedent. A council of twelve was chosen by the Great Council of magnates on 17 July, the day after the coronation. It was not strictly speaking a Council of Regency, for the king was supposed to rule. Its composition shewed that the plan was to conciliate the various interests. The court circle—Gaunt's following and that of the Black Prince alike—and the magnates of the aristocratic opposition were represented. The household of the Black Prince was perhaps predominant, and as time passed Gaunt's power tended to decline. Even before the council was formed, the reconciliation of Gaunt with the Londoners and with Wykeham, and the release of Peter de la Mare, shewed that the concordat between Gaunt and the Princess of Wales was effective. Burley, a soldier-follower of the Black Prince, controlled the inner circle of the king's servants.

This method of government by a continual council to advise the great officers of State lasted only till 1380. It was not a great success. The expeditions made each year in France or Brittany cost money and brought no credit. English fortunes went steadily back; the sea was unsafe; the coasts were ravaged. Parliament met frequently, once a year at least. Though it voted money fairly freely, it profited by the weakness of the government to advance its claims. The first Parliament, with de la Mare again as Speaker, secured a promise that no law ordained in Parliament should be repealed without Parliament and that during the king's youth the ministers should be elected in Parliament. The lords, however, did not support the commons in their further request that the king's household staff should also be nominated in Parliament, and this was not granted. Constant changes of chancellors indicated the instability of the government, but Parliament had no constructive policy except to call for committees to investigate abuses and check the spending of revenue. By 1380 the commons, weary of voting money for an unsuccessful government, asked that Parliament rather than the council should have more direct control of the principal officers of State, and by a novel proposal included knights and burgesses in the commission to investigate the administration.

The continuity of problems and of policy from the last years of Edward's reign was illustrated by the Parliament held at Gloucester in October 1378. It marks perhaps the moment when the suspicion of the court rose highest in the minds of churchmen. Clerical opinion had been inflamed by a more flagrant breach of sanctuary than had occurred since the days of St Thomas of Canterbury. Two Englishmen, Hawley and Shakell, in 1367 at the battle of Nájera had captured the Count of Denia, and eleven years later, his ransom being unpaid, were still holding his son as hostage. Fearing to lose their money when the King of Aragon was thought to be making representations to the English government on behalf of the count, they hid their hostage and were thrown into the Tower for concealing him. Breaking loose, they took sanctuary in Westminster Abbey. The lieutenant of the Tower, Boxhill, at the order of the council went to arrest them. He took Shakell, but Hawley resisted violently. As Boxhill's men tried to drag Hawley from the altar during Mass he was killed and a sacristan was mortally wounded. The abbey was closed; Sudbury denounced the greater excommunication against all concerned; Courtenay three times a week published the excommunication, and ignored a royal request to cease. Not unnaturally blame fell on Gaunt, for, though he was away on the St Malo expedition, his Spanish interests were known. London was much

moved and Westminster was no place for a Parliament. When it met at
Gloucester, the archbishop demanded satisfaction for the outrage. Wyclif,
though condemned by papal bull in the preceding year, was introduced
among other doctors of theology and law to defend the king and to shew
that sanctuary might be an abuse of God's law. This indicated the attitude of the circle of the Princess of Wales as well as Gaunt's, but was not
likely to appease clerical suspicion. The clerical chancellor, Houghton of
St David's, resigned; and the height of the feeling of suspicion of the
court at this time shewed itself by the persistent rumours (whether with
foundation or not) that sweeping measures of confiscation or taxation of
Church property formed part of the government's programme. It was
said even that secret statutes were made without the knowledge of the
bishops. Whatever may have been discussed in court circles, no campaign
against ecclesiastical privilege followed and no conclusion of the sacrilege
controversy was reached. Next year sanctuary for felony was confirmed,
but protection of debtors was withdrawn. This Parliament recognised
Urban VI as the true Pope.

Trouble with London—in itself a sign of a weak government—was to
be a constantly recurring feature of the reign. It had broken out against
Gaunt in 1377, when a threat to city liberties coincided with Gaunt's
support of Wyclif against Courtenay. It was renewed later in the contest
of John of Northampton and Nicholas Brember for the mayoralty; and
towards the end of his reign Richard was personally involved in undignified
quarrels with the city.

It was this government more directly in touch with Parliament after
the breakdown of the council system that provoked the Peasants' Revolt;
for financial needs, though they did not cause that attack on ecclesiastical
property which had been feared, led to the use of a new kind of taxation.
In the last year of Edward's life a poll tax of a groat a head had been
given to the king by Parliament and Convocation, and in 1379 a graduated
poll tax varying from ten marks from the Duke of Lancaster to a groat
from the poor was voted. This produced only half what was expected,
but provided some record of the tax-paying population. In 1380 a new
variant was tried: three groats per head from all over fifteen, the wealthier
to help the poor in each district, provided that none paid more than £1
or less than a groat for man and wife. The graduation was made only inside individual districts; in a poor district the poor got no relief. The
collection would have been difficult in any circumstances, but the government's urgent need of cash made it more so. In the winter and spring
of 1380–81 one set of authorities after another received instructions to
expedite payment; they were more effective in producing confusion. Two-
thirds of the tax was due by 27 January and the balance by Whitsuntide,
but the disappointing results and the immediate necessities led the
government to demand that final accounts should be made by 22 April.
The attempts at evasion were gross, but the behaviour of the government

was stupid; and it is significant that the revolting districts were almost the same as those for which special commissions of inspectors were appointed in March and May.

The Peasants' Revolt has a unique place in English history. Risings and riots occurred at almost the same time in all the south-eastern part of England, and in some isolated regions as far distant from the principal areas as the Wirral and Yorkshire. The risings, though marked by some common characteristics, have the appearance of being rather the spontaneous and sympathetic responses to the same general causes than a closely organised movement definitely directed towards one end. They did not synchronise very exactly, and they did not throw up one leader or a uniform programme. Yet, at least in some of the regions affected, mysterious semi-allegorical messages, often in verse, passed through the countryside as signals that the time for action had come. Breaking out at the end of May, the revolt reached its height when rebel hordes from Essex and Kent occupied London for four days in mid-June, but the crisis was over there before the corresponding risings had reached their acutest stages farther afield. The main outline is tolerably clear, but many details are not yet beyond dispute.

In Essex in May 1381 there were troubles about the collection of the poll tax, and at the very end of the month three villages on the Thames-side resisted the authorities by force. When the chief justice of the Common Pleas went down to punish the rioters, he went without adequate force to command the situation. He escaped, but clerks and jurors were murdered. Then in the first week of June riots occurred throughout the county. These the government could not easily suppress, because in north Kent, which had easy communication across the Thames with Essex, a rising had also begun. Armed rebels moving from Dartford entered Rochester on 6 June and plundered the castle. On 10 June Canterbury was occupied and the prison opened. The leader of the rebels, Wat Tyler—it is uncertain whether he was originally from Essex or Kent—maintained some sort of order, and was perhaps an ex-soldier. He had the spiritual support of John Ball, a priest released from the archbishop's prison. Ball had preached in a semi-political manner against social inequalities and wickedness in high places in Church and State for some twenty years, and had frequently been in trouble with his ecclesiastical superiors. On 11 June the host set out for London, and on the next day reached Blackheath. It repeated its earlier actions by releasing prisoners at the Marshalsea and the King's Bench prison and by sacking the archbishop's manor house at Lambeth. At the same time rebels from Essex were approaching London. Walworth, the mayor, prepared to defend the city, and, had he been adequately supported, could have kept the rebels outside. But there was strange indecision and lack of plan in the royal council gathered at the Tower for safety, and there was definite treachery in the city government itself. On the 13th the king with Sudbury and others of the council made

an indecisive attempt to parley with the rebels from a barge off the
Rotherhithe bank, but it came to nothing. By the connivance of
certain aldermen the drawbridge on London Bridge was let down for
the men from Kent, and Aldgate was opened for the men from Essex. The
rebels found many sympathisers in London. These joined them in opening prisons and in sacking the Temple, the palace of the Savoy, and the
Priory of St John's, hated for their connexion with lawyers, Gaunt, and
the treasurer, Hales, respectively.

The policy that prevailed in the Tower was to try to disperse the rebels
by concessions rather than to resist them by force, and, on Friday 14 June,
Richard with a group of courtiers met a body of the rebels by appointment at Mile End. What they asked was granted: villeinage and feudal
services to be abolished throughout the realm ; land held by villein tenure
to be held at a rent of 4*d.* an acre as freehold; monopolies and restrictions
on buying to be ended. An amnesty for the rebels and punishment of
such ministers and others as could be proved traitors were also promised.
Charters confirming these concessions to particular localities were at once
drawn up. But before the meeting at Mile End was over those whom the
rebels regarded as traitors met their end. Sudbury and Hales had remained at the Tower, and by accident or design the protection there was
inadequate. Rebels broke in. They dragged Sudbury from the chapel and
beheaded him with Hales on Tower Hill. It was as a politician that Sudbury
was murdered, though a monastic chronicler saw in his death a judgment
on one who had been too lax towards heretics. So far there had been little
bloodshed, but other murders now followed. There was a massacre of
Flemings, and among other victims was Lyons. Anarchy reigned in the
city.

It was, therefore, at considerable personal risk that Richard resumed
negotiations next morning at Smithfield. Tyler, it seems, increased his
demands, and shewed scant respect for the king and his party. Walworth
struck Tyler, wounding him mortally. Then Richard, helped for once by
his dramatic instincts, did precisely the right thing, and shewed that,
though only a boy of fourteen, he was no unworthy son of the boy who
had won his spurs at Crécy, and no unworthy grandson of that other boy
who had rid England of his mother's paramour. Riding forward to the
rebels, as they were still wavering and confused by their leader's fall, he
offered himself as their chief and captain, promising what they sought and
calling them to follow him. While he led them north to the open fields
of Clerkenwell, Walworth returned to the city. Despite the efforts of
disloyal aldermen, he brought out to the king a substantial band of soldiers and citizens determined to end the anarchy. Without bloodshed the
rebels dispersed. The Essex men went home. The Kentish men were led
through London to London Bridge. The sequence and interpretation of
the incidents of the Rising still present mysteries, in particular the
unguarded state of the Tower and precisely what took place at the inter-

views with the rebels. But the general attitude of the Kent and Essex men is clear. They shewed no disloyalty to Richard personally, but besides political dissatisfaction with his advisers, Gaunt, Sudbury, and Hales, there were radical social demands: an end of villeinage and partial dis-endowment of the Church.

Risings in the neighbouring counties followed quickly on the success of the Essex and Kentish men in London: in East Anglia on 12 June; in Cambridgeshire and Hertfordshire on 14 June; in some districts farther afield even later. In Cambridgeshire and East Anglia the rebels were particularly bitter and violent. Generally the local gentry put up little or no resistance, but from 18 June the government began to organise repression and the restoration of order. By the end of the month the situation was well in hand. Sporadic disturbances continued for some months. The Bishop of Norwich alone shewed fight from the first, and in a regular battle defeated Litster, "the king of the commons," who had established himself in rude state in Norwich. The suppression of the revolt followed the course of law in the ordinary courts, and, though severe, it did not provide displays of the brutality which had followed the Jacquerie.

The causes and the consequences of the revolt, in particular its relation with the Black Death, have been and still are the subjects of controversy. Until detailed evidence from the manors is known in bulk, and not merely in selections, it is impossible to generalise with confidence or justification. The one thing that seems certain is that there was great unevenness of agricultural and social development both before and after 1349. No general formula is to be looked for. It appears that villein services, though in many districts being commuted gradually, had not disappeared, as used to be thought, before the Black Death. On the contrary, in much of the south-east of England in particular (where the revolt was mainly centred) they formed a very important part of manorial life and economy on many estates, both lay and ecclesiastical. The Black Death violently disturbed the relations existing between the land and the population living on it, relations which in so far as they had been hitherto modified by the evolu-tion of the manor and the development of commerce and industry had been modified gradually. Labour, whether rendered in the form of villein services or free and paid for in cash, became suddenly much more valuable. For work which had been done previously by hired labour landlords were asked to pay perhaps twice as much as before the pestilence, while to get the same number of days work done by feudal service they had now to press much harder on the smaller population that remained. The im-mediate result of the Black Death was, therefore, a not unnatural attempt to regulate the price of labour. This attempt was neither so unfair nor so ineffective as it has sometimes been represented. An Ordinance of 18 June 1349 forbade labourers to receive, or employers to give, wages higher than those paid in 1346 or the immediately preceding years. All men and women under sixty having no means of support might be compelled to work at these rates. Food prices were to be reasonable. The first Parliament after the pestilence on 9 February 1351 gave greater precision to the arrangement by fixing a definite tariff of wages for different occupations. After some preliminary experiments combining the duties of enforcing the Statute of Labourers with those of the guardians of the peace, came a period (1352–59) when justices of labourers were appointed by distinct commissions; but a little before a general review of the office of the guardians of the peace in 1361 the justices of labourers were superseded, and in the end the justices of the peace took over their duties. The statutes were enforced vigorously, and, though they could not prevent a rise in wages, probably moderated it. In themselves they are evidence of the break-up of the manorial system. The lord did not rely on his own court; even for the problems of his own land he was coming to rely rather on agents of the central government commissioned to maintain a national policy. Competition among the lords for the services of free labourers and runaway villeins was mainly responsible for the comparative failure of the statutes. The persistent efforts to put them into force, clamoured for in almost every Parliament, had perhaps their main effect in adding to that widespread sense of grievance which provoked the Peasants' Revolt.

In other ways the lords tried to meet the new situation. As there had been before the Black Death some commutation of services, so there had been some landholding for rent; and in the half century after the Black Death the leasing of land for money rents increased. Sheep farming also increased, but it is doubtful if the Black Death had much immediate effect in greatly increasing the amount of land dealt with in these ways. After momentary disorganisation the old system continued in many manors, and then was gradually changed in the same direction as it had already been changing before the Black Death came. The Black Death by its first and later visitations helped to accelerate the change. It made the villeins at once more anxious and more able to throw off such services as remained.

The changes that had come over rural England since the Black Death, partly as a result of it and partly independent of it, provided, then, a considerable grievance for many who found conditions altering less quickly than they desired. It is most significant that on the social and economic side the demands of the rebels were not to be rid of new wrongs; they frankly called for a change from the old to a better state of things. This open desire to break with the past—an unusual thing in the Middle Ages—shewed itself also on the Continent in similar risings of artisans and peasants in the fourteenth century. In England it was provoked mainly by the Statutes of Labourers. But the political reasons for the revolt, represented sometimes as the mere occasion, were effective causes too. The Black Death was not the only disaster which had happened in the middle of the fourteenth century; the government was to pay for twelve years of unsuccessful war since 1369, a crushing burden to be borne by a population that was perhaps something like two-thirds of what it had been when Edward III began the war. The poll tax set the pile of discontents ablaze, but it added to the pile too. The later stages of the revolt gave an opportunity for mere looters, and in particular districts, as at St Albans, particular grievances, urban or rural, were worked off. In its earlier stages, however, the revolt was not wild communism, but a concrete demand for the improvement of rural conditions and a protest against the ministers of the Crown. That it had any direct connexion with Wyclif is a hypothesis lacking evidence and in itself unlikely.

There is little to be said for the old opinion that, though Parliament annulled the concessions made to the rebels in London, the villeins got what they wanted as a result of the revolt. They wanted an immediate end of some parts of the manorial system where it still existed, but the manorial system which had been gradually dissolving before the revolt continued to dissolve gradually after it. The main importance of the revolt is as an indication of what already existed in England, not as a cause of future things. The rebels had indeed no policy and no worthy leader. They had grievances and desires, and the weakness of the government gave them an opportunity to make a demonstration.

The rising of 1381, dramatic as it was, produced no sudden change in economic or political life. The period of feeble government, hampered by the French war, continued. The king was treated as a minor still, and Gaunt had still a varying amount of power in determining policy. His plans for a loan to enable him to conduct war in Spain and Portugal began to be considered, and this became his main preoccupation. Courtenay had succeeded Sudbury as chancellor as well as Archbishop of Canterbury, but he was soon followed at the chancery by Scrope, a friend of Gaunt. On 20 January 1382 Richard married Anne, sister of Wenceslas, King of the Romans. For Richard personally it was a happy marriage, though it did not fulfil the hopes of the politicians and bring Wenceslas into the war against the French. For Europe its importance lay in the new fostering of communication between England and Bohemia and the introduction of Wyclif's writings to the Bohemian Church.

The five years 1381–86 continued to be full of Parliaments. Two were summoned most years. War schemes also continued to illustrate the incompetence of the administration and the divided mind of the nation. The enthusiastic unity in following a strong lead from a king who knew his own mind—that was gone. The ministers were uncertain whether to conduct the war by the way of Flanders or by the way of Portugal. In Flanders, until his death in November 1382, Artevelde was resisting Count Louis whom the French supported; in Portugal it seemed possible that the national resistance to the Castilian claim to the Portuguese crown could be made to serve Gaunt's ambitions in Castile. For each campaign crusading privileges were offered, since both Louis and the Castilians supported the Pope of Avignon. These privileges served not only to attract recruits but also to ease the financing of the campaign. The commons preferred the nearer and cheaper campaign, and, despite opposition from Lancaster and other lords, the way of Flanders was chosen. Despenser, Bishop of Norwich, in the summer of 1383 headed an army which went too late to be effective, and came back covered with dishonour yet lucky to have suffered no greater disaster. Impeachment and temporary loss of his possessions punished the bishop, and Wyclif's tract *Cruciata* shewed that there was at least some revulsion against this shameless use of the crusading motive.

In 1384 the discords at home continued: magnates against the court, the commons against the lords, Gaunt against Northumberland, John of Northampton against Brember. De la Pole, who had been appointed with Arundel governor of the king's person in 1381, was now chancellor. He pressed the commons for an expression of opinion about the desirability of peace, even at the price of Richard doing homage for his possessions; and drew from them a general expression in favour of a peace policy, though they shewed extreme reluctance to take responsibility for definitely advising it. Peace was now the policy of the court. A truce for nine months was arranged at Leulighen, but as yet no permanent settlement could be arranged, because neither side would abandon its extreme claims. A group of the king's intimate counsellors began to appear more prominently. Among them was Vere, the young Earl of Oxford, and attacks on the court by Arundel, who had been dismissed from his governorship in 1383, roused Richard to a display of violent passion.

Gaunt held a position of comparative isolation. He was on bad terms with the court, and during the Salisbury Parliament in the spring of 1384 occurred an incident which puzzled contemporaries and has not yet ceased to puzzle historians. An Irish Carmelite, Latimer, claimed to be able to reveal a plot by Gaunt against the life of the king. Richard after violent threats against his uncle was somewhat appeased. Before the charges could be cleared up the friar was tortured to death with peculiar brutality, still refusing to reveal the names of any who knew his secret. To estimate the significance of the incident is the more difficult because, though he was introduced to the king through Vere, the followers of Gaunt and the king were jointly responsible for his death. A few months later the parts were reversed: in February 1385 Gaunt charged Richard with worthless conduct and the court with attempts on his life. Even Courtenay spoke for Gaunt, and suffered from a violent outbreak of the king's temper in consequence. One of the charges brought against Richard was a lack of spirit in not going personally to the wars, but his campaign against the Scots in 1385 brought him no credit. He found no organised opposition, and in less than a fortnight re-crossed the Border, having done nothing but ravage and burn. The outrageous murder of the son of the Earl of Stafford, a young friend of the king, by the king's half-brother John Holland, indicated the completely unsatisfactory and uncontrolled society in which Richard spent his youth.

It was during this Scottish campaign that there occurred in the Spanish peninsula an event which was greatly to influence English affairs. In August 1385 the victory of the Portuguese at Aljubarrota delivered them from Castilian domination. This made possible the campaign by the way of Portugal which had previously been regarded as hopeless. Gaunt, at the end of 1385, secured parliamentary support for his darling scheme, and in the following July sailed with a considerable force. No sooner had Gaunt's forces gone than a new threat of invasion, the last, scared England. But incompetence was by no means confined to the English side of the Channel, and nothing came of the grandiose French schemes.

The real significance of these wretched, confused years was the slow gathering around Richard, as he approached the age of twenty, of a new court party in opposition both to Gaunt and to the magnates. Its better side was shewn by the less frequent change of ministers. Segrave, an old officer of the Black Prince, was treasurer from 1381 to 1386 and de la Pole chancellor from 1383 to 1386. Both were good officials; de la Pole, created Earl of Suffolk, was perhaps the most competent of all Richard's advisers. Even Vere was idle and incompetent rather than vicious; but Richard's extravagant advancement of him to the "strange name" of Marquis of Dublin and the grant of all royal lands and authority in Ireland made him hated as a "favourite," though he came of an old house. The factious divisions in the aristocratic opposition and the uncertain attitude of Gaunt, its natural leader, gave an opportunity for the strengthening of the new court party. In the years immediately preceding Gaunt's departure, Richard began not merely to be truculent to the magnates personally, but to shew to the commons that he was not disposed to submit to new claims from Parliament. Parliament met less frequently, once only instead of twice in each of the years 1385 and 1386. In 1385, in reply to a request for a review of his household, Richard told the commons that his present servants satisfied him and that he would change them only when he pleased. He chose that moment to commit Ireland at great expense to Vere. The freer use after 1383 of the signet seal by the king's "secretary" was also a sign that the new personal policy of the king was finding new forms of expressing itself along the traditional lines of administrative inventions. Richard's intervention in London affairs points in the same direction.

Thus at the close of this first period, through the years of faction and weakness, a preparation for a change had come. That policy of compromise between all interests with which the reign had opened was ending. The great offices had been for some years in the hands—the not incompetent hands—of the court party. Gaunt, who had played a changing and often ineffective part, sometimes influential by alliance with the king or the magnates, sometimes in surly isolation from both, never to be relied on by either, had now ceased to try to control English politics, because he had got what he hoped the control of English politics would give him. His disappearance left the court face to face with the aristocratic party. Richard was trying to do what Edward III had done when he emerged from the period of tutelage. But the national situation and the personal factors were now less favourable. Edward's easy-going policy had strengthened the force of the opposition, and the compromise which was to be reached after a time of stress in 1389 was to prove less permanent than that which had followed the stormy years 1340–41.

The period of struggle between Richard and his new court party and the magnates' opposition may be taken as covering the time between July 1386, when Gaunt sailed, and 3 May 1389, when Richard dramatically, as his manner was, assumed full responsibility for the government. The removal of Gaunt left his two brothers naturally more prominent, but the temperamental ineffectiveness of York meant that in fact Gloucester took the lead. Himself only thirty, he was neither very wise nor very generous. He had, however, popularity: men remembered that he had revived the military reputation of the royal house by his remarkable, if rather useless, march from Calais through northern France to Brittany in 1380. Prominent in the party of magnates that he led were Gaunt's son Henry of Derby, Arundel, personally alienated from the king, Thomas Beauchamp, Earl of Warwick, and Thomas Mowbray, Earl of Nottingham. Among the prelates were Arundel's brother, the Bishop of Ely, Brantingham, Courtenay, and Wykeham. The contest opened at once by a challenge to the court party in the Parliament of October 1386. From that time the opposition was open and articulate. Gloucester's friends used Parliament as the best instrument for controlling the king, whilst the king spoke constantly of his prerogative as something beyond the control of any authority.

England was still nervous about the possibility of an invasion when Parliament met, and the chancellor Suffolk asked for a subsidy to enable the king to take the field in person. Instead of a subsidy came an attack from the commons on the ministers. Richard shewed fight. Having retired to Eltham, he made Vere Duke of Ireland, and, in the same tone as in 1385, bade Parliament mind its own business, declaring that he would not at its request dismiss a scullion. He reminded it that it might be dissolved. Parliament declined to proceed until Suffolk were dismissed and Richard should return to London. Instead of the forty commoners whom Richard had asked for to explain its demands, it sent Gloucester and Arundel. They asserted that an ancient statute made necessary annual Parliaments at which administration should be discussed. If the king kept away for forty days Parliament might dissolve itself. Richard threatened to appeal to the King of France if there were rebellion, and was threatened in turn with the fate of Edward II[1]. This broke his opposition. He returned and

---

[1] Knighton, *Chronicon*, ii, p. 219.

changed his ministers, dismissing Suffolk and making Arundel's brother, the Bishop of Ely, chancellor. Suffolk was impeached; but it was difficult to convict so good a public servant. He was found guilty of but three out of seven charges. Condemned to fine and imprisonment, he was in fact not severely treated. The prosecution was a political move; it was followed by the favourite device for controlling kings, a council to supervise all royal actions. This Commission consisted of eleven persons and included, beside rigid opponents of the court like Gloucester and Arundel, moderate men with official experience like Courtenay, Brantingham, and Wykeham. The Commission had unusually wide powers to regulate the royal household and revenue and to control the administration. The king was forced to accept it in order to get a grant, but he secured a limitation of its powers to the year November 1386 to November 1387. He closed Parliament with an unusually explicit note of defiance declaring his intention that "for nothing done in that Parliament should any prejudice arise to himself or his crown or prerogative."

He had, however, lost control for the present of the great offices of State. The Commission remained in authority at Westminster. Its mixed composition might have induced him to try gradually to construct a new ministerial party inside and in touch with it. He chose to have as little as possible to do with it, and all he could do in the circumstances was to try to organise an opposition in the country based on his household officials and supported by the armed forces that he might hope to rely on from Cheshire, Wales, and Ireland. He left London on 9 February 1387, and until the eve of the expiry of the authority of the Commission moved round the midlands. He called no Parliament, but held several Councils, and secured his position by enrolling troops personally devoted to his cause. It became clear that, apart from such special forces, he could count on little general support. At a Shrewsbury council the sheriffs reported that the commons were on the side of the barons and would not fight against them, nor would they be willing to see the election of the knights tampered with in order to secure those friendly to the king. The judges were more helpful. On 25 August at Nottingham they gave written opinions in favour of Richard's view of his prerogative and the Commission's attempt to control it[1]. Later they pleaded that they gave the opinions under pressure, and this seems likely. The opinions were not published, but kept for future use. Richard also made a bid for popularity in London by pardoning John of Northampton, and on 10 November 1387 entered a capital apparently loyal to him.

[1] In answer to ten questions the Chief Justices Tresilian and Bealknap, and others, declared that the Commission was derogatory to the prerogative and that all who had helped to procure it deserved capital punishment; that Parliament should follow business as prescribed by the king; that it had no power without his consent to impeach his servants; that the judgment on Suffolk was erroneous and revocable; and that the person who had moved for the production of the statute deposing Edward II was guilty of treason.

CH. XV.

Seeing their danger as the period of the Commission's authority drew to an end, Gloucester, Arundel, and Warwick, the backbone of the Commission, became very active. They gathered with armed forces at Waltham, and on 14 November "appealed" five of the king's most prominent supporters: Neville, Archbishop of York, the Duke of Ireland, Suffolk, Tresilian, and Brember. Richard, apparently to his surprise, found that in London he had no chance of opposing the appellants' forces. The more moderate members of the Commission arranged for a meeting between the king and the appellants on 17 November. Richard had to agree to call a Parliament for 3 February to deal with the appeal. Meanwhile Suffolk and Neville fled abroad; Tresilian and Brember hid themselves; and the Duke of Ireland went to rouse Cheshire and the west to save the king. He tried to return to London by way of the Severn and the Cotswolds with the force he had raised. But when his force met the appellants' force at Radcot Bridge on 20 December it made little resistance and dispersed. Vere fled to the Continent, where he died in 1392. Before Vere's defeat Gloucester is said to have discussed deposing Richard, but to have found no support for this plan from Nottingham and Derby. With his army dispersed and the alternatives of deposition or surrender, Richard had no choice but to submit completely. Yet there is considerable uncertainty about the last week of December. There was much negotiation and a crisis that seems to have lasted for some days. Possibly the rival claims of Gloucester and Derby explain why Richard was not deposed or, if he was deposed, why he was restored after two or three days. He was made to withdraw writs that he had issued while his force was still in being under Vere, asking that knights *in debatis modernis magis indifferentes* should be chosen for the Parliament. Then a great number of his loyal household officers were removed, some being accused of treason, others simply banished from court. Richard had tried to defy the aristocratic opposition by force of arms, and he had failed utterly. He was to pay the price in full. The severity of the proceedings of 1388 compared with those of 1386 indicates the difference between the end of a political and of a military campaign between the magnates and the court. In Gloucester the triumphant opposition had a leader unusually persistent and even malicious.

The "merciless" Parliament met on 3 February, and sat with breaks till 4 June. No epithet was ever better earned: in most matters the Parliament shewed itself the willing agent of the appellants. A feature of the crisis was the care taken to appeal to public opinion against the king. After Gloucester had protested his loyalty to Richard, the articles of the appeal against the five members of the court party were read. They amounted to little more than a condemnation of recent policy; the five had misled the king and opposed the Commission. The king attempted to dispose of the articles by a legal opinion that they were not conformable to civil law or to the law of the land. The Lords ruled, however, that the lords of Parliament were judges of such charges against peers, with the king's assent, and according to the law and course of Parliament were bound neither by civil law nor by the usages of inferior courts, since other courts were only the executors of ancient laws and customs and of the ordinances of Parliament. This declaration was notable as an assertion of the sovereignty of Parliament against both the theory of the prerogative contained in the Nottingham judicial opinions and the view recently expressed by the lawyers of the sovereignty of law. It was also notable as another step in the definition of the claims of the House of Lords; the declaration contained its claim to be the supreme law-court, and foreshadowed the method of bill of attainder. Found guilty of treason by an examination of the articles, Suffolk, Vere, Tresilian, and Brember were condemned to execution, Archbishop Neville to the loss of his temporalities and to further judgment. Tresilian and Brember were executed. The judges who had given opinions against the Commission were impeached, condemned to death, and banished to Ireland. Minor servants of the king suffered death.

Gloucester now began to lose his hold on his party; it wearied of vengeance before he did. Yet he secured the execution of Burley, despite the opposition of the king, York, Nottingham, and Derby, for he and Arundel and Warwick were the men ultimately in control. The Pope complaisantly translated Neville to St Andrews, a see, in fact, held by a schismatic supporter of the anti-Pope. He also rewarded or punished other bishops by suitable translations, as required—an interesting commentary on the legislation about provisors. The appellants received £20,000 for their services to the nation; the king, on request, renewed his coronation oath; and the Parliament ended after oaths had been taken from all in authority to prevent the disturbance of its work.

For eleven months England remained mainly under the control of the appellants' party. The arrangements made in the "merciless" Parliament had more effect than those of most Parliaments because they had behind them the sanction of military force. Once their opponents had been destroyed, the appellants shed no more blood. A short Parliament at Cambridge in the autumn made a grant for continuing the war, and re-enacted and enlarged the Statutes of Labourers in a sense that shewed some regard for the tenant farmer as well as the landlord, but none for the labourer. The plan of the later Acts of Settlement was sketched in an attempt to prevent the movement of labourers from their hundreds, except by the permission of justices of the peace. No one was to leave husbandry after the age of twelve. Impotent beggars were to be maintained in their own towns and parishes. The justices were to meet quarterly and to receive salaries. An attempt to abolish "liveries called cognizances" revealed, not for the first time, a division of interest between the great and the small landowners; compromise and postponement resulted. A statute was also made against Provisors.

The great officers carried on the government. Some useful reforms and reorganisations were made. The Chancery Ordinances of 1388–89 are at once a codification of practice and plan of reform; they indicate the steady growth of a trained lay bureaucracy with professional feeling. Its business was to administer, whoever might be in control, and it survived not only political changes in the great offices, but political revolutions too. The eclipse of the personal influence of the king meant the end of the use of signet letters. Yet the king's household and chamber still contained some of his friends. He had never given way completely to the "merciless" Parliament about all appointments, and, as the storm abated, those who had dispersed began to come back to court. The change from Richard's acquiescence in the rule of the magnates in 1388 to their acquiescence in his rule in 1389 was not, therefore, unprepared or altogether revolutionary. Many of the same men conducted the business of State in the same spirit before and after Richard's assumption of power on 3 May 1389. Foreign policy provided an example of this. Under the appellants the war continued against both France and Scotland: there were naval exploits by Arundel and the famous battle of Chevy Chase at Otterbourne. But the appellants in power continued the war unwillingly as Richard had done, and their negotiations for peace come into line with those which he had conducted in 1386 and would conduct again in 1389.

"For eight years Richard governed England as, to all appearance, a constitutional and popular king."[1] The eight years which followed Richard's assumption of power on 3 May 1389 have sometimes been so sharply differentiated from the period preceding them that the difficulty of relating them to the rest of Richard's reign has been artificially increased. Was Richard shamming a belief in "constitutional" government in order to lull his enemies into a carelessness that would bring them to their death? Or was he truly a changed man? Or was Gaunt the miracle-worker? The task of choosing one of several improbable solutions to the problem would disappear if it should seem that the problem had been overstated. There was less change in Richard personally than has been often said. It is not impossible to trace a thread of consistency in his character and actions throughout his reign. Moody, violent, with melodramatic tastes, and a high notion of his prerogative, he pursued in a somewhat new style the old policy of the kings of England. He tried to get his own way, but he used different methods at different times according to his mood and the circumstances of the moment. The real problem of these years is not so much the conduct of Richard—that grew out of the past not unnaturally—but the conduct of Gloucester and his colleagues, especially Arundel. That Richard should wish to take on his responsibilities when the crisis of 1388 was comfortably over, and that for some years with little provocation he should not act outrageously, was not in itself very surprising; but that the men who had acted so

[1] Stubbs, *Constitutional History*, ii, p. 507.

violently and so cruelly in 1388 should be edged out of power and should make so little resistance needs explaining. Perhaps they were less wanton than at times they have been pictured. Having destroyed their enemies, they were content to help the king to rule, especially since, in more normal times, they could no longer count on the universal dereliction of the king and his circle. For English public life could not continue indefinitely a mere duel between the king and the three principal appellants. Appeals to public opinion made by both sides indicate that no policy was hopeless which could convince people of influence that it was reasonable and deserved a trial. It was not unreasonable in the fourteenth century that a king of twenty-two should rule as well as reign, and so when Richard asked the chancellor and treasurer to resign and appointed two veterans, Wykeham and Brantingham, in their places no revolution followed. So supported, he felt strong enough to dismiss Gloucester and Arundel from the council, and to replace Arundel as admiral by his own half-brother Holland. He also recast the judicial bench. But since he punished no one for the acts of the recent administration and called back no one who had been banished by the "merciless" Parliament, but postponed the collection of part of the last subsidy and raised salaries, there was no case for resistance. The dramatic seizure of power on 3 May 1389 was meant to impress public opinion, but it was not unprepared for—the king had already a hold on the officials—and it was followed by no reversal of policy.

The Commission of 1386, by which his earlier attempt at personal rule had been upset, had always contained two elements: aristocratic magnates and conservative ecclesiastics with a knowledge of official life. There was the possibility of a cleavage. In 1386 Richard had not taken advantage of it. In 1389, perhaps having learnt something, he did so. His exhibition of displeasure with Gloucester and Arundel was not unnatural, nor perhaps unwise; but he put the ecclesiastical appellants into office, and tried to win Nottingham and Derby. Gaunt returned six months after Richard had assumed power. He had been urged to do so by the king, and his presence helped to give stability to the new rule. Gaunt had satisfied his continental ambitions. For the rest of his life he played a dignified and useful part in strengthening the government and, if favourable chroniclers are to be believed, in influencing his nephew's mind. In 1390 he was made Duke of Guienne and at last brought about a definite cessation of hostilities in France. Most important of all, his return in itself destroyed much of Gloucester's importance, just as his departure had thrust Gloucester forward as leader of the magnates. Gloucester and Arundel in a few months reappeared in the council. Gloucester, still very popular, was used by Richard in important work, and Arundel's brother in 1391 succeeded Wykeham as chancellor. He held office for five years, and then in 1396 he followed Courtenay at Canterbury. He seems to have had not only office, but the king's confidence. Richard, now maturer, was

building up an official party, but it had a wider base than in the days of
Suffolk and Vere.

Yet he was the same king with the same weaknesses. His passionate
grief at the death of Queen Anne in 1394 and his violence in striking
Arundel to the ground in Westminster Abbey at her funeral shewed his
old unbalanced temperament. He had not abated his opinion about his
prerogative, and did not pretend that he had done so. At the first
Parliament which met after he had resumed power the chancellor,
treasurer, and council resigned to give Parliament an opportunity of
judging them. Parliament having judged them satisfactory, the king
reappointed them, but he stated that he did not regard this as a precedent
limiting his freedom to remove and appoint at pleasure. Still more
significant was the declaration of the Parliament of 1391 that "our lord
the king should be as free in his royal dignity as any of his predecessors,
despite any statute to the contrary, notably those in the days of Edward II,
and that if any such statute had that effect under Edward II it should
be annulled." His old spirit was shewn in his renewed quarrel with
London in 1392, when he removed the administration to York and
Nottingham, suspended the liberties of the city, imprisoned the mayor
and sheriffs, and restored all on payment of a fine.

The council, too, which had been prominent before 3 May 1389 did
not cease to be so. Parliament was meeting less frequently[1] and the small
working council of ministers was becoming a place for administrative
decisions rather than consultation. This small council really ruled
England. On occasion it resisted the personal wishes of the king, who
did not always attend it. Parliament, now sharply differentiated from an
enlarged council, produced some notable legislation: in 1390 a more
stringent Statute of Provisors; in 1393, in response to papal opposition to
that statute, the "second" Statute of Praemunire. In 1390, alleging many
complaints in Parliament, Richard made an ordinance in council designed
to end the practice by which "maintainers" of other men's quarrels per-
verted the course of justice. Such maintenance was encouraged by the
undue grant of livery by magnates: the circumstances in which livery
might be granted were therefore narrowly restricted. In 1393 Parliament
legislated on the same subject. The most notable achievement of these
years was the peace with France. This made the general situation easier,
and in itself would almost account for the success of the government, the
lighter taxation, and the less frequent Parliaments. The treaty also opened
a way for more ambitious action by Richard.

The years were not entirely without troubles. There was disorder in the
north, mixed, it was thought, with the ambitions and jealousies of the
great magnates towards one another and the king. Partly as a result of
this, the old dislike of Gaunt and Arundel flared out in a violent quarrel

---

[1] Between 1380 and 1388 thirteen Parliaments met; between 1388 and 1397 seven met,
lasting on an average only half as long as in the earlier years. Tout, *Chapters*, III, p. 473.

in 1394. Arundel's real grievance was the close alliance of the house of Lancaster and the king, and several events went to strengthen this. On the death of his second wife Constance in 1394, Gaunt married his mistress Catherine Swynford, and Richard recognised her children as legitimate members of the royal family. The death of Derby's wife removed a personal link between him and Gloucester, who had married another of the Bohun sisters. Signs were not wanting that Gloucester and Arundel, the unbending remains of the appellants, would not hold indefinitely to the compromise that had marked politics since 1389. Gloucester, appointed in 1392 as lieutenant in Ireland, had had his authority at once recalled.

Meanwhile Richard was moving in the direction of more personal exercise of power. The death of Anne removed a good influence from him. His experiences in Ireland and his friendship with France encouraged him. From August 1394 till May 1395 Richard was in Ireland. This was Richard's first considerable experience of military life, for conditions in Ireland made his journey from Waterford to Dublin "of the nature of a campaign rather than a royal progress." His companions, except Gloucester, were his loyal friends. He saw no considerable fighting, but the possibility of the use of forces drawn from Ireland, Wales, Cheshire, and the west had a larger place henceforth in royal schemes. The Parliament held in Richard's absence probably marked the high-tide of Lollard influence on public opinion. A petition, supported by several prominent members, was presented, and was published by being fixed to the doors of St Paul's and Westminster Abbey. The petition represented the most radical criticism of the clergy and rites of the Roman Church which Wyclif had uttered in the *Trialogus*, but it was expressed in a manner even more uncompromising than his. The Lollards were now beginning to organise themselves as a sect with ministers specially ordained.

Richard sealed the new friendship with France by his marriage on 12 March 1396 with the seven-year-old daughter of Charles VI. The marriage was his own policy, and was not altogether popular. It left open the question of the succession. Richard's thoughts had turned to France since the death of Anne. He still played with the notion of getting French help against rebels if need arose. He had blurted out the suggestion to Gloucester in 1386, and it reappeared in the stipulation made in the preliminary negotiations early in 1396 that the French king should support Richard with all his power against any of his subjects.

But it was not upon France that Richard principally depended. His position at home was much improved. Gloucester alone of the royal magnates was hostile to the peace. Gaunt was held by new ties. The ministers were competent and trustworthy. Gilbert (1389–91), Waltham (1391–95), and Walden (1395–98) succeeded one another at the Treasury. Arundel was chancellor 1391–96. He was followed by Stafford, who had proved his worth as keeper of the Privy Seal. Longer tenure of office was in itself a sign of the strength of the government. The king had also in Bushy, Bagot, and Green representatives of the class of knights devoted to court interests. Bushy was especially valuable as a Speaker who was adept at managing the commons. Richard was spending considerably in organising military support for himself. He had, like the magnates, his own livery and badge of the white hart, and the followers of his household were attached to him by personal ties. The next step in improving his control was to be dramatic, but it was not out of harmony with the policy of recent years. Gloucester, though he had now only Arundel and Warwick to support him, had not grown less offensive to the king; and every year made it less necessary to endure him.

When, in January 1397, Parliament met, it was three years since Richard had had dealings with it, the last having met during his Irish visit. In this Parliament the issue became clearer: Richard saw at once how great his power now was and how at the same time it was definitely limited by certain obstacles. The next step was to remove the obstacles. It was in doing this that Richard passed from seeking to build a strong royal power without breach of precedent to something that approached a royal revolution.

On the one side Parliament was submissive. The commons had included in their rather familiar grievances against the administration one which roused the king's special fury: the cost of his household swollen by bishops and ladies. In response to Richard's enquiry, the Speaker, Bushy, named Haxey as responsible for submitting this complaint to the commons[1]. The commons apologised for their interference in the household, and the lords resolved that it was treason to excite the commons to reform anything touching the person, government, or regality of the sovereign. Haxey was condemned for treason, but was pardoned. Richard had made his point. His announcement that as "emperor of the realm" he had legitimated the Beauforts sounded the same note of prerogative. With the assent of Parliament he restored the justices banished to Ireland in 1388, but his confirmation of the other acts of the "merciless" Parliament shewed that he recognised the need of proceeding slowly.

For by its successful opposition to his foreign policy this Parliament had shewed not less clearly the limits to his power. As a sign of his friendship with France, he had promised to send Rutland and Nottingham on an ill-conceived expedition against the Visconti. Now, though he made a personal appeal and used rather wild language about his freedom and his intentions, he could get no support, and dropped his request for a

[1] Haxey was a clerk, but there is no reason to suppose that he was a member of Parliament summoned under the *praemunientes* clause. He was in royal service as a clerk of the common bench, and the bill which he handed to the commons was not a bill in the modern technical sense, but a complaint such as non-members could put before Parliament. Such discussion of the constitutional importance of his case as turned upon his being a member of Parliament is therefore irrelevant. Tout, *Chapters*, IV, p. 18.

subsidy. Later it was said that there had been plots against the king, but the opposition in itself was a reason for removing the king's opponents. Besides the check in the Parliament and Gloucester's constant hostility to the royal foreign policy, Richard had to suffer from his reproaches when, in accordance with treaty obligations, Brest was evacuated on 12 June. Gloucester and Arundel refused also to attend the council.

In July Richard struck decisively. He invited Gloucester, Arundel, and Warwick to a banquet at the chancellor's house on the 10th. Warwick alone came, and was arrested. Gloucester pleaded ill-health. Arundel without an excuse retired to Reigate. This did not save them. Gloucester on the next day was compelled to come to London, and was sent to Calais. Arundel was induced by his brother to surrender to the king. These arrests were made on the advice of eight lords: Nottingham, Huntingdon, Kent, Rutland, Somerset, Salisbury, Despenser, Scrope. They represented the younger elements in the king's party. Several were kinsmen of Richard; almost all had been promoted in his reign. Gaunt, York, and Derby were said to have approved the arrests. The reason given for them was the extortions and misdeeds to be laid bare in Parliament.

The procedure of 1388 was not unnaturally followed. The eight lords "appealed" Gloucester, Arundel, and Warwick. In the Parliament which met on 17 September, the opposition had no leaders, lay or clerical; but by this time only very determined opposition would have sufficed to check the king. He made use of his military preparations. His Cheshire archers and white hart retainers were summoned. Only his friends were allowed to bring their armed supporters. Parliament met in an open wooden building, a temporary shelter necessary perhaps because of rebuilding at Westminster, but one that conveniently left the archers in sight. Bushy produced from the commons exactly what was wanted, and in fourteen days Richard's opponents were destroyed. The act appointing the Commission of 1386 and the pardons of 1388 were repealed, pardons being given afresh to those who were now on the king's side. The eight lords then made their charges. Arundel, unmannerly to the last, was executed. Warwick was banished to the Isle of Man. Gloucester, it was announced, had already died before Parliament met after making a confession at Calais, but he was nevertheless condemned. There is little room for doubt that he was murdered. To make a clean sweep, even Archbishop Arundel, as one of the appellants of 1388, was condemned to exile. Walden, the treasurer, succeeded him at Canterbury, and Arundel, like Neville, was translated to St Andrews. In the lavish bestowal of honours on his friends Richard raised Nottingham and Derby to be Dukes of Norfolk and Hereford. Parliament was adjourned to meet at Shrewsbury on 27 January 1398.

Was Richard satisfied? If not, how much farther would he go? In a conversation in December, if Hereford's word could be believed, Norfolk stated his fear that in the end Gaunt and Hereford and himself would suffer, as the king had not forgotten or forgiven the original appellants. The matter is obscure. Hereford had been away crusading in the Baltic and visiting Jerusalem in the critical years, and had not hitherto had the confidence of Richard to the same extent as Norfolk. He laid the matter before Parliament in circumstances which did no credit to his good faith.

At Shrewsbury there was carried out what Stafford in his opening speech pronounced to be the object of the Parliament: to make one ruler, not many. The acts of the "merciless" Parliament were repealed as trenching on the prerogative. The Nottingham opinion of the judges became good law. By an unprecedented act the customs on wool were given to the king for life, and any attempt to undo any of the work of that Parliament was included in a new definition of treason. Not so great a breach of precedent as has sometimes been represented was made, however, when Parliament referred certain petitions to a committee of eighteen of its members, giving the committee power to determine them and also to deal with the charges laid against Norfolk by Hereford.

For a year and a half Richard ruled England with the powers given him at Shrewsbury. There was no constitutional revolution, and it is still possible to trace development in his policy. Richard had so effective a control over the ordinary machinery of State that he had no need to disturb or attack the public services or to invent new instruments of autocracy. There was no conflict between the public and private officers; the signet did not now challenge the seals. This is not to say that Richard's rule was popular. It was not. He tried to enforce his will on the local administration by complaisant sheriffs; there were complaints about the undue use of prerogative courts; and above all there was financial oppression. Despite peace, Richard's court cost more than Edward III's, and, despite the Shrewsbury grant, he had to have recourse to loans, fines, blank charters, and the like. This alarmed the middle as well as the noble classes. Behind all stood his army, held to him by personal rather than by official ties. It at least kept order in these months, and perhaps it helped to prevent the king from realising the slenderness of the foundations of his authority.

The parliamentary committee met on 19 March to settle petitions, and on 29 April, augmented by magnates, considered the charges against Norfolk. Trial by combat on 16 September was ordered, since, though Norfolk made some admissions, the evidence was held to be insufficient for a judgment. In the most melodramatic scene of his reign Richard stopped the contest as it was on the point of beginning at Coventry in crowded lists. Two hours later he announced that, "by the full advice and assent of Parliament," he banished Norfolk for life and Hereford for ten years. Norfolk had confessed some matters which might nourish troubles in future; Hereford's absence was needed for the peace and tranquillity of the realm. Norfolk's property, except £1000 a year, was confiscated. The sentence on Norfolk proclaimed the injustice of that on Hereford. The fact was that Richard now stood face to face with the house of Lancaster. He was still placating Gaunt; by a very flagrant manoeuvre Buckingham, for thirty-five years Bishop of Lincoln, had been translated to Lichfield to make a vacancy for Henry Beaufort, a mere youth; and Richard thought to be rid of Hereford before a schism in his party occurred. It was a crazy act, but it was the inevitable result of the deserved triumph of an unbalanced king over a factious and unworthy opposition. Richard had no capacity for strong rule; he feared to be left in England with the house of Lancaster. The strength of his position at the moment was shewn by the obedience of Norfolk and Hereford; but the death of Gaunt at the age of 58 on 3 February 1399 presented a problem which required greater political ability than Richard's for its solution.

Richard faced the problem of the future of the Lancaster estates with the folly of one whose head was turned by a mixture of success and suspicion. He falsified the Rolls of Parliament so as to make it appear that the Shewsbury committee, so far from having been limited to the two definite objects which it had achieved, had authority also to terminate all other matters and things named in the king's presence in accordance with what seemed best to them. On 18 March 1399 the committee revoked the patent by which, on his banishment, Hereford had been allowed to appoint an attorney to receive any inheritance coming to him. Richard took possession of the Lancastrian estates. This act made loyalty impossible for Hereford, whatever he might have wished. It was the more foolish inasmuch as some months earlier Roger, Earl of March, had been killed in Ireland, and his six-year-old son now stood alone between Hereford and the throne. By his injustice to Hereford Richard had given to the opposition what it had not had since Gaunt returned from Spain to eclipse Gloucester—a leader.

For Richard to leave England at such a moment shewed his total failure to understand public opinion[1]. Yet in May he left London for Ireland to avenge Roger's death and to restore royal authority. He left the incompetent York in charge as regent, and took his army with him. Its removal was the sign for an outbreak of disorder. On 29 May Richard left Milford Haven; early in July Henry of Lancaster, with Archbishop Arundel and a small party, landed in Yorkshire. Declaring that he sought only his own inheritance, he was warmly received in northern England. The regent with some delay tried to raise a force through the sheriffs, but failed, and the regency government in its flight west towards Bristol to meet the king was cut off by the forces of Lancaster coming south by way of the Severn valley. York made his peace, and three of

[1] These paragraphs concerning the end of Richard's reign follow the conclusions contained in the important article, "The Deposition of Richard II," by M. V. Clarke and V. H. Galbraith, in *Bulletin of John Rylands Library*, xiv (1930), pp. 125 sqq.

Richard's immediate agents, including Bushy, were beheaded on 30 July after Bristol had fallen into Lancaster's hands. Richard himself, who had only had time to struggle from Waterford to Dublin, left Ireland on 27 July and landed in South Wales. A part of his army he had sent to North Wales from Dublin; the rest accompanied him. His behaviour did nothing to save a lost cause. Finding little promise of support in South Wales, he disbanded his army, and made his way along the coast to join his forces in North Wales and Cheshire. Lancaster also went north by Shrewsbury, and was at Chester on 9 August. The incompetence of Salisbury, the vigour of Henry, and rumours of Richard's death had sufficed to make the loyalist forces disperse. When Richard arrived he found only a tiny band with Salisbury at Conway. His handling of such troops as had been at his disposal when in Ireland he first heard of Henry's landing had proved most unfortunate, and it is possible that both in Ireland and in South Wales his advisers were treacherous rather than foolish.

There seems no reason to doubt that in what followed he was tricked into putting himself into Henry's hands. The Lancastrian story was that at Conway he willingly agreed to resign on condition that his life was spared, but the true account appears to be that Henry offered fair terms, proposing that he should be hereditary steward of England whilst Richard remained king. Archbishop Arundel and Northumberland are said to have sworn on the host to the terms, which after some hesitation Richard accepted. Henry then met Richard at Flint, and from that moment the king was treated as a captive. None of his later acts was the act of a free man. By 16 August he was at Chester, and on 19 August Parliament was summoned for 30 September. It was announced in Richard's name that the Duke of Lancaster had come to redress defects in the government of England. Richard's attempt to escape at Lichfield failed, and reaching London on 1 September he went to the Tower. On 29 September he executed a deed of abdication, absolving his subjects from obedience and acknowledging that he was not worthy to govern. That this was wrung from him and that he claimed in vain to appear before Parliament is, however, more worthy of credence than the account of his cheerful demeanour and ready acceptance of his fate. When Parliament received the abdication there was some protest that it was not the king's free act and that he was entitled to a hearing, but the Lancastrian majority overruled the objection. To remove suspicion, a list of thirty-three counts of indictment against him was read. This dealt with his injustices to individuals, notably the Arundels, Warwick, Gloucester, and Lancaster, with general abuses, and more particularly with exaltations of the prerogative since his resistance to the parliamentary commission of 1386. Sentence of deposition followed. Then Henry of Lancaster claimed the throne in a statement of his rights by descent, conquest, and election. The statement was ambiguous and perhaps inconsistent, but appropriate enough to his own character, the situation, and the genius of what we may begin to call the English constitution. There was general assent, and the two archbishops enthroned Henry.

On 23 October the lords, in the new king's first Parliament, resolved on the secret imprisonment of Richard for the rest of his life. He was taken at once into the country, and a rising of the appellants of 1397 in January 1400 led to such treatment of him that before the end of February his corpse was taken from Pontefract to London and exhibited in St Paul's before burial. The brutal prophecy that Richard might suffer his great-grandfather's fate had been fulfilled almost to the letter in circumstances almost as squalid, if slightly less revolting.

Though it is not possible to regard the events of 1399 as the seventeenth-century Whigs regarded them, and though the significance of the reign of Richard II is still far from clear, certain developments and decisions of capital importance in the constitutional and social history of England can be traced in the period that separated his deposition from that of Edward II.

In the first place it was in this period that there emerged and definitely established itself Parliament, in which two houses were crystallising and gaining distinct constitutions and powers. When Edward III came to the throne the elements which were to go to the final composition of Parliament had indeed been assembled. His predecessors had wished to make use of the new social forces, as well as the old, for the support of their policies, and they had called to their Great Council beside the lay and clerical magnates the representatives of the lesser gentry, the lower clergy, and the towns. But as yet the Great Council was one assembly. Its competence for business did not come to an end if certain elements in it had not been summoned or had gone home. No one had an incontrovertible right to be summoned either by individual writ or otherwise; and, though the Statute of York in 1322 may have shewn the importance placed on the presence of the commons on certain occasions, there was as yet no clear distinction drawn between statutes made when they were present and ordinances made when they were not.

By the end of the century, however, a process of definition and differentiation had proceeded so far as to disintegrate this variable Great Council. As previously it had thrown off judicial courts without losing all its judicial powers, so now it threw off Parliament without ceasing to be competent to deal with some of the financial, legislative, and judicial business which normally came before the fuller assembly. By the end of Richard II's reign there are to be distinguished, first, a small efficient body of ministers, in part administrative experts, meeting almost daily, directing the day to day government of the kingdom; second, the Great Council of the magnates, summoned under the Privy Seal; and third, Parliament, summoned under the Great Seal. Parliament is still an aspect of the

Council, and is in theory and for some purposes one assembly, but its two parts are fairly sharply defined. The lords temporal and spiritual, summoned by individual writ, are well on the way to establishing a right to be considered as a special class in society; they claim that they have a right to be summoned, that they can be judged only by those who have the same right, and that (so far as laymen are concerned) these rights are hereditary. The old moral claim of the magnates that they are the natural counsellors of the king is crystallising into legal privilege. The commons came into existence as a mere appendage. Only when they met with the lords were they in Parliament, though the separate estates of which they were composed might withdraw to discuss the business laid by the king before Parliament. A decisive development began when the knights of the shire and the representatives of the towns consulted not apart, but together. This habit grew up between the years 1332 and 1339; and in this union was the foundation of the bi-cameral system. The English commons made one strong representative house, not several weaker estates sharply divided by class feeling and less capable of effective action. The social standing of the knights made it not unnatural for the commons to consult with representatives of the magnates before presenting petitions or returning answers to the king. The election of a speaker to represent them when they returned to the king and the lords with the result of their deliberations was a sign, however informal, of some corporate consciousness and organisation.

If by the end of the century the form of Parliament in two houses was thus distinguishable from the Council, so were its powers. The presentation of private petitions still formed a large part of its activities, but the common, public petition was becoming more important. Parliament was trying, too, to secure that its petitions should be put into effect in the form in which they were made without modification. It was in fact maintaining that all important legislation should require its consent and take the form of statute. The struggle of 1340 had put a very general control of taxation in the hands of Parliament, and though the king not infrequently evaded this control, it was recognised as evasion. The constant demands for money for the war gave Parliaments many opportunities for bargaining with the king, and after 1340 they often put forward grievances to be redressed as a condition of making a grant. They earmarked grants for specific purposes. They appointed commissioners to enquire into the way in which grants had been spent. Already in the early part of the century the lower clergy had withdrawn to Convocation, for all but exceptional occasions. There they voted their own taxes, but Parliament so commonly made its grants conditional upon corresponding action by Convocation that Archbishop Courtenay protested against this destruction of the liberty of the clergy. The king's making statutes by assenting to the petitions of the clergy, like his making private bargains with assemblies of merchants, Parliament regarded with hostility. Yet there were effective, irregular ways of taxation and legislation, and even if Parliament were used, it was easily made the convenient instrument of the king or the magnates. It was very much open to their influence and leadership, and on occasion could be packed or overawed by armed forces.

The influence of Parliament over national policy was less clear and less direct than its influence in legislation and finance. It often shewed reluctance in committing itself to the responsibility of advising the king even when he asked it. But, on the other hand, the beginning of the practice of impeaching unpopular ministers and the demand that the principal officers of State, the council, the king's household, or even minor administrative officials like the justices of the peace, should be nominated in Parliament indicated an interest in controlling the agents by whom policy was determined and executed. These claims met with less success than the claims to control finance and legislation.

The growth of Parliament was but one feature of fourteenth-century England. Beside Parliament the monarchy continued to develop a body of professional administrators, attached to the court and taking instructions from it alone. By these men whose whole career was in the service of the Crown, rather than by independent magnates, the king preferred to be advised, and through them he preferred to give effect to his decisions. From them came reforms in administration, and imperceptibly they came to be responsible for more and more of the government that had once been carried out by feudal machinery. The machinery of the central government was so comparatively competent and powerful that the smaller gentry came to rely on it rather than on the feudal courts, as, for example, in the wages crisis following the Black Death. The greater lords saw that their object should be to capture, not to destroy or frustrate it. We can, then, begin to discern the features of the secular State of Tudor times. As yet it was manned for the most part, at least in high offices, by churchmen; but there was a considerable and increasing society of professional lay clerks. There were signs that the State would separate itself from the Church in personnel as it was already doing in its conception of its functions. Church revenues, like churchmen, were used indirectly for national services. There was talk of direct appropriation of some Church property. The State had in fact endowed itself with power which might be used to subject the Church, if it should suit the king's purpose and public opinion to do so. For the present it suited neither, but the beginnings of an independent secular administration on the one side and the doctrines of the divine right of monarchy on the other formed a double basis for a challenge of the position of the Church in medieval society.

But if the practice of fourteenth-century Parliaments foreshadowed seventeenth-century claims, and if fourteenth-century administration foreshadowed the sixteenth-century State, this was not the whole of the matter. Neither the king's administration nor the Parliament was yet to have the decisive influence in English affairs. Though feudal methods of local government might be increasingly inadequate, the way was not clear for parliamentary or monarchical rule from the centre. The magnates were still the most effective part of public opinion and their "displeasure was like a sentence of death." The great estates were amassed by a few families. The average number of barons summoned had sunk from 74 in Edward II's time to 43 in Edward III's. Nor was the development of effective professional administration confined to the king's court. The greater magnates too had household services, not so much modelled on the king's as called into being for similar purposes in similar circumstances. Moreover many of the forces employed in the Scottish and French wars, and later turned loose on England, were not in any full sense the king's forces. The magnates raised them, and often continued to control them. Men trained in war, wearing their master's livery, with no ties but his wages and no aim but his pleasure, were in effect so many private standing armies. In these many of the lesser gentry served as knights, and the possession of such forces enabled the magnates not merely to overawe but rather to control and use their smaller neighbours for their own purposes, to pervert the judicial machinery of the State, and to pack Parliament itself. In Edward III's time the evil was partly undeveloped and partly hidden, but Richard II had to face it. He saw no means of controlling the new bastard feudalism except by exalting his *regalie* against its local influence and by imitating its methods, if possible, on a larger scale. His love of ceremony was not mere bombast; it expressed the new doctrine of monarchy based on Roman Law. In Cornwall, Wales, Cheshire, and perhaps Ireland there was a base for a private royal estate. The badge of the white hart and the use of the Cheshire archers were the only practical response to the danger that Richard could make. At the end he made a bid for annexing the Lancastrian estates to the Crown, but personal factors modified the plan and in the event Henry annexed the Crown to the Lancastrian estates. Henry V's victories postponed the evil day, as Edward III's had done, but Henry VI had to face in an exaggerated form the evils that had destroyed Richard II. Meanwhile, however, the full machinery of Parliament which the fourteenth century had elaborated had definitely established itself as part of the constitution of the State.

The danger from which the events of 1399 saved England was, then, scarcely a present danger; for if it checked a too impetuous king, it did nothing to check the more deep-seated evils of the new feudalism. England was in the end to be saved from those evils by an alliance of the monarchy and the lesser gentry, by a Crown exalted on doctrines of *regalie* and the spoils of the Church, such as the fourteenth-century kings seemed at times to be feeling after. Had Richard II succeeded as Charles V of France succeeded, it is indeed possible that the English Parliament would have collapsed beneath royal authority. From such an event the revolution of 1399 may have saved England. But this is doubtful speculation. What is clear is that the end of the fourteenth century found monarchy, magnates, and Parliament vigorous and active, but with their final positions in the constitution still to be decided.

The England of Edward III and Richard II is not seen truly if it is seen only or chiefly as a country of warfare, pestilence, and rebellion. The narrative of these things must occupy the chronicler, but beside the highly coloured story of catastrophe and distress, which almost inevitably looms too large, there is another side of English life more sober, but not less important. This spendthrift age, for all its tinsel, false glitter, and war neurosis, has to its credit achievements in literature second only to the greatest, if to them. It was the age of Rolle and Wyclif, Langland and Gower, Froissart and Chaucer. It was an age that told men abundantly about its doings and its thoughts, its pieties and its frivolities, its ambitions and its regrets, its hopes for the future and its judgments on itself. In the works of Langland and Chaucer—to name only the greatest—we have the authentic voices of the two chief sections of the English people. In Langland we have, it seems, the voice of the poor parson of the town, making articulate the conscience, the pathos, the indignation of the plain godly men who paid in their labour and their lives the monstrous price of pomp and war, revolted by the injustice, the callousness, the hypocrisy of the powerful in Church and State, but at heart conservative, lovers of old ways, suspicious of the new age, untouched by any foreign influences, the permanent substratum of English life. It is a voice from the very depth of the English countryside and the crooked little towns that hide there. In Chaucer, in sharpest contrast, we have the voice of the fashionable go-ahead world, of the society that did the king's business and made his court brilliant. This was the society that moulded and used the men for whom Langland spoke. It was a society where the number of educated laymen was increasing, a society secular in its temper and cosmopolitan in its outlook. Its culture and its language, its codes and its interests owed hardly less to France and Italy than to English tradition. In its vivacity, in its humour, in its combination of kindliness and cynicism, as in its occasional shallowness, it represents a civilisation that was already ripe and waiting for a change. The society for which Chaucer spoke, by virtue of its close touch with France, had forced on England a full share in West European culture. England was to be a part of that West European society of nations which, as Byzantine civilisation was slowly extinguished in blood and misery, was to continue and to expand the priceless traditions of Mediterranean life.

CHAPTER XVI

WYCLIF

THE story of the life of Wyclif, as if to foreshadow all that follows, begins with ambiguous references in a mutilated record. Leland in his *Collectanea* mentions Wiclif, a north-Yorkshire village, as the place *unde Wigclif haereticus originem duxit*. In his *Itinerary* he says that Wyclif was born at Hipswell, some miles to the south-east. The contradiction is apparent only. One note mentions the seat of the family; the other records the birthplace of an individual. For at least half a century before his birth the family had had some local importance, holding the advowson and the manor. Wiclif was part of the honour of Richmond granted to John of Gaunt in 1342, and if (as is possible) Wyclif himself became lord of the manor, Gaunt was his overlord for some thirty years.

Wyclif was born about 1330, and went to Oxford. Three of the six colleges then founded have claimed connexion with him, but how he entered the university is uncertain. The first thing tolerably clear is that in 1360 he was Master of Balliol, succeeding the second Master some time after 1356. On 14 May 1361 he was instituted at Holbeach to the College living of Fillingham, Lincolnshire, valued at 30 marks. This made resignation of the Mastership necessary. The place and time of his ordination are uncertain. Described later as a priest of York, he was probably ordained by Thoresby.

Wyclif's connexion with Queen's is now as generally accepted as his connexion with Balliol. A John Wyclif rented rooms at 20s. per annum from 1363–64 to 1366, again in 1374–75, and in 1380–81; there is no adequate reason for doubt that this was the ex-Master of Balliol, but it does not follow that he was more than a tenant. Connected with Queen's as tenants or Fellows or both were several men intimately associated with Wyclif's principal enterprises: William Middleworth and William Selby with his wardenship of Canterbury Hall, and Nicholas Hereford with his later teaching.

About Merton there is less agreement. The name Wyclif appears for 1356 among the Fellows responsible for provisioning the Fellows' table, and in the oldest list of the Fellows (*c.* 1422) is a note that points to a definite, though shortened, association which the College later wished to minimise as much as possible. To be unable to give reasons for Wyclif's removal from Merton to Balliol is not to prove that it did not occur.

There was yet another Oxford society with which Wyclif probably had to do: Canterbury Hall, founded by Archbishop Islip in 1361 as a joint house for secular and regular clergy to accommodate monks sent from

Canterbury and to increase the number of clergy depleted by the plague. The endowments were of two kinds: private donations made or procured by Islip, and the rich appropriated living of Pagham, which belonged to Islip as archbishop, given as Canon Law required with the consent of the prior and chapter. The first statutes provided that the Warden and three Fellows should be monks, while the eight secular students were in a distinctly subordinate position. The first warden, Henry de Wodehull, did not avert a clash between the privileged regular minority and the seculars, and on 9 December 1365 Islip appointed "John de Wyclyve" warden. No special reason is alleged, but the struggle over the claim of the regulars to obtain the doctorate in theology without proceeding in arts was then very intense, and Wodehull had taken this course. Islip's appointment of a secular warden may have been only a matter for discussion with the chapter, but his next step in replacing the three monastic Fellows by three seculars, Selby, Middleworth, and Benger, possibly violated Canon Law and plainly contravened the licence in mortmain which had contemplated a mixed society. Islip prepared new statutes for a wholly secular society uncontrolled by the chapter, but died on 26 April 1366 before the king or the chapter had approved them.

Islip's successor, Langham, a Benedictine, promptly challenged the new plan, and after some temporary arrangements reappointed Wodehull on 22 April 1367. The new secular Hall refused to receive him; Langham decided to dispossess the seculars completely, and the revenues of Pagham were sequestrated when Wyclif and his colleagues failed to shew their title to them. Wyclif and the seculars appealed to the Pope. They had a poor case, presented ineffectively and rather disingenuously by Benger, who put in only one appearance. The case against Wyclif, based on the original statutes, was stronger and was better handled. There is no reason to represent him as an aggrieved individual over-ridden by a powerful corporation; the badness of his case explains its failure. Cardinal Androin, instructed in no event to permit a re-establishment of a mixed society, decided for Wodehull on 23 July 1369. Androin's death delayed execution of the sentence, but on 30 June 1371 two Canterbury monks were appointed to expel all the seculars. The latest settlement, like Islip's reconstitution of the Hall, contravened the licence in mortmain for a mixed society, and not till 8 April 1372, for a fine of 200 marks, did Edward III confirm the papal judgment. Was the warden of Canterbury the schoolman Wyclif? The traditional identification has been questioned, and a rival put forward in John Whytclif, whom Islip presented to the vicarage of Mayfield in 1361. There are two explicit contemporary statements in favour of the schoolman; to overthrow these more is needed than the circumstantial evidence that can be adduced in favour of the vicar of Mayfield. Wyclif's own reference to the matter in *De Ecclesia*, though impersonal, shews exactly the same spirit as the *expositio* at the Curia.

For most of his life Wyclif had the normal career of a distinguished scholar. He appears to have been a regent master in 1360 at Balliol, but not in 1356 at Merton. He took his B.D., it seems, between April 1368 and May 1370, and his D.D. probably in 1372. He received in turn three livings with the cure of souls: Fillingham, Ludgershall, and Lutterworth. The residence needed for a doctorate, the rooms in Queen's, licences for non-residence for periods of study for two years in 1363 and 1368, indicate that for much of the time he did not discharge his duties in person. On 12 November 1368 he exchanged Fillingham for Ludgershall in Buckinghamshire, worth only 10 marks, but nearer Oxford.

As was usual for a man of his distinction, Wyclif's income was supplemented by a prebend not entailing residence. On 24 November 1362 the university included him among the masters for whom it asked the Pope to provide, and the Pope granted him the prebend of Aust in the collegiate church of Westbury-on-Trym, near Bristol. He had responsibility only for the chancel of Aust and for his share in the services at Westbury, but like his colleagues he sometimes neglected these. On 27 June 1366 all five canons were reported as non-resident from the time of obtaining their prebends, only one having provided a vicar; for a year Wyclif had withdrawn his chaplain, and like the rest he had neglected his chancel. All were ordered to appear before the bishop, but there is no record of their appearance. The other four canons made the returns of benefices held in plurality demanded by the constitution *Horribilis* in May that year, but though the Lincoln records contain the others due from Westbury, Wyclif's is missing. Did he evade enquiries, uneasily conscious of his neglect? In 1377, though non-resident, all canons had vicars. Wyclif appears to have held Aust till his death. That he should accept a canonry by papal provision, should hold it as a non-resident with a cure of souls elsewhere, and should neglect its small duties at times, does not prove him incapable of zeal above the average or hypocritical in professing it; but it shews him to have been in most ways in the main part of his career a typical scholarly clerk of the fourteenth century.

In 1371, probably from Gregory XI, Wyclif received a provision of a canonry in Lincoln; the grant was renewed 26 December 1373, with permission to retain Westbury. Thus only eleven years before his death he was at the height of his ecclesiastical success. He appears never to have received the prebend and made a considerable grievance of not getting Caistor in 1375. Caistor was valuable, and went to the illegitimate son of Thornbury, an English leader of papal troops whose services the Pope wished to retain. Wyclif never forgot this promotion of an unqualified youth, born out of England. Wyclif had hitherto followed the usual course of promotion through university and papal influence. In the second part of his career he passed to the active service of the Crown. As yet he shewed no dislike of the influence of the Pope in the Church, or of the king's use of beneficed clergy.

On 7 April 1374 the king, acting in the minority of the patron, Henry de Ferrers, presented Wyclif to the rectory of Lutterworth, and Wyclif resigned Ludgershall. This presentation may be regarded as a retaining fee; and on 26 July Wyclif was appointed to the commission to discuss with papal representatives at Bruges questions outstanding between England and the Curia and made more urgent by the second refusal of tribute on 21 May. Wyclif, the only distinguished theologian on the commission, ranked second. By the middle of September the commission returned after indecisive proceedings. We have no record of Wyclif's impressions, nor do we know why he was not put on the second commission in the following year. He now returned to Oxford, and worked out those theories which grew into *De Dominio Divino* and *De Civili Dominio*. A reflexion of academic controversies on this subject appears in the *Deter-minatio de Dominio*, published probably early in 1375. The first part courteously combats Uhtred of Boldon's opinions about the superiority of priestly to lay rule and the sin of secularising Church property in any circumstances. Uhtred had served the Crown before Wyclif in negotiations with the Pope. The second part is a more bitter reply to Binham, a monk of St Albans. Binham had tried to bring the burning political question of papal tribute into an academic discussion about dominion, with the object, Wyclif complained, of discrediting him at the Curia in order that he might lose his benefices. Wyclif, therefore, put his views into the mouths of seven anonymous lords, a literary device which has caused wild speculation. On 22 September 1376 he was summoned from Oxford to appear before the King's Council. After the death of the Black Prince and the end of the Good Parliament, Gaunt had an opportunity of carrying out his anti-clerical policy. Wyclif's Oxford teaching had shewn him to be the most eminent English representative of that school of thought in the Church which favoured partial disendowment. By preaching in London, "running about from church to church," he lent moral support to Gaunt's party.

On 12 September 1375 William Courtenay at the age of 33 became Bishop of London. To him passed the effective leadership of the clerical opposition, and he determined to silence Gaunt's scholastic henchman. In answer to a summons Wyclif appeared before Sudbury and Courtenay at St Paul's on 19 February 1377. Four friars accompanied him to give scholastic support to opinions about Church property that they shared. Gaunt and Percy, the king's marshal, with followers, provided temporal support. Instead of an examination there was altercation between the bishops and the lords; this degenerated into personal affronts to Courtenay by Gaunt, and the assembly was broken up because of a report of a bill in Parliament to put the city within the jurisdiction of the king's marshal. In the riots and reconciliation which followed Wyclif disappeared from view.

What Wyclif had feared for some time now happened. Some fifty conclusions from his teaching were sent to Rome, and on 22 May 1377

Gregory XI issued five bulls: three to Sudbury and Courtenay, one to the University of Oxford, and one to Edward III. He complained of the sloth, of the official watchmen, and stated that he had heard on the information of several persons very worthy of credence that Wyclif had dogmatised and publicly preached propositions erroneous, false, contrary to the faith, threatening to overthrow the status of the whole Church. In part his teaching resembled that of Marsilio of Padua and John of Jandun already condemned. A schedule of eighteen errors[1], mostly from *De Civili Dominio*, Wyclif's chief published work, followed. As the careful wording of the bull indicated, the errors were political rather than theological: they dealt with dominion founded on grace, the secularisation of ecclesiastical property, and the opinion that Church discipline was valid only if it were in conformity with the law of Christ. Sudbury or Courtenay must learn privately if Wyclif taught such theses. If he did, he should be imprisoned by papal authority. If possible, a confession should be obtained and sent secretly to the Pope, whilst Wyclif was kept in chains pending further instructions. A second bull instructed the bishops, if Wyclif should flee, to cite him to appear before Gregory within three months. A third bull urged them to convince the king, his family, and the nobility that the conclusions menaced polity and government not less than faith. To Oxford Gregory expressed surprise at the sloth which allowed tares to ripen; upon pain of loss of all privileges the university was ordered to deliver Wyclif and his followers to the bishops. Finally, Gregory besought King Edward to favour the bishops in their efforts against Wyclif. The bulls attempted to set up a papal inquisition in England. The ordinary courts were not appealed to; the king was to help rather than to act; the bishops were made papal commissioners. It is likely that possessioners, probably the Benedictines, had aroused the Pope.

Before the bull reached him Edward died on 21 June 1377. The redirection to Richard was made as soon as possible, but the reluctance of the government to follow the Pope's wishes was shewn in two ways. The new Parliament pressed for the use of the revenues of foreign clergy for the war; and Wyclif, who had lately published the oath of Garnier, the papal collector, with comments, gave a written opinion on a question put to him by the king and council in the first year of the new reign: whether for national defence it were lawful to prevent treasure from going to foreign nations, even if the Pope demanded it on pain of censure. Wyclif argues that the law of nature, the Gospel, and conscience all allow this,

---

[1] The conclusions state (1) the temporary and conditional nature of civil dominion, (2) kings and temporal lords may dispossess the Church of wealth in certain circumstances, and it is improper to use ecclesiastical censures in connexion with temporal goods, (3) ecclesiastical judgments are not absolute: they depend on the state of the individual judged and their conformity to Christ's law, (4) every priest can absolve from every sin and every ecclesiastic, even the Pope, can be called to account by laymen.

but the consent of the whole people should be obtained for such a course. On 28 November Parliament ended, and on 18 December Sudbury and Courtenay published the bulls. They did not do all that was required. They called on the chancellor of Oxford to report secretly if Wyclif taught these conclusions, and to cite him to appear at St Paul's within thirty days.

The university acted even less decisively. Wyclif, for the sake of the privileges of the university, went into a sort of voluntary detention. The chancellor, Adam de Tonworth, after receiving the opinions of the masters regent in theology, "for all and by the assent of all," declared publicly in the schools that the conclusions, though sounding badly, were true. Wyclif, fearing violence, did not go to St Paul's, but some time before Gregory's death on 27 March 1378 appeared before the bishops at Lambeth. There they had no free hand. The king's mother ordered that no formal judgment should be given, and a London crowd broke into the chapel. Without definite condemnation, the bishops prohibited Wyclif from canvassing such theses in the schools or in sermons because of the scandal given to the laity. Wyclif issued several papers, very moderate in tone, explaining the conclusions; he sent an explanation of his teaching to Rome, and published in English and Latin a summary of *De Civili Dominio*, entitled *Thirty-Three Conclusions on the Poverty of Christ*. His last appearance in politics, still in alliance with Gaunt against Courtenay, occurred in the autumn of 1378. At the Parliament of Gloucester in October, Sudbury demanded satisfaction for the breach of the privileges of Westminster Abbey on 11 August, when, in connexion with the Spanish prisoners' case treated elsewhere, Hawley had been killed with a sacristan beside the Confessor's shrine. Wyclif was one of the doctors of theology who put the king's case before Parliament. The substance of the defence, a mixture of bad history, scholastic exegesis, and a genuine perception of the evils caused by certain privileges, found a place later in *De Ecclesia* which Wyclif was then writing. The matter was abandoned rather than settled. At Gloucester, as at Bruges and before the Council, the scholar's part was not decisive. He left the political arena having accomplished little except perhaps his own disillusionment. Yet it was the friendship of the royal circle which made his later work possible by protecting his person.

This same summer came the beginning of the Schism. On 8 April Urban VI was elected; on 30 September Clement VII was elected; and on 29 November Urban excommunicated him. In Urban, a scholar with a reputation for austere piety, Wyclif welcomed "a catholic head, an evangelical man," who might be expected to live "in conformity with the law of Christ." To the end he remained for Wyclif *Urbanus noster*, while Clement was "Robert of Geneva"; but the Schism contributed decisively to a change in Wyclif's attitude to the Papacy. Gregory he had disliked personally as a "horrible devil," but the continuing scandal of the Schism set him against the institution itself. It helped to turn him from a critical member of the Church who used its regular machinery for his own career into something like a rebel against the system in which he had hitherto lived. But it is easier to exaggerate than to define this change.

Soon after the papal Schism, perhaps early in 1379, Wyclif gave more explicit expression to opinions about the Eucharist which had been implicit only in his earlier teaching. From this came the hostility of the friars, who had sympathised with his attack on the endowed clergy. Oxford began to divide into definitely friendly and unfriendly parties, soon called "Lollards" and "Catholics." The Lambeth trial had shewn how little even Courtenay could do about the conclusions condemned in the bulls; for criticism of current Eucharistic doctrine there was to be less lay support.

From the autumn of 1379 to the spring of 1381 Berton, who had opposed Wyclif in the schools, was chancellor of Oxford. Late in 1380, or early in 1381, he arranged for a scrutiny of Wyclif's Eucharistic teaching by twelve doctors, four seculars, two monks, and six friars. The verdict of this body might have been foreseen, but to call it packed seems too strong. Wyclif says he was condemned by seven votes. Two opinions were declared erroneous: first, that the substance of material bread and wine "really" remain after consecration; second, that the Body and Blood of Christ are not *essentialiter nec substantialiter nec etiam corporaliter* in the sacrament, but only *figurative seu tropice*. The greater excommunication was threatened against all who taught or heard such doctrine.

Irregularly, but in accordance with what he was teaching about the king's religious authority and responsibility, Wyclif appealed to the king. Sudbury was chancellor, and no official action followed; but Gaunt came to Oxford and urged Wyclif to be silent about the Eucharist. Wyclif, however, defended his views scholastically in a *Confessio* dated 10 May 1381. We have no record of his renting rooms at Queen's after the summer of 1381, and his retirement to Lutterworth probably took place about this time, for in the following summer Hereford, not Wyclif, was the leader of the party in Oxford.

The Peasants' Revolt in June 1381 had less direct effect on Wyclif's work than has been represented by those who exaggerate his political importance. Its indirect effect was very great, for by the murder of Sudbury the supreme influence in the Church in England passed to the new Archbishop of Canterbury, the far more energetic Courtenay. Courtenay found Wyclif's friends in control of Oxford and a number of priests moving about the country teaching his doctrine in a popular way. Apart from what they taught, their indiscriminate preaching was in itself a breach of order, and as early as 1377 or 1378 they were in trouble with the bishops. These preachers were not another "private sect" in the Church or a body of dissenters outside. Some were Oxford scholars;

others had little learning, and for them Wyclif prepared tracts and sermons; only after his death does it seem that laymen appeared among these preachers. That they had any responsibility for the rising is extremely unlikely, but not unnaturally some saw in the general danger to property an opportunity of discrediting Wyclif's attacks on one kind of property. The revolt did not affect Wyclif's teaching; he issued papers appealing to the king and the Parliament which met on 7 May 1382 for disendowment and the end of imprisonment for excommunication[1]. Meanwhile Courtenay received the pallium on 6 May and straightway summoned a specially chosen assembly of clergy to meet on the 17th at Blackfriars hall. Besides the archbishop nine bishops, sixteen doctors and seven bachelors of theology, eleven doctors and two bachelors of law attended the first session. The assembly was undoubtedly eminent, but the presence of sixteen friars and the absence of secular doctors of theology gave it an unbalanced appearance. Wyclif, it appears, was not personally condemned, but twenty-four conclusions which came from his writings were examined. Ten were found heretical and fourteen erroneous[2]. The sitting was ended by an earthquake, which Courtenay and Wyclif interpreted in different ways. Courtenay's next step was to obtain the help of the temporal power. He obtained first an ordinance, later ineffectually de-

[1] The petition asked for the ending of obedience and payments to Rome or Avignon unless proved to be according to Scripture, of the evils of non-residence, of the employment of the clergy in the royal service, and of the imprisonment of excommunicated persons. The duty of confiscating the temporalities of delinquent clergy was urged; no unaccustomed tallages should be imposed until the whole endowment of the clergy has been exhausted.

An English *Complaint* in the form of a petition to Parliament adds to the representations about ecclesiastical property two more radical demands: members of religious Orders are to be allowed to leave them, and the true doctrine of the Eucharist is to be taught in opposition to modern error. The *Complaint* is also in Latin.

[2] The ten heretical conclusions state (1) the nature of the consecrated elements and the absence of Christ's authority for the Mass, (2) ecclesiastical rites are worthless or superfluous according to the state of the person using them: a "foreknown" Pope has no authority, a bishop or priest in mortal sin does not ordain, consecrate, or baptise, a contrite man needs no outer confession, (3) God ought to obey the devil, (4) after Urban VI the West, like the Greeks, should have no Pope, (5) according to the Bible ecclesiastics should have no temporal possessions.

The fourteen erroneous conclusions state (1) excommunication, except of those known to be excommunicated by God, injures only the prelate concerned; to excommunicate one who has appealed to the king or council is traitorous; to cease to hear or to preach the Word of God for fear of excommunication excommunicates a man; deacons and priests need no authorisation for preaching; (2) no man is lord or prelate while in mortal sin; goods and tithes may be withdrawn from delinquent ecclesiastics; the commonalty may correct delinquent lords; (3) special prayers have no special value; particular orders were instituted in error; and, friars being bound to earn their living, alms given to them bring excommunication on the giver and receiver.

The conclusions represent aspects of Wyclif's teaching; most, if not all, of them were capable of defence subject to scholastic interpretation, but such interpretation left them almost without distinctive meaning.

CH. XVI.

nounced by the Commons as unauthorised by them, and then, on 26 June, letters patent. The ordinance ordered sheriffs to arrest and imprison upon a bishop's certificate; the letters patent empowered the archbishop and his suffragans to imprison defenders of the condemned doctrines. On 30 May Courtenay ordered the condemnation of the conclusions to be published in every church in his province.

The archbishop then turned to Oxford, where a friend of Wyclif, Rigg, had replaced Berton as chancellor. Two days before the Blackfriars assembly Hereford, the Ascension Day preacher appointed by the chancellor, had vigorously defended Wyclif in an English sermon. A Carmelite opponent of Wyclif, Stokes, had it reported. For the Corpus Christi Day sermon on 5 June Rigg appointed Repingdon, a young Austin canon of Leicester, attractive but volatile, not yet a doctor, but known as a defender of Wyclif's ethical doctrine. The opponents of Wyclif urged that the Blackfriars condemnation should be published before the sermon; but Rigg deliberately neglected the archbishop's instructions and the sermon was a Lollard triumph. Stokes, whom Courtenay had made his special commissioner to read the condemnation, wrote a pitiful report to Courtenay protesting that he could do nothing for fear of death. The Oxford defiance of the archbishop was quickly ended. A week afterwards, on 12 June, Rigg and Stokes appeared at a second session of the Blackfriars assembly, and Rigg, charged with contempt of the archbishop and a leaning to suspect persons and doctrines, secured pardon only by submission. The king's council charged him to carry out a humiliating mandate of Courtenay, and his new resistance led only to new humiliation. The principal Lollards fled, and in time almost all made their peace with the Church. Hereford and Repingdon appealed personally to Gaunt; he ordered them to obey the archbishop when he learnt of their views on the Eucharist, though he made clear his sympathy with the more political side of their teaching.

Though no judgment was passed on him at Blackfriars, it is not accurate to say that no action was taken against Wyclif personally. By Courtenay's mandate of 12 June Rigg, as chancellor, was ordered to prevent Wyclif, "as notoriously suspected of heresies," from preaching or performing any academic act until his innocence was proved before the chancellor. On 13 July letters patent ordered a general search in the university for any who had communication with Wyclif or other suspects; the books of Wyclif and Hereford were to be sent to the archbishop. In November Courtenay completed his triumph by holding Convocation in Oxford. In six months by vigorous, skilful work he had destroyed the Lollard hold on Oxford. Without risking set-backs such as had nullified the early proceedings against Wyclif, he had isolated him personally; and the dangerous academic teaching condemned in Gregory's bulls had ended. Courtenay owed his success partly to his own judgment, partly to a modification in the political situation, but most to Wyclif's Eucharistic doctrine. This last limited the active friendliness of Gaunt.

Wyclif remained incumbent of Lutterworth for the remaining two and a half years of his life. The supposition that he made some recantation at the Oxford Convocation lacks foundation; he had not been formally convicted, for he had not been tried. It is possible, but far from certain, that attempts were made to renew Gregory XI's citation of him to Rome. He states that he promised not to use the terms substance of material bread and wine outside the schools, but he continued to write in Latin and English, and his most violent attacks on the friars date from this period. He had some apprehension about his safety, but his eulogistic references in very late writings to Gaunt as friend of poor priests and as the innocent victim of friars' plots indicate one reason for his personal immunity. In the last two years of his life he was partly paralysed, and on 28 December 1384 whilst hearing Mass at Lutterworth church he collapsed as the result of a severe stroke, from which he died on 31 December. Dying in communion with the Church Wyclif was buried at Lutterworth, but thirty years later, when the full consequences of his teaching had shewn themselves in Bohemia, the Council of Constance condemned him, and ordered his bones to be cast out of consecrated ground. The ex-Lollard, Repingdon, then Bishop of Lincoln, on whom the duty devolved, took no action; but Fleming, who had himself played with heresy in his youth, moved by the urgent demand of Martin V, executed the order. In 1428 Wyclif's bones were disinterred, burnt, and cast into the Swift.

Wyclif's literary work falls under three heads: Latin writings, English writings, work in connexion with the translation of the Bible. The English writings and the translation, however significant for the future, have been made to appear unduly prominent. The Latin works are Wyclif's main personal achievement, but to relate them exactly with the incidents in his career is at present impossible. They have been pronounced prolix, dull, and obscure, violent without being animated, and vulgar without being picturesque. They are said to betray a mind cold, rationalistic, abounding in negative criticism, destitute of constructive faith. Such a judgment is too harsh. Wyclif's was the silver age of scholastic Latin, and to the general reader his philosophical works are obscure; but at most times he expressed himself with complete clarity and some force. He often wrote tersely, and not seldom came a rush of simple earnest eloquence. At times in his love for Oxford, his hope for the Church, his contemplation of the mystery of divine love in the Incarnation, his words rang with deep and tender passion. He was a master of irony, and no account of him is balanced which omits his elephantine playfulness. To say that at the end of life, exiled from Oxford, he was unfair is to say that he was a controversialist in hardship. To say that his language at times offends modern taste is to say that he was a contemporary of Urban VI and Clement VII. Even the violence with which he parodied his opponents' doctrine of the Eucharist shews him a true son of his age. The worst fault in his writing—bad arrangement—comes

CH. XVI.

from his attempt to preserve the form of a scholastic discussion, when he is in truth not arguing but denouncing some abuse or announcing some conviction. The literary vehicle was unsuited for the purpose of a reformer, but in many treatises produced very rapidly in the last ten years of his life he used material in the same shape that it had had in the schools.

Though no little of Wyclif's philosophical work remains unedited, it is clear that his theology stood firmly on his realist philosophy. It seems legitimate to date in the late sixties and early seventies of the century the *Summa de Ente*, and the separate philosophical works, *De Compositione Hominis*, *De Actibus Animae*, *De Logica*, and *De Materia et Forma*. The occasional laments about defects in the Church were such as any serious churchman might make, but already in these works Wyclif was pressing his attack on the nominalist "sign-doctors." In his opinions that all being is one and is good, and that evil *per se* does not exist, as in his attempt to reconcile man's free-will and the will of God, Wyclif worked over fairly familiar ground. Yet his intense realism led him even in these early works to positions from which it was inevitable that he should make an assault on the dominant theology of his day. Though he had that acute sense of God as will which marked most fourteenth-century thinkers, the divine will was never for Wyclif an arbitrary will. The contrast between what God could do by His absolute power and what in fact He does in the universe—though in his earlier days Wyclif allowed it—was not for him valid. In truth God willed the best; nothing better could be conceived, for had a better conception been possible God would have willed it instead of the existing universe. To annihilate any part would therefore so far worsen it. Moreover, since universals are real, being itself is real and is one; and to annihilate that which any one thing is, is to annihilate being itself. The notion of annihilation is then absurd and contrary to God's goodness. Wyclif did not fail to notice that this opinion had a bearing on the doctrine of the Eucharist, and referred more than once to it without pursuing a theological enquiry. He asserted that the sensible world of our observation is to be depended on and is not delusive; there is no need for that intellectual agnosticism which Duns had used to prepare the way for unquestioning submission to ecclesiastical authority. In Wyclif's opinion what distinguishes the "sect of Christ" from the sect of Mahomet or from other false sects is the way in which the Christian faith can bear rational examination and finds support from it.

The first of Wyclif's important theological works was *De Benedicta Incarnatione*, his sententiary treatise which may be dated *c.* 1370. In it Wyclif appears as the theologian proper. He has not yet descended to the dust and sweat of ecclesiastical and political controversy. This book shews that of him, hardly less than of St Augustine, St Anselm, and St Thomas Aquinas, it was true that *pectus facit theologum*. *De Benedicta Incarnatione* is closely linked with Wyclif's philosophical work, for its object is to shew that the Catholic doctrine of the Incarnation finds better expression in realist than in contemporary nominalist philosophy. There was nothing arbitrary in the assumption of human nature by the second Person in the Godhead: it was a metaphysical necessity. Wyclif turns with disgusted horror from speculations about the possibility of mankind being saved in some other way; these, though much indulged in by the followers of Duns, are as unnecessary to the philosopher as they are shocking to the devout. The most important feature in the book, probably indeed the most distinctive contribution of Wyclif to the development of Christian thought, is his emphasis on the true humanity of Christ and his exposition of the implications of this. Christ is *verissime et univoce* our friend and our brother, no demi-god. Wyclif anticipates Erasmus and Luther in the tenderness of his contemplation of the human Son of Man; for him, to the end of his life, to comprehend the reality of the Incarnation was the key to almost all theological problems. The terms in which he states the doctrine are also a key to his own mind. The contemplation of the humiliation, *summa minoracio*, of the Word, he says, should kindle in us pilgrims the theological virtues. That is not the word of the "twice-born"; it reveals Wyclif as outside the main stream of Western evangelical experience. His realism tended to make sin unreal, and his own experience did not supplement his philosophy. That is why it has been truly said that, for all his veneration of St Augustine, he never understood St Augustine's doctrine of grace. In later controversies Wyclif, like Marsilio, drew from the doctrine of the humanity of Christ deductions that sometimes look like special pleading on behalf of the temporal power which represents His divinity as opposed to the priesthood which represents His humanity. This book makes clear that Wyclif did not emphasise the humanity of Christ for the use that could be made of it in politics; it was central in the faith which he had expressed in passionate words before the political controversy arose. *De Benedicta Incarnatione*, his most beautiful book, is a piece of great religious writing. It is a measure of the sacrifice made when the divine became the reformer.

The doctrine of dominion, the most famous, though almost the least original, part of Wyclif's teaching, provided the main reason for the issue of Gregory XI's bulls, and the books in which it is set out, *De Dominio Divino* and *De Civili Dominio*, stand with *De Mandatis* and *De Statu Innocenciae* as the introduction and head of his theological *Summa*[1]. Wyclif's work on the problem of lordship[2]—a subject much discussed in the fourteenth century in connexion with the friars' use of property—was

---

[1] For contents of this *Summa*, distinct from the *Summa de Ente*, see Bibliography.

[2] In *dominium* Wyclif was employing a familiar technical term borrowed from feudal land law. Feudal lawyers distinguished absolute ownership of land (*dominium eminens*) from possession with the right of use (*dominium utile*) which the owner might grant, on terms of service, to some other person. Such a person had legal possession, to be distinguished from mere occupation which might be entirely indefensible. Cf. *supra*, Vol. III, Chap. XVIII, p. 462.

the first result of that re-dedication of his life to study which is recorded at the beginning of *De Dominio Divino*. That work defines the problem. Lordship and service are two relations that began with creation; lordship, as distinct from possession, is in the primary sense God's; man is God's steward only. In the state of innocence he had the use of all things in common with all other men; private property came with sin. In *De Civili Dominio* two theses are maintained: no one in mortal sin can hold lordship; everyone in a state of grace has real lordship over all creation. The righteous ought in strictness to hold all goods in common to the exclusion of all others, but Wyclif allows that since the Fall the establishment of private property and the protection of it by secular law has been useful in a mixed society. The taint of sin remains nevertheless in secular law and the possession that it ensures. Secular law and canon law (which since Constantine endowed the Church is its ecclesiastical equivalent) are therefore inferior to evangelical law contained in the Bible. The obvious practical conclusion is that since the Church rests its claim to exist on the evangelical law, it must not make the best of both worlds by also claiming property under the secular law. It must be judged by its own higher standard; if churchmen abuse endowments or tithes they lose the right to them by the only law to which they can appeal—the evangelical. In such circumstances the temporal power has a duty of disendowment, but it is not for the theologian to do more than lay down these general principles. The temporal power must judge if the particular circumstances of the day call for action. The later books of *De Civili Dominio*, written apparently after his appearance at St Paul's, defend and develop the theses of the first book. The tone is respectful to the Pope and friendly to the friars.

To compare these works with *De Pauperie Salvatoris*, written some twenty years before by Fitzralph, makes it clear that Wyclif's doctrine of dominion was adopted almost without alteration from Fitzralph. God's lordship since the creation, man's delegated lordship before and after the Fall, private property and secular lordship as a result of sin—the governing notions are Fitzralph's, and his not less is that irritating refusal to adjust theories to practice for which Wyclif has received much censure. Wyclif, despite the incoherence of his scheme, carried Fitzralph's doctrine at least one stage farther by applying it to the endowed part of the Church. The Church stands for a return to the state of innocency; Christ undid what Adam did. That sort of lordship which is well enough in secular affairs is unworthy of a society founded on grace. Let the Church at least live by the law of Christ in a sub-Christian world. Wyclif has been charged with inconsistency in teaching that dues must be paid to laymen whether in a state of grace or not, but withheld from clergymen whose state is doubtful; but it was not inconsistent to demand that the Church should be judged by a different standard from the world. The doctrine of the Eucharist provides a particular example of the way in which Wyclif carried

Fitzralph's thought a stage farther. Fitzralph denied emphatically that annihilation is an act of God's lordship, and was well aware that the conversion of the elements in the Eucharist presents a difficulty if it is thought of from the side of the bread and wine. He observed the difficulty, and declined to face it. Wyclif was not content to leave the problem in the air.

That the opinions contained in this first section of the theological writings produced the bulls of 1377 is not surprising. Wyclif had indeed so stated a doctrine of dominion as to turn it against the Papacy and those interests in the Church which hitherto it had been made to serve. Since the time of St Augustine it had been a commonplace that without *iusticia* earthly rule was mere injustice; dominion over any temporal goods similarly needed *iusticia*, and the defence of the extreme papal claims made in *Unam Sanctam* rested on a coherent exposition of these views[1]. To the Church, and in particular to the Pope, has been given full dominion over all temporal things; to temporal rulers and other lords the Church grants an inferior kind of dominion, but by such grants the Church does not lose its dominion or its right to withdraw from the unworthy what it has granted. Only faithful Christians can have dominion; or, in other words, outside the communion of the Roman Church there is no valid title to anything. In this line of thought everything plainly depends on the nature of that *iusticia* which makes true dominion. The official interpretation since *Unam Sanctam* was that it meant obedience to the Roman Pontiff: St Augustine's thought had been completely legalised. One effect of Wyclif's treatment was to restore a moral content to *iusticia* and to make dominion depend on that. Following another line of St Augustine's thought he found in the eternal counsel of God, not in external communion with the Roman See, that which gave to some men, and denied to others, essential righteousness. On this righteousness, independent of and untouchable by ecclesiastical processes, turned human rights of every kind. Starting from this relation of the individual soul and the will of God, Wyclif used the familiar antithesis of righteous dominion and mere unrighteous occupation as a criterion by which to judge the use which the Church was making of its temporal possessions. The Papacy had reason to fear the issue of opinions which tended towards such a readjustment of the relation of the spiritual and temporal powers as Marsilio had demanded. On two lines the ecclesiastical system was threatened: by the secularisation of Church property and by the undercutting of Church authority in a world where every man was predestined for salvation or foreknown for damnation. Yet the second part of the problem, the function of a visible Church where all is determined by God's will, Wyclif shared with orthodox thinkers; without

---

[1] This strictly legal conception of *iusticia* and its application to *dominium* was first made into a system by Aegidius Romanus in his *De Ecclesiastica Potestate,* which appears to have been written as a preliminary to *Unam Sanctam.*

his call for disendowment this would have caused less commotion. No suspicion of the issue of his opinions on the Eucharist appeared.

In a group of books following the bulls Wyclif examined some aspects of the Church[1], and there was now far more conscious defence of personal opinions. In *De Veritate Sacrae Scripturae* he defended the Bible against "modern theologians." It is entirely true, and its main sense is the literal sense. Apparent discrepancies disappear if it is considered as a whole— an approach to the historical method—or by allegory. It is the final authority. All Christians should study it, and priests should preach it in the vulgar tongue. The significance of this book is its recognition that nominalist criticism was disturbing the harmony which St Thomas had maintained between the Bible and Church customs and dogmas. Faced by this criticism most of Wyclif's contemporaries in the schools proposed to confirm custom and dogma by admitting that the Bible was in a certain degree "false to the letter" and in need of interpretation. Wyclif offered another solution: if, as criticism indicated, practice and dogma seemed not to harmonise with the Bible, these must be judged by the literal sense of Scripture.

In *De Ecclesia, De Officio Regis*, and *De Potestate Papae*, Wyclif considered particular aspects of medieval society from this point of view. *De Ecclesia*, a peculiarly interesting medley of papers assembled in 1378, defended the definition of the Church as consisting of all those predestined for salvation, whose head is Christ, and contrasted them with the body of those foreknown for damnation, whose head is the devil. As it is impossible to know whether any particular individual belongs to the Church, the bearing of this definition on practical affairs is unsatisfactory. Rites are not to be neglected; even the sacraments of the "foreknown" are useful; but ecclesiastical authority is not in itself binding or deserving of more than conditional respect. To make of the Pope a god on earth (the phrase comes from Alvarus Pelagius) is to make him like Anti-Christ, who exalts himself above all that is called God[2].

De Officio Regis (c. 1379), a neater work, expounded the rights and duties of the civil power, especially in relation to the Church. Refusing to decide which power is the older or more necessary, Wyclif noted that in this world the king has the advantage, for he represents the divinity of Christ, while the priest represents His humanity. The king is above human laws, which he respects for the sake of example only. His duty is to see that the Church in his kingdom does its work; at the moment his main duty is disendowment, the provision of poorer, fewer, more godly clergy. Cruder and more confined in view than the *Defensor Pacis*, this book heralds the rule of the same "godly prince," and is decidedly national in temper.

[1] Wyclif's opinions, considered below, on the literal sense of the Bible, on St Peter's primacy and claims built upon it, and on the nature of the ministry, coincided precisely with those of Marsilio.   [2] II Thessalonians ii. 4.

In *De Potestate Papae* (c. 1379), at great length but without excessive violence, Wyclif destroyed most of the claims of the contemporary Papacy by a consideration of dogma and history which left little for the Renaissance scholars to add. The Pope's salvation is as uncertain as any other man's. His acts are to be judged by their conformity to God's law. He is entitled for historical reasons to respect but to nothing more. He may, easily, as one exalting himself, be among those who deserve the name of Anti-Christ. Claims based on St Peter's personal priority are null. Bishops and priests are essentially the same, and their work should be thought of in terms of preaching and pastoral care, not of jurisdiction.

With *De Eucharistia*, which probably represents the lectures that caused Berton to summon his council of twelve, we pass to the final stage. The definitive statement of the Council of 1215 concerning transubstantiation had ended one series of debates, but had left to subsequent generations of theologians the extremely elusive problem of defining exactly what were the relations of the earthly and the divine constituents of the consecrated host. Wyclif like any other schoolman devoted himself to this problem; he had at the beginning no new "scriptural" doctrine to proclaim and no crusade against popular superstition. Many of his works published before *De Eucharistia* refer to the matter, and shew that he was sufficiently influenced by current criticism of St Thomas Aquinas to find his explanations unconvincing. Yet St Thomas' critics seemed to Wyclif even less satisfying than St Thomas himself. At a very early stage Wyclif's philosophy made any doctrine involving the annihilation of the substance of bread and wine impossible. Though at one time he accepted the view that the accidents were upheld by *quantity*, he came to feel that the arguments advanced against *quality* could be equally advanced against *quantity*. Duns' doctrine of absolute accidents, resting on an arbitrary use of God's power and making the phenomena of the universe delusive, he could not accept. By a process of elimination he was driven, therefore, to the opinion that the substance of bread and wine remained after consecration, and the farther he looked into the history of Eucharistic doctrine the better it satisfied him. His later writings record his astonishment and irritation on finding that any other view could commend itself to anyone.

De Eucharistia defends this doctrine from many angles. It is the teaching of Christ, of the Bible, of the Fathers, of the liturgy, of the universal Church until the loosing of Satan about the middle of the eleventh century. The best doctors since have inclined to it. The doctrine of *accidens sine subiecto* is a new heresy. The *Confessio* which Berengar made before Nicholas II, *Ego Berengarius*[1], plainly speaks of bread and wine, not of the accidents of bread and wine, being the Body and Blood of Christ. Even Innocent III's *Cum Marthae* and St Thomas

---

[1] This Confession, enforced on Berengar at the Roman Synod of 1059, was incorporated by Gratian, and thus formed part of the *Corpus Iuris Canonici* (Decreti Pars Tertia, dist. II, c. XLII). Cf. *supra*, Vol. VI, Chap. XIX, p. 679.

himself may be read in the same sense, and we ought to suppose that words patient of orthodox meaning are orthodox. When Wyclif turned to explain how Christ's Body was in the host he had a less satisfactory reply, though his thought is neither so confused nor so unintelligible as has often been said. After consecration the host is two things: naturally bread, spiritually Christ's Body. What we see and what the priest "makes" is the sacrament of Christ's Body, not the Body itself; that is sacramentally, but not corporally, present. St Thomas had distinguished two ways of receiving: (1) sacramentally, without effect, as when the wicked communicate; (2) spiritually, with effect, as when the communicant is in a state of grace. Wyclif similarly distinguished two ways of receiving, but he only calls that a reception of Christ's Body which St Thomas had called spiritual. Whereas St Thomas said the wicked receive Christ's Body sacramentally, Wyclif said they receive only the sacrament of Christ's Body. The gap between the two views may be represented almost as a difference of emphasis, but two quite different attitudes to the host itself are involved. From the one came the crude materialism of popular mass legend, from the other a denial of the real presence. The one is a travesty of St Thomas and the other of Wyclif. Inevitably Wyclif emphasised more and more the danger of superstition surrounding the elements, until he could say that his main intention was to prevent idolatry and to call men to a remembrance of that spiritual union with Christ which, as St Thomas taught, was the effect of the sacrament rightly used. The host may be adored, but there is grave danger of its being wrongly adored as long as the vulgar are not plainly taught that what they see is as truly bread as what the faithful receive in it is Christ's Body. In *De Apostasia* Wyclif denies that this makes the Eucharist only a sign as the crucifix is a sign; the crucifix has not behind it the effectual words of Christ which give the Eucharist its unique value. The doctrine of the Incarnation helps us to explain how two natures can co-exist, how bread is *bene, miraculose, vere et realiter, spiritualiter, virtualiter et sacramentaliter Corpus Christi*, but they are too gross who demand that it shall be *substantialiter et corporaliter Corpus Christi*. In a passionate phrase that is reminiscent of *De Benedicta Incarnatione* he denies that Christ's Body is degraded by becoming truly bread; on the contrary *totum sonat in bonitatem largifluam Iesu nostri*.

   De Simonia, *De Apostasia*, and *De Blasphemia*, standing last in the *Summa*, cover a period of rapid change in Wyclif's mind. He had not hitherto denounced the friars, but the fuller exposition of his Eucharistic doctrine, to which these books refer, had alienated them. In *De Simonia*, written some time after September 1378, which treats of abuses in the Church due to love of temporal gain, the main attack is on the Pope, the bishops, and the possessioners; the friars are blamed for silence and complicity only. In *De Apostasia* his condemnation of friars is not unqualified; but, though he mentions some with affection, he finds it hard now to distinguish friars from possessioners. In *De Blasphemia*, written apparently in the early part of 1382, the tone is greatly altered. The Council of Twelve has been held. Wyclif is consciously at variance with authority. The penitential system and hierarchy are now assaulted; the parochial system is almost the only part of the working institutions of the Church that escapes censure. He says that his adversaries attack him on three lines concerning religious Orders, endowments, and the sacraments of the Eucharist and penance, but that they make the last charge for the sake of the former; it is his criticism of endowments that rouses most fury. This remark at a time when his Eucharistic doctrine was modifying Gaunt's attitude has special significance; it may have direct reference to the attempt to alienate Gaunt from the Lollards.

The *Trialogus* (c. 1382), printed as early as 1525, is deservedly Wyclif's best known work. Succinct, orderly, and for the most part written without violence, it is the best single account of his fully matured opinions. It aims at being a compendium of theology, and, with one long excursus on the friars, it traverses the whole field. It is Wyclif's only sustained attempt at literary artifice, a discussion between three clearly distinguished characters sustained with considerable spirit to the end. In the *Dialogus*, a short discussion of disendowment, the device was less successful. Though the *Trialogus* shews little change in his philosophy and fundamental theology, Wyclif examines in it many more current practices and doctrines, and so develops a more comprehensive criticism of the Church than in any earlier book. The decree *Omnis utriusque sexus*, the treasury of merit, canonisation, confirmation, and extreme unction, he judges to have no sufficient warrant. He denies that his doctrine means that a layman may consecrate the elements, or that the use of sacraments is a blemish in spiritual religion; as a matter of opinion, though not of faith, he would reserve the celebration of the Eucharist to priests. The most bitter part of the book is the attack on the friars; they are mainly responsible for false Eucharistic doctrine, and for the Blackfriars decisions. The same character marks the *Opus Evangelicum* left unfinished at Wyclif's death. In form a commentary on parts of St Matthew and St John, it is in great part an attack on the friars and the Papacy. The priesthood with its special offices of preaching and administering the sacraments Wyclif accepts, but the conception of ecclesiastical law, the whole hierarchy which enforces it, great buildings, elaborate services, indulgences, and many other things not authorised by a rather literal interpretation of the Bible, suffer attack. His mind is as acute as ever; he does not regard himself as an outcast from Christian society. The Schism is an indication that the worst is past. Wyclif died regarding himself as a member of the Western Church, which was, he hoped, on the eve of accepting his views.

Towards the end of his life, perhaps mainly after leaving Oxford, Wyclif wrote in English, it seems, some three hundred sermons and a number of tracts. The language and the comparative rareness of appeals to authorities for support shew that he had in view a more general public than that likely to be reached by his Latin works. Criticism has reduced the number of the English tracts which may certainly be called Wyclif's, and by attributing some of the more bitter and radical to his followers of the next generation has reduced also the difference in tone and emphasis which used to be observed between his Latin and his English works. *The Holy Prophet David Seith*, one of the most interesting tracts probably written by him, argues, for instance, in the manner of *De Veritate Sacrae Scripturae*, that the Bible is in no sense false and that all men should study it. Since it refers to no translations as then existing, it has been dated as early as 1378–80. Some of the other English tracts are translations, more or less free, of Latin tracts; some express briefly for the unacademic reader the conclusions presented in the *Trialogus* and the late Latin works. Christ, who is God and man, has given a law and an example; any deviation from these must be the work of Anti-Christ. Examined from this point of view, endowment, religious Orders, Pope, cardinals, and hierarchy enjoying worldly state, merit condemnation. Priests have no control of the fate of the soul in the next world; their binding and loosing are declaratory, effective only if they agree with God's. The new doctrine of the Eucharist is heretical; the Pope should declare what his doctrine is. The Papacy is not identified with Anti-Christ, but a Pope who works the works of Anti-Christ, as many do, may bear his name. The temporal power is urged to amend the Church by renewing its primitive poverty, and individuals are advised to withhold alms from friars. In general the true followers of Christ are pictured as living by His written law, using those ministrations of the parish church which the Bible authorises but neglecting those which rest on the authority of the hierarchy. The sermons, many of which bear signs of being intended as helps to preachers, present the same lessons. They contain much translated scripture, and this is expounded in several ways: sometimes simply and literally, sometimes with the richness of scholastic allegory. Most sermons contain simple practical advice, sometimes concerning the general practice of virtue, perhaps more often concerning the need for avoiding the errors of the hierarchy and the friars. As elsewhere, there is no general attack on the secular clergy. Wyclif's English works add nothing to our knowledge of his mind, but they shew that he shared the belief of his contemporaries in the value of the vernacular. It was an age of translation, and Wyclif in effect translated and adapted his own works.

General opinion from his own day onwards has considered the translation of the Bible Wyclif's most important literary achievement, and this verdict, though it needs interpretation, may still stand. Two complete versions made from the Vulgate are associated with his name. One is a literal version, reproducing as nearly as may be the Latin idiom, often almost unreadable and sometimes obscure. The other is a free translation into running English, far more intelligible to readers who were unfamiliar with the construction of Latin sentences; this has also orthodox prefaces translated from the Vulgate and a more tendencious general prologue specially written. The relations of these versions with one another and with the lengthy translations contained in Wyclif's English sermons have been much debated. It is likely that Wyclif made translations at sight for use in his own writings and that these have no integral connexion with either version. The more literal translation, apparently the earlier, may be dated with some confidence as having been made in the years round about 1382. Several persons seem to have been concerned in it; and prominent among them was Hereford, whose personal work broke off at Baruch iii. 20, when after appearing before the Blackfriars assembly in June 1382 he fled to Rome. That Wyclif himself did any of the actual work of translating there is no evidence to prove, and it is in itself unlikely. His part is best described in Arundel's words: he "devised the expedient" of at least this earlier version; *quod fecit per alium fecit per se*. This version was unglossed and accurate. The complaint made against Wyclif was that he made the Bible available for the vulgar, not that he corrupted or annotated it. The freer of the two versions may have been begun in Wyclif's lifetime. It was finished before 1395–97, when the general prologue was written by Purvey, who had been Wyclif's secretary and was the last of the eminent Oxford scholars to remain faithful to his teaching. This version naturally attained a greater popularity than the other. Contemporary official opinion judged rightly that, by making the whole of the Bible available even for laymen, Wyclif had done something new and something very different from the work of those who at the same time, especially in the north of England, were translating portions of the Bible for private devotional purposes. Beside the Bible in English went Wyclif's teaching that in its literal sense men had the whole of that evangelical law by which the Church should live. The translations made under his influence could be used, and in fact were used, by the orthodox without harm, but for men who had been taught to believe that current custom in the Church differed from God's law the vernacular Scriptures proved a weapon of unmeasured possibilities. His tracts and sermons do not entitle Wyclif to be called the father of English prose, but he was the first and chief "deviser" of the English Bible.

The work of Wyclif cannot be squeezed into a single formula. No sect or school remained in England to embody his influence with completeness; it was in another country that they were to find the fullest expression and by the death of another man that they were to receive the seal of martyrdom. In most of his thought Wyclif was a typical scholar of the fourteenth century. His erudition and his manner of using it, his knowledge of the Bible, of the Fathers, of the great schoolmen of the West, mark him as a later schoolman with the defects and the qualities of a later schoolman. Though he deplored the dominant tendencies of theological thought since St Thomas, he combated his opponents with their own weapons, and never shewed more relish for his work than when he piled subtlety on subtlety and refinement on refinement. There were contemporary thinkers with whom he was in sympathy: to Bradwardine and Fitzralph in particular he directly acknowledged his debt. But his master was St Augustine. "John, son of Augustine" his disciples called him; and his references to St Augustine not only far outnumber his references to any other writer, they give a faithful indication of the source from which he drew the essentials of his interpretation of Christianity. The Bishop of Hippo once more proved his power to stir later thinkers to a new inspiration and to place them in a new field of thought. The prevailing quality of Wyclif's mind is often said to be rationalism. This is true if by rationalism is meant not a reliance on reason to the disparagement of faith, but a re-assertion of the reasonableness of the Christian faith. Wyclif tried to rescue the orthodox from a combination of intellectual scepticism with unreasoning acceptance of ecclesiastical authority, by a return to the older opinion that, in so far as they touch, faith and reason support each other. Like most rebels, therefore, Wyclif conceived that he was calling for a return to the healthier outlook of an earlier age. In the dissolution of St Thomas' synthesis of reason, the Bible, and Church custom and belief, Wyclif does not fall back on ecclesiastical authority. He proposes to re-establish equilibrium by the more arduous method of adjusting Church custom and belief so as to agree with a reasoned interpretation of the Bible, for the Bible is the most authoritative statement of God's law.

But the attainment of this position along the lines of conservative scholastic theology put Wyclif not very far from the revolutionary attitude of the heretics of the thirteenth century. This appears in his attack at the end of his life on customs not readily derived from the Bible, his repudiation of the division of Christians into "religious" and "secular," his assertion that the rule of "the sect of Christ," without addition or subtraction, is the rule for all, and his consequent denunciation of all religious Orders. It was natural, therefore, that he should renew the attempt to provide Bible translations. This emphasis on the Bible as God's law is easily made to appear as a colder and more legalistic presentation of Christianity than in truth it was. For Wyclif the Christian life was best understood in terms of the imitation of the human life of Christ, a conception which links him on the one side with St Francis and on the other with the contemporary Rhineland mystics, though in general he was destitute of specifically mystical sympathies.

On the political side Wyclif's teaching heralded the modern State, freed from the embarrassing co-operation and competition of the Church in many fields of human activity. But it is better to see Wyclif in relation to his own times. He is indeed less the prophet of the future than the conscience of his own generation. The Western Church had welcomed the codification of moral laws in the dark ages and the systematisation of theology in the twelfth and thirteenth centuries, but in the fourteenth it found itself in some danger of thinking of Christian morality as a penal code and theology as dialectic. The triumph of the Papacy, the penetration of society by the Canon Law, the use of the most sacred mysteries on occasion as sanctions for mundane claims enforced without reference to moral considerations, were making the Christian dispensation take on the aspect of mechanical legalism. Theologians still spoke of grace, but it was a grace so exactly and so certainly confined in official channels that it seemed rather to deserve the name of law. In the last ten years of his life Wyclif gave expression to feelings, doubts, and hopes gathered from many quarters and shared by many of his contemporaries. The Church of the fourteenth century was feeling after something nearer to the historic origins of Christianity, something with less legalism and more conscience, something which put religion again into direct and obvious touch with the heart and will, a new exposition of the *caritas* which, as Wyclif said, is in one word the whole law of God.

CHAPTER XVII

WALES, 1066 TO 1485

THE Norman invasion of 1066 caught Wales, no less than England, at a disadvantage. She was in the trough of the reaction which followed the downfall in 1063 of Gruffydd ap Llywelyn, the strong ruler who, in spite of weak hereditary claims, had made himself master of all Wales and the terror of the English border. The country fell once more into its four ancient divisions of Gwynedd, Powys, Deheubarth, and Morgannwg; a new dynasty arose in Powys, founded by Bleddyn ap Cynfyn, while in the other three realms the ancient ruling stocks, submerged during the usurper's reign, came once more to the surface. These were conditions which made the way easy for foreign conquest: though the enemy had still to contend with the physical difficulties of the country, the crags of Eryri, the marshes of Rhuddlan and Aber Glaslyn, the universal forest, and with a people well used to the business of national defence, he was not faced with a united resistance; rather, he found means to pit Welshman against Welshman, as when Caradog ap Gruffydd of Wentloog in 1072 received Norman help in his attack on Maredudd ab Owain of South Wales. The situation was somewhat improved by the decisive victory won in 1081 by Gruffydd ap Cynan and Rhys ap Tewdwr at Mynydd Carn in the Precelly Mountains; the former was the representative of the ancient line of Gwynedd, the latter that of the stock of Hywel the Good in South Wales, and their triumph finally established the two houses in their respective dominions. But neither of them, nor yet the house of Bleddyn in Powys, was strong enough to oppose an effective barrier to the progress of the all-conquering Norman.

The first menace to the independence of Wales was the setting up along the border of three powerful earldoms. Hereford was given to William Fitz Osbern, Shrewsbury to Roger Montgomery, Chester to Hugh of Avranches. Thus in Mercia the house of Leofric, whose alliance with the Welsh had survived the change of dynasty in England, was replaced by three hostile wardens of the march, whose task was not merely defensive but included, as far as practicable, the subjugation of the Welsh. At the time of the compilation of Domesday, much of the work of conquest had been achieved. Earl Hugh of Chester had carried his border to the Clwyd, where his relative, Robert of Rhuddlan, was installed in the stronghold which had once been held by the formidable Gruffydd. Robert himself, with a commission to conquer Gwynedd, was making his way westward and was already firmly seated at Degannwy on the estuary of the Conway. Farther south, Earl Roger of Shrewsbury had won the valley of the Dee as far as Corwen; his lieutenant held Oswestry and he himself had built a new Montgomery on the Severn, in the midst of the waste country left by Gruffydd's ravages; from this point he had pushed on to the skirts of Plynlimon. In South Wales the tide had not flowed so rapidly; the earldom of Hereford, which under William Fitz Osbern had subdued Gwent, proved dangerous in the hands of his son and was suppressed in 1075. Moreover, the king seems, as the result of a visit to St David's in 1081, to have recognised the title of Rhys ap Tewdwr and to have protected his lands from attack. Yet even here the onslaught was merely delayed; Normans at Caerleon were ready for the conquest of Glamorgan, others at Clifford had their eyes upon the Wye valley and the acquisition of Brecknock.

It was in the reign of Rufus that the most determined and vigorous attempt was made to reduce the Welsh. The king's own expeditions in 1095 and 1097 were little more than demonstrations of might; the type was one with which Wales grew very familiar and learnt not unduly to dread. Mountain ramparts, such as faced William at Tomen y Mur (near Festiniog), the mobility of the Welsh, who in their retreat carried off with them all their belongings, and commissariat difficulties usually set a limit to what could be accomplished in these summer campaigns; they were costly and yielded little result. But the raids of the barons of the march were in a different category, and seemed likely at this time to bring the whole of Wales under foreign rule. The Earl of Chester, in no wise daunted by the vengeance taken by the Welsh upon Robert of Rhuddlan in 1088, had gained a footing in Anglesey and built castles at Bangor and Carnarvon; Gruffydd ap Cynan, the rightful lord of the district, was his prisoner. In the south, the death of Rhys ap Tewdwr in 1093 opened the floodgates of invasion; no claims were now recognised in that region and the country was rapidly parcelled out among soldiers of fortune. Builth and Radnor went to the Braiose family, Brecknock to Bernard of Neufmarché, Glamorgan to Robert Fitz Hamon. The men of the Earl of Shrewsbury poured into West Wales and erected there the first castles of Cardigan and Pembroke. Even the ancient peace of St David's was rudely disturbed, as one may read in the "Lament" of Rhigyfarch, son of the learned Bishop Sulien; his tale of horrors vividly brings before us what the "gens Britanna" suffered at the hands of the "Francigenae" in the way of extortion, imprisonment, mutilation, and death[1]. The noble were set to menial tasks, the heir had nothing to live for, the courts of princes were deserted, music had lost its charm—heaven was the only hope and consolation of the Britons.

Rhigyfarch suggests that the British race had lost its ancient valour. The chronicles speak, on the other hand, of fierce resistance and some measure of success under the escaped Gruffydd ap Cynan and under Cadwgan ap Bleddyn. From 1094 to 1100 Wales was in active revolt and

[1] *Psalter and Martyrology of Ricemarch*, ed. H. J. Lawlor (1914), pp. 121-3.

many of the newly built castles were destroyed. But Welsh independence was preserved from total extinction rather by natural advantages than by the courage of its defenders. Earl Hugh of Chester, with the aid of Earl Hugh of Shrewsbury, had conquered Anglesey in 1098, when the sudden appearance in "Anglesey Sound" of King Magnus of Norway with a pirate fleet revealed to him the essential insecurity of his position. Desirable as were the cornlands of Môn and Arfon, they could not be controlled from Chester except by way of the sea, and the want of naval power induced the Normans at this stage, when the battle appeared to be won, to abandon North and Mid Wales to the foe and to make the best of their substantial gains in the south. Gruffydd ap Cynan regained his power in the region to the west of the Conway; Cadwgan ap Bleddyn was recognised as chief ruler of Powys. But along the shores of the Bristol Channel there was no turning back; Glamorgan never again passed into the hands of a Welsh overlord, and Pembroke Castle, amid all the tumults of the next two hundred years, remained inviolably Norman.

During the long reign of Henry I, the process of conquest was continued by less violent, though equally effective methods. The king's two Welsh expeditions (1114, 1121) were not of much account, conforming as they did to the usual pattern. But in other ways Henry shewed himself the undisputed master of Wales, "the man," to quote the Welsh chronicler of Llanbadarn Fawr, "with whom none may strive, save God Himself, who hath given him the lordship."[1] Early in his reign, the revolt and ruin of the great Montgomery family destroyed the second of the Conqueror's border earldoms. Instead of an earl, Henry placed a cleric in charge of the middle march; at the same time, he brought Pembroke under the direct rule of the Crown. Not many years afterwards Carmarthen began its long career as a royal stronghold; the ancient church of Llan Deulyddog which had marked this spot was given to the monks of Battle, and a new castle was built hard by, at the head of the Towy estuary. A feature of this period is the temporary importance of Powys, which Henry increased by the grant of Ceredigion to Cadwgan ap Bleddyn in 1102. It was, however, a greatness of brief duration; the rivalries of the sons and grandsons of Bleddyn led to continual intrigues and conspiracies, which were carefully fostered by Bishop Richard of London, the royal representative at Shrewsbury, and which ultimately reduced the house to a single member, Maredudd ap Bleddyn, prince of all Powys at his death in 1132. Ceredigion was taken from Cadwgan in 1110 and bestowed upon Gilbert Fitz Richard, of the house of Clare, under whose sway it was tilled by English and Flemish settlers and guarded by many castles. Cantref Bychan, with its castle of Llandovery, also became at this time a Norman lordship and an appurtenance of the house of Clifford. Only in Cantref Mawr, the rough forest land to the north of the Towy, did Henry allow the Welsh a limited degree of independence; its windswept moorlands, its valleys

[1] *Brut y Tywysogion* (ed. Williams, J., Rolls Series, 1860), p. 128.

choked with scrub, offered few temptations to the invader, and it was here that Gruffydd, heir to the claims of his father Rhys ap Tewdwr, is found at the end of the reign, after more than one fruitless attempt to assert his hereditary rights, in possession of nothing more than the little commote of Caeo.

In one remote corner of Wales the even pressure of Henry's rule does not seem to have been felt. Yet it was a capital error to neglect Gwynedd, for it was here that Welsh independence, driven back into its last refuge, always rallied, to furnish liberators for the rest of Wales. Gruffydd ap Cynan, after many vicissitudes, had at last found a firm foothold; while Henry was holding the chieftains of Powys and Deheubarth in check, the northern prince was slowly pushing eastward and southward, across the Conway and the Mawddach, and re-establishing the larger Gwynedd. Hence, when the opportunity came with the death of the great king, the Snowdonian State was able at once to assume the leadership. It is true that by that time Gruffydd, a blind old man of eighty, was nearing his end (he died in 1137), but he left able and energetic successors in his two sons, Owain and Cadwaladr. Immediately the news arrived of the death of Henry, there was a general uprising throughout South Wales; Owain and Cadwaladr came south with a very large force, and in three successive expeditions (1136-37) so ravaged Ceredigion as to leave the Clare family nothing in that region save the strong castle of Cardigan. The death of Gruffydd ap Rhys in 1137 was a further advantage for Gwynedd; his four young sons were no match for the northern leaders, who established themselves securely in Ceredigion. Meanwhile, Stephen's efforts to restore the authority of the Crown in Wales were intermittent and futile, and when the civil war began the Welsh had a free course, for the barons of the march, led by the Lord of Glamorgan, Earl Robert of Gloucester, were active supporters of Matilda and, for the most part, allowed their zeal as partisans to outweigh their interests in Wales. It is not too much to say that during the nominal reign of Stephen a large part of the work of the preceding seventy years was undone, and that, while the whole country was not recovered from the Normans, enough achieved its liberty to form henceforth a solid block of independent territory.

This was the problem which faced Henry II in 1154. He found Owain Gwynedd holding Tegeingl (North Flintshire) and the border fortress of Mold, both included in Cheshire under the earlier Norman kings. Madog ap Maredudd, sole ruler of Powys, had made himself master of Oswestry. Rhys ap Gruffydd, the only survivor of the stock of South Wales, held, in addition to Cantref Mawr, the Clare lordship of Ceredigion and the Clifford lordship of Cantref Bychan. The successes of the Welsh had filled them with a new daring and confidence; they had learnt from their Norman rulers the arts of horsemanship and castle-building; a martial order of minstrels inspired them to valiant deeds. In this situation, the king's earlier policy was to deal with each local problem separately: in

1157 he had the help of Powys against Gwynedd and, after marching as far as the Clwyd, induced Owain to give up Tegeingl and Mold; in 1163 he penetrated South Wales as far as Pencader, and reduced the power of the Lord Rhys within very narrow limits. But his plans were ruined by the quarrel with Archbishop Thomas; in this conflict he lost prestige so heavily that the Welsh were emboldened to unite in a national revolt against his power. In 1165 the forces of Gwynedd, Powys, and Deheubarth combined to meet him at Corwen; though the main armies never met, he suffered a decisive repulse, for wind and rain drove him back from the Berwyn moorlands to his base at Oswestry, and he had to abandon the campaign in high dudgeon. Soon afterwards, the Welsh took the castles of Cardigan, Cilgerran, and Rhuddlan; it was clear that Henry's schemes of reconquest had failed and that the resistance of the Welsh was not to be overcome.

A new element now entered into the question of the attitude of the Crown towards Wales. The Anglo-Norman conquest of Ireland entirely transformed the relations between the Lord Rhys and Henry II. Largely brought about by the foreign colony in West Wales, it relieved the prince of persistent and dangerous enemies and created for the king the menace of an independent Norman State across the channel. Henry lost no time in asserting his own authority in Ireland over the Earl of Pembroke and his followers, and at the same time (1171–72) he concluded, with the same end in view, an alliance with the South Wales chief which lasted during the rest of the reign. By the death of Owain Gwynedd in 1170, followed by that of Cadwaladr in 1172, Rhys had become the foremost man in Wales; Gwynedd was once more divided (as Powys had been since the death of Madog ap Maredudd in 1160), and for a quarter of a century the unusual spectacle was witnessed of a southern leadership of the Welsh people. The alliance with Rhys and the minor Welsh chieftains stood Henry in very good stead, for they remained faithful to him in the great upheaval of 1173–74 and gave him substantial military aid. In spite of border affrays, such as arose in Gwent after the massacre of Welsh notables in Abergavenny Castle by William de Braiose in 1175, the normal relations between England and Wales were at this time peaceful. The king was well content to allow Rhys to dominate Wales, so long as he kept the lesser princes in order and brought them from time to time, as at Gloucester in 1175 and at Oxford in 1177, to the royal presence to pay their humble duty.

One of the men used by Henry to weave the threads of this alliance deserves something more than a passing mention. Gerald de Barry, to give the true family name of "Giraldus Cambrensis," was primarily a student and scholar, the author of works which mirror the age in which he lived, a keen and resourceful controversialist. But he also has his place in the history of Wales, notably as the dauntless champion of the independence of the see of St David's. He belonged to the Anglo-Norman colony in Dyfed, where the Barry family held the castle of Manorbier in the earldom of Pembroke, and in him the power of adaptation of the Norman type, its intellectual vigour, and its devotion to the Church are vividly illustrated. But he was also, through his mother, a descendant of Rhys ap Tewdwr, and he never forgot the connexion. Sometimes, as in his ambition to be Bishop of St David's, he sought to turn his Welsh origin to profitable account; sometimes it was used by others, as when Henry II made him his envoy to the Lord Rhys; sometimes it was an unconscious influence, as when it gives a sympathetic tone and outlook to his account of Wales and the Welsh in the "Itinerary" (1191) and the "Description" (1194). Gerald had a long and busy life (1146–1223); he studied at Oxford, Paris, and Lincoln, twice visited Ireland (1183, 1185), where his Pembrokeshire kinsmen were much in evidence, and for some ten or more years was in the service of the Crown. But he is best remembered in Wales as the companion of Archbishop Baldwin in 1188, when the crusade was preached from end to end of the country, and as the hero of the great fight in the reign of John for the metropolitan rights of St David's. Gerald was an unsuccessful candidate for the see in 1176, when he hoped to succeed his uncle David Fitz Gerald, but it was in 1198, on the death of Peter of Lee, his successful rival, that he secured election by the chapter in defiance of the Crown and of Archbishop Hubert, and took up zealously, as part of his own cause, that of the independence of St David's. Three times did he visit Rome, hoping to enlist the powerful aid of Innocent III, but, although the great Pope heard him with courtesy and, indeed, if we may believe Gerald, with some sympathy, he did not win his case; in 1203 he was obliged to acquiesce in the election of Geoffrey, prior of Llanthony, who made the usual profession of obedience to Canterbury. It cannot be doubted that the struggle, in spite of its unfavourable issue, appealed strongly to the imagination of the Welsh people; well might Llywelyn ap Iorwerth say it would be remembered "as long as Wales should stand."

The death of Henry II produced almost as great a turmoil in Wales as that of his grandfather; no attempt was made under Richard I to continue the policy of conciliation, and the last years of the Lord Rhys were spent in fierce attacks upon Norman strongholds which recalled the stormy days of his youth. He died in 1197, the last great ruler of South Wales; though his descendants were princes in that region until the end of the thirteenth century, none arose to compare with him in statesmanship and power. The primacy of Wales passed to its customary seat in Gwynedd, with the rise at this juncture of Llywelyn ap Iorwerth. Llywelyn, a grandson of Owain Gwynedd, had been early left an orphan, but at the age of twenty-one had swept aside his uncles, David and Rhodri, and had become prince of Eastern Gwynedd (1194). Turning towards the English border, he had in 1199 proved his mettle by the conquest of Mold, an outpost of Cheshire from which he ejected the barons of Montalt. Shortly afterwards, he was able to annex Western Gwynedd; here he made Aber, near Bangor, one of his chief residences, and liberally endowed the adjacent Cistercian abbey of Aberconwy. In Gwynedd he had now no serious rival; Powys, however, for a few years furnished him with a formidable competitor in the person of Gwenwynwyn, prince of the land south of the Tanat, who had some of the gifts of a national leader. It was John who, after some attempts to play the two leaders against each other, finally cleared the way for the triumph of Llywelyn by giving him his natural daughter Joanna in marriage, and by striking down his two chief opponents, Gwenwynwyn and William de Braiose (1208). The prince of Gwynedd had still to pass through one testing experience: in 1211 John invaded Wales, got as far as Aber, and reduced his son-in-law to complete submission. But, through the influence of Joanna, the terms imposed on him were not hard; the fabric of Llywelyn's power was shaken but not overthrown, and in 1212 the lesser princes, whom jealousy had driven into the enemy camp, rallied round him once more, as they realised that he alone could secure their independence. Llywelyn, with the whole of North Wales under his control, now took an active part in the English movement against John and entered into a working alliance with the barons of the march, in virtue of which he occupied Shrewsbury. Certain articles in the Great Charter[1] shew that his services were appreciated; their stipulations had no effect, however, upon the course of the war in Wales, which was only brought to an end by the Peace of Worcester, concluded with Llywelyn by the government of the young Henry III in 1218.

By this peace, won from an exhausted and still troubled England, Llywelyn secured recognition of all his conquests and was allowed to retain the lands of Gwenwynwyn, who had died in exile in 1216, and the royal castles of Cardigan, Carmarthen, and Montgomery. He had during the war won for himself a strong position in South Wales; the sons and grandsons of the Lord Rhys had willingly accepted him as their leader and, at Aberdovey in 1216, he divided among them, as their feudal superior, the liberated lands in the south. This was a new position for the lord of Gwynedd; contemporary manuscripts of the Welsh laws assert it to be the undoubted right of the lord of Aberffraw (in Anglesey), and from 1230 onwards Llywelyn emphasised the claim by styling himself "prince of Aberffraw and lord of Snowdon," but, historically, the ascendancy of Gwynedd over the rest of Wales was the result of the events which have just been described.

From this time until his death Llywelyn's power suffered no serious eclipse; he was the one man in Wales with whom the English government had to reckon. He was faced, first by the regents of England during Henry's minority, and afterwards by the feeble king himself, so that he may be regarded as fortunate in the enemies he had to encounter; yet a close study of his career reveals statesmanship which fully justifies his title of Llywelyn the Great. A characteristic example of his skill is the

[1] Nos. 56, 57, 58.

alliance he formed in 1220 with Earl Ranulf of Chester, like himself a territorial magnate with wide interests who looked with distrust upon the growth of the central authority; the bond was drawn tighter by the marriage of the earl's nephew and heir, John the Scot, to Llywelyn's daughter Helen, and it protected North Wales from attack until the death of Earl John in 1237. In South Wales Llywelyn had more ado to maintain his supremacy; in 1223 the Earl Marshal brought over an army from Ireland and recaptured Cardigan and Carmarthen; the castle of Montgomery was at the same time rebuilt by Hubert de Burgh on a new site. Five years later, there was war again on the border; Hubert attempted to build another great sentinel fortress at Kerry, but this time he was decisively repulsed (1228). After a brief interval of peace, Llywelyn again took the field in 1231 and succeeded in winning back Cardigan; about the same time he received Builth from the Braiose family as the dowry of Isabella, the wife of his son David. He was actively concerned in the war of 1233–34 between Earl Richard and the king's foreign advisers, but thereafter kept the peace until his death on 11 April 1240. Llywelyn was an enlightened ruler, whose activities were far from being confined to the sphere of politics and war. He secured the election of Welshmen as Bishops of St David's (1215) and Bangor (1215), issued charters to the Cistercian abbeys of Aberconwy (1198?) and Cymer (1209), and founded a house of Franciscan friars at Llanfaes near Beaumaris (1237). He was a liberal patron of the bards, and it is probably to him that we are to attribute the North Wales recension of the Law of Hywel, commonly known as the Venedotian Code.

The one difficulty which harassed the closing years of Llywelyn was that of the succession. He had by Joanna a son David, whose royal connexions and marriage alliance with the house of Braiose made him the natural heir to his father's greatness. But Welsh custom gave an equal place to his elder (though not legitimate) brother Gruffydd, and on his father's death David only secured the undivided principality by keeping Gruffydd in close confinement. He won without difficulty the recognition of the king, but soon found that it was not intended to leave him in possession of all that his father had held; a royal campaign in 1241 reduced him to the confines of Gwynedd and forced him to give up his prisoner Gruffydd. With this hostage in his hands Henry for a time had peace, but the death of Gruffydd, who broke his neck while trying to escape from the Tower of London (1244), left David without a rival and free to engage in a war, the issue of which was still in doubt when he died at Aber in 1246.

A period of ten years now follows in which Wales is paralysed by internal divisions and English authority is pressed to its farthest limits. Eastern Gwynedd, in particular, is annexed by the Crown, with its castles of Diserth[1] and Degannwy, and becomes, with the county of Chester and

---

[1] Diserth took the place of Rhuddlan from 1241 to 1263.

much of South Wales, a part of the inheritance of the young Edward (1254). Western Gwynedd is divided between Owain and Llywelyn, two sons of Gruffydd ap Llywelyn. At last, in 1255, a quarrel between the latter disturbs the equilibrium of forces in Wales; the decisive victory of Bryn Derwin (near Clynnog) brings to the front in the person of Llywelyn the man who is to repeat the achievements of his grandfather and for a brief space to unite the Welsh nation once again. For a quarter of a century Llywelyn ap Gruffydd dominates Wales; he keeps his elder brother, Owain the Red, a prisoner, and in spite of the wayward attitude of his younger brother David, who is sometimes his enemy and sometimes his ally, maintains a firm hold upon power.

Llywelyn's opportunity was furnished by the baronial quarrel with Henry III, now ripening for the open breach of 1258. In 1256 the men of Eastern Gwynedd appealed to him to rescue them from the clutches of Edward's officials; he won the district in a week and thus restored the Gwynedd of his grandfather. No help was afforded to the Crown by the dissident barons, who heard of the victories of the Welsh with equanimity. Llywelyn lost no time in pushing home his advantage; crossing the Mawddach, he occupied Meirionydd and thence advanced to the conquest of Builth and Aberystwyth. In 1257 he drove Gruffydd ap Gwenwynwyn from Southern Powys, and in a very short time had won complete ascendancy in South Wales, the princes of which became his vassals. At the Parliament of Oxford, the idea of opposing the Welsh was, in view of the constitutional crisis, set aside in favour of a truce, and Llywelyn was emboldened to take two further steps of importance: he created for himself the title of "Prince of Wales" and concluded a formal alliance with the barons of Scotland (1258). The reality of his power as overlord was shewn in 1259, when Maredudd ap Rhys, holder of Dinefwr, the South Wales "caput," was tried for treason by his fellow-princes and suffered imprisonment in Criccieth Castle. In three years Llywelyn had made himself a power in the realm and his truce with the Crown became a virtual peace.

With the outbreak of civil war in England new prospects offered themselves. Llywelyn, having captured the long-besieged castles of Diserth and Degannwy, entered in 1263 into an alliance with Earl Simon—an immediate advantage for the earl, but perhaps the key to his ultimate overthrow. For the marcher lords, hitherto solid for reform, now deserted in their anger to the royalist side; in spite of the victory of Lewes, the earl was not able to break up their opposition and it eventually bore ample fruit in the catastrophe of Evesham. Had the fortunes of battle been reversed on that day, Llywelyn would have been a large gainer, in virtue of his treaty with the earl, concluded at Pipton, near Hay (1265); the disaster, on the other hand, entailed little loss, for he had taken care to risk as little as possible. When, in the course of the general settlement, the Crown was ready for peace with Wales, Llywelyn obtained in the

Peace of Montgomery (1267) the confirmation of his title of Prince of Wales, the suzerainty of the other Welsh princes, and the recognition of all his conquests. No Welsh prince since the Norman Conquest held a prouder position than he did at the death of Henry III.

His relations with Edward I form something of an enigma. He began by persistently refusing fealty and homage, as though he hoped to revive the Barons' War and shake off finally the English overlordship, a scheme shadowed forth in his proposed marriage to Eleanor, daughter of Earl Simon. Edward countered this design by securing the lady and hemming Llywelyn in his natural stronghold of Snowdonia, until he was forced to submit and agree to the Peace of Conway (1277), which reduced him to Western Gwynedd and threw down the house of cards erected by the Peace of Montgomery. The Prince of Wales (he still kept that title) had made two serious miscalculations: he had not reckoned on the unity of an England weary of civil strife, and he had underestimated the military skill of the first English monarch who applied naval resources to the problem of the conquest of Wales. What is remarkable is that he fell twice into the same errors. Edward, believing that he had fully learnt the lesson of 1277, gave him his affianced bride (1278) and otherwise treated him with consideration, in the hope that he would accept his now diminished, but still far from despicable, place in the realm. The outbreak of 1282, due in the first instance to the restless David but soon involving Llywelyn also, shewed that he was wrong, and Edward entered on the campaign with the conviction that an end must be put to the Welsh trouble once for all. He brought all the resources of the realm, including a fleet from the Cinque Ports, to bear upon the situation, easily subdued Llywelyn's allies in Powys and South Wales, and beset the prince himself in his rocky citadel. Realising that the blockade of Snowdonia must be broken, Llywelyn slipped south, to organise a counter-movement in the Wye valley. But here, on 11 December 1282, not far from the town of Builth, he was killed in a chance encounter with a border force, and with him fell the fabric of Welsh independence. By his wife Eleanor he left an infant daughter only, who was captured and spent her days as a nun; his brothers were without his hold upon the loyalty of the Welsh people, and David, after prolonging the struggle for a few months, was seized, tried as a traitor, and executed (1283).

Edward had now on his hands the problem of the settlement of the conquered country. He had been well supported by the marcher lords, with the result that there was no diminution of the extent of Wales occupied by them; marcher ground was, in fact, considerably extended. Denbighland was given to Henry, Earl of Lincoln, Ruthin to Reginald de Grey, Bromfield and Yale to the Earl of Surrey, Chirkland to Roger Mortimer. The princes who had sided with the king against Llywelyn were not disturbed, and thus the house of Powys continued to rule over Welshpool and the north of our Montgomeryshire, while the house of

South Wales was represented at Dryslwyn in the Towy valley by Rhys ap Maredudd, son and successor of the rebel of 1259. The Crown did indeed take possession of the domains of the house of Gwynedd, but, as these had been much reduced in 1277, the political status of Wales was less altered than might be imagined; it still remained a land of small, independent areas, collectively outside the English shire and parliamentary system, each one with its own customs and traditional organisation, a source of revenue and a reservoir of troops for its usually non-resident lord. The barons of the march kept a tight hold upon their ample privileges, as was seen when Edward in 1290 endeavoured to prevent Gilbert de Clare, lord of Glamorgan, and Humphrey de Bohun, lord of Brecknock, from fighting out a local quarrel on the border of their lordships; the king obtained a temporary victory, but in the long run the "custom of the march," the right of private war, was effectively asserted. These conditions were favourable to the maintenance of the Welsh language and Welsh traditions; Welsh literature flourished, the old Welsh law was administered in the local courts. The conquest of Wales by Edward, in short, produced no social revolution or change of culture; its chief result was to deprive the Welsh of a national head and a centre of national life.

In the area of Llywelyn's principality a new system of administration was set up. By the Statute of Rhuddlan (19 March 1284) it was annexed to the Crown, divided into the three shires of Anglesey, Carnarvon, and Merioneth, and provided with a justice, sheriffs, coroners, and commote bailiffs[1]. A new system of justice was introduced, which may be broadly described as a combination of English criminal and Welsh civil law. Five castles were built to control the district, at Carnarvon, Harlech, Criccieth, Conway, and (after the rising of 1294) Beaumaris, and in each case a borough of the English type, a colony of English traders, was established at the castle gates, to serve the needs of the garrison and to be, through its fairs and markets, an economic centre of English influence. At Criccieth (and also at Bere, near Towyn, which disappeared after 1294), a Welsh stronghold was made use of; the other four castles were new and elaborate structures of the "concentric" type. Beaumaris (Fair Marsh) was laid out on an entirely fresh site; at Conway, the Cistercian abbey was removed to Maenan to make room for the new settlement; Carnarvon, a seat of the Welsh princes, becomes the capital of the whole district, with its independent chancery and exchequer. Minor results of the Statute of Rhuddlan were the grouping of Tegeingl and Maelor Saesneg as the county of Flint, in dependence on the administrative centre of Chester, and the formal organisation, in "West Wales," of the two ancient shires of Cardigan and Carmarthen.

The first settlement of Wales was followed by two considerable revolts. In June 1287 Rhys ap Maredudd, lord of Dryslwyn and Newcastle

---

[1] The old Welsh local area known as the commote (in Welsh, *cymwd*) was accepted as the equivalent of the English hundred. Merioneth is Meirionydd.

Emlyn, broke into rebellion and seized castles in the vale of Towy. His motive would seem to have been jealousy of the power exercised in the district by Robert de Tibetot (*ob.* 1298), justice of Carmarthen, whose commission made him virtual viceroy of South Wales. Not without difficulty, the rising was suppressed and Rhys himself, after long wandering in the forests of Cantref Mawr, captured and put to death. The second upheaval was of a more general character; it was a concerted outbreak at the end of September 1294, throughout all Wales, due to no special grievance of a Welsh magnate, but to widespread popular discontent at the levy of troops and taxes in Wales to defend English interests in Gascony. New leaders appeared: Madog ap Llywelyn in North Wales, who claimed to be hereditary prince in succession to Llywelyn and was probably of the line of Meirionydd, Cynan ap Maredudd and Maelgwn ap Rhys in West Wales, representing the old stock of that region, and Morgan ap Maredudd, of the line of Caerleon, in Glamorgan. So serious was the situation that the king abandoned the French expedition and appeared at the end of the year in Gwynedd, to face once more the task of the subjugation of Wales. January saw him in serious difficulties in Conway Castle, but with the advent of spring matters improved; on 5 March 1295 the Earl of Warwick defeated Madog in a pitched battle at Maes Moydog, in Caer Einion[1], and thereafter resistance gradually died down, enabling the king to finish the campaign in July. He convinced himself that the Welsh had not risen without provocation, for he treated most of the captured chieftains with leniency and in September authorised an enquiry into the grievances of the men of North Wales. It was a further concession to the Welsh that in February 1301 he revived the title of Prince of Wales, dormant since 1282, in favour of his eldest son, Edward, who had been born at Carnarvon in April 1284[2]. The lords marchers were required to do homage to the new prince instead of to the king, and with them great numbers of Welsh gentlemen tendered their obedience; the event may be said to signalise the complete settlement of Wales as a dependency of the Crown.

Under Edward II, whose title of Prince of Wales was merged in the dignity of the kingship, the power of the Crown notably declined, and Wales shared to the full in the disorder of the reign. It was at this time that the only surviving Welsh principality of consequence became an English marcher lordship. Gruffydd ab Owain of Southern Powys died in June 1309, while still a minor; the succession, in accordance with English (though not Welsh) law, was presumed to have passed to his sister Hawise the Strong, who was forthwith married to John Charlton, a

---

[1] *Annals of Worcester*; *EHR.* xxxix, pp. 1–12.

[2] The story of his presentation to the Welsh magnates as their prince at the time of his birth is a late fable, first found in Powel (1584). He was not born in the present castle, the building of which began in 1285 (C. R. Peers in *Cymmrodorion Transactions*, 1915–16).

Shropshire knight in high favour with the king. Thenceforward, the lordship of Powysland, with its centre at Welshpool, was held by the Charltons, despite the opposition of Hawise's uncle, Gruffydd "de la Pole," who took his stand on the Welsh rules of inheritance. Another marcher lordship was thrown into confusion in 1314 by the death of the Earl of Gloucester on the field of Bannockburn; Gilbert left no children and his possessions were divided in 1317 among three co-heiresses, his sisters, with the result that Glamorgan fell to the lot of the younger Hugh Despenser, who had married Eleanor de Clare. There was serious trouble even before the partition: the measures of Payn Turberville, keeper of the lordship at the beginning of 1316, drove the Welsh into revolt under Llywelyn ap Rhys of Senghenydd, commonly known as Llywelyn Bren, and, though the movement was soon put down and Llywelyn captured, Despenser succeeded to a heritage of discontent, which his methods did nothing to appease. His execution of Llywelyn in 1317 alienated his Welsh subjects; his attempt to secure for himself the reversion of the lordship of Gower led to a coalition against him of the barons of the march, who in May 1321 overran Glamorgan and captured Cardiff and Newport. Despenser secured a respite as the result of Boroughbridge and the fall of Lancaster (1322), but he never recovered the good will of his men of Glamorgan, and he was captured in their midst, not far from Neath, on 16 November 1326. His companion, the king, was taken with him; Edward was not unpopular in Wales and took pride on occasion, as in the remedial Ordinances of 1316, in the fact that he was a native of the country; but the Welsh were not ready to rally in his defence, notwithstanding that he had some loyal Welsh supporters, such as Sir Gruffydd Llwyd of Tregarnedd in Anglesey, who gave him substantial help in the struggles of 1322 and was imprisoned after his fall as a dangerous adherent to the royal cause[1].

Another great border lord, Roger Mortimer of Wigmore, who became Earl of March in 1328, now succeeded to the commanding position of the younger Despenser and, like him, set himself to dominate England from the vantage-ground of an absolute control of Wales. But the second attempt had no greater success than the first; Mortimer's Welsh troops could not protect him from the blow which fell upon him in 1330. What was needed to safeguard the interests of the Crown in the west was the re-establishment of the principality, and in May 1343 this was brought about; Edward III's twelve-year-old son, known to history as the Black Prince, was raised to the dignity of Prince of Wales and invested with the symbols of that office, the gold diadem or chaplet, the gold ring, and the silver rod. The diadem or "talaith" had been worn by princes of Wales since the middle of the thirteenth century, if not earlier; the silver rod was a very ancient token of sovereignty among the Welsh. In one respect,

[1] For the true story of Gruffydd, which has been much obscured by legend, see EHR. xxx, p. 589.

the dignity of the Black Prince fell short of that held by his grandfather: the great marcher lords were not required to hold their lands of him, but continued to be tenants in chief of the Crown; any doubt which might be entertained on this point was set at rest by an Act of Parliament of 1354 (28 Edward III, c. 2), which stipulated that all the lords of the Marches of Wales should be "perpetually attending and annexed to the crown of England...and not to the principality of Wales." Edward does not seem to have visited his principality, but the country was efficiently governed by his ministers, who have left one valuable memorial of their activity in the "Record of Carnarvon," an extent of the counties of Anglesey and Carnarvon taken by the deputy of Richard, Earl of Arundel, justice of North Wales, in the summer of 1352.

The fourteenth century was an epoch of slow social and economic change in a country hitherto hardly touched by movements of the kind. A first impression of the extents and other records would no doubt suggest that the old institutions had great vitality. The commote was still the effective local area; dues were still paid to the prince and other lords under the old names; land was divided equally among sons, under the old Welsh rules; marcher privileges were jealously guarded. True, the native princes had gone; but their place as leaders of Welsh society and patrons of Welsh culture was taken by gentlemen not greatly inferior to them in wealth and influence. Such were Sir Howel ap Gruffydd ap Iorwerth, known as "Sir Howel of the Horseshoes," who came of the noble Anglesey stock of Hwfa ap Cynddelw; Sir Howel ap Gruffydd ap Hywel of Eifionydd, who fought at Poitiers and was known as "Sir Howel of the Battleaxe"; Llywelyn ap Gwilym of Emlyn, uncle of the poet Dafydd ap Gwilym and deputy for Gilbert Talbot in his native district; Ifor the Generous of Gwynllwg, whose mother was of the line of Caerleon; the Tudurs and Gronws of the line of Ednyfed Fychan, who were seated at Penmynydd and Trecastell in Anglesey; Sir Rhys ap Gruffydd ap Hywel, of the same stock, who was a leading figure in South Wales during the first half of the fourteenth century. But, if in many respects Wales was little altered, the life of the countryside was nevertheless passing through a silent revolution. The establishment everywhere of castles and towns produced its inevitable effect; the self-contained rural communities began to find in borough and market town, alien colonies though they were, the natural centre for the sale of farm produce and the purchase of luxuries. Town and country still stood apart in all conflicts between the two races, as well as in law and administration, but economically they had become mutually dependent.

In the French wars which fill so large a space in the reign of Edward III, Welshmen played an active part. The origin of the tactics which won the battle of Crécy may, indeed, be found in the adaptation to general warfare of the long-bow which, as we learn from Giraldus Cambrensis, was the traditional and most effective weapon of the men of South Wales.

But, apart from this, large numbers of Welshmen fought in the campaigns, such as the men raised from time to time by Sir Rhys ap Gruffydd as royal agent in the Towy district. It was at Crécy, according to Welsh tradition, that Welshmen first wore the leek as a distinctive national symbol. But more remarkable than any native of Wales who served in the English ranks was Owain ap Thomas ap Rhodri, known to the French as Yeuain of Wales and to his fellow-countrymen as Owain Lawgoch (of the Red Hand), who at the end of this reign fought with conspicuous success on the French side. His grandfather, a brother of the last Llywelyn, had accepted the reverses of 1282 and settled down as an English landowner. Thomas occupied the same position and, on his death in 1363, left to Owain land in Surrey and the manor of Plas yn Dinas (a part of the ancient Mechain) on the Vyrnwy. Owain, however, had no mind for the quiet life of his father and grandfather; he broke out into rebellion against the English government, assumed the title of Prince of Wales, and from 1370 until his death in 1378 fought with distinction as a soldier of fortune in the forces of Charles V. An attempt was made to use him as an instrument to raise Wales in favour of the French; this proved futile, for storms broke up the expedition which he led from Rouen; but he nevertheless rendered great service to the French cause, seizing Guernsey in 1372, capturing Sir Thomas Percy and the Captal de Buch, and aiding Du Guesclin in the struggle which drove the English from Brittany. The English government determined to use the assassin's dagger against so dangerous a foe; he was murdered at Mortagne on the Gironde by a squire named John Lamb, who was in due course rewarded for the deed. Needless to say, his memory lived long in Wales, and the tradition of his achievements was one of the sources of inspiration of the rising of Glyn Dŵr.

Upon the death of the Black Prince, Richard of Bordeaux succeeded to the principality, but it was not long ere his accession to the throne once more merged the lower in the higher title. Father and son were not unpopular among their Welsh subjects, and there was in Wales no more than the usual disorder of the marches during their time. Iolo Goch, a well-known bard of the period, tells how the two bonny fighters of the Conway valley, Hywel Coetmor of Gwydir and his brother Rhys Gethin, kept the peace under Richard, but made open war upon the English under his successor. During the fatal weeks at the end of the reign, when Richard's power was slowly slipping from him and Henry of Lancaster was daily winning supporters, the king having returned from Ireland spent some time in Wales, where he had hopes of a general movement in his favour. But, as in the case of Edward II, these hopes proved delusive; Welsh acquiescence in his rule did not rise to the height of enthusiasm on his behalf or willingness to die in his defence. Left to fight his own battle, he accepted at Conway the terms of his antagonist, found himself a prisoner on Penmaen Rhos, and at Flint was confronted with Lancaster.

The reign of Henry IV is made memorable in Welsh history by the rising of Owain Glyn Dŵr ("Glendower"), the recollection of which has never died out in Wales and which was, in fact, at one point nearer success than is generally imagined. It had its origin in a personal quarrel between Owain ap Gruffydd, lord of Glyn Dyfrdwy and Cynllaith Owain in the Berwyn region, and Reginald de Grey, lord of Ruthin. That this private difference grew to the dimensions of a national revolt was due to the high character and the exceptional claims of the Welsh protagonist. Owain was one of the few Welsh landowners who had a princely pedigree and a hold upon the territories once ruled by their ancestors; he was the direct heir of the princes of Northern Powys and had lands in Cardiganshire also, which he inherited, through his mother, from the ancient dynasty of South Wales. Add to this that he had been trained to the law at Westminster, was married to the daughter of an English judge (Sir David Hanmer), and had fought with gallantry in the armies of Richard, notably in the Scottish campaign of 1385, and it will be realised that Henry could not, by a refusal of justice, have driven into rebellion any more dangerous representative of the Welsh national spirit. He was no mere lawless bandit, but in character, talents, and popular estimation well fitted to grace the dignity of Prince of Wales.

The original outbreak took place on 16 September 1400, when Glyn Dŵr, his relatives, and friends raised the banner of revolt in Glyn Dyfrdwy. They first attacked and burnt Grey's town of Ruthin and then ravaged in succession Denbigh, Rhuddlan, Flint, Hawarden, Holt, Oswestry, and Welshpool. On 24 September they were defeated near the last-mentioned town by Hugh Burnell with the forces of the nearest English counties, and the movement was for the time being checked. But it was far from being crushed: Glyn Dŵr's estates were forfeited and given to John, Earl of Somerset; the king shewed his power by marching through North Wales with an army; but the Welsh leader was not captured and, with hosts of sympathisers in every part of the country, he was still able to hold out in the mountainous west. Offers of pardon (which did not, of course, extend to the prime mover in the rebellion) had little effect, and Parliament, in February 1401, shewed serious concern, pointing out that great numbers of Welsh scholars at Oxford and Cambridge and of Welsh labourers in England had all of a sudden given up work and gone home, arming themselves for battle. A series of penal statutes (2 Hen. IV, cc. 12, 16–20) was enacted which vividly reflects the alarm felt at the position in Wales, where Welshmen, who might be presumed friendly to Glyn Dŵr, were burgesses, officers, and landholders in the various boroughs of the principality and the march. In the spring, two cousins of Glyn Dŵr, William and Rhys ap Tudur of Anglesey, of the stock of Ednyfed Fychan, effected a surprising coup in the capture of Conway Castle (1 April), which they seized by stratagem when the garrison were all at church. Hotspur, who was the royal lieutenant in the district, regained the fortress in a few months and the affair had no immediate sequel. But it was typical of the daring and enterprise of the followers of the Welsh chief, who in the summer appears in a new region, winning at Hyddgen in Plynlimon a decisive victory over a royalist force drawn from south-west Wales. The king again led an army into Wales (September 1401), but with little real success, and in August Percy had relinquished his ungrateful task, which he had been left to prosecute largely with his own resources. It would seem that Glyn Dŵr might at this point have been placated with the redress of his personal grievances; he had not yet burnt his boats or formally claimed the principality of Wales. But Grey was a close friend of the king, and Henry would hear of no negotiations.

In 1402 the fortunes of Glyn Dŵr visibly improved. In April a raid upon Ruthin delivered his arch-enemy, Reginald de Grey, into his hands; he was far too shrewd to treat him otherwise than as a very valuable prisoner and, after much bargaining, finally set him free in November in return for a ransom of 10,000 marks. On 22 June he met the Herefordshire levies under Sir Edmund Mortimer, uncle of the fifth Earl of March, at Pilleth in Maelienydd, and won a signal victory; Robert Whitney and Kinard de la Bere were slain, and Edmund was taken prisoner. The Mortimers could advance a clearer title than Henry to the English crown; hence there was no such haste to ransom Edmund as had been shewn in the case of Grey, and Glyn Dŵr had an opportunity for diplomacy, of which he was not slow to make use. Before the end of the year, Mortimer had married his captor's daughter and was deeply committed to his cause. The king led another fruitless expedition, much hampered by bad weather, into Wales in September, while Glyn Dŵr appeared on the Severn estuary and ravaged Newport and Caerleon.

It was intended in 1403 to renew the attack upon Owain, but in the summer all plans were upset by the rising of the Percies, culminating in the battle of Shrewsbury (21 July). That an understanding had been reached between the English and the Welsh insurgents is most probable, but there is nothing to shew that Glyn Dŵr was expected to effect a junction with the Percies, and the story that he watched the battle from the branches of the great oak at Shelton is a baseless myth. He was, in fact, busily engaged about this time in South Wales, where he had raised the Welsh of the Towy valley and captured Carmarthen. The overthrow of Hotspur and his uncle the Earl of Worcester, no doubt, destroyed some hopes, but it did not seriously injure the position of the Welsh leader, who advanced in 1404 to still more important successes. He now had the whole of Wales in his grip: the town and castle of Cardiff were at his mercy, Beaumaris and Carnarvon were closely beset and, more important than all, Harlech and Aberystwyth fell into his hands, enabling him to establish himself strongly in Central Wales. It was at this point that he assumed the title of Prince of Wales and, therewith, the status of an independent ruler, with a great and a privy seal, a chancellor, and envoys accredited to foreign courts. He summoned to Machynlleth a parliament representative of the area of his obedience, and received, there is reason to think, formal investiture of his office. In May he sent his chancellor and John Hanmer, his brother-in-law, to France to conclude an alliance with Charles VI. They were well received and a treaty was concluded in July which provided for military help for the Welsh insurrection. It came in August 1405, somewhat belated, but substantial in character, a force of about 2500 men which landed in Milford Haven. Glyn Dŵr had suffered some reverses earlier in the year, notably at Pwll Melyn near Usk (5 May), but he was now on the crest of the wave, and he summoned a second parliament to Harlech, hoping with its aid and that of the French army to secure his recognition by the English government. But the results of the French alliance were disappointing; though the troops remained for some months in the country and on one occasion penetrated into England as far as Woodbury Hill in Worcestershire, no solid victory was won, and their withdrawal marks the beginning of Glyn Dŵr's decline. He was still looking for further assistance from the same quarter and agreed, with this object in view, to transfer his allegiance from the Roman to the Avignon pontiff; the letter (Pennal, 31 March 1406) is well known for its proposal to make St David's an archbishopric and to establish two universities in Wales. But the king was now extricating himself from his other difficulties; the war in Wales was, moreover, passing into the capable hands of his heir, now twenty years of age, and the operations of the young Henry in a short time deprived Glyn Dŵr of his foothold as a ruling prince by the successful siege of Aberystwyth and Harlech (1408). The death of Mortimer and the capture of Owain's family at the latter place marked the final ruin of the Welshman's more ambitious designs; he now reverts to his former status of outlaw, with friends in abundance and considerable powers of resistance, but none of the outward show of sovereignty. After many years of this existence, he died in some obscure hiding-place on the Herefordshire border at the beginning of 1416, just after Henry V had offered him a free pardon.

While the courage and the statesmanship of Glyn Dŵr will always command admiration, it is beyond doubt that the failure of his rising left Wales in a worse plight than it had been for many years. Economically, the country had suffered heavily; the fifteen years of pillage and disorder left upon it an indelible mark. Relations between the two races were much embittered; it had been a common cry during the rebellion that Owain aimed at the extirpation from Wales of the English tongue, and Adam of Usk was equally certain that the destruction of Welsh was intended on the other side. Thus, on the one hand, a rigorous series of statutes, passed in 1401 and 1402, excluded Welshmen from all positions of power and authority and closely limited their activities; and that it was no dead letter is proved by the cases of David Holbach of Oswestry and Gruffydd ap Nicholas of Dynevor (Dinefwr), in which exemption was granted from its restrictions. On the other hand, hostility to the English grew deeper among the Welsh, and found fierce expression in the bardic poetry of the period, notably that of Lewis Glyn Cothi. One link there was between the two races in the French wars of Henry V and Henry VI, in which Welshmen took an honourable part; David Gam of Brecknock, an old enemy of Glyn Dŵr, was killed at Agincourt, and Matthew Gough (*i.e.* Goch, the Red) of Maelor (*ob.* 1450) fought with great honour in the last stages of the struggle in Normandy.

The Wars of the Roses inevitably weakened the hold of the Crown upon Wales and opened the door for a revival of activity among the native Welsh. Yorkist and Lancastrian alike relied on the warriors they were able to draw from the Welsh highlands, and the battle of Mortimer's Cross (2 February 1461), though fought on English soil, was largely an encounter between rival Welsh armies. The Duke of York and Edward IV, inheriting the Mortimer estates, could command the allegiance of Central Wales, while in the west, from Anglesey to Pembroke, the name of Tudor was powerful. Owen Tudor (*ob.* 1461), a nephew of the captors of Conway Castle, had by a secret marriage with the widow of Henry V two sons: the elder, Edmund, died young (1456), but left, by Margaret Beaufort, a posthumous son, the future Henry VII. The younger, Jasper, became the protagonist of the Lancastrian cause in Wales, where he was Earl of Pembroke, and carefully watched over the fortunes of his nephew. During the reign of Edward IV, the Lancastrian cause was reduced to great straits, though Harlech Castle held out for seven years (1461–68). The ultimate escape of the young Henry, Earl of Richmond, was for Wales the decisive event which ensured that, when the time was ripe, the house of Lancaster should recover the crown in the person of a scion of Ednyfed Fychan, born in Pembroke and nursed by a Welsh foster-mother. Welsh sentiment has always persisted in regarding Bosworth as a Welsh victory, placing a genuine Welshman on the English throne and thus ending happily the long quarrel between the two races; nor is this view a mere patriotic flourish, for an Italian, writing about 1500, makes the remark that "the Welsh may be said to have recovered their independence, for Henry VII is a Welshman."[1]

[1] *Italian Relation,* ed. Sneyd (Camden Society, 1847), pp. 18–19.

CHAPTER XVIII

IRELAND TO 1315

IRELAND was never subjected to the discipline of Imperial Rome, and her people missed the early lesson in orderly government which the subject races of the Empire never quite forgot; but in the early part of the fifth century, when the Western Empire was beginning to crumble under its own weight, Ireland received from Romanised Britain and Gaul the message of Christianity together with some of the civilising influences that followed in its train. Popular tradition has fixed upon St Patrick as the Apostle of Ireland, and in so doing has had good grounds. He was certainly an historical character, and his *Confessio*, recognised as an authentic work of his hand, shews him an unassuming servant of God whose whole heart was in his work; but it also shews—what indeed vague traditions indicate—that there were other workers in the field in Southern Ireland, more learned perhaps than he, but not so single-minded or so free from jealousy. The new faith was not enforced by the sword; it gradually gained adherents through precept and example, and there was no disturbance of the existing tribal organisation. There is, however, little positive evidence about this early period. The earliest extant Life of St Patrick was written by Muirchu Maccu Machtheni near the close of the seventh century, and the Memoirs of Tirechan a little later. It would seem that here and there a tribal chief who had accepted the new teaching would grant some land, a fort or an island, to the founder saint, who with his companions would build a primitive church and necessary habitations thereon. Disciples would be attracted, and the Christian community thus formed was regarded as the separate *finé* or family (in an extended sense) of the saint, existing side by side with the *finé* of the land. The successors (*comarbs*) of the founder were selected from his *finé* in much the same way as the successor of the tribal chief. Women were welcomed in the work of evangelisation, the most famous being St Brigit of Kildare, called the "Mary of the Gael." In some such way, in the course of the next century and a half, numerous churches were founded and primitive monastic communities and schools were formed, in which the civilising influences of the new religion were centred and fostered. With the religion of the Book, writing and the Latin language were introduced, and through such means of communication came some of the art and learning of the Old World.

The missionary effort was not confined to Ireland. In 563 Columba carried the Christian faith from Derry to the island of Hy (Iona), the mother church of Scotland, and to the Northern Picts, and from thence in 635 his disciples brought it to Lindisfarne, whence it spread over Northumbria. Columba's success was followed by a great missionary movement among the barbarian kingdoms of Western Europe. The most famous missionary there was Columbanus, a monk of Bangor on Belfast Lough. He made his way to Burgundy and founded a monastery at Luxovium (Luxeuil) in 590, where for many years his missionary efforts prospered. At length, however, having come into conflict with Brunhild, the Queen Regent, and having estranged the Gallican clergy by his adherence to Celtic usages, he was forced to leave the country. Afterwards he went up the Rhine to Lake Constance (where his follower, St Gall, remained to found the monastery known by his name), and thence passing into Lombardy he founded the famous monastery of Bobbio. Here in 615 he died. From these and other centres many daughter houses issued, and communication was kept up between these foreign monasteries and those in Ireland to the advancement of learning. From the middle of the seventh century there were also reflex waves of immigrants from Britain and the Continent to the monastic schools of Ireland. Moreover, the influence of Italo-Byzantine art, and more particularly of Lombardic art, has been traced in the wonderful development of interlaced work as shewn in Irish and Hiberno-Saxon manuscripts, such as the Books of Kells, Lindisfarne, and Durrow, about the close of the seventh century, and at a later period in metal, as on the shrines of bell, book, and crozier; and though at least one important *motif* of Irish art, the divergent spiral, has been traced back to what is known as the late Celtic or La Tène period, it seems probable that an important channel of influence in art as in learning was the inter-communication of foreign and Irish monasteries. Certainly the results in Ireland were mainly confined to monastic institutions.

According to traditions preserved in the older heroic literature, Ireland was at one time divided into five independent kingdoms, corresponding roughly to the present four provinces with the kingdom of Meath cut out of Leinster to make the fifth. Later writers often speak of "the five-fifths of Ireland" to designate the whole. There was also an old traditional division of Ireland into two halves, which came to be known respectively as Conn's Half (*Leth Cuinn*), and Mogh's Half (*Leth Mogha*), and were separated by a line through the great central plain from the Bay of Dublin to that of Galway. This division, originating in all probability in a racial difference, was deep-seated. It never quite lost its hold on popular memory, and in later ages it often inspired political aims and ideals and influenced military efforts. In the historical period, however, prior to the Scandinavian invasions and up to the coming of the Normans, Ireland appears as a Heptarchy acknowledging at most a shadowy high king (*ard-rí*). Accordingly in the Book of Rights, compiled (in the form that has come down to us) at the opening of the tenth century, when Cormac son of Cuilennan was King of Cashel, with additions made about a century later in the time of King Brian Bórumha, the numerous subordinate kingdoms and territories of Ireland are grouped under the following seven chief kings: (1) the king of Cashel, representing Munster and part of King's County; (2) the king of Cruachan, representing Connaught and Cavan; (3) the king of Ailech, representing Donegal, Derry, Tyrone, and part of Fermanagh; (4) the king of Uriel (*Oirghialla*), representing Armagh, Monaghan, the rest of Fermanagh, and part of Louth; (5) the king of *Ulaidh*, representing Antrim, Down, and part of Louth; (6) the king of Tara, representing Meath, Westmeath, Longford, and parts of King's County and Kildare; (7) the king of *Laighin*, representing Leinster, less the kingdom of Tara and Louth. In the addition to the Book of Rights ascribed to Brian, it is claimed that "when the king of Cashel is not king of Ireland the government of the (southern) half of Ireland is due to him," and further that "the supreme sovereignty of Ireland ought to be in him"; but the poetical version naïvely admits that the history on which this right is founded "is not taught by the Leinster-men" or "preserved in Conn's Half." As a matter of fact, during the historic period up to the time of King Brian, with one or two disputed exceptions, the Kings of Ailech and Tara, representing two branches of the Ui Neill family, supplied between them the generally recognised high kings of Ireland. In the descent of kingship all males of the family to which the existing king belonged were eligible. Each was known as a *rigdamna*, "the makings of a king." The family (*derb finé*) consisted of a single head (whether living or dead) and his sons, grandsons, and great-grandsons, but on the birth of a member of the next generation it became sub-divided into as many families as there were sons of the first head. Such at least appears to have been the theory. In practice, at any rate, so wide a choice often led to intrigues, violence, and bloodshed, and to minimise these the plan was adopted in the thirteenth century of naming a *tánaiste* or successor in the lifetime of the ruling prince.

From the beginning of the sixth to the close of the eighth century, Ireland, though split up into a number of petty kingdoms often at variance with each other, was free from the ravages of external invasion. This, indeed, was the period of her "Golden Age of art and learning." But early in the ninth century this comparative peace was at an end. From about the year 807 sporadic bands of raiders commenced to ravage the mainland, and in the course of the next 150 years "countless sea-belched shoals of foreigners" penetrated up the estuaries and rivers of Ireland and plundered and burned the monasteries—many of them over and over again—in all parts of the country. No general resistance was organised, and though the invaders met with defeats here and there from particular clan-groups, new hordes came to fill the gap. Uniting under a leader called Turgeis, these predatory bands succeeded in dominating the northern half of Ireland until, in 845, their leader was captured and drowned. This domination was contemporary with attempts by Felimy, son of Criffan, King of Cashel, to contest the supremacy of the recognised *ard-rí* in the north—the first, but not the last, example of internal dissensions facilitating the work of invaders of Ireland.

The first invaders seem to have been Norwegians, but in the middle of the ninth century there came *Dubhgaill* (or Danes) who fought against and subdued the *Finngaill* (or Norwegians) there, though in general no clear distinction can be gathered from the annalists. In 853 Olaf (Amhlaibh), "son of the king of Lochlann," believed to be "Olaf the White" of the Landnamabok, "came to Ireland, when the foreigners submitted to him and a tribute was given to him by the Gael." He is repeatedly mentioned as fighting and plundering along with Ivar (Imhar) and sometimes with Carrol (Cerball), King of Ossory. He flits from Ireland to Alba and Britain. In 866 he is fighting in Fortrenn (Pictland); in 867 he is at the battle of Caer Ebroc (York); and in 870 with Ivar at the siege of Ail Cluathe (Dumbarton). Next year they return to Dublin with captives and booty, but Olaf is heard of no more. Then in 873 "Ivar, king of the Northmen of all Ireland and Britain, died." This and other entries indicate that the leaders of the Northmen, who at this time and later were carving out a kingdom for themselves in the north of England, were using the harbours of Ireland as bases for their operations against the sister kingdom.

From this time, for a period of about forty years, no fresh invasion of foreigners is recorded, though several examples are noted of their plundering churches and of conflicts between them and the native clans. But in 914 and following years fresh fleets of foreigners came to Waterford. In 917 their leaders were Ragnall (Regnald), King of the *Dubhgaill*, and Sihtric, both "grandsons of Ivar," and they gained a victory over the King of Leinster at Cenn Fuait (near St Mullins, County Carlow). Next year Ragnall fought against the men of Alba on the Tyne, but Sihtric went to Dublin, and on 15 September 919 defeated and slew Niall Black-knee (*Glundubh*), *ard-rí* of Ireland, at Cell-mo-samog on the Liffey immediately west of Dublin. He was probably the Sihtric who married Aethelstan's sister and died in 927. Ragnall died in 921 and was succeeded by Guthfrith, another grandson of Ivar, who died in 934. Then in 937 Olaf son of Guthfrith left Dublin to join the combination of the Northumbrian Danes and Constantine the Scottish King against Aethelstan which met with the signal defeat of Brunanburh. Olaf escaped and "fled o'er the deep water, Dublin to seek." But there was another Olaf, a son of Sihtric and son-in-law of Constantine, who also escaped from the battle-field. Both successively appear at times as King of Northumbria and of Dublin. Olaf Guthfrithson died in 941, but Olaf Sihtricson (who is also called Olaf Cuaran) lived to 980, when he met with a severe defeat from Malachy II (Maelsechlainn), King of Tara, and retreated to Iona, "where he died in holiness and penance." Malachy's victory was followed by the release of the hostages held by the Danes of Dublin and the freedom of the Ui Neil from tribute and exaction.

About this time a new outstanding figure appears in the south in the person of Brian, son of Kennedy, commonly called, from a fort near Killaloe, Brian Bórumha. He was leader of the Dál Cais, a group of clans in Thomond or North Munster now beginning to rival the Eoghanachta, who had hitherto supplied the kings of Cashel. Three of these kings, Felimy mac Criffan, Cormac mac Cuilennain, and Cellachan of Cashel, had claimed to be supreme kings of Leth Mogha and even beyond, but their power had waned, and Munster seems to have become dominated by the Danes of Limerick. In 967, however, Brian and his elder brother, Mahon, defeated the Danes in a battle near Tipperary, and followed up their victory by the sack of Limerick. Mahon was now King of Munster, but a conspiracy formed against him by the Eoghanacht leaders, Molloy and Donovan, in alliance with the foreigners, resulted in his murder in 976 and the eventual accession of Brian as King, not only of Munster but of all Leth Mogha. Then began the rivalry between Brian and the *ard-rí* Malachy. In 982 Malachy plundered Thomond and cut down the sacred tree at Magh Adhair, the inauguration hill of the Dál Cais, and in the following year defeated Donnell Claen, King of Leinster, and the foreigners of Waterford and plundered Leinster to the sea. Brian's retort was to bring a fleet of boats to Lough Ree and plunder the west of Meath and Connaught. And so the bickering went on between the rivals until 998, when, according to a tract which may be regarded as "the Brian Saga," Malachy came to meet Brian on the shores of Lough Ree, and a treaty was concluded by which Malachy surrendered to Brian the hostages he held of Leth Mogha and even those of the southern clans of Connaught, while Brian acknowledged that the sole sovereignty of Leth Cuinn belonged to Malachy. Though this treaty is not mentioned in the regular annals, its result is seen in the joint action of Brian and Malachy against the foreigners in that year, and also in the next, when they together defeated the united forces of the Danes of Dublin, under Sihtric son of Olaf, and the Leinstermen, under their King Maelmora, at Glenmama (probably Glen-Saggart near Dublin) and entered Dublin and pillaged it.

But the concord between Brian and Malachy did not last long. Next year (1000) Brian made terms with Sihtric, gave him his daughter in marriage, and led a hosting of the men of Leinster and South Connaught accompanied by the Danes of Dublin "to proceed to Tara." As was his custom, he avoided a pitched battle with Malachy, but he soon practically gained his end. He obtained the hostages of Connaught and Meath and in 1003 was reckoned King of Ireland. In 1005 he was at Armagh, and, as *Imperator Scotorum*, recognised its ecclesiastical supremacy, as a marginal entry in the Book of Armagh testifies. He had more difficulty in securing the submission of the northern clans. Year after year he led armies against them, but not till 1010 did he receive the hostages of all Leth Cuinn.

Brian's reign, as the annals shew, was far from the peaceful time alleged by his shanachies, but he went nearer to uniting Ireland under one head than any native king before or since. It was moreover a time of recuperation. Churches and ecclesiastical towers were built or restored, and there was some revival of art and learning. Henceforth the Danes were normally confined to their seaport towns and the districts immediately adjoining. They had become Christians too, and intermarried with the Gael. Indeed the protagonists in the drama at this time were curiously connected by marriage with one another. Gormflaith, sister of Maelmora King of Leinster, called in the Njal Saga "the fairest of women," but one "who did all things ill over which she had any power," was, it seems, first the wife of Olaf Cuaran and mother of Sihtric King of Dublin. Next, probably after 980, she was the wife of Malachy II and mother of his son Conor, but repudiated by him she became wife of Brian Bórumha and mother of his son Donough. Perhaps in each case she was the prize of the victor. But the complication was greater still, for Malachy's wife Maelmaire, who died in 1021, was daughter of Olaf, Sihtric's father, and finally, as we have mentioned, Sihtric married Brian's daughter.

In spite of these alliances, Maelmora and Sihtric with their forces revolted against Brian and Malachy in 1013, and this led in the next year to the great attempt by "the foreigners of the West of Europe" to recover and complete their domination of Ireland. The battle of Clontarf was fought on Good Friday, 23 April 1014. Brian brought with him the men of Munster and some of the southern clans of Connaught, and he was supported by the men of Meath under Malachy, but the King of Connaught and all the northern kings held aloof. On the other side were the Leinstermen under Maelmora, the Danes of Dublin under Sihtric, and "the foreigners of Lochlann" whom Sihtric had invited to his aid. These last were said to be a thousand mail-clad men. Their principal leaders were Sigurd, Earl of Orkney, and Brodir, a viking, called "chieftain of the Lochlann fleet," which then lay at the Isle of Man. It was a desperate fight. Most of the leaders on both sides were killed, including Brian himself, his eldest son and grandson, and both Sigurd and Brodir as well as Maelmora. Sihtric indeed still held Dublin, but the few surviving invaders were driven to their ships, and the attempted conquest failed.

If Brian's aim, as has been thought, was to establish political unity in Ireland under a strong monarchy, the hope was shattered at his death, if not defeated by the very course he adopted. His surviving sons quarrelled among themselves and were opposed by some of the Eoghanacht clans. Malachy's resumption of his former position was not indeed disputed, but he never had much power, and after his death in 1022 there was no recognised *ard-rí* for many years. Curiously enough, it is stated in the Annals of Clonmacnois (of which the Irish original is lost) that the land was governed for twenty years "like a free State, and not like a monarchy," by a poet and an anchorite. Whatever that may mean, it is certain that

Brian's action in breaking the monopoly of the high-kingship hitherto vested in the two branches of the Ui Neill had a lasting effect. If one king of Munster could gain the supremacy by the sword, the way was open for another king of Munster, or of Leinster, or of Connaught, to attain the same position by the same means; and as a matter of fact the political history of the next century and a half is a record of the attempts of one or other of the provincial kings to subdue the rest. None of them, however, succeeded. At best the most powerful became *ard-rí co fressabhra*, "high-king with opposition," which meant that at least one province held out against him. The consequence was that, besides the usual border raids between hostile clans, whole provinces were often engaged in devastating one another. The usual policy of an aspirant for supremacy was to divide a province which he had subdued and set up two or more kings in it. These arbitrary divisions were most frequent in Meath and Munster, but all the provinces were at various times temporarily split up, either by internal dissensions or by external compulsion.

Yet during this long period of anarchy the Viking terror was no longer present. The Scandinavian sea-rovers settled down in the seaport towns they had formed and exchanged piracy for trade, thus gradually reviving a more healthy communication with England and Western Europe. They became zealous Christians and from about the middle of the eleventh century had bishops of their own in Dublin, Waterford, and Limerick, who received consecration from Canterbury and professed canonical obedience to that see, and not to Armagh. From this beginning indeed may be traced the movement to bring the Church of Ireland into conformity with that of England and through it with that of Rome. Early in the twelfth century Gilbert, Danish Bishop of Limerick, a friend of Anselm, was appointed papal legate, and in a treatise which is still extant he expounded the hierarchical system as developed in Canterbury and Rome. Malchus, consecrated by Anselm in 1096 as Bishop of Waterford, presided over the famous school of Lismore, where one of his pupils was Maelmaedog O'Morgair, afterwards known as St Malachy. He went to Rome in 1139 and was appointed papal legate in succession to Gilbert. He became the principal instrument in the reform of the Irish Church, and to his efforts was doubtless due the constitution by the Pope in 1152 of the four metropolitan sees of Armagh, Dublin, Cashel, and Tuam. To Malachy, who was the lifelong friend of St Bernard of Clairvaux, is also to be attributed the first introduction of the Cistercians into Ireland, and among the earliest houses of the Order were St Mary's Abbey in Dublin and Mellifont near Drogheda (1142).

From 1156 to 1166 Murtough O'Loughlin, representative of the northern Ui Neill, was the most powerful king in Ireland. He was consistently supported by Dermot MacMurrough, King of Leinster, but was at first vigorously opposed by Rory O'Conor, King of Connaught. Each of these rivals repeatedly fought for supremacy over Munster, Meath, and

North Leinster. Each would set up his own nominees in these districts, to be immediately replaced by the nominees of the rival party. In 1159 Tiernan O'Rourke, King of Breffny, a country bordering on the territories of both rivals, threw in his lot with O'Conor. It was inevitable that he should take the side opposed to MacMurrough, who in 1152 had carried off his wife, an insult he never forgot. But the united forces of O'Conor and O'Rourke were utterly defeated, and in 1161 O'Conor gave hostages to O'Loughlin. He was, however, merely biding his time. In 1166 by a gross breach of faith O'Loughlin alienated both the clergy and his own people, and later in the same year he fell a victim to the avenging arm of one of his sub-kings.

O'Conor now seized the opportunity of his rival's disgrace or death. He led an army to Dublin, where the citizens made him their king. Then, after receiving the hostages of Uriel, he advanced into Leinster. There the northern clans submitted to him, and he forced Dermot to give him hostages for his own territory of Okinselagh (represented by the diocese of Ferns). With this submission O'Conor seems to have been satisfied, and he passed into Ossory and Munster and took their hostages. But O'Rourke did not let his personal enemy escape so easily. He led an army composed of the men of Breffny and Meath and of Dermot's own revolted subjects against Dermot, who, deserted by all, fled from Ireland by sea. Whether Rory O'Conor would have been more successful than the previous provincial kings in founding a permanent dynasty and bringing political unity to Ireland, if it had not been for foreign interference, is one of those speculations which it seems futile to entertain. All that can be said is that he began well, but he was not a resolute man, and subsequent history shews that the O'Conors were hopelessly divided amongst themselves even as regards the succession to their own province.

Dermot MacMurrough, on the other hand, shewed great pertinacity in the steps he took to recover his position. He landed at Bristol, where he was well received by Robert Fitz Harding, a personal friend of Henry II. Probably it was by his advice that Dermot sought aid from the King of England, and after much journeying, early in 1167, found him in Aquitaine. Henry, as is well known, on coming to the throne had conceived the design of annexing Ireland and had sought and obtained the sanction of Pope Hadrian IV, but at the time had laid the project aside; and though he now received the exiled king courteously, he put him off with vague promises and an open letter assuring the royal favour to such of his subjects as should be willing to aid Dermot to recover his dominions. Dermot then returned to Bristol, where after some time he got a conditional promise from Richard Fitz Gilbert, Earl of Striguil, commonly known as "Strongbow," on Dermot's agreeing to give him his daughter in marriage and (according to Giraldus) the succession to the kingdom of Leinster. It may, however, be doubted if this latter promise was made, in this bald form at least, as such a devolution of an Irish kingdom was quite unknown to Irish custom. Dermot then went to St David's, where he secured further promises of assistance from the descendants of Gerald, former castellan of Pembroke, or (to speak more correctly) of Nest, daughter of Rhys ap Tewdwr, last independent king of South Wales.

From this remarkable lady indeed were sprung most of those leaders in the Cambro-Norman invasion of Ireland who have been styled "the first conquerors." By a royal lover, Henry I, she had a son known as Henry Fitz Henry, who was slain in 1157. His sons, Meiler and Robert, took part in the invasion. She was married to Gerald, castellan of Pembroke, about 1100 and bore him three sons and one daughter: (1) William de Carew, whose sons were Odo, ancestor of the Carews, Raymond called "le gros," and Griffin; of these, Raymond took the most prominent part; (2) Maurice, ancestor of the barons of Naas, the earls of Kildare, the earls of Desmond, and other families, all more or less famous in the subsequent history of Ireland; (3) David, Bishop of St David's, whose son Miles was the first baron of Iverk; (4) Angarad, who by William de Barry of Manorbier was mother of Gerald, the historian of the Conquest, and ancestress of the numerous families of the Barrys in Ireland. Finally (as far as we are concerned), Nest had a son, Robert, by Stephen constable of Cardigan, and he was the first of the adventurers to set foot in Ireland.

Dermot did not wait for this promised aid, but about August returned to Ferns with only a few troops under Richard, son of Godibert, a Fleming from Rhos near Haverford. O'Conor and O'Rourke came to Cill Osnadh (Kellistown, Co. Carlow) to oppose him, where after some skirmishing Dermot gave hostages to O'Conor for Okinselagh, and 100 ounces of gold to O'Rourke in atonement for the wrong done to him fifteen years previously. Dermot, however, had no intention of submitting, and was only awaiting the expected help from Wales, and as this did not come in the ensuing spring (1168) he sent his *latimer* or secretary, Maurice Regan, to Wales with offers of rewards for armed aid. To this Maurice Regan, as being the principal informant of the author of the rhymed chronicle known as "the Song of Dermot," we are indebted for much of our knowledge of this period up to the taking of Limerick in October 1175.

At length, in May 1169, Robert Fitz Stephen landed at Bannow with thirty men-at-arms (*milites*) of his kinsmen and sixty others clad in mail and about 300 archers, "the flower of the youth of Wales." With them came Hervey de Montmorency, Strongbow's uncle (*i.e.* son of his paternal grandmother by a second marriage), and on the following day Maurice de Prendergast, another Fleming from Rhos. All told, they were not more than 600 men, but they were well armed, inured to warfare in Wales, and the archers carried a weapon for which the Irish had no counterpart and no defence. Having been joined by Dermot with 500 men, they proceeded to assault the walled town of Wexford. On the second day the Ostmen (as the Northmen, whether Danes or Norwegians, are now usually called) surrendered on terms, and afterwards supplied a

CH. XVIII.

contingent to Dermot's army. This success was followed by the return of many Leinster clans to their allegiance, and by more or less successful forays against such as still held out in Ossory and North Leinster.

These operations did not pass unnoticed by O'Conor and O'Rourke. They led their forces, accompanied as before by the Meathmen and the Ostmen of Dublin, into Leinster. This was a critical moment for Dermot, more especially as Maurice de Prendergast, perhaps despairing of success, had returned with his men to Wales. But once more peace was made. Dermot was to hold Leinster of the *ard-rí* and to give his son Conor as a hostage, while by a secret agreement he is said to have promised to introduce no more foreigners and to dismiss those already with him as soon as Leinster was pacified. But Dermot preferred to keep faith with the foreigner rather than with his countrymen. Soon afterwards Maurice Fitz Gerald arrived with a further contingent, and he and Dermot ravaged the country about Dublin. So confident did Dermot become that he sent Fitz Stephen with his followers to distant Limerick to assist his son-in-law Donnell O'Brien, who had turned against the *ard-rí*, and now, with Fitz Stephen's help, for the time successfully resisted him.

Strongbow, encouraged by the success of the "first conquerors," and urged on by Dermot who was already aspiring to the position of *ard-rí*, was now preparing an expedition on a larger scale. About the beginning of May 1170, he sent on before him Raymond Fitz William, nicknamed le Gros, with a small force of ten *milites* and seventy archers. Raymond landed at a rocky headland then known as Dundonnell, but now called Baginbun, on the southern coast of Wexford. Here he was joined by Hervey de Montmorency, but it was thought better to make no move before Strongbow arrived. Accordingly they formed an entrenched camp, cutting off the entire headland by a large double rampart which still remains. Here they beat off a formidable attack organised by the Ostmen of Waterford, and here they awaited the arrival of the earl. At the last moment, when Strongbow was ready to embark, messengers came from the king forbidding the expedition, but it was too late to draw back, and on 23 August 1170 the earl landed near Waterford with about 1200 men. Here he was at once joined by Raymond, and on Tuesday 25 August they took the city by assault. Dermot now came to meet the earl, and the nuptials of his daughter Eva (Aoife) with Strongbow were duly solemnised—a sign that the invaders had come to stay.

The next objective was Dublin, towards which, after leaving a garrison at Waterford, the united forces now marched. That city was under the rule of "Asgall mac Raghnaill mic Turcaill," who had submitted to O'Conor. Anticipating an attack, he had sent for assistance to his over-lord, who promptly came with O'Rourke and O'Carroll and encamped at Clondalkin. Moreover, the usual approaches to Dublin were "plashed" and guarded. Informed by his scouts of this, Dermot led the army over the mountains of Glendalough and reached the city without opposition.

Through the mediation of the Archbishop Lawrence O'Toole, Dermot's brother-in-law, the Ostmen prepared to submit, but while the terms were being arranged, on 21 September, Raymond le Gros and Miles de Cogan with a band of youths rushed the walls and captured the town. Many of the citizens were slain, but Asgall and others escaped in their ships. O'Conor, seeing that the Ostmen had deserted him, left the city to its fate and departed.

MacMurrough now plundered Meath and Breffny, territories of his old enemy O'Rourke. In reply O'Conor and O'Rourke put to death the hostages they held, including Dermot's son Conor. Dermot had regained his kingdom and something more, and in Munster O'Brien was his ally, so that at his death he is called in the Book of Leinster "King of all Leth Mogha and also of Meath." But he did not live long to enjoy his triumph. He died at Ferns in the spring of 1171 in the sixty-first year of his age. His death was the signal for the Leinster clans to rise under Murtough MacMurrough, Dermot's nephew. It was also the signal for all Ireland, except the northern Ui Neill, to send contingents to the *ard-rí* for the siege of Dublin, while Godred, King of Man, was invited to blockade the port. To add to the earl's difficulties he could get no supplies or reinforcements from Wales, for earlier in the year King Henry, on hearing of the earl's doings, had placed an embargo on shipping to Ireland, and had even ordered all his subjects who were already there to return before Easter. Raymond, who had been then sent to the king with Strongbow's assurance that whatever he should acquire in Ireland he would hold at the king's disposal, had recently returned without a favourable reply, and Hervey de Montmorency was now sent on a further mission to the king. The siege lasted nearly two months when, as provisions were nearly exhausted, a desperate sortie was made by three small companies. They took O'Conor's camp at Castleknock by surprise, and the Irish, stript of everything, "fled away like scattered cattle." It was an astounding feat. The rest of the besiegers at once dispersed, and thus ended the last attempt of the *ard-rí* to expel the invaders.

Hervey seems to have found Henry at Argentan in July, where he had summoned a council with a view to his expedition to Ireland, and it was about the end of August when Hervey reached Waterford with letters from the king bidding Strongbow to come to meet him in England. The earl met Henry in Wales or on its border, and made his peace with the king on the terms that he should surrender Dublin with the adjoining cantreds and the other seaport towns to Henry and hold the rest of Leinster from the king. While the earl was absent from Dublin, Miles de Cogan, who was left in charge of the city, had to meet two attacks on it, one by the late ruler, Asgall son of Turcall, and the other by O'Rourke. The latter seems to have been easily repulsed, but the Scandinavian attack was a more formidable affair. Asgall had collected a large viking force from the Isles and Man, including a notable berserker named John "the

Wode" (*furiosus*) from Norway, and while they were attacking the east
gate Richard de Cogan, brother of Miles, issued from the west gate and
took the attackers in the rear. Ultimately, with the aid of the local
chieftain, Donnell MacGillamocholmog, the Norsemen were put to flight.
John the Wode was killed and Asgall was taken prisoner and beheaded.
This was the last attempt of the Scandinavians on Ireland.

Henry landed at Crook near Waterford on 17 October 1171 with a
well-equipped army of about 4000 men. He did not come prepared to
make any extensive campaign at that late season of the year, and in fact
he had no occasion to unsheathe a sword. His primary aim was to secure
the supremacy of the Crown over the lands already acquired by the earl.
He saw clearly the danger of allowing an independent feudal State to
arise on England's flank. He further hoped to conciliate the Irish and
win them over to accept him as their overlord. He entered Waterford
the next day, and Strongbow formally surrendered the city to him and
did homage for Leinster. Dermot MacCarthy, King of Desmond, at once
came and swore fealty to him. Then, knowing how essential it was to gain
the favour of the clergy, Henry went to Lismore, where the papal legate,
Christian O'Conarchy, was bishop, and with him, no doubt, arranged for
the holding of the synod of prelates which met some months later under
the legate's presidency. Next he visited Cashel, the seat of the southern
archbishopric, where the synod was afterwards actually held. Near Cashel
Donnell O'Brien, King of Thomond, came to meet him and gave in his
allegiance, and to both Cork and Limerick the king sent officers of his
own to govern the towns. Having left a garrison at Waterford, Henry
moved through Ossory to Dublin, which he reached on 11 November,
receiving either on the way or at Dublin the submission of all the
principal chieftains of Ossory, Leinster, Meath, Breffny, Uriel, and Ulidia
(*Ulaidh*) or North-East Ulster. Rory O'Conor met the king's messengers,
Hugh de Lacy and William Fitz Audelin, on the Shannon, but while acknowledging the King of England as his supreme lord, he appears to have
insisted on his position as *ard-rí* with respect to all the other kings of
Ireland; this view was met by a compromise four years later, but the
arrangement did not last long. Of all Ireland only the Kings of Tirowen
and Tirconnell held completely aloof.

Henry kept Christmas in Dublin in a palace constructed of wattlework
in the fashion of the country, and entertained there numerous Irish princes
who came to visit him. It was probably after Christmas that the Synod
of Cashel was held under the presidency of the papal legate. It was
attended by the Archbishops of Cashel, Dublin, and Tuam, and their
suffragans, together with many abbots, priors, and other dignitaries,
while Ralph, Abbot of Buildwas, Ralph, archdeacon of Llandaff, and
Nicholas, the king's chaplain, were present on behalf of the king. The
Archbishop of Armagh was in his eighty-fifth year and was unable to
attend, but he afterwards assented to the arrangements made. Either now

or previously all these prelates made full submission to Henry. The synod issued several decrees directed towards the reformation of certain irregularities in ritual and conduct, the improvement of the status of the Church in Ireland, and its conformity with that in England.

⌐ Unfortunately few of Henry's charters or grants of this period survive or have been recorded. His grant of the city of Dublin (Duvelina) to his men of Bristol (Bristowa), with the liberties and free customs that they had at Bristol and throughout his land, has been exceptionally preserved. But though several men of Bristol took advantage of Henry's charter to settle in Dublin, it is clear from the names on the earliest rolls of citizens that have been preserved that immigrants, mostly merchants and traders, came from numerous towns in England and Wales and some from Scotland and France. The Ostmen inhabitants that remained appear to have been settled in the northern suburb about St Mary's Abbey, which came to be known as the Villa Ostmannorum, Ostmaneby, or (corruptly) Oxmantown. Similarly in Waterford, Cork, and Limerick there was an Ostmen's quarter.

On 1 March Henry left Dublin for Wexford. Owing to contrary winds no news had come from England during the winter, and when at last, about 26 March, news did come it was so serious that he determined to wait no longer. Before leaving he granted Meath to Hugh de Lacy for the service of fifty knights and appointed him justiciar—an appointment which seems to shew that he still felt a certain distrust of the Earl of Striguil. On Easter Monday, 17 April 1172, Henry left Ireland.

Strongbow and Hugh de Lacy now set about securing their respective fiefs, but about a year later Henry summoned both of them to his assistance in Normandy and sent William Fitz Audelin as his representative to Ireland. By this time the replies had been received from Pope Alexander III, dated 20 September 1172, to the letters sent to him from the Synod of Cashel. They were addressed to the prelates, to Henry, and to the kings and princes of Ireland, respectively. They expressed complete approval of what had been done, and contained commands to the clergy and admonishments to the kings to be faithful in their allegiance to the King of England. According to Giraldus, the Pope also sent an express confirmation of Hadrian's privilege, and these two *privilegia* were now publicly read before a synod at Waterford. Without here attempting to review the somewhat heated controversy that has arisen concerning the authenticity of these *privilegia* as given by Giraldus, we may note three points not always observed: (1) Hadrian's letter does not purport to be a grant of Ireland (though from the first loosely described as such), but only a sanction to Henry's project; (2) its publication was not delayed beyond what might be expected, considering Henry's strained relations with the Papacy at the time of his entry into Ireland; (3) if with most scholars of repute we admit as genuine the statement of John of Salisbury in the *Metalogicon* and Alexander's three letters, the question of the authenticity of *Laudabiliter* becomes merely an academic one.

About the close of August 1173 Henry allowed Strongbow to return, and shewed confidence in him by entrusting to him the government of Ireland, while recalling the garrisons he had left there. From the time of Strongbow's first landing to his death was not quite six years. Within this period the settlement of the Crown lands about Dublin and the sub-infeudation of the greater part of Leinster took place. To his principal followers Strongbow granted large fiefs, lying for the most part in the rich lands about the rivers Liffey, Barrow, and Slaney. He had more difficulty with the land about the Nore, for here he came into conflict with Donnell O'Brien. In 1174, indeed, a combination of O'Conor and O'Brien and a revolt of the Ostmen of Waterford reduced him to great straits, from which he was relieved by Raymond le Gros, who was rewarded by the hand of the earl's sister in marriage and a large fief about the upper waters of the Slaney. On 6 October 1175 a treaty was made at Windsor between Henry and the envoys of O'Conor, by which O'Conor was to hold Connaught of the king as long as he should faithfully serve him, subject to a tribute of hides, and to be overlord of the rest of the land (except what was held in demesne by the king and his barons), and to remove any sub-king who should refuse to pay his share of tribute or withdraw from his fealty, and for this purpose, if necessary, to call for the aid of the king's constable. This treaty soon proved unworkable. Rory O'Conor had not the power to enforce the obedience of his sub-kings or even, as the event shewed, of members of his own family, and his attempt to do so by calling in Norman troops was probably the cause of his unpopularity and subsequent dethronement. Within eight months from the date of this treaty Strongbow died of blood-poisoning. He was buried in the church of the Holy Trinity at Dublin—a church which, founded in his time on the site of the Norse cathedral and added to, altered, and injured many times since, has been restored in our own days to its original lines, and may well be regarded as a monument of the higher civilisation which Strongbow introduced. By his death the Anglo-Norman colony lost their most prudent leader, one who had thrown in his lot with the country in a constructive spirit and had done much to check the mere filibustering of some of his followers.

Henry now again sent William Fitz Audelin as his representative to Ireland. Acting evidently on instructions, he endeavoured to keep the Geraldines in check. But there was another adventurous spirit who would not be restrained. Setting out from Dublin early in 1177 with a small band of followers, John de Courcy marched rapidly northwards and took by surprise the city of Down, and in the course of the next few years in a series of battles, sometimes "facing fearful odds," made himself master of the district lying east of the Newry River, Lough Neagh, and the Bann. Here he encastled and organised a feudal principality for himself, and was not disturbed until after King John came to the throne. But meantime, in May 1177, Henry made an entirely new disposition of Ireland. His son John, then in his tenth year, was created *Dominus Hiberniae*. Hugh de Lacy was given the custody of Dublin and William Fitz Audelin that of Wexford, while the services of Leinster were divided between the two. But more important than these arrangements, necessitated by the minority of Strongbow's heir, were the grants now made of the "kingdom of Cork" to Robert Fitz Stephen and Miles de Cogan jointly, and of the "kingdom of Limerick" to Philip de Braiose. These grants were obviously inconsistent with the Treaty of Windsor. Presumably Donnell O'Brien was regarded as having withdrawn from his allegiance. Certainly O'Brien, who claimed to be King of Leth Mogha, had fought against Strongbow in Ossory and had been expelled by O'Conor from his kingdom. The city of Cork was still in the hands of an English garrison, and the grantees seem to have come to terms with Dermot MacCarthy, and for the present were satisfied to divide the seven cantreds nearest Cork between themselves. But Philip de Braiose, finding on arrival that the citizens of Limerick set fire to their city rather than surrender it, preferred to return home and not risk his life among such determined enemies.

Hugh de Lacy was a capable and prudent governor. He occupied himself in restoring peace and order, in encouraging Irish cultivators to return to their lands, and in building castles both in Meath and Leinster. These early castles, which were hastily erected in all districts occupied by the Normans, were not substantial stone buildings, but, as is now generally recognised, wooden towers erected on earthworks called "mottes." A motte was a steep mound or hillock of earth surrounded by a fosse, with generally a bailey or court-yard enclosed within palisaded earthen ramparts at its base. These motte-castles were often replaced by stone castles, but at nearly all the known early manorial centres such earthworks, or traces of them, are to be seen, while they are not found in purely Celtic districts. We hear of no filibustering expeditions under Hugh de Lacy. He married as his second wife a daughter of Rory O'Conor. Indeed it was this marriage and his popularity with the Irish which aroused in Henry's mind suspicions, probably quite unfounded, of his aiming at becoming King of Ireland. He was superseded in 1184 by Philip of Worcester, and two years later he fell a victim to the vengeance of an Irish assassin.

Meantime, in 1184, Henry conceived the unfortunate plan of sending his son John, then in his eighteenth year, to Ireland as *Dominus*. John landed at Waterford on 25 April 1185 with some 300 men-at-arms and a large force of horsemen and archers. Among his followers were Bertram de Verdun and Gilbert Pipard, to both of whom he gave lands in County Louth. With him also came Gerald de Barry (Giraldus Cambrensis), to whose writings we owe much of our knowledge of the preceding period.

Unfortunately he gives no adequate account of John's actual doings in Ireland, though in general language he scathingly censures his mis-management of affairs, and intimates that he exasperated the native chieftains and alienated the existing settlers. From other sources we know that John made a large speculative grant to Theobald Walter, ancestor of the Ormonde family, in North Tipperary, and similar grants to William de Burgh and Philip of Worcester in South Tipperary, but his efforts to give possession to his grantees were not successful. Indeed an English chronicler tells us that the greater part of John's army deserted to the Irish who were about to fight against him, while the Irish annals shew that in this year Connaught was torn by a general war among the princes (*rigdamna*) of the house of O'Conor, and that there were foreign mercenaries (presumably the deserters from John's army) fighting on behalf of some of the rivals. Eventually Rory O'Conor was banished by his son Conor "of Maenmagh." No wonder that Henry recalled the *Dominus Hiberniae* before the year was out.

From this period to the accession of King John we are largely dependent on the bald entries in the Irish annals. In 1189 Conor "of Maenmagh" was killed by his own kinsmen, and after another unsuccessful attempt by Rory O'Conor to recover his throne, his younger brother, Cathal Red Hand (*Crobhderg*), was generally recognised as king. He was opposed by Cathal Carragh, son of the former king, until in 1202 the latter was slain. In the parts of Ireland already dominated by the Normans this appears to have been a period of peaceful consolidation. Leinster in 1189 passed with the marriage of Strongbow's heiress to William Marshal, Earl of Pembroke. For many years he managed his great fief through seneschals, and it was not until 1207 that he came to reside there, but to his tact, ability, and loyalty the increasing prosperity of the province was largely due. In 1192 an important advance was made by William de Burgh and Philip of Worcester to take possession of the "speculative" fiefs granted to them by Prince John in the Suir valley, and this was continued and extended until by 1197 Limerick was finally in Norman hands, and with the acquiescence of the sons of Donnell O'Brien the lands of their Eoghanacht rivals to the south of the Shannon were divided among the leaders of the expedition. The Norman barons were no doubt rapacious and unscrupulous, but their encroachments were seldom made without both royal warrant and some native encouragement. It seems clear too that John before coming to the throne made a grant of lands in Connaught to William de Burgh, and this, together with a call for his aid by Cathal Carragh, was the ground of William's interference there in the year 1200. Soon afterwards, however, Cathal Red Hand was recognised by the Crown as a vassal-king, and finally, by a charter dated 13 September 1215, he was to hold his land of Connaught during good service, and so that he should not be disseised thereof without judgment of the king's court, rendering yearly 300 marks. On the same date a grant was made to Richard, son of William de Burgh, of all the land of Connaught which William his father held, but apparently this grant was to come into operation only if Cathal made default.

John's attitude towards his barons was always capricious. Thus, after making numerous grants in Counties Limerick and Tipperary, he sought in 1201 to subject the grantees to William de Braiose, to whom for a large fine he granted the honour of Limerick. This naturally provoked opposition, and William de Braiose gained little or nothing by the transaction. Next, John confiscated the lands of John de Courcy, who certainly seems to have been a contumacious subject, and on 29 May 1205 gave them to the younger Hugh de Lacy and created him Earl of Ulster. Then in 1208 John fell out with William de Braiose and pursued him with relentless hostility. In fact, if we are to believe the king's own account, his great expedition to Ireland in the summer of 1210 was undertaken because William owed the enormous fine of 40,000 marks for regaining the king's peace. Certain it is that all John's military actions when in Ireland were directed towards punishing the de Lacys for having harboured William, whom he had outlawed, and who was Walter de Lacy's father-in-law. He expelled the de Lacys and confiscated all their lands in Meath and Ulster, and he succeeded in capturing Maud de Braiose, William's wife, and one of her sons, and starved them to death in prison. He was even suspicious of that most loyal of men, Earl William Marshal, and did what he could to injure him. Only towards the close of his reign, when his enemies were threatening him, did he acknowledge the earl's sterling worth, and under his influence begin to make restitution to those whom he had despoiled in Ireland. John's expedition, however, had the wholesome effect of increasing the power of the Crown in Ireland, and under the governors whom he appointed much was done to improve the administration by the formation of counties and sheriffs' courts, and the institution of itinerant justices outside the great liberties, and by restricting the powers of the courts of the liberties themselves. Under the influence of William Marshal restitution was made to Walter de Lacy and others, but it was not until after Hugh de Lacy had recourse to "direct action" that in 1227 he was restored to his earldom.

Cathal O'Conor remained loyal up to his death in 1224. His son Aedh succeeded to him, but was opposed by a son of Rory, the last *ard-rí.* Aedh now, like some other Irish potentates, was faced with this dilemma: without seeking English aid he could not overcome his rival, but unless he attacked the English he could not retain the allegiance of his *urriaghs* (sub-kings). He foolishly tried both alternatives, with the result that he forfeited his position, and Connaught lost its independence. After having regained the crown with English help, Aedh was summoned to the justiciar's court on a charge of forfeiture. He ignored the summons, and at a subsequent conference near Athlone he seized the English envoys and burned the town. In May 1227 the grant of Connaught to Richard de Burgh was confirmed, five cantreds on the eastern border being retained by King Henry out of which provision was to be made for the Irish king. The province was repeatedly subdued, but several years elapsed before peace was finally established. The main difficulty was to find a king who would remain satisfied with the restricted territory assigned to him. At last in 1235 Felim, another son of Cathal, accepted the five cantreds, and the remaining 25 cantreds were parcelled out by Richard de Burgh among the leaders who had assisted him in his campaigns.

In 1254 Henry gave Ireland to his son Edward on his marriage, but so that it should never be separated from the Crown, and retaining to himself all matters relating to the Church. Before this, in 1243, on the death of Hugh de Lacy, his land of Ulster reverted to the Crown and was managed by seneschals, while by 1245 the liberties of both Meath and Leinster, owing to failure of male heirs, had become sub-divided and thereby weakened. Edward paid more attention to Gascony and Wales than to Ireland, and relations with the semi-independent kings there grew worse. In 1258 Brian O'Neill attempted to revive in his own person the extinct high-kingship, and Aedh, the warlike son of Felim, confederated with him and gave him hostages; but his neighbour O'Donnell rejected O'Neill's overtures, quoting the proverb "Every man should have his own world." This indeed is the sentiment which has ever stood in the way of Irish unity. Next year Aedh O'Conor married a daughter of Dugald MacSorley (*Somhairle*), a descendant of Somerled, lord of the Isles, and with her brought back 160 warriors called *óglāigh* under Dugald's brother Alan. This was the first of many bands of *gall-óglāigh*, or "galloglasses" as the name came to be written, that took service as heavy-armed foot-soldiers under Irish chieftains and did much to increase their military power. But, in spite of this foreign aid, the confederates were defeated at the battle of Down in 1260 and Brian O'Neill was killed. In or shortly before 1264, when the struggle with Simon de Montfort was coming to a head, Edward enfeoffed Walter de Burgh in the land of Ulster, and the earldom was revived in his favour. In Earl Walter's time there was peace in Ulster. Aedh *Buidhe* O'Neill, the new King of the Cenel Eoghain, was friendly to him. He married a cousin of the earl and acknowledged that he held his regality of him. But in Connaught the earl was not so successful at this time. He had a quarrel about tenure with Maurice Fitz Maurice which caused great disturbance, and he was much harassed by Aedh O'Conor who, on the death of Felim in 1265, became king of a still more restricted territory. He died in 1271 without having been able to subdue his formidable opponent.

During the long reign of Henry III the area of English domination in Ireland had greatly increased, and the peace and prosperity of the more settled districts in the east and south were well maintained. Numerous small towns grew up under the shelter of the castles, and many of these received charters from their lords, formed trade gilds, and became centres of industry and commerce. Rivers were bridged. Cathedrals and monastic and parish churches were built, several of which remain and, whether still in use or in ruins, bear witness to the beauty and strength of thirteenth-century architecture. In Connaught, Thomond, and Desmond, the plan of treating the native chief as a quasi-feudal tenant of the Crown in a restricted part of his former territory had at first some measure of success. These chiefs remained loyal and repeatedly fought beside the king's forces. But towards the close of the reign some expectant successor would chafe against the restrictions and take the more popular course of heading a raid against his English neighbours.

When Edward I came to the throne, Thomond (*i.e.* the present County Clare) was being torn between the rival factions of the O'Briens. Brian Roe O'Brien, son of the late King Conor, who held a moiety of Thomond under the Crown, had been expelled by his nephew Turlough. Edward in 1276 sought to put an end to these disturbances by granting the whole of Thomond to Thomas de Clare, brother of the Earl of Gloucester, and by an arrangement with the former Norman owner the castle of Bunratty and the adjoining cantred were given to him in possession. De Clare restored King Brian and expelled Turlough, but next year Brian was defeated by Turlough and de Clare's brother-in-law slain. In a fit of frenzy de Clare caused Brian to be executed. According to the *Caithréim Toirdelbaig*, de Clare afterwards repented of this deed and aided Donough, son of Brian, in recovering his father's throne. A savage warfare ensued, however, between the rival O'Briens until in 1284 Donough was killed. De Clare died on 29 August 1287, when the manor of Bunratty was fairly prosperous, but the vendetta between the O'Brien factions broke out again at intervals until 1318, when Richard, son of Thomas de Clare, was killed, and not long afterwards all hope of maintaining English rule in Thomond was abandoned. The ultimate failure was largely due to the de Burghs of Connaught who, through jealousy of the de Clares, habitually supported the O'Brien party opposed to them.

In Connaught, after the death in 1274 of Aedh son of Felim, the old quarrels between the rival O'Conor factions again broke out, and in the next four years four successive aspirants to the throne were killed by their kinsmen. The fighting, however, was confined to the cantreds reserved for them, and at first the English did not interfere. According to the story of a late chronicler, Edward in 1278 called his justiciar, Robert d'Ufford, to account for permitting "such shameful enormities," and he replied that "in policie he thought it expedient to winke at one knave cutting off another," whereat "the king smiled and sent him back to Ireland." Whether true or false, the story is *ben trovato* and seems applicable to other periods in Irish history, but such is not the policy by which good government can be maintained. Robert d'Ufford, however, built the great Edwardian castle of Roscommon and repaired those of Athlone and Randown to protect the southern part of the county now in the hands of English settlers.

In Ulster after 1280, when Earl Richard de Burgh, son of Earl Walter, was given seisin of his lands, the disturbances which often accompanied a minority ceased, and by 1286 the young earl was supreme in all his dominions both in Connaught and Ulster. In Connaught indeed the old quarrel with the Geraldine feoffees broke out in 1294, but ultimately John Fitz Thomas, head of the Geraldines, was obliged to surrender his Connaught lands to the earl, whose supremacy was now undisputed over the whole north of Ireland from Carlingford Lough to Galway Bay. He took an important part in the Scottish campaigns of 1296 and 1303, and up to the period of Bruce's invasion was by far the most powerful man in Ireland, but probably just because of his great power he was never actually made justiciar. The most successful justiciar appointed by Edward I was John de Wogan, lord of Picton Castle near Haverford, who retained his post almost continuously from 1295 for eighteen years. In 1297 he summoned the first council that can properly be called a parliament, to which, in addition to the lords temporal and spiritual usually summoned by writ, two knights for each shire and liberty were to be elected "by the assent of the county or liberty," and in subsequent parliaments in 1300 and 1310 the cities and boroughs were also represented. Unfortunately the experiment of summoning the principal Irish chieftains was not tried.

All the great legislation of Edward I in England, framed for the improvement of the law and the reform of its administration, was extended to Ireland. The justiciars held their courts throughout Meath, Leinster, and Munster. The increasing wealth of the orderly districts is shewn in many ways: by the growth of numerous towns, by the largely increased revenue, by the produce of the tax on the export of wool and the great variety of articles subject to customs duties, by the considerable subsidies granted and the large quantities of corn and other supplies purchased for Edward's foreign wars. The farming accounts of the Earl of Norfolk's estates in Counties Carlow and Wexford shew in detail the careful way in which landed property was managed, and many inquisitions attest the large acreage "under the lord's plough." All this prosperity was rendered possible by the comparative order which went hand in hand with Norman domination, and in the latter part of Edward's reign it seemed as if a *Pax Normannica* was about to extend throughout the length and breadth of the land.

But there was another side to the picture. There were large districts where Gaelic clans continued to live in their old independent way under their antiquated customs and were little affected by the material progress beyond their borders. The ideal of Norman feudalism was incompatible with that of the Celtic clan-system. The clansmen would not part with their liberty for a peace and order they did not value. Their chieftains would not willingly subordinate themselves to any superior, whether Gael or Norman. These characteristics had always operated against the political unity of Ireland, and they operated still. Notwithstanding some intermarriages, the races as a whole did not amalgamate. The incomers regarded the natives as an inferior race, whereas in reality they were only in an earlier stage of the evolution of civilisation. The Geraldines understood them best, and saw that if they lacked some of the elements essential to the vitality of a nation, they had many good qualities, such as physical courage, intelligence, and a taste for literary culture of their own. The natives, on the other hand, thought the foreigners proud and rapacious, as indeed, like most conquerors, they often were. Thus the Gaelic clans were for the most part ever ready to take advantage of any governmental weakness to plunder and destroy the wealth of their neighbours which they had not the qualities to create or maintain for themselves. The opportunity came with the weak rule of Edward II and the invasion of Edward Bruce.

CHAPTER XIX

SCOTLAND TO 1328

THE racial basis of Scottish nationality presents a problem obscure, perhaps insoluble, and, apart from the question of language, relatively unimportant. No convincing evidence associates Scotland with a palaeolithic population. But thereafter, as in England, successive waves of immigrant Celts, Goidelic and Brythonic, reached her shores, and, ahead of them, a Mediterranean neolithic race whose presence along the western coast, in the Clyde valley, and elsewhere in the Lowlands, is discovered by distinctive long barrows or cairns. The sixth century added other racial ingredients, Saxon immigrants; and it is probable that nordic settlers were drawn to the northern mainland and islands long before their subsequent predatory exodus from Scandinavia. Late in the Roman occupation the Picts are named. That the word connoted an observed racial content cannot be supposed. In the use of Bede and the *Anglo-Saxon Chronicle* it distinguishes an assumed aboriginal Scottish population from the Irish Scots and Strathclyde Britons. But modern investigation is not in agreement upon the Picts' racial identity. The theory that they represented a pre-Aryan immigration is challenged by the ascription to them of a Celtic origin, a hypothesis supported by their personal, tribal, and geographical names recorded by Ptolemy and classical writers, by an eloquent, though meagre, *corpus* of sepulchral inscriptions ranging from the fourth or fifth to the eighth or ninth centuries, and by the facile union of the Scottish and Pictish kingdoms under Kenneth MacAlpin. Unlike contemporary inscriptions within Romanised Scotland below the Forth, which exhibit mixed Latin and Celtic, these northern examples are pure vernacular and declare a Goidelic speech akin to Erse, Manx, and Gaelic.

Upon a population preponderantly Celtic, Rome descended towards the close of the first Christian century, and nowhere else enforced so faint an impress of her genius. The theory of Roman continuity, which vexes the institutional history of Saxon England, has no counterpart in Scotland's experience. Neither have there survived material evidences of Rome's constructive genius, nor, to the same degree as elsewhere, did her industry improve the physical conditions of the soil. Her beneficent activity was confined to the region between Hadrian's Wall and the Vallum of Antoninus Pius. Excavations within it, at Newstead, near Melrose, Balmuildie, and elsewhere, reveal the amenities of a military garrison. But outside this narrow area Rome's power was demonstrated only intermittently, as at Mons Graupius (A.D. 84?) over Calgacus; and though the footsteps of the Romans can certainly be traced at Ythan Wells, it is a credible but unverified tradition that Severus led his legions to the

Moray Firth (208–11). Certainly the population of North Britain was never Romanised nor submitted to the municipal organisation Rome elsewhere established. Throughout the fourth century her hold upon Caledonia was increasingly precarious, till the tramp of Alaric's Goths, reverberating through Western Europe, incited Picts, Irish Scots, and English to challenge a weakening giant. Early in the fifth century Rome abandoned a remote country she had never tamed.

After a darkened interval, the sixth century discovers four political systems ethnically distinguished, whose slow fusion created the Scottish nation and kingdom. (1) Most considerable in area, the kingdom of the Picts extended from the Pentland Firth to the central plain, including, apparently, a number of vassal provinces whose locality and nomenclature are preserved in the ancient earldoms of Angus, Atholl, Fife, Lennox, Mar, and Menteith, subject to a monarch whose principal seat was on the Ness. (2) What impulse drove Fergus Mor and his brothers Loarn and Angus, sons of Erc, from the Irish main is not recorded. The event (*c.* 498) laid the foundation of Dalriada, a Scottish State which at its largest extent embraced Argyllshire and the islands Jura and Islay. Subject for half a century to the Irish *ard-rí*, interlopers and Christians, the newcomers provoked the enmity of their pagan neighbour. About the year 559 the Pictish King Brude (*c.* 555–84), son of Maelchon, inflicted on them a defeat from which they had not recovered when St Columba came among them four years later. His intervention saved the stricken colony from extinction; the third generation of Fergus' line was already on the throne, and every one of its princes had died a violent death. (3) Meanwhile, the Anglian advance into the interior of South Britain drove before it Brythonic, Welsh-speaking refugees who settled in Strathclyde, dominating or expelling into the shires of Wigtown and Kirkcudbright an aboriginal Pictish population which maintained its distinctive language there until after the union of the crowns in 1603. Circumstances decreed the isolation of the newcomers from the national system out of which they were expelled, and linked their future with Scotland's fortune. Having in 573 fixed their seat at Dumbarton on the Clyde, Aethelfrith of Bernicia's victory at Daegsastan (603) thirty years later cut them off conclusively from their Welsh kindred. (4) Eastward of Strathclyde, in the same period, Ida of Bernicia laid his hand upon the rich pastoral region between Tweed and Forth, whose possession embroiled the English with the Scottish monarchy till the eleventh century, and profoundly affected the economy of the Scottish kingdom.

Full thirty years before Augustine's arrival in Kent, the coming of Columba (521–97) to Scotland invited North Britain to a similar profession of Christian ideals and endeavour. "Angelic in appearance, polished in speech, holy in work, excellent in intelligence, great in resourcefulness,"[1] a busy founder of religious houses throughout his middle

---

[1] Adamnan, quoted in Anderson, *Early Sources*, I, 27.

years, he still could involve himself in the secular feuds of his countrymen. A banished and excommunicated man, he landed on Iona with twelve companions in 563. Two years later the indomitable apostle stood before the Pictish palace on the Ness. Its gates, fast locked against him, flew open at the holy sign. Thaumaturgic contests, in which the royal magicians met their master, completed the sovereign's conversion. Brude declared himself a Christian and led his people to the font. Ethical considerations probably influenced his decision but little, and moral standards were not immediately raised. But touch was established with Ireland's riper culture, and forces were loosed which in time evolved a consolidated kingdom and a united people. The conversion of the Picts may be held to be the governing factor in early Scottish history. For more than thirty years it was Columba's absorbing task. Monastic colonies ("families of Iona"), tribal in organisation, centres of light, examples of noble purpose, were planted throughout the territory of the northern Picts. To the Minch, by Eigg, Tiree, and Applecross, the apostles of Iona made their way; thence to the Black Isle (Rosemarkie) and the coastal plain bordering Moray Firth, at Mortlach, Forglen, Aberdour, Deer, and Turriff; and, by another route, through Glen Dochart, to Strath-Tay, Dunblane, Abernethy, and Kilrimont (St Andrews). Disciples of Columba—Machar, Ternan, Serf, Devenick— expanded their leader's work; while southward, in Strathclyde, Kentigern (Mungo) gleaned a harvest of souls in a field his predecessor Ninian (*c.* 397) had tilled.

Scotland received her first impulse towards a cultured Christian life through Columba from Ireland, whose sons in Dalriada eventually made her speech dominant. But the forces that moulded Scotland's political development came from across the English border. Sixty-seven years after Columba's death England rejected the rule of Iona, which, carried by Aidan thence to Lindisfarne (635), threatened to sever England and Scotland from Latin Christendom. Boasting neither the traditions, authority, nor cultural promise of the Roman Church, that of Iona practised rites which its rival denounced as barbarous, followed a calendar which Rome had abandoned, and tonsured its clergy from ear to ear instead of upon the scalp. Its supremacy involved rejection of a system and ideals competent to advance the political no less than the ethical welfare of the island kingdoms. Forbidding the threatened isolation, the Synod of Whitby (664) decisively linked England with Rome and the continental churches. A generation later, Nechtan, King of the Picts (706–24), admitting, like Oswy, the superior authority of the See of St Peter and the poverty of the Scoto-Irish Church in apostolic tradition, also imposed the Roman use upon his subjects. In 716 Iona herself adopted the Roman tonsure and calendar; though, down to the four- teenth century, the Culdees perpetuated certain obstinate Celtic usages.

An event of political moment preceded Nechtan's decision. Oswy of Northumbria's victory over Penda at Winwaed (655) laid England at his feet, and thereafter subjugated the Pictish kingdom dominant beyond the Forth. For a generation Picts and Scots owned her supremacy, till his successor, Ecgfrith, headstrong and ill-counselled, was shamefully overthrown at Dunnichen (Nechtansmere), near Forfar (685). The event broke English power in Scotland. The Picts, Scots, and Britons of Strathclyde recovered their independence, and the nascent kingdom of which they were the embryo, no longer impeded from outside, was free to pursue the stubborn process of consolidation. To this endeavour the closing years of the eighth century contributed a new and disturbing factor. Impelled by economic conditions and the Saxon wars of Charles the Great, Scandinavian exiles fared westward along the not unfamiliar path to Orkney and the Shetlands, whence the Hebrides, the plains of Caithness, the southern shores of Moray Firth, and the sea lochs of Ross, Sutherland, and Inverness were accessible to them. In 794 the *Annals of Ulster* record the devastation of "all the islands of Britain" by "the gentiles." In 795 Skye was pillaged. In 798 the Hebrides were wasted. In 802 Iona was again in ashes, and four years later its whole community perished. For a generation every coast was at the mercy of Viking war-keels, till the Pictish kingdom was drained of its strength in wearying warfare with an enemy already possessed of its islands and northern provinces. Its plight stirred the cupidity of the Dalriada princes or invited them to press a claim to a disputed and tottering throne. Succeeding a father who died fighting the Picts in Galloway, Kenneth MacAlpin, "when Danish pirates had occupied the shores, and with the greatest slaughter had destroyed the Picts who defended their land, passed over into and turned his arms against the remaining provinces of the Picts; and, after slaying many, drove [the rest] into flight. And so he was the first of the Scots to obtain the monarchy of the whole of Albania, which is now called Scotia."[1] Circumstances facilitated the union (844[2]) achieved in his person. In Iona lately, and soon in Dunkeld, the conjoined kingdoms owned a common ecclesiastical capital. In blood probably, in language certainly, they were akin, and the Scandinavian assault advised the need to compose the futile rivalries of three centuries. That the union proved permanent declares it opportune. Its achievement reduced the four systems to three. In less than two centuries the three were compressed into one, and, excepting the Norse regions, Scotland geographically was complete.

The central fact in the history of Scotland after 844 is the clear intention of the new kingdom, whose sovereigns are distinguished as *Rí Alban*, to emerge from the Highland table-land to which for the most part it was as yet confined. No deterring physical barrier proscribed its expansion, and over the central plateau, extending from Dumbarton to Dunnottar, from Girvan to Dunbar, it was imperative to assert its ownership. Only in this district, richer in soil and more accessible to

---

[1] *Chronicle of the Canons of Huntingdon,* printed in Skene, *Chronicles of the Picts* etc., I, 209. [2] The date is not precisely ascertained.

commerce, could an ordered polity be developed. Its attachment to the Scottish system was the achievement of Alpin's dynasty. Kenneth I (*ob.* 858), who significantly planted his seat at Forteviot in Perthshire[1] and established the religious centre at Dunkeld in the same county, six times invaded English territory, raiding Dunbar and Melrose. But the depredations of the Danes and Norsemen, subjecting England and Scotland to a common experience, invited defensive co-operation. Kenneth's grandson Constantine II (900–43) made a pact with Alfred the Great's daughter Aethelfleda, Lady of the Mercians, and in 921, "with his whole nation,"[2] chose her brother Edward the Elder for lord. The obligation weighed lightly on him. To punish his disregard of it, Aethelstan, asserting the imperial pretensions of the house of Wessex, wasted Scotland to the Mearns in 934 and shewed his fleet off the coast of Caithness. Three years later (937) Constantine, in alliance with Norse and Northumbrian princes dispossessed by Aethelstan, sought to throw off the yoke imposed on him and was overthrown at Brunanburh[3].

Scottish policy at this juncture, involved on two fronts, sought to turn a shifting situation to its advantage, hoping to gain the coveted territories beyond the Forth. As his "helper both by land and sea,"[4] ally or vassal, Malcolm I (943–54) received Cumbria from Edmund in 945 and undertook arduous responsibilities with its possession; the district formed the highway between the Northumbrian Danes and their kinsmen in Galloway, Wales, and Ireland. A generation later, Malcolm's son, Kenneth II (971–95), is declared to have received the Lothians from Edgar; if so, the obligation of service cannot fail to have been exacted. The significance of this cession is heightened by the fact that Kenneth's predecessor, Indulf (954–62), had already acquired Edinburgh[5], and Kenneth himself had taken measures to strengthen the defences of the Forth. From that vantage-ground the rich Bernician plains, the granary of the north, were the more coveted. The *Annals of Ulster* record in 1006 a Scottish defeat, apparently upon the contested territory. Twelve years later (1018) the decision was reversed by the victory of Malcolm II (1005–34) over Eadulf at Carham, which added Lothian to the domains of the Scottish crown, an acquisition[6] destined to transform the polity of the Scottish State. The date is otherwise memorable; in the same year died Owen the Bald, prince of Strathclyde. His kingdom passed to Malcolm's grandson, "gentle Duncan," on whose accession in 1034 it was attached to Scotland in a bond thereafter not broken. The union of the four original kingdoms

---

[1] Traditionally, Angus MacFergus (729–61) built a church here.
[2] *Anglo-Saxon Chronicle.*
[3] Burnswark (Birrenswark), in Annandale.
[4] *Anglo-Saxon Chronicle.* The *Chronicle* says that the land was "commended."
[5] *Oppidum Eden.*
[6] The authorities imply that Canute exacted some sort of submission within the following seven years.

was achieved, and Scotland, saving the Norse districts, was geographically complete.

Scotland exhibited in 1034 neither political nor racial homogeneity. Her Isles and northern coasts remained under Scandinavian lordship, while her English neighbour, imminently to fall to a Norman invader, aimed at submitting her to the rigid obligations of vassalage. But the most urgent need was to assimilate her populations and reconcile their cultural and political standards. The Anglo-Norman polity was well adapted to develop her backward state. But for two centuries there was hardly any Scottish king that did not feel the anger of his Celtic subjects at his preference for it; Alexander III was the first whom the true Scots took to their hearts. The two hundred and fifty years between his death (1286) and Duncan I's accession (1034) were consequently a period of racial and civil turmoil. For the first ninety years (1034–1124) Celt and Teuton, Scot and Englishman, contended for mastery of the kingdom. Under David I (1124–53) the issue at length was decided: Scotland abandoned the polity of ancient Alba, received from England the apparatus of a feudal monarchy, and qualified herself to enter the system of European States.

The familiar tragedy of Duncan's death (1040) becomes significant in the light of these reflections. His is the first example of direct succession to the Scottish throne. For nearly two centuries the crown had alternated between the elder and younger branches of Kenneth MacAlpin's line. The younger became extinct in 997, and thereafter the succession promised to alternate within the elder line exclusively. Thus, while Kenneth III (997–1005) was succeeded by his cousin Malcolm II (1005–34), Malcolm's heir, in the eyes of Celtic legitimists, was to be found in Kenneth III's family, according to the custom of alternation hitherto unbroken. But Malcolm challenged the rule. His heir was his grandson Duncan by his daughter's marriage with Crinan, lay Abbot of Dunkeld. Kenneth's heir, preferred by the legitimists, was an unnamed infant who fell into Malcolm's hands in 1033 and was conveniently removed. The feud thus provoked persisted for generations and immediately involved Duncan in its tragedy. Her nephew's removal made Kenneth's granddaughter Gruoch heiress of his line. She was already, or soon became, the wife of Macbeth, Mormaer of Moray, himself through his mother descended from Malcolm II[1], chieftain of a house that claimed the throne itself, behind whom was the patriotic fervour of Celtic Scotland. On that constituency his marriage to Gruoch established another claim. Behind Duncan, on the other hand, were forces which the Celtic pretenders could not command. English aid pulled down Macbeth, his stepson Lulach the Fatuous, who briefly succeeded him, and Donald Bane (1093–97), who championed the interests that supported him. Donald was the last king of pure Celtic birth who sat on Scotland's throne. But in remote Morayshire, in touch with a

---

[1] Macbeth's mother, however, may have been a daughter of Kenneth II.

rebellious Scandinavian element, Macbeth (or Macheth)[1] pretenders were not extinguished till the reign of Alexander III[2].

A new chapter opens with the accession of Malcolm Canmore (1058–93), Duncan's son and avenger. An exile since early youth at the Confessor's court, he grew to manhood in an English atmosphere, married first the Norse Ingeborg, and in 1070[3], after her death, Margaret, sister of the English heir to the Confessor's crown, like herself exiled to Scotland before the Conqueror's fury. Malcolm made her quarrel his own, using it to pursue his kingdom's advantage and gain an increment of English territory. Before the year of his marriage was out, he was over the border, carrying fire and sword southward to Yorkshire. Two years later the Conqueror retaliated, marched unresisted to the Tay, and at Abernethy Malcolm *homo suus devenit*. The transaction was the first of many of similar character which compromised Scotland's independence, founded the Plantagenet claim upon her fealty, and provoked her later to a struggle which won her freedom. Taking advantage of the Conqueror's preoccupation in Normandy, Malcolm again invaded England in 1079 and laid waste the country between Tweed and Tyne. In 1091, following the familiar road, he found in Rufus an antagonist as stout as his father and repeated his homage; the castles of Newcastle (1080) and Carlisle (1092) were raised to exclude him. Rufus' insistence upon their feudal relationship brought Malcolm a last time into England. Returning from a stormy interview with his suzerain at Gloucester, he was intercepted at Alnwick and fell there (1093). His warfare added no territory to Scotland, but altered the texture of her population. English exiles and captives of war settled in the Lothians among their own race. Beyond the Forth English speech, population, and culture entered in the wake of commercial intercourse, strengthening that racial element on which the sovereign relied to impose English ideas and institutions.

[1] Macbeth = macc-bethad = one of the elect. Macheth = (?) macc-Aeda = son of Aed = Mackay, or, possibly, son of Heth. The two names are confused in the chronicles, and the less familiar is probably correct.

[2]

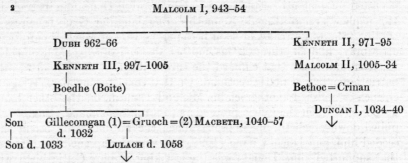

MALCOLM I, 943–54

DUBH 962–66   KENNETH II, 971–95

KENNETH III, 997–1005   MALCOLM II, 1005–34

Boedhe (Boite)   Bethoc = Crinan

DUNCAN I, 1034–40 ↓

Son   Gillecomgan (1) = Gruoch = (2) MACBETH, 1040–57
           d. 1032
Son d. 1033   LULACH d. 1058 ↓

For a fuller pedigree table see Terry, *History of Scotland*, p. xiv. Cf. Anderson, I, 580.

[3] The date is not precisely established.

In any circumstances the fortunes of the Scottish State must have been profoundly affected by English infiltration. But the consequences were deeper and more immediate because, for a quarter of a century, Malcolm's queen was the unflagging missionary and pattern of English culture. Turgot's (?) life of her, written shortly after her death for her daughter's comfort, pictures a saintly, masterful woman, whose chamber, littered with chasubles, stoles, altar cloths, and priestly raiment worked by herself and her attendants, seemed "a workshop of celestial art." None was more intent in prayer, more given to works of mercy and almsgiving. In Lent her devotion was unremitting, her abstinence so rigid that all her life she suffered acute abdominal pain. Every day she washed and fed the poor, whose marshalling was her chamberlain's principal daily duty. Over Malcolm her influence was unbounded. Unable to read, he cherished the books she used and bound them in rich covers studded with jewels of price. At all times he courted her counsel, and Turgot declares the adventure that cost him his life a rare exception of failure to obey her admonition. No less was she the monitor of her children. She transformed the ceremonial of a rude court and multiplied the adornment of the royal palace. At her bidding and example her courtiers adopted refinement of dress and "seemed indeed to be transformed by this elegance." The laws were submitted to her judgment, merchants had her patronage and protection, precious wares till then unfamiliar began to circulate, prosperity followed in the wake of commerce, and a rude society assumed a veneer of culture. Upon the Church especially Margaret left her mark: she purged the ritual of the Mass of "barbarous" practices, reformed the lax observance of Lent, Easter, and Sunday, and suppressed irregular degrees of matrimony. Thus she completed the work of Nechtan and brought the Scottish Church into union with Roman Christendom.

For nearly sixty years, three of Margaret's sons, holding rule in succession, continued the process of Anglicisation, after an interlude of Celtic revolt suppressed by English arms in 1094 and 1097. The population of Lothian, which otherwise must have been attracted into the English system, was repelled from it by the Norman conquest and well-disposed to a Scottish sovereign who, on the spindle side, represented the dispossessed house of Cerdic. Celtic irreconcilables in Ross, Moray, and Galloway were ever ready to advance a pretender. But on the Lothians the royal hold was secure. Edinburgh, superseding Canmore's Dunfermline, became the capital, a fact which, along with Edgar's (1097–1107) measures for the devolution of his authority, declares the dominance of English Scotland in what so recently had been a Celtic State. For, while his brother Alexander I (1107–24) succeeded him in the territories above the Forth, his younger brother David was placed as Earl over Lothian and Strathclyde, an administrative device which confessed the uneasy relations of those provinces with ancient Alban, and also promised to elude England's intention to compromise the dignity of the Scottish crown.

No similar separation was attempted in the ecclesiastical sphere. Alexander, faithful to his mother's preference, committed his Church to English direction. To the bishopric of St Andrews, sole see beyond the Forth, vacant since 1093, he appointed in succession three Englishmen, the first two of whom, however, incurred his anger and their dismissal by acknowledging the metropolitan authority of York or Canterbury. A priory of Augustinian canons superseded the Culdee society at St Andrews, and similar brotherhoods were established in Scone, Inchcolm, and elsewhere. Dunkeld and Moray received episcopal foundations.

Only the reign of Mary Stewart approaches that of David I (1124–53), youngest and greatest of Margaret's sons, in its vital contribution to Scotland's development. His purpose was to weld into an effective unity the diverse populations that called him lord by subjecting them to the Crown's authority. Norman England offered her experience, and David's reign has been termed aptly a "bloodless Norman Conquest" of his kingdom. In both countries a new aristocracy was introduced as the agent, and eventually the tyrant, of the monarchy. But whereas in England a feudal polity riveted the subjugation of a conquered people, only in Moray was David able to use rebellion as a pretext for the confiscation of the soil and settlement of an Anglo-Norman aristocracy upon it. Neither Pictish Galloway nor Highland Alban as yet succumbed. But elsewhere Anglo-Norman families—Morevilles, Somervilles, Bruces, Balliols, Lindsays, Fitz Alans (Stewarts), and others—received the land and planted an alien culture upon it. The aboriginal Celtic population was not expelled; tenure by charter merely replaced the customary lordships hitherto vested in the senior kindred of the sept. But ultimately the texture of Scottish society was radically changed. The cadets and servitors of the Anglo-Norman proprietor received parcels of his estate upon conditions of feudal tenure and, like himself, propagated a new culture and language. Performing prescribed services to his superior upon the security of a charter, the new proprietor was ready to accord as much to others upon a similar obligation. Before Scotland was provoked by Edward I to defend her liberties, the greater part of the kingdom outside the Highlands was owned by powerful vassals of the Crown fulfilling the obligations feudal custom prescribed and, in their turn, imposing them upon sub-vassals of Celtic stock. The smoothness with which the transformation was accomplished was due, it may be assumed, to the fact that in Scotland, as in England, an archaic polity was already shaping itself to the institutions feudalism employed.

David I, his descendant complained, was a "sair sanct for the crown." A true son of his mother, the Church acquired from him a disproportionate share of the national wealth. Holyrood, Kinloss, Jedburgh, Cambuskenneth, Newbattle, Dundrennan, and Dryburgh owed their foundation to his munificence and contributed, as was his purpose, to cement the fabric of Anglo-Norman culture. Of the four dioceses then existing he already was founder of one (Glasgow); as king he added five more—Dunblane, Brechin, Aberdeen, Ross, and Caithness. Lothian, as yet grouped within the diocese of St Andrews, was administered by an archdeacon. Ninian's twice desolated see of Candida Casa was revived[1], perhaps under the stimulus of David's example at Glasgow, by Fergus of Galloway (*ob.* 1161), distant ancestor of the Balliols and Comyns of the War of Independence. The bishops of the Orkneys and the Sudreys were suffragans of Nidaros; not until 1472 were they brought under the Scottish primate by the Bull of Sixtus IV. Thus, excepting Argyll, which was constituted a diocese apart from Dunkeld about the close of the twelfth century, the sometime embracing authority of St Andrews was completely subdivided by David and his predecessor in a period (1106–53) marked by larger and more abiding ecclesiastical changes than any other in Scotland's history except the Reformation.

Accompanying these developments in the social and ecclesiastical fabric of the nation proceeded a transformation of its administrative apparatus. Already in Alexander I's reign a Constable, Justiciar, and Chancellor make their appearance, the nucleus of a royal Council which perhaps superseded the Celtic council of Mormaers, if that body ever existed. To these high officials David added a Chamberlain, Marshal, and Steward, the last becoming hereditary in the family of Fitz Alan, cadets of the English house of Arundel, ancestors of the royal Stewarts. Like his English brother, the Scottish sovereign exercised the administrative functions of the Crown with the advice of his principal vassals, though as yet no organised system of Estates was established. Till David I's reign Scotland adhered to her Celtic judicial customs. Mormaers, rendering uncertain homage to their sovereign, held supreme jurisdiction within their provinces, delegating their judicial functions to subordinate Toisecs (Toshachs) and judges. Into this simple scheme David introduced the office of sheriff, associating its holder invariably with one of the royal castles, which thus became the capitals of their respective areas. Charged with the duties attached to the office in England, David's sheriffs were appointed for military and fiscal purposes rather than with the object of supplanting the archaic Celtic machinery. Toshachs and Brehons continued in office, the former ranking as thanes, next below the earl in dignity, and exercising authority which the sheriff gradually absorbed. A system of jury trial, the *visnet* or *voisinage*, has its origin in David's reign, and in that of Alexander II (1214–49) trial by ordeal of water and iron disappeared. The number of sheriffdoms was in the same period increased, though the institution of Regalities conferred upon their owners judicial rights on which the sheriff might not trespass[2], the pleas of the crown (murder, rape, arson, robbery) being reserved for the

---

[1] It remained under York's jurisdiction until the Bull of Sixtus IV (1472) which established the primacy of St Andrews over the other sees.

[2] *The Sheriff Court Book of Fife,* Scott. Hist. Soc., Introduction.

cognisance of justiciars sitting twice a year in Lothian, Galloway, and the Lowland districts above the Forth[1]. Thus Scotland was equipped to stand beside her neighbours in feudal Europe, clogged no longer by the obstinate conservatism of her Celtic traditions.

Simultaneously with these processes of consolidation, the relations of Scotland with England moved surely towards a breach. David, like his father, was brought up at the English court. His sister was the wife of Henry I; his brother Alexander I was Henry's son-in-law. David's own marriage as clearly marked the new orientation of Scottish policy: in the winter of 1113–14 he wedded Matilda, elder daughter of Earl Waltheof of Northumbria, widow of Simon de Senlis, recently deceased on crusade, to whom, after Waltheof's execution (1076), the Conqueror had granted the earldom of Northampton and Huntingdon, with which David was invested on his marriage. Through his wife he could advance claims to the earldom of Northumbria, and also to Cumbria, in which her grandfather Siward had dominion. To establish them and coincidently advance the frontier of his kingdom was David's purpose, though their possession involved his vassalage to the English Crown. The civil commotions of Stephen's reign gave him the opportunity he desired. By supporting his niece, the Empress Matilda, David attached himself at first to the weaker side. A compact with Stephen in 1136, however, obtained his son Henry's (*ob.* 1152) recognition as Earl of Huntingdon, possession of the castles of Doncaster and Carlisle, and a promise that his claims to Northumberland should have preference over those of Simon de Senlis' son. Not content with the agreement, David again took arms, and, though defeated in the battle of the Standard (1138), obtained from Stephen (1139) recognition of young Henry's claim to the coveted earldom. Its concession advanced the Scottish frontier to the Tees, as already by the pact of 1136 it had moved to Carlisle and the Eden. In subsequent warfare these successes were not maintained; for the vigorous Henry II recovered much of the territory in 1157, leaving to Malcolm IV only the Honour[2] of Huntingdon, and to his brother William the Liberty of Tynedale.

Between the death of David in 1153 and that of his great-great-grandson Alexander III in 1286, an interval of one hundred and thirty years, four reigns intervened. The period was one of steady and, upon the whole, quiet consolidation, in which, while Scotland's relations with England moved inexorably towards the impending collision, the separatist inclination of the Norse and Celtic populations was as steadily overborne. So far from being the cradle of the Scottish nation, as it has been represented,

---

[1] *The Scottish King's Household*, Scott. Hist. Review, XLIV, 42.
[2] *I.e.* the territories pertaining to the earldom. After Malcolm the earldom was held by William I, who, after its reconfirmation to him in 1185, gave it to his brother David, the ancestor of the Balliol, Bruce, and Hastings competitors in 1291.

the War of Independence tested a system already close welded in the generations that preceded it. Of the four kings—David's two grandsons, great-grandson, and great-great-grandson—only the last was untroubled by factious revolt in Moray or Galloway. A union of Norse and Celtic irreconcilables at once faced David's successor Malcolm IV (1153–65) upon his accession. Somerled of the Isles, "regulus" of Argyll, uniting with his kinsman Donald, son of Malcolm Macheth[1], disturbed the peace. In 1156 Donald joined his father in confinement; Somerled remained at large till 1164, when, landing in the Clyde with a miscellaneous host from Ireland and the Isles, he was overcome and slain at Renfrew. Thrice within those years Malcolm fought in Galloway and, by 1160, quelled its disobedience; Fergus, its lord, surrendered his son Uchtred as a hostage and himself took the habit of a canon in David's abbey of Holyrood, where he died (1161). Thirteen years later, William the Lion's capture at Alnwick in 1174 invoked renewed disturbance in the province. It was not quelled until 1185, when Uchtred's son Roland made submission. Simultaneously, under Donald MacWilliam (or Bane), alleging himself to be a great-grandson of Malcolm Canmore's Norse marriage, Moray and Ross also raised the flag of revolt and were not subdued until 1187. In 1215 MacWilliam's son Donald appeared in Moray along with Kenneth Macheth, probably the son of Somerled's ally. With their defeat and death the line of Celtic pretenders comes to an end[2]. For half a century Galloway remained passive, till Roland's son Alan, dying in 1234, left his lordship to his three daughters, wives of Anglo-Norman husbands. "Preferring to have one lord rather than several,"[3] the Galwegians desired Alexander II (1214–49) to assume direct rule over them. Upon his refusal, they set up an illegitimate brother of the co-heiresses and were reduced to obedience. Galloway thereafter made no effort to assert her particularism.

Equally significant was the period in the Crown's assertion of Scottish authority over Norse separatism. Since Kenneth MacAlpin's reign a princely alliance between the two races had been not infrequent. Malcolm II gave his daughter to Earl Sigurd of Orkney, who died at Clontarf (1014). On their son Thorfinn he conferred Caithness and Sutherland with the title of earl, designing to detach an ally from the Macbeth faction. Thorfinn, however, proved a stubborn enemy, whose defeats of Duncan I rendered easier Macbeth's overthrow of his sovereign (1040). Thorfinn's collusion with Macbeth is not exposed in the Saga, but Malcolm Canmore's marriage with his widow Ingeborg clearly was

---

[1] Malcolm is stated to have been a son of Alexander I and so heir under the Celtic rule of alternation. His wife was either the sister or daughter of Somerled.

[2] The *Melrose Chronicle*, which records this event, also mentions an attempt by Godfrey, or Guthred, MacWilliam's son, in 1211. This pretender, according to Fordun, was beheaded *c.* 1212.

[3] *Melrose Chronicle.*

planned to enlist Norse friendship. For the moment it did so; but from
it sprang pretenders to the throne who troubled Scotland for more than
a century, until 1215[1]. Earl Thorfinn, who died *c.* 1065, held sway also
in Galloway, where Norse power was so firmly settled that its timber
was felled to build Manx fortresses. In 1098 and 1102 a more formidable
enemy appeared in Magnus Bareleg, King of Norway, who came to assert
his distant authority and wrested from Edgar (1097–1107) all the western
islands between which and the mainland a vessel could sail with rudder
shipped. Landing in Kintyre, he caused his long-ship to be drawn across
the isthmus at Tarbert, himself grasping the rudder, and so added the
peninsula to his spoils. Somerled's activities, already remarked, and his
collusion with the Moray pretenders, declared Scotland's danger from
this exposed flank, and, in the last year of the twelfth century, Scottish
authority began to assert itself. In 1197 and 1198 William the Lion
reduced Harold, "Earl of Orkney, Caithness, and Shetland," who took
arms at the instigation of his wife, sister of the Donald Macheth whom
Malcolm IV overthrew in 1156. These successes, and his peaceful relations
with England, stimulated Alexander II (1214–49) to accomplish an
exploit not yet attempted. In 1222 he subjugated Argyll; a sheriffdom
planted there *c.* 1226 brought the district within the operation of royal
writs. Alexander next demanded the Hebrides, and, upon Hakon of
Norway's refusal to surrender or sell them, prepared a fleet for their recovery, but died at Kerrera, his purpose unfulfilled. His son Alexander III
(1249–86) resumed the negotiation and provoked Hakon to assert his
sovereignty. Sailing in 1263, "to avenge the warfare the King of Scots
had made in his dominions," his armada was scattered near Largs off
the Cumbraes; he died in the Orkneys, whither he withdrew to refit.
Alexander pressed his advantage, subdued the Hebrides, and in 1266
received from Magnus of Norway the surrender his father had refused.
On payment of 1000 marks of refined silver for four years and 100
annually in perpetuity, Man and the Hebrides passed[2] under Scottish
sovereignty. The marriage of Alexander's daughter Margaret to Magnus'
son and successor Eric in 1281 clinched the bargain.

Very different is the English aspect of the period. Two of David's
successors, sons-in-law of the English monarch, by their eager quest of
the Northumbrian earldom afforded England occasion to assert her
suzerainty. Malcolm IV did homage for Huntingdon in 1157, and, to
his people's dismay, attended his liege's banner in Toulouse. He surrendered Northumberland and Cumberland, for whose recovery the more
intemperate William the Lion fatally compromised the status of his

[1] The MacWilliams were descended from William the Nobleman, grandson of
Malcolm and Ingeborg.
[2] The treaty, signed at Perth by Norwegian plenipotentiaries on Friday 2 July
1266, surrendered "Man, with the other islands of the Hebrides, and all the other
islands on the western and southern side of the great sea."—Anderson, *op. cit.* II, 655.

crown. Made prisoner in 1174 when campaigning on the soil he coveted, he was conveyed to Falaise in Normandy and accepted terms which strictly defined Scotland's feudal dependence on England. Edinburgh, Berwick, and Roxburgh castles were delivered to English garrisons, hostages were surrendered, and at York Minster, in 1175, in token of his unqualified allegiance, William offered his casque, lance, and saddle upon the high altar. Till the death of Henry II (1189) Scotland was a vassal fief over which he exercised his suzerainty with inexorable punctilio. The autonomy of the Scottish Church also was compromised, till Pope Clement III declared it *filia specialis* and immediately subject to the Holy See. At the price of submission to papal authority it eluded that of York, which claimed metropolitan jurisdiction *ad extremos Scotiae fines*. But Henry II's death relieved Scotland of her humiliation. Needing money for his Crusade, and fearing to leave an enemy on the flank of his kingdom, Richard I gave William acquittal (1189) of the obligations imposed in 1174, saving that "he shall do us, entirely and fully, all that the King of Scotland, Malcolm, his brother, did by right to our predecessors, and ought by right to have done." Whatever were Malcolm's obligations, Scotland was absolved from an unqualified admission of English suzerainty. When Edward I revived the claim, other precedents needed to be invoked.

Meanwhile John shewed as strong a will as his grandson to assert English paramountcy, erected a castle at Tweedmouth to overawe Berwick, and in 1209 received William's daughters to dispose of in marriage[1]. Three years later (1212) William entrusted to him the marriage of his son Alexander also, whose union (1221) with Henry III's sister Joan, and his own sister's marriage to Hubert de Burgh, established relations which permitted Alexander to plan the reduction of Argyll, the principal achievement of his reign. Having accomplished it, he vainly revived his father's demand for Northumberland, and accepted at York a definitive settlement (1237) of the old controversy. Alexander abandoned his hereditary claims upon Northumberland, Westmorland, and Cumberland, and received instead two hundred librates of rural land in the first and last of those counties, for which he did homage and swore fealty. But his second marriage, with Marie de Coucy, as suspicious to English eyes as the Ancient League of a later generation, disturbed the prospects of peace and stirred Henry to demand renewed submission. At Newcastle (1244) the pact of 1237 was confirmed and Henry contracted his infant daughter to Alexander's heir. For the remainder of Alexander's reign his relations with England were cordial.

Alexander III (1249–86), last king of Canmore's line in male descent, came to the throne a boy of eight. Married two years later (1251) to his English wife, it was not until 1261 that his daughter Margaret's birth

[1] John's failure to give one of them to one of his sons founded a claim for compensation which Alexander II abandoned in the settlement of 1237.

assured direct succession to the throne; the succession consequently stood in dangerous uncertainty. Three years before his son's birth Alexander II had recognised (1238) Robert Bruce as heir apparent, a natural choice of the male representative of David, Earl of Huntingdon (*ob.* 1219), among whose descendants the king was to be sought upon the extinction of the elder line. Bruce's prospects were revived by the tardy birth of Alexander III's heir. Other interests also were concerned: Alan the Doorward, husband of Alexander II's natural daughter Marjorie, had a daughter whose claims, if legitimated, could be advanced[1]; a third interest was represented by Walter Comyn, Earl of Menteith, whose influence in the north and Galloway and his descent from Donald Bane (1093–97) made him the representative of the nationalist party lately headed by the Macbeth pretenders. Alternately these jealous interests coerced the youthful sovereign, until in 1258, for the quiet of the realm, Henry III set up a Council of Regency which included the Doorward and Comyn factions. Concurrently (1262) the birth of Alexander's daughter Margaret settled the succession, and his coming of age terminated his tutelage. Ten years later Henry's death (1272) called Alexander to renew his homage to his brother-in-law Edward I: he performed it in 1278 for his English lands, "reserving" his kingdom, a qualification which Edward, too, on his side, "reserved." Events inexorably demanded a settlement. In 1281 Alexander's younger son died. The deaths of his remaining son and daughter extinguished his issue in 1284. Only his granddaughter Margaret, Maid of Norway, survived, and in February 1284 a council of his vassals declared her heiress to the throne. Her prospects of succession seemed remote; for Alexander, a hale man of forty-four, took a second wife (1285), Joleta of Dreux, and could expect children by her. In fact she bore him none, and less than six months after his marriage he died (March 1286). Anglo-Scottish relations had reached a crisis.

On 2 July 1286[2] the Council of Regency, on which the Comyns were prominent, proclaimed the Maid of Norway queen. The sovereign was an infant, resident abroad, heiress to a foreign throne, and of a sex that never yet had ruled Scotland. Her father Eric therefore took steps to establish her authority. For two generations the royal houses of England and Scotland had sought each other in marriage, and Edward I welcomed an exceptional opportunity to unite the crowns by that means and so establish English paramountcy. The Holy See was invited to legalise the union of the Scottish Queen with her cousin, the English heir-apparent, and plenipotentiaries from Norway and Scotland assembled at Salisbury (1289) to examine the conditions upon which it might be concluded. In the following July (1290) a numerously attended council of the Scottish vassals *in capite*, convened at Birgham, sanctioned the projected union subject to conditions which amply safeguarded Scotland's

[1] The Doorward's grandson, in fact, was a competitor in 1291.
[2] The delay was due to uncertainty as to Queen Joleta being pregnant.

autonomy. A last calamity, however, befell Canmore's fated house. In September 1290 the youthful queen sailed from Bergen. On the voyage to Scotland she died, and the peace of Scotland passed with her.

The death of the queen invited competition for the throne from among the nobility, Anglo-Normans or Normanised Celts, whose genealogies alone revealed a Scottish descent. The comparative remoteness of even the chief candidates from the royal stem, the frequent intermarrying of the nobility with illegitimate offspring of the sovereign, and a situation to which the experience of Europe afforded no parallel, all combined to encourage even those remotely allied with royalty to come forward. The War of Independence was primarily an issue between the Scottish people and their alien baronage. Undeterred by patriotic scruples, and in many cases already involved in feudal relations with an English suzerain, his assistance was not repugnant to them. On the news of the queen's death, Bruce and his most formidable rival, John Balliol, directly or through their partisans, put themselves in touch with Edward. It is idle to discover "no evidence that the Scots as a nation invited [his] interference in the affairs of their country."[1] Neither in Edward's view nor in that of his petitioners were popular suffrages involved. Nor had medieval law evolved the impartial arbitrator. A situation had arisen for whose solution the feudal code afforded no guide; to determine the dispute in which he was invited to intervene Edward needed to be accorded the status which alone, short of naked force, could make his verdict authoritative. English paramountcy, often asserted, fostered by the ambition of Scotland's rulers for generations, encouraged by her baronage, needed first to be admitted. Edward moved to obtain it.

Careful to establish a preliminary historical foundation, Edward ordered exhaustive search of documents to elucidate the past relations of the two crowns. Much fantastic material, credible to an uncritical age, was laid before the Scottish vassals at Norham in May 1291, and, though it elicited a protest from the minor vassals, was elsewhere accepted as authoritative. The competitors already in the field, including Bruce and Balliol, put their seals in June to a document binding them to accept Edward's award as lord paramount, being satisfied that "the sovereign lordship of Scotland and right to determine our several pretensions" belonged to him. The legal suit opened two months later (August 1291) and terminated in November 1292. It adjudicated on the claims of thirteen competitors[2], only one of whom was related to the royal house by paternal descent. Six were the issue of illegitimate children of Alexander II and William the Lion. One traced from Canmore's brother Donald Bane. Two were descended from David I's son, Prince Henry. Three—John Balliol, Robert Bruce, and John Hastings—were respectively great-grandson, grandson, and great-grandson of the Lion's brother, David, Earl of

[1] Hume Brown, I, p. 137.
[2] See Pedigree Table II in Terry, *Hist. of Scotland,* p. xvi.

Huntingdon (*ob.* 1219), through the marriages of his three daughters. Bruce, the son of the second daughter, stood one degree nearer to the common ancestor than Balliol or Hastings, grandsons respectively of the eldest and youngest; whether his seniority outweighed Balliol's descent from Huntingdon's eldest daughter was a novel point of law which Edward's award determined. Hastings, otherwise without a case, contended that the kingdom was partible and claimed a share.

The procedure which determined the most famous suit of the Middle Ages was formed upon the ancient *centumvirale iudicium* and was charged to explore a cause closely related to its prerogative. Like the Roman court, Edward's consisted of 105 assessors, including the sovereign— eighty nominated by the Scottish interests concerned, twenty-four by the lord paramount. Early in August 1291 the court assembled at Berwick to receive statements of claim from the competitors, and adjourned. Reassembling in June 1292, the pleadings of all but Bruce and Balliol were dismissed, and, after a further adjournment, those of Bruce also were rejected. It remained to test Hastings' submission that the kingdom was partible, and the contention having been negatived, Edward made his award in the hall of Berwick Castle on 17 November 1292. He gave the kingdom, whole and undivided, to John Balliol, who swore fealty to his suzerain, and before the end of the month was crowned at Scone.

Unwelcome to the true Scots, Edward's intervention saved the country from civil war. On the other hand, it gave Scotland an indifferent sovereign, from whom his suzerain was resolved to exact the last ounce of feudal obligation. A summons to attend him abroad, however, exceeded the limits of Balliol's acquiescence. More than a century earlier, Malcolm IV, obeying a similar call, was threatened with death by his indignant subjects on his return. Balliol refused to obey, and in 1295 sought the support of France in a defensive alliance which for three centuries profoundly influenced Scotland's cultural and political development. Edward's vengeance was swift. Descending upon Scotland, in July 1296 he compelled Balliol's submission at Stracathro, near Brechin. Leaving English garrisons to assert his authority, and a triumvirate of Englishmen to administer it, Edward marched out of a country apparently subdued, taking with him, to point the significance of Balliol's degradation, the Stone of Destiny, on which Scottish sovereigns were wont to be crowned, and a cargo of the nation's archives.

In the moment of her humiliation the voice of Scotland's commonalty found utterance. Hardly had Edward turned his back before William Wallace appears, a second Calgacus. History records few examples of so meteoric a rise, an achievement so striking, a fate so swift and heroic. The younger son, apparently, of Malcolm Wallace of Elderslie, near Paisley, he emerges in the spring of 1297 as the leader of guerrilla patriots pledged to recover Scotland for her king. Before the autumn

English authority was in the dust, its officers in flight, and Wallace and his colleague Andrew of Moray masters of the kingdom in the name of King John. But their success was brief. In 1298 Edward came in person and at Falkirk overthrew Wallace's authority. France, seduced from the Scottish cause, afforded no help; Bruce and Comyn watched their own fortunes; and Pope Boniface VIII's warning (1300) to Edward to respect a vassal of the Holy See went unheeded. In 1304 Edward was again in possession of Stirling. Wallace, becoming his prisoner a few months later (1305), died a patriot's death. The way was clear to a settlement, and in September 1305, three weeks after Wallace's execution, Edward revealed his policy. Abandoning the experiment of a puppet State, he assumed direct lordship over the kingdom, naming his nephew John of Brittany as his viceroy. Precautions were taken to secure the loyalty of officials, and the castles were received into English hands. Scotland's ancient legal customs were abolished, and, attentive to her historical divisions, efficient plans were drawn for the administration of Anglo-Norman law. But Edward reckoned without the spirit Wallace had stirred. Within six months the Constitution of 1305 was a dead letter, and under a new leader Scotland received the crowning mercy of Bannockburn.

Wallace's mantle descended upon Robert Bruce, chief of an Anglo-Norman house whom David I had established in Annandale with princely possessions two centuries earlier, a man whose career exhibits to this point duplicity and self-seeking remarkable even in an age not scrupulous. Grandson of the competitor, his father's death in 1304 encouraged him to sustain the ambitions Balliol's nomination had disappointed. After Wallace's defeat at Falkirk he joined himself to John (Red) Comyn in Scotland's cause. In 1302 he was Edward's sheriff in Lanarkshire, attended his campaigns in 1303 and 1304, and early in 1306 left London ostensibly to aid the newly constituted English executive in Scotland. With Bishop William Lamberton of St Andrews, however, he was already in collusion for the overthrow of what he professed to serve, and an encounter with Red Comyn at Dumfries removed an impediment from the path of his ambition. Thence he rode to Glasgow, sought absolution for his sacrilegious deed, and, meagrely attended, was crowned at Scone. Three months later he was a hunted fugitive. But in May 1307 he scattered his enemies at Loudon Hill, and Edward's death in July made his fortunes secure. By the end of August 1307 Edward's worthless son was out of Scotland and Bruce free to establish his authority. First he subdued the Comyns—his "herschip" of Buchan was a proverb for vindictive destruction for half a century—and when the clergy owned his sovereignty in 1310 the north had passed under his authority. Edward II retaliated with a feeble invasion that never passed the Forth. Upon his withdrawal Bruce assailed the English garrisons with unrelaxing pressure. Roxburgh and Edinburgh surrendered early in 1314, when the English flag flew only above Stirling beyond the Forth. Even the spiritless Edward was spurred to succour the surviving evidence of English supremacy. On Midsummer Day (1314) at Bannockburn the issue was decided. Had Bruce been defeated, the history of Britain must have run another course. As it was, Scotland survived to contribute her individuality and experience to the United Kingdom of a later day.

Bannockburn planted Bruce firmly upon the throne and gave him the heart of his people as no king before or after him possessed it. "Like another Judas Maccabaeus," his council declared to the Pope in 1320, he had "rescued his people and inheritance out of the hands of their enemy." But England stubbornly withheld acknowledgment of the defeat of Plantagenet imperialism. The Papacy also refused recognition of Bruce's sovereignty. To compel it was the purpose of the king's remaining years. Sir James Douglas' name became a terror on the Marches. Berwick passed to Scottish hands in 1318, and Douglas raided Yorkshire. Foiled in his intention to abduct the English queen, he won the White Battle or Chapter of Mytton (1319). In Ireland Edward Bruce, aiding the O'Neills against English oppression, was crowned king and fought a stubborn fight till his death in 1318. Five years later (1323) Edward II accepted a truce for thirteen years, and his son's preoccupation in France at length gave Scotland her liberty. The Treaty of Northampton (1328) explicitly surrendered England's claim to suzerainty and put the seal upon Bruce's life-work. A few months later he died (1329), a man of rare force, sagacity, and decision. The greatness of his achievement cannot be exaggerated. In material advantage Scotland was the poorer by the postponement of her economic union with England till the eighteenth century. But her loss was amply compensated by the opportunity to develop her national life and character under the independent conditions Bannockburn secured for her.

CHAPTER XX

SPAIN, 1252–1410

THE period treated in chapter XII of the last volume comprised the main movement in Spanish history from the early part of the eleventh century to the middle of the thirteenth, that is to say the reconquest from the Muslims of the greater part of southern and eastern Spain. The men who carried through the decisive efforts were Ferdinand III of Castile, who died in 1252, and James I of Aragon, who survived until 1276. Accordingly in that chapter the story was carried somewhat later than 1248, the date of the capture of Seville. The period now to be treated begins, in Castile, with Alfonso X, under whose sceptre the ancient kingdoms of Asturias, Leon, and Castile were now united, together with the conquests south of the Tagus as far as the Guadalquivir. The new period in Aragon starts with Peter III.

Logically, Alfonso X and his successors in Castile should have continued the peninsular policy of Ferdinand III, by mastering the Moorish kingdom of Granada and thus completing the reconquest, and by confirming it afterwards by dominating the coast of Morocco in order to check any fresh offensive on the part of the Muslims. Aragon could do no more in this direction, since the treaties with Castile, ratified in 1244, had closed the south to her, leaving the future conquests of the small territory which remained in the hands of the Muslims exclusively to the care and to the advantage of Castile. But the kings of Castile did not pursue continuously or decisively the policy laid down by their forerunners, nor did the opinion of their subjects urge them to do so. They considered that, after the great victories of the thirteenth century, the military power of the enemy was no longer formidable or able to take the offensive. Moreover, a struggle now so remote from their homes no longer interested the inhabitants of Leon and Castile, and was consequently reduced for the most part to frontier strife, chiefly carried on by the people of Andalusia—a circumstance which gives a special character to the expeditions against the Moors in the fourteenth and fifteenth centuries till the reign of Isabella. Only kings such as Sancho IV and Alfonso XI shewed that they had not forgotten the fundamental importance of completing the reconquest and, perhaps even more clearly, the question of neutralising the African peril by the conquest, not only of the Andalusian coast at the Straits, but also of the coast of Morocco. On their side the Moors of Granada, changing the old policy of the kings of the Taifas, who had sought direct aid from the Moroccan kingdoms and had thereby brought about the invasions of the Almohades and Almorávides, restricted themselves to making an *entente* with the Banū-Marīn, the then masters of the region of Maghrib, and to strengthening the armies of the kingdom of Granada with African elements, the Zeneteh, which enabled them to resist for a long time the occasional attacks of the Christians.

The progress of the reconquest was checked by these causes, but still more by two crucial questions which preoccupied the Castilian monarchy, dynastic struggles and the anarchy of the nobles, who resisted the efforts of the Crown for discipline, order, and centralisation of power. During the second half of the thirteenth century and the whole of the fourteenth, these two questions distracted and absorbed the strength of the community, and had the disastrous effect of driving the contending parties into frequent alliances with the Moors of Granada—a fact which prolonged the existence of that kingdom. This provides an additional explanation for the intermittent character of the reconquest and the rarity of any decisive advance southward.

Meantime the Aragonese monarchy, no longer concerned with war against the Moors, directed its military energies and ambitions towards other lands. Expansion to the north of the Pyrenees having been checked by the victory of Simon de Montfort, the Aragonese kings turned again towards that Mediterranean movement which had been pursued by the independent Counts of Barcelona and had received a great impulse from the conquests of James I and the Aragonese occupation of all the eastern coast as far as Gandía together with the Balearic Islands. It was natural that this eastward movement should extend to the other Mediterranean islands and to Italy, where it was sure to clash once again with the ambitions of the French kings.

Such is the purely political outline of the period. The cultural background is supplied by the steady extension of the Castilian element over the rest of Spain, and by the prevalence of the culture already developed through the contributions of Moorish and Jewish influence and the penetration throughout the peninsula of the literary, artistic, and juridical renaissance. This followed Spanish lines and encouraged the development of the Spanish character in its distinct regional traits and its various spiritual expressions.

The reign of Alfonso X of Leon and Castile (1252–84) is characterised in the political sphere by two features. One of these is the struggle carried on between the king and the ever rebellious nobility; the other his aspiration to the imperial crown. Success in the latter, which was almost attained, would have anticipated by three centuries, though it is impossible to say whether with similar consequences, the achievement of Charles V. Many and various circumstances produced these two movements, circumstances which interacted upon one another. The consequent complexity was increased by a strong personal element, the principal cause of the misfortunes which embittered the life of the king and which rendered unfruitful for the time his political work. In theory this work was sound, as is shewn by the king's juridical labours, especially in his great book, *Las Partidas*. His failing was indecision in the question of succession to the crown and in dealing with the ambitions and wilful character of his second son, Sancho.

Alfonso X, largely brought up on the books of the contemporary writers of Roman Law, believed in absolute monarchy and the sub-ordination to it of the power then enjoyed by the nobles. This brought him face to face with the aristocracy, rebellious, proud, and unscrupulous in its public conduct, ever ready for revolt, and a natural enemy to the authority of the monarch. In the struggle he found himself weakened by two factors of great influence upon public opinion, namely, the exhaustion of the treasury greatly impoverished by the previous wars, and his own wasteful, careless, and somewhat ostentatious character. The opponents of the king took full advantage of these two causes of un-popularity. Reduction of the tribute paid by the King of Granada, debasement, on two occasions, of the coinage, a measure which always disturbs the economic life of a country, and other ineffective fiscal measures aroused protests and disapproval, all the more alarming as the king increased his expenditure upon servants and courtiers and spent enormous sums on entertainments and presents. To these causes of discontent were added others of a strictly political nature, which clearly shewed Alfonso's conception of the royal authority. These were the cession of the Algarves to the King of Portugal (1254), the renunciation of the feudal tie which bound that monarch to the King of Castile, and the abandonment of the claims of the Crown of Castile to the duchy of Gascony (1254), which had been the dowry of the wife of Alfonso VIII, Alfonso X's great-grandfather.

The nobility considered these acts as an abuse of the royal authority and as a sign of a tendency towards absolutism, and made this a pretext for repeated rebellions, which usually took the unpatriotic form of aiding the Moors of Granada against the Christian king, or forsaking the service of the latter by denaturalising themselves—that is to say "changing their nationality," as one would say nowadays, and offering their services to the Kings of Navarre and Aragon. These disturbances were promoted principally by the house of Haro, whose head was lord of Biscay, and by the king's brothers Don Henry and Don Frederick. Alfonso attempted to avert civil war, by granting extensive privileges to the nobles in the Cortes of Burgos in 1271, or again by the execution of some rebel leader; but the efficacy of both measures was slight and merely temporary.

He was not more fortunate in his efforts to acquire the imperial crown, which was his main political ambition. Besides other factors of an inter-national nature, the king's indecision was as usual most damaging to his cause. The military reputation of certain of the Kings of Leon and Castile in the twelfth and thirteenth centuries had opened up direct relations with the Emperors, and alliances by marriage were formed between the two reigning houses. The decisive event in these relations was the marriage of Ferdinand III with Beatrix the Younger, daughter of King Philip, Duke of Swabia (1199–1208). Alfonso X, as their son, claimed the duchy of Swabia. During the Great Interregnum, after the deaths of Conrad IV in 1254 and William of Holland in 1256[1], the opportunity arose for Alfonso X to become a candidate for the Empire. The republic of Pisa took the initiative by sending an embassy to the King of Castile in 1256 with the object of recognising him as Emperor and of negotiating a military and commercial treaty with him. Alfonso accepted the offer, and in spite of the fact that Richard of Cornwall, brother of Henry III of England, presented himself as a rival candidate, the King of Castile soon obtained by means of bribes the support of four of the Electors to the imperial crown. The majority having been thus obtained, the election took place on 1 April 1257, in spite of the active opposition of Richard's partisans. A few months later a German embassy arrived at Burgos to offer the imperial crown to Alfonso, who accepted it; but Spanish opinion, far from rejoicing at this high honour, which might have greatly enhanced the political position of a Spanish kingdom in Europe, shewed itself hostile. The obvious reason for this hostility was the great expenditure of the king, not only on the election but also on the presents to the ambassadors. Very probably the spontaneous aversion of certain important elements in Castilian politics to any adventures abroad influenced this attitude, coupled perhaps with a lack of clear conception on the part of the Castilian people of the position in Europe which the Empire represented and which at a later date Charles V and Philip II were to understand, each in his own way. In any case, the election to the Empire was unpopular in Castile, and this unpopularity produced a series of vacillations and subterfuges on the part of the weak-willed king which gravely compromised his position with regard to the Empire.

It should be added that the opposition of Pope Alexander IV and his three successors was as potent a factor in the final failure of Alfonso. The Popes, for various reasons connected with their Italian policy, inclined to Richard of Cornwall, and then supported Rudolf of Habsburg, who was elected on Richard's death (1272). The culminating point was reached in the interview between Pope Gregory X and Alfonso at Beaucaire (June, July 1275). The King of Castile left this interview a beaten man, and was obliged to renounce the Empire, first verbally and later (October 1275) in a formal and decisive document. It is true that in the last stage of the struggle for the imperial crown the situation of the king was most unfavourable, for to his enemies abroad, who were both numerous and powerful, were soon added his domestic foes. The fresh rising of the nobles in 1272, an invasion of the Banū-Marīn from Morocco in conjunction with the Moors of Granada (1275), and the death of

[1] See *supra*, Vol. VI, Chap. IV.

Ferdinand de la Cerda (1275), Alfonso's eldest son, profoundly affected both the spirit and the public position of the king.

The unexpected death of the heir brought yet another conflict upon him. The Crown of Castile had succeeded in obtaining the legalisation of the hereditary principle, which had been in practice since the beginning of the eleventh century. Alfonso, so careful in converting juridical principles into legal rules, had established as one of his laws in *Las Partidas* an order of succession upon the basis of the Roman law of representation, by virtue of which the eldest son transmitted the right of inheritance to his children. By this law, when the Infante de la Cerda died, his firstborn, Ferdinand, should have been recognised as heir to the throne; but Don Sancho, Alfonso's second son, refused to abide by the law and insisted upon being recognised as heir to the throne, relying upon the nobility, who were hostile to the king. The latter, on his return from Beaucaire, instead of maintaining the law which he himself had formulated, gave way to the demands of Don Sancho. The Infantes de la Cerda fled to Aragon with their mother Blanche, a French princess, daughter of St Louis and sister of Philip III of France.

Shortly afterwards Alfonso repented under strong pressure from the King of France, who urged him to remedy the illegality committed. Alfonso now proposed to create for the Infante Ferdinand de la Cerda a new kingdom, feudatory to Castile, out of the territories of the old Moorish kingdom of Jaen. Don Sancho would not agree to this, and when Alfonso persisted in his scheme, civil war broke out between father and son (1281). In this war we have again the spectacle of the contending parties allying themselves with Moorish kings, a situation which recurs in Spanish history, as we have already seen, and which shews how the reconquest was not mainly religious but rather a political war on the part of the ruling classes in Spain. Alfonso allied himself with the Banū-Marīn, Sancho with the Moors of Granada and with the majority of the nobility, who in this way sought to satisfy their resentment against the king. The Cortes which were assembled at Valladolid (1282) by the partisans of Sancho deposed Alfonso. The Pope intervened this time on the side of the legitimate king, who, however, was not able to continue the struggle long, as he died in 1284. He left a will in which he disinherited Sancho, bestowing the throne of Castile upon Don Ferdinand de la Cerda. Out of the territories of Seville and Badajoz on one side and Murcia on the other he formed two new kingdoms, one for the Infante Don John and the other for the Infante Don James, his younger sons; but Sancho was strong enough to prevent the execution of the will, and the civil war dragged on for many years, as we shall see, with the usual complications in respect of relations with the Moors of Granada and Morocco. The only positive advantages gained by Alfonso for the reconquest were the occupation of the district round Cadiz, from Morón to Medina Sidonia and Rota, Niebla and part of the Algarves (1262), and Cartagena

(1263). By these conquests the coast of the kingdom of Granada was further restricted. Alfonso fortified afresh both of these districts, and moreover encouraged the settlement in Cadiz of Christians, especially Cantabrian sailors. The unfortunate picture which, apart from these military advantages, is presented in the political sphere by the reign of Alfonso the Learned, is only counterbalanced by his contribution to learning and his considerable influence on Spanish culture, especially with regard to jurisprudence and the introduction of theories of Roman Law, the protection of Moorish and Jewish culture, the production of lyrical poetry in the Galician idiom, and the writing of national history.

The eleven years' reign of Sancho IV, who was recognised as king by the majority of the nobles and the towns, was very turbulent. On the one hand, those who remained loyal to the Infantes de la Cerda and to the testament of Alfonso X did not resign themselves to the violation of the will and continued in rebellion against the new king. As usual, some nobles took advantage of the situation, and once again we have the case of one of the pretenders, the Infante John, Sancho's brother, seeking the aid of the Banū-Marīn, as Alfonso X had done, and of Don Alfonso de le Cerda seeking aid from the Moors of Granada and from the King of Aragon. Consequently Sancho was obliged to fight at the same time against rebellious subjects, who were, however, supporting a better legal claim, and against the Moors of Africa. Sancho defeated the latter, dispersing the fleet which they had prepared at Tangier in order to invade Spain, and thus prevented the stronghold Tarifa, conquered some years earlier from the Banū-Marīn, from falling into the hands of Don John and his Moorish auxiliaries. In the defence of this stronghold occurred the heroic deed of the Governor Guzmán el Bueno, who refused to purchase the life of his son, a prisoner in the hands of Don John, by an act of infidelity towards his king and country.

A most important episode in this reign in respect of international politics was the change of attitude on the part of the new King of Aragon, James II, towards Castile. Alfonso III, the late King of Aragon, had helped, as we have said, the Infante de la Cerda, Don Alfonso, who was proclaimed King of Castile at Jaca in 1288, whence followed a short war between Alfonso III of Aragon and Sancho IV of Castile. The latter, ever intent on diminishing the number of his enemies, now succeeded in obtaining an alliance with James II, the successor of Alfonso III, and made a pact with him whereby the territories of North Africa were divided between the two kingdoms, Castile reserving for herself the eastern part from Melilla as far as Bougie and Tunis. This agreement, which shews clearly the determination to secure the African coast, was initiated by the afore-mentioned capture of Tarifa, an enterprise in which Sancho IV received military aid from James II.

The premature death of Sancho IV entailed on Castile the difficulties of a minority, since the heir, Ferdinand IV, was a child nine years old.

The crisis which had occurred during the minority of Alfonso VIII was now to be repeated. In those days a king's word and a king's friendship counted for little. The King of Aragon, James II, turned once again to the side of Don Alfonso de la Cerda, who was receiving aid from the King of Granada, Muḥammad II, and from many Castilian nobles. For his part, the Infante Don John reasserted his claims, supported by King Denis of Portugal. The situation would have been hopeless for Ferdinand IV had it not been for the great qualities of his mother, Doña Maria de Molina, granddaughter of Ferdinand III, queen-regent for the young king. She was a woman of courage, endowed with presence of mind in the face of dangers and with ready skill in dealing with the ambitious politicians of the time. In the midst of the war, not only civil but international, with Aragon, Portugal, Granada, and France, whose king seized the opportunity to gain advantages in Navarre, Doña Maria contrived gradually to detach the towns from their support of the Infante de la Cerda or of Don John by means of donations and promises of fresh *fueros* and privileges and by a policy of mildness and the great prestige of her word and presence. At the same time she strove to win over the Castilian nobles by granting them concessions, and by other modes of enlisting them on the king's side. She also worked to win the Kings of Aragon and Portugal to her cause. No less arduous was her struggle to obtain from the Cortes and the towns funds with which to prosecute the war. For this end, she herself sold her jewels and continually sacrificed herself for her son. The position held by the queen-mother in the court resembled that held by Guzmán el Bueno in the army. He continued to defend bravely and loyally the stronghold of Tarifa and the surrounding territory against all attacks, especially on the part of the Moors of Granada aided by the Banū-Marīn, and he resisted all the proposals of treason against the king which were made to him. So the ground was held until the king, now sixteen, was declared of age in 1303; and shortly afterwards peace was made with the Kings of Portugal and Aragon. With the latter Ferdinand IV concerted a campaign against Granada and the possessions of the Banū-Marīn in the south-east of Andalusia (1309). In this campaign, which was favoured by a political revolt in Granada, James II laid siege to the fortified city of Almería, and Ferdinand IV to that of Algeciras, but the only result achieved was the capture of Gibraltar, effected by the initiative of Guzmán el Bueno with the help of an Aragonese squadron. The defeat of a Castilian expedition against Granada led by Guzmán, in which he lost his life, compelled James II to raise the siege of Almería, and shortly afterwards Ferdinand was obliged to abandon the siege of Algeciras and arrange a peace and alliance with Nasr, the new King of Granada. This peace was short-lived. But Aragon afterwards took little part in the reconquest of Andalusia.

On the death of Ferdinand IV in 1312, another minority occurred; for his son Alfonso XI was only one year old. This minority was even more serious and disturbing than that of the previous reign, since various members of the royal family, supported respectively by the nobles and by the towns, disputed the regency. This situation lasted until 1325, when the Cortes, meeting at Valladolid, declared the king of age, but it became singularly grave when a fresh war broke out with the Moors of Granada, in which the Christians suffered various defeats (1319–25) and lost several strongholds in the south, amongst others Baza (1324). When Alfonso XI assumed the government, he shewed himself to be endowed with great military and political ability. He soon overcame the internal anarchy, reducing the nobles to order; he favoured the municipalities, protecting them against the nobles; he reformed the public finances and succeeded in imposing the principle of equality in the eyes of the law. But he also longed to complete the reconquest, and vigorously attacked the Moors as soon as he took the reins of power. The struggle was again complicated by the help which the Banū-Marīn, desirous of regaining Gibraltar, gave to the Moors of Granada. At first the Moors gained advantages, recapturing Gibraltar (1333) and defeating the Christians at Algeciras (1340), but Alfonso XI was not discouraged by these defeats and in the same year, 1340, going to the relief of Tarifa which was again besieged by the Banū-Marīn and Moors of Granada, gained a brilliant victory in the battle of the Salado, followed by another in 1343 in the battle of the river Palmones. The consequence was the capture of Algeciras, which the king entered in March 1344. In this second enterprise he was aided by various English, German, and Gascon knights and by the King of Navarre, Philip of Évreux. To complete these victories, Alfonso XI laid siege to Gibraltar in 1349, and died in his camp a victim of the Black Death, which was then desolating Spain. If this misfortune delayed the reconquest of that stronghold, the preceding victories on the other hand averted the possibility of any further invasions from Morocco. Another advantage gained by Alfonso XI was the final incorporation of the Biscayan province of Alava under the crown of Castile in 1332, the king undertaking to respect the *fueros* or special laws of that district.

Alfonso XI at his death left one legitimate son, Peter, issue of his marriage with Doña Maria of Portugal, and five bastards by a lady of Seville, Doña Leonor de Guzmán, who had been his mistress for twenty years. The bastard sons of Alfonso XI were Don Henry, Count of Trastamara, Don Frederick, Master of the Order of Santiago, Don Ferdinand, Don Tello, and Don John. The mere existence of this double line in the royal house was conducive to internal strife. The widowed queen, as soon as her husband was buried, imprisoned Doña Leonor and the struggle began, though at first not openly. Indeed the bastards and their half-brother Peter were apparently reconciled, though with intermittent revolts on one side and persecution on the other. At this time none of the bastards put forward any pretension to the throne, nor in

spite of their wealth and their many powerful friends did anyone consider them in that light. This was clearly shewn by the fact that when
Peter fell so gravely ill that his life was despaired of, two parties of
nobles were formed with a view to the succession. While one of these supported the candidature of the Marquess of Tortosa, nephew of Alfonso XI,
the other supported Don Juan Nuñez de Lara, lord of Biscay and a
descendant of one of the Infantes de la Cerda. The king recovered and
matters returned to their normal course, which meant a constant struggle
on the part of the Crown against the nobles and the prelates, who continued their lawless and deplorable custom of oppressing the weak and of
taking justice into their own hands whenever it suited them. Things
being thus, Doña Leonor was murdered by order of the widowed queen—
whether with Peter's consent is unknown, as he was still almost a boy, but
certainly with the complicity of the king's favourite, Don Juan Alfonso de
Albuquerque, a noble of Portuguese origin. In spite of this heinous deed,
the sons of Doña Leonor did not revolt immediately. However, it was to
be expected that some, if not all of them, would finally revolt, although
others, for instance the second, Don Frederick, were almost constantly
loyal to Peter. The occasion came a little later when one of the frequent
episodes of anarchy produced the customary repression on the part of
the king. In the first place certain citizens of Burgos, stirred up by a
noble of that city, Garcilaso de la Vega, revolted and killed one of the
king's tax-collectors; shortly afterwards the lord of Aguilar, Don Alfonso
Fernández de Coronel, also revolted, seeking alliance with other nobles and
with the Moors of Granada and Africa. Peter put down the revolt at Burgos
and put to death Garcilaso and other people of the city. He then attacked and took the town of Aguilar, put Coronel to death together with
his principal followers, and declared the town to be the property of the
Crown in perpetuity. Thereupon the bastards Don Henry and Don
Tello attempted to stir up a rebellion; the former was obliged to flee
to Aragon and the latter, defeated at Gijón by Peter, was pardoned by
the king and reinstated in all his castles and lands in Asturias.

A fresh occurrence added to the motives for the struggle thus begun.
In 1353 Peter married Blanche de Bourbon of the royal house of France,
a marriage negotiated by the queen-mother and by the favourite,
Albuquerque. Peter, who was then only seventeen years old, had previously had relations with a lady of good family, Doña Maria de Padilla.
So great was the love which the king had for her that he accompanied
her everywhere, much as his father had done previously with Doña Leonor.
Three days after the celebration of his marriage with Blanche de Bourbon
the king abandoned her, leaving the palace and rejoining Doña Maria.
The reasons for this step are unknown. It has been supposed that it was
on account of his passion for Doña Maria; also that the king suspected
some previous intrigue between Blanche and the bastard Don Frederick.
It has also been suggested that the main reason was the non-payment of

the dowry of Blanche which had been promised by the King of France. In any case, the event caused great scandal in the Court and amongst the nobles; it also aroused the apprehensions of Albuquerque, who feared that the relatives of Doña Maria would supplant him in the king's favour. On the other hand, other nobles and among them the bastard brothers of the king took Peter's side, thinking thereby perhaps to compass the fall of Albuquerque. The situation grew worse when Peter had Blanche imprisoned in the castle of Arévalo and changed all the officials of the Court. Some disaffected nobles whom the king had meant to execute owed their lives to the intercession of Maria de Padilla. Albuquerque had taken refuge in the fortress of Carvajales near the Portuguese frontier. Peter, regarding him as a rebel, marched against him. Thereupon Albuquerque planned a rising, with the connivance of the bastards Henry and Frederick, intending to dethrone Peter and offer the crown to a Portuguese prince. This rising gathered strength, being supported by various nobles in Galicia and in other districts, and also by the city of Toledo and by the queen-mother herself. They all demanded that Peter should give up Maria de Padilla. Some alleged feelings of pity for Blanche; but the majority were merely intent upon supplanting the relatives of Doña Maria in the king's favour. Inveigled by his mother, Peter went to Toro to confer with her and certain of the nobles. They promptly seized him and treated him with scant respect (1354); but the king succeeded in escaping, got together some troops, and attacked the rebels, who were clearly guilty of treason. He defeated them; many were executed, and the civil war was ended for the time. Don Frederick and Don Tello submitted, and Don Henry fled to France. Peter pardoned his mother, who retired to Portugal.

The peace was of but short duration. It was broken by the personal rivalry between Peter and the King of Aragon, Peter IV, who had succeeded to the throne in 1336. Both kings were wilful, short-tempered, and but little disposed to abandon their whims. War broke out in 1356 concerning a discourtesy towards the King of Castile on the part of a captain of the Catalan squadron at Sanlucar. The importance of this war, stopped soon after it had started by a truce arranged by the legate of Pope Innocent VI (1357), lay in the fact that Henry of Trastamara immediately went over to the side of Peter IV and that several Castilian nobles who had been loyal to Peter went with him. From that time Trastamara always found support in the King of Aragon; but six years were yet to elapse before he could openly aim at the throne of Castile. The truce of 1357 lasted but a little while. Both the King of Castile and the King of Aragon were aware of their perpetual and irremediable enmity and sought alliances with a view to future warfare. Peter I succeeded in obtaining the support of King Edward III of England. Peter IV, in addition to the aid of Trastamara and his party, got help from the Kings of Granada and Morocco. The King of Castile, suspicious of everybody, not without reason in view of the constant disloyalty, had been deserted by some of his partisans, among them his bastard brother Frederick. Peter had him executed in the royal palace at Seville, believing him to be in league with Trastamara, although he had just conquered for Castile the town of Jumilla in Murcian territory (1358). Peter's cousin Don Juan, and many other nobles and knights of Cordova, Salamanca, and other cities were also alienated from him. The murder of Don Frederick angered Trastamara so much that he broke the truce and invaded Castile. The Pope intervened again, and Peter was ready to give way, but not so Peter of Aragon. This so much irritated the King of Castile that he ordered fresh assassinations, that of his aunt Doña Leonor, of Don Tello's wife and her sister, of the bastards Don John and Don Tello, and of various castellans and others. The defeat of Trastamara at Nájera caused the Aragonese King to sue for peace, but the struggle was not ended until May 1361. This peace also was of short duration. During this time Peter intervened in the dynastic struggle in Granada between the King Muḥammad V and a pretender who had dethroned him in 1359, called Abū-Saʿīd or Bermejo. Peter aided Muḥammad V, and attacking the territory of Granada took possession of Iznajar, Cerna, Sagra, and Benameji. These victories forced Abū-Saʿīd to come and sue for peace in person. Peter killed the suppliant with his own hand in revenge for the help given to the King of Aragon in the late war.

Once again war broke out between the two Christian kings and once again Trastamara fought on the side of Peter IV. These two now signed the pact of 1363 in which Trastamara appears as pretender to the throne of Castile. In a later agreement Trastamara undertook to hand over to the King of Aragon the kingdom of Murcia and various important Castilian strongholds near the Aragonese frontier. Trastamara started the struggle with the aid of the celebrated bands of German, Gascon, English, and Spanish adventurers, so well known by the name of the White Companies, whose outrages at that time filled the south of France with terror. These were under the command of the French knight Bertrand du Guesclin; and in order to get rid of them, not only the King of France but also the Pope, then residing at Avignon, encouraged them to pass into Spain. The latter gave them 100,000 gold florins; the King of Aragon also gave them 100,000 gold florins and bestowed the title of Count of Borja upon du Guesclin. With these troops Trastamara first of all entered Calahorra (March 1366) and then Burgos, Toledo, and Seville. At Burgos he had himself proclaimed King of Castile.

Peter, without sufficient means to defend himself, fled to Bayonne and negotiated there for help from the King of England, to whom he promised the cession of various ports, castles, and lands along the Cantabrian coast. He also sought the aid of the King of Navarre. From the King of England he obtained an army under the command of the Black Prince, by whom Trastamara was again defeated at the battle of Nájera (1367).

In spite of the chivalrous protection which the Black Prince wished to accord to the prisoners taken in this battle, Peter had a number of them executed and insisted that others should be handed over to him. This disgusted the Black Prince. In Toledo, Cordova, and Seville the king also put to death a number of his enemies. These fresh cruelties, in addition to the fact that Peter had not given the pay promised to the English troops nor handed over the promised towns to the Black Prince, caused the English to abandon him and withdraw to France. Various cities of Castile at once rose in favour of Trastamara; he again took the field, and gained the crowning victory of Montiel over the troops which remained loyal to Peter. The latter took refuge in the castle, where he was besieged by Trastamara. Peter proposed to du Guesclin that he should be allowed to escape; du Guesclin refused out of loyalty to Trastamara, but then pretending to agree he induced Peter with several followers to visit him in his tent. They were all made prisoners. Trastamara came to see the prisoners, and the two brothers joined in a hand to hand struggle. Trastamara fell beneath his adversary but one of his followers, whether the Count of Rocaberti or another is uncertain, helped him to get on top; and Trastamara, thus getting the advantage, killed his brother (23 March 1369). Such was the end of the king whom historians and tradition have called alternately Peter the Cruel and Peter *el Justiciero*. The recent examination of Peter's skull has given rise to the opinion that he was abnormal, and certainly most of his punishments and acts of vengeance have the appearance of insanity; many of his executions, however, which shock our present conceptions, were only the application of the contemporary penal code and an example of the cruelty and violence of public morality at that time. We find numerous similar examples in the political history of all medieval kings and of many nobles. The struggle between the nobility and the monarchy was violent and presupposed the destruction of one or the other.

Don Henry of Trastamara, who became king as Henry II after the defeat and murder of Peter and was not less cruel than he, at once shewed the truth of what has already been stated. Although after the victory of Montiel the majority of the nobles, cities, and towns of Castile and Leon recognised Peter's bastard brother as king, certain important cities, such as Zamora, Ciudad Rodrigo, Carmona, Morlina, Vitoria, Salvatierra, Cañete, Requena, and others remained loyal to the memory of Peter I and continued the civil war for some time. But this resistance was useless against the superiority of the new king's military forces. On the surrender of Carmona Henry II promised to respect the life of the governor, Martin López de Córdoba, who was the guardian of Peter's two daughters, but after the custom of the time he broke his word and had him executed; the daughters of Peter I were imprisoned. Henry was soon involved in war with the King of Aragon, who had now turned against him, also with the Kings of Portugal, Navarre, Granada, and even England. The Portuguese King, as protector of Peter's daughters, invaded Galicia, where partisans hostile to Henry were gathered. The King of Navarre, Charles II, attacked the frontiers of Castile and took Logroño and other places in the Rioja.

With regard to England a serious dynastic question arose. The Dukes of Lancaster and York, sons of Edward III of England, had married respectively Doña Constance and Doña Isabella, daughters of Peter the Cruel by Doña Maria de Padilla. At the Cortes held in Seville in the year 1362 Peter had declared that before his marriage to Blanche of Bourbon he had married Doña Maria de Padilla and that consequently his issue by her was legitimate; thus their claims had some legal basis. This right in the first place descended to Don Alfonso, Doña Maria's son, but he died in 1367 and consequently his rights went to his sisters, who had in fact been recognised as heiresses to the throne by the Cortes of Briviesca in 1363. This was the basis of the Plantagenet claims to the throne of Castile, legally vacant on the death of Peter, and they were championed by the Duke of Lancaster, John of Gaunt, who assumed the title of King of Castile. For Henry it was important not only to repel these claims but also to weaken the power of England as much as possible. For this purpose his friendship with Charles V of France, a constant enemy of the English King, supplied a pretext. Accordingly, while Henry himself invaded Portugal, besieged Lisbon, and forced the Portuguese King to sue for peace, he also sent to the coast of Guienne a Castilian fleet which defeated the English fleet, under the Earl of Pembroke, off La Rochelle (23 June 1372); the earl, with seventy knights, was made prisoner and brought to Spain. On land Henry crossed the Bidasoa and laid siege to the fortress of Bayonne, but without success. However, he thereby succeeded in averting the invasion of Spain which was being prepared by the Duke of Lancaster. Henry also held in check the attacks made by the Kings of Navarre and Aragon. With the latter he formed an alliance by means of marriages between Don John, the heir of Castile, and a daughter of Peter IV of Aragon, and between Charles (III) the heir of Navarre and one of his own daughters. Peace with England followed as a consequence of the truce arranged by the mediation of the Pope between the Kings of England and France (Bruges, 27 June 1375), to which Castile was also a party. This truce and the peace also renewed with the Moors of Granada initiated a period of calm such as had not been known for many years in Castile, and which was only broken for a short time at the end of Henry's reign by a brief war with Navarre.

Henry spent the last four years of his life (1375–79) in strengthening his dynasty by a policy of amity, even towards his former enemies. To this end he showered honours and gifts of lands and lordships, a type of favour which, from its abundance and the name of him who bestowed it, became known as *Mercedes enriqueñas*. Henry himself was called *El de las mercedes* (gifts). His son John I succeeded him at the age of twenty.

John's reign is marked by two important political events: the alliances with Portugal and with England. The former might have brought about the union of the two crowns of Castile and Portugal in one sovereign, the latter effected the legitimisation of the illegitimate dynasty of Trastamara through the union with the legitimate branch of Peter. Alliance with Portugal came as a consequence of a fresh war in which Castile had the advantage and negotiated a treaty of peace; one condition of this was the marriage of the Infanta Doña Beatriz, heiress to the Portuguese crown, with the second son of John I, but the king having become a widower in the meantime married Doña Beatriz himself. It was agreed that on the death of the Portuguese King, Ferdinand I, the Kings of Castile should assume the title of "King of Portugal," but that they should not become so in fact except in the person of the son or daughter who should attain fourteen years of age. This condition was never fulfilled, since at the death of Ferdinand I in 1383 the Portuguese people, and particularly the nobility, refused to recognise the validity of his promise and elected for their king the Master of the Military Order of Avis founded in the thirteenth century. The King of Castile determined to assert his treaty rights by force, but the war thus begun, although at first favourable to the Castilians, ended with the decisive Portuguese victory of Aljubarrota (15 August 1385). Thus the proposed union of the two crowns came to nothing, and the Master of Avis reigned as John I of Portugal. The alliance between Castile and England came about from the renewal of the pretensions of the Duke of Lancaster, who invaded Galicia with the help of the King of Portugal and took possession of several strongholds. John I of Castile, instead of venturing on a doubtful war, preferred to negotiate with Lancaster, and finally concluded in 1387 the Treaty of Troncoso, which arranged for the marriage of Henry, heir to the Castilian throne, with Catherine, daughter of the Duke of Lancaster and granddaughter of Peter I. The newly-married couple thenceforward assumed the title of Princes of Asturias (1388), which was used by the heirs to the throne of Leon and Castile and later of Spain. Thus the two rival branches, that of Peter and that of Henry II, were united, and the memory of the fratricide of 1369 was wiped out.

On the death of John I in 1388 Henry III, who was still a minor, succeeded to the throne. During his minority the political upheavals of the time of Ferdinand IV and Alfonso XI were repeated, a proof that neither Henry II's gifts nor those afterwards granted by John I had solved the problems of strife between royal discipline and the anarchical ways of the nobles. The regents governed rather to their personal advantage than in the interests of the State. The nobles, divided into factions as usual, fought amongst themselves, filling the cities and countryside with sanguinary strife as, for example, in Seville, where the Count of Niebla and the Ponce family fought for mastery, and in Murcia where the Fajardos and Manuales did likewise. Moreover, assaults on the ghettos and massacres of Jews, which had been occasional episodes in the time of Alfonso VIII and of Peter the Cruel, now, as in other parts of Europe, became regular proceedings, beginning in Seville and spreading thence over most of Andalusia and Castile. The king, although of a weak constitution, as is evident from his nickname "el doliente" (the invalid), had great force of character. Hardly had he been declared of age in his fifteenth year than he began to remedy the evils introduced by the regents and nobles. To this end he revoked many of the gifts which the regents had granted to the detriment of the royal treasury. He insisted on the return of rents and lands usurped from the Crown and chastised the factions of nobles. The ever-latent strife with Portugal broke out again through an unexpected act of aggression without previous declaration of war on the part of the Portuguese King, whose forces took possession of Badajoz, but the Castilian troops soon recovered the stronghold (1397). The African Moors still disturbed the coasts of Andalusia by their piratical expeditions. To put an end to these Henry III ordered a naval expedition against Tetuan. The Castilian navy forced the bar of the river Martín and destroyed the city (1400), which had been the lair of the pirates. He attempted to make a truce with the Moors of Granada, but without success, and consequently in 1405 prepared to undertake a war against them.

Henry also turned his attention to international relations, aiming at a peaceful understanding with the most powerful and influential kings of the time. This policy, very probably connected with the importance of commercial relations with the East, induced him to send embassies to the celebrated conqueror, Tamerlane, ruler of Persia and Turkestan (1376–1405), and to the Sultan of the Ottoman Turks, Bāyazīd I (1360–1403). In these embassies there were among others two Castilian nobles and a monk. One of the Castilian ambassadors, Ruy González de Clavijo, wrote a curious account of the visit to Tamerlane, entitled *Historia del Gran Tamerlán*. Tamerlane sent to Henry among other presents two maidens mentioned in poems collected fifty years later and published in the *Cancionero de Baena* (compiled about 1445). Henry also encouraged the capture and colonisation of the Canary Islands in the Atlantic, already known and a matter of dispute in the time of Alfonso XI, but not yet taken by any European power. In 1402 the conquest was undertaken by the Spaniard Rubín de Bracamonte and the French adventurer Jean de Béthencourt, who had sworn fealty to the King of Castile. The islands conquered, not without great resistance on the part of the inhabitants, were then named Hierro, Fuerteventura, Gomera, and Lanzarote. But their definite possession and incorporation with the Crown of Castile did not take place until the end of the fifteenth century.

Henry died prematurely in 1407. All his efforts on behalf of internal peace, social order, and the aggrandisement of Castile were insufficient to solve the political problems of the period. And indeed the difficulties were insuperable. This was to be shewn by the wars during the fifteenth century, at the end of which the firm hand of Isabella, as we shall see later, and other favourable factors, were at last able to change the face of things.

While the history of the Castilian part of the Peninsula was developing along these lines, on the eastern side, in the united realms of Aragon and Catalonia, events were taking place which partly corresponded to the same social and political problems as in Castile and in some measure opened the way to Spanish expansion beyond the Peninsula. Seven kings occupy the period under discussion, four of whom are of capital importance in the history of Aragon and Catalonia.

The partition by James I of his dominions into the kingdoms of Aragon and Majorca, inherited by his sons Peter and James respectively, brought about the political independence of the Balearic Islands for a number of years, but the bonds between the kingdoms of Majorca and Aragon were not completely severed, especially when James of Majorca declared himself a feudatory of the Crown of Aragon (1278). If the policy of James I in this direction does not appear very wise, since it weakened the power of the monarchy which he had increased by the conquest of Valencia and the Balearic Islands, yet he deserves credit for his diplomatic aggrandisement of Aragon by the marriage of his son Peter to Constance, daughter of Manfred, King of Sicily. The rights of the Aragonese kings to parts of Italy were derived from this marriage. James I proposed at the same time to counteract in this way the alliance advantageous to France brought about by the marriage of the Countess of Provence with Charles of Anjou, the perpetual rival of the Catalans and Aragonese in the south of France.

The first act of the new king, Peter III, was to affirm his political independence with regard to the Papacy, thus denying the validity of the vassalage contracted by his grandfather[1] Peter II. Peter III expressed this doctrine in the declaration which he made at his coronation at Saragossa that he was not receiving the crown from the hands of the archbishop in the name of the Church, and was neither for her nor against her (16 November 1276). James I had been the ally of Mustanṣir, King of Tunis, who paid tribute to Aragon. On the death of Mustanṣir the throne was usurped by one of his sons, and Peter III seized the opportunity to intervene in Tunisian affairs. To this end he sent an expedition in 1280 under the command of a Sicilian captain, Coral or Corrado Lancia, with the result that a sort of Aragonese protectorate was established over Tunis, which comprised the right of levying direct tribute and half of the taxation imposed on the country, the establishment of consuls in Bougie and Tunis, and a governor for the Christian residents in the district. This governor, who was to be an Aragonese or Catalan, enjoyed the privilege of flying the Aragonese flag, to which equal honours

[1] See *supra*, Vol. vi, Chap. xii.

were to be paid as to the Tunisian flag. This important diplomatic success, which laid the foundation of Aragonese influence in the north of Africa, was the forerunner of new events of which the kingdom of Sicily was the scene and in prevision of which Peter III probably undertook the expedition to Tunis.

The kingdom of Sicily was composed of the island of that name and of the territory of Naples on the mainland. It was then ruled by the Hohenstaufen in the person of Manfred, father-in-law of Peter III and son of the Emperor Frederick II[1]. The long struggle between the Papacy and the Hohenstaufen was drawing to its close, and the Pope was resolved to wrest the kingdom, of which he was the lawful suzerain, from the enemy house. For this end, the Pope enfeoffed Charles of Anjou with the kingdom of Sicily on condition that he should conquer it as papal vassal and champion. Charles invaded the kingdom (1264), and Manfred perished at the battle of Benevento. A similar fate befell Manfred's nephew Conradin, the last of the Hohenstaufen. Overcome by Charles of Anjou, Conradin was taken prisoner and beheaded at Naples. Thus Peter III remained the legitimate representative of the rights of the house of Swabia in Sicily and the last hope of the Ghibelline party, persecuted by the Guelf or papal party. The most important members of the Ghibelline party in Sicily fled from the cruel persecutions of Charles of Anjou, now master of Sicily, and sought refuge with Peter III. It is not known for certain whether the King of Aragon planned the conquest of Sicily independently at this time or whether he made an agreement with the Sicilians to that end. It may, however, be affirmed that Peter conducted negotiations through the Sicilian John of Procida to concert a league against Charles of Anjou into which the Kings of Aragon and Castile were to enter, together with the Emperor of Constantinople, many of the Sicilian nobles, and even Pope Nicholas III himself. The Pope appears to have designed the establishment of two kingdoms in Italy, one in Lombardy and the other in Tuscany, for two of his nephews and to have found that Charles of Anjou was an obstacle to this plan.

The death of Nicholas III and the election in 1281 of the Frenchman Martin IV, who immediately shewed opposition to Peter III, caused the projected alliance to fail. But the King of Aragon did not abandon his scheme. He made sure of peace at home by an alliance with Sancho IV of Castile, and coming to an agreement with the Count of Pallars and the Viscount of Cardona who might have caused disturbances in Catalonia, he made Constance queen-regent of the kingdom in case of his own absence. At the same time he made great preparations for war, assembling on the coast of Catalonia and Valencia a fleet which counted as many as 140 ships and 15,000 men. The King of France in alarm sent ambassadors to Peter to learn what the reason of these preparations might be. But the King of Aragon gave an evasive answer. The ostensible motive was to

[1] See *supra,* Vol. vi, Chap. vi.

make a crusade to Constantine in Africa, where the governor had sought help from Peter against the King of Tunis, promising to hand over the city and to become a Christian. The fleet put to sea with the troops in June 1282 and made towards Collo on the Barbary coast. The Aragonese took the city, where they fortified themselves and continued for some time the war against the natives of the country.

Shortly before, there had taken place in Sicily the rising against the French known as the Sicilian Vespers (31 March 1282); and an embassy from the Sicilians now offered to Peter, as representative of the house of Swabia, the crown which Charles of Anjou had wrested from Manfred. Peter III accepted, fully convinced of his rights. Notwithstanding the opposition of many of the nobles in his host, he ordered Collo to be burnt as well as other towns in the district, and embarked his army for Sicily. On 30 August he arrived at Trapani, and soon afterwards defeated the French fleet and made himself master of the whole island. Charles of Anjou, who was then engaged in besieging Messina, abandoned that enterprise and withdrew towards the north of Calabria, whose coasts however fell into Peter's hands in February 1283. Charles, in despair at these defeats, had recourse to a measure frequent at that time and challenged the King of Aragon to a duel. The challenge was accepted, and the combat was arranged to take place at Bordeaux on 1 June 1283. When the time came, Peter learnt that the King of France, in agreement with the King of England to whom Bordeaux belonged, was preparing an ambush for him and for the nobles who were to accompany him. To avoid this danger and to keep his word, Peter went to Bordeaux in disguise and learnt that the plot was a fact, and that the governor could give no guarantee for the person of the king and his company. Peter thereupon made himself known at the place appointed for the combat and had it certified that he had been there. He then immediately rode back to Spain, not without grave peril of capture by the partisans of the King of France. He entered Spain by way of Guipuzcoa and proceeded to Tarragona.

In the meanwhile the war continued in Italy with favourable results for the King of Aragon, whose admiral Roger Loria gained a great reputation as a sailor and warrior. He defeated the French fleet twice off Malta and off Naples, taking prisoner Charles the Lame son of Charles of Anjou (1284). In the January of the following year Charles of Anjou died, leaving the Angevin cause in the kingdom of Sicily without a leader; but Pope Martin IV on the other hand, who did not forgive the King of Aragon for having conquered the island of Sicily and who maintained his claims to the feudal rights over Aragon repudiated by Peter III, excommunicated the latter and, declaring him to be deprived of his possessions, absolved his subjects from their oaths of fealty, and granted his dominions to Charles of Valois, third son of Philip III of France (May 1284). King Philip III invaded Catalonia at the head of an army of 1800 horse and countless foot. The Holy See declared this war to be a crusade and gathered contributions to support it, while the invaders found support in James II, King of Majorca, the brother of Peter III and also lord of Roussillon, who allowed passage through that territory. Accordingly the French penetrated through Ampurias (Ampurdan), notwithstanding the fact that some fortresses in Roussillon such as Salces and Coplliure held out for Peter. The French took possession of places in Ampurias and then laid siege to Gerona. Charles of Valois was crowned king in the castle of Lleis with the support of certain Catalan nobles and ecclesiastics and of various towns of Ampurdan.

Peter III was hard pressed. His preparations to beat back the invasion, which had obliged him to temporise with some political claims of the nobles and of the city of Barcelona, were insufficient. Fortunately the fortress of Gerona held out long enough to allow Roger Loria, who had been summoned by Peter, to arrive with his ships. He defeated the French fleet at the battle of the Islas Hormigas. This victory, which stopped the provisioning of the French army by sea, together with an epidemic which broke out amongst the troops through lack of food and excessive crowding in the camp, forced the French King, Philip the Bold, to retire. His retreat was disastrous. The Aragonese and Catalan forces posted on the pass of Panisars allowed Philip to go by, but fell upon the rest of the troops and slaughtered them. The war went on for some time in Roussillon, but the towns which had been taken by the French soon surrendered to Peter III. Shortly afterwards (2 November 1285) Peter died, at the moment when his son Alfonso was leading an expedition against Majorca to punish the disloyalty of King James II. Before his death Peter III had asked the Archbishop of Tarragona to remove the excommunication which the Pope had laid upon him, declaring at the same time that he was willing to hand over the kingdom of Sicily to the Holy See. But Peter's successor Alfonso III did not carry out his father's intentions. Having gained possession of Majorca he retained it during the whole of his reign, as a punishment for the conduct of his uncle at the time of the French invasion, and soon afterwards he took Minorca, which from the time of James I had been only a vassal-State. Peter's second son James, who during the life-time of his father had been accepted as the heir to Sicily, kept the island with the connivance of his brother Alfonso and was crowned its king in 1286. Consequently the war continued between the Sicilians and the French in Italy; but Aragon was not directly concerned in it, since Sicily was now a separate kingdom. This fact aided Alfonso III in composing his differences with France and with the Papacy, under pressure from other European States, especially England.

Peace was finally made at Canfranc in 1288, the principal conditions of which with regard to Aragon were: the revocation of the investiture of the kingdom of Aragon made by the Pope in favour of Charles of Valois in 1284; the recognition of the sovereignty of the Crown of

Aragon over Majorca and Roussillon; and the liberation of Charles the Lame, a prisoner since June 1284, in exchange for indemnities and fresh securities and the possession of the island of Sicily for James the brother of Alfonso III. When Charles the Lame was set at liberty, neither the King of France nor the Pope fulfilled the pact, the former renewing his menaces with the connivance of the dethroned King of Majorca; and the struggle went on both in Sicily and Calabria. A new peace signed at Tarascon in 1291 put an end to the struggle, but greatly to the prejudice of Aragon, seeing that Alfonso now undertook to pay to the Holy See the tribute promised by Peter II with all arrears in return for the Pope's renewed withdrawal of his grant of the kingdom to Charles of Valois; this is very clear evidence of the moral force which the Papacy still exercised upon secular politics. By the Treaty of Tarascon Alfonso undertook to prevent Aragonese and Catalans from serving under James of Sicily, to require of the latter the surrender of Sicily to the Pope, and in the case of his refusal to declare war upon him. Shortly afterwards Alfonso III died without issue and the throne passed to his brother James, who had been deprived of his rights over Sicily by the terms of the Treaty of Tarascon. Events shewed that, in spite of everything, the aims of France and the Papacy could not be realised. James II left Sicily in order to be crowned King of Aragon, Catalonia, and Valencia, but he appointed his brother Frederick governor in Sicily. This open violation of the Treaty of Tarascon, to which James had never consented when reigning in Sicily, provoked a fresh war with France. But James desired peace, and now accepted the terms of Pope Boniface VIII. Accordingly a third treaty was soon made at Anagni in 1295, in which once again the King of Aragon renounced his claims to Sicily, as Alfonso III had done in 1291, and undertook to make war upon the Sicilians and upon Frederick, should they not agree to restore the island to the Pope. On his side the Pope raised all sentences of excommunication from the Aragonese sovereigns. The King of France also renounced for himself and Charles of Valois their claims on Aragon, and the marriage was arranged of Blanche, daughter of Charles the Lame, to the King of Aragon. Finally, two years later, by way of compensation for the loss of Sicily, James obtained from the Papacy the grant of dominion over the islands of Sardinia and Corsica, provided that he should conquer them and pay a tribute to the Pope.

Alfonso, heir to the Aragonese throne, undertook (1323–24) the conquest of Sardinia, but met with great resistance on the part of the islanders, and failed to effect complete occupation. The dispute with France over the Pyrenean Val d'Aran was settled by arbitration in favour of the Aragonese King, who adduced documentary proof of his rights. But the Treaty of Anagni did not solve the question of Sicily. Neither Frederick nor—what was more important—the people of Sicily would surrender their independence. The war was reopened, and James fought against his brother, now Frederick II of Sicily, with varying fortunes, although brilliant naval victories were won by the famous admiral Roger Loria, now in James' service. Finally, however, all being weary of such a prolonged struggle and the great invasion of Sicily by Charles of Valois having failed, peace was made in 1302, by which Boniface VIII and Charles the Lame recognised Frederick as King of island Sicily (Trinacria), but on the condition that the latter should marry Eleonor Charles' daughter and that on Frederick's death the island should be reunited with Naples, which had been all the time Angevin. In compensation for this promised concession, the King of Naples undertook to pay Frederick's children 100,000 ounces of gold and to induce the King of Aragon to allow them to conquer a kingdom, either Cyprus or else Sardinia, which he had not yet attacked. In spite of this new treaty, Sicily remained in the power of the house of Aragon even after Frederick's death[1].

While James was thus intervening in Sicily in a way so contrary to the political interests of Aragon, he aimed at extending his dynastic influence by marriages. He himself married Blanche of Anjou, and, after her death, Mary, daughter of the King of Cyprus. Their daughter Isabella married Frederick the Handsome, Duke of Austria, later the rival of Lewis IV for the Empire, a union of far-reaching consequences in the struggle with the Papacy. His second son Alfonso married a niece of the Count of Urgel and inherited his estates. His third son Peter inherited the counties of Ribagorza and Ampurias. Finally, a granddaughter of James was married to his cousin James III, King of Majorca; Majorca had been restored in 1295 to James III's grandfather James II, who had betrayed Peter III, but on condition that it was a fief of the Crown of Aragon. James also acquired the northern part of the kingdom of Murcia in return for his intervention in the war of succession between Sancho IV and the Infante de la Cerda in Castile. Thus James II of Aragon can be considered as a king solicitous for the aggrandisement of his possessions in spite of his weakness with regard to Sicily.

Before beginning the account of the reign of Alfonso IV who succeeded to the throne on the death of James in 1327, it is necessary to mention an episode of great importance in the history of south-east Europe which resulted from the termination of the war in Sicily in 1302, an exploit which can be considered glorious amongst the military achievements and adventures of that time, and which is known to history as the "Catalan Expedition to the East," although, as we shall see, there were recruits from Navarre and from other countries as well. Owing to the lack of regular armies paid by the State or maintained by compulsory military service as at the present day, it happened that when some war was finished for which thousands of men had been got together in a certain district, a great number of them were left without occupation. This became a veritable menace to the country, particularly if they were not natives, as

[1] See *supra*, Chap. I.

was frequently the case. These unemployed troops often formed themselves into companies of robbers or conquerors who fought on their own account or sold their services to the highest bidder. It may be easily understood that every country attempted to shake off such a plague, facilitating their departure to other lands, as we have already seen in the case of the White Companies in southern France in the time of Peter I of Castile. Frederick II, King of Sicily, wishing to get rid of the numerous adventurers who had remained in the island after the peace of 1302, suggested to one of the captains, Roger de Flor of Brindisi, that he should go to the aid of Andronicus, Emperor of Constantinople, who was then hard pressed by the Turks, already masters of all the Byzantine possessions in Asia Minor[1]. Roger agreed, and in ships lent by Frederick sailed to Constantinople in 1303, with 1500 horse, 1000 infantry from various parts, and 4000 almogávares ("raiders"), picked troops so called because they followed the Moorish tactics of incursions and raids in enemy country. The Emperor received them with joy, bestowed upon Roger de Flor the title of megaduke, and married him to a daughter of the King of Bulgaria. Roger and his troops invaded Asia Minor and won great victories over the Turks. The news of these victories and of the honours and gifts bestowed upon the leader of the expedition attracted fresh adventurers from Catalonia, Aragon, and Navarre, who made two new expeditions to Asia Minor under Berengar de Rocafort and Berengar de Entenza. The Emperor in reward for these successes, which freed him for the time from the Turkish peril, gave the exalted title of Caesar to Roger de Flor; on Entenza he bestowed the title of megaduke. He also granted the whole of Anatolia to be parcelled out among those who took part in the expedition (1305).

Such great favours, although well earned, roused the jealousy of the Greek courtiers and of Michael the heir to the throne. They formed a conspiracy. Roger de Flor, many of his officers, and 1300 of their followers were murdered at a banquet. A body of Catalans and Aragonese stationed in the town of Gallipoli were also massacred, as well as those under the command of Admiral Fernando de Ahones in Constantinople. Thereby the expeditionary force was reduced to some 3300 men and 200 horses. However, so far from being intimidated, these survivors, furious for revenge, rose against the Byzantines, defeated them repeatedly, and set fire to several towns. Rivalry broke out between the leaders of the various bands, which were joined for a time by the Infante Ferdinand of Majorca, appointed commander-in-chief by his cousin, Frederick of Sicily, in order to turn the situation to account. This rivalry rendered their victories politically useless, and gave a new direction to the action of the Spanish and other warriors in the East. The Catalans and Aragonese, with some Turkish auxiliaries, entered the service of Walter, Duke of Athens, who was hard pressed by his enemies. They delivered him from this peril. But the

[1] Cf. *supra*, Vol. IV, Chaps. XV and XXI.

treacherous duke attempted to make away with his deliverers after the example of Constantinople. The adventurers thereupon stormed the city of Athens and placed themselves under the protection of the King of Sicily. The latter seized the opportunity and sent his second son Manfred, who became sovereign of the Sicilian duchy of Athens, which however owed its origin to Catalans and Aragonese. The duchy, which lasted from 1326 to 1387, was a singular conclusion to the exploits of those adventurers who, leaving Sicily in 1303, not only carried the banner of Aragon for the first time triumphantly through Asia Minor and Greece, but introduced Spanish culture into those countries, especially Greece.

The short reign of Alfonso IV of Aragon (1327–36) was marked in foreign affairs by the continued effort to conquer Sardinia and at home by family disputes. Alfonso's second wife, Leonor of Castile, sister of Alfonso XI, strove to favour her own children at the expense of those by her husband's first marriage. These resisted vigorously, especially the eldest, Peter, who from his earliest years shewed remarkable energy. He won the support of the people, and succeeded to the throne on his father's death without serious opposition from Leonor.

The new king Peter IV, whose struggles with Peter I of Castile and whose intervention in the civil wars of that country we have already related, was, although energetic, treacherous and cruel like his contemporary in Castile. Less harsh than the latter, he was more hypocritical and observant of outward appearances, whence his name Peter the Ceremonious. The first years of Peter IV's reign were occupied with the above-mentioned war against the Banū-Marīn and the Moors of Granada, in which he gave his aid to Alfonso XI of Castile, and with the struggle to effect the annexation of Majorca in order to restore the unity of the possessions of the Crown which had been divided by the testament of James I. Peter IV sought a pretext in the claims of the French King to the stronghold of Montpellier, which belonged to James III, King of Majorca. Instead of aiding the latter against the King of France, Peter drew up a list of charges against James, accusing him of the infraction of his feudal duties to the Crown of Aragon. James III was willing to submit the question to trial and went to Barcelona, but Peter IV, bent on gaining his ends, alleged that James III had conspired against his life, and accused him of high treason. The natural result was a war between the two kings, easily won by Peter IV, who seized Majorca and Roussillon; James was killed in battle. To flatter the national pride, Peter promised solemnly in the Cortes of March 1354 never to separate the two recovered States from the kingdom of Aragon. Majorca thenceforth formed part of the Aragonese kingdom. Roussillon was retained by the kings of Aragon until 1462, when John II ceded it to France, although shortly afterwards he tried to regain it, thus bequeathing a new political problem to his successors.

The war in Sardinia continued, causing serious trouble to the kings of Aragon. The Republic of Genoa in conjunction with Pisa and other Italian States stirred up frequent revolts amongst the islanders against the Aragonese dominion. Peter IV decided to attack the evil at its root, and so allying himself with Venice, the perpetual enemy of Genoa, he declared war on the latter. Two naval victories gained by the Aragonese and Venetians did not suffice to pacify Sardinia. The king himself, at the head of a strong army, took several important places on the island, but not even so did he succeed in overcoming the local disorders of the Sardinians, who were always in a state of insurrection. However, as a contrast to this unfortunate state of affairs, Peter IV in 1381 had a pleasant surprise. The duchy of Athens—so far a Sicilian dependency—was offered to him by an embassy of nobles and burghers of the city. Peter accepted their offer and in return granted Athens the same civic privileges as those enjoyed by Barcelona, which was the most autonomous and powerful of all Catalan municipalities. Moreover, from his intervention in the dynastic wars of Castile, Peter IV obtained in addition to certain material advantages a union with the victorious house of Trastamara, through the marriage of the Aragonese Infanta Leonora with the Infante Don John of Castile. Upon this marriage were based the claims of the Castilian dynasty which some forty years later was to rule in Aragon. The last years of Peter IV were embittered by family dissensions and by an unfortunate attempt to subjugate the peasant vassals of the Archbishop of Tarragona. The king died in January 1387, abandoned by his wife and children.

More valuable perhaps to his country than all his territorial acquisitions was his decisive victory over the anarchical nobility, principally Aragonese and Valencian, and over those municipalities which had made common cause with them. The struggle, already of long standing, had reached a serious crisis in the reign of Peter III. The great nobles of Aragon and their retainers, together with the above-mentioned municipalities, more interested in the increase of their particular privileges than in the political task of breaking the power of the nobles which was really more formidable than that of the Crown, had formed a league known as the "Union" which possessed an organisation and armed force of its own. Confident of its strength, the Union had presented to the king in 1282 a list of petitions and complaints to which Peter III was obliged to agree, being hard pressed at that moment with other political troubles, notably the war in Sicily with Charles of Anjou. The whole body of privileges and promises made by the king was termed *Privilegio General*. This document was both a statute recognising an aristocratic oligarchy of nobles and citizens and also a charter which defined the immunities and class privileges obtained by the nobility, particularly in the reign of James I (1265), and the civic liberties obtained in successive steps by the municipalities. Alfonso III, who succeeded Peter III, less energetic and resolute than his father, gave way still farther and granted in 1288 to the revolted nobles and municipalities the *Privilegio de la Unión*, still more irksome to the royal authority than the *Privilegio General*. One clause gave to the Cortes the right of deposing the king if he omitted to fulfil certain of the privileges granted. Obviously matters could not rest there. The accession of a vigorous and resolute king, tenacious of royal prerogatives as they were then conceived, was certain to renew the struggle.

And so it was when Peter IV came to the throne: the struggle soon broke out, since the king, as we have seen, was not a man of a complacent disposition. The trouble began when Peter, being without male heirs, appointed his daughter Constance regent and heiress to the throne, whereas the Aragonese and Valencian nobles preferred the claim of Peter's brother James, Count of Urgel. For the time being the king was obliged to give way, for only the Catalan nobility and four Aragonese municipalities, Huesca, Daroca, Calatayud, and Teruel, took his side in the Cortes of 1347 at Saragossa. He confirmed the *Privilegio de la Unión* and agreed to change his council and the high officials of the palace, dismissing the Catalan nobles. But this submission on the part of the king was only provisional. Peter IV was waiting for the moment of his revenge, and for this purpose he strove to divide the nobles and form a strong party of his own. The members of the Union in Valencia gave him an excellent opportunity by sacking the houses of those whom they suspected of being partisans of the king. Peter attacked them, but failed in this first attempt (1348). He was himself for some time practically a prisoner in the hands of the Valencians, and suffered treatment but little compatible with his authority. About midsummer he escaped to Aragon, where the Union troops under the command of his brother Ferdinand were besieging the town of Epila. Loyal troops came to the assistance of the besieged, and in the battle which ensued the Union suffered a crushing defeat (21 July 1348). The king entered Saragossa, abolished the *Privilegio de la Unión*, and punished many of the delinquents with death. He did the same in Valencia shortly afterwards. The ferocity of these struggles and of the legal penalties of that age appears in the torments inflicted upon the Valencian unionists by the king. They were even compelled to drink the molten metal of the very bells which had called them to the meetings of the Union.

However, the abolition of the *Privilegio* went no farther than the actual contents of the document. The rights of the nobility as a social class remained intact, also those of the municipalities just as they existed in the ancient laws of the kingdom and in the local *fueros*; a fact which shews that Peter IV did not move against the fundamental political organisation of Aragon, but against the unwarrantable pretensions of the nobility and municipalities. Consequently, if the political power which the nobles had acquired by the Union was shattered, in other respects the Aragonese aristocracy retained their former power and social influence, and did not acquiesce, as did the Castilian nobility a century later, in the total abolition of their political importance and their privileges over the plebeian classes.

The two kings who succeeded Peter IV, and with whom the fourteenth century in Aragon comes to a close, are of but slight importance in the political history of the country. The first of them, John I (1387–95), son of Peter IV, had to contend with the Count of Armagnac and the Count of Foix, who made vague claims to the crown, and had to quell another insurrection in Sardinia and a rising in Sicily. During his reign the duchy of Athens was lost to Aragon. John I was succeeded by Martin I (1395–1410), regent of Sicily, who left his only son, also named Martin, as king of that island. The latter died in 1409, leaving the kingdom to his father Martin I of Aragon; but he also died in less than a year without surviving issue or leaving any other will than that by which he had bequeathed his throne to his son Martin of Sicily. Thus uncertainty as to the succession raised a serious question which might have been calamitous if the usual appeal to arms had been made. Fortunately this did not occur.

The period of about a century so far covered in this chapter is a brief space in the nation's history. Yet in Castile the period from Alfonso X to Henry III and in Aragon that from Peter III to Martin I brought some interesting and sometimes radical changes both in political and in civil institutions.

With regard to social and economic life we see on the one hand in Leon and Castile an evolution towards personal freedom among the rural and urban lower classes, and on the other hand the growth of municipalities, centres of free civic life. We have little detailed knowledge concerning the former tendency. Documents of the thirteenth and fourteenth centuries contain evidence of servile insurrections and of protests against seignorial excesses—proof that in some districts the liberating movement was slow and met with strong resistance. The movement received legal support through the extension to the whole country of the law granted by Alfonso IX[1] in 1215 to the serfs, known as *foreros*, in the royal manors of Leon and in those subject to the Archbishop of Santiago. On the other hand it appears that the right of asylum in municipal territory enjoyed by fugitive serfs from the seignories was restricted; also there was a change for the worse in the status of a certain class, known as *behetrías*, who had to pay tribute and services to a lord. This change seems to have consisted of a restriction, in many cases, of the right possessed by some of these *behetrías* to choose any noble as their lord, this right being now restricted to choice among the members of some specified noble family. But apart from the *behetrías*, the number of free labourers must have become greater as the cultivation of the land spread and as the general wealth increased.

[1] See *supra*, Vol. vi, Chap. xii, p. 417.

This increase of wealth was furthered in the twelfth and thirteenth centuries by the formation of important industrial and commercial urban centres, first Santiago de Galicia, and later, after the conquests of Ferdinand III and Alfonso X, Seville and other towns in Andalusia. Moreover, the greater security of the strictly Castilian and Leonese districts, once the frontier reached and passed the line of the Guadalquivir, allowed the normal development of economic life in the north. In rural life and the extension of tillage the monasteries still played an important part, while at the same time they gave military aid to the kings, sending bodies of slaves, labourers, and dependants under the command of the abbot or of some layman appointed by him. Indeed so great was the civilising influence of the monastic system that the progress of the reconquest and the successive prosperity of the kingdoms so recovered can be traced on the map by counting the number of monasteries as exactly as by following the dates of Christian victories and the conquest of Moorish territories. The Military Orders founded in Leon and Castile during the Middle Ages, especially those of Calatrava and Alcántara, played a similar part to the monasteries in the colonisation of territory reconquered from the Arabs.

With regard to urban and municipal life, in proportion as the middle class increased, either entirely plebeian or possessing something of aristocratic privilege (*los caballeros de villa* or *colación*), the manual workers organised themselves in *gremios*, an institution similar to the gilds and corporations of other European countries. The professions or trades grouped in *gremios* were composed of the *menestrales* or workmen in manual industries, merchants, sailors, and *artistas* or workers in industrial arts. Protected by the municipalities and also by the kings, the gilds increased in importance and became an influential social element in city life. From the fourteenth century particularly, the kings made general laws, *ordenanzas de menestrales*, to regulate not only the inner life of the *gremios* but also the wages, the working day, the technical conditions of production in each trade. The development of commerce, especially the commerce of Castile and of the Cantabrian coast with France, Flanders, and other northern countries is shewn, among other things, by the existence of consuls, representatives in various foreign cities of the Spanish producers and exporters.

With regard to the nobility, the introduction of new titles is noticeable, replacing the old names of *ricoshombres*, *infanzones*, etc. From the time of Henry II the newer titles of marquess and duke are added to the ancient title of count. The title of Constable of Castile, the head of the army, appears to have been created during the reign of John I. Other important innovations were the fixing of the order of succession to titles by a law of the *Partidas* of Alfonso X and the institution of *mayorazgos*, an entail on real estate generally in favour of the eldest son. These *mayorazgos* soon extended to the upper middle class and caused a rigidity in the ownership of landed property. The wealth of the nobles, originally founded on land, which by the progress of economic life, the freedom of the labourers, and the ever increasing importance of movable property was becoming less lucrative than formerly for the landowners, was however increased by the above-mentioned gifts or *mercedes* of the kings. These *mercedes* were often known as *encomiendas*. They were of two kinds: *encomiendas de honor*, when the king ceded to the noble the fiscal rights of a town or district; and *encomiendas de tierra*, when the king granted a rent or sum to be raised from one or various places or from the Jewish or Moorish quarter of a city.

The principal innovation in the social sphere was in respect of the Jews, as we have already indicated. They were strongly protected in the interests of science and literature in the time of Alfonso X and other kings, and played a great part in financial affairs both public and unofficial. Thenceforward we find mention of their economic privileges, as for instance the regulation by Alfonso X of the rate of usury. At the same time religious intolerance, stirred by pulpit oratory, was increasing among the people. In the Cortes of Burgos (1396) it was petitioned that the Jews should be deprived of the fortresses they held, of their public offices, of the farming of the royal revenues, and of the posts which certain of them held in the council of Henry III. The king granted only the last demand. But assaults on the ghettos and massacres by the populace became more frequent, and aggravated the situation.

Social innovations in Aragon and Catalonia were unimportant during this time. In the new kingdom of Valencia constituted by James I and inherited by Peter III, there was no servile Christian class of cultivators, but a class of Moorish slaves and tenant-farmers bestowed by the king upon the conquerors who obtained grants of land. As the majority of these were Aragonese nobles, rural life in Valencia was dominated by these lords and regulated according to the customs of Aragon. On the other hand, the middle class and the popular element predominated in the cities and important towns, giving to the Valencian municipalities a markedly democratic character, which received legal sanction from the *fuero* or charter granted by James I to the capital. This charter is one of the best models of municipal legislation of the late thirteenth and early fourteenth centuries, and was imitated later at Tarragona.

Social history in Majorca resembled that of Catalonia, with the difference that the aristocratic element was not represented there by the nobles and clergy but by the burghers or rich citizens of the capital who were the chief landowners. Their exploitation of the country folk (*forenses*) provoked a ferment of protests and tumults which at a later date degenerated into sanguinary revolts.

The chief political movement in Leon and Castile is the struggle between the monarch and the nobility, of which some account has been already given. As to public administration, a reform introduced by Ferdinand III was extended and securely established, the old *condados* or *mandationes* (counties) being replaced by new territorial divisions known as *adelantamientos*, ruled by *adelantados*, divided into two classes, *mayores* and *menores*. Alfonso X defined their functions by law. If an *adelantamiento* touched the Moorish frontier, the governor was called *adelantado de frontera*. The legislative tendency, also initiated by Ferdinand III and greatly developed by Alfonso X, was more important and progressive. This tendency took two directions: the unification or steps towards the unification of law, and the introduction of the doctrines of the Justinianean Code. Unification was prepared by extending to various towns, by way of a municipal code, the application of the Visigothic *Liber Iudiciorum*, translated with some modifications into Castilian under the name of *Fuero Juzgo*, which was in force as the law of appeal in the royal tribunal. The same use was made of the so-called Royal *Fuero* promulgated by Alfonso X in 1254 and based on that of Soria. This was meant to be a typical or model municipal code and was extended to various cities such as Burgos, Valladolid, Avila, and Segovia. But this method was slow, and moreover clashed to a certain degree with the Romanising tendency favoured by the lawyers, which naturally tended towards juridical doctrines of a more modern character. Accordingly the late thirteenth century and the early fourteenth century is a time of erudite juridical compilations, sometimes the work of individual jurisconsults, sometimes the result of official orders, but seldom attaining legal authority. Nevertheless these compilations often had greater weight in jurisdiction than the very laws promulgated by the kings. Such was the case notably with the juridical encyclopedia, 1256–63, of Alfonso the Learned, drawn up in the form of a code and generally known by the name of the *Siete Partidas* because it is divided into seven books. Although composed by jurisconsults, some of whose names are known, the king himself directed the work, wrote a great amount of it, and revised the compilation of his collaborators. It draws upon the *fueros* and customs of Leon and Castile, but much more upon the Justinianean Code, the Italian commentators, and the Canon Law. Even these elements were not slavishly copied, but rather remodelled with modifications, which in some matters, such as the doctrine of royal authority, rectify the Caesarism so prevalent in the writers and the religious and political theories of the time. The *Partidas*, though not promulgated as law, were immediately established as a text-book in the universities, not only in the kingdom of Castile but in those of Aragon and Portugal as well, and through the students of law it exercised great influence upon jurisprudence.

Another compilation less extensive, known as the *Espéculo*, composed either during the reign of Alfonso the Learned or that of Sancho IV, had a similar influence. While these innovations were being made in juridical principles, the municipal institutions were developing in the direction of self-government. The first municipal organisations, whose *fueros* or charters contain economic and iuridical privileges and the recognition of individual rights, worked under the authority of the king and the immediate direction of the count representing the king. The judges who administered justice were appointed by the king either directly or through the *juntas* or judicial assemblies presided over by the count. In addition to these judicial assemblies, there were also others composed of all the householders, which like the ancient rural *juntas* of the Visigoths (*concilium vicinorum*) concerned themselves with local affairs connected with land, irrigation, and cattle. Some of these assemblies are called *concilios* in documents of the period, whence the Castilian word *concejo*, which later came to mean the corporate entity of the town.

By degrees the cities obtained, either from the king or from their seigniors, the right of electing their own judges as distinct from the royal judges in order to reduce litigation and to settle questions of general interest to the citizens. The exercise of this right, which gained ground during the period we are considering, gave to the *concejos* or municipalities a more democratic tendency and a growing feeling of strength and importance, particularly in the principal towns such as Burgos, Toledo, Valladolid, Seville; and it strengthened their influence in the Cortes on matters of general policy. But the equality imposed by the *fuero* on all citizens, of whatever class, could not prevent strife between the classes for the exercise of power, especially when the assemblies were replaced by town-councils or *Cabildos*, executive corporations composed necessarily of smaller numbers than the assemblies and elected by the householders. These struggles were less violent in Leon and Castile than in Catalonia, Valencia, and other regions. Nevertheless in the long run the result was that the *Caballeros* of noble or plebeian origin took possession of the town-councils or dominated them.

In the kingdom of Aragon, through special circumstances of a social and economic nature, the two cities most typical and most advanced in their autonomy were Barcelona and Valencia, the former being the capital of the ancient county and the latter the capital of the new kingdom created by James I. But on the other hand these cities were the scene of the hottest political struggles between the rich burghers and the plebeians.

The importance of the Cortes also increased during this period through the combined effect of all the afore-mentioned circumstances and of the struggles between the nobility and the king, who sometimes from motives of policy and frequently of necessity sought the support of the municipalities and of the Cortes which represented them, particularly in Leon and Castile. For some time these two ancient kingdoms, definitely united as we have seen under Ferdinand III, had separate Cortes; but already in the time of Alfonso X they met together, and the fusion was finally established in the fourteenth century. But the existence of three separate Cortes for the three great territories of the Crown of Aragon was maintained, except in certain exceptional cases. There were therefore separate

Cortes in Aragon, Catalonia, and Valencia. Among their functions was the singular right known as the *derecho de greuges* or *agravios*, which meant the presentation of protests made by the municipalities or by other bodies attending the Cortes against the king or his officers for infringements of law. As time went on they also enjoyed a greater share in legislation than the Cortes of Leon and Castile. The origin of this does not appear to be earlier than 1283, that is to say than the reign of Peter III. Unanimity was necessary for the passing of any resolution. The principal cities disposed of a number of votes, while the less important had only one. Saragossa and Barcelona had five votes each.

When, on account of the death of the king and the extinction of the dynasty through lack of direct heirs, a new king had to be elected, the Cortes held a special meeting which took the name of Parlamento. Such a meeting was first held at Borja in 1134 and elected Ramiro the Monk as King of Aragon. During the intervals between the sessions of the Cortes, a Junta or Committee, appointed by the Cortes, sat, called *Diputación General* in Aragon and *Diputación General* or *Generalidad* in Catalonia. The formal existence of this Junta cannot be clearly traced before the fourteenth century. Navarre and Valencia had similar permanent committees of the Cortes. The duty of the Junta was to watch over the observance of the laws and the expenditure of public funds.

In the reign of James II, and even more so in that of Peter IV after the defeat of the Unionists, the special institution, which probably originated in the twelfth century, known as the *Justicia Mayor de Aragón*, became particularly important. James I on the petition of the nobles granted to this judge, who was a member of the Curia or Royal Tribunal, the power of holding a court of first instance and also of hearing appeals from the courts of the local justices. In the Cortes of 1348, Peter IV made the office tenable for life, with the special function of interpreting the *fueros* and acting as judge of *contrafuero* or violation of *fueros*. In this capacity the *Justicia Mayor* saw to the fulfilment of the *fuero de manifestación*, a sort of legal guarantee by which the accused was kept in a special prison while the competent judge dealt with the case. The *Justicia* also saw to the enforcement of the *fuero de firma de derecho*, which guaranteed the personal liberty and the property of the litigant, except in cases of serious offences, during the time he remained uncondemned, a guarantee similar to the *mesures conservatoires* of the present law. These two powers of the *Justicia* played an important part in later centuries, when the struggle developed between the absolute monarchy and the *fueros*. On the other hand, the power also granted to him of acting as mediating judge between the king and the nobles was no more than a moral guarantee which has been compared to a sheathed sword. Only once, in the time of James II, did the *Justicia* settle a question of that nature between the king and the nobility.

Finally, a fact of considerable importance from the economic as well

CH. XX.

as from the legislative point of view was the creation, in Valencia in 1283, Majorca in 1343, and Barcelona in 1347, of a court to deal with commercial affairs, known as the Court of the Consulate of the Sea. Simultaneously, there appeared at Barcelona (in, or shortly before, 1283) a collection of commercial law (*Llibre del Consolat de Mar*), thus giving legal form to the customary maritime law which had been elaborated during the preceding centuries along the eastern coasts of Spain.

CHAPTER XXI

RUSSIA. 1015–1462

By accepting, in 988, Christianity from the Greeks, St Vladimir did nothing more than give a new expression to an existing state of things. Constantinople was already the economic metropolis of Russia; it was now explicitly recognised as its religious metropolis. The new-born Russian Church became an ecclesiastical province of the patriarchate of Constantinople, with all the cultural consequences implied by such a dependence. This state of things continued for some time to correspond to the economic and political situation. But even when, after the middle of the eleventh century, the commercial relations of Kiev with Constantinople were severed by the nomads of the South Russian steppe, the cultural and ecclesiastical connexion remained. Russia had definitely become a part of Eastern Christendom. When the breach between the Greek and Latin Churches became final, Russia remained with the Greeks, and thus outside the pale of Western Christendom. Isolated geographically from the Greeks and the Orthodox Balkans, she was isolated culturally and religiously from her neighbours in the West. This isolation is the main fact in the subsequent history of Russia.

On the death of Vladimir in 1015[1] his power devolved on all the surviving members of his family. These included Svyatopolk, son of Vladimir's elder brother Yaropolk, and his own stepson; the children of Vladimir's eldest son Izyaslav, who had been made Prince of Polotsk in his father's lifetime and had died in 1001; and several sons by different mothers, for in his heathen days Vladimir had had many wives and concubines. Svyatopolk, who was married to a daughter of Boleslav, Duke of Poland, became Great Prince[2] of Kiev; the sons of Izyaslav remained in their patrimony of Polotsk; the others retained as princes the several cities where they had been installed by their father as his lieutenants. Immediately after Vladimir's death Svyatopolk attempted to restore his uncle's monarchy by eliminating his brothers. He caused Boris, Prince of Rostov, and Gleb, Prince of Murom, to be murdered (July–September 1015). But Yaroslav, Prince of Novgorod, rose to avenge them, and a war began in which Svyatopolk called in the help of his Polish father-in-

[1] For an account of the reign of Vladimir (Vladímir) see *supra*, Vol. IV, Chap. VII, pp. 208 sqq.

[2] In accordance with its meaning in modern Russian it is customary to translate the Old Russian *knyaz'* by *Prince*. This, however, for the earliest period is not correct. Not only is the word (old Slavonic *kŭnĕdzĭ*) identical with the old Norse *konung*, Anglo-Saxon *cyning*, but Latin writers of the eleventh–twelfth century invariably translate it by *rex*. As late as 1227 Honorius III addresses a bull *universis regibus Russiae*.

law, but was ultimately defeated and fled abroad, where he perished obscurely (1019). Yaroslav became Great Prince of Kiev, but his brother Mstislav of Tmutarakan', a warrior who remained long famous in literary and oral tradition for his adventurous bravery, claimed his part in the succession of his deceased kinsmen. He defeated Yaroslav, and ruled over the whole country east of the Dnieper. Only on Mstislav's childless death in 1035 did Yaroslav become sole ruler of Russia as his father had been.

The years of Yaroslav's undivided rule and those immediately following are the golden age of Byzantine Kiev. The work of Byzantinisation, scarcely begun by Vladimir, was now carried on apace. The Church spread its influence. In the martyred Princes Boris and Gleb, now canonised, Russia received her first national saints, for St Vladimir seems to have been canonised only in the thirteenth century. The great monastery of Pechersk was founded, and Ilarion, first Russian Metropolitan of Kiev, in his sermons rivalled the most sophisticated Greek orators. Yaroslav was a great builder. The churches of Kiev, especially the cathedral of St Sophia, their frescoes and mosaics, are among the most characteristic monuments of eleventh-century Byzantine art. Commerce flourished, and Kiev became, next to Constantinople, the wealthiest and most beautiful city of Eastern Christendom, "clarissimum decus Graeciae et aemula sceptri Constantinopolitani," says Adam of Bremen. This period of intense Byzantinisation also saw the last Russo-Byzantine war (1043–46), in which the Russians, led by Yaroslav's eldest son Vladimir, were at first successful by sea, but a Russian army which landed at Varna was completely destroyed by the Greeks. The peace, however, was followed by the marriage of Yaroslav's son Vsévolod to a Byzantine princess[1]. At home these years were a time of peace. Russian rule was extended and solidified along the frontiers, especially in the direction of Livonia, Lithuania, and Poland. In the south conditions were also exceptionally favourable: the Patzinaks had moved westwards (they are heard of on the Dnieper for the last time in 1034), and were replaced by the much less dangerous Torks (Uzz Turks), who gave little trouble to the Russian marches. Yaroslav's dynastic relations extended also to the west of Europe his daughter Anne was married to Henry I, King of France. Yaroslav was the last Russian prince to keep in close touch with the Scandinavian North. Northmen gave him active help in the struggle with Svyatopolk; Harald Hardrada married his daughter; and his son Izyaslav's wife was the daughter of Harold of England.

On Yaroslav's death (1054) authority once again devolved on the whole family: Izyaslav-Demetrius, his eldest surviving son, occupied the throne of Kiev, while the younger brothers, Svyatoslav and Vsévolod, received the other principal cities, Chernigov and Pereyaslavl. Vseslav, Prince of Polotsk, who had kept quiet as long as his uncle Yaroslav lived, and Yaroslav's grandson Rostislav (the son of Vladimir Yaroslavich, who had

[1] See *supra*, Vol. IV, p. 111.

died before his father), dissatisfied with their share in the partition, rose in arms, but were easily suppressed and Vseslav was brought a prisoner to Kiev. The conditions of Yaroslav's time might have continued but for the introduction of a new factor: in 1061 the Cumans (in Russian *Pólovtsy*), a powerful and warlike nation, made their first appearance in the South Russian steppe, forced the Torks to retire behind the Russian frontier, and, in 1068, inflicted a crushing defeat on the united armies of Izyaslav, Svyatoslav, and Vsévolod (near Pereyaslavl). This victory of the nomads had lasting consequences, for it assured their mastery of the South Russian steppe, and put an end to the commercial connexion of Kiev with Constantinople by closing the Dnieper waterway. It had a more immediate effect, too: the defeated Kievian militia, returning home on the heels of the flying Izyaslav, deposed him and proclaimed his prisoner Vseslav of Polotsk Prince of Kiev. Izyaslav fled abroad, but returning the following year with a Polish army instituted a reign of terror against all whom he suspected of having favoured Vseslav. Svyatoslav and Vsévolod were alarmed at the success of Izyaslav, who had acted all the time on his own, introducing foreigners without consulting his brothers. The citizens of Kiev were indignant at Izyaslav's methods of suppression, and opened their gates to his brothers. Svyatoslav was proclaimed Great Prince. Izyaslav escaped abroad and for several years wandered an exile in the West, trying to interest in his cause first the Emperor and then the Pope, promising to the former the submission of Russia to the Empire, to the latter its adhesion to the Latin Church. Ultimately he once again secured a Polish army, and marched with it into Russia. By that time Svyatoslav had just died, and Vsévolod allowed his elder brother to enter Kiev unopposed (1076). The sons of Svyatoslav found themselves excluded from their patrimony of Chernigov. One of them, Roman, was Prince of Tmutarakan' and in that outlying sanctuary beyond the reach of their uncles he gave hospitality to his eldest brother, Oleg. In 1078 Oleg issued forth to assert his rights to Chernigov. He brought with him an army of Cumans, thus establishing a precedent that was followed in the following century and a half by countless princes. In the battle that ensued Oleg was defeated, but Izyaslav was killed, and Vsévolod succeeded to the throne of Kiev.

Vsévolod's reign (1078–93) was comparatively quiet, though Oleg and the disinherited princes, established at Tmutarakan', gave ceaseless trouble. So did the Cumans, but they were held in check and often severely chastised by Vsévolod's son Vladimir Monomakh, grandson on his mother's side of the Emperor Constantine Monomachos, a prince who early began to acquire a universal popularity. Vsévolod himself, a good Christian and a generous lord to his companions and citizens, was much loved by the people of Kiev and approved of by the clergy, who had a predominant influence on the moulding of general opinion.

On Vsévolod's death the Kievians wanted to have Monomakh for his successor, but the latter, respecting the rights of seniority, withdrew to his patrimony of Pereyaslavl, and Svyatopolk-Michael, son of Izyaslav, became Great Prince. Oleg again emerged from Tmutarakan', and once more marched on Chernigov with an army of Cumans. He succeeded in establishing himself at Chernigov, but this did not stop the war. It continued with varying fortunes and great devastation till 1096, when on the initiative of Monomakh all the princes were convoked to a peace conference at Lyúbech on the Dnieper, north of Kiev. The conference proclaimed the doctrine that each prince was entitled to inherit his patrimony (*otchina*), that is to say, the city and territory that had been his father's, and in accordance with it Oleg and his brothers were allowed to keep Chernigov, the other disinherited princes also receiving adequate shares.

The agreements of Lyúbech had a lasting effect on the territorial constitution of Russia; by identifying the several branches of the house of St Vladimir with the various principalities of Russia they gave official consecration to the growing importance of the latter. They are an important formal landmark in the process which changed the Russia of St Vladimir and Yaroslav centred round Kiev to the Russia of the later twelfth century with its numerous local centres of roughly equal importance.

In the tenth and eleventh centuries the Russian State, founded by Oleg and Igor', was the common inheritance of the princely family. As long as the family consisted of a father and his sons, with perhaps a nephew or two of distinctly inferior importance, the distribution of authority was simple: the father was the head of the house, and his sons were his limbs rather than independent persons. He "sat" in Kiev, and they acted as his lieutenants in the other towns. But when the father died and the paternal authority devolved on an eldest surviving brother (or cousin as was the case with Svyatopolk) the situation became different. The authority of an elder kinsman of the same generation was much weaker than a father's. His younger brothers regarded him as no better than a *primus inter pares*. His every attempt to assert or extend his authority aroused opposition, and the situation invariably ended in war. On the other hand, the surviving brothers were inclined to exclude from a share in the succession their nephews whose fathers were dead; the orphaned nephews claimed their father's share, and this was another cause of dispute. The territorial principle proclaimed at Lyúbech introduced a new element of stability, but also increased the mutual independence of the princes and favoured centrifugal tendencies.

Russia (*Rus'*) was at first the name of the country round Kiev. The Eastern Slavs, a politically amorphous congeries of tribes, had originally no common name, until they were conquered by the "Russians" of Kiev and gradually adopted the name of the conquering group. The conquests of Svyatoslav and Vladimir, and the consolidating work of Yaroslav, extended the Russian State so as to coincide with, and partly to overlap, the ethno-graphical area of the Eastern Slavs. In the twelfth century the term *Rus'* is used in two senses, a narrower to denote the Kiev country, and a wider covering the whole country ruled by the house of St Vladimir. Afterwards the narrower sense was lost, and the wider alone subsisted.

The domination of Kiev over the other lands was at first purely pre-datory; only the towns round Kiev and along the great north-to-south waterway (especially Novgorod) were the associates of Kiev, being allied to it by common interests. The hinterland east and west of the waterway was a field of exploitation. Its rôle in the economic system of Kiev was purely passive; an eloquent illustration of this is the fact that in the tenth century the main article of export from Russia was slaves. But in the eleventh century this is replaced by a more settled system of tributes and fees, and the hinterland is drawn into more regular and less one-sided relations with Kiev. The multiplication of the ruling family was one of the causes that led to a more intensive and economic system of exploita-tion; the local princes began to see their interest in the development of their territories; the foundation of every new principality was the forma-tion of a self-dependent financial centre that had not to feed Kiev, or any other city. The multiplication of principalities destroyed the political cohesion of Russia, but favoured the development of the resources of the land.

After the death of Yaroslav, Kiev ceased to be the administrative metropolis of Russia, but it retained a precedence over the other towns. Its prince was the Great Prince. The oldest surviving member of the house of St Vladimir had a vague right to the throne of Kiev, and more often than not was able to assert it. This right to the throne of Kiev continued to give a unity to the princely family as a whole. But at the same time it was dissolving into secondary families, in each of which the same state of things was repeated on a diminishing scale: as long as it was a father and sons the family remained one; as soon as the father died, it budded out into as many new family-units as there were fatherless princes, and each of these tended to identify itself with one of the towns or districts of the principality. This natural process of multiplication transformed in less than two centuries the quasi-centralised kingdom of Vladimir and Yaroslav into an infinity of greater and smaller territories ruled by closely related, but mutually independent, princes.

The founders of the two principal branches of the house of St Vladimir were Yaroslav's third and fourth sons, Svyatoslav of Chernigov and Vsévolod of Pereyaslavl. From the names of their two most famous sons the two branches came to be known as the Ol'govichi and the Mono-makhovichi. It is characteristic of the conditions of the mid-eleventh century, when all interest centred round Kiev, that the residences of the two princes next in seniority to the Great Prince were both situated within easy reach of Kiev, while their hinterlands stretched far away into the east and north, a distribution similar to that of the residences of the Merovingian kings.

Chernigov was the key to all the basin of the Desna and of the country situated east of it. Its territory included the whole or the greater part of the later provinces of Chernigov, Kursk, Orel, Kaluga, Tula, Ryazán', the south of Moscow and Vladimir, and the west of Voronezh and Tambov. Its eastern part was the land of the Vyátichi, the last of the Russian tribes to be drawn into the Kievian system, and not finally Christianised before the twelfth century. A younger branch of the house of Chernigov became Princes of Ryazán' and Murom on the Oká in the north-east of the territory, and were eventually drawn into the north-eastern political system, becoming vassals of the Princes of Suzdal'.

The immediate territory of Pereyaslavl was less extensive. It included the steppe-land east of the Dnieper and south of the Desna (roughly co-extensive with the modern province of Poltava), but its princes also ruled the territory of Smolensk, the important junction-land of all the Russian waterways, where the headwaters of the Dvina, Volkhov, and Volga basins are within easy reach of the Dnieper; and the vast land of Rostov, which included all the upper Volga basin, and was destined to become the birth-place of the Muscovite Empire.

Novgorod, the northern terminus of the great waterway and the metropolis of the north, was from an early date closely connected with Kiev. Of primary political and economic importance, it was, in the eleventh and twelfth centuries, usually governed by a son of the Great Prince and thus failed to identify itself with any particular branch of the family.

The north-western branch of the great waterway formed the principality of Polotsk, and included the northern part of what is now White Russia. It was the first part of the Russian territory to become the patrimony of a separate house of princes—the descendants of St Vladimir's eldest son, Izyaslav. With the exception of Vseslav, they took little part in the common affairs of Russia, and their country sank to the level of a provincial backwater. The same may be said of the other White Russian principalities, Gorodno (Grodno) and Pinsk, which in the twelfth century became the patrimonies of princes who had failed to uphold their rights of seniority in the general competition for Kiev and other coveted places.

Much more important were the south-western lands of Volhynia and Galicia. The former included the western part of the later province of Volhynia and had for its capital Vladimir (called Vladimir-Volynski to distinguish it from the northern Vladimir that was to become so important later on). After some vicissitudes it became the possession of a branch of the Monomakhovichi. Galicia, called so from the town of Galich (Halicz), which became the capital only in the twelfth century, was at first a bone of contention between Russia and Poland, but became finally Russian in the eleventh century. It was recognised at Lyúbech as the patrimony of the descendants of Rostislav, son of Yaroslav's eldest son Vladimir. But Galicia began to play a prominent part only in the later twelfth century. Between Volhynia and Kiev, near the modern towns of Berdichev and Vinnitsa, was situated the curious little land of Bolokhovo, which is still something of a puzzle to historians. It seems to have been inhabited by a peculiar, though Russian, population, and to have had princes of its own that did not belong to the house of St Vladimir.

The metropolitan territory of Kiev, the ancient Russia in the strict sense, included, round the capital and south of it, a strip of steppe or semi-steppe, the land of the Polyane (steppemen), and north-west of it a large tract of forest-land, the land of the ancient Derevlyane (woodmen). This included the town of Turov, which at times was an independent principality. But on the whole the Kiev country was not subdivided as the other lands were into minor principalities; the "by-towns" (*prigorody*) of Kiev were usually held by the sons of the Great Prince or by his lieutenants. The southern part of the territory, like that of Pereyaslavl, was exposed to nomad inroads and was strongly fortified. In the twelfth century its population consisted largely of nomads, hostile to the Cumans and in the service of the Prince of Kiev. Kiev did not succeed in becoming identified with a definite line of princes. The people of Kiev were devoted to the Monomakhovichi and did their best to keep them, but the attraction of the metropolis, of its riches, and of its prestige of seniority was too great for the other princes to abandon attempts to possess it.

Russian society in the eleventh century was urban and aristocratic. The part of the rural population (*smerdy*) was entirely passive. At first the object of predatory exploitation on the part of the princes, and of the armed merchants whose interests the princes represented, with the opening-up of the hinterland and the development of agriculture the rural districts became organised into manors belonging to the princes and to the urban aristocracy. Their inhabitants instead of being systematically raided now became the object of protection on the part of the ruling class, as the source of their revenues. Especially in the south they had to be defended from the ever-menacing nomads, and, among his other virtues, Monomakh was universally praised for his solicitude for the *smerdy*. The general term for the aristocracy was *boyare* (singular *boyarin*). They consisted of two main groups: one were the prince's *muzhi* (singular *muzh*, "vir," opposed to *lyudin*, "homo," as the commoners were called), who followed their prince in his movements, acted as his captains and lieutenants, and forming as they did a permanent following round him (*druzhina*) made him a political and military power. Practically the only expenditure of the prince, except the expenditure prescribed by his Christian duties, was on the maintenance of his *druzhina*. The other section of the aristocracy was the local magnates, connected not with the shifting prince but with the stable town. Originally they were mainly commercial capitalists, but with the opening-up of the hinterland and the progress of agricultural exploitation their main power came to reside in their rural possessions. The local, territorial aristocracy were in principle distinct from the prince's *druzhina*, but individually many of the prince's companions came from the territorial families, and in later times, at any rate in the north-east, the identification of the two became the rule. But in other parts the aristocracy appear as a distinct group opposed to the prince, as in Galicia, or quite independent of him, as in Novgorod.

A political force at least as active and as important as the boyars were the people of the large towns. From the beginning they formed a militia distinct from the prince's *druzhina*, the urban *tysyacha* (thousand). At its head stood an elective magistrate, the *tysyatski* (chiliarch). It is precisely in the form of an armed militia returning home from battle that the people of Kiev make their first appearance as an active political force, on the occasion of the deposition of Izyaslav in 1068. The militia was the nucleus of the *vêche*, the general gathering of citizens, which becomes a regular institution in the twelfth century. In Kiev we see it chiefly in moments of emergency treating with rival princes, deposing and proclaiming them. But this may be due to the nature of our evidence, the annalists being interested in events rather than in institutions, and paying little attention to normal administrative proceedings. We have no Kiev charters, but two Smolensk charters have come down to us (1150 and 1229) which shew the Smolensk *vêche* acting as a regular part of the political body in normal and peaceful circumstances. But until we come to Novgorod, we find no attempt on the part of the *vêche* to eliminate or supersede the prince.

The prince was the born and natural executive power. Only he could defend the town and the land, for he was inseparable from his *druzhina*, the only trained military force in the country, and only he could administer justice. In return for this he was entitled to large revenues, consisting of judicial fees, of duties on trade, of various tributes and levies, and of the incomes of his manors, the latter item growing in importance with the general growth of the importance of agriculture and decline of commerce. The prince's dependants, his *muzhi*, and minor followers (*otroki*, "boys"), and his tenants formed a privileged group specially protected by law.

Our knowledge of Old Russian law comes chiefly from the *Russkaya Pravda*, which has come down to us in numerous and varying redactions. It was not an official code, but a private compilation of the practice and principles of Russian secular law. Its nucleus goes back to the times of Yaroslav. Being the creation of the urban classes and intended for their use, it contains few regulations concerning landed property, but many concerning slavery, and various forms of semi-slavery arising out of debts. Its penal system is entirely based on fines. In general it presents a society ruled mainly by economic relations, where power went with money. Slavery continued to be a prominent feature in Russian society until in the seventeenth and eighteenth centuries it was merged in the much more recent institution of serfdom. The Church had a jurisdiction of its own which extended on the one hand over the clergy and other classes dependent on them, on the other over certain categories of offences (heresy, crimes against chastity, etc.). The law applied by the Church was Byzantine Canon Law. The dependants of the Church like those of the princes formed a "peculiar" inside Russian society ruled by different laws. The Church began to acquire property from the outset, but it was only in post-Tartar times that it grew into an independent political and economic force.

However lasting their effects on the territorial constitution of Russia, the agreements of Lyúbech did not put an end to the constant feuds of the princes, and were even followed by a particularly notorious outbreak of fratricidal strife. Immediately after the conference, David of Volhynia, suspicious of his neighbour the Galician Prince Vasil'ko, treacherously seized him with the connivance of Svyatopolk and had him blinded. Monomakh tried to organise a punitive war against David, but the latter, largely availing himself of Cuman help, defended himself for four years against the avengers of Vasil'ko. At last, again on the initiative of Monomakh, a second conference was called at Vitichev (1100), where David finding himself under the boycott of all his kin had to resign his throne of Vladimir in Volhynia and content himself with some minor towns.

This inaugurates a comparatively long period of relative peace (1100–32). The dominating spirit of the period is Vladimir Monomakh, Great Prince of Kiev from 1113 to 1125; before 1113 he was only Prince of Pereyaslavl, Smolensk, and Rostov, but his influence, due to his achievements at Lyúbech and Vitichev and to his successes against the Cumans, was already paramount. He answered exactly to the ideal of a prince as conceived by the best part of Kievian society, the peaceful middle class of the towns, represented mainly by the clergy and with the annalists as their mouth-piece. A brave and able warrior, Monomakh applied his military virtues not to self-seeking aims but to the defence of the Russian borderland from the Cumans. Brave but not ambitious, manly and pious, a good Christian, a generous lord to his companions, and a practical man both in conciliating princes and in opening up his distant northern possessions, Monomakh stands out as the most attractive figure of a prince of the Kievian period. He is also the one we know best, for the annalists like to speak of him, and his own *Instruction* to his sons has also been preserved. It is one of the most remarkable of Old Russian literary documents, a self-portrait drawn with manly dignity and Christian humility.

The *pax Monomachica* continued under the reign of Monomakh's eldest son Mstislav (1125–32), who was the last ruler of Kiev to exercise an effective moral authority over the other princes. With Mstislav's younger brother Yaropolk (1132–39) a new period of feuds begins. The house of Monomakh becomes divided against itself: Mstislav's sons Izyaslav and Rostislav, ambitious for the throne of Kiev, begin an endless struggle against their uncles, the younger brothers of Mstislav, of whom the most powerful was Yuri Dolgoruki (George Long-Arm) of Suzdal'. The Ol'govichi of Chernigov lost no time in profiting by the new situation: on Yaropolk's death, Vsévolod Ol'govich occupied Kiev, and was recognised as Great Prince by the Kievians, in spite of their traditional devotion to the Monomakhovichi. Vsévolod (1139–46) was an able and redoubtable prince, but on his death his younger brother Igor' proved unequal to the task. The hostility of the Kievians to the house of Chernigov broke forth. They rose against Igor', looted his palace, deposed and imprisoned him, and opened the gates to Izyaslav Mstislavich. Izyaslav was a warrior prince with a strong sense of honour and a religion of the pledged word, but his one aim in life was to advance the personal ambitions of himself and his brothers. His reign (1146–54) was a ceaseless war against his uncles and against the Ol'govichi. The people of Kiev stood staunchly by him. In 1147 when he was away fighting, news came that some younger princes of the house of Chernigov, who had been fighting on Izyaslav's side against their elder cousins, had gone over to the enemy. Infuriated by this treachery, the people of Kiev dragged the unfortunate Igor', who since his deposition had been shorn monk, out of his prison and tore him to pieces, in spite of the sincere but ineffective protests of Izyaslav's brother and lieutenant, Vladimir. The account of this episode in the chronicle is a most powerful and poignant picture of a mob goaded into senseless cruelty by bad news from the front. The intense local feeling that was growing and centring round the local dynasties is illustrated by the fact that, after being murdered in Kiev, Igor' almost immediately came to be venerated as a saint in Chernigov.

In 1154 Izyaslav died. His uncle Yuri of Suzdal' at length was able to become Great Prince of Kiev. But his reign was short, for he died in 1157. The struggle continued, until having turned out a Chernigov prince the Kievians invited Izyaslav's brother Rostislav to be their ruler. Rostislav, Prince of Smolensk and also of Novgorod, was thus able to unite under one rule the whole length of the great waterway from Novgorod to Kiev. He was one of the most able and far-sighted princes of his time. He ruled in Kiev from 1159 to 1168, and these were once more years of comparative peace. In the meantime Yuri Dolgoruki's son Andrey Bogolyubski had built up in his north-eastern land of Suzdal' a first-class military power. As soon as Rostislav died and his nephew succeeded to him in Kiev, Andrey decided to assert his supremacy in the south. A Suzdalian army led by Andrey's son, and including eleven princes, marched against Kiev. The citizens, who since the short reign of Yuri had learned to dislike the north-eastern princes, shut their gates and offered resistance. The city was stormed by the Suzdalians and pitilessly sacked, churches were burned and looted, the male population massacred, women and children led into captivity. To add to the humiliation of the old capital, Andrey, in whose name it was taken, did not transfer his residence to Kiev, but, while assuming the title of Great Prince, remained in his northern residence of Vladimir, deputing his son to rule the southern metropolis as his lieutenant (1169).

The events of 1169 mark an important epoch in Russian history, and recent historians are inclined to regard them and not the Tartar invasion as closing the Kievian period. In the tenth and eleventh centuries Kiev was the natural centre of Russia towards which, fanwise, converged all the routes from west, north, and east; it was their junction and outlet towards the sea and Greece, as well as the centre of the principal agricultural region of the whole country. But two factors militated against this state of things: the opening-up of the hinterland which made immense progress in the later eleventh and early twelfth centuries, and the loss of the lower Dnieper route owing to the final establishment of the Cumans in the southern steppe. Galicia and the land of the upper Volga became rival agricultural centres with growing populations. The latter was inferior to Kievian "Russia" in fertility, but this defect was amply made up by its complete security from the nomads behind the Oká and its belt of forests and marshland. Galicia's and Suzdal's economic connexions were not exclusively with Kiev, but, respectively, with the west and with the middle and lower Volga. These ties grew, and contributed to make the new peripheric centres less and less dependent on intercourse with Kiev. So the growth of Galicia and of Suzdal' made Kiev relatively less important in the general economy of Russia. At the same time the constant pressure of the nomads gradually diminished its absolute importance and wealth. The decisive turning-point in the history of Kiev is the last third of the eleventh century, when the Cumans, favoured by the feuds of the princes, some of whom led them as allies into Russia, secured their control over the steppe. It was then that the lower Dnieper ceased to be an avenue to Greece. By 1100 the trans-steppe colony of Tmutarakan' was finally lost. Even Monomakh, for all his organising energy and all his successes, could only laboriously keep up the *status quo* on the agricultural marches, but could not recover the control of the steppe. After the death of Mstislav (1132) the advance of the steppe is again resumed. The agricultural area recedes. Pereyaslavl, the capital of the borderland, one of the most coveted cities in the eleventh century, becomes a disagreeable and precarious outpost. The Kievian borderland is settled mainly by nomads in the Russian service (Torks, Berendeys, and the Black Kalpaks—*Chërnye Klobukí*) who play an increasingly important rôle in local Kievian politics. The sack of Kiev and the refusal of Andrey to fix his residence there is only a dramatic moment in a long process of degradation. But even after 1169 Kiev, though no longer the political or economic centre of Russia, retains its cultural and sentimental prestige as the "mother of Russian towns," the most beautiful in its buildings, the see of the metropolitan, and the site of the greatest of Russian monastic houses, the nursery garden of all ecclesiastical culture, the Catacomb or Pechersky monastery. But its political rôle is over. The centrifugal powers of Suzdal' and Galicia are now chief in the field. So far as there remains a more or less powerful centripetal force at all it is represented by the principality of Smolensk.

Smolensk had been an important town ever since the dawn of Russian history, but only in the middle of the twelfth century did it become an independent principality with a permanent dynasty of its own. Its founder was Rostislav, younger son of Mstislav Monomakhovich, whom we have already mentioned as Great Prince of Kiev in 1159–68. His descendants up to the Tartar invasion were able and powerful rulers. More often than not they were also Princes of Kiev, and sometimes also of Novgorod. The Princes of Polotsk were also in their sphere of influence. More than any other princes of their times they preserved the family tradition and the idea of the unity of the house of St Vladimir. In this respect the most notable was a cadet of the house of Smolensk, Mstislav of Torópets (*ob.* 1228). His activity extended from Novgorod to Galicia; he was always intervening in disputes, defending the Novgorod democracy from the encroachments of Suzdal', protecting orphaned minors (*e.g.* Daniel of Galicia), and winning martial renown. He may be regarded as the last in the race of princes that includes Svyatoslav, Mstislav of Tmutarakan', and his own great-uncle Izyaslav Mstislavich. Under the descendants of Rostislav, Smolensk flourished. Owing to the preservation of two charters that are among the oldest extant, we know more of the interior constitution of Smolensk than of any other Russian territory of the time. The earlier of the two (1150) is the act of endowment of the see of Smolensk with tithes from the princely revenues. It is our principal source of knowledge of the financial administration of Old Russia. The later, a treaty with Riga and Wisby (1229), shews Smolensk as a thriving commercial centre with a numerous population of foreign merchants. Both shew us the citizens—the *véche*—taking regular part in the government.

The real founder of the Galician power was Vladimirko (*ob.* 1152), nephew of the unfortunate Vasil'ko. He was a grasping and unscrupulous, often perjured prince, much disapproved of by the chroniclers, but he succeeded in building up a great military power. His work was continued by his son Yaroslav Osmomysl ("the Eight-witted"), one of the most powerful rulers of his time, who is described by the *Slovo o polku Igorevê* with little exaggeration as extending his jurisdiction as far as the Danube. After his death and the short reign of his son, the old Galician dynasty became extinct, and the country was annexed by the prince of the neighbouring Volhynia, Roman, grandson of Izyaslav II. Henceforward Volhynia and Galicia became one whole. Roman (1198–1205) was the most powerful, ambitious, and able South Russian Prince of his time. Besides Volhynia and Galicia he ruled in Kiev, and thus controlled practically the whole south. He treated as an equal with the Greek Emperor and with the

Pope, who offered him a crown, kept the Cumans in check and severely chastised the Lithuanians, a savage people that were then beginning to emerge out of their backwoods and become a serious danger to Russia. The chronicle gave him, alone of all princes, the title of *Samodérzhets* ($a\dot{v}\tau o\kappa\rho\dot{a}\tau\omega\rho$, Emperor). But his death in 1205 put an end to the first golden age of Galicia, and a period of exceedingly complicated strife followed, which ended only with the final triumph of Roman's son Daniel over all his foes (1235).

In the twelfth and thirteenth centuries Galicia was, as it is now, the most densely peopled part of the whole East European plain. It combined fertility of land with a greater security from the steppe than was the case with Kiev, with mineral wealth, and with commercial importance as the corridor to the West. Its urban development was in advance of the rest of Russia; some fifty Galician towns are mentioned by the chroniclers in the thirteenth century. Its agricultural wealth gave rise to a territorial aristocracy more ambitious and more independent than elsewhere. These boyars were as active a political force in Galicia as the urban mob was in Kiev. They could force the powerful Yaroslav Osmomysl himself to do their will; they burned at the stake his favourite mistress, and excluded from the succession his bastard son. They came to still greater prominence during the wars that followed the death of Roman. On one occasion they tried and executed two princes, on another they proclaimed prince one of their own class, Volodislav. He was promptly deposed, but these facts were without parallel in the rest of Russia. The southern part of Galicia, which extended over a large part of what is now Moldavia and Bessarabia, was an open steppe where stood the town of Berlad' (modern Bîrlad). In the twelfth century Berlad' played the part that had been played by Tmutarakan' in the eleventh, that of a sanctuary where dissatisfied Russians mixed with every kind of steppe people. This population was a ready-made army for disinherited and ambitious princes trying to recover their share in the family pie. Such a prince was Ivan Berladnik (a cadet of the house of Galicia) who gave much trouble to his cousin Yaroslav. But the most distinctive feature of Galicia's history is the constant intercourse with its Western neighbours, Poland, and especially Hungary, then by far the greater power of the two. Hungarian intervention played a large part in the feuds that followed the death of Yaroslav Osmomysl and that of Roman. With the decline of the centripetal forces in Russia the influence on Galicia of her Latin neighbours became increasingly marked.

The north-east of Russia, including the basin of the upper Volga (above Nizhni) and those of the Oká's left tributaries, the Klyaz'ma and the Moskvá-reka, had for its centres the two ancient towns of Rostov and Suzdal'; Rostov became the episcopal see, Suzdal' the political capital. The principality included the northern part of the modern provinces of Moscow and Vladimir, the north-west of Nizhni, the west of Kostromá, the whole of Yaroslavl, the south-east of Tver', and the east of Novgorod. Originally inhabited by sparsely settled Finnish tribes (Ves' and Merya), it was colonised at first, as appears from philological evidence, from the north-west. But it was opened up in the later eleventh and early twelfth centuries by its princes (whose main residence was in Pereyaslavl) Vsévolod and his son Monomakh. Monomakh founded many new towns, including the northern Pereyaslavl and Vladimir on the Klyaz'ma, which his son Yuri, the founder of the independent house of Suzdal', made his chief residence. Yuri did much for the advancement of his Suzdal' principality, but spent his last years in the struggle, crowned by a Pyrrhic victory, to win the throne of Kiev. The real founder of the greatness of the Suzdal' principality was Yuri's son and successor Andrey Bogolyubski. Like the Galician princes, but unhampered by a Galician aristocracy, he strove to build up a centralised territorial power. He definitely disregarded the idea of Russian unity and even attempted to make Vladimir an ecclesiastical province independent of Kiev. Unpopular for his policy of financial extortion, contempt of tradition, and inclination to favourites of low birth, he was killed as the result of a palace conspiracy (1174). His death was followed by two years of feuds between his nephews, the sons of his elder brother who had died before him, and his younger brother Vsévolod. The nephews had on their side the old cities of Rostov and Suzdal' with their aristocratic and municipal traditions, Vsévolod had the newer towns of Vladimir and Pereyaslavl. Vsévolod was victorious, and his reign (1176–1212) marks the height of the power of the Great Prince of Vladimir. After his death the land was divided between his numerous sons (whence his surname of "Big-Nest"), and its unity was only restored after two centuries of uphill work by the rulers of Moscow.

Like Andrey, Vsévolod, whose only rivals in power were Yaroslav of Galicia and Roman of Volhynia, aimed at creating a local power and paid scant attention to the south and to the possession of Kiev. Forestalling the policy of the post-Tartar princes, he tried to establish his overlordship over his nearest neighbours, forcing the Princes of Murom and of Ryazán' to enter into treaties of vassalage, and severely repressing their vain efforts at independence. Thus the nucleus of an upper Volga State was being formed, the basis of the future Muscovy. Unlike the rest of Russia, which opened out on Europe, the new State, situated in the upper basin of a tributary of the Caspian, faced east. It was closely connected by commerce, and at times by war, with its eastern neighbours the Bulgars of the middle Volga, a civilised, Muslim nation with extensive trading connexions in the East. The oriental connexion of Vladimir and Suzdal' is illustrated by the beautiful churches dating from this period: they are built of stone quarried in the Urals, and are closely related in style to the contemporary architecture of Georgia and Armenia. We also find that one of Andrey's sons married the Georgian queen, Tamara. But relations also existed with the West, and the chronicle mentions colonies of Greek,

German, and Czech artisans and merchants in Vladimir, as well as Jews and Armenians.

In spite of the growth of centrifugal forces, the unity of the Russian nation was still keenly felt by the contemporaries of Roman of Volhynia and of Vsévolod Big-Nest. A common language, a common dynasty, and a common ecclesiastical organisation were enough to keep the feeling alive. It found expression in the all-Russian activities of princes like Mstislav of Torópets, but above all in literature. The principal literary monument of the time is the chronicles or annals (*létopisi*). Begun in Kiev probably about 1040, the chronicles were continued in various parts of the country, but wherever they wrote the chroniclers kept an eye on happenings in the whole of Russia, and continued to regard war against the nomads and other aggressive foreigners as the chief duty of the princes and their feuds as crimes. The greater part of the chronicle is by monks and clerics, but some of it, as the remarkable account of the reign of Izyaslav Mstislavich (1146–54), is obviously by lay hands. To the end of the twelfth century belongs the masterpiece of Old Russian literature, *The Campaign of Igor'* (*Slovo o polku Igorevê*), which has for its subject the disastrous and comparatively insignificant campaign (1185) of a secondary prince of the house of Chernigov, Igor' of Novgorod-Sêversk, against the Cumans. Apart from its high poetical merits, the poem is remarkable for the keen sense of national unity inspiring it, and for the patriotic feeling with which the anonymous author blames the princes for their feuds, and exhorts the great rulers of Suzdal', Smolensk, and Galicia to come to the rescue of the brave prince who had gone out single-handed against the enemy.

In the late twelfth and early thirteenth centuries the relations of the Southern Princes with the Cumans were by no means exclusively hostile. Proximity often turned into good-neighbourliness, and marriages between Russian and Cuman ruling families were increasingly frequent. So, when in 1224 a Tartar[1] army sent by Jenghiz Khan under the command of Jebe and Subatai invaded the Cumanian steppe, it was quite natural for the Cumans to ask for Russian help, which was granted them. Mstislav of Torópets (then also of Galicia) and other South Russian Princes marched with them against the invaders. The allied Russo-Cumanian host met the Tartars at the Kalka (now Kalmius, a northern tributary of the Sea of Azov), and suffered a crushing defeat (16 June 1224). Most of the Russian princes were taken captive and put to death. The disaster produced a terrible impression, which is reflected in the contemporary chronicles. The Tartars turned back east and were not heard of for several

---

[1] The Russians called the Mongols "Tatars," which has been turned into "Tartars" in Western Europe. The name was extended to all the direct subjects of the Khans. It was primarily a political name. It has been retained by several groups of Turkish-speaking peoples. See *supra*, Vol. IV, Chap. xx, p. 630.

years. But when they reappeared it was no longer as a reconnoitring advance-guard, but as an army bent on lasting conquest, led by Bātu son of Juji and grandson of Jenghiz Khan. In 1236 Bātu conquered the land of the Volga Bulgars. In the late autumn of the following year he entered the Russian principality of Ryazán', destroyed that city, marched on to the Great Prince's residence Vladimir, destroyed that, defeated the united Northern Princes on the Sit', north-west of Yaroslavl, on 4 March 1238, and advanced in the direction of Novgorod; but deterred by the swampy nature of the country and the advancing spring, he turned south. On his southern march the only town which valiantly opposed him, Kozel'sk, was drowned in blood. In 1239 Bātu again raided the land of Suzdal'. In 1240 he started on a campaign for the conquest of the West. Kiev was taken and destroyed, and the inhabitants massacred. The Tartars swept through Volhynia and Galicia, and penetrated into Silesia. But the death of the Great Khan, rather than the very partial successes of the Latin armies, saved Europe from further invasion; Bātu had to hasten to Mongolia to take part in the election of a new Emperor (1242). In the partition that followed, Bātu received as his *ulus* the north-west of the Mongol Empire, including the Russian plain. He fixed his residence near the bend of the lower Volga, at Saray (near the modern Tsarev). The Khanate of Bātu and his successors is referred to by Muslim writers as Kipchak, by the Russians as the Golden Horde (*Zolotáya Ordá*, in Turki *Altyn Ordu*).

The Tartar invasion coincided in time with the rise of another alien race, the Lithuanians. Under Mindovg (*c.* 1235–60) they emerged from their original state of primitive anarchy and became an organised and aggressive power. Mindovg extended his authority over large tracts of purely Russian territory, including Vilna, Minsk, and Grodno. In the south-west the Lithuanians were kept in check by Daniel of Galicia, but in all other directions their devastating raids penetrated far into Russian territory, reaching as far as Novgorod, Moscow, and Kiev, so that intercourse between the north-east and south-west became difficult and precarious. The only remaining Russian power that was at all central, the principality of Smolensk, rapidly declined, crippled both by Lithuanian aggression and the destruction of Kiev, from constant contact with which Smolensk had derived much of its importance. All vitality was drawn towards the extreme periphery of the Russian territory; the only centres of population and of political action were now the Great Principality of Vladimir and Novgorod in the north and east, Lithuania in the west, and Galicia in the south-west. The centrifugal tendencies of the twelfth century now reached their natural conclusion. The Kievian unity was at an end, and the several parts of Russia were henceforward to develop along diverging roads. The thirteenth century is the age when the three modern Russian nationalities begin to take form, as distinct from each other: the Great Russians are the people of the north-east, of the lands dependent on Vladimir (and later on Moscow) and the closely connected Novgorod, the future Muscovy; the White Russians are the Russian population absorbed into the Lithuanian State; the Ukrainians are the people of Galicia and Volhynia and the other lands of the south-west.

But besides its purely disruptive effects the Tartar invasion had for its consequence the subjection of the greater part of Russia to the Golden Horde. This subjection is known in Russian historical tradition as the "Tartar Yoke" (*tatarskoe ígo*). The weight of the "yoke" varied in various parts of the country, but the only part that escaped it altogether was the lands that became subject to another alien race, the Lithuanians. The "yoke" was light in Galicia and in Novgorod, which was only indirectly subject to the Khan, in so far as it was subject to the Great Prince of Vladimir. It weighed much heavier in the north-eastern principalities, the centre of the future development of the Empire. At last a large belt of borderland in the south and south-east, more or less coextensive with the "park-land" or "semi-steppe" belt between the Dniester and the Don, and including the land of Bolokhovo, Pereyaslavl, and a large part of Kiev and Chernigov, became the actual grazing-ground of the nomads held by minor chiefs and *murzas* under the Khan of Saray. This tract was largely depopulated. But a part of the Russian population survived, and even some of the princes remained ruling over them, vassals themselves of some Tartar *murza*. As for the little anomalous land of Bolokhovo, it seems to have sided whole-heartedly with the Tartars and become their advance-guard against the Galician princes.

Galicia does not appear to have suffered very much from Bātu's invasion. Its Prince Daniel, who had been reigning since 1235, had to recognise the Tartar supremacy, but the Tartars treated him more considerately than they did his northern kinsmen; they felt behind his back the constant menace of Latin support. For a time Daniel, without openly breaking with the Tartars, cherished the hope of throwing off their yoke with the help of his western neighbours. To this end he recognised the papal supremacy and was crowned by the papal legate King of Galicia and Vladimiria (from Vladimir, capital of Volhynia). But Innocent IV proved powerless to raise the Poles and Hungarians against the heathen, and at length Daniel, disgusted by the bad faith of the Latins, renounced his allegiance to Rome. He retained, however, his title of king (in Russian, *korol'*) and transmitted it to his successors. In the latter part of his reign his attitude towards the Tartars was one of conciliating submission. This gave him a free hand against the Lithuanians, whom he kept in check; and he even at one time succeeded in making his son Shvarno their duke. In spite of the Tartar overlordship, Daniel's reign was a brilliant age for Galicia, the most brilliant in the whole history of that part of Russia. He was a great builder of churches and founder of towns, and a great encourager of commerce and industry.

After his death (*c.* 1265) the cultural conditions continued for a time unchanged. Galicia was in close contact with the West. Marriages with Western dynasties were frequent. But the political greatness of Galicia, divided between several princes, came to an end. The Lithuanians got the upper hand. In 1282 the Tartars under Khan Tulubugha invaded Galicia on their way to Poland and laid it waste. For some time the country became a grazing-ground for the nomads. The invasion seems to have been more destructive than that of Bātu, and is an important landmark in the decline of Galicia. The entries of the so-called Volhynian Chronicle[1], which relates the events of the reign of Daniel and his sons and stands out as one of the most remarkable Old Russian histories, stop after 1293. For the next half century we have practically no sources for Galician and Volhynian history. Isolated from the other Russian powers, Galicia became the prey of Western expansion. It was finally incorporated in Poland in 1347. The aristocracy went over to Rome and Polish civilisation. But the middle and lower classes remained staunchly Russian and Orthodox, and the Russian burgesses of Lvov were destined to play a principal part in the first stages of the Ukrainian revival of the sixteenth–seventeenth century.

The decline of Galicia gave the leadership in the Russian West to Lithuania, which under the successors of Mindovg became increasingly powerful. Though the majority of the subjects of the Lithuanian dukes were Russian, the Russian element failed to become dominant. The dynasty remained heathen till the middle of the fourteenth century and ultimately became Roman Catholic. Lithuania never became a consciously Russian State, and this justifies its exclusion from the present account of Russian history. But it must be borne in mind that in the fifteenth century, at the height of their power, the Dukes of Lithuania extended their suzerainty over the whole of White Russia and Ukraine (except Galicia), and far into the heart of Great Russia, as far as Tula and Orel.

The decline of the commercial importance of Kiev had gone hand in hand with a general decline of the commercial importance of Russia, due to the shifting of the great trade routes. Even the revived commercial importance of the South Russian steppe, due to the new stability given it by the Tartars, did not affect the Dnieper land; the new trade routes converged towards the lower Don, leaving the Russian lands outside the transit movement. The commercial decline of Russia is illustrated by the scarcity of precious metal which increased from the eleventh century onwards, making living cheaper, and by the decline of the relative importance of the towns. The only part of the Russian territory which retained an international commercial importance and a constitution based on urban supremacy was Novgorod.

Novgorod was the metropolis of the North. Its immediate territory

---

[1] The Volhynian Chronicle is not annalistic in form, but presents a continuous pragmatic narrative, with few dates. Hence the difficulty of an exact chronology. Even the date of Daniel's death can be only approximately fixed.

included the basin of the Neva and other southern tributaries of the Finnish Gulf. Except the south-west section of this territory, with Pskov, which ultimately grew into an independent polity, the country was largely unfit for agriculture and sparsely populated. So for its existence Novgorod had to rely on imported grain, which came chiefly from the upper Volga country, known to the Novgorodians as the *Niz* (Lower country), because at an early date they had made themselves masters of the portages from the Baltic into the Volga basin and held all the north-western headwaters of the latter. Their principal settlement in the Volga basin was Torzhók. In spite of the possession of these strategical vantage points, its economic dependence on the Niz was a very serious handicap for Novgorod, and ultimately doomed it to become the prey of Moscow.

The real foundation of the wealth and greatness of Novgorod was its northern possessions, the immense territories stretching north and east of the Baltic-Arctic divide which the Novgorodians called the "land beyond the portages" (*Závoloch'e*). Závoloch'e extended north to the Murman coast and east beyond the Urals to the mouth of the Obi. It was not so much a possession of the city of Novgorod as of individual Novgorodians. Only in the western part, especially on the White Sea and along the Dvina and its affluents, were there any permanent Novgorodian settlements. The vast north-east, inhabited very sparsely by Samoyeds and Zyryans, was only periodically raided for tribute. The chief article supplied to Novgorod by Závoloch'e was precious furs, and these were the foundation of Novgorod's economic importance. Other northern commodities distributed by Novgorod to the West were fish, whale and walrus bone, hunting falcons, salt, mica, and silver. On the whole the economic system of Novgorod may roughly be formulated thus: Novgorod sold the produce of Závoloch'e to the West, and on the money thus obtained bought grain from the Niz. But of course the produce of its export trade shewed a large surplus over what it required to pay for its grain, and Novgorod in the thirteenth, fourteenth, and even fifteenth century was by far the richest place in all Russia. The commercial greatness of Novgorod begins in the twelfth century and is closely connected with that of Wisby and of the Hansa. A characteristic feature of Novgorodian trade is that it was active in the Niz and in Závoloch'e, and passive in the West. Novgorodian merchants monopolised not only the north, but practically all the trade of the Niz. They did not as a rule trade in the West; the "Goths and Germans" came to Novgorod, but were not allowed to go any farther east or north. All Novgorodian export to the West went through the hands of the Hanseatic factory in Novgorod (St Peters Hof).

While relations with the Germans of the Hansa were friendly, Novgorod's nearer Latin neighbours, the Teutonic Knights and the Swedes, were often its enemies. This was especially so in the years following the settlement of the Knights in Livonia and the expansion of the Swedes in

South Finland. In the second quarter of the thirteenth century, influenced by papal policy, both these powers contemplated the complete reduction of Novgorod. Coming as it did at the same time as the Tartar and Lithuanian invasions, the Latin menace to Novgorod was a very real one. Fortunately the Swedes and the Teutonic Knights acted apart, and Novgorod had at the time a military leader equal to the occasion. This was Alexander, son of Yaroslav, Great Prince of Vladimir. In 1240 he defeated the Swedes under Earl Birger on the Neva, not far from the present site of Leningrad. This victory gave him the surname of Nevski. Two years later he routed the Teutonic Knights on the ice of Lake Peipus (1242). These victories fixed the territorial *status quo* for the next three centuries. The legend of these battles and of Alexander Nevski helped to keep Novgorod aloof from Western cultural influences. Its immunity from all Latin infection was quite as great as that of the Niz, and is more striking if one considers its constant intercourse with the Latins. In the century and a half following the Tartar invasion, Novgorod was the cultural and artistic metropolis of Great Russia. Much of its wealth was spent on the building and decoration of churches and monasteries. In architecture it developed a style of its own, based on the Byzantine tradition, but manifesting considerable originality, while the religious painting of Novgorod is a direct introduction to the great Muscovite renaissance of the fifteenth century.

The constitutional history of Novgorod, and of its "younger brother" Pskov, gives these two cities a unique place in Russian history. It is a development to their logical end of the republican possibilities inherent in the institutions of Kievian Russia. As has been said, Novgorod owing to its close political connexion with Kiev failed to identify itself with any branch of the house of St Vladimir. So the prince, in Novgorod, was always a stranger with no roots in the country. At first the Novgorodians seem to have resented this fact, and tried to secure for themselves a local dynasty, but before long they took advantage of the situation. The first important step towards "republicanism" was made as early as 1126, when the Posadnik, originally the prince's lieutenant and the chief civil officer in the town, became an elected magistrate. Precedent soon established that he could not be dismissed by the prince. In 1156 the bishop, contrary to the usage of other dioceses, came to be elected by the citizens, and only consecrated by the metropolitan. At the end of the twelfth century Novgorodian liberty found a dangerous enemy in the rising power of the Princes of Suzdal' and Vladimir. But from the long struggle that followed the Novgorodians emerged victorious. An important date is their victory over Andrey Bogolyubski under the walls of Novgorod on 27 November 1170. It was ascribed to a miracle of the Holy Virgin, and its anniversary has paradoxically enough become a feast for the whole Russian Church. In the early thirteenth century the Novgorodian liberties found a powerful champion in the person of the ubiquitous Mstislav of

Torópets, who was long Prince of Novgorod and whose reign may be regarded as the final establishment of the republican principle there. After Mstislav, force of circumstances made Novgorod almost invariably choose the Great Prince of Vladimir, or a near kinsman of his, for their prince, but they were now sufficiently strong to reduce him to the status of a mere magistrate (*uryádnik*) with rights strictly defined by treaty. If he attempted to infringe them he was promptly "shewn the way out." In the later thirteenth century, the princes, whose pride suffered in Novgorod from constant pinpricks, adopted the policy of not coming there in person but only sending their lieutenants. Still the dependence of Novgorod on the Niz, owing to economic reasons, was definite. When the Great Prince of Vladimir became the subject of the Khan, Novgorod was itself involved, indirectly, in subjection to the Tartars. No Tartar army ever approached Novgorod, but in 1257 the Novgorodians on the insistence of the Great Prince of Vladimir had to consent to pay the Tartar poll-tax. It is true that this Prince, Alexander Nevski, was exceptionally popular in Novgorod; and the situation did not last long.

At the height of its power Novgorod was practically a republic. The prince was a foreign potentate invited by treaty to act as chief judge and military commander. His authority was limited by the treaties meticulously and jealously. Without the elected Posadnik he could "neither pronounce judgment, nor grant land, nor issue charters." Commercial law was administered without his assistance. He could not acquire property within the jurisdiction of Novgorod, and the tribute he was allowed to collect for himself in the country districts was jealously controlled by the civic authorities. On the other hand, he was obliged to concede the right of free trade to Novgorodians in his hereditary possessions.

All authority was vested in the "sovereign people" gathered in the *véche*. It was unlimited in power. In the thirteenth century, especially under the distinctly democratically-minded Mstislav of Torópets, the influence of the lower classes, of the social democracy, seems to have been real and decisive, but, in the fourteenth and fifteenth, the capitalist aristocracy became the only real political factor, and the *véche* an instrument in the hands of individual boyars or parties of boyars. There was no procedure in the *véche*. It could only say Aye or No to the proposals put before it. These were usually prepared by a sort of unofficial cabinet (the Germans called it the *Herrenrat*) which was presided over by the archbishop and consisted of the acting and the former magistrates, Posadniks and Tysyatskies. If a party of the *véche* was sufficiently loud to shout down the other party it carried the day; if not, the parties had recourse to arms, and the bridge over the Volkhov was the scene of these judgments by battle. The executive magistrates were, like the prince, limited in power, elected for short terms, and subject to removal; the

Novgorodians were "masters of their Princes and Posadniks." The Posadnik was the chief executive, though the archbishop took precedence over him. The tysyatski (chiliarch) was originally commander of the city militia, but in later times his chief function was that of president of the commercial court.

The social constitution of the Novgorodian polity was distinctly plutocratic. The boyars were an aristocracy of capitalists, bankers, and landowners. They had enormous estates, especially in the outlying territories of Závoloch'e, and in the fourteenth and fifteenth centuries they controlled all affairs and held all the magistracies. Beneath them were the merchants, who did the actual trading and were organised into gilds. One of these, "St John's hundred"(*Ivanskoe sto*), was of special importance and exercised control over weights and measures. The common people were the chief actors at the *vêche*, but generally only as pawns in the hands of the rich. The city of Novgorod was organised into an infinity of small communities, each quarter and each street having its own organisation. The country districts (*pogosty*), the smaller towns (*prigorody*—"by-towns"), and the outlying colonies had no voice in the politics of Novgorod, but enjoyed a large amount of self-government, which was also in the hands of the local rich. When in the fifteenth century the struggle of Novgorod with Moscow entered on its final stage, the plutocratic nature of its society was fatal to it; the lower classes had no interest in supporting the oligarchy, and very largely sided with Moscow.

Pskov, at first a mere "by-town" of Novgorod, in the fourteenth century became independent, had princes of its own, and obtained the style of "younger brother" of Novgorod. Unlike Novgorod, it was agricultural rather than commercial; its country is still the principal flax-growing district of Russia. Though in the main also an oligarchy, there was less difference in wealth and more equality. Alone of all Russian lands Pskov had no slaves. Its constitution was similar to that of Novgorod, but better codified. The rights of the prince, of the two Posadniks, of the *vêche*, and of the minor townships were better defined. Pskov did not succeed in becoming an independent bishopric, and remained part of the diocese of Novgorod, but the rights of the archbishop were also strictly defined and limited by treaty, and the ecclesiastical affairs managed by an elective board representing all the parishes and monasteries of the town, of which there were eighty-five. Like Novgorod, Pskov was a home of the arts and its small churches have a charm and distinction entirely their own. Situated on the Livonian frontier, Pskov was a fighting city, Russia's farthest outpost against the Latin. Its walls were, till the sixteenth century, the best in Russia, and often withstood the Germans and the Lithuanians. Its Russian patriotism was kept alive by this border-position, and when in the struggle against Moscow Novgorod shewed itself so prone to seek help from the alien and Latin Lithuanian, Pskov invariably supported

Moscow. And it is no chance that the imperial Muscovite theory of Moscow—the Third Rome—was first voiced by a man of Pskov.

While Novgorod, Pskov, and the south-west remained comparatively unaffected by Tartar dominion, it was otherwise with the land that was to become the cradle of the Russian Empire. This was the land ruled by the princes of the houses of Suzdal' and Ryazán', with the adjoining northern and eastern parts of the lands of Chernigov and Smolensk. For two hundred and forty years it bore the chief weight of the "Tartar Yoke." The land was unfit for nomads, and the Tartars made no attempt to take direct possession of it. They only made it a tribute-paying dependency and organised its financial exploitation. In the first half-century or so following the invasion, the Khans appointed Tartar lieutenant; (*baskaki*) to Russia, whose principal office was to collect the poll-tax which the Tartars imposed on their subjects. The poll-tax was paid by all the population except the clergy, and for this end censuses were taken in 1257 and in 1275. Except for occasional punitive inroads, the poll-tax and the census were the only form in which the Yoke affected the common people. The princes were much more closely affected by it. They had to be invested with the Khan's *yarlyk* (charter) and this *yarlyk* cost much money, for the only means of obtaining it was a liberal expenditure of cash at the Horde, to the Khan, his wives, his kinsmen, and his *murzas*. It was also quite precarious, for no prince was at any moment guaranteed against his kinsman getting a *yarlyk* for the same principality by paying a higher price. Besides their money the princes had to spend much of their time in journeys to Saray, and in the earlier years even to Karakorum. Many of them never returned from these journeys, and it was customary to draw up one's testament before starting for the Horde. The Horde became a school of shameless intrigue and corruption. These conditions lasted till the decline of the Tartar power in the fifteenth century.

It is impossible to discuss here what was the cultural influence of the Tartars, and whether its effect was for the worse or not; too much depends on the values that are taken as standards. But two political results of the Tartar dominion are quite apparent, and destroy the myth of an uninterrupted evolution: it was the Tartars who made the Church an independent political force, and it was they who by constituting the Great Princes of Vladimir farmers of the Tartar tribute gave them the political instrument by which to subject the other princes and lands of Russia.

The position of the Church in Kievian Russia was analogous to its position in the Eastern Empire. It was an overwhelmingly important cultural and moral influence, but, politically, it was dependent on the secular power. Only the fact that, with two anomalous exceptions, the Metropolitans of Kiev were invariably Greeks, together with their dependence on the Patriarch of Constantinople, gave them a position of relative independence in regard to the Russian princes. The other bishops had not even this degree of independence. With the growth of monastic and episcopal land-owning, the economic importance of the Church grew, but that this in itself was insufficient to make the Church an independent political power is shewn by the example of those Russian lands which remained outside the Tartar influence—Novgorod and Lithuania, where the Church remained as dependent (in the former case on the citizens, in the latter on the dukes and magnates) as it had been before the invasion. The Tartars changed the situation. Their religious policy was one of tolerance and protection towards the priests of all religions, whom the animist Tartars regarded as having control over supernatural forces which it was prudent to propitiate. So the clergy of all religions were given a privileged treatment, in return for which they were expected to pray to their several deities for the welfare of the Khan. In Russia, the clergy were from the outset exempted from taxes and the Church given immunity from all secular jurisdiction. These privileges were embodied in special *yarlyks* issued to the Metropolitan, whose authority was thus greatly increased[1]; the Church not only became independent, but its government grew more centralised and monarchical, while its economic wealth gave it a stable basis. Throughout the Tartar period the Metropolitan must not be regarded as a subject of the Great Prince, but as an independent power. When the two became allies, as they did in the early fourteenth century, it was an alliance of two equal powers. The power of the Great Prince ultimately grew more rapidly than that of the Church, and by the middle of the fifteenth century had certainly outstripped it. But in the earlier period the situation was different, and till about the time of the death of St Alexis (1378) the Church was the predominant partner in the alliance.

After the destruction of Kiev the Metropolitans remained at first nominally attached to their old see, but its absolute degradation forced them to look for a new residence. At first they were attracted westwards, but ultimately they settled in the north. In 1300 Vladimir became the official see, and a little later St Peter (1308-26), the first regularly appointed Metropolitan of Russian birth, chose for his residence a secondary town of the archiepiscopal diocese, Moscow. It was only in the fifteenth century that Moscow became the official seat of the metropolitans. The fact that the Metropolitan of Russia had become a vassal of the Khan, and cast in his lot with the Princes of Vladimir and Moscow, made the western dioceses try to emancipate themselves from his authority. As early as 1303 the kingdom of Galicia seems to have been created a separate ecclesiastical province, but this did not last. The Dukes of Lithuania made repeated and temporarily successful efforts towards the same end, but it was only

---

[1] A bishopric, subject to the Metropolitan of Russia, was founded at Saray in 1261.

late in the fifteenth century (1458) that the western dioceses were finally separated from Moscow.

The Tartar period, especially the fourteenth century, in Great Russia (but not in West Russia) was also a period of great religious revival, of great individual religious and ascetic achievement. In Kievian times Russian monasticism was purely urban, and all the oldest Russian monasteries were situated in or near the larger towns. Great monasteries continued to be founded, and flourished in the cities, after the Tartar invasion. But at the same time there began a movement, which reached its highest point in the fifteenth century, away from human centres into the wilderness of the North Russian forest. The movement originated in the purest ascetic and spiritual impulse, but it resulted in the opening-up of the forest land and in the growth of great and wealthy monastic communities, endowed with extensive lands and immune feudal jurisdiction, which became the social and economic centres of vast regions. The greatest monasteries were those founded by the holiest and most venerated hermits, who combined ascetic purity with great organising ability. The most important of these houses were: the Trinity Monastery (Troitsa), forty miles north-east of Moscow, founded (*c.* 1335) by St Sergius of Rádonezh, the most venerated of Russian saints; the Kirilov-Belozersky Monastery, founded (1397) by St Cyril near the White Lake; and the monastery founded (in 1429) by SS. Zosima, German, and Savatiy on the island of Solovki in the White Sea.

The second political effect of the "Tartar Yoke," the growth of a centralised monarchic power, began to shew only in the fourteenth century. The end of the thirteenth on the contrary saw the decline of all central authority. The age of Alexander Nevski (1246–63) was a period of some recuperation. He spent most of his reign in journeys to Saray, and farther east to Karakorum, trying every means to alleviate the burdens of his ruined land. His policy was one of unqualified submission to the Horde. It emphasises the growing "eastward" tendency of Russia that this victorious enemy of the Latins was an obedient vassal of the Mongols. After his death (1263) he was canonised.

The following sixty years were a period of continuous strife between the princes for the "Great Principality of Vladimir." The principal rivals were the Princes of Tver', Nizhni-Novgorod, and Moscow. Those of Ryazán', who did not belong to the house of Vsévolod Big-Nest, were excluded from the competition, but remained important potentates at home. The princes who succeeded in obtaining the Khan's *yarlyk* for the Great Principality adopted the policy of not coming to Vladimir, but remaining in their original residences. Thus Vladimir sank to the level of a merely symbolic capital. But the territory and revenues attached to its possession were more important than those of any of the local principalities, even before it became linked with the right to collect the Tartar tribute.

A main feature of North-Eastern Russia in the Tartar period is the continuous multiplication of princes and principalities. Each prince was entitled to his share in the paternal domain, and where sons were numerous the principalities rapidly split up into an infinity of tiny patrimonies. This was particularly the case in the northern principalities of Rostov, Yaroslavl, and Bêlozero. But however small the principality, the prince retained in full his rights as territorial sovereign. Apart from the Great Prince of Vladimir's authority as tax-collector and lieutenant of the Khan, a prince's sovereignty could be limited only by voluntary contract. The great inequality of real distribution of power forced the lesser princes to enter into contracts of a feudal character with the greater. They commended[1] themselves to a more powerful neighbour, and became his "younger brothers" or even his "servants." Contract became the only source of obligation, and no distinction was made between public and private law. The character of the prince as judge and guardian of the peace was obscured by his quality of proprietor of lands and rights. Beneath the princes stood the untitled landowners, the boyars. Though no boyar could ever become a prince, there was little difference, beyond the title, between the two. The boyars were also privileged landowners, possessors of extensive juridical and financial immunities. They were "free servants" (*vól'nye slúgi*) of the prince. They served him at will, and could always leave him, after giving proper notice, and transfer their homage to another prince. The clause of the "free passage" of servants is included in all the inter-princely treaties of the time. The lands of the departing "servant" could not be confiscated; the personal feudal tie of the boyar was independent of the territorial subjection of his lands; and this, the lands being as a rule immune, was of the loosest kind. It is obvious that the clause of the "free passage" was advantageous to the more powerful and richer princes who could thus attract numerous and important followers. The prince was the *gospodín* of his free servants, a word more or less answering to suzerain, and opposed to *gosudár'* ("master," "owner," *dominus*) which described his relation to his inferior servants, slaves, and other possessions. The term *gosudár'*, originally a purely economic conception, grew in the fifteenth century to denote the absolute power of the unlimited monarch. It ultimately became the current and official name for the Russian monarch, and its derivative *gosudárstvo* came to denote the State in general.

Both the princes and boyars had numerous military retainers, who formed their political and military force, and tenants who provided an economic basis. The latter were called the "black people" (*chërnye lyúdi*) and played a very inferior part in fourteenth-century society; they did all the paying. Still they were free men, for there was no servitude of the glebe, and in the larger or more outlying manors they enjoyed a certain degree of self-administration, which increased in Muscovite times. There

[1] The Russian term is *zalozhít'sya*.

was also a numerous unfree population, the descendants of the older slaves, or the result of feudal surrender of liberty. The unfree class included men of a higher standing than mere domestic servants or labourers, stewards for instance and military retainers. These unfree retainers were akin to the *ministeriales* of early medieval Germany. They were better off than the free tax-paying tenant, and afterwards played an important part in the making of the Russian gentry. In general, this structure of society bears a strong likeness to the early forms of Western feudalism, but Russia never developed anything like a complete system of feudal law.

Moscow is first mentioned in 1147. Its situation on the extreme south-west border of the Suzdal' land, near the Chernigov frontier, is still reflected in the fact that near it passes the dividing line between the two principal dialects of Great Russia. This border situation became a central one when the Smolensk and Chernigov lands that had not been devastated by the Tartars or annexed by the Lithuanians became parts of the north-eastern social and economic system. The founder of the Muscovite branch of the house of Vsévolod Big-Nest was Daniel (*ob.* 1304), youngest son of Alexander Nevski. At first his possessions included only four of the thirteen districts of the modern province of Moscow, but by his death they included the important principality of Pereyaslavl bequeathed to Daniel by his childless nephew. Under Daniel's son Yuri (George) began the struggle between Moscow and Tver' for the throne of Vladimir. It was chiefly a struggle of intrigue at the Khan's court, in which Yuri proved himself more skilful than his reckless rival, Michael of Tver'. At Yuri's instigation and with his direct concurrence, Michael was put to death by the Tartars (1319). How little Moscow had yet the sympathy of Russian opinion is shewn by the fact that Michael was canonised by the Church as a martyr. A little later Yuri was in his turn killed by the Tver' party (1324). His younger brother Ivan Kalitá (John the Pouch) succeeded him in Moscow, and by dint of lavish expenditure at the Horde obtained the *yarlyk* for the Great Principality (1328). What was more, he was en-trusted with the collection of the Tartar tribute, a turning-point of primary importance for the creation of a centralised monarchy. Henceforward, except for one insignificant interval, the Great Principality, and with it the power to collect the tribute, remained with the house of Moscow.

Ivan Kalitá inaugurated the policy that was to make the fortune of his dynasty. Its main points were alliance with the Church, thrift at home, and, above all, the maintenance of friendly and peaceful relations with the Horde by constant expenditure and complete submission, in order to secure by every means the throne of Vladimir in the family. The Khan's friendship cost much, but it paid; it meant, besides the rich revenues of the Great Principality, the control of the Tartar tribute of which a large part naturally remained in Moscow. On their increased income Kalitá and his successors bought up lands and jurisdictions, and forced contracts of "younger brotherage" and vassalage on minor princes. Besides, the administration of the tribute gave a powerful means of control over the other princes, and Kalitá and his successors did not hesitate to use the Khan's armies against insubordinate rivals. Though the alliance with the Khan gave power and wealth, it did not give popularity or moral authority. In this respect a far more profitable ally of the Princes of Moscow was the Church. The Church more than any other force in Russia was inspired with the idea of national unity; the Metropolitan was in fact the only all-Russian authority, the only visible symbol of unity. In order that the ideal of unity might also materialise in the secular sphere, he had no choice but to select one among the rival princes on whom to bestow his influence. When St Peter chose Moscow rather than Tver' or Ryazán', he had two main reasons. The first was of a formal nature: Moscow was a town of the metropolitan diocese, while the capitals of the other important princes had bishops of their own, and the metropolitan could not exercise in them his episcopal rights. Secondly, the Church was closely linked with the Khans whose *yarlyks* were the foundation of its political independence, and the loyalty of the Moscow Princes made them preferable to the restless and ambitious Princes of Tver'. So, after St Peter, his successor the Greek Theognost (1328–53) followed his example, stayed in Moscow, and continued his pro-Muscovite policy.

Ivan Kalitá died in 1341. He was a far more powerful prince at his death than he had been at his accession, but how little conscious he was of his work of unification is shewn by his will, the oldest document of its kind that has come down to us: he divided his possessions in almost equal parts between his three sons and his widow; Moscow itself with all its revenue and jurisdiction was divided between the three brothers. The wording of the document is highly typical of the domestic and private attitude of the princes of the time to their possessions of whatever kind; towns, manors, jurisdictions, jewels, furs, and clothes are treated exactly in the same way and in the same language. Taken by itself the effect of the will would have been the breaking-up of Moscow into a new succession of petty principalities. But it was not in their quality of Princes of Moscow that these princes did their work of unification, but as Great Princes of Vladimir, and the *yarlyk* for the Great Principality was easily obtained by Kalitá's eldest son Simeon (1341–53), and after his death by his younger brother Ivan II (1353–59). Ivan was a weak-minded and feeble prince, and if the future of Moscow had depended as much as is sometimes supposed on the character of its princes he would certainly have jeopardised it. But it did not. A Russian prince, in the fourteenth century, was not an autocrat, except in his own manors where alone he was *gosudár'* (*dominus*), but a "Prince in Council." His councillors were the boyars, and without them he did nothing. Simeon in his will enjoined his successors to "obey them," next to "our father the Metropolitan," and a generation later Dimitri of the Don on his death-bed said to them: "your title was not boyars but princes of my land."[1] It was in the Muscovite boyars that the continuity of Muscovite policy resided, so that neither the feebleness of Ivan II nor the minority of his son Dimitri seriously endangered it. But besides the boyars there was another man who saw to the future of Moscow and of Russian unity, St Alexis, himself a member of a family of Moscow boyars, who after the death of Theognost succeeded to the metropolitan see (1354). Till his death in 1378 he remained virtual ruler of Russia, secular and spiritual. After Ivan II's death the Prince of Suzdal' succeeded in obtaining the *yarlyk* for the throne of Vladimir, but owing to the boyars at home and to the influence of St Alexis at the Horde this was promptly set aside, and the infant Dimitri once again united the possession of Moscow with that of the Great Principality. They were never again separated.

The years of the administration of St Alexis and the reign of Dimitri (who came of age about 1369) were a period when the power of Moscow received its final confirmation and consecration. Alexis exercised his spiritual authority in the interests of unity, bringing the princes to mutual peace and obedience to Moscow. Tver' and Ryazán' were humbled and reduced to vassalage, while Nizhni-Novgorod became an unequal ally. The only serious rival power, Lithuania, was now also making rapid progress under the leadership of Olgierd (1345–77) and Jagiello. In relation to the Horde the old policy of obedience was continued, but the Horde was in a state of dissolution. The dynasty of Bātu had lost all vitality and prestige. The vizier (*temnik*) Mamay became Khan-maker and was finally proclaimed Khan. Meanwhile a movement of Russian colonisation south-east of the lower Oká in the Mordvá country became a source of frontier incidents with the Tartars. When Mamay decided to retaliate and chastise the Russians, it was resolved in Moscow, for the first time, to meet him with open force. The first victory over a Tartar army was won in 1378. Mamay prepared for a more serious invasion. St Alexis was now dead, but his spiritual successor St Sergius of Rádonezh, who had refused the succession of the metropolitan see offered him by Alexis, realised that a policy of submission was no longer necessary, and gave his benediction to Dimitri's army and all his moral support to the cause of resistance. The army led by Dimitri against the Tartars included all the northern princes except those of Ryazán'. For the first time the Prince of Moscow appeared in the rôle of a national leader. Dimitri's and Mamay's armies met in the field of Kulikovo on the upper Don (8 September 1380). The battle was furious and the losses on both sides very heavy. But the Russian victory was decisive. It determined Moscow as the leader and the symbol of national unity, and became legendary. Dimitri became known by the surname of Donskoy (of the Don). But it

---

[1] One of the boyars of Simeon was Andrey Kobyla, the earliest known ancestor of the Romanovs.

caused little change in Russia's relation to the Tartars. Mamay, it is true, was overthrown. But two years later Tuqtāmish, a vassal of Tamerlane, appeared in the Volga steppe, took possession of Saray, and marched into Russia. Moscow, abandoned by Dimitri, was besieged by Tuqtāmish and surrendered. The Princes of Tver', Ryazán', Nizhni hastened to pay homage to the victor. After laying waste the lands of Moscow and Vladimir, Tuqtāmish retired to the Horde (1382). The result of his campaign was a complete reassertion of the Tartar Yoke. When Dimitri died, his son Vasili I (Basil, 1389–1425) had to go, as his fathers had gone, to the Horde, there to obtain the *yarlyk* for the Great Principality.

In Vasili's reign Russia again had to suffer from Tartar invasion. In 1395 Tamerlane, on a punitive expedition against Tuqtāmish, who had rebelled against him, entered Russia, took and destroyed Eléts, and raided the open country in the direction of Ryazán' and Kolomna; but he soon retired into the steppe, not to return. Tamerlane's invasion did not mean any increase of Tartar power in Russia, and in the following years the authority of the Horde sank to such a low level that Vasili attempted a new policy: he stopped sending the tribute to the Khan, while continuing to collect it for his own benefit. This lasted for several years, until the Khan-maker and virtual Khan Edigey, a more efficient and resolute soldier than the degenerate Khans, decided to put an end to it. In 1408 he invaded Russia and besieged Moscow. Like his father in 1382, Vasili abandoned his capital in the hour of danger, but the citizens defended themselves valiantly, shewing that in time of emergency the old municipal spirit of self-help was still alive in them. The Tartars after a fruitless siege were forced to withdraw, devastating the open country. The result of the invasion was a new reassertion of the "yoke." But the power of the Horde was irrevocably sinking, and Vasili's journey to Saray in 1412 was the last of its kind undertaken by a Russian prince. His son Vasili II and his grandson Ivan III still received investiture from the Horde, but did not go there personally; it was brought to them to Moscow by ambassadors. But attempts to shake the Yoke off by force were given up, until it became too weak to be maintained.

The period from the death of St Alexis to that of Vasili I (1378–1425) was not so uniformly propitious to Moscow as the preceding one. The invasions of 1382 and 1408 were serious setbacks to Muscovite power. In particular Moscow's hold on Tver' and Ryazán' was much weakened. The further rise of the Lithuanian power was another menace. Under the rule of Vitovt (Vitold, 1388–1430) Lithuania became a great European power. Its suzerainty extended over most of the old lands of Smolensk and Chernigov, while Ryazán' and Tver' looked up to it as a more desirable suzerain than Moscow. But Vitovt had more neighbours than Moscow to quarrel with, and his relations with Vasili I, who was married to his daughter, were more often friendly than hostile.

On the whole, however, the power of Moscow grew steadily. The

Church under the metropolitan Cyprian, a Bulgarian (1390–1406), and Photius, a Greek (1408–31), continued the policy of St Alexis though neither of his two successors had his personal influence. They gave support to Vasili's aggressive policy against Nizhni-Novgorod and against Novgorod. The annexation of the former principality (1391) was the chief territorial advance made under Vasili I. It is a characteristic example of Muscovite methods. Vasili began by purchasing at the Horde a *yarlyk* for the principality of Nizhni which dispossessed the ruling prince in favour of himself. The Prince of Nizhni on hearing this news asked his boyars if they would stand by him against the Muscovite aggression; they pledged their support. But they had already been secretly corrupted by Vasili, who had promised them advancement and rewards. As soon as the Tartar and Muscovite envoys arrived at Nizhni with the *yarlyk*, the boyars threw off the mask and placed themselves at the disposal of Vasili. The Prince of Nizhni was seized and deported to a remote Muscovite possession, and his territory incorporated in the Great Principality. Vasili's attempt against Novgorod, though vigorously supported by Cyprian, was less successful. In this case Tartar help could be of little avail. He adopted the policy of attacking Novgorod's most vital possession, the Dvina land, the heart of Závoloch'e, which was also the most exposed, as the headwaters of the Dvina were in the possession of princes dependent on Vasili. In 1396 a Muscovite army occupied the Dvina land with the aid of the local landlords who, in a charter that has been preserved, were granted autonomy under Muscovite suzerainty. But in 1398 the Novgorodians coming in force drove off the Muscovites, and the Dvina boyars were severely chastised for their treachery.

The principal aspect of Muscovite progress in these years was that St Alexis and St Sergius had given Moscow a moral and spiritual halo, and the battle of Kulikovo had consecrated it the leader of the nation. This idea of Moscow as the centre and symbol of national unity, indefatigably propagated by the Church, did as much as the aggressive policy of its princes, and even counterbalanced those aspects which worked against their popularity. Moscow now superseded Novgorod also as the cultural and artistic capital. Stone architecture, which had died out since the Tartar invasion, was revived. Literature, under the influence of Cyprian and other South Slav clerics, became ambitious and more elaborately rhetorical. But the greatest achievement of Muscovite culture was in religious painting: the age of Cyprian is also that of Andrey Rublev, the greatest painter ever produced by Russia.

In social history the reign of Vasili I is marked by the rapid growth of a new class, the "serving princes" (or "princelings," *sluzhílye knyazháta*). Ever since the time of Kalitá and Simeon, the minor princes, especially of the houses of Rostov, Yaroslavl, and Bêlozero, were entering in increasing numbers on contracts of vassalage with Moscow. At first these were contracts of "younger brotherage" under which the princes retained their sovereign rights inside their domains, only pledging themselves to follow their "elder brother" in war. Later on they began to commend their lands to the Great Prince, receiving them back from him as fiefs, and in return for good service obtaining other grants of land in other parts of the country. They retained their titles, but except for that became practically the same as the boyars. Like these latter they were "servants" (*slúgi*) of the Great Prince. The same process went on in Lithuania, and on a much smaller scale in Tver' and Ryazán'. This new element began to take precedence over the older boyars, and to throw them into the shade. The princes arriving from Lithuania and from the Chernigov lands under Lithuanian suzerainty were especially important, and as, under the clause of the "free passage of servants," they retained their lands and revenues in Lithuania, besides receiving new grants from the Great Prince of Moscow, they were far richer than any boyars. Under Vasili II these princes definitely became the upper class of the Muscovite aristocracy. Under his successors they constituted a formidable opposition to autocracy. But in the beginning it flattered the Muscovite ruler to have so many and such brilliant princes for his followers and servants.

In the reign of Vasili I's son, Vasili II (1425–62), the Muscovite power passed through the last great crisis before it finally emerged on the path of unity and autocracy. It was the struggle of the Great Prince with his nearest relatives, his uncle and first cousins. Vasili II was himself a man of no merits, no talents, and no virtue. He was universally unpopular. But as the lawful heir to the Muscovite throne he had behind him the support of the Church, of the Muscovite boyars, of Russian public opinion in general, and, last but not least, of the Golden Horde. His opponents were his uncle Yuri, and after the latter's death (1432) his sons, among whom the most energetic was Dimitri Shemyáka. It is unprofitable to follow the details of the struggle. It came to a climax in 1446 when Shemyáka succeeded in seizing Vasili and blinding him, which gave Vasili II his surname of "the Dark" (*Tëmny*). Shemyáka became master of Moscow and kept his blinded cousin in captivity. But the metropolitan, St Jonas, prevailed on him to release Vasili from prison and to give him in fief the principality of Vologda. As soon as Vasili was free and installed in his new residence, the boyars and "servant" princes began to gather round him and the struggle recommenced. He was soon victorious and Shemyáka had to take refuge with his allies, the Novgorodians. It was in Novgorod that the emissaries of Vasili succeeded in poisoning him (1453). Vasili followed up this success by a campaign against the northern city in which he was completely victorious. The conditions he imposed on Novgorod were the first step towards the loss of Novgorodian independence: the judicial fees were to go to the Great Prince, and charters to be issued in his name and not in that of the city. About the same time the Prince of Ryazán', a minor and a ward of Vasili, was transferred to Moscow, and Muscovite lieutenants were sent to govern his principality.

The year 1453, the date of Shemyáka's death, marks the end of the heavy up-hill period of Moscow's history; henceforward its successes were to be practically unopposed. By a significant coincidence 1453 is also the date of another event of primary importance for Moscow—the fall of Constantinople. The Greek Emperor gone, Moscow was now the first Orthodox power, and the head of the Orthodox world. The Muscovites were not slow in taking stock of the fact. The fall of Constantinople had been preceded in 1439 by an event which greatly emphasised its significance—the Council of Florence, at which the Greeks had consented to unite with Rome. The Metropolitan of Russia, the Greek Isidore, had accepted the Union. This on his return to Moscow led to his deposition, and, after some hesitation, to the decision to throw off obedience to Constantinople and to put up a Russian metropolitan by the sole authority of the Russian Church: this was St Jonas (1448–61). Independence from Constantinople increased the prestige of the Russian Church, but also its dependence on the secular power; and though it retained its immunities and its position as the greatest and wealthiest land-owning power in the country, and also its enormous moral and cultural influence, it ceased by degrees to be what it had been in the fourteenth century and once more became like the Byzantine Church dependent, politically, on the State.

When in 1462 Vasili II died and his son Ivan III became Great Prince and *Gosudár'* (he was the first officially to adopt the style) "of all Russia," the task before him was clear and easy. It was to assert his absolute, sovereign independence by casting off the Tartar Yoke; to assert the primacy of Russia as the heir to the Greek Emperor, and the only Orthodox monarchy in the world; to merge in a complete Muscovite unity the local particularisms of the other Great Russian polities; and to advance against Lithuania Moscow's rights to the legacy of Kiev in Western Russia. The first of these tasks was easiest of all: Ivan III had hardly to move a finger, and certainly did not hasten the event; the Tartar supremacy disappeared almost imperceptibly in 1480. The legacy of Byzantium was taken up by the marriage with a Palaeologus princess in 1471; by the adoption of the title of *Samodérzhets (autokrator)*, and, in the political consciousness of Russian society, by the theory of "Moscow—the Third Rome," first voiced by the monk Philotheus of Pskov. The independence of the old rival, Tver', was put an end to in 1484, and that of Novgorod in 1478; both demanded very little effort. Ryazán' and Pskov, loyal and not dangerous, were allowed to retain a measure of autonomy till early in the next century. At last Lithuania was forced back into the West and all the old lands of Smolensk and Chernigov became Muscovite, as the result of the war that culminated in the battle of Vedrosha (1500). The complete formal consequences of the new state of things were not, however, reached till the following century when Ivan III's grandson and namesake was crowned Tsar (from *tsêsari*—Caesar) in 1547, and the Metropolitan of Moscow raised to the rank of Patriarch in 1589.

CHAPTER XXII

THE JEWS IN THE MIDDLE AGES

The capture of Jerusalem by Titus had been no more than an episode in Jewish history. Perhaps, in the long run, the nation gained in powers of expansion and of resistance through the loss of a territorial centre. In the immediate sequel, however, its life continued without any great change save for the cessation of sacrificial worship; and Jewish culture enjoyed another period of productivity, first in its ancient seat in Palestine, and then in the newer centres of population in Mesopotamia. The fifth century, which witnessed the disruption of the Roman Empire in the West, was the period of the redaction of the Talmudic literature and of the final settlement of the forms of Rabbinic observance which gave medieval Judaism its characteristic imprint as well as its phenomenal resilience and cohesion. For, while the new peoples of Western Europe were struggling into existence, the Jew was entering into a fresh phase of his history which was to link his fate decisively with theirs.

Already before the destruction of Jerusalem, the Diaspora had been a familiar phenomenon in Europe. The prisoners captured in innumerable wars in the East and spread through the Empire as slaves had been followed (if not preceded) by merchants and traders. Philo, Seneca, and Josephus all give evidence of the extent to which Jewish observances were spread through the civilised world of their day. From early times there had been extensive colonies in Egypt, Syria, and Mesopotamia, from which there was a constant expansion. Flaccus and Mithridates had been able to enrich themselves at the expense of those in Asia Minor and the Archipelago. Paul had found them in large numbers in Greece; and the infant Church advanced consistently where the Synagogue had blazed the way. Progressively, settlers penetrated farther west. The capital itself preserved without any serious break the community against which Cicero had inveighed and Juvenal sneered; and in other places in Italy, especially along the lines of communication with the Levant, they were similarly established at an early date. The proscriptive measures of the provincial Council of Elvira, which began the tradition of Iberian intolerance, attest the strength of the settlement in Spain as early as the first decade of the fourth century. The regulations of Constantine prove the existence of regularly constituted communities in the Rhineland at the same period; and it is not likely that they were absent from the rest of Gaul, or even from the more remote provinces. Indeed, it is probable that, before the Roman Empire had begun to decay, Jews were to be found in all of its greater cities. In any case, it is highly suggestive that their presence in some numbers through Western Europe is attested from precisely the period at which the medieval world may be considered to begin.

With the Christianisation of the Empire, however, a change came about in their condition. From the period of its triumph, the Church was able to advance beyond the stage of mere polemics and to concentrate upon differentiation, which finally degenerated into oppression. With the conversion of Constantine, the ecclesiastical outlook came to be adopted almost in its entirety, though with less discrimination, by the State. From an *insignissima religio, certe licita,* as it had been to earlier jurists, Judaism became the *secta nefaria* or *sacrilegi coetus* which figure in the edicts of the first Christian Emperors. The difference of language marks a fundamental change of attitude. It is true that there were at first no juridical repercussions, the Jews being comprised in the toleration accorded by the Edict of Milan. But, while they lost none of their privileges immediately, their status became profoundly different. For the first time, there arose the conception (unknown to pagan antiquity) that civic rights were dependent upon adhesion to certain articles of belief. Judaism was changed almost in a moment into a proscribed faith, existing only on sufferance. From full citizens, suffering from only one or two minor disabilities, its followers became transformed into a recalcitrant minority which both Church and State deemed it necessary to segregate and to humiliate.

The ecclesiastical policy was far from being merely persecutory. The victory of Christianity was not yet secure; and the line of demarcation from Judaism was still in many places so indefinite as to be perilous. It was unthinkable therefore that the infidel should be allowed to exercise any semblance of authority; hence the Jew must be excluded from all office, and (whatever the economic disadvantage entailed) should not either purchase Christian slaves or retain pagan ones if they became baptised. At the same time, he should not be permitted to contaminate the purity of the faith by entering into close social relations with Christians. For this reason, feasting together and intermarriage were prohibited, and it was forbidden even to make use of the services of Jewish physicians. With the Council of Chalcedon, in the middle of the fifth century (451), this policy was finally enunciated. It must be realised that, like so much else in medieval legislation, it remained in many ways an ideal rather than a standard of conduct. Nevertheless, it set up a code to which the Church inevitably reverted at moments when circumstances rendered her peculiarly suspicious: in the twelfth century, under the menace of the Albigenses; in the fifteenth, in consequence of the Hussite movement; and, finally, in the sixteenth, in the wake of the Reformation. Thus, paradoxically enough, it was only after the Renaissance that the regulations of the early Councils were consistently enforced even by the Popes themselves.

There was, however, a positive side to the ecclesiastical attitude accompanying these restrictions. The preservation of the Jew, though in ignominy, provided in Christian eyes standing testimony to the truth of

Scripture and the punishment of guilt; while the more enlightened thought of him as custodian of the text and interpretation of Holy Writ. At the same time, while the ideal of conversion was inevitably present, it was an ideal to be achieved by peaceful persuasion, and the employment of force was deprecated. A corollary of this was that the Jews might enjoy liberty of worship and maintain their synagogues, though they should be allowed neither to erect new ones nor to embellish the old. Toleration, however, was essentially for the Jew by race. Hence the Christian who apostatised (not an uncommon occurrence even in the Middle Ages), or the Jew who received him into his faith, was liable to the penalty of death. Gregory the Great summed up the ecclesiastical policy in its double aspect. He figures in his epistles alternately as the protector of Jews far and near against injustice and as repressor of their "insolence." This was the ideal generally followed by his successors, who tended to depart from it rather on the side of lenience. It is noteworthy that, until the period of the Reformation, the rôle of patron was assumed more consistently and more frequently than the reverse. Down to modern times, the grosser libels and attacks upon the Jewish people were generally discouraged, or even prohibited, by the Papacy, save in a very few exceptional cases where a tardy and unwilling acquiescence was forced upon it by popular action. It is significant that, under the papal aegis, the community of Rome, almost alone in the whole of Europe, was enabled to continue its existence undisturbed from classical times down to the present day[1].

The delicate balance of the official ecclesiastical policy was seldom, however, appreciated by secular rulers, who generally carried it to what appeared to be its logical conclusion in the one direction or the other. The theological predilections of Byzantium in particular translated themselves into discriminatory action. The embodiment of the ecclesiastical attitude towards the Jews in the Codex Theodosianus ultimately permeated the whole of Western law with the idea of their inferiority. It was Theodosius II, too, who finally abolished the Jewish Patriarchate in Palestine on the death of Gamaliel VI without male heirs, after an existence which had continued for nearly four centuries (425). Justinian, however, besides proclaiming the Jews ineligible for any public office whatsoever (537), was the first Emperor who interfered with their religious institutions, forbidding them to celebrate the Passover before Easter or to interpret the Bible in public worship according to their traditions. Under Heraclius, the dwindling communities of Palestine were driven to a last revolt in support of the Persian invasion (614); and it seems as though the Emperor, embittered and disquieted at this or at the subsequent rise of Islām, tried

---

[1] The most memorable papal charter of liberties for the Jews was the protective Bull *Etsi Judaeis,* condemning the exercise of violence against them. Originally issued by Calixtus II in 1120, it was confirmed at least fourteen times by the middle of the fifteenth century.

to procure a general persecution throughout Europe. From this period, it became regular to attempt to procure the conversion of the Jews by force when persuasion failed, Basil I (867–886) being especially notorious in this respect. The degrading special Jewish form of oath, which continued till very recently in some countries of Europe, goes back to Constantine VII (912–959). The devastations caused by Byzantine intolerance were to be traced as far off as Apulia and northern Africa, where the very existence of the ancient communities was jeopardised.

In Western Europe, the Jews, belonging as they did essentially to the older culture, became associated after the barbarian invasions with the inferior position which was now the lot of the Roman; and this persisted as far as they were concerned when it had otherwise disappeared. Religiously, indeed, the new rulers displayed at first that tolerance which arises from indifference; while those who adopted the Arian form of Christianity were sympathetically inclined towards the adherents of a stricter monotheism, if only to enlist support against their opponents. But, with the triumph of Catholicism, the Jews were made in almost every case to feel the fervour of the neophyte, or served as the offering which proved his sincerity. It was only in Italy, under the patronage of the Ostrogoths, succeeded by the qualified protection of the Popes, that no general reaction took place, though local persecutions were not unknown.

Conditions were worst, however, in Spain, where the Jews had come to be an important element in the population. Under the Arian rulers, they enjoyed remarkable freedom and influence. After the conversion to Catholicism, the inevitable change came about. The disabilities at first imposed developed progressively into oppression[1]. Sisebut (612–621) and his more fanatical successors, at the Councils of Toledo, utterly proscribed the practice of Judaism, and gave its adherents the alternative of baptism or banishment. The repetition of these or even crueller regulations by later rulers seems to indicate that they were none too rigidly enforced; and the converts actually secured proved anything but a strength to their new faith, setting the example for the characteristically Spanish product of crypto-Judaism. In the end, there seems to have been a slight reaction in their favour. Nevertheless, it is hardly a cause for wonder that the Jews warmly sympathised with the Arab invasion, even if they did not actually invite it.

The rise of Islām had spelled disaster for the independent Jewish tribes in Arabia, which had attained the zenith of their importance in the previous century. Though his teaching owed so much to the older religion, Mahomet had exterminated, expelled, or reduced to tribute those of its adherents with whom he came into contact[2]. His successors continued his policy with even greater rigour, and Omar in particular imposed the most severe restrictions upon the Jews of his new conquests. But,

[1] *Supra*, Vol. ii, pp. 173 sqq.   [2] *Supra*, Vol. ii, pp. 306 sqq., 318 sqq.

once their original missionary enthusiasm had declined, the Caliphs shewed themselves willing to accord an almost boundless toleration in return for a slender poll-tax. Mesopotamia, where the greatest Jewish masses were still to be found, fell victim to the first wave of attack. The persecutions which had disturbed Jewish life in the Persian and Byzantine Empires, in the name of Zoroaster or of Jesus, came to an end. Judaism became almost Arabianised; and there resulted a brilliant revival, centred about Baghdad. The glories of the office of Exilarch, or Prince of the Captivity— the secular head of local Jewry—were revived after a period of abeyance, which had lasted since the execution of Mar Zutra II for revolt in the previous century (520). Bostanai (c. 660), the first of the new line, could trace his descent, like his predecessors, to the house of David; and the office continued to be filled by his descendants until its extinction[1]. A graphic account has come down of the brilliant ceremonies usual at the time of installation, when homage was paid by the heads of the two great Rabbinical colleges, each of whom was known at this period as *Gaon*. The most prominent of these was without doubt Saadiah (882–942), who first exemplified in his philological and philosophical writings the fruitful combination of the Helleno-Arabic and Jewish cultures. It was his activity which was principally responsible for the check of the anti-traditional Karaite schism which seemed at this time to be threatening the existence of Judaism.

The Muslim conquest of Spain marks a new stage in the history of the Jews in Europe. Hitherto, their importance had been comparatively slight, in relation to their own people or to the Western world as a whole. Their numbers were relatively small, and they had as yet made no contribution of any importance to Jewish or to general culture. The centre of the national life was still in Asia—particularly in Mesopotamia. But the same economic causes which made the Arabs leave their peninsula to overrun the Mediterranean world were operative with the Jews of those regions. It was only a minority which turned its footsteps to the East, founding the ancient settlements in India and China. Others had already begun to push northwards, to Persia and Armenia; and, crossing the Caucasus, perhaps laid the foundations of the great nuclei in the later Russian Empire. It was through these that the ruling classes at least of the Chazar kingdom were brought to accept Judaism in the eighth century. But more important than all of these in the history of civilisation as well as of Judaism (probably also in point of number, though of this there is no definite proof) were those who turned to Western Europe. Records of the transition are virtually non-existent, and even the date cannot be

---

[1] The importance of the office came to an end with the great persecution culminating in the death of the exilarch Hezekiah (1040). The Gaonate declined at about the same period, the last noteworthy figure being Hai (939–1038). Both offices continued sporadically however under various names in Mesopotamia, Syria, Palestine, or Egypt down to the thirteenth century, or even later.

given with any degree of certainty. But the vast Arab Empire, stretching from the Indian Ocean to the Atlantic, provided an easy and natural bridge whereby the influence of Mesopotamian Jewry was indefinitely widened. It was possible to travel from Baghdad to Cordova without any change of ruler, culture, or language. Jews must have flocked in the wake of the conquering tribes as immigrants, as traders, even as warriors. The immemorial settlements in Egypt, in fullest decadence since the repressive activities of the patriarch Cyril (415), awakened to a new life. Farther east, great communities sprang up again at Qairawān, Fez, and elsewhere in the northern provinces of Africa. In Sicily and Apulia, the phenomenon was repeated. But above all, the Jew took root and flourished in Muslim Spain. No restrictions were placed upon his activity. At the court of Cordova, and in those of the minor States which arose upon its ruins, he attained the highest offices of State, his linguistic or medical abilities usually serving as his introduction. Intellectual and cultural activities, stimulated by Moorish example, followed in the wake of freedom and numbers. Thus it came about that the academies of Mesopotamia, united at last with the West by the ties of a living language, were able to transmit the torch of learning to worthy successors before their decay.

In the result, Spain became the seat of a Jewish culture hardly equalled before or since in the Diaspora. Ḥasdai ibn Shabrut (*c.* 915–970), court physician to ʿAbd-ar-Raḥmān III, and described by John of Göritz as the acutest diplomat he had met, was the Maecenas of the new era. Under his encouragement all branches of Jewish intellectual activity, but especially poetry and philology, took root in the country. The ancestral traditions of the East, the manifold interests of the Moors, and the rediscovered sciences of ancient Greece were marvellously blended. The age was summed up in Samuel ibn Nagdela, called haNagid, or the Prince (993–1055), vizier to the King of Granada, a position which he characteristically attained by virtue of his Arabic style. A generous and discriminating patron of letters, he was himself distinguished as lexicographer, Talmudist, and poet. With his name is inseparably associated that of Solomon ibn Gabirol (1021?–56?), his protégé, a poet and philosopher of the first importance, whose *Fons Vitae* became a classic of medieval Catholic literature. Ibn Nagdela's son Joseph was unable to maintain his father's political position; and, on his fall, the Jews of Granada were associated in his fate and subjected to a ruthless massacre (1066)[1]. A majority of the local emirs continued a benevolent policy. Ministers at the courts of Seville, Saragossa, and Cordova kept alive the traditions of Ibn Shabrut and Samuel haNagid. Nevertheless, the record was no longer an unchequered one. Under the rule of the first of the

---

[1] This, however, was not the first persecution under Muslim rule in Spain. Thus, on the fall of Hishām II in 1013, the Jews were expelled from Cordova. It is necessary to accentuate this in view of the impression that the period of Muslim predominance was one of unqualified happiness for Spanish Jewry.

Almorávides, an attempt was made to force the Jews of Lucena to embrace Islām (1107). His successors were more tolerant; but they gave way (1148) to the fanatical Almohades, whose rule had spelled disaster for the communities of Morocco. Under their authority, the practice of the Jewish religion was completely prohibited, so that crypto-Judaism again became common in the peninsula. It was in consequence of this persecution that the father of Moses Maimonides (1135–1204) went into exile with his family, and that the son's remarkable powers distinguished Cairo instead of Cordova. The fall of the Almohadic power at the battle of Las Navas de Tolosa (1212) was hailed by the Jews of Spain as a deliverance.

Meanwhile, those of the northern countries had grown in numbers and importance. Settlements had indeed been found in Gaul from early times, but the conversion of the Franks to Christianity had necessarily made a difference in their position. The provincial councils from the middle of the fifth century tried to enforce the strict separation of Jew and Gentile; and the Merovingians, especially from Chilperic onwards, shewed themselves fanatically submissive. Mass baptisms were sporadically enforced by local prelates, of whom Avitus of Auvergne, Bishop of Clermont, was the most prominent (576). Though Gregory the Great had roundly condemned this unofficial ecclesiastical policy, it was adopted in its entirety by Dagobert, who, following the example of his neighbours to the south of the Pyrenees, gave his Jewish subjects the alternative of baptism or banishment (629). For a century and a half to come, the Jews entirely disappear from view in northern France. To the south, in Septimania, the later Visigothic rulers attempted to enforce the same uniformity as in Spain, though, it seems, with exceptionally small success.

In Lombardy, in the middle of the seventh century, King Perctarit gave the Jews a similar alternative shortly after his conversion. The details are all vague, and obscured with legend; and it is far from certain that, as later chroniclers report, it was at the invitation of Heraclius that Dagobert acted as he did. Nevertheless, the simultaneous wave of forced conversion which swept all over Europe, from Constantinople to Toledo, in the course of the seventh century, is significant to a degree. It was one of the great hours of crisis for Judaism; and it might well have succumbed but for the strength it still possessed outside the boundaries of the Christian world.

With the decline of the Merovingians, conditions in the Frankish dominions changed. It was from the eighth century, the period of the Muslim invasions to the south and the rise of the Carolingians to the north, that the Jews of Western Europe began to assume the importance which characterised them in the later Middle Ages, and to eclipse by degrees the older settlements of the East. By the period of the Crusades, they had attained absolute cultural, if not numerical, supremacy in the Jewish world. Thus it may be said that it was in the period from the middle of the eighth century to the middle of the eleventh that the Jews became a European people. The origin of the new settlement in the Frankish dominions is difficult to trace. Wherever there was a commercial route of any importance, there existed a potential road for Jewish expansion and penetration. To any survivors who may have been left from Roman times were added refugees who came from beyond the Pyrenees during the Visigothic persecutions. Some originated from Italy, a country which has always been most important in Jewish history as a bridge or a refuge; though its settlement remained uninterrupted, and acquired a disproportionate importance owing to its nearness to the nerve-centres of the Christian world. Others penetrated directly into Central Europe along the valley of the Danube. From the Carolingian monarchs they received consistent encouragement; for strong rulers were less amenable to the influence of the Church, and statesmen could realise the importance of the Jews in the extension of commerce and of culture. They were not indeed excessively favoured, and the principles of the ecclesiastical restrictions were sternly enforced. Nevertheless, Jewish merchants invariably received protection and privileges, while Jewish factors, physicians, and interpreters were employed at court or sent on diplomatic missions. Jewish legend long preserved the name of Charles the Great—the personification of his house—in connexion with favours and patronage bestowed upon their fathers[1]. The temper of the Church was indeed unchanged. Agobard, Archbishop of Lyons (*ob.* 840), with his successor Amulo (*ob.* 852), the fathers of medieval anti-Semitism, inveighed against the favour shewn by the ruling house to the infidels. Their writings, and the recommendations of successive synods under their influence, had however very little effect in practice; and the earlier rulers of the house of Capet continued in the main the favourable policy of their predecessors.

Under these auspices, the Jews of the Frankish dominions increased in numbers and in importance. The earliest settlements were apparently to be found in Provence and spread up the valley of the Rhone to those of the Loire and the Seine, penetrating thus to Champagne. The communities of the Rhineland were probably in the main an offshoot of these

---

[1] Thus a "Charlemagne" is said to have invested one Makhir (a scholar of the seed of David whom he had requested the Caliph Hārūn ar-Rashīd to send him) with the dignity of *Nasi*, or Prince, over the Jews of Narbonne, in recognition of their assistance in the recapture of the city. Similarly, he is reported to have founded the traditions of Jewish scholarship in Germany by settling Kalonymus (or Moses ben Kalonymus) of Lucca at Mayence. Considering that Jewish savants were frequently physicians, and that the Carolingians had an interest in medicine which certainly was not shared by the Talmud, it is tempting to imagine that the two persons in question were medical experts as well as mere Rabbinists. That Charlemagne had a Jewish physician, Ferragut, is known. All this may perhaps be brought into connexion with the embassy to the East of 797–801, in which the Jew Isaac took an important part.

and were closely connected with them culturally, thus compensating for the intellectual subordination of Provence to Spain. Other congregations were to be found along the valleys of the Danube and the Elbe. Farther to the east, the importance of the Jews was as yet inconsiderable, though a settlement was established at an early date in Bohemia. Northward, to Scandinavia, they never penetrated to any appreciable extent. By the middle of the eleventh century, when the ancient seats of learning in Mesopotamia were nearing their end, the communities of northern France and the Rhineland, forming one intellectual unit, were able to co-operate with those of Spain in keeping alight the torch of Jewish learning, excelling in legalistic studies as others did in the humanities. It is to be imagined that the ideas from East and West, exchanged together with merchandise at the great fairs of Champagne (without doubt one of the main attractions to the newcomers), must have been largely responsible for this remarkable revival. The first important figure was Gershom of Mayence, "the Light of the Exile" (960–1040), chiefly remembered for the ordinance which forbade among Western Jews the polygamy which had long been abandoned in practice. Local tendencies were summed up in the work of Solomon ben Isaac of Troyes (1040–1105), universally known by the abbreviation of "Rashi," whose writings preserved the older traditions of Talmudic scholarship for after generations. An extensive body of *Tosaphists*, or "supplementers," whose activities extended to almost every township of north-eastern France, and even beyond, carried on his work.

The last important region of Western Europe to be penetrated was England, where the Jews came over in the wake of the Conqueror; though that they were entirely absent previously is hardly probable. This country, brought at last into the orbit of European affairs, was attractive territory to the pioneer. As yet, it lacked a middle class, and needed the capital which the Jews could bring. The ambitious policy and frequent emergencies of the new régime made their presence definitely welcome to the sovereign. William Rufus, indeed, favoured them somewhat too exuberantly, in words at least. Henry I began to regularise their position by charter. Before long, there were settled communities in London, York, Lincoln, Norwich, Bristol, Oxford, and, indeed, almost all of the more important towns. The pioneers came from Rouen; but they were followed before long by others, attracted by the fresh field of activity or fleeing from persecution abroad. This was the culmination of the westward sweep of the Jewish masses, which had lasted from the fourth century and had been intense since the eighth. The next four hundred years were to witness the reversal of the process, which drove the vast mass of the Jewish people back again towards the East.

The First Crusade marks an epoch in Jewish no less than in general history. The story is familiar how the crusading hosts, marching to wrest the Holy Sepulchre from the hands of the Muslims, considered it their duty to exterminate the infidel whom they found on their path[1]. Here and there in France, and especially at Rouen, the pilgrims began their work by murdering individuals or forcing them to the font. Further outrages took place in Lorraine, particularly at Metz. But the horrors were greatest in the Rhineland, where each successive mob of crusaders massacred the Jews as it passed through. The bishops of the various cities worked, characteristically, to protect them both by their spiritual authority and by force of arms. In the case of Cologne and of Spires, they met with considerable success; but in most instances their efforts were fruitless. The community of Trèves sought refuge in baptism; those of Mayence, Worms, and many other places "sanctified the Name" almost to a man by a resolute death. Many committed suicide after slaying their wives and children with their own hands to save them from the temptations of abjuration. In more than one spot, the first historical record of the presence of Jews is that of a massacre at this period. The numbers of the victims may have been exaggerated; but the extent of the disaster may be gauged by the fact that over 350 martyrs belonging to the community of Worms were subsequently remembered by name. Popular fantasy saw in this calamity the tribulations which were to prelude the coming of the Messiah.

These were not the first persecutions which the Jews had undergone in Europe after the outburst of intolerance in the seventh century. About the year 1010, apparently in consequence of the passions aroused by the profanation of the Holy Sepulchre (at the instigation of the Jews, as it was alleged), there were persecutions at Limoges, Rouen, and Mayence. In 1065 the Viscount and Bishop of Narbonne earned the gratitude of the Pope by protecting the Jews of their city against the troops on their way to help the Christians on the south of the Pyrenees. It was, however, with the outrages of 1096 that the age of martyrdom began. Hitherto, persecution had been merely sporadic. Henceforth, it was to become more and more general, and, down to the close of the Middle Ages and after, it was the rule rather than the exception. Rabbinic codes gravely prescribed the prayer to be recited at the moment of martyrdom. The example became contagious, spreading from the Rhineland to the adjacent countries; and to religious passion there was added the commercial jealousy of the mercantile class which was now springing up. The horrors of the Second Crusade rivalled those of the First. Whereas in 1096 the danger had principally come from an ill-disciplined and superstitious rabble on the march, and the Jews could look almost invariably to the local authorities for protection, in 1146 it began at the point of assembly, and was due in large measure to the deliberate rousing of the passions of the populace. The noble efforts of Bernard of Clairvaux, who had inspired the Crusade, were partially successful in

---

[1] *Supra*, Vol. v, pp. 276-7.

restricting the massacres; but, nevertheless, northern France suffered on this occasion equally with the Rhineland.

The example was rapidly followed elsewhere, and the pretext of a crusade soon became superfluous. Thus in England, where this movement had as yet aroused only slight enthusiasm, a different justification was found. The supposed martyrdom of William of Norwich at the hands of the Jews (1144) was the first recorded case of the infamous Blood Accusation[1]; and it was followed by a long series which has continued down to the present day, notwithstanding the opinion of scholars, the authority of rulers, the declarations of the Papacy, and the dictates of common-sense. After the recognition of the doctrine of transubstantiation in 1215, another pretext was made available. The desecration of the Host was a libel even more ridiculous than the other, if such a thing were possible, because it postulated a degree of regard for the consecrated elements which would have been self-contradictory in a Jew; yet this did not prevent countless martyrs from being put to death on the charge. The first instance was that of Belitz, near Berlin, where the entire Jewish population was burned alive for the alleged offence (1243). It has recently been conjectured that the *micrococcus prodigiosus*, a scarlet microscopical organism which sometimes forms on stale food kept in a damp place, may have been responsible for the phenomenon of the "bleeding host," and for the wholesale massacres frequently perpetrated in consequence.

The wave of intolerance which passed through Christendom as a result of the Crusades and of the Albigensian movement received formal expression in the enactments of the Third and Fourth Lateran Councils (1179, 1215), after a period of comparative quiescence which had lasted for seven centuries. The former, besides renewing old restrictions, absolutely forbade Jews to have Christians in their service, even as nurses or midwives. In addition, it forbade true believers even to lodge amongst the infidel, thus laying the foundation of the Ghetto system. The latter enforced for the first time the payment of tithes by the Jews, and strictly prohibited the secular government from employing them in any position which might afford any semblance of authority over Christians. These were accompanied by other provisions which reduced the Jews almost to the position of social pariahs. Above all, the regulations instituted by certain Muslim rulers, by which all unbelievers were compelled to wear a distinguishing badge, were introduced for the first time into the Christian world, ostensibly in order to prevent the unthinkable offence of unwitting sexual intercourse between adherents of the two faiths. In

---

[1] Socrates, the fifth-century Church historian, reports, however, something similar at Inmestar in Syria about 415 (*Hist. Eccl.* vii, 16). All the earlier instances allege the crucifixion of a child in mockery of the Passion, generally at Easter. From the middle of the thirteenth century, we find the elaboration that the "sacrifice" was committed for the sake of the blood to be used in the manufacture of unleavened bread for the Passover (which generally coincided with Easter), or for other purposes.

practice, the badge consisted of a piece of yellow or crimson cloth, in England in the form of the Ten Commandments, in France, Germany, and elsewhere of a wheel, the *rotella* or *rouelle*. In Italy, where a simple badge was found inadequate, the wearing of a hat of distinctive colour was subsequently prescribed. The result of this was to stigmatise the Jews in perpetuity as a race apart, and to single them out for insult and massacre in any outburst of popular feeling. It must not be thought that all of these regulations were immediately and consistently enforced, even in the Papal States themselves. Nevertheless, they remained a standard of conduct to which it was always possible to revert with increasing severity, and which in fact formed the basis of the repressive policy of the Counter-Reformation. The Fourth Lateran Council is as crucial in Jewish history as it is in that of Europe as a whole. It marked the high-water mark of medieval legislative anti-Semitism in theory. The rest of the Middle Ages witnessed the gradual translation into action.

There was another direction in which the provisions of the Lateran Councils vitally affected the Jews. The year 1179 marked the culmination of the Church's attack upon usury, the laws against it being increased in severity, and Christian burial being refused to those dying in the sin. Though the success of these regulations was imperfect, they nevertheless tended to throw the business of money-lending more and more into the hands of those to whom canonical prescriptions did not apply.

In the earliest days of their settlement in Europe, many Jews had been agriculturalists. But the peaceful immigrant into a country already inhabited cannot easily settle on the soil. Moreover, the communal character of Jewish religious observance rendered desirable a constant contact which cannot easily be secured in rural solitude. This fact reinforced the natural tendency of newcomers to remain where colonies of their compatriots were already to be found. Besides, the growing differentiation made it necessary to enter walks of life where they were indispensable and need fear no boycott; while their increasing unpopularity rendered it advisable to settle where it was easy to band together, not only for prayer, but also for self-defence.

This tendency to concentration was reinforced, as time went on, by a further important consideration. The whole of feudal society was built up upon a military and agricultural basis, in which actual service was supplemented only by payments in kind. In this system the Jew, like the merchant or the priest, could find no place. There was a tradition dating back to the earliest days of the Christian Empire which excluded him from a military career[1]. In later times, an inevitable distrust and un-

---

[1] In emergencies, however, his services were used without compunction, and with considerable effect: to cite only one instance in our period, at the siege of Naples in 537. In Spain, he regularly figured as a soldier down to a comparatively late period.

popularity, as well as the facts of his urban life, combined to discriminate against him. In England, indeed, the *Assize of Arms* categorically forbade him to possess any weapon. Moreover, in consequence of his religion, he could neither give nor receive like other men the Christian oath of fealty which formed an inseparable element of the bond between superior and inferior. Hence there was absolutely no place for him in the growing feudal economy, and his exclusion from agricultural life became in consequence more and more complete as time went on.

All these causes combined to make the Jews congregate more and more in the towns. Many were artisans; and in some places, especially in Spain and Sicily, this remained common till the end. In the medieval gild organisation, indeed, based as it was partly on a religious bond, and wholly on feelings of solidarity and good will, there was no opening for the Jew. As a merchant, however, he had unusual qualifications, by reason both of his acumen and of his ubiquity. It was as merchants, without doubt, that many of the pioneers penetrated to the western countries, and laid the foundations of the later settlements. The "Syrian" traders who almost monopolised the trade of Western Europe after the Barbarian invasions must have comprised Jews; and the *lingua franca* spoken, for example, in Bordeaux in the sixth century[1], was as a matter of fact almost identical with that in which the Jewish legalistic correspondence between East and West was carried on in the early Middle Ages. A majority of the older settlements, until they were displaced by persecution, lay along the lines of the major trade-routes. Ibn Khurdādhbih, the Postmaster of the Caliphate of Baghdad, gives in his *Book of the Ways* (*c.* 847) a remarkable picture of the activities of the so-called "Radanite" Jewish traders, from China to Spain, in the ninth century. In the Carolingian cartularies, "Jew" and "merchant" are used as almost interchangeable terms. Despite the indignation of the Church (based of course on religious and not humanitarian grounds), the infidels controlled the slave-trade, purchasing their human merchandise in the Slavonic countries or the Byzantine Empire, and selling it as far afield as Andalusia to supply the harem or the body-guard of the Caliphs.

The growth of the mercantile spirit in Europe from the tenth century, and especially from the period of the Crusades, tended to displace the Jew from the favourable position which he formerly enjoyed. He suffered from obvious disadvantages where a Christian competitor offered himself; and he could not emulate the grandiose co-operative enterprises which the Italian and other commercial cities were able to organise. Moreover, as a general rule, he was excluded from the Merchant Gild when it came into being, and, naturally, from the privileges which it enjoyed. His growing insecurity brought about another result of hardly less importance. It was advisable for him to have his capital in a form in which it could soon be liquidated and would not easily be jeopardised by any sporadic

[1] *Supra*, Vol. ii, p. 156.

outburst of mob violence. The merchant excluded from trade can more-over hardly find an outlet for his capital except as a financier. For this the Jew enjoyed one great advantage in his widespread literary and family connexions. It was not that he necessarily invented "credit" in its technical sense (though a good case can be made out to support the hypothesis), but that he enjoyed it as a social reality. Accordingly, he had every facility for supplying medieval society with the capital which it considered disgraceful to provide, but with which it found itself unable to dispense. The Jewish authorities disapproved, and, where a co-religionist was in question, they flatly forbade; but they had to yield to circumstances. The action of the Third Lateran Council in endeavouring to extirpate usury among the Christians tended to concentrate the occupation more and more in the hands of the Jews; even though the Fourth tried to control their activities, limiting the interest they were allowed to charge and remitting it where any crusader was concerned.

For a period, therefore, the Jew was almost the sole capitalist in some countries. Whenever any great scheme was on foot, his services had to be sought out. For the two characteristic occupations of the Middle Ages, fighting and building, his aid was indispensable. The Crusades, fatal as they were to him, were in part made possible only by his financial aid. Aaron of Lincoln, the greatest Anglo-Jewish financier of the twelfth century, assisted in the construction of no less than nine of the Cistercian monasteries of England, as well as the great abbey of St Albans. The growth of the system of scutage made the capital which the Jew could alone provide all the more necessary even in times of peace; and the transition would perhaps have been impossible had it not been for his co-operation.

As yet it was the upper classes with whom he was principally concerned; not so much the greater nobles, who could dispense with his services, as the lesser feudal baronage, or the patricians of the continental cities. He earned, in consequence, unpopularity from all classes: from his clients, who fell deeper and deeper into debt, and from their enemies, who re-sented this financial succour; and the time inevitably came when this hatred expressed itself in massacre, whatever the ostensible cause. The heyday of this period of predominance in finance was from the middle of the twelfth century, when on the one hand the displacement from trade had come to be effective, and on the other the canonical restrictions against Christian usury were more rigidly enforced. A century later, the Cahorsins and the Lombards, availing themselves of legal fictions, and enjoying both a closer cohesion and a higher patronage, including that of the Popes themselves, began to make their competition increasingly felt. From this point, the Jews tended to abandon money-lending on a large scale and to engage in pawnbroking, in which the more centralised foreigners would not compete even if it had been worth their while.

The rate charged was high; necessarily so, in view of the scarcity of coin and the general unruliness. Even when fixed by law, it was in the northern countries rarely less than 43 per cent., unless exceptional security was available[1]. The chances of violence and expropriation were extreme, and it was inevitable that there should be taken into account the high probability of losing both capital and interest. But if this were obviated, profits were so enormous as to arouse general jealousy and to add another incitement to violence. It was a vicious circle, any peaceful escape from which was impossible. Yet the Christian usurer, although he did not have to safeguard himself to anything like the same extent against the chances of murder and pillage, was no less exacting. When the Jews were expelled from France, the common people were far from approving:

> Car Juïfs furent débonères
> Trop plus, en fesant telz affères
> Que ne sont ore crestien. ...
>   (GEOFFREY OF PARIS, *Histoire de France*, xii.)

An inevitable result of a special occupation in the Middle Ages was a special status; for any persons who could not be included in the feudal scheme of things had necessarily to find some place in the organisation of society outside it. It would perhaps have been natural to include the Jews with the other inhabitants of the towns; but this would have presumed a degree of sympathy and solidarity between the two elements which was in fact generally absent. Besides, since the Jew was so frequently a stranger, he had to find some external safeguard against the jealousy which he was sure to encounter. Accordingly, he looked for protection to the king— the lord of all men who had no other, and the traditional protector of the merchant and the foreigner. Especially in Germany, appeals to the Emperor for protection during the period of the Crusades were continuous, and had much to do with the growth of the later theories of subjection. But there was another side to the question. After the destruction of Jerusalem, Vespasian had ordered the voluntary levy which every Jew had hitherto contributed each year to the sanctuary of Jerusalem, in obedience to Biblical precept, to be continued as an annual poll-tax for the benefit of the temple of Jupiter Capitolinus, under the name of the *Fiscus Iudaicus*. This had indeed been abolished, as an indirect consequence of his anti-Christian attitude, by Julian the Apostate. It had never been revived; but Theodosius II, when he put an end to the Jewish Patriarchate in Palestine, ordered the *aurum coronarium* which it had hitherto received year by year as a voluntary offering from every Jew throughout the Diaspora to be paid henceforth by the heads of the community to the imperial treasury[2]. The later history of the levy is not clear; but it is

---

[1] In Italy, however, the rate generally varied from 23 per cent. to 37 per cent., according to security.

[2] G. Krakauer, *Die rechtliche und gesellschaftliche Stellung der Juden in sinkenden Römerreiche* (*Magazin für Geschichte und Wissenschaft des Judenthums*, xxiii, 53 sqq.), suggests that this is the prototype of the characteristic Jewish *communal* fiscal responsibility of later times.

more than probable that the special right of taxation was revived by the Carolingian Empire and taken over imitatively by other sovereigns; and that, instead of the Crown deriving its power to mulct the Jews from their special relationship, this theory was in part a legalistic invention intended to justify the royal claims. The payments to the Emperor in return for his protection, especially during the Third Crusade, helped to revive the old ideas. The *Opferpfennig* imposed by Lewis the Bavarian in 1342 was thus explained as being in theory the poll-tax which was due to the Roman Emperor since the days of Vespasian in testimony of perpetual servitude to the imperial throne. On a similar line of reasoning, it was possible to put forward a claim to the ultimate suzerainty over all the Jews of Europe. Such pretensions, while they were not likely to be conceded, were easy to imitate[1]. Whatever the reason for it, the Jews were reckoned *servi camerae regis* (*Kammerknechte*). It is this special relationship to the Crown which explains a great deal of their characteristic position in the national life of the Middle Ages.

In each town they formed a unit enjoying a considerable degree of judicial and fiscal autonomy—the *universitas*, or *schola, Iudaeorum*; the latter term was not yet restricted to the synagogue building, nor did it have any educational significance. Their relations with the government were essentially as a collective body. A Jewish "Parliament" representing all of the Jewries of the realm could sometimes be summoned for purposes of taxation; and such gatherings might assume a legislative side and in virtue of their spiritual authority make regulations for the general guidance. Of the manifold corporations of the Middle Ages, that of the Jews was perhaps the closest and the most rigidly controlled, for there was no way out of it except through apostasy. A logical consequence of the proprietary rights of the Crown was that it might pledge or alienate its Jews individually or collectively to some other party for the sake of an immediate monetary consideration, or that it might expel them from the country without any cogent reason.

Being the king's men, they were subject to him in every way. When it was to his interest, he attempted to enforce the appointment of rabbis and even lesser officials in the same fashion as he did that of the bishops. In England at least, appeals overseas on questions of Jewish law could be prevented by a sort of counterpart to *praemunire*. Though permitted to settle internal disputes according to their own traditions, they were subject in other matters to the exclusive jurisdiction of the Crown—greatly indeed to its profit, though not a little to their security. Above all, the king found in them a source of income. Unlike the Christian usurer, who was breaking the law, the Jew was able to sue his debtors in the royal courts; and the profits of justice accrued to the king. The wealth

---

[1] The theory of territorial as against imperial overlordship over the Jews was strenuously championed in the thirteenth century by Innocent III and Thomas Aquinas.

of the dead usurer, whether Jew or Gentile, legally escheated to the Crown: though the reality was not so drastic, as it was to the king's advantage to leave the heirs sufficient to carry on the business. If a Jew became converted to Christianity, his property, or a large proportion of it, would be confiscated; for it was not equitable that he should continue to enjoy the profits which he had amassed in sin. Besides all this, there were certain "extraordinary" amercements, such as the tallage of 60,000 marks on the occasion of an alleged ritual murder at London in 1244, or the 14,000 which the wealthy Aaron of York was fined on a suspicion of forgery six years later. All of this was quite apart from the ordinary taxation by arbitrary tallage. The average revenue derived from the Jews in northern countries has been reckoned at about one-twelfth of the total royal income. The amount is not so large; but it is wholly disproportionate to their numerical importance, which was never great[1]. Above all, the levies were entirely arbitrary. It was possible to raise what were for those days enormous sums without any customary pretext, merely to suit the royal convenience. Naturally, therefore, it was to the king's interest to protect the Jews and encourage their activities. So much of their profits came into his coffers that he became, in a certain sense, the arch-usurer of the realm. Very frequently, he came into possession of their claims as well. It was only short-sighted rulers (though there were many of them) who would display their authority by a wholesale remission of interest, or even of the whole debt, on condition that a certain proportion should be paid into the treasury. This had the automatic effect of increasing the rate of usury for future occasions. But, besides this, it was illogical in the extreme; for it was obvious that the Crown stood to gain more by a few years of sleeping partnership than by the most drastic measure of wholesale confiscation.

It is of the highest importance to realise that the description given above is not universal. Generalisation is even more difficult in Jewish than in general history. The nearest approach to the typical medieval Jewish organisation was to be found in England. In France and Germany, the communities approximated to the same economic, and therefore constitutional, position; but, by reason of the antiquity of their settlement and of their gradual evolution, as well as by the lack of uniformity through the two countries, it is less easy to generalise. Thus, in Narbonne, the Jews remained allodial proprietors until their expulsion, in consequence, according to legend, of a grant made by Charlemagne. Viticulture was similarly practised in the south of France until late in the thirteenth century. In Germany especially, the position of the Crown with regard

---

[1] The Jewish population of England in 1290 is given circumstantially as 16,511, which would represent about 1 per cent. of the population. The number is not likely to err on the side of underestimation. If it is even approximately correct, however, the Jews contributed at least ten times more to the royal income than their numbers warranted.

to the Jews, as in so many other matters, was usurped by the nobility; and Charles IV sanctioned the alienation of his rights in the Electoral territories by the Golden Bull (1356). Here, moreover, the Jewish financial hegemony came comparatively late; for loans were made until the twelfth century principally by the clergy, and thereafter by the citizens and nobles, the Jews coming to the fore only after 1300. In a few handicrafts the Jews long retained their predominance, especially in the south and east of Europe. Down to a late period, they almost monopolised the dyeing and silk-weaving industries in Sicily and Greece, as well as farther east; and they were little less prominent as tanners and glassblowers. The art of the goldsmith, facilitated by foreign intercourse, and above all desirable for a nomad who needed his possessions in the most easily transferable form, was represented even in England. In Spain, owing to its peculiar circumstances, this development was least. The Jews never abandoned the practice of handicrafts on a large scale; many remained addicted to commerce; and, though money-lending was the calling of a minority, it never widely degenerated into pawnbroking.

In Italy, the position of the Jews faithfully reflected the bewildering political condition of the country, and three, or even four, separate zones may be distinguished. In the independent mercantile cities of the north, where their commercial rivalry was feared, they were generally admitted towards the close of the Middle Ages, by a special temporary "condotta," for the specific purpose of opening loan-banks when local scruples or disorganisation rendered it necessary; and they were liable to expulsion when the immediate need had passed, or when a *monte di pietà* was erected to supply the want. Thus the important community of Venice existed down to modern times on a recurrent ten-year tenure, not always renewed; and the Jews were admitted to Florence, under similar conditions, only as late as 1437. In the States of the Church, matters were much the same where the towns enjoyed any degree of independence, though the influence of the Papacy and the example of Rome made for a greater tolerance and stability. The kingdom of Naples approximated to the type of the feudal countries of the North, as in other things. Ecclesiastical restrictions were strenuously enforced; and the settlement in Apulia was interrupted by persecution under the Angevin rulers at the end of the thirteenth century. The economic position of the Jewish capitalist in the rural centres of Calabria was, however, so important that the country is said not to have recovered even now from the effects of his ultimate disappearance. In Sicily, finally, the community approached the Spanish type politically and economically, its rigid control and high centralisation compensating in part for the bewildering complexity which was the rule in the rest of the country. The complete economic and social degradation of the Jew did not come about, in those parts of Italy where he was ultimately allowed to remain, until the Middle Ages were at an end.

Even in those places where they were utterly excluded from the ordinary walks of life, the Jewish communities could not be restricted to a single occupation. The principal householders, indeed, might be financiers. These would represent, however, only a small proportion of the total numbers. Dependent upon them, directly or indirectly, there would necessarily be numerous subordinates—agents and clerks—to help in their business; synagogal officials to carry out divine worship; scribes to draw up their business documents and to copy out their literary or liturgical compositions; tutors for the instruction of their children; physicians to care for their sick; attendants to perform household services, forbidden by the Church to Gentiles; butchers and bakers to prepare their food in accordance with ritual requirements; even a bath-keeper to facilitate the cleanliness which was reckoned an integral part of godliness. In any considerable community, however restricted in its activities by ecclesiastical and governmental prescriptions, all of these occupations were necessarily represented, though occasionally more than one might be filled by a single individual. Their very multiplicity, however, prevented a rigorous control on the part of the authorities, and facilitated evasion of the statutory restrictions.

Even before the formal institution of the Ghetto, there was a natural tendency for the Jews to forgather in one street or quarter of the town—the *Jewry, Juiverie, Judería, Via dei Giudei,* or *Jüdengasse,* as it was called in the various countries[1]. Within it, a difference might be noted in the construction of the houses; for the Jews were among the pioneers in domestic architecture, and, for security's sake, were driven to make considerable use of stone[2]. The whole would be grouped about the synagogue, which reflected faithfully in its architectural style the current fashions of the environment, though Christian zeal ensured that it remained, externally at least, modest and unassuming to a degree. To this would inevitably be added the school and bath-house, together with, in larger communities, a hall for wedding festivities, a work-room, and even a hospital which served also as a hostelry for strangers.

In spite of all restrictions, and of occasional outbursts of fanaticism, the relations between the Jewish and Christian population were generally intimate, though they tended to become more embittered as time went on. The language spoken in Western Europe was invariably the vernacular, with perhaps a few dialectal differences, though in writing it Hebrew characters were usually employed. The glosses of Rashi and his contemporaries thus preserve some of the oldest specimens of the Langue d'oïl vocabulary. In all else, the outward similarity with the Gentile must have been close to justify the institution of the Badge, though a cha-

[1] The corresponding Arab term, which was long retained in Sicily and Spain even under Christian rule, was *Aljama,* or "The Assemblage," later giving place in northern Africa to *Mellah,* which more nearly corresponds to the Ghetto.

[2] It is noteworthy that old stone houses are frequently associated with the Jews in popular lore in England, especially at Lincoln.

racteristic pointed head-dress was common. Life was profoundly influenced by the environment. The severe Gothic of the oldest German synagogues contrasts strikingly with the flowing Arabesques of Toledo. Hebrew codices were illuminated in the same manner as the Church missals, and sometimes, perhaps, by the same artists. On the other hand, a Jewish *minnesinger* such as Süsskind von Trimberg (*c.* 1200) might enter the service of a German court; and a poet like Immanuel of Rome (1270–1330), who introduced something of the careless spirit of Italian verse into Hebrew literature, could exchange sonnets in the vernacular with his Christian contemporaries, and is conjectured to have been an intimate of Dante himself, whose *Divina Commedia* he parodied.

However much he was depressed by force of circumstances, the Jew could not discard his intellectual interests. The only calling in which he is universally found besides finance is medicine, and this in spite of innumerable ecclesiastical ordinances forbidding recourse to infidel care, which the Popes themselves were the first to evade. Many courts, especially in Spain, employed a Jewish astrologer, whose activities extended to astronomy and cartography; Vasco da Gama's dependence upon astronomical tables prepared by Jews was fully as characteristic as Columbus' recourse to financiers of the same race for funds. At a period at which the vast majority of Europeans were illiterate, the Jews insisted as a religious duty upon a system of universal education of remarkable comprehensiveness. In every land to which they penetrated, schools of Rabbinical learning sprang up, in which the shrewd financiers became transmuted into acute scholars while their clients sat toping in their castles. The rolls of the various Exchequers bear ample witness to the wide secular activities of men whose names are immortalised in the annals of Hebrew literature; even England, backward as she was in this respect, is proved by recent discoveries to have exemplified it to a far greater extent than was formerly suspected. The office of rabbi became professionalised, so far as it ever was, only at a comparatively recent date.

Even where legalistic studies were most cherished, the humanities were not altogether neglected; and in the Latin countries they sometimes predominated. To philosophic studies there was indeed some resistance, particularly in France and Germany. It was long before the rationalistic tendencies even of Maimonides obtained anything like universal acceptance. On one occasion the reactionary party secured the help of the newly-founded Dominicans to burn his writings (1233); but it subsequently suffered and repented for its action. The speculative tendency, however, found its outlet in a vast mystical literature, afterwards grouped about the Zohar, which afforded a refuge from the tribulations of daily existence.

For a considerable time to come, the Christian world, with rare exceptions like Roger Bacon, shewed very little interest in Jewish learning.

CH. XXII.

From time to time, indeed, especially after the rise of the Dominican Order, disputations would be staged, usually by apostates, in which the imbecility of the Talmud and its testimony to the truth of Christianity would alternately or simultaneously be argued. All possibility of fair debate was, however, stifled by the fact that any outspoken reply on the part of the Jewish protagonists would be characterised as blasphemy. These disputations generally took place under the highest patronage, such as that of Louis IX, who presided over the debate of Nicholas Donin and Jehiel of Paris in 1240; of James I of Aragon, before whom Pablo Christiani argued with Moses Nahmanides at Barcelona in 1263; and the anti-Pope Benedict XIII, under whose auspices Jerónimo de Santa Fé pitted himself against the philosopher Joseph Albo and others at Tortosa in 1413–14. The results of these encounters were all necessarily adverse, and led to a general attack upon the traditional literature. In obedience to the ecclesiastical injunction that the Jews were not to be permitted to have in their possession works containing blasphemies against the Christian faith, twenty-four cartloads of Talmudic writings were burned in Paris after the disputation of 1240; and the example was followed intermittently elsewhere. It was not, however, until after the Reformation that a systematic censorship of Hebrew books was introduced. A further means of persuasion was by conversionist sermons, for which the Jews were sometimes forced to lend the hospitality of their synagogues.

There was one side of Jewish intellectual activity which was, however, of supreme importance to the Christian world. When Western Europe was wrapped in darkness, the learning of ancient Greece had been acquired by the Muslims. In Moorish Spain, this had brought about the great intellectual revival which is associated with the names of Avicenna and Averroës. The Jews were not slow to be affected by the new intellectual movement. Moses Maimonides, familiar to the schoolmen as Rabbi Moses of Egypt, was far from being a solitary phenomenon, though his influence surpassed that of all others both in his own community and outside[1]. But it is in a different direction that Jewish influence was of most importance. The medieval world, ignorant of Arabic as it was of Greek, gained access to the intellectual treasures rediscovered in Spain largely through the medium of translations from the Hebrew versions which the Jews had prepared from the Arabic for their own use. At a later period, especially under the patronage of Frederick II, Robert of Anjou, and Alfonso the Learned, a systematic series of renderings was carried out by Jewish scholars in Naples, Provence, and Castile. The share of the Jew in bringing about the earlier, Aristotelean, phases of the Renaissance is symbolic of his intermediary position in medieval life. It was only as late as the fifteenth century that Pico della Mirandola and Marsilio Ficino, eager disciples of the Jewish *littérateurs* in Florence, taught the Christian world the importance of direct acquaintance with Hebrew

[1] See *supra*, Vol. v, p. 817.

literature for its own sake; but their example, followed by John Reuchlin, was of considerable moment in the growth of the Reformation.

From the many-sided activity described above, England was to a certain extent isolated. As has already been pointed out, her settlement was late and artificial. She did not possess, like France, Spain, Italy, and Germany, any nucleus of what may perhaps be termed autochthonous Jews. Those who were admitted were intended to fill a very definite gap in the economy of the country; others were not likely to be encouraged. In addition, the authority of the Crown under the Norman monarchs was so strong as to ensure their continuance in the functions for which they were introduced. England's was therefore the type of a feudal Jewry; for it knew no survivals, and few exceptions, to qualify the general rule. The history of the Jews in medieval England is indeed so compact, so fully documented, and so well defined, that it has a "typical" value disproportionate to its real importance.

The community had steadily grown under the Normans, when England, as yet comparatively unaffected by the Crusades, provided a tranquil haven of refuge from the growing storms of the Continent. A majority of its members hailed from France, or from the western provinces of Germany; but we find Spain and Italy, and even Russia and the Muslim countries, represented to a minor extent. Their tranquillity was not indeed without qualification. In the course of the war of succession between Stephen and Matilda, both sides mulcted them to the limit of their ability, the Oxford community suffering especially. In 1130 the Jews of London were fined the enormous sum of £2000 on the pretext that one of their number had killed a sick man—a drastic expression, it would seem, of primitive ideas of medical responsibility. The prototype of the Blood Accusation at Norwich in 1144 was followed at Gloucester in 1168, before it had time to be imitated outside England, and, subsequently, at Bury St Edmunds in 1181. Nevertheless, the position of the English Jew was as yet on the whole enviable compared with that of his co-religionists in the adjacent parts of the Continent.

This comparative tranquillity came to an end with the rise in England of the full tide of the crusading enthusiasm. At the coronation of Richard I (1189), a riot began which ended in the sack of the London Jewry and the murder of many of its inhabitants, the work of violence being carried on overnight and into the next day by the light of the burning buildings. The example was followed throughout the country immediately the king had crossed the Channel; notably at York, where the steadfastness of the victims added a glorious page to the history of Jewish martyrdom (1190). The ringleaders were in many cases members of the lesser baronage, whose religious ardour was heightened if not occasioned by their financial indebtedness.

Such outbreaks were in every way against the interest of the government. Any breach of order was naturally distasteful to it; and immediate vassals had a special title to the royal protection. The rioters had moreover been careful to destroy wherever possible the records of their indebtedness, threatening thereby heavy loss to the Crown, to which the claims of those who had perished legally reverted. For their unruliness the ringleaders were punished, though none too severely. The financial question was, however, so important that it was deemed necessary to take steps against any possible recurrence. Accordingly, after his return from captivity (to his ransom from which the Jews of the realm had been made to contribute three times as much as the burghers of London), Richard ordered the establishment in the principal cities, under the charge of Jewish and Christian "chirographers," of "archae" in which were to be deposited records of all debts contracted with Jews. Thus, whatever might happen, the Crown and its rights would henceforth be secure. As co-ordinating authority over these provincial centres, ultimately twenty-six in number, there came into being the "Exchequer of the Jews," an institution mainly judicial, though not without its financial side. In close connexion with this was the office of *Presbyter Iudaeorum*, or Chief Rabbi: not so much in the modern sense of the supreme spiritual head of the Jews of the country as of an official representative appointed by the Crown without any necessary regard for the individual qualifications or the general desire. Through their Exchequer, the Jews of medieval England acquired an organisation (by no means, indeed, to their advantage) equalled probably in no other country of Europe; and it is by its records that we are so minutely informed as to their position.

The English communities never fully recovered from the blow they had received at the accession of Richard I. John, indeed, whether from his perennial neediness or his natural sympathy for unpopular causes, conceded them in 1201 a comprehensive charter of liberties in return for a considerable subsidy. But later in his reign his attitude changed, and he began to squeeze money out of them by a series of expedients as typical of his short-sightedness as anything in his reign. During the minority of Henry III, the condition of the Jews improved; but, from the beginning of his personal rule, it became worse and worse. Tallage succeeded tallage with fatal regularity, allowing no time for recovery. The rapacity of the Crown overreached itself. If the figures given are correct, the annual revenue derived from the Jews went down from about £3000 in the second half of the twelfth century to less than £700 at the close of the thirteenth. So far did the spoliation go that in 1254 the Presbyter Elias appealed for permission for his people to leave the country, as they had no more left to give. When nothing further could be extorted from them directly, Henry exercised his right as suzerain by mortgaging them to his brother, Richard of Cornwall. They were subsequently made over to Prince Edward, and by him to their competitors, the Cahorsins. Religious intolerance meanwhile came to a head. The oppressive decrees of the Fourth Lateran Council were early enforced. The Blood Libel and similar accusations again blazed out, coming to a head with the classical case of Little Hugh of Lincoln in 1255. From several cities the Jews were entirely excluded. With the outbreak of the Barons' War, there was a recrudescence of massacre all over the country.

In this condition the Jews were found by Edward I on his accession. It was a state of affairs which obviously could not be allowed to continue. They were so impoverished that their importance to the treasury, the needs of which were increasing, had become negligible. Moreover, the foreign bankers, who enjoyed a higher patronage, had begun to render the services for which they were formerly essential. It was necessary to make a fundamental alteration. Edward shewed in his treatment of the question many of his finest qualities. He was perhaps the first European statesman before Napoleon who tried to face the Jewish problem; and his *Statutum de Iudaismo* of 1275 is deserving of a good deal more notice than it has generally received. In the previous year, at the Council of Lyons, Pope Gregory X had urged the Christian world to make a strenuous effort to suppress usury. Edward obeyed implicitly, adding to his proceedings against Christian money-lenders an attempt to effect a complete change in the Jewish economic position and mode of life. The practice of usury was utterly forbidden, the consequent financial loss to the Crown being in part made good by the establishment of a poll-tax on every adult. On the other hand, the Jews were to be empowered to engage in commerce and handicrafts, and (for an experimental period) to rent farms on short leases. That there was no essential tenderness in the measure was proved by the strict enforcement simultaneously of all the ecclesiastical restrictions[1].

This was a courageous attempt to grapple with the Jewish problem; but it did not go far enough. Restrictions could be removed, yet prejudices on either side were more obstinate. The Jew might have been diverted from his enforced activities, but only by removing the causes which had driven him to them. He would perhaps have turned his attention to agriculture if he had been granted security of tenure, and if he had been admitted to it on terms of equality with other persons. He would assuredly have embraced commerce if he could have been included in the Gild Merchant. But to hope to change his manner of life while he remained subject to the same insecurity, to the same prejudices, and to the same differentiation of treatment as before was impossible: the habits of a lifetime and the hereditary influence of past generations

---

[1] A similar policy had been adumbrated, however, by Grosseteste, and subsequently by Thomas Aquinas, *Opusculum ad Ducissam Brabantiae*, xxi: "If rulers think that they harm their souls by taking money from usurers, let them remember that they are themselves to blame. They ought to see that the Jews are compelled to labour, as they do in some parts of Italy." A feeble attempt to put a similar policy into execution seems to have been made by Louis IX of France in instructions from the Holy Land in 1253.

CH. XXII.

could not be so easily cancelled. A Bull of Honorius IV of 1286 insisting upon a stricter segregation cut off the possibility of further concessions. As a result, Edward's scheme failed utterly. A few of the wealthier, indeed, entered into commerce, particularly the export of wool. The money-lending now prohibited by law continued, however, to be carried on in a clandestine manner; while it appears that some, prevented from following their old profession, attempted to continue to eke a living out of their capital by clipping the coinage. For a moment, Edward contemplated, if he did not execute, a relaxation of his own measure, by permitting a resumption of usury for a limited period of years. On second thoughts, however, he preferred to sweep away the problem which he had failed to solve. Already the Jews had been expelled or excluded from a number of cities in the country[1]. On more than one occasion, they had been temporarily banished from the narrow royal domains in France. The expulsion from England in 1290, however, was the first general measure of the sort which the Jews had known since their establishment in Europe. The exclusion was not, indeed, absolute, and individuals continued to appear in the country intermittently. The re-establishment of a settled community was, however, impossible until the seventeenth century[2].

Closest akin to the Jews of England in culture, in condition, and in history were those of France. Here, since the outbreaks which had accompanied the Second Crusade, they had lived a chequered existence. From the close of the twelfth century, the house of Capet developed an anti-Jewish attitude which was perhaps unparalleled in Europe as a dynastic policy. At the beginning, their sphere of influence was so limited that the effects were not much greater than the enmity of any major baron would have been; and the condition of the communities of Languedoc in particular remained very similar from every point of view to that of their more fortunate brethren in Spain. The history of the Jews in France is hence to be understood only in relation to the expansion of the royal authority, which spelled for them utter disaster. Philip Augustus set the example to his successors by driving the Jews from his possessions after cancelling the debts due to them, save for one-fifth payable to himself, and confiscating their property (1182). Sixteen years later, however, on his return from crusade, he invited them back and regularised their activities (1198). From this period dates the establishment of the *Produit des Juifs* as a department of the treasury, and the assimilation of the Jews to the position of serfs in both the royal and the baronial domains.

Louis VIII followed his father's example, remitting all interest due on

[1] *E.g.* Bury St Edmunds (1190), Leicester (1231), Derby (1263), Cambridge and the other dower-towns of Queen Eleanor (1275).
[2] A tale of a second expulsion in 1358, repeated by many modern historians, seems to be a mere fable; though it is not out of the question that a few surreptitious immigrants were escorted out of the country in that year.

current loans in his *Établissement sur les Juifs* (1223). With Louis IX, however, religious zeal reinforced ancestral prejudice. The prescriptions of the Fourth Lateran Council were rigorously enforced. A personal interest was taken in securing converts. It was under his auspices that the Disputation of Paris was held and the Talmud condemned to the flames[1]. Not only the interest, but also a third part of the capital of all debts was remitted. Finally, before setting out for the East, he decreed the expulsion of the Jews from his realms (1249), though the order was not apparently carried out. Philip the Bold continued his father's policy. But the sufferings of the Jews reached their culmination under Philip the Fair. From the moment of his accession, he shewed that he considered them merely as a source of gold. Spoliation succeeded spoliation, wholesale imprisonment being resorted to in order to prevent evasion. The climax came in 1306, when the policy of Edward I of England was imitated with the usual significant differences. On the anniversary, as it happened, of the destruction of the Temple of Jerusalem, he had all the Jews of his realm arrested; and in prison, they were informed that they had been sentenced to exile and that the whole of their property was confiscated to the Crown. The real object of this measure, and the entire lack of religious motive, shewed itself in the fact that the king took over, not only their property, but also their usurious claims in full. By this time, the royal authority extended over the majority of France proper, including Champagne, where the schools of Rabbinic learning had especially flourished. This banishment spelled accordingly the end of the ancient and glorious traditions of French Jewry, except in part of Provence. The recall of some financiers for a few years from 1315, and on a somewhat larger scale after the financial crisis which followed the battle of Poitiers, from 1359 to 1394, cannot be counted a real restoration, and failed to revive to any appreciable extent the old tradition of Franco-Jewish culture.

From Germany, by reason of its special political conditions, there was no general expulsion. It figures instead as the classical land of Jewish martyrdom, where banishment was employed only locally and sporadically to complete the work of massacre. The example set in the First Crusade was followed with fatal regularity. When external occasion was wanting, the Blood Libel or a charge of the desecration of the Host was always to hand to serve as pretext. As long as the central authority retained any strength, the Jews enjoyed a certain degree of protection. On its decay, however, they were at the mercy of any wave of popular prejudice. Thus, in 1298, a charge of desecrating the Host at Röttingen proved the pretext for wholesale massacres throughout Franconia, Bavaria, and Austria by a band of fanatics led by one Rindfleisch. Forty years later, the example was imitated in Franconia, Swabia, and Alsace by a mob frankly calling themselves *Jüdenschläger*, led by two nobles, named Armleder, from a strip

[1] *supra*, p. 652.

of leather which they wore round their arms (1336–38). But popular prejudice came to its height at the period of the Black Death. Some time before, the first resettlement of the Jews in France had ended after a wave of massacre which had swept through the country, in consequence of an accusation that the Jews and lepers had poisoned the wells at the instigation of the King of Granada (1321–22). Now, in the face of a great general scourge, a similar indictment was almost universally made and obtained general currency. The ridiculousness of the charge should have been apparent even to fourteenth-century credulity; for the plague raged virulently even in those places where the Christian population was absolutely unadulterated; and elsewhere the Jews suffered with the rest, though their manner of life and their superior medical knowledge may have reduced their mortality. Nevertheless, a wave of general and pitiless massacres, usually carried out under some semblance of judicial form, started in Savoy and spread through Switzerland until it had swept the whole of Germany (1348–49). Something like 350 places where massacres occurred at this time were remembered; 60 large and 150 small communities were utterly exterminated. This was the climax of disaster for the Jews of that country, just as the great expulsions had been for those of England and France. When the storm had died down, a large number of the cities thought better of the vows made in the heat of the moment and summoned Jews back again to supply their financial requirements. The period which followed was one of comparative quiescence, if only for lack of victims. King Wenceslas, however, initiated the short-sighted policy of periodical cancellation of the Jewish debts in return for some monetary consideration. It was impossible therefore for the remnant which returned to recover the position held by their predecessors; and the hegemony of German Jewry passed, with the refugees, to the East.

There followed a period when the Jews of Austria, who had received a model charter in 1244, enjoyed a certain degree of comparative prosperity and intellectual pre-eminence. The Hussite wars, however, reviving the worst passions of religious intolerance, brought in their train a further wave of massacre at the hands of the degenerate successors of the crusaders, which affected the eastern part of the country in particular. This interlude came to an end with the great expulsion following upon a trumped-up accusation of ritual murder and Host-desecration at Vienna in 1421.

In the bewildering turmoil of massacre and banishment which followed, down to the close of the Middle Ages and after, it is difficult to steer a clear path. Isolated handfuls continued to live here and there throughout the country. Larger aggregations were to be found in the semi-Slavonic territories on the eastern borders of the Empire. No important communities in Germany proper managed, however, to protract their existence unbroken down to modern times save those of Frankfort-on-Main and Worms[1].

[1] The last of the great expulsions of this period was that of the ancient community of Ratisbon in 1519.

For the refugees, only one way of escape really lay open. A small minority crossed the Alps into the cities of northern Italy, to which they were admitted under strict regulation. But the vast majority turned towards the East. The massacres in the Rhineland contributed to spread the area of settlement in the outlying provinces of the Empire. In Bohemia, the history of the Jews followed ominously upon that of their brethren in Germany, but there was never any general expulsion. In Hungary, conditions were much the same, though the massacres at the period of the First Crusade, which had decimated the community of Prague, were here checked; subsequently, however, the story was more chequered, and there was more than one temporary interruption. But the great haven of refuge was Poland. Here Jews had without doubt penetrated from the ancient settlements on either side of the Caucasus and in the Crimea, where they had been settled from Roman times; and it may well be that the Chazar converts of the eighth century contributed to their numbers. However that may be, the immigrants from the West were able to impose their superior culture upon their indigenous brethren, with the result that the vast majority of the Jews of Russia and Poland still speak to-day the Low German dialect which they brought with them. In the twelfth century, Jews were in control of the mints, as is proved by the existence of a large number of coins with Hebrew lettering.

The Tartar invasions which devastated the whole country, especially the towns, from 1241 onwards mark the starting-point of a more systematic immigration, in which Jewish and Gentile settlers from Germany were equally encouraged. The concessions to the former of Boleslav the Chaste (1264) formed the charter of the new settlement. The Christian newcomers, however, brought with them something of the persecuting spirit of their native country; this was reflected in the decrees of the provincial synod of Breslau, whereby an attempt was made to enforce the policy of the Lateran Councils (1266). Nevertheless, the new settlement grew apace, each fresh outbreak in Germany driving before it a new wave of refugees. Under the favour of Casimir the Great (1333–70), Jewish prosperity reached its climax. Thereafter, indeed, their tranquillity was not undisturbed. Accusations of ritual murder and of the desecration of the Host began to claim their victims. In the middle of the fifteenth century, the inflammatory sermons of Giovanni da Capistrano, personifying the anti-Hussite reaction, brought about a recrudescence of massacre here as in most other places on his road, from Sicily northwards. Nevertheless, the lot of the Jews of Poland was happy by comparison with those of the rest of Northern Europe. There was little restriction upon their economic activity. Their numbers grew rapidly; and scholarship followed as usual in the wake of population. In Lithuania, their history was very similar, though it dated from a somewhat later period. When, at the close of the Middle Ages, almost the whole of Northern Europe was closed to the Jews, they had thus secured in this last corner a haven of refuge which ensured their preservation even if not an undisturbed tranquillity.

In Spain, the Christian reconquest had originally involved obvious peril for the Jews. Closely assimilated to the Muslims as they were in language and mode of life, they were classed with them as infidels and enemies of Christendom. Accordingly, the early phases of the advance had been stained by massacre and maltreatment. As early as the tenth century, however, a change of attitude began to shew itself. If the Christian hold upon the country was to be secure, it was obviously necessary to conciliate so important an element of the population. At the same time, by reason of their linguistic qualifications, it was found convenient to employ Jews on important diplomatic missions, while their inherent aptitude won them high office in the financial administration. Thus the golden age of Jewish life in Spain, while without doubt largely due throughout to the propinquity and example of the Moors, was by no means exclusively under their rule; and, indeed, over a prolonged period Christian tolerance compared most favourably with Almohadan fanaticism. It was under Christian rule, though to some extent under Muslim intellectual influence, that some of the greatest figures of Spanish Jewry flourished: Jehudah haLevi (*c.* 1086–1141), the sweetest singer of Zion; Abraham ibn Ezra (1092–1167), traveller, poet, and exegete, who shewed more than a glimmering of the principles of modern criticism; and many others of a later date. But as the Moorish rivalry progressively grew less dangerous, the Christian attitude towards the Jews correspondingly stiffened; till finally the disappearance of the last vestiges of Muslim rule was closely followed by the final disaster.

It was in the reign of Alfonso VI of Castile (1065–1109) that the acme of prosperity was reached. His armies contained large numbers of Jews, on whose behalf (it was reported) military operations were on one occasion postponed until the conclusion of the Sabbath. By his *fueros*, despite the admonitions of Gregory VII, they were left in possession of all the privileges they had enjoyed under the Mohammedans, and were placed in a position of legal equality with the general population. His body-physician, the Jew Cidelo, enjoyed high influence at his court; and co-religionists were employed on delicate diplomatic missions. Even before Alfonso's death, the inevitable reaction set in, accompanied as usual by massacres; and his successors considerably restricted the privileges which the Jews were theoretically allowed to enjoy. But in fact this period of special favour only came to an end with the final breaking of Muslim power at the battle of Las Navas de Tolosa (1212). The crusaders on their way thither had followed the example set in the Rhineland, beginning the Holy War with an attack on the Jews of Toledo. The repressive policy of the Lateran Councils now began to gain a foothold in the Peninsula. Even Alfonso the Learned (1252–84), though his court was one of the greatest centres of the Jewish activities in translation and in the sciences, subjected the Jews in his *Siete Partidas* to the most minute and galling restrictions. In spite of this, Spain remained the solitary haven of comparative tranquillity in the west of Europe. Though there were occasional local outbreaks, massacre did not become the rule. The restrictive enactments of the Church were reflected in legislation, but they were never fully enforced. Tax-farming was largely in Jewish hands. Through the medium principally of medicine or of finance, individuals attained great influence in the State. Yet at the same time the Jews were not divorced from agriculture, and continued to figure largely as merchants and as craftsmen. If they were restricted to their *Aljama* in a single quarter of the town, they enjoyed in it an unusual degree of autonomy. As a natural consequence, the standard of intellectual life was high; and science, philosophy, and letters continued to flourish by the side of Rabbinic studies.

From the fourteenth century, however, there were signs that the violence which had become rife in the rest of Europe was spreading to the peninsula. The *Pastoureaux* of southern France, beginning the redemption of the Holy Sepulchre amongst the restored communities of their own region, continued their ravages on the south of the Pyrenees (1320). The massacres at the time of the Black Death extended into Catalonia, though with nothing like the virulence with which they raged in Germany (1348). The excessive favour of Peter the Cruel naturally led to a reaction under his rival, Henry of Trastamara, whose wild mercenaries sacked the *Aljama* of every city they entered (1355 onwards). But the crucial year was 1391, when political provocation was virtually absent. It is from this date that the glory of Spanish Jewry may be said to end. Following the inflammatory Easter sermons of the archdeacon Fernán Martínez, the wealthy *Judería* of Seville was attacked by a fanatical mob on Ash Wednesday 1391. Hence the movement spread like wild-fire through the country, from the Pyrenees to the Balearic Islands. Except in Granada and Portugal, hardly a single community was spared. The solitary way of escape from death lay through baptism. For the only time, perhaps, in the whole of their long history, the morale of the Jews broke. Elsewhere, it had only been a small and weak remnant which saved its life by apostasy. But in Spain, there seems to have been something in the atmosphere which predisposed their brethren to a lesser fortitude. As we have seen, there was a tradition of crypto-Judaism dating back to Visigothic times. The long association with the country may have weakened their power of resistance. The calamities in the neighbouring lands had deprived them of any haven of refuge, and perhaps made them doubt after so many centuries of their future. However that may be, a very large proportion of the Jews, when offered the alternative of baptism or death, chose the former.

When the storm died down—only to break out again with similar results a couple of decades later (1411) under the influence of Fra Vincent Ferrer—Spanish Jewry found itself in an entirely new position. By the side of those who had managed to escape massacre while remaining true to their old faith, there was now an immense number of *nuevos cristianos*. Some indeed were sincere enough, and, like Paul de Santa Maria, later Archbishop of Burgos, took the lead in baiting their former co-religionists. But the vast majority remained unaffected by the mere fact of baptism, though they feared to return formally to their old faith. Whatever characteristics had earned their previous unpopularity remained unchanged. With the removal of the disabilities from which they had formerly suffered by reason of their religion, they entered into every walk of life and pushed their way into the highest offices of State. They thronged the financial administration. Some entered the Church, and attained high rank. Many contracted family alliances with the proudest nobility of the land. But the majority intermarried amongst themselves, consorted familiarly with Jews, observed almost without concealment the practices of their old religion, and spoke with open disparagement of their new one. Moreover, and this was the distinguishing characteristic of Iberian crypto-Judaism, they were able to transmit their traditions to their children, who were in most cases Christians only by the accident of baptism.

These *Marranos*, as they were disparagingly called[1], became a real problem for a State in which religion was taken so seriously as in medieval Spain, as was shewn by a frequent recrudescence of massacre. The passage of years proved that the problem was not likely to be solved by time. In an age which could not admit the idea of release from the sacrament of baptism, there was only one solution. The genuine piety of Isabella the Catholic rendered her a willing tool in the hands of her spiritual advisers. A Bull authorising the appointment of Inquisitors in the Spanish dominions was obtained from Sixtus IV in 1478. The Holy Office was set up in Castile in 1480, and in Aragon four years later; and it began to extirpate the canker of heresy with all the horrors of which it was capable. But the position was hopelessly illogical. A *converso*, Christian only in name, would be burned alive for practising in secret only a fraction of what his unconverted brethren were doing every day in public with impunity. It seemed impossible to root out this Judaising heresy from the land while the Jews were still present to teach their relapsed kinsmen, by precept and by example, the practices of their old faith. Moreover, the tide of nationalism as well as of fanaticism was rising in Spain, and the time was ripe for her to follow the example of the neighbouring countries. The conquest of Granada, to which the Jews had liberally contributed, did away with all further need for their support. Seven months after that event, Ferdinand and Isabella issued the edict of expulsion which put an end to the settlement of the Jews in Spain after so many centuries (31 March 1492). In this were included the more distant possessions of the crown of Aragon—Sicily and Sardinia—in spite of the

---

[1] For the history of the name (probably meaning originally "pig") see A. Farinelli, *Marrano: storia di un vituperio*, Geneva, 1925.

fact that in them the problem of the crypto-Jew was absent. In vain were the prayers and inducements of Isaac Abrabanel (1437–1508), the last of the long line of Jewish scholar-statesmen in the Peninsula. The edict was imitated in Portugal (1496) and in Navarre (1498) after a very brief interval. Almost simultaneously, the last remnant of the ancient French communities was banished from Provence.

Thus ended, with the Middle Ages themselves, the immemorial Jewish connexion with South-Western Europe. The easterly movement of population, which had begun with the First Crusade, was complete. The Marranos, indeed, continued a surreptitious existence in the Peninsula, handing on their traditions secretly from generation to generation at the risk of their lives. It was their descendants, fleeing from the fires of the Inquisition, who founded the modern communities in France, Holland, England, and even America. Their forcible assimilation to European standards brought about the inception of the modern, individualistic attitude towards their race, hitherto considered and treated as a distinct and inferior branch of humanity.

The whole of the west of Europe was now closed to the Jew, except for northern Italy[1] and a few regions of Germany. Of the refugees, a vast majority made their way with indescribable difficulty to the Muslim countries of the Mediterranean littoral, where they found at least toleration. With them, they brought their native Spanish tongue, which is spoken by their descendants to the present day. Many fled to the ancient settlements of Morocco and northern Africa, which had gone through a prolonged period of decadence, but had been recruited and awakened to a new, if degraded, life by the Spanish fugitives of 1391. In Palestine itself, the exiles re-established the ancient connexion, which had been almost extinct since the period of the Crusades and the Tartar invasions. But by far the greatest number made their way to the central provinces of the Turkish Empire, with the sedulous encouragement of Bāyazīd II. Here, their superior culture and numbers soon assimilated the remnants of the old Byzantine communities, which had managed to protract a decadent and uninspired existence from ancient times. Thus Turkey became, with Poland, the greatest centre of population for the whole Jewish people, which was now overwhelmingly concentrated in the two great empires of the Near East. The Western European phase of Jewish history, which had begun with the Middle Ages, ended with them. The stage was set for a new act of the age-long drama to be played.

---

[1] An expulsion from the kingdom of Naples followed the Spanish occupation (1510, and, more completely, 1548). A handful of Jews was tolerated also in Avignon and the other French possessions of the Holy See—a symptomatic fact.

CHAPTER XXIII

MEDIEVAL ESTATES

THE word "feudalism" is little more than a rough generalisation or formula under which we try to include such conditions, economic, social, and governmental, as are found to be common and uniform throughout the lands and peoples which were once parts of the Western Roman Empire, in that obscure period of rapid change between the dismembering of the Carolingian Empire and the growth of national States.

In a period so long as this, when conditions were changing so rapidly, it is inevitable that many conflicting elements, forces, and tendencies should be found together at every stage of the development, and still greater differences between different historical stages of the growth even of a single common institution or idea.

It is fortunately not within the scope of this chapter to discuss the vexed and disputed questions of the origin of these varying elements or of their relative importance. From the establishment of the Frankish Empire a development may be clearly traced which in time superseded the régime of the personality of law resulting from the "wandering of the peoples," and substituted for it the restored Roman idea of territoriality; and later, when the cohesive force of the Frankish Empire became weakened and that Empire again fell in pieces, these pieces retained the main characteristic they had acquired under their Frankish rulers, the principle of territoriality. The primitive Germanic conception of law as tribal custom was by no means obliterated, but it was now the law of peoples who had settled homes and determinate geographical boundaries, whose jurisdiction was complete over all the inhabitants within those boundaries, of whatever race, and limited only by those boundaries themselves. It was a period of the complete territoriality of law, in the absence more or less complete of all coercive central authority, a régime when small territories, each practically independent of all the rest and of all central authority, and each with its own customary law binding upon all within its boundaries, were the rule; and for a time the process of subdivision was making these little territorial units ever more numerous and more minute.

When this process of subdivision reached its limit, and the counter-process began of the gradual accretion of fiefs which was ultimately to develop into the great national States of Western Europe, the course and direction of that development were determined by the institutions and ideas which had become established within the scattered territorial units from which the later States were ultimately formed. Prominent among these institutions and ideas was that of law as the custom of the people within a territory, the *mos utentium*, a *ius non scriptum* whose beginning was beyond memory and whose transmission was by oral tradition. Since the law was the usage of the people, it was the people alone who could know it. Hence, when concrete cases arose requiring the application of the law, it was the people of the district alone who could "find" it, and this became one of the chief functions of the "courts" of the district. As Gneist points out, however, it was an equally marked characteristic of all these assemblies or courts that there was in them no differentiation of functions, such as we know in modern times, and no conscious distinction between finding a law in general and administering it in an individual case. No doubt these general duties had been performed in earlier times by all, or at least by all who were regarded as qualified. But later there was a tendency everywhere to restrict these duties to a smaller number, as in the *scabini* on the Continent, or the reeve, the priest, and the four men from each township, as mentioned in English documents of the reign of Henry I. The finding and the administering of law alike were then both communal and territorial, and a survey of European procedure at this time shews how widely it differed from the Roman procedure with its normal trial by a single *iudex*. This difference is of fundamental importance and lies at the very roots of modern constitutionalism. The Roman *iudex* was a real judge in our modern sense, even though he was guided by the *formula* of a magistrate in his decision. He weighed both sides of the case, and pronounced a real judgment upon the weight of the evidence. The whole rationale of the judicial system of Western Europe in the feudal period was strikingly different. In imitation of Rome, the suitors who administered these courts might be called *iudices*, as they are, for example, in the *Leges Henrici Primi*, in the case of England, early in the twelfth century; but their functions are in reality markedly different. They weigh no evidence, for properly speaking there is no evidence. They reach no judgment, for there is no place for any judgment. They merely "award the proof." Judicial discretion and a rational system of weighing evidence are the marks of the matured judicial procedure of the Roman Empire, and judicial discretion may be exercised by a single *iudex* as well as by a number, if not better. But the cruder law of the feudal age knew no discretion, and very little rationalism. If ever there was "a government of laws and not of men," it was at that time. It was a formal, rigid, one-sided procedure. Nothing was left to the discretion of any human judge, as is immediately disclosed by an inspection of the tariffs of compositions in such a "code" as the *Lex Frisionum*, or of the mechanical list of formal *essonia*, or lawful excuses for non-appearance at court, even as late as Bracton's time. It was not the business of the members of these medieval courts to give a judgment. It was not their discretion that was wanted; it was their knowledge, the knowledge of the unwritten law of the district of which they alone were possessed, or the acquaintance with the local reputation of an accused man, which might affect the award of proof. That proof once awarded, whether it was a trial by reputation, as in compurgation, or some form of the *Iudicium Dei*, as the ordeal or duel, the rest was mechanical. If the accused succeeded, he was free; if not, he was guilty. There was an equal lack of discretion whether the trial was civil or criminal, as we should say. Trial by witnesses, when possible, was not, as now, the admission of witnesses to inform an impartial arbiter; it was merely the introduction of persons who had been officially present as formal witnesses when the original transaction took place. And their introduction was as final and decisive as the result of an ordeal or of trial by battle. Such witnesses swore only a formal oath. They were never sworn to tell the truth on their consciences. They appeared to swear *with* the defendant. They could not possibly be introduced to swear against him.

In this system the duties of the presiding officer were as mechanical as those of the members of the court over whom he kept order, and whose findings he pronounced. Not till a comparatively late period did he begin to acquire, mainly, I think, by delegation from the king, a discretionary power, which in time gradually developed into that of the Roman *iudex* or the modern judge.

The judicial work of these medieval courts was performed by the members of the community, or by a selected portion of them "representing" the community and necessarily fairly large in numbers. Had their duties required discretion, one "judge" might have been enough, but since instead they required knowledge—a knowledge of the customs and of the people of the district—a considerable number became necessary, and these had to be "representative" in the sense that they would be persons of the district who knew their neighbours and were acquainted with the customary law in force there from time immemorial, *more utentium*; an acquaintance, as Glanville says of the Grand Assize in England in the twelfth century, which they have gained from what they themselves have seen and heard, "vel per verba patrum suorum et per talia quibus fidem teneantur habere in propriis."

The point is that the general business of these undifferentiated "courts" was everywhere such that it could be carried on only by those acquainted with the men and the customs of the country. Thus it was that when the *inquisitio* or inquest was in time introduced among the older forms, at the instance of the king in England, it retained the old communal basis. It still required, like the older procedure to which it was in many respects closely akin, knowledge rather than judgment, and a knowledge which could not safely be got from one but only from many. Though the true jury, when it came, came from above and not below, as Maitland shews, and though it implied an answer on oath to a question which unlike the older procedure might be either Yes or No, still it was, as its name implies, like its communal predecessors, a trial *per patriam, per pais*, by "the countryside."

The striking contrast between all these pieces of medieval judicial machinery and the *iudex* of Rome lies in the fact that it was knowledge, not judgment, that a medieval court wanted; and that knowledge of the things needed for a decision required a considerable number of neighbours, while *judgment* may be safely exacted from a single individual regardless of his knowledge. Thus medieval procedure was based on a knowledge of the community by the community, and this could safely be found only from that community. When the practice arose of drawing this knowledge from a number selected from this community *pro omnibus*, the earliest foundations of modern representative institutions were laid. The great fact is that the procedure of the Middle Ages required a fairly consider-able number of "representatives" of the community to make it really effective, under the ideas of law and of proof as they existed at that time.

Early in the eighth century the Lombard laws furnish an interesting illustration of these Germanic ideas of fixed customary law and of the struggle for the mastery between them and the Roman conception of the arbitrament of the *iudex*. Among the Lombards, it is recited in the laws— "alii per consuitutinem, alii per arbitrium iudicare aestimabant"; and the resulting uncertainty was so great that it was found necessary to call together the *iudices et fideles* in the fourteenth year of King Liutprand, "ut nullus error esse deberet, sed omnibus manifesta clariscere lex."[1] The Lombards, of course, were far in advance of most Germanic nations in their legal development at this time.

These general characteristics of medieval procedure are to be found in all parts of Western Europe at this time and in all kinds of courts, feudal, seignorial, communal, or royal. In some places the development of feudalism tended at times to turn communal courts into seignorial ones, and often also to shift the burden of attendance at the court from the community as a whole upon the tenants of definite pieces of land within it. But, in any case, that burden of suit remained, and in all the courts of whatever kind the procedure continued to be one requiring the concerted action of a considerable number of the men of the neighbourhood. Thus whether it was the custom of the manor or the feudal law of the fief that was to be found, that law would be ascertained from a sufficient number of men of the district who knew it.

Locally this required, in the court of the district, "representatives" from the community if they were not all present in person. The presence of these representatives in early times does not, of course, imply their "election" in our modern sense. Till a comparatively late date we know little of how they were chosen, but it is as likely, if not more likely, that they were appointed as that they were "elected." *Eligere* is an elastic word in medieval documents, from which too much should not be inferred. Further-more, these representatives of the community were chosen—however they

---

[1] *Edictus ceteraeque Langobardorum leges* (Ed. Bluhme), SGUS, Liutprandi Leges, de anno quartodecimo, pr.

were chosen—to perform a duty, to acquit their community of a burden. It was no privilege they enjoyed. Sometimes, indeed, this has been compared to modern representative institutions, and it has something in common with them. But this representing of the community was not then an honour. If it must be compared with something modern to which it has little practical resemblance, it would be fitter to compare it with our jury service than with membership in a modern legislative body. Nevertheless, burden though it was, it contained and it continued the practice, and even the theory, that lies at the roots of modern representative institutions—not the practice alone, but the theory as well. A proof of this exists in the wording of English official documents of the eleventh and early twelfth centuries. We know absolutely that at that time, in both the hundred and the county court, each township was "represented" by six persons at most. Yet, for both hundred and hundred court, there was used but one word, the word *hundredus*; while in like fashion a single word, *comitatus*, had to do duty alike for the shire and the shire court. In short, the *hundredus* was both the hundred and the hundred court— they were theoretically the same, though in actual fact widely different; and the *comitatus* meant equally the county and the county court, though but a small proportion of the whole county actually attended that court. Theoretically the county and the county court were the same. Actually they were not. The fiction of "representation" alone can explain this identity. There must have been in existence some theory of representation as well as the fact.

Possibly an even clearer indication of this may be seen in the statement made by the author of the *Leges Henrici Primi* written in the reign of Henry I of England. After a statement that a lord or his steward who has a right to do so may acquit the lord's demesne lands in the hundred of the suit in the hundred court due from them, he goes on to say that if the lord or his steward is unable to be present, then "prepositus et sacerdos et IIII de melioribus ville assint *pro omnibus* qui nominatim non erunt ad placitum submoniti."[1]

When the courts began in England to feel the strong hand of the Norman kings and the process of administrative centralisation started, these germs of representation, instead of dying out, developed a stronger growth. The documents of this period prove that the kings retained the old communal courts of the hundred and shire of set purpose[2]. They also began the process of unifying them, chiefly through the activity of the royally appointed sheriff and later through the justices in eyre. With the growth of the eyre system and largely through the increasing practice of

[1] Liebermann, *Gesetze der Angelsachsen*, I, p. 553.
[2] For example: "Requiratur hundred et comitatus, sicut antecessores nostri statuerunt," William the Conqueror, Liebermann, *op. cit.*, I, p. 488; "Sciatis, quod concedo et precipio, ut amodo comitatus mei et hundreta in illis locis et eisdem terminis sedeant, sicut sederunt in tempore regis Eadwardi, et non aliter," Henry I, Liebermann, *op. cit.*, I, p. 524.

drawing cases by royal writ from other courts to the King's Court, it became increasingly necessary that these royal courts should be certified of the proceedings already taken in the other courts from which the cases were drawn away. The King's Courts required a bringing up of the "record" from the court, whether manorial or communal, in which the case had begun. In the days before the proceedings of these courts were written, this "record" was only in the minds of the men of the court, not in writing. Hence the "bringing up of the record" was the bringing up of a man or men, not of a written document.

So section 4 of Henry II's *Assize of Clarendon,* in 1166, prescribes that when the sheriff brings violators of the assize before the itinerant justices for trial, he shall bring along with them "from the hundred and the township where they were arrested 'duos legales homines ad portandum recordationem comitatus et hundredi, quare capti fuerint.'"[1] Professor G. B. Adams has pointed out a number of cases of the same practice in Bracton's *Note Book,* one in 1226 where four discreet knights of the county and four of the king's *servientes* were to come "ad certificandum Dominum Regem"[2]; another in 1219 when the sheriff is directed to have before the royal justices the record "per quatuor milites de comitatu qui recordo illi interfuerunt"[3]; another in 1220 when the knights are said to speak *pro comitatu*[4]; one in 1230 where three knights are said to come *pro toto comitatu*[5]; and several more[6]. The number might easily be increased. "Here," says Professor Adams, "was certainly a direct line of connexion between the county court and the king's council, already established and in frequent use."[7] He sees in the first recorded appearance of the knights of the shire in parliament, in 1254, a repetition of this procedure in matters of parliamentary grant instead of in a trial, and he finds in these earlier judicial practices the precedent and the justification for the extra-feudal practice initiated in 1254 of summoning the representative knights as well as the tenants-in-chief to a parliament. This acute suggestion of Professor Adams, a suggestion amply supported by contemporary records, really enables us to trace a continuous development of the practice and the theory of representation in England from the end of the Anglo-Saxon period through the fundamental reforms of William I, Henry I, and Henry II, by which the royal administration was unified and extended, down to the period of the appearance of the first surviving record of a summons of representative knights of the shire to parliament in 1254. It is a matter of the greatest consequence.

This development, however, seems not to have been confined to the

---

[1] Stubbs, *Select Charters* (9th edition), p. 170.
[2] Bracton's *Note Book,* plea 1730.
[3] *Ibid.,* plea 40.
[4] *Ibid.,* plea 1436.
[5] *Ibid.,* plea 445.
[6] Adams, *Origin of the English Constitution,* p. 321.
[7] *Ibid.,* pp. 321–2.

representative knights. It appears, though considerably later and much less clearly, in the representation of burgesses as well, long before the time of the Earl of Leicester's parliament of 1265, when we have the first record of the appearance of representative burgesses in a parliament for the whole realm. In section 12 of John's charter, after the promise that scutage and extraordinary aids should be imposed only with the common assent of the realm, provision is made that in case of aids from the city of London the procedure shall be *simili modo*. From the time of Sir Henry Spelman to the present, the meaning of *simili modo* has been an enigma. Spelman himself seemed to think the words implied representation in the king's Curia, and was therefore surprised to find no appearance of any burgesses in the records of the years following 1215[1]. Professor Adams, on the other hand, believes that these words indicated merely that London and London alone of all English towns had a commune, and therefore an independent feudal status which placed it on a par feudally with the tenants-in-chief already mentioned in this section of the document, and that this of course implies the necessity of consent to aids, but apparently not necessarily any representative from the city in any Curia where the collective consent of the tenants-in-chief was obtained.

However this may be, the fact is that there is no surviving record of the presence of these borough representatives before the parliament of Simon de Montfort in 1265. But as in the case of the representative knights, there is a long local history behind this first known appearance of burgesses in a central assembly. For example, in 1231 the sheriff of Yorkshire is directed by writ to present before the justices itinerant on their coming into the county, not only the nobility and higher clergy, the knights and the free tenants of the county, but twelve legal burgesses from each borough and all others "who usually are and ought to be" there, to assist in the trial of the pleas of the Crown and others[2]. Cases might be multiplied, and it is clear that the words of Stubbs applied to the knights of the shire are almost equally applicable to the townsmen as well: "a consolidated body of men trained by a century and a half of common interests and common work."[3]

In recent years a tendency has appeared in certain quarters to criticise the masterly account of these developments by Bishop Stubbs, on the ground that he understates the importance of the clergy in shaping their course and attaches "too much weight in comparison to the old communal institutions of England, such as the attendance of the four men and the reeve at hundred and shire court, and to the influence of the judicial procedure of Henry II."[4] The *reductio ad absurdum* of Professor Barker's

[1] *Of Parliaments, Reliquiae Spelmannianae*, p. 64.
[2] Stubbs, *Select Charters* (9th edition), p. 354.
[3] Stubbs, *Constitutional History of England*, II, p. 195.
[4] Ernest Barker, *The Dominican Order and Convocation*, p. 53.

temperate thesis on this subject is found in a recent American study of representative government where it is baldly declared that: "The Church originated representative institutions; the State adopted them."[1] To make such a declaration one must either be totally ignorant of the meaning and significance of the striking and continuous series of evidences of representative ideas and institutions running back to the very Conquest in England and even beyond, or he must consider himself able to explain them as not really representative in character. One way of doing the latter is to attempt, as Dr Barker does, to distinguish between the mere representation "to give information" (*ad recognoscendum*) in the earlier English instances and the true representation "to take action" (*ad faciendum*), supposed to occur only at a later period and as the result of clerical ideas and institutions.

But against this view several serious objections may be urged. It implies a distinction between central and local institutions which is too sharp and too modern; it depends upon a sharp cleavage between the ideas of representation for information and representation for action, for which there is little contemporary evidence in the thirteenth century and before; and it is greatly weakened by the fact that there were no Dominicans in England before 1221, yet it is to the Dominicans that the institutions of representation are mainly attributed. It is true enough, as has been urged in support of this view, that our earliest surviving official record of the idea of representation on anything like a national scale, the writ of King John in 1213 for the return of "four discreet knights" from the counties of England, probably had no practical result, since we have no record of their actual meeting; but the writ itself nevertheless is evidence of the existence of the idea in 1213, some years before the development of the Dominican constitution or its transfer to England; and it is noteworthy that the four discreet knights were summoned not merely *ad recognoscendum*, but *ad loquendum nobiscum de negotiis regni nostri*[2]. In local matters it is equally impossible to distinguish clearly between information and action in numberless cases, and the distinction between the local occurrence of representation and its use in a national assembly is one that strikes us as it does only because we know its later developments; to contemporaries it was insignificant and unimportant. The contemporary chroniclers give no attention whatever to the first English case of borough representation which we consider so epoch-making. To them it was only a slight modification of ideas and practices long familiar to them in the county court. Knights

---

[1] Henry J. Ford, *Representative Government* (New York, 1924), p. 111.

[2] Stubbs, *Select Charters* (9th edition), p. 282. The impossibility of making such clear-cut distinctions comes out plainly, for example, in the ordinance for the assessment of the Saladin tithe in 1188, where four or six legal men were to swear to the amount any taxable person should have returned if it was suspected that his return was too low. Stubbs, p. 189. This is in effect an assessment of a tax. Dare we say that these men are employed solely *ad recognoscendum* and in no sense *ad faciendum?* The line between the two was very shadowy.

and burgesses had been co-operating for generations with the *iusticiarii* on their circuits throughout the counties of England, and these *iusticiarii* were in fact, if not in theory, members of the king's central Curia. The clergy no doubt contributed a large part of the later development of representation; truly to assert that they "originated" it is impossible in face of the overwhelming evidence to the contrary.

In 1254 in England, for the first time so far as we have evidence surviving, these local practices and ideas were incorporated in the national assembly or Curia, and in order to understand the working of the "estates" that resulted, a brief review of the earlier history of the Curia itself is necessary.

Though in an earlier period the English national assembly—and the local assemblies as well—had in all probability been a real *folc mote* in the same sense and of much the same kind as the meetings of the warriors of the *civitas* or tribe as described in the *Germania* of Tacitus, long before the Norman Conquest it had turned into a select body of comparatively few magnates, elders, or *sapientes*, a *witenagemot*, in which the "wisdom" which constituted the supposed qualification for membership was coming more and more to consist in royal favour and wide estates. This body survived the Conquest and is frequently referred to in the gradually expiring "Anglo-Saxon Chronicle" by the old names of *Witan* or *Mickel-gemot*. But its character was changed. Even before the Conquest, if we may accept the brilliant suggestions of Professor H. M. Chadwick, feudal tendencies had long been at work upon it, and the Conquest at a stroke completed the development. The drastic confiscation of the lands of the greater English lords and the wholesale transfer of these lands by the Conqueror to a completely new set of Norman tenants-in-chief are not only the beginning of the English land law; they mark the complete transformation of the English national assembly. It became completely feudalised. Tenure became the single basis of the vassals' obligation which entitled the king as their feudal overlord to demand the services of such of them as he chose in the administration of the fief, and the fief was a kingdom; hence the court was the *Curia Regis*. The list from which he might choose in 1086 is the list of tenants-in-chief set forth in Domesday Book, as printed in Sir Henry Ellis' *Introduction*. In fact, he chose few, and some of these, for practical reasons, he could not well omit. But the regularity of the summons to great officials, such as the Chancellor or Treasurer, is owing, not to any constitutional rule that gives them a "right" to be present, but only to the practical necessity of their presence with their records and seals in order to get business done. No one, in fact, had any right to attend. All tenants-in-chief were bound to do so. It was the king's right to summon them all, and he summoned whom he would or whom practical necessity required.

Thus the first and oldest medieval estate emerges in England. It is the estate of the *barones* or feudal tenants-in-chief, both spiritual and lay, a fraction of which, and not always the same fraction, was summoned by the king from time to time to his Councils. Thus it remained in general till the afforcement in 1254 by the introduction of representative knights of the shire. But it would be premature to attach the name "estate" to such a body in the Norman period. Such a term was not applied, and could hardly be applied to the body of tenants-in-chief in England, before that body began to act and to think collectively. In the eleventh and twelfth centuries these tenants are referred to simply as *barones*. That word is not found in the singular, nor is the collective noun *baronagium* or *barnagium* used as yet. Such *barones* were simply a number of persons who happened to be *pares*, because they held of the same lord and of the same fief, *convassalli*; and, at the same time, any one of them might hold other lands in other fiefs or of other lords and thus be a member of other courts and the "peer" of other bodies of men.

So long as these centrifugal tendencies remained unchecked, the conception of corporateness among the English tenants-in-chief was difficult to realise, and history shews little collective action of a permanent kind. The feudal *diffidatio* by which a vassal repudiated his lord was an individual thing, as were the original homage and fealty which it renounced. In certain senses feudalism in its unchanged form was extremely individualistic.

In England it was not till the thirteenth century that the barons began to act as a collective unit, but as early as the reign of John they are found doing so. It is in that reign that we find the first royal recognition of the baronial right collectively to coerce the king by force, in the final sections of Magna Carta. From that reign, too, comes the first known instance of a "parliamentary grant" to the king by the barons, acting in their collective capacity, and it is but a few years afterward, as Matthew Paris tells us, that *totius Angliae nobilitas*, when importuned by the king for money, took an oath each to the other that they would give the king no answer except a *communis responsio*[1], an early instance of "collective bargaining."

An indication of the absence of any idea of a definite corporate character in the baronage may possibly be seen in section 14 of Magna Carta, in which it is promised that an assessment of a scutage or extraordinary aid shall bind all tenants-in-chief who have been summoned, even if all these have not appeared, provided it is agreed to by those who are present. The tacit exception here made of those who had not been summoned seems to indicate that assent is still several rather than joint, though it is given when all are assembled together instead of separately. Probably one not summoned was not bound by their action[2]. This provision as to summons had not been demanded by the barons in their Articles; and it, together with the whole of the provisions of 1215 concerning aids, was entirely omitted from all later reissues of the Charter, while scutage was by the terms of the second reissue of 1217 to be thereafter imposed as was the custom in the time of Henry II.

[1] In 1242. Matt. Paris, *Chron. Maj.* (Rolls Series), iv, 181–2. [2] See *infra*, p. 675.

Professor Powicke has shewn how John's loss of Normandy had resulted in the surrender of their Norman lands by the barons of England, who were thus for the first time left "free to devote themselves to English affairs." There can be no doubt that this was a great impetus to the growth among the English barons, not only of a feeling of nationality, but of their corporate character as a real baronage or estate of the realm of England. John was one of the first kings regularly to style himself *Rex Angliae* instead of *Rex Anglorum*; in a few years we find the contemporary chronicler speaking of his barons also as *nobilitas Angliae*.

It is a commonplace that the units of political or legal thought in the later Middle Ages are groups rather than individuals. When the barons then began in practice to have common interests, aims, and actions, it was natural that they should be regarded, first rather loosely, later much more definitely, as a *universitas* or commune; and as such we may consider them as the first of the communes which in time combined to form the English Parliament.

Up to 1254 the commune of these barons or royal tenants-in-chief constituted the only element in the national assembly, and up to the end of the first quarter of the fourteenth century the only invariable and essential element. The basis of the membership was military tenure tempered by royal summons. The greater barons were entitled to a special summons, the lesser ones, whom Round has shewn not to be the same as mere knights, must attend if merely summoned generally by the sheriff. Thus they assisted in the general business of the Curia, which was at once consultative, administrative, and judicial; and it included the promulgation of administrative assizes as well as the issuing of original writs in judicial matters—until the increasingly onerous and technical burden of the last of these was gradually delegated to the chancellor alone—and the trial of such cases as found their way, on account of difficulty or importance, to the whole Council for determination. On feudal principles, these members collectively also gave judgment in cases involving any of their own number, and each of them was entitled to such a *iudicium parium suorum* in his own case. The growing definition of the feudal incidents in feudal custom had made certain of these incidents a matter of course which the lord might levy without consent when occasion arose, but in all other or extraordinary cases no assessment of aids could be made under feudal custom without the assent of the body of tenants upon whom it would directly fall. This was as true of the tenants-in-chief of the English king as it was of the vassals of any lord, and it was the meetings of these tenants in the royal Curia and their consent to such aids, beginning on a national scale apparently in 1207 in England, that must be considered the source of the later parliamentary grants which played so large a part in the development of English constitutionalism. The barons in 1215 formally demanded that all such extraordinary aids as well as scutages should be imposed only "per commune consilium regni"—with the common assent of the realm[1]—and in conceding this demand the king promised in addition that all the tenants-in-chief should be summoned to a meeting for the purpose, and that those there present should be able to decide the matter even in the absence of the rest who had not obeyed the summons[2]. These provisions, their wording, and other documents of this period, warrant us in assuming that the barons are by this time in a sense acting as an estate of the realm and that their assent alone is referred to as the assent of the *realm*; and elsewhere in documents and chronicles of this time they are frequently spoken of and speak of themselves and themselves alone as the *populus*. This is the more significant when we remember that by this time the rôle of the Roman *populus* as the ultimate source of the authority of Roman law was known in England through the law books of Justinian, as is shewn clearly by statements made in the preface of Glanville's treatise on the laws of England, written before the end of the twelfth century, and repeated by Bracton. The meaning of *populus* was understood and the baronage was as yet the whole *populus*; it was the only estate of the realm; its consent alone was the *commune consilium regni*. It was, however, an estate in which there existed no representation in any definite constitutional sense.

To such a meeting "for obtaining the common assent of the realm" all the individuals to whom that assent directly applied were summoned; all barons upon whom the burden of the aids or scutage there assessed directly fell were actually present or had an opportunity to be present. The body thus represented no one. Their decision was their own, it directly affected none but themselves, and they alone were considered competent to make it.

It may even be assumed that a baron, had he been omitted from the summons, would not have been bound by their action; and we have some additional evidence that this was the rule[3]. But this is only the formal or legal aspect of the matter. Though a baron who had failed to receive a summons was probably not bound by the action of the rest, one who had received a summons and ignored it certainly was, and this in itself is a striking evidence of the growing idea of corporateness. Furthermore, though these barons alone were the whole *populus* whose assent would be enough to conclude all others, at least for assessments whose original incidence fell upon them alone, there was a vague sense in which even in these matters they did act for the classes below them upon whom they were constantly shifting the actual burden of these exactions.

An illustration of this is found on the Close Rolls of Henry III in 1237, in which the fact is recited that a *colloquium* had met at Westminster composed of "the archbishops, bishops, abbots, priors, earls, and barons

---

[1] *Articles of the Barons*, section 32, Stubbs, *Select Charters* (9th edition), p. 288.
[2] Stubbs, *op. cit.*, p. 295.
[3] S. K. Mitchell, *Studies in Taxation under John and Henry III*, pp. 127, 131–2 note, 141, 156–7, 161–2, 208–9, 282 sqq.

of our whole realm," and apparently none beyond these; yet there follows immediately the statement that "the same archbishops, bishops, abbots, priors, and ecclesiastics holding lands which do not belong to their churches, earls, barons, knights, and free men, for themselves *and their villani*," had granted to the king in aid a thirtieth of their movables[1].

And a time was to come, and that before long, after the *milites* or "country gentry" had gradually grown to sufficient importance, strength, and political self-consciousness, when the uneasiness aroused by these conditions would force the barons to begin to doubt their own unaided ability, if not their right, to consent to burdens whose chief weight must fall in the last instance upon estates lower in the feudal hierarchy, and even to suggest to the king that the estate of the knights should be consulted as well as their own in the imposition of such burdens[2].

An interesting example of such doubts on the part of the magnates occurs in 1290 in the case of an aid for the marriage of the king's daughter. The lords did, it is true, profess to make the grant "for themselves and for the community of the whole realm," but their growing doubts of their own unaided ability to do so appear in the phrase immediately following: "quantum in ipsis est."[3] As a result of these doubts the king summoned representative knights of the shire to consult on this matter, and in the writs he distinctly says that he is issuing them at the special request of the magnates—"cum per comites, barones, et quosdam alios de proceribus regni nostri, nuper fuissemus super quibusdam *specialiter requisiti*,...tibi praecipimus, etc."[4]

In like manner the "lords spiritual" were becoming less certain of their ability by their assent alone to bind all the clergy. Thus the assembly of the clergy which met at the king's command at Northampton in 1282 to make a grant to the king, though it contained proctors from the cathedral chapters, alleged, as a cause of its failure to make any grant, the lack of consent by the parochial clergy. As a result, in 1283 the writs to the archbishop to a second meeting remedied this defect by directing that proctors of the parochial clergy should be summoned, and the reason given was that at the previous convocation, "partly through the absence of the greater part of the clergy who according to the usual practice at that time prevailing had not been summoned, partly for other reasons, *ad plenum non potuit responderi*."[5]

Thus it is evident that the monopoly of the *barones*, both ecclesiastical and lay, as the sole element in the *populus*, was gradually wearing away, and that strong tendencies were at work which were widening the basis

[1] Stubbs, *Select Charters* (9th edition), p. 358.

[2] For the best account of the relations of these classes with the magnates and with the king, see E. F. Jacob, *Studies in the period of baronial reforms and rebellion, 1258–1267.*

[3] *Rot. Parl.*, I, 25, Stubbs, *Select Charters* (9th edition), p. 472.

[4] Stubbs, *op. cit.*, p. 472.

[5] Wilkins, *Concilia*, II, 93; Stubbs, *Select Charters* (9th edition), p. 459.

of the State and rapidly creating the necessity for the emergence of additional "estates" as sharers at least in the burdens imposed by the increasing demands of the king. Later, a sharing of burdens must of necessity lead to a sharing in other things as well.

Thus new elements were in time added to the older Curia, but the Curia itself remained through all the changes. This has been well expressed by M. Pasquet when he says, speaking of the House of Commons: "That convocation is in short merely the extension to some of the new classes of society—the *bourgeoisie* of the towns and the class of free tenants of the country—of 'the service of the court' which had hitherto been demanded by the king only from his barons. The delegates of the *communautés* then came to take their place in an organisation already in existence; for an understanding of the real significance of the innovations which were made in the reign of Henry III and of Edward I, it is necessary to recall the essential features of that organisation."[1]

The real motives behind these "innovations" of Henry III and more especially of Edward I, and their immediate causes, have been the occasion of considerable discussion in recent years. The traditional view, still generally held, and admirably set forth in detail by Bishop Stubbs, attributes these new developments almost solely to the increasing demands of the king for money, and the participation of these additional "estates" in the parliamentary grants which resulted. In recent years, several other alternative explanations have been offered. In 1888 Ludwig Riess, the author of the history of English parliamentary elections in the Middle Ages, contended that the chief purpose of Edward I was not so much this, as the better control and oversight of the county administration in the hands of the sheriffs, and the centralisation of a system employing the aid of the knights of the shire in local administration including the local assessment and collection of aids[2]. M. Pasquet, while admitting the existence of all these causes, would find the principal motive of Edward I in calling new estates to his councils in his determination not only to be the suzerain of his vassals, but the king of all his subjects; and he connects the king's summoning of these new elements with his inquests *quo warranto* and the statute of *Quia Emptores*, as all parts of a general design of destroying the distinction existing in feudal custom between his tenants-in-chief and the mesne lords or *arrière-vassaux*[3]. Professor Pollard sees in the fact that in so many of Edward's parliaments no financial supply was granted or asked for, a proof that it was its judicial and not its financial activity that must furnish the explanation at least of the frequency of its meetings, and he believes this frequency to be due less to the king than to his subjects[4].

[1] D. Pasquet, *Essai sur les origines de la chambre des communes*, p. 1.

[2] *Der Ursprung des englischen Unterhauses*, in Sybel's *Historische Zeitschrift*, LX, pp. 1–33.

[3] *Essai*, pp. 242 sqq. [4] *The Evolution of Parliament*, pp. 42–3.

CH. XXIII.

A famous case of such a demand by the barons for reasons largely judicial occurs in the twenty-ninth ordinance of the "Lords' Ordinances" in 1311, where a parliament is required once a year or oftener, and the reason given is that defendants had alleged that they were bound to reply only *coram Rege,* and that the king's ministers had been guilty of acts of oppression against law, for which there was no redress without a parliament. It was therefore ordained that a parliament should meet at least once a year where these delayed cases might be terminated, as well as those in which the justices were of conflicting opinions, and final action taken on bills brought into parliament according to law and reason[1]. But these circumstances were to say the least exceptional, if not to be termed revolutionary.

Without doubt there is much to be said for each of these factors, and this modern discussion has considerably widened and deepened our understanding of the development of parliament. If we confine ourselves to the beginnings of these innovations, while Henry III was still alive, the contemporary evidence is strongly in favour of Bishop Stubbs' view that the original motive behind the beginning of these changes was almost entirely fiscal. But the reigns of Edward I and Edward II are a period of almost bewildering development, and new forces, unknown or latent before, then began to operate. Certainly before 1327, the representative knights who had originally come to parliament only to grant, were remaining to do much more, and a part of this transformation must be placed in Edward I's reign if not attributed to his initiative. The Rolls of Parliament, which have by this time begun, prove the activity of the representative estates in framing petitions, and in 1322 the well-known statute of York provides that enactments touching the estate of the whole realm—"pour lestat de nostre seigneur le Roi, et de ses Heirs, et pour lestat du roialme et du poeple"—must have their participation[2]. In 1290, when the statute of *Quia Emptores* was enacted, this had probably not been so, and this rapid change may have been owing in part at least to Edward's policy of advancing the *arrière-vassaux,* or his attempts to consolidate the local administration with the central. It seems probable that most of these great changes were in the beginning at least the result of the king's initiative—occasionally but only in exceptional circumstances the barons'— rather than of the desires of the new classes represented; but, even admitting this, the effect of the changes upon those classes is not far different from what it would have been had they originated with themselves. These classes do now in time gradually grow to be an integral part of parliament, the parliament to which *Fleta* referred when he said, "The king has his court in his council in his parliaments." And they are becoming some-

[1] *Rot. Parl.,* i, p. 285.

[2] The investigations of Mr J. Conway Davies, in his *Baronial Opposition to Edward II,* confirm the interpretation given here, which is adopted in preference to the view of Mr G. T. Lapsley accepted by Professor Tout in his *Place of Edward II in English History,* restricting the application of the statute to "constitutional" matters only.

thing more than a mere addendum to the Curia as they seemed to be at
first, summoned only to participate in an aid demanded by the king and
then summarily sent home; they are now remaining to do many important
things beyond the granting of supply, though they continue to be in many
things subordinate to the lords. Edward I's famous dictum of 1295, "quod
omnes tangit ab omnibus approbetur," applied to them, and it cannot be
wholly waved aside as the unimportant verbiage of some minor official, as
is sometimes done; but it originally included only grants and nothing
more. By 1322, however, it had come in effect to include enactment as
well as grant, and possibly in practice much besides. Whatever then may
have been the true proximate cause or causes of the beginning of this
important development, its remoter causes lie far back in the earlier
history, and the main features of the system of representation thus
established are fairly clear.

In the first recorded instance of a summons of knights to a parliament,
in 1254, election in the county court is clearly referred to, as well as precise
instructions, and the clear principle that these representatives both act
for and can bind the whole body of the county ; and it may safely be inferred that these ideas and practices were already thoroughly familiar
through long usage in local matters in these courts. For certain specific
things election was employed at least as early as 1215. Chapter 18 of
John's charter had prescribed the assistance of four knights elected *per
comitatum* in the assizes of novel disseisin and mort d'ancestor, and
chapter 48 had provided even more definitely that the twelve knights
who were to investigate the wrongdoing of the king's foresters "ought to
be elected by the good men" in the county court. It is true, as M. Pasquet
has pointed out, that the expedients of 1254 in one respect fall far short
of our modern complete idea of representation. The representatives are
not empowered by their constituents to represent them for a long period,
and have no authority to bind them in any matter that may happen in future
to come before them; they are definitely restricted to the matter of which
the county court has received notice in the king's writ. As representatives,
in their consent in parliament they are confined *ad hoc*. This, however,
does not mean that they have no discretion, for they have power *ad
tractandum*. The limits of their discretion are probably fixed in their instructions, and on this they are to have power to answer *praecise*, but
within these limits they are left free. This is, as M. Pasquet says, a
system of procuration rather than one truly and entirely representative
in our modern sense[1], but many of the essentials of modern representation
are there, and of the others a beginning may be seen. The representatives
bind their constituents, they have a "mandate," they have some discretionary power, and before long they acquire a greater permanence.
Medieval English parliaments never lasted longer than a few weeks at the
most, but we may easily see slight but more and more definite indications

[1] *Essai*, pp. 78–81.

of the growth of a more general delegation of power, and for a longer
time, in the writs of summons that we find from time to time in the later
years of the thirteenth century; and in the next century these delegations
of power become more extensive still, though it was hardly before the
Tudor period, with its parliaments occasionally lasting several years and
divided into several sessions, that the full modern idea can be said to have
become completely established.

Space will not permit of a detailed examination of the growth of the
different estates of the knights, burgesses, cathedral and parochial clergy.
When summoned to parliament, the knights of one county in one writ of
summons are directed to treat with the representatives of the other counties
upon the matters on which the magnates shall have agreed. The matter
thus agreed upon was of course a grant, and the writ implies that all
the knights were to deliberate together upon it, and do so separately
from the magnates, and there is other full evidence that this was the
practice. When burgesses were summoned, they too deliberated together,
but apart from the other estates, and the same was true of the "communes" of the cathedral and the parish clergy, whether these were present
in person or by proctors, in the few cases of their presence in English
parliaments of the late thirteenth century.

Thus the new representative element in the parliaments of that period
really consisted of several collective units or *universitates*, each consisting
of representatives who acted for the class as a whole from which it was
drawn, and no more. They were summoned *ad tractandum*, but the
"treating" was only in common with their fellow-representatives from
the same estate. Hence the answers of these several estates to the king's
request for supply might be and usually were different. In the same
parliament the knights collectively might agree to grant a tenth, while
the parochial clergy might promise only a thirteenth, and so on. The
lower clergy in a few years disappeared as an estate in parliament but
continued till the seventeenth century to make grants in their convocations, a remarkable proof of the separation of clergy and laity in the later
Middle Ages, since a similar tendency on the part of the merchants was
successfully and permanently checked by the House of Commons about
the middle of the fourteenth century. Thus the parliament in its deliberations upon the king's requests was really not one body, and in the early
period not two bodies, but often three, four, or even five, according as
knights, burgesses, cathedral and parochial clergy were present or not.
Ad tractandum it was strictly a combination of several separate communes
or estates, deliberating apart from each other and often returning different
answers to the king's demands, and estates whose number actually varied
widely from year to year. Before the reign of Edward III it would be
more accurate to call the representative portion of the parliament a house
of communes than a house of commons.

But there is another side to all this. As M. Pasquet says, the representatives are the delegates of separate communes, "but they come to take their place in an organisation already in existence." They did not take this place at once. In the reign of Henry III, or even the early years of Edward I, when they participated in grants and nothing more, it is questionable whether they could properly be considered a part of that organisation; a few years later there can be no question. True, the various communes continue to deliberate apart, and *for deliberation* parliament remains a body of several almost distinct parts. But by the end of Edward's reign these communes have taken their place as parts of *one* parliament. Organically it is one and they have become members of it. At the solemn opening of parliament, when the king's demands are made known in the *pronunciatio*, the representatives are present with the lords in the same chamber to hear it. This was probably not the case so late as 1290; it becomes invariable in the fourteenth century. It is only for deliberation that parliament is now separated. For its formal acts it is one. Thus the estates continue, but they have become merged in one official body. In 1297 Edward I had recognised that new customs duties might be levied only with the assent of all the realm, and that in parliament, for this touched all. In 1322 it was established that common law as well as common grants needed the assent of "all," and a statute which enacted a common law required the assent of "all," including the representatives as well as the lords. By 1348 the Commons were able to assert their control even over grants that appeared to touch not all but particular classes only, and Edward III was compelled to desist from his attempts to treat for a grant with assemblies composed of the merchants[1].

In the meantime, Convocation had gone its separate way, and the communes of the knights and the burgesses were gradually coalescing into a true "House of Commons," a process that was almost complete by the middle of the fourteenth century[2]. By 1365 a chief justice of England could say, "Everyone is considered to know what is done in parliament: for so soon as parliament has concluded anything, the law presumes that everybody has notice of it; for the parliament represents the body of all the realm."[3] The feudal estates have become the "body of all the realm." Edward I's design of being king rather than mere lord has largely been fulfilled. Modern political ideas are supplanting the medieval ones, and a national "House of Commons" is rapidly replacing the medieval house of communes.

[1] F. R. Barnes, *The Taxation of Wool*, and G. Unwin, *The Estate of Merchants*; both in *Finance and Trade under Edward III*.

[2] This development is of the greatest importance. It is one of the most fundamental of the differences between English and French constitutional history. Stubbs' admirable account remains the best general statement of our existing knowledge, *Constitutional History*, II, pp. 193–8. The beginning of a more detailed study has been made in the excellent papers of Mr Richardson, Mr Sayles, and Mr Edwards.

[3] *Year Book*, Pasch., 39 Edward III, p. 7.

The above sketch of the development of the English communes is brief and inadequate, but it was necessary to choose the growth of a single system as an illustration, in order to bring out the fact that these institutions everywhere were really the result of a gradual development, not of a sudden creation; and the English system is best adapted to that purpose on account of the greater richness of English records, especially of a local character, in the earlier period.

But developments somewhat like this were by no means confined to England. Almost everywhere in Western Europe, out of much the same original materials and ideas and under the stimulus of circumstances generally similar though often specifically different, a development not unlike this had taken place; and by the end of the thirteenth century we find all over the Continent conditions and ideas sometimes less developed than those of England, sometimes in some respects apparently even more developed. These ideas and institutions are neither of sudden occurrence nor the product of imitation to any great degree. They are everywhere the result of a slow growth which no doubt might be followed step by step elsewhere as we have tried briefly to follow it in England, if other countries were as fortunate as England in the preservation of the contemporary records of their earlier history. The universality of these institutions is the sufficient answer to any theory of their exclusively "Anglo-Saxon" origin and character. They are owing neither to English blood nor to English political genius, but rather to the common stock of institutions with which most of the Western nations started, and the operation of definite historic events upon the development of these, which was in its larger aspects much the same everywhere. The unique character of English constitutional development began far back in English history, but its most striking manifestations, as far as they are exclusively English, lie on this side of the thirteenth century rather than on the other, and even they must be attributed to definite historic conditions and events which demand only detailed knowledge to explain them; they are not the result of some mysterious quality in the blood of England. At the most, the factors are cultural rather than racial, but historical rather than either.

By the latter part of the thirteenth century, a development analogous to England's had produced institutions and ideas not fundamentally different from hers in almost all parts of Christendom. From Scandinavia to the Adriatic they are found, and in the east of Europe as well as the west; in Hungary, Poland, and Bohemia, no less than in Italy, Spain, and the Low Countries. Those of Eastern Europe treated in other chapters in this work are not included in this sketch, but even in the West alone their wide distribution is sufficiently remarkable.

In France, the historic connexion of these remarkable constitutional developments with the earlier institutions of the Frankish monarchy is fairly clear. The tradition of the old Frankish régime, its royal power, its enactments, and its assemblies had remained[1]; but in the tenth and eleventh centuries the powerlessness of the kings and the parcelling out of royal authority among great lords, whose dependence was little more than nominal, had gone so far as to make this scarcely more than a memory. With Louis VI, as Luchaire points out[2], this striking contradiction between the king's great claims and his actual feebleness began to grow less, and a new tradition was founded which was ultimately gradually to grow into the absolutism of Louis XIV. In France, however, conditions were at first less favourable for its rapid development than in England. The twelfth century was in reality the critical period for both countries, and England was then able to lay the foundations of later constitutionalism in her national system of administration, while in France similar conditions were hardly approximated before the reign of Philip the Fair. These things gave to England and Normandy an administrative development in advance of France by more than a century[3], and that difference in time determined the difference between England's subsequent constitutionalism and the absolutism of France. Otherwise, conditions were roughly much the same on both sides of the Channel. As in England, though more rarely than in England, the French king from time to time assembled in his Curia varying numbers of the great feudatories owing him suit, and by the reign of Louis VII their activity often resulted in administrative enactments or *établissements* of considerable importance. Such enactments, except in the crises of war or invasion, Beaumanoir says, must, however, be for sufficient cause, for the common profit, not against God and good customs; and they must be made *par grant conseil*[4].

It was to the appearance of a great national emergency, together with the continuance of these earlier institutions and practices, that we must attribute the unusual developments in France in the time of Philip the Fair, which resulted in the first assembling of the feudal estates on a national scale; and the inclusion in these assemblies of the *bourgeoisie* was, in the first instance at least, due to the enfranchisement of so many of the communes during the thirteenth century, which thus brought them within the feudal hierarchy and imposed upon them the burden of the suit generally incident to feudal tenure whenever it was demanded of them by their feudal overlord, together with the other customary obligations of *auxilium* and military service. In common with the other vassals of the king they owed him counsel and they owed him aid, and these, or the second of them at least, had been demanded and received by the kings of the thirteenth century from their *villes*, in assemblies of which the great lords had formed no part. The rapid differentia-

---

[1] Luchaire, *Institutions Monarchiques*, I, pp. 47–59.

[2] In Lavisse, *Histoire de France*, tome II, IIe partie, liv. II, c. 5.

[3] *Ibid.*, tome III, I[e] partie, p. 49.

[4] *Coutûmes de Beauvaisis*, edited by Salmon, Chapter XLIX, section 1515 (Vol. II, p. 264).

tion in the central administration of the latter part of the thirteenth century is no doubt an important cause of this separate action. The judicial function of the old Curia had already passed in large part to the *Parlement*, while *consilium* had become one of the chief functions of the king's private council, though this was, as Viollet says, a matter of fact rather than of legal definition. When the communes were summoned, it was usually *auxilium* and that alone that was wanted, and before the opening of the fourteenth century, in all cases where it was demanded from them collectively, it was in assemblies to which no other feudatories were summoned. No doubt the reason why they had been summoned at all was the force of the feudal principle that all specific aids beyond the few accustomed ones could be assessed only with the consent of the vassals upon whom they fell. Instances of these separate assemblies of representatives of the *villes* are to be found a good while before the opening of the fourteenth century[1], and separate they might have remained much longer but for the great national questions brought up by the conflict between Pope Boniface VIII and Philip the Fair. For such a national emergency the old feudal revenues were inadequate. Feudalism was dying and its revenues drying up none the less surely, even if more gradually, than in England, and, as in England, the national power was rising and with it a national activity that required for its support a larger revenue than could be drawn from sources strictly feudal in character. The king was driven to treat on extra-feudal terms with his vassals, the barons and the enfranchised *villes*. Thus the estates are feudal, but they are extra-feudal also. Philip probably called to him in 1302 none who did not owe him feudal suit, but he did it in a way unprecedented in feudal custom. The departure from precedent might seem less striking in the occasional *assemblées de notables* to which none but great nobles lay or spiritual were summoned, but the greater assemblies of Philip the Fair were certainly an innovation, though their feudal basis is evident; and later meetings mark a far more radical departure from feudal institutions and ideas.

The first instance seems to have been in the year 1301 at an assembly held by Philip at Senlis, in which was demanded the counsel "clericorum et laicorum, doctorum *et aliorum proborum virorum*," on the difficult question raised by the king proceeding against the Bishop of Pamiers for breach of faith and *lèse-majesté*[2].

But other differences arose between the Pope and the French King which finally became so serious that on 10 April 1302 Philip called a great meeting of the Estates at Paris. This assembly is usually regarded

---

[1] Viollet, *Histoire des institutions politiques et administratives de la France*, III, pp. 180–2.

[2] A. Esmein, *Cours élémentaire d'histoire du droit français* (11th edition), p. 543; Lavisse, *Histoire de France*, tome III, IIᵉ partie (Langlois), pp. 142 sqq.

as the beginning of the States General, and the documents edited by
the late M. Georges Picot[1] enable us to draw with some confidence certain
conclusions as to the character, powers, and activities of its members. The
assembly was composed of tenants-in-chief of the king, lay and spiritual,
as had long been the custom; and it also included *arrière-vassaux*, "representatives" of enfranchised *villes*. All these *arrière-vassaux* were bound in
a general way by the fealty they owed their liege lord, but direct negotiations with them were an addition to feudal custom which could be made
regular only by the assent of their overlords who held of the king *in
capite*. In England, an aid had already been asked of the mesne lords, as
we have seen, but "at the instance" of their feudal superiors. This was
now done for France by Philip in 1302, and it illustrates the gradually
widening basis of the State on both sides of the Channel, a process
observable earlier in England than in France. In both, fealty is gradually
becoming wider, more national, and less feudal, as wealth, power, and
political self-consciousness diffuse themselves beyond the circle of the
greater land-holders. But the development is a gradual one which proceeds without any distinct break with feudal custom. The mesne lords—
a term including communes outside the royal demesne—are now summoned,
but it is on account of an obligation which may be called as much feudal
as national, and the innovation of summoning them is softened by obtaining
the assent of the direct vassals who had hitherto concluded their tenants
by their own unassisted decisions. This assent was forthcoming no doubt
because the participation which was now first extended beyond the immediate circle of the king's tenants-in-chief was not a privilege to be
guarded, but rather a burden which might be borne more easily when more
widely shared.

Changing economic and social conditions were making increasingly
difficult the older shifting of the incidence of the burden of *auxilia*
sanctioned by regular feudal custom. The consent of the tenants-in-chief
was necessary if such a change was to be made, but it was a consent probably not hard to obtain in view of the crisis which faced the nation in
1302. Thus it is clear that the basis of the membership of the first
Estates was obligation and not right, an obligation arising out of fealty;
while the growing forces of nationalism were now imposing upon it the
necessity of direct negotiations between the king and his *arrière-vassaux*,
hitherto unnecessary but now accepted by the chief tenants in the
prospect of unusually heavy demands for aid in the impending struggle
with the Pope, and accepted the more willingly no doubt because of their
decreasing confidence in their ability longer to shift these burdens from
their own shoulders to those of their tenants. That the real basis of the

[1] *Documents relatifs aux États Généraux et assemblées réunis sous Philippe le Bel,*
publiés par M. Georges Picot, Paris, Imprimerie Nationale, 1901.

CH. XXIII.

summons was obligation rather than right is made plain by the surviving summonses to the Estates themselves. In the very first of these, addressed by the king to the seneschal of Beaucaire on 15 February 1302, the purpose of the meeting is set forth in language which echoes the famous phrase of Edward I of England seven years before—"quod omnes tangit ab omnibus approbetur": Since on "many difficult matters" which touch in no small degree the status and liberty of himself and his realm no less than of the churches, ecclesiastics, nobles, secular persons, and all and singular the inhabitants of the said realm, the king wishes to "treat and deliberate" with his prelates, barons, and others the subjects and lieges of him and of the said realm (et aliis nostris et eiusdem regni fidelibus et subiectis), he commands to be summoned under their obligation of fealty and any other obligation whatsoever by which they are bound to him (sub debito fidelitatis et quocumque vinculo quo nobis tenentur astricti) to appear at Paris on 8 April then next ensuing, the "consules et universitates civitatum et villarum praedictarum" (in this case seven *villes*) through two or three "de maioribus et pericioribus singularum universitatum predictarum," who are to have full power from the afore-said consuls and communes among other things "to hear, receive, and carry out, and to consent to everything ordained by the king in this regard without the excuse of a referendum," their presence being for the purpose "of treating and deliberating upon these matters, of hearing, receiving, and carrying out" all of them, and of giving their assent "in the name of the consuls and communes aforesaid" to all those things ordained by the king in the premises or connected therewith. The docu-ment here summarised clearly indicates that this summons grew out of the *obligations* incident to fealty. There appear also the instructions to "representatives" such as are to be found a generation earlier in England, but there is no definite reference to any election[1].

But an important question arises at the outset in regard to those things which touch the status and liberty of all the inhabitants of the realm. Must all actually approve of what touches all? Whom must the king include when he asks assent in matters thus touching all? How far beyond the prelates and barons does the obligation of fealty extend; or the additional phrase *quocumque vinculo*? How much of this "representation" is only "virtual"? Shall we translate the important words "aliis nostris et eiusdem regni fidelibus et subiectis" with M. Picot, as "*les autres sujets du royaume*,"[2] or with the late Professor Esmein, as "*d'autres fidèles sujets du royaume*," thus including among the "others" none beyond the inhabitants of enfranchised *villes*?[3] How far is this important experiment of Philip "national" and novel, how far is it merely feudal and traditional? It is a difficult question. There can be no doubt that there was a great development of these matters between 1300 and the

---

[1] Picot, *Documents*, pp. 1–2.   [2] *Ibid.*, Introduction, p. viii.
[3] *Histoire du droit français* (11th edition), p. 549 note.

great meeting of the Estates in 1484 for which Masselin's journal gives us such detailed information, but on the whole, though the paucity of documents for the first meeting makes certain conclusions impossible in regard to it, if we may judge from the history of earlier assemblies in France and elsewhere, the more conservative interpretation of Esmein seems to offer an explanation of these important transactions more in accordance with the facts and the political habits and ideas of the time than the "conséquences exagérées" of M. Picot. It is important, however, to bear in mind that this applies wholly only to the earliest meetings of the Estates.

Several times in 1303, at Paris, Montpellier, Nîmes and Carcassonne, and again in 1308 in the struggle with the Templars, the Estates were called together; and many of the documents have survived from which some conclusions may be drawn as to the general character of the assemblies in the early fourteenth century. They met again in 1314, in 1356, when there were two assemblies, one for the South at Toulouse and one for the North at Paris; in 1413, and in 1484, and several times between; often in times of national defeat and civil disorder which make their actions seem more revolutionary than constitutional. The last meeting before the fateful one of 1789 was in 1614.

In the beginning the prelates and barons were required to appear in person, and such of the members of these assemblies as were ordered to come and gave their assent only *nomine consulum et universitatum* doubtless lacked many of the powers characteristic of the more fully developed representatives of modern times. The attendance of both classes was *sub debito fidelitatis* and under threat of punishment for failure. But even the prelates and barons owing personal attendance might find it impossible to answer the summons in person, and in such cases they might appear by attorney, as was possible in all the royal courts at this time in both England and France, provided the royal licence could be had. The reasons given for these procurations or letters of attorney issued by the clergy for the meeting in Paris in 1303—here suspiciously numerous—which M. Picot has printed, shew conclusively that this appearance by attorney was at the time of that meeting regarded as an exception to be admitted only when sufficient cause was shewn. So one abbot prays this privilege "propter infirmitatem,"[1] the Prior of Saint-Léon of Sens is prevented from coming "gravi proprii corporis infirmitate."[2] "We have started on our journey," says another, "though very weak, but are not strong enough to appear in person, as God is our witness, without grave danger to our health."[3] Another is so poor and so burdened with his duties at home that he begs to be excused[4]. Another has got as far as Troyes but the journey is too much for a man of almost eighty, wherefore he begs "vestre regie maiestati quatenus super hoc pro excusato dignemini me habere."[5]

[1] Picot, *Documents,* p. 63.   [2] *Ibid.,* p. 65.
[3] *Ibid.,* p. 67.   [4] *Ibid.,* p. 69.   [5] *Ibid.,* p. 70.

Another is so ill that he is not able to ride[1]. The Abbot of Chantoin cannot come because his monastery is so poor that he must come afoot, which he could not do without grave danger to his health[2]. Another has broken his leg, "as is well known in the whole neighbourhood."[3] Another is deaf[4]. In these exceptional cases, the attorney was usually given power first of all to present the excuses of his principal, which were probably not always acceptable—"full power to excuse our absence from your presence for the reasons aforesaid, and to take oath on the excuse given," as in one instance[5]. This was accompanied by a grant of authority to the attorney to conclude his principal as fully as though he himself were present in person, sometimes in all the king's demands, but quite as often with important reservations; "salva fide," in the case of the Abbot of Longuay[6], and in another instance only so far as the acts agreed to should be done "de iure," and even then with the proviso that they must be referred to the principal for ratification[7]. One letter limits the attorney's consent to those things alone to which the majority of the prelates shall have agreed[8]. Sometimes the attorneys are empowered to consent, "if necessary," or "to consent" and if necessary "to affix their seals." Others are only to give assent subject to ratification by the superior of the Order to which the monastery belongs. In one case power is given merely to excuse and to take oath that the excuse is genuine, but no power whatever to act[9]. The Bishop of Rodez expressly delegates authority to join in all acts against Boniface, "quondam papam octavum,"[10] while the Abbot of Villemagne and the Prior of Sainte-Énimie are careful to except always the status, honour, and revenue of the Holy See[11]. The persons designated in these letters of procuration are usually referred to as "procurator ac nuncius specialis,"[12] "exhibitor presencium nostrum,"[13] "latores presencium,"[14] "excusator specialis"[15]; and in some cases several are appointed, in others a single individual. When several are chosen, usually any one of them may act for the whole[16]. Most of the appointments of these proctors were made directly by abbots or priors, but in one case it was by a chapter[17], in another by the dean and chapter[18], and in another, where the abbot of the monastery was absent, it was authorised by the prior and monks[19].

In July 1303 an assembly was held at Montpellier which marks some notable developments in representation beyond those of a few months before. The summons addressed to the *viguier* of Béziers prescribes the attendance of all prelates and barons of the district, together with chapters, collegia, the *conventus* as well as the priors of important collegiate and conventual as well as cathedral churches, together with "syndicos et

[1] *Ibid.*, p. 72. [2] *Ibid.*, p. 77. [3] *Ibid.*, p. 79. [4] *Ibid.*, p. 85.
[5] *Ibid.*, p. 67. [6] *Ibid.*, p. 70. [7] *Ibid.*, p. 71. [8] *Ibid.*, p. 72.
[9] *Ibid.*, p. 81. [10] *Ibid.*, p. 84. [11] *Ibid.*, pp. 89, 91. [12] *Ibid.*, p. 63.
[13] *Ibid.*, p. 64. [14] *Ibid.*, p. 73. [15] *Ibid.*, p. 75. [16] *Ibid.*, p. 71.
[17] *Ibid.*, pp. 92–3. [18] *Ibid.*, p. 66. [19] *Ibid.*, p. 76.

universitates civitatum et castrorum aliarumque villarum insignium." Of these the prelates, barons, priors, and *consules* must appear in person, the rest by suitable proctors with adequate power and instructions[1]. The notices of the choice of proctors in the cities, *châteaux*, and *villes* are particularly interesting. In one, the Château d'Aimargues near Nîmes, the *universitas* of the men of the Château were summoned by the trumpet and the public crier, and they or a majority of them "as appears and is declared," "nobles as well as non-noble," "representing that universitas," proceeded to elect (fecerunt, constituerunt, et elegerunt) four men, two noble, two non-noble, to act "on behalf of the universitas and everyone of the said universitas," its authority inhering in all or each of the proctors in such way that anything begun by one or more of them might lawfully be carried on and determined by the others, one or more; an authority, too, which extended far beyond the narrow mandates earlier in the year, to include *generaliter* everything the *universitas* could do, say, treat of, and accomplish, if all its members were present in person[2]. Even where the election was the act of the *consules* alone, as in the Château de Capdenac, the representative was sometimes "general" as well as special, and was empowered to do not only the things specified but "all others."[3] The *procuratores* are in one mandate designated as "our certain general and special proctors,"[4] in others authority to prosecute and defend legal actions against the commune is specifically mentioned. At Lunel "the people of the university of the men" of the *ville*, three hundred and thirty-six in number, were called together by crier and trumpet in the churchyard where it was the custom of the people to assemble, and there, "all and singular and each of them" appointed four proctors, with "full, general, and liberal power" to act, two of them noble, one a lawyer, and one a draper of Lunel. Later in the day fifty-three more of the inhabitants ratified the action already taken[5].

At Viviers "those men of the *universitas* who were present declaring that they constituted two parts and more of the men of that *universitas*, as seemed very probable," proceeded in the name of the whole *universitas* to elect their two representatives and to promise ratification of their acts[6]. At Lodève the assembled inhabitants, five hundred and forty-four in number, whose names are all set down, after hearing the letters of convocation translated for them, "as a *universitas* and in the name of the *universitas* of Lodève," unanimously chose three syndics to represent them[7]. Occasionally *procuratores* were empowered to substitute others for themselves[8], and there is at least one case in which this was actually done[9]. In 1308, for the assembly at Tours, two proctors were to be chosen at

---

[1] Picot, *Documents*, p. 101. A contemporary list of those summoned to Montpellier in person from Rouergue is printed by M. Picot at page 105. They were thirty-eight in number.

[2] *Ibid.*, pp. 137–8.   [3] *Ibid.*, p. 146.   [4] *Ibid.*, p. 147.
[5] *Ibid.*, pp. 162–6.   [6] *Ibid.*, pp. 167–8.   [7] *Ibid.*, p. 177.
[8] *Ibid.*, p. 248.   [9] *Ibid.*, pp. 498–9.

Beaucaire, one "pro parte nobilium," the other "pro parte popularium personarum," and the election of the latter occurred in an assembly of the "burgenses et homines populares," who chose a doctor of laws as the representative "pro popularibus personis et nomine universitatis earum."[1]

Such specific instances as these indicate far more clearly than any amount of detailed comment the nature and the extent of representative institutions and ideas in France at the opening of the fourteenth century. Several points seem clear. The attendance is not a right but a duty, and a duty imposed primarily by the obligation of fealty. Those summoned to appear in person must do so, at the beginning of the century at least, unless they have an excuse, of whose sufficiency the king will judge. With the king's permission they may in such cases appear by an attorney. This Esmein considers exceptional and existing only in 1302. Normally, he says, they might appear by proctor if they chose. This was certainly not the case, however, at the first meeting in 1303, but obviously soon became the general practice. Such proctors when appointed were attorneys or *mandatarii*, and usually little more. They represented in most cases no one but their principal. They were his personal agents and bound none beyond him by their acts. "Each appeared in virtue of an obligation that was personal."[2] Collective bodies such as *villes* or chapters of necessity had to appear by a proctor or proctors, who were likewise regarded oftentimes as little more than *mandatarii*, as is indicated among other things by their being occasionally allowed to appoint substitutes, a power hardly consistent with the existence of the discretionary power necessarily incident to representation in any developed sense. But many cases go far beyond this. There were other proctors who were general as well as special, empowered in advance legally to bind their principals in any way whatsoever, and there were cases where several prelates or barons agreed to employ the same proctor in common, and one instance at least where several bishops of a single province are authorised to choose one of their own number "to act as representative in place of all and to have the full power of all."[3] In the *villes* the developments are particularly interesting. For purposes of representation they are conceived in the usual manner of the time as collective wholes, *universitates* or communes, and the proctors they chose represent the *universitas*. Apparently the franchise is wide, and the decision is sometimes made by the vote of a majority. This body of the *ville* usually includes nobles and non-nobles, but in one case in 1308 there are two communes in a single *ville*, the nobles and the *populares personae*, the second of which separately chose a proctor for their own *universitas*[4]. Seemingly none but the inhabitants of the towns are

[1] Picot, *Documents*, pp. 712–13.
[2] Esmein, *Histoire du droit français*, p. 548.
[3] Picot, *Documents*, p. 489; cited by Esmein, *op. cit.*, p. 548.
[4] This dual system as found at Beaucaire was not unusual, and marks the jealousy between the aristocratic *cité* and the developing more democratic *bourg*. See Luchaire, *Manuel des institutions françaises*, p. 370.

represented in these assemblies of 1303 and 1308. The inhabitants of the open country are not mentioned till long afterward.

In fact, the most striking difference between France and England in the local representation at this time and before undoubtedly lies in the continuance of the old county court in England and the absence of anything comparable to it in France. Thanks to the circumstances of the Conquest, the vigour of William I and Henry I, and the obvious advantage to them in continuing the older system of the hundred and the shire, it became the settled policy of the Norman Kings of England to retain them[1]. Thus in England the sheriff, the king's chief local officer, remained a part of the court over which he presided. He remained the *shire*-reeve to the end, and though he was the king's *praepositus*, his authority increasing in proportion to the increasing growth of royal power itself, yet he never became detached from his county or its court or independent of it. Its authority as a whole did not decline as his advanced, though his authority was partly gained at the expense of the old suitors of the court itself. And when in turn the sheriff's authority gave way to that of the justices itinerant, the vigorous communal life of the shire was not affected. The justices were strong, but they were active in and through the machinery of the county court. In France, on the contrary, the *praepositus*, in developing into the *prévôt* as royal power increased, tended to lose touch with the community and become more a royal minister than a local officer, and the later *baillis* were even more markedly so. Neither the *prévôté* nor the *bailliage* ever came to be the full equivalent of the English county. The difference is profound, and it had results no less decisive on the development of the rural representative institutions in the two countries. In the early fourteenth century the only local representation in France is in the *universitates* of the *villes*. In England at the same time, and probably until the passage of the forty-shilling freehold act, the participation in elections of representatives extended to all the members of the county court, including much of the agricultural population of the open country, as seems the better opinion, supported by Homersham Cox[2], Riess[3], and Stubbs[4].

For the towns, on the other hand, though there is a vast practical difference between the frequent meetings of an English Parliament and the rare and exceptional assemblies of the French Estates, the theory and practice of representation in France certainly seems no less advanced than in England in the early fourteenth century; and in the period following, at times of great political excitement, it occasionally advanced far beyond the earlier precedents. In fact there were several significant changes whose results were of the greatest importance.

[1] *Supra*, p. 668.
[2] *Antient Parliamentary Elections.*
[3] *Geschichte des Wahlrechts zum englischen Parlament im Mittelalter.*
[4] *Constitutional History*, Chapter xv, sections 216–17.

Gradually the nobles and the prelates ceased to attend the meetings of the Estates in person or to be required to do so. It became their practice, contrary to that of England, to appear only by deputy; and a further step of the greatest importance followed when the prelates and the nobility of a general district began regularly to elect a small number of proctors to represent them all. Equally important was the extension of the franchise to the people of the whole *bailliage* including the open country as well as the *villes*, as is found in 1484 at the meeting of the Estates at Tours. This was no doubt exceptional, but it seems to indicate the existence, temporarily at least, of conditions in some respects not greatly different from those in the English shire. Unlike England, however, the representatives of each order in the French districts were chosen, not by all the electors together as in the county court but separately, each of the orders, clergy, nobility, and "third estate" choosing deputies to represent none but their own order in the *bailliage* at the general meeting of the Estates. In 1484, in the case of the third estate, the suffrage for these elections seems to have been almost universal; but, taking the later Middle Ages in general, the basis remained on the whole municipal rather than general, though at times of crisis it was occasionally extended in theory at least to cover the whole *bailliage*. So, as Augustin Thierry says, however restricted may have been the representation of the third estate on account of its exclusively municipal character, it nevertheless had the merit of feeling itself charged with the duty of pleading the cause, "not of this or that fraction, nor of this or that class of the people, but the cause of the whole body of the non-nobles, of the people without distinction of free or serf, of bourgeois or peasant."[1]

There were thus in 1484 deputies for and from each order or estate, but all represented one "electoral district"; and the *bailliage* for which they all appeared included the *villes* and, theoretically at least, the *campaniae* as well. For electoral purposes these were not separate and distinct as were the boroughs and the counties in England. Jean Masselin speaks of the assembly of 1484 as disposed "per nationes et turmas," and specifically mentions the representatives of Paris, Picardy, and Normandy, the "chief nations" of France in the University of Paris[2]. In the famous oration given in the assembly by Philippe Pot, he speaks of "his nation," by which he undoubtedly means Burgundy, in which there were nine *baillivati* or *bailliages*, no doubt the *turmae* or subdivisions of that "nation," from whom representatives were returned[3]. As a general rule, says Masselin, each *bailliage* returned one deputy for each of its three estates, the Church,

---

[1] *Essai sur l'histoire du tiers état* (edition of 1882), pp. 50–1. "Les élections des députés du tiers état, bornées, durant le quatorzième siècle et une grande partie du quinzième, à ce qu'on nommait les *bonnes villes*, furent, vers la fin du quinzième siècle, étendues aux villes non murées et aux simples villages." *Ibid.*, p. 51, note.

[2] Masselin's *Journal*, p. 2.

[3] *Ibid.*, p. 154.

the nobility, and *status plebeius*; but occasionally from places of great size or dignity there were two or three and in rare cases fewer than one for each estate, though this he felt was inadequate[1]. From the *bailliage* of Senlis there was but one[2], from a few others two. But this inequality is of less significance because the votes in the assembly were not by individuals but by the *bailliages* as collective units.

In most national assemblies of the later Middle Ages a distinction should be noted more clearly than is sometimes done between their formal acts and the less formal proceedings of which the formal acts are often only the preliminary or the result, a distinction roughly analogous to the difference between a regular session of the House of Commons and a committee of the whole House in our own day. The difficulty in distinguishing the two was one cause of the momentous struggle with which the French Revolution opened. It was probably the chief cause of the series of conflicts between the two English Houses of Parliament in the seventeenth century. In more recent times it has led to serious misapprehension and frequent misstatement of the relations of the various parts of these medieval assemblies one to the other. Professor Pollard in his *Evolution of Parliament* has emphasised the fact, well known but often insufficiently attended to, that organically the English Parliament was a single body; only informally and for deliberation did it gradually become bicameral during the Middle Ages. In the formal sessions with which it opened and closed, the only ones in which the king was present in person or by deputy, the whole body was present in one room there to hear the formal *pronunciatio* in which the subjects were laid before them for their separate deliberation, or to learn at the end which of their decisions had obtained the royal favour and were to be made effective by the final sanction of the king. Not till the reign of Edward VI did the Commons have an official "House" set aside for their exclusive use in the Palace of St Stephen, and their journals begin only at the beginning of the same reign.

At the formal opening of parliament, while the Council sat on the woolsacks in the middle of the house and the Lords along the sides, the whole body of the Commons stood uncovered at the foot of the room below the bar, their speaker at their head. This over, the Commons withdrew for deliberation apart on this medieval "speech from the throne" to wherever they could find a suitable place, usually the chapter house of the Abbey across the street, and only returned when they were ready for the final formal ceremonies of the royal assent and dissolution.

The practice was somewhat the same in the early French assemblies. Masselin's detailed description of the assembly chambers in 1484 shews that the third estate were segregated in the lower part of the room[3]

[1] Masselin's *Journal*, p. 8. [2] *Ibid.*, p. 18.
[3] *Ibid.*, pp. 4–6.

though they were probably seated[1]. The meeting was opened as in England
by a speech of the Chancellor announcing the reasons for their summons
and the action expected of them[2]. Then the deliberation followed, all
the Estates remaining at times where they were, as they seem to have
done in 1467[3], contrary to the English practice; or sometimes separately,
as is indicated at times in the Assembly of 1484[4], until a decision (*conclusio*)
was reached on each part of the king's demands, which seems then to have
been reduced to writing. There was thus a considerable difference between
the French practice in which the three estates at times deliberated together
but never really fused, and the English, in which the knights of the shire
and the burgesses regularly withdrew together and apart from the lords
for common discussion.

The French Estates in times of crisis exercised unusual and enormous
power, as in 1420, and Glasson believes that it was the very extravagance
of their acts at such times that caused their later weakness[5]. But the
reasons for this weakness, and for the long intervals between their meetings
as compared with the frequent parliaments in England, lie much deeper,
and have their roots, some of them, in a past already distant in the
fifteenth century. Some of the results of these same causes were clearly
seen by Sir John Fortescue, and they are closely connected with the ones
with which we are concerned. The French king, he says, has taken upon
him "to sett tayles and other imposicions upon the commons without the
assent of the III estates; but yet he wolde not sett any such charges, nor
hath sette, uppon the nobles for fere of rebillion."[6] The growth of these
impôts permanents which the king might take without consent is a sign
of the increasing tendency toward absolutism in practice and theory; and
this, together with the exemption of the nobility from such burdens, is
at once a striking difference, noticeable to Fortescue between England
and France in his day, and an argument in favour of the more limited
monarchy which he believed to exist at home. The great difference between
the two countries in these two things, whether itself a cause or only the
result of deeper differences, certainly was a practical factor of increasing
importance in determining the future difference between parliamentary
and constitutional England and the absolutism of eighteenth-century
France. The Estates in 1484 struggled against this fatal tendency, but
in vain. The theory insisted upon by the Estates survived in part in
Bodin's *Six Livres de la République*, but the practice became far otherwise.
As Esmein sums it up: "In a word, the institution of the States General

---

[1] Masselin's *Journal*, p. 36.   [2] *Ibid.*, p. 36.
[3] Esmein, *Histoire du droit français* (11th edition), p. 563, note, with references
there cited.
[4] "Congregatis singulis scilicet suis in locis."
[5] *Histoire du droit et des institutions de la France*, v, p. 433.
[6] Sir John Fortescue, *The Governance of England* (Plummer's edition), Chapter III,
p. 114.

had proved abortive. They had no regular time of meeting but came into existence as the last resort of the royal government in times of crisis. As for their powers, the king demanded of them the vote of subsidies which he might impose without them, and the giving of counsel which he was free to disregard....But the absolute monarchy, with an instinct that was sure, mistrusted the States General even when so weakened: it had a sense of the existence in them of latent forces, which favouring events might well let loose. Hence, without abolishing the institution, it carefully refrained from calling them together. Their whole activity occurred under *la monarchie tempérée*, between 1302 and 1614. The meeting of 1614 was the last before the Revolution."[1]

If the States General are the most interesting French parallel with English constitutional development, probably the history of the provincial estates would furnish the most interesting French analogy to the development of representative institutions in countries such as Germany and Italy, where the postponement of political unity to more modern times restricted the activity of their representative bodies to local affairs during the Middle Ages. These provincial estates were for single provinces what the States General were for the whole realm; and in general, where they were suffered to remain, they retained the form, the powers, and the general procedure found in the general estates of the fourteenth century. Varying in origin in the different provinces before their absorption in the Crown domains, some of these estates remained, particularly on the borders of the kingdom, long after the States General had fallen into abeyance; but since the ideas and practices to be found in them, as well as the general conditions out of which they grew, do not differ essentially from those already described for the realm as a whole, our limited space might better be employed by a brief consideration of representative institutions elsewhere in Western Europe[2].

In no country, not even excepting England and France, are these developments illustrated more clearly than in the Spanish peninsula. The remarkable development and maturity of representative institutions and ideas found in Spain, arising in the thirteenth century or before, reaching their climax in the fourteenth and fifteenth centuries, and declining during the late fifteenth century and the sixteenth, might well furnish the material for many volumes. These developments abundantly prove the careful statement of Professor Merriman: "The claim of the people to a share in the government was considerably more fully recognised, theoretically

---

[1] *Histoire du droit français* (11th edition), pp. 575–6.

[2] The Provincial Estates are treated comprehensively in the following places, with bibliographies more or less full: Viollet, *Histoire des institutions politiques et administratives de la France*, III, pp. 236–46; Glasson, *Histoire du droit et des institutions de la France*, v, pp. 448–59; Esmein, *Cours élémentaire d'histoire du droit français* (11th edition), pp. 665–85.

at least, in Spain than in England, at that stage of their development."[1] The difficulty is to deal with so large and so important a subject in small compass. This difficulty is increased by the fact that the great constitutional age of Spain preceded the union of the crowns and must therefore be studied separately for Castile and Leon, and for the eastern kingdoms, while even among the latter there are often found differences that are fundamental. In such circumstances the only course open— though one rather unsatisfactory—is to choose the representative institutions of one kingdom for treatment and indicate the chief differences found in other kingdoms as variants from this. For this purpose the institutions of Catalonia will here be taken, because, as Professor Merriman says, "the Cortes of Catalonia in this period resembled a modern legislative body perhaps more closely than any other in the peninsula"[2]; and since the main purpose of this chapter is to make clear medieval representative institutions and ideas in general, rather than to trace their history in detail, it would seem better to choose as an illustration the more perfect forms of Catalonia rather than those of Castile, though the latter probably had an earlier beginning and certainly exercised a greater influence upon subsequent institutions and events. Catalonia is chosen instead of Aragon because the documentary history of its Cortes is now fully covered for our period in the *Cortes...de Aragón y de Valencia, y Principado de Cataluña*, whose magnificent volumes, still in process of publication by the Spanish Royal Academy of History, have not yet included any of the records of the kingdoms of Aragon and Valencia[3].

The assemblies in Christian Spain had come down from Visigothic times and were in their earlier development not unlike those of the same early period in England or France, especially in the fact that they included none beyond the nobles and the clergy. Conflicting statements have been made by Spanish historians early and modern as to the first appearance of representatives from the towns, but the first official mention of such representatives seems to have been in the decrees promulgated in the kingdom of Leon in 1188, where the presence of the archbishop, the bishops, and the magnates of the realm is noted—"cum electis civibus ex singulis civitatibus."[4] It is almost a century after this before certain indications are found of the appearance of such additional representatives

---

[1] *The Cortes of the Spanish Kingdoms in the later Middle Ages*, AHR, Vol. xvi, p. 495. To this valuable paper and to the first two volumes of Professor Merriman's *Rise of the Spanish Empire* I wish to make general acknowledgment for many of the statements which follow, to which special references could not always be added.

[2] *The Cortes of the Spanish Kingdoms in the later Middle Ages*, AHR, xvi, p. 492.

[3] The United General Cortes of the three kingdoms of Aragon, Catalonia, and Valencia offer few peculiarities worthy of note, and are not separately treated.

[4] *Cortes de León y de Castilla*, i, 39; Colmeiro, *Introducción*, Vol. i, pp. 11–12; Merriman, *op. cit.* pp. 478–9; *The Rise of the Spanish Empire*, i, p. 219; Hallam, *Middle Ages*, Part II, Chapter iv.

in the other kingdoms, but by the end of the thirteenth century they are found in all.

Before the middle of the fourteenth century these representative institutions had assumed a form in Catalonia which is impressive in its definiteness and maturity, as well as in its completeness. In the case, for example, of the Cortes or *Curia Generalis* which met at Tortosa in 1331, we find summonses requiring the personal attendance of seven high secular ecclesiastics, of nineteen abbots, and of the Prior of the Order of Hospitallers in Catalonia, together with several members of the royal family and the King of Majorca. In addition to these, forty-three "nobiles" are summoned, thirty-eight of whom must appear in person and five are permitted to appear by proctor; forty-two "milites," one of whom may appear by proctor. To six cities, Barcelona, Lérida, Tarragona, Gerona, Vich, and Manresa instructions are given to send syndics or proctors with full powers, and similar instructions are given in twelve towns to "probis hominibus ex universitate Cervarie," as in the case of Cervera, or to "iuratis probis hominibus."[1]

There were three estates or *brazos* in the Cortes of Catalonia as in Castile, instead of four as in Aragon: the clergy, the "nobiles" and knights, and the proctors of the cities and towns. The nobles—in Castile usually called *ricos hombres* (*richi homines*)—corresponded rather closely to the *barones* in England (the word *ricos* as used here retaining its original meaning in all Indo-European languages, of "powerful," "mighty," "exalted," "noble," rather than our modern "rich"). The "milites" or *caballeros*, like the magnates, received individual summonses to appear in person, and when they did so, joined with the *ricos hombres* as one *braç*, or estate. This is a difference of great consequence from the practice at this time growing up in England by which the knights of the shire were associating themselves not with the barons but with the burgesses, in the discussion of the matters they were called together to treat. And even in Aragon, where there was a separate *brazo de caballeros*, it never coalesced with the burgesses as in England.

The obligation of personal attendance in Catalonia, and apparently elsewhere in Spain, was as in England more lasting than in France. Though attendance in person was required in France by Philip the Fair, the magnates both lay and clerical were soon able to substitute an attendance by representatives, and regularly absented themselves, thus no doubt greatly weakening the influence of the Estates. In England this was avoided by the greater power of the king in the earlier period, and later by the greater importance of parliament, in which it gradually became an advantage and in time an honour to be present. In Catalonia it is clear that personal attendance was rigidly insisted upon except when a sufficient excuse could be given and sworn to. In the Cortes of 1331, for example, the king on learning that the Bishop of

[1] *Cortes...de Aragón y de Valencia,* I, pp. 281–91.

Barcelona intended to be represented by a proctor for reasons "non bene sufficientibus," separately commanded him to appear in person, especially because he was "bound to take part in person" in the making of constitutions by the Cortes[1].

The representative element in the Cortes of Catalonia in 1331 consisted of syndics or *procuratores* chosen by the deans and chapters of the seven cathedral churches and the representatives from the cities and towns. Abbots were required to be present in person and were the sole representatives of their abbeys, since no summons issued for the attendance of monastic proctors. There was none for representatives of the parish clergy. Thus the practice in Catalonia in 1331 differed from that of the Estates in France to which monastic proctors were summoned, and from similar assemblies in England to which the parish clergy were summoned in the *praemunientes* clause in 1295 and occasionally thereafter until Convocation became separate from Parliament. But the most interesting and important feature of the Catalan and other Spanish Estates is in the representation of cities and towns—in 1331 respectively six and twelve in number in Catalonia—and in the peculiarities of this representation when compared with those of France and England in the same general period.

Mention of the presence of a third estate appears in Leon, as we have seen, as early as 1188, and about a century later references to the *hombres buenos* become common in all the kingdoms. "Many good men" of Barcelona are recorded as attending the Cortes in Catalonia as early as 1251[2], but, as it was to a meeting in Barcelona itself, and as no other burghers are mentioned, its significance might easily be overrated. By the year 1283, however, from two to four representatives were summoned from each of the cities and from "many" of the towns throughout Catalonia[3], and among the constitutions enacted and sealed by the king at that meeting, one provides that in future no general constitution for Catalonia shall be made by the king without the consent of the *cives* of Catalonia, as well as of the barons and knights, "vel......maioris et sanioris partis eorundem."[4] Another provision promises that in future the king and his successors will convene a meeting of the Cortes in Catalonia once in every year in which to treat of the condition and reform of the country with the clergy secular and regular, with barons, knights, and "cum...civibus et hominibus villarum."[5]

Though "just cause" may often have been found for less frequent meetings, the latter of these provisions is remarkable, and it precedes by more than a quarter of a century the first similar enactment in England in the famous ordinances of 1311, assented to by the king only under compulsion. England can shew nothing comparable to the Catalan provision for

[1] *Cortes...de Aragón y de Valencia*, I, p. 289.
[2] *Ibid.*, p. 137.
[3] *Ibid.*, p. 141.
[4] *Ibid.*, p. 145.
[5] *Ibid.*, p. 147.

the assent of the burgesses to new constitutions before the year 1322 in the well-known statute of York by which the ordinances of 1311 were repealed.

Thus from the opening of the fourteenth century and before, the regularity and the constitutional character of municipal representation is established by law in Catalonia, and all existing evidence seems to point to an actual practice conforming with the law. In 1300 it is distinctly stated that the ordinances made in the Cortes of that year are made with the counsel and assent and at the request not only of nobles and knights but of the citizens and men of the towns as well[1]; it is further provided that no interpretation of the constitution should be made in future except with the help of jurists and in the presence of four *ricos hombres* and four citizens[2]; and provision is made even for local committees consisting of one knight, one man of the law, and one citizen, to keep watch for breaches of the constitution[3].

In the summonses of this period in Catalonia, the *procuradores* of the towns are to have full power from their constituents, "tractandi, consenciendi, faciendi, et firmandi," in all that shall be ordained there[4]. In 1322 it is recorded that such differences of opinion arose in the Cortes that nothing could be agreed to, but nevertheless that the proctors of the cities and towns made a grant[5]. It is this participation of the third estate alone in grants that marks one of the greatest of the differences between Spain and France on the one hand and England on the other, and this important difference played no small part in the great contrast between the continuance of representative institutions and the further development of constitutional principles in England a little later, at the same time that Spain and France, from beginnings often even more remarkable, were gradually lapsing into absolutism.

It seems clear from a general survey of the official documents of the Catalan Cortes of the fourteenth century that the representation of the cities and towns was very uniform from year to year. Thus the cities and the towns as well as the individual clergy, barons, and *caballeros*, obtained what might be called a prescriptive right to be summoned, a right which seems to have been respected by the king and prized by the burgesses. There is not in Catalonia at this time such a variation in the towns summoned as may be found in Castile or in England, where the king's discretion alone seems to have determined what towns should send deputies. There is ample justification for Professor Merriman's statement that the Catalan assemblies more nearly resembled a modern legislative body than any other in the Peninsula. One is tempted to substitute for "the Peninsula," "the world."

In definiteness of organisation and regularity of procedure neither the English Parliament nor the French Estates can compare with the Cortes of Catalonia at this time. Their nearest rival seems to have been

---

[1] *Cortes...de Aragón y de Valencia,* i, p. 168; also pp. 193, 229–30.
[2] *Ibid.,* p. 177.   [3] *Ibid.,* p. 179.   [4] *E.g., ibid.,* p. 183.   [5] *Ibid.,* p. 277.

in the sister kingdom of Aragon, in which a right of attendance similar to that in Catalonia was recognised by the king. A proof of this definiteness is found in the elaborateness of the procedure of *habilitación*, or determination of the qualification of members, which fills many pages of the records of the Cortes, in striking contrast with the Rolls of Parliament in England at the same period. Those summoned individually could substitute a proctor only in exceptional cases and for "just cause"; while chapters of churches and the *universitates* of towns, which of necessity appeared by deputy, were under obligation to see that their proctors were both *idonei* and entrusted with sufficient power to bind their principals in all the matters of which they were called together to treat, or for which their common consent, enactment, and confirmation were necessary. This formal determination of the *poderes* (credentials and instructions) of the members regularly preceded the principal business of the Cortes, and its importance and minuteness seem to prove that the representative constitution of the Catalan Cortes had no rival for definiteness in any national assembly outside the Spanish peninsula at this time. In the Cortes held at Perpignan in 1350 and 1351, for example, a committee of twelve was elected by the Cortes to examine the *poderes* of the members in conjunction with two jurists of the royal council, consisting of two bishops, two nobles, one abbot, one canon, two knights, a doctor of laws of Barcelona, another of Perpignan, and one citizen from each of the two cities of Lérida and Gerona[1].

It is true that this third estate in Catalonia, and in fact in all the Spanish kingdoms, seems to be in composition more closely allied to the third estate of France than to the "commons" of England. No Spanish *procuradores* represented such a body of constituents as we find in the English county court. They were all deputed as in France by the *universitates* of the cities and *villes*, and none came as in England from the body of a rural county. This difference is fundamental and its results are of great consequence. "There were two essential defects in the constitution of Castile, through which perhaps it was ultimately subverted," says Hallam. "It wanted those two brilliants in the coronet of British liberty, the representation of freeholders among the commons, and trial by jury. The Cortes of Castile became a congress of deputies from a few cities, public-spirited indeed and intrepid, as we find them in bad times, to an eminent degree, but too much limited in number, and too unconnected with the territorial aristocracy, to maintain a just balance against the crown."[2] In Catalonia the cities represented were not so few in relation to the size of the realm as they became in Castile, but in neither is there anything like the English county court whose representatives were probably chosen by all the suitors in common whether they were knights or of lower status. While this is undoubtedly true and of an importance not easily overestimated, a part—though only a part—of the significance

[1] *Cortes...de Aragón y de Valencia*, I, pp. 337 sqq.   [2] *Middle Ages*, Part II, Chapter IV.

of this contrast loses its sharpness from the fact that the jurisdiction of the cities and *villae* of all the Spanish kingdoms, as in the *banlieue* of the towns in France, extended in most cases far into the *campaniae* beyond their walls, often including many hamlets as well as much open country. From such an extended jurisdiction it would be rash and probably incorrect to assume that the rural inhabitants had any such direct participation in elections as the members of an English county which included all the territory as far as the boundaries of the next shire. Many parts of the open country in Spain, as in France and unlike England, must have been wholly unrepresented. But there still remained considerable portions of it, within the jurisdiction of the greater towns, for which this was not the case, formally at least. And beginning early in the thirteenth century in Castile, the *hombres buenos* were often directed to appear *por personeros de los concejos*, not only *de las cibdades et de las villas* but *de los logares* as well[1]. What amount of actual participation the inhabitants of a *lugar* may have had the words of these *formulae* are far from making clear. It may have been very small, and was probably greater in the early fourteenth century than later. Colmeiro's opinion that the choice of the town was construed as the act of all the inhabitants under its jurisdiction[2], which most of the French parallels seem to corroborate, may be accepted as the most probable explanation; but these expressions are not wholly without significance. In Catalonia, the ordinances of the Cortes of 1307 were made in an assembly that included none below the syndics of the cities and *villae*, but their ordinances were expressly extended not to these cities and towns alone, but "civitatibus et villis et locis nostris Chatalonie, et habitatoribus eorundem"[3]; while in the Cortes of Barcelona in 1311 both the presence and the advice, as well as the approbation and consent to the ordinances made, extended to the syndics of the cities, the *villae*, "et locorum Chatalonie, qui ad nostram generalem curiam predictam pervenerunt."[4]

The *procuradores* from the Catalan towns varied in number, Barcelona usually having a larger deputation than any other, but as in the French Estates the voting units in the Cortes of Catalonia and the other Spanish kingdoms were towns and not individual proctors. There were of course many differences in the mode of electing these proctors between the cathedral chapters and the *universitates* of the cities and towns, and even among the latter alone[5]. The actual power of the Cortes in the Spanish

[1] *Cortes de León y de Castilla*, I, pp. 45, 49, 99–101, 173, 372, 389–90.
[2] *Introducción*, Vol. I, p. 18.
[3] *Cortes...de Aragón y de Valencia*, I, pp. 200–1, 203.   [4] *Ibid.*, pp. 216–17.
[5] An interesting account of an election of two proctors by the "consiliarii et iurati" of Barcelona is given in *Cortes...de Aragón y de Valencia*, I, pp. 194–7. For an account of the municipal institutions of Barcelona, see Merriman, *The Rise of the Spanish Empire*, I, pp. 488–92, and the authorities there cited. For a comprehensive account of the methods of election of proctors, see Merriman, in AHR, Vol. XVI, pp. 481, 491.

kingdoms in the great constitutional age were very great, and nowhere so great as in Aragon and Catalonia.

As in all representative bodies found in the developing national States of the West in this great constitutional period from the thirteenth to the fifteenth century, the ordinary powers of the Cortes in the Peninsula were exhibited most strikingly, on the one hand, in their control over enactments of law, less frequently in the necessity for their assent to measures of national policy; and on the other, in the great practical power involved in their theoretical right of making voluntary grants of supply in support of government. To these might be added an exceptional authority as in times of national crisis or of royal minority. No doubt it was largely this control over grants that brought about their control over enactment, and for a time the latter is found probably more explicitly recognised in Aragon and Catalonia than in any other Western State. Its gradual disappearance there, as in France in the later Middle Ages, is to be accounted for chiefly by the inability of the Cortes permanently to retain their earlier control over the national finances, and by the gradual growth of *impôts permanents*, which the kings were more and more collecting without their assent. Though the Cortes of the Peninsula at the height of their power were able to exact from their kings more striking formal recognition of their legal rights and powers than even England can shew in this period, they were eventually stripped of these powers mainly because of their inability to make permanent the financial dependence of the Crown upon them, as the English Commons were able in the long run to do, chiefly on account of the continuous association of the gentry and burgesses in parliamentary grants from which all were exempt in Spain and France except the representatives of the towns. This fundamental difference in turn resulted mainly from the peculiar nature, extensive powers, and wider constituency of the county courts in England, which have no parallel on the Continent; a peculiarity which goes back in its historical causes to the character of the Norman Conquest of England itself, and the resulting consistent and astute policy of the strong Norman Kings and Henry II of retaining the old machinery of the county courts as a part of their scheme of establishing a vigorous and centralised royal administrative system at the expense of the power and jurisdiction of the feudal lords.

But if the powers of the Spanish Cortes were short-lived, they were impressive in their extent while they lasted. In Catalonia as well as in Aragon no laws were valid to which their assent had not been given, and they were able repeatedly to exact from their kings formal recognition of extensive popular rights of which even the concessions of Magna Carta fall short[1]. To these they regularly required the king to promise his adherence under oath and seal, and this was done in Aragon

---

[1] R. Altamira, *Magna Carta and Spanish Mediaeval Jurisprudence, Magna Carta Commemoration Essays*, pp. 227 sqq.

and Catalonia, though probably not in Castile, at the formal session with which the Cortes closed. A consideration of the *fueros* ratified in these assemblies, and the constitutions enacted and included in the records of the Cortes, shews that the rights to which they were able to compel the king's assent were in general more extensive and far more popular than any similar concessions then found in England, and the assumption is warranted that the proctors of the towns had a more direct and influential part in obtaining them than any such representatives had in England until a period considerably later. An illustration of their power in this respect is to be found in varying forms in an institution of the greatest importance common to all the greater kingdoms of Christian Spain, known in Catalonia as the *Diputación General*, a committee chosen in the Cortes to keep watch in the intervals between their sessions over the administration of the grants and constitutions to which they had assented, and consisting of members from each of the Estates[1].

In matters of grant the powers of the Cortes were as extensive as in the enactment of law. The principle was recognised as fully as in England that no new or unaccustomed dues could be levied by the king without the consent of the Cortes, and much of the revenue of the government came in the form of the grant or *donativo* made by the Cortes. The burden of it fell, however, on the towns alone, as the nobles and knights were supposed to acquit themselves of their obligation by personal service, and this in time proved one of the greatest points of practical weakness in the Spanish constitutions and contributed in large measure to the later development, so fatal to the liberties of the Peninsula, by which the kings were able gradually to obtain money without consent of the Estates and thus to dispense with their regular sessions.

But in the great age of Spanish constitutionalism this right was jealously guarded by the Cortes, and the grants were accompanied by petitions for redress of grievances—*gravamina* or *greuges*—of which the king was prayed to give redress, which are closely analogous to the *cahiers* of the French Estates and the petitions of the Commons in England. These were often complaints of particular nobles or towns and sometimes came from the whole *brazo* of the nobles and knights. Frequently they disclose serious contentions among the different Estates between which the king had to mediate. The king, as in England, gave separate *responsiones* to the several *gravamina*, and seems to have had much the same latitude in his replies as is found in the similar *responsiones* on the English Rolls of Parliament[2].

[1] Though the complete organisation of the *Diputación General* in Catalonia is probably not found till much later, there is an interesting example as early as 1301 of local committees for the same general purpose chosen by the king and each composed of one knight, one burgess, one jurist, and one notary. *Cortes...de Aragón y de Valencia,* I, p. 192.

[2] For an interesting series of such *greuges* in 1350 in Catalonia, see *Cortes...de Aragón y de Valencia,* I, pp. 403 sqq.

CH. XXIII.

In the fifteenth century these great powers of the Spanish Cortes began to decline. In Castile the number of towns summoned to the Curia rapidly shrank, and the privileged classes were sometimes not summoned at all. The differences between the orders were cunningly used by the kings, and revenues were obtained from other sources which rendered the meetings of the Estates less and less necessary. Thus after the union of Castile and Aragon a development which had begun before was rapidly accelerated, and without formally destroying the various Cortes as institutions the sovereigns were at length able gradually to dispense with them as the Kings of France did with the Estates. "All in all, the Catholic Kings had managed to drive the Cortes of their various realms a long way on the road to destruction; but with all their efforts they were unable entirely to exterminate the ancient Spanish love of freedom and democracy, as the revolt of the *comuneros* in the succeeding reign was to prove in dramatic fashion."[1]

While the Estates in England, France, and Spain are probably the most instructive in the later Middle Ages to a student of the growth of political institutions in general, on account of the relatively early development of centralised and national monarchies, some of the other Western European States where centralisation came later than the period included in this chapter furnish remarkable instances of similar institutions and ideas, of a few of which space remains only for briefer mention.

As might be expected from the place and the man, it is in Italy and in the time of the Emperor Frederick II that we find what has been called the "first example of the modern representative system."[2] In 1232 he summoned two representatives of the "third estate" from each city and *castello* to an assembly to treat concerning "the utility of the realm and the common good."[3] Two years later, in 1234, he ordained that a *curia* should be held in each of the provinces of the realm twice in the year, in which should be present, in addition to nobles and prelates, from each great city four men "de melioribus terre, pro parte universitatis," and two from each of the smaller cities and *castelli*, for the purpose of presenting *gravamina* or complaints of injuries done by any official[4]. Another instance similar to that in 1232 is found in 1240. Early in the fourteenth century instances of representation of the third estate became fairly common in many parts of Italy. In Savoy, beginning with the fourteenth century or a little before, assemblies both general and pro-

---

[1] Merriman, *The Rise of the Spanish Empire*, II, pp. 130-1. For an excellent general account of the course and causes of the decline of the Spanish Cortes, see the whole passage (pp. 126–31).

[2] Pertile, *Storia del Diritto Italiano* (2nd ed.), Vol. II, Part I, p. 338.

[3] Huillard-Bréholles, *Historia diplomatica Friderici II*, IV, p. 390.

[4] *Ibid.*, pp. 460–1; Pertile, *op. cit.*, Vol. II, Part I, pp. 338-9.

vincial are found which include representatives of the third estate[1]. Before the end of the thirteenth century and frequently during the fourteenth and fifteenth in the States of the Church, meetings of provincial estates were held to which towns owing fealty to the Pope were bound to send syndics with their mandates[2]; and even as early as the papacy of Innocent III (1207) there is mention of a summons to Rome of *consules* from cities within the papal jurisdiction[3].

So general had representation of the third estate become by the middle of the fourteenth century that Bartolus in his commentary on the term "consilium," occurring even in a constitution of the year 392, assumes it as a matter of course. "Note," he says, "that the heads of provinces assemble a council or universal parliament of the province. Which you must understand is not that all from the province are bound to go to it...but from all the cities certain persons are deputed as ambassadors or syndics who represent the city."[4]

In Naples and Sicily the tradition of Frederick II was revived under the Spanish monarchs by the transfer to them as well as to Sardinia of a representative system on the model of the Spanish Cortes[5].

In Germany, during the Middle Ages, the development of representative institutions was delayed by the persistence of feudal decentralisation and by the autocracy of the separate princes and nobles, but many indications are found of the activity of representatives, both as parts of the *Landstände* and on a wider scale in the *Reichstag*. In the *Landtag*, the vassals of the princes, including the towns, were often able to enforce against their lord the customary law of the district, and to make good their right of consent to impositions and to important questions of policy. In the *Reichstag*, from the time of William of Holland (1247–56), the towns were at times represented[6]. In 1254 the promise was made that in future assemblies both lords and cities should send four "sollempnes nuncios" with full power[7], and in the next two years several *colloquia generalia* were held in which these were included, the royal confirmation of the great *Landfriedensbund* of the Rhenish cities in 1255 formally acknowledging the unanimous consent of nobles "et eciam civitatum."[8] In the troubled

---

[1] Pertile, *op. cit.*, Vol. ii, Part i, pp. 319 sqq., with references.

[2] Pertile, *op. cit.*, Vol. ii, Part i, pp. 330 sqq.

[3] Theiner, *Codex Diplomaticus Dominii Temporalis S. Sedis*, i, p. 41; Pertile, *op. cit.*, Vol. ii, Part i, p. 332.

[4] *Code*, 10, 65, 5.

[5] Calisse, *Storia del Parlamento in Sicilia*; Giannone, *History of Naples*, English translation by Ogilvie; Pertile, *op. cit.*, Vol. ii, Part i, pp. 337–47; Merriman, *The Rise of the Spanish Empire*, i, pp. 507 sqq.

[6] Brunner, *Grundzüge der deutschen Rechtsgeschichte* (5th ed.), p. 152.

[7] MGH, *Constitutiones*, ii, number 428; Zeumer, *Quellensammlung zur Geschichte der deutschen Reichsverfassung*, p. 80.

[8] MGH, *Constitutiones*, ii, number 375; Zeumer, *op. cit.*, p. 85; Schröder, *Lehrbuch der deutschen Rechtsgeschichte* (5th ed.), pp. 659–60, and references.

times that followed the death of William and in the reign of Rudolf of Habsburg, there is little evidence of any representation of the third estate as contemplated by William. In fact it was not until the great struggle between Lewis of Bavaria and Pope John XXII that this element of the nation was called upon in general to give support to the imperial claims, as Philip IV of France had done against Boniface VIII thirty-six years before. In the call to the assembly at Frankfort in 1338, in which Lewis issued his famous law *Licet Iuris*, are included not merely secular and ecclesiastical princes, *comites*, and *barones*, but *civitates et communitates*, the latter to appear by two representatives "with sufficient mandate."[1] Such instances, however, are the exception, that of 1338 being the result of a crisis in the history of the Empire, as the first French Estates were of a similar conflict between the Papacy and the French kingdom ; and complete recognition of the claims of the German cities to representation was not obtained within the period covered by this chapter, and in fact hardly before the *Ewige Landfriede* of Maximilian I in 1495 and the great *Regiments-Ordnung* of 1500—provisions which were not unlike the ordinances obtained by the French Estates in 1357 after the battle of Poitiers, not only in their both containing unprecedented recognition of the rights of the towns, but in the fact that both were followed by periods of reaction toward an absolutism greater than any which had preceded.

Further illustrations of developments similar in many ways to those in the countries already mentioned might be given from various other parts of Western Europe within our period, particularly from Sweden, with its system of four estates, from the other Scandinavian kingdoms and Iceland, the peculiar institutions of the Isle of Man, or the "States" of Jersey and Guernsey which have preserved a surprising number of their medieval institutions even to our own day, from Switzerland, the Netherlands, and locally from many others. The medieval Estates of the Irish Parliament, composed as they were exclusively of Anglo-Irish, were probably modelled too closely upon English precedents to furnish independent characteristics worth noting here, but, in closing, brief notice must be taken of a few of the peculiarities of the Estates of medieval Scotland, some of which were unusual if not unique.

The contrast in parliamentary institutions north and south of the Tweed is striking, but the chief difficulty in coming to a real understanding of the former for the medieval period lies in the constant influence of English constitutional ideas upon those of Scotland and the regular employment, especially after the reign of James I, in Scottish official documents of words and phrases borrowed from England. Are such phrases to mean what they mean in England, or are they mere formulae little more than meaningless, foreign importations never really naturalised in Scotland, probably little understood at the time, and never now to be given the full meaning they undoubtedly have for England? The latter

[1] Zeumer, *Quellensammlung*, p. 154.

is the view of the leading present-day historian of the Scots Parliament[1].
In Scotland the strength of the kings was never as in England great
enough to check the power of the feudal lords in the medieval period and
thus to establish a strong administrative system as a foundation of constitutional development. Nationalism when it came in Scotland took
other forms than constitutional; it was concentrated neither in the king
as in France nor in parliament. Its first real organ was the Kirk. The
earlier parliaments in Scotland were of the type usual in feudal Europe
at that time, composed of the king's tenants-in-chief. Innes believed that
the addition of burgesses is to be dated from the Parliament of Cambuskenneth in 1326[2], but Professor Rait holds that this is not borne out
by the records[3]. At all events, they were occasionally present before the
end of the fourteenth century, frequently in the fifteenth, and invariably
in the latter half of it. Originally the smaller tenants of the king were
bound to attend his councils as fully as the greater ones, but it is a sign
of the weakness of the Scottish monarchs that they were never able to
compel them to attend. James I attempted to secure their attendance
by representatives without result; about the middle of the fourteenth
century the lesser of them were exempted by law, and at least from that
time they practically ceased to come and their influence is negligible in
the Scottish Parliament. This is one of the greatest of the differences
between its constitution and the institutions of England, and for Scotland
one of the most unfortunate. In their powers, the Scottish Parliaments
differed little theoretically from those of the other European national
assemblies, including enactment of law and the grant of supply, but in
the exercise of these powers they were greatly weakened, not only by their
incompleteness of *personnel* but by the peculiarities of their procedure.
Medieval parliaments everywhere were in the beginning regarded by their
members as a burden, and attendance was only obtained by rulers strong
enough to compel it.

Thus the king in Scotland had found it impossible to force his lesser
tenants to appear, and even such members as did appear would not remain
long enough to do the necessary business of a parliament. From the
second of these facts arose one of the most peculiar and most unfortunate
of Scottish institutions, the Lords of the Articles. In 1367 the Estates
chose certain persons "to hold the parliament" (ad parliamentum te-
nendum) and the rest obtained leave to go home for the harvest. This
precedent was followed with increasing frequency and by the early sixteenth
century the only functions left to the Estates as a whole were the choosing
of the Lords of the Articles at the opening of a parliament and the

[1] Robert S. Rait, *The Scottish Parliament before the Union of the Crowns* (1901);
The Parliaments of Scotland (1924).
[2] *Acts of the Parliament of Scotland*, I, preface p. 8; *Lectures on Scotch Legal Antiquities*, pp. 104–5, 116.
[3] *The Scottish Parliament before the Union*, pp. 28–30.

perfunctory ratification of their work as a matter of course at the end. Thus the parliament willingly and regularly handed over its whole power, even at times in the matter of voting a grant, to this committee. While they sat at all, the whole of the Estates met together in one house, but these sessions were so short, though they were fairly frequent, that nothing of importance could be done. Compared with the national assemblies of England, the Scottish Parliaments throughout the Middle Ages in general are utterly insignificant in importance, though of considerable interest on account of their peculiarity. "We possess no writs summoning a Parliament, no report of a debate in the Scottish Estates....Between 1437 and 1513 it is not easy to discover any single token of definite constitutional development, either in the direction of absolute government or in that of popular liberty. Not only does Scotland fail to produce a constitutional movement like that which characterizes the history of England; she does not develop any kind of constitution at all. No absolute monarch, no oligarchical council, no democratic parliament occupies the stage of her history for any length of time, nor does she know any free cities or any independent duchies. This constant condition of unstable equilibrium is not precisely analogous to the history of any other European country, and least of all is it like that of England, where we are apt to judge of national, by constitutional progress. Yet advance there certainly was, if not unbroken, still persistent, and persistently unconnected with questions relating to the constitution."[1]

The fate of these representative institutions, so widely spread and so surprisingly alike, was very different in different parts of Western Europe. In some, as in Germany, the continuance of feudal decentralisation and the long-belated appearance of an effective central authority caused these feudal Estates to remain with many of their essential features unchanged, and prevented their fusion into the national assembly of a State, often until modern times. In others, when the like feudal decentralisation gave way or was absorbed in a strong central authority at a comparatively early period, that authority was the authority of a monarch who soon made himself practically absolute and excluded the representatives of the people from all direct participation in the government of the State. This happened in Spain and France, where the Cortes and the Estates disappeared entirely, or became so occasional that their importance was lost as a regular organ of government. England is no doubt the most striking and far the most important instance of a third development, in which feudalism early gave way not to absolutism but to constitutionalism; where the representative Estates remained but became national instead of feudal, and were never so far weakened by monarchy that they could be suppressed by it, or prevented from exerting a strong and continuous influence which preserved the participation of the people in government

---

[1] Rait, *The Scottish Parliament before the Union of the Crowns*, pp. xvi–xx.

and consequently limited the power of the monarch and protected his subjects from the arbitrary exercise of that power.

Space will not permit the detailed examination of the later development of all the medieval Estates, even for the west of Europe alone. It is probably more important to try to determine the general factors at work on the Estates by a comparison, in greater detail than would be otherwise possible, of two countries whose development was strikingly different but where these developments occurred nearly enough together, and therefore amid general surroundings sufficiently alike to enable us to discover the real causes of their dissimilarity.

For such a purpose the contrast of France and England is the most valuable. In both, the transition from feudal to what we usually call modern conditions took place before the Renaissance. In both, the changes are nearly enough contemporary to be comparable; and though the results were very different in the two countries, they were brought about amid conditions of the same age and of the same general kind. In no other country, with the possible exception of Spain, do these fundamental changes come early enough safely to illustrate by their peculiarities the factors that created the modern out of the medieval political world, and the constitutional history of Spain has not been sufficiently studied.

"England, after the Norman Conquest, began in a monarchy almost absolute; and it is perhaps for that reason that in the seventeenth century it emerged as a monarchy representative. Feudal France began with a royal authority almost totally powerless; and it is probably on that account that she ended in the seventeenth century in the monarchy absolute."[1] In these words the late Professor Esmein has pointed out the first and greatest of the factors which turned the institutions of France and England into channels so different from each other. But this statement is an apparent paradox whose profound truth becomes apparent only when examined in greater detail. Elsewhere the same author indicates another of these factors in the growing community of interest between the feudal nobility in England and the rising "middle class."[2] But the second of these factors with all its vast importance came in part as a result of the first. The broadest lines of distinction in constitutional development between France and England lie ultimately in the fact that in the former kingdom the feudal monarchy passed into the absolute monarchy while in England it became a constitutional monarchy. Why did one become absolute while the other became constitutional? It was because the English monarchy became national before it ceased to be feudal, at a time when the French monarchy still remained feudal only. When then the feudal element disappeared, as it ultimately did in both kingdoms, in England its place was taken by a government in which the

---

[1] Esmein, *Droit constitutionnel* (5th ed.), p. 65.
[2] *Ibid.*, p. 64.

Estates had already begun to share; in France there was no power in existence to replace the feudal monarchy but the uncontrolled power of an absolute king. The difference is owing to the regular participation of the Estates in England before the feudal monarchy disappeared, a participation which existed in that period of French history, with one exception, only on the rare occasions of popular unrest. On the decline of feudalism in France there was no authority, and no body of men, politically prepared permanently to take over or even to share with the king in the centralised government that was replacing feudal decentralisation. That place could be taken only by an authority that was at once centralised and national, and the only one then in existence to do it was a strong, national, but practically absolute monarch. To put it otherwise, in England there was participation and there was representation while feudal conditions still remained, and therefore when these conditions disappeared the strong centralised national power which emerged was one which retained the participation of the Estates. In France, since this participation had not begun during the period when feudal conditions flourished, so it could not continue when they began to decline, and the feudal monarchy was replaced by one practically, even if not theoretically, absolute. These results are inherent in feudal monarchy itself, and partly owing to the unusual strength of the feudal monarchs in England after the Norman Conquest, partly to the circumstances of that conquest itself. As Professor Dicey says, "A King who is forced to receive advice, means, at the present day, a King who is a King in name alone, who 'reigns but does not govern.' According to the ideas prevailing in the eleventh century, it was rather the King's privilege than his duty to receive counsel from the great men of his kingdom.... The more powerful the monarch, the more frequent the conventions of his barons. In England these assemblies were constantly held, whilst in France, where the royal power was feeble, they became more and more rare. The reason of this is clear. A feudal monarch had to dread the isolation, not the union, of his liege men. A feudatory who threw off his sovereign's rule, withdrew from his counsels. The Dukes of Burgundy, or Normandy, gradually dropped attendance at the royal court. For once let the barons attend their lord, and his authority was secure, since attendance was an acknowledgement of his sovereign rights...."[1]

The decisive factor in determining these results for England was the *early* centralisation of administration, a centralisation which came far sooner there than elsewhere. It was this that made England the only Western country with a common law little influenced by Rome, and this too ultimately made her a constitutional instead of an absolute monarchy. The great founders of this strong central administration, William I, Henry I, and Henry II, were the first great builders of modern constitutionalism. They laid in their administrative reforms the foundation on

[1] *The Privy Council*, p. 3.

which the superstructure of the English "representative monarchy" was later to rise. Save for the permanent foundations they laid, the outbursts of popular discontent at arbitrary rule would have been as ephemeral in England as the protests of the French *États Généraux* in the fourteenth century.

It was not so much mere centralisation that had these important results, it was *early* centralisation. France became centralised too, but too late to save constitutionalism or to secure for her a common law based almost wholly on the customs of the land. England, on the other hand, received at the strong hands of her kings before the eleventh and twelfth centuries were over an administrative system so extensive, so strong, and so uniform, that it created the immediate necessity for a uniform procedure and ultimately for a system of legal principles common to the whole realm, and this at so early a period that the gradually recovering Roman Law was not yet strong enough to make its bid to be that common system. When the law of Rome had again become strong enough in Western Europe, for England the opportunity had passed, and England was already inoculated against it; she already had a common law of her own, which Rome was never afterwards able to replace. England had been forced by her early centralisation of judicial administration to build a general system of common law from materials then at hand, and at that early time it was not yet Roman but English materials alone that were at hand. England and her descendants alone of all the Western nations have to-day a common law almost entirely independent of Rome, on account of the great centralising work of her kings in the eleventh and twelfth centuries; and mainly for the same reason, England alone preserved for the Western world the continuity of the development from feudalism to constitutionalism. This could not have been merely because England became centralised, for other nations became centralised too. It was because she became centralised *early*, earlier than any of the other national States of the West. It was in part the consequences of the nature of the Conquest itself and in part the masterful character of the line of kings the Conquest gave to England, that led to this early centralisation of administration at the expense of the jurisdiction of the feudal lords; and the monarchy that resulted, though in character feudal, was the strongest of its day. But the strength resulted not only in the earliest centralisation of jurisdiction, procedure, and law; to it we must attribute that other characteristic which Professor Dicey considers the chief badge of royal authority in feudal times, the regularity of the attendance of the *barones* in answer to the royal summons to the *Curia Regis*. Thus the *barones* became the first "estate"; and, thanks to the strength of the king, an estate which was never suffered long to absent itself from the work of his councils. And it was with this estate, when the *populus* was extended to include the *milites* and the burgesses, beginning with the thirteenth

CH. XXIII.

century, that the representatives of these classes gradually merged, as new parts "dans une organisation préexistante."[1]

In the beginning it was the feudal obligation of the barons to attend their lord's court, and it is the unusual vigour with which the English king was able to exact it with regularity, rather than the strength of these barons or their independent spirit, to which we must trace back the causes of English constitutionalism. But in order to make the whole of this development clear, it is not only necessary to understand its beginnings, but its results as well. The work of the early kings may be summarised as: (1) a centralisation of administration stronger and earlier than any found elsewhere, (2) a regularity in the meetings of the Curia, which the strength of the English king made unique in Western Europe, (3) a consequent sharing in the tasks of administration between king and barons, which in time became continuous, permanent, and regular. And this sharing in the burdens of administration became of greater and greater constitutional importance the more closely it brought the members of the King's Council, as *iusticiarii itinerantes,* in closer and closer touch with the knights in the county courts, whose political development had been steadily going on locally side by side with that of the central Curia. Thus began the *rapprochement* of the estate of the barons and those knights who were later to be incorporated with them as an added estate in a representative parliament.

It was the encroachment of a centralised authority upon the powers and jurisdiction of the feudal lords that marked the development of both England and France in the later Middle Ages. But in England this had started earlier and was becoming national and constitutional even while it yet remained in many respects feudal. The individual *barones* became a *baronagium,* an estate of the realm, though still feudal vassals of a common lord, while their feudal *auxilia* gradually became parliamentary grants, without wholly losing at once their original feudal character; and the nature of these gradual transitions is typical of the whole development from feudalism to nationalism, and in this case to constitutionalism.

Originally the king was both *dominus* and *Rex.* In the Norman period he had been able largely to "live of his own." These strictly feudal revenues as *dominus* sufficed for most of his needs. But every advance of the central administration tended to increase his revenues as *Rex,* and an increase of these revenues was, we may suspect, as often as not the real reason for administrative reforms, rather than any desire for justice. In general, the extension of this central administration meant a corresponding transformation of the king's revenues: it was more to the king as *Rex* and less and less as mere *dominus* that they were coming. The fact is that on its economic side feudalism was declining, and the ordinary revenues properly to be called feudal were gradually drying up. It was partly resentment against this that led to the baronial uprising which produced

[1] Pasquet, *Essai,* p. 1.

Magna Carta. The barons rightly attributed part of this result to the reforms of Henry II, and among their demands were included several which would have undone some important parts of his work if the designs of the barons had been fully realised.

This drying-up of feudal revenue necessarily affected the king, whose demesne was involved, no less than the lands in the hands of tenants. Thus John and Henry III were driven more and more to depend on grants, which as we have seen were truly national in scope even though their origin is to be traced to feudal custom. The strong kings of the eleventh and twelfth centuries, in adding to their strength by extending their claims as *Rex*, could hardly have foreseen that in this nationalising of the administration they were imposing upon their weaker successors the necessity of taking the nation into partnership in that administration. But the proof that they were actually doing so is seen in the baronial claims in the reign of Henry III, as well as the baronial demand for a control of administration in the Provisions of Oxford, and the ordinances of the barons in 1311, in the concessions of Edward I in the confirmation of the charters of 1297, in the distinction made in the reign of Edward II between the king and the Crown, in the extension of baronial control over the Exchequer and even over the King's Wardrobe, and finally in the rapid enlargement of the powers and claims of parliament which reached their height at the time of the Lancastrians.

By making English administration national, the kings of the eleventh and twelfth centuries also made inevitable national participation in that administration, just so soon as the nation should become conscious of itself, and just so far as classes or "estates" of the people strong enough and politically self-conscious enough should arise to demand their proper share in this participation. This consciousness of nationalism began to be effective in the thirteenth century, particularly in the long weak reign of Henry III, and by the fourteenth century it had extended down from the barons to knights and burgesses who, in theory if not entirely in fact, had become the commons of the whole realm—*communa totius Angliae*.

Thus constitutionalism in England took the place of feudalism and gradually grew out of it. In France, on the contrary, the original estate of the barons never became so closely connected with the administration of the kingdom as in England, largely because the king was unable to compel them regularly to attend him. Neither was there in France that early strengthening and centralising of administration to be seen in England, nor the equally important linking up of the central Curia and the local courts by a systematic and periodical employment of itinerant members of the Curia. Without this encroachment of royal power as in England, feudal decentralisation in France remained longer and while it remained was less affected by the growing tendency toward nationalism. Thus when feudalism finally did decline in France, the royal power that replaced it was the power of a king who did in fact become national, but in doing so did not to the same degree become constitutional as in England. No Estates were in France so closely interwoven with the royal administration that they could not be dispensed with without endangering that administration itself or destroying its national character. In the seventeenth century Loyseau could say of the French monarchy that it was a monarchy royal and not seignorial, "a perfect sovereignty in which the estates have no part."[1] "Est igitur pura monarchia, nulla populi aut optimatum potestate confusa."[2]

Elsewhere, for local reasons, the developments were somewhat different. In Scotland, for example, no powerful kings appeared during the earlier development, as in England, and in later times no constitutional monarchy really worthy the name. But the latter result was not, as in France, owing to the growth of an absolute monarchy, but rather to the longer continuance of feudal anarchy. To the very end of the Middle Ages and long afterward, the kings of Scotland were both irresponsible and weak. Though parliaments were frequent, they were too little representative of the nation to impose any constitutional limitations upon the king of lasting importance, while at the same time the monarchy was so completely at the mercy of factions of the nobles that it was never able to establish itself on an independent basis. Scotland produced neither strong monarchy nor constitutionalism; she retained feudal anarchy so long that neither of these had a chance to develop in the Middle Ages. Even locally her constitutional life was weaker than in most continental countries, though by no means non-existent. The representative institutions of the burghs, particularly in the conventions of the royal burghs, have no doubt been given an exaggerated importance by some Scottish constitutional writers of modern times[3], and a greater antiquity has been attributed to them than contemporary evidence seems to warrant. Nevertheless, before the Reformation, there can be little doubt that it was in these burghs that Scotland's chief constitutional life was to be found, and the burghs are at last beginning to receive the attention from constitutional historians that they have long deserved.

In most other Western States, where neither royal absolutism nor constitutional monarchy developed, this lack of development was the result of the lateness of the unification. Effective centralised administration and a common law go hand in hand as a rule. Germany, for example, got neither of these before the late fifteenth century. This meant, however, merely that the communes remained local; they were never merged in an effective centralised but constitutional monarchy as in England nor destroyed by an effective centralised absolutism as in France. These institutions survived, but survived only locally, until modern times. In many places, however, the local constitutional life remained strong and

[1] Quoted in Esmein, *Droit constitutionnel*, p. 58.
[2] Bodin, *De Republica*, Lib. II, Cap. I, p. 182 (in edition of 1586).
[3] For example, by Cosmo Innes.

vigorous and outlasted the Middle Ages to contribute to an important degree, when later combined with parliamentary institutions borrowed from England, to Continental constitutionalism in modern times and under modern conditions, when central authority had finally become established and revolution had destroyed the most important remnants of feudal particularism which had burdened it hitherto.

The later history of the medieval Estates thus varied widely from country to country. In some they remained merely local, in others they for a time shewed promise of combining with the growing centralised power of the nation, only to be later suppressed by the monarchy. In England, circumstances were more favourable, and constitutional monarchy resulted. But amid all these variations, it may be said that, whenever constitutionalism arose out of an earlier feudalism, its rise and its continuance alike were conditioned upon a corresponding appearance and participation in government of the medieval Estates or their descendants.

CHAPTER XXIV

PEASANT LIFE AND RURAL CONDITIONS (*c.* 1100 TO *c.* 1500)

THE student of medieval social and economic history who commits himself to a generalisation is digging a pit into which he will later assuredly fall, and nowhere does the pit yawn deeper than in the realm of rural history. It is of the nature of trade to overflow the bounds of geography and race, but the rustic world is a local world; it does what sun and soil demand and it is ruled by a custom which may vary from one village to the next. There is little enough in common between the daily lives of the wandering shepherds of Spain, Apulia, and the Carpathians, the vine-growers of the Rhineland and Bordelais, the men who tended seed gardens round Erfurt, the toiling plowmen of the English midlands, the Flemings draining their sea marshes, and the pioneers beyond the Elbe. Moreover, rural society was in a state of flux during the centuries to be considered here (roughly from 1100 to 1500). Estates were coalescing and breaking up, towns were rising, land was being brought under cultivation or becoming exhausted, the population was growing, men were struggling out of serfdom or falling into it, new forms of landholding were being evolved; and all this was happening unevenly in different parts of Europe. It is necessary, therefore, to consider first the chief differences in the local framework and then the changes, which were slowly metamorphosing the rural world during the last four centuries of the Middle Ages, before any general picture of village life can be attempted.

The peasant's existence was unrolled in a double framework, the work in part of nature and in part of man. The geographical lie of the land, the climate, and the dominant occupation forced upon the district by these facts largely dictated the type of settlement, the field systems, even the personal status of the peasantry. For the organisation of estate and manor, and the complicated personal and tenurial relations between lords and peasants, which formed the artificial framework of rural life, were profoundly modified by the physical framework into which they were fitted, and elaborate historical explanations are sometimes given for differences which were simply due to geographical conditions. It is possible to observe certain economic equations which have a rough validity, despite the variations which race and history may introduce from place to place. Wide plains, which lend themselves readily to arable cultivation, usually lead to the clustered type of settlement known as the village, with houses lying together and open fields stretching round them. The home of the two and three field system is in country of this type, the south and centre of England, the great belt of north and north-eastern France, Germany from the basin of the Seine and the Swiss Alps across to the plains of the Slavonic north-east, and over the Danish peninsula to the Scandinavian lowlands. It usually breeds big estates and a strong feudal system, for feudalism ever thrives best in cornlands; it breeds a peasantry which, though often economically very prosperous, is strongly bound to the soil; labour services are numerous and serfdom is tenacious. It is the country of the typical, one might almost call it the "textbook" manor, the main characteristics of which are too well known to need further description.

On the other hand, hilly country and pasture-farming lead to different types of settlement and different social conditions. The people live not in large villages or rural bourgs but in scattered hamlets or separate farms, for their flocks and herds are spread over a wide area and water is usually abundant. Labour services are much less numerous, and payments in kind are correspondingly more important, for generally speaking it is more convenient for the lord of a manor to take his profits in the form of labour in an arable district, where he has his own demesne farm to cultivate, and of produce or money in a pastoral district, since how shall he utilise week work from all his peasants on a sheep farm and what profession is more essentially skilled and permanent than the shepherd's? In these hilly pastoral lands, moreover, the feudal system in general and manorialism in particular are apt to be weak and serfdom is rarely onerous and disappears rapidly. In the most remote mountain districts, indeed, the peasants are often quite free; the lord exacts compulsory hospitality for himself and his servants when hunting or riding on business over these wild lands, but though such rights of *gîte* and *albergue* are sometimes oppressive and exacted by violence, they are more often rigidly fixed by custom and early commuted for rents. In general, the control of the lords is slight and in some parts, as for example in the high valleys of the Pyrenees, the villages are actually independent. The valley of Aspe, disputing with Gaston Phébus, Viscount of Béarn, declared that "the valley of Aspe was before the lord was and the lord has only that which they have given him"; and the lord never entered the valley without exacting two hostages for his personal safety. The Pyrenean villages were in practice little republics, governing themselves according to the custom of the valley, and making pastoral treaties with the men of other valleys on both slopes of the mountains. The peasants of certain Alpine valleys were equally independent, and in the later Middle Ages the term Swiss became a synonym for freedom. "We will be Switzers," cried the insurgent peasants at Spires in the great revolt of 1502.

Marsh and forest lands, which have to be drained or cleared for cultivation, and frontier lands which must be settled by pioneers, bring about yet another combination of circumstances. In many cases settlements in these newly reclaimed areas are planned in a sense that the old casual villages and hamlets were not. The *Waldhufen* in the forest districts of Germany and elsewhere and the *Merschhufen* in the Low Countries and the marshes of the Weser and Elbe are long rectangular blocks, lying along the road as an axis and stretching to the edge of the forest or the dyke. Such villages, especially in the Eastern colonial areas where they were laid out by promoters, have an economical and logical ground-plan often suggestive on a small scale of a modern American town. Just as the conditions of reclamation and colonisation influenced the form of settlement, so they influenced methods of cultivation and social status. Individual cultivation was the rule in the fertile polders reclaimed from the sea along the Flemish coast, and *Waldhufen* and *Merschhufen* were usually enclosed, though in the colonial East the open field system was common. Moreover, from a social point of view reclaimed land and frontier land is free land. If freedom dwells in the mountains, she likewise flourishes in marsh and forest, because no man will bring them under cultivation save for an inducement and there are no inducements more potent than freedom and cheap land. The *hosti* who reclaim Brittany after the ravages of the Northmen, the settlers on the Jura plateau, the Flemings who drain their own flats and those of the colonial East, the wild clansmen of Ditmarschen, the backwoodsmen and cowboys of the Eastern frontier, the Castilian *behetrías* who settle the lands reconquered from the Moor and have the right to change their lord "up to seven times in one day," all are free; and even in areas where serfdom prevails the man who makes an assart holds it by free tenure, though the rest of his land be servile and he a bondsman by blood. Serfdom is unknown in colonial areas, except where an aboriginal population cultivates the land of an alien ruling class side by side with free alien settlers, or where occasional owners of frontier *latifundia* import a few serfs from home, or where serfdom arises by retrogression after the frontier period is over.

Finally, it should be observed that certain specialised crops are usually associated with small holdings, individual cultivation, and a free or mainly free peasantry. This is notably the case in the vine and olive-growing districts of the Mediterranean, and the reason is to be found in the fact that vine-tending is a skilled occupation and that wine is, in the main areas of its cultivation, produced for a wide market. The peasant can find a ready sale for his vintage and even small holdings are profitable; the lord, on the other hand, finds rent-paying tenants and wage labour better suited than cultivation by unfree labour to an estate run for profit. But when we speak of a market we introduce a factor which is historical rather than natural, and historical and racial as well as geographical factors must always be taken into account in analysing the development of a district. The historical factors which most profoundly modified the life of the rural districts were the growth of towns and the consequent extension of the trade in foodstuffs, for an exchange economy invariably brings with it agrarian specialisation and in the long run freedom. The growth of towns led to the increasing devotion of land in their neighbourhood to dairy farming and market gardening, to meet the demand of the town population for food. The rise of industries led to the cultivation of certain industrial crops, such as the woad of Toulouse and the madder of Albi.

More intensive farming and smaller individual holdings characterised such districts; and freedom came quickly to serfs in the vicinity of towns, which were the homes of free burgesses.

Thus the physical framework in which the medieval peasant passed his life, modified sometimes by racial and historical circumstances, conditioned not only his occupation but the kind of settlement in which he lived, his personal status, and his relations with his lord. The artificial framework of his existence was the institution known in England as the manor, the character of which was largely modified by geography. In general, a manor in a pastoral district consisted in rights over a large number of scattered homesteads and a heavy exaction of dues in kind, while a manor in an agricultural district usually contained a more or less large home-farm cultivated in part by the labour of servile tenants. The home-farm and the peasant tenures were bound together in a single economic system by these labour services and also by the fact that the lord, no less than the peasants, was subordinated to a common routine of cultivation in the open fields and bound to recognise rights of usage in the waste. The organisation of production differed. The lord of a single manor dwelt there and lived on the produce of his farm, the working of which he probably superintended himself. The lord of ten, fifty, or a hundred manors, had his seneschal to supervise his whole estate, and each of the manors was farmed by a bailiff, who sometimes lived at the manor house. The large landowner employed several methods of turning the produce of all these home-farms and peasant rents to his own use. Three in particular followed each other in rough chronological sequence, though they co-existed until a comparatively late date. These were the system of the travelling household, the system of delivering food rents from the different manors to a central place, and finally the much more convenient system of selling the surplus produce and delivering money instead of goods to the lord.

As to the status of the peasantry it may be said that at the beginning of the twelfth century the mass of them were serfs, though free tenants were to be found everywhere and in certain districts predominated, and there still existed, especially in the mountainous south of Europe, little pockets of *allodiers*, who owned no lord but their king. Serfdom, however, involved two different relationships, one of status and one of tenure, which were not necessarily concentrated upon a single lord. A man might be a serf by blood, handing down his serfdom to all his brood, the personal chattel of some body-lord (*Leibherr*). He might, again, be a servile tenant, holding his land by bondage tenure of a landlord (*Grundherr*), but personally free. He might be the bondsman of one lord and the bond-tenant of another. He might be a bondsman holding a piece of free land. There was, however, a tendency for the relationships of status and tenure to be combined and a tendency also to transfer servile obligations from the person of the bondsman to the land. When payments were thus first transferred and then fixed and deprived of the uncertainty which clung to status-payments, by reason of the lord's theoretical right to do what he would with his own, two steps had been taken on the road to freedom. Henceforth it was the *mansa* and not the man that was liable to tallage, the virgate and not the virgin that owed *leyrwite* for a slip from grace; and the land knew what it had to pay. The transference might, of course, be turned to the disadvantage of freemen, as in Germany in the later Middle Ages, when mere residence on certain land made a man a serf on the principle of *Luft macht Eigen,* and a revival of personal bondage took place; but in the early Middle Ages the transference of obligations from the person to the land was undoubtedly a step forward. Important as was the distinction between bond and free it was, however, a legal and not an economic one. The bondsman might, economically speaking, be a prosperous small farmer employing labour, while the freeman owned only a cottage and a croft and worked upon the bondsman's land. Moreover, it is exceedingly difficult to say which of the many dues and services to which the medieval peasant was subject were characteristically servile, for there is hardly one which was not somewhere paid by freemen as well as serfs. The serf was usually marked by his inability to move from his holding without his lord's permission, by his liability (in agricultural districts) to weekwork, by the payment of certain onerous dues on death and marriage, and sometimes also of a tallage which was theoretically arbitrary, though in practice usually fixed; while the freeman held his land at a rent in money or in kind and was liable only to occasional boons and less onerous payments. But freemen as well as serfs are sometimes found subject to *mainmorte* or to the *maritagium.*

Apart from the various "bans" by which the lords forced their tenants (sometimes free as well as bond) to grind corn at their mill, bake bread in their oven, and press grapes in their winepress, the peasantry was subject to a whole series of regular and irregular payments. The regular annual payments included ground-rent, payment for the use of commons, and tallage; the irregular payments fell due on death, marriage, and inheritance, or when the land changed hands. In addition, there were labour services, which varied with the nature of the land, some being regular weekwork or taskwork, others "boons" performed at certain seasons. The serf was also burdened by special obligations which differed from place to place: in England, for example, he was often obliged to fold his sheep on the lord's acres for the sake of manure; in forest districts he had to do hunting services; in some parts he paid when he sold any of his livestock. All these payments had become fixed in the course of time, and although in theory the serf might own (as an Abbot of Burton once claimed) *nihil praeter ventrem,* in practice he enjoyed complete security of tenure while he paid his dues, and knew as exactly as the freeman what those dues were, the lord's demands being more or less restricted by the custom of the manor. Occasional amenities softened the irksomeness of forced services; boonworks were frequently rewarded by an armful

of the crop harvested and by a meal and, with the fall in the value
of money, these "beanfeasts" came to cost the lord more than the
services were worth. Still, taken all together, the dues and services to
which the serfs of many manors were subject were exceedingly heavy. He
who is disposed to idealise the medieval peasant's lot should study the
list set forth in the famous *Conte des vilains de Verson* by the *trouvère*
Estout de Goz in the middle of the thirteenth century, and borne out by
the official extent of the revenues of the abbey of Mont-Saint-Michel at
Verson and Bretteville, which Delisle has printed, or the customs of the
bond-tenants of Darnell and Over, as recorded in the Ledger Book of
Vale Royal Abbey in 1326.[1] It is not surprising that the serfs of both
these abbeys were in revolt at the time.

Of the irregular payments to which the serf was subject the most
bitterly resented were those which entered his inmost life and cast the
shadow of a ravening hand over bridal bed and death-bed alike. The
payment of the *maritagium* (*merchet, formariage, Bedemund*) was sometimes
exacted only when marriage was contracted outside the manor, but it was
everywhere one of the dues which serfs were most anxious to evade, for it
was a check upon their freedom of movement. The payments for incon-
tinence, such as the English *leyrwite* exacted from a serf when his daughter
sinned, and the Catalonian *cugucia* which gave the lord the whole or part
of the property of any peasant's wife guilty of adultery, were no less
resented. Much more onerous, however, was the *mortuarium* (*heriot,
mainmorte, Sterbfall, Buteil, Kurmede, Besthaupt*) which was also almost
universal. In France it was usually exacted only when a serf died without
heirs living with him in his household, but elsewhere it was payable
whenever a tenant died. A study of the different forms taken by the
Sterbfall as recorded in the German *Weistümer*, or village "dooms,"
provides some entertaining reading and a very strong impression of the
burdensomeness of the tax. In some places it was levied on the capital
value of the holding, and often amounted to as much as a third, sometimes
even to a half. More often it was the best beast and best suit of clothes
which a man possessed; if he had no son his weapons and sometimes his
sharpened tools were taken, leaving the widow only a chopper to cut her
wood. A woman owed her best dress and kerchief which she had been
wont to wear on Sundays or at market, and her marriage bed, unless she
left an unmarried daughter, who was allowed to keep it. Occasionally the
husband was permitted to retain the bed as long as he remained unmarried, but if he took a second wife the lord's steward might go and drag
it out of the back door, while the peasant brought in his bride at the
front, leaving her (like Anne Hathaway) with the second-best bed. When
it is remembered that the Church also exacted its mortuary from the dead

---

[1] See Delisle, *Études sur la condition de la classe agricole...en Normandie au moyen
âge*, pp. 668–90; *Ledger Book of Vale Royal Abbey*, ed. J. Brownbill (Lancs. and
Cheshire Rec. Soc.), pp. 31–42, 117–22.

parishioner, taking the second-best beast and garment after the lord had taken the best, it is small wonder that the moralists of the age sometimes (but all too rarely) turned in disgust from lord and priest feeding like vultures on the poor man's corpse.

Mention of the ecclesiastical mortuary calls attention to another aspect of the question of peasant dues. These were not payable solely to his lord. As a parishioner he owed the Church not only the irregular mortuary, but regular annual tithes, which were a heavy burden, though they often in the course of time fell into the hands of the landlord and merely added another item to the rent. But besides these payments the peasants on many parts of the Continent owed dues and allegiance to a third type of lord beside the *Leibherr* and *Grundherr*. Sometimes it was the lord's suzerain; sometimes a *Gerichtsherr*, who acquired jurisdictional rights over a territory and was responsible for its protection and for the public peace. This type of lord is not found in England, but on the Continent, particularly on ecclesiastical estates where the landlords were unable themselves to provide military protection, the *Vogt* or *Avoué* was an almost universal phenomenon. In theory his business was protection. "If a villager asks for the support of the Vogt," says the custom of Nieder-Ranspach in Alsace, "the Vogt ought to come to his help so speedily that if he have but one foot shod he should take the other boot in his hand and fly to the defence of right." At Neuillers the serfs of St Peter had the right to emigrate to Dossenheim and "if on the road a wheel come off their cart, the Vogt ought to dismount and give them bodily aid." In return, the people of the villages over which he exercised his authority attended his court and gave him and his suite hospitality when it was held. But the exactions of the Vogt grew both in France and Germany; the maintenance claim developed into a regular tax (the *Vogtbede*), he took his share in death and succession dues and exacted his corvée from the people. In both countries Vogtei taxes were often heavier than those due to the landlord, and as a rule they fell on free as well as on bond. Moreover, free peasants were also liable to State taxes, which grew steadily as the centuries advanced, though they were sometimes merged with the *Vogtbede*. Inama-Sternegg calculated that in Germany towards the end of the Middle Ages the fourfold payment of rent to the landowner, ecclesiastical tithe, Vogtei dues, and State taxes amounted on an average to two-thirds of the gross product of the land; he works out the case of a free leaseholder paying an annual rent of one-third of his produce (not the worst form of lease), which shews that the ground rent amounted to 33.4%, the tithe to 6.6%, the Vogtei dues to 20% and the territorial tax to 4%, making a total of 64%, not counting labour dues, irregular payments such as the marriage and death dues, and fines, which probably raised his annual rent by another 5%.

It has already been stated that throughout the Middle Ages changes were at work in the countryside; but at certain periods the process was accelerated, and the twelfth and thirteenth centuries are pre-eminently one of these periods of hastened change. Three movements in particular affected the life of the rural districts: the rise of towns, the impetus to clearance and colonisation, and the disintegration of the manor. All were connected with a still more fundamental economic movement, the growth of the population.

The steady growth of the population shewed itself in a number of ways. One was the rise of towns, which was marked all over Western Europe. To take Germany alone, the researches of Püschel, based upon a study of town walls, streets, and buildings as well as upon written records, have shewn that the old German towns of the West became too small for their inhabitants in the course of the eleventh century, grew very rapidly during the twelfth and thirteenth, and usually stopped growing some time in the fourteenth, from which time their area in most cases sufficed for their inhabitants until the nineteenth century[1]. Such a phenomenon speaks eloquently of a crowded countryside, for the town population was obviously being fed by immigration from outside, and it is significant that the period of growth coincides with the period when the colonisation movement of the German people beyond the Elbe was most active. In the countryside the increase shewed itself in the subdivision of holdings, in a steady rise in land values, and in the carrying of cultivation as far as the technical knowledge of the time allowed, even to land from which the economic return was poor and which sometimes had to be abandoned later in the Middle Ages. Checked though it was by famines and pestilences, this upward movement of the population continued and is at the bottom of most of the economic changes of the time.

The growth of towns, one of its most important manifestations, inevitably reacted upon conditions in the surrounding countryside, for the town looked to the country to provide it with population, with food, and with some at least of the commodities of its export trade. It was to its interest to attract the more enterprising members of the peasant class within its walls, and it was easy to do so, since town air, as the proverb ran, made a man free. But besides the tendency thus set up for a flow of population from the country into the towns, they had a far-reaching effect upon the organisation of the countryside itself, for manorial lords found it increasingly expedient to supersede travelling households and food rents by the sale of their surplus produce in the market for cash. This fact provides a key to the nature of manorial economy during the central period of the Middle Ages. It was not, as it has often been represented, a closed economy, a kind of subsistence farming, aiming only at self-sufficiency. Marx's epigram that the walls of his stomach set the limits to the lord's exploitation of his peasantry rests upon a misconception.

[1] See A. Püschel, *Das Anwachsen der deutschen Städte in der Zeit der mittelalterlichen Colonisation* (Berlin, 1910), *passim*.

The acquisition of landed property by lay and ecclesiastical lords went far beyond the limits necessary for self-support, and landownership was organised for profit at a very early date. An international trade in certain agrarian products (notably in corn, wine, and wool) was already in existence in the Dark Ages; in the twelfth and thirteenth centuries it was active and brought great profits to landowners as well as to merchants. The same chapter in the *Rules of St Robert* (*c.* 1240), which bids the Countess of Lincoln travel with her household from place to place, adds: "so arrange your sojourns that the place at your departure shall not remain in debt, but something may remain on the manor, whereby the manor can raise money from increase of stock and especially cows and sheep, until your stock acquit your wine, robes, wax, and all your wardrobe," and proceeds to give details as to the sale of wool. Nor was it only in the pastoral districts that English manors were profit-making concerns. Almost every manor in the corn-growing areas sold its surplus grain in the market, and that grain came from the peasants' holdings as well as from the demesne farm; a regular market organisation was developing early in the twelfth century, and well-defined market areas may be detected in the thirteenth. England was a land of comparatively small towns; the effect of this evolution upon the countryside was even more marked in those parts of the Continent where town life was more highly developed. Everywhere towns were a magnet for the peasant who wanted to leave the land and a market for the peasant who remained upon it.

No less far-reaching than the rise of towns was the effect of another and simultaneous movement. At the beginning of the period a large part of the soil of Europe was still uncultivated and uninhabited, sodden with marsh and fen or overgrown with forests. A steady work of drainage and colonisation had been going on piecemeal during the Dark Ages, but in the eleventh century it was pushed forward with new vigour. Nowhere was it more active than in the Low Countries, where the Counts of Flanders, the great abbeys, lay landowners, and peasants all combined to stem the encroachments of the sea along the coast, drain the marshes of the Lower Scheldt and Meuse, and bring the heaths of Brabant and Hainault under cultivation. In maritime Flanders associations called *wateringues* were formed to organise the control of the dykes and water channels. All the way from Flanders to Frisia they built up a wall against the sea and behind it cultivated a long line of fertile polders, where fat cattle grazed. In the thirteenth century the towns took a leading share in the work, and many polders to this day bear the names of the capitalist "undertakers" who drained them in that age of activity. A similar work of reclamation was going on in other countries, and harsh were the penalties on the man who failed to do his part in maintaining the defences against the invading waters. In one district in Germany it was laid down that if a man barked one of the willows which held the dykes together, "his belly shall be ripped up and his bowels taken out and wound round the harm he has done, and if he can get over that the willow also can get over it." An equally energetic war was also waged against heath and forest; indeed, the attack on the forests was so relentless that towards the end of the Middle Ages rulers and landowners and sometimes the peasant communities themselves were obliged to make regulations for their protection. In this work of reclaiming the soil of Europe due credit must be given to the monastic houses, which had both the capital to undertake large-scale operations and the intelligence to supervise them. An additional motive came in the twelfth century, when the newly-founded Cistercian and Premonstratensian Orders deliberately settled in wild and savage places, far from the haunts of man, and slowly brought them under cultivation. The Cistercians in particular were great sheep and cattle farmers.

The work of reclamation was thus going on steadily in Europe throughout the Middle Ages, but for the Western nations it was a question of settling and bringing under cultivation land within their own national boundaries. With Germany it was different. The Germans were the colonising people *par excellence* of the Middle Ages, not merely on account of their intrinsic industry and enterprise (which were great), but because they alone of West-European nations had a movable frontier to the East. In character and achievement the eastward expansion of the German people over the Slav lands has aptly been compared with the westward expansion of the American people from Atlantic seaboard to Pacific, with the Slav in the rôle of the Red Indian; many centuries earlier, it passed through the same stages and bred the same types. Its fundamental cause was the growth of the population in old Germany, and the first stirrings of a new activity came early in the twelfth century. After Adolf of Holstein's conquest of the Wagri in 1142, Helmold, whose *Chronica Slavorum* is the epic of the Saxon frontiersman, tells how he sent into the Low Countries, Westphalia, and Frisia, for settlers and how "there rose up an innumerable multitude of divers nationalities and they took with them their households and all their possessions and came into the country of the Wagri." The Wendish Crusade of 1147 was followed by a similar rush of settlers to the East, "with horses and oxen, with ploughs and wains and labourers fit for the work," which in places was a true mass emigration. At a later date (towards the end of the thirteenth century) German peasant settlers began to follow the Teutonic Knights into Prussia. Nor was the movement only across the Saale and the Elbe, for colonists also pressed into Poland and Silesia, Bohemia, Austria, and parts of Hungary[1].

[1] It must be borne in mind that a great deal of this colonisation was not a mass immigration from outside, but "internal colonisation," carried on by the original population. This seems to have been notably the case in Bohemia, Moravia, and Silesia, where Germans were living side by side with the Slavs long before the twelfth century. The established view as to the colonisation and Germanisation of Mecklenburg in the thirteenth century has recently been attacked by a Russian scholar Egorov, who argues, on the basis of detailed researches, that the office of the *locator* was unknown there, and that there was no policy of Germanisation but simply internal colonisation and reclamation carried on mainly by the local Slavonic lords and peasants. (See D. N. Egorov, *Kolonizatsiya Meklenburga v xiii v.* 2 vols. Moscow, 1915.)

The chief colonising peoples of Germany were the Saxons and Bavarians, but a remarkable part was also played in the movement by peasants from Flanders and Holland. Their readiness to transport themselves so far from home was doubtless due to the over-population of the Low Countries and partly perhaps to the fact that they were weary of their incessant struggle with the ravenous ocean, "a people," as Helmold said, "who bear the brunt of the sea." They sought to find a better land in the East, and the often-quoted ballad, "Naer Oostland willen wy ryden," may well enshrine the spirit in which they went. Their hereditary capacity for drainage and irrigation alike made them particularly valuable colonists in marsh and heath lands, and the lords and bishops of the East were anxious to obtain them as settlers. Gradually Dutch and Flemings reclaimed the marshlands of the Weser, Elbe, Havel, and even of the Oder and Vistula, taking their own law with them, sometimes even (as at Bitterfeld and Jüterbog) using a special coinage, *moneta nova Flamingorum Jutreboc*, and leaving an indelible mark on place-names and on the architecture of barn and farmhouse. The Cistercians imported them into the morasses of the Thuringian basin, where under the leadership of the monks of Walkenried they reclaimed the famous Goldene Aue. They were even to be found in the mountainous south, scattered here and there as far as Transylvania.

It may well be wondered how these treks of colonists from West to East were managed, how they knew where to go, and who laid out their villages, for the business clearly needed organisation. The most common method was the employment by landowners of a *locator*, or professional agent, who was given a commission to settle a piece of unoccupied land. He would lay it out in large rectangular blocks of 125 acres or more, then set off westward to gather his colonists and bring them back with him, planting each family upon one of these big holdings, the "manses of Dutch measurement" referred to in so many charters, and setting aside one for the church and one for himself as *Bauermeister*. Each colonist paid a small premium in cash, but as a rule lived rent-free for a period of four to sixteen years while engaged in the work of reclamation, after which he paid an annual rent. They held by free hereditary tenure and usually brought with them their own law, "German law" or "Dutch law" as the case might be, and this law was spread through the East, and the villages of the aboriginal Wends and Poles and Prussians were sometimes assimilated to it. It is easy to see what an attraction the cheap land and freedom of these Eastern countries were to the more energetic peasants of the over-crowded and servile West; indeed, the colonisation movement, like the rise of towns, promoted emancipation at home, since the lords of old Germany were obliged to improve conditions lest their peasants should flee to the frontier. The *locator* was well paid for his work; he often received a holding rent-free in perpetuity in each village settled, and became the *Bauermeister* or *Schulze*, that is to say, the judicial and administrative head of the village, taking as a rule two-thirds of the fines in the village court (the other third going to the lord), and having the right to keep the village tavern and other privileges.

The rise of towns and the colonial movement were perhaps the most far-reaching economic events of the twelfth and thirteenth centuries and were closely connected with a third change at work during the period, the slow disintegration of the manor, which substituted for demesne farming a totally different method of exploiting landed property for profit. The lord cultivating his home-farm in part by means of labour services under the direction of a bailiff became a landlord, living upon rents and cultivating his home-farm (if he retained one at all) entirely with the help of hired wage-earners. The process was accompanied by a marked change in the proportion of land in demesne and land in the hands of peasant farmers, the former shrinking steadily at the expense of the latter, and by the steady emancipation of the peasantry.

It has already been shewn that the nature of the dominant economy brought about this change at an earlier date in some parts of Europe than in others. It appeared first in places where the demesne farm was small or labour services unimportant (as in pastoral districts), or where specialised crops (such as vines) were being grown for an international market, or where uncultivated land was leased on easy terms for purposes of reclamation. The spread of the system into the big corn-growing areas which were the main strongholds of manorialism was due to the economic revolution which was taking place during the twelfth and thirteenth centuries. On the one hand, the market for manorial produce was growing steadily and putting money into the pockets of the peasantry; and on the other, the towns and the colonial East were offering an asylum to discontented serfs. The lords tried to stem the increasing number of flights by repressive measures, concluding treaties among each other against the reception of runaways, or incorporating a clause to the same effect in town charters; but the tide was too strong, and in order to keep their peasants at home they had in the end to emancipate, to lighten burdens, and to commute labour services. Sometimes the process went on piecemeal by the emancipation of individuals, but there was an increasing number of regional emancipations, notably in the vicinity of towns. In Italy the freeing of the peasantry was one of the chief weapons of the cities in their struggle with the landed nobility, and in parts of France there was a tendency to form bourgs and villages into rural communes, with charters modelled on those of some town in the vicinity; the charters of Lorris and Beaumont, for instance, had a great vogue. Emancipation usually but not always carried with it the abolition of the more deeply resented servile disabilities, such as the *mortuarium* and the *maritagium*. From the point of view of manorial organisation the most interesting phenomenon was the disappearance of servile tenure and in particular of labour services. The process went on very unevenly in different parts of Europe, but in the end the result was everywhere much the same. The lords went over wholesale to the rental system, serfs were transformed into customary tenants, paying a fixed annual quit-rent, and more and more free leaseholders appeared. The leases were of an infinite variety as to conditions and terms, some hereditary, some for life, some for shorter periods. The main types were two: by the one the tenant paid an unvarying rent, usually in money, by the other (*métayage, mezzadria*) he paid a proportion of his harvest or stock in kind. In the long run *métayage*, which was common in the Mediterranean countries, paid the landlord best, for though he shared his tenant's loss in a bad year, the price of land was rising and a fixed quit-rent or a long lease worked in favour of the tenant. At the same time, there was also an increase in the number of free proprietors who were able to buy their land outright, and especially in the South of Europe a considerable part of the soil began to pass into the hands of the peasants.

It must not be supposed that this process of emancipation accomplished itself swiftly or evenly throughout Europe. In France, for instance, serfdom was strongest in the east, in Lorraine and Franche Comté, parts of Burgundy, Berry, and Nivernais, where it lasted until the fifteenth century, and in some parts until the eighteenth; in the Midi, a mountainous land of small properties, it was never strongly rooted, and most of the serfs of Provence and Languedoc had disappeared by the end of the thirteenth century; in the west it was weaker still and Normandy, Brittany, and Poitou were almost entirely free by the end of the eleventh. Serfdom came to an end early in Flanders and Italy largely on account of the prevalence of towns. In England it was always less prevalent in the north and west than in the south and east, where the process of emancipation was not complete until the end of the Middle Ages. In Spain feudalism was never firmly rooted except in Catalonia; in Leon and Castile the need for population (as the reconquest proceeded) and the protection of the towns had brought about an almost complete emancipation of the serfs during the thirteenth century; in Catalonia, on the other hand, a very heavy form of serfdom prevailed and was only brought to an end in the course of the fifteenth century. In Germany serfdom decreased most rapidly in the north-west (Lower Saxony and Westphalia) and in the Rhineland, but it was still to be found there at the end of the Middle Ages and was even more prevalent in the south-west, while it was actually increasing in the once free east in the fifteenth century, for reasons which will be explained later.

The change to a rental system meant something more than the spread of personal emancipation and an alteration in the terms on which the mass of the peasantry held their land. It did not, of course, preclude the lord from continuing to exploit his home-farm himself, with the help of hired instead of villein labour, but nevertheless the tendency grew for him to retire to a great extent, if not altogether, from the management of his demesne. This would rarely happen in the case of a small knight living on a single manor, but it became increasingly common on large estates where bailiff farming prevailed. On such estates the lords began to lease their demesne farms, now piecemeal, now *en bloc*. Even big stock farms were let out. In the thirteenth century the Earls of Lincoln had vaccaries in the Forest of Rossendale, which they managed themselves through local bailiffs supervised by a chief Instaurator; but in the course of the fourteenth century the new owners of the Honour of Clitheroe gradually abandoned their personal interest in cattle-raising and let out the farms to farmers. Many monastic stock-farms on the Continent were similarly leased instead of being directly cultivated by lay brothers or hired servants. This practice of "farming the demesne" was more subversive of the old manorial system than was the practice of letting out the tenant's holdings at a money rent. Sometimes the farmers were the whole community of tenants, sometimes two or three rich peasants, sometimes the bailiff or the reeve, sometimes a speculator from outside. It is interesting to observe the part played in the process in certain parts of Europe by the lord's bailiff (*villicus, Meier, maire*). In Lower Saxony in the eleventh and twelfth centuries the Meiers began to try to convert their position from an office into a tenure by making it hereditary, and they made use of the prevalent practice of exacting a produce rent from each manor to appropriate the surplus yield, and sometimes more than the surplus, to their own use. In the course of time the Meier often became *de facto* a leaseholder of the demesne, and the lords, making the best of the situation, began to separate the demesne farm from the rest of the manor and let it out by the same relatively free form of tenure (*Meierrecht*), at the same time converting the dues and services of the peasants into money payments or making them over to the Vogt. The next stage came when the lords began to throw together peasants' holdings into larger blocks and let these out in *Meierrecht* also. This created a number of cottagers and landless men, but the Meiers (many of whom had thus no connexion with that office) formed a class of free leaseholders who were the most prosperous peasants of Northern Saxony and whose life tenure steadily tended to become hereditary. In France a similar process began, and from the twelfth century many *mairies* were hereditary and an important feudal property, but the process never went so far as in Saxony, nor had it the same repercussion upon peasant tenure.

Thus throughout Europe a metamorphosis was gradually taking place in the exploitation of land ownership. The change was not entirely a beneficial one from the point of view of agriculture, for the large estates had often been pioneers of progress, and they could introduce improvements and undertake works of drainage and reclamation on a large scale, which were beyond the means of the peasant. It was the great landowners who studied the treatises on agriculture which had come down from classical times, and it was they for whom new works on the same model were drawn up, based in part upon Cato, Varro, Columella, or Palladius and in part upon practical experience. Such works are the famous thirteenth-century

English group which comprises Walter of Henley's *Husbandry*, the *Rules* of Robert Grosseteste, and two anonymous treatises on *Husbandry* and *Seneschaucie*; such too the *Opus Ruralium* of Petrus Crescentius of Bologna (1230–1307) and the delightful handbook for shepherds called *Le Bon Berger* written at the request of the King of France in 1379 by Jehan de Brie. In the exchange economy of the day, moreover, the new system must have been responsible for the great increase in the number of middlemen in rural areas, always a necessity for the small owner. The French or Rhenish monastery of old could employ its own *negotiator* to sell its wine and its own boats to freight the produce of its manors to port or market; the big English landlord could sell his wool wholesale to Lombard or Flemish merchants. But such organisation was beyond the small farmer. The dealer in agrarian produce had appeared at an early date (as town regulations against forestalling and regrating shew), but the growth of tenant farming at the expense of demesne farming inevitably paved the way for that multiplication of corn-bodgers, wool-broggers, and other middlemen, decried as caterpillars of the commonwealth by sixteenth-century moralists, who failed to understand that they were now not merely convenient but essential.

The dissolution of the old manorial organisation and the emancipation that went with it were accompanied by a marked improvement in the position of the peasantry. Probably at no time in the Middle Ages was agriculture more flourishing and the mass of the rural classes better off than during the twelfth and thirteenth centuries. Brunetto Latini speaks of the open manor houses of the Île de France, surrounded by gardens and orchards and a peaceful countryside, and Froissart in the next century admires the rich Cotentin, so soon to be desolated by war: "si trouvèrent le pays gras et plentureux de toutes choses, les granges pleines de blé, les maisons pleines de toutes richesses, riches bourgeois, chars, charrettes et chevaux, pourceaux, brebis, moutons et les plus beaux bœufs du monde que on nourrit en ce pays."[1] The prosperity of the French peasantry appears occasionally in the literature of the time, as in Bertran de Born's savage *sirvente* against the rich peasant, and in those pictures of well-to-do *vilains* with wide lands which occur in certain of the *fabliaux*. German literature throws an even more favourable light on the prosperity of the peasantry of that country in the thirteenth century. It is the age of the satirical peasant-epic *Meier Helmbrecht*, of the charming tale *Der Arme Heinrich*, and of the school of courtly *Dorfpoesie*, which is best represented by Neidhart von Reuental and Seifried Helbling. Neidhart shews the well-to-do Bavarian and Austrian peasants aping the gentry, village dandies with spices in their pockets for scent and pomade in their long curling locks, wearing silk-lined caps and coats of fine foreign cloth and carrying swords at their sides and clinking spurs at their heels, as though they were knights.

[1] Froissart, *Chroniques*, Lib. i, Ch. CCLXVIII (1346).

The causes of this rural prosperity must be sought elsewhere than in the progress of emancipation, which was only one of its symptoms. It was due in part to favourable external conditions. It is true that famine and pestilence took their toll as of old, but the latter at least was less deadly in the earlier centuries than the great series of visitations of bubonic plague which began with the Black Death (1347–49). The peasantry suffered considerably from time to time from war; the misery of England under Stephen and of Italy during the struggle between Frederick II and the Pope was great, and the crusading movement brought with it the harrying of the humble and backward Slav peasants in Eastern Europe and of the prosperous and enlightened Moorish peasants of Spain, as well as the terrible devastation of Languedoc in the Albigensian Crusade. Still the loss of Slav and Moor was the gain of German and Castilian peasants, and Languedoc at least rapidly recovered its prosperity. In general, the Crusades diverted fighting energy away from the Western peasantry, and there was nothing during this period as serious for them as some of the struggles of the Dark Ages or as the long horror of the Hundred Years' War. Moreover, it has already been shewn that the rise of the towns and the needs of reclamation, especially in the East, were during these centuries providing an outlet for the surplus population and raising both the status and the income of the rural classes as a whole. But there were yet more fundamental movements at work on the peasants' behalf. Between the tenth and thirteenth centuries the growth of the population, the development of *défrichement* and of agricultural technique, and the rise in the price of agrarian produce increased the economic rent of the soil to a very considerable extent. Lamprecht has calculated that land in the Rhine and Mosel districts was worth at the end of this period about seventeen times what it had been worth at the beginning, but the old customary rents remained the same, with the result that something like four-fifths of the unearned increment was going into the peasant's pocket. At the same time the purchasing power of money was steadily falling during the same period, and wherever payments were fixed in money the peasant benefited by this too. It is these facts which account for the shipwreck of large-scale demesne farming in the twelfth and thirteenth centuries, and for the desperate straits of so many of the great abbeys; they explain also the readiness of the lords to sell emancipation and the ability of the peasants to buy it.

The advance of the rural classes was not, however, everywhere maintained during the later Middle Ages. In France the Hundred Years' War undid a great deal of the benefit gained and some of the most fertile lands in Europe were reduced to the utmost misery, a prey alike to *routiers* and wolves. The wretched people whom Louis XI saw, as he rode from the prosperous Flemish countryside through the half-deserted fields of his own land, seemed to him gaunt and emaciated as though they had just emerged from dungeons, and Fortescue's celebrated comparison of the French and English peasants draws a similar picture. It was only after the middle of the fifteenth century that the work of clearance and agricultural improvement could begin again in France, and in many places lords let their lands to peasants on terms as favourable as in the early days of *défrichement* and settlement, and for the same reason. In Germany, again, the rise of the small territorial States on the ruins of the Holy Roman Empire was far from a blessing to the peasantry, which suffered (with all other classes) from their burdensome regulations and increased taxation. Moreover, the territorial rulers turned the *Gerichtsherrschaft* into an instrument of oppression, by everywhere using these jurisdictional lords as their representatives and by greatly extending the office. In Italy the peasantry, emancipated largely through the support of the towns in a common struggle against the landed nobility, often found that they had exchanged one bondage for another, and if the lords had chastised them with rods the burgesses chastised them with scorpions. For the city republics subordinated the countryside to their own interests. They invested their money in it; in the whole territory of Florence in the fourteenth century there was hardly a rood of land which was not owned by merchants, bankers, and even artisans. They strictly regulated agriculture, forcing labourers to work at fixed wages, insisting on leases on the *mezzadria* system, burdening the peasants with heavy taxation, and above all regulating the price and forbidding the export of agricultural produce in order to secure the food supply of the town, a policy which severely hit the small peasant proprietor. Refusals by peasants to pay not only public imposts but also private debts to town merchants became more and more common and flights once again became general, amounting sometimes to an exodus *en masse*. Everywhere in Europe, moreover, the town shewed itself an implacable enemy to the country in the matter of rural industry. In Flanders, where Bruges, Ghent, and Ypres sought, like the Italian cities, to dominate the countryside in the interests of their food supply, the townsmen made constant sorties to break the looms of the peasants; but both in Flanders and in England rural industry had triumphed by the end of the Middle Ages, though it was none the less subject to the economic control of capitalist clothiers.

But if the special circumstances of war, of State taxation and policy, or of urban interests worked in particular districts to the undoing of a peasantry whose prospects had seemed so bright in the thirteenth century, there were other and more fundamental conditions working in the same direction. In general the disintegration of the manor was a benefit to those classes which succeeded in keeping their hold upon the land. But all classes did not so succeed. That this was so, was due less to a breakdown of the old security of tenure in the framework of the manor than to the development of economic inequalities among the peasantry, as the increasing market for agricultural produce offered opportunities for enterprise, and in some districts perhaps to a continued pressure of population.

In some parts of Europe, it is true, the growth of the population (so striking during the twelfth and thirteenth centuries) was arrested and static; towns and deserted holdings bear witness to a relatively sparse population. In others the rapid *morcellement* of peasant farms seems due to something more than a mere redistribution, and suggests a still over-crowded countryside. It is possible that there would in any case have been an agrarian crisis in the later Middle Ages, apart altogether from the break-down of the manor, which merely dictated the particular form it assumed. That it was not more serious was due to the fact that from time to time pestilence and famine still acted as external checks upon the growth of the population, notably the Black Death of 1347–49, which, temporarily at least, gave rise to a severe under-population crisis throughout Western Europe.

In the countryside during the later Middle Ages two phenomena may be remarked, which were present within the manor from an early date, but which only assumed serious proportions towards the end of the thirteenth century. These were the steady subdivision of holdings and the rise of a class of landless labourers. The subdivision of holdings had been going on for a long time, but it had to some extent been held in check by the interest of the lords in maintaining their integrity as a basis for labour and other dues. It naturally went farthest in those regions where the customary law of inheritance allowed division among heirs, and it was watched with anxiety by the lords, who sometimes insisted on joint cultivation by all the heirs living under one roof, the eldest or youngest being responsible for all obligations on behalf of the rest (*aînesse, Trä-gerei*). The lords also tried to promote the practice of individual in-heritance, whether by primogeniture or ultimogeniture, and in other cases limited the number and laid down the minimum size of subdivisions. But the tendency towards *morcellement* increased with the dissolution of the manor, which weakened the direct concern of the lord in the peasant holdings, and with the growth in the number of hereditary tenures, and a great deal of subdivision and even more subletting was taking place during the later Middle Ages. The process no doubt promoted the formation of a prosperous rural *bourgeoisie*; the rich peasants bought up tenures and increased their own holdings and in some places (as in Holstein and Jutland) they voluntarily adopted the principle of majority or minority succession, instead of division among heirs. But while the Kulak was thus as familiar in the medieval as in the modern Russian village, the other side of the process was the formation of a rural proletariat, which was already making its appearance by the end of the Middle Ages.

Cotters and wage-earners had been found from very early times upon the undissolved manor, where they were employed by lords and wealthy tenants alike, and they were common in districts where the intensive cultivation of vines and other commercial crops brought with it an earlier recourse to wage labour. But the number of persons dependent on wages increased with the commutation of labour services, and the result was a new element in the social problem of the countryside. The main labour problem of the thirteenth century had been the question of serfdom; that of the fourteenth and fifteenth centuries was the modern question of free labour, its wages and conditions of employment; and the new employer was no less bent on controlling wage labour than the old lord had been bent on controlling his serfs. Everywhere there now appeared attempts to regulate rural labour, which became extremely vigorous when the Black Death, by temporarily depopulating the countryside, created such a scarcity as to give the wage-earners the whip hand. Wages rose to unprecedented heights and labourers left their employers and went wherever they were paid most. The landowners were in a difficult position, since flights of villeins (in those regions where villeinage still existed) were also frequent for the same reasons. The situation was met, both in France and England, by government legislation fixing wages, imposing severe penalties on those who gave or accepted more than the legal maximum, and forcing all who were not fully employed on their own land to take service. Similar wage tariffs were issued at different times by the Teutonic Order in Prussia and by the Italian cities. They gave rise to a long and bitter struggle, and in England the Statutes of Labourers were among the causes of the Peasants' Revolt of 1381. But the nature of the legislation must not be misunderstood. In Prussia (a country of big capitalist estates) and in Italy (where the land was in the hands of bourgeois capitalists) it was class legislation in the interests of landed capital against the wage-earners. But the position was not quite the same in England and France, where the people most severely hit by the rise in wages were not the big landowners but the small ones and above all the innumerable little peasant farmers who now employed hired labour.

The appearance of a large class of landless labourers and with it of an acute labour problem was not the only mark of deterioration in the position of the peasantry. In the course of the fifteenth century there appeared in Eastern Europe a manorial reaction, which brought about a recrudescence of serfdom in those parts, just as Western Europe was witnessing its final extinction. This reaction was the product of two movements working together. The first was that extension of the powers of the jurisdictional lord, or *Gerichtsherr*, to which reference has already been made. The second was the evolution of a new type of great estate, capitalistically organised for market production and worked by servile labour, but unlike the old manor by landless labour, production being concentrated on a demesne farm. This new type of estate (*Gutsherrschaft*), which was most common east of the Elbe, thus differed essentially both from the old manor (*Villikation*), in which the land in demesne was usually smaller than the land held by the peasants, and from the new *Grundherrschaft*, in which the landlord's profits were derived from rents and the market was fed almost entirely by the tenant farmers.

The spread of the *Gerichtsherrschaft* may be observed in most parts of Germany during the later Middle Ages, often taking the form of an extension of the powers and exactions of the Vogt. The demands of these jurisdictional lords upon their subjects became increasingly onerous and were often modelled on old servile dues; the universal exaction of the Vogt's hen, for example, was a recognition due based on the "bondage hen" paid by serfs to their personal lords. It was often easy to transform the control thus obtained over the peasantry into personal bondage, so tenuous was the line which separated the two relations. Such a transformation was easiest in places where the *Gerichtsherr* was also the *Grundherr*, and the peasant who was both his subject and his tenant could slip with tragic ease into the third relationship of dependence and become his bondsman, owning him as *Leibherr* too. Where the two lordships were distinct and often antagonistic the peasant had a better chance of maintaining his freedom. In western Germany the distinction was usually maintained, but in the east the landlord almost always possessed *Gerichtsherrschaft* as well, and the position of the peasantry was correspondingly worse. The whole movement was intensified by the hold which these jurisdictional lords began to get upon the waste, and the appearance or extension of all sorts of forest and hunting services as a result. The effect of this granting away of State functions to great lords was everywhere the same, a steady pressure upon the peasantry, which forced the landless class into personal bondage and too often amalgamated with them the less fortunate of the small proprietors. The new class of *Leibeigene* thus formed reached its lowest depths in the post-medieval period, but the process of decline was at work all through the fifteenth century.

The fate of the *Leibeigene* reacted on that of the remaining serfs of the old type and of the free leaseholders. The tendency to shift burdens from the person of the serf onto his land, which had once been a step in the process of emancipation, was now turned against the peasantry by the evolution of the doctrine of *Luft macht Eigen*, and in France too there came to be *mainmortable* districts in which every immigrant became subject to that due. Inheritance payments and burdensome dues which had long been dropped began to be exacted again. Landlords as well as Vogts increased their claims, and more precarious forms of tenure began to be substituted for those which had given security to the peasant leaseholder. The more fortunate retained their position as a prosperous rural middle class; but the mass of the peasantry became what they are so often called in the German literature of the fifteenth and sixteenth centuries, the *Arme Leute*, the poor folk.

The formation of the new territorial bondage and the depression of the peasantry went farthest in those trans-Elbian lands which in the first period of colonisation had been essentially the home of free German settlers. Here the grant of jurisdictional and State powers over wide districts was usually made to the landowners, and those landowners were engaged in capitalistic farming on a large scale, which meant that they were in constant need of labour. From the very beginning in Prussia and other Eastern lands knights had held compact estates, side by side with the free German villages, but at first these estates were rather small and mostly engaged in cattle farming, so that their demand for labour was limited and could usually be met by employing the servile Slav villagers. There were, however, enough estates which did not contain such villagers to call into existence a class of landless labourers and small cotters, both Slav and German, called *Kossaths* in Prussia and Pomerania and *Gärtner* in Silesia. From the fourteenth century corn-growing for export was becoming increasingly common and the estates or *Rittergüter* were growing greatly in size, and in the fifteenth century they were being increased by the purchase of peasant farms and the seizure of commons. The inevitable result was the appearance of an acute labour problem, especially in Prussia. Here there was a numerous class of free labourers, made up of the *Gärtner*, the hired servants in husbandry, and a body of so-called *Austlohner*, or harvesters, which was fed by the seasonal migration of Polish labourers. The wages of these workers were regulated by the tariff of the Order, and at the beginning of the fifteenth century the Grand Master was already fulminating against excessive wages paid in defiance of the rates. The Polish War of 1409–11 seriously depopulated the rural districts and the rise of towns had the same effect. The landed interests petitioned the Order to make agricultural labour compulsory upon "idlers who roam on the roads and in the towns," and a series of statutes was passed fixing penalties for the exaction or payment of more than the maximum rate; but the labour shortage continued and the wars of the end of the century caused still more depopulation, while the policy of the Polish government in finally fixing its peasants to the soil (1496) brought to an end the seasonal migration of *Austlohner* to get in the Prussian harvest.

The result of this growing shortage of labour was that increasingly throughout the fifteenth century the farmer-knights turned their attention to the free German peasants and sought to solve the labour problem by reducing them to serfdom. Restrictions were gradually introduced on freedom of movement: a tenant could not leave unless he provided some-one else to farm his holding and obtained a document of quittance from his landlord; those who went without the document could be forced back, and the Order entered into treaties with neighbouring countries for their extradition in 1436, 1472, and 1481. The work of the big estates came to be done more and more by exacting labour services from the once free peasantry and by settling servile *Gärtner*, and the German peasant was gradually forced into a bondage indistinguishable from that of the Slav. This development only, it is true, reached its climax in the sixteenth and seventeenth centuries, but it had begun much sooner. Already in the fifteenth century the big corn-growing estates across the Elbe con-trasted strongly with the rent-gathering estates of old Germany and the process of asservation was well on its way. It was generally characteristic of Prussia, Pomerania, Silesia, and Brandenburg and was to be found also in certain districts of Saxony, Brunswick, Hanover, and Thuringia. In England also, it may be observed, the *Gutsherrschaft* was making its appearance during the latter part of the fifteenth century, swallowing up peasant farms and engaging in large-scale production. But the English *Gutsherrschaft* was not, as in Prussia, a corn-growing estate but a sheep-farm which required little labour, and the problem to which it gave rise was not, therefore, a recrudescence of serfdom but a certain amount of depopulation and unemployment in the regions affected by the enclosure movement. In any case the dominant form of landownership in England remained the *Grundherrschaft*, and the chief cause of distress in sixteenth-century England was not enclosure but rack-renting and excessive entry fines.

The two factors mainly responsible for the recrudescence of serfdom and the depression of the peasantry in Eastern Europe were thus the extension of the powers of the *Gerichtsherr* and the appearance of a new type of capitalist estate. To these factors it has been usual to add a third, the adoption of Roman Law, which subjected the peasant, for generations ruled by local custom, to a strange law which he had no share in making and which tended to intensify the proprietorial rights of the landlord, particularly over the waste. In some parts the change to Roman Law did no doubt increase the distress of the peasantry, but the researches of von Below and Aubin have now shewn conclusively that this was not always and everywhere the case and that the Roman Law affected different classes and localities in different ways. In Lower Saxony and Westphalia, for example, the position of the peasantry suffered no decline and the new law contributed to the evolution of *Meierrecht* from a free time-lease into a hereditary tenure which gave the maximum of security to the small farmer. In general there was probably little direct connexion between the adoption of Roman Law and the manorial reaction, which had already advanced far upon its way before the adoption became general.

Thus peasants of all classes had cause for discontent at different times and in different places, especially during the last two centuries of the Middle Ages. Some were prosperous, resented feudal oppression, and were fain to hasten the process of emancipation; others were driven desperate by war, or by wage regulations, or by the growing demands of Vogt or lord, or by the exactions of city usurers, or by the loss of commons. National, political, and religious discontents often reinforced their economic grievances and they sometimes found allies among other classes and powers, now making common cause with the towns against the rural nobility (as in Flanders and Italy), now with the nobility against the towns (as in Wurtemberg and Baden), now with a native against a foreign landlord class (as in Bohemia and Denmark), now with the Crown against the Church and the nobles (as in Catalonia), now with industrial workers and poor priests against the bourgeois and ecclesiastical hierarchy (as in the English Peasants' Revolt). A few general peasant risings took place on the eve of the period under discussion, notably that of the Breton and Norman peasants at the beginning of the eleventh century and that of the Low Countries at the end, but on the whole the twelfth and thirteenth centuries were free of them. It was an age of increasing prosperity for the peasantry and emancipation was making steady progress. Risings were sporadic and local, and most of them seem to have been upon monastic lands, though whether this is due to the fact that monastic chroniclers naturally recorded disturbances on their own estates, or to any particular severity on the part of monastic lords, it is hard to say. There is some reason to believe that monasteries were conservative landlords, slow to grant freedom and exceedingly tenacious of their rights. Moreover, the combination of ecclesiastical and territorial rights in the hands of one lord, who took your best beast as a heriot and your second-best as a mortuary when you died and annually exacted his tithe as well as his rental from your fields, may well have made monastic landlords seem harsher than lay lords and concentrated a double resentment on their heads. The peasants who rose were often prosperous, some of them themselves employers of labour, and it is a commonplace that such revolts are usually the work of those to whom economic prosperity makes their servile status seem doubly irksome, or who are threatened with unaccustomed burdens, rather than of men sunk in the lowest stage of depression. The revolt of the peasants of maritime Flanders in 1322–28 is a case in point; they were both free and well-to-do, and rose against the attempt to force serfdom upon them, and they were successful. Similarly in England Froissart was not far wrong when he attributed the rebellion of 1381 to "the ease and riches that the common people were of."

It was not until after the middle of the fourteenth century that peasant risings became both frequent and general, sometimes assuming the proportions of a real "green revolution." The long series began with the Jacquerie in France (1358), which was caused by the ravages of war and the resentment of the peasantry against a nobility which not only loaded them with exactions, but could not even perform its own business successfully and clear the English from the land; for Poitiers had just been lost. The Peasants' Revolt in England (1381), perhaps the most interesting of all, was precipitated by an unfairly graduated poll-tax, but it united villeins who wanted the abolition of serfdom with free labourers who wanted the abolition of the Statutes of Labourers, and gradually drew into its scope every smouldering grievance of the working-classes in town and country alike. It was suppressed with far less violence than had been shewn by the French nobles after the Jacquerie, probably because the peasants had been guilty of few excesses, and it had little effect upon the disappearance of villeinage. In Spain the method of revolt was more successful: the serfs of Upper Catalonia rose three times between 1395 and 1471 and finally won their freedom with the assistance of the Crown; in Majorca, on the other hand, four insurrections were directed between 1351 and 1477 against the town capitalists who had concentrated the bulk of the rural property in their hands, and were unsuccessful. In Scandinavia the free peasants of Sweden rose in 1437–40, as those of maritime Flanders had done a century previously, to prevent themselves from being reduced to serfdom, and were successful; but three great revolts in Denmark between 1340 and 1441 only increased the hold of the German aristocracy upon the peasantry. All these risings were to culminate in the slow-gathering resentment of the German peasant in the grip of the feudal reaction. The long struggle of the peasants of the Kempten estates against their Prince-Abbot began in 1423; there were risings in Saxony, Silesia, Brandenburg, and the Rhineland in 1432, and (as Dr Coulton has pointed out) at least eleven serious revolts in various parts of Germany during the thirty years before Luther's appearance in 1517. The great Peasants' Revolt of 1524 was only the climax of a long movement.

This effervescence in the rural world was accompanied by the appearance of a new spirit in the countryside, something of more universal significance than the old revolt against burdensome dues and services. This new spirit, half religious and half socialistic, is very marked in the English Peasants' Revolt and in some of the German movements. Dreams of a reform of the Church were in the heads of English peasants in 1381, long before Hussite and German revolts linked agrarian discontent with the nascent Reformation. Moreover the peasant himself began to be idealised and his figure to take on a kind of mystic significance. Men quoted the words of the Psalmist, *Labores manuum tuarum quia manducabis beatus es,* and of Christ Himself, *Pater meus agricola.* It was labourer and not priest who was the type of holiness, whose sweat quenched hell fire and washed the soul clean. The remarkable English poem of *Piers Plowman* sounds a new note in medieval literature. No less marked was the growing class consciousness of the peasantry and the rise of egalitarian and socialistic doctrines. The German peasants marched with the wooden *Bundschuh* for their banner and the English repeated a doggerel couplet:

> When Adam delved and Eve span
> Who was then the gentleman?

Froissart's description of the preaching of the wandering priest John Ball in the villages is a *locus classicus* in the history of the democratic movement:

Ah, ye good people, the matters goeth not well to pass in England, nor shall not do till everything be common and that there be no villains nor gentlemen, but that we may all be united together, and that the lords be no greater masters than we be. What have we deserved or why should we be kept thus in servage? We be all come from one father and one mother, Adam and Eve; whereby can they say or shew that they be greater lords than we be, saving by that they cause us to win and labour for that they dispend? They are clothed in velvet and camlet furred with grise and we be vestured with poor cloth: they have their wines, spices, and good bread and we have the rye, the bran, and the straw, and drink water: they dwell in fair houses and we have the pain and travail, rain and wind in the fields; and by that that cometh of our labours they keep and maintain their estates. We be called their bondmen and without we do readily them service, we be beaten; and we have no sovereign to whom we may complain, nor that will hear us nor do us right.

Froissart, lover of chivalry and hanger-on of princes, had no sympathy for what he was reporting, but its tremendous import comes through him, in spite of himself, and all the clash of arms in his chronicle cannot hide that ominous note, the clatter of the *Bundschuh* on the road to freedom.

It is perhaps an inevitable result of the fact that economic history has been to such a great extent written by legal historians that the medieval peasant is usually considered primarily in relation to his lord. The profusion of manorial documents and the fact that all we know of medieval farming is concerned (save by implication) with demesne farming, have led to the same result. Yet the peasant was not only the inhabitant of a manor (and the manorial hold over him was often loose enough); he was a villager, the member of a community with a close and active life of its own. It was this village community which made rules for the common routine of husbandry, into which lord no less than tenant had to fit. Occasionally its regulations for such matters as the harvest are found enrolled upon court rolls; more often there have survived its customary rules for the use of forest and waste; and these are of great interest where there was an intercommoning of several vills over the same land, and often a *Markgenossenschaft,* with its own officials elected by the constituent villages to enforce the agreed regulations. The lords steadily encroached upon these organisations in the course of time, but they played an important part in rural life and many of their regulations may be read in the German *Weistümer.*

The religious, the social, the family life of the villager all elude the historian who confines his attention to estate books and manorial documents, save in so far as court rolls throw their light on his less reputable moments, his often sanguinary feuds and hues and cries, his burglaries, and his daughter's peccadilloes. But there is ample other material from which to reconstruct it. Contemporary literature is rich in pictures of village life. What a familiar collection of types—*mutatis mutandis* still to be found in the countryside—is assembled in the thirteenth-century French *lai,* which prefaces "a rhymed octosyllabic curse" of peculiar force and comprehensiveness with a description of the twenty-three types of *vilains* to be stricken by it. There is the headman who announces feast days under the elm tree in front of the church, and the pious villagers who sit with the clerks and turn over the book of hours for them and who carry the cross and the holy water in procession. There is the surly vine-dresser who will not point out the way to travellers; and the grumbler, who sits before his cottage-door on Sundays and mocks the passers-by, and if he sees a gentleman coming along with a hawk on his wrist, he says, "Ho, that screech-owl will get a hen to eat to-night that would have given my children their bellyful"; and there is the embittered fellow who hates God, Holy Church, and the gentry. There is the accommodating ass (Vilain Asnin) who carries the cakes and wine to the feast and if the weather is fine he carries his wife's cloak too, but if it is wet he strips himself to his breeches and covers her up. There is the country bumpkin, who goes to Paris and stands in front of Notre Dame, gaping up at the kings and saying, "Look, there's Pepin! There's Charlemagne!" while a pickpocket cuts his purse behind. There is the village leader, who speaks for the others to the bailiff and says, "Sir, in my grandfather's and great-grandfather's time, our cows used to go in that meadow and our sheep in that copse," and so gains a hundred sous for the villeins. There are also the miser; and the poacher who leaves his work at morn and eve to steal his lord's conies; and the "cowled vilain, that is the poor married clerk who goes to work with the other vilains"; and the wood-gatherer, who brings his load in backwards because his cottage-door is so low; and the marl-spreader, who upsets the last cartload over himself, "and he lies there and does not trouble the graveyard." Finally, there is "Vilain Graft, to wit he that taketh a gentlewoman to wife, even as a garden pear is grafted on a wild pear tree, or a cabbage, or a turnip," a witness to the fact that in France at least rich peasants occasionally married above them. Similar pictures are to be found in the *fabliaux* and they abound, likewise, in German and English literature. Meier Helmbrecht's family; Chaucer's "povre widwe somdel stope in age," in whose yard dwelt Chantecler and Pertelote, that incomparable pair; the village taverns in *Piers Plowman* and *The Tunnyng of Elynour Rummynge* (genre pictures as robust and redolent of the soil as Breughel's paintings); all these linger in the memory. Langland's great epic, indeed, is a whole gallery of peasant types, from the labourers who deigned not to dine on bacon and last night's vegetables, but must have hot fried fish, to "the wo of these women that wonyeth in cotes" and the poor man's pride that will not let his neighbours see his need. This last passage—too well known for quotation—is equalled in pathos only by the poignant vignette in *Pierce the Plowman's Crede* which shews the poor peasant and his wife plowing, with their little babe in a crumb-bowl at the end of the acre, and two-year-old twins tumbling beside it, all crying one cry, "a careful note." One is reminded of the sentence, so significant and so devoid of sympathy, in Pelagius' *De Planctu Ecclesiae* where he sets forth, among the sins of the peasant folk, that "they often abstain from knowing their own wives lest children should be born, fearing that they could not bring up so many, under pretext of poverty."

Another particularly valuable source of evidence for medieval village life, in its non-manorial aspects, is to be found in certain ecclesiastical documents, more particularly in those dealing with the parochial visitations, which took place from time to time. Records of several of such visitations have survived, notably those of four Norman parishes made by the Abbot of Cerisy's Official in the fourteenth century and those made by the Archdeacon of Josas in the Île de France between 1458 and 1470, both of which are particularly valuable in covering a number of consecutive years. The picture which they give of village life with its immorality and violence and dilapidation is a sombre one, and has sometimes been ascribed in part to the effect of the Hundred Years' War upon the countryside. That effect is, indeed, marked in the Josas series, a picture of desolation relieved only by the care with which, in place after place, the people are made to elect a village midwife, who is then sworn and licensed by the archdeacon. Nevertheless the general impression derived from those Cerisy visitations which belong to the period before the war is not very different from that derived from the later reports, although it is undeniably less gloomy, and there is much in common between both the Cerisy and the Josas series and the reports of the visitations of the diocese of Hereford in 1397, which have recently come to light.

These Hereford returns give a picture of English village life which is unsurpassed by that to be obtained from any other class of record. Here parish after parish is unrolled, with its superstitions, manners, morals, its village quarrels and its relations with the church. It is the border country, where Welsh and English mingle and occasionally the parson does not understand the language of his flock, as they complain. They are, indeed, nothing loath to complain of their parson if they have anything against him. The vicar of Eardisley is at feud with the whole parish; he has failed to supply a parish clerk, and his two maid-servants ring the bells and help him in the celebration of Mass, and his relations with them are gravely suspect; several men have died without the last sacrament by his default, and when he was burying one John Boly in the churchyard, he said publicly in the hearing of those present, "Lie you there, excommunicate!" He refuses to give the sacrament at Easter to the labourers of the parish, unless they agree with him for a tithe of their wages, and would not absolve a certain woman after confession unless she gave him 12*d.* towards the repair of the church books, so that she went into Hereford to get herself shriven. The church is befouled with flax and hemp, and he is a common trader in corn and other goods and a usurer. *Differuntur omnia contravencia Vicarii sub spe concordie*, runs a note in the Register; but the hope seems faint. Even when Hodge had no complaint against his parson, he was not a particularly devout son of the Church. He grumbled over mortuaries and tithes, tried to evade his turn to provide the *panis benedictus*, and was reported for not coming to church on Sundays or for working in the fields on holy days. Nevertheless the church was obviously the centre of village life. There the people went to be christened, married, and buried. They might or might not learn something of the truths of religion from their priest, but they got a rough familiarity with the lives of the saints and with the Bible from statue or storied capital or from wall-paintings, St Christopher opposite the door to befriend the traveller, the Last Judgment over the chancel, and the Virgin in her lady chapel at the side. Nor did the people only use the church for their devotions; they were apt to do their buying and selling in the porch, and the priest himself sometimes stored and even threshed his grain there. The churchyard, too, was a convenient open space for village festivities. This was well and good if a miracle play came round, which might be considered edifying, but the fairs which grew up round the churches were apt to encroach on the churchyards, to the wrath of ecclesiastical authorities, and sometimes the people came there for dances and revels.

One thing is certain, whether pious or not, the villagers, like country people in all parts of the world, were exceedingly superstitious and ready believers in charms and ghosts and witches. The *Poenitentiale* of Bartholomew Iscanus, Bishop of Exeter (1161–84), sets forth a list of such village superstitions[1]. Whosoever has prepared a table with three knives for the service of the fairies, that they may predestinate good to such as are born in the house; whosoever shall pollute New Year's Day by magic enquiries into the future; whosoever, labouring in wool or otherwise, shall lay spells thereon that the work may prosper, or who shall forbid the carrying away of fire or aught else from his house, lest the young of his beasts perish; whosoever shall cast into his barn or cellar a bow or any plaything soever wherewith "the devils called fairies" should play that they may bring greater plenty; whosoever shall believe that a man or woman may be changed into shape of a wolf or other beast; whosoever shall spy out the footsteps of Christian folk, believing that they may be bewitched by cutting away the turf whereon they have trodden. Many other superstitions are set forth, and readers of medieval *exempla* will remember too the peasant women who steal the consecrated Host, to sprinkle it among their cabbages or in their beehives as a charm against disease.

It is from the villages, one feels sure, that there come those tales of marvels which find their way into medieval chronicles. They smack of the rustics on the alehouse bench, or under the haystack at midday, or warming themselves around the fire at night. Villages in the West Country, where the Celtic strain was strong, were particularly prone to such tales, and many of them are collected in that most enchanting of books, Walter Map's *De Nugis Curialium*, where may be read the story of the man who married a fairy and others full of a graceful imagination not always found in folk tales. The villages of the diocese of Hereford visited in 1397 were full of the same superstitions and not even the priests were always blameless. John the chaplain, say the villagers of Kilpeck, "seemeth to them by no means firm in the faith, for he hath oftentimes conjured by night with familiar spirits" (*fecit pompam suam tempore*

---

[1] Printed in *Reliquiae Antiquae*, ed. T. Wright and J. O. Halliwell, I, 285, and translated in *Life in the Middle Ages*, ed. G. G. Coulton, I, 33–5.

nocturno cum spiritis fantasticis). There is even a ghost: "the parishioners [of Shrawardine] say that a certain Nicholas Cutler of Ruwardyne (*sic*) on his father's death publicly put it about that his father walked by night in the aforesaid parish and he watched at his father's tomb one night, to the great scandal of the Catholic Church." A group of really admirable village ghost stories comes from Yorkshire, where a monk of Byland Abbey wrote them down about the year 1400. The best tells of the man who was camped with a group of pilgrims beside a lonely road at night, and suddenly heard a neighing and screaming and galloping in the air and saw to his horror all the last year's dead coming hell-for-leather down the road towards him riding upon their mortuaries, horses, cows, and sheep, a motley and grisly crew, with his own abortive and unchristened infant rolling along the ground in an old stocking in which his wife had buried it[1]. The Hereford visitations shew us witches too. Amice Daniel useth sorcery in Cradley, and in Bromyard Alison Brown so practises that when she puts her curse on a man God forthwith visits vengeance upon him, which (say the villagers) is against the Catholic faith and tempting the Lord, and what can be expected of a woman who sells her hemp inside the church itself?

In general, however, the witch was much less unpopular than the village usurer, that still universal figure in rural society, from the gombeen-man of Ireland to the bániah of India. The small farmer is often hard up just before he gets in his harvest (when Langland shews the peasants tightening their belts and living on poor fare), or if the crops are bad, or if storm and flood destroy his little possessions; and to tide him over hard times he must borrow. In the Middle Ages the Church, of course, strictly forbade usury, but the rich neighbour who lent would not lend for nothing; so the peasants used him and hated him and when there was a visitation hurried to accuse him. Thus the villagers of Dymock say "that Henry Cece is a common usurer, viz. he lent to a certain Jak atte Hull 12*s*., the which he received back in full together with four bushels of wheat for the delay and he lent Proserpine Wele 10*s*. and received from her three bushels." Sometimes it was the parish priest himself who lent out money at interest to his flock. At Yazor "Sir Thomas, vicar there, lent a certain Gylym of Erdeshope 40*d*. and took by way of usury twelve pullets; the same lent to him 20*d*. and received in usury two pounds of oats." The village of Church Stoke (Montgomery) was full of usurers, and Jevan ap David ap Joris had lent Madoc ap David 15*s*. at 5*s*. per annum and had already received 30*s*. in this way.

A particularly vivid picture of German peasant life is to be found in the *Weistümer*, or customs drawn up in the village courts, mostly during the period when manorial organisation was breaking up and the lords were anxious to preserve their rights against the inroads of the peasants; they reflect a changing world and sometimes represent more than one stage of

---

[1] These Yorkshire ghost stories have been edited by the Provost of Eton; see *Twelve Medieval Ghost-stories*, ed. M. R. James, EHR, xxxvii (1922), pp. 413–23.

evolution. In these documents peasant speech is preserved and peasant life mirrored more clearly perhaps than in the custumals of any other country; they have a perfectly distinctive note, an atmosphere (as Professor Levett has observed) of Grimm's fairy tales which is unmistakable, if only for the part played in them by animals. Here is the steward of the Provost of St Alban's at Basle receiving the rent at Brattellen: "He shall come there, and after sunset when the night falls and the stars begin to shine he shall sit under the open sky and thus wait for the tenants to bring their rent. If they be slow and pay not promptly, he may rise and go into the inn and whosoever is behindhand and maketh not payment at the place where the steward sat, he owes twice as much next day and four times as much if he delay a day and a night; so let all be warned and pay their rent before they go to bed." But in other places the steward must fetch the rent and the peasant pays it "over his hedge," and the rent-hen must be sought "so softly and quietly that the child is not waked in the cradle, nor the cock frightened on the perch." This matter of rents and payments is one that calls for care. The hen due to the lord must be lively enough to fly "from the ground to the ladder, from the ladder to the manger, and from the manger to the roost"; the cheese "of such a hardness that if it be thrown against a wall it rebounds without breaking"; and if the Meier of Hengwiller suspects the quality of a grain rent, "let him take his stand at the door by which the swineherd passes and spread some of the corn on the ground; when a sow with seven piglings after her stops and eats thereof the Meier must be content, when the sow passes without stopping the villager must provide corn of a better quality." The sow, one feels, was probably on the tenant's side, and other definitions in his interest are found, such as that which bids the lord of Bischholz be content with the wine grown by his tenants, even if it be so sour that it would corrode a horse's hoof, and directs that the cartload of wood gathered for the Count of Stolberg at Born be so loosely packed "that a hare could run through with his ears erect."

The records are full of Gargantuan feasts. When the men of Huningue take a boat-load of wine down the river to Basle, the provost serves them with food and drink, and "they shall be made to drink so well that they can only stagger back to the boat"; and when wine has been carried by villagers on the estates of a Schwarzwald monastery, they are to be regaled with some of it until "no two men can carry the third to bed." The foresters of Colmar, on their Martinmas inspection of the Waltmark, pass the night with the Abbot of Münster, "and he shall give them two kinds of bread, two kinds of wine (white and red), and a new tablecloth, and the loaves must be of such a size that when they set them on end upon their feet, the foresters can cut enough above the knee to glut themselves, and on their departure they can make a parcel of the cloth and the fragments and take the lot, unless the abbot pay them five shillings instead. When night falls, straw shall be strewn for them round the fire and a minstrel shall be sent to play them to sleep on the viol. A servant must keep watch over the clothes, lest the fire harm them; if the sleepers burn in front it is their affair, if they burn behind they shall receive compensation. When the foresters take leave of the abbot in the morning he shall cause each of them to be given a pair of new shoes and they shall go on and breakfast at the manor house of Wihr." Here too we find the kindliness which remits the shrovetide hen to the pregnant bondswoman and makes her husband shew up its head, to be sure she has dined off it, or allows her to fish for herself in the lord's brook; but also the cruelty which lays down that the man who has removed his neighbour's landmark shall be buried up to his chin in the place where it stood, and the field plowed by a plough and four oxen, "and the buried man may help himself as best he can."

The peasants with whose life and work this chapter has been concerned have been those who formed the vast majority of medieval farmers and labourers, sedentary persons living in their villages, hamlets, or separate farms. It is true that the medieval peasant was much less sedentary than has sometimes been supposed. Under the food-rent system, carrying services often obliged the villein to travel far beyond the confines of his native village. The man whose lord owned but a single manor probably remained there and saw but a hundred or two hundred faces in all his life, but not so the tenants of St Paul's carrying their food-rents from Essex up to London, the bondsmen of Darnell doing carriage with sack and pack throughout Cheshire, or the men of Huningue taking wine for the Meier of Ystein by boat down the Rhine to Basle. It is an interesting reflection that for a large part of the peasantry the growth of a money economy, the commutation of labour services, and the restriction of demesne farming probably made travel less rather than more frequent and considerably restricted their horizon. They had now only to take their rent up to the manor house and carry their produce to market, or wait until the travelling middleman collected it. Economically they were tied to the soil, if legally they were free; save for the congenital wanderer, compulsory travel came to an end with serfdom. In many places, too, manorial custom permitted the serf to live off the manor on payment of a fine, *traités de parcours* between lords provided for the intermarriage of their respective serfs, and in some parts of France the unfree peasant possessed the right of *désaveu*, allowing him to leave his tenement on giving his lord notice and abandoning his goods. The records of the time shew that apart from the movement thus legitimised there were constant flights, and the steady recruitment of the towns from the countryside, to say nothing of the great mass emigrations of German and Flemish pioneers to the Eastern frontier, bears witness to a considerable mobility. Indeed the immobile medieval peasant, like the self-sufficing medieval manor, is something of a myth. It is interesting that in Wittenweiler's poem *Der Ring*, written by a fifteenth-century Bavarian satirist, a peasant enumerating the ten points of good education puts first that his boy should serve God and second that he should visit a foreign land.

Certain classes of rural workers, moreover, were forced by the nature of their work to be nomads, wandering from place to place. The seasonal harvest workers who migrated from Poland into Prussia, or came down from Wales and the north of England to gather in the harvest in the agricultural midlands, are cases in point. But more interesting and more truly nomadic were the migrant shepherds who drove their great flocks of sheep every year from summer pasture in the mountains to winter pasture in the plains. This regular seasonal migration, which is usually known by the name of *transhumance*, has taken place from very early times in lands where changes of climate are extreme and where there exists a combination of low-lying plains, too dry to support flocks and herds in summer, with high mountain pastures, which are under snow in winter. The practice is found in a modified degree in many hilly districts. It was carried on in Scotland and Wales and even in parts of England, where a Bishop of Lichfield and Coventry in the early thirteenth century laid down that the tithes of wool taken by churches in his diocese were to be divided "if the sheep be fed in one place in winter and another place in summer." In many of the Alpine valleys the peasants had a more or less permanent winter settlement in the valley, where their few cultivated fields were situated, but moved to summer huts in the mountains when the snow melted. In others they were more nomadic still, owning only temporary dwellings and moving from fief to fief with their sheep, so that in one charter, hailing from the Briançonnais district, it was laid down that a man who passed Christmas Day on a lord's land was to be held that lord's man for a year.

The home of transhumance proper, however, is in the Mediterranean region, where from an early period it has been characteristic of Spain, southern France, south-eastern Italy and the Roman Campagna, and northern Greece. The most remarkable example of the industry is certainly provided by Spain. Spanish wool had a great reputation in the Middle Ages, being considered second only to the fine Cotswold wool of England, and the merino sheep became the pivot of Spanish economic life. It has been calculated that the total number of sheep on the move in Spain at the close of the Middle Ages (1477) was over two and a half millions. They travelled very long distances along the *cañadas* or sheepwalks, the flocks from Leon often going 350 to 450 miles from their summer to their winter pastures; nor were Spanish sheep the only animals upon the road, for the ordinances of the town league of Daroca deal with "French, Gascon, Basque, and foreign herdsmen" coming from the South of France over the Pyrenees and down the Ebro valley to winter in southern Aragon. By the end of October all the flocks were in their winter camps in the sunny lowland plains and the lambing season began soon after their arrival. They stayed there until the middle of April and then began to depart. The sheep-shearing was done in sheds along the way, by clippers working in gangs of 125, each of which clipped a thousand sheep a day. The wool was either sold at once or stored in central warehouses, the chief of which was at Segovia, and then dispatched to the great fairs or to the ports. By the end of May the sheep were back in their home pastures in the northern uplands. The shepherds, who were a much favoured class in Castilian society, were engaged for the year, beginning on St John the Baptist's Day (24 June), and were paid, usually in kind, at the close of a year's service. In the middle of the fourteenth century the legal wage was 12 bushels of grain, one-fifth of the lambs born during the year, one-seventh of the cheese produced, and six maravedis in coin for every hundred sheep under the care of the shepherd, who was also allowed to keep a certain number of his own sheep free of charge with his master's flock.

Wherever it existed on a large scale, migratory sheep-farming had certain common characteristics. The routes followed by the flocks were fixed and the pasturages were communally owned. In southern Italy and Spain they were mainly Crown lands, but the Provençal flocks, whether they migrated westward into the Pyrenees or eastward into the Alps, had to depend mainly on the common lands of the upland valleys, the use of which they obtained by agreements with the lords concerned or with the virtually independent mountain villages. In one village in upper Dauphiné the people say in 1354 that sheep from Provence have long frequented the Alpine heights above them, and when one of the nomad shepherds falls ill, the curé of their village goes up to him in the mountains and gives him the sacraments, and if he die the villagers fetch down his body at their own cost and bury him in their graveyard. But the transhumants were never as welcome to the people as to their lords, for the lords profited by the taxes which the visitors paid, while the local inhabitants sometimes suffered from over-crowded pastures. These local taxes levied on the passing flocks, under different names (*pulvérage* in Provence, *carnal* in the Pyrenees, *montazgo* and *montadigo* in Spain and Portugal), are an early and important form of the taxation of movables, and out of them there developed in the Spanish kingdoms and in southern Italy a system of taxation by the central government which led to the protection of flocks and maintenance of highways by the State and to the development of an elaborate machinery of administration. Another common characteristic of the migratory sheep industry is the deep-rooted antagonism to which it gave birth, between the sedentary husbandman of the plain and the nomadic herdsman who passed through his lands. The shepherds were everywhere blamed for deforestation and the ruin of husbandry, and all sorts of regulations were laid down to protect the latter. At the end of the twelfth century, when the Castilian kings granted wide privileges for sheep migrations, the flocks were forbidden to trespass upon the "five forbidden things," to wit, pastures reserved for local animals, cornfields, vineyards, orchards, and mown meadows, though they were occasionally allowed to graze on the stubble after harvest. The hostility of the settled town and village dwellers often took the form of oppressive taxation and the formation of leagues of towns to protect themselves against transhumants.

These characteristics of the migratory sheep industry had two interesting consequences. In certain districts, notably in southern Italy and Spain, they led to the appointment of special itinerant officials and judges, whose business it was to protect the interests of the flocks. More important still, the need to deal with common routes, common taxes, and a common hostility brought about the organisation of great protective associations among the sheep-owners themselves. Of these associations the most famous was the Castilian Mesta, which by the end of the Middle Ages completely dominated the economic organisation of Spain and ultimately proved fatal to Spanish agriculture. The Mesta was first definitely organised as a single national association by Alfonso the Learned in 1273. It had some two or three thousand members, mostly small men driving their own sheep, though a few owners of big flocks, like the Duke of Béjar and the monastery of Escorial, belonged to it. Its meetings were held three times a year, and were attended as a rule by two hundred or three hundred owners, women often being present and having full rights. At these meetings the duties and behaviour of the shepherds were regulated, negotiations were carried on with towns over local taxes and with the Crown over privileges, and in general the migrations were organised and the interests of members protected. There were similar associations in Aragon and Apulia[1].

Such were the main features of peasant life and rural conditions during the last four centuries of the Middle Ages. From his contemporaries, or at least from those whose opinions have come down to us, the peasant received but little appreciation. Clerkly writers scorned him, and he was the butt of many half-proverbial rhymes and epigrams. "Servi qui non timent, tument"; "rustica gens optima flens, pessima gaudens"; "oignez vilain, il vous poindra, poignez vilain il vous oindra"; "Knechte schlagen wenn sie nicht zagen"; "Der Bauer ist an Ochsen statt, nur dass er keine Hörner hat." Very few are the writers who suggest that villein is as villein does, and express any sympathy for the hard lot of those who labour in the fields:

> Cil enduront les grefs tormenz,
> Les nefs, les pluyes è les venz;
> Cist ovrent la terro od lur mains,
> Od granz mesaises e od fains;

[1] For sheep-farming in Spain, see the admirable work of J. Klein, *The Mesta. A study in Spanish economic history*, 1273–1836 (Cambridge, Mass., 1920), to which I am much indebted. An excellent account of transhumance in the French Alps will be found in T. Sclafert, *Le Haut Dauphiné au moyen âge* (Paris, 1926). Both books contain valuable bibliographies.

> Icist r'ont assez aspre vie,
> Povre, soffraitose è mendie.
> Senz cest ordre, senz cest gent,
> Ne sai mie com faitement
> Li autre peüssent durer.

It is not until the later Middle Ages that there appears the idealised peasant type and the mystical exaltation of manual labour performed not by monk but by husbandman. Yet these inarticulate and despised masses had two achievements to their credit which are worthy to be set beside the greatest works of art and literature and government produced by the Middle Ages. They fed and colonised Europe; and slowly, painfully, laboriously they raised themselves from serfdom to freedom, laying hands as they did so upon a good proportion of that land which they loved with such a passionate and tenacious devotion.

CHAPTER XXV

THE EARLY RENAISSANCE

THE term "Renaissance" is commonly and conveniently used to denote the transition from the medieval to the modern world, and it implies that this transition has special features which distinguish it from other historical periods. It has been portrayed as a whole by many able writers, but they have sometimes forgotten that in the long course of its gradual development its features did not always present the same appearance. A truer idea of it may perhaps be obtained by treating it on historical lines, a method which will not prevent us from taking note of its special characteristics—its eager curiosity, its questioning of tradition and authority, its insistence on the human side of man, its love of beauty for beauty's sake, its cult of the ancient world.

The difficulty in dealing with such a movement is to know where to begin, for, wherever you begin, you will find it heralded by premonitions and precursors. Thus for the Renaissance there is St Francis with his love of nature and his sense of the importance of self-development, whose sermon to the birds marks, according to M. Sabatier, the dawn of individualism; there is Frederick II with his passion for intellectual discovery, his devotion to beauty, and his undying hatred of the Papacy; there is Roger Bacon with his scientific spirit and his zeal for educational reform; and there is Dante. How far is he a precursor of the Renaissance? On the one hand, is not his great poem a synthesis of medieval thought and the crown of medieval art? And is not his attitude towards the great writers of antiquity, with all its reverence, that of the medieval world rather than that of the Renaissance? On the other hand, his interest in individual character and above all the marked individuality of his treatment of nature and natural phenomena seem to be Renaissance characteristics. But we must not confuse individuality with individualism; still less must we forget that there is individuality in every work of genius, and that works of genius, as well in literature as in art, were not unknown in the Middle Ages. It is rather in the sphere of political thought, in his attitude towards the Papacy, in his indictment of individual Popes, and in his claim so nobly expressed in the *De Monarchia* for the independence of the temporal power that Dante appears most truly as a precursor.

It is noticeable that in the very year (1300) which Dante selects as the date of his great vision of the other world, the jubilee was celebrated for the first time at Rome with singular magnificence by that Boniface VIII who declared in his bull *Unam Sanctam* that it was necessary to salvation to believe that every human being should be subject to the Pope. A year after this declaration (1303) the same Boniface VIII was insulted and mal-treated at his native Anagni by adherents of Philip IV of France without a finger being raised in his defence. He died broken in spirit a few weeks later. Eight years more, with the death of Henry of Luxemburg, the hero of the *De Monarchia*, the medieval Empire may be said to have come to an end. At any rate its glory departed, for the violent conflict between the new Emperor, Lewis of Bavaria, and Pope John XXII which broke out in 1322, the year after Dante's death, lessened the prestige of both combatants, though the claims of the temporal power were supported by two powerful thinkers and writers, Marsilio of Padua and William of Ockham, and by a bold and revolutionary dreamer, Pierre Dubois.

All these were heralds of the dawn, rather than the dawn itself. Yet in Avignon, that "Babylon of the West," where John XXII had his extravagant court, and whence William of Ockham fled in 1328, there was living a man who is generally regarded as the real "begetter" of the Renaissance, for he was the first to unite in his own person most of the characteristics that we associate with that movement. This was Petrarch, and, in order to understand the spirit which underlay these characteristics, it is well to turn to his *De contemptu mundi* or *Secretum*, that intimate work which takes the form of three dialogues between the author and St Augustine. Here we have brought face to face the man who may be said to have inaugurated the medieval world and "the first modern man," the representative of the ascetic self-suppression of the Middle Ages and the representative of the cultivated individualism of the Renaissance. Throughout the discussion Petrarch shews the greatest reverence for St Augustine, whose *Confessions* were for forty years his constant companion, and the victory is nominally with his antagonist. But though Petrarch is ready at St Augustine's bidding to sever one of the two "chains" which hold him in bondage, namely his love for Laura, he still clings to the chain of Glory—"the glory conferred by men and immortal fame," the glory which he hoped to win by his *De viris illustribus* and *Africa*, but which he really won by the poems in the vernacular inspired by this very love for Laura.

Francesco Petrarca (1304–74) was born at Arezzo, where his father, an exile from Florence, had found a temporary refuge, but he spent his boyhood with his family at Avignon and Carpentras. Later he studied law at Montpellier and Bologna, returning to Avignon on his father's death in 1325 with a view to an ecclesiastical instead of a legal career. On a day in Holy Week 1327, he saw and loved Laura, who has been doubtfully identified with the wife of Hugues de Sade. His love was unrequited, but it made him an immortal poet.

The *Canzoniere* impresses one at once with its modern character. It is the intimate record of a real love-story, and thus has a living interest which is lacking to many of the sonnet-sequences that it inspired. It is true that we have no clear vision of Laura beyond her golden hair and her white skin, but she is at any rate a living woman. And Petrarch is a real human lover. Being artist as well as lover, he has arranged and revised his poems in the interests of art, but, in spite of some exaggerations and some reticences, his record is sincere. It is a record of alternating moods, of joy and melancholy, of discontent and resignation, of glory in his love and of shame for his bondage. The years pass by; his love grows colder, and his conscience reproaches him more loudly. He writes the fine *canzone, I' vo pensando,* and soon afterwards his *Secretum* (1342). He promises to break his "chain," but it still holds him, though less firmly. Then he hears of Laura's death (1348) and his tone changes. His grief for her loss is mingled with his praise of her perfections. His conscience no longer pricks him, and his love, purified from earthly desires, soars triumphantly into the region of spirit.

If Petrarch's verse is modern in its content, it is also modern in its language. Nearly six hundred years have elapsed since he wrote, and his speech has not become antiquated. Though some of the sonnets, at any rate in the first part of the *Canzoniere,* are marred by the abuse of anti-thesis, by conceits, even puns and other rhetorical devices, in the majority the poetic style is maintained at a high artistic level. Indeed at his best Petrarch is one of the great masters of style; he can be consistently elevated without being over-emphatic or bombastic, he can be concise and pregnant without being obscure. But he is more than a master of style; he is a true poet. He does not habitually think in images, but when he uses a metaphor he does it with arresting effect. He not only calls up a picture, but he appeals to our deepest emotions, as for instance in the well-known sonnet, *Movesi 'l vecchierel* (xii).

The poems of the second part, on the death of Laura, are as a whole superior to those written during her life. Artifice and rhetoric have now vanished. Petrarch's mind is no longer divided between allegiance to his love and allegiance to his duty as a Christian. Moreover, if his earthly love is deficient in passion, as a spiritual lover he is truly in-spired. It is his sonnets that have been chiefly if not exclusively imitated by his followers; but his genius moves most freely in his *canzoni.* In *Chiare, fresche e dolci acque* (xi), in *Nella stagion che il ciel rapido inchina* (iv), in *Si è debile il filo* (iii), in *I' vo pensando* (xvii), as in the beautiful sonnet addressed to the Virgin Mary, and in the two patriotic sonnets, *Spirto gentil* and *Italia mia,* he shews himself a great lyrical poet. By far the least successful of his poems are his *Trionfi,* the illustrations to which, executed in every conceivable form of art, had an immense popularity from the last years of the fifteenth century onwards.

Another modern feature that distinguishes Petrarch's poetry is his ob-servation of nature, and we even find in it examples of what has been called "the pathetic fallacy," namely the idea that nature sympathises with the joys and sorrows of the poet. His appreciation of natural scenery is also exemplified in the famous account of his ascent of Mont Ventoux (1335), and in a letter to Giacopo Colonna (*Ep.* I, 7) in which he describes the scenery of his beloved Vaucluse.

Partly from honest curiosity and partly from restlessness Petrarch was a great traveller. In 1333 he visited northern France, including Paris, and Flanders. In 1337 he paid his first visit to Rome, and four years later he was solemnly crowned on the Capitol with the laurel crown of poetry. From 1342 to 1353 he was continually moving from place to place, visiting Naples, Parma, where he spent some time, Verona, Florence, where he made the acquaintance of Boccaccio, Rome, and Padua, and returning from time to time to Avignon and Vaucluse. From 1352 to 1353 he made a considerable stay at Vaucluse and then, wearied with the "western Babylon," he left it for ever. On arriving at Milan he took service with the Visconti, and he was employed by them as ambassador to Venice (1353), to the Emperor (Charles IV) whom he found at Prague (1356), and to the King of France (1360). From 1361 to 1371 he spent his time between Padua and Venice, and in the latter year he settled at Arquà (near Padua), where he died in 1374.

Petrarch had many interests: he loved music and played the lute with skill; he was a friend of the Sienese painter, Simone Martini, who worked in the Palace of the Popes at Avignon; and he was an enthusiastic gardener, labouring with his own hands. But he had an enquiring mind as well as a receptive one. He was not content to accept traditional views without questioning them. Rather he attacked with vigour most of the learning of his day—its astrology, its jurisprudence, its medicine, its logic, its theology—and he shewed that he apprehended the true principles of historical criticism by declaring in the preface to his *De viris illustribus* that he followed only those historians "whose greater credibility or superior authority commands respect."

Petrarch is rightly termed the first humanist, for he was the first to find in ancient literature a larger measure than elsewhere of that learning and training in virtue which are peculiar to man. Moreover, he prized classical literature as a form of intercourse with great men. He found in the pages of Virgil and Horace, of Cicero and Seneca, especially in those of Cicero, a consecration of human aims and aspirations and a guide to human endeavour. He also learnt from them the true meaning of style, regarding it not as a mere rhetorical trick, as did the Ciceronians of a later period, but as the expression of the individual man. Thus his own Latin style, incorrect though it often is, has the merit of individuality. Especially it expresses his idea of beauty, his feeling for artistic perfection. Both his *Africa* and his *De viris illustribus* have come down to us in an incomplete state because he was for ever touching and retouching what he had written.

With Petrarch's devotion to Latin literature it was natural that he should throw himself heart and soul into the search for manuscripts of new authors and new works. It must be remembered that a considerable number of the more important Latin authors were widely known in the Middle Ages—Terence, Sallust, Cicero (philosophical works and four rhetorical works), Virgil, Livy (decades I, III, and IV), Ovid (especially the *Metamorphoses*), Horace (*Satires* and *Epistles*), Valerius Maximus, Lucan, Persius, Seneca (tragedies and philosophical works), Pliny—the two Plinies, like the two Senecas, were regarded as one and the same—Martial, Statius (except the *Silvae*), Juvenal, Suetonius. Less widely known were Caesar and Quintilian, the latter chiefly in a mutilated form, while rarer still were Plautus (eight comedies only), Lucretius, Propertius, Tibullus, Vitruvius, and Apuleius.

In the fascinating pursuit of discovering new manuscripts and new works Petrarch had some predecessors—notably, Albertino Mussato of Padua (1262–1329), who has been called "the initiator of humanism," Benzo of Alessandria (*ob. c.* 1330), who lived for some time at Milan and in its neighbourhood, and above all several enthusiasts at Verona, of whom the chief was Guglielmo da Pastrengo (*ob.* 1363). It was an obscure Veronese copyist, named Francesco, who at the close of the thirteenth century brought back from distant lands his "exiled compatriot" Catullus. This precious manuscript found a home in the chapter library of Verona, which, being one of the richest in classical works, made Verona the chief centre of nascent humanism in the first half of the fourteenth century. Among its leading humanists was Piero di Dante, the commentator on his father's *Divina Commedia*, who lived there from 1332 to 1347.

Other early libraries which contained classical works were those of the Visconti at Pavia, which Galeazzo Visconti established in 1360 and which was greatly increased by his son Gian Galeazzo, and that of the Gonzaga at Mantua, the catalogue of which in 1407 contained the names of about 300 Latin volumes.

Petrarch's passion for collecting books began when he was a student of law at Montpellier in 1319 and it continued throughout his life. Already at Vaucluse he possessed a considerable classical library and in Italy he made numerous additions to it. Some of the volumes were presents from his many friends and admirers, some he purchased, and some were copies which he made with his own hand or had made for him by professional copyists. On each of his numerous journeys—in France, in Flanders, at Rome, at Verona, at Genoa, at Mantua—he systematically visited monasteries and chapter-houses. He discovered a copy of Propertius in France, and he had a copy made of the Verona Catullus. But his chief quarry was Cicero. In 1333 he discovered at Liège the *Pro Archia*. Four speeches, all new to him, he acquired from his friend and rival collector, the Florentine Lapo di Castiglionchio. In 1345 he copied the whole of the *Letters to Atticus* with his own hand at Verona. At the end of his life he possessed practically all that we now have of Cicero, except eight speeches, the *Brutus*, the *Epistolae ad Familiares*, and the fragmentary *De republica*. He also had copies of Varro's *De re rustica* and *De lingua latina* and of Vitruvius.

In 1350 Petrarch and Boccaccio met, as we have seen, for the first time, but it was not till some years later that this acquaintance, which ripened into a close friendship, led to important results. Giovanni Boccaccio (1313–75), when he met Petrarch, was known as the author of several works—of two prose romances, the *Filocolo* and the *Fiammetta*, the latter a psychological novel with a large autobiographical element, and of several narrative poems, of which the chief are the *Teseide* and the *Filostrato*. They all deal with love and they are all founded on Boccaccio's own love-story. When he met Petrarch he was engaged on the work by which he is chiefly known to posterity, the famous *Decameron*. It was begun in 1348, the year of the Black Death, and was completed in 1353. The hundred stories of which it is composed are told in turn by seven young women and three young men, who, having met by chance in the Church of Santa Maria Novella at Florence, had agreed to leave the almost deserted city for a villa in the surrounding hills. The stories, as might be expected, vary in length, character, and merit. Some are compact little dramas dealing with a single action; some are long narratives of strange adventures; the majority are witty or at least amusing; a few, such as the beautiful story of Federigo degli Alberighi and his falcon (v. 9), are deeply pathetic. But nearly all alike are instinct with life and movement, and reveal the born story-teller. And they are set off by an incomparable gift for style, which is only occasionally marred by outbursts of misplaced rhetoric. Boccaccio has disciplined the vernacular Italian, as regards both language and syntax, in the school of ancient Rome, and the result is singularly successful. Few writers, even of modern times, handle a periodic and comparatively long sentence with greater ease and apparent simplicity. Italian critics have objected that, save in occasional conversations, the language has in Boccaccio's hands lost some of its national flavour, but for the purpose of telling a story for the story's sake, of carrying forward the reader without hindrance or effort, as on a gently flowing river, the style of the *Decameron* at its best, with its harmony, its graceful dignity, and its undercurrent of malice and humour, is a miracle of that art which resembles nature.

There is, however, a reverse side to the medal. The *Decameron* is frankly immoral, and that not so much because the author relates the doings of villainous monks and amorous women with evident relish as because he is an avowed apologist for free love and adultery. As a picture of Florentine society it would be unfair to take it too seriously; rather, it represents the experience of a man who, having been separated at an early age from his unwedded and deserted mother—a Frenchwoman of good family—had grown up without any home influence, and had spent his youth in the dissolute Court of Naples. His own relations with women account for the irony and cynicism which underlie the seemingly naïve directness of his narration.

The year 1361 was a turning-point in Boccaccio's life. He began to think of religion, and even of becoming a religious. However, on his friend Petrarch's advice, he determined not to give up his literary life altogether, but to turn it into a new channel. Accordingly, down to his death in 1375, he devoted himself with amazing zeal, industry, and patience to the study and spread of ancient literature. His *De claribus mulieribus* and *De casibus illustrium virorum*, both written with a moral purpose, achieved a wide popularity and helped greatly to stimulate that interest in human nature which was one of the characteristics of the Renaissance. They were both printed (in Germany) at a comparatively early date, and the *De casibus illustrium virorum* was translated by John Lydgate into English verse and by Pierre Faivre into French prose. His *Genealogia deorum* with all its faults is the earliest modern handbook on mythology.

As a book-collector he was a worthy rival of Petrarch. His library, considerable for the time, could boast of some volumes more or less unknown to his friend, as for instance, Martial, a complete Ausonius, and the *Ibis* of Ovid. But his great discovery was the manuscript of Tacitus containing books XI–XVI of the *Annals* and books I–V of the *Histories*, which he "rescued" from the monastery of Monte Cassino and copied with his own hand.

At the beginning of the fourteenth century a knowledge of Greek, except in some parts of southern Italy, where it still survived as a spoken language, was very rare in Western Europe. Greek classical literature was scantily represented by translations of Plato's *Timaeus*, of some of the works of Aristotle, and of Diogenes Laertius. Petrarch made a vain effort to learn Greek from a Calabrian monk named Barlaam. When a friend sent him a manuscript of Homer, he could only gaze at it with reverence and delight. But Boccaccio, urged by Petrarch, attained a greater measure of success. Hearing of the arrival at Venice of another Calabrian, Leontius Pilatus, who had spent some time at Constantinople, he brought him to Florence, had him appointed to a professorship, entertained him in his own house for three years—an act of real heroism, for the man was of a morose temper and repulsive in his habits—kept him at his work on a Latin translation of Homer, and, when it was finished, sent a transcript, which he made himself, to Petrarch. It was a bad piece of work, for Pilatus was as ignorant as he was pretentious.

Eight months before Boccaccio's death (1375), Coluccio Salutati (1331–1406) was appointed Latin Secretary to the Florentine Republic. He was a correspondent of Petrarch and Boccaccio, both of whom he greatly revered, and after the death of the latter he became the leader of the humanist movement at Florence. Grave and even severe in appearance, he had a genial and kindly nature and was always ready to give help and encouragement to others. He diligently carried on the search for manuscripts, and he was rewarded by finding at Vercelli a manuscript of the whole sixteen books of Cicero's *Familiar Epistles*. For Cicero he had a special cult, but his own Latin style was neither classical nor, like Petrarch's, expressive of his own individuality.

Contemporary with Salutati was the Augustinian monk, Luigi Marsigli (*c.* 1330–94), to whom Petrarch had given, shortly before his death, that precious volume of St Augustine's *Confessions* which for forty years had been his constant companion. Marsigli had studied at Padua and at Paris, where he took a doctor's degree, but in 1382 he returned to his native city of Florence, with a high reputation for learning. At Santo Spirito he formed a sort of Academy, where his fellow humanists assembled to hear from his lips eloquent discourses on theology, philosophy, and the wisdom of the ancients.

Next to Florence, the city which responded most warmly to Petrarch's call to the study of Latin literature was Padua. Its university since the decline of Bologna about 1320 had risen to be the first in Italy, and though the Italian universities were not as a rule particularly favourable to the new studies, Padua, thanks partly to the enlightened patronage of the Carrara family, of whom Francesco I was a close friend of Petrarch, was an exception. Added to this, the spirit of Petrarch, who had spent the last four years of his life at Arquà, ten miles distant, was still a potent influence. In 1392 Giovanni Conversini of Ravenna (1347–1406)—not to be confused with Giovanni Malapighi, also of Ravenna (*b.* 1346), who lived with Petrarch as copyist for three years—was appointed to the Chair of Rhetoric. He only held the post for a year, but as Chancellor to the new lord, Francesco II, he had considerable influence, which he exercised for the benefit of humanism. In 1397 Gasparino da Barzizza, who was accounted the greatest Latin scholar of his day, became Professor of Rhetoric. He inaugurated the critical study of Cicero, paying special attention to the *De Oratore*, and he founded the Ciceronian tradition of style, without however becoming a slavish imitator of him. When Padua was captured by Venice in 1405 he still remained professor, till in 1422 he was succeeded by Vittorino da Feltre, who except for an absence of eighteen months at Venice had lived at Padua as student and teacher, and for part of the time in Gasparino's house, since 1396.

The one thing lacking at Padua was Greek, and it is significant of this want that in 1397 Pier Paolo Vergerio, Professor of Logic since 1391, gave up his post in order to attend the lectures of Manuel Chrysoloras, who had recently been appointed to a newly established Greek chair in the Studium or University of Florence. The appointment was a momentous event in the history of humanism, for it marks the re-introduction to Western Europe of that Greek thought and learning which Byzantine civilisation had guarded so faithfully. Chrysoloras left Florence in 1400, and between that date and his return to his native Constantinople in 1403 he lectured at Milan and Pavia. Later he paid several visits to Venice, and in 1414 he was sent as an envoy to the Council of Constance. He died in the following year, and his epitaph, written by Vergerio, may be read to-day in the old monastery at Constance. The three men who profited most by his teaching were Leonardo Bruni, Giannozzo Manetti, and Guarino da Verona, and of these the last-named accompanied him on his return to Constantinople and lived in his house for five years. He returned home in 1408, bringing with him a rich prize of 54 volumes, of which some contained Greek manuscripts. But the most successful Italian collector of Greek manuscripts was the Sicilian, Giovanni Aurispa (1374–1450), who travelled in the East from 1405 to 1413 and again from 1421 to 1423, his second journey being far more fruitful than his first. From Constantinople he sent to Florence the famous Aeschylus, Sophocles, and Apollonius Rhodius which are now among the glories of the Laurentian library, and he brought back with him no less than 238 manuscripts. He had a friendly rival in Francesco Filelfo, who spent seven years in the Byzantine capital as secretary to the Venetian ambassador, married the great-niece of Chrysoloras, and returned in 1427 with some 40 manuscripts and a better knowledge of Greek than any of his countrymen. In a letter to Ambrogio Traversari, written from Bologna the year after his return, he gives a complete list of all his manuscripts that had already arrived, and he says that he is expecting a few more. We have also three interesting letters from Aurispa to Traversari, in which he in his turn records several of his finds.

In March 1438 an important stimulus was given to the study of Greek in Italy by the arrival of 500 Greeks, including the Emperor and the Patriarch of Constantinople, to attend the Council of Ferrara. Owing to the outbreak of the plague, it was transferred in the following January to Florence, where it carried on its labours till the following July. It was at the prompting of the most learned of the Greek envoys, Georgios Gemistos Plethon (1356–1450), that Cosimo de' Medici founded the famous Florentine Academy. Another envoy, Plethon's most illustrious pupil, Joannes Bessarion (1403–72), Bishop of Nicaea and afterwards Cardinal, remained in Italy to become the leader of Greek scholarship in that country and to bequeath his valuable library to the Venetian Republic. A third envoy, Theodore Gaza (1400–75), who had fled from his home at Thessalonica just before its capture by the Turks in 1430, was the author of the well-known Greek grammar, the best of the fifteenth century. An earlier arrival was George of Trebizond (1396–1484), a native of Crete, whom we find at Venice and Padua before 1418. Together with Bessarion and Gaza he was later employed at Rome by Nicholas V to translate the works of Aristotle. Younger men were Demetrius Chalcondyles (1424–1511) of Athens, the editor of the *editio princeps* of Homer, who lectured successively at Perugia, Padua, Florence, and Milan; and Joannes Argyropoulos (1416–86), who first visited Italy in 1441, but did not take up his abode there till after the fall of Constantinople. After Chrysoloras he was the ablest of the Greeks who came to Italy. He lectured at Florence from 1456 to 1471, and at Rome from 1471 to 1486, where he died. He too was an active translator of Aristotle, but he was also a distinguished Platonist, and in his lectures he tried to reconcile the two philosophers.

The merit of inviting Manuel Chrysoloras to Florence, the only Italian city in which Greek learning took real root, mainly belongs to Palla Strozzi, the noblest Florentine of his day. Learned, wealthy, and generous, he was, till his banishment in 1434, the mainstay of humanism in his native city. After the death of Salutati, the leading Florentine humanist was Niccolò Niccoli (1364–1437), of whom we have a charming and vivid, if over-indulgent, picture from the pen of Vespasiano da Bisticci, famous as a bookseller and copyist and as the biographer of all the humanists and patrons of humanism who were his contemporaries. Though Niccolò Niccoli had a caustic tongue and an irritable and suspicious temper, he was the friend, says his biographer, of all the learned men of Italy. He had wide interests, especially in everything connected with the ancient world, and he had the *flair* and the critical appreciation of a born collector. Pictures, mosaics, sculptures, vases, gems, coins, medals—he loved them all, and he carried his feeling for beauty into his daily life. His food was served in antique vases, and he drank from a crystal cup. Clad in a red gown which swept the ground, he was a conspicuous figure in the streets of Florence. Above all he loved manuscripts, and he spared neither pains nor expense in collecting them, purchasing some and making copies of others, either with his own hand or by those of professional copyists. When he had exhausted his own patrimony, the liberality of Cosimo de' Medici, who allowed him to draw at will on his bank, enabled him to continue his work.

Another leading member of the Florentine circle of humanists was Leonardo Bruni of Arezzo (1370–1444), generally known as Leonardo Aretino, who was Chancellor of Florence, first in 1410, and again from 1427 to his death. He was a close friend of Niccolò Niccoli, though their friendship was interrupted for a time by a violent quarrel. His chief service to learning was the translation into Latin—he prided himself on his Latin style—of five of Plato's dialogues, half-a-dozen of Plutarch's *Lives*, and the *Ethics*, *Politics*, and *Economics* of Aristotle. He also left an unfinished Latin history of Florence in twelve books. He was buried with great honour in Santa Croce, where his tomb by Bernardo Rossellino is one of the glories of the early Renaissance.

In the same church is the equally beautiful tomb which Desiderio da Settignano made for Leonardo's successor in the chancellorship, Carlo Marsuppini (*c.* 1399–1453), also of Arezzo, who, though he wrote little, was regarded as Leonardo's equal in learning. He was a cold and dour man, his only intimate friend being Niccolò Niccoli, and, unlike the rest of the humanists of his generation, was an avowed disbeliever in the Christian religion.

His contemporary, Giannozzo Manetti (1396–1459), is remarkable as the most distinguished Hebrew scholar of Italy in the first half of the fifteenth century. To multifarious learning he united a marked capacity for the conduct of affairs. He was frequently employed on embassies to various courts and he held numerous administrative posts, in all of which he made a deep impression by the justice of his decisions and the uprightness of his character. He was for a short time secretary to Nicholas V, and he spent three years in the service of Alfonso, King of Naples, who held him in the highest esteem. He had, like Niccolò Niccoli, a fine library, in which Greek and Hebrew manuscripts were largely represented.

A favourite meeting-place of these Florentine humanists was the Camaldulensian convent of Santa Maria degli Angeli just outside Florence, the Superior of which was Ambrogio Traversari (1386–1439). Much of his time was spent in translating the Greek Fathers, and he regarded pagan literature with some disquietude. When Cosimo de' Medici bade him translate the *Lives* of Diogenes Laertius, he complied with reluctance and misgiving. His correspondence edited by Mehus, with the life prefixed to it, is one of our chief sources of knowledge for Italian humanism. For the last eight years of his life he was General of his Order.

Though he was born at Terranuova, a little distance from Florence, and though he spent most of his life at Rome, Gianfrancesco Poggio Bracciolini (1380–1459) was proud to call himself a Florentine. While earning his livelihood as a notary and copyist, he attracted the attention of Salutati and Niccolò Niccoli, and through Salutati's interest he obtained early in 1404 a post in the Papal Chancery, but, though his duties for the next fifty years kept him chiefly at Rome, he continued to maintain friendly relations with his Florentine friends, especially with Niccolò Niccoli, whom he regarded with the affectionate piety of a son, and with Leonardo Bruni. His services to humanism in the course of his long life were manifold: he inaugurated the serious study of Roman topography, and wrote a rapid but impressive survey of its ancient monuments as they existed at the close of the pontificate of Martin V; he copied inscriptions, collected coins and sculptures (chiefly torsos and noseless busts), and formed a small but select library of Latin authors. But the work by which he is best known is the discovery of new manuscripts of classical authors. It was indeed a happy chance which sent him as Apostolic Secretary to the Council of Constance in 1414, for it enabled him to undertake four highly successful journeys in pursuit of his quarry. On his first journey, made in the first half of 1415, he found in the abbey of Cluny a manuscript of Cicero which contained three speeches, known in France but unknown in Italy. His second journey (1416) brought him to the abbey of St Gall, where "in a filthy and dark dungeon at the bottom of a tower" he

unearthed manuscripts of Valerius Flaccus (three and a half books) and
Asconius, and a complete text of Quintilian. This last discovery aroused
enthusiasm and from this time Quintilian's influence was considerable,
particularly on Valla, Vittorino da Feltre, Battista Guarino, and later on
Erasmus. The third journey (1417) was even more fruitful, for he added
to his trophies Lucretius, Manilius, Silius Italicus, and Ammianus
Marcellinus—all probably discovered in the monastery of Fulda. Later
in the same year he found the *Pro Caecina* at Langres, and seven other
new speeches of Cicero at Cologne. Two other finds, Columella and the
Silvae of Statius, belong either to the third or the fourth journey.

A little later (1421) Gherardo Landriani, Bishop of Lodi, discovered
in his cathedral a manuscript of Cicero's rhetorical works, including the
Brutus, which was absolutely new, and the *De Oratore* and the *Orator*,
which had hitherto been known only through imperfect copies. The
precious manuscript was entrusted to Barzizza and greatly rejoiced his
heart. It was lost soon afterwards, but not till copies of it had been made.
In 1429 Poggio was permitted to borrow from Monte Cassino for the
purpose of transcription a manuscript of Frontinus' *De aquaeductibus*, and
in the same year Nicholas of Cusa forwarded to Cardinal Orsini, in whose
service he was, a manuscript containing twelve new plays of Plautus.
The Cardinal kept it for some time under lock and key, greatly to the
indignation of Poggio, who had spared no pains to get hold of it.

By 1429 the tale of Latin classical authors, as we now have it, was nearly
complete. But a prolonged search in the library of Bobbio, the famous
Lombard monastery founded by St Columbanus, where the saint died and
was buried, which was carried out during the years 1493 to 1506, resulted
in the discovery of various minor authors, of whom the most important
was the Christian poet Prudentius. A little later—about the year 1500—
Fra Giocondo of Verona, scholar and architect, discovered at Paris a
manuscript of the hitherto unknown correspondence between Pliny and
Trajan, and this was followed in 1508 by one of the greatest of the
Renaissance acquisitions.

The *Histories* of Tacitus and books xi–xvi of the *Annals* had, as we
have seen, been discovered by Boccaccio at Monte Cassino, and in 1426
the manuscript came mysteriously into the hands of Niccolò Niccoli, who
lent it to Poggio. It is now in the Laurentian library (Mediceus II). In
1427 Poggio heard from a monk of Hersfeld of a manuscript of Tacitus'
three minor works, but it did not reach Rome till 1455. Finally in 1508
the first six books of the *Annals* (Mediceus I) were discovered in the
Westphalian monastery of Corvey. Lastly, in 1527 Simon Grynaeus
discovered books i–v of the fifth decade of Livy in the monastery of
Lorsch near Worms, one of the most famous of medieval German libraries.

The discovery of manuscripts naturally stimulated the formation of
libraries. The modest collection formed by Poggio was far surpassed by that
of Niccolò Niccoli, who at his death in 1437 possessed 800 volumes. These

he bequeathed to sixteen trustees, among whom were Cosimo de' Medici, Leonardo Bruni, and Poggio, with the view of their being preserved in a library accessible to the public. Accordingly Cosimo, who, as we have seen, had advanced to Niccoli considerable sums of money, placed 400 of the manuscripts in the library which he had recently built for the monastery of San Marco, and added the remainder to his private collection. He also formed a third library in the Badia of Fiesole. The Medicean library received accessions from Cosimo's grandson, Lorenzo, especially of Greek manuscripts collected for him by Janus Lascaris. When after Lorenzo's death it was joined to that of San Marco, the united collection, which came to be known as the Laurentian library, consisted, according to an inventory made in 1495, of 1039 manuscripts, of which about 460 were Greek.

Older than the library of San Marco was that founded by Galeazzo Visconti (*ob.* 1378) at Pavia, and considerably increased, first by his son Gian Galeazzo (*ob.* 1402), and then by his grandson Filippo Maria, who ruled from 1412 to 1446. In 1426 it contained 988 manuscripts, and it went on increasing under Francesco Sforza and his son Galeazzo Maria, who was a pupil of Filelfo. Another famous library was that of Federigo of Montefeltro, Duke of Urbino and Captain-General of the forces to Francesco Sforza. The catalogue, which was in process of making when the duke died in 1482, enumerates 772 manuscripts, of which 73 were Hebrew, 93 Greek, and 604 Latin.

One of the greatest of private collectors was Cardinal Bessarion. In 1468, four years before his death, his collection, which he bequeathed to the republic of Venice, consisted of 482 Greek and 264 Latin manuscripts. Another collection was that made by Domenico Malatesta Novello, lord of Cesena, who built for it, in 1452, a library which still exists and is an interesting example of a chained library.

But by far the greatest of these Renaissance libraries was that of the Vatican, which was practically founded by Pope Nicholas V. According to the inventory made at his death in 1455 it contained 353 Greek manuscripts and 824 Latin ones. By 1481, according to the catalogue made by Platina, the librarian of Sixtus IV, the total number of manuscripts had increased to 2527, of which 770 were Greek and 1757 Latin. At the death of Sixtus IV in 1484, about 1100 more had been added. Unlike the other Renaissance libraries, with the exception of that of Urbino, the Vatican was essentially a theological library. But, by reason that the search for manuscripts had been carried on by humanists who were mainly interested in pagan literature, it does not contain many novelties. In the Latin library we find Cyprian, Tertullian, and Lactantius, the last author being a favourite with the humanists by virtue of his style, and various Latin versions, new as well as old, of the Greek Fathers. The Greek library is described by Dr James as "commonplace" and "disappointing." The earliest ages of Christian literature are hardly represented at all; there is only one volume of Origen; and there is no complete Greek Bible.

The formation of these libraries necessitated the extensive employment of copyists, who had greatly increased both in numbers and efficiency since the days of Petrarch. Both he and Boccaccio, and later Niccolò Niccoli, Manetti, and Poggio, had to copy many manuscripts with their own hands. But the demands of eager and wealthy collectors called forth a supply of competent professionals. Copyists of Greek manuscripts commanded a high rate of pay, and in this branch of the work the first place was held by Theodore Gaza. Cosimo de' Medici employed for his library at Fiesole 45 copyists, who turned out 200 volumes in 22 months. The Duke of Urbino kept 30 to 40 at work for fourteen years. "There was not a single printed book in his library; he would have been ashamed to have one," says his biographer, Vespasiano da Bisticci (1421–98), who had helped him to form the library, as he had already helped Cosimo de' Medici, and as he had probably helped Nicholas V, with whom he was on the friendliest of terms. It was his business to find the copyists, and to some extent, for he was not devoid of scholarship, to superintend their work. The services of Nicholas V were of a higher order. He was not only responsible for the Vatican library, but he wrote out for Cosimo de' Medici with his own hand a classified list of desirable works, and he performed the same office for the Duke of Urbino, for Malatesta Novello of Cesena, and for Alessandro Sforza of Pesaro. The Canon of Parentucelli, as it is called, still survives to bear witness to his learning.

It will be seen that all these libraries, except those of Niccolò Niccoli and Cardinal Bessarion, were due to the munificence of various despots, of the Visconti and Sforza, of the Duke of Urbino, of Cosimo and Lorenzo de' Medici, who were none the less despots for being nominally private citizens, and of Nicholas V and his successors, who may be fairly counted in the same category. So in general the development of humanism owed far more to the enlightened enthusiasm of these powerful and wealthy patrons than to the action of the universities. These were mainly devoted to professional studies—law, medicine, theology. At more than one university there were sometimes as many as twenty professorships of law. Latin and Greek, on the other hand, were only provided for by occasional teachers, and humanist professors wandered from one university to another, or often to a town which did not possess a university, according as stipends were forthcoming. Padua, the leading university, was an exception, for its Chair of Rhetoric was held by a succession of distinguished humanists. Next to it in reputation were Pavia and, later, Pisa, whither the Florentine Studium, which, in spite of Manuel Chrysoloras and other distinguished professors, never attained great distinction, was transferred in 1472. For Florence, like Venice and Milan, discovered that it was far easier to find lodgings for students in a comparatively small town than in the capital itself. Ferrara, which was revived about 1420, obtained a brief renown from the presence of Guarino da Verona, for whom it founded a professorship in 1436. Among the students whom he attracted were a small band of English humanists. Bologna during the decade 1420–30 shewed a marked interest in humanist studies, among those who profited by its hospitality being Aurispa, Guarino and his pupil Lamola, Beccadelli, Filelfo, and the future Pope Nicholas V. But it was not till the second half of the fifteenth century that it appointed professors of Greek or Latin for any considerable period. Naples, unlike all the other Italian universities, except that of the Roman Curia, was entirely dependent on its ruling sovereign. Happily it had in Alfonso I an enthusiastic and liberal supporter of humanism.

In another essential development of humanism, namely education, the despots did good service. It was to the lords of Ferrara and Mantua —princes of the houses of Este and Gonzaga—that we mainly owe the work of the two great schoolmasters of the Renaissance, Guarino da Verona and Vittorino da Feltre.

The first in the field was Guarino (1370–1460), who, having returned, as we have seen, from Greece in 1408, lived at Florence from 1410 to 1414, and in the latter year established a school on humanist lines at Venice. But in 1419 he transferred it to Verona, his native town, where he had been appointed Professor of Rhetoric. Then in 1429 he accepted an offer from Nicholas III d'Este, the lord of Ferrara, to superintend the education of his eldest son Leonello, and at Ferrara he spent, with hardly a break, the remaining thirty-one years of his life. With the young prince were associated a large number of resident pupils, so that Guarino was able to carry on his essential work, and to develop more completely his methods of education.

The activities of his long life of ninety years were by no means confined to education; there were few, if any, sides of humanism which he did not represent with marked distinction. His interest in the search for manuscripts continued after his return from Constantinople, and he was closely associated with the discoveries of Plautus, Cicero, and Celsus. He wrote letters, like so many of the humanists, with a view to publication; he rivalled Manetti as an orator, and was in great demand for inaugural, matrimonial, and funeral speeches. His contribution to the translation of Greek authors consisted of several *Lives* of Plutarch, two orations of Isocrates, three works of Lucian, and the whole of Strabo. He also did good work as a textual critic, chiefly on Caesar, Cicero's speeches, the two Plinies, Aulus Gellius, and Servius. Nor must it be forgotten that his studies embraced sacred as well as pagan authors, and that, ardent humanist though he was, he regarded humanism as an evolution from the medieval world rather than as a revolt against it.

Vittorino (1378–1446) began his life-work a few years later than Guarino, for though he joined him at Venice, probably in 1415, he does not appear to have helped in the conduct of his school. But in 1420 we find him receiving a number of students in his house at Padua, and three years later he was carrying on the same work at Venice with the difference that many, if not most, of his pupils were not university students. Then, before the year was out, he received an offer from Gianfrancesco Gonzaga, the lord of Mantua, to superintend the education of his children. He accepted the offer and remained at Mantua till his death in 1446. To the three Gonzaga boys, whose ages ranged from nine to three—another boy and a girl, Cecilia, were born later—were added the sons of the leading Mantuan families, of some of the other princes of northern Italy, and of personal friends, and lastly, free of charge, the promising sons of poor parents, these amounting at one time to as many as forty. The greater number were lodged in a palace of the Marquess, known as La Gioiosa, but which Vittorino preferred to call La Giocosa; the rest lived in a house close at hand.

The story of this greatest school of the Renaissance has been well and fully told by Professor Woodward, and it will be described in the general account of Renaissance education in the next volume of this *History*. But some of its features may be referred to here, so far as they throw light on the character of the Renaissance spirit. In the first place, it was before all things a classical education, an education based on the study of Greek and Roman literature. Latin was the ordinary language of conversation, and the writing of Latin prose was sedulously practised. But the importance of Greek literature by the side of Latin was steadily insisted upon—by Vittorino even more than by Guarino. Vittorino was not, indeed, Guarino's equal as a Greek scholar, but he called to his assistance such proficients as George of Trebizond and Theodore Gaza.

As the result of this humanist education, Guarino's son Battista could write in his treatise *De ordine docendi et studendi* (1459), which is based on the practice of his father's school, that "as to my own conviction, without a knowledge of Greek, Latin scholarship itself is, in any real sense, impossible." Christian authors were read as well as pagan—Lactantius, whose classical style, as we have seen, made him a favourite with the humanists, Augustine, Jerome, and Cyprian. Other subjects besides Latin and Greek literature found a place in the curriculum, especially history and ethical philosophy, and Vittorino, at any rate, paid considerable attention to mathematics. Religious and moral training was regarded as of primary importance, and both Vittorino and Guarino insisted upon daily attendance at worship. Neither of them seems to have been in the least embarrassed by a sense of contradiction between pagan and Christian ideals, and their whole method was a practical answer to such a protest against the revival of classical learning as the *Regola del governo di cura familiare* of Giovanni Domenici of the Dominican convent of Santa Maria Novella (*c.* 1400–05).

This education was not confined to boys. Among Guarino's pupils were Isotta and Ginevra Nogarola of Verona; among Vittorino's Cecilia

Gonzaga (*b.* 1425), whose features are familiar to us from Pisanello's beautiful medal, and Ippolita, daughter of Francesco Sforza and wife of Alfonso II of Naples. Both Isotta and Cecilia attained considerable distinction as humanists, being learned in Greek as well as Latin. Both took the veil at an early age. But the first of the learned women of the Renaissance was Battista di Montefeltro (1383–1450), to whom Leonardo Bruni dedicated his treatise *De studiis et literis* soon after her marriage in 1405 to Galeazzo Malatesta, heir to the lordship of Pesaro. The marriage was an unhappy one, and after her widowhood she too took the veil. This record of women who studied the humanities is a scant one, but it serves to shew that the Renaissance, even in its early days, was not averse to the higher education of women. Moreover, those eager students who retired from the world to the cloister were the forerunners of Eleonora of Aragon, the wife of Ercole d'Este, and her daughters Isabella, the wife of Francesco Gonzaga, and Beatrice, the wife of Ludovico il Moro, who helped to make the courts of Ferrara, Mantua, and Milan important centres of art and culture; of Elisabetta Gonzaga, sister of Francesco and wife of Guid' Ubaldo of Montefeltro, who did the same for the Court of Urbino; of Catarina Cornaro, the Queen of Cyprus; of Vittoria Colonna and Olympia Morata.

When Tommaso Parentucelli (1398–1455), to the surprise of everybody, was elected Pope in March 1447, and took the title of Nicholas V, all the humanists were filled with joy. Poggio spoke of him as a "heaven-sent" Pope, and Guarino wrote him a long, laudatory letter of congratulation. If he was not in the first rank of scholars, he was a voracious reader both of Christian and pagan literature and had, as we have seen, a great knowledge of books. After studying at Bologna for seven years, he went to Florence and acted as tutor to the sons, first of Rinaldo degli Albizzi, and then of Palla Strozzi. Returning to Bologna he entered the service of the Bishop, Niccolò Albergata, afterwards Cardinal, and accompanied him on his many embassies. He thus became acquainted with other countries than his own, and, what he must have valued most, with the leading scholars of Italy. He had only been a short time Bishop of Bologna and Cardinal when he was elected Pope. He at once conceived and proceeded to put into execution the idea of making Rome the material and intellectual capital of Italy, and to this end he was stimulated by two ruling passions, a passion for building and a passion for books. He rebuilt the walls and a great part of the Capitol, he restored several churches, he began to rebuild St Peter's from the foundations, and he planned and partly carried out extensive additions to the Vatican. His intellectual schemes were equally ambitious, and in the furtherance of them he gave his patronage freely to the leading humanists. He attracted them to his Court all the more readily because since the death of Bruni (1444) Florence, largely owing to the preoccupation of Cosimo de' Medici with political affairs, had ceased for a time to be the chief centre of Italian humanism. Poggio was already a papal secretary, and the Pope's personal friend, Manetti, who was to become his biographer, came at his invitation from Florence, and having been made a secretary with an annual stipend of 600 ducats was set to the double task of writing an Apology for Christianity and of translating the Bible into Latin. But the chief work upon which the Pope employed the humanists was the translation of Greek prose writers. The Greek Fathers were allotted to George of Trebizond; Aristotle to Bessarion and Theodore Gaza. As for the Greek historians, Diodorus Siculus was entrusted to Poggio, who had previously translated Xenophon's *Cyropaedia*; Strabo to Guarino and Gregorio of Città di Castello (Gregorius Tifernas); and Appian to Pier Candido Decembrio (1399–1477), who had lived for thirty years at Milan as secretary to the Visconti dukes, and whom the Pope now took into his own service. Polybius fell to Niccolò Perotti (1430–80), who was a pupil of Valla, and Valla himself received 500 ducats for a translation of Thucydides. The same scholar began a translation of Herodotus, but did not live to complete it.

The Pope's latest recruit was Francesco Filelfo (1398–1481), who visited him in 1453 in the course of a triumphal journey from Milan to Naples and presented him with a copy of his filthy satires. Nicholas V read them with approval, and offered their author a house in Rome, an estate in the country, and 10,000 ducats for a Latin translation of the *Iliad* and the *Odyssey*. But the Pope's death in 1455 prevented the proposal from being carried out. Filelfo had been professor at Florence, but when Cosimo de' Medici, whom Filelfo had violently opposed, was recalled from exile in 1434, he fled to Siena. In 1439 he took service first with Filippo Maria Visconti, and then with the new lord of Milan, Francesco Sforza. But on the latter's death (1466) his star set, and, after fifteen years of a wandering life, he died in poverty at Florence. He had glaring faults, but his vigour, alike physical and intellectual, was amazing, while his knowledge of Greek and Latin literature and his power of composing in both languages did not fall far short of his pretensions.

A different and higher type of humanism is represented by Flavio Biondo (1392–1463), a native of Forlì, who had been appointed a papal secretary by Eugenius IV. He was the true founder of classical archaeology, for in *Roma triumphans*, *Roma instaurata*, and *Italia illustrata* he treated the several topics of Roman antiquities, Roman topography, and Italian geography in a really scientific spirit. His *Roma instaurata*, written in 1446 and first printed in 1474, kept the field unchallenged till the appearance of the second edition of Marliani's work seventy years later. Lacking Biondo's critical faculty, but an ardent worker in the field of archaeology, was Ciriaco of Ancona (*c.* 1391–*c.* 1451), who spent his time in transcribing inscriptions and exploring archaeological remains, not only in Italy but in many countries of the East.

A greater name is that of Lorenzo Valla (1405–57), the founder of critical scholarship and historical criticism. He learnt Greek at Florence from Aurispa, and in 1431 he was appointed Professor of Rhetoric at Pavia, where he had as fellow-professors Antonio Beccadelli (1394–1471), generally known as "il Panormita," the author of the scandalous *Hermaphroditus*, and Maffeo Vegio (1406–58), an upright, tolerant, and sincere Christian, whose early devotion to Virgil had been succeeded by an even greater devotion to St Augustine and St Monica. In 1432 Valla published a treatise entitled *De voluptate*, in which under the form of a dialogue between Leonardo Bruni, Beccadelli, and Niccolò Niccoli he examined in turn the ethical doctrines of the Stoics, the Epicureans, and Christ. Valla's mouthpiece is Niccolò Niccoli, who, while defending the Epicureans against the Stoics, maintains the inferiority of both systems to Christianity, which he declares to be a religion, not of gloomy asceticism, but of joyous freedom. From 1435 to 1448 Valla was in the service of Alfonso of Naples, and it was there that he translated sixteen books of the *Iliad* and wrote the famous treatise in which he proved the spuriousness of the Donation of Constantine (1440). Seeing that he had also denounced as spurious the writings of Dionysius the Areopagite, and had questioned the traditional composition of the Apostles' Creed by the Apostles in person, it argued great courage on the part of Nicholas V to give him a post at his Court. Valla's criticism was by no means confined to the cherished traditions of the Church; he attacked the logic of Aristotle and the jurisprudence of Bartolus, thus following in the footsteps of Petrarch. He made a scientific study of the Latin language, and gave his results to the world in that abiding monument of his scholarship, the *Elegantiae latinae linguae*, which, first printed at Venice in 1471, went through fifty-nine editions between that date and 1536, and even at the present day may be consulted with profit.

If humanism is rightly defined as the cult of antiquity, then Alfonso of Aragon (1385–1458), who by the capture of Naples in 1442 finally dispossessed René of Anjou of the Neapolitan crown, was the ideal humanist. There was something of superstition in his cult. Every day he had read to him, besides a portion of the Bible, a few pages of Seneca and Livy, and when the supposed bones of the Roman historian were discovered at Padua, he sent Beccadelli to Venice to beg for an arm. As a patron of humanists he maintained an honourable rivalry with Nicholas V, and his patronage is said to have cost him 20,000 ducats a year.

Among the recipients of his bounty were Poggio, Theodore Gaza, George of Trebizond, and (after the death of Nicholas V) Manetti. But the humanists who were most closely associated with him were Valla, Bartolommeo Fazio (*c.* 1400–57), a pupil of Guarino and a fine Latinist, and Il Panormita, who spent thirty-six years at his Court and that of his successor. In spite of Il Panormita's high reputation, he was no more than a facile and agreeable writer of Latin verse and prose. It was a disquieting feature of humanism, and one which justified the apprehensions of Ambrogio Traversari, that his scandalous volume, which he wrote when he was past thirty, was received with favour, and even with acclamation, by good men like Guarino and King Alfonso.

The excuse is that these ardent humanists suffered from more than a touch of that pedantry which regards language and literature as having little relation to real life. The same pedantry was at the bottom of the scurrilous invectives, founded upon classical models, which they hurled against each other. Poggio, Valla, Filelfo, George of Trebizond, Guarino, Niccolò Niccoli, and Leonardo Bruni all figured in encounters of this sort; but the three who most distinguished themselves by the vigour of their attacks and the indecency of their personal allusions were Poggio, Valla, and Filelfo.

The great favour shewn to the humanists was largely the result of that inordinate desire for fame which, starting from Petrarch, became so pronounced a feature of the Renaissance. The humanists, naïvely confident in the immortality of their writings, succeeded in persuading their patrons that they could confer on them eternal glory or eternal shame—or, worse still, consign them to oblivion. Thus there sprang up between princes and humanists a brisk traffic, in which no one was more successful than Filelfo. He even got money out of that shrewd *condottiere*, Francesco Sforza, for an epic poem, the *Sfortias*, which celebrated his illustrious deeds.

Another charge that has been brought against the humanists as a class is that they were hostile to the Christian religion. But this, at any rate for the period we are now considering, is not supported by the facts. It is true that Poggio attacked the corrupt practices of the Church, especially of the Roman Curia, with acrimony and irreverence. But he was not a disbeliever in Christianity. It is true that Valla brought his critical artillery to bear on some of the Church's most cherished traditions; but he never waged war on the essential doctrines of the faith. Even Filelfo, who was as inimical as Poggio to the monks and friars, and who admitted none but pagan authors to his library, professed an almost zealous orthodoxy. In fact, almost the only humanist who openly proclaimed himself a pagan was Carlo Marsuppini. On the other hand, the two great schoolmasters, Vittorino da Feltre and Guarino da Verona, whose influence through their scholars must have reached far and wide, were, as we have seen, very sincere and orthodox Christians. The same may be said of Pier Paolo Vergerio, the author of the first treatise on humanist education, *De ingenuis moribus*, which, written in 1403 or soon after, remained a classic till the middle of the sixteenth century. Leonardo Bruni's *De studiis et literis*, written a year or two later, shews the same Christian spirit. And of the humanists in general at this time it may be said that in spite of their devotion to Cicero and Seneca—Lucretius was hardly known to them—they were neither sceptics nor rationalists. In fact down to the very close of the fifteenth century the Church and humanism were in close alliance. It was not till 1516 that Pomponazzi published his famous treatise, *On the immortality of the soul.*

Thus much of humanism. But humanism was not the whole of the Renaissance, and we must now take into account another manifestation of the Renaissance spirit which is equally well known to us in detail and in which the primacy of Florence was equally pronounced. The announcement of the competition for the second doors of the Florence Baptistery in the first year of the fifteenth century marks the beginning of a great revival of Italian art. The successful competitor, Lorenzo Ghiberti (1381–1455), had all the many-sidedness of the great Renaissance artists; but though there is, perhaps, no great exaggeration in his remark that "there are few important works in our country which have not been designed and executed by my hand," he had a less powerful and a less far-reaching influence than either Filippo Brunelleschi (1377–1446) or Donatello or Masaccio.

In spite of the story, told with such picturesque detail by Antonio Manetti (who was only twenty-three at the time of Brunelleschi's death) and repeated by Vasari, of the visit paid by Brunelleschi and Donatello to Rome, and of the former's long sojourn in that city, it may be said that the four great Florentines owed less to antiquity than to their medieval predecessors. Ghiberti in his *Commentaries* praises highly not only Giotto, but Taddeo Gaddi and Orcagna and the Sienese painters, Ambrogio Lorenzetti, Simone Martini, and Duccio; and though he speaks with enthusiasm of certain recently discovered specimens of classical art, nothing can be more unclassical than his later doors (the "Gates of Paradise") with their four separate planes of relief and their strong pictorial effect. Donatello's statues, with one exception, owe nothing to antiquity, and it must be remembered that in his day all that was known of classical sculpture did not amount to much more than five or six bronzes in or around the Lateran palace, the bronze horses at Venice, and a few sarcophagi at Florence, Pisa, and elsewhere, and that nearly all these belonged to the Graeco-Roman period, none to the great age of Greek sculpture. Only in the horse of his Gattamelata statue, which he began about 1445, can Donatello be said to have been helped by a classical model—the bronze horses at Venice. It is true that his Annunciation in Santa Croce, one of the most beautiful works of the early Renaissance, is set in a carved frame which shews rich Renaissance decoration; but it is not till nearly the close of his life, when he executed the pulpits of San Lorenzo, that he makes much use of classical forms in his architectural backgrounds.

Masaccio learned much from Giotto and much from Donatello, but, according to Leonardo da Vinci, it was the study of nature, "the mistress of all masters," which enabled him to bring back painting to the true path upon which Giotto had set it. Similarly Ghiberti, speaking of his second doors, says that he strove to imitate nature as closely as possible.

Donatello's statues were inspired by the study of living models, and several of his prophets are evidently portraits of his fellow-citizens. Even Brunelleschi, the parent of Renaissance architecture, had reached middle age before he built a complete Renaissance building. The problem which occupied his mind during the earlier part of his career was how to finish a medieval one.

The great church of Santa Maria del Fiore still lacked a cupola to complete the work of Arnolfo and his successors, and owing to the immense span this was a problem of very great difficulty. After many years of pondering and investigation, in which he was helped far more by the neighbouring Baptistery than, as one story goes, by the Pantheon of Rome, Brunelleschi arrived at a solution, and in 1420 his model, which shewed a double cupola without centering, was accepted by the Opera del Duomo (the Building Committee). In 1436 the cupola was finished and there only remained the lantern; Brunelleschi's design for this was accepted, but the work was not begun till shortly before his death. His palaces, the Palazzo Pitti (altered and added to in the seventeenth century) and the finer Palazzo Pazzi (now Quaratesi), shew little departure from medieval tradition, and it is only in his churches that he works out after his own fashion the principles which he had studied in Rome. But here again he was largely influenced by the Romanesque work of his own Florence, such as the SS. Apostoli, San Miniato, and the old Badia at Fiesole. In the old sacristy of San Lorenzo and in the Pazzi chapel of Santa Croce the classical work is merely decorative; on the other hand, in the churches of San Lorenzo and Santo Spirito the classical pilasters and entablature have for the first time a real structural importance.

While profiting to the full by medieval tradition and practice, Brunelleschi was always improving upon them. Throughout his work on the Duomo he was perpetually hampered by the pedantry and prejudices of the Opera, and its successful completion was the triumph of individual genius over authority and tradition. In fact the most striking characteristic of Florentine art during the early Renaissance is the individualism and the enquiring spirit of its greatest exponents. All were occupied with important and difficult problems, whether of engineering or perspective or light. Brunelleschi is said to have "rediscovered the art of perspective," and it was the master-passion of Paolo Uccello.

Later Piero de' Franceschi (1416?–92), who, though not a Florentine, was born in Tuscany and worked under Domenico Veneziano at Florence, and who was reputed to be the first geometrician of his time, studied the subject scientifically and embodied his results in an unpublished treatise. He also paid close attention to problems of light and shade, as may be seen in his famous frescoes at Arezzo (begun in 1453), especially in the Vision of Constantine.

Another feature of the Florentine painters and sculptors was their sympathy with human nature and their belief in the high calling of man.

Much of their work is an embodiment of Hamlet's "What a piece of work is a man! how noble in reason! how infinite in faculty! in form and moving how express and admirable!" Energy, sometimes restrained, sometimes animated, but always combined with dignity is a noticeable characteristic of Donatello's work. His St George, his Gattamelata, and some of his Madonnas are models of dignified restraint, while his bronze reliefs on the altar of Sant' Antonio at Padua and on the pulpits of San Lorenzo at Florence, and his glorious "Cantoria" are no less remarkable for their lively and rhythmical animation. It is the same with Masaccio. Note the massive dignity of his Madonna in our National Gallery, and the contrast in the fresco of the Tribute-money between the calm dignity of Christ and the energetic indignation of St Peter. Indeed, all his frescoes in Santa Maria del Carmine shew the same sense of the essential nobility of the human form and the same power of representing the character of an action by gesture as well as by expression. So too, going outside Florence, we find in the reliefs which Giacopo della Quercia (1374?–1438), the great Sienese sculptor, executed for the portal of San Petronio at Bologna, a feeling for the human figure in dramatic and energetic action which proclaims him as the forerunner of Michelangelo.

But the beauty of woman and the joyousness of childhood appealed as powerfully to many of the Renaissance artists as the vigour and energy of man. Giacopo della Quercia was also the sculptor of the lovely figure of Ilaria del Carretto in the cathedral at Lucca. The charm of Filippo Lippi (1406–69), the favourite painter of the Medici, is largely due to the delicate beauty of his women and children, and those of a greater artist than Lippi, Luca della Robbia (1400–82), shew equal beauty, and beauty of a more intellectual type. His "Cantoria" with its glorious dancing and singing children is a worthy companion to that of Donatello, the supreme sculptor of childhood.

The study of man in general leads to the study of individual man, and when this coincides with a strong desire for posthumous fame, portraiture rapidly develops. Yet during the first half of the fifteenth century avowed portraits of living persons were rare at Florence. Donatello immortalised his friends under the guise of prophets, and made busts of women and boys as Magdalens or John the Baptists. Masaccio and Filippo Lippi introduced portraits of Florentine citizens into their frescoes. Even Fra Angelico adopted this method of portraiture. But in the Courts of northern Italy and of Naples portraiture was open and avowed, and those despotic, art-loving princes found in Antonio Pisano, commonly known as Pisanello (1397–c. 1450), a portraitist of rare genius. His medals of Filippo Maria Visconti, Francesco Sforza, Sigismondo Malatesta and his younger brother Malatesta Novello, of Gianfrancesco Gonzaga and his daughter Cecilia, Leonello d'Este, and the numerous medals of Alfonso of Naples, all executed between 1440 and 1450, form a remarkable record which may be completed by those of Vittorino da Feltre, the great schoolmaster of Mantua, and of Pier Candido Decembrio, who served the Visconti so long and so faithfully.

Remarkable as are the obverses of Pisanello's medals, even more remarkable are the reverses. The best of these, notably those of the medals of Cecilia Gonzaga, Malatesta Novello, and Leonello d'Este (the marriage medal), shew all the power of design, the sense of the capacities and the limitations of the artist's medium, the economy, the restraint, the simplicity, the perfect workmanship of the best Classical art. Yet they owe little, if anything, to Classical influence. So in Luca della Robbia's work, whether it be his bronze doors, or his terra-cotta reliefs, or his "Cantoria," or his monument to Bishop Federighi, we find the same felicity of artistic expression, the same instinctive perception of the treatment appropriate to his medium. And his debt to antiquity is even less than Pisanello's.

Luca della Robbia's work, if less mystical than Fra Angelico's, is just as instinct with Christian sentiment. Donatello's few authentic Madonnas, less winning than Luca's, arrest us by their look of yearning tenderness and sad foreboding. In the painters the religious feeling is less marked. Masaccio certainly has it, but Paolo Uccello was too much occupied with the scientific side of his art to care for its spiritual side, and Filippo Lippi, though he owed much to the influence of Masaccio and something to that of Fra Angelico, had but a small share of their religious spirit. His pictures charm us by their grace and geniality and the evident pleasure with which he painted them, but they are eloquent of his love for the things of this world.

In the Courts of northern Italy the secularisation of art proceeded more rapidly than at Florence. At Verona the fresco of the Crucifixion, painted towards the close of the fourteenth century by Altichiero and Avanzo, shews that the painters are chiefly interested in the contemporaneous figures with which the canvas is crowded. The same interest in the world around him is manifest in the half-dozen existing pictures and in the sketch-books of their follower and fellow-citizen, Pisanello, who became famous as a painter by his work at Venice, Rome, Verona, Mantua, Pavia, and Milan, long before he made his first medal. He was partly influenced by Gentile da Fabriano (*ob.* 1428), whose work in Venice he was called on to complete, and whom we know best by the Adoration of the Magi, painted at Florence in 1423. The long procession of sumptuously dressed figures proclaims that the painter, unlike his fellow-Umbrians, was above all things interested in the pageant of life.

This early emancipation from the tutelage of the Church in the cities of northern Italy is due mainly, if not entirely, to the despots who ruled them. Like every other class of men, they differed greatly in character. It is a mistake to regard Sigismondo Malatesta as a normal type. We do, however, find in the despots certain common traits which help to throw light on the general character of the Renaissance. In the first place, they were, on the whole, generous and intelligent patrons of art and learning, even if their love of art was sometimes a mere taste for magnificence, and if their sympathy with learning was largely prompted by a desire for posthumous fame. Another characteristic was their abundant energy and vitality. Knowing that their tenure of power depended mainly on success, they were ruthless towards their opponents and unscrupulous in their dealings with their neighbours, but they governed their States well and justly. The family crimes which were almost traditional in the annals of the Carraras, the La Scalas, and the Estes, and which were not uncommon in other princely families, were more or less a matter of indifference to their subjects. But this very indifference is significant, for it testifies to a general feeling that the despot was above law and morality, and was free to shape his conduct according to his own pleasure. The same feeling is shewn in the scant regard paid by the despot and his subjects to legitimate birth. In default of legitimate issue, illegitimate sons succeeded their fathers as a matter of course. Alfonso I of Naples, in many respects a model of virtue, had only two children, an illegitimate son who succeeded him, and an illegitimate daughter whom he married to Leonello d'Este, the successor and eldest of the eight bastards of Nicholas III. Federigo of Montefeltro, another just and admirable ruler, was illegitimate himself, and the father of illegitimate children.

There were some despots whose power rested, not on birth at all, but solely on the right of conquest. Machiavelli's example is Francesco Sforza, who "from a private individual became Duke of Milan through great *virtù*," and by *virtù* the author of *The Prince* means, not virtue, but vigour, ability, and, above all, success—the qualities which the Renaissance prized most, and which Marlowe's Mortimer, a true Renaissance figure, sums up in the line:

> Who now makes Fortune's wheel turn as he please.

Such was the Renaissance—not a re-birth, not a sudden transformation from darkness to light, but a gradual transition from the medieval to the modern world. And this transition was stimulated by the advent of a new spirit—a spirit of enthusiasm, of adventure, of pride in the dignity of man, of belief in individual effort, of criticism of old traditions, of search for new knowledge, a spirit guided and sustained by intercourse with the great writers of antiquity—poets, philosophers, historians—many of whom had been recently disinterred from dust-laden repositories, and who were all studied with a new reverence and a more enlightened understanding. Thus humanism, or the belief in the supreme value of ancient literature and culture, exercised a widespread influence. Art, however, remained to a large extent unaffected by it. Painting, except in mere decorative accessories, was untouched by it; sculpture was influenced by it only to a slight extent; even the transition from Gothic to Classical architecture was gradual, and when Brunelleschi at last produced his first complete building in the Classical style, he did so in no

CH. XXV.

spirit of slavish imitation. Like the painters and the sculptors, he made observation and experiment his starting-point, and if he profited by Classical models he adapted them to the needs of his individual genius.

For it was a note of the Renaissance that the individual claimed to express, not only his artistic personality, but his ideas and opinions, unhampered by tradition or authority. He claimed, in fact, the right of criticism and free enquiry. And, provided this claim was limited by a regard for the individuality of others and for the social organism of which the individual was part, it was individualism in the best sense. Another note of the Renaissance was belief in the goodness of human life and in the dignity, even in the perfectibility, of man. And this belief was the ultimate basis of humanism, that is to say, of the study of that classical literature which provided better than any other subject that training in knowledge and virtue which is the prerogative of man.

CHAPTER XXVI

MEDIEVAL MYSTICISM

THE intense medieval interest in religion discharges itself mainly along two parallel paths: the intellectual and the intuitive. These, though distinct in their methods and sometimes pursued in isolation, yet frequently react upon one another; for the mystic and the theologian seek the same ultimate goal. The intellectual and speculative vigour of the time produced on the one hand the scholastic philosophy, and the great theological constructions of St Thomas Aquinas and his successors, devoted to the justification and explication of traditional dogma; on the other hand, it inspired anxious questioning and daring explorations, which opened the door to heresy and prepared the path of the Reformation. So too the intuitive and experimental religious temper produced that great efflorescence of mysticism which is one of the most striking characteristics of medieval Christianity; and which has, like the corresponding intellectual activity, important historical results both within and without the Catholic fold. Too various in its manifestations to be comprehended in any single formula, this mystical temper expresses itself not only in the personal experiences of spiritual genius, but also in corporate and democratic movements. It profoundly influences religion and art, and instigates both religious rebellion and religious reform. Appearing in history at the latter part of the eleventh century, it is at first closely associated with the Benedictine Order and completely orthodox in outlook and activities. From the twelfth century onwards, however, it inspires, on the one hand, an increasing number of mystical sects proclaiming the liberty of the individual soul, and, on the other, the best activities of those who oppose them, and seek to regenerate the Church from within. Thus on the extreme left we have the wild libertinism of such mystical sects as that of the Free Spirit, tending to moral and religious anarchy; and on the extreme right the unimpeachable orthodoxy of such great constructive mystics as Bernard, Francis, Catherine of Siena. Between these two points every gradation of feeling and doctrine can be found. The history of medieval Catholicism includes the perpetual friction of the mystical heretics with their criticism of ecclesiastical authority; and the tonic influence of the orthodox mystics, seeking to restore that authority to its primitive purity. This orthodox mysticism receives immense development through the practice and teaching of the Mendicant Friars. It has its golden age in the fourteenth century, and gradually recedes from the centre of the stage before the approach of the Renaissance.

Mysticism, the claim to an immediate apprehension of God and the craving for union with Him, is of course an element in all developed religion. It is present in Christianity from the first. But, though it is essentially the "religion of the heart" and so may conceivably exist at any level of religious culture, if it is to exert an influence on thought and action and so achieve historical importance, it requires a considerable intellectual equipment. The mystic needs abstract conceptions wherewith to communicate his doctrine and experience; and wherever a mystical movement arises through the influence of great spiritual personalities, it soon acquires a philosophy suited to its needs. With hardly an exception, the great mystics of history have been educated men, fed by tradition as well as by direct experience. Though doubtless hidden contemplatives were always numerous, those who achieved historical significance did so because of their acquaintance with the great mystical tradition ot Christendom, which enabled them to nourish their mental life, express their intuitions, and so affect the religious life of their time. Therefore the primary fact for the student of medieval mysticism is the existence within the Church of this tradition, which guaranteed the classic phenomena of the interior life, explained them, and provided a symbolism in which they could be given literary form. Any carefully annotated mystical text will shew the close dependence on authority even of the most apparently personal outpourings. Because the genuine mystic is a realist and speaks from experience, he often gives the impression of intense religious spontaneity. Nevertheless he is always in the truest sense a historical figure imbedded in the religious culture of his time. We have constantly to strike the balance between the often vigorous originality of the individual, and the strong tradition by which he was nurtured and which gave him his technique; and to be on our guard against discovering novelty in sayings and doctrines which are often adopted without acknowledgment from an earlier source. The Bible, and especially the Psalter—the daily food of the professed religious—is the dominant literary influence of medieval mysticism; and intimate Scripture knowledge is required of those who would understand its literature. Next in importance is St Augustine, through whom Neoplatonism entered Christian theology. Behind St Augustine, whose lofty genius has affected every great mystic of this period, stands Plotinus who—though only known by them at second-hand—is yet a determining influence in their development. The *Dialogues* of Cassian, which carried forward into medieval monasticism the teaching of the Fathers of the Desert on contemplative prayer and the works of St Gregory the Great, are also fundamental for an understanding of Benedictine spirituality and its offshoots. But the event which, above all, made possible the great development of mystical religion that culminated in the fourteenth century was the translation into Latin of the works of the so-called "Dionysius the Areopagite" by John Scotus Eriugena (*ob.* 877). Through these writings, which became gradually diffused throughout the Catholic world, and affected the spiritual outlook of all its greatest religious personalities, the mystics obtained a philosophy which justified and explained their experiences, and a theological landscape within which to place them. Their influence is especially to be felt in the Dominican and Franciscan schools. Though here mysticism will be studied mainly as a religious and social phenomenon and not in its doctrinal or philosophic implications, these cultural influences—Scriptural, Neoplatonic, and Patristic—must be remembered if we are to understand its manifold surface activities.

Since mysticism is essentially religious realism, claiming and emphasising first-hand intuitive experience of those spiritual realities which theology describes, and requiring their application to life, it is plain that where this type of religion prevails and is taken seriously it will act in one of two ways. (1) It will impart a more vivid actuality and meaning to traditional symbols and more fervour to traditional practices, heightening their spiritual content, colour, and significance. Thus the widespread medieval cultus of the Holy Name, the development of Eucharistic devotion, are in part the expression of the mysticism of the time. (2) Where these symbols and practices are felt to have become inadequate, formal, or unreal, the mystic may lead a revolt against them, involving a more or less complete rejection of tradition and claim to spiritual liberty: as in the Brethren of the Free Spirit. These opposing tendencies run right through medieval history. Where mysticism enters into an alliance with orthodoxy and expresses itself through orthodox symbols, it purifies and deepens the institutional life, opposes the constant tendency to degenerate, undertakes the reform of abuses, fills practices with fresh fervour, and inspires artistic and liturgic development. Thus Francis, Ruysbroeck, Catherine of Siena, while exerting a transforming influence on the religious life of their time, were valuable allies of the Church. On the other hand, where the intensely spontaneous element inherent in mystical feeling is out of harmony with its environment, and comes into conflict with authority—as in the "Spiritual" Franciscans; where it rejects the outward in favour of the inward, is associated with an extreme type of intellectual speculation—as in Eckehart—or enters into alliance with social unrest, mysticism may shew itself as the inspiration of revolt and become the parent of heresy. Thus, though the great mystic is above all a man of prayer and contemplation, his social importance is considerable, and he often plays the part of reformer and prophet. The modern tendency to draw a hard line between active and contemplative life is not justified by history, which constantly shews their intimate connexion; and this especially in the period under review.

In their written works—and by these, after all, they are chiefly known to us—the medieval mystics constantly trespass on the ground of the moralists and speculative theologians; while their history is closely connected with that of the religious Orders and other group-formations. We cannot restrict the name "mystic" to those who write or teach on the

degrees of contemplation or similar themes. Many are deeply concerned
to impress on the world their own vision of holiness, or to remodel the life
of the Church nearer to their heart's desire. Thus the mystical and
realistic temper of medieval religion first appears in that movement
towards the reform of monasticism which is characteristic of the eleventh
century. This is fully discussed as part of the history of the monastic
Orders[1]. Here we are only concerned with it in its mystical aspect, as the
work of certain great personalities, filled with an enthusiasm for the
other-worldly life of unimpeded communion with God which had been
sought both by the Fathers in the Desert and the first monks of the
West. In its pure form, monasticism is a life which gives the first place
to these transcendental interests. Its ascetic disciplines, its liturgic,
philanthropic, and intellectual activities, are all subservient to this. It
was therefore pre-eminently the institution through which the mystical
impulse of the period was likely to find its first path of discharge. The
formation during the eleventh century of reformed Benedictine Congregations under the influence of saintly personalities witnesses to a genuine
revival of mystical religion; even though this revival has left few literary
memorials, but was mainly expressed in terms of actual life.

The movement is first seen in Italy, where St Romuald (*c.* 950–1027)
effected in the early years of the century what is usually counted as the
second Benedictine reform. His career is typical of many others. After
seven years in the abbey of Sant' Apollinare in Classe, which he sought to
restore to exact observance, Romuald went to Venice, where he received
an intensive ascetic training from a hermit. A period of wandering
finally brought him to Camaldoli in the Casentino, where he founded
the still-existent Hermitage—a little walled village of solitary contemplatives. This pioneer experiment in communal mysticism anticipated
in many respects the great creation of St Bruno. Romuald's follower,
St Peter Damian (1007–72), Abbot of Fonte Avellana, though best
known for his love of asceticism and his campaigns against ecclesiastical
corruption, was also a contemplative at heart. The third of the Italian
reformers, St Giovanni Gualberti (985–1073)—the hero of the beautiful
legend of the Merciful Knight—was driven by the same impulse from
the Benedictine monastery of San Miniato to Vallombrosa; there he lived
in solitary communion with God, until the fame of his holiness drew so
many disciples that he was obliged to organise them upon monastic lines.
Thus was founded about 1020 the Order of Vallombrosa.

During the second half of the century, similar tendencies appear in
France, and result in the foundation about 1080 of the Poor Men of
Grandmont under St Stephen Muret (1048–1124); in 1084, of the
Carthusian Order under St Bruno (*c.* 1032–1101); and finally, in 1098,
of the Cistercian reform under St Robert of Molesme and St Stephen
Harding. The Poor Men of Grandmont did not long maintain the purity

[1] *Supra*, Vol. v, Chap. xx.

of their rule after their heroic founder's death; but the setting up of the Carthusian and Cistercian Orders were events of capital importance for the subsequent development of medieval mysticism. St Bruno's desire was to combine the perfect solitude of the hermitage with the mutual support given by the common life, a conception that could only have come to a mind for which contemplative interests were paramount, and is alone enough to prove St Bruno a mystic. With six companions, he established himself under conditions of great poverty and hardship at the Grande Chartreuse. Thus began an institution which exerted a great though not manifest influence on the development of mysticism during the succeeding centuries. The Carthusians lived and live still so hidden a life that we have few means of knowing the degree and way in which mysticism was cultivated in their houses. But we do know that they were the contemplative Order *par excellence*, each Charterhouse being by intention a community of practical mystics; and that they played a definite part in the maintenance of a lofty spiritual tradition. This they did by practice rather than by propaganda. The essence of mysticism being not a doctrine but a way of life, its interests require the existence of groups of persons who put its principles into effect. The early Carthusians seem to have fulfilled this office. Their houses were recognised places of resort for spiritual persons; and though they produced few mystical writers, Carthusian influence is constantly discovered in the lives of the great medieval mystics. The monks, who were educated men, studied mystical literature with eagerness, and collected it in their libraries. They also devoted much time to the copying of MSS; and many mystical works were thus preserved and disseminated by them.

The relations between the first Carthusians and Cistercians were close. St Bruno had received his early discipline from St Robert, the future founder of Cîteaux; and in the following century St Bernard was on intimate terms with the monks of the Grande Chartreuse, visiting them, and exchanging letters upon spiritual themes. A Carthusian abbot was one of the first recipients of his mystical commentary on the Song of Songs—one of the great source-books of mystical doctrine in the later Middle Ages. These facts already shew the beginning of a phenomenon of great importance in this phase of religious history: the degree in which mysticism was fostered and imparted through social intercourse, personal instruction, and discipleship. Often conceived as a solitary adventure of the spirit, it has as a matter of fact a strongly marked social aspect, well seen in the relationship existing between some of its outstanding personalities and their followers.

Of such personalities, one of the most influential for the eleventh century revival of mysticism was St Anselm (1033–1109), Abbot of Bec and Archbishop of Canterbury. Anselm is one of those great figures, peculiarly characteristic of Catholic culture at its best, which exhibit in

action the fruits of contemplation. It is this type, balancing spirituality
by immense intellectual and practical ability, which gives the Christian
mysticism of the West its historical importance. Driven by a strongly
religious temperament, Anselm after some years of wandering found
at the abbey of Bec in Normandy a "heaven on earth." He was professed at the age of twenty-seven, and lived there for thirty-three years,
successively becoming prior and abbot. The charm and greatness of his
character are well known to us from contemporary notices. In spite of the
vast influence and permanent value of his theological writings and his important ecclesiastical work, it is a mistake to regard Anselm mainly as
a theologian or administrator. His real interest and the efficacious cause
of his ceaseless labours was the personal passion of the mystic. Thus while
on the one hand rightly considered the father of scholasticism, on the other
hand he anticipates St Bernard as a teacher of contemplative love. The
genuine prayers and meditations which modern criticism has separated
from the many spurious pieces passing under his name reveal the nature
of his secret life. They were widely circulated and became one of the
great formative influences of the medieval school, especially in England.
It does not appear that St Anselm was acquainted with the works of
"Dionysius the Areopagite." As a mystic he depends chiefly upon
St Augustine, whose philosophic and devotional fervour he reproduces
in the terms of his own time, blending with it that personal and intimate
feeling which was characteristic of medieval piety. His clear and critical
mind rejected the elaborate and often ridiculous symbolism which
weighed down the religious expression of the early Middle Ages, and
dwelt by preference upon those first principles which are the food of
the contemplative life.

Anselm's life overlaps that of St Bernard of Clairvaux (1091–1153),
the outstanding name in twelfth-century mysticism. St Bernard was at
once the son and the support of the Cistercian reform, which had at its
outset a contemplative character afterwards lost. Behind him, and somewhat obscured by his many-sided brilliance, stands the beautiful figure
of the true founder, Stephen Harding, the English saint, who combined
great administrative gifts with a passionate love of poverty and an unfailing spirit of joy that anticipate St Francis of Assisi. Stephen was a
convinced and realistic mystic, who saw the whole of life in terms of work
and contemplation. The monks were consecrated peasants. The record
of his rule at Cîteaux is an epic of heroic other-worldliness and serene
courage, in the face of the famine and pestilence which almost wiped out
the community. It was saved from extinction in 1113 by the arrival of
Bernard, a brilliant and attractive young noble of twenty-two, leading
a band of thirty disciples. The party had spent six months in retreat
together before asking admission at Cîteaux, a sufficient tribute to the
personal influence of their youthful leader, whose fragile body was
possessed by an intrepid will to holiness.

Spiritual genius matures swiftly. At twenty-five, Bernard was sent to found the daughter house of Clairvaux, of which he remained abbot till his death. He entered almost at once on a career of boundless activity which finally made him the dominant spiritual and ecclesiastical influence of his time. Monastic founder and reformer, preacher, statesman, and director of souls, he is characteristic of the varied and vigorous religious life of the twelfth century. Yet he remained to the end a solitary and contemplative at heart, his many outward works the expressions of an interior devotedness. His personal charm and talent for friendship, the energy which triumphed over persistent ill-health produced by his early and immoderate austerities, the practical abilities which balanced his profound spiritual absorption, are all made plain to us by contemporary sources, which include considerable remains of his voluminous correspondence.

As a mystic, Bernard's influence was on the whole conservative and anti-intellectual. His contemporary Richard of St Victor was making pioneer researches into the psychology of contemplation; but Bernard had no interests of this kind. His view of the mystical life was devotional and practical; he stressed affection rather than intellect, and continued the Benedictine tradition, based on the meditation of Scripture and on the writings of St Gregory and Cassian. Yet, adding nothing new to the doctrine of the contemplative life, he impressed on the developing mysticism of the Middle Ages a distinctive form and colour, and became one of the major authorities on whom all later mystics depend. Bernard's spirituality emerges from the Benedictine tradition, as early Gothic art emerges from the Romanesque. It adds to inherited qualities a new graciousness, responds to a new emotional demand. The position given to him by Dante in the *Paradiso* correctly represents the place which he occupied in the religious development of the Middle Ages. The treatise *On the Love of God*, written in 1126 before the beginning of his great public career, and the sermons on the Canticles, composed in later life for the edification of his monks, are the chief literary expressions of his mysticism.

If the specific medieval tradition of spiritual life descends on one side from St Bernard, on the other it takes its departure from the Augustinian abbey of St Victor at Paris. Here about 1108 a theological school, which soon became an important centre of intellectual life, was founded by William of Champeaux (*ob.* 1121), one of Bernard's personal friends. St Bernard, a man of prayer and action, had little interest in the speculative side of religion. The Victorines, who were Platonists and students of St Augustine's works, supplied together with a deep spiritual fervour the necessary intellectual backbone to the growing science of the mystical life. For medieval thought, scholastic and mystical theology were closely related; and in the best Victorine writings an endeavour is made to harmonise rational and intuitive knowledge. Hugh of St Victor (*c.* 1096–1141), a great and influential thinker, is the chief theologian of the school. The poet Adam (*ob.* 1192), in his sequences, brought the learning and spirituality of the community to bear on the liturgic life of the Church. More important for the subsequent history of mysticism was Hugh's Scottish—or perhaps Irish—disciple, the fervent and learned Richard (*ob.* 1173). Richard of St Victor was the first Christian thinker to attempt a psychological account of mystical experience, and is the originator of some of its most important distinctions. His remarkable analysis and description of the stages in the development of the contemplative consciousness—the expansion, the uplifting, and the transfiguration of the mind—exercised a decisive influence on the great mystical teachers of the thirteenth and fourteenth centuries, especially the vernacular writers of the English and Flemish schools. His personal holiness is said to have been great; and though his writings are entirely objective and nothing is known of his own experience, for Dante he was the typical mystic "superhuman in contemplation." Richard regarded the heart and not the head as the organ of spiritual knowledge; and he rivalled St Francis in his expressions of contempt for secular learning. Yet it is largely due to his penetrating intellect that the mystical fervour of the time was saved from an easy and general descent into the abyss of religious emotionalism. Thus the Victorines, though cloistered scholars, profoundly influenced the religious life of the Middle Ages. Much of their teaching was conveyed by way of mystical commentaries on Scripture, and with an abundant—often extravagant—use of symbolic imagery. Nevertheless, with them begins the great part played by the Dionysian writings, with their resolute rejection of symbol and image, in the development of medieval religion.

France was a chief centre of the great spiritual revival of the twelfth century; and French influence was at this period dominant in the spheres of monastic reform, religious art, and learning. We might therefore expect to find it at work in the religious movement which arose in England during the reign of Stephen, when a wave of spiritual enthusiasm comparable to the Puritan and Evangelical revivals spread over the country. The history of this movement is not yet fully made out. Its beginning apparently coincided with the coming of the Cistercians to England, and the rapid foundation—mostly under circumstances of poverty and hardship—of the great Yorkshire abbeys; but the form which it assumed was less monastic, more individualistic, than in France. It is significant that its chief literary monument, the *Ancren Riwle*, witnesses to that cult of the solitary or anchoretic life which had already arisen in late Saxon times, and was afterwards so closely associated with the classic age of English mysticism. Perhaps the first English medieval mystic of whom we have certain knowledge is St Wulsi (*ob. c.* 1097), originally a monk of Crowland, whose longing for a contemplative life drove him to seek refuge in a cave near Evesham, where he lived for over seventy years, becoming one of the chief spiritual influences of the West. In the following century, the general dissatisfaction with the lax state of the nunneries and unreformed Benedictine houses led to numerous experiments in the solitary life being made by those who desired to give themselves to contemplation. Northern France at this time was said to be "full of hermits," and although the Carthusians were not established in England till 1174, their fame had preceded them; and spiritual minds were drawn to seek means of imitating their methods. We hear frequently of small groups of hermits, or solitaries of either sex, established in lonely places in order to lead a life of contemplation. Some of these hermits exerted a widespread influence on the pupils and clients who resorted to them. Such were St Godric of Finchale (*ob.* 1170), who lived for seventy years in a lonely spot on the banks of the Wear, and is credited with the Franciscan power over animals; and St Wulfric (*ob.* 1154), who lived in a cell adjoining the church of Haselbury near Crewkerne. St Wulfric was much venerated as a prophet and wonder-worker, and Henry I and Stephen came to him for counsel. At Markyate, between Dunstable and St Albans, dwelt in the first half of the century the holy hermit Roger, a mystic whose soul "conversed with the invisible" and who was called the "friend of God." His disciple St Christina of Markyate, a prophetess and clairvoyante, became one of the most notable women of her time. Henry II in 1155 made provision for her support out of the Exchequer; and Abbot Robert of St Albans, seeking to win the favour of Hadrian IV, could find no better gift than sandals and two mitres embroidered by "Lady Christina of the Wood." Less famous figures, but equally significant of the religious outlook, are the visionary Seleth, supernaturally led from the south to set up a company of hermits in Airedale, and thence evicted by the ruthless founder of Kirkstall Abbey; Bartholomew, the hermit of the Farne (1120–93); or the two women brought in from the woods about 1140 by Abbot Geoffrey of St Albans to form the nucleus of Sopwell Priory. Though this widespread movement has left few literary remains, its chief personalities probably imparting their spiritual knowledge by direct intercourse with visitors and disciples, it is here that we must look for the origins of English mysticism. The beautiful Middle English rhapsody, *A Talking of the Love of God*—now recognised as a conflation of earlier materials—suggests something of the realistic spiritual passion which irradiated these solitary lives. So too the *Meditations* of St Aelred (Abbot of Rievaulx 1146–66)—often confused with those of St Anselm—and the *Rule* of a Recluse, which he composed for the use of his sister, must be reckoned among its characteristic products.

Especially in the *Ancren Riwle* we have a document which reflects the religious temper of this time. It is a spiritual directory written for three girls of noble birth, who had left the world to be enclosed as anchoresses, independently of the established religious Orders, and desired a rule by

which to live[1]. Though it deals much with the externals of their existence, there is implied throughout the mystical object for which they have
been enclosed, and the contrast which exists in the writer's mind between
the formalism of the older religious Orders and the realistic spirituality
which is required of the true anchoress. Here it is probably representative
of the religious outlook which found expression in the cult of the solitary
life. At about the time that the *Ancren Riwle* was written, the Gilbertine
Order began (1131-35) with the enclosure by St Gilbert of Sempringham of seven village girls in a church-anchorage. We must remember,
in estimating such events, that they are at once an implied criticism of
the older religious establishments, and the outward expression of a vigorous
interest in the things of the spirit; the same desire to cultivate the invisible side of life, and subdue all external circumstances to its demands,
which had inspired the heroic founders of Cîteaux and the Grande
Chartreuse.

Both in England and France the mysticism of this period was as a
whole sober, austere, and comparatively free from sensational and apocalyptic characters. Devotional rather than intellectual, it expressed itself
outwardly in a life of intense asceticism and tended little to speculation.
In Germany and Italy, however, the mystical impulse took a more
startling form; and, in the prophetic activities of St Hildegarde and the
Abbot Joachim of Flora, entered into close relations with secular history.
Hildegarde (1098-1179), the "Sibyl of the Rhine," was the first of those
strange women of genius who played so great a part in the history of the
medieval Church, her manifest psychic abnormality contributing to her
spiritual prestige. Born in 1098, she entered the religious life as an oblate
when only eight years old; and was educated by Jutta, an anchoress of
noble birth, whose disciples formed the nucleus of the Benedictine convent
of Mount St Disibode. Hildegarde took the vows here in 1117, becoming
abbess in 1130. Subject to visions from childhood, and reputed to possess
healing and other abnormal powers, Hildegarde laid claim to direct
inspiration and believed the obligation was laid upon her to denounce
the abuses of contemporary life. Her great prophetic period began in
1141, when she was divinely ordered to tell her revelations to the world.
It continued for about ten years, during which time the series of symbolic
visions described in her *Scivias* were received by her. As a result of her
prophecies, which dealt in vigorous terms with the corruption of the
Church and of society, and greatly disturbed the contemporary mind, she
entered into relations with all the chief personages of her time, to whom
she wrote with the authority of one who literally believed herself the
"agent of the Living Light." Her correspondents included four Popes,

[1] The view put forward by Miss Hope Allen that these were the three hand-
maidens of Queen Matilda—Emma, Gunilda, and Christina—established in Kilburn
Priory about 1130, is probable but awaits confirmation. (Cf. *The Origin of the Ancren
Riwle* by H. E. Allen. Mod. Lang. Assoc. of America, 1918.)

two Emperors, and numerous royal and ecclesiastical persons. She consulted St Bernard on the validity of her experiences, and his guarded letter of reply still survives. The latter part of her life, like that of St Teresa, was spent in ceaseless activities. She founded two convents, and travelled hundreds of miles in a country and time which were ill-adapted to women's journeyings. Her intellectual interests ranged from medicine to music, and her literary works include a long physical treatise in nine books and over sixty hymns. Her friend and neighbour, the Benedictine nun St Elizabeth of Schonau (1129–65), was an ecstatic whose trance utterances and symbolic visions were also directed to the reform of ecclesiastical corruption. Her influence, however, was small in comparison with that of St Hildegarde.

St Hildegarde and St Elizabeth, like earlier mystics of their type, had denounced with violence the increasing wealth and political preoccupation of the Church, the glaring contrast between the worldly lives and the spiritual obligations of the priesthood. Their reputation for sanctity protected them; but their protests had little real effect. The religious revival of the early twelfth century, which had given to the mystical fervour of the great monastic reformers and solitaries so favouring an environment, was now nearly spent. As a result, when that fervour appeared in individuals, instead of driving its possessor to a monastery or anchorhold, it tended more and more to emphasise the contrast between institutional and interior religion, and to find new expression outside the ecclesiastical frame. Especially in North Italy, the Rhineland, and France, groups and individuals were beginning to appear among the laity, filled with a craving for spiritual perfection which the average institutionalism did not satisfy; and seeking, as the monastic contemplatives had done—though with different results—an outward life consistent with the aspiration of their souls. Some of these spiritual realists managed to retain their Catholic status. Others, more logical and less submissive to authority, were driven into heresy. Although in the strict sense we cannot perhaps give the name of "mystic" to any of these movements and their founders, there was yet a definite mystical element in their teaching. Its theological basis was a pantheistic doctrine of the divine nature of the soul, which derived from the works of Eriugena and the Neoplatonists and tended to undermine the authority of the official Church. Its social impetus came from the manifest disorders and shortcomings of ecclesiastical life. Its devotional bias was quietist. If, from the point of view of Church history, these heretical mystics are precursors of the Reformation, seen from a more purely religious angle they represent the working under changed conditions and without institutional safeguards of that same realistic spiritual temper which had inspired the Catholic solitaries and reforming saints. While these had expressed their other-worldly passion by means of a vigorous and penetrating use of Catholic discipline and symbolism, perpetually seeking to restore their purity and power, the heretical mystics reacted with more or less violence against institutional religion, and sought the inward by the rejection of the outward. In them first appear the characters which afterwards distinguished the orthodox mysticism of the thirteenth and fourteenth centuries, namely, the ever greater part played by the devout laity and by the formation of free associations or groups; the abandonment of the old tendency to identify mysticism with a special class vowed to the "religious" life; and that use of the vernacular for religious writings which played so great a part in the development of European literature.

The general method of these sects was the substitution of religious experience for religious authority, and a return to the apostolic life of poverty. Their aim was the same liberation from an unspiritual world and initiation into the life of God which had been offered by the ascetic discipline of the cloister, the anchorite's cell, or the Victorine mystic's "elevation of the mind." They attracted adherents, because this mystical craving for spiritual realities was at work in the medieval world, and was now assuming a democratic form. The support given by the Papacy to the Mendicant Orders in the next century was at least partly inspired by a recognition of this fact, and of the need of meeting the threatening tide of heretical mysticism by the counter-attractions of a popular spiritual movement embodying many of its principles but arising within and controlled by the Catholic Church. When Innocent III approved the First Rule of St Francis, he was announcing to the world that the life of the Gospel could still flourish within its walls.

The history of the numerous heretical sects and groups which appeared in North Italy, Germany, Flanders, and France during the twelfth century is still imperfectly known. Their literature is lost, and we now see them only through the eyes of their ecclesiastical critics. Some, particularly the dualistic Cathari and Albigenses and their offshoots, seem to have had little or no mystical character; and these need not be considered here. But in many others we find that combination of speculative freedom, moral earnestness, devotional fervour, and anti-clerical feeling which is in all periods characteristic of the Christian mystical sect. Two distinct but really complementary influences lie behind these movements. The first is that desire for a return to the pure apostolic life of the New Testament— and especially the evangelical poverty which is the price of spiritual freedom—which always tends to appear in times of ecclesiastical decadence, and was widespread in the latter part of the twelfth century. The second is the enormous impetus given to mystical speculation by the renewed study of the works of Dionysius the Areopagite and of Eriugena, which were much read and discussed—often with intoxicating effect—in the University of Paris in the twelfth and early thirteenth centuries. The Neoplatonic philosophy, that unfailing stimulant of the mystical sense, was thus brought into the current academic life, offering a vision of spiritual reality which seemed to satisfy men's deepest cravings. Actually, it tended to the encouragement of that "pure" mysticism which is in the end indistinguishable from pantheism; and, where it achieves concrete expression, commonly means a more or less complete revolt from authority and tradition, and a consequent reduction of religious practice to quietism.

This strand in the spiritual complex of the twelfth century appears early in Flanders, where the speculative religious temper was always at home. Mystical groups, at first orthodox but tending to degenerate into heresy, are already found at Arras in the mid-eleventh century. At the beginning of the twelfth, Tauchelin of Zeeland was teaching a pantheistic mysticism in Antwerp and Bruges, which survived into the next century. Mild tendencies of this sort within the Catholic fold have been detected in the *Letter to the Brethren of Mont Dieu* probably written *c.* 1145 in North France or Flanders by Abbot William of St Thierry, the friend of St Bernard. Addressed to the monks of a newly established Charterhouse, and afterwards widely circulated, this beautiful little treatise suggests how thin a line already divided the orthodox and the heretical mystic. In the following century we find its doctrine reproduced, with guarded ecclesiastical approval, by the daring *Mirror of Simple Souls* apparently written in French in the Liège district. In France, Amaury of Chartres (*ob.* 1205) had pushed to extreme lengths the Neoplatonic doctrine of divine immanence. His teaching was condemned, and he retracted before his death; but his disciples, variously known as the Amaurists or "Spiritual Society," survived him, and promulgated his ideas in a more popular and excessive form. They held that all men were potentially divine, and hence emancipated from all rites and ceremonies; and also that the universal reign of the Holy Ghost—fixed for the year 1210—was at hand. This notion suggests Joachist influence, though it may have arisen independently. Groups holding similar pantheistic and quietist doctrines appeared about the same time in the Rhineland and Flanders, one of the chief distributing centres of medieval mysticism. Here, at the end of the twelfth century, Lambert le Bégue founded at Liège the lay associations of Béguins and Beghards which played so large a part in the promulgation of mystical religion, both orthodox and heretical, during the later Middle Ages. These communities represented a definite revolt from Monasticism; and, after the coming of the friars, the orthodox groups were frequently under mendicant direction. Of those which departed from Catholic normality some—the Beghards—became closely allied with the Fraticelli; and others—the Béguins—with the Brethren of the Free Spirit. By the mid-thirteenth century, béguinages had multiplied in all the Rhenish cities; that at Malines is described as "a little town." Many of the occupants being educated, they provided a favouring soil for that pantheistic mysticism, involving the claim to an inner light absolving its possessor from ecclesiastical and ultimately even from moral law, which was the common doctrine of the quietist sects; and so dangerous did they become in the eyes of the Church that in 1311 the Council of Vienne ordered their suppression.

The most celebrated and widespread association of heretical mystics, the Brethren of the Free Spirit, first appear in Augsburg in 1262; and for over a century they are prominent in German and Flemish religious history. By the beginning of the fourteenth century they were also numerous in Central Italy, where Boniface VIII and Clement V attempted their suppression. Historically descended from the followers of Ortlieb of Strasbourg, their ultimate ancestry is Neoplatonic. Other groups sought rather to revive the primitive Christian life. Among these were the Waldensians, who arose in the Lyons district under the leadership of Peter Waldo in the last quarter of the twelfth century, the Apostolics of Cologne, and the Humiliati of North Italy. The Humiliati, who seem originally to have been a gild or fraternity vowed to a life of prayer and evangelical poverty, anticipated in many respects—especially their "third order" of married laity—the creation of St Francis. Their tenets included pacificism, and the refusal to take oaths or wear dyed clothing. They early split into two divisions: the "true" Humiliati, who remained within the Church, and tended under clerical influence to become more and more monastic in character, and the "false," whose defiance of the prohibition against lay-preachers and the holding of conventicles finally drove them into schism. By the late thirteenth century all these various bodies of spiritual experimentalists and dissidents, including the Fraticelli and Brethren of the Free Spirit, had become closely interconnected, and formed a heretical movement so strong and widely spread that it persisted in the teeth of persecution until the Reformation finally absorbed its constituent elements. In estimating the mysticism of the Middle Ages and interpreting its literature, we have always to remember this fact, and the thin line which often separated mystical rebel from mystical saint. Many of the works of the orthodox mystics can only be understood in the light of the heresies they were concerned to rebuke or to avoid.

Meanwhile there had arisen in South Italy a mystic and prophet who was to influence profoundly the religious history of the West. Joachim of Flora (1132–1202) was born in Calabria, a district remote from the spiritual and secular interests and conflicts of the north. While spiritual and political unrest was filling North Italy and France with heretical movements, in Calabria Latin Christianity had developed in continuous contact with the Byzantine Church. Here the hermits of the tenth century still represented the spiritual ideals of the fervent; and the Basilian monks, though in union with Rome, still used the Greek rite.

The familiar characteristics of the mystical saints are seen in the Abbot Joachim, who is rightly placed by Dante among the great contemplatives in the Heaven of the Sun. His revelation of the "Eternal Gospel," which shall wholly supersede the temporal gospel and bring in the age of the Holy Ghost, was the intuition of a mystic, who found in the Scriptures that which he longed to find there—the promise of a spiritual renovation, the coming of the Kingdom of God. His career was determined by a revelation received during a pilgrimage to the Holy Land, in which he believed that the true meaning of the Scriptures was disclosed to him. Returning to Calabria, he became first a wandering preacher, then a Cistercian monk, and in 1178 Abbot of Corazo. Obtaining papal permission to adopt the hermit's life, he retired first to Pietralata and finally to the remote mountain-retreat of Flora, where with his disciples he lived in extreme austerity, absorbed in communion with the unseen world, and composing his great prophetic books. Occasionally he emerged to visit the Italian monasteries and urge them to reform. Universally revered as a great prophet, and enjoying papal approval throughout his life, the destructive element in Joachim's revelations was not at first realised. For these revelations, astonishing in their vastness and daring, meant nothing less than the supersession of institutional by mystical Christianity. He declared that the epochs of Father and Son—the Old and the New Testament—were nearly over. The monks, and especially the hermits, restored to their primitive perfection of life, were about to bring in the epoch of the Spirit, that "new age" of love and freedom when the Church should be ruled by its contemplative souls. Joachim, in fact, solemnly announced from within the Church the precise consummation which the various heretical sects were seeking outside the fold. By a series of calculations he fixed the coming of the new era in the year 1260, and declared that it would be established through two new Orders, one of laymen, the other of priests, who would live in apostolic poverty the spiritual life. This prophecy, apparently fulfilled in the coming of the friars, probably contributed to the prompt success of the Mendicant Orders; and the friars in their turn demonstrated in the eyes of the world the truth of Joachim's revelation.

In Italy during the thirteenth century, and indeed later, all spiritual minds were in some degree influenced by Joachist ideas, and by the spurious revelations which soon became attributed to him. In the general unrest of that vigorous time of transition, the apocalyptic longings of dissatisfied piety found in his visions a certain justification of their hopes. Though the Trinitarian doctrine of the "Eternal Gospel" was condemned by Rome in 1215, the holy life of the abbot and his followers was commended. The prestige of his prophecies increased, and after the death of St Francis they became a principal support of the Spiritual Franciscans in the struggle against the *relaxati*. In Paris a Joachist circle, marked by vigorous criticism of the Papacy and belief in the coming of the New Age, formed round the friar Gerard of San Donnino, author of the notorious *Introduction to the Eternal Gospel*. This *reductio ad absurdum* of Joachist teaching, made in the interests of the Franciscan extremists, was solemnly condemned in 1256, and its destruction ordered. But its influence lingered for many years, and may be estimated by the fact that the Abbot Joachim is the only non-Biblical prophet to whom Dante gives a place in Paradise.

Francis of Assisi (1182–1226), who was to give the mysticism of the thirteenth century its most original characteristics, was twenty when the Abbot Joachim died. The son of a prosperous Umbrian merchant, living on the highway between North Italy and Rome, he can hardly have grown up without some knowledge of the prophecies of the Eternal Gospel on the one hand, and on the other of those heretical movements which anticipated his own cult of evangelical poverty. Similarities between certain doctrines of the Cathari and Humiliati and primitive Franciscanism have indeed been traced; but the unquestioning adherence of Francis to the Church and his life-long veneration for its sacraments preclude any suggestion of deliberate borrowing from this or any other anti-clerical sources. What Francis gave the world—or those who would listen to him—was rather a satisfaction from within the Catholic fold of those spiritual needs which the best and most sane of the heretical movements had sought to meet outside it. He was a mystic and poet, who insisted with the simple logic of a child or an artist on embodying his spiritual intuitions in the stuff of practical life. He obliged his first followers—and only these were in the full sense Franciscan—to live that "mixed life" of action and contemplation which the Middle Ages had accepted from St Gregory as its spiritual ideal, but had only practised in the rare persons of its saints. Basing his First Rule on three texts from the Gospels, and imitating as closely as possible the life therein described, he was by turns itinerant preacher, hermit, penitent, and troubadour. With him mysticism definitely comes out from the cloister into the open air, irradiates the natural scene, speaks the common language of the people, and accepts inspiration from the literature of romance; yet retains that contact with Catholic tradition and practice which had been deliberately broken by the heretical sects. Thus the "New Religion" of St Francis conserves the positive values of the evangelical reaction whilst avoiding its negative extravagances.

The spiritual genius of the Founder is shewn especially in two directions. First, in the degree in which not only religion, but also literature and art, were affected by him; for it is not too much to say that the realistic fervour, the tender human quality which transformed late-medieval paintings and religious poetry, especially in Italy, are largely of Franciscan origin. Next, in the number of diverse strands woven into his practice and teaching: the penitential outlook of the Christian ascetic, the romantic outlook of the poet, the love of all living creatures which could serve the lepers and preach to the birds, the intense Christocentric fervour which controlled his whole career, found its consummation in the episode of the Stigmata, and left its mark on the devotional life of succeeding centuries. It is true that the life-long effort of St Francis to maintain his followers at his own level of spiritual realism ended in disappointment and frustration, and that his Order as a whole failed to reproduce his ideals. But the extraordinary impression made by his life—for the "relaxed" friars, who did not attempt to follow, still admired it—is shewn by the common and quite literal belief that in him the earthly life of Christ had been lived again. This conviction, which is worked out in detail in the early Lives of Francis, had an enormous effect on the religious imagination of the time, and gives the Franciscan mysticism of the following generation its peculiar note of personal enthusiasm.

It is usual to say that Franciscan mysticism is mainly distinguished by this ardent personal feeling, while the Dominican school is marked by a more speculative and philosophic temper; but this contrast is too absolute. On the one hand, an intense fervour certainly enters into Dominican mysticism. On the other, the Franciscan contemplatives, while emphasising the emotional and volitional element in personal religion—and in their more extreme representatives continuing the founder's hostility to secular and even theological learning—shew in their greatest works close dependence on traditional sources, especially on St Augustine and Dionysius the Areopagite. The difference of temper between the two schools is better understood if we remember that one is primarily the expression of Latin, the other of Teutonic spirituality. The real marks of thorough-going Franciscan mysticism are (1) a sense of the unique commission of St Francis, and hence of his spiritual descendants, to restore within the Church the primitive evangelical life; (2) a continuance of his belief in the absolute spiritual worth and obligation of Poverty; (3) an adoring devotion to the earthly life, and especially the passion, of Christ. It is obvious that a mystical doctrine composed of these three elements may have revolutionary effects, both social and spiritual, on those who accept it literally. It permeated all the early Franciscan writings, especially the Lives and legends of the patriarch, and operated in various degrees of intensity over the wide area which was by the middle of the thirteenth century included in the Franciscan sphere of influence. At one end of the scale, the lives of the Conventual friars, who had accepted a mitigated rule, were but little affected by it. It appears in a reasonable and tempered form in the writings of St Bonaventura (1221–74), who nevertheless became, with St Bernard and Richard of St Victor, one of the chief literary sources of the fourteenth-century mystics. Whilst emphasis on evangelical poverty soon became the peculiar mark of the Spiritual extremists, the Christocentric side of Franciscan mysticism found its classic expression in the celebrated and popular *Meditations on the Life of Christ*, long attributed to St Bonaventura, but now recognised as the work of an unknown thirteenth-century Minorite, in whom ardent feeling and creative imagination have combined to produce a devotional masterpiece. The influence of this book, not only on the literature, but on the sacred art and drama of the later Middle Ages, was enormous. Ludolf the Carthusian, writing in the late fourteenth century his *Life of Christ*, which became a standard manual of meditation for the religious, merely copied its methods. Thus the contributions of the mitigated Franciscans to mysticism, though sober in method, were important and had permanent results.

At the other end of the scale were the "Spiritual" friars of the extreme left, who were driven by their own passionate logic into fanaticism, and finally into conflict with the Church. The history of the Spiritual party as a whole is complicated first by a lack of documents, and next by the extraordinary variety of interests and personalities which became included in it. But there can be little doubt that, even in its most turbulent manifestations, the movement was in essence a mystical one. It was born of the desire to actualise the spiritual vision of St Francis, and was supported by the influence of those saintly friars of the Primitive Observance—many of them the companions of the patriarch— who were still living in the latter part of the thirteenth century. These deeply-venerated brothers, who had refused to accept the mitigated rule, now dwelt in remote hermitages in Umbria and the March of Ancona. There they lived the life of poverty and contemplation, sometimes emerging to preach in the Umbrian cities, and constantly visited by the more fervent members of the Spiritual party. Among them were Brother Leo (*ob.* 1271), the close friend of Francis and unrelenting apostle of Franciscan rigorism; the great visionaries Conrad of Offida (1237–1306) and Peter of Monticello; and the mystics, John of Parma (1209–1288), who had ruled the Order for ten years, and John of La Verna (*ob.* 1322), a celebrated preacher who is said to have been the spiritual father of Jacopone da Todi. The diversity of interests and cultural level among those who resorted to these hidden mystics and were inspired by their teachings was great, for the Spiritual party contained both lay and clerical elements and had political, doctrinal, and revolutionary, as well as purely mystical objectives. All these appear in the poetry of Jacopone da Todi (1228–1306), a man of education and of fierce enthusiasms, who had been by turns lawyer, penitent, wandering preacher, contemplative, and poet, and became one of the leaders of the Spiritual friars during the last quarter of the thirteenth century. The subjects of Jacopone's *laude*, extending from the heights of Neoplatonic contemplation, through every phase of mystical fervour, to the depths of social and political satire, indeed invective, may be considered representative of the many types of feeling included in the Spiritual ranks. On the extreme left were those Franciscan zealots whose devotion to the prophecies of the Abbot Joachim and the principle of unmitigated poverty involved personal squalor, and an apocalyptic propaganda which at last drove them into schism. Joachist ideas began to spread in the Order during John of Parma's rule (1247–57), mainly in Italy and the south of France. In Provence Hugues de Digne (*ob.* 1285) and his sister the ecstatic

St Douceline (born 1214) became the leaders of a widespread mystical movement intimately connected with the Joachist dream of a Spiritual Church. This was continued by Petrus Johannis Olivi of Languedoc (1248–98), a man of much learning and devout life, and a convinced believer in the Joachist prophecies. Twice summoned before the General Chapter of the Order, Olivi successfully defended himself against charges of heresy, and died faithful to his ideals. In Italy Angelo Clareno (1247–1337), a disciple of Brother Leo and friend of Conrad of Offida and Jacopone, was the leader of those Spirituals who had placed all their hopes on the hermit-Pope Celestine V, and were ruined by his abdication. All these had believed, on the authority of the Prophecies, that they were called to purge the Church of its manifest corruption and bring in the new era of the Holy Ghost, and in pursuit of this end mingled political intrigue with mystical enthusiasm. After Celestine's fall, some recanted, some retired to their hermitages, others were imprisoned or exiled. The rest, known as Fraticelli, refused to submit to the Church. They spread northwards, tending to merge with other insurgent and Illuminist groups, and by the opening of the fourteenth century were intimately concerned with the heterodox béguins of Germany and Flanders. Yet the Spirituals had their belated triumph. It was a disciple of Angelo Clareno, the Blessed Giovanni Valle (1351), who brought back into the life of the Order the ideals of Francis, in that great Reform of the Strict Observance which restored to the fourteenth-century Minorites something of the glory of primitive times. Combining the contemplative life of the hermitages with the missionary activities proper to the friars, the Strict Observance provided a frame within which some of the spirit of Franciscan mysticism could survive, and gradually absorbed into its ranks all that was best in the Order.

The most characteristic products of that mysticism, however, and our best clues to its character, are found in the vernacular writings which were produced in Central Italy, mainly in connexion with the Tertiary movement. The Tertiaries, who were devout lay-folk bound to an austere rule of life, were numerous in most of the cities of North and Central Italy by the middle of the thirteenth century, while in the Rhineland they formed the inhabitants of many of the orthodox béguinages. They were in fact a loosely-knit religious society, usually in close touch with those friars of the Spiritual Party who were struggling in the teeth of official discouragement to maintain the Primitive Rule, and occupied an important position in the religious life of Italy, where their groups provided a particularly favourable environment for the development of mystical enthusiasm. We recover their atmosphere in such relics of Spiritual literature as the *Speculum* and the *Fioretti*; in the works of the remarkable ecstatic and religious teacher Angela of Foligno (1248–1309), whom her admirers did not hesitate to call a Mistress of Theologians; in the personal confessions of her disciple, the tempestuous

Ubertino da Casale; and in the *laude* of Jacopone da Todi, many of which were probably composed to be sung at their meetings. Angela, Jacopone, and Ubertino were all converts from a life of ease to absolute destitution, and in this exhibit the power operating in Franciscan mysticism of the second generation. The thought of Jacopone, while keeping close to the evangelical fervour of St Francis, is deeply tinctured with Neoplatonism; and it is perhaps from his *laude*, or a similar source, that Angela has obtained the Dionysian language in which some of her great visions are described. The work of both these mystics, which circulated rapidly, greatly affected the later development of mysticism; while many scholars find in Jacopone's dramatic *lauda*, "Donna del Paradiso," the origin of the Italian religious drama.

Such facts as these indicate how wide a variety of mystical phenomena was produced in Tertiary circles, and how high was the level of spiritual culture and enthusiasm presupposed in those whom the Franciscan vernacular writers addressed. Here the vision of Francis indeed survived, and was embodied in a democratic lay-movement, anticipating in many points that of the Friends of God, which arose in Germany in the next century under Dominican influence, and, like that movement, producing its own vernacular literature. Among the Tertiaries, social origin, learning, and ecclesiastical office appear to have been little considered. Only spiritual aristocracy was acknowledged; and this seems to have shewn itself in many humble and nameless saints. Thus it was from the holy Sienese comb-seller Pier Pettignano (*ob.* 1289) that the brilliant friar Ubertino da Casale first learned "seraphic contemplation"; while Angela of Foligno, an elderly widow of the middle class, completed his education.

In Germany during the second half of the thirteenth century mysticism assumed two sharply contrasting forms: the first associated with the Preaching Friars, the second with the old Benedictine monasticism. In the great Dominican scholars, Master Eckehart (*c.* 1260–1327) and Theodore of Freiburg (living in 1310), we see the vigorous beginnings of an entirely new movement, destined to colour the spirituality of the next century, in which bold theological speculation and profound mystical fervour are combined with pastoral zeal. In the exuberant visionary, St Gertrude the Great (1256–1301), and her associates at the aristocratic Cistercian convent of Helfde in Saxony—Gertrude of Hackeborn (1232–91) and her sister St Mechthild of Hackeborn (1240–98)—we have the final flower of that Benedictine tradition which had nourished the genius of St Hildegarde. The mysticism of the Cistercians of Helfde owes its peculiar quality to the blending of two streams of influence. The first is that daily liturgic routine and sequence of the Christian year, which was the framework of the nuns' religious lives, and inspired the vividly pictorial visions of Christ and the Saints which abound in their writings. The second is the romantic vernacular poetry of the Minnesingers, which reached them through the inspiring genius of the group, the exquisite poet and visionary, Mechthild of Magdeburg (c. 1212–80). Born near Magdeburg, of the ruling class, Mechthild renounced her rank and property in girlhood, and lived for many years under Dominican direction the unenclosed but dedicated life of a béguine. Her vigorous criticisms of the clergy provoked reprisals which at last drove her to take refuge at Helfde, where she was received by the Abbess Gertrude of Hackeborn in 1268. Her prophecies and denunciations of contemporary morals, in which Joachist influence has been detected, continue the tradition of St Hildegarde, but do not constitute her chief claim to remembrance. A true "Minnesinger of the Holy Ghost," she resembles the Franciscan *laudisti* in her power of adapting the poetry of Chivalry to the purposes of spiritual passion. She wrote, in the Low German dialect of the day, her great *Book of the Flowing Light of the Godhead*: a collection of lyrics, visions, and dramatic dialogues in prose and verse, filled with the romantic idealism, the tender feeling, the fresh delight in natural beauty, which characterised the new-born secular poetry. In her we see again the mystical genius of the laity entering and transforming the traditional spirituality of the cloister, and contributing to the beginnings of a national literature. The contrast between Mechthild of Magdeburg and the three Helfde nuns is striking; but her influence can be detected in those poetic passages which—especially in St Mechthild of Hackeborn—relieve their more conventional visions and rhapsodies. The school had more than a local influence. The beginnings of the Catholic cultus of the Sacred Heart have been traced to the visions of St Gertrude; and her meditations have a permanent place in Catholic literature. Mechthild of Magdeburg—whose works were translated into Latin before her death—disputes with Mechthild of Hackeborn the honour of providing Dante with the model for the Matilda of the Earthly Paradise.

The lives of these nuns—who were, with the exception of the poetess Mechthild, "inheritors of a dying world"—overlapped the rise of that vigorous school of mysticism, at once so wide in its philosophic sweep and so practical in application, which was to inspire in the next century the great movement of the Friends of God. Mechthild of Hackeborn in one of her visions saw the two real founders of this school—the Dominican doctors Albert the Great and his pupil St Thomas Aquinas—entering Paradise. Though Franciscan mysticism in its later developments is by no means independent of literary and philosophic culture, and its great writers shew thorough acquaintance with Christian Neoplatonism, its inspiration is mainly evangelical. But the mysticism which developed in the Rhineland under Dominican influence explores, and subordinates to the requirements of orthodoxy and the needs of the devout laity, those religious speculations which had been inspired by the study of Dionysius the Areopagite and Eriugena. Thus one school proceeded mainly by the enhancement and spiritualisation of religious feeling, the other by the enhancement and spiritualisation of religious thought. In so far as they retained their Catholic status, and avoided capitulation, the first to the extravagant logic of the Fraticelli, the second to the pantheistic tendencies of the German religious temper, they formed together the Church's answer to the demands and declarations of the heretical sects. The Dominican mystics have an intellectual background, a solid mental culture, hardly to be found in the Franciscans of the first generation. They all depend upon St Thomas Aquinas, whose unquestioned authority governs the orthodox mysticism of the later Middle Ages. St Thomas had learned from his master Albert the Great (who wrote a commentary on the Dionysian writings[1]) to appreciate the Areopagite and Richard of St Victor, both of whom he frequently and respectfully quotes in the *Summa*, placing their doctrine in precise and orderly relation with the general theological scheme. This, perhaps more than any other single fact, assured to Dionysius his prominent place among the sources of later Catholic mysticism. Though his treatment of mysticism in the *Summa* is entirely objective, and his real place is in the history of scholastic philosophy, St Thomas' Eucharistic hymns are enough to prove that he had a strong mystical side. For medieval thought, the sharp modern distinction between philosophy, theology, and mysticism did not exist; and in the great mind of Aquinas, as afterwards in that of Dante, these three avenues to one Truth were harmonised.

Both Albert the Great and St Thomas had taught in the schools of Cologne, which retained the impress of their powerful personalities; and here German Dominican mysticism began in the person of Master Eckehart (*c.* 1260–1327), the dominant and in many respects the most enigmatic personality of the school. After centuries of neglect, modern students of mysticism have tended somewhat to over-estimate Eckehart's originality. He should perhaps be regarded as the most brilliant and powerful representative of a school to which his contemporary Theodore of Freiburg also belonged. Theodore, who was studying at Paris in 1285, was, like Eckehart, in philosophy a Neoplatonist, in religion a profound and daring mystic. Both men passed their lives in the Dominican Order, in which Eckehart rose to the rank of Provincial for Saxony and Vicar General of Bohemia. Probably entering on his studies at Cologne about the year of Albert the Great's death, in later life he spent two periods, in 1302 and 1311, at the University of Paris. Thence in middle-age he returned, soaked in the mystical philosophy of Dionysius and Eriugena, to begin his great career as a preacher at Strasbourg, at that time the chief

[1] Albert the Great's claim to a place among the mystics has been reduced by the fact that the mystical tract *De Adhaerendo Deo*, long attributed to him, is now regarded as a Benedictine work of the early fifteenth century (cf. Dr M. Grabmann, *Der Benediktines Mystikes; Joannes von Kastl*, in *Tübingen. Theol. Quart.* 1920, pp. 186–235).

religious centre of Germany, and much affected by heretical mysticism. About 1320, being now at the height of his power and reputation, he returned to Cologne, where he taught until his death, inspiring a group of disciples, which appears to have included Suso (1295–1365) and Tauler (*c.* 1290–1361), the two chief Dominican mystics of the next generation. Both Eckehart and Theodore of Freiburg shew the workings of the speculative Teutonic mind on the transcendental doctrines of Christian Neoplatonism. Both embodied their teachings in vernacular sermons which are surprising in their profundity, when we consider the degree of theological intelligence presupposed in the congregations to which they are addressed. In his sermons—which only survive in transcripts of doubtful accuracy—we see Eckehart as a teaching mystic, full of pastoral zeal. In his fragmentary Latin writings he appears as a daring speculative philosopher, expounding a doctrine which may possibly be justified as a legitimate development of Thomism, but is certainly susceptible of a pantheistic interpretation. Indeed, forty-nine propositions drawn from his works were condemned at Rome in the year of his death, and the heretics of the next generation frequently appealed to his authority. There is, however, no doubt that in spite of excessive language Eckehart's intentions were strictly orthodox; and his memory was revered by his disciples as that of a saint. Moreover, careful comparison of his teaching with the most mystical poems of his Italian contemporary, Jacopone da Todi, reveals a close identity of doctrine between the most advanced Franciscan and Dominican mysticism, both in fact depending directly on Dionysius the Areopagite, and suggests that we must attribute Eckehart's influential position far more to intellectual vigour and impressive personal qualities than to the novelty of his teaching. Here the point of interest for the historian of religion is the existence among the laity and in the béguinages and Dominican convents of the Rhineland— as among the Franciscan Tertiaries of Central Italy—of a public capable of assimilating the profound and abstract doctrines of Eckehart and his contemporaries and followers. They offered from within the Church food to that vigorous appetite for religious fundamentals which sought satisfaction in the heretical mysticism—often an exaggeration of orthodox teaching—flourishing in the Rhenish cities at the opening of the fourteenth century. This heretical mysticism, which infested the béguinages, was the object of persistent attack on the part of the great Dominican preachers. Cologne was an important centre of the Brethren of the Free Spirit, who actually extracted from Eckehart's sermons many propositions in support of their own teaching.

It was mainly, however, through the work of his immediate disciples, the Dominicans Johann Tauler and Heinrich Suso or Seuse, that Eckehart's genius bore fruit. They, like their master, were both philosophers and teaching mystics; and in them his spiritual realism and metaphysical passion for ultimates transfigure the ordinary materials of Catholic devotion. Even the intensely emotional Suso combines intimate fervour with strongly Platonic passages; while the impressive quality of Tauler's sermons arises from his power of placing against the vast Eckehartian background the directly ethical and spiritual demands of the Christian life.

Born at Strasbourg, and probably a fellow-student with Suso and Nicholas of Strasbourg at Cologne, Tauler—who calls Eckehart his "most holy Master"—became the greatest German preacher of his time. His sermons, which unite the lofty mystical doctrine of Eckehart with simple Christian teaching, were mostly delivered at the orthodox béguinages and Dominican nunneries. They are his only authentic works. During the Interdict imposed by John XXII in 1324, he removed to Basle, at that time the headquarters of the Friends of God. Thence he returned in 1347 to Strasbourg, and finally to Cologne, where he died in 1361. Tauler was a thinker, teacher, and religious leader. As a mystic, he tells us nothing of his own experience. His contemporary Suso, though his exuberant symbolism conceals the degree in which he too has assimilated Eckehart's philosophic doctrine, is pre-eminently subjective and emotional. His *Life* is one of the most important documents for the history of personal religion in this period. Like Eckehart of aristocratic origin, Suso was born by Lake Constance in 1295, and studied at Strasbourg and Cologne. Poetic and impressionable, he is the Minnesinger of the Dominican, as Mechthild of Magdeburg had been of the Benedictine, mystics, combining the two strands which run through the history of German religion—metaphysical speculation and pietistic sentiment. His devotion is given to the Eternal Wisdom, but is expressed in the terms of romantic love. His writings, which shew close acquaintance with Dionysius and Aquinas, are partly addressed to his immediate disciples and fellow-members of the Friends of God, partly directed against the heresies of the Brethren of the Free Spirit. If Tauler is pre-eminently the preacher of the school, Suso's teaching was chiefly imparted in personal ways. Trained in the cloister and practising for many years an extreme asceticism, he became a trainer and director of souls; and under his influence the Dominican nunneries of Switzerland and western Germany, especially Tösz, Unterlinden, Adalhausen, and Engelthal, became hotbeds of an intensive religious culture, closely connected with the movement of the Friends of God. The best known of these women mystics were Christina Ebner (*ob.* 1356) and Adelaide Langmann (*ob.* 1375) of Engelthal, and Margaret Ebner (*ob.* 1351) of Medingen.

The Friends of God, the chief fourteenth-century expression of group mysticism, came into existence as the result of the conjunction of various tendencies and events, local, political, and spiritual. The conditions surrounding institutional religion were of the most distressing kind. The removal of the Papacy to Avignon in 1309 had troubled all pious minds. In 1324 those German cities which supported Lewis of Bavaria in his struggle against the Pope had been placed under an Interdict. Heresy was increasing. The lives of many of the clergy were corrupt. The Black Death, which swept over Western Europe in 1347–48, inevitably left behind it a sense of the divine wrath, increased by the series of earthquakes which visited the Rhine valley about the middle of the century, Basle being almost destroyed in 1356.

Circumstances were favourable for a vigorous revival of mystical religion; and this in fact took place, largely under the influence of devout laymen of the middle class, such as Rulman Merswin of Strasbourg, but also in close association with the work of the great Dominican mystics. The Friends of God drew their inspiration on the one hand from the older German mysticism, especially the apocalyptic prophecies of St Hildegarde and St Elizabeth of Schonau, which they applied to the disorders of their own time as the Franciscan Spirituals had done with the Joachist prophecies. On the other hand, they absorbed through Eckehart's disciples something of his exalted Neoplatonic mysticism, and thus obtained a theological landscape within which their reforming efforts could be staged. The movement appears to have penetrated all ranks of society, and bound together all religious realists in a concerted effort for the revival of the Christian life. It included sober citizens, friars, visionaries, anti-clerical agitators, and ecstatic nuns; and produced a mass of tendency-literature of a visionary and prophetic character. Essentially a movement of reform from within the Church, it presented the familiar features of lay-control, group-formation, a vernacular literature, and a great variety of mystical and inspirational phenomena; in all these points resembling the Franciscan lay-mysticism of Central Italy. The moral standard was austere, many Friends of God practising an extreme asceticism and detachment. The chief centres of the movement lay along the banks of the Rhine, especially at Strasbourg, Basle, and Cologne; but it was also strong in Bavaria. The members formed open groups in the chief towns, though some lived in brotherhood-houses like those of the Beghards. The circles were visited by itinerant prophets; and a considerable literature, which included Suso's and Tauler's works, was circulated amongst them. Apart from the sermons of Tauler, who is its greatest figure, the chief literary monument of the movement is Rulman Merswin's *Book of the Nine Rocks*, which contrasts, in a series of apocalyptic visions, the spiritual ascent to which the Friend of God is called with the corrupt condition of the official Church. This and similar documents shew clearly that the Friends of God considered themselves an "inner church" of spiritual men, acting under direct divine guidance; but in spite of this exalted illuminism, and the critical attitude which they adopted towards the secular clergy, they were and remained orthodox Catholics. Possibly under the influence of their Dominican directors, they combined emphasis upon personal mysticism with great reverence for the sacraments, and carried on a vigorous campaign against the doctrinal and moral excesses of the Brethren of the Free Spirit. The movement produced one literary masterpiece, the exquisite *Theologia Germanica*, attributed to an unknown priest of the Teutonic Order in Frankfort, in which the doctrine of Eckehart is re-interpreted in terms of love and will.

The corporate activities of the Friends of God do not exhaust the history of the German mystical revival. Contemporary with them, and equally significant of the religious temper of the time, are many forgotten visionaries and saints, such as the Franciscan tertiary Luitgarde (*c.* 1290–1348), who, after twenty years as a béguine, founded "in great courage and poverty" the convent of Wittichen in the Black Forest. Luitgarde's immoderate cult of poverty and ignorance suggests the influence of the Fraticelli. Her life abounds in abnormal incidents, and she is said to have travelled, like Catherine of Siena, to Avignon to plead with John XXII. In Flanders too, where the situation was much like that in Germany, mystical religion, fostered by social misery and clerical decadence, flourished both in its orthodox and in its heretical forms. Pious souls retreated to the béguinages, where mystical notions, often of an extravagant kind, were cherished, as we can see from the opening chapters of Ruysbroeck's *XII Béguines*. In 1310 a béguine of Hainault, Marguerite Porette, leader of the sect of Porettists, was burnt in Paris; in Brussels, a few years later, the heretical mystic Bloemardine, a Sister of the Free Spirit, seems to have obtained a great following. Both taught those extreme doctrines of deification and quietism which easily tend to moral and religious anarchy, and are so vigorously denounced by Ruysbroeck (1293–1381), the greatest of the Flemish mystics.

The contemporary of Suso and Tauler, and probably in touch with the leaders of the Friends of God, Ruysbroeck lived till middle age as a secular priest in Brussels, at that time seething with the heresies of Beghards, Lollards, and Béguins. He was active in the campaign against them, especially attacking Bloemardine. In 1343 he retired to the hermitage of Groenendael, where with a few companions he took the Augustinian rule; and here most of his works were composed. Writing in Flemish, in order to reach the public the heretical mystics addressed, Ruysbroeck combined lofty spiritual qualities with a powerful and well-equipped mind. He takes from his predecessors, especially Dionysius, the Victorines, Eckehart, and Aquinas, what he requires for the expression of his own doctrine; and this doctrine corrects the most advanced mysticism of the time in such a sense that, while maintaining its transcendental quality, it remains within the frame of Catholic belief. The Franco-Flemish *Mirror of Simple Souls*, which its fifteenth-century English translator Methley actually attributed to him, shews how far it had once been possible to go without sacrificing orthodoxy. Nevertheless, the prevalence of pantheistic mysticism, and the narrow line between orthodox and heretic, caused a nervous scrutiny and even adverse criticism of some of Ruysbroeck's more profound works. *The Book of Truth*, one of his last writings, was devoted, at the instance of the Carthusians of Herinnes, to clearing himself of the charge of pantheism. Yet in the next generation his doctrines were denounced as excessive by the mystical theologian Gerson, who involved them in a general criticism including the Letter to the Brethren of Mont Dieu.

The fourteenth century witnesses the transition from monastic mysticism, stated in precise theological and philosophical terms and addressing itself to the professed religious, to a more popular type of mystical religion, spread by means of vernacular writings, stated in terms of feeling and experience, and directed to practical results. In this revolution, initiated by the Mendicant Orders, and pursued with violence by the heretics and with more prudence by the orthodox mystics of the Church, Ruysbroeck occupies an important place, as a chief intermediary between traditional and empirical Catholic mysticism. His works, inspired by the Neoplatonists and scholastics, yet convey the impression of a personal experience exceeding that of normal minds. His teaching was spread partly through his vernacular writings, many of which were translated into Latin during his lifetime and widely distributed. In the next century the Franciscan Harphius (*ob.* 1477) and the Carthusian Denys Ryckel (1402–71) wrote under his immediate inspiration. But his chief influence upon religious history was exerted through his personal disciples, who included the most spiritual contemporary minds; and especially through Gerard Groote (1340–84), the founder of the New Devotion.

Gerard is a figure of great importance for the history of late-medieval religion. He was a brilliant and versatile scholar, and had taught at Cologne, where he was probably influenced by the Friends of God; his conversion being completed by the Carthusian Henry de Kalkar—the leader of a group devoted to mystical piety—and by Ruysbroeck, whom he frequently visited at Groenendael. He first became a lay-preacher, his eloquence drawing crowds to hear him; but his biting criticisms of the clergy having cost him his licence, in 1381, with his disciple Florent Radewyns, he founded at Deventer the Brothers of the Common Life. It was largely through this community, with its many schools and houses in the Flemish cities, and that of the Augustinian Canons of Windesheim which sprang from it, that the teaching of the Flemish mystics was disseminated, and initiated a genuine renaissance of personal religion within the Church. Though the "New Devotion" of the Brothers was in essence a simple and practical pietism, it drew its spirit of profound interiority from the works of Ruysbroeck and the classics of Christian mysticism, which were studied and copied in the houses of the Fraternity. It produced a literature of its own. The mystical tracts of Henry de Mande (*c.* 1360–1415), a disciple of Gerard who was known as the Ruysbroeck of the North, the beautiful *Fiery Soliloquy with God* of Gerlac Petersen (1378–1411), and the Lives of the founders by his friend

Thomas à Kempis (1379–1471), shew well the practical yet transcendental temper of its spirituality. But its chief gift to the world was the *Imitatio Christi*, in which we recapture its very spirit, and with it the interior trend characteristic of the best mystical religion at the end of the fourteenth century. Through this book—much of it a *catena* of Biblical and Patristic passages harmonised by one informing spirit—Flemish mysticism became an enduring influence in the religious life of Europe. It is needless to insist on the unique position which it occupies in Christian literature, but more important to recollect that in it we have the fruit of a spirituality derived from the school of Ruysbroeck, and perhaps embodying the actual notes and meditations of his pupil Gerard Groote[1]. Thus the reform which began at Deventer looks back to the genius of Ruysbroeck—its main link with the Catholic mystic tradition—and forward to Nicholas of Cusa and the philosophic mystics of the next century.

In contrast to the philosophic character of German and Flemish mysticism and the tendency towards political action which marks that of Italy and Central Europe, the English fourteenth-century mystics were closely connected with that solitary life which was still the natural refuge of contemplative souls. Hence they appear to have exerted little or no influence on social and ecclesiastical affairs. One unfortunate result of this is that, with the exception of the exuberant and subjective Rolle, the personalities of the English mystics have left no mark on contemporary history. While much has come down to us concerning the character and life of Hildegarde, the first Franciscans, Suso, or Catherine of Siena, we are entirely ignorant of the origin and personal life of Hilton, or the writer of *The Cloud of Unknowing*, and know little of that of Juliana of Norwich. No doubt the roots of English fourteenth-century mysticism, with its emphasis on devotion and neglect of philosophy, and its strong Christocentric bias, go down into that religious stratum which produced such early medieval rhapsodies as the *Orison* and *Wooing of Our Lord*. Much of its writing reproduces on levels of experience the emotional temper of those Middle English religious lyrics based on the *Iesu dulcis memoria* and connected with the cult of the Holy Name. But the school as we know it arises, independently of monastic influence, in the north-eastern and eastern counties; and its works have a marked reference to the solitary life. There seems to have been in this country no inclination within the Church to form lay-groups or inspire lay-movements, such as the Humiliati or the Friends of God. The first definitely mystical writer who has been identified, Margery Kemp (late thirteenth century),

---

[1] Thomas à Kempis still remains on the whole the most probable author of the Latin text. But in a lecture delivered before the Royal Flemish Academy at Ghent, 24 June 1928, P. van Ginneken S.J. gave reasons based on the examination of numerous MSS for the belief that Bk. I was first composed in Dutch by G. Groote and circulated in that form.

was an anchoress of Lynn. Richard Rolle of Hampole (*c.* 1300–49) was a wandering hermit. The two great mystical treatises of the next generation—the anonymous *Cloud of Unknowing* and Walter Hilton's *Scale of Perfection*—were written for recluses. Finally, Juliana of Norwich (1343–died after 1413) was an anchoress. English mysticism, then, is mostly concerned with individual spiritual culture. Its main works being either confessional, or intended for the instruction of lay persons—especially women—unable to read Latin, it is intimately connected with the beginnings of vernacular literature. The number of early MSS surviving, and also the quantity of anonymous mystical pieces found in MS collections, prove that its products were deeply appreciated, especially perhaps in Brigittine and Carthusian houses. But its work in the religious complex was quietly done. Though Rolle attacked monastic luxury and deeply desired the reform of the clergy, he led no movement for these ends. Again, the English mystics are little interested in speculation; and thus both avoid the metaphysical excesses of German and Flemish mysticism and fall short of its greatest achievements. Though Rolle, Hilton, and the writer of the *Cloud* were trained theologians, and Juliana of Norwich shews remarkable understanding of Christian Platonism, all are content to take their philosophic conceptions from St Augustine, Dionysius the Areopagite, the Victorines, St Bernard, and Aquinas. Richard of St Victor was particularly appreciated here, and has strongly influenced Hilton and the writer of the *Cloud*. But the ruling intention of these writers is practical; they abound in shrewd advice and homely imagery. A peculiar characteristic is the almost total absence of Eucharistic references, a feature which sharply distinguishes them from their Continental contemporaries.

Nevertheless, the English school, though so national in character, is influenced by Continental mysticism and articulated to the great Catholic tradition of the contemplative life. Means of contact were not lacking. The works of the Franciscan and Dominican mystics quickly circulated through the houses of those Orders. Early translations of Suso, Tauler, and Catherine of Siena survive. At Knaresborough in 1315, Edward II had established four Flemish hermits from Ypres. Rolle, a layman and vigorous religious individualist, whose anti-clerical temper and claim to direct inspiration first caused collision with the clergy, and afterwards recommended his writings to the Lollards, was a trained scholar, sent to Oxford as a boy. Recent research shews that he may also have spent one if not two periods at the Sorbonne, where he would receive the influences of contemporary European mysticism and learn something too of the prevalent heresies. The works of the Spiritual Franciscans—who may well have affected him—were well known in Paris at that time. He cannot entirely have escaped contact with Joachism, the ideas of Eckehart, or the spirit that produced the Friends of God.

In Rolle's exuberant character the prophet, devotee, and lyrical poet combine; as in some of those Franciscan mystics to whom he is temperamentally akin, and whose passion for poverty he shares. Like them he blends mystical emotion with moral austerity, and like them seems to have led by turns the life of wandering preacher and recluse. His emotional and poetic mysticism is intimately connected with the cult of the Holy Name, at that time the favourite expression of Christocentric fervour. He attracted disciples, and his works were quickly and widely circulated; but his large and learned commentaries on the Psalter, and the fact that surviving MSS are chiefly from monastic libraries, suggest that his reading public was mainly of the religious class. Syon House, which had Yorkshire founders, and the Shene Charterhouse, which was in touch with Mount Grace, were peculiarly rich in Rolle MSS. During the 150 years preceding the Reformation, he was widely read both here and on the Continent, where he was known before the end of the fourteenth century. The contagious quality of his emotional fervour, the beautiful rhapsodies addressed to the Name of Jesus, and the entire absence of abstract and difficult doctrine, are enough to account for his popularity. His authentic English works are three epistles and a Commentary on the Psalms, written for women disciples, with five prose fragments and a few poems. His more important mystical writings, the *Melum* and *Incendium Amoris*, are in Latin. The first is mainly a glorification of the hermit's career, which is sharply contrasted with that of the regular clergy, in terms which explain and even excuse his unpopularity with the authorities. In this distinctly egoistic work Rolle claims already to have attained the height of sanctity; but in the *Incendium*, written perhaps ten years later, he describes more humbly and attractively his spiritual course. Rolle's reputation as a saint stood so high in the North that after his death an Office—our chief though not wholly reliable source for the facts of his early life—was composed in his honour; and though he was never canonised, a cultus survived at his shrine for over 200 years.

Rolle owes his historical importance, however, more to his religious and literary influence than to his quality as a mystic. Here he is outdistanced by his chief followers, especially the writer of *The Cloud of Unknowing*, and Walter Hilton, an Austin Canon of Thurgarton near Nottingham (*ob.* 1395–96). *The Cloud of Unknowing*, a remarkable treatise on contemplation addressed to a young recluse, represents the introduction of the Dionysian writings into English literature; and the number of surviving MSS attests its popularity. We have four epistles and a free translation of the *Mystical Theology*, entitled *Dionise Hid Divinite*, by the same unknown author, a mystic who writes in a North Midland dialect, is acquainted with Rolle's work, but otherwise gives us no clue to his identity. His work, which shews much philosophic and psychological knowledge, deals with levels of spiritual experience untouched by Rolle, and is addressed exclusively to those called to contemplation. We note in him, as characteristic of the English school, that the use made of

Neoplatonism is always practical, never speculative. Walter Hilton, whose *Scale of Perfection* became and remained a devotional classic second only in popularity to the *Imitatio*, is more general in his appeal; and is, perhaps, in his mingled practical and transcendental teaching, the most typical mystic of the English school. The rapid circulation of all these works shews the continued existence, here as elsewhere, of a tradition of spiritual culture within the Catholic Church, vigorously opposed both to Quietism and to Lollardy, which Hilton attacks in the strongest terms. Juliana of Norwich, one of the most individual products of this tradition, certainly depends on it. Traces of Hilton's influence have been noted in her *Revelations of Divine Love*; and it is possible that they may have met, for she was over fifty when he died. Either by reading or oral instruction, Juliana had absorbed much theological knowledge, which has mingled with the fruits of intuition in her singularly poetic and sensitive mind to produce the spiritual masterpiece by which she is known. This in its developed form—for two versions exist—seems to represent her meditations upon a single mystical experience, occurring at the crisis of an illness in her thirtieth year. Juliana appears never to have enjoyed the popularity of Rolle and Hilton, and so far only one early MS of her *Revelations* has come to light. Until a critical text is possible we cannot estimate her sources, or her place in the history of English religion. Her connexion with the Benedictine house of Carrow links her with the monastic tradition; while the intimate relation of Norwich with the Low Countries makes us suspect the possible influence of Flemish and German mysticism, for the works of Suso and Ruysbroeck were in circulation before her *Revelations* were composed. Apart from a few notices in her book, however, we are completely ignorant of her life and origin. Yet she is the first English woman of letters; and through her we learn what the life of the anchorhold could be and produce at its best.

The religious history of Italy in the second half of the fourteenth century is dominated by another woman of genius, the Dominican tertiary St Catherine of Siena (1347–80). In St Catherine we see mysticism in action, the spiritual realist at grips with the disorders of contemporary life. We incline, however, to attribute to her political action a unique character it did not really possess. The scandals she attacked were patent; and the particular aims she set before herself were the objects of all who had the welfare of Christianity at heart. The continued exile of the Papacy and the condition of the clergy created chronic dissatisfaction in all religious minds; and produced within the Church a series of reforming mystics whose denunciations exceed in violence anything uttered by its enemies. In Siena itself Giovanni Colombini (*ob.* 1367) had founded the congregation of Gesuati, devoted to absolute poverty and evangelical ideals, who surrounded Urban V with their ragged and disconcerting enthusiasm on his return to Rome. The preaching of the Gesuati caused a transient revival in Siena and Tuscany, especially among the friars, and helped to form St Catherine's religious environment. From another point of view, Catherine took over and completed the work begun by Birgitta (Bridget) of Sweden (1303–73). Birgitta, a mystic and visionary of the Hildegardian type, believed herself called by God to purify the Church and end the exile of the Papacy. After founding the Brigittine Order in 1346, she went in 1349 to Rome, where she ended her days. When Urban V retired to Avignon in 1370, she prophesied with accuracy his coming death. Driven by her revelations, she visited Gregory XI at Avignon, denouncing the immorality of the clergy, demanding his return to the Vatican, and warning him of the price of refusal. Her final appeal reached Gregory in 1373. Four months later she died, and St Catherine of Siena—whose political letters begin in 1372—took up her unfinished task.

At this time, aged twenty-six and at the height of her reputation, Catherine had only seven years to live. During a four-hour trance in which she nearly died, she believed that she had received a divine command to leave her cell and city and "witness before small and great," including the Supreme Pontiff. Travelling now to Avignon in her turn, she pleaded with the Pope to such effect that he sailed from Marseilles in September 1376, she going overland to Genoa, where he visited her secretly and received from her courage to enter Rome. When we consider the initiative and self-sacrifice involved in the decision of a French Pope, knowing no Italian, to leave his country and family and establish himself in strange and hostile surroundings at the behest of a young woman recommended by nothing but her sanctity and simple-mindedness, we obtain from this incident a vivid impression of Catherine's power. Though ecstatic and other abnormal phenomena abound in her life, she was no mere visionary, but a woman of genius controlled by her strong sense of vocation, whose astonishing public career only represents one aspect of her greatness. Born of the people and with little education, her spiritual power matured early; and at twenty she was already the centre of a group of disciples, including priests, scholars, and aristocrats, over whom she exercised an unquestioned authority. In private life an extreme ascetic, the transforming influence she exerted, the courage with which she opposed vested interests and attacked apparently impossible tasks, the mingled authority and humility of her writings—which are among the masterpieces of early Italian literature—all prove her spiritual transcendence. Her follower Barduccio called her with reason the "Mother of thousands of souls," and at the culmination of her career the sight of her face was enough to effect a conversion. St Catherine's letters, of which over 400 survive, shew the range of her interests and influence, extending from an intimate care of individuals to the pacification of Italy and the regeneration of the Church. Her aim was nothing less than the purging and spiritualising of political and ecclesiastical life, by applying to it the standards of contemplation and inspiring its rulers with that invincible spirit of charity and courage which possessed her own soul. The words with which her *Dialogue* begins: "Wishing to follow the truth in a more virile way"—shew well the temper of her mind, which was doubtless cultivated by the Dominican and other scholars in her immediate circle. By the time her public career began, she had obtained from this or other sources considerable theological knowledge, and was well acquainted with the ruling ideas and symbolism of Christian mysticism. While her heart-broken accounts of clerical corruption are among the most terrible we possess, her vision of the Church and its destiny has an almost epic greatness. She was a militant mystic; and though her political work was soon undone, the impress of her amazing personality remained. "This poor little woman shames us by her valour!" said Urban VI when she appeared before him in 1378, racked by illness, but intrepid still.

In Ruysbroeck, Juliana of Norwich, and Catherine of Siena, we have three differing yet typical manifestations of the developed mysticism of the fourteenth century, with its often sublime transcendentalism, tender feeling, and moral and reforming zeal. It represents the reaction of really religious natures to the miseries of society and manifest disorders of the Church. It is probable that in this period the only monastic houses in "spiritual good health" were those where mystical piety flourished; and, in addition to these, we have evidence of the existence of many individual mystics, of whom most achieved only a local reputation. As the century matured, the character of its mysticism had gradually changed. The strict schools of monastic contemplation, the Benedictine and Augustinian ideals of the twelfth and early thirteenth centuries, were more and more criticised. The anchoretic life was no longer taken for granted. The more humanistic religious outlook encouraged by the friars shewed itself on the one hand in the steady increase of such Christocentric devotions as the cults of the Precious Blood and the Holy Name, with their strong emotional emphasis. On the other hand, it encouraged a democratic effort to bring into the common life a realistic spirituality which might or might not find nourishment in ceremonial and sacramental religion, but could flourish independently of the often corrupt institutional life. In the Franciscan Tertiaries, the Friends of God, and the *Devotio Moderna* we see the orthodox side of this movement. The often extravagant mystical heresies of the fourteenth and early fifteenth centuries shew the inevitable results of an uncontrolled popularisation of principles too abstract for general use, coupled with a rejection of the safeguarding influences of tradition. The final positions reached by many of these heresies were equally repugnant to normal morality and to common sense. Thus the history of mysticism in the fourteenth century is punctuated by the burnings of those—including some of the less prudent Friends of God—who had crossed the narrow line between an exalted and an insurgent spirituality.

The position of Catholic mysticism at the opening of the fifteenth century is well shewn in the significant figure of the chancellor Gerson, at once a mystic in his own right and a keen and discriminating critic of the mass of religious writings, movements, and phenomena claiming the title of mysticism. Gerson was a second Bonaventura, a man of true and humble sanctity, a born psychologist, a lover in all things of the golden mean. Much experience had given him a dread of extravagances in religion, and an intense distrust of the visionaries and pseudo-mystics who swarmed in Flanders and France at the end of the fourteenth century. His hostile reference to the women whose visions brought back Gregory XI to Rome, and so gave rise to the Great Schism, reminds us that two opinions were possible about the activities of St Bridget and St Catherine of Siena. Yet Gerson's sincerity and discriminating power is proved by two facts. First, that in spite of his anti-feminist and anti-visionary bias, he was one of the two theologians who guaranteed the authenticity of the voices of St Joan of Arc (1412–31). Next, that though a severe critic of Ruysbroeck's more extreme doctrines, he defended at the Council of Constance (1418) the Brothers of the Common Life, whom a Dutch Dominican had charged with heresy. Gerson's own works are partly concerned with the criticism of false mysticism, and also of the Neoplatonic and pantheistic tendencies in the Catholic mystics; partly with rules for the "discernment of spirits"; and partly with his own theory of the contemplative life, in which he keeps close to the Victorines and St Bonaventura. The fact that he has been regarded as a probable author of the *Imitatio* indicates the character and tone of his spirituality.

Save for a few scattered stars, of whom only one is of the first magnitude, we reach with Gerson the end of the classic period of medieval mysticism. The fifteenth century witnesses its gradual decline before the growing forces of humanism. A tendency to repetition, a failure to make fresh devotional discoveries, mark the dropping temperature characteristic of a transitional epoch. In Flanders the long life of Thomas à Kempis (1379–1471) covers the careers on the one hand of such merely reminiscent mystics as Harphius (*ob.* 1477) or the pathological visionary St Lydwine of Schiedam (1380–1432), and on the other of the saintly scholars, Denis the Carthusian (1402–71) and Cardinal Nicholas of Cusa (1401–64). In England in the same period, religious pieces inspired by Rolle and his followers continued to be produced; and the numerous fifteenth-century MSS of their works and those of other fourteenth-century mystics shew that mysticism was still a living interest in the Church, though no longer producing great and creative personalities. In Italy the exquisite yet entirely traditional spirituality revealed in the paintings of Fra Angelico (1387–1455) shews us the mystical piety of the early fifteenth century at its best. It is characteristic of the period that we find the older and truly medieval types of spiritual feeling and endeavour continuing side by side with those which look towards newer embodiments. Thus we still have reforming mystics, intent on the regeneration of religious Orders or religious practice. Such are the Franciscans St Colette of Corbie (1381–1447), St Bernardino of Siena (1380–1444), and St Catherine of Bologna (1413–63). St Colette, who combined mystical fervour with immense practical energy, began life as a béguine. At twenty-two she was enclosed at Corbie as an anchoress, but was driven by her visions to leave her cell and undertake the reform of the Poor Clares. Travelling to Nice, she received the authority of Benedict XIII for this work, and founded thirteen houses of the Colettine reform before her death. St Bernardino of Siena, through whose preaching a wave of spiritual fervour passed over Central Italy, was glad to call himself her disciple. He shares with her, and with his compatriots St Giovanni da Capistrano (1385–1456) and the ecstatic Clarisse, St Catherine of Bologna, the credit of the transient revival of Franciscan mysticism, with its evangelical enthusiasm and moral demands, which marked the first half of the fifteenth century.

Side by side with this, the current of spirituality arising in the New Devotion, and ultimately derived from the great mind of Ruysbroeck, is found operative in such typical scholars of the early Renaissance as Cardinal Nicholas of Cusa and his friend Denis the Carthusian. Here both intellectual speculation and reforming energy are transfused by the spiritual realism of the mystic. Denis, one of the great figures of fifteenth-century religion, was first an obscure secular priest; but in 1423 he entered the Charterhouse of Roermond, of which he became prior. His combination of ascetic and intellectual intensity—his works fill 45 large volumes, and he claimed with reason "an iron head and steel stomach"—gave him a European reputation for learning and sanctity. A mystic, subject to visions and ecstasies, and a profound student of Dionysius and Ruysbroeck, he was yet keenly interested in contemporary life. He advised from his cell the chief personages of the State, and accompanied Nicholas of Cusa on his reforming missions. Many of his visions were apocalyptic; and he steadily prophesied calamity for the Church if she delayed the work of reform. Yet Denis was not spiritually creative; and here he is typical of his period. His works, immense in range, mainly simplify and make accessible the lofty teachings of his predecessors, as Deventer had made accessible to ordinary men the monastic discipline of meditation and prayer.

Nicholas of Cusa was trained at Deventer, where sound learning no less than mystical piety flourished. He was an enthusiastic student of Eckehart and the Neoplatonists; and was also influenced by the writings of the Majorcan scholar-mystic Raymond Lull (*ob.* 1315). These studies, congenial to his profoundly metaphysical intellect, at first gave Nicholas' mysticism a coldly speculative character. But later, when beset by the many exacting duties of a great ecclesiastic, his vision of Reality was brought into more immediate relation with the demands of practical life. As between the intense intellectualism of the scholastics and the anti-intellectualism of those who identified mystical knowledge with the "wise ignorance"

of the Areopagite, Nicholas, as we see in his *De Visione Dei*, takes an
intermediate position, recognising the claims of both mind and heart.
This little masterpiece—the final flower of Flemish mysticism—was written
for the Benedictines of Tegernsee, who had applied to him for spiritual
help. In its combination of intimate and metaphysical feeling, it expounds
a mysticism too profound to be popular, but which was the inspiration of
a life spent partly in scholarship, partly in the struggle that has called
so many of the mystics to restore the purity and force of a Christianity
which in Nicholas' eyes had "degenerated into an appearance."

Though nourished on the medieval tradition, Nicholas of Cusa is not
truly a medieval figure. With him we are definitely moving away from
the Middle Ages; and with the last great mystical saint of the period—
St Catherine of Genoa (1447–1510)—we finally part company with them.
While her compatriots, the widely venerated Dominican *beati*, Columba
of Rieti (1430–1501) and Osanna Andreassi of Mantua (1449–1505),
merely continue in their visions and denunciations the tradition of St
Catherine of Siena, bringing no contribution of their own, Catherine of
Genoa lifts Christian Platonism to fresh levels of fertility. She is a lady
of the Renaissance with a genius for the spiritual life. She joins no religious Order, leads no campaign, performs no miracles. Her contemporary
Savonarola (of whose existence she betrays no knowledge) is led from
contemplation to a hopeless conflict with society; and at last to martyrdom. But Catherine Fieschi is content to teach her sublime doctrine to
a small group of disciples, and to establish and rule with admirable
common sense the first modern hospital. In her, mystical religion com-
pletes its transition from the medieval to the modern world.

LIST OF ABBREVIATIONS OF TITLES
OF PERIODICALS, SOCIETIES, ETC.

(1) The following abbreviations are used for titles of periodicals:

AB.   Analecta Bollandiana. Paris and Brussels. 1882 ff.

AHR.   American Historical Review. New York and London. 1895 ff.

AKKR.   Archiv für katholisches Kirchenrecht. Innsbruck. 1857–61. Mayence. 1862 ff.

AOG.   Archiv für Kunde österreichischer Geschichts-Quellen. Vienna. 1848–65; *continued as* Archiv für österreichische Geschichte. 1865 ff.

Arch. Ven.   (*and* N. Arch. Ven.; Arch. Ven.-Tri.). Archivio veneto. Venice. 40 vols. 1871–90; *continued as* Nuovo archivio veneto. 1st series. 20 vols. 1891–1900. New series. 42 vols. 1901–21. *And* Archivio veneto-tridentino. 10 vols. 1922–6. *And* Archivio veneto. 5th series. 1927 ff., in progress.

ASAK.   Anzeiger für schweizerische Alterthumskunde. Zurich. 1869 ff.

ASI.   Archivio storico italiano. Florence. Ser. I. 20 vols. and App. 9 vols. 1842–53. Index. 1857. Ser. nuova. 18 vols. 1855–63. Ser. III. 26 vols. 1865–77. Indexes to II and III. 1874. Supplt. 1877. Ser. IV. 20 vols. 1878–87. Index. 1891. Ser. V. 50 vols. 1888–1912. Index. 1900. Ser. VI. Anni 71–81. 22 vols. 1913–23. Ser. VII. Anni 82 etc. 1924 ff., in progress. (Index up to 1927 in Catalogue of The London Library. Vol. I. 1913, and Supplts. 1920, 29.)

ASL.   Archivio storico lombardo. Milan. 1874 ff.

ASPN.   Archivio storico per le province napoletane. Naples. 1876 ff.

ASRSP.   Archivio della Società romana di storia patria. Rome. 1878 ff.

BEC.   Bibliothèque de l'École des chartes. Paris. 1839 ff.

BISI.   Bullettino dell' Istituto storico italiano. Rome. 1886 ff.

BRAH.   Boletin de la R. Academia de la historia. Madrid. 1877 ff.

CQR.   Church Quarterly Review. London. 1875 ff.

DZG.   Deutsche Zeitschrift für Geschichtswissenschaft. Freiburg-im-Breisgau. 1889–98. *Continued as* HVJS. *See below.*

DZKR.   Deutsche Zeitschrift für Kirchenrecht. Freiburg-im-Breisgau. 1891 ff.

EHR.   English Historical Review. London. 1886 ff.

FDG.   Forschungen zur deutschen Geschichte. Göttingen. 1860 ff.

HJ.   Historisches Jahrbuch. Munich. 1880 ff.

HVJS.   Historische Vierteljahrsschrift. Leipsic. 1898 ff.

HZ.   Historische Zeitschrift (von Sybel). Munich and Berlin. 1859 ff.

JQR.   Jewish Quarterly Review. London. 1889–1908. New series. Philadelphia. 1910 ff.

JTS.   Journal of Theological Studies. London. 1900 ff.

MA.   Le moyen âge. Paris. 1888 ff.

MGWJ.   Monatsschrift für die Geschichte und Wissenschaft des Judenthums. Dresden, and later Breslau. 1851 ff.

MIOGF.   Mittheilungen des Instituts für österreichische Geschichtsforschung. Innsbruck. 1880 ff.

Neu. Arch.   Neues Archiv der Gesellschaft für ältere deutsche Geschichtskunde. Hanover and Leipsic. 1876 ff.

NRDF (*and* RDF).   Nouvelle Revue hist. de droit français et étranger. Paris. 1877–1921; *continued as* Revue hist. de droit français et étranger. Paris. 1922 ff.

QFIA.   Quellen und Forschungen aus italienischen Archiven und Bibliotheken. Rome. 1898 ff.

RBén.   Revue bénédictine. Maredsous. 1890 ff.

RDF.   *See above*, NRDF.

REJ.   Revue des études juives. Paris. 1880 ff.

RH.   Revue historique. Paris. 1876 ff.

RHE.   Revue d'histoire ecclésiastique. Louvain. 1900 ff.
RQH.   Revue des questions historiques. Paris. 1866 ff.
RSH.   Revue de synthèse historique. Paris. 1900 ff.
SBAW.   Sitzungsberichte der (kön.) bayerischen Akademie der Wissenschaften.
            [Philos.-philol.-hist. Classe.] Munich. 1891 ff.
SKAW.   Sitzungsberichte der (kaiserlichen) Akademie der Wissenschaften.
            [Philos.-hist. Classe.] Vienna. 1848 ff.
SPAW.   Sitzungsberichte der (kön.) preussischen Akademie der Wissenschaften.
            Berlin. 1882 ff.
TRHS.   Transactions of the Royal Historical Society. London. 1871 ff.
ZDMG.   Zeitschrift der deutschen morgenländischen Gesellschaft. Leipsic. 1846 ff.
ZKG.   Zeitschrift für Kirchengeschichte. Gotha. 1877 ff.
ZR.   Zeitschrift für Rechtsgeschichte. Weimar. 1861–78. *Continued as*
ZSR.   Zeitschrift der Savigny-Stiftung für Rechtswissenschaft. Weimar. 1880 ff.
            [Each vol. contains a Romanistische, a Germanistische, and after
            1911, a Kanonistische Abteilung.]
ZWT.   Zeitschrift für wissenschaftliche Theologie. Frankfort-on-Main. 1858 ff.

     (2) Other abbreviations used are:

AcadIBL.   Académie des Inscriptions et Belles-Lettres.
AcadIP.   Académie Impériale de Pétersbourg. (*Now* Acad. des sciences de l'Union
            des républiques soviétiques socialistes. Leningrad.)
AllgDB.   Allgemeine deutsche Biographie. *See Gen. Bibl.* i.
ASBen.   *See* Mabillon and Achery *in Gen. Bibl.* iv.
ASBoll.   Acta Sanctorum Bollandiana. *See Gen. Bibl.* iv.
BAW.   (Königliche) bayerische Akademie der Wissenschaften. Munich.
BGén.   Nouvelle Biographie générale. *See Gen. Bibl.* i.
BHE.   Bibliothèque de l'École des Hautes Études. *See Gen. Bibl.* v.
Bouquet.   *See* Rerum Gallicarum...scriptores *in Gen. Bibl.* iv.
BUniv.   Biographie universelle. *See Gen. Bibl.* i.
Cal.SP.   Calendars of State Papers, Close Rolls, Patent Rolls, etc., issued by the
            State Paper Office, Public Record Office, and General Register House.
Class. hist. Classiques de l'histoire de France au moyen âge. *See Gen. Bibl.* iv.
Coll.doc.   Collection de documents inédits sur l'histoire de France. *See Gen. Bibl.* iv.
Coll.textes. Collection de textes pour servir à l'étude et à l'enseignement de l'histoire.
            See Gen. Bibl. iv.
CSEL.   Corpus scriptorum ecclesiasticorum latinorum. *See Gen. Bibl.* iv.
CSHB.   Corpus scriptorum historiae Byzantinae.
DNB.   Dictionary of National Biography. *See Gen. Bibl.* i.
EcfrAR.   Écoles françaises d'Athènes et de Rome. Paris.
EETS.   Early English Text Society. *See Gen. Bibl.* iv.
EncBr.   Encyclopaedia Britannica. *See Gen. Bibl.* i.
Fonti.   Fonti per la storia d' Italia. *See Gen. Bibl.* iv.
KAW.   (Kaiserliche) Akademie der Wissenschaften. Vienna.
Mansi.   *See Gen. Bibl.* iv.
MGH.   Monumenta Germaniae Historica. *See Gen. Bibl.* iv.
MHP.   Monumenta historiae patriae. Turin. *See Gen. Bibl.* iv.
MPG.   Migne's Patrologiae cursus completus. Ser. graeco-latina. [Greek texts
            with Latin translations in parallel columns.] *See Gen. Bibl.* iv.
MPL.   Migne's Patrologiae cursus completus. Ser. latina. *See Gen. Bibl.* iv.
PAW.   (Königliche) preussische Akademie der Wissenschaften. Berlin.
P.R.O.   Public Record Office.
RAH.   Real Academia de la Historia. Madrid.
RC.   Record Commissioners. *See Gen. Bibl.* iv.
Rolls.   Rerum Britannicarum medii aevi scriptores. *See Gen. Bibl.* iv.
RR.II.SS.   *See* Muratori *in Gen. Bibl.* iv.
SGUS.   Scriptores rerum Germanicarum in usum scholarum. *See* Monumenta
            Germaniae Historica *in Gen. Bibl.* iv.
SHF.   Société de l'histoire de France. *See Gen. Bibl.* iv.
SRD.   Scriptores rerum Danicarum medii aevi. *See Gen. Bibl.* v.

Abh.	Abhandlungen.	mem.	memoir.
antiq.	antiquarian, antiquaire.	mém.	mémoire.
app.	appendix.	n.s.	new series.
coll.	collection.	progr.	programme.
disc.	discourse, discurso.	publ.	published, publié.
diss.	dissertation.	R. ⎫	real, reale.
ed., edn.	edited, edition.	r. ⎭	
enl.	enlarged.	repr.	reprinted.
hist.	history, histoire, historical,	rev.	revised.
	historique, historisch.	roy.	royal, royale.
Jahrb.	Jahrbuch.	ser.	series.
	⎧kaiserlich.	soc.	society, société, società.
k.	⎨königlich.	stor.	storico, storica.
	⎩koninklijk.	Viert.	Vierteljahrsschrift.

GENERAL BIBLIOGRAPHY.

I. DICTIONARIES, BIBLIOGRAPHIES, AND GENERAL WORKS OF REFERENCE.

Allgemeine deutsche Biographie. Ed. Liliencron, R. von, and Wegele, F. X. (Hist. Commission BAW.) 56 vols. Leipsic. 1875–1912. (AllgDB.)

Annuario bibliografico della storia d' Italia. 1902 ff.

Ballester, R. Bibliografía de la historia de España. Gerona. 1921. [Select.]

Balzani, U. Le cronache italiane nel Medio Evo. 3rd edn. Milan. 1909.

Below, G. von, and Meinecke, F. edd. Handbuch der mittelalt. und neu. Geschichte. Munich. 1903 ff., in progress. (Below-Meinecke.)

Bernheim, E. Lehrbuch der historischen Methode und der Geschichtsphilosophie. 5th and 6th enl. edn. Leipsic. 1908.

Biographie nationale de Belgique. Brussels. 1866 ff., in progress. (Acad. Roy. des sciences, des lettres, et des beaux arts.)

Biographie universelle, ancienne et moderne. Ed. Michaud, L. G. and others. 45 vols. (Publ. by Desplaces.) Paris. 1843–65. [Greatly improved edn. of earlier work, 1811–28, and supplt., 1832–62.] (BUniv.)

Boüard, A. de. Manuel de diplomatique, française et pontificale. Vol. i. Paris. 1929, in progress.

Bresslau, H. Handbuch der Urkundenlehre für Deutschland und Italien. 2nd edn. enl. 2 vols. in 3 pts. Leipsic. 1912–31.

Cabrol, F. and Leclercq, H. Dictionnaire d'archéologie chrétienne et de liturgie. Vols. i–x. i (in 19 pts.). Paris. 1907 ff., in progress.

Calvi, E. Bibliografia generale di Roma medioevale e moderna. Pt. i. Medio Evo. Rome. 1906. Supplt. 1908.

Capasso, B. Le fonti della storia delle provincie napolitane dal 568 al 1500. Ed. Mastrojanni, E. O. Naples. 1902.

Cappelli, A. Dizionario di abbreviature latine ed italiane (Lexicon abbreviaturarum). 3rd edn. Milan. 1929.

Ceillier, R. Histoire générale des auteurs sacrés et ecclésiastiques. 23 vols. Paris. 1729–63. New edn. 14 vols. in 15. Paris. 1858–69.

Chevalier, C. U. J. Répertoire des sources historiques du moyen âge. Bio-bibliographie. Paris. 1883–8. Rev. edn. 2 vols. 1905–7. Topo-bibliographie. Montbéliard. 1894–1903.

Dahlmann, F. C. and Waitz, G. Quellenkunde der deutschen Geschichte. 9th edn. Haering, H. Leipsic. 1931. Index. 1932.

Dictionary of National Biography. Ed. Stephen, L. and Lee, S. 63 vols. London. 1885–1900. 1st supplt. 3 vols. 1901. Errata vol. 1904. Re-issue. 22 vols. 1908–9. 2nd supplt. 3 vols. 1912. 3rd supplt. 1927. (DNB.)

Dictionnaire de biographie française. Ed. Balteau, J. and others. Paris. 1929 ff., in progress.

Du Cange, C. du Fresne. Glossarium ad scriptores mediae et infimae Latinitatis. Edns. of Henschel, 7 vols. Paris. 1840–50; and Favre, 10 vols. Niort. 1883–7.

—— Glossarium ad scriptores mediae et infimae Graecitatis. 2 vols. Lyons. 1688.

Egidi, P. La storia medioevale. (Guide bibliografiche, 8–9.) Rome. 1922. [Publications on Italy.]

Encyclopaedia Britannica. 11th and 13th edn. 32 vols. Cambridge. London and New York. 1910–26. 14th edn. 24 vols. London and New York. 1929. (EncBr.)

Encyclopaedia of Islam. A dictionary of the geography, ethnography, and biography of the Muhammadan peoples. Ed. Houtsma, M. T., Arnold, T. W., and Basset, R. Leiden and London. 1913 ff., in progress.

Ersch, J. S. and Gruber, J. G. Allgemeine Encyklopädie der Wissenschaften und Künste. Berlin. 1818–90. (Ersch-Gruber.) [Incomplete.]

Giry, A. Manuel de diplomatique. 2nd edn. 2 vols. Paris. 1925.

Giuseppi, M. S. Guide to the Manuscripts preserved in the Public Record Office. 2 vols. London. 1923–4.

Grässe, J. G. T. Lehrbuch einer allgemeinen Litterärgeschichte aller bekannten Völker der Welt von der ältesten bis auf die neueste Zeit. 4 vols. Leipsic. 1837–59.

Gröber, G. *ed.* Grundriss der romanischen Philologie. 2 vols. Strasbourg. 1888–1902. 2nd edn. Vol. I. 1904–6. Neue Folge. I. iv. 1914.

Gross, C. Bibliography of British Municipal History including Gilds and Parliamentary Representation. (Harvard Hist. Studies. v.) New York. 1897.

—— Sources and Literature of English History from the earliest times to about 1485. 2nd edn. enl. London. 1915.

Hardy, T. D. Descriptive catalogue of materials relating to the history of Great Britain and Ireland to the end of the reign of Henry VII. 3 vols. in 4. (Rolls.) 1862–71.

Hastings, J. and Selbie, J. A. Encyclopaedia of Religion and Ethics. 13 vols. Edinburgh and New York. 1908–26.

Herre, P., Hofmeister, A., and Stübe, R. Quellenkunde zur Weltgeschichte. Leipsic. 1910.

Herzog, J. J. and Hauck, A. Real-Encyklopädie für protestantische Theologie und Kirche. 3rd edn. 24 vols. Leipsic. 1896–1913.

Holtzendorff, F. von. Encyklopädie der Rechtswissenschaft. 5th edn. Leipsic. 1890. 6th edn. Kohler, J. 2 vols. Leipsic. 1904. Vol. I. 7th edn. 1913. (Holtzendorff-Kohler.)

Jahresberichte für deutsche Geschichte. Ed. Brackmann, A. and Hartung, F. Jahrg. 1925 ff. Leipsic. 1927 ff., in progress.

Jansen, M. and Schmitz-Kallenberg, L. Historiographie und Quellen der deutschen Geschichte bis 1500. 2nd edn. (Meister's Grundriss, I. vii. *See below.*) 1914.

Krumbacher, K. Geschichte der byzantinischen Literatur. *See below,* v.

Lichtenberger, F. Encyclopédie des sciences religieuses. 13 vols. Paris. 1877–82.

Lorenz, O. Deutschlands Geschichtsquellen im Mittelalter seit der Mitte des 13 Jahrhts. 3rd edn. 2 vols. Berlin. 1886–7.

Maigne d'Arnis, W. H. Lexicon manuale ad scriptores mediae et infimae Latinitatis. (Publ. by Migne.) Paris. 1858. Repr. 1866 and 1890.

Manzoni, L. Bibliografia statutaria e storica italiana. 2 vols. in 3. Bologna. 1876–92. I. Bibl. d. statuti, ordini, e legge dei municipii. 2 pts. II. Bibl. storica municipale, etc. A–E. [No more publ.]

Meister, A. *ed.* Grundriss der Geschichtswissenschaft zur Einführung in das Studium der deutschen Geschichte des Mittelalters und der Neuzeit. Leipsic. 1906 ff. 2nd edn. 1912 ff., in progress.

Molinier, A. Les Sources de l'histoire de France des origines aux guerres d'Italie (1494). 6 vols. (Manuels de bibliographie historique, III. i.) Paris. 1901–6.

Monod, G. Bibliographie de l'histoire de France depuis les origines jusqu'en 1789. Paris. 1888.

Nouvelle Biographie générale,...avec les renseignements bibliographiques. Ed. Höfer, J. C. F. 46 vols. (Publ. by Didot frères.) Paris. 1854–66. (BGén.)

Oudin, Casimir. Commentarius de scriptoribus ecclesiae antiquae illorumque scriptis tam impressis quam manuscriptis adhuc extantibus in celebrioribus Europae bibliothecis a Bellarmino, etc. omissis ad annum MCCCCLX. 3 vols. Frankfort-on-M. and Leipsic. 1722.

Paetow, L. J. Guide to the study of Medieval History. Rev. edn. (Mediaeval Acad. of America.) New York; and London. 1931.

Paul, H. *ed.* Grundriss der germanischen Philologie. 3rd edn. Strasbourg. 1911 ff.

Pirenne, H. Bibliographie de l'histoire de Belgique. 3rd edn., with the collaboration of Nowé, H. and Obreen, H. Brussels. 1931.

Potthast, A. Bibliotheca historica medii aevi. Wegweiser durch die Geschichtswerke des europäischen Mittelalters bis 1500. 2nd edn. 2 vols. Berlin. 1896.

Redlich, O. and Erben, W. Urkundenlehre. Pts. I and III. (Below-Meinecke. *See above.*) Munich. 1907, 11.

Rivista storica italiana. Turin. 1884 ff., in progress. [Up to 1921 contained quarterly classified bibliography of books and articles on Italian history.]

Sánchez Alonso, B. Fuentes de la historia española. Vol. i. Madrid. 1919.
Solmi, A. La storia del diritto italiano. (Guide bibliografiche, 10.) Rome. 1922.
Thompson, E. M. Introduction to Greek and Latin Palaeography. London. 1912.
Vacant, A. and Mangenot, E. Dictionnaire de théologie catholique. Paris. 1909 ff.
Victoria History of the Counties of England. London. 1900 ff., in progress. (Vict. Co. Hist.)
Vildhaut, H. Handbuch der Quellenkunde zur deutschen Geschichte bis zum Ausgange der Staufer. 2nd edn. Werl. 1906.
Villien, A. and Magnin, E. Dictionnaire de droit canonique. Paris. 1924 ff., in progress.
Wattenbach, W. Deutschlands Geschichtsquellen im Mittelalter bis zur Mitte des 13 Jahrhunderts. 6th edn. 2 vols. Berlin. 1893-4. Vol. i. 7th edn. Dümmler, E. Stuttgart and Berlin. 1904.
Wetzer, H. J. and Welte, B. Kirchenlexikon oder Encyklopädie der katholischen Theologie. 1847-60. 2nd edn. Kaulen, F. Freiburg-i.-B. 1882-1903. Index. 1903. (Wetzer-Kaulen.) French transl. Goschler, I. 26 vols. Paris. 1869-70.
Whitney, J. P. Bibliography of Church History. (Historical Assoc. Leaflet 55.) London. 1923.

II. ATLASES AND GEOGRAPHY.

Baudrillart-Vogt-Rouziès. Dictionnaire d'histoire et de géographie ecclésiastique. Paris. 1911 ff., in progress.
Droysen, G. Allgemeiner historischer Handatlas. Bielefeld. 1886.
Freeman, E. A. Historical Geography of Europe (with Atlas). London. 1881. 3rd edn. revised and ed. Bury, J. B. 1903.
Kretschmer, K. Historische Geographie von Mitteleuropa. (Below-Meinecke. *See above*, i.) Munich. 1904.
Longnon, A. Atlas historique de la France depuis César jusqu'à nos jours. (Text separate.) Paris. (1885-9.) 1912. [Incomplete.]
Muir, R. and Philip, G. Philip's Historical Atlas, mediaeval and modern. 6th edn. London. 1927.
Poole, R. L. *ed.* Historical Atlas of Modern Europe. Oxford. 1902. [With valuable introductions.]
Putzger, F. W. Historischer Schul-Atlas. Ed. Baldamus, A. and others. 43rd edn. Bielefeld and Leipsic. 1922.
Schrader, F. *ed.* Atlas de géographie historique. New edn. Paris. 1907.
Shepherd, W. R. Historical atlas. 7th edn. New York and London. 1929.
Spruner-Menke. Hand-Atlas für die Geschichte des Mittelalters und der neueren Zeit. Gotha. 1880. (3rd edn. of Spruner's Hand-Atlas, etc. Ed. Menke, T.)

(For place-names :—)

Bischoff, H. T. and Möller, J. H. Vergleichendes Wörterbuch der alten, mittleren, und neuen Geographie. Gotha. 1892.
Deschamps, P. Dictionnaire de Géographie. (Supplt. to Brunet, J. C. Manuel du Libraire.) Paris. 1870. 2nd edn. 2 vols. 1878, 80.
Grässe, J. G. T. Orbis Latinus. Dresden. 1861. Ed. Benedict, F. Berlin. 1909. [Part i only.]
Martin, C. T. The Record Interpreter. London. 1892. 2nd edn. 1910. [For the British Isles.]
See also above, i. Chevalier, C. U. J. Répertoire etc., Topo-bibliographie.

III. CHRONOLOGY, NUMISMATICS, AND GENEALOGY.

(Chronology :—)

L'Art de vérifier les dates et les faits historiques. 2ᵉ partie. Depuis la naissance de J.-C. 3rd edn. Paris. 3 vols. 1783 ff., and other edns. and reprints. Also 4th edn. by Saint-Allais. 18 vols. 1818-19.
Beviglieri, C. Tavole sincrone e genealogiche di storia italiana dal 306 al 1870. Florence. 1875. Repr. 1885.

Bond, J. J. Handybook of rules and tables for verifying dates. 4th edn. London. 1899.

Calvi, E. Tavole storiche dei comuni italiani. Pts. i–iii. Rome. 1903–7. i. Liguria e Piemonte. ii. Marche. iii. Romagna. [Also useful bibliographies.] [No more publ.]

Cappelli, A. Cronologia, cronografia, e calendario perpetuo dal principio dell' Era Cristiana ai giorni nostri. 2nd edn. Milan. 1930.

Eubel, C. Hierarchia catholica medii aevi. Vol. i. 2nd edn. Münster. 1913.

Gams, P. B. Series episcoporum ecclesiae catholicae. (With supplt.) Ratisbon. 1873, 86. Repr. 1931.

Grotefend, H. Taschenbuch der Zeitrechnung des deutschen Mittelalters und der Neuzeit. 3rd enl. edn. Hanover. 1910.

—— Zeitrechnung des deutschen Mittelalters und der Neuzeit. 2 vols. Hanover. 1891, 98.

Janus: ein Datumweiser für alle Jahrhunderte. By Doliarius, J. E. Leipsic. *n.d.*

Lane-Poole, S. The Mohammadan Dynasties. London. 1894. Repr. 1925.

Mas Latrie, J. M. J. L. de. Trésor de chronologie, d'histoire, et de géographie pour l'étude des documents du moyen âge. Paris. 1889.

Nicolas, Sir N. H. The chronology of history. Revised edn. London. 1838.

Poole, R. L. Medieval reckonings of time. (Helps for Students of History.) S.P.C.K. London. 1918.

Rühl, F. Chronologie des Mittelalters und der Neuzeit. Berlin. 1897.

Savio, F. Gli antichi vescovi d' Italia dalle origini al 1300. Piemonte. Turin. 1899. Lombardia. Pt. i. Florence. 1913. Pt. ii. 2 vols. Bergamo. 1929, 32.

Schram, R. Hilfstafeln für Chronologie. Vienna. 1883. New edn. Kalendario-graphische und chronologische Tafeln. Leipsic. 1908.

Stokvis, A. M. H. J. Manuel d'histoire, de généalogie, et de chronologie de tous les États du globe, etc. 3 vols. Leiden. 1888–93.

Stubbs, W. Registrum sacrum Anglicanum. 2nd edn. Oxford. 1897.

Wallis, J. E. W. English regnal years and titles, hand-lists, Easter dates, etc. (English Time-books. Vol. i.) (Helps for Students of History.) S.P.C.K. London. 1921.

(*Note:*—Much information in such works as Gallia Christiana; Ughelli, Italia sacra, for which see iv, *below.*)

(Numismatics:—)

Blanchet, A. and Dieudonné, A. Manuel de numismatique française. Vols. i, ii. Paris. 1912, 16, in progress.

Brooke, G. C. English Coins. London. 1932.

Corpus nummorum italicorum. Vols. i–xi. Rome. 1910 ff., in progress.

Dieudonné, A. Les Monnaies françaises. (Collection Payot, 34.) Paris. 1925.

Engel, A. and Serrure, R. Traité de numismatique du moyen âge. 3 vols. Paris. 1891–1905.

Grueber, H. A. Handbook of the Coins of Great Britain and Ireland in the British Museum. London. 1899.

Hill, G. F. Coins and Medals. (Helps for Students of History.) S.P.C.K. London. 1920. [Bibliographical guide.]

Luschin von Ebengreuth, A. Allgemeine Münzkunde und Geldgeschichte des Mittelalters und der neueren Zeit. (Below-Meinecke. *See above,* i.) Munich. 1904. 2nd edn. 1926.

Martinori, E. La Moneta. Rome. 1915. [Dictionary of names of coins.]

(Genealogy:—)

Cokayne, G. E. Complete Peerage of England, Scotland, Ireland, Great Britain and the United Kingdom. 8 vols. Exeter. 1887–98. New enl. edn. Gibbs, V. and others. London. 1910 ff., in progress.

Fernandez de Bethencourt, F. Historia genealógica y heráldica de la Monarquía Española, Casa Real, y Grandes de España. Madrid. 1897 ff., in progress.

Foras, E. A. de, and Mareschal de Luciane. Armorial et Nobiliaire de l'ancien duché de Savoie. Vols. i–v. Grenoble. 1863 ff., in progress.

George, H. B. Genealogical Tables illustrative of Modern History. Oxford. 1873. 5th edn. rev. and enl. Weaver, J. R. H. 1916.

Grote, H. Stammtafeln mit Anhang calendarium medii aevi. (Münzstudien. Vol. IX.) Leipsic. 1877.

Guasco di Bisio, F. Dizionario feudale degli antichi stati sardi e della Lombardia dall' epoca carolingica ai nostri tempi (774–1909). 5 vols. (Biblioteca della soc. storica subalpina. Vols. 54–58.) Pinerolo. 1911.

Institut héraldique de France. Le Nobiliaire universel. 24 vols. Paris. 1854–1900.

Litta, P. (and continuators). Famiglie celebri italiane. 11 vols. Milan and Turin. 1819–99. 2nd series. Naples. 1902-23. [No more publ.]

Moreri, L. Le grand dictionnaire historique. Latest edn. 10 vols. Paris. 1759. English version, Collier, J. 2nd edn. with supplts. and app. 4 vols. London. 1701–16.

Voigtel, T. G. and Cohn, L. A. Stammtafeln zur Geschichte d. europäischen Staaten. Vol. I. Die deutschen Staaten u. d. Niederlande. Brunswick. 1871.

See also L'Art de vérifier les dates (*above*), Lane-Poole, Mohammadan Dynasties (*above*), and Stokvis (*above*).

IV. SOURCES AND COLLECTIONS OF SOURCES.

Achery, L. d'. Spicilegium sive collectio veterum aliquot scriptorum. 13 vols. Paris. 1655(1665)–77. New edn. Barre, L. F. J. de la. 3 vols. Paris. 1723.

Acta Sanctorum Bollandiana. Jan.–Oct. VI. Antwerp, Brussels, and Tongerloo. 1643–1794. Oct. VII–XIII. Brussels, Paris and Rome, Paris. 1845–83. Nov. Paris and Rome, Brussels. 1887 ff., in progress. [The reprint of Jan.–Oct. x published by Palmé at Paris and Rome, 1863 ff., among other variations, has 3 instead of 2 vols. of Jan., and re-arranges the contents of the 7 vols. of June.] (ASBoll.) [Supplemented by Analecta Bollandiana. 1882 ff. (AB.)]

Amari, M. *See under* Muratori.

Archivio storico italiano. (ASI.) *See List of Abbreviations* (1).

Baluzius, S. Vitae paparum Avenionesium. New edn. by Mollat, G. 4 vols. Paris. 1914–27.

Biblioteca della società storica subalpina. Ed. Gabotto, F. and Tallone, A. Pinerolo, etc. 1899 ff., in progress. [Contains charters and monographs.]

Böhmer, J. F. Regesta imperii.
  Regesten d. Kaiserreichs...1246–1313. Stuttgart. 1844. Additamenta I and II. 1849, 57.
  Regesten d. Kaiserreichs...1314–1347. Frankfort. 1839. Additamenta I–III. 1841–65.

——Regesta imperii. (New edn. in several parts by various editors.) Innsbruck. 1877 ff. [*See also Gen. Bibl. of Vol.* v, p. 838.]
  v. Regesten d. Kaiserreichs...1198–1272. Ed. Ficker, J. and Winkelmann, E. 3 vols. 1881–1901.
  VI. Regesten d. Kaiserreichs...1273–1313. Ed. Redlich, O. Abtlg. 1 (1273–91). 1898, in progress.
  VIII. Regesten d. Kaiserreichs...1346–78. Ed. Huber, A. 1877. Additamentum I. 1889.

Bouquet. *See* Rerum Gallicarum...scriptores.

Camden Society. Publications. London. 1838 ff., in progress. (Now publ. by the Roy. Hist. Soc.)

Chartes et diplômes relatifs à l'histoire de France. AcadIBL. Paris. 1908 ff., in progress.

Classiques de l'histoire de France au moyen âge. General editor: Halphen, L. Paris. 1924 ff., in progress. (Class. hist.) [Texts and French translations.]

Collection de chroniques Belges inédits. Brussels. 1836 ff., in progress.

Collection de documents inédits sur l'histoire de France. Paris. 1835 ff., in progress. (Coll. doc.)

Collection de textes pour servir à l'étude et à l'enseignement de l'histoire. 49 vols. Paris. 1886–1913. (Coll. textes.)

Corpus Iuris Canonici. Vol. I. Decretum Gratiani. Vol. II. Decretales Gregorii Papae IX, etc. Ed. Friedberg, E. Leipsic. 1879, 81. [Critical edition.]

Corpus Iuris Canonici (*cont.*). (Edition of Gregory XIII.) 3 vols. Lyons. 1584; and
    other 16th century edns. also. [Contains the medieval glosses.]
Corpus Iuris Civilis. 3 vols. Berlin. [Critical modern edn.]
    Vol. i. Institutiones. Ed. Krueger, P. Digesta. Ed. Mommsen, T. 15th
      edn. 1928.
    Vol. ii. Codex Iustinianus. Ed. Krueger, P. 10th edn. 1929.
    Vol. iii. Novellae. Ed. Schoell, R. and Kroll, W. 5th edn. 1928.
    —— Ed. Gothofredus, D. 3rd edn. 6 vols. Cologne. 1612; and other edns.
    [Contains the medieval glosses and additions, such as the Libri Feudorum.]
Corpus scriptorum ecclesiasticorum latinorum. Vienna. 1866 ff., in progress. (CSEL.)
Dugdale, W. Monasticon Anglicanum. 3 vols. London. 1655–73. New edn. by
    Caley, J. and others. 6 vols. in 8. London. 1817–30. Repr. 1846.
Early English Text Society. Publications. London. 1864 ff., in progress. (EETS.)
España Sagrada. Ed. Florez, H. and others. 51 vols. Madrid. 1747–1879.
Fejér, G. Codex diplomaticus Hungariae ecclesiasticus et civilis. (Chronological
    table by Knauz, F. Index by Czinár, M.) 45 vols. Buda-Pest. 1829–66.
Fonti per la storia d' Italia. Publ. by Istituto storico italiano. Rome. 1887 ff., in
    progress. (Chronicles, 36 vols. Letters, 7 vols. Diplomas, 7 vols. Statutes,
    7 vols. Laws, 1 vol. Antiquities, 3 vols. Poems, 1 vol.) (Fonti.)
Gallia Christiana (Vetus). Ed. Sainte-Marthe, S. de, and others. 4 vols. Paris.
    1656.
—— (Nova). Vols. i–xiii. Ed. Sainte-Marthe, D. de, and others. Vols. xiv–xvi.
    Ed. Hauréau, B. Paris. 1715–1865. 2nd edn. Revised by Piolin, P. Vols. i–v,
    xi, xiii. Paris. 1870–8. Provincia Tolosana. New edn. Vol. i. Toulouse. 1892.
—— (Novissima). Ed. Albanès, J. H. and Chevalier, C. U. J. 7 vols. Montbéliard
    and Valence. 1895–1920.
Germania sacra. Publ. by Kaiser-Wilhelm-Institut für deutsche Geschichte. Berlin.
    1929, in progress.
Geschichtschreiber der deutschen Vorzeit etc. Ed. Pertz, Wattenbach, and others.
    New series. Leipsic. 1884, in progress. [German translations.]
Graevius, J. G. and Burmannus, P. Thesaurus antiquitatum et historiarum Italiae
    etc. 30 vols. Leiden. 1704–23.
—— Thesaurus antiq. et histor. Siciliae, Sardiniae, Corsicae, etc. 15 vols.
    Leiden. 1723–5. [Forms a continuation of the preceding.]
Guizot, F. P. C. Collection des mém. relatifs à l'hist. de France...jusqu'au 13ᵉ siècle.
    Paris. 1823–35. [French translations.]
Haddan, A. W. and Stubbs, W. Councils and ecclesiastical documents relating to
    Great Britain and Ireland. Ed. after Spelman and Wilkins. 3 vols. Oxford.
    1869–78.
Hinschius, P. Decretales pseudo-Isidorianae et Capitula Angilramni. Leipsic. 1863.
Historiae patriae monumenta. *See* Monumenta historiae patriae.
Mabillon, J. Annales Ordinis S. Benedicti. 6 vols. Paris. 1703–39. 2nd edn.
    Lucca. 1739–45.
Mabillon, J. and Achery, L. d'. Acta Sanctorum ord. S. Benedicti [A.D. 500–1100].
    9 vols. Paris. 1668–1701. Repr. Venice. 1733–40. (ASBen.)
Mansi, J. D. Sacrorum conciliorum collectio. 31 vols. Florence and Venice. 1759–
    98. Repr. Martin, J. B. and Petit, L. (With continuation, vols. 32–50.) Paris.
    1901 ff., in progress. (Mansi.)
Marrier, M. and Quercetanus (Duchesne), A. Bibliotheca Cluniacensis. Paris. 1614.
Martène, E. and Durand, U. Thesaurus novus anecdotorum. 5 vols. Paris. 1717.
Mémoires et documents publiés par la Société de l'École des chartes. Paris. 1896 ff.,
    in progress.
Migne, J. P. Patrologiae cursus completus. Series graeco-latina. Paris. 1857–66.
    161 vols. in 166. (MPG.) Indices, Cavallera, F. Paris. 1912; *also* Hopfner, T.
    Paris. 1928 ff., in progress. [This is the series containing Greek texts with
    Latin translations in parallel columns. The so-called Series graeca (81 vols.
    in 85. 1856–67) contains Latin translations only.]
—— —— Series latina. 221 vols. Paris. 1844–55. Index, 4 vols. 1862–4. (MPL.)
Mirbt, C. Quellen zur Geschichte des Papsttums und des römischen Katholizismus.
    4th edn. Tübingen. 1924. (Mirbt. Quellen.)

Monumenta Germaniae Historica. Ed. Pertz, G. H., Mommsen, T., and others. Hanover and Berlin. 1826 ff. Index. 1890. [For full list of the different series *see Gen. Bibl. of Vol.* v, pp. 840–1.] (MGH.)

Deutsche Chroniken (Scriptores qui vernac. lingua usi sunt). i–vi. 1892 ff., in progress.

Epistolae saec. xiii e regestis pontificum Romanorum. i–iii. 1883–94.

Epistolae selectae. i–iv. 1916 ff., in progress. 8°. (Epp. select.)

Legum sectiones quinque. 4°.
  Sect. iii. Concilia. 2 vols. in 4. 1893–1924.
  Sect. iv. Constitutiones etc. i–v, vi. i, viii. 1893 ff.

Libelli de lite imperatorum et pontificum (saec. xi, xii). i–iii. 1891 ff.

Scriptores. Vols. i–xxx. Fol. 1826–1929. And 4°. Vols. xxxi, xxxii. 1903, 1913. In progress. (Script.)

Scriptores rerum Germanicarum in usum scholarum. Hanover. 1839 ff. Fresh series. 1890–1920. 8°. (SGUS.) [Contains revised editions of many of Scriptores in Fol. edition.]

Scriptores rerum Germanicarum. Nova Series. i–iv. i, v–viii. Berlin. 1922 ff., in progress. (MGH. Script. N.S.)

Monumenta historiae patriae. 19 vols. Fol. 2 vols. 4°. Turin. 1836 ff., in progress. (MHP.)

Muratori, L. A. Rerum Italicarum scriptores. 25 vols. Milan. 1723–51. Supplements: Tartini, J. M., 2 vols., Florence, 1748, 70; and Mittarelli, J. B., Venice, 1771; and Amari, M., Biblioteca arabo-sicula, versione italiana, and Appendix. Turin and Rome. 1880–1, 1889. Indices chronolog. Turin. 1885. New enl. edn. with chronicles printed as separate parts. Carducci, G., Fiorini, V., Fedele, P. Città di Castello and Bologna. 1900 ff., in progress. (RR.II.SS.)

—— Antiquitates italicae medii aevi. 6 vols. Milan. 1738–42. Indices chronolog. Turin. 1885.

Papal Documents (*for earlier Popes see Gen. Bibl. of Vol.* vi, p. 852).

Registres de Boniface VIII. Ed. Digard, G., Fauçon, M., and Thomas, A. Pts. i–xiv. EcfrAR. Paris. 1884 ff., in progress.

Registre de Benoît XI. Ed. Grandjean, C. EcfrAR. Paris. 1905.

Regestum Clementis papae V ex Vaticanis archetypis,...cura et studio monachorum ordinis S. Benedicti. 8 vols. Rome. 1884–92.

Jean XXII. Lettres communes. Ed. Mollat, G. Vols. i–viii. EcfrAR. Paris. 1904 ff., in progress.

Benoît XII. Lettres communes. Ed. Vidal, J. M. 3 vols. EcfrAR. Paris. 1903–11.

Benoît XII. Lettres closes et patentes intéressant les pays autres que la France. Ed. Vidal, J. M. Pts. i–iii. EcfrAR. Paris. 1913 ff., in progress.

Auszüge aus den Urkunden des Vatikanischen Archivs von 1315–34. Ed. Reinkens, J. H. *in* Abh. d. BAW. xvi. Abt. ii, pp. 156–284; xvii. Abt. i, pp. 161–338; Abt. iii, pp. 571–93. Munich. 1882–6.

Vatikanische Akten zur deutschen Geschichte in der Zeit Kaiser Ludwigs des Bayern. Ed. Riezler, S. (Hist. Commission. BAW.) Innsbruck. 1891.

Vatikanische Quellen zur Geschichte der päpstlichen Hof- und Finanzverwaltung 1316–78, etc. Ed. Göller, E. and Schäfer, K. H. 4 vols. Paderborn. 1910–20.

Analecta Vaticano-Belgica. Documents relatifs aux anciens diocèses de Cambrai, Liège, Thérouanne, et Tournai. (Institut hist. belge de Rome.) Rome, Brussels, etc. 1906 ff.
  ii, iii. Lettres de Jean XXII. Ed. Fayen, A. 2 vols. 1908, 12.
  iv. Lettres de Benoît XII. Ed. Fierens, A. 1910.
  vi. Lettres de Clément VI. Ed. Van Isacker, P. and Berlière, U. Vol. i. 1924.
  i. Suppliques de Clément VI. Ed. Berlière, U. 1906.
  v. Suppliques d'Innocent VI. Ed. Berlière, U. 1911.
  vii. Suppliques d'Urbain V. Ed. Fierens, A. 1924.
  ix. Lettres d'Urbain V. Vol. i. Ed. Fierens, A. and Tihon, C. 1928. Vol. ii. Ed. Tihon, C.
  viii, xii. Documents relatifs au Grand Schisme. Vol. i. Suppliques de Clément VII. Ed. Hanquet, K. 1924. Vol. ii. Lettres de Clément VII. Ed. Hanquet, K. and Berlière, U. 1930.

x. Les Collectories pontificales dans les anciens diocèses de Cambrai, Thérouanne, et Tournai au xive siècle. Ed. Berlière, U. 1929.
Monumenta Vaticana res gestas Bohemicas illustrantia. Prague. 1903 ff.
   i. Acta Clementis VI. Ed. Klicman, L. 1903.
   ii. Acta Innocentii VI. Ed. Novák, J. F. 1907.
   v. Acta Urbani VI et Bonifatii IX. Ed. Krofta, C. 2 pts. 1903, 5.
Lettres des Papes d'Avignon se rapportant à la France.
   Jean XXII. Lettres secrètes et curiales. Ed. Coulon, A. Pts. i–v. EcfrAR. Paris. 1900 ff., in progress.
   Benoît XII. Lettres closes, patentes, et curiales. Ed. Daumet, G. 2 vols. EcfrAR. Paris. 1899–1920.
   Clément VI. Lettres closes, patentes, et curiales. Ed. Deprez, M. Pts. i, ii. EcfrAR. Paris. 1901 ff., in progress.
   Innocent VI. Lettres closes, patentes, et curiales. Ed. Deprez, E. Pt. i. EcfrAR. Paris. 1909, in progress.
   Urbain V. Lettres secrètes et curiales. Ed. Lecacheux, P. Pts. i, ii. EcfrAR. Paris. 1902 ff., in progress.
Documents pontificaux sur la Gascogne d'après les Archives du Vatican. Pontificat de Jean XXII. Ed. Guérard, L. 2 vols. (Archives hist. de la Gascogne. 2nd ser. ii, vi.) Paris and Auch. 1896, 1903.
Calendar of entries in the Papal Registers relating to Great Britain and Ireland. Papal Letters. Vols. i–vi. Ed. Bliss, W. H. and others. (Cal. SP.) London. 1893–1904.
   Petitions to the Pope. Vol. i. Ed. Bliss, W. H. (Cal. SP.) London. 1896.
Potthast, A. Regesta Pontificum Romanorum inde ab anno 1198 ad annum 1304. 2 vols. Berlin. 1874–5.
Record Commissioners, Publications of the. London. 1802–69. (RC.)
Regesta chartarum Italiae. Publ. by K. Preuss. Histor. Instit. and Istituto storico italiano. Rome. 1907 ff., in progress.
Regesta Pontificum Romanorum. *See above under* Potthast, A.
Rerum Britannicarum medii aevi scriptores. (Chronicles and Memorials of Great Britain and Ireland during the Middle Ages.) Published under direction of the Master of the Rolls. London. 1858 ff. (Rolls.) [For convenient list see Gross (Section i, *above*), App. c.]
Rerum Gallicarum et Francicarum scriptores. (Recueil des hist. des Gaules et de la France.) Ed. Bouquet, M. and others. 24 vols. Paris. 1738–1904. Vols. i–xix re-ed. by Delisle, L. 1868–80. New series. 4°. AcadIBL. Paris. 1899 ff., in progress. (Bouquet.)
Rymer, T. Foedera. [1101–1654.] 20 vols. (xvi ff. by Sanderson, R.) London. 1704–35. 3rd edn. The Hague. 1739–45. New edn. [1069–1383] by Clarke, A., Holbrooke, F., and Caley, J. 4 vols. in 7 pts. (RC.) London. 1816–69. Syllabus by Hardy, T. D. 3 vols. London. 1869–85. Report (App. a–e only) by Cooper, C. P. (RC.) London. [1836?] Publ. 1869.
Scriptores rerum Danicarum medii aevi. Ed. Langebek, I. and others. 9 vols. Copenhagen. 1772–1878. (SRD.)
Scriptores rerum Germanicarum in usum scholarum. (SGUS.) *See above*, Monumenta Germaniae Historica.
Selden Society. Publications. London. 1888 ff., in progress.
Société de l'histoire de France. Publications. Paris. 1834 ff., in progress. (SHF.)
Stevenson, J. Church Historians of England. London. 1853–8. [Translations.]
Stubbs, W. Select Charters and other illustrations of English Constitutional History to the reign of Edward I. Oxford. 1870. 9th edn. rev. Davis, H. W. C. Oxford. 1913.
Theiner, A. Codex diplomaticus dominii temporalis S. Sedis. 3 vols. Rome. 1861–2.
Ughelli, F. Italia sacra. 2nd edn. Coleti, N. 10 vols. Venice. 1717–22.
Vic, C. de, and Vaissete, J. J. Histoire générale de Languedoc. New edn. Dulaurier, E. 16 vols. Toulouse. 1872–1904.
Wilkins, D. Concilia Magnae Britanniae et Hiberniae. 4 vols. London. 1737.
Winkelmann, E. Acta imperii inedita seculi xiii et xiv. Urkunden und Briefe zur Geschichte des Kaiserreichs und des Königsreichs Sicilien (1198–1400). 2 vols. Innsbruck. 1880, 85.

V. MODERN WORKS.

Altamira, R. Historia de España y de la civilización española. 3rd edn. 4 vols. Barcelona. 1913–14.

Alzog, J. Universalgeschichte der Kirche. Mayence. 1841. Best edn. 10th by Kraus, F. X. 1882. Transl. (from 9th German edn.) Pabisch, F. J. and Byrne, T. S. Manual of Church History. 4 vols. Dublin. 1895–1900.

Baronius, C. Annales Ecclesiastici una cum critica historico-chronologica P. A. Pagii. [–1198.] Contin. by Raynaldus, O. [1198–1565.] Ed. Mansi, J. D. Lucca. 34 vols. 1738–46. Apparatus and Index, 4 vols. 1740, 1757–9. New edn. 37 vols. Bar-le-duc. 1864–83. [Not completed.]

Bédier, J. and Hazard, P. *edd.* Histoire de la littérature française illustrée. 2 vols. Paris. 1923–4.

Bibliothèque de l'École des Hautes Études. Paris. 1869 ff., in progress. (BHE.)

Bréhier, L. L'Église et l'Orient au moyen âge. Les Croisades. 5th edn. Paris. 1928. (Bibliothèque de l'enseignement de l'histoire ecclésiastique.) [With bibliography.]

Brown, P. Hume. History of Scotland to the present time. (Library edn.) 3 vols. Cambridge. 1911.

Brunner, H. Deutsche Rechtsgeschichte. 2 vols. Leipsic. 1887, 92. Vol. I. 2nd edn. 1906. Vol. II, ed. Schwerin, C. von. 1928.

—— Grundzüge der deutschen Rechtsgeschichte. 8th edn. Schwerin, C. von. Munich. 1930. [Bibliographies.]

Bryce, J. The Holy Roman Empire. New edn. London. 1906, and reprints.

Cambridge History of English Literature. Ed. Ward, A. W. and Waller, A. R. 15 vols. Cambridge. 1907–27.

Cánovas del Castillo, A. *ed.* Historia general de la España. (By members of R. Acad. de la Hist.) Madrid. 1892 ff., in progress.

Carlyle, R. W. and A. J. A history of Mediaeval Political Theory in the West. Vols. I–V. Edinburgh and London. 1903 ff., in progress.

Coulton, G. G. Five Centuries of Religion. Vols. I, II. Cambridge. 1923 ff., in progress.

Cunningham, W. The growth of English Industry and Commerce. [Vol. I.] Early and Middle Ages. 5th edn. Cambridge. 1910.

Davidsohn, R. Geschichte von Florenz. Vols. II–IV. Berlin. 1908–27.

Denifle, H. Die Universitäten des Mittelalters bis 1400. Vol. I. Die Entstehung der Universitäten. Berlin. 1885. [No more publ.]

England, A History of, in seven volumes. Ed. Oman, C. 7 vols. London. 1905–13.

—— The Political History of. Ed. Hunt, W. and Poole, R. L. 12 vols. London. 1905–10.

Erben, W. Kriegsgeschichte des Mittelalters. (HZ. Beiheft 16.) Munich and Berlin. 1929. [Valuable bibliographies.]

Ficker, G. and Hermelink, H. Das Mittelalter. 2nd edn. (Handbuch d. Kirchengesch. für Studierende. Ed. Krüger, G. Vol. II.) Tübingen. 1929.

Fleury, C. Histoire ecclésiastique. 20 vols. Paris. 1691–1720. Continued to end of 18th century under Vidal, O. Many editions. (Orig. edn. to 1414. 4 add. vols. by Fleury to 1517, publ. Paris. 1836–7.)

Gebhardt, B. Handbuch der deutschen Geschichte. 7th edn. by Holtzman, R. 2 vols. Stuttgart. 1930–1.

Gibbon, E. The History of the Decline and Fall of the Roman Empire. 1776–81. Ed. Bury, J. B. 7 vols. London. 1896–1900; best edn., rev. and illustrated. 7 vols. London. 1909–14. [Notes essential, especially for bibliography.]

Gierke, O. Das deutsche Genossenschaftsrecht. 4 vols. Berlin. 1868–1913.

—— Political Theories of the Middle Age. Transl. and ed. Maitland, F. W. Cambridge. 1900. [Translation of a section of the preceding.]

Gieseler, J. C. L. Lehrbuch der Kirchengeschichte. Vols. I–III (in 8 pts.). 4th, 2nd, and 1st edns. Bonn. 1844–8; 35–53. Engl. transl. Davidson, S. and Hull, J. W. Vols. I–III. Edinburgh. 1853 ff.

Gilson, E. La philosophie au moyen âge. 2 vols. Paris. 1922. [Bibliographies.]

Gregorovius, F. Geschichte der Stadt Rom im Mittelalter. 5th edn. 8 vols. Stuttgart. 1903–8. (Engl. transl. from 4th edn. by Mrs A. Hamilton. 8 vols. in 13. London. 1894–1902.)

Hanotaux, G. *ed.* Histoire de la nation française. 15 vols. Paris. 1920–9.

Harnack, C. G. A. Lehrbuch der Dogmengeschichte. 4th edn. 3 vols. (Sammlung theolog. Lehrbücher.) Tübingen. 1909–10. Engl. transl. of the 3rd edn Buchanan, N. and others. 7 vols. London. 1894–9.

Hartmann, L. M. *ed.* Weltgeschichte in gemeinverständlicher Darstellung. Vol. v. Kaser, K. Das späte Mittelalter. Gotha. 1921.

Haskins, C. H. Studies in the history of Mediaeval Science. Cambridge, Mass 1924.

Hauck, A. Kirchengeschichte Deutschlands. 5 vols. Leipsic. 1887–1920. Vols. i–iv. 4th edn. 1906–13. Vol. v. 2nd edn. 2 pts. 1911, 20.

Heeren, A. H. L. and others, *edd.* Geschichte der europäischen Staaten. Hamburg and Gotha. 1829 ff. Continued as section 1 of Allgemeine Staatengeschichte. Ed. Lamprecht, K. and Oncken, H. *Cited sub nom. auct.* (Heeren.)

Hefele, C. J. v., contin. Hergenröther, J. A. G. Conciliengeschichte. 9 vols. Freiburg-i.-B. 1855 ff. 2nd edn. 1873 ff. French transl. Delarc, O. 1869. New rev. Fr. transl. Leclercq, H. Vols. i–viii (in 18 pts.). Paris. 1907 ff., in progress. (Hefele-Leclercq.)

Heyd, W. Histoire du Commerce du Levant au moyen-âge. 2nd edn. (in French transl. by Raynaud, F.). 2 vols. Leipsic. 1885–6. Reprinted. 2 vols. Leipsic. 1923.

Hinojosa, E. de. Historia general del derecho español. Vol. i. Madrid. 1887 [No more publ.]

Hinschius, P. Das Kirchenrecht der Katholiken und Protestanten in Deutschland. Pt. i. System des kathol. Kirchenrechts, mit besonderer Rücksicht auf Deutschland. Vols. i–vi. i. Berlin. 1869–97.

Historische Studien. Ed. Ebering, E. Berlin. 1896 ff., in progress.

Holdsworth, W. S. History of English Law. 3rd edn. Vols. i–iii. London. 1922–3.

Jahrbücher der deutschen Geschichte. (Hist. Commission BAW.) Berlin and Leipsic. 1862 ff., in progress.

Kirchenrechtliche Abhandlungen. Ed. Stutz, U. Stuttgart, 1902 ff., in progress.

Köhler, G. Die Entwicklung des Kriegswesen und der Kriegsführung in der Ritterzeit von der Mitte des 11 Jahrhunderts bis zu den Hussitenkriegen. 3 vols. Breslau. 1886–90.

Kraus, F. X. Geschichte der christlichen Kunst. 2 vols. in 4. Freiburg-i.-B. 1896–1908.

Kretschmayr, H. Geschichte von Venedig. Vols. i, ii. (Heeren. *See above.*) Gotha. 1905, 20.

Krumbacher, K. Geschichte der byzantinischen Literatur. (527–1453.) 2nd edn. (Handbuch d. klass. Altertums-Wissenschaft. Ed. Müller, I. von. Vol. ix. i.) Munich. 1897.

Lamprecht, K. Deutsche Geschichte. 12 vols. in 16. Berlin. 1891–1909. Vols. i–v. 3rd edn. 1902–6. Supplts. 2 vols. in 3. 1902–4.

Langen, J. Geschichte der römischen Kirche. 4 vols. Bonn. 1881.

Lavisse, E. *ed.* Histoire de France jusqu'à la Révolution. 9 vols. in 18. Paris. 1900–11. Vols. i–iv.

Lavisse, E. and Rambaud, A. *edd.* Histoire générale du iv⁰ siècle jusqu'à nos jours. Vols. i–iii. Paris. 1893–6.

Lea, H. C. History of the Inquisition of the Middle Ages. 3 vols. New York. 1887. French transl. Reinach, S., with introdn. by Frédéricq, P. 3 vols. Paris. 1900–2.

—— History of Sacerdotal Celibacy in the Christian Church. 3rd edn. 2 vols. London. 1907.

Lloyd, J. E. History of Wales from the earliest times to the Edwardian Conquest. 2nd edn. 2 vols. London. 1912.

Loserth, J. Geschichte des späteren Mittelalters von 1197 bis 1492. (Below-Meinecke. *See above*, i.) Munich. 1903.

Luchaire, A. Manuel des institutions françaises; période des Capétiens directs Paris. 1892.

Manitius, M. Geschichte der lateinischen Literatur des Mittelalters. Vols. i–iii. (Handbuch d. klass. Altertums-Wissenschaft. Ed. Müller, I. von. Vol. ix. ii. 1–3.) Munich. 1911 ff., in progress.

Merriman, R. B. The rise of the Spanish empire in the old world and in the new. Vols. i and ii. New York. 1918.

Miller, W. The Latin Orient. (Helps for Students of History.) S.P.C.K. London. 1920. [Contains a bibliography.]

Moeller, W. Hist. of the Christian Church (A.D. 1–1648). Transl. Rutherfurd and Freese. 3 vols. London. 1892–1900.

Mollat, G. Les Papes d'Avignon. 6th rev. edn. Paris. 1930. [Bibliographies.]

Mosheim, J. L. von. Institutionum historiae ecclesiasticae antiquae et recentioris libri iv. 4 vols. Helmstedt. 1755. Transl. Murdock, J., ed. Soames, H. 4 vols. London. 1841. 2nd rev. edn. 1850.

Müller, K. Kirchengeschichte. Vols. i, ii. Freiburg-i.-B. 1892.

Muratori, L. A. Annali d' Italia. 12 vols. Milan. 1744–9. Also other editions.

Norden, W. Das Papsttum und Byzanz. Berlin. 1903.

Oman, C. W. C. History of the Art of War in the Middle Ages. 2nd edn. enl. 2 vols. London. 1924.

Oncken, W. *ed.* Allgemeine Geschichte in Einzeldarstellungen. 45 vols. Berlin. 1879–93. *Cited sub nom. auct.* (Oncken.)

Orpen, G. H. Ireland under the Normans (1169–1333). 4 vols. Oxford. 1911–20.

Pertile, A. Storia del diritto italiano dalla caduta dell' impero Romano alla codificazione. 2nd edn. Del Giudice, P. 6 vols. Turin. 1892–1902. Index. Eusebio, L. Turin. 1893.

Petit de Julleville, L. *ed.* Histoire de la langue et de la littérature française. 8 vols. Paris. 1896–1900.

Pirenne, H. Histoire de Belgique. Vol. i. 5th edn. Brussels. 1929. Vol. ii. 3rd edn. 1922.

Pollock, F. and Maitland, F. W. The history of English Law before Edward I. 2nd edn. 2 vols. Cambridge. 1898.

Poole, R. L. Illustrations of the history of Medieval Thought and Learning. 2nd edn. London. 1920.

Previté-Orton, C. W. Outlines of Medieval History. Rev. repr. of 2nd edn. Cambridge. 1932.

Rambaud, A. Histoire de la Russie depuis les origines jusqu'à nos jours. 6th edn. rev. by Haumant, E. Paris. 1914. Engl. transl. Lang, L. B. Rev. edn. 3 vols. Boston, Mass. 1886.

Ranke, L. von. Weltgeschichte. 9 vols. Leipsic. 1881–8. And later edns.

Rashdall, H. The Universities of Europe in the Middle Ages. 2 vols. in 3. Oxford. 1895. [A new edn. is in preparation.]

Reichel, O. J. The elements of Canon Law. London. 1887.

Salembier, L. Le Grand Schisme d'Occident. 5th edn. Paris. 1922.

Savigny, F. C. von. Geschichte des Römischen Rechts im Mittelalter. 2nd edn. 7 vols. Heidelberg. 1834–51. French transl. Guenoux, C. 4 vols. Paris. 1839.

Schaube, A. Handelsgeschichte der romanischen Völker des Mittelmeergebiets bis zum Ende der Kreuzzüge. (Below-Meinecke. *See above,* i.) Munich. 1906.

Schröder, R. Lehrbuch der deutschen Rechtsgeschichte. 6th edn. Ed. Künnsberg, E. von. Berlin and Leipsic. 1922.

Schulte, J. F. v. Die Geschichte der Quellen und Literatur des Canonischen Rechts von Gratian bis auf die Gegenwart. 3 vols. Stuttgart. 1875–80.

Storia letteraria d' Italia scritta da una società di professori. Milan. 1900 ff.

Storia politica d' Italia scritta da una società d' amici. Ed. Villari, P. Vols. iii (Lanzani, F.), iv (Cipolla, C.). Milan. 1882, 81.

Storia politica d' Italia scritta da una società di professori. Vols. iii (Romano, G.), iv (Gianani, F.), v (Orsi, P.). Milan. [1900 ff.]

Stubbs, W. Constitutional history of England. 3 vols. Oxford. 1873–8. (Frequently reprinted.) French transl. Lefebvre, G., with notes and studies by Petit-Dutaillis, C. 3 vols. Paris. 1907–27. English transl. of notes, etc. Ed. Tait, J. and Powicke, F. M. *as* Studies and notes supplementary to Stubbs' Constitutional history. Vol. i. Transl. Rhodes, W. E. Vol. ii. Transl.

Waugh, W. T. Vol. iii. Transl. Robertson, M. I. E. and Treharne, R. F. Manchester. 1908–29.

Tiraboschi, G. Storia della letteratura italiana. New edn. 9 vols. in 16. Florence. 1805–13. Milan. 1822–6.

Ueberweg, F. Grundriss der Geschichte der Philosophie. 12th edn. Ed. Frischeisen-Köhler, M. and Praechter, K. 5 vols. Berlin. 1926–8. [Bibliography.]

Valois, N. La France et le Grand Schisme d'Occident. 4 vols. Paris. 1896–1902.

Vinogradoff, P. Roman Law in Mediaeval Europe. 2nd edn. Oxford. 1929. [Bibliographies.]

Viollet, P. Droit public. Histoire des institutions politiques et administratives de la France. 3 vols. Paris. 1890–1903.

—— Histoire du droit civil français. 3rd edn. Paris. 1905.

Waitz, G. Deutsche Verfassungsgeschichte. Vols. v–viii. Vol. v. 2nd edn. Zeumer, K. Berlin. 1893; Vol. vi. 2nd edn. Seeliger, G. Berlin. 1896; Vol. viii. Keil. 1878.

Weil, G. Geschichte der islamitischen Völker von Mohammed bis zur Zeit des Sultans Selim. Stuttgart. 1866.

Werminghoff, A. Geschichte der Kirchenverfassung Deutschlands im Mittelalter. Vol. i. Hanover and Leipsic. 1905.

Zeller, J. Histoire d'Allemagne. Vols. i–ix. Paris. 1872–91. [No more publ.]

CHAPTER I.

ITALY IN THE TIME OF DANTE.

I. SPECIAL BIBLIOGRAPHIES.

Allen, A. M. History of Verona. *See below*, III B.
Capasso, B. Le Fonti della storia delle provincie napolitane dal 568 al 1500. *See Gen. Bibl.* I.
Caro, G. Genua und die Mächte am Mittelmeer. Vol. II. *See below*, III B.
Davidsohn, R. Geschichte von Florenz. Vols. II–IV. *See Gen. Bibl.* V. [Useful also for other Italian states.]
Kretschmayr, H. Geschichte von Venedig. Vol. II. *See Gen. Bibl.* **v.**
Mollat, G. Les Papes d'Avignon. *See Gen. Bibl.* v.
Spangenberg, H. Cangrande I della Scala. Vol. I. *See below*, III B.

II. SOURCES FOR POLITICAL HISTORY.

A. GENERAL. (Connected mainly with Henry VII.)

Acta Aragonensia. Ed. Finke, H. 3 vols. Berlin. 1908 ff., in progress.
Acta Henrici VII. Ed. Bonaini, F. 2 vols. Florence. 1877.
—— Ed. Dönniges, W. 2 pts. Berlin. 1839.
Cermenate, Johannes de. Historia. Ed. Ferrai, L. A. (Fonti.) 1889.
Constitutiones et Acta publica imperatorum et regum. Vols. III–V. MGH. Legum Sect. IV. 1904–13.
Ferretus Vicentinus. Historia rerum in Italia gestarum. Ed. Cipolla, C. 3 vols. (Fonti.) 1908–20.
Mussatus, Albertinus. Historia Augusta. Ed. Muratori. RR.II.SS. 1st edn. Vol. x.
—— De gestis Italicorum post Henricum VII. *Ibid. Also* Sette libri inediti del De gestis Italicorum post Henricum VII. Ed. Padrin, L. and Medin, A. (R. Dep. Veneta di stor. pat. Monumenti. Ser. III. Vol. III.) Venice. 1903.
Nicolaus episcopus Botrontinensis. Relatio. Ed. Heyck, E. Innsbruck. 1888. *Also in* Baluzius, S. Vitae paparum Avenionensium; ed. Mollat, G. Vol. III, pp. 491–561. Paris. 1921.
Pipinus, Franciscus. Chronicon. Ed. Muratori. RR.II.SS. 1st edn. Vol. IX.

B. NORTH ITALY.

Annales Ianuenses (Jacobus Auriae). Vol. v. Ed. Imperiale di S. Angelo, C. (Fonti.) 1929.
Annales Mantuani (1183–1299). Ed. Pertz, G. H. MGH. Script. XIX. 1866.
Annales Mediolanenses anonymi auctoris. Ed. Muratori. RR.II.SS. 1st edn. Vol. XVI.
Annales veteres Mutinensium. Ed. Muratori. RR.II.SS. 1st edn. Vol. XI.
Annales Parmenses maiores (1165–1335). Ed. Jaffé, P. MGH. Script. XVIII. 1863. *Also* ed. Bonazzi, G. *as* Chronicon Parmense. RR.II.SS. New edn. Vol. IX, pt. 9.
Annales Patavini. Ed. Bonardi, A. *with* Rolandinus Patavinus. RR.II.SS. New edn. Vol. VIII, pt. 1.
Annales Placentini Gibellini (1012–1317). Ed. Pertz, G. H. MGH. XVIII. 1863. *Also* ed. Huillard-Bréholles, J. L. A. *as* Chron. de rebus in Italia gestis, *in* Chronicon Placentinum. Paris. 1856.
Annales Vincentiae (1200–1312). Ed. Soranzo, G. RR.II.SS. New edn. Vol. VIII, pt. 5.
Anonymi Itali Historia (1250–1454). Ed. Muratori. RR.II.SS. 1st edn. Vol. VIII.
Anonymi Ticinensis liber de laudibus civitatis Ticinensis (Pavia). Ed. Maiocchi, R. and Quintavalle, F. RR.II.SS. New edn. Vol. XI, pt. 1.

Antiche cronache Veronesi. Ed. Cipolla, C. and F. Vol. I. (R. Dep. Veneta di stor. pat. Monumenti. Ser. III. Vol. II.) Venice. 1890.
    Cronachetta in volgare.
    Chronica illorum de la Scala.
    Marzagaia. Opusculum. Gli Scaligeri ed i Veronesi.
    —— De modernis gestis.
Azarius, P. Liber gestorum in Lombardia. Ed. Cognasso, F. RR.II.SS. New edn. Vol. XVI, pt. 4.
Codice diplomatico Cremonese. Ed. Astegiano, L. MHP. XXI–XXII. 1895–8.
Corpus chronicorum Bononiensium. Ed. Sorbelli, A. RR.II.SS. New edn. Vol. XVIII, pt. 1.
Pagliarino, B. Croniche di Vicenza. Vicenza. 1663.

C. Tuscany.

Annales Senenses (1107–1479). Ed. Böhmer, J. F. MGH. Script. XIX. 1866.
Cronache Senesi. Ed. Lisini, A. and Jacometti, F. RR.II.SS. New edn. Vol. XV, pt. 6.
Dante Alighieri. Opere. Ed. Moore, E. and Toynbee, P. 4th edn. Oxford. 1924.
—— Opere. Testo critico della Società Dantesca Italiana. Ed. Barbi, M., etc. Florence. 1921.
Dino Compagni. Cronica. Ed. Del Lungo, I. RR.II.SS. New edn. Vol. IX, pt. 2. Original edition. 3 vols. Florence. 1879–87. Engl. transl. (Temple Classics). London. 1906.
—— Del Lungo, I. Storia esterna, vicende, avventure d' un piccol libro de' tempi di Dante. 2 vols. Milan. 1917.
Istorie Pisane di Rafaele Roncioni e Cronache varie. Ed. Bonaini, F. ASI. VI. 1844–5.
Leonardus Aretinus. Historiarum Florentini populi libri XII. Ed. Santini, E. and Di Pierro, C. RR.II.SS. New edn. Vol. XIX, pt. 3.
Marchionne di Coppo Stefani (Bonaiuti). Cronaca Fiorentina (from 1306). Ed. Rodolico, N. RR.II.SS. New edn. Vol. XXX, pt. 1.
Storie Pistoresi (1300–1348). Ed. Barbi, S. A. RR.II.SS. New edn. Vol. XI, pt. 5.
Tholomeus Lucensis. Annales. Ed. Schmeidler, B. MGH. Script. N.S. VIII. 1930. *Also* ed. Minutoli, C. *in* Documenti di storia italiana, VI : Cronache dei secoli XIII e XIV. (R. Dep. Toscana di storia patria.) Florence. 1876.
Villani, Giovanni. Historie Fiorentine. Ed. Muratori. RR.II.SS. 1st edn. Vol. XIII. And later edns. [Valuable also for other Italian states.]
Vita Castruccii Antelminelli auctore Nicolao Tegrimo. Ed. Muratori. RR.II.SS. 1st edn. Vol. XI.

D. Papacy and Papal States.

[For Registers and Letters of the Popes *see Gen. Bibl.* IV *under* Papal Documents.]

Annales Forolivienses. Ed. Mazzatinti, G. RR.II.SS. New edn. Vol. XXII, pt. 2.
Biscaro, G. Le relazioni de' Visconti con la Chiesa. ASL. XVI. 1919.
—— Dante Alighieri ed i sortilegi di Matteo e Galeazzo Visconti contro Papa Giovanni XXII. ASL. XVII. 1920.
Bullarium Franciscanum. Vol. v. Ed. Eubel, K. Rome. 1898.
Cantinelli, Petrus. Chronicon (1228–1306). Ed. Torraca, F. RR.II.SS. New edn. Vol. XXVIII, pt. 2.
Chronicon Estense. Ed. Bertoni, G. and Vicini, E. P. RR.II.SS. New edn. Vol. XV, pt. 3, in progress.
Ciatti, F. Delle memorie annali et istoriche delle cose di Perugia. 2 vols. Perugia. 1638.
Cronache Malatestiane (1295–1385). Ed. Massèra, A. F. RR.II.SS. New edn. Vol. XV, pt. 2.
Ephemerides Urbevetanae, etc. Ed. Fumi, L. RR.II.SS. New edn. Vol. XV, pt. 5. (Of this collection the Annales Urbevetanae are also ed. Bethmann, L. C. MGH. Script. XIX. 1866.)
Hieronymus de Bursellis. Cronica gestorum ac factorum civitatis Bononie. Ed. Sorbelli, A. RR.II.SS. New edn. Vol. XXIII, pt. 2.
Platina. Liber de Vita Christi et omnium pontificum. Ed. Gaida, G. RR.II.SS. New edn. Vol. III, pt. 1.

Potthast, A. Regesta Pontificum Romanorum, 1192–1304. *See Gen. Bibl.* iv.
Ptolomaeus [Tholomeus] Lucensis. Historia ecclesiastica (1–1312). Ed. Muratori. RR.II.SS. 1st edn. Vol. xi.
Raynaldus, O. Annales ecclesiastici. Vols. iv, v. *See Gen. Bibl.* v *under* Baronius.

E. Naples and Sicily.

Bartholomeus de Neocastro. Historia Sicula (1250–1293). Ed. Paladino, G. RR.II.SS. New edn. Vol. xiii, pt. 3. *Also* ed. Gregorio, R. Vol. ii. *See below.*
Capasso, B. Archivio di Stato. Inventario cronologico dei registri angioini. Naples. 1894.
Carini, I. Gli Archivi e le biblioteche di Spagna in rapporto alla storia d' Italia in generale e di Sicilia in particolare. 2 vols. Palermo. 1884, 97.
Chronicon Siciliae (820–1327). Ed. Muratori. RR.II.SS. 1st edn. Vol. x. *Also* ed. Gregorio, R. Vol. ii. *See below.*
Desclot, Bernat. Crónica del Rey En Pere e dels seus antecessors passats. Ed. Berchon, J. A. C. *in* Chroniques étrangères relatives aux expéditions françaises du xiiie siècle. Paris. 1840. Engl. transl. (1276–85). Critchlow, F. L. Princeton. 1928.
Gregorio, R. Bibliotheca scriptorum qui res in Sicilia gestas sub Aragonum imperio retulere. 2 vols. Palermo. 1791–2.
La Mantia, G. Codice diplomatico dei re aragonesi di Sicilia. Vol. i (1282–1320). Palermo. 1917.
Muntaner, Ramón. Cronica catalana. Ed. Bofarull, A. de. Barcelona. 1860. Engl. transl. Goodenough, Lady. 2 vols. (Hakluyt Soc.) London. 1920–1.
Simonsfeld, H. Documenti angioini (1316–17). Arch. Ven. xiii. 1887.
Specialis, Nicolaus. Historia Sicula (1282–1337). Ed. Muratori. RR.II.SS. 1st edn. Vol. x. *Also* ed. Gregorio, R. Vol. i. *See above.*

III. MODERN WORKS.
A. General.

Blandini, G. La Tirannide italiana nel Rinascimento. Catania. 1889.
Cipolla, C. Storia delle Signorie Italiane, 1313–1530. (Storia politica d' Italia scritta da una società d' amici. Vol. iv.) Milan. 1881.
Del Lungo, I. I Bianchi e i Neri. Milan. 1921. (2nd edn. of Da Bonifazio VIII ad Arrigo VII. Milan. 1899.)
—— Dante nei tempi di Dante. Bologna. 1888.
Israel, W. Robert König von Neapel und Kaiser Heinrich VII. Hersfeld. 1904.
Kraack, E. Rom oder Avignon? Die römische Frage unter den Päpsten Clemens V und Johann XXII. (Marburger Studien zur ält. deutsch. Gesch.) Marburg. 1929.
Lanzani, F. Storia dei Comuni italiani dalle origini al 1313. (Storia politica d' Italia scritta da una società d' amici. Vol. iii.) Milan. 1882.
Litta, P. Famiglie celebri italiane. *See Gen. Bibl.* iii.
Manfroni, C. Storia della marina italiana dal trattato di Ninfeo alla caduta di Constantinople. Pt. i. Leghorn. 1902.
Orsi, P. Signorie e Principati, 1300–1530. (Storia politica d' Italia scritta da una società di professori. Vol. v.) Milan. 1901.
Petit, L. Charles de Valois. Paris. 1900.
Poole, R. L. Illustrations of the history of Medieval Thought and Learning. *See Gen. Bibl.* v.
Renan, E. Guillaume de Nogaret. *In* Hist. littéraire de la France. Vol. xxvii. AcadIBL. Paris. 1877.
Schneider, F. Kaiser Heinrich VII. 3 pts. Greiz-im-Vogtland. 1924–8.
Toynbee, Paget. Dante dictionary. Oxford. 1898.
—— Concise Dante dictionary. Oxford. 1914.

B. North Italy.

Affò, I. Storia di Parma. 4 vols. Parma. 1792–5.
Allen, A. M. History of Verona. London. 1910.
Arco, C. d'. Storia di Mantova. Mantua. 1871.

Brown, H. F. Venice. An historical sketch. London. 1895.
—— Venetian studies. Vol. I. London. 1887.
Butler, W. F. The Lombard Communes. London. 1906.
Cappelletti, G. Storia di Padova. 2 vols. Padua. 1874–5.
Caro, G. Genua und die Mächte am Mittelmeer. Vol. II. Halle-a.-S. 1899.
Castellini, S. Storia della città di Vicenza. 5 vols. Vicenza. 1783–1823.
Cipolla, C. Compendio della storia politica di Verona. Verona. 1899.
Davari, S. Notizie storiche topografiche della città di Mantova nei secoli XIII e XIV.
    ASL. XXIV. 1897.
Foligno, C. The story of Padua. (Medieval Towns Series.) London. 1910.
Frati, L. La contesa fra Matteo Visconti e Papa Giovanni XXII. ASL. XV. 1888.
Gabotto, F. Storia del Piemonte nella prima metà del secolo XIV, 1299–1349. Turin.
    1891.
Hodgson, F. C. Venice in the thirteenth and fourteenth centuries. London. 1910.
Kretschmayr, H. Geschichte von Venedig. Vol. II. *See Gen. Bibl.* v.
Mazzi, A. Studi bergomensi. Bergamo. 1888.
Merores, M. Der grosse Rat von Venedig und die sogenannte Serrata vom Jahre
    1297. *In* Viert. für Sozial- und Wirtschaftsgesch. XXI. Stuttgart. 1928.
Molmenti, P. Storia di Venezia nella vita privata. Pt. I. La grandezza. 5th edn.
    Bergamo. 1910. Transl. Brown, H. F. Venice, its individual growth, etc.
    Pt. I. The Middle Ages. 2 vols. London. 1906.
Monti, G. M. La Dominazione angioina in Piemonte. *In* Bibl. d. soc. stor. subalpina.
    CXVI. Turin. 1930.
Muir, D. History of Milan under the Visconti. London. 1924.
Poggiali, C. Memorie storiche di Piacenza. Piacenza. 1789.
Romanin, S. Storia documentata di Venezia. Vols. II, III. Venice. 1855.
Sommerfeldt, G. König Heinrich VII und die Lombardischen Städte. DZG. II.
    1889.
Soranzo, G. La guerra fra Venezia e la Santa Sede per il dominio di Ferrara, 1308–
    1313. Città di Castello. 1905.
Spangenberg, H. Cangrande I della Scala. 2 vols. Berlin. 1892, 95.
Verci, G. B. Storia della Marca Trivigiana e Veronese. 20 vols. Venice. 1786–91.
Volta, C. Storia di Mantova. Mantua. 1807.
Wychgram, J. Albertino Mussato. Ein Beitrag zur italienischen Geschichte.
    Leipsic. 1880.

C. Tuscany.

Caggese, R. Firenze dalla decadenza di Roma al risorgimento d' Italia. Vol. II.
    Florence. 1913.
Capponi, G. Storia della repubblica di Firenze. Vol. I. Florence. 1876.
Davidsohn, R. Geschichte von Florenz. Vols. II, pt. ii–iv. *See Gen. Bibl.* v. [Useful
    for all Italian history of this period.]
—— Forschungen zur Geschichte von Florenz. Vol. III. Berlin. 1901.
Del Lungo, I. Dell' esilio di Dante. Florence. 1881.
Douglas, R. L. History of Siena. London. 1902.
Manucci, A. Le Azioni di Castruccio Castracane degli Antelminelli. Lucca. 1843.
Peruzzi, S. L. Storia di commercio di Firenze, 1200–1345. Florence. 1868.
Salvemini, G. Magnati e popolani in Firenze, 1280–95. Florence. 1899.
—— La dignità cavalleresca nel comune di Firenze. Florence. 1896.
Sforza, G. Castruccio Castracani. *In* Mem. della R. Accad. di Torino. 2nd ser.
    XLII. Turin. 1891.
Silva, P. Giacomo II d' Aragona e la Toscana, 1307–9. ASI. LXXI. 1913.
Vigo, P. Uguccione della Faggiuola. Leghorn. 1879.
Villari, P. I primi due secoli della storia di Firenze. 2nd edn. Florence. 1905.
    Engl. transl. Villari, L. London. 1901.

D. Papacy and Papal States.

Antonelli, M. Vicende della dominazione pontificia nel Patrimonio. ASRSP. XXV–
    XXVII. 1902–4.

Arias, G. Studi e documenti della storia del diritto. Florence. 1901. [Relates to Tuscan bankers and Papacy, 1300–4.]
—— I banchieri Toscani e la Santa Sede sotto Benedetto XI. ASRSP. xxiv. 1901.
—— Le Società di Commercio medievali in rapporto con la Chiesa. *Ibid.* xxix. 1906.
Baluzius, S. Vitae paparum Avenionensium. *See Gen. Bibl.* iv.
Bonazzi, L. Storia di Perugia. Perugia. 1875.
Ciatti, F. Delle memorie annali et istoriche delle cose di Perugia. 2 vols. Perugia. 1638.
Döllinger, J. J. von. Addresses on historical and literary subjects (on the outrage of Anagni). Transl. Warre, M. London. 1894.
Dupuy, P. Histoire du différend d'entre le Pape Boniface VIII et Philippes le Bel. Paris. 1655.
Eitel, A. Der Kirchenstaat unter Clemenz VII. Berlin and Leipsic. 1907.
Finke, H. Aus den Tagen Bonifaz VIII. Münster-i.-W. 1902.
Frati, L. La Vita privata di Bologna dal secolo xiii. Bologna. 1900.
Frizzi, A. Memorie della storia di Ferrara. 2nd edn. Ferrara. 1847.
Funke, P. Papst Benedikt XI. (Kirchengesch. Studien. Ed. Knöpfler, A., etc. i. i.) Münster-i.-W. 1891.
Gorreta, A. La lotta fra il Comune Bolognese e la Signoria Estense. Bologna. 1906.
Gregorovius, F. Geschichte der Stadt Rom im Mittelalter. *See Gen. Bibl.* v.
Heywood, W. History of Perugia. London. 1910.
—— Palio and Ponte. London. 1909.
Holtzmann, R. Wilhelm von Nogaret. Freiburg-i.-B. 1898.
Huyskens, A. Kardinal Napoleone Orsini. Marburg. 1902.
James, E. E. C. Bologna: its history, antiquities, and art. London. 1909.
Levi, G. Bonifazio VIII. Le sue relazioni col Comune di Firenze. ASRSP. v. 1882.
Lizerand, V. G. Clément V et Philippe le Bel. Paris. 1910.
Mollat, G. Les Papes d'Avignon. *See Gen. Bibl.* v.
Pellini, P. Historia di Perugia. Venice. 1664.
Reumont, A. von. Geschichte der Stadt Rom. Vol. ii. Berlin. 1868.
Scholz, R. Die Publizistik zur Zeit Philipps des Schönen und Bonifaz VIII. (Kirchenrechtliche Abhandlungen. Ed. Stutz, U., 6–8.) Stuttgart. 1903.
Verlagne, G. Jean XXII, sa vie et ses oeuvres. Paris. 1883.
Vitale, V. Il dominio della Parte Guelfa in Bologna, 1280–1327. Bologna. 1901.
Wenck, C. Clement V und Heinrich VII. Halle. 1882.

E. NAPLES AND SICILY.

Amari, M. La Guerra del Vespro Siciliano. 9th edn. 3 vols. Milan. 1886.
Baddeley, R. St Clair. Robert the Wise. London. 1897.
Bozzo, S. V. Note storiche siciliane del secolo xiv, 1302–7. Palermo. 1882.
Cadier, L. Essai sur l'administration du royaume de Sicile sous Charles I et Charles II d'Anjou. EcfrAR. Paris. 1891.
Caggese, C. Roberto d'Angiò. 2 vols. Florence. 1922, 31. [Gives political narrative and is especially important for institutions and economics.]
Carabellese, F. Le relazioni commerciali tra la Puglia e la Repubblica di Venezia. Trani. 1897.
—— Saggio di storia del Commercio della Puglia. Trani. 1900.
Giannone, P. Istoria civile del Regno di Napoli. Vol. vii. Naples. 1823.
Goetz, W. König Robert von Neapel. Tübingen. 1910.
Haberkern, E. Der Kampf um Sizilien in den Jahren 1302–1337. (Abh. zur mittl. und neueren Gesch. Ed. Below, G. von, etc. 67.) Berlin. 1921.
Jordan, E. Les origines de la domination angevine en Italie. Paris. 1909.
Minieri Riccio, C. Genealogia di Carlo II. ASPN. vii, viii. 1882–3.
Rohde, H. E. Der Kampf um Sizilien in den Jahren 1291–1302. (Abh. zur mittl. und neueren Gesch. Ed. Below, G. von, etc. 42.) Berlin. 1913.
Schipa, M. Carlo Martello. ASPN. xiv, xv. 1889–90.
Yver, G. Le commerce et les marchands dans l'Italie méridionale au xiiie et au xive siècle. Paris. 1903.

CHAPTER II.

ITALY, 1313–1414.

I. BIBLIOGRAPHIES.

Bianchi, N. Materie politiche degli archivi piemontesi. Turin. 1876.
Capasso, B. Le fonti della storia delle provincie napolitane dal 568 al 1500. *See Gen. Bibl.* i.
—— Inventario dei registri angioini, etc. Naples. 1894.
Egidi, P. La storia medioevale. *See Gen. Bibl.* i.
Fontana, L. Bibliografia statutaria comunale. Turin. 1907.
Mazzatinti, G. Gli archivi della storia d' Italia. 5 vols. Rocca S. Casciano. 1897–1906.
Reumont, A. Bibliografia dei lavori pubblicati in Germania su la storia d' Italia. Berlin. 1863.

II. SOURCES.

A. DOCUMENTS, ETC.

[For Registers and Letters of the Popes *see Gen. Bibl.* iv *under* Papal Documents.]

Acta Aragonensia. Ed. Finke, H. 3 vols. Berlin. 1908 ff., in progress.
Baluzius, S. Vitae paparum Avenionensium. *See Gen. Bibl.* iv.
Böhmer, J. F. Regesta imperii. *See Gen. Bibl.* iv.
Briefwechsel des Cola di Rienzo. Ed. Burdach, K. and Piur, P. 5 vols. (PAW.) Berlin. 1912–29.
Bullarium Franciscanum, etc. Vols. v, vi. Ed. Eubel, K. Rome. 1898, 1902.
Codex Italiae diplomaticus. Ed. Lünig, J. C. 4 vols. Frankfort. 1725–35.
Constitutiones et Acta publica imperatorum et regum. Vols. v, vi. i. MGH. Legum Sect. iv. 1909–27.
Costituzioni egidiane del 1357. Ed. Sella, P. *in* Corpus Statutorum Italiae. Rome. 1912.
Documenti di storia italiana. Publ. by R. Deputazione Toscana di storia patria. Florence. 1867 ff., in progress.
Epistolario di Cola di Rienzo. Ed. Gabrielli, A. (Fonti.) 1892.
Epistolario di Coluccio Salutati. Ed. Novati, F. 4 vols. (Fonti.) 1891–1905.
Epistolario di Pellegrino Zambeccari. Ed. Frati, L. (Fonti.) 1929.
Luchaire, J. Documenti per la storia dei rivolgimenti politici del comune di Siena dal 1354 al 1369. Paris. 1906.
Monumenta historiae patriae. *See Gen. Bibl.* iv.
Monumenta Hungariae historica. Ser. iv. Acta extera. Vols. i–iii. (Magyar Tudományos Akad.) Buda-Pest. 1874–6.
Osio, L. Documenti diplomatici tratti dagli archivi milanesi. 3 vols. Milan. 1864.
Repertorio diplomatico visconteo. Vols. i, ii. (Soc. stor. Lombarda.) Milan. 1911 ff., in progress.
Vatikanische Akten. Ed. Riezler, S. *See Gen. Bibl.* iv *under* Papal Documents.
Vatikanische Quellen zur Geschichte der päpstlichen Hof- und Finanzverwaltung 1316–78, etc. Ed. Göller, E. and Schäfer, K. H. *Ibid.*

B. CHRONICLES, ETC.

Annales Mediolanenses. Ed. Muratori. RR.II.SS. 1st edn. Vol. xvi.
Annales Parmenses maiores. Ed. Jaffé, P. MGH. Script. xviii. 1863. *Also* ed. Bonazzi, G. *as* Chronicon Parmense. RR.II.SS. New edn. Vol. ix, pt. 9.
Azarius, P. Liber gestorum in Lombardia. Ed. Cognasso, F. RR.II.SS. New edn. Vol. xvi, pt. 4.
Bazano, Joannes (de). Chronicon Mutinense. Ed. Casini, E. RR.II.SS. New edn. Vol. xv, pt. 4.
Camera, M. Annali del Regno delle Due Sicilie. 2 vols. Naples. 1842, 60.

Campanus, J. A. De vita et gestis Braccii. Ed. Valentini, R. RR.II.SS. New edn. Vol. xix, pt. 4.

Chronicon Estense. Ed. Bertoni, G. and Vicini, E. P. RR.II.SS. New edn. Vol. xv, pt. 3, in progress.

Chronicon Parmense. Ed. Bonazzi, G. RR.II.SS. New edn. Vol. ix, pt. 9.

Chronicon Placentinum. Ed. Muratori. RR.II.SS. 1st edn. Vol. xvi.

Conforto da Costoza. Frammenti di storia vicentina. Ed. Steiner, C. RR.II.SS. New edn. Vol. xiii, pt. 1.

Corpus chronicorum Bononiensium. Ed. Sorbelli, A. RR.II.SS. New edn. Vol. xviii, pt. 1.

Cronache Catalane del secolo xiii e xiv. Ed. Moisè, F. Florence. 1844.

Cronache Malatestiane dei secoli xiv e xv. Ed. Massèra, A. F. RR.II.SS. New edn. Vol. xv, pt. 2.

Dei, Andrea. Cronica Sanese. Ed. Muratori. RR.II.SS. 1st edn. Vol. xv.

Ephemerides Urbevetanae. Ed. Fumi, L. RR.II.SS. New edn. Vol. xv, pt. 5.

Ferreto dei Ferreti. Le Opere. Ed. Cipolla, C. 3 vols. (Fonti.) 1908-20.

Ghirardacci, Cherubino. Della Historia di Bologna. Ed. Sorbelli, A. RR.II.SS. New edn. Vol. xxxiii, pt. 1.

Gravina, Dominicus de. Chronicon de rebus in Apulia gestis. Ed. Sorbelli, A. RR.II.SS. New edn. Vol. xii, pt. 3.

Griffonibus, Matthaeus de. Memoriale historicum de rebus Bononiensium. Ed. Frati, L. and Sorbelli, A. RR.II.SS. New edn. Vol. xviii, pt. 2.

Historia Cortusiorum. Ed. Muratori. RR.II.SS. 1st edn. Vol. xii.

Leonardus Aretinus. Historiarum Florentini populi libri xii. Ed. Santini, E. and Di Pierro, C. RR.II.SS. New edn. Vol. xix, pt. 3.

Marchionne di Coppo Stefani (Bonaiuti). Cronaca Fiorentina. Ed. Rodolico, N. RR.II.SS. New edn. Vol. xxx, pt. 1.

Minuti, A. Vita di Muzio Attendolo Sforza. Ed. Lambertenghi, G.P. *in* Miscell. di storia italiana. vii. (R. Dep. di stor. pat.) Turin. 1869.

Morigia, Bonincontro. Chronicon Modoetiense. Ed. Muratori. RR.II.SS. 1st edn. Vol. xi.

Neri di Donato. Cronica Sanese. Ed. Muratori. RR.II.SS. 1st edn. Vol. xv.

Raynaldus, O. Annales ecclesiastici. *See Gen. Bibl.* v *under* Baronius.

Sercambi, Giovanni. Le Croniche. Ed. Bongi, S. (Fonti.) 1892.

Stella, G. Annales Genuenses. Ed. Muratori. RR.II.SS. 1st edn. Vol. xvii.

Storie Pistoresi. Ed. Barbi, S. A. RR.II.SS. New edn. Vol. xi, pt. 5.

Velluti, D. Cronica. Ed. Manni, D. M. Florence. 1731.

Ventura, G. Memoriale. Ed. Muratori. RR.II.SS. 1st edn. Vol. xii.

Villani, Giovanni and Matteo. Historie Fiorentine. **Ed.** Muratori. RR.II.SS. 1st edn. Vols. xiii, xiv. And later edns.

III. MODERN WORKS.

A. General.

Arias, G. Il sistema della costituzione econ. e sociale italiana nell' età dei Comuni. Turin. 1905.

Balbo, C. Sommario della storia d' Italia. Ed. Solmi, A. Milan. 1927.

Cipolla, C. Storia delle Signorie italiane. (Storia politica d' Italia scritta da una società d' amici. Vol. iv.) Milan. 1881.

Emerton, E. Humanism and Tyranny. Studies in the Italian Trecento. Cambridge, Mass. 1925.

Emiliani-Giudici, P. Storia politica dei municipi italiani. 2 vols. Florence. 1851.

Ercole, F. Dal Comune al Principato. Florence. 1929.

Luchaire, J. Les démocraties italiennes. Paris. 1916.

Mirot, L. La politique pontificale et le retour du Saint Siège à Rome. Paris. 1899.

Mollat, G. Les Papes d'Avignon. *See Gen. Bibl.* v.

Orsi, P. Signorie e Principati, 1300-1530. (Storia politica d' Italia scritta da una società di professori. Vol. v.) Milan. 1901.

Ricotti, E. Storia delle compagnie di ventura in Italia. Turin. 1893.

Salzer, E. Über die Anfänge der Signorie in Oberitalien. Berlin. 1900.

Schulte, A. Geschichte des mittelalterlichen Handels und Verkehrs zwischen Westdeutschland und Italien. 2 vols. Leipsic. 1900.
Segre, A. Storia del commercio. 2nd edn. 2 vols. Turin. 1923.
Tocco, F. La questione della povertà nel secolo xiv. Naples. 1910.
Volpe, G. Il Medioevo. Florence. 1927.
Weber, M. Zur Geschichte der Handelsgesellschaften im Mittelalter. Stuttgart. 1889.

B. SPECIAL.

Baddeley, W. St Clair. Robert the Wise. London. 1897.
Baldasseroni, F. La guerra tra Firenze e G. Visconti. *In* Studi storici. Ed. Crivellucci, A. Vols. xi, xii. Pisa. 1902–3.
Barbadoro, B. Le finanze della repubblica fiorentina. Florence. 1930.
Broglio d' Ajano, R. Tumulti e scioperi a Siena nel secolo xiv. *In* Viert. für Sozial- und Wirtschaftsgesch. v. Stuttgart. 1907.
—— Lotte sociali a Perugia nel secolo xiv. *Ibid.* viii. 1910.
Caggese, R. Firenze dalla decadenza di Roma al risorgimento d' Italia. 3 vols. Florence. 1912–21.
—— Roberto d' Angiò e i suoi tempi. 2 vols. Florence. 1922, 31.
Canale, M. G. Nuova storia della repubblica di Genova. Vols. i–iv. Florence. 1858–64.
Cerasoli, F. Clemente VI e Giovanna I di Napoli. ASPN. xxi, xxii. 1896–7.
—— Innocenzo VI e Giovanna I. *Ibid.* xxii, xxiii. 1897–8.
—— Gregorio XI e Giovanna I. *Ibid.* xxiv, xxv. 1899–1900.
Ciasca, R. L' Arte dei Medici e Speziali nella storia e nel commercio fiorentino. Florence. 1927.
Cibrario, L. Storia della monarchia di Savoja. 3 vols. Turin. 1841–2.
Cognasso, F. Amedeo VIII. 2 vols. (Collana storica Sabauda.) Turin. 1930.
—— Il Conte Rosso. (*Ibid.*) Turin. 1931.
—— Il Conte Verde. (*Ibid.*) Turin. 1926.
Collino, L. La guerra viscontea contro gli Scaligeri. ASL. xxxiv. 1907.
—— La preparazione della guerra veneto-viscontea contro i Carraresi. *Ibid.*
Cutolo, A. Per una storia di Re Ladislao. Naples. 1926.
—— Maria d' Enghien. Naples. 1929.
Davidsohn, R. Geschichte von Florenz. Vols. iii, iv. *See Gen. Bibl.* v.
—— Forschungen zur Geschichte von Florenz. Vol. iii. Berlin. 1908.
Doren, A. Studien aus florentiner Wirtschaftsgeschichte. 2 vols. Stuttgart. 1901, 8.
Falletti, P. Il tumulto dei Ciompi. Turin. 1882.
Filippini, F. La prima legazione del cardinale Albornoz in Italia (1353–7). *In* Studi storici. Ed. Crivellucci, A. Vol. v. Pisa. 1896.
—— La riconquista dello stato della Chiesa per opera di Egidio Albornoz (1353–7). *Ibid.* vi–viii. 1897–9.
—— La seconda legazione del cardinale Albornoz in Italia (1358–67). *Ibid.* Vols. xii–xiv. 1903–5.
Frati, L. La contesa fra Matteo Visconti e Giovanni XXII. ASL. xv. 1888.
Gabotto, F. Storia del Piemonte nella prima metà del secolo xiv. Turin. 1894.
Gherardi, A. La guerra degli Otto Santi. ASI. Ser. iii. Vols. v–viii. 1867–8.
Gregorovius, F. Geschichte der Stadt Rom im Mittelalter. *See Gen. Bibl.* v.
Heynen, R. Zur Entstehung des Kapitalismus in Venedig. Stuttgart. 1905.
Kretschmayr, H. Geschichte von Venedig. *See Gen. Bibl.* v.
Maranini, G. La costituzione di Venezia dalle origini al 1297. Venice. 1927.
Michel, R. Le procès de Matteo et Galeazzo Visconti. *In* Mélanges d'archéol. et d'hist. xxix. (École franç. de Rome.) 1909.
Müller, C. Der Kampf Ludwigs des Baiern mit der römischen Curie. 2 vols. Tübingen. 1879–80.
Otto, H. Zur italienischen Politik Johanns XXII. Rome. 1911.
Paoli, C. Della signoria di Gualtieri Duca d'Atene in Firenze. *In* Giornale stor. degli Archivi Toscani. vi. Florence. 1862.
Pirchan, G. Italien und Kaiser Karl IV in der Zeit seiner zweiten Romfahrt. 2 vols. Prague. 1930.

Piur, P. Cola di Rienzo. Vienna. 1931.
Pöhlmann, L. Die Wirtschaftspolitik der florentiner Renaissance. Leipsic. 1878.
Professione, A. Siena e le compagnie di ventura. Civitanova-Marche. 1898.
Ratti, A. (S.S. Pio XI). Intorno all' anno della scomunica di Matteo Visconti.
    In Rend. del R. Istit. Lombardo di Scienze e Lettere. Ser. ii. Vol. xxxvi.
    Milan. 1903.
Rodolico, N. Dal Comune alla Signoria. Bologna. 1898.
—— La democrazia fiorentina nel suo tramonto. Bologna. 1904.
Romanin, S. Storia documentata di Venezia. 10 vols. Venice. 1853–61.
Romano, G. Niccolò Spinelli da Giovinazzo. Naples. 1902.
Sapori, A. La crisi delle compagnie mercantili dei Bardi e dei Peruzzi. Florence.
    1926.
Schäfer, K. H. Deutsche Ritter und Edelknechte in Italien während des 14 Jahrht.
    (Quellen u. Forsch. aus d. Gebiete d. Gesch. xv, xvi.) Paderborn. 1911, 14.
Sieveking, H. Studio su le finanze genovesi nel medioevo. Genoa. 1906.
Sighinolfi, L. La signoria di Giovanni Oleggio in Bologna. Bologna. 1905.
Silva, P. Il governo di Pietro Gambacorta a Pisa. Pisa. 1911.
Sorbelli, A. La signoria di Giovanni Visconti a Bologna e le sue relazioni con la
    Toscana. Bologna. 1902.
Steele, F. M. The beautiful Queen, Joanna I of Naples. London. 1910.
Villari, P. Niccolò Machiavelli e i suoi tempi. 3rd edn. 2 vols. Milan. 1927.
Wenck, K. Clemens V und Heinrich VII. Halle. 1882.
Werunsky, E. Geschichte Kaiser Karls IV und seiner Zeit. 3 vols in 4. Innsbruck.
    1880–92.
Zerbi, L. I Visconti di Milano e la signoria di Lucca. Como. 1894.

CHAPTER III.

GERMANY, 1273-1313 (*by* Professor W. T. Waugh).

I. BIBLIOGRAPHIES.

Bresslau, H. Handbuch der Urkundenlehre für Deutschland und Italien. *See Gen. Bibl.* I.

Dahlmann-Waitz. Quellenkunde. *See Gen. Bibl.* I.

Lorenz, O. Deutschlands Geschichtsquellen im Mittelalter seit der Mitte des 13 Jahrhts. *See Gen. Bibl.* I.

Potthast, A. Bibliotheca historica medii aevi. *See Gen. Bibl.* I.

II. DOCUMENTS.

Baumgartenberger Formelbuch. Ed. Bärwald, H. (Fontes rerum Austriacarum. Abt. II. Vol. xxv.) Vienna. 1866.

Bodmann, F. J. Codex epistolaris Rudolfi I Romanorum regis. Leipsic. 1806.

Böhmer, J. F. Acta imperii selecta. Ed. Ficker, J. Innsbruck. 1870.

—— Regesta imperii, 1246-1313. *See Gen. Bibl.* IV.

—— —— (New edn.) Vol. VI. i (1273-91). *Ibid.*

Bonaini, F. Acta Henrici VII Romanorum imperatoris et monumenta quaedam alia suorum temporum historiam illustrantia. 2 vols. Florence. 1877.

Constitutiones et Acta publica imperatorum et regum. Vols. III, IV. i, ii. MGH. Legum Sect. IV. 1904-11.

Dönniges, G. Acta Henrici VII imperatoris Romanorum et monumenta quaedam medii aevi. 2 pts. Berlin. 1839.

Finke, H. Acta Aragonensia. 3 vols. Berlin. 1908 ff., in progress.

Formelbuch König Albrechts I. Ed. Chmel, J. AOG. II.

Gerbert, M. Codex epistolaris Rudolphi I Romanorum regis. St Blasien. 1772.

Kaltenbrunner, F. Aktenstücke zur Geschichte des Deutschen Reiches unter den Königen Rudolf I und Albrecht I. (Mitteilungen aus dem Vatikan. Archive, I.) Vienna. 1889.

Kern, F. Acta Imperii, Angliae, et Franciae ab anno 1267 ad annum 1313. Tübingen. 1911.

Krammer, M. Quellen zur Geschichte der deutschen Königswahl und des Kurfürstenkollegs. Leipsic. 1911.

Martène, E. and Durand, U. Thesaurus anecdotorum novus. *See Gen. Bibl.* IV.

Raynaldus, O. Annales ecclesiastici. Vols. III, IV. Ed. Mansi, J. D. *See Gen. Bibl.* V *under* Baronius.

Regesta Habsburgica. Abt. I. Die Regesten der Grafen von Habsburg bis 1281. Ed. Steinacker, H. Innsbruck. 1905.

Regesten der Bischöfe von Strassburg. Vol. II. Ed. Hessel, A. and Krebs, M. Innsbruck. 1924-8.

Regesten der Erzbischöfe und des Domkapitels von Salzburg, 1247-1343. Pt. II (1270-1290). Ed. Martin, F. Salzburg. 1928.

Regesten der Erzbischöfe von Köln im Mittelalter. Vol. III (1205-1304), ed. Knipping, R. Vol. IV (1304-1332), ed. Kisky, W. Bonn. 1909, 15.

Regesten der Erzbischöfe von Mainz, 1289-1396. Ed. Vogt, E. and Vigener, F. 2 vols. Leipsic. 1907-14.

Regesten der Markgrafen von Brandenburg aus askanischem Hause. Ed. Krabbo, H. 8 vols. Leipsic and Berlin. 1910-26.

Riezler, S. Urkunden zur bairischen und deutschen Geschichte aus den Jahren 1256-1353. FDG. xx. 1880.

Schwalm, J. Formulare aus Rudolf von Habsburgs Kanzlei. Neu. Arch. xxviii.

Schwalm, **J.** Neue Aktenstücke zur Geschichte der Beziehungen Clemens V und Heinrich VII. QFIA. v. 1904.

Stengel, E. Nova Alamanniae. Urkunden, Briefe, und andere Quellen besonders zur deutschen Geschichte des 14 Jahrhunderts. 2 pts. Berlin. 1921, 30.

Summa curiae regis [Formulary of reigns of Rudolf I and Albert I]. Ed. Stobbe, O. AOG. xiv.

Winkelmann, **E.** Acta imperii saeculi xiii et xiv. 2 vols. *See Gen. Bibl.* iv.

III. NARRATIVE AUTHORITIES.

Albertinus Mussatus. Historia Augusta sive de Gestis Henrici VII libri 16. Ed. Muratori. RR.II.SS. 1st edn. Vol. x.

Albertus de Bezanis. Cronica pontificum et imperatorum. Ed. Holder-Egger, O. SGUS. 1908.

Annales Basileenses. MGH. Script. xvii.

Annales Colmarienses Maiores. MGH. Script. xvii.

Annales Heinrici de Heimberg. MGH. Script. xvii.

Annales Lubicenses. MGH. Script. xvi.

Annales Mellicenses, with continuations. MGH. Script. ix.

Annales Sancti Rudberti Salisburgenses, with continuations by Weichard von Polhain and others. MGH. Script. ix.

Annales Wormatienses, with continuation to 1298. MGH. Script. xvii. *Also* ed. Boos, H. *in* Quellen zur Geschichte der Stadt Worms. Vol. iii. Berlin. 1886 ff.

Bairische Fortsetzungen der Sächsischen Weltchronik. Ed. Weiland, L. MGH. Deutsche Chroniken. ii.

Benesch Krabice of Weitmühl. Chronicon. Ed. Emler, J. *in* Fontes rerum Bohemicarum. Vol. iv. Prague. 1882.

Böhmische Reimchronik by "Dalimil" (in Czech). *Ibid.* Vol. iii. 1878. German transl. in prose (of *c.* 1320) and in verse (of *c.* 1346) ed. Hanka, V. *in* Bibl. des literar. Vereins in Stuttgart. Vol. xlviii. 1859.

Chronica Sancti Petri Erfordensis moderna. MGH. Script. xxx. *Also* ed. Holder-Egger, O. *in* Monumenta Erphesfurtensia. SGUS. 1899.

Chronica Reinhardsbrunnensis. MGH. Script. xxx.

Chronicae Bavaricae saec. xiv. Ed. Leidinger, G. SGUS. 1918.

Chronicon Colmariense. MGH. Script. xvii.

Eberhard von Regensburg. Annales, 1273–1305. MGH. Script. xvii.

Fritsche Closener. Strassburgische Chronik. Ed. Hegel, C. *in* Chroniken der deutschen Städte. Vol. viii. Leipsic. 1870.

Gesta Boemundi archiepiscopi Treverensis. MGH. Script. xxiv.

Heinrich Taube von Selbach. Chronica. Ed. Bresslau, H. MGH. Script. N.S. i. 1922.

Henricus de Hervordia. Liber de rebus memorabilioribus. Ed. Potthast, A. Göttingen. 1859.

Hermannus Altahensis. Annales, Continuations of. MGH. Script. xvii.

Jacob von Mainz. Gesta Adolfi, Alberti, Heinrici VII. Ed. Waitz, G. FDG. xiii, xiv, xv. 1873–5.

Jacob Twinger von Königshofen. Chronik. Ed. Hegel, C. *in* Chroniken der deutschen Städte. Vols. viii, ix. Leipsic. 1870–1.

Johann von Winterthur. Chronica. Ed. Baethgen, F. MGH. Script. N.S. iii. 1924.

Johannes abbas Victoriensis. Liber certarum historiarum. Ed. Schneider, F. 2 vols. SGUS. 1909–10.

Johannes de Cermenate. Historia. Ed. Ferrai, L. A. (Fonti.) 1889.

Konrad von Halberstadt. Chronicon. Ed. Wenck, K. FDG. xx. 1880.

Konrad von Mure. Commendatitia [Poem in praise of Rudolf I]. Ed. Bendel, F. J. MIOGF. xxx. 1909.

Lübecker Chronik. Ed. Koppmann, K. *in* Chroniken der deutschen Städte. Vol. xix. Leipsic. 1884.

Mathias von Neuenburg. Chronica. Ed. Hofmeister, A. MGH. Script. N.S. iv, 1. 1924, in progress.

Monachus Furstfeldensis. Chronica de gestis principum. Ed. Böhmer, J. F. *in* Fontes rerum Germanicarum. Vol. I. Stuttgart. 1843.
Nicolaus de Butrinto. Relatio de Henrici VII itinere Italico. Ed. Heyck, E. Innsbruck. 1888. *Also in* Baluzius, S. Vitae paparum Avenionesium; ed. Mollat, G. Vol. III, pp. 491–561. Paris. 1921.
Otto and Peter von Zittau. Chronica Aulae regiae libri tres. Ed. Emler, J. *in* Fontes rerum Bohemicarum. Vol. IV. Prague. 1882. *Also* ed. Loserth, J. *as* Die Königsaaler Geschichtsquellen, *in* Fontes rerum Austriacarum. Abt. I. Script. VIII. Vienna. 1875.
Ottokars Österreichische Reimchronik, 1250–1309. Ed. Seemüller, J. MGH. Deutsche Chroniken. v. i, ii.
Rhythmus über die Schlacht auf dem Marchfelde. Ed. Huemer, J. AOG. LXVIII.
Villani, Giovanni. Historie Fiorentine. Ed. Muratori. RR.II.SS. 1st edn. Vol. XIII. *Also* ed. Dragomanni, F. G. 6 vols. Florence. 1844–6.
Vita Brunonis Olomucensis. Ed. Dudik, B. AOG. LXV.
Les Voeux de l'épervier [Poem on the Italian expedition of Henry VII]. Ed. Wolfram, G. and Bonnardot, J. *in* Jahrb. der Gesellsch. für Lothringische Gesch. VI. Metz. 1896.

IV. MODERN WORKS.

A. GENERAL.

Hauck, A. Kirchengeschichte Deutschlands. Vol. v. *See Gen. Bibl.* v.
Kern, F. Analekten zur Gesch. des 13 u. 14 Jahrhts. MIOGF. XXX, XXXI. 1909–10.
Kopp, J. E. Geschichten von der Wiederherstellung und dem Verfalle des heiligen Römischen Reiches. 5 vols. Berlin and Basle. 1845–82.
Krammer, M. Wahl und Einsetzung des Deutschen Königs im Verhältnis zu einander. Weimar. 1905.
Lichnowsky, E. M. Fürst von. Gesch. des Hauses Habsburg. 8 pts. Vienna. 1836–44.
Lindner, T. Deutsche Geschichte unter den Habsburgern und Luxemburgern. 2 vols. (Bibliothek deutscher Geschichte. Ed. Zwiedineck-Südenhorst, H. von.) Stuttgart. 1888–93.
Lorenz, O. Deutsche Geschichte im 13 und 14 Jahrht. 2 vols. Vienna. 1863, 67.
Michael, E. Geschichte des deutschen Volkes vom 13 Jahrht. bis zum Ausgang des Mittelalters. 5 vols. Freiburg. 1897–1911.
Papsttum und Kaisertum. Forschungen zur polit. Geschichte und Geisteskultur des Mittelalters (Festschrift für Paul Kehr). Ed. Brackmann, A. Munich. 1926.
Samanek, V. Kronrat und Reichsherrschaft im 13 und 14 Jahrht. Berlin and Leipsic. 1910.
Stutz, U. Der Erzbischof von Mainz und die deutsche Königswahl. Weimar. 1910.

B. SPECIAL.

Baethgen, F. Der Anspruch des Papsttums auf dem Reichsvikariat. ZSR. XLI. Kanon. Abt. 1919.
—— Die Promissio Albrechts I für Bonifaz VIII. *In* Aus Politik u. Gesch. Gedächtnisschrift für G. von Below. Berlin. 1928.
—— Ein Versuch Rudolfs von Habsburg die Reichsrechte in Toskana wahrzunehmen. HVJS. XXII.
Barthold, F. W. Der Römerzug König Heinrichs von Lützelburg. 2 vols. Königsberg. 1830–1.
Beckmann, G. Thronbesteigung Papst Bonifaz' VIII und König Adolf von Nassau. Neu. Arch. XXXII. 1906.
Bergengrün, A. Die politischen Beziehungen Deutschlands zu Frankreich während der Regierung Adolfs von Nassau. Strasbourg. 1884.
Bresslau, H. Zur Vorgeschichte der Wahl Rudolfs I. MIOGF. xv. 1894.
Busson, A. Der falsche Friedrich. SKAW. CXI. 1885.
—— Die Wahl Adolfs von Nassau. SKAW. CXIV. 1887.
Dobenecker, O. König Rudolfs I Friedenspolitik in Thüringen. *In* Zeitschr. des Vereins für Thüringische Gesch. und Altertumskunde. n.s. IV. Jena.
Fournier, P. Le royaume d'Arles et de Vienne (1138–1378). Paris. 1891.

Gössgen, G. Die Beziehungen König Rudolfs von Habsburg zum Elsass. Strasbourg. 1899.

Gräfe, K. Die Persönlichkeit Kaiser Heinrichs VII. Leipsic. 1911.

Grauert, H. Zur Vorgeschichte der Wahl Rudolfs von Habsburg. HJ. xiii. 1893.

Haering, H. Der Reichskrieg gegen Graf Eberhard den Erlauchten von Württemberg…1310–16 und seine Stellung in der allgemeinen deutschen Geschichte. *In* Württemberg. Jahrb. f. Statist. und Landeskunde. Stuttgart. 1910.

Havet, J. La frontière d'Empire dans l'Argonne. Enquête faite par ordre de Rodolphe de Habsbourg à Verdun en Mai 1288. BEC. xlii. 1881.

Heller, J. Deutschland und Frankreich in ihren politischen Beziehungen vom Ende des Interregnums bis zum Tode Rudolfs von Habsburg. Göttingen. 1874.

Henneberg, H. Die politischen Beziehungen zwischen Deutschland und Frankreich unter König Albrecht I. Strasbourg. 1891. [diss.]

Hessel, A. Jahrbücher des Deutschen Reichs unter König Albrecht I von Habsburg. (Hist. Commission BAW.) Munich. 1931.

—— Die Politik König Albrechts I. *In* Historische Blätter. Herausg. von Haus-, Hof-, und Staatsarchiv in Wien. i. Vienna. 1922.

Hörneke, W. Albrecht I und die Kurfürsten. Halle. 1908.

Hovedissen, H. König Albrechts I Verhältnis zu Böhmen. Erlangen. 1891. [diss.]

Huber, A. Rudolf von Habsburg vor seiner Thronbesteigung. Vienna. 1873.

Kienast, W. Die deutschen Fürsten im Dienste der Westmächte bis zum Tode Philipps des Schönen von Frankreich. Vol. i. Utrecht, etc. 1924.

Köhler, G. Die Schlacht auf dem Marchfelde am 26 August 1278. FDG. xix–xxi. 1879–81.

Kraussold, M. Die politischen Beziehungen zwischen Deutschland und Frankreich während der Regierung Heinrichs VII. Munich. 1900. [diss.]

Krebs, M. Konrad III von Lichtenberg, Bischof von Strassburg. Frankfort. 1926.

Leroux, A. Recherches critiques sur les relations politiques de la France avec l'Allemagne de 1292 à 1378. Paris. 1882.

Mücke, J. F. A. Albrecht I von Habsburg. Gotha. 1866.

Neumann, W. Päpstliche Reichsreformpläne im 13 Jahrht. *In* Festschrift für Hermann Reincke-Bloch. Breslau. 1927.

Niemayer, A. Untersuchungen über die Beziehungen Albrechts I zu Bonifaz VIII. Berlin. 1900.

Otto, H. Die Beziehungen Rudolfs von Habsburg zu Papst Gregor X. Innsbruck. 1894.

Preger, W. Albrecht von Österreich und Adolf von Nassau. 2 vols. Leipsic. 1869.

Redlich, O. Rudolf von Habsburg. Innsbruck. 1903.

Renken, W. Hat König Albrecht I dem Papste Bonifaz VIII einen Lehnseid geleistet? Halle. 1909.

Reuter, E. Der Feldzug Rudolfs I…gegen Burgund, 1289. Halle. 1901. [diss.]

Roeder, H. Rudolf von Habsburg als römischer König. Bonn. 1926. [diss.]

Roth, F. W. E. Geschichte des römischen Königs Adolf von Nassau. Wiesbaden. 1879.

Ryll, G. Die böhmische Politik bei der Königswahl Adolfs von Nassau. Marburg. 1909. [diss.]

Samanek, V. Studien zur Geschichte König Adolfs. SKAW. ccvii. 1930.

Schneider, E. Der Kampf Graf Eberhards des Erlauchten von Württemberg gegen König Rudolf von Habsburg. Stuttgart. 1886.

Schneider, F. Kaiser Heinrich VII. 3 pts. Greiz-im-Vogtland. 1924–8.

Welvert, E. Philippe le Bel et la maison de Luxembourg. BEC. xlv. 1884.

Wenck, K. Clemens V und Heinrich VII. Halle. 1882.

—— Französische Werbung um die deutsche Königskrone zur Zeit Philipps des Schönen und Clemens V. HZ. lxxxv. 1900.

Werminghoff, A. Zur Geschichte der politischen Beziehungen zwischen Deutschland und Frankreich unter Albrecht I. Neu. Arch. xxvi. 1901.

Zeissberg, H. von. Rudolf von Habsburg und der österreichische Staatsgedanke. Vienna. 1882.

—— Ueber das Rechtsverfahren Rudolfs von Habsburg gegen Ottokar von Böhmen. AOG. lxix.

Zisterer, A. Gregor X und Rudolf von Habsburg in ihrer beiderseitigen Beziehungen. Freiburg-i.-B. 1891.

CHAPTER IV.

GERMANY: LEWIS THE BAVARIAN.

I. BIBLIOGRAPHIES.

Bresslau, H. Handbuch der Urkundenlehre für Deutschland und Italien. *See Gen. Bibl.* i.
Dahlmann-Waitz. Quellenkunde. *See Gen. Bibl.* i.
Lorenz, O. Deutschlands Geschichtsquellen im Mittelalter seit der Mitte des 13 Jahrhts. *See Gen. Bibl.* i.
Potthast, A. Bibliotheca historica medii aevi. *See Gen. Bibl.* i.

II. DOCUMENTS.

A. General.

Böhmer, J. F. Acta imperii selecta. Ed. Ficker, J. Innsbruck. 1870.
Martène, E. and Durand, U. Thesaurus anecdotorum novus. Vol. ii. *See Gen. Bibl.* iv.
Raynaldus, O. Annales ecclesiastici. Vols. iv–vi. Ed. Mansi, J. D. *See Gen. Bibl.* v *under* Baronius.
Riezler, S. Urkunden zur bairischen und deutschen Geschichte aus den Jahren 1256–1353. FDG. xx. 1880.
Stengel, E. Nova Alamanniae. Urkunden, Briefe, und andere Quellen besonders zur deutschen Geschichte des 14 Jahrhunderts. 2 pts. Berlin. 1921, 30.
Winkelmann, E. Acta imperii saeculi xiii et xiv. Vol. ii. *See Gen. Bibl.* iv.

B. Special.

Böhmer, J. F. Regesta imperii, 1314–1347. *See Gen. Bibl.* iv.
Briefe Ludwigs des Bayern. Ed. Böhmer, J. F. *in* Fontes rerum Germanicarum. Vol. i. Stuttgart. 1843.
Constitutiones et Acta publica imperatorum et regum. Vols. v, vi. i, viii. MGH. Legum Sect. iv. 1909–27.
Häutle, C. Beiträge zum Itinerar König Ludwigs. FDG. xiii. 1873.
Jacobi, T. Codex epistolaris Johannis regis Bohemiae. Berlin. 1841.
Kaiser Ludwigs Baierisches Landrecht. Ed. Freyberg, M. von. (Sammlung historischer Schriften. iv.) Stuttgart. 1827.
Landesgesetze des K. Ludwigs des Bayern. Ed. Rockinger, L. *in* Denkmäler des baierischen Landesrechts. Vol. ii. i. Munich. 1891.
Löher, F. von. Vatikanische Urkunden zur Geschichte König Ludwigs des Bayern. *In* Archivalische Zeitschr. v, vi. Munich. 1880–1.
Regesta Habsburgica. Abt. iii. i, ii. Die Regesten der Herzöge von Österreich sowie Friedrichs des Schönen als deutschen Königs von 1314–1330. Ed. Gross, L. Innsbruck. 1922, 24.
Regesten der Erzbischöfe von Köln im Mittelalter. Vol. iv. Ed. Kisky, W. Bonn. 1915.
Regesten der Erzbischöfe von Mainz, 1289–1396. Ed. Vogt, E. and Vigener, F. 2 vols. Leipsic. 1907–14.
Schwalm, J. Reiseberichte, 1894–6. Neu. Arch. xxiii. 1897–8.
—— Reise nach München und Koblenz im Sommer 1897. *Ibid.*
—— Beiträge zur Reichsgeschichte des 14 Jahrht. Aus dem Vatikanischen Archiv mitgeteilt. *Ibid.* xxv. 1899.
—— Reise nach Italien im Herbst 1898. *Ibid.* xxv, xxvi. 1899–1900.
—— Reise nach Oberitalien und Burgund im Herbst 1901. *Ibid.* xxvii. 1901.

Schwalm, J. Reise nach Frankreich und Italien im Sommer 1903. *Ibid.* xxix. 1904.
—— Nachlese zu früheren Reiseberichten. *Ibid.* xxx. 1905.
[These seven articles contain valuable documents not previously printed.]
—— Die Appellation König Ludwigs des Bayern von 1324 in ursprünglicher Gestalt herausgegeben. Weimar. 1906.
Urkunden zur Geschichte des Römerzuges König Ludwigs des Baiern. Ed. Ficker, J. Innsbruck. 1865.
Urkunden Ludwigs des Baiern. Ed. Oefele, A. F. *in* Rerum Boicarum scriptores. Vol. i. Augsburg. 1763.
Urkundliche Beiträge zur Geschichte König Ludwigs IV und anderer baierischen Fürsten. Ed. Höfler, C. *in* Oberbaierisches Archiv für vaterländische Gesch. i. Munich. 1839.
Vatikanische Akten. Ed. Riezler, S. *See Gen. Bibl.* iv *under* Papal Documents.
Weech, F. von. Sechzig Urkunden König Ludwigs. *In* Oberbaierisches Archiv für vaterländische Geschichte. xxiii. Munich.
Zeissberg, H. von. Der Register No. 318 des Archivs der aragonesischen Krone in Barcelona, enthaltend die Briefe König Jacobs II von Aragon an Friedrich den Schönen... SKAW. cxl. 1898.

III. CHRONICLES, ETC.

Albertinus Mussatus. Ludovicus Bavarus. Ed. Böhmer, J. F. *in* Fontes rerum Germanicarum. Vol. i. Stuttgart. 1843. *Also* ed. Muratori. RR.II.SS. 1st edn. Vol. x.
Annales Mellicenses: Continuatio Novimontensis. Ed. Wattenbach, W. MGH. Script. ix.
Annales S. Rudberti Salisburgensis. Ed. Wattenbach, W. MGH. Script. ix.
Annales Zwetlenses. *Ibid.*
Bairische Fortsetzungen der Sächsischen Weltchronik. Ed. Weiland, L. MGH. Deutsche Chroniken. ii.
Chronica de ducibus Bavariae. Chronica de gestis principum. Chronica Ludovici imperatoris. Ed. Leidinger, G. *in* Chronicae Bavaricae saeculi xiv. SGUS. 1918.
Chronicon S. Petri vulgo Sampetrinum Erfurtense. Ed. Stübel, B. *in* Geschichtsquellen der Provinz Sachsen. i. Halle. 1870.
Fritsche Closener. Strassburgische Chronik. Ed. Hegel, C. *in* Chroniken der deutschen Städte. Vol. viii. Leipsic. 1870.
Gesta Baldewini archiepiscopi Treverensis. Ed. Wyttenbach, H. and Müller, M. F. *in* Gesta Trevirorum. Vol. ii. Trèves. 1838.
Heinrich Taube von Selbach. Chronica. Ed. Bresslau, H. MGH. Script. N.S. i. 1922.
Heinrich Truchsess von Diessenhoven. Historia ecclesiastica *or* Chronicon. Ed. Böhmer, J. F. *in* Fontes. Vol. iv.
Henricus de Hervordia. Liber de rebus memorabilioribus. Ed. Potthast, A. Göttingen. 1859.
Hermannus Gygas. Continuation of Flores temporum. Ed. Meuschen, J. G. Leyden. 1743.
Historiae Reinhardsbrunnenses. Ed. Wegele, F. X. *as* Annales Rein. *in* Thüringische Geschichtsquellen. Vol. i. Jena. 1854.
Jacob Twinger von Königshofen. Chronik. Ed. Hegel, C. *in* Chroniken der deutschen Städte. Vols. viii, ix. 1870-1.
Johann von Winterthur. Chronica. Ed. Baethgen, F. MGH. Script. N.S. i. 1924.
Johannes abbas Victoriensis. Liber certarum historiarum. 2 vols. Ed. Schneider, F. SGUS. 1909-10.
Kalendarium Zwetlense. Ed. Wattenbach, W. MGH. Script. ix.
Konrad von Halberstadt. Chronicon. Ed. Wenck, K. FDG. xx. 1880.
Magdeburger Schöppenchronik. Ed. Janicke, K. *in* Chroniken der deutschen Städte. Vol. vii. Leipsic. 1869.
Mathias von Neuenburg. Chronica. Ed. Studer, G. Bern. 1866. *Also* ed. Böhmer, J. F. *in* Fontes. Vol. iv. *Also* ed. Hofmeister, A. MGH. Script. N.S. iv, 1. 1924, in progress.

Nicolaus Minorita. De controversia paupertatis Christi, *as* Johannes Minorita *in* Baluze, E. Miscellanea; ed. Mansi, J. D. Vol. III. Lucca. 1761.
Oberrheinische Chronik. Ed. Grieshaber, F. K. Rastatt. 1850.
Otto and Peter von Zittau. Chronica Aulae regiae libri tres. Ed. Emler, J. *in* Fontes rerum Bohemicarum. Vol. IV. Prague. *Also* ed. Loserth, J. *as* Die Königsaaler Geschichtsquellen, *in* Fontes rerum Austriacarum. Abth. I. Script. VIII. Vienna. 1875.
Villani, Giovanni and Matteo. Historie Fiorentine. Ed. Muratori. RR.II.SS. 1st edn. Vols. XIII, XIV. *Also* ed. Dragomanni, F. G. 6 vols. Florence. 1844–6.
Vita Caroli quarti ab ipso conscripta. Ed. Böhmer, J. F. *in* Fontes. Vol. I. *Also* ed. Emler, J. *in* Fontes rerum Bohemicarum. Vol. III. Prague. 1878.

IV. CONTROVERSIAL TREATISES, ETC.

Lupold von Bebenburg. De iure regni et imperii. Ed. Schardius, S. *in* De iurisdictione, auctoritate, et praeeminentia imperiali ac potestate ecclesiastica. pp. 328–409. Basle. 1566.
—— Libellus de zelo catholicae fidei veterum principum Germanorum. *Ibid.* pp. 410–65.
—— Rimaticum querulosum et lamentosum dictamen de modernis cursibus et defectibus regni ac imperii Romanorum. Ed. Böhmer, J. F. *in* Fontes. Vol. I.
Marsilius of Padua. Defensor Pacis. Ed. Previté-Orton, C. W. Cambridge. 1928.
—— Defensor minor. Ed. Brampton, C. K. Birmingham. 1922.
—— Tractatus de translatione imperii. Ed. Goldast, M. *in* Monarchia S. romani imperii. Vol. II. Frankfort. 1614.
Michael of Cesena. Tractatus (Epistolae) tres contra errores Johannis XXII. *Ibid.*
Unbekannte kirchenpolitische Streitschriften aus der Zeit Ludwigs des Bayern. Ed. Scholz, R. 2 vols. (Bibl. d. K. Preuss. Hist. Inst. in Rom. IX, X.) Rome. 1912, 14.
William of Ockham. Compendium errorum Johannis XXII papae. Ed. Goldast, M. *in* Monarchia. Vol. II.
—— De iurisdictione imperatoris in causis matrimonialibus. *Ibid.* Vol. I.
—— Defensorium contra errores Johannis XXII papae. *In* Baluze, E. Miscellanea; ed. Mansi, J. D. Vol. III. Lucca. 1761.
—— Dialogus. Ed. Goldast, M. *in* Monarchia. Vol. II.
—— Octo quaestiones. *Ibid.*
—— Opus nonaginta dierum. *Ibid.*
—— Traktat gegen die Unterwerfungsformel Clemens' VI. Ed. Müller, K. *in* Festschrift dem Grossherzog von Hessen Ludwig IV zum 25 Aug. 1888 gewidmet. Giessen. 1888.

V. MODERN WORKS.

A. GENERAL.

Burdach, K. Von Mittelalter zu Reformation. Vol. I. Halle. 1893.
Hauck, A. Kirchengeschichte Deutschlands. Vol. V. *See Gen. Bibl.* V.
Höfler, C. Aus Avignon. *In* Abh. d. Böhmischen Gesellsch. der Wissensch. Ser. VI. Vol. II. Prague. 1868.
Kopp, J. E. Geschichten von der Wiederherstellung und dem Verfalle des heiligen Römischen Reiches. Vols. IV, V. Berlin and Basle. 1871, 82.
Krammer, M. Wahl und Einsetzung des deutschen Königs im Verhältnis zu einander. Weimar. 1905.
Lichnowsky, E. M. Fürst von. Geschichte des Hauses Habsburg. 8 pts. Vienna. 1836–44.
Lindner, T. Deutsche Geschichte unter den Habsburgern und Luxemburgern. 2 vols. (Bibliothek deutscher Geschichte. Ed. Zwiedineck-Südenhorst, H. von.) Stuttgart. 1888–93.
Samanek, V. Kronrat und Reichsherrschaft im 13 und 14 Jahrht. Berlin and Leipsic. 1910.
Schultz, A. Deutsches Leben im 14 und 15 Jahrht. Leipsic. 1892.
Stutz, U. Der Erzbischof von Mainz und die deutsche Königswahl. Weimar. 1910.

B. SPECIAL.

Altmann, **W.** Der Römerzug Ludwigs des Baiern. Berlin. 1886.

Bachmann, **A.** Nochmals die Schlacht bei Mühldorf. *In* Forschungen zur Geschichte Bayerns. XIV. Munich. 1907.

Chroust, **A.** Beiträge zur Geschichte Ludwigs des Bayers und seiner Zeit. Gotha. 1887.

Dormann, **H.** Die Stellung des Bistums Freising im Kampfe zwischen Ludwig dem Bayern und der römischen Kurie. Wiesbaden. 1907.

Erben, **W.** Die Schlacht bei Mühldorf. Graz. 1923.

—— Berthold von Tuttlingen, Registrator und Notar in der Kanzlei Kaiser Ludwigs des Baiern. *In* Denkschr. der KAW. LXVI, Abh. 2. 1924. *Also* publ. separately. Vienna. 1924.

Felten, **W.** Die Bulle "Ne pretereat" und die Reconciliationsverhandlungen Ludwigs des Baiern mit dem Papste Johann XXII. 2 pts. Trèves. 1885, 87.

—— Forschungen zur Geschichte Ludwigs des Bayern. Neuss. 1900. [diss.]

Ficker, **J.** Zur Geschichte des Kurvereines zu Rense. Vienna. 1853.

Finke, **H.** Die Stellung der westfälischen Bischöfe und Herren im Kampfe Ludwigs des Bayern mit Papst Johann XXII. *In* Zeitschr. für vaterländische Geschichte und Alterthumskunde. XLVIII. Münster.

Fischer, **J.** Das ältere Rechtsbuch Ludwigs des Bayern. Landshut. 1909.

Hetzenecker, **J.** Studien zu Reichs- u. Kirchenpolitik des Würzburger Hochstiftes in den Zeiten Kaiser Ludwigs des Bayern (1333–47). Augsburg. 1901. [diss.]

Höhlbaum, **K.** Der Kurverein von Rense im Jahr 1338. Berlin. 1903.

Hoffmann, **K.** Die Haltung des Erzbistums Köln in den kirchenpolitischen Kämpfen Ludwigs des Bayern. Bonn. 1911. [diss.]

Kisky, **W.** Die Domkapitel der geistlichen Kurfürsten in ihrer persönlichen Zusammensetzung im 14 und 15 Jahrht. Weimar. 1906.

Kothe, **W.** Kirchliche Zustände Strassburgs im 14 Jahrht. Freiburg. 1902.

Kupke, **G.** Das Reichsvikariat und die Stellung des Pfalzgrafen bei Rhein. Halle. 1891. [diss.]

Lehleiter, **Á.** Die Politik König Johanns von Böhmen in den Jahren 1330–4. Bonn. 1908. [diss.]

Meyer, **H.** Lupold von Bebenburg. Studien zu seinen Schriften. Freiburg-i.-B. 1910.

Moeller, **R.** Ludwig der Bayer und die Kurie im Kampf um das Reich. Berlin. 1914.

Mühling, **C.** Die Geschichte der Doppelwahl des Jahres 1314. Munich. 1882.

Müller, **C.** Der Kampf Ludwigs des Baiern mit der römischen Curie. 2 vols. Tübingen. 1879–80.

Pfannenschmid, **H.** Die Schlacht bei Mühldorf. FDG. III, IV. 1863–4.

Pflugk-Harttung, **J.** von. Anhang, Gegner, und Hilfsmittel Ludwigs des Bayern in seinem Kampf mit der Kurie. ZKG. XXI. 1900.

—— Die Johanniten und der Deutsche Orden im Kampf Ludwigs des Bayern mit der Kurie. Leipsic. 1900.

—— Die Wahl des letzten kaiserlichen Gegenpapstes. ZKG. XXII. 1901.

Preger, **W.** Beiträge und Erörterungen zur Geschichte des Deutschen Reichs, 1330–4. Munich. 1880.

—— Der kirchenpolitische Kampf unter Ludwig dem Baier. Munich. 1877.

—— Die Politik des Papstes Johann XXII in Bezug auf Italien und Deutschland. Munich. 1885.

—— Die Verträge Ludwigs des Baiern mit Friedrich dem Schönen in den Jahren 1325 und 1326. Munich. 1883.

—— Ueber die Anfänge des kirchenpolitischen Kampfes unter Ludwig dem Baier. Munich. 1882.

[All these articles are in the Abh. der BAW.]

Priesack, **J.** Die Reichspolitik des Erzbischofs Balduin von Trier in den Jahren 1314–28. Göttingen. 1894.

—— Zur Sachsenhäuser Appellation. ZKG. XVII. 1896.

Riedner, **O.** Die Rechtsbücher Ludwigs des Bayern. Heidelberg. 1911.

Riezler, **S.** Die literarischen Widersacher der Päpste zur Zeit Ludwig des Baiers. Leipsic. 1874.

Rohrmann, **A.** Die Prokuratorien Ludwigs des Baiern. Göttingen. 1882.

Rümler, K. Die Akten der Gesandtschaften Ludwigs des Baiern an Benedict XII und Klemens VI. *In* Quellenstudien aus dem hist. Seminar der Universität Innsbruck. Vol. ii. Innsbruck. 1910

Salchow, G. Der Uebergang der Mark Brandenburg auf das Haus Wittelsbach. Halle. 1893. [diss.]

Schönach, L. Zum tirol-brandenburg. Tauschprojekt c. 1336. *In* Mitteil. d. Vereins für die Geschichte der Deutschen in Böhmen. xliii. Prague. 1905.

Schötter, J. Johann Graf von Luxemburg und König von Böhmen. 2 vols. Luxemburg. 1865.

Schrohe, H. Der Kampf der Gegenkönige Ludwig und Friedrich um das Reich bis zur Entscheidungsschlacht bei Mühldorf. Berlin. 1902.

Schwalm, J. Die Landfrieden in Deutschland unter Ludwig dem Bayern. Göttingen. 1889.

Sievers, G. Die politischen Beziehungen König Ludwigs des Bayern zu Frankreich in den Jahren 1314–37. Berlin. 1896.

Steinberger, A. Kaiser Ludwig der Bayer, ein Lebensbild. Munich. 1901.

Stengel, E. E. Avignon und Rhens. Forschungen zur Geschichte des Kampfes um das Recht am Reich in der ersten Hälfte des 14 Jahrhts. (Quellen und Studien zur Verfassungsgesch. des Deutschen Reiches. vi. i.) Weimar. 1930.

Tebbe, H. Kaiser Ludwig der Bayer, Erzbischof Heinrich III von Mainz, und die Beschlüsse des Kurfürstentages von Rense. Breslau. 1919. [diss.]

Ueding, P. Ludwig der Bayer und die niederrheinischen Städte. Paderborn. 1904.

Uhl, G. Untersuchungen über die Politik Erzbischofs Heinrichs III von Mainz und seines Kapitels in den Jahren 1337–1346. *In* Archiv für hessische Geschichte. xv. Darmstadt. 1926.

Vogt, E. Die Reichspolitik d. Erzbischofs Balduin von Trier in den Jahren 1328–34. Gotha. 1901.

—— Erzbischof Mathias von Mainz (1321–38). Berlin. 1905.

Waldeyer, K. J. Walram von Jülich, Erzbischof von Köln und seine Reichspolitik. 2 pts. Bonn. 1890–1.

Weech, F. von. Kaiser Ludwig der Bayer und König Johann von Böhmen. Munich. 1860.

—— Die Schlacht bei Mühldorf. FDG. iv. 1864.

Weiland, L. Ueber die Sprache und die Texte des Kurvereins und des Weisthums von Rense. Neu. Arch. xviii. 1893.

Weiss, H. Frankreichs Politik in den Rheinlanden am Vorabend des hundertjährigen Krieges. Reval. 1927.

Wilhelm, B. Die Verhandlungen Ludwigs des Bayern mit Friedrich von Österreich in den Jahren 1325–1326, und die deutsche Erzählung über den Streit zu Mühldorf. MIOGF. xlii. 1927.

Würdinger, J. Ueber die von K. Ludwig gewonnene Schlacht bei Mühldorf. SBAW. 1872.

Zeissberg, H. von. Elizabeth von Aragonien, Gemahlin Friedrichs des Schönen von Österreich. SKAW. cxxxvii. 1898. *Also* publ. separately. Vienna. 1898.

Zeumer, K. Das Königswahlgesetz "Licet iuris." Neu. Arch. xxx. 1904.

—— Zur Kritik der Appellationen Ludwigs des Bayern. *Ibid.* xxxvii. 1911.

CHAPTER V.

GERMANY: CHARLES IV.

[*See also* Bibliography to ch. VI.]

I. BIBLIOGRAPHIES.

See Bibliography to ch. IV.

II. DOCUMENTS.

A. GENERAL.

Raynaldus, O. Annales ecclesiastici. Vols. VI, VII. *See Gen. Bibl.* v *under* Baronius.
[For other sources *see* Bibliography to ch. IV.]

B. SPECIAL.

Acta Karoli IV imperatoris inedita. Aus italienischen Archiven gesammelt und
herausgegeben von F. Zimmermann. Innsbruck. 1891.
Böhmer, J. F. Regesta imperii. Vol. VIII (1346-78). *See Gen. Bibl.* IV.
Cancellaria Johannis Noviforensis episcopi Olomucensis. Ed. Tadra, F. AOG.
LXVIII. 1886.
Collectarius perpetuarum formarum Johannis de Geylnhusen. Ed. Kaiser, H.
Innsbruck. 1900.
Constitutiones et acta publica imperatorum et regum. Vol. VIII. MGH. Legum
Sect. IV. 1910-26.
Diplomatarium Caroli IV. Ed. Mencken, J. B. *in* Script. rerum Germanicarum,
praecipue Saxonicarum. Vol. III. Leipsic. 1730.
Golden Bull. Critical edition by Zeumer, K. Die goldene Bulle Kaiser Karls IV.
2 pts. (Quellen und Studien zur Verfassungsgeschichte des Deutschen Reiches.
II. i, ii.) Weimar. 1908. *Also* ed. Harnack, O. *in* Das Kurfürstenkollegium
bis zur Mitte des 14 Jahrhts. Giessen. 1883.
Lindner, T. Das Urkundenwesen Karls IV und seiner Nachfolger (1346-1437).
Stuttgart. 1882.
—— Urkunden Günthers und Karls IV. Neu. Arch. VIII. 1882.
Maiestas Carolina. Ed. Palacky, F. *in* Archiv Cesky. III. Prague. 1844.
Neumann, T. Ein Formelbuch Kaiser Karls IV (Summa cancellariae). Görlitz. 1846.
Regesten der Erzbischöfe von Mainz, 1289-1396. Ed. Vogt, E. and Vigener, F.
2 vols. Leipsic. 1907-14.
Werunsky, E. Excerpta ex registris Clementis VI et Innocentii VI historiam sancti
Romani imperii sub regimine Caroli IV illustrantia. Innsbruck. 1885.

III. CHRONICLES, ETC.

Bairische Fortsetzungen der Sächsischen Weltchronik. *See* Bibl. to ch. IV.
Chronica de ducibus Bavariae. *Ibid.*
Chronicon...Sampetrinum Erfurtense. *Ibid.*
Continuatio Zwetlensis IV. Ed. Wattenbach, W. MGH. Script. IX.
Entreveues de Charles IV empereur...et de Charles V roy de France. Ed. Godefroy,
T. Paris. 1614.
Fritsche Closener. Strassburgische Chronik. *See* Bibl. to ch. IV.
Heinrich Truchsess von Diessenhoven. *Ibid.*
Heinricus de Hervordia. Liber de rebus memorabilioribus. *Ibid.*
Jacob Twinger von Königshofen. *Ibid.*
Johannes dictus Porta de Annoniaco. Modus coronationis Caroli Romani imperatoris
IV. Ed. Höfler, C. *as* De coronatione Caroli IV. (Beiträge zur Geschichte
Böhmens. Abth. I. ii.) Prague. 1864.
Kalendarium Zwetlense. *See* Bibl. to ch. IV.
Konrad von Halberstadt. Chronicon. *Ibid.*
Magdeburger Schöppenchronik. *Ibid.*
Mathias von Neuenburg. Chronica. *Ibid.*

Moralitates Caroli quarti imperatoris. Ed. Wotke, K. *in* Zeitschr. des Vereins für
   Geschichte Mährens und Schlesiens. I. 1897.
Tractatus de coronatione imperatoris. Ed. Werminghoff, A. ZSR. xxiv. Germ.
   Abt. 1903.
Villani, Matteo. *See* Bibl. to ch. IV.

IV. MODERN WORKS.

A. GENERAL.

See Bibliography to ch. IV.

B. SPECIAL.

Fischer, E. Die Landfriedensverfassung unter Karl IV. Göttingen. 1883. [diss.]
Friedjung, H. Kaiser Karl IV und sein Antheil am geistigen Leben seiner Zeit.
   Vienna. 1876.
Gottlob, A. Karls IV private u. polit. Beziehungen zu Frankreich. Innsbruck. 1883.
Grotefend, S. Die Erwerbungspolitik Kaiser Karls IV. Berlin. 1909. [diss.]
Hoeniger, R. Der schwarze Tod in Deutschland. Berlin. 1882.
Huber, A. Geschichte des Herzogs Rudolf IV von Oesterreich. Innsbruck. 1865.
—— Geschichte der Vereinigung Tirols mit Oesterreich. Innsbruck. 1864.
Jansen, M. Eine chronikalische Erwähnung der goldenen Bulle. HJ. xvi. 1895.
Janson, K. Das Königthum Günthers von Schwarzburg. Leipsic. 1880.
Kaiser, H. Der Collectarius perpetuarum formarum des Johann von Gelnhausen.
   Strasbourg. 1898.
Klein, W. Kaiser Karls IV Jugendaufenthalt in Frankreich und dessen Einfluss auf
   seiner Entwicklung. Berlin. 1926. [diss.]
Kröger, H. Der Einfluss und die Politik Kaiser Karls IV bei der Besetzung der
   deutschen Reichsbistümer. Münster. 1835. [diss.]
Lechner, K. Das grosse Sterben in Deutschland in den Jahren 1348–51 und die
   folgenden Pestepidemien bis zum Schlusse des 14 Jahrhts. Innsbruck. 1884.
Lindner, T. Karl IV und die Wittelsbacher. MIOGF. xii. 1891.
Matthes, J. Der zweite Römerzug Kaiser Karls IV. Halle. 1880. [diss.]
Mendl, B. and Quicke, F. Les relations politiques entre l'empereur et le roi de France
   de 1355 à 1356. *In* Revue belge de philol. et d'hist. viii. 1929.
Menzel, T. Italienische Politik Kaiser Karls IV, 1355–1368. Halle. 1880. [diss.]
—— Italienische Politik Kaiser Karls IV, 1347–1368. (Progr. Blankenb.) 1885.
Nuglisch, A. Das Finanzwesen der Deutschen Reiches unter Kaiser Karl IV.
   Strasbourg. 1899.
Reincke, H. Machtpolitik u. Weltwirtschaftsplane Kaiser Karls IV. Lübeck. 1924.
Scheffler, W. Karl IV und Innocenz VI. Berlin. 1912.
Steinherz, S. Die Beziehungen Ludwigs I von Ungarn zu Karl IV. MIOGF. viii,
   ix. 1887–8.
—— Margareta von Tirol und Rudolf IV. *Ibid.* xxvi. 1905.
—— Ein Fürstenspiegel Karls IV. Reichenberg. 1925.
Stoy, S. Die polit. Beziehungen zwischen Kaiser u. Papst. Strasbourg. 1881. [diss.]
Stutz, U. Die Abstimmungsordnung der goldenen Bulle. ZSR. xliii. Germ. Abt.
   1922. Also publ. separately. Weimar. 1922.
Theuner, E. Der Uebergang der Mark Brandenburg vom wittelsbachischen an das
   luxemburgische Haus. Berlin. 1887. [diss.]
Tumbült, G. Kaiser Karl IV und seine Beziehungen zu den schwäbischen Reichs-
   städten vom Jahr 1370 bis zur Gründung des Städtebundes im Jahre 1376.
   Münster. 1879. [diss.]
Vigener, F. Kaiser Karl IV und der mainzer Bistumsstreit (1373–8). Trèves. 1908.
—— König Wenzel und der rotenburger Landfriede. Neu. Arch. xxxi. 1906.
Warnecke, G. Der zweite Römerzug Kaiser Karls IV. Jena. 1881. [diss.]
Werunsky, E. Der erste Römerzug König Karls IV. Innsbruck. 1878.
—— Die italienische Politik Papst Innocenz' VI und König Karls IV in den Jahren
   1353–54. Innsbruck. 1878.
—— Geschichte Kaiser Karls IV und seiner Zeit. 3 vols. Innsbruck. 1880–92.
Winckelmann, O. Die Beziehungen Kaiser Karls IV zum Königreich Arelat.
   Strasbourg. 1882.
Worthmann, L. Die Wahl Karls IV zum Römischen Könige. Breslau. 1875.

CHAPTER VI.

BOHEMIA IN THE FOURTEENTH CENTURY.

I. BIBLIOGRAPHIES.

Zíbrt, Č. Bibliografie české historie. (Bibliography of Czech history.) Vol. II Prague. 1902.

Kazimour, J. Bibliografie české historie. (Bibliography of Czech history.) [For the years 1904–14 published with the Czech Historical Review, for the years 1915–25 published independently. Prague. 1926.]

Krofta, K. Novější bádání o Husovi a hnutí husitském. Kapitola I: Dějinné základy hnutí husitského. Předchůdcové husitství. (The recent investigations about John Huss and the Hussite movement. Ch. I: The historical foundation of the Hussite movement.) [Critical review of literature from the death of F. Palacký, 1876. Contained in the Czech Historical Review, 1915.]

II. SOURCES.

Acta i[illegible] consistorii Pragensis. Ed. Tadra, F. Vols. I–III. Prague. 1893–1900. [Documents from the years 1373–1398.]

Archivium coronae regni Bohemiae. Vol. II. 1346–1355. Ed. Hrubý, V. Prague. 1928. [Documents from the Czech State Archives.]

Cancellaria Arnesti. Formelbuch des ersten Prager Erzbischofs Arnošt von Pardubic. Ed. Tadra, F. AOG. LXI. 1880.

Cancellaria Johannis Noviforensis episcopi Olomucensis. 1364–1380. Ed. Tadra, F. *Ibid.* LXVIII. 1886.

Codex diplomaticus et epistolaris Moraviae. Ed. Boček, A. and others. Vols. V–XII. Brno (Brünn). 1850–90. [These volumes contain documents from the years 1294–1399.]

Codex epistolaris des Erzbischofs von Prag Johann von Jenzenstein, 1374–1388. Ed. Loserth, J. AOG. LV. 1877.

Codex epistolaris Johannis regis Bohemiae. Ed. Jacobi, T. Berlin. 1841.

Collectarius perpetuarum formarum Johannis de Geylnhusen. Ed. Kaiser, H. Innsbruck. 1900. [The collection of formularies from the chancery of King Charles IV.]

Concilia Pragensia. 1353–1413. Prager Synodalbeschlüsse. Ed. Höfler, C. *in* Abh d. K. Böhmischen Gesellsch. d. Wiss. Ser. V. Vol. XII. Prague. 1862.

Fontes rerum Bohemicarum. Vols. III–V. Ed. Emler, J. Prague. 1882–93.

Königsaaler Geschichtsquellen. Ed. Loserth, J. (Fontes rer. Austriacarum. Script. VIII.) Vienna. 1875.

Libri confirmationum ad beneficia ecclesiastica Pragensem per archidioecesim. Ed. Tingl, F. and Emler, J. Prague. 1865–89. [Entries from the years 1354–1436.]

Libri erectionum archidioecesis Pragensis saeculo XIV et XV. Vols. I–V (1358–1407). Ed. Borový, C. Prague. 1875–89.

Monumenta Vaticana res gestas Bohemicas illustrantia. Vol. I. Acta Clementis VI. Vol. II. Acta Innocentii VI. Vol. V. Acta Urbani VI et Bonifatii IX. *See Gen. Bibl.* IV. *under* Papal Documents.

Regesta diplomatica necnon epistolaria Bohemiae et Moraviae. Vols. II–V (1253–1346). Ed. Emler, J. Prague. 1882–92. Vol. VI (1355–1363). i, ii. Ed. Mendl, B. Prague. 1928, 9.

Regesta imperii. Vol. VIII (1346–78). *See Gen. Bibl.* IV *under* Böhmer, J. F.

Reichstagsakten, Deutsche. Vols. I–III. Ed. Weizsäcker, J. Munich. 1867–77.

Summa cancellariae (Cancellaria Caroli IV). Ed. Tadra, F. Prague. 1895.

Summa Gerhardi. Ein Formelbuch aus der Zeit des Königs Johann von Böhmen. (1336–1346.) Ed. Tadra, F. AOG. LXIII. 1882.

III. MODERN WORKS.

A. General History of Bohemia.

Bachmann, A. Geschichte Böhmens. Vol. i (to 1400). (Heeren. *See Gen. Bibl.* v.) Gotha. 1899.

Chaloupecký, V. Jan IV z Dražic, poslední biskup pražský. (John IV of Dražice, the last bishop of Prague.) Prague. 1908.

Dudík, B. Mährens allgemeine Geschichte. Vols. vii–xii (1278–1359). Brünn. 1876–88.

Franz, A. Der Magister Nikolaus Magni de Jawor. Freiburg. 1898.

Grünhagen, C. Geschichte Schlesiens. Vol. i (to 1527). Gotha. 1884.

Jakubec, J. Dějiny české literatury. (History of Czech literature.) Prague. 1929.

Kalousek, J. Karel IV, Otec vlasti. (Charles IV, father of his country.) Prague. 1878.

Kybal, V. Matěj z Janova; jeho život, spisy a učení. (Matthias of Janov, his life, works, and doctrine.) Prague. 1905.

Lindner, T. Deutsche Geschichte unter den Habsburgern und Luxemburgern (1273–1437). 2 vols. Stuttgart. 1888–93.

—— Geschichte des Deutschen Reiches unter König Wenzel. 2 vols. Brunswick. 1875–80.

Lützow, Francis, Count. Bohemia, an historical sketch. London. 1896. Reprinted *in* Everyman's Library. London. 1909; and 1920.

Maurice, C. E. Bohemia from the earliest times to the fall of national independence in 1620. (Story of the Nations.) London. 1896.

Novotný, V. Náboženské hnutí české ve 14 a 15 století. Část i: Do Husa. (Czech religious movement in the 14th and 15th centuries. Pt. i: To John Hus.) Prague. 1915.

Palacký, F. Dějiny národa českého v Čechách a na Moravě. (History of the Czech nation in Bohemia and Moravia.) Vol. ii. i, ii. Prague. 1875–6.

—— Geschichte von Böhmen. Vols. ii and iii. Prague. 1839, 45.

Pelzel, F. M. Kaiser Karl der Vierte. 2 vols. Prague. 1780–1.

—— Lebensgeschichte des römischen und böhmischen Königs Wenceslaus. 2 vols. Prague and Leipsic. 1788, 90.

Šimák, J. V. Kronika československá. (Czechoslovak Chronicle.) Vol. iii (1306–1378). Prague. 1925.

Šusta, J. Dvě knihy českých dějin (1300–1320). (Two books of Czech history, 1300–1320.) 2 vols. Prague. 1917, 19.

Tadra, F. Kulturní styky Čech s cizinou až do válek husitských. (Cultural relations of Bohemia with foreign countries up to the Hussite wars.) Prague. 1897.

Tomek, V. V. Děje království českého. (History of the kingdom of Bohemia.) 6th edn. Prague. 1891. German transl. Prague. 1865.

—— Dějepis města Prahy. (History of the city of Prague.) Vols. ii and iii. 2nd edn. Prague. 1892 ff.

—— Děje university pražské. (History of the university of Prague.) Prague. 1849.

Werunsky, E. Geschichte Kaiser Karl IV und seiner Zeit. Vols. i–iii. Innsbruck. 1880–3. [A very detailed history of Charles IV's period, but only till the year 1368.]

B. Legal, Economic, and Social History.

Čelakovský, J. Povšechné české dějiny právní. (Sketch of Czech legal history.) Prague. 1900.

Kapras, J. Právní dějiny zemí koruny české. (Legal history of the lands of the Bohemian crown.) Vols. i and ii. Prague. 1913.

Krofta, K. Přehled dějin selského stavu v Čechách a na Moravě. (Sketch of the history of the peasantry in Bohemia and Moravia.) Prague. 1919.

Lippert, J. Social-Geschichte Böhmens in vorhussitischer Zeit. Vols. i and ii. Prague, Vienna, and Leipsic. 1896, 98.

Mendl, B. Sociální krise a zápasy ve městech čtrnáctého věku. (Social crises and conflicts in the cities of the 14th century.) Prague. 1926.

Peterka, O. Rechtsgeschichte der böhmischen Länder. Vol. i. Prague. 1923.

Winter, Z. Dějiny řemesel a obchodu v Čechách v xiv a xv století. (History of handicraft and commerce in Bohemia in the 14th and 15th centuries.) Prague. 1906.

CHAPTER VII.

THE SWISS CONFEDERATION IN THE MIDDLE AGES.

I. BIBLIOGRAPHIES.

Haller, G. E. von. Bibliothek der Schweizer-Geschichte. 7 vols. Bern. 1788.

Brandstetter, J. L. Repertorium über die in Zeit- und Sammelschriften der Jahre 1812–90 enthaltenen Aufsätze und Mitteilungen schweizergeschichtlichen Inhaltes. Basle. 1892.

Barth, H. Repertorium über die in Zeit- und Sammelschriften der Jahre 1891–1900 enthaltenen Aufsätze und Mitteilungen schweizergeschichtlichen Inhaltes. Basle. 1906.

—— Bibliographie der Schweizer-Geschichte enthaltend die selbständig erschienenen Drückwerke zur Geschichte der Schweiz bis Ende 1912. (Quellen zur Schweizer-Geschichte. Abteil. IV. i–iii.) 3 vols. Basle. 1914–15.

Bibliographie der Schweizer-Geschichte, 1913–19. Issued as supplts. to the Anzeiger für schweizerische Geschichte. Neue Folge. XII–XVIII. Bern. 1914–20.

—— 1920 ff. Issued as supplts. to the Zeitschr. für schweizerische Geschichte. Zürich. 1921 ff., in progress.

See also bibliographies in Dierauer, J. Geschichte der Schweizerischen Eidgenossenschaft. *See below,* III A.

II. SOURCES.

For list of sources *see* Barth, H. Bibliographie der Schweizer-Geschichte. *See above,* I.

Wyss, G. von. Geschichte der Historiographie in der Schweiz. Zürich. 1895.

Oechsli, W. Quellenbuch zur Schweizergeschichte. Kleine Ausgabe. 9th edn. Zürich. 1918.

Inventare schweizerischer Archive. 3 pts. (Ed. by Veranstaltung der Allgemeinen Geschichtforschenden Gesellschaft der Schweiz.) Bern. 1895–9. Aarau. 1917.

III. MODERN WORKS.

A. GENERAL.

Blumer, J. J. Staats- und Rechtsgeschichte der schweizerischen Demokratien oder der Kantone Uri, Schwyz, Unterwalden, Glarus, Zug, und Appenzell. 2 vols. St Gall. 1850, 59.

Dändliker, K. Geschichte der Schweiz, mit besonderer Rücksicht auf die Entwicklung des Verfassungs- und Kulturlebens. Vol. I. 4th edn. Zürich. 1901. Vol. II. 3rd edn. 1901.

Dierauer, J. Geschichte der Schweizerischen Eidgenossenschaft. Vols. I and II. 3rd edn. (Heeren. *See Gen. Bibl.* v.) Gotha. 1919–20. French transl. Reymond, A. Vol. I. 2nd edn. Lausanne. 1927. Vol. II. 1912.

Gagliardi, E. Geschichte der Schweiz von den Anfängen bis auf die Gegenwart. Vol. I. Zürich. 1920. French transl. Reymond, A. Vol. I. Lausanne. 1925.

Geschichte der Schweiz. Ed. by Dürr, E., Feller, R., Muralt, L. v., and Nabholz, H. Zürich. 1930, in progress.

Heusler, A. Schweizerische Verfassungsgeschichte. Basle. 1920. French transl. *in* Histoire des constitutions fédérales, Vol. I, by Abravanel, G. and Favey, J. G. Lausanne and Geneva. 1924.

Hilty, C. Les Constitutions fédérales de la Confédération Suisse. Bern. 1891. Also appeared in German.

Müller, J. von, Gloutz-Blozheim, R., and Hottinger, J. J. Histoire de la Confédération Suisse. French transl. Monnard, C. and Vulliemin, L. 18 vols. Paris and Geneva. 1837–51.

Oechsli, W. Orte und Zugewandte. Eine Studie zur Geschichte der schweizerischen Bundesrechte. *In* Jahrb. für schweizerische Geschichte. xiii (1888). 1–486.
—— Schweizergeschichte für Sekundar-, Real-, und Mittelschulen. 3rd edn. Zürich. 1907. [Admirable maps.]
Reymond, M. Histoire de la Suisse des origines jusqu'à nos jours. Ses gloires, sa civilisation. Vol. i. Lausanne. 1931.

B. Special.

Arx, I. von. Geschichten des Kantons St Gallen. 3 vols. St Gall. 1819.
Below, G. von. Die Entstehung der Schweizerischen Eidgenossenschaft. *In* Zeitschr. für schweizerische Geschichte. 3te Jahrg. (1923). 129–63.
Berchem, V. van. Genève et les Suisses au xve siècle. La Folle Vie et le premier traité de combourgeoisie (1477). *In* Jahrb. für schweizerische Geschichte. xliv and xlv. 1920.
—— Guichard Tavel, évêque de Sion. *Ibid.* xxiv (1899). 27–397.
Bernouilli, A. Die Schlacht bei St Jakob an der Birs. Basle. 1877.
Bonhôte, J. E. Essai sur la bataille de Grandson. *In* Musée Neuchâtelois. xxxi (1894). 25–52.
Breslau, H. Das älteste Bündnis der schweizer Urkantone. *In* Jahrb. für schweizerische Geschichte. xx (1895). 1–36.
Büchi, A. Freiburgs Bruch mit Oesterreich, sein Uebergang an Savoyen und Anschluss an die Eidgenossenschaft. (Collectanea Friburgensia. Vol. vii.) Fribourg. 1897.
—— Kardinal Matthäus Schiner als Staatsmann und Kirchenfürst. Ein Beitrag zur allgemeinen und schweizerischen Geschichte von der Wende des 15–16 Jahrhts. Zürich. 1923.
Castella, G. Histoire du canton de Fribourg. Fribourg. 1922.
Dändliker, K. Geschichte der Stadt und Kantons Zürich. Vol. i. Zürich. 1908.
—— Hans Waldmann und die züricher Revolution von 1489. Zürich. 1889.
Durrer, R. Bruder Klaus. 3 vols. Sarnen. 1917–21.
—— Premiers combats de la Suisse primitive pour la liberté. *In* Hist. militaire de la Suisse, i. Bern. 1915. pp. 29–106. Also appeared in German.
Escher, H. Der Verrat von Novara, 1500. *In* Jahrb. für schweizerische Geschichte. xx (1896). 73–194.
Favre, É. La Confédération des huit cantons. Étude historique sur la Suisse au 14e siècle. Leipsic. 1879.
Furrer, Y. Geschichte, Statistik, und Urkundensammlung über Wallis. 3 vols. Sion. 1850–2.
Gagliardi, E. Der Anteil der Schweizer an den italienischen Kriegen, 1494–1516. Vol. i. Von Karls VIII Zug nach Neapel bis zur Liga von Cambrai. Zürich. 1919.
—— Dokumente zur Geschichte des Burgermeisters Hans Waldmann. (Quellen zur Schweizergeschichte. Abteil. ii.) 2 vols. Basle. 1911, 13.
—— Novara und Dijon. Hohepunkt und Verfall der schweizerischen Grossmacht. Zürich. 1907.
Gasser. Der Schwabenkrieg mit Hervorhebung der Ereignisse im Klettgau und Hegau. Schaffhausen. 1899.
Gingins, F. de. Épisodes des guerres de Bourgogne. *In* Mém. et documents publiés par la Soc. d'Hist. de la Suisse romande. viii (1849). 113–510.
Heer, G. Geschichte des Landes Glarus. 2 vols. Glarus. 1898–9.
—— Zur 500jährigen Gedächtnisfeier der Schlacht bei Näfels (Festschrift). Glarus. 1888.
Hungerbühler, H. Étude critique sur les traditions relatives aux origines de la Confédération Suisse. *In* Bulletin de l'Institut national génevois. xv (1869). 221–340.
Jecklin, C. and F. Der Anteil Graubündens am Schwabenkrieg. *In* Festschrift zur Calvenfeier. Davos. 1899.
Kohler, C. Les Suisses dans les guerres d'Italie, de 1506 à 1512. *In* Mém. et documents publiés par la Soc. d'hist. et d'archéol. de Genève. xxiv. 1896.

Kopp, J. E. Geschichte der Eidgenössischen Bünde. 5 vols. Leipsic, Berlin, etc. 1845–82.

Liebenau, T. de. Die Schlacht bei Sempach. *In* Gedenkblatt zur fünften Säcular-feier. Lucerne. 1886.

Mandrot, B. de. Étude sur les relations de Charles VII et de Louis XI, rois de France avec les cantons suisses. *In* Jahrb. für schweizerische Geschichte. v (1880). 57–182.

Meyer, K. Politique transalpine et expédition des Confédérés au delà des Alpes, jusqu'à la victoire de Giornico. *In* Hist. militaire de la Suisse, iii. Bern. 1915. pp. 35–78. Also appeared in German.

—— Italienische Einflüsse bei der Entstehung der Eidgenossenschaft. *In* Jahrb. für schweizerische Geschichte. xlv (1920). 1–76.

—— Die urschweizer Befreiungstradition in ihrer Einheit, Überlieferung, und Stoffwahl. Zürich. 1927.

Meyer von Knonau, G. Des origines à l'an 1218. *In* Hist. militaire de la Suisse, i. Bern. 1915. pp. 13–28. Also appeared in German.

Nabholz, H. Les origines de la Confédération Suisse d'après des travaux récents. *In* Étrennes génevoises. Geneva. 1929. pp. 3–33.

Ochsenbein, G. F. Die Urkunden der Belagerung und Schlacht von Murten. Fribourg. 1876.

Oechsli, W. Die Anfänge der Schweizerischer Eidgenossenschaft. Zürich. 1891. French transl. Ducommun, J. E. Bern. 1891.

Plattner, W. Die Entstehung des Freistaates der drei Bünde. Davos. 1895.

Pupikofer, J. A. Geschichte des Thurgaus. Vol. i. 2nd edn. Frauenfeld. 1886.

Rilliet, A. Les origines de la Confédération Suisse, histoire et légende. 2nd edn. Geneva and Basle. 1869. German transl. Aarau. 1873.

Rodt, E. von. Die Kriege Karls des Kühnen...und seiner Erben. 2 vols. Schaff-hausen. 1843–4.

Rott, É. Histoire de la représentation diplomatique de la France auprès des cantons suisses. Vol. i (1430–1559). Bern. 1900.

Schupfli, K. E. Geschichte der Stadtverfassung von Solothurn. Basle. 1897.

Segesser, A. P. von. Rechtsgeschichte der Stadt und Republik Lucerne. 4 vols. Lucerne. 1851–8.

—— Sammlung kleiner Schriften. 2 vols. Bern. 1879.

Tatarinoff, E. Die Beteiligung Solothurns am Schwabenkriege bis zur Schlacht bei Dornach, 22 Juli 1499. Soleure. 1899.

Tillier, A. von. Geschichte des eidgenössischen Freistaates Bern. 6 vols. Bern. 1838–40.

Vallière, P. E. de. Le Régiment des Gardes Suisses en France. Les Suisses en Italie (Campagne de Marignan). Lausanne and Paris. 1912.

—— Morat. Le Siège et la Bataille, 1476. Lausanne. 1926.

Vaucher, P. Les commencements de la Confédération Suisse. Revised edn. Geneva and Basle. 1891.

—— Les traditions nationales de la Suisse. *In* Mém. de l'Institut national génevois. xvi (1886). 50.

Wackernagel, R. Festschrift zum vierhunderten Jahrestage des ewigen Bundes zwischen Basel und der Eidgenossen, 13 Juli 1901. Basle. 1901.

—— Geschichte des Kantons Schaffhausen zur Bundesfeier. Schaffhausen. 1901.

—— Geschichte der Stadt Basel. 2 vols. Basle. 1907, 16.

Wartmann, H. Die geschichtliche Entwicklung der Stadt St. Gallen bis zu ihrem Bunde mit der schweiz. Eidgenossenschaft. *In* Archiv für schweizerische Geschichte. xvi (1868). 3–58.

Wattelet, H. Die Schlacht bei Murten. *In* Freiburger Geschichtsblätter. i (1894). 1–84.

Wattenwyl-Diesbach, E. Geschichte der Stadt und Landschaft Bern. 2 vols. Schaffhausen and Bern. 1867–72.

Wirz, H. G. Der Sieg von Sempach im Lichte der Überlieferung. *In* Neujahrsblatt der Feuerwerker-Gesellschaft in Zürich. 1922.

Zellweger, J. C. Geschichte des appenzellischen Volkes. Vol. i. Trogen. 1830.

Zschokke, E. Historische Festschrift für die Centenairfeier des Kantons Aargau. Die Geschichte des Aargaus dem aargauischen Volke erzählt. Aarau. 1903.

CHAPTER VIII.

THE HANSA.

I. BIBLIOGRAPHIES.

There is no independent bibliography of Hansa history in existence. The most complete list is to be found in Dahlmann-Waitz, Quellenkunde (*see Gen. Bibl.* 1), where separate sections are allotted to it. References to collections of sources, legal and commercial history etc. are given in the divisions appropriated to them. The foregoing should be supplemented by periodicals such as the Jahresberichte für deutsche Geschichte. 1927 ff. (*see Gen. Bibl.* 1), the Historische Vierteljahrsschrift (HVJS), and, above all, the Hansische Geschichtsblätter (*see below,* iii); since 1920–1 the last mentioned has published short critical notes upon all current publications dealing with the Hansa.

II. ORIGINAL DOCUMENTS, SOURCES, AND CHRONICLES.

Adam of Bremen. Gesta Pontificum Hammaburgensium. Ed. Lappenberg, J. M. MGH. Script. vii. *Also* ed. Schmeidler, B. SGUS. 3rd edn. 1917.
Arnold of Lübeck. Chronica Slavorum (1172–1209). Ed. Lappenberg, J. M. MGH. Script. xxi. *Ibid.* SGUS. 1868.
Bremisches Urkundenbuch. Ed. Ehmeck, D. R. and Bippen, W. von. Vols. i–v (–1433). Bremen. 1863–93.
Breslauer Urkundenbuch. Ed. Korn, G. A. W. Pt. i. Breslau. 1870.
Chroniken der deutschen Städte vom 14 bis ins 16 Jahrht. (Hist. Commission BAW.) Leipsic. 1862–1917. The following important Hansa towns are included:
  Brunswick (1279–1514). Vols. vi and xvi.
  Cologne (1277–1499). Vols. xii–xiv.
  Dortmund (750–1550). Vol. xx.
  Lübeck (1105–1482). Vols. xix, xxvi, xxviii–xxxii.
  Magdeburg (b.c. 47–a.d. 1556). Vols. vii and xxvii.
  Soest (1417–59). Vols. xxi and xxiv.
Codex Diplomaticus Lubecensis. Abt. i. Urkundenbuch der Stadt Lübeck. 11 vols (Verein für Lübeckische Geschichte.) Lübeck. 1843 ff.
Dortmunder Urkundenbuch. Vols. i, ii, ed. Rübel, K. and Roese, E.; iii. i (–1410), ed. Rübel, K. Dortmund. 1881 ff.
Ennen, L. and Eckertz, G. Quellen zur Geschichte der Stadt Köln. 6 vols. Cologne. 1860–79.
Hagedorn, A. and Höhlbaum, K. Das Hansekontor zu Brügge-Antwerpen. Verzeichnis der Urkunden. Hamburg. 1875.
Hamburgische Chroniken in niedersächsischer Sprache. Ed. Lappenberg, J. M. 4 pts. Hamburg. 1852–61.
Hamburgisches Urkundenbuch. Ed. Lappenberg, J. M. Vol. i (–1300). Hamburg. 1842. [No more publ.]
Hansische Geschichtsquellen. (Verein für Hansische Geschichte.)

  Erste Folge.
  I. Das Verfestungsbuch der Stadt Stralsund. Ed. Francke, O. Halle. 1875.
  II. Die Rathslinie der Stadt Wismar. Ed. Crull, F. Halle. 1875.
  III. Dortmunder Statuten und Urteile. Ed. Frensdorff, F. Halle. 1882.
  IV. Das Buch des Lübeckischen Vogts auf Schonen. Ed. Schäfer, D. Halle. 1887.
  V. Revaler Zollbücher und Quittungen. Ed. Stieda, W. Halle. 1887.
  VI. Hanseakten aus England, 1272–1412. Ed. Kunze, K. Halle. 1891.
  VII. Berichte und Akten der hansischen Gesandtschaft nach Moskau im 1603. Ed. Blümcke, O. Halle. 1894.

Neue Folge.
  I. Geschichte und Urkunden der Rigafahrer in Lübeck im 16 und 17 Jahrht. Ed.
       Siewert, F. Berlin. 1897.
 II. Die Lübecker Bergenfahrer und ihre Chronistik. Ed. Bruns, F. Berlin.
       1900.
III. Die Bürgersprachen der Stadt Wismar. Ed. Techen, F. Leipsic. 1906.
 IV. Die Lübecker Schonenfahrer. Ed. Baasch, E. Lübeck. 1922.
  V. Deutsch-russische Handelsgeschichte des Mittelalters. Ed. Goetz, K. Lübeck.
       1922.
 VI. Der Wendische Münzeverein. Ed. Jesse, W.
VII. Die Zinngiesser in Liv-, Est-, und Kurland. Ed. Gahlnbäck, J. In the press.
Hansisches Urkundenbuch. Vols. i–iii, ed. Höhlbaum, K.; iv–vi, ed. Kunze, K.;
       viii–x, ed. Stein, W. Leipsic. 1876–1907.
Hasse, P. Freibrief für Lübeck. Lübeck. 1893.
Helmold. Chronica Slavorum (–1172). Ed. Lappenberg, J. M. MGH. Script. xxi.
       Also ed. Schmeidler, B. SGUS. 2nd edn. 1909.
Inventare Hansischer Archive. Vols. i and ii. Kölner Inventar (1531–91). Ed.
       Höhlbaum, K.; iii. Danziger Inventar (1531–91). Ed. Simson, P. (Verein für
       Hansische Geschichte.) Leipsic. 1896–1913.
Knipping, R. Die Kölner Stadtrechnungen des Mittelalters mit einer Darstellung der
       Finanzverwaltung. 2 vols. Bonn. 1897.
Koppmann, K. Johann Tölners Handlungsbuch von 1345 bis 1350. (Geschichts-
       quellen der Stadt Rostock.) Rostock. 1885.
—— Kämmereirechnungen der Stadt Hamburg. 7 vols. 1869–97.
—— Leitfaden für die Älterleute des deutschen Kaufmanns zu Brügge. Hamburg.
       1875.
Korner, H. Die Chronica Novella. Ed. Schwalm, J. Göttingen. 1895.
Lappenberg, J. M. Geschichtsquellen des Erzstiftes und der Stadt Bremen. Bremen.
       1841.
—— Urkundliche Geschichte des Londoner Stahlhofes. Hamburg. 1851.
Liv-, Esth-, und Curländisches Urkundenbuch nebst Regesten. Vols. i–vi, ed.
       Bunge, F. G. von; vii–ix, ed. Hildebrand, H.; x–xi, ed. Schwartz, P.; xii (–1472),
       ed. Schwartz, P. and Bulmerincq, A. von. Abt. ii. Vols. i–iii (1494–1510), ed.
       Arbusoff, L., etc. Reval. 1852–73; Riga. 1881–1914.
Mecklenburgisches Urkundenbuch. Ed. by Verein für Mecklenburgische Geschichte
       und Altertumskunde. 24 vols. Schwerin. 1863 ff.
Mollwo, C. Das Handlungsbuch von Hermann und Johann Wittenborg. Leipsic.
       1902.
Niederländische Akten und Urkunden zur Geschichte der Hanse. Ed. Häpke, R.
       Vols. i, ii (–1669). (Verein für Hansische Geschichte.) Munich and Lübeck.
       1913, 23.
Nirrnheim, H. Das Handlungsbuch Vickos von Geldersen. (Verein für Hamburgische
       Geschichte.) Hamburg. 1895.
Ostfriesisches Urkundenbuch. Ed. Friedländer, E. 2 vols. (–1500). Emden. 1878, 81.
Pommersches Urkundenbuch. Ed. Klempin, R. and others. (K. Staatsarchiv zu
       Stettin.) 6 vols. Stettin. 1868 ff.
Prahl, F. Chronica der Stadt Kiel. Stettin. 1856.
Recesse und andere Akten der Hansetage von 1256–1430. Pt. i. Ed. Koppmann, K.
       8 vols. (Hist. Commission BAW.) Leipsic. 1870–97; Pt. ii (1431–76). Ed.
       Ropp, G. von der. 7 vols. (Verein für Hansische Geschichte.) Leipsic. 1876–92;
       Pt. iii (1477–1530). Ed. Schäfer, D. 8 vols. 1881–1910.
Rigische Stadtbuch. Ed. Hildebrand, H. St Petersburg (Leningrad). 1872.
Sattler, K. Handelsrechnungen des Deutschen Ordens. Leipsic. 1881.
Stralsunder Stadtbuch. Das älteste (1270–1310). Ed. Fabricius, F. Berlin. 1872;
       Das zweite (1310–42). Pt. i. Ed. Reuter, C., Lietz, P., and Wehner, O.
       Stralsund. 1893. Pts. ii and iii. Ed. Ebeling, R. 1896, 1903.
Tratziger, Adam. Chronica der Stadt Hamburg bis 1557. Ed. Lappenberg, J. M.
       Hamburg. 1865.
Urkundenbuch der Stadt Braunschweig. Ed. Hänselmann, L. Brunswick. 1862.
Urkundenbuch zur Geschichte der Herzöge von Braunschweig und Lüneburg. Ed.
       Sudendorf, H. 11 vols. Hanover. 1859–83.

Urkundenbuch der Stadt Goslar. Ed. Bode, G. 4 vols. (Geschichtsquellen d. Provinz Sachsen. xxix–xxxii. Hist. Commission d. Provinz Sachsen.) Halle. 1893–1905.
Urkundenbuch der Stadt Hannover. Ed. Grotefeld, C. L. and Fiedler, F. L. (Urkundenbuch des hist. Vereins für Niedersachsen, v.) Hanover. 1860.
Urkundenbuch der Stadt Lüneburg. Ed. Volger, W. F. Vols. i, ii (–1387). (*Ibid.* viii, ix.) Hanover. 1872, 75. Vol. iii (–1402). Lüneburg. 1877.
Urkundenbuch der Stadt Magdeburg. Ed. Hertel, G. Vols. i–iii. (Geschichtsquellen d. Provinz Sachsen. xxvi–xxviii. Hist. Commission d. Provinz Sachsen.) Halle. 1892.
Urkundenbuch für die Geschichte des Niederrheins. Ed. Lacomblet, T. J. 4 vols. Düsseldorf. 1840–56.
Weinrich, C. Danziger Chronik. Ed. Hirsch, T. and Vossberg, F. A. Danzig. 1855.

III. MODERN WORKS.

A. General.

Agats, A. Der hansische Baienhandel. (Abh. zur mittleren und neuern Gesch. v.) Heidelberg. 1904.
Bahr, K. Handel und Verkehr der deutschen Hanse in Flandern während des 14 Jahrhts. Leipsic. 1911.
Baltische Monatsschrift. Vol. xxii. Riga. 1872.
Barthold, F. W. Die Geschichte der deutschen Hanse. New edn. 2 vols. Magdeburg and Leipsic. 1909.
Berg, F. E. Die Nederlanden en het Hanseverbond. (Provinciaal Utrechtsch Genootschap van Kunsten en Wetenschap. Nieuwe Verhandelingen. ix.) Utrecht. 1833.
Berg, G. Lübecks Stellung in der Hanse bis zur Mitte des 14 Jahrhts. Rostock. 1889. [diss.]
Buck, W. Der deutsche Handel in Nowgorod bis zur Mitte des 14 Jahrhts. St Petersburg (Leningrad). 1895.
—— Der deutsche Kaufmann in Nowgorod bis zur Mitte des 14 Jahrhts. Berlin. 1891. [diss.]
Christensen, W. Unionskongerne og Hansestaederne, 1439–66. Copenhagen. 1895.
Daenell, E. R. Die Blütezeit der deutschen Hanse. Hansische Geschichte von der zweiten Hälfte des 14 bis zum letzten Viertel des 15 Jahrhts. 2 vols. Berlin. 1905–6.
—— Geschichte der deutschen Hanse in der 2ten Hälfte des 14 Jahrhts. Leipsic. 1897.
—— Die Hansestädte und der Krieg um Schleswig. *In* Zeitschr. d. Gesellsch. für Schleswig-Holstein. Gesch. xxxii. Kiel. 1903.
—— Die Kölner Konföderation vom 1367 und die Schonischen Pfandschaften, 1367–85. (Leipziger Studien aus dem Gebiet der Gesch. i, 1.) Leipsic. 1894.
—— Polen und die Hanse um die Wende des 14 Jahrhts. DZG. Neue Folge. 1897–8.
Denicke, H. Die Hansestädte, Dänemark, und Norwegen von 1369 bis 1376. Halle. 1880.
Dittmer, G. W. Geschichte des Krieges der See- oder Wendischen Städte mit Dänemark und Norwegen in Folge der Kölner Konföderation vom Jahre 1367. Lübeck. 1853.
Erslev, K. Dronning Margarethe og Kalmarunions Grundlaeggelse. Copenhagen. 1882.
—— Erik af Pommern. Copenhagen. 1901.
Eschebach, E. Die Beziehungen der niedersächsischen Städte zur deutschen Hanse bis 1477 und 1478. Halle. 1901. [diss.]
Frensdorff, F. Das Reich und die Hansestädte. ZSR. xx. German. Abt. 1899.
—— Das statuarische Recht der deutschen Kaufleute in Nowgorod. *In* Abh. d. k. Gesellsch. der Wissensch. Göttingen. 1886–7.

Girgensohn, P. Die skandinavischen Politik der Hanse, 1375–95. (Upsala Universitets Årsskrift.) Upsala. 1898. [diss.]

Häpke, R. Brügges Entwicklung zum mittelalterlichen Weltmarkt. (Abh. zur Verkehrs- und Seegesch. Ed. Schäfer, D. i.) Berlin. 1908.

Hansische Geschichtsblätter. (Verein für Hansische Geschichte.) Leipsic, and later Lübeck. 1871 ff., in progress.

Hansische Volkshefte. (Verein für Hansische Geschichte.) Bremen. 1923 ff., in progress. [Short popular studies.]

Harttung (Pflugk-Harttung), J. von. Norwegen und die deutschen Seestädte bis zum Schluss des 13 Jahrhts. Berlin. 1877.

Hill, M. Margaret of Denmark. London. 1898.

Hoffmann, M. Ueber allgemeine Hansetage in Lübeck. Lübeck. 1884. [progr.]

Keutgen, F. Die Beziehungen der Hanse zu England im letzten Drittel des 14 Jahrhts. Giessen. 1890.

Kiesselbach, G. A. Die wirtschaftlichen Grundlagen der deutschen Hanse und die Handelsstellung Hamburgs bis in die 2te Hälfte des 14 Jahrhts. Berlin. 1907.

Levin, L. Das Kommissionsgeschäft im Hansegebiet. Berlin. 1887. [diss.]

Lindner, T. Die deutsche Hanse. 4th edn. Leipsic. 1911.

Mantels, W. Beiträge zur lübisch-hansischen Geschichte. Ed. Koppmann, K. Jena. 1881.

—— Der im Jahre 1367 zu Köln beschlossne zweite hanseatische Pfundzoll Lübeck. 1862.

Nanninga, J. G. Het Handelverker der Oesterlingen door Holland in de dertiende eeuw. Bussum. 1921.

Nirrnheim, H. Hamburg und Ostfriesland in der ersten Hälfte des 15 Jahrhts. Strasbourg. 1890. [diss.]

Pfingstblätter des hansischen Geschichtsvereins. (Verein für Hansische Geschichte.) Leipsic and Munich. 1905 ff., in progress. [Short popular studies.]

Riesenkampff, N. G. Der deutsche Hof zu Nowgorod bis zu seiner Schliessung durch Ivan III im Jahre 1494. Dorpat. 1854.

Rörig, F. Hansische Beiträge zur deutschen Wirtschaftsgeschichte. Breslau. 1928.

Rogge, H. Der Stapelzwang des hansischen Kontors zu Brügge im 15 Jahrht. Kiel. 1913. [diss.]

Ropp, G. von der. Zur deutsch-skandinavischen Geschichte des 15 Jahrhts. Leipsic. 1876.

Sartorius, G. F. Geschichte des hanseatischen Bundes. 3 vols. Göttingen. 1802–8.

—— Urkundliche Geschichte des Ursprungs der deutschen Hanse. Ed. Lappenberg, J. M. 2 vols. Hamburg. 1830.

Schäfer, D. Die Hanse. (Monographien zur Weltgesch. Ed. Heyck, E. xix.) Leipsic and Bielefeld. 1903.

—— Die Hanse und ihre Handelspolitik. Jena. 1885.

—— Die Hansestädte und König Waldemar von Dänemark. Hansische Geschichte bis 1376. Jena. 1879.

—— Wisby und Gothland. *In* Aufsätze, Vorträge, und Reden. Jena. 1913.

—— Wisby und Gothland. Zur Geschichte des deutschen Handels nach Finland. Lübeck. 1878.

Schanz, G. Englische Handelspolitik gegen Ende des Mittelalters. 2 vols. Leipsic. 1881.

Schlözer, K. von. Die Hanse und der Deutsche Ritters-Orden in den Ostseeländern. Berlin. 1851.

—— Livland und die Anfänge deutschen Lebens im baltischen Norden. Berlin. 1850.

—— Verfall und Untergang der Hanse und des Deutschen Ordens in den Ostseeländern. Berlin. 1851.

Schulz, F. Die Hanse und England von Edwards III bis auf Heinrichs VIII Zeit. (Abh. zur Verkehrs- und Seegesch. Ed. Schäfer, D. v.) Berlin. 1911.

Stein, W. Beiträge zur Geschichte der deutschen Hanse bis um die Mitte des 15 Jahrhts. Giessen. 1900.

—— Die Genossenschaft der deutsch. Kaufleute in Brügge. Berlin. 1890. [diss.]

—— Die Hanse und England. Ein hansische-englischer Seekrieg im 15 Jahrht. (Pfingstblätter d. hansisch. Gesch. i.) Leipsic. 1905.

Stieda, W. Hansisch-venetianische Handelsbeziehungen im 15 Jahrhts. *In* Festschrift der Univ. Rostock zur 2ten Säkularfeier der Univ. Halle. Rostock. 1894.
—— Hildebrand Veckinhusen. Briefwechsel eines deutschen Kaufmanns im 15 Jahrht. Leipsic. 1921.
Vogel, W. Kurze Geschichte der deutschen Hanse. (Pfingstblätter d. hansisch. Gesch. xi.) Munich. 1915.
Wehrmann, K. Die Gründung des hanseatischen Hauses in Antwerpen. Lübeck. 1874.
Weiner, A. Early commercial intercourse between England and Germany. *In* Economica. No. 5. London. 1922.
Winckler, A. Die deutsche Hanse in Russland. Berlin. 1886.
Zimmern, H. The Hansa Towns. (Story of the Nations.) London and New York. 1889.

B. SINGLE TOWNS.

(Only the more important are included.)

Bippen, W. von. Geschichte der Stadt Bremen. 3 vols. Bremen. 1892–1904.
Deecke, E. Geschichte der Stadt Lübeck. Lübeck. 1844.
Dürre, H. Geschichte der Stadt Braunschweig im Mittelalter. Brunswick. 1875.
Duntze, J. H. Geschichte der freien Stadt Bremen. 4 vols. Bremen. 1845–51.
Ennen, L. Geschichte der Stadt Köln. 5 vols. Cologne. 1863–80.
Hirsch, T. Handels- und Gewerbegeschichte Danzigs unter der Herrschaft des Deutschen Ordens. Leipsic. 1858.
Hoffmann, M. Geschichte der freien und Hansestadt Lübeck. 2 pts. Lübeck. 1889, 92.
King, W. Chronicles of three Free Cities (Hamburg, Bremen, and Lübeck). London and New York. 1914.
Koppmann, K. Aus Hamburgs Vergangenheit. Hamburg and Leipsic. 1885.
Mettig, C. Geschichte der Stadt Riga. Riga. 1897.
Mönckeberg, C. Geschichte der freien und Hansestadt Hamburg. Hamburg. 1885.
Rübel, C. Geschichte der Grafschaft und der freien Reichstadt Dortmund. Dortmund. 1917.
Simson, P. Geschichte der Stadt Danzig. 4 vols. Danzig. 1913–18.
Techen, F. Geschichte der Seestadt Wismar. Wismar. 1929.

858

CHAPTER IX.

THE TEUTONIC ORDER.

I. BIBLIOGRAPHIES.

Dahlmann-Waitz. Quellenkunde der deutschen Geschichte. *See Gen. Bibl.* i.
Finkel, L. Bibliografia historyi polskiej. 3 vols. and suppl. Cracow. 1891–1910.
Potthast, A. Bibliotheca historica medii aevi. *See Gen. Bibl.* i.
Winkelmann, E. Bibliotheca Livoniae historica. St Petersburg (Leningrad). 1870.

II. DOCUMENTS.

Acta Borussica ecclesiastica, civilia, literaria. Ed. Lilienthal, M. 3 vols. Königsberg. 1730–2.
Akty unii horodelskiej. *In* Volumina legum. i. *See below.*
Altpreussische Monatsschrift. Königsberg. 1864 ff.
Brestiae, Literae pacis inter Ordinem Teutonicum et Poloniam. *In* Volumina legum. i. *See below.*
Brock, J. De controversiis quae post pacem Thorunensem exortae sunt. Breslau. 1871.
Bunge, F. G. von. Liv-, Esth-, und Curländische Urkunden-Regesten bis 1300. Leipsic. 1881.
—— and others. Liv-, Esth-, und Curländisches Urkundenbuch nebst Regesten. 12 vols. Reval. 1852–73; Riga. 1881–1909.
Casimirus rex ius Culmense per totam Prussiam servari iubet. *In* Volumina legum. i. *See below.*
Concordia dominorum de Prussia cum rege Poloniae. SKAW. ii. 1850.
Corpus constitutionum Prutenicarum. Königsberg. 1721.
Dogiel, M. Codex diplomaticus regni Poloniae et Lithuaniae. Vilna. 1758–9.
Dolliner, T. Codex epistolaris Premislai Ottocari. Vienna. 1803.
Hennes, J. H. Codex diplomaticus ordinis sanctae Mariae Teutonicorum. Mayence. 1845–61.
Hildebrand, H. Das Rigische Schuldbuch. St Petersburg (Leningrad). 1872.
Jacobi, T. Codex epistolaris Joannis regis Bohemiae. Berlin. 1841.
Jacobson, T. Geschichte der Quellen des kathol. Kirchenrechtes der Provinzen Preussen und Polen. Königsberg. 1837.
Kętrzyński, W. O przywileju księcia Mściwoja. *In* Przewodnik nauk. i. lit. Lemberg. 1877.
Kriegszüge der Nowgoroder in Esthland. *In* Mittheil. Liv-, Esth-, und Kurlands. iv. Riga. 1847.
Lampe, E. Beiträge z. Geschichte Heinrich von Plauen. Danzig. 1889.
Lindaus, G. Geschichte d. dreizehnjährigen Krieges. *In* Script. rerum Prussicarum. iv. *See below,* iii.
Listy Gedimina. *In* Narbutt, T. Dzieje Litwy. iv. *See below,* iv.
Literae pacis perpetuae inter Poloniam et Ordinem Teutonicum. *In* Volumina legum. i. *See below.*
Lites ac res gestae inter Polonos Ordinemque Cruciferorum. Poznań (Posen). 1855.
Mittheilungen aus dem Gebiete der Geschichte der Liv-, Esth-, und Kurlands. (Gesellsch. f. Gesch. u. Alterthumskunde d. russisch. Ostsee-Provinzen.) Riga. 1840 ff.
Monumenta medii aevi historica res gestas Poloniae illustrantia. Ed. Academia Cracoviensis. 13 vols. Cracow. 1874 ff.
Mülverstedt, G. A. Zur Geschichte und Chronologie älterer Bischöfe von Pomezanien und Culm. *In* Zeitschr. des hist. Vereins für...Marienwerder. ii. 1889.
Nadanie cesarza Fryderyka krzyżakom Litwy, Kurlandyi, i Semigalii. *In* Narbutt, T. Dzieje Litwy. iv. *See below,* iv.
Najstarszy dokument Torunia 1231. *In* Przegląd bibliog. arch. Warsz. Warsaw. ii. 1881.

Napierski, C. E. Index Corporis diplomatici Livoniae, Esthoniae, Curoniae. Riga. 1833–5.
—— Monumenta Livoniae antiqua. Riga. 1839.
Perlbach, M. Die ältesten preussischen Urkunden kritisch untersucht. Königsberg. 1873.
—— Königsberger Regesten (1256–1524). *In* Altpreuss. Monatsschr. XVII, XVIII. Königsberg. 1881.
—— Preussisch-polnische Studien. Halle. 1886.
—— Preussische Regesten. Königsberg. 1875–6.
—— Quellen-Beiträge zur Geschichte der Stadt Königsberg. Göttingen. 1878.
—— Das Urkundenwesen Mestwins II von Pomerellen. *In* Preussisch-polnische Studien. Halle. 1886.
Philippi, R. and Wölky, C. P. Preussisches Urkundenbuch. Königsberg. 1882.
Potthast, A. Regesta Pontificum Romanorum 1198–1340. *See Gen. Bibl.* IV.
Prochaska, A. Codex epistolaris Vitoldi. *In* Monumenta medii aevi historica. VI. *See above.*
Raczyński, E. Codex diplomaticus Lithuaniae. Breslau. 1845.
Romanowski, J. N. De Conradi, ducis Mazoviae, conditione. Poznań (Posen). 1857.
—— O zakonie braci dobrzyńskich. *In* Biblioteka Warszawska. Warsaw. 1857.
Russko-livonskiya Akty. Ed. Napierski, C. E. (Arkheograf. Kommissiya). St Petersburg (Leningrad). 1868.
Schirren, C. 25 Urkunden zur Gesch. Livlands im 13 Jahrht. Dorpat. 1866.
Smith, L. Toulmin, *ed.* Expeditions to Prussia...by Henry earl of Derby. (Camden Soc., n.s. LII.) London. 1894. [Account of receipts and expenses.]
Strehlke, E. Tabulae Ordinis Teutonici. Berlin. 1869.
Szymeński, B. P. Wykaz praw i przywilejów dyecezyi chelmskiej. *In* Przegląd poznański. XXXII. Poznań (Posen).
Theiner, A. Vetera monumenta Poloniae et Lithuaniae ex tabulariis Vaticanis Romae. I, II. Rome. 1860–1.
Töppen, M. Acten der Ständetage Preussens unter dem Deutschen Orden. Leipsic. 1878–88.
Voigt, J. Codex diplomaticus Prussicus. 5 vols. Königsberg. 1836–61.
—— Geschichte Preussens. Vol. IX. Königsberg. 1839.
—— and Schubert, F. Editio Lindenblatts Jahrbücher. Königsberg. 1823.
Volumina legum. Vol. I. Ed. Konarski, S. H. Warsaw. 1732.
Wölky, C. P. Urkundenbuch des Bisthums Culm. Danzig. 1884–7.
—— and Saage, M. Codex diplomaticus Warmiensis. Mayence. 1860–74.
Zeitschrift des Westpreuss. Geschichtsvereins. Danzig. 1880 ff.
Zuccalmaglio, F. Urkundenbuch d. Stadt Mitau. Mitau. 1845–7.
Zwölf Urkunden zur livländischen Geschichte. *In* Mittheil. Liv-, Esth-, und Kurlands. VIII. Riga. 1855.

III. CHRONICLES, ETC.

A. COLLECTIONS.

Monumenta Germaniae Historica. Scriptores. *See Gen. Bibl.* IV.
Monumenta historiae Warmiensis. Ed. by Hist. Verein für Ermland. 8 vols. Mayence. 1860–9.
Monumenta Livoniae antiquae. Riga and Leipsic. 1835–47.
Monumenta Poloniae Historica. Vols. I–VI. Ed. Bielowski, A. and others. Lemberg. 1864–88.
Polnoe Sobranie russkikh lêtopisey. I, II. (Arkheograf. Kommissiya.) St Petersburg (Leningrad). 1846, 63.
Scriptores rerum Livonicarum. 2 vols. Riga and Leipsic. 1848, 53.
Scriptores rerum Prussicarum. Ed. Hirsch, T., Töppen, M., and Strehlke, E. 5 vols. Leipsic. 1861–74.

B. SEPARATE CHRONICLES.

Acta de interceptione castri Allenstein (1455–61). *In* Monumenta hist. Warmiensis. I. *See above,* III A.
Aeltere Hochmeisterschronik. Ed. Töppen, M. *Ibid.* III.

Aeneas Sylvius. De Polonia, Lithuania, et Prussia. *In* Pistorius, J. Polonicae historiae Corpus. Basle. 1582.
—— De situ et origine Pruthenorum. *In* Script. rerum Prussicarum. IV. *See above*, III A.
Annales canonici Sambiensis. MGH. Script. XIX.
Annales Cuiavienses (1202–1376). Ed. Bielowski, A. *in* Monumenta Poloniae Hist. III. *See above*, III A.
Annales Dunamundenses (1211–48). Ed. Strehlke, E. *in* Script. rer. Prussicarum. II. *Also* MGH. Script. XIX.
Annales expeditialis Prussici (1253–1414). Ed. Strehlke, E. *in* Script. rerum Prussicarum. III.
Annales Joannis Marienwerder decani (1391–8). Ed. Töppen, M. *Ibid.* V.
Annales Majoris Poloniae. Ed. Bielowski, A. *in* Monumenta Poloniae Hist. II, III.
Annales Masovienses (967–1370). Ed. Bielowski, A. *Ibid.* III.
Annales Minorum Prussicorum. Ed. Strehlke, E. *in* Script. rerum Prussicarum. V.
Annales Pelplinenses (1190–1293). Ed. Töppen, M. *Ibid.* I.
Annales Polonorum. MGH. Script. XIX. *Also in* Annales Poloniae. SGUS. 1866.
Annales Prussici breves (1190–1337). *In* Script. rerum Prussicarum. III.
Annales terrae Prussiae (1029–1450). MGH. Script. XIX.
Arnold of Lübeck. Chronica Slavorum (1171–1209). *Ibid.* XXI.
Bitschin, Conrad. Fortsetzung zu P. von Dustwigs Chronik (1326–1435). Ed. Töppen, M. *in* Script. rerum Prussicarum. III.
Blumenau, Laurentius. Historia de Ordine Theutonicorum (1226–1455). Ed. Töppen, M. *Ibid.* IV.
Catalogus abbatum monast. de Oliva (1224–1641). Ed. Hirsch, T. *Ibid.* V.
Chronicon Gedanense (1190–1422). *Ibid.*
Chronicon Oliviense (1170–1353). Ed. Hirsch, T. *Ibid.* I.
Czarnków, J. de. Chronicon Polonorum (... –1384). Ed. Sommersberg, F. W. de, *in* Script. rerum Silesiacarum. Leipsic. 1729–32.
Die Dantziger Chronik (1190–1526). *In* Script. rerum Prussicarum. V.
David, Lucas. Preussische Chronik. Ed. Henning, E. Königsberg. 1812–17.
De magna strage 1410. Ed. Kętrzyński, W. *in* Monumenta Poloniae Hist. IV.
De primordiis Ordinis Teutonici narratio. *In* Script. rerum Prussicarum. I.
Die Ermländischen Anniversarienbücher (1393–1611). *In* Monumenta hist. Warmiensis. I.
Die Ferber Chronik (1511–25). *In* Script. rerum Prussicarum. V.
Dlugosz, Jan. Opera omnia. Ed. Przezdziecki, A. Cracow. 1863–87.
—— Banderia Pruthenorum. Ed. Vossberg, F. A. Berlin. 1849.
Dusburg, Peter. Cronica terrae Prussiae (1190–1326). Ed. Töppen, M. *in* Script. rerum Prussicarum. I.
Fontes Olivienses (1356–1545). Ed. Kętrzyński, W. *in* Monumenta Poloniae Hist. V.
Francisci Thorunensis annales Prussici (941–1410). Ed. Strehlke, E. *in* Script. rerum Prussicarum. III.
Geschichte von wegen eines Bundes 1422–1462. Ed. Töppen, M. *Ibid.* IV.
Grunau, S. Preussische Chronik. Ed. Perlbach, M. Leipsic. 1876.
Hanseatische Chronik (1216–1525). *In* Script. rerum Prussicarum. V.
Hartknoch, C. De scriptoribus historiae Prussiae. Leipsic. 1679.
Henricus Lettus. Chronicum Livonicum vetus seu Chron. Lyvoniae. *In* Script. rerum Livonicarum. I. *See above*, III A. *Also* MGH. Script. XXIII. *Also* SGUS. 1874.
Henricus Sbigneus de Gora. Tractatulus contra Cruciferos. Ed. Balzer, O. *in* Monumenta Poloniae Hist. IV.
Historia brevis magistri Teutonici (1190–1469). *In* Script. rerum Prussicarum. IV.
Höhlbaum, K. Beiträge zur Quellenkunde Alt-Livlands. Leipsic. 1873.
Horn, A. Nachtrag zur Schlacht von Tannenberg. *In* Altpreuss. Monatsschr. XXIII. 1886.
Jeroschin, N. von. Di Kronike von Pruzinlant. Ed. Strehlke, E. *in* Script. rerum Prussicarum. I. *Also* Leipsic. 1861.
Jüngere Hochmeisterchronik (... –1467). Ed. Hirsch, T. *in* Script. rerum Prussicarum. V.
Jüngere livländische Reimchronik (1315–48). Ed. Höhlbaum, K. Leipsic. 1872.
Kadlubek, V. Historia Polonica (... –1203). *In* Monumenta Poloniae Hist. II.

Kętrzyński, W. Magistri Ordinis Teutonicorum. *Ibid.* IV.
—— Prussica. *Ibid.*
Königshofens Bericht über die Schlacht bei Tannenberg. *In* Altpreuss. Monatsschr. IX.
Lindaus, J. Geschichte des 13-jährigen Krieges. *In* Script. rerum Prussicarum. IV.
Livländische Reimchronik. Ed. Napierski, K. *In* Script. rerum Livonicarum. I.
Lubbes, F. Familienchronik (1400-1518). *In* Script. rerum Prussicarum. IV.
Pole, P. Preussische Chronik (1422-1532). Ed. Töppen, M. *In* Script. rerum Prussicarum. V.
Posilge, J. von. Chronik des Landes Preussen (1360-1419). Ed. Voigt, J. and Schubert, T. W. Königsberg. 1823.
Registri damnorum a Cruciferis factorum. Ed. Kętrzyński, W. *In* Monumenta Poloniae Hist. v.
Schutzius, C. Historia rerum Prussicarum. Leipsic. 1599.
Series episcoporum Culmensium, 1276-1688. *In* Monumenta Poloniae Hist. IV.
Series episcoporum Pomezaniensium. *In* Script. rerum Prussicarum.
Series episcoporum Varmiensium. *In* Monumenta hist. Warmiensis.
Stryjkowski, M. Kronika. Ed. Malinowski, M. Warsaw. 1846.
Töppen, M. Kleine chronikalische Aufzeichnungen zur Geschichte Preussens im 16 Jahrht. *In* Altpreuss. Monatsschr. XXXII, XXXIII. 1896-7.
Walsingham, Thomas. Historia Anglicana. Ed. Riley, H. T. Vol. II. pp. 197-8, 202. (Rolls.) 1864. [The expeditions of the earl of Derby (Henry IV) and the duke of Gloucester.] Transl. in Hakluyt, R. Navigations. Vol. I. pp. 304, 306. (Hakluyt Soc., extra ser.) Glasgow. 1903.
Wartberge, H. von. Chronicon Livoniae (... -1378). Leipsic. 1863.
Weinreich, C. Dantziger Chronik (1461-1495). Ed. Hirsch, T. Berlin. 1855. *Also in* Script. rerum Prussicarum. IV.
Wigand von Marburg. Cronica nova Prutenica (1293-1394). Ed. Hirsch, T. *in* Script. rerum Prussicarum. II.

IV. MODERN WORKS.

Altpreussische Monatsschrift. Königsberg. 1864 ff.
Ambrassat, A. Die Provinz Ostpreussen. Königsberg. 1896.
Archiv für d. Geschichte Liv-, Esth-, und Curlands. Reval. 1842 ff.
Baczko, L. Geschichte Preussens. Königsberg. 1792.
—— Versuch einer Gesch. Königsbergs. Königsberg. 1804.
Barbashev, A. Tannenbergskaya bitva. *In* Zhurnal Ministerstva narodnago prosveshcheniya. CCLIV. St Petersburg (Leningrad). 1887.
—— Vitovt i yego politika. St Petersburg (Leningrad). 1885.
Bielenstein, A. Die Grenzen des lettischen Volksstammes. St Petersburg (Leningrad). 1893.
Bienemann, F. Die Kolonialpolitik des Deutschen Ritterordens. *In* Zeitschr. für Kulturgeschichte. II. Weimar. 1895.
Bock, F. S. Leben Albrechts von Preussen. Königsberg. 1745.
Bogorya, J. La bataille de Grunwald. Paris. 1878.
Boldt, F. Der Deutsche Orden und Littauen 1370-86. Königsberg. 1870.
Breiter, E. Wladyslaw książe Opolski. Lemberg. 1889.
Bujack, G. Der Deutsche Orden und Witold von Littauen. Königsberg. 1869.
Bunge, F. G. Der Orden der Schwertbrüder. Leipsic. 1875.
—— Die Stadt Riga im 13 und 14 Jahrht. Leipsic. 1878.
Celichowski, Z. Spory i sprawy pomiędzy Polakami a Zakonem. Poznań (Posen). 1890, 92.
Cheshykhin, E. Istoria Livonii. Riga. 1885.
Choiseul-Gouffier, S. Vladislav Jagellon et Hedvige. Paris. 1824.
Croeger, C. Geschichte Liv-, Esth-, und Kurlands. 2 pts. Leipsic. 1867, 70.
Dehio, G. Geschichte des Erzbistums Hamburg-Bremen. Vol. II. Livländische Mission. Berlin. 1877.
Engelhardt, H. von. Beitrag zur Entstehung der Gutsherrschaft in Livland während der Ordenzeit. Riga. 1897.
Engelmann, A. Khronologicheskiya izsledovania v oblasti russkoy i livonskoy istorii v XIII i XIV stoletiakh. St Petersburg (Leningrad). 1858.

Ewald, A. L. Die Eroberung Preussens durch die Deutschen. Halle. 1872–84.
Fabricius, C. G. Die Herrschaft der Herzöge von Pommern und Dantzig. *In* Studien z. Gesch. der wendischen Ostseeländer. Berlin. 1856–9.
Fleischer, F. Bischof Heinrich IV von Ermland (1401–15). *In* Zeitschr. für d. Gesch. Ermlands. xii. 1897.
Froelich, X. Geschichte des Graudenzer Kreises. Graudenz. 1868, 72.
Gadebusch, F. K. Livländische Jahrbücher. i (1030–1561). Riga. 1780.
Geschichte d. Ostseeprovinzen Liv-, Esth-, und Kurland. Mitau. 1879.
Gołębiowski, L. Dzieje Polski za panowania Jagiellonów. Warsaw. 1846–8.
Goll, J. Čechy a Prusy ve středověku. Prague. 1897.
Gorski, K. Bitwa pod Grunwaldem. *In* Biblioteka Warsz. iii. Warsaw. 1888.
Gorzycki, K. J. Wplyw stolicy apostolskiej na rokowania Kazimierza W. z Czechami i Zakonem. Lemberg. 1893.
Gralath, D. Versuch einer Geschichte Danzigs. Berlin. 1791.
Hartknoch, C. Alt- und Neues Preussen. Leipsic. 1684.
—— Dissertatio de Curonorum et Semigallorum republica. Leipsic. 1698.
Henneberger, K. Beschreibung des Landes zu Preussen. Königsberg. 1584.
Hirsch, T. Handels- und Gewerbsgeschichte Danzigs unter der Herrschaft des Deutschen Ordens. Leipsic. 1858.
Höhlbaum, K. Die Gründung der deutschen Kolonie an der Düna. *In* Hansische Geschichtsbl. Leipsic. 1872.
Joachim, E. Die Politik des letzten Hochmeisters in Preussen. Leipsic. 1892, 95.
Kaczkowski, S. Krzyżacy i Polska. Poznań (Posen). 1845.
Kętrzynski, W. Prusy a Polska przed przybyciem Krzyżaków. *In* Przewodnik nauk. lit. Lemberg. 1881.
Koch, A. Hermann von Salza, Meister des Deutschen Ordens. Leipsic. 1885.
Koneczny, F. Jagiello i Witold. Lemberg. 1893.
—— Polityka Zakonu, 1389–90. Cracow. 1889.
—— Walter von Plettenberg, landmistrz inflancki wobec Zakonu, Litwy, i Moskwy. Cracow. 1891.
Korzon, T. Grunwald. Warsaw. 1910.
Koyalovich, M. O. Grunvaldenskaya bitva. St Petersburg (Leningrad). 1885.
Kruse, F. Urgeschichte des esthnischen Volksstammes. Leipsic. 1846.
Kujot, S. Piotr Swięca a Wladyslaw Lokietek. *In* Warta. iii. Poznań (Posen). 1876–7.
Kurtzenbaum, K. A. Kurze Darstellung der Regierung des Ordenmeisters Walter von Plettenberg. Riga. 1836–8.
Lampe, E. Beiträge zur Gesch. Heinrichs von Plauen. Danzig. 1889.
Lavisse, E. Récit de l'histoire de Prusse. Paris. 1879.
Lęgowski, J. Der Hochmeister Konrad von Wallenrod. Königsberg. 1879.
Lelewel, J. Ocalenie Polski za króla Lokiekta. *In* Dziennik Warszawski. v. Warsaw. 1826.
Lengnich, G. Geschichte der preuss. Lande. 9 vols. Danzig. 1722–55.
Leniek, J. Kongres Wyszegradzki w roku 1335. Lemberg. 1884.
Liek, G. Die Stadt Löbau. Marienwerder. 1892.
Löschin, G. Geschichte Danzigs. Danzig. 1816.
Lohmeyer, K. Geschichte von Ost- und West-Preussen. Gotha. 1880–1.
—— Herzog Albrecht von Preussen. Danzig. 1890.
—— Witowd, Grossfürst von Littauen. Königsberg. 1885.
Lorenz, O. Deutsche Geschichte im 13 und 14 Jahrht. Vienna. 1863.
Mettig, C. Geschichte der Stadt Riga. Riga. 1897.
Mittheilungen aus d. Gebiete d. Gesch. Liv-, Esth-, und Kurlands. *See above*, ii.
Mollerup, W. Daenemarks Beziehungen zu Livland. Berlin. 1884.
Murawski, B. Kurzes Lebensbild des heil. Adalbert, Apostels der Preussen. Gnesen. 1897.
Napierski, C. E. Reihenfolge der livländ. Landmeister. Riga. 1850.
Narbutt, T. Dzieje Litwy. Vilna. 1836–41.
Pabst, E. Die Anfänge d. deutschen Herrschaft in Livland. *In* Archiv für d. Gesch. Liv-, Esth-, und Curlands. iii, v. Reval. 1844–7.
—— Meinhart, Livlands Apostel. Reval. 1847–9.

Paprocki, B. Herby rycerstwa polskiego. Cracow. 1858–9.
Pauli, D. C. F. Allgemeine preussische Staatsgeschichte. Halle. 1760.
Pauli, R. Graf Heinrich von Derby in Danzig. *In* Zeitschr. d. Westpreuss. Geschichts-
vereins. VI. Danzig. 1882.
Pawlowski, J. N. Geschichte der Provinzial-Hauptstadt Danzig. Danzig. 1893.
Perlbach, M. Preussisch-polnische Studien. Halle. 1886.
Podczaszyński, M. O rycerzach Jaszczurkòwych w Prusiech. *In* Dziennik warsz. III.
Warsaw. 1825–6.
Pokój toruński 1466. *In* Warta. II. Poznań (Posen). 1875–6.
Potkański, K. Walka o Poznań (1306–13). Cracow. 1899.
Prochaska, A. Konrad Wallenrod w poezyi a w dziejach. *In* Szkice historyczne.
Warsaw. 1884.
—— O prawdziwości listów Gedymina. Cracow. 1895.
—— Spór o mitrę w Rydzie 1395–7. *In* Kwartalnik hist. Cracow. 1895.
—— Stosunki Krzyżaków z Gedyminem i Lokietkiem. *Ibid.* 1896.
—— Szkice historyczne z XV wieku. Cracow. 1884.
—— Warmia w czasie 13-letniej wojny. *In* Kwartalnik hist. Cracow. 1898.
Prutz, H. Rechnungen über Heinrich von Derbys Preussenfahrten (1390–91 und
1392). Leipsic. 1894.
Rathlef, G. Das Verhältniss des livl. Ordens zu den Landesbischöfen in der Stadt
Riga im 13 und 14 Jahrht. Dorpat. 1875.
Reicke, R. and Meyer, W. Altpreussische Bibliographie. Beilagheft zur Altpreuss.
Monatsschrift. *See above.*
Richter, A. von. Geschichte der dem Russischen Kaiserthum einverleibten deutschen
Ostseeprovinzen. Riga. 1857–8.
Richter, J. W. O. Geschichten aus der Zeit des preussischen Ordenstaates. 2 vols.
Hanover. 1892.
Roczniki Towarzystwa naukowego w Toruniu. Toruń (Thorn). 1878 ff.
Röhrich, A. Die Theilung der Diözese Ermland. *In* Zeitschr. für Gesch. Ermlands.
XII. 1899.
Röpell, R. und Caro, J. Geschichte Polens. Gotha. 1863–88.
Rüssow, B. Chronica der Provintz Lyfflandt. Rostock. 1578. *Also* in Script. rerum
Livonicarum. II. *See above,* III A.
Sattler, C. Handelsrechnungen des Deutschen Ordens. Leipsic. 1887.
Sbornik materialov i statey po istorii pribaltiyskago kraya. Riga. 1881 ff.
Schiemann, T. Russland, Polen, und Livland bis ins 17 Jahrht. (Oncken. *See Gen.
Bibl.* v.) Berlin. 1886–7.
Schlözer, K. Die Hansa und der Deutsche Ritterorden in den Ostseeländern. Berlin.
1851.
—— Livland und die Anfänge deutschen Lebens im baltischen Norden. Berlin.
1850.
Schultz, F. Geschichte der Stadt und d. Kreises Kulm bis 1479. Danzig. 1876.
Schutzius, C. Historia rerum Prussicarum. Zerbst. 1592.
Schwartz, P. Kurland im 13 Jahrht. Leipsic. 1875.
Seraphim, E. Geschichte Liv-, Esth-, und Kurlands. 2nd edn. 3 vols. Reval. 1897–1904.
Sieniawski, D. Biskupstwo warmińskie. Poznań (Posen). 1878.
Simson, P. Danzig im 13-jährigen Kriege (1454–64). Berlin. 1891.
Smolka, S. Witold pod Grunwaldem. Szkice hist. Vol. I. Warsaw. 1882.
Sokolowski, A. Konrad, książe na Mazowszu i Zakon niemiecki. Poznań (Posen).
1873.
Soloviev, S. Krestonostsy i Litva. *In* Otechestvenniya Zapiski. LXXXII. St Petersburg
(Leningrad). 1852.
Steinbrecht, C. Thorn im Mittelalter. Berlin. 1885.
Stier, H. Heinrich von Plauen. Chemnitz. 1874.
Sutowicz, J. Zjazd lucki. Cracow. 1875.
Szajnocha, K. Jadwiga i Jagiello, 1374–1413. *In* Dziela. Vols. IV–VIII. Warsaw. 1877.
—— Odrodzenie Polski za w Lokietka. Lemberg. 1859.
Szujski, J. Warunki traktatu kaliskiego 1343. *In* Dziela. Ser. II. Vol. VII. Cracow. 1888.
—— Dzieje Polski. Cracow. 1866.
Thunert, F. Der grosse Krieg, 1410–11. *In* Zeitschr. des Westpreuss. Geschichts-
vereins. XVI. Danzig. 1886.

Tikhomirov, T. Torgoviya i mirniya snoshenia russkikh knyazestv z Livoniey v XIII stol. *In* Zhurnal Ministerstva narodnago prosveshcheniya. CLXXX. St Petersburg (Leningrad). 1876.

Töppen, M. Aufsätze zur Gesch. Preussens. Danzig. 1866.

—— Die Deutschen in Livland. *In* Preuss. Prov. Blätter. v. 1848.

—— Elbinger Antiquitäten. Danzig. 1871–3.

—— Geschichte der Stadt Marienwerder.

—— Geschichte Masurens. Danzig. 1870.

—— Historisch-comparativ Geographie von Preussen. Gotha. 1858.

Voigt, J. Die Eroberung der Neumark. Berlin. 1863.

—— Geschichte des Deutschen Ritterordens in seinen zwölf Balleien in Deutschland 2 vols. Berlin. 1857–9.

—— Geschichte Preussens. 9 vols. Königsberg. 1827–39.

Wagner, P. Urkundliche Nachrichten von der Kreuzfahrt rheinischer Herrn nach Preussen. *In* Altpreuss. Monatsschr. XXV. Königsberg. 1889.

Watterich, J. M. Die Gründung des Deutschen Ordenstaates im Preussen. Leipsic. 1857.

Wegner, R. Ein pommersches Herzogthum, Kulturgeschichte des schwetzer Kreises. Posen. 1872.

Wernicke, E. J. Geschichte Thorns aus Urkunden. Thorn. 1839–42.

Werunsky, E. Geschichte Kaiser Karls IV und seiner Zeit. 3 vols. Innsbruck. 1880–92.

Winckelmann, E. Livländische Forschungen. Riga. 1868.

Zeitschrift des historischen Vereins für den Reg.-Bez. Marienwerder. Marienwerder. 1876 ff.

Zeitschrift des Westpreussischen Geschichtsvereins. Danzig. 1880 ff.

Zeitschrift für Geschichte und Alterthumskunde Ermlands. Braunsberg. 1858 ff.

CHAPTER X.

THE POPES OF AVIGNON AND THE GREAT SCHISM.

PART I. THE PAPACY AT AVIGNON.

I. SPECIAL BIBLIOGRAPHIES.

Camozzi, G. Il papato Avignonese. Palermo. 1912. [Unfinished: mainly for older works.]

Chevalier, C. U. J. Répertoire des sources historiques du moyen âge. Topo-bibliographie. Coll. 284, 2248–52. *See Gen. Bibl.* I.

Mollat, G. Les Papes d'Avignon (1305–1378). 6th rev. edn. Paris. 1930.

II. ORIGINAL AUTHORITIES.

A. DOCUMENTARY SOURCES.

[For complete list of papal documents *see* Mollat, G. *op. cit.,* pp. 5–19. For Registers and Letters of the Popes *see Gen. Bibl.* IV *under* Papal Documents.]

Baumgarten, P. M. Aus der Kanzlei und Kammer. Freiburg-i.-B. 1907.
—— Untersuchungen und Urkunden über die Camera collegii cardinalium für die Zeit von 1295 bis 1437. Leipsic. 1898.
—— Von der apostolischen Kanzlei. Cologne. 1908.

Du Chesne, F. Histoire de tous les cardinaux françois. 2 vols. Paris. 1660, 66.

Ehrle, F. Historia bibliothecae romanorum pontificum tum Bonifatianae tum Avinionensis. Rome. 1890.

Eubel, K. Bullarium Franciscanum. Vols. V and VI. Rome. 1898, 1902.
—— Der Registerband des Gegenpapstes Nikolaus V. *In* Archivalische Zeitschrift. 2nd ser. Vol. IV. Munich. 1893. pp. 123–212.

Faucon, M. La Librairie des papes d'Avignon. 2 vols. Paris. 1886–7.

Finke, H. Papsttum und Untergang des Templerordens. Münster. 1907.
—— Acta Aragonensia. 3 vols. Berlin. 1908 ff., in progress.

Kirsch, J. P. Die päpstlichen Annaten in Deutschland während des 14 Jahrhts. Paderborn. 1903.
—— Die päpstlichen Kollektorien in Deutschland während des 14 Jahrhts. Paderborn. 1894.
—— Die Rückkehr der Päpste Urban V und Gregor XI von Avignon nach Rom. Paderborn. 1898.

Ottenthal, E. von. Die päpstlichen Kanzleiregeln von Johannes XXII bis Nicolaus V. Innsbruck. 1888.

Prynne, W. The history of King John, Henry III, and...Edward I. London. 1670.

Raynaldus, O. Annales ecclesiastici. Vols. IV–VII. *See Gen. Bibl.* V *under* Baronius.

Rymer, T. Foedera. Vols. I–IV. *See Gen. Bibl.* IV.

Tangl, M. Die päpstlichen Kanzleiordnungen von 1200–1500. Innsbruck. 1894.

Vatikanische Quellen zur Geschichte der päpstlichen Hof- und Finanzverwaltung 1316–1378. Ed. Göller, E. and Schäfer, K. H. *See Gen. Bibl.* IV *under* Papal Documents.

Wadding, L. Annales minorum. Vols. VI–VIII. Rome. 1734.

B. CHRONICLES, ETC.

[Almost all the chronicles of the time refer to the Papacy at Avignon. Complete lists for the separate countries are given in the bibliographies by Balzani, Gross, Lorenz, Molinier (*for which see Gen. Bibl.* I). *See also* Mollat, G. Les Papes d'Avignon, pp. 19–24; and Mollat, G. Étude critique sur les vitae paparum Avenionensium d'Étienne Baluze. Paris. 1917.]

Baluzius, Stephanus. Vitae paparum Avenionensium. *See Gen. Bibl.* IV.
Böhmer, J. F. Fontes rerum Germanicarum. Vol. IV. Stuttgart. 1868.
Caterina da Siena, Santa. Lettere. Ed. Tommaseo, N. 4 vols. Florence. 1860.
Durandus, Gulielmus. De modo concilii generalis celebrandi. Lyons. 1531.
Fasciculus rerum expetendarum et fugiendarum. Ed. Brown, E. Vol. II. London.
    1690.
Le Maire, Guillaume. Gesta. Ed. Port, C. *in* Mélanges historiques. Vol. II. (Coll.
    doc.) Paris. 1877.
Murimuth, Adam. Continuatio chronicarum. Ed. Thompson, E. M. (Rolls.) 1889.
Pelagius, Alvarus. De planctu Ecclesiae. Venice. 1560.
Petrarch. Opera. Ed. Herold, J. 4 vols. Basle. 1554.
Villani, Giovanni and Matteo. Historie Fiorentine. Ed. Muratori. RR.II.SS.
    1st edn. Vols. XIII, XIV.
Walsingham, Thomas. Historia Anglicana. Ed. Riley, H. T. 2 vols. (Rolls.)
    1863–4.

III. MODERN WORKS.

A. General.

Christophe, J. B. Histoire de la papauté pendant le XIVe siècle. 3 vols. Paris. 1853
    [Somewhat antiquated.]
Hefele-Leclercq. Histoire des Conciles. Vol. VI. *See Gen. Bibl.* v.
Mollat, G. Les Papes d'Avignon (1305–1378). 6th rev. edn. Paris. 1930.
Pastor, L. von. Geschichte der Päpste im Zeitalter der Renaissance bis zur Wahl
    Pius II : Martin V, Eugen IV, Nikolaus V, Kalixtus III. 5th edn. Vol. I. Frei-
    burg-i.-B. 1925.

B. Special.

Albanès, J. H. and Chevalier, U. Actes anciens et documents concernant le bien-
    heureux Urbain V. Paris. 1897.
Albe, E. Autour de Jean XXII. Les familles du Quercy. 2 vols. Rome. 1903, 6.
Bréhier, L. L'Église et l'Orient au moyen âge. Les Croisades. 5th edn. Paris.
    1927.
Chaillan, M. Le bienheureux Urbain V. Paris. 1911.
Clergeac, A. La Curie et les bénéficiers consistoriaux. Paris. 1911.
Delaville Le Roulx, J. Les Hospitaliers à Rhodes. Paris. 1913.
Fumi, L. Eretici e ribelli nell' Umbria. Studio d'un decennio (1320–30). Todi. 1916.
Gardner, E. G. Saint Catherine of Siena. London. 1907.
Gasquet, F. A. The Black Death of 1348 and 1349. London. 1908.
Gay, J. Le pape Clément VI et les affaires d'Orient. Paris. 1904.
Göller, E. Die päpstliche Pönitentiarie von ihrem Ursprung bis zu ihrer Ungestaltung
    unter Pius V. Rome. 1907.
—— Der Liber taxarum der päpstlichen Kammer. QFIA. VIII. 1905.
Guiraud, J. L'église romaine et les origines de la Renaissance. Paris. 1911.
Haller, J. Papsttum und Kirchenreform. Berlin. 1903.
Jacob, K. Studien über Papst Benedikt XII. Berlin. 1910.
Jensen, O. Der englische Peterspfennig und die Lehenssteuer aus England und Irland
    an der Papststuhl im Mittelalter. Heidelberg. 1903. *Also* The Denarius Sancti
    Petri in England. TRHS. n.s. xv (1901). 201 ff., and *Ibid.* XIX (1905). 209 ff.
Levett, A. E. The Black Death. *In* Oxford Studies in Social and Legal History.
    Ed. Vinogradoff, P. Vol. v. Oxford. 1916.
Lizerand, G. Clément V et Philippe IV le Bel. Paris. 1910.
Marx, J. L'Inquisition en Dauphiné. Paris. 1914.
Mirot, L. La politique pontificale et le retour du Saint-Siège à Rome en 1376. Paris.
    1899.
Mollat, G. La collation des bénéfices ecclésiastiques sous les papes d'Avignon. Paris.
    1921.
—— La fiscalité pontificale en France au XIVe siècle, période d'Avignon et du Grand
    Schisme d'Occident. Paris. 1905.
Scheffler, W. Karl IV und Innocenz VI. Berlin. 1912.

Schelenz, E. Studien zur Gesch. d. Kardinalats im 13 u. 14 Jahrht. Marburg. 1913.
Vidal, J. M. Bullaire de l'inquisition française au xiv⁰ siècle. Paris. 1913.
Wenck, C. Clemens V und Heinrich VII. Halle. 1882.

PART II. THE GREAT SCHISM.

I. SPECIAL BIBLIOGRAPHIES.

Chevalier, C. U. J. Répertoire des sources. Topo-bibliographie. Coll. 2895–6. *See Gen. Bibl.* i.
Salembier, L. Le Grand Schisme d'Occident. 5th edn. Paris. 1922.
Valois, N. La France et le Grand Schisme d'Occident. 4 vols. Paris. 1896–1902. [Especially introduction to Vols. i and iii.]

II. ORIGINAL AUTHORITIES.

A. DOCUMENTARY SOURCES.

[A full list is given in Valois, N. *op. cit.* Only the more important are mentioned below.]

Baluzius, Stephanus. Vitae paparum Avenionensium. *See Gen. Bibl.* iv.
Bulaeus, C. E. Historia Universitatis Parisiensis. 6 vols. Paris. 1665–73.
Denifle, H. and Chatelain, É. Chartularium Universitatis Parisiensis. Vols. iii, iv. Paris. 1894, 97.
Ehrle, F. Aus den Acten des Afterconcils von Perpignan 1408. *In* Archiv für Lit.- und Kirchengeschichte des Mittelalters. v and vii. 1889, 91.
—— Neue Materialien zur Geschichte Peters von Luna. *Ibid.* vi, vii. 1890–1.
Erler, G. Der Liber cancellariae apostolicae vom Jahre 1380 und der Stilus palatii abbreviatus Dietrichs von Nieheim. Leipsic. 1888.
Finke, H. Acta concilii Constanciensis. 4 vols. Münster-i.-W. 1896–1928.
Gayet, L. Le Grand Schisme d'Occident. 2 vols. Rome. 1889.
Göller, E. Repertorium Germanicum. Clemens VII von Avignon. Berlin. 1916.
Hanquet, K. and Berlière, U. Documents relatifs au Grand Schisme. 2 vols. (Analecta Vaticano-Belgica. viii, xii. *See Gen. Bibl.* iv *under* Papal Documents.) 1924 ff., in progress.
Krofta, C. Acta Urbani VI et Bonifatii IX. (Monumenta Vaticana res gestas Bohemicas illustrantia. v. *See Gen. Bibl.* iv *under* Papal Documents.) 1903, 5.
Lesquen, G. de, and Mollat, G. Mesures fiscales exercées en Bretagne par les Papes d'Avignon à l'époque du Grand Schisme d'Occident. Paris. 1903.
Mansi, J. D. Sacrorum conciliorum collectio. Vols. xxvi, xxvii. *See Gen. Bibl.* iv.
Martène, E. and Durand, U. Thesaurus novus anecdotorum. *See Gen. Bibl.* iv.
Raynaldus, O. Annales ecclesiastici. Vols. vii, viii. *See Gen. Bibl.* v *under* Baronius. [This contains documents of all kinds, especially treaties and business of the cardinals.]

B. CHRONICLES.

Ailly, Peter d'. Epistola Leviathan ad pseudoprelatos Ecclesie pro scismate confirmando. Ed. Tschackert, P. *in* Peter von Ailli. Gotha. 1877.
Alpartils, Martin de. Chronica actitatorum temporibus Benedicti XIII. Ed. Ehrle, F. Paderborn. 1906.
Bliemetzrieder, P. Literarische Polemik zu Beginn des grossen abendländischen Schismas. Vienna. 1909. [Contains treatises by cardinals Peter Flandrin and Peter Ameilh, and the famous Epistola Concordiae of Conrad of Gelnhausen.]
—— Traktat des Minoriten provinzials von England Fr. Nikolaus de Fakenham (1395) über das grosse abendländische Schisma. *In* Archivum Franciscanum historicum. i, ii. Quaracchi. 1908–9.
Chronique du religieux de Saint-Denys. Ed. Bellaguet, L. (Coll. doc.) Paris. 1839.
Clemangis, Nicolas de. De corrupto ecclesiae statu. *In* Opera. Ed. Lydius, J. M. Leyden. 1613.
Cracovia, Matthaeus de. De squaloribus Romanae curiae. Ed. Walch, C. W. F. *in* Monumenta medii aevi. Vol. i, pt. i. Göttingen. 1757.

Ferrer, Vincent, Saint. Oeuvres. Ed. Fages, H. 2 vols. Paris. 1909.
—— De moderno ecclesiae schismate tractatus. Ed. Sorbelli, A. *in* Il trattato di san Vincenzo Ferrer intorno al Grande Scisma d' Occidente. 2nd edn. Bologna. 1906.
Hardt, H. van der. Magnum oecumenicum Constantiense concilium. 6 vols. Frankfort and Leipsic. 1697–1700. [Contains writings of Henry of Langenstein, Gerson, Peter d'Ailly, and others.]
Hutten, Ulrich de. De schismate extinguendo. *n.p.* 1520.
Le Fèvre, Jean. Journal. Ed. Moranvillé, H. 2 vols. Paris. 1887–92.
Niem, Theodoricus de. De schismate libri iv. Ed. Erler, G. Leipsic. 1890.
—— Historia de vita Johannis XXIII. Ed. Hardt, H. van der. *Op. cit.* Vol. ii.
—— Nemus unionis. Ed. Schard, S. Basle. 1560.
Reichert, B. M. Registrum litterarum Raymundi de Capua, 1386–1399. (Quellen und Forschungen zur Geschichte der Dominikaner-Ordens in Deutschland. vi.) Leipsic. 1911.

III. MODERN WORKS.

A. General.

Bruce, H. The age of Schism, 1304–1503. London. 1907.
Gayet, L. Le Grand Schisme d'Occident. *See above*, pt. ii, sect. ii a.
Pastor, L. von. Geschichte der Päpste. *See above*, pt. i, sect. iii a.
Salembier, L. Le Grand Schisme d'Occident. *See above*, pt. ii, sect. i.
Valois, N. La France et le Grand Schisme d'Occident. *Ibid.* [This supersedes all the preceding works.]

B. Special.

[Only the most important are mentioned here.]

Bliemetzrieder, F. Das Generalkonzil im grossen abendländischen Schisma. Paderborn. 1904.
Degert, A. La fin du Schisme d'Occident en Gascogne. *In* Mélanges Couture. Toulouse. 1900.
Doizé, J. Le dernier pape d'Avignon. *In* Études. Revue fondée par des Pères de la Compagnie de Jésus. Feb. 5, Mar. 20, May 15. Paris. 1903.
Droste, M. von. Die kirchenpolitische Tätigkeit des heiliges Vincente Ferrer. Freiburg-i.-B. 1904.
Eubel, K. Die avignonesische Obedienz der Mendikanten-Orden sowie der Orden der Mercedarier und Trinitarier zur Zeit des grossen Schismas. Paderborn. 1900.
Hirsch, K. Die Ausbildung der konziliaren Theorie im 14 Jahrht. Vienna. 1903.
Holtermann, P. Die kirchenpolitische Stellung der Stadt Freiburg im Breisgau während des grossen Papst-Schismas. Freiburg-i.-B. 1925.
Jansen, M. Papst Bonifaz IX und seine Beziehungen zur deutschen Kirche. Freiburg-i.-B. 1903.
Kehrmann, C. Frankreichs innere Kirchenpolitik von der Wahl Clemens VII und dem Beginn des grossen Schismas bis zum Pisaner Konzil. Leipsic. 1890.
Kitts, E. J. In the days of the Councils: a sketch of the life and time of Baldassare Cossa, afterwards pope John XXIII. London. 1908.
Kneer, A. Die Entstehung der konziliaren Theorie. Rome. 1893.
Kummer, F. Die Bischofswahlen in Deutschland zur Zeit des grossen Schismas. Jena. 1892.
Miebach, A. Die Politik Wenzels und der rheinischen Kurfürsten in der Frage des Schismas von der Thronbesteigung des Königs bis zum Jahre 1380. Münster. 1912.
O'Callaghan, R. Terminación del Cisma de Occidente y concilio provincial de Tortosa. Tortosa. 1911.
Reinke, G. Frankreich und Papst Johann XXIII. Munich. 1900.
Scheuffgen, F. J. Beiträge zu der Geschichte des grossen Schismas. Freiburg-i.-B. 1889.
Stinco, E. Politica ecclesiastica di Martino I in Sicilia (1392–1409). Palermo. 1921.
Zanutto, L. Il pontefice Bonifazio IX. Memorie friulesi sullo Scisma d' Occidente. Udine. 1904.

CHAPTER XI.

FRANCE: THE LAST CAPETIANS.

I. SPECIAL BIBLIOGRAPHIES.

Bibliographies or bibliographical notes will be found in Lavisse, E., Histoire de France, vol. III, pt. 2 and in Lavisse, E. and Rambaud, A., Histoire générale, vol. III (*see Gen. Bibl.* v). Also in the works of Boutaric, Langlois, Lehugeur, and Wenck, mentioned below (III A). For Flanders *see* Pirenne, H., Bibliographie de l'histoire de Belgique. *See Gen. Bibl.* I.

II. ORIGINAL AUTHORITIES.

A. CHRONICLES.

i. The most convenient collection of narratives by French authors is in Bouquet (*see Gen. Bibl.* IV) as follows:

Vol. xx, pp. 466–724. Especially the Gesta Philippi III by Guillaume de Nangis, pp. 466–559: the relevant portion of the same author's Chronicon to 1300, pp. 563–82; and its continuation, pp. 583–646.

Vol. xxi, pp. 1–219, 630–734, 802–14. Especially the continuation of the chronicle of Géraud de Frachet, pp. 5–70; a series of short anonymous chronicles, pp. 80–158; the chronicle of Yves, monk of Saint Denis, here wrongly attributed to Guillaume the Scot, who copied one of the manuscripts, pp. 201–11; the Memoriale Historiarum of Jean of Saint Victor, pp. 630–76; and its continuation to 1329, pp. 676–89.

Vol. xxii, pp. 6–11, 14–20, 84–166, 171–300, 349–429. Especially the rhymed chronicle attributed to Geoffroi of Paris, pp. 87–166; Guillaume Guiard's La branche des roiaus lignages, pp. 171–300, specially interesting for the Flemish wars; and a Flemish chronicle, probably of the fifteenth century, but embodying earlier matter, pp. 349–429.

Vol. xxiii, pp. 85–106, 192–212, 341–52. Especially Jean de Vignay's French translation of the lost Latin chronicle of Primat, monk of Saint Denis, pp. 85–106.

Molinier, A. Les sources de l'histoire de France, vol. III (*see Gen. Bibl.* I) should be consulted for criticism of these, and for more modern editions; *e.g.* the continuation of Géraud de Frachet's chronicle from 1268–1285 was printed by Lemoine, J. at the end of his Chronique de Richard Lescot. (SHF.) Paris. 1896.

ii. Other chronicles.

Anelier, Guillem. Histoire de la guerre de Navarre [1274–6]. Ed. Michel, F. (Coll. doc.) Paris. 1856.

Duples, Agier. Chronique de Saint Martial de Limoges. (SHF.) Paris. 1874.

Muisis, Gilles li. Chronique et Annales. Ed. Lemaître, H. (SHF.) Paris. 1906.
[By Gilles, monk and afterwards abbot of St Martin at Tournay, 1272–1352. Well informed. This edition supersedes that of Smet, J. J. de *in* Corpus chronicorum Flandriae. Vol. II. Brussels. 1841.]

B. DOCUMENTS.

Brevis nota eorum quae in secundo concilio Lugdunensi acta sunt. *In* Mansi. xxxiv, pp. 61–8. Paris. 1759 ff.

Champollion-Figeac, J. J. Lettres de rois, reines, et autres personnages des cours de France et d'Angleterre. 2 vols. (Coll. doc.) Paris. 1839, 47.

Finke, H. Acta Aragonensia. Quellen aus der diplomatischen Korrespondenz Jaymes II (1291–1327). Vols. I–III. Berlin. 1908, 22.

Funck-Brentano, F. Documents pour servir à l'histoire des relations de la France avec l'Angleterre et l'Allemagne sous Philippe le Bel. RH. XXXIX. 1889.

Kern, F. Acta Imperii, Angliae, et Franciae (1267–1313). Tübingen. 1911.

Langlois, C. V. Textes relatifs à l'histoire du Parlement. (Coll. textes.) Paris. 1888.

Laurière, E. J. de. Ordonnances des Rois de France de la troisième race. Vol. I. Paris. 1723.

Lizerand, G. Le dossier de l'affaire des Templiers. (Class. hist.) Paris. 1923.

Picot, G. Documents relatifs aux États Généraux et assemblées réunis sous Philippe le Bel. (Coll. doc.) Paris. 1901.

III. MODERN WORKS.

A. GENERAL.

Boutaric, E. La France sous Philippe le Bel. Paris. 1861.

Langlois, C. V. Le règne de Philippe III le Hardi. Paris. 1877.

—— *In* Lavisse, E. Histoire de France. Vol. III, pt. 2, pp. 103–352. *See Gen. Bibl.* v.

Lehugeur, P. Histoire de Philippe le Long. Paris. 1897.

Wenck, C. Philipp der Schöne von Frankreich, seine Persönlichkeit und das Urteil der Zeitgenossen. Marburg. 1905.

B. STUDIES ON SPECIAL SUBJECTS

(i) *Ecclesiastical.*

Finke, H. Papsttum und Untergang des Templerordens. Münster. 1907.
[A popular account, based on printed material only, is given by Martin, E. J. The Trial of the Templars. London. 1928.]

Lizerand, G. Clément V et Philippe IV le Bel. Paris. 1910.

Mollat, G. Les Papes d'Avignon (1305–78). 6th rev. edn. Paris. 1930.

(ii) *Constitutional and Administrative.*

Borrelli de Serres, L. L. Recherches sur divers services publics du XIIIᵉ au XVIIᵉ siècle. 3 vols. Paris. 1895–1909.

Langlois, C. V. La Chancellerie royale depuis l'avènement de Saint Louis jusqu'à celui de Philippe de Valois. Paris. 1895.

Perrichet, L. La grande Chancellerie de France des origines à 1328. Paris. 1912.

Valois, N. Le Conseil du roi au XIVᵉ, XVᵉ, et XVIᵉ siècles. Paris. 1888.

Viollet, P. Droit public. Histoire des institutions politiques et administratives de la France. Vols. II, III. *See Gen. Bibl.* v.

(iii) *Miscellaneous.*

Artonne, A. Le mouvement de 1314 et les chartes provinciales de 1315. Paris. 1912.

Rothwell, H. Edward I's case against Philip the Fair over Gascony in 1298. EHR. XLII (1927). 572–82.

CHAPTER XII.

FRANCE: THE HUNDRED YEARS' WAR (TO 1380).

I. BIBLIOGRAPHIES.

Chevalier, C. U. J. Répertoire des sources historiques du moyen âge. *See Gen. Bibl.* I.

Coville, A. Les premiers Valois et la guerre de Cent Ans. *In* Lavisse, E. Histoire de France. Vol. IV, pt. 1. *See Gen. Bibl.* v.

Molinier, A. Les sources de l'histoire de France. Vol. IV. *See Gen. Bibl.* I.

II. CHRONICLES.

Avesbury, Robert of. De Gestis mirabilibus regis Edwardi III (1303–1396). Ed. Thompson, E. M. (Rolls.) 1889.

Ayala, P. Lopez de. Crónica del Rey Don Pedro...(1350–1396), con las enmiendas de G. Zurita y las correcciones...por E. de Llaguno Amirola. (Colección de las crónicas y memorias de los reyes de Castilla. I.) Madrid. 1779.

Baker, Geoffrey le. Chronicon Galfridi le B. de Swynebroke (1303–1356). Ed. Thompson, E. M. Oxford. 1889.

Baluzius, S. Vitae paparum Avenionensium. Ed. Mollat, G. *See Gen. Bibl.* IV.

Bel, Jean le. Chronique (1326–61). Ed. Viard, J. and Déprez, E. 2 vols. (SHF.) Paris. 1904–5.

Chandos Herald. Life of the Black Prince by the herald of Sir John Chandos. Ed. (with prose transl.) Pope, M. K. and Lodge, E. C. Oxford. 1910.

Chronicle of London (1089–1483). Ed. Nicolas, N. H. London. 1827.

Chronicon Angliae, 1328–88, auctore monacho quodam Sancti Albani. Ed. Thompson, E. M. (Rolls.) 1874.

Chronique Normande du XIVe siècle (1294–1376). Ed. Molinier, E. (SHF.) Paris. 1882.

Chronique Parisienne anonyme (1206–1339). Ed. Hellot, A. *in* Mém. de la Soc. de l'Hist. de Paris. XI. Paris. 1884.

Chronique des quatre premiers Valois (1327–93). Ed. Luce, S. (SHF.) Paris. 1862.

Chronographia regum Francorum (1270–1405). Ed. Moranvillé, H. 3 vols. (SHF.) Paris. 1891–7.

Cochon, Pierre. Chronique Normande (1198–1430). Ed. Beaurepaire, C. de. (Soc. de l'Hist. de Normandie.) Rouen. 1870.

Cuvelier, Jean. La vie de Bertrand Du Guesclin. Ed. Charrière, E. 2 vols. (Coll. doc.) Paris. 1839.

[Dezcoll, Bernat.] Crónica del Rey de Aragon, D. Pedro IV. Spanish transl. ed. Bofarull, A. de. Barcelona. 1850.

Eulogium historiarum sive temporis, chron. ab orbe condito usque ad A.D. 1366 a monacho quodam Malmesburiensi exaratum. [With a continuation to 1413.] Ed. Haydon, F. S. Vol. III. (Rolls.) 1863.

Fordun, John of. Chronica gentis Scotorum [to 1383]. Ed. Skene, W. F., with Engl. transl. (Historians of Scotland. Vols. I and IV.) Edinburgh. 1871–2.

Fragment de Chronique (1346). Ed. Moisant, J. *in* Le Prince Noir en Aquitaine. Paris. 1894. p. 157.

Froissart, Jean. Chroniques (1307–1400). Ed. Kervyn de Lettenhove. 25 vols. Brussels. 1867–79. *Also* ed. Luce, S. and Raynaud, G. 11 vols. (SHF.) Paris. 1869–99. Engl. transl. Bourchier, J., Lord Berners. 6 vols. (Tudor Transl. Library.) London. 1901–3.

Gesta Edwardi III. Gesta Edwardi de Carnarvon, auctore canonico Bridlingtoniensi cum continuatione ad A.D. 1377. Ed. Stubbs, W. *in* Chronicles of the reigns of Edward I and Edward II. Vol. II. (Rolls.) 1883.

Grandes chroniques de France (...–1380). Ed. Paris, P. Vols. v, VI. Paris. 1836–8.

Grandes chroniques de France. Chronique des règnes de Jean et Charles V (1350–80). Ed. Delachenal, R. Vols. I–III. (SHF.) Paris. 1910–20.

Gray, Thomas. Scalacronica. A Chronicle of England and Scotland from A.D. 1066 to A.D. 1362. Ed. Stevenson, J. (Maitland Club.) Edinburgh. 1836.

Hemingburgh, Walter of. Chronicon...de gestis regum Angliae (1048–1346). Ed. Hamilton, H. C. Vol. ii. (English Hist. Soc.) London. 1849.

Istore et chroniques de Flandre (...–1383). Ed. Kervyn de Lettenhove. 2 vols. (Collection des chroniques belges inédites.) Brussels. 1879–80.

Jan de Klerk (Jan Boendaele). Van den Derden Edewaert, coninc van Engelant. Rymkronyk geschreven 1347. Ed. Willems, J. F. (Belgisch Museum, iv.) Ghent. 1840. French transl. Delepierre, O. Édouard III, roi d'Angleterre en Belgique. Ghent. 1841.

Knighton, Henry. Chronicon (959–1395). Ed. Lumby, J. R. 2 vols. (Rolls.) 1889, 95.

Lescot, Richard. Chronique (1328–1344–1364). Ed. Lemoine, J. (SHF.) Paris. 1896.

Muisis, Gilles li. Chronique et Annales (1272–1352). Ed. Lemaître, H. (SHF.) Paris. 1906.

Murimuth, Adam. Continuatio Chronicarum (1303–1347). Ed. Thompson, E. M. (Rolls.) 1889.

Orville, Jean Cabaret d'. La chronique du bon duc Loys de Bourbon. Ed. Chazaud, A. M. (SHF.) Paris. 1876.

Pisan, Christine de. Le livre des faits et bonnes meurs du sage roy Charles le Quint. Ed. Lebeuf, J. *in* Dissertations sur l'histoire...de Paris. Vol. iii. Paris. 1743.

Récits d'un bourgeois de Valenciennes (1254–1366). Ed. Kervyn de Lettenhove. Louvain. 1877.

Saint-André, Guillaume de. Le livre du bon Jehan, duc de Bretaigne. Ed. Charrière, E. Vol. ii. (Coll. doc.) Paris. 1839.

Venette, Jean de. Continuationis Chronici Guillelmi de Nangiaco pars tertia (1340–68). Ed. Géraud, H. Vol. ii. (SHF.) Paris. 1843.

Villani, Giovanni and Matteo. Historie Fiorentine (...–1364). Ed. Muratori. RR.II.SS. 1st edn. Vols. xiii, xiv.

III. DOCUMENTS.

Aumale, duc d'. Notes et Documents relatifs à Jean roi de France et à sa captivité en Angleterre. (Philobiblion Society.) London. 1856.

Bardonnet, A. Procès-verbal de délivrance à Chandos, commissaire du roi d'Angleterre, des places abandonnées par le traité de Brétigny. *In* Mém. de la Soc. de Statistique des Deux Sèvres. Niort. 1867.

Boudet, M. Registres consulaires de Saint-Flour (1376–1405). Vol. i. Paris. 1898.

Brutails, J. Documents des archives de la Chambre des Comptes de Navarre. (BHE. 84.) Paris. 1890.

Champollion-Figeac, J. J. Lettres de rois, reines, et autres personnages des cours de France et d'Angleterre depuis Louis VII jusqu'à Henri IV. 2 vols. (Coll. doc.) Paris. 1839, 47.

Cosneau, E. Les grands traités de la guerre de Cent Ans. (Coll. textes.) Paris. 1889.

Delachenal, R. Journal des États-Généraux réunis à Paris au mois d'Octobre 1356. NRDF. 1900.

Delaville Le Roulx, J. Registres des comptes municipaux de Tours (1358–1389). 2 vols. Tours. 1878.

Delisle, L. Actes normands de la Chambre des Comptes sous Philippe de Valois. (Soc. de l'Hist. de Normandie.) Rouen. 1881.

—— Mandements et Actes divers de Charles V. (Coll. doc.) Paris. 1874.

Delpit, J. Collection générale des documents français qui se trouvent en Angleterre. Paris. 1847.

Demay, G. Inventaire des sceaux de la Collection Clairambault à la Bibliothèque Nationale. 2 vols. (Coll. doc.) Paris. 1885–6.

Deschamps, E. Poésies complètes. Ed. Queux de Saint Hilaire, A. le, and Raynaud, G. 11 vols. (Société des anciens textes.) Paris. 1878–1901.

Douët d'Arcq, L. Comptes de l'argenterie des rois de France au xive siècle. (SHF.) Paris. 1851.

—— Nouveaux comptes de l'argenterie des rois de France. (SHF.) Paris. 1874.

Duckett, G. F. Original documents relating to the hostages of John, King of France, and the treaty of Bretigny in 1360. London. 1890.

Forestié, E. Le livre de comptes des frères Bonis, marchands montalbanais. 3 vols. (Archives hist. de la Gascogne, xx, xxiii, xxvi.) Paris and Auch. 1890–4.

Gilliodts van Severen, L. Archives de Bruges. Inventaire des Chartes. 7 vols. Bruges. 1871–8.

Guérin, P. Documents concernant le Poitou, contenus dans les registres de la chancellerie. (Archives du Poitou, xi, xii, xiii, xvii, xix, xxi.) Poitiers.

Guesnon, A. Documents inédits sur l'invasion anglaise et les États au temps de Philippe VI et Jean le Bon. *In* Bulletin du Comité des travaux hist., Section d'hist. et de philol. Paris. 1897.

Hauréau, J. B. Relation de la mort de Charles V. *In* Notices et extraits de manuscrits de la Bibliothèque Nationale. xxxi. 2 vols. Paris. 1892.

Jousselin, M. Comment la France se préparait à la guerre de Cent Ans. BEC. lxxiii. 1912.

Labarte, J. Inventaire du mobilier de Charles V. (Coll. doc.) Paris. 1879.

Lettres des papes d'Avignon se rapportant à la France. *See Gen. Bibl.* iv *under* Papal Documents.

Luce, S. Pièces inédites relatives à Étienne Marcel. BEC. xxi. 1860.

Mirot, L. and Déprez, E. Les ambassades anglaises pendant la guerre de Cent Ans. Catalogue chronologique (1327–1450). BEC. lix, lxi. 1898, 1900.

Moranvillé, H. Rapports à Philippe VI sur l'état de ses finances. BEC. xlviii. 1887.

Morice, P. H. Mémoires pour servir de preuves à l'histoire civile et ecclésiastique de Bretagne. Vol. i. Paris. 1742.

Ordonnances des Rois de France de la troisième race. Vols. i–vi. Paris. 1723 ff.

Pauw, N. de, and Vuylsteke, J. Rekeningen des Stad Gent (1336–49). Ghent. 1874–85.

—— Cartulaire historique et généalogique des Artevelde. Brussels. 1920.

Perroy, É. Charles V et le traité de Brétigny. MA. 2nd ser. xxix. 1928. [18 documents.]

Petit, E. Itinéraires de Philippe le Hardi et de Jean Sans Peur, ducs de Bourgogne. (Coll. doc.) Paris. 1888.

Rymer, T. Foedera. *See Gen. Bibl.* iv.

Secousse, D. F. Mémoires pour servir à l'histoire de Charles...le Mauvais. Vol. i. Paris. 1758.

Thalamus Parvus. Le Petit Thalamus de Montpellier. (Société archéol. de Montpellier.) Montpellier. 1836.

Varin, P. Archives administratives de la ville de Reims. Vol. ii. (Coll. doc.) Paris. 1849.

Viard, J. Les journaux du Trésor de Philippe VI de Valois (1338–39). (Coll. doc.) Paris. 1899.

—— Documents parisiens du règne de Philippe VI. 2 vols. (SHF.) Paris. 1899–1900.

—— Lettres d'état enregistrées au Parlement sous le règne de Philippe VI. *In* Ann. Bulletin de la SHF. Paris. 1897–8.

IV. MODERN WORKS.

Ashley, W. J. James and Philip van Artevelde. London. 1883.

Barnes, J. History of Edward III. Cambridge. 1688.

Benoist, C. La politique du roi Charles V. Paris. 1886.

Boudet, M. Thomas de la Marche, bâtard de France, et ses aventures. Paris. 1900.

Breuils, J. Jean I d'Armagnac. RQH. lix. 1896.

Bridrey, E. Nicole Oresme, étude d'histoire des doctrines et des faits économiques. Paris. 1906.

Chérest, A. L'archiprêtre, épisodes de la guerre de Cent Ans. Paris. 1879.

Clément, S. G. La rupture du traité de Brétigny et ses conséquences au Limousin. Paris. 1898.

Cordey, J. Les comtes de Savoie et les rois de France pendant la guerre de Cent Ans, 1329–91. Paris. 1911.

Coville, A. Les États de Normandie, leurs origines et leur développement au XIVᵉ siècle. Paris. 1894.
—— Les premiers Valois et la guerre de Cent Ans (1328–1422). *In* Lavisse, E. Histoire de France. Vol. IV, pt. 1. 1902. *See Gen. Bibl.* v.
Czeppan, R. Die Schlacht bei Crécy. Berlin. 1906.
Daumet, G. Étude sur l'alliance de la France et de la Castille au XIVᵉ et au XVᵉ siècle. (BHE. 118.) Paris. 1898.
Delachenal, R. Premières négociations de Charles le Mauvais avec les Anglais. BEC. LXI. 1900.
—— Histoire de Charles V, 1338–64. 5 vols. Paris. 1909–31.
Delaville Le Roulx, J. La France en Orient au XIVᵉ siècle. EcfrAR. Paris. 1885–6.
Delisle, L. Histoire de Saint-Sauveur le Vicomte. Valognes. 1867.
—— Recherches sur la librairie de Charles V. 2 vols. Paris. 1907.
Denifle, H. La désolation des églises, monastères, et hôpitaux en France pendant la guerre de Cent Ans. Vol. I (1337–84). Paris. 1899.
Denys d'Aussy. Campagnes de Du Guesclin en Poitou et en Saintonge. *In* Revue de Saintonge. X. Saintes. 1890.
Déprez, E. La conférence d'Avignon (1344). L'arbitrage pontifical entre la France et l'Angleterre. (Essays in Medieval History presented to T. F. Tout, no. 23.) Manchester. 1925.
—— Les préliminaires de la guerre de Cent Ans. La Papauté, la France, et l'Angleterre (1328–1422). EcfrAR. Paris. 1902.
Dessales, L. La rançon du roi Jean. Paris. 1850.
Dufourmantelle, C. La marine militaire en France au commencement de la guerre de Cent Ans. Paris. 1878.
Finot, J. Recherches sur les incursions des Anglais et des Compagnies en Bourgogne. Paris. 1874.
Flammermont, J. La Jacquerie en Beauvaisis. RH. IX. 1879.
Fournier, P. La Royaume d'Arles et de Vienne, 1138–1378. Paris. 1891.
Garcia, J. C. Castilla y Leon durante los reinados de D. Pedro I, Enrique II, Juan I, y Enrique III. Vol. I. (Hist. gen. de España.) Madrid. 1891.
Gasquet, F. A. The Great Pestilence. London. 1893.
Guibal, J. Histoire du sentiment national en France pendant la guerre de Cent Ans. Paris. 1875.
Guiffrey, J. Histoire de la réunion du Dauphiné à la France. Paris. 1868.
Guigue, G. Les Tard-Venus en Lyonnais. Lyon. 1886.
Jorga, N. Philippe de Mézières, 1327–1405. (BHE. 110.) Paris, 1896.
La Borderie, A. de. Études historiques bretonnes. 2ᵉᵐᵉ série. Paris. 1888.
—— Le règne de Jean IV, duc de Bretagne, 1364–99. Rennes. 1893.
—— Histoire de Bretagne. Vol. III. Rennes. 1899.
Labroue, E. Le Livre de Vie. Les seigneurs et les capitaines du Périgord blanc au XIVᵉ siècle. Bordeaux. 1891.
Landry, A. Essai économique sur les mutations des monnaies dans l'ancienne France de Philippe le Bel à Charles VII. (BHE. 185.) Paris. 1910.
La Roncière, C. de. Histoire de la marine française. Vols. I, II. Paris. 1899, 1900.
Legrand, H. Paris en 1380. (Histoire générale de Paris.) Paris. 1868.
Leroux, A. Recherches critiques sur les relations politiques de la France avec l'Allemagne de 1292 à 1378. (BHE. 50.) Paris. 1882.
—— Le Sac de la ville de Limoges. Limoges. 1908.
Longman, W. Life and times of Edward III. 2 vols. London. 1869.
Lucas, H. S. The Low Countries and the Hundred Years' War, 1326–47. Ann Arbor. 1929.
Luce, S. La France pendant la guerre de Cent Ans. 2 vols. Paris. 1890, 93.
—— Du Guesclin en Normandie. Le siège et la prise de Valognes. RQH. XLIX. 1893.
—— La jeunesse de Bertrand Du Guesclin. Paris. 1876.
—— Histoire de la Jacquerie. 2nd edn. Paris. 1894.
Mackinnon, J. History of Edward III, 1327–77. London. 1900.
Ménard, L. Histoire de la ville de Nîmes. 7 vols. Nîmes. 1750–8.
Mérimée, P. Histoire de Don Pedro I, roi de Castille. Paris. 1865.

Mirot, L. Une grande famille parlementaire aux xive et xve siècles. Les d'Orgemont. Paris. 1913.

Moisant, J. Le Prince Noir en Aquitaine, 1335-70. Paris. 1894.

Molinier, E. Étude sur la vie d'Arnoul d'Andrehem, maréchal de France, 1330-70. *In* Mém. AcadIBL. 2nd ser. Vol. vi. Paris. 1883.

Mollat, G. Les Papes d'Avignon, 1305-78. 6th edn. Paris. 1930.

Moranvillé, H. Étude sur la vie de Jean Le Mercier, 13..-1397. *In* Mém. AcadIBL. 2nd ser. Vol. vi. Paris. 1888.

Nicolas, N. H. History of the Royal Navy [to 1422]. 2 vols. London. 1847.

Oman, C. W. C. History of the art of war in the Middle Ages. *See Gen. Bibl.* v.

Périer. Hugues Aubriot, prévôt de Paris. *In* Mém. Société Bourguignonne d'hist. et géog. ,xv. Dijon. 1908.

Perrens, E. Étienne Marcel. 2nd edn. (Histoire générale de Paris.) Paris. 1875.

Petit, E. Les séjours de Charles V, 1364-80. *In* Bulletin du Comité des travaux hist., Section d'hist. et de philol. Paris. 1887.

—— Ducs de Bourgogne de la maison de Valois. Philippe le Hardi, 1363-80. Paris. 1909.

Petit-Dutaillis, C. and Collier, P. La diplomatie française et le traité de Brétigny. MA. 1897.

Picot, G. Histoire des États Généraux. Vol. i. 2nd edn. Paris. 1888.

Pirenne, H. Le soulèvement de la Flandre maritime de 1323-28. Brussels. 1900.

—— Histoire de Belgique. Vol. ii. *See Gen. Bibl.* v.

Plancher, U. Histoire générale et particulière de Bourgogne. 4 vols. Dijon. 1739-81.

Poëte, M. Paris de sa naissance à nos jours. Vol. i. Paris. 1924.

Prentout, H. Les États provinciaux de Normandie. 3 vols. (Mém. de l'Acad. Nat.... de Caen. n.s. i-iii.) Caen. 1925-7. Also publ. separately.

Prou, M. Étude sur les relations politiques du pape Urbain V avec les rois de France (1362-70). (BHE. 76.) Paris. 1888.

Puymaigre, de. Jean de Bohème en France. RQH. lii. 1892.

Ramsay, Sir J. H. The Genesis of Lancaster, or the reigns of Edward II, Edward III, and Richard II. 2 vols. Oxford. 1913.

Rouquette, J. Le Rouergue sous les Anglais. Millau. 1887.

Secousse, D. F. Mémoires pour servir à l'histoire de Charles le Mauvais. Vol. ii. Paris. 1755.

Sitges, J. B. Las mujeres del Rey D. Pedro I de Castilla. Madrid. 1910.

Smith, S. Armitage. John of Gaunt. London. 1904.

Smyttere, P. J. É. de. La bataille du Val-de-Cassel en 1328. Lille. 1883.

Tauzin. Les débuts de la guerre de Cent Ans en Gascogne. *In* Revue de Gascogne. n.s. vi. Agen. 1905.

Terrier de Loray. Jean de Vienne. Paris. 1878.

Tout, T. F. History of England, 1216-1377. New edn. (Polit. Hist. of England. Ed. Hunt, W. and Poole, R. L. Vol. iii.) London. 1920.

Unwin, S. Finance and trade under Edward III. Manchester. 1918.

Valois, N. Le conseil du roi aux xive, xve, et xvie siècles. Paris. 1888.

Varenbergh, E. Histoire des relations diplomatiques entre le comté de Flandre et l'Angleterre au moyen âge. Brussels. 1874.

Vernier. Philippe le Hardi, duc de Bourgogne, et son mariage avec Marguerite de Flandre. *In* Bulletin de la commission hist. du Nord. xxii.

Viard, J. La France sous Philippe de Valois. RQH. lix. 1896.

—— Un chapitre d'histoire administrative. Les ressources extraordinaires de la royauté sous Philippe VI. RQH. xliv. 1888.

—— Itinéraire de Philippe de Valois. BEC. lxxiv. 1913.

Vic, C. de, and Vaissete, J. J. Histoire générale de Languedoc. *See Gen. Bibl.* iv.

Wrottesley, G. Crecy and Calais. London. 1898.

CHAPTER XIII.

FRANCE: ARMAGNACS AND BURGUNDIANS (1380-1422).

I. BIBLIOGRAPHIES.

See Bibliography to ch. xii.

II. CHRONICLES.

Baye, Nicolas de. Journal. Ed. Tuetey, A. 2 vols. (SHF.) Paris. 1885, 88.

Berry, Le Héraut (Gilles le Bouvier). Chronique du roi Charles VII (1402–1455). Ed. Godefroy, D. *in* Histoire du roi Charles VI. Paris. 1653.

Cagny, Perceval de. Chroniques. Ed. Moranvillé, H. (SHF.) Paris. 1902.

Capgrave, John. Liber de illustribus Henricis. Ed. Hingeston, F. C. (Rolls.) London. 1858. Engl. transl. Hingeston, F. C. London. 1858.

Chronicon Angliae, 1328–88, auctore monacho quodam Sancti Albani. Ed. Thompson, E. M. (Rolls.) 1874.

Chronicon Angliae de regnis Henrici IV, Henrici V, Henrici VI [1399–1455]. Ed. Giles, J. A. London. 1848.

Chronique des quatre premiers Valois (1327–1393). Ed. Luce, S. (SHF.) Paris. 1862.

Chronique rimée des troubles de Flandres à la fin du xiv⁰ siècle. Ed. Pirenne, E. (Soc. d'hist. et d'archéol. de Gand.) Ghent. 1902.

Chroniques des religieux de Dunes, Jean Brandon, Gilles de Roye, Adrien de But. Ed. Kervyn de Lettenhove *in* Chroniques relatives à l'hist. de la Belgique sous la domination des ducs de Bourgogne. Vol. i. (Collection des chroniques belges inédites.) Brussels. 1870.

Chronographia regum Francorum (1270–1405). Ed. Moranvillé, H. 3 vols. (SHF.) Paris. 1891–7.

Cochon, Pierre. Chronique Normande (1198–1430). Ed. Beaurepaire, C. de. (Soc. de l'Hist. de Normandie.) Rouen. 1870.

Cousinot, Guillaume. La geste des nobles françois. Fragments. Ed. Vallet de Viriville, A. Paris. 1859.

Créton, Jean. Histoire du roy d'Angleterre Richard, traictant particulièrement la rebellion de ses subiectz. Ed. with Engl. transl. Webb, J. *in* Archaeologia. xx. (Soc. of Antiq. of London.) London 1824.

Eulogium historiarum sive temporis, chron. ab orbe condito usque ad A.D. 1366 a monacho quodam Malmesburiensi exaratum. [With a continuation to 1413.] Ed. Haydon, F S. Vol. iii. (Rolls.) 1863.

Fauquembergue, Clément de. Journal, 1417–1435. Ed. Tuetey, A. Vol. i. (SHF.) Paris. 1903.

Fénin, Pierre de. Mémoires, 1407–1427. Ed. Dupont, F. (SHF.) Paris. 1837.

Froissart, Jean. *See* Bibliography to ch. xii.

Geste des ducs Philippe et Jehan de Bourgoigne (1393–1411). Ed. Kervyn de Lettenhove *in* Chroniques relatives à l'hist. de Belgique sous la domination des ducs de Bourgogne. Vol. ii. (Collection des chroniques belges inédites.) Brussels. 1873.

Henrici quinti Angliae regis gesta. Ed. Williams, B. (English Hist. Soc.) London. 1850.

Journal d'un bourgeois de Paris (1405–1449). Ed. Tuetey, A. (Soc. de l'hist. de Paris.) Paris. 1881.

Knighton, Henry. Chronicon (959–1395). Ed. Lumby, J. R. 2 vols. (Rolls.) 1889, 95.

Le Beau, Jean. Chronique de Richard II, 1377–1399. Ed. Buchon, J. A. (Collection des chroniques nationales françaises, xxv. Suppl. ii.) Paris. 1826.

Le Fevre de Saint-Remy, Jean. Chronique (1408–1435). Ed. Morand, F. 2 vols. (SHF.) Paris. 1876, 81.

Le Livre des faicts du Mareschal Boucicaut. Ed. Buchon, J. A. *in* Choix de chroniques...sur l'hist. de France. Vol. iii. Paris. 1836.

Le Livre des trahisons de France. Ed. Kervyn de Lettenhove *in* Chroniques relatives à l'hist. de la Belgique sous la domination des ducs de Bourgogne. Vol. ii. (Collection des chroniques belges inédites.) Brussels. 1873.

Memorials of Henry V. Ed. Cole, C. A. (Rolls.) 1858.

Meuillon, Guillaume de. Faits et Gestes. Ed. Maignien. Grenoble. 1897.

Monstrelet, Enguerrand de. Chroniques. Ed. Douët d'Arcq, L. 6 vols. (SHF.) Paris. 1857–62. Engl. transl. Johnes, T. 5 vols. Hafod. 1809.

Morosini, Antonio. Chronique. Ed. Lefèvre-Pontalis, G. Vols. i, ii. (SHF.) 1898–9.

Orville, Jean Cabaret d'. La Chronique du bon duc Loys de Bourbon. Ed. Chazaud, A. M. (SHF.) Paris. 1876.

Page, John. Poem on the siege of Rouen. Ed. Gairdner, J. *in* Historical Collections of a citizen of London in the fifteenth century. (Camden Society.) London. 1876.

Partie inédite des chroniques de Saint-Denis. Ed. Pichon, J. (Soc. des Bibliophiles français.) Paris. 1864.

Pisan, Christine de. Le Livre des faits et bonnes meurs du sage roy Charles le Quint. Ed. Lebeuf, J. *in* Dissertations sur l'histoire...de Paris. Vol. iii. Paris. 1743.

Religieux de Saint Denis. Chronique de Charles VI. Ed. Bellaguet, L. F. 6 vols. (Coll. doc.) Paris. 1839–52.

Rijmkronijk van Vlaenderen. Ed. Smet, J. J. de, *in* Corpus Chronicorum Flandriae. Vol. iv. (Collection des chroniques belges inédites.) Brussels. 1865.

Salmon, Pierre le Fruitier dit. Les demandes faites par le roy Charles VI. Ed. Crapelet, G. A. Paris. 1833.

Le Songe véritable. Ed. Moranvillé, H. *in* Mém. de la Soc. de l'Hist. de Paris. xvii. Paris. 1891.

Walsingham, Thomas. Historia Anglicana. Ed. Riley, H. T. 2 vols. (Rolls.) 1863, 64.

—— Ypodigma Neustriae. Ed. Riley, H. T. (Rolls.) 1876.

Waurin, Jehan de. Recueil des croniques et anchiennes istories de la Grant Bretaigne. Ed. Hardy, W. and Hardy, E. L. C. P. 5 vols. (Rolls.) 1864–91.

Zantfliet, Cornelius. Chronicon. Ed. Martène, E. and Durand, U. *in* Amplissima Collectio. Vol. v. Paris. 1729.

III. DOCUMENTS.

Besse, G. Recueil de diverses pièces servant à l'histoire de Charles VI. Paris. 1660.

Bourquelot, F. Correspondance entre le corps municipal de la ville de Paris et celui de la ville de Noyon en 1413. BEC. vii. 1845–6.

Champollion-Figeac, J. J. Lettres des rois, reines, et autres personnages des cours de France et d'Angleterre depuis Louis VII jusqu'à Henri IV. 2 vols. (Coll. doc.) Paris. 1839, 47.

Cosneau, E. Les grands traités de la guerre de Cent Ans. (Coll. textes.) Paris. 1889.

Coville, A. L'ordonnance Cabochienne (26–27 mai 1413). (Coll. textes.) Paris. 1891.

Delpit, J. Collection générale des documents français qui se trouvent en Angleterre. Paris. 1847.

Demay, G. Inventaire des sceaux de la Collection Clairambault à la Bibliothèque Nationale. 2 vols. (Coll. doc.) Paris. 1885–6.

Denifle, H. and Chatelain, E. Chartularium Universitatis Parisiensis. Vols. iii and iv. Paris. 1894, 97.

Documents pour servir à l'histoire de Lyon, tirés des archives de cette ville. Lyons. 1839.

Douët d'Arcq, L. Choix de pièces inédites relatives au règne de Charles VI. 2 vols. (SHF.) Paris. 1863–4.

—— Comptes de l'hôtel des rois de France au xiv et au xv siècles. (SHF.) Paris. 1865.

Duplès-Agier, H. Registre criminel du Châtelet (6 sept. 1389—18 mai 1392). 2 vols (Société des Bibliophiles français.) Paris. 1861, 64.

Dupont, E. Registre des recettes et dépenses de la ville de Boulogne-sur-Mer (1415–16). *In* Mém. de la Soc. acad. de l'arrondissement de Boulogne-sur-Mer. vii. Boulogne-sur-Mer. 1882.

Ellis, H. Original letters illustrative of English history. 11 vols. London. 1824–46.

Garnier, J. Correspondance de la mairie de Dijon. (Analecta Divionensia, i.) Dijon. 1868.

Gilliodts van Severen, L. Archives de Bruges. Inventaire des Chartes. 7 vols. Bruges. 1871–8.
—— Le Cotton Manuscrit Galba, B. I. (Collection des chroniques belges inédites.) Brussels. 1896.
Godefroy, D. Histoire du roy Charles VI. Paris. 1653.
Grave, F. M. Quelques pièces relatives à la vie de Louis, duc d'Orléans, et de Valentine Visconti. Paris. 1913.
Hingeston, F. C. Royal and historical letters during the reign of Henry IV. Vol. I. (Rolls.) 1860.
[La Barre, L. F. J. de.] Mémoires pour servir à l'histoire de France et de Bourgogne. 2 vols. Paris. 1729.
Laborde, L. E. S. J. de. Les ducs de Bourgogne. Études sur les lettres, les arts, et l'industrie pendant le xv⁰ siècle. Preuves. 3 vols. Paris. 1849–51.
Leroux de Lincy, A. J. V. and Tisserand, L. M. Paris et ses historiens. (Histoire générale de Paris.) Paris. 1868.
Marion, J. Rapport adressé au roi sur les doléances du clergé aux États-Généraux de 1413. BÉC. VI. 1844–5.
Mirot, L. and Déprez, E. Les ambassades anglaises pendant la guerre de Cent Ans. Catalogue chronologique (1327–1450). BÉC. LIX, LXI. 1898, 1900.
Moranvillé, H. Remontrances de l'université et de la ville de Paris à Charles VI sur le gouvernement du royaume. BÉC. LI. 1890.
Nicolas, N. H. Proceedings and ordinances of the Privy Council of England. Vols. I, II. (RC.) London. 1834, 5.
Ordonnances des Rois de France de la troisième race. Vols. VII–XII. Paris. 1741 ff.
Petit, E. Itinéraires de Philippe le Hardi et de Jean Sans Peur, ducs de Bourgogne. (Coll. doc.) Paris. 1888.
Prost, B. and H. Inventaires mobiliers et extraits de comptes des ducs de Bourgogne. 2 vols. Paris. 1902, 8.
Raymond, P. Enquête du prévôt de Paris sur l'assassinat de Louis, duc d'Orléans (1407). BÉC. XXVI. 1864–5.
Rôles des actes de Henry V, roi d'Angleterre, pour la Normandie (1415–22), publiés d'après les copies et extraits de Bréquigny. *In* Mém. de la Soc. des Antiquaires de Normandie. XIII. Caen. 1858.
Roman, J. Inventaires et documents relatifs aux joyaux et tapisseries des princes d'Orléans-Valois. (Recueil d'anciens inventaires, I.) Paris. 1894.
Rymer, T. Foedera. *See Gen. Bibl.* IV.
Tuetey, A. Testaments enregistrés au Parlement de Paris, sous Charles VI. (Coll. doc.) Paris. 1880.
Van den Broeck, H. Extraits analytiques des anciens registres des Consaux de Tournai de 1385 à 1422. 2 vols. Tournai. 1861, 63.
Vuylstoke, J. Die Rekeningen der Stad Gent. Tijdvak van Philips van Artevelde (1370–89). Ghent. 1891–3.

IV. MODERN WORKS.

Ashley, W. J. James and Philip van Artevelde. London. 1883.
Aubert, F. Le Parlement de Paris de Philippe le Bel à Charles VI. 2 vols. Paris. 1890–7.
Barante, A. G. B. P. de. Histoire des ducs de Bourgogne. Ed. Reiffenberg, F. de. 10 vols. Brussels. 1835–6.
Batiffol, L. Jean Jouvenel, prévôt des marchands de la ville de Paris, 1360–1431. Paris. 1894.
Beaucourt, G. D. F. de. Histoire de Charles VII. Vol. I. Le Dauphin, 1403–22. Paris. 1881.
Belleval, R. de. Azincourt. Paris. 1865.
Bess, B. Frankreichs Kirchenpolitik und der Prozess des Jean Petit. Marburg. 1891.
Boudet, M. La Jacquerie des Tuchins, 1363–84. Paris. 1895.
Bourquelot, F. Jean des Marés. *In* Rev. étrangère et française. 1838.
Brachet, A. Pathologie mentale des rois de France. Louis XI et ses ascendants. Paris. 1903.

Camus, J. La venue en France de Valentine Visconti. *In* Miscellanea di Storia Italiana. Ser. III. Vol. v. Turin. 1900.

Caro, J. Das Bündniss von Canterbury. Gotha. 1880.

Cartellieri, O. Geschichte der Herzöge von Burgund. Vol. I. Philipp der Kühne. Leipsic. 1910.

—— Beiträge zur Geschichte der Herzögen von Burgund. Heidelberg. 1912–13.

Champion, P. Vie de Charles d'Orléans, 1394–1465. Paris. 1911.

Chavanon, J. Renaud VI de Pons (vers 1348–1427). (Soc. des Archives hist. de l'Aunis et de la Saintonge.) La Rochelle. 1903.

Chéruel, P. A. Histoire de Rouen sous la domination anglaise au xvᵉ siècle. Rouen. 1840.

Circourt, de. Le duc d'Orléans, frère du roi Charles VI : ses débuts dans la politique, origine de sa rivalité avec les ducs de Bourgogne, ses entreprises en Italie, Savone, et Gênes. RQH. XLII, XLV, XLVI. 1887, 89.

Collas, E. Valentine de Milan, duchesse d'Orléans. Paris. 1911.

Cordey, J. Les comtes de Savoie et les rois de France pendant la guerre de Cent Ans, 1329–91. Paris. 1911.

Cosneau, E. Le Connétable de Richemont, Artur de Bretagne, 1393–1458. Paris. 1886.

Coville, A. Les États de Normandie, leurs origines et leur développement au xivᵉ siècle. Paris. 1894.

—— Les Cabochiens et l'ordonnance de 1413. Paris. 1888.

—— Les premiers Valois et la guerre de Cent Ans (1328–1422). *In* Lavisse, E. Histoire de France. Vol. iv, pt. 1. 1902. *See Gen. Bibl.* iv.

Daumet, E. Étude sur l'alliance de la France et de la Castille au xivᵉ et au xvᵉ siècles. (BHE. 118.) Paris. 1898.

Delaville Le Roulx, J. La France en Orient au xivᵉ siècle. EcfrAR. Paris, 1885–6.

Durrieu, P. Le royaume d'Adria. Épisode de la politique française en Italie sous le règne de Charles VI. RQH. XXVIII. 1880.

—— Les Gascons en Italie. Études historiques. Auch. 1885.

Finot, J. La paix d'Arras. *In* Annales de l'Est et du Nord. Nancy. 1906.

Frédéricq, P. Essai sur le rôle politique et social des ducs de Bourgogne dans les Pays-Bas. Ghent. 1875.

Guibal, G. Histoire du sentiment national en France pendant la guerre de Cent Ans. Paris. 1875.

Haller, J. Papsttum und Kirchenreform. Vol. I. Berlin. 1903.

Jarry, E. La vie politique de Louis de France, duc d'Orléans, 1372–1407. Paris. 1889.

—— La voie de fait et l'alliance franco-milanaise, 1386–95. BEC. LIII. 1892.

—— Les origines de la domination française à Gênes, 1392–1402. Paris. 1896.

—— Actes additionnels au contrat de mariage de Louis d'Orléans et de Valentine Visconti. BEC. LXII. 1901.

Jorga, N. Thomas III, marquis de Saluces. Saint-Denis. 1893.

—— Philippe de Mézières, 1327–1405. (BHE. 110.) Paris. 1896.

Kervyn de Lettenhove, J. M. B. C. Histoire de Flandre. Vols. III, IV. Brussels. 1847, 49.

La Borderie, A. de. Hist. de Bretagne. Vol. IV. (Cont. by Pocquet, B.) Rennes. 1906.

La Roncière, C. de. Histoire de la marine française. Vol. II. Paris. 1900.

Lefranc, A. Olivier de Clisson, connétable de France. Paris. 1898.

Leroux, A. Nouvelles recherches critiques sur les relations politiques de la France avec l'Allemagne de 1378 à 1461. Paris. 1892.

Lindner, T. Der Feldzug der Französen gegen Jülich und Geldern im Jahre 1388. *In* Monatsschr. für Rhein.-Westfäl. Geschichtsforschung und Alterthumskunde. II. Trèves. 1876.

—— Geschichte des Deutschen Reiches unter König Wenzel. 2 vols. Brunswick. 1875–80.

Luce, S. La France pendant la guerre de Cent Ans. 2 vols. Paris. 1890, 93.

Margry, P. La conquête et les conquérants des Canaries. Paris. 1896.

Mémoire sur Pierre de Craon. *In* Mélanges de littérature et d'histoire. (Société des Bibliophiles français.) Paris. 1856.

Ménard, C. Histoire de la ville de Nîmes. 7 vols. Nîmes. 1750–8.

Merlet, L. Biographie de Jean de Montagu. BEC. xiii. 1851–2.
Mirot, L. Les insurrections urbaines au début du règne de Charles VI (1380–3), leurs causes et leurs conséquences. Paris. 1906.
—— Isabelle de France, reine d'Angleterre (1380–1409). RHD. xviii. 1904.
—— Le Procès de maître Jean Fusoris, chanoine de Notre-Dame de Paris (1415–16). *In* Mém. de la Soc. de l'Hist. de Paris. xxvii. Paris. 1901.
—— Une grande famille parlementaire aux xive et xve siècles. Les d'Orgemont. Paris. 1913.
Moranvillé, H. Étude sur la vie de Jean Le Mercier, 13..–1397. *In* Mém. AcadIBL. 2nd ser. Vol. vi. Paris. 1888.
—— Conférences entre la France et l'Angleterre, 1390–93. BEC. l. 1889.
Mowat, R. B. Henry V. London. 1919.
Nicolas, N. H. History of the battle of Agincourt. 3rd edn. London. 1833.
Oman, C. History of England…, 1377–1485. (Polit. Hist. of England. Ed. Hunt, W. and Poole, R. L. Vol. iv.) London. 1906.
—— The Great Revolt of 1381. London. 1906.
Owen, L. V. D. England and the Low Countries (1405–13). EHR. xxviii. 1913.
Petit, E. Les séjours de Charles VI, 1380–1400. *In* Bulletin du Comité des travaux hist., Section d'hist. et de philol. Paris. 1893.
Pirenne, A. Histoire de Belgique. Vol. ii. *See Gen. Bibl.* v.
Plancher, U. Histoire générale et particulière de Bourgogne. 4 vols. Dijon. 1739–81.
Portal, C. Les insurrections des Tuchins dans les pays de Languedoc. *In* Annales du Midi. iv. Toulouse. 1892.
Postel, R. Siège et capitulation de Bayeux en 1417. Caen. 1873.
Puiseux, L. Siège et prise de Caen par les Anglais en 1417. *In* Mém. de la Soc. des antiq. de Normandie. xxii. Caen. 1856.
—— Étude sur le siège de Rouen par Henri V, roi d'Angleterre, en 1418–19. *Ibid.* xxvi. 1867.
Romano, S. Valentina Visconti e il suo matrimonio con Luigi di Turania. ASL. xxv. 1898.
Salembier, L. Le Grand Schisme d'Occident. 5th edn. Paris. 1922.
Saltel, J. La folie de Charles VI. Toulouse. 1907.
Schwab, B. Johannes Gerson, Professor der Theologie und Kanzler der Universität. Paris. Würzburg. 1858.
Skalweil, G. Der Kreuzzug des Bischofs Heinrich von Norwich im Jahre 1383. Königsberg. 1898.
Terrier de Loray. Les frères de Charles V, examen des accusations dont ils ont été l'objet. RQH. xxv. 1879.
Thibault, M. Isabeau de Bavière, reine de France, sa jeunesse, 1370–1405. Paris. 1903.
Tschackert, P. Peter von Ailli. Gotha. 1877.
Vallet de Viriville, A. Notes sur l'état civil des princes et des princesses nés de Charles VI et d'Isabeau de Bavière. BEC. xix. 1857–8.
—— Isabeau de Bavière. Paris. 1859.
—— Histoire de Charles VII. Vol. i. Paris. 1862.
Valois, N. La France et le Grand Schisme d'Occident. 4 vols. Paris. 1896–1902.
—— Le conseil du roi aux xive, xve, et xvie siècles. Paris. 1888.
Vanderkindere, L. Le siècle des Artevelde. 2nd edn. Brussels. 1907.
Varenbergh, E. Histoire des relations diplomatiques entre le comté de Flandre et l'Angleterre au moyen âge. Brussels. 1874.
Vernier, J. J. Le duché de Bourgogne et les compagnies dans la seconde moitié du xive siècle. *In* Mém. de l'Acad. de Dijon. 4th ser. Vol. viii. Dijon. 1902.
Vic, C. de, and Vaissete, J. J. Histoire générale de Languedoc. *See Gen. Bibl.* iv.
Vickers, K. H. England in the later Middle Ages. London. 1913.
Wallon, H. Richard II. Épisode de la rivalité de la France et de l'Angleterre. 2 vols. Paris. 1864.
Wylie, J. H. History of England under Henry the Fourth. 4 vols. London. 1884–98.
—— and Waugh, W. T. The reign of Henry the Fifth. 3 vols. Cambridge. 1914–29.

CHAPTER XIV.

ENGLAND: EDWARD I AND EDWARD II.

I. SPECIAL BIBLIOGRAPHIES.

Professor Tout has made a critical survey of authorities in the appendix to his
History of England, 1216–1377 (*see below*, III A); a useful list of sources, mainly for
Edward II's reign, is appended to J. Conway Davies' Baronial Opposition to
Edward II (*see below*, III B (ii)).

II. ORIGINAL AUTHORITIES.

A. CHRONICLES AND ANNALS.

[A fairly full list of these is given, because they deserve more careful and constant
reading than the present zeal for record material makes fashionable.]

Annales Londonienses (1194–1330, with gap 1293–1301). Ed. Stubbs, W. *in* Chronicles
    of the reigns of Edw. I and Edw. II. Vol. I, pp. 3–251. (Rolls.) 1882. [Specially
    valuable 1301–16.]
Annales monasterii de Oseneia (1016–1347). Ed. Luard, H. R. *in* Annales Monastici.
    Vol. IV, pp. 1–352. (Rolls.) 1869.
Annales Paulini (1307–41). Ed. Stubbs, W. *in* Chronicles of...Edw. I and Edw. II.
    Vol. I, pp. 255–370 (Rolls.) 1882.
Annales monasterii de Waverleia (to 1291). Ed. Luard, H. R. *in* Annales Monastici.
    Vol. II, pp. 127–411. (Rolls.) 1865.
Annales prioratus de Wigornia (to 1377). *Ibid.* Vol. IV, pp. 353–564. (Rolls.) 1869.
Annales monasterii de Wintonia (519–1277). *Ibid.* Vol. II, pp. 1–125. (Rolls.) 1865.
Baker, Geoffrey le. Chronicon (1303–56). Ed. Thompson, E. M. Oxford. 1889.
    [The portion 1307–27 was wrongly ascribed to Baker's patron Thomas de la More
    and printed by Stubbs as Vita et Mors Edwardi II. *See below.*]
Blaneford, Henry de. Chronica (1323–24). Ed. Riley, H. T. *in* Chronica et Annales
    J. de Trokelowe, pp. 131–152. (Rolls.) 1866.
Commendatio lamentabilis in transitu magni regis Edwardi...secundum Johannem
    de Londonia. Ed. Stubbs, W. *in* Chronicles of...Edw. I and Edw. II. Vol. II,
    pp. 1–21. (Rolls.) 1883.
Cotton, Bartholomew. Historia Anglicana (449–1298). Ed. Luard, H. R. (Rolls.)
    1859. [Valuable and contemporary, 1291–8.]
Flores Historiarum. Vol. III (1265–1326). Ed. Luard, H. R. (Rolls.) 1890. [For the
    authorship of the later portion of this *see* T. F. Tout, The Westminster Chronicle
    attributed to Robert of Reading. EHR. XXXI (1916). 450–64.]
Gesta Edwardi de Carnarvan auctore canonico Bridlingtoniensi (1307–27). Ed.
    Stubbs, W. *in* Chronicles of...Edw. I and Edw. II. Vol. II, pp. 25–92. (Rolls.)
    1883.
Gray, Thomas. Scalacronica. [Ed. Stevenson, J.] (Maitland Club.) Edinburgh.
    1836. Engl. transl. Maxwell, Sir H. Glasgow. 1907.
Hemingburgh, Walter de. Chronicon. Vol. II, pp. 1–296 (1274–1315). Ed.
    Hamilton, H. C. (English Hist. Soc.) London. 1849.
Higden, Ranulf. Polychronicon. Vol. VIII, pp. 260–326. Ed. Lumby, J. R. (Rolls.)
    1882. [A late compilation. Contains the much-quoted sketch of the character of
    Edward II (p. 298).]
Lanercost, Chronicon de (1201–1346). [Ed. Stevenson, J.] (Bannatyne Club.)
    Edinburgh. 1839. Engl. transl. Maxwell, Sir H. Glasgow. 1913.
Langtoft, Peter. Chronicle, in French verse. Vol. II, pp. 164–382 (1272–1307). Ed.
    Wright, T., with transl. (Rolls.) 1868.

Liber de Antiquis Legibus *containing* Cronica maiorum et vicecomitum Londoniarum. Ed. Stapleton, T. (Camden Soc.) London. 1846. [Appendix, pp. 250–3, has annals of Edw. II's reign with important details concerning the publication of the Ordinances.]

Mannyng, Robert. Translation of Peter Langtoft's chronicle. Ed. Hearne, T. Vol. II, pp. 235–341. Oxford. 1725. *Also in* Hearne's Works. Vol. IV. London. 1810.

Murimuth, Adam. Continuatio Chronicarum (1303–47). Ed. Thompson, E. M. (Rolls.) 1889.

Opus Chronicorum (1259–96). Ed. Riley, H. T. *in* Chronica et Annales J. de Trokelowe, pp. 3–59. (Rolls.) 1866.

Oxenedes *or* Oxnead, John de. Chronica (449–1293). Ed. Ellis, Sir H. (Rolls.) 1859.

Rishanger, Willelmi, et quorundam Anonymorum Chronica et Annales (1259–1306). Ed. Riley, H. T. (Rolls.) 1865. [The portion from 1272 was written later than 1327, and almost certainly not by Rishanger.]

Trevet *or* Trivet, Nicholas. Annales Sex Regum Angliae, 1135–1307. Ed. Hog, T. (English Hist. Soc.) London. 1845.

Trokelowe, John de. Annales (1307–23). Ed. Riley, H. T. *in* Chronica et Annales J. de Trokelowe. (Rolls.) 1866.

Vita Edwardi Secundi. Ed. Stubbs, W. *in* Chronicles of...Edw. I and Edw. II. Vol. II, pp. 155–290. (Rolls.) 1883. [The author was stated, on slender evidence, to be a monk of Malmesbury, and the work is often referred to as "Malmesbury."]

Vita et Mors Edwardi Secundi. *Ibid.* Vol. II, pp. 297–319. *See above*, Geoffrey le Baker.

Wykes, Thomas. Chronicon (1066–1289). Ed. Luard, H. R. *in* Annales Monastici. Vol. IV, pp. 6–319. (Rolls.) 1869.

B. Records.

(i) *General Collections.*

Bémont, C. Chartes des Libertés anglaises, 1100–1305. (Coll. textes.) Paris. 1892.

Cole, H. Documents illustrative of English history in the thirteenth and fourteenth centuries. (RC.) London. 1844.

Rymer, T. Foedera. Vol. II, pt. I. *See Gen. Bibl.* IV.

Statutes of the Realm. Vol. I. (RC.) London. 1810.

Stubbs, W. Select Charters. 9th edn. *See Gen. Bibl.* IV.

[Documents relating to the English Customs System have been edited by Gras, N. S. B. *in* The early English Customs System. *See below*, III B (ii).]

(ii) *Letters.*

Letters of Edward, Prince of Wales, 1304–5. Ed. Johnstone, Hilda. (Roxburghe Club.) 1931.

Edward II, the Lords Ordainers, and Piers Gaveston's Jewels and Horses (1312–1313). Ed. Roberts, R. A. (Roy. Hist. Soc., Camden Miscellany. xv.) London. 1929. [A mutilated but interesting record in the Vatican archives, containing the report to Pope Clement V of two envoys sent to England to compose the quarrel between Edward II and the magnates after Gaveston's death.]

Lettres des rois, reines, et autres personnages de France et d'Angleterre. Ed. Champollion-Figeac, J. J. 2 vols. (Coll. doc.) Paris. 1839, 47.

(iii) *Chancery Enrolments.*

[It should be noted that the full texts of many Chancery enrolments for these reigns are printed in Sir F. Palgrave's Parliamentary Writs, *see below*, II B (v).]

Bémont, C. Rôles Gascons. Vols. II, III, 1273–1307. (Coll. doc.) Paris. 1900, 6.

Calendar of Chancery Rolls, Various, 1277–1326. (Cal. SP.) London. 1912.

Calendar of Chancery Warrants preserved in P.R.O., 1244–1326. (Cal. SP.) London. 1927. [A valuable supplement to the other calendars, since it contains all warrants under the Privy Seal for letters under the Great Seal which have not left their trace in the Chancery enrolments or inquisitions.]

Calendar of Charter Rolls. Vol. II, Hen. III—Edw. I; vol. III, Edw. I—Edw. II. (Cal. SP.) London. 1906, 8.

Calendar of Close Rolls. Edw. I (5 vols.); Edw. II (4 vols.). (Cal. SP.) London. 1892–1908.
Calendar of Fine Rolls. Vol. i, Edw. I; vols. ii, iii, Edw. II. (Cal. SP.) London. 1911–13.
Calendar of Inquisitions, Miscellaneous (Chancery). Vol. i, Hen. III and Edw. I; vol. ii, Edw. II and Edw. III. (Cal. SP.) London. 1916.
Calendar of Inquisitions post Mortem. Vols. ii–iv, Edw. I; vols. v, vi, Edw. II. (Cal. SP.) London. 1906–13.
Calendar of Patent Rolls. Edw. I (4 vols.); Edw. II (5 vols.). (Cal. SP.) London. 1893–1904.
Calendarium Genealogicum. Hen. III and Edw. I. Ed. Roberts, C. 2 vols. (Cal. SP.) London. 1865.

(iv) *Records preserved in the Exchequer.*

Book of Fees, commonly called Testa de Nevill. Pts. ii, iii. (Cal. SP.) London. 1923, 31.
Feudal Aids, Inquisitions, and Assessments relating to, 1284–1431. 6 vols. (Cal. SP.) London. 1899–1920.
Issues of the Exchequer. Ed. Devon, F. London. 1837. [Contains translated extracts from liberate, issue, memoranda, and household rolls.]
Kirkby's Quest. A survey made in various counties, probably in 1284–85. For portions printed *see* Gross, C. Sources. § 55, p. 482. *See Gen. Bibl.* i.
Liber Niger Scaccarii. Ed. Hearne, T. 2nd edn. 2 vols. London. 1771; repr. 1774.
Liber quotidianus contrarotulatoris garderobae, 1299–1300. (Soc. of Antiq. of London.) London, 1787. [The only printed specimen for the period of a complete wardrobe book.]
Memoranda Roll for 1297. Extracts printed in TRHS. n.s. iii (1886). 281–91.
Nomina Villarum (Returns as to boroughs and townships made in 1316). Printed in Parl. Writs. Vol. ii, div. iii, pp. 301–416. *See below,* ii b (v).
Pipe Roll for 1295. Surrey membrane. Ed. Mills, M. H. (Surrey Record Soc. xxi.) Guildford. 1924. [Though confined to Surrey membrane, invaluable as the only printed text of a Pipe Roll available for period. Has a long and valuable introduction.]
Red Book of the Exchequer. Ed. Hall, H. 3 vols. (Rolls.) 1896.
Rotulorum Originalium in Curia Scaccarii Abbreviatio. [Ed. Playford, H.] Vol. i, Hen. III—Edw. II. (RC.) London. 1805.
Taxatio ecclesiastica Angliae et Walliae auctoritate P. Nicholai IV *circa* a.d. 1291. Ed. Astle, T., Ayscough, S. and Caley, J. (RC.) London. 1802.

(v) *Records illustrating Parliamentary history.*

Maitland, F. W. Memoranda de Parliamento (1305). (Rolls.) 1893.
Palgrave, F. Parliamentary Writs and Writs of Military Summons. Vol. i, Edw. I; vol. ii, Edw. II. (RC.) London. 1827, 34.
Rotuli Parliamentorum. [Ed. Strachey, J. and others.] Vol. i. [London. 1767.] Index. (RC.) London. 1832.
Rotuli Parliamentorum Anglie hactenus inediti, 1279–1373. Ed. Richardson, H. G. and Sayles, G. (Roy. Hist. Soc., Camden 3rd ser. li.) London. 1935.
Rotulus Parliamenti anno 12 Edw. II. Ed. Cole, H. *in* Documents, pp. 1–54. *See above,* ii b (i)

(vi) *Legal Records and Law-Writers.*

Britton. French text ed. and transl. Nichols, F. M. 2 vols. Oxford. 1865. Re-publ. (without text) with introd. by Baldwin, S. E. Washington. 1901.
Court Baron, The. Ed. Maitland, F. W. and Baildon, W. P. [Precedents and pleas, with transl.] (Selden Soc. iv.) London. 1891.
Fleta, seu Commentarius juris Anglicani. Ed. Selden, J. 2nd edn. London. 1685. Book i. Ed. Clarke, Sir T. London. 1735.
Placita coram rege [1297]. Ed. Phillimore, W. P. W. (British Record Soc., Index Library, xix.) London. 1898.
Placita de Quo Warranto. [Ed. Illingworth, W.] (RC.) London. 1818.

Placitorum abbreviatio. Rich. I—Edw. II. [Ed. Rose, G. and Illingworth, W.] (RC.) [London.] 1811.

Public Works in Mediaeval Law. Ed. Flower, C. T. 2 vols. (Selden Soc. XXXII, XL.) London. 1915, 23.

Rotuli Hundredorum. [Ed. Illingworth, W.] 2 vols. (RC.) London. 1812, 18.

Select Bills in Eyre, 1292–1333. Ed. Bolland, W. C. (Selden Soc. XXX.) London. 1914.

Select Cases from the Coroners' Rolls, 1265–1413 (with transl.). Ed. Gross, C. (*Ibid.* IX.) 1896.

Select Cases before the King's Council, 1243–1482. Ed. Leadam, I. S. and Baldwin, J. F. (*Ibid.* XXXV.) Cambridge, Mass. 1918.

Select Pleas...from the rolls of the Exchequer of the Jews, 1220–84. Ed. Rigg, J. M. (*Ibid.* XV.) London. 1902.

State Trials of the reign of Edward I, 1289–93. Ed. Tout, T. F. and Johnstone, Hilda. (Roy. Hist. Soc., Camden 3rd ser. IX.) London. 1906.

Year Books, 20–22, 30–35 Edw. I. Ed. Horwood, A. J. 5 vols. (Rolls.) 1866–79.

Year Books of Edw. II. Ed. Maitland, F. W., and others. (Selden Soc., Year Books Series. I–XIX.) London. 1903 ff., in progress. [Until this new series is complete, reference will still be necessary to the folio edition—Les reports des cases argue et adjudge en le temps del roy Edward le Second. London. 1678.]

(vii) *Ecclesiastical Records.*

[For Registers and Letters of the Popes *see Gen. Bibl.* IV *under* Papal Documents. For the Decrees of English Councils *see* Wilkins, D., Concilia Magnae Britanniae et Hiberniae. Vol. II (1268–1349). London, 1737, which also contains extracts from episcopal registers and other records.]

Registers of Archbishops and Bishops.

Bath and Wells.
    Walter Giffard (1265–66). Ed. Holmes, T. S. (Somerset Record Soc.) London. 1899.
    John of Drokenesford (1309–29). Ed. Hobhouse, E. (*Ibid.*) 1887.

Canterbury.
    John Peckham (1279–92). Ed. Martin, C. T. 3 vols. (Rolls.) 1882–5. [Selections only.] New edn. [complete]. Ed. Jenkins, C. (Cant. and York Soc.) London. 1908 ff., in progress.
    Robert of Winchelsey (1294–1308). Ed. Graham, Rose. (*Ibid.*) 1917 ff., in progress.

Carlisle.
    John of Halton (1292–1324). Ed. Thompson, W. N. and Tout, T. F. 1913. 2 vols. (*Ibid.*)

Coventry and Lichfield.
    Roger of Northburgh (1322–59). Ed. Hobhouse, E. (Will. Salt Archaeol. Soc., Collections. Vol. I, pp. 241–88.) Birmingham. 1881. [Abstract of contents only.]

Durham.
    Richard of Kellawe (1311–16). Ed. Hardy, T. D. 4 vols. (Rolls.) 1873–8.

Exeter.
    Walter Bronescombe (1257–80) and Peter Quivil (1280–91). Walter of Stapledon (1307–26). All ed. Hingeston-Randolph, F. C. London. 1889, 92. [These editions are arranged as indexes with long illustrative extracts. Some records of the episcopate of Thomas Bitton (1292–1309), who left no register, are included.]

Hereford.
    Thomas of Cantilupe (1275–82). Ed. Griffiths, R. G. and Capes, W. W. (Cantilupe Soc.) Hereford; *and* (Cant. and York Soc.) London. 1907.
    Richard of Swinfield (1283–1317). Ed. Capes, W. W. (*Ibid.*) 1909.
    Adam of Orleton (1317–27). Ed. Bannister, A. T. (*Ibid.*) 1908.

Lincoln.
  Richard Gravesend (1258–79). Ed. Davis, F. N., and others. (Cant. and York
    Soc.) London. 1925.
London.
  Ralph Baldock (1304–13); Gilbert Segrave (1313–16); Richard Newport (1317–18);
    Stephen Gravesend (1318–38). Ed. Fowler, R. C. (*Ibid.*) 1911.
Rochester.
  Hamo de Hethe (1319–52). Ed. Johnson, C. (*Ibid.*) 1914 ff., in progress.
Salisbury.
  Simon of Ghent (1297–1315). Ed. Flower, C. T. (*Ibid.*) 1914 ff., in progress.
Winchester.
  John de Pontissara (1282–1304). Ed. Deedes, C. 2 vols. (*Ibid.*) 1915, 24.
  Henry Woodlock (1305–1316). Ed. Goodman, A. W. (*Ibid.*) In preparation.
  John of Sandale (1316–19) and Rigaud de Asserio (1320–23). Ed. Baigent, F. J.
    (Hampshire Record Soc.) London. 1897.
Worcester.
  Godfrey Giffard (1268–1301). Ed. Willis-Bund, J. W. 2 vols. (Worcs. Hist. Soc.)
    Oxford. (1898–)1902.
  William de Geynesburgh (1302–7). Ed. Willis-Bund, J. W., introd. by Wilson, R. A.
    (*Ibid.*) 1907, 29.
  Walter Reynolds (1308–13). Ed. Wilson, R. A. (*Ibid.*) London. 1927.
  Thomas de Cobham (1317–27). Ed. Pearce, E. H. (*Ibid.*) 1930.
  Sede vacante (1301–1435). Ed. Willis-Bund, J. W. 4 pts. in 5. (*Ibid.*) Oxford.
    1893–7.
York.
  Walter Giffard (1266–79). Ed. Brown, W. (Surtees Soc.) Durham. 1904.
  William Wickwane (1279–85). Ed. Brown, W. (*Ibid.*) 1907.
  John le Romeyne (1286–96) and Henry of Newark (1296–99). Ed. Brown, W.
    (*Ibid.*) 1914, 17.
  Thomas of Corbridge (1300–1304). Ed. Thompson, A. Hamilton. (*Ibid.*) 1925, 28.
Historical papers and letters from the northern registers. Ed. Raine, J. (Rolls.)
  1873.

III. MODERN WORKS.

A. GENERAL.

Jenks, E. Edward Plantagenet. London. 1902.
Ramsay, Sir J. H. The Dawn of the Constitution, 1216–1307. London. 1908.
—— The Genesis of Lancaster. Vol. I, pp. 1–182. Oxford. 1913.
Tout, T. F. History of England, 1216–1377. New edn. (Political History of England.
  Ed. Hunt, W. and Poole, R. L. Vol. III.) London. 1920.
—— Edward the First. London. 1896.
—— The Place of Edward II in English History. Manchester. 1922. New edn. by
  Johnstone, Hilda, in preparation.

B. STUDIES ON SPECIAL SUBJECTS.

(i) *Ecclesiastical.*

Deeley, Ann. Papal Provision and Royal Rights of Patronage in the early fourteenth
  century. EHR. XLIII (1928). 497–527.
Graham, Rose. English Ecclesiastical Studies. London. 1929. [Sixteen reprinted
  studies on medieval subjects, of which nos. XI–XV inclusive are relevant to this
  chapter.]
Graves, E. B. Circumspecte agatis. EHR. XLIII (1928). 1–20. [Prints as appendix
  a better text of the Writ and Addition than that in Statutes of the Realm.]
Johnstone, Hilda. Archbishop Pecham and the Council of Lambeth of 1281. (Essays
  in Medieval History presented to T. F. Tout, no. 14.) Manchester. 1925.
Lunt, W. E. The Account of a Papal Collector in England in 1304. EHR. XXVIII
  (1913). 313–21.

Lunt, W. E. Collectors' Accounts for the clerical tenth levied in England by order of
      Nicholas IV. EHR. xxxi (1916). 102–19.
—— The first Levy of Papal Annates. AHR. xviii (1912). 48–64.
—— Papal Taxation in England in the reign of Edward I. EHR. xxx (1915).
      393–417.
—— A papal tenth levied in the British Isles from 1274–80. EHR. xxxii (1917).
      49–89.
—— William Testa and the Parliament of Carlisle. EHR. xli (1926). 332–57.
Maitland, F. W. Roman Canon Law in the Church of England. London. 1898.
Mollat, G. La collation des bénéfices ecclésiastiques sous les papes d'Avignon (1305–
      78). Paris. 1921.
Stubbs, W. Registrum sacrum Anglicanum. *See Gen. Bibl.* iii.
Waugh, W. T. Archbishop Peckham and Pluralities. EHR. xxviii (1913). 625–35.

(ii) *Administrative, constitutional, and legal.*

Baldwin, J. F. The King's Council in England during the Middle Ages. Oxford. 1913.
Broome, D. M. Auditors of the Foreign Accounts of the Exchequer, 1310–27. EHR.
      xxxviii (1923). 63–71.
—— Exchequer Migrations to York in the thirteenth and fourteenth centuries.
      (Essays in Medieval History presented to T. F. Tout, no. 22.) Manchester. 1925.
Cam, H. M. Studies in the Hundred Rolls. (Oxford Studies in Social and Legal
      History. Vol. vi. No. 11.) Oxford. 1921.
—— The Hundred and the Hundred Rolls. London. 1930.
Chew, H. M. The Ecclesiastical Tenants-in-chief and Writs of Military Summons.
      EHR. xli (1926). 161–9.
—— Scutage under Edward I. EHR. xxxvii (1922). 321–36.
—— Scutage in the fourteenth century. EHR. xxxviii (1923). 19–41.
Davies, J. Conway. The Baronial Opposition to Edward II. Cambridge. 1918.
—— The First Journal of Edward II's Chamber. EHR. xxx (1915). 662–80.
Dibben, L. B. Secretaries in the thirteenth and fourteenth centuries. EHR. xxv
      (1910). 430–44.
Dowell, S. History of Taxation and Taxes in England. 2nd edn. Vol. i. London.
      1888.
Edwards, J. G. The Personnel of the Commons in Parliament under Edward I and
      Edward II. (Essays in Medieval History presented to T. F. Tout, no. 16.) Man-
      chester. 1925.
Ehrlich, L. E. Proceedings against the Crown (1216–1377). (Oxford Studies in Social
      and Legal History. Vol. vi. No. 12.) Oxford. 1921.
Gras, N. S. B. The early English Customs System. (Harvard Econ. Studies. xviii.)
      Cambridge, Mass. 1918.
Hall, H. History of the Customs revenue in England. New edn. London. 1892.
Holdsworth, W. S. History of English Law. 3rd edn. Vols. i–iii. *See Gen. Bibl.* v.
Jacob, E. F. The Reign of Henry III. Some suggestions. TRHS. 4th ser. x (1927).
      21–53. [Prints as appendix Memoranda of the parliament of 1279.]
Jenkinson, C. H. The First Parliament of Edward I. EHR. xxv (1910). 231–
      42, 416.
Johnson, C. The Exchequer Chamber under Edward II. EHR. xxi (1906). 726–7.
—— The System of Account in the Wardrobe of Edward I. TRHS. 4th ser.
      vi (1923). 50–72.
Johnstone, Hilda. The Parliament of Lincoln of 1316. EHR. xxvi (1921). 53–
      57, 480.
Lapsley, G. T. The Commons and the Statute of York. EHR. xxviii (1913). 118–24.
—— Knights of the Shire in the Parliaments of Edward II. EHR. xxxiv (1919).
      25–42, 152–71.
Lees, B. A. The Statute of Winchester and Villa Integra. EHR. xli (1926).
      98–103.
Mills, M. H. Adventus Vicecomitum, 1272–1307. EHR. xxxviii (1923). 331–54.
—— Exchequer Agenda and Estimate of Revenue, Easter term 1284. EHR. xl (1925).
      229–34.

Morris, W. A. The Medieval English Sheriff to 1300. Manchester. 1927.

Pasquet, D. Essai sur les origines de la Chambre des Communes. Paris. 1914. Engl. transl. by Laffan, R. G. D., preface and additional notes by Lapsley, G. T. Cambridge. 1925.

Plucknett, T. F. T. Statutes and their interpretation in the first half of the fourteenth century. Cambridge. 1922.

Pollard, A. F. The Evolution of Parliament. 2nd edn. London. 1926.

Pollock, F. and Maitland, F. W. History of English Law before the time of Edward I. *See Gen. Bibl.* v.

Reid, R. R. Barony and Thanage. EHR. xxxv (1920). 161–99.

Richardson, H. G. The Origins of Parliament. TRHS. 4th ser. xi (1928). 137–83.

—— and Sayles, G. The early Records of the English Parliaments. *In* Bulletin of the Institute of Hist. Research. Vol. v, pp. 129–54. Vol. vi, pp. 71–88, 129–55. London. 1928–9.

—— —— The King's Ministers in Parliament, 1272–1377. EHR. xlvi (1931). 529–50. xlvii (1932).

Stevenson, W. H. A letter of the Younger Despenser on the eve of the Barons' Rebellion (21 March 1321). EHR. xii (1897). 755–61.

Stubbs, W. Constitutional History. *See Gen. Bibl.* v.

Tout, T. F. Chapters in Medieval Administrative History. 6 vols. Manchester. 1920–32.

—— The Chief Officers of the King's Wardrobe down to 1399. EHR. xxiv (1909). 496–505.

Vinogradoff, Sir P. Ralph of Hengham as Chief Justice of Common Pleas. (Essays in Medieval History presented to T. F. Tout, no. 15.) Manchester. 1925.

Willard, J. F. The Memoranda Rolls and the Remembrancers, 1282–1350. (*Ibid.* no. 17.)

—— The Taxes upon Moveables of the Reigns of Edward I and Edward II. EHR. xxviii (1913). 517–21. xxix (1914). 317–21.

(iii) *Biographical and personal.*

Dimitresco, M. Pierre de Gavaston, comte de Cornouailles. Paris. 1898.

Gough, H. An Itinerary of Edward I. 2 vols. Paisley. 1900.

Rhodes, W. E. Edmund, earl of Lancaster. EHR. x (1895). 19–40, 209–37.

Robinson, C. Was King Edward II a degenerate? *In* American Journ. of Insanity. lxvi (1910). 445–64.

Studer, P. An Anglo-Norman poem by Edward II, King of England. *In* Modern Language Review. xvi (1921). 34–46.

Tanquerey, F. J. The Conspiracy of Thomas Dunheved, 1327. EHR. xxxi (1916). 119–24.

Tout, T. F. The Captivity and Death of Edward of Carnarvon. Manchester. 1920.

(iv) *English lands in France.*

Black, J. G. Edward I and Gascony in 1300. EHR. xvii (1902). 518–27.

Johnson, C. The Homage for Guienne in 1304. EHR. xxiii (1908). 728.

Johnstone, Hilda. The County of Ponthieu, 1279–1307. EHR. xxix (1914). 435–52.

Lodge, E. C. Gascony under English rule. London. 1926.

Rothwell, H. Edward I's case against Philip the Fair over Gascony in 1298. EHR. xlii (1927). 572–82.

Salt, M. C. L. List of English Embassies to France, 1272–1307. EHR. xliv (1929). 263–78.

Stuart, E. Pole. The Interview between Philip V and Edward I at Amiens in 1320. EHR. xli (1926). 412–15.

Tout, T. F. France and England; their relations in the Middle Ages and now. Manchester. 1922.

CHAPTER XV.

ENGLAND: EDWARD III AND RICHARD II.

I. SPECIAL BIBLIOGRAPHIES.

Tout, T. F. History of England, 1216–1377. *See below*, III A. [Contains a critical account of the chief authorities for Edward III's reign.]

Oman, C. History of England, 1377–1485. *See below*, III A. [Discusses those for Richard II's reign.]

Gross, C. Sources and Literature of English History...to about 1485. 2nd edn. enl. London. 1915.

Winfield, P. H. The chief Sources of English Legal History. Cambridge, Mass. 1925.

[A complete bibliography of the administrative sources and literature is given in Tout, T. F. Chapters in the Administrative History of Mediaeval England. Vol. VI. *See below*, III C.]

II. ORIGINAL AUTHORITIES.

A. NARRATIVE SOURCES.

Annales monasterii de Bermundeseia (1042–1432). Ed. Luard, H. R. *in* Annales Monastici. Vol. III. (Rolls.) 1866.

Annales monasterii de Oseneia (1016–1347). *Ibid.* Vol. IV. (Rolls.) 1869.

Annales Paulini (1307–41). Ed. Stubbs, W. *in* Chronicles of the Reigns of Edward I and Edward II. Vol. I. (Rolls.) 1882.

Annales prioratus de Wigornia (to 1377). Ed. Luard, H. R. *in* Annales Monastici. Vol. IV. (Rolls.) 1869.

Annales Ricardi Secundi. Ed. Riley, H. T. *in* Chronica et Annales J. de Trokelowe. (Rolls.) 1866.

Anonimalle Chronicle, The, 1333 to 1381. Ed. Galbraith, V. H. Manchester. 1927.

Avesbury, Robert of. De gestis mirabilibus regis Edwardi Tertii (to 1359). Ed. Thompson, E. M. (Rolls.) 1889.

Baker, Geoffrey le. Chronicon (1303–1356). Ed. Thompson, E. M. Oxford. 1889.

Brut, The, or the Chronicles of England. Ed. Brie, F. W. D. 2 pts. (EETS. Orig. ser. Nos. 131, 136.) London. 1906, 8. [There is a continuation *in* The English Chronicle of the reigns of Richard II, Henry IV, etc. Ed. Davies, J. S. *See below.*]

Burton, Thomas of. Chronica monasterii de Melsa (1150–1396, with a continuation to 1406). Ed. Bond, E. A. Vols. II, III. (Rolls.) 1867–8.

Capgrave, J. Chronicle of England (to 1417). Ed. Hingeston, F. C. (Rolls.) 1858.

Chandos Herald. Life of the Black Prince by the herald of Sir John Chandos. Ed. (with prose transl.) Pope, M. K. and Lodge, E. C. Oxford. 1910.

Chronicles of London. Ed. Kingsford, C. L. Oxford. 1905.

Chronicon abbatiae de Evesham ad annum 1418. Ed. Macray, W. D. (Rolls.) 1863.

Chronicon Angliae (1328–88). Ed. Thompson, E. M. (Rolls.) 1874.

Chronique de la traïson et mort de Richart Deux, Roy d'Engleterre (1397–1400, with Engl. transl.). Ed. Williams, B. (English Hist. Soc.) London. 1846.

Chronique du religieux de Saint-Denys (1380–1422) (with a French transl. of the Latin text). Ed. Bellaguet, L. 6 vols. (Coll. doc.) Paris. 1839–52.

Créton, J. Histoire du roy d'Angleterre Richard [II], traictant particulièrement la rebellion de ses subiectz. Ed., with Engl. transl., Webb, J. *in* Archaeologia, XX. (Soc. of Antiq. of London.) London. 1824. A better text, ed. Buchon, J. A. C. (*as* Poème sur la déposition de Richard II) *in* Collection des chroniques nationales françaises, XXIV. pp. 321–466. Paris. 1826.

Croniques de London depuis l'an 44 Hen. III jusqu'à l'an 17 Edw. III. Ed. Aungier, G. J. (Camden Soc. xxviii.) London. 1844. Transl. by Riley, H. T. : The French chronicle of London, 1259–1343. London. 1863.

English Chronicle of the reigns of Richard II, Henry IV, Henry V, and Henry VI. Ed. Davies, J. S. (Camden Soc. lxiv.) London. 1856. *See above,* Brut, The, or the Chronicles of England.

Eulogium historiarum sive temporis (to 1366, with continuation to 1413). Ed. Haydon, F. S. Vol. iii. (Rolls.) 1863.

Favent, Thomas. Historia...de modo et forma mirabilis parliamenti apud West-monasterium a.d. millesimo ccclxxxvi [*sic*]...Ricardi II...anno decimo. Ed. McKisack, M. *in* Camden Miscellany. xiv (Roy. Hist. Soc., Camden 3rd ser., xxxvii.) London. 1926.

Froissart, Jean. Chroniques (1307–1400). Ed. Luce, S. and Raynaud, G. 11 vols. (to 1385). (SHF.) Paris. 1869–99. For the remaining years *see* the edition of Kervyn de Lettenhove. 25 vols. in 26. Brussels. 1867–77. Engl. transl. Bourchier, J., Lord Berners. Chronicles of England, France, etc. Ed. Ker, W. P. 6 vols. (Tudor Transl. Library.) London. 1901–3. *See also* Coulton, G. G. The Chronicler of European Chivalry. *See below,* iii a.

Gesta abbatum monasterii Sancti Albani. Ed. Riley, H. T. Vols. ii, iii. (Rolls.) 1867, 69.

Gesta Edwardi de Carnarvan auctore canonico Bridlingtoniensi, cum continuatione ad a.d. 1377. Ed. Stubbs, W. *in* Chronicles of the Reigns of Edward I and Edward II. Vol. ii. (Rolls.) 1883.

Gray, Thomas. Scalacronica. Ed. Stevenson, J. (Maitland Club.) Edinburgh. 1836. Engl. transl. Maxwell, Sir H. Glasgow. 1907.

Graystanes, Robertus de. Historia de statu ecclesiae Dunelmensis, 1214–1336. Ed. Raine, J. *in* Historiae Dunelmensis scriptores tres. *See below.*

Hemingburgh, Walter de. Chronicon (1048–1346). Ed. Hamilton, H. C. Vol. ii. (English Hist. Soc.) London. 1849. [New edn. in preparation in the Camden Series of the Roy. Hist. Soc.]

Higden, Ranulf. Polychronicon (to 1352, with a continuation to 1394). Ed. Lumby, J. R. Vols. viii, ix. (Rolls.) 1882, 86.

Historia Aurea. Extracts from the Historia Aurea and a French "Brut" (1317–47). Ed. Galbraith, V. H. *in* EHR. xliii (1928). 203–17.

Historia et cartularium monasterii Sancti Petri Gloucestriae. Ed. Hart, W. H. 3 vols. (Rolls.) 1863–7.

Historia vitae et regni Ricardi II a monacho quodam de Evesham consignata. Ed. Hearne, T. Oxford. 1729.

Historiae Dunelmensis scriptores tres. Ed. Raine, J. (Surtees Soc. x.) London. 1839. [Contains, besides Robertus de Graystanes, *see above,* Continuatio historiae Dunelmensis, 1336–1571, attributed in part to Willelmus de Chambre.]

Historians of the Church of York and its Archbishops. Ed. Raine, J. Vols. ii, iii. (Rolls.) 1886, 94.

Historical Papers and Letters from the Northern Registers. Ed. Raine, J. (Rolls.) 1873.

Jan de Klerk (Jan Boendaele). Van den Derden Edewaert, coninc van Engelant. Rymkronyk geschreven circa 1347. Ed. Willems, J. F. Ghent. 1840. French transl. Delepierre, O. Édouard III, roi d'Angleterre, en Belgique. Ghent. 1841. [Delepierre, O. Édouard III, roi d'Angleterre, en Flandre, *in* Philobiblon Society Miscellanies, x, 1866–7, gives an account of the poem.]

Knighton, Henry. Chronicon (959–1366, with a continuation 1377–95). Ed. Lumby, J. R. 2 vols. (Rolls.) 1889, 95.

Lanercost, Chronicon de (1201–1346). Ed. Stevenson, J. (Bannatyne Club.) Edinburgh. 1839. English transl. Maxwell, Sir H. Glasgow. 1913.

Le Beau, Jean. Chronique de Richard II, 1377–1399. Ed. Buchon, J. A. C. (Collection des chroniques nationales françaises, xxv. Supplt. ii.) Paris. 1826.

Le Bel, Jean. Chronique de Jean le Bel (1272–1361). Ed. Viard, J. and Déprez, E. 2 vols. (SHF.) Paris. 1904–5.

Literae Cantuarienses. Ed. Sheppard, J. B. 3 vols. (Rolls.) 1887–9.

Memorials of St Edmund's Abbey. Ed. Arnold, T. Vols. ii, iii. (Rolls.) 1892, 96

Murimuth, Adam. Continuatio Chronicarum (1303–1347). Ed. Thompson, E. M. (Rolls.) 1889.
Otterbourne, Thomas. Chronica regum Angliae (to 1420). Ed. Hearne, T. *in* Duo Rerum Anglicarum Scriptores Veteres. Vol. I. Oxford. 1732.
Reading, John of. Chronica Johannis de Reading et Anonymi Cantuariensis, 1346–1367. Ed. Tait, J. Manchester. 1914.
Speculum regis Edwardi III [attributed erroneously to Simon Islip]. Ed. Moisant, J. Paris. 1891.
Thorne, William. Chronica de rebus gestis abbatum S. Augustini Cantuariae (578–1397). Ed. Twysden, R. *in* Historiae Anglicanae Scriptores, x. London. 1652.
Usk, Adam of. Chronicon, 1377–1421. Ed. with transl. Thompson, E. M. 2nd edn. (Roy. Soc. of Literature.) London. 1904.
Walsingham, Thomas. Historia Anglicana (1272–1422). Ed. Riley, H. T. 2 vols. (Rolls.) 1863–4.
—— Ypodigma Neustriae. Ed. Riley, H. T. (Rolls.) 1876.
Worcester, William of. Annales rerum Anglicarum (1324–1468). Ed. Stevenson, J. *in* Letters and Papers illustrative of the Wars of the English in France during the Reign of Henry VI. Vol. II. (Rolls.) 1864.

[Mr V. H. Galbraith is preparing for the Clarendon Press from MS. Bodley 462 an edition of the full or great chronicle of St Albans for the years 1406–1420, a portion hitherto unprinted. Mr Galbraith kindly allows me to state that among his conclusions it will appear that, so far as they concern the period of this chapter, the chronicles in the Rolls Series printed as *Historia Anglicana* to 1392 and *Annales Ricardi II et Henrici IV* (1392–1406) form the earlier part of this full chronicle, which was very largely, if not entirely, the work of Thomas Walsingham himself. Of this full chronicle Walsingham made an abridgement, parts of which are printed as *Chronicon Angliae* (1328–1388) and as *Historia Anglicana* (1392–1420). The *Scandalous Chronicle* (1376–77), printed in the *Chronicon Angliae*, was thus the work of Walsingham, and was later excised from his *Chronica Majora. See* Galbraith, V. H. Thomas Walsingham and the St Albans Chronicle. EHR. XLII (1932). 12–30.]

B. RECORD SOURCES.

For a note on the history of the Records *see supra*, Vol. VI, p. 890; and Gross, C., *op. cit.*, pp. 77–9; 691–7, *see above*, I.

(i) *Guides.*

Giuseppi, M. S. Guide to the Manuscripts...in the P.R.O. *See Gen. Bibl.* I.
Hall, H. Repertory of British Archives. Pt. I, England. London. 1920.
—— Studies in English Official Historical Documents. Cambridge. 1908.
—— ed. Formula Book of English Official Historical Documents. 2 pts. Cambridge. 1908–9.
Holdsworth, W. S. Sources and Literature of English Law. Oxford. 1925.
Willard, J. F. A brief guide to the records dealing with the taxes upon moveables, 1290–1350. *In* Bulletin of the Institute of Hist. Research. III (1925–6). 27–37.
Winfield, P. H. Chief Sources. pp. 103–44. *See above*, I.

(ii) *General Collections.*

Adams, G. B. and Stephens, H. M. Select documents of English Constitutional History. New York. 1921.
Rymer, T. Foedera. Vols. II, pt. 2, III, IV. *See Gen. Bibl.* IV.
Statutes of the Realm. Vols. I, II. (RC.) London. 1810, 16.

(iii) *Chancery.*

Calendarium rotulorum chartarum (1199–1483) et inquisitionum ad quod damnum (1307–1461). (RC.) London. 1803.
Calendar of Charter Rolls. Vol. IV, Edward III; Vol. V, Edward III—Richard II. (Cal. SP.) London. 1912, 16. [Complete.]
Calendar of Close Rolls. Edward III (14 vols.); Richard II (6 vols.). (Cal. SP.) London. 1896–1927. [Complete.]

Calendar of Fine Rolls. Vols. iv–viii, Edward III; Vols. ix–xi, Richard II. (Cal. SP.) London. 1913–29. [Complete.]
Calendar of Inquisitions, Miscellaneous (Chancery). Vol. ii (1307–1348). (Cal. SP.) London. 1916.
Calendar of Inquisitions post Mortem and other analogous documents. Vols. vii–x, 1–34 Edward III. (Cal. SP.) London. 1909–21.
Calendar of Patent Rolls. Edward III (16 vols.); Richard II (6 vols.). (Cal. SP.) London. 1891–1916. [Complete.]
[*See also* P.R.O. Lists and Indexes (set out in Gross, C., *op. cit.*, pp. 81–2, *see above*, 1) for Chancery Rolls, Inquisitions ad quod damnum, Early Chancery Proceedings.]

(iv) *Exchequer.*

Feudal Aids, Inquisitions and Assessments relating to, 1284–1431. 6 vols. (Cal. SP.) London. 1899–1920.
Issue Roll of Thomas de Brantingham, 44 Edward III, 1370. Ed. Devon, F. London. 1835.
Issues of the Exchequer (Henry III—Henry VI). Ed. Devon, F. London. 1837.
Nonarum Inquisitiones in Curia Scaccarii temp. Regis Edwardi III. (RC.) London. 1807.
Palgrave, F. The antient kalendars and inventories of the treasury of his majesty's exchequer, together with other documents illustrating the history of that repository. 3 vols. (RC.) London. 1836.
Rotulorum originalium in curia scaccarii abbreviatio. Vol. ii. (RC.) London. 1810.
[*See also* P.R.O. Lists and Indexes (set out in Gross, C., *op. cit.*, pp. 81–2, *see above*, 1) for Foreign Accounts enrolled on the great Rolls of the Exchequer, and for Various Accounts formerly preserved in the Exchequer.
See also (not included in Gross):
Diplomatic Documents. P.R.O. List xlix. 1925.
Typed List, 1926, for Exchequer K. R. Memoranda Rolls; and Exchequer L. T. R. Chancellor's Rolls, Memoranda Rolls, Originalia Rolls, and Pipe Rolls.]

(v) *Legal Records and Law-Writers.*

Court Baron, The. Ed. Maitland, F. W. and Baildon, W. P. (Selden Soc. iv.) London. 1891.
(Novae Narrationes.) Herein is conteined the booke called Novae Narrationes. *R. Tottell*: London. 1561.
Olde teners newly corrected. *R. Pynson*: London. 1525 (and later editions).
Placita de Quo Warranto. Edward I—Edward III. [Ed. Illingworth, W.] (RC.) London. 1818.
Public Works in Mediaeval Law. Ed. Flower, C. T. 2 vols. (Selden Soc. xxxii and xl.) London. 1915, 23.
Select Bills in Eyre, 1292–1333. Ed. Bolland, W. C. (*Ibid.* xxx.) London. 1914.
Select Cases before the King's Council, 1243–1482. Ed. Leadam, I. S. and Baldwin, J. F. (*Ibid.* xxxv.) Cambridge, Mass. 1918.
Select Cases from the Coroners' Rolls, 1265–1413. (With translation.) Ed. Gross, C. (*Ibid.* ix.) London. 1896.
Select Cases in Chancery, 1364–1471. Ed. Baildon, W. P. (*Ibid.* x.) London. 1896.
Select Pleas in the Court of Admiralty. Vol. i, pt. i (1390–1404). Ed. Marsden, R. G. (*Ibid.* vi.) London. 1894.
Year Books, 11–20 Edward III. Ed. Horwood, A. J. and Pike, L. O. 15 vols. (Rolls.) 1883–1911.
Year Books of Richard II. (Ames Foundation publns.) [To be completed in 8 vols.]
12 Richard II (1388–89). Ed. Deiser, G. F. Cambridge, Mass. 1914.
13 Richard II (1389–90). Ed. Plucknett, T. F. T. London. 1929.
For other years of Edward III it is still necessary to refer to the edition, Les Reports des Cases, London, 1679, and earlier edns.; for other years of Richard II, since the Year Books of his reign have never yet been printed, to Anthony Fitzherbert's Graunde Abridgement, London, 1516 (and many later edns.), and Robert Brooke's

Graunde Abridgement, London, 1568 (and later), a revised and enlarged edition of Fitzherbert's work. For an account of the Year Books, full bibliographical notes, and a discussion of their value for historical study *see* Bolland, W. C. Manual of Year Book Studies. Cambridge, 1925; and Richardson, H. G. Year Books and Plea Rolls as sources of historical information, *in* TRHS. 4th ser. Vol. v. 1922. pp. 28–70.

[*See also* P.R.O. Lists and Indexes (set out in Gross, C., *op. cit.*, pp. 81–2, *see above*, i) for Plea Rolls.]

[Feet of Fines. Indexes and Calendars printed by many County Societies. *See* index volumes to their Transactions; and Gross, *op. cit.*, especially pp. 457–63.]

(vi) *Records illustrating Parliamentary History.*

Dugdale, W. A perfect copy of all summons of the nobility to the great councils and parliaments of the realm. London. 1685.

Modus tenendi parliamentum. Ed. Hardy, T. D. (RC.) London. 1846. Extracts *in* Select Charters. Ed. Stubbs, W. *See Gen Bibl.* iv.

Prynne, W. A brief register, kalendar, and survey of the several kinds of all parliamentary writs. 4 pts. London. 1659–64. [The third part is entitled: Brevia Parliamentaria Rediviva.]

Reports from the Lords' Committees appointed to search the Journals of the House, Rolls of Parliament, and other records for all matters touching the dignity of a peer. 5 vols. London. 1820–9.

Rotuli Parliamentorum. [Ed. Strachey, J. and others.] Vols. ii, iii. [London. 1767.] Index. (RC.) London. 1832.

Rotuli Parliamentorum Anglie hactenus inediti, 1279–1373. Ed. Richardson, H. G. and Sayles, G. (Roy. Hist. Soc., Camden 3rd ser. li.) London. 1935.

(vii) *Ecclesiastical Records.*

(a) *General.*

[For Registers and Letters of the Popes *see Gen. Bibl.* iv *under* Papal Documents.]

Anglia Sacra. Ed. Wharton, H. London. 1691. [Contains Vitae Archiepiscoporum Cantuariensium, doubtfully attributed to Stephen Birchington.]

Dugdale, Sir W. Monasticon Anglicanum. *See Gen. Bibl.* iv.

Lyndwood, W. Provinciale. Oxford. 1679.

Neve, J. Fasti Ecclesiae Anglicanae. Ed. Hardy, T. D. Oxford. 1854.

Stubbs, W. Registrum sacrum Anglicanum. *See Gen. Bibl.* iii.

Wilkins, D. Concilia Magnae Britanniae et Hiberniae. *See Gen. Bibl.* iv. [Contains extracts from episcopal registers and other records.]

(b) *Registers of Archbishops and Bishops.*

[Fowler, R. C. Episcopal Registers of England and Wales. (Helps for Students of History.) S.P.C.K. London. 1918.]

Bath and Wells.
Ralph of Shrewsbury (1329–63). Ed. Holmes, T. S. (Somerset Record Soc.) London. 1896.

Chichester.
Robert Rede (1397–1415). Ed. Deedes, C. 2 pts. (Sussex Record Soc.) London. 1908, 10.

Coventry and Lichfield.
Roger de Norbury (1322–58). Ed. Hobhouse, E. (Will. Salt Archaeol. Soc., Collections. Vol. i, pp. 241–88.) Birmingham. 1881. [Abstract of contents.]
Robert de Stretton (1358–85). Ed. Wilson, R. A. 2 vols. (*Ibid.* new series. Vols. viii and x, pt. 2. Vol. viii contains the later part; Vol. x contains the earlier part including the *sede vacante* register.) London. 1905, 7. [Abstract.]

Durham.
Richard of Bury (1338–45). The Register of Richard de Kellawe. Ed. Hardy, T. D. Vol. iii. (Rolls.) 1875. [Contains lists of ordinations 1341–5; 1334–40; and a portion of the Register of Richard of Bury 1338–45. Vol. iv (1878) contains some relevant material.]
Richard d'Aungerville, of Bury, Fragments from his Register and other documents. (Surtees Soc. cix.) Durham and London. 1910.

Ely.
Abstract of Registers ed. by Crosby, J. H. *in* Ely Diocesan Remembrancer, November 1889–December 1914. Cambridge.
Simon de Montacute (1337–45). *Ibid.* November 1889–June 1892.
Thomas Lisle (1345–61). *Ibid.* to October–November 1894. [Registers of Langham and Barnet are wanting.]
Thomas de Arundel (1374–88). *Ibid.* to March–April 1897.
John de Fordham (1388–1425). *Ibid.* to May–June 1902.
Ely Episcopal Records: a calendar of the episcopal records in the muniment room of the palace of Ely. Ed. Gibbons, A. Lincoln. 1891. [Contains extracts from registers 1375–1587.]

Exeter.
John de Grandisson (1327–69). 3 vols. London. 1894–9.
Thomas de Brantyngham (1370–94). 2 vols. 1901, 6.
Edmund Stafford (1395–1419). 1886.
All ed. Hingeston-Randolph, F. C. [Mainly indexes of the contents of the registers, with extracts.]

Hereford.
Thomas Charlton (1327–44). Ed. Capes, W. W. 1912.
John de Trillek (1344–61). Ed. Parry, J. H. 2 pts. 1910, 12.
Lewis Charlton (1361–69). Ed. Parry, J. H. 1913.
William Courtenay (1370–75). Ed. Capes, W. W. 1913.
John Gilbert (1375–89). Ed. Parry, J. H. 1913.
John Trefnant (1389–1404). Ed. Capes, W. W. 2 vols. 1914–15.
Issued jointly by the Cantilupe Society (Hereford) and Canterbury and York Society (London).

Lincoln.
Thompson, A. Hamilton. Registers of John Gynewell, Bishop of Lincoln, for the years 1347–1350. *In* Archaeol. Journ. Vol. LXVIII (*or* 2nd ser., Vol. XVIII). pp. 301–60. London. 1911. [Examines evidence for the effect of the Plague, especially on institutions of clergy. Gynewell was bishop from 1347 to 1362.]

London.
Stephen Gravesend (1319–38). *In* Registrum Radulphi Baldock,...et Stephani Gravesend. Ed. Fowler, R. C. (Cant. and York Soc.) London. 1911.
Simon Sudbury (1362–75). Ed. Fowler, R. C. Vol. I. (*Ibid.*) 1927.

Rochester.
Hamo de Hethe (1319–52). Ed. Johnson, C. (*Ibid.*) 1914 ff., in progress.

Winchester.
William of Wykeham (1366–1404). Ed. Kirby, T. F. 2 vols. (Hampshire Record Soc.) London. 1896, 99.
Chartulary of Winchester Cathedral. Ed., in English, Goodman, A. W. Winchester. 1927. [Contains documents of public interest.]

Worcester.
Sede vacante (1301–1435). Ed. Willis-Bund, J. W. 4 pts. in 5. (Worcs. Hist. Soc.) Oxford. 1893–7.

York.
See Historical Papers and Letters from the Northern Registers. Ed. Raine, J. under II A, *above*.

[For the many important cartularies and registers of religious houses which have been published *see* Gross, C., Sources (*see above*, 1), and the chapters on religious history in the Vict. Co. Hist. *See Gen. Bibl.* I. Cf. *supra*, Vol. VI, p. 894.]
[For Wyclif *see* Bibliography to ch. XVI.]

(viii) *Miscellaneous.*

Black Book of the Admiralty. Ed. Twiss, T. 4 vols. (Rolls.) 1871–6.
Calendar of Letter Books...of the City of London. Letter Books E, F, G, and H (1314–1399). Ed. Sharpe, R. R. London. 1903–7.

Catalogue of Ancient Deeds. 6 vols. (Cal. SP.) London. 1890–1915. [Chancery and Exchequer.]
Charters of the Duchy of Lancaster. Ed. Hardy, W. London. 1845. [*See also* Gross, C., *op. cit.*, pp. 546–8, *see above*, I.]
Expeditions to Prussia and the Holy Land made by Henry, earl of Derby (afterwards king Henry IV), in 1390–1 and 1392–3 : being the accounts kept by his treasurer. Ed. Smith, L. Toulmin. (Camden Soc. n.s. LII.) London. 1894.
John of Gaunt's Register (1371–75). Ed. Armitage-Smith, S. Vols. I, II. (Roy. Hist. Soc., Camden 3rd ser., xx, xxi.) London. 1911. [Vol. III in preparation.]
Lettres de rois, reines, et autres personnages de France et d'Angleterre. Ed. Champollion-Figeac, J. J. Vol. II. (Coll. doc.) Paris. 1847.
Liber regalis seu ordo consecrandi regem solum, etc. (Roxburghe Club.) London. 1870.
Proceedings and Ordinances of the Privy Council of England. Ed. Nicholas, H. Vol. I. (RC.) London. 1834.
Register of Edward the Black Prince. 2 vols. (Cal. SP.) London. 1930–1.
[*See also* P.R.O. Lists and Indexes (set out in Gross, C., *op. cit.*, pp. 81–2, *see above*, I) for Ancient Correspondence (Chancery and Exchequer), Ancient Petitions (Chancery and Exchequer), Court Rolls, Ministers' Accounts, Duchy of Lancaster, Chester, Durham, etc., Lists of Sheriffs for England and Wales.
See also (not included in Gross) P.R.O. List XLIX, 1925 for Papal Bulls.]
[For local records of national importance, *e.g.* Taxation and Subsidy Rolls, and for Deputy Keeper's Reports, *see* Gross, C., *op. cit.*, *see above*, I.]

C. POETICAL WORKS.

Chaucer, G. Works. Ed. Skeat, W. W. 7 vols. Oxford. 1894–7.
Gower, J. Works. Ed. Macaulay, G. C. 4 vols. Oxford. 1899–1902.
Langland, W. Vision of William concerning Piers the Plowman together with Richard the Redeless. Ed. Skeat, W. W. 2 vols. Oxford. 1886.
Minot, Laurence. Poems. Ed. Hall, J. Oxford. 1897.
Political poems and songs relating to English history, from the accession of Edward III to that of Richard III. Ed. Wright, T. 2 vols. (Rolls.) 1859, 61.
Twenty-six political and other poems. Ed. Kail, J. Pt. I. (EETS. Orig. ser. No. 124.) London. 1904.

III. MODERN WORKS.

A. GENERAL.

Coulton, G. G. Chaucer and his England. London. 1908.
—— The Chronicler of European Chivalry. London. 1930.
Davis, H. W. C. *ed.* Mediaeval England. (A new edn. of Barnard's Companion to English History.) Oxford. 1924.
Hughes, D. A study of social and constitutional tendencies in the early years of Edward III. London. 1915.
Humphreys, A. L. Handbook to County Bibliography. London. 1917.
Oman, C. History of England, 1377–1485. (Political History of England. Ed. Hunt, W. and Poole, R. L. Vol. IV.) London. 1918.
Pauli, R. Geschichte von England. *In* Lappenberg, J. M. and Pauli, R. Geschichte. Vols. III–v. Hamburg. 1834–58.
Ramsay, Sir J. H. Genesis of Lancaster, 1307–1399. 2 vols. Oxford. 1913.
Tout, T. F. History of England, 1216–1377. (Political History of England. Ed. Hunt, W. and Poole, R. L. Vol. III.) London. 1920.
Trevelyan, G. M. England in the age of Wycliffe. London. 1899; and reprints.
Vickers, K. H. England in the later Middle Ages. London. 1913.
Victoria County History. *See Gen. Bibl.* I.

B. BIOGRAPHICAL, MILITARY, AND POLITICAL.

Armitage-Smith, S. John of Gaunt. London. 1904.
Barnes, J. History of Edward III. Cambridge. 1688.

Crump, C. G. The arrest of Roger Mortimer and Queen Isabel. EHR. xxvi (1911). 331–2.

Longman, W. The life and times of Edward III. 2 vols. London. 1869.

Lowth, R. Life of William of Wykeham, bishop of Winchester. 3rd edn. Oxford. 1777.

Mackinnon, J. The history of Edward III. London. 1900.

Magrath, J. R. Sir Robert Parvyng, Knight of the Shire for Cumberland, and Chancellor of England. *In* Trans. of the Cumberland and Westmoreland Antiq. and Archaeol. Soc. n.s. xix (1919). 30–91.

Moberly, G. H. Life of William of Wykeham. 2nd edn. London. 1893.

Myres, J. N. L. The Campaign of Radcot Bridge in December 1387. EHR. xlii (1927). 20–33.

Nicholas, N. H. *ed.* An account of the army with which Richard II invaded Scotland in 1385. *In* Archaeologia. xxii. (Soc. of Antiq. of London.) London. 1829. pp. 13–19.

Prince, A. E. The strength of English Armies in the reign of Edward III. EHR. xlvi (1931). 353–71.

Stamp, A. E.; Atkinson, R. L.; Wright, H. G. Richard II and the death of the Duke of Gloucester. EHR. xxxviii (1923). 249–51; 563–4. xlvii (1932).

Walcott, M. E. C. William of Wykeham and his colleges. London. 1852.

Wallon, H. Richard II. 2 vols. Paris. 1864.

C. Constitutional and Administrative.

Adams, G. B. Constitutional History of England. London. 1921.

Baldwin, J. F. The Chancery of the Duchy of Lancaster. *In* Bulletin of the Institute of Hist. Research. iv (1926–7). 129–43.

—— The King's Council in England during the Middle Ages. Oxford. 1913.

Beard, C. A. The Office of Justice of the Peace in England. *In* Columbia University Studies in Hist. Vol. xx. New York. 1904.

Bird, W. H. B. Taxation and representation in the County Palatine of Chester. EHR. xxx (1915). 303.

Bock, F. Bericht über archivalische Arbeiten in England. Neu. Arch. xlviii (1930). 435–40.

—— Some new documents illustrating the early years of the Hundred Years' War (1353–1356). *In* Bulletin of the John Rylands Library. xv (1931). 60.

—— An unknown Register of the reign of Edward III. EHR. xlv (1930). 353–72.

Bolland, W. C. Manual of Year Book Studies. Cambridge. 1925.

Broome, D. M. Exchequer migrations to York in the thirteenth and fourteenth centuries. (Essays in Medieval History presented to T. F. Tout, no. 22.) Manchester. 1925.

Chew, H. M. Scutage in the fourteenth century. EHR. xxxviii (1923). 19–41.

Clarke, M. V. and Galbraith, V. H. The deposition of Richard II. *In* Bulletin of the John Rylands Library. xiv (1930). 125.

Crump, C. G. What became of Robert Rag, or some Chancery blunders. (Essays in Medieval History presented to T. F. Tout, no. 25.) Manchester. 1925.

Dowell, S. History of Taxation and Taxes in England. 2nd edn. 4 vols. London. 1888.

Edwards, J. G. The Parliamentary Committee of 1398. EHR. xl (1925). 321–33.

Ehrlich, L. Proceedings against the Crown (1216–1377). *In* Oxford Studies in Social and Legal History. Ed. Vinogradoff, P. Vol. vi. Oxford. 1921.

Fitzroy, A. The history of the Privy Council. London. 1928.

Galbraith, V. H. Articles laid before the parliament of 1371. EHR. xxxiv (1919). 579–82.

Gibson, S. T. The Escheatries, 1327–41. EHR. xxxvi (1921). 218–25.

Hall, H. History of the Custom-Revenue in England. 2 vols. London. 1885. New edn. in 1 vol. 1892.

Holdsworth, W. S. History of English Law. Vols. i–iii. *See Gen. Bibl.* v.

Jenkinson, H. and Mills, M. H. Rolls from a Sheriff's Office of the fourteenth century. EHR. xliii (1928). 21–32.

Lapsley, G. T. Archbishop Stratford and the parliamentary crisis of 1341. EHR.
xxx (1915). 6–18; 193–215.
—— The County Palatine of Durham. (Harvard Hist. Studies. viii.) New York.
1900.
Levett, A. E. Baronial Councils and their relation to Manorial Courts. *In* Mélanges
d'hist....offerts à Ferdinand Lot. pp. 421–41. Paris. 1925.
Lewis, N. B. Article vii of the impeachment of Michael de la Pole in 1386. EHR.
xlii (1927). 402–7.
—— The "Continual Council' in the early years of Richard II, 1377–80. EHR.
xli (1926). 246–51.
McIlwain, C. H. The High Court of Parliament and its supremacy. New Haven.
1910.
McKisack, M. Borough representation in Richard II's reign. EHR. xxxix (1924).
511–25.
—— The parliamentary representation of King's Lynn before 1500. EHR. xlii
(1927). 583–9.
Maitland, F. W. The Constitutional History of England. Cambridge. 1908.
Maxwell-Lyte, H. C. Historical notes on the use of the Great Seal of England.
London. 1926.
Pasquet, D. Essai sur les origines de la Chambre des Communes. Paris. 1914.
Engl. transl. by Laffan, R. G. D., preface and additional notes by Lapsley, G. T.
Cambridge. 1925.
Petit-Dutaillis, C. (and Lefebvre, G.). Studies and notes supplementary to Stubbs'
Constitutional History. Vols. ii, iii. *See Gen. Bibl.* v *under* Stubbs.
Pike, L. O. Constitutional History of the House of Lords. London. 1894.
Plucknett, T. F. T. Statutes and their interpretation in the first half of the four-
teenth century. (Camb. Studies in English Legal Hist.) Cambridge. 1922.
Pollard, A. F. The Evolution of Parliament. 2nd edn. London. 1926.
Putnam, B. H. The Justices of Labourers in the fourteenth century. EHR. xxi
(1906). 517–38.
—— The transformation of the Keepers of the Peace into the Justices of the Peace,
1327–80. TRHS. 4th ser. Vol. xii (1929). 19–48.
Ramsay, Sir J. H. The Revenues of the Kings of England, 1066–1399. Vol. ii.
Oxford. 1925. [*See* review by Miss M. H. Mills *in* EHR. xli (1926). 429–31.]
Rezneck, S. The early history of the Parliamentary Declaration of Treason. EHR.
xlii (1927). 497–513.
Richardson, H. G. Year Books and Plea Rolls as sources of historical information.
TRHS. 4th ser. Vol. v (1922). 28–70.
—— and Sayles, G. The King's Ministers in Parliament, 1272–1377. EHR. xlvi
(1931). 529–50; xlvii (1932).
—— The Parliaments of Edward III. *In* Bulletin of the Institute of Hist.
Research. viii (1930–1). 65–82; ix (1931–2). 1–18.
Sharp, M. The Administrative Chancery of the Black Prince before 1362.
(Essays in Medieval History presented to T. F. Tout, no. 24.) Manchester.
1925.
Steel, A. B. The distribution of assignment in the Treasurer's Receipt Roll, Michael-
mas, 1364–5. *In* Camb. Hist. Journ. ii (1926–8). 178–85.
—— The marginalia of the Treasurer's Receipt Rolls, 1349–1399. *In* Bulletin of the
Institute of Hist. Research. vii (1929–30). 67–84; 133–43; viii (1930–1). 1–13.
—— The practice of Assignment in the later fourteenth century. EHR. xliii
(1928). 172–80.
—— Some aspects of English Finance in the fourteenth century. *In* History. n.s.
xii (1928). 298–309.
Stubbs, W. Constitutional History of England. Vol. ii. *See Gen. Bibl.* v.
Thornley, I. D. The Act of Treasons, 1352. *In* History. n.s. vi (1922). 106–8.
Tout, T. F. The beginnings of a modern capital.—London and Westminster in the
fourteenth century. *In* Proceedings of the British Acad. xi. 1923.
—— Chapters in the Administrative History of Mediaeval England: The Wardrobe,
the Chamber, and the Small Seals. Vols. iii–vi. Manchester. 1928–32. [Vol. vi
contains bibliographies and indexes.]

Tout, T. F. The English Civil Service in the fourteenth century. *In* Bulletin of the John Rylands Library. III (1916). 185–214.

—— The English Parliament and public opinion, 1376–88. *In* Mélanges d'hist. offerts à Henri Pirenne. pp. 545–62. Brussels. 1926.

—— Some conflicting tendencies in English Administrative History during the fourteenth century. *In* Bulletin of the John Rylands Library. VIII (1924). 82–106.

—— and Broome, D. M. A national balance sheet for 1362–3, with documents subsidiary thereto. EHR. XXXIX (1924). 404–19.

Waugh, W. T. The Great Statute of Praemunire. *In* History. n.s. VIII (1924). 289–92.

Wedgwood, J. C. John of Gaunt and the Packing of Parliament. EHR. XLV (1930). 623–5.

Wilkinson, B. The authorisation of Chancery Writs under Edward III. *In* Bulletin of the John Rylands Library. VIII (1924). 107–39.

—— The Chancery under Edward III. Manchester. 1929. [Contains a useful bibliography.]

—— Letter of Edward III to his Chancellor and Treasurer. EHR. XLII (1927). 248–51.

—— The Protest of the Earls of Arundel and Surrey in the crisis of 1341. EHR. XLVI (1931). 177–93.

—— The Seals of the two benches under Edward III. EHR. XLII (1927). 397–401.

Willard, J. F. The Assessment of Lay Subsidies, 1290–1332. *In* Annual Report of the American Hist. Assoc. for 1917. pp. 281–92. Washington. 1920.

—— The Crown and its creditors. EHR. XLII (1927). 12–19.

—— Edward III's negotiations for a grant in 1337. EHR. XXI (1906). 727–31.

—— The English Church and the lay taxes of the fourteenth century. *In* University of Colorado Studies. IV. pp. 217–35. Boulder, Colorado. 1907.

—— The Memoranda Rolls and the Remembrancers, 1282–1350. (Essays in Medieval History presented to T. F. Tout, no. 17.) Manchester. 1925.

—— Sidelights upon the assessment and collection of the Mediaeval Subsidies. TRHS. 3rd ser. Vol. VII (1913). 167–89.

—— The Scotch Raids and the fourteenth century taxation of northern England. *In* University of Colorado Studies. V. pp. 237–42. Boulder, Colorado. 1908.

—— The taxes upon movables of the reign of Edward III. EHR. XXX (1915). 69–74.

Wood-Legh, K. L. Sheriffs, lawyers, and belted knights in the Parliaments of Edward III. EHR. XLVI (1931). 372–88.

D. ECONOMIC AND SOCIAL.

Beardwood, A. Alien Merchants and the English Crown in the later fourteenth century. *In* Economic History Review. II (1929–30). 229–60.

—— Alien Merchants in England, 1350 to 1377; their legal and economic position. Cambridge, Mass. 1931.

Bennett, H. S. The Reeve and the Manor in the fourteenth century. EHR. XLI (1926). 358–65.

Bird, W. H. B. The Peasants' Rising of 1381: the king's itinerary. EHR. XXXI (1916). 124–6.

Campbell, A. M. The Black Death and Men of Learning. New York. 1931.

Coulton, G. G. The Black Death. London. 1929. [Useful bibliographical note.]

—— Social Life in Britain from the Conquest to the Reformation. Cambridge. 1918.

Creighton, C. History of Epidemics in England. Vol. I. Cambridge. 1891.

Davenport, F. G. The decay of villeinage in East Anglia. TRHS. n.s. Vol. XIV (1900). 123–41.

Gasquet, F. A. The Black Death of 1348–49. London. 1908.

Gras, N. S. B. The early English Customs System. (Harvard Econ. Studies. XVIII.) Cambridge, Mass. 1918.

Gray, H. L. The commutation of Villein Services in England before the Black Death. EHR. XXIX (1914). 625–56.

Gray, H. L. The production and exportation of English Woollens in the fourteenth century. EHR. xxxix (1924). 13–35.

Jusserand, J. J. English Wayfaring Life in the Middle Ages. (14th century.) Transl. by Smith, L. Toulmin. New edn. rev. and enl. London. 1920.

Kriehn, G. Studies in the sources of the social revolt in 1381. AHR. vii (1902). 254–85; 458–84.

Levett, A. E. and Ballard, A. The Black Death on the estates of the see of Winchester. *In* Oxford Studies in Social and Legal History. Ed. Vinogradoff, P. Vol. v. Oxford. 1916.

Miller, F. The Middleburgh Staple, 1383–88. *In* Cambridge Hist. Journ. ii (1926–8). 63–5.

Oman, C. The Great Revolt of 1381. Oxford. 1906. [*See* review by Tait, J. *in* EHR. xxii (1907). 161–4.]

Page, F. M. The Customary Poor-Law of three Cambridgeshire Manors. Cambridge Hist. Journ. iii (1929–31). 125–33.

Page, T. W. The end of Villainage in England. (American Econ. Assoc.) New York. 1900.

—— Die Umwandlung der Frohndienste in Geldrenten. Baltimore. 1897.

Petit-Dutaillis, C. Les causes sociales du soulèvement des travailleurs en 1381. *In* Séances et travaux de l'Acad. des sciences morales et politiques. n.s. xlix (1893). 161–91.

—— Les prédications populaires, les Lollards, et le soulèvement des travailleurs anglais en 1381. *In* Études d'histoire du moyen âge dédiées à Gabriel Monod. pp. 373–88. Paris. 1896.

Petruševski, D. Vozstanie Uota Tailera. [Wat Tyler's Rebellion.] 2 vols. in 1. St Petersburg (Leningrad). 1897–1901. [*See* review by Savine, A. *in* EHR. xvii (1902). 780–2.]

Postan, M. Credit in medieval trade. *In* Economic History Review. i (1927–8). 234–61.

Powell, E. The Rising in East Anglia in 1381: with an appendix containing the Suffolk poll-tax lists for that year. Cambridge. 1896.

Power, E. E. The effects of the Black Death on Rural Organisation in England. *In* History. n.s. iii (1919). 109–16.

Putnam, B. H. The Enforcement of the Statutes of Labourers during the first decade after the Black Death, 1349–59. New York. 1908.

Réville, A. Le soulèvement des travailleurs d'Angleterre en 1381. Études et documents, publiés avec une introduction hist. par C. Petit-Dutaillis. (Soc. de l'École des chartes. Mém. et Documents. ii.) Paris. 1898.

Robo, E. The Black Death in the Hundred of Farnham. EHR. xliv (1929). 560–72.

Salzman, L. F. English Industries of the Middle Ages. New edn. Oxford. 1923.

—— English Trade in the Middle Ages. Oxford. 1931.

Tout, T. F. Literature and learning in the English Civil Service in the fourteenth century. *In* Speculum. iv (1929). 365–89.

Trevelyan, G. M. and Powell, E. The Peasants' Rising and the Lollards [1381–93]: a collection of documents forming an appendix to "England in the age of Wycliffe." London. 1899.

Unwin, G. *ed.* Finance and Trade under Edward III. Manchester. 1918.

E. Ecclesiastical and Religious.

Allen, H. E. Writings ascribed to Richard Rolle, Hermit of Hampole, and materials for his biography. (Mod. Lang. Assoc. of America, Monograph series, iii.) New York and London. 1927.

Capes, W. W. The English Church in the fourteenth and fifteenth centuries. (History of the English Church. Ed. Stephens, W. R. W. and Hunt, W. iii.) London. 1900.

Deeley, A. Papal provision and royal rights of patronage in the early fourteenth century. EHR. xliii (1928). 497–527.

Gairdner, J. Lollardy and the Reformation. Vol. i. London. 1908.

Graham, Rose. English Ecclesiastical Studies. London. 1929. [Nos. iii, v, and ix are relevant to this chapter.]
—— The Great Schism and the English Monasteries of the Cistercian Order. EHR. xliv (1929). 373–87.
Loserth, J. Studien zur Kirchenpolitik Englands im 14 Jahrht. 2 pts. SKAW. cxxxvi and clvi. 1897, 1907.
Maitland, F. W. Roman Canon Law in the Church of England. London. 1898.
Makower, F. The Constitutional History and Constitution of the Church of England. (Transl. from the German.) London. 1895.
Mollat, G. La collation des bénéfices ecclésiastiques à l'époque des papes d'Avignon. (1305–78.) Paris. 1921.
Owst, G. R. Preaching in medieval England. Cambridge. 1926.
Power, E. E. Medieval English Nunneries, 1275–1535. Cambridge. 1922
Richardson, H. G. The Parish Clergy of the thirteenth and fourteenth centuries. TRHS. 3rd ser. Vol. vi (1912). 89–128.
Snape, R. H. English monastic finances in the later Middle Ages. Cambridge. 1926.
Wood-Legh, K. L. The appropriation of Parish Churches during the reign of Edward III. *In* Cambridge Hist. Journ. iii (1929–31). 15–22.

CHAPTER XVI.

WYCLIF.

I. SPECIAL BIBLIOGRAPHIES.

For a view of the historic growth of the Wyclif literature *see* bibliographies in the following encyclopaedia articles:

Loserth, J. Article: Wiclif und der Wiclifismus *in* Herzog-Hauck. Real-Encyklopädie. Vol. XXI. 1908. *See also* Vol. XXIV (Ergänzungen). 1913. *See Gen. Bibl.* I.

—— Article: Wyclif, John, *in* The New Schaff-Herzog Encyclopedia of Religious Knowledge. Vol. XII. New York and London. 1912.

Workman, H. B. Article: Wyclif *in* Encyclopaedia of Religion. Ed. Hastings, J. Vol. XII. 1921. *See Gen. Bibl.* I. [A comprehensive view of the literature is more readily obtained from this bibliography than from the selective one in Workman, H. B. John Wyclif. Vol. I. *See below*, III A.]

Loserth, J. Geschichte des späteren Mittelalters. pp. 389–92. *See Gen. Bibl.* V.

—— Neuere Erscheinungen der Wiclif-Literatur. HZ. LIII (1885). 43–62; LXII (1889). 266–78; XCV (1905). 271–7.

—— Neue Erscheinungen der Wiclif- und Huss-Literatur. HZ. CXVI (1916). 271–82.

Whitney, J. P. A note on the work of the Wyclif Society. *In* Essays in History presented to Reginald Lane Poole. Ed. Davis, H. W. C. Oxford. 1927.

II. ORIGINAL AUTHORITIES.

A. WYCLIF'S WRITINGS.

(i) *Latin.*

(a) *Publications of the Wyclif Society, London* (*except where otherwise stated*).

De Ente sive Summa Intellectualium. Book I.
1. Tractatus de Ente in communi.
2. Tractatus de Ente primo in communi.
   Ed. Thomson, S. H. *in* Summa de Ente. Libri primi tractatus primus et secundus. Oxford. 1930.
3. Tractatus purgans errores circa veritates in communi.
4. Tractatus purgans errores circa universalia in communi.
   Ed. Dziewicki, M. H. *in* De Ente librorum duorum excerpta. 1909.
   [For the missing parts of chapters 2 and 3 *see* Thomson, S. H. A "lost" chapter of Wyclif's Summa de Ente. *In* Speculum. IV (1929). 339–46.]
5. De Universalibus. Edn. by Thomson, S. H. in preparation: *see* his Summa de Ente, p. ix, *op. cit.*
6. Tractatus de Tempore. Edn. by Thomson, S. H. in preparation: *see* his Summa de Ente, p. ix, *op. cit.*
De Ente sive Summa Intellectualium. Book II.
1. Tractatus de Intellectione Dei. Ed. Dziewicki, M. H. *in* De Ente librorum duorum excerpta. 1909.
2. Tractatus de Sciencia Dei. Dr Thomson will print this and the three other unprinted tractates of Book II. *See* his Summa de Ente, p. ix, *op. cit.*
3. Tractatus de Volucione Dei. Ed. Dziewicki, M. H. *in* De Ente librorum duorum excerpta. 1909.
4. Tractatus de Personarum Distinccione sive de Trinitate. Unprinted.

5. Tractatus de Ideis. Unprinted.
6. Tractatus de Potencia productiva Dei ad Extra. Unprinted, except a fragment: De Annihilatione [ch. xii–xiv], ed. Dziewicki, M. H. *in* De Ente librorum duorum excerpta. 1909.
De Ente predicamentali. Ed. Beer, R. 1891. [Beer and Thomson consider this as Part 5 of Book i of De Ente sive Summa Intellectualium, reckoning De Universalibus and Tractatus de Tempore as Parts 6 and 7. *See* Thomson, S. H. A "lost" chapter of Wyclif's Summa de Ente. *In* Speculum. iv (1929). 339–46.]

Summa Theologiae. Books i, ii. Tractatus de Mandatis Divinis. Accedit Tractatus de Statu Innocencie. Ed. Loserth, J. and Matthew, F. D. 1922.
Summa Theologiae. Books iii–v. Tractatus de Civili Dominio. Liber primus. Ed. Poole, R. L. 1885. Liber secundus. Ed. Loserth, J. 1900. Liber tertius. Ed. Loserth, J. 2 vols. 1903–4.
Summa Theologiae. Book vi. De Veritate Sacrae Scripturae. Ed. Buddensieg, R. 3 vols. 1905–7.
Summa Theologiae. Book vii. Tractatus de Ecclesia. Ed. Loserth, J. 1886.
Summa Theologiae. Book viii. Tractatus de Officio Regis. Ed. Pollard, A. W. and Sayle, C. 1887.
Summa Theologiae. Book ix. Tractatus de Potestate Pape. Ed. Loserth, J. 1907.
Summa Theologiae. Book x. Tractatus de Simonia. Ed. Herzberg-Fränkel and Dziewicki, M. H. 1898.
Summa Theologiae. Book xi. Tractatus de Apostasia. Ed. Dziewicki, M. H. 1889.
Summa Theologiae. Book xii. Tractatus de Blasphemia. Ed. Dziewicki, M. H. 1893.

De Compositione Hominis. Ed. Beer, R. 1884.
De Dominio Divino libri tres. Ed. Poole, R. L. 1890. [Includes Richard Fitzralph's De Pauperie Salvatoris, Books i–iv.]
De Eucharistia et Poenitentia sive de Confessione. Ed. Loserth, J. *in* De Eucharistia Tractatus Maior. 1892.
De Eucharistia Tractatus Maior. Accedit Tractatus de Eucharistia et Poenitentia sive de Confessione. Ed. Loserth, J. 1892.
Dialogus sive Speculum Ecclesie Militantis. Ed. Pollard, A. W. 1886.
Differentia inter Peccatum Mortale et Veniale. Ed. Loserth, J. and Matthew, F. D. *in* Tractatus de Mandatis Divinis. 1922.
Logica. Ed. Dziewicki, M. H. *in* Tractatus de Logica. Vol. i. 1893.
Logicae continuacio. Tractatus primus et secundus. *Ibid.*
Logicae continuacio. Tractatus tercius. *Ibid.* Vols. ii, iii. 1896, 99.
Opus Evangelicum. Books i, ii. De Sermone Domini in Monte. Books iii, iv. De Antichristo. Ed. Loserth, J. 2 vols. 1895–6.
Quaestiones xiii Logicae et Philosophicae. [*See* Unauthentic and Contested Writings, *below*, ii a (iii).]
Questio ad Fratres de Sacramento Altaris. Ed. Loserth, J. *in* De Eucharistia Tractatus Maior. 1892.
Tractatus de Benedicta Incarnatione. Ed. Harris, E. 1886.

Miscellanea Philosophica. Ed. Dziewicki, M. H. 2 vols. 1902, 5.
1. De Actibus Animae (in Vol. i).
2. De Materia et Forma (in Vol. i).
    [Of the nine pieces in these volumes these two alone appear to be Wyclif's. *Cf.* Dziewicki's Introductions and Thomson, S. H. Some Latin Works erroneously ascribed to Wyclif. *In* Speculum. iii (1928). 382–91.]

Opera Minora. Ed. Loserth, J. 1913.
1. Missives and letters:
    (*a*) Litera missa pape Urbano VI.
    (*b*) Epistola missa archiepiscopo Cantuariensi.
    (*c*) Epistola missa episcopo Lincolniensi.
    (*d*) Epistola missa ad simplices sacerdotes.

    (e) De Amore sive ad quinque questiones.
    (f) Litera ad quendam Socium.
    (g) De Peccato in Spiritum Sanctum.
    (h) De Octo Questionibus Pulcris.
    (i) De Fratribus ad Scholares.
2. Conclusiones triginta tres sive de Paupertate Christi.
3. Speculum secularium dominorum.
4. De prelatis contencionum sive de incarcerandis fidelibus.
5. De Fide Catholica.
6. De Ordine Christiano.
7. De Gradibus Cleri Ecclesie.
8. De Servitute Civili et Dominio Seculari.
9. De Vaticinacione seu Prophetia.
10. Responsiones ad argumenta Radulfi Strode.
11. Responsiones ad xliv conclusiones sive ad argucias monachales.
12. Responsiones ad argumenta cuiusdam emuli veritatis.
13. Exposicio textus Matthei xxiii sive De Vae Octuplici.
14. Exposicio textus Matthei xxiv sive De Antichristo.
15. De Oracione Dominica.
16. De Salutacione Angelica.
17. Responsio ad decem questiones magistri Ricardi Strode.
18. Determinacio ad argumenta magistri Outredi de Omesima monachi.
19. Determinacio ad argumenta Wilhelmi Vyrinham. [The second part is some-
    times known separately as De Dominio determinacio contra unum monachum.
    See Loserth, J. Die ältesten Streitschriften Wiclifs. SKAW. clx. No. 2.
    1909.]
20. Labora sicut bonus miles Christi. ii Tim. ii. 3.
21. De Graduacionibus sive De Magisterio Christi.

Polemical Works. Ed. Buddensieg, R. 2 vols. 1883. [Contains twenty-six tracts,
    classified as twenty against the sects, six against the Pope. Buddensieg doubts
    the authenticity of De Religione Privata i only. Loserth expresses no doubt in
    his revision of Shirley's Catalogue. *See below,* iii c.]

Vol. i. [Against the sects.]
  1. De Fundatione Sectarum.
  2. De Ordinatione Fratrum sive De Concordatione Fratrum cum secta simplici
     Christi sive De Sectis monachorum.
  3. De Nova Praevaricantia Mandatorum.
  4. De Triplici Vinculo Amoris.
  5. De Septem Donis Spiritus Sancti.
  6. De Quattuor Sectis Novellis.
  7. Purgatorium Sectae Christi.
  8. De Novis Ordinibus.
  9. De Oratione et Ecclesiae Purgatione.
10. De Diabolo et Membris eius.
11. De Detectione Perfidiarum Antichristi.

Vol. ii.
12. De Solutione Satanae.
13. De Mendaciis Fratrum.
14. Descriptio Fratris.
15. De Daemonio Meridiano.
16. De Duobus Generibus Haereticorum.
17. De Religionibus Vanis Monachorum sive de Fundatore Religionis.
18. De Perfectione Statuum.
19. De Religione Privata i.
20. De Religione Privata ii.

    [Against the Pope.]
21. De Citationibus Frivolis.
22. De Dissensione Paparum sive de Schismate.

23. Cruciata.
24. De Christo et suo Adversario Antichristo.
25. De Contrarietate Duorum Dominorum.
26. Quattuor Imprecationes.

Sermones. 4 vols. Ed. Loserth, J. 1887–90.
  I. Super Evangelia Dominicalia.
  II. Super Evangelia de Sanctis.
  III. Super Epistolas.
  IV. Sermones Miscellanei.

(b) *Published otherwise and unpublished.*

[For MSS. of unpublished works *see* Loserth's revision of Shirley's Catalogue, *below*, III c.]

Ad Parliamentum Regis. *In* Fasciculi Zizaniorum. pp. 245–57. *See below*, II B.
Ad quesita regis et concilii. *Ibid.* pp. 258–71.
Bonus et utilis tractatus secundum magistrum Johannem. *See* Stein, I. H. The Wyclif Manuscript in Florence. *In* Speculum. v (1930). 95–7.
Contra Killingham Carmelitam. [Two tracts, one incomplete.] *In* Fasciculi Zizaniorum. pp. 453–76; 477–80. *See below*, II B.
De Captivo Hispanensi sive De filio comitis de Dene. Included as ch. VII *in* De Ecclesia. *See above*, (a). Summa Theologiae. Book VII.
Declarationes. *In* Walsingham, T. Historia Anglicana. Vol. I. pp. 357–63. *See below*, II B.
De Clavibus Ecclesie id est De Potestate Ligandi sive De Clave Celi. Ed. Thomson, S. H. *in* Speculum. III (1928). 251.
De Condemnatione XIX Conclusionum. *In* Appendix to Fasciculi Zizaniorum. pp. 481–92. *See below*, II B.
De Dotatione Ecclesiae sive Supplementum Trialogi. Ed. Lechler, G. V. *in* Trialogus. *See below.*
De Eucharistia conclusiones quindecim. *In* Fasciculi Zizaniorum. pp. 105–6. *See below*, II B.
De Eucharistia Confessio. *Ibid.* pp. 115–32.
De Eucharistia Confessio. Unprinted. [A separate work from preceding.]
De Insolubilibus. Unprinted. Edn. by Thomson, S. H. in preparation.
De Iuramento Arnaldi. *In* Lechler, G. V. Johann von Wiclif. Vol. II. pp. 575–9. *See below*, III A.
De Officio Regis Conclusio. Ed. Thomson, S. H. *in* Speculum. III (1928). 251–3.
De Versuciis Anti-Christi. Ed. Stein, I. H. EHR. XLVII (1932). 95–103.
Errare in Materia Fidei quod potuit Ecclesia militans. Ed. Thomson, S. H. *in* Speculum. III (1928). 248–50.
In omnes Novi Testamenti libros, preter Apocalypsin, Commentarius. Unprinted.
Summa de Ente. Libri primi tractatus primus et secundus. Ed. Thomson, S. H. Oxford. 1930.
Tractatus de Officio Pastorali. Ed. Lechler, G. V. Leipsic. 1863.
Trialogus cum Supplemento Trialogi. Ed. Lechler, G. V. Oxford. 1869.

(ii) *English.*

[Some of these are translations or popularisations of Latin writings.]

Select English Works of John Wyclif. Ed. Arnold, T. 3 vols. Oxford. 1869–71. [Mostly sermons; some authentic and some unauthentic tracts.]
The English Works of Wyclif hitherto unprinted. Ed. Matthew, F. D. (EETS. Orig. ser. No. 74.) London. 1880. [Contains a valuable biographical introduction. For a discussion of the genuineness of contents, *see* Jones, E. D. The authenticity of some English works ascribed to Wycliffe (*below*, III c). A great part is of doubtful authenticity.]
The holi prophete Dauid seith. Printed by Deanesly, M. *in* The Lollard Bible. pp. 445–56. *See below*, III B.
Wyclif: Select English Writings. Ed. Winn, H. E. Oxford. 1929. [A source book.]

(iii) *Unauthentic and contested writings, Latin and English.*

Antichrist and his Meynee. Ed. Todd, J. H. *in* Three Treatises by John Wycklyffe D.D. Dublin. 1851.

An Apology for Lollard Doctrines. Ed. Todd, J. H. (Camden Soc. xx.) London. 1842.

De Imaginibus. Unprinted. [*See* Loserth's revision of Shirley's Catalogue. p. 8 (*below,* III c).]

De Necessitate Futurorum. Unprinted. [*See* Loserth, J. Die ältesten Streitschriften Wiclifs. SKAW. CLX. No. 2. 1909.]

De Triplici Ecclesia. Ed. Thomson, S. H. *in* Speculum. III (1928). 387–91.

The Holy Bible...with the Apocryphal Books in the earliest English Versions made ...by John Wycliffe and his followers. Ed. Forshall, J. and Madden, Sir F. 4 vols. Oxford. 1850.

The Last Age of the Church. Ed. Todd, J. H. Dublin. 1840.

Quaestiones XIII Logicae et Philosophicae. Ed. Beer, R. *in* De Ente predicamentali. (Wyclif Society.) London. 1891. [*See* Thomson, S. H. *in* Speculum. III (1928). 385–7.]

Super Cantica Canticorum. Unprinted. [*See* Loserth, J. Die ältesten Streitschriften Wiclifs. SKAW. CLX. No. 2. 1909.]

A Treatise against the orders of Friars. [Probably by Purvey.] Ed. James, T. *in* Two Short Treatises against the Orders of the Begging Friars. Oxford. 1608.

Wycklyffes Wycket: whych he made in Kyng Rychards Days the Second. Nuremberg [?]. 1546. Reprinted Oxford. 1828.

B. NARRATIVE SOURCES FOR WYCLIF'S LIFE.

[*See also* Narrative Sources for ch. xv, *above.*]

Anonimalle Chronicle, The. Ed. Galbraith, V. H. Manchester. 1927.

Bale, J. Illustrium majoris Britanniae Scriptorum Summarium. Ipswich. 1548. Another version publ. *as* Index Britanniae Scriptorum. Ed. Poole, R. L. and Bateson, M. Oxford. 1902.

Capgrave, J. Chronicle of England. Ed. Hingeston, F. C. (Rolls.) 1858.

Chronicon Angliae. Ed. Thompson, E. M. (Rolls.) 1874.

Eulogium historiarum sive temporis. Ed. Haydon, F. S. Vol. III. (Rolls.) 1863.

Fasciculi Zizaniorum, ascribed to Thomas Netter of Walden. Ed. Shirley, W. W. (Rolls.) 1858.

Higden, R. Polychronicon. Ed. Lumby, J. R. Vols. VIII, IX. (Rolls.) 1882, 86.

Knighton, H. Chronicon. Ed. Lumby, J. R. Vol. II. (Rolls.) 1895.

Leland, J. Commentarii de Scriptoribus Britannicis. Ed. Hall, A. Oxford. 1709.

—— De rebus Britannicis. Collectanea. Ed. Hearne, T. 6 vols. London. 1770.

—— The Itinerary of John Leland. Ed. Smith, L. Toulmin. 4 vols. London. 1907–10.

Walsingham, T. Historia Anglicana. Ed. Riley, H. T. 2 vols. (Rolls.) 1863–4.

—— Ypodigma Neustriae. Ed. Riley, H. T. (Rolls.) 1876.

C. RECORD AND LEGAL SOURCES FOR WYCLIF'S LIFE.

[*See also* Record Sources for ch. xv, *above.*]

Articuli Johannis Wiclefi Angli, impugnati a Wilhelmo Wodfordo. *In* Brown, E. Fasciculus Rerum Expetendarum et Fugiendarum. Vol. I. London. 1690.

Articuli Johannis Wiclefi Angli, damnati per Concilium Constantiense. *Ibid.*

Rationes et Motiva, ac Reprobationes Articulorum Wiclefi, et sequacis ipsius Johannis Hus, in Concilio Constantiensi damnatorum. *Ibid.*

Sententia Damnationis Doctrinae Johannis Wiclefi, et articulorum quadraginta-quinque lata per sacrosanctam synodum Constantiensem. *Ibid.*

Calendar of Close Rolls. Edw. III (14 vols.). Rich. II (6 vols.). (Cal. SP.) London. 1896–1927.

Calendar of entries in the Papal Registers relating to Great Britain and Ireland. Papal Letters *and* Petitions to the Pope. *See Gen. Bibl.* IV *under* Papal Documents.

Calendar of Patent Rolls. Edw. III (16 vols.). Rich. II (6 vols.). (Cal. SP.) London. 1891–1926.

Foxe, J. The Acts and Monuments. Ed. Pratt, J. Vols. II and III. London.
 [1877 ff.] [Valuable collection of documents in vol. II. Appendix and addenda.]
Historical MSS. Commission. London. 1874–83.
 2nd Report. pp. 141–2. (Queen's College, Oxford.)
 4th Report. pp. 447–8. (Balliol College, Oxford.)
 6th Report. p. 547. (Merton College, Oxford.)
 8th Report. pp. 324 and 342. (Dean and Chapter of Canterbury.)
 9th Report. p. 89. (*Idem.*)
Issues of the Exchequer. Ed. Devon, F. (RC.) London. 1837.
Literae Cantuarienses. Ed. Sheppard, J. B. Vol. II. (Rolls.) 1888.
Lyndwood, W. Provinciale. Oxford. 1679.
Mediaeval Archives of the University of Oxford. Ed. Salter, H. E. 2 vols. (Oxford
 Hist. Soc. LXX, LXXIII.) Oxford. 1920–1.
Merton Muniments. Ed. Allen, P. S. and Garrod, H. W. (*Ibid.* LXXXVI.) Oxford.
 1928.
Oxford City Documents. Ed. Rogers, J. E. T. (*Ibid.* XVIII.) Oxford. 1891.
Raynaldus, O. Annales Ecclesiastici. Vol. VII. 1752. *See Gen. Bibl.* IV *under*
 Baronius.
Rotuli Parliamentorum. [Ed. Strachey, J. and others.] Vols. II, III. [London.
 1767.] Index. (RC.) London. 1832.
Rymer, T. Foedera. Vols. II pt. 2, III, IV. *See Gen. Bibl.* IV.
Snappe's Formulary and other Records. Ed. Salter, H. E. (Oxford Hist. Soc. LXXX.)
 Oxford. 1924.
Wilkins, D. Concilia Magnae Britanniae et Hiberniae. Vol. III. *See Gen. Bibl.* IV.

III. MODERN WORKS.

A. BIOGRAPHICAL.

Böhringer, F. Johannes von Wykliffe. *In* Die Vorreformatoren des 14 und 15
 Jahrhts. Zürich. 1856.
Buddensieg, R. Johann Wiclif und seine Zeit. Gotha. 1885.
Burrows, M. Wiclif's place in History: three lectures. London. 1882.
Cronin, H. S. John Wycliffe, the Reformer, and Canterbury Hall, Oxford. TRHS.
 3rd ser. Vol. VIII (1914). 55–76.
—— Wycliffe's canonry at Lincoln. EHR. XXXV (1920). 564–9.
Lechler, G. V. Johann von Wiclif und die Vorgeschichte der Reformation. 2 vols.
 Leipsic. 1873. Transl. and abridged by Lorimer, P. John Wycliffe and his
 English precursors. London. [1884.]
Lewis, J. History of the life and sufferings of...John Wicliffe. London. 1720.
 Rev. edn. Oxford. 1820.
Loserth, J. The beginnings of Wyclif's activity in ecclesiastical politics. EHR.
 XI (1896). 319–28.
—— Studien zur Kirchenpolitik Englands im XIV Jahrht. i. Bis zum Ausbruch des
 grossen Schismas (1378). SKAW. CXXXVI. No. 1. 1897. ii. Die Genesis von
 Wiclifs Summa Theologiae und seine Lehre vom wahren und falschen Papsttum.
 SKAW. CLVI. No. 6. 1908.
Manning, B. L. Wyclif and the House of Herod. *In* Cambridge Hist. Journ.
 II (1926). 66–7.
Matthew, F. D. The date of Wyclif's attack on Transubstantiation. EHR. V (1890).
 328–30.
Poole, R. L. Wycliffe and movements for reform. London. 1911.
Rashdall, H. Article: Wycliffe, John, *in* DNB.
Salter, H. E. John Wyclif, Canon of Lincoln. EHR. XXXV (1920). 98.
Sergeant, L. John Wyclif. (Heroes of the Nations.) New York. 1892.
Twemlow, J. A. Wycliffe's Preferments and University Degrees. EHR. XV (1900).
 529–30.
Vattier, V. John Wyclyff: sa vie, ses oeuvres, sa doctrine. Paris. 1886.
Vaughan, R. John de Wycliffe, D.D. London. 1853.
Whitney, J. P. Religious Movements in the fourteenth century [Rolle and Wyclif].
 In Camb. Hist. of English Literature. Vol. II, ch. II. Cambridge. 1908.

Wilkins, H. J. Was John Wycliffe a negligent pluralist? *Also* John de Trevisa. London. 1915. Appendix. Bristol. 1916.
—— Westbury College. Bristol. 1917.
Workman, H. B. The dawn of the Reformation. Vol. I. The Age of Wyclif. London. 1901.
—— John Wyclif: a study of the English Medieval Church. 2 vols. Oxford. 1926.

B. STUDIES ON SPECIAL ASPECTS OF WYCLIF'S WORK AND TEACHING.

Cannon, H. L. The Poor Priests, a study in the rise of English Lollardry. *In* American Hist. Assoc. Annual Report. I (1899). 449–82.
Deanesly, M. The Lollard Bible and other medieval biblical versions. Cambridge. 1920.
Förster, E. Wiklif als Bibelübersetzer. ZKG. XII (1891). 495–518.
Fürstenau, H. Johann von Wiclifs Lehren von der Einteilung der Kirche und von der Stellung der weltlichen Gewalt. Berlin. 1900.
Heine, D. Wiclifs Lehre vom Güterbesitz. Gütersloh. 1903.
Lewald, E. A. Die theologische Doctrin Johann Wycliffe's nach den Quellen dar-gestellt und kritisch beleuchtet. *In* Zeitschr. für hist. Theologie. 1846–7.
Lindsay, J. Studies in European philosophy. Edinburgh. 1909.
Loserth, J. Die ältesten Streitschriften Wiclifs. Studien über die Anfänge der kirchenpolitischen Tätigkeit Wiclifs und die Überlieferung seiner Schriften. SKAW. CLX. No. 2. 1909.
—— Hus und Wiclif. 2nd rev. edn. Munich. 1925. English transl. of 1st edn. Evans, M. J. London. 1884.
—— Johann von Wiclif und Guilelmus Peraldus. Studien zur Geschichte der Entstehung von Wiclifs Summa Theologiae. SKAW. CLXXX. No. 3. 1917.
—— Johann von Wiclif und Robert Grosseteste, Bischof von Lincoln. SKAW. CLXXXVI. No. 2. 1921.
—— Wiclifs Lehre vom wahren und falschen Papsttum. HZ. XCIX (1907). 237–55.
Maitland, F. W. Wyclif on English and Roman Law. *In* Collected Papers. Vol. III, pp. 50–3. Cambridge. 1911.
Matthew, F. D. The authorship of the Wycliffite Bible. EHR. x (1895). 91–9.
Odložilík, O. Wycliffe's influence upon Central and Eastern Europe. *In* Slavonic Review. VII (1928–9). 634–48. [Bibliographical note at end.]
Poole, R. L. Illustrations of the history of Medieval Thought and Learning. (Ch. x. Wycliffe's Doctrine of Dominion.) *See Gen. Bibl.* v.
Thomson, S. H. The philosophical basis of Wyclif's Theology. *In* The Journal of Religion. XI (1931). 86–116.
Wiegand, F. De Ecclesiae Notione quid Wiclif docuerit. Leipsic. 1891.

C. ON THE WYCLIF CANON.

Jones, E. D. The authenticity of some English works ascribed to Wycliffe. *In* Anglia. XXX. Halle-a.-S. 1907. pp. 261–8.
Loserth, J. Das vermeintliche Schreiben Wiclif's an Urban VI und einige verlorene Flugschriften Wiclif's aus seinen letzten Lebenstage. HZ. LXXV (1895). 476–80.
—— Wiclif's Sendschreiben, Flugschriften, und kleinere Werke kirchenpolitischen Inhalts. SKAW. CLXVI. No. 6. 1910.
—— Zur Kritik der Wyclif-Handschriften. *In* Zeitschr. des deutschen Vereins für die Gesch. Mährens und Schlesiens. XX. pp. 247–57.
Shirley, W. W. Catalogue of the Original Works of John Wyclif. Oxford. 1865. Rev. edn. by Loserth, J. (Wyclif Society.) London. [1924.]
Stein, I. H. Two notes on Wyclif. *In* Speculum. VI (1931). 465–8.
—— The Wyclif Manuscript in Florence. *In* Speculum. V (1930). 95–7.
Tanner, T. Bibliotheca Britannico-Hibernica sive de scriptoribus, etc. Ed. Wilkins, D. London. 1748.
Thomson, S. H. A "lost" chapter of Wyclif's Summa de Ente. *In* Speculum. IV (1929). 339–46.

Thomson, S. H. The order of writing of Wyclif's Philosophical Works. *In* Českou Minulosti. [Festschrift to V. Novotný.] Prague. 1929. pp. 146–66.
—— Some Latin Works erroneously ascribed to Wyclif. *In* Speculum. III (1928). 382–91.
—— Three unprinted Opuscula of John Wyclif. *In* Speculum. III (1928). 248–53.
Wells, J. E. Manual of the Writings in Middle English. Yale. 1920.

D. PHILOLOGICAL.

Carr, J. W. Ueber das Verhältnis der Wiclifitischen und der Purvey'schen Bibelübersetzung zur Vulgata und zu Einander. Hampstead, N. H. (U.S.A.). *n.d.* [Leipsic diss.]
Fischer, H. Ueber die Sprache John Wycliffs. Halle. 1880.
Gasner, E. Beiträge zum Entwicklungsgang der neuenglischen Schriftsprache auf Grund der mittelenglischen Bibelübersetzung, wie sie auf Wycliffe und Purvey zurückgehen soll. Göttingen. 1891. [diss.]
Ortmann, F. J. Formen und Syntax des Verbs bei Wycliffe und Purvey. Berlin. 1902. [Bibliography.]
Skeat, W. W. On the dialect of Wycliffe's Bible. *In* Trans. of the Philol. Soc., Lond. (1895–8.) 212–19.
Smith, H. Syntax der Wycliffe-Purveyschen Uebersetzung und der "Authorised Version" der vier Evangelien. Marburg. 1907.
Thamm, G. A. W. Das Relativpronomen in der Bibelübersetzung Wyclifs und Purveys. Berlin. 1908. [Bibliography.]
[*See also* for useful summary, Workman, H. B. John Wyclif. Vol. I. Appendices c and D (*above*, III A).]

E. GENERAL AND MISCELLANEOUS.

Brodrick, G. C. Memorials of Merton College. (Oxford Hist. Soc. IV) Oxford. 1885.
Ehrle, F. Der Sentenzenkommentar Peters von Candia, des Pisaner Papstes Alexanders V. Ein Beitrag zur Scheidung der Schulen in der Scholastik des 14 Jahrhts. und zur Geschichte des Wegestreites. Münster-i.-W. 1925.
Harnack, A. Lehrbuch der Dogmengeschichte. *See Gen. Bibl.* v.
Jensen, O. The "Denarius Sancti Petri" in England. TRHS. n.s. Vols. xv (1901). 171–247; xix (1905). 209–77.
Laun, J. F. Thomas von Bradwardin, der Schüler Augustins und Lehrer Wiclifs. ZKG. xlvii (1928). 333–56.
Lechler, G. V. De Thoma Bradwardino Commentatio. Leipsic. 1862.
Little, A. G. Studies in English Franciscan history. Manchester. 1917.
—— The Grey Friars in Oxford. (Oxford Hist. Soc. xx.) Oxford. 1892.
Magrath, J. R. The Queen's College. 2 vols. Oxford. 1921.
Manning, B. L. The People's Faith in the time of Wyclif. Cambridge. 1919.
Pantin, W. A. A Benedictine opponent of John Wyclif. EHR. xliii (1928). 73–7.
Thomas Waldensis. Doctrinale Antiquitatum Fidei Catholicae Ecclesiae. Ed. Blanciotti, F. B. 3 vols. Venice. 1757–9.
Thompson, A. Hamilton. Notes on the Ecclesiastical History of the Parish of Henbury. *In* Bristol and Gloucestershire Archaeol. Soc. Trans. xxxviii (1915). 99–186.
Troeltsch, E. Die Soziallehren der christlichen Kirchen und Gruppen. Tübingen. 1923.
Victoria History of the Counties of England. *See Gen. Bibl.* I.
Wood, Anthony à. Fasti Oxonienses. Ed. Gutch, J. Oxford. 1790. [This is vol. II of History and Antiquities of the Colleges and Halls. *See below.*]
—— Historia et antiquitates Universitatis Oxoniensis. Oxford. 1674.
—— The History and Antiquities of the Colleges and Halls in the University of Oxford. Ed. Gutch, J. 2 vols. Oxford. 1786, 90.
—— Survey of the Antiquities of the City of Oxford. Ed. Clark, A. 3 vols. (Oxford Hist. Soc. xv, xvii, xxxvii.) Oxford. 1889–99.

CHAPTER XVII.

WALES, 1066 TO 1485.

I. SPECIAL BIBLIOGRAPHIES.

Bibliography of the History of Wales. Ed. for the Guild of Graduates of the University of Wales by Jenkins, R. T. and Rees, W. Cardiff. 1931.
Lloyd, J. E. Brief Bibliography of Welsh History. (Historical Association Leaflet no. 49.) London. 1921.
Phillips, D. R. Select Bibliography of Owen Glyndwr. (Welsh Bibliog. Soc.) Swansea. 1915.
[See also the Reports on Welsh MSS. of the Historical MSS. Commission. 2 vols. in 7 pts. London. 1898–1910; and Owen, E. Catalogue of MSS. relating to Wales in the British Museum (Cymmrodorion Record Series). London. 1900 ff., in progress.]

II. ORIGINAL AUTHORITIES.

(i) From 1066 to 1282.

Annales Cambriae. Ed. Williams ab Ithel, J. (Rolls.) 1860.
Brut y Tywysogion ; or, the Chronicle of the Princes. Ed. with Engl. transl. Williams ab Ithel, J. (Rolls.) 1860.
Buchedd Gruffydd ap Cynan (Life of Gruffydd ap Cynan). Ed. with Engl. transl. Jones, A. Manchester. 1910.
Calendar of Welsh Rolls, 1277–94. In Calendar of various Chancery Rolls. (Cal.SP.) London. 1912.
Giraldus Cambrensis. Opera. Ed. Brewer, J. S. and others. 8 vols. (Rolls.) 1861–91. [Vol. vi contains the Itinerary and the Description of Wales. Transl. in Historical works of Giraldus Cambrensis. Ed. Wright, T. (Bohn's Antiq. Hist. Library.) London. 1863.]
—— De Invectionibus. Ed. Davies, W. S. in Cymmrodor. Vol. xxx. London. 1920.
Haddan, A. W. and Stubbs, W. Councils and Ecclesiastical Documents. Vol. i, sect. iii. See Gen. Bibl. iv.
Liber Landavensis. The Text of the Book of Llan Dâv. Ed. Evans, J. G. and Rhys, J. Oxford. 1893. [Best edn.]
Map, Walter. De Nugis Curialium. Ed. James, M. R. (Anecdota Oxoniensia, Mediaeval Series, xiv.) Oxford. 1914. [Best edn.] Transl. James, M. R., with notes by Hartland, E. S. and Lloyd, J. E. (Hon. Soc. of Cymmrodorion.) London. 1923.
Myvyrian Archaiology of Wales. Ed. Jones, O. and others. 3 vols. London. 1801–7. 2nd edition. Denbigh. 1870. [Largely superseded by later works, but still needed for the text of the early poetry (separately issued as The Poetry of the Gogynfeirdd, ed. Anwyl, E. Denbigh. 1909) and some other sources.]
Welsh Laws. Ancient Laws and Institutes of Wales. Ed. Owen, A. 2 vols. 8vo, or 1 vol. fol. (RC.) London. 1841. [Supersedes for most purposes Cyfreithieu Hywel Dda ac Eraill. Ed. Wotton, W. London. 1730.]
    Particular MSS. have been edited as follows :
    Harleian MS. 4353. Ed. and transl. Wade-Evans, A. W. as Welsh Medieval Law. Oxford. 1909.
    Llanstephan MS. 116. Ed. Lewis, T. as The Laws of Howel Dda. (Univ. of Wales. Welsh texts, no. 1.) London. 1912.

[For general authorities on English history containing references to Wales, see Lloyd, J.E. History of Wales, index of authors, etc., cited in the notes. See below, iii a.]

(ii) *From* 1282 *to* 1485.

(a) *Chronicles.*

Adam of Usk. Chronicon (1377–1421). Ed. Thompson, E. M. 2nd edn. London. 1904.
Annals of Owain Glyn Dŵr (Welsh). Printed, from Panton MS. 22, in Hist. MSS. Commission, Report on Welsh MSS. Vol. II. pp. 830–1. London. 1905.
Brut y Tywysogion (*see above,* (i)). Continuation in Peniarth MS. 20 from 1282 to 1332. Welsh text printed in Report on Welsh MSS. Vol. I. pp. 342–6. London. 1898.

(b) *Records.*

The bulk of the material at the Public Record Office (*see,* especially, no. XL of Lists and Indexes. London. 1914) and elsewhere has not yet been made available for general use, but the following are in print:

Black Book of St David's. Ed. Willis-Bund, J. W. (Hon. Soc. of Cymmrodorion.) London. 1902. [An extent of the lands of the bishopric in 1326.]
Cartae et Alia Munimenta quae ad dominium de Glamorgancia pertinent. Ed. Clark, G. T. 4 vols. Dowlais and Cardiff. 1885–93. Re-issued in 6 vols. Cardiff. 1910.
Cartularium S. Johannis Bapt. [*recte* Evang.] de Caermarthen. (Privately printed for Sir Thomas Phillipps.) Cheltenham. 1865.
Episcopal Registers of the Diocese of St David's, 1397–1518. 3 vols. (Hon. Soc. of Cymmrodorion.) London. 1917–20.
Flint Pleas, 1283–5. Ed. Edwards, J. G. (Flintshire Hist. Soc.) Chester. 1921. [Introdn., text, and transl.]
Flintshire Ministers' Accounts, 1301–28. Ed. Jones, A. (Flintshire Hist. Soc.) Prestatyn. 1913. [Introdn. and Engl. transl. only.]
Registrum vulgariter nuncupatum The Record of Caernarvon. Ed. Ellis, Sir H. (RC.) London. 1838.
Ruthin Court Rolls of the reign of Edward I. Ed. Roberts, R. A. (Hon. Soc. of Cymmrodorion). London. 1893.
Survey of the Honour of Denbigh, 1334. Ed. Vinogradoff, P. and Morgan, F. (British Acad., Records of the Social and Econ. Hist. of England and Wales, I.) London. 1914.

[Many original documents have from time to time been printed in Archaeologia Cambrensis; Bulletin of the Board of Celtic Studies; Byegones (Oswestry); Cymmrodor; Montgomeryshire Collections; and Transactions of the Hon. Soc. of Cymmrodorion.]

III. MODERN WORKS.

A. GENERAL.

Edwards, O. M. Wales. (Story of the Nations.) London. 1901.
Lloyd, J. E. History of Wales to the Edwardian Conquest. 2nd edn. 2 vols. London. 1912.
Powel, David. The Historie of Cambria. London. 1584; repr. 1811. Ed. Wynne, W. London. 1697. 8th edn. 1832.
Price, T. (Carnhuanawc). Hanes Cymru. Crickhowel. 1842.
Rhys J. and Jones, D. B. The Welsh People. London. 1900.
Warrington, W. History of Wales. 3rd edn. 2 vols. London. 1791.
Woodward, B. B. History of Wales. 2nd edn. 2 vols. London. [1856.]

B. SPECIAL.

(i) *From* 1066 *to* 1282.

Bridgeman, G. T. O. History of the Princes of South Wales. Wigan. 1876.
Lloyd, J. E. The Welsh Chronicles. (Proc. Brit. Acad. XIV.) London. [1929.]
Newell, E. J. History of the Welsh Church. London. 1895.
Owen, H. Gerald the Welshman. London. 1889.
Powicke, F. M. Gerald of Wales. (Repr. from Bull. John Rylands Library.) Manchester. 1928.

(ii) *From* 1282 *to* 1485.

Bradley, A. G. Owen Glyndwr. New York and London. 1901.

Clark, G. T. The Land of Morgan. (Cambrian Archaeol. Assoc.) London. 1883.

Davies, J. C. The Despenser War in Glamorgan. TRHS. 3rd ser. ix (1915). 21–64.

Edwards, J. G. The site of the battle of "Meismeidoc," 1295. EHR. xlvi (1931). 262–5.

Evans, H. T. Wales and the Wars of the Roses. Cambridge. 1915.

Jones, M. C. The Feudal Barons of Powys. (Repr. from Montgomeryshire Collections.) London. 1868.

Lewis, E. A. The Mediaeval Boroughs of Snowdonia. (Univ. of Wales Lit. and Hist. Studies, no. 1.) London. 1912.

Lloyd, J. E. Owen Glendower (Owen Glyn Dŵr). Oxford. 1931.

Lloyd, J. Y. W. The History...of Powys Fadog. 6 vols. London. 1881–7. [A collection of pedigrees and other material of varying value.]

Matthews, T. Welsh Records in Paris. Carmarthen. 1910. [Mostly connected with the rising of Glyn Dŵr.]

Morris, J. E. The Welsh Wars of Edward I. Oxford. 1901.

Owen, E. Owain Lawgoch—Yeuain de Galles. *In* Trans. Hon. Soc. of Cymmrodorion, 1899–1900. London. 1901. pp. 6–105.

Pennant, T. Of Owen Glyndwr, being appendix no. vii to 1810 edition (London) of Tours in Wales (vol. iii. pp. 310–92). [Originally appeared in text of First Part, pp. 302–69. London. 1778.]

Rees, W. South Wales and the March, 1284–1415. A social and agrarian study. Oxford. 1924.

Williams, Ifor. Dafydd ap Gwilym a'r Glêr. *In* Trans. Hon. Soc. of Cymmrodorion, 1913–14. London. 1915. pp. 83–204.

Wynne, Sir John [1553–1626]. History of the Gwydir Family. Oswestry, 1878. New edn. by Ballinger, J. Cardiff. 1927. [Valuable for social conditions in the late fifteenth century.]

CHAPTER XVIII.

IRELAND TO 1315.

I. BIBLIOGRAPHIES.

Abbott, T. K. and Gwynn, E. Catalogue of Irish MSS. in Trinity College, Dublin. Dublin. 1921.

Best, R. I. Bibliography of Irish philology and Irish printed literature. Dublin. 1913.

Catalogue of Irish MSS. in the British Museum. Vol. i, by O'Grady, S. H. [London. 1892.] Vol. ii, by Flower, R. London. 1926. Vol. iii, in progress.

Kenney, J. F. The sources for the early history of Ireland: an introduction and guide. Vol. i (Ecclesiastical). (Columbia Univ. Records of Civilization.) New York. 1929, in progress.

Maxwell, Constantia. Short Bibliography of Irish History (Historical Association leaflet No. 23, revised). London. 1921.

Murray, R. H. The Public Record Office, Dublin. (Helps for Students of History, No. 7.) S.P.C.K. London. 1919.

Nicolson, William, Bp of Derry. The Irish Historical Library, pointing at most of the authors and records in print or manuscript which may be serviceable to the compilers of a general history of Ireland. Dublin. 1724.

O'Curry, E. Lectures on the manuscript materials of ancient Irish history. Dublin. 1861. [A pioneer study of Irish narrative MSS., useful, but lacking in critical judgment.]

Wood, H. Guide to the records deposited in the Public Record Office of Ireland. Dublin. 1919. [Now unhappily a guide to a cenotaph!]

II. ORIGINAL AUTHORITIES.

A. PRE-NORMAN PERIOD.

Adamnan. Life of St Columba. Ed. Reeves, W. (Irish Archaeol. and Celtic Soc.) Dublin. 1857. *Also* ed. Fowler, J. T. Oxford. 1894.

Ancient Irish Law. The law of Status or Franchise. By MacNeill, E. *In* Proc. Roy. Irish Acad. xxxvi (c), pp. 265–316. Dublin. 1923.

Ancient Laws of Ireland. [Ed. Hancock, W. N. and others.] 6 vols. Dublin. 1865–1901.

Anglo-Saxon Chronicle. Ed. with transl. Thorpe, B. 2 vols. (Rolls.) 1861. *Also* Two of the Saxon Chronicles, parallel. Ed. Plummer, C. 2 vols. Oxford. 1892, 99.

Annala Locha Cé (1014–1590). Ed. with transl. Hennessy, W. M. 2 vols. (Rolls.) 1871.

Annala Rioghachta Eireann. (Annals of the kingdom of Ireland by the Four Masters to 1616.) Ed. with transl. O'Donovan, J. 7 vols. Dublin. 1851.

Annala Uladh (Annals of Ulster) (431–1541). Ed. with transl. Hennessy, W. M. (and MacCarthy, B.). 4 vols. Dublin. 1887–1901.

Annales Cambriae (447–1288). Ed. Williams ab Ithel, J. (Rolls.) 1860.

Annals of Clonmacnoise (to 1408), transl. from the Irish by Conell Mageoghegan. Ed. Murphy, D. (Roy. Soc. Antiq., Ireland.) Dublin. 1896.

Annals of Ireland. Three Fragments (573–913) copied from ancient sources by Dubhaltach MacFirbisigh. Ed. with transl. O'Donovan, J. (Irish Archaeol. and Celtic Soc.) Dublin. 1860.

Annals of Tigernach (including continuation to 1178). Ed. with transl. Stokes, W. *in* Revue Celtique. xvi–xviii. Paris. 1895–7.

Brut y Tywysogion; or, the Chronicle of the Princes (681–1282). Ed. with transl. Williams ab Ithel, J. (Rolls.) 1860.

Caithreim Cellachain Caisil. Ed. with transl. Bugge, A. Christiania (Oslo). 1905.

Chronicum Scotorum (to 1135). Ed. with transl. Hennessy, W. M. (Rolls.) 1866.

The Circuit of Ireland by Muircheartach MacNeill in 941. Ed. with transl. O'Donovan, J. (Irish Archaeol. Soc.) Dublin. 1841. [A contemporary Irish poem.]

Cogadh Gaedhel re Gallaibh. Ed. with transl. Todd, J. H. (Rolls.) 1867.

Ionas. Vitae S. Columbani, Vedastis, Johannis. Ed. Krusch, B. SGUS. 1905.

Leabhar na g-Ceart (Book of Rights). Ed. with transl. O'Donovan, J. (Celtic Society.) Dublin. 1847.

Liber Ardmachanus. Ed. Gwynn, J. (Royal Irish Acad.) Dublin. 1913. [Contains the oldest Patrician documents, etc. with valuable introductions.]

O'Dubhagain, J. and O'Huidhrin, G. na N. Topographical poems. Ed. with transl. O'Donovan, J. (Irish Archaeol. Soc.) Dublin. 1862.

Veterum Epistolarum Hibernicarum Sylloge. Ed. Ussher, J. *In* Works. Vol. IV. Ed. Elrington, C. R. Dublin. 1847.

B. From 1169 to 1315.

(i) *Calendars of Records and Collections of Deeds and Documents.*

The Black Book of Limerick. Ed. MacCaffrey, J. Dublin. 1907.

Calendar of Ancient Records of Dublin. Vol. I. Ed. Gilbert, J. T. Dublin. 1889.

Calendar of Christ Church Deeds. Ed. McEnery, M. J. in appendices to 20th, 23rd, 24th, and 27th Reports of the Deputy Keeper of the Public Records of Ireland. Dublin. 1888-96. [Originals destroyed as below.]

Calendar of Documents relating to Ireland (1171-1307). Ed. Sweetman, H. S. 5 vols. (Cal.SP.) London. 1875-86. [Contains abstracts of most of the entries relating to Ireland in the records preserved in the P.R.O., London, for the above period; but the published transcripts and Calendars of the English Patent, Close, Charter, Fine, and Pipe Rolls and, in cases of doubt, the originals themselves should be consulted.]

Calendar of entries in the Papal Registers relating to Great Britain and Ireland. Ed. Bliss, W. H. and others. *See Gen. Bibl.* IV *under* Papal Documents.

Calendar of the Gormanston Register. Ed. Mills, J. and McEnery, M. J. Dublin. 1916.

Calendar of Justiciary Rolls, 23-35 Edw. I. Ed. Mills, J. 2 vols. (Cal.SP.) Dublin. 1905, 14.

[Of the various classes of Plea Rolls Mr Wood informs me that Justiciary Rolls 6 and 7 Edw. II, 6 Edw. IV, and a fragmentary roll of Henry VII, remain undamaged; that a few original rolls, much damaged by fire and water, have been recovered; that the Record Commissioners' Transcripts 1265-1306 and 1318, and a Calendar of a portion of Iter Roll 34 Edw. I, have been preserved. Also that of the Memoranda Rolls of the Exchequer (31 Edw. I-1784) Rolls 3 Edw. II and 13 and 14 Edw. II are undamaged; and that the following MS. collections have been preserved (1) Record Commissioners' Transcripts 6 Edw. I-Hen. VI; (2) MS. Calendars (made in P.R.O.) 22-3 Edw. I, 31-35 Edw. I, 1 Edw. II, 3 Edw. II, and 1 Hen. IV (mm. 1-48); (3) MS. collection by J. F. Ferguson, being volumes of selected entries from the Memoranda Rolls, 1 Edw. I-Anne; and (4) Repertories and Indexes by J. F. Ferguson, Edw. III-Chas. II. The site of the Record Treasury has not yet been cleared, but there is no expectation of any further documents being found there.]

Calendar of the Liber Niger and Liber Albus of Christ Church, Dublin. Ed. Lawlor, H. J. *in* Proc. Roy. Irish Acad. XXVII (c), pp. 1-93. Dublin. 1909.

Catalogue of Accounts on the Great Rolls of the Pipe of the Irish Exchequer, Hen. III-15 Edw. III. Ed. McEnery, M. J. in appendices to the 35th and subsequent Reports of the Deputy Keeper. Dublin. 1903 ff. [Originals of these and subsequent Pipe Rolls destroyed as above. Mr Herbert Wood, late Deputy Keeper, informs me that MS. Calendars of 16, 18, and 22 Edw. III, and a fragment (?) of 30 Edw. III have been preserved.]

Chartae, Privilegia, et Immunitates, being transcripts of Charters and Privileges to Cities, Towns, Abbeys, and other Bodies Corporate (1171-1395). (Irish Record Commission.) Dublin. 1889. [Of the originals, the majority, being from Patent Memoranda and Plea Rolls, have been destroyed as above.]

Charters of the Abbey of Duiske, Co. Kilkenny. Ed. Bernard, J. H. *in* Proc. Roy. Irish Acad. xxxv (c). pp. 1–188. Dublin. 1918.

Chartularies of St Mary's Abbey, Dublin, with the Register of its House at Dunbrody and Annals of Ireland. Ed. Gilbert, J. T. 2 vols. (Rolls.) 1884.

Crede Mihi. The most ancient Register Book of the archbishops of Dublin. Ed. Gilbert, J. T. Dublin. 1897.

Historic and Municipal Documents of Ireland, 1172–1320, from the archives of the city of Dublin. Ed. Gilbert, J. T. (Rolls.) 1870.

The Earle of Kildare's Redde Book. A MS. compiled in 1503 and preserved by the Duke of Leinster. For table of contents, as stated (not quite accurately) in a copy made in 1633, *see* Pt. ii (App.) of 9th Report, Historical MSS. Commission. London. 1884.

Register of the Abbey of St Thomas, Dublin. Ed. Gilbert, J. T. (Rolls.) 1889.

Registrum (or Liber Niger) Alani. MS. compiled from ancient documents by Archbishop Alan *c.* 1530, in the custody of the present Archbishop of Dublin. Transcripts in Marsh's Library, Dublin, and Trin. Coll., Dublin.

Registrum Prioratus Omnium Sanctorum iuxta Dublin. Ed. Butler, R. (Irish Archaeol. Soc.) Dublin. 1845.

Rotulorum Patentium et Clausorum Hiberniae Calendarium, Hen. II–Hen. VII. Ed. Tresham, E. 1828. [The originals of these and of subsequent Patent Rolls, together with countless other invaluable documents, were destroyed by the explosion at the Record Treasury on 30 June 1922.]

Royal and other Historical Letters, Henry III. Ed. Shirley, W. W. 2 vols. (Rolls.) 1862, 66.

Statutes and Ordinances of the Parliament of Ireland. King John to Henry V. Ed. Berry, H. F. (Rolls.) 1907.

Vetera Monumenta Hibernorum et Scotorum Historiam illustrantia (1216–1264). Ed. Theiner, A. Rome. 1864.

(ii) *Annals and Narrative Sources.*

(Irish Annals as in ii A, *above.*)

Annales Hiberniae (1162–1370) from Laud MS. 526. Bodleian Library, Oxford. Ed. Gilbert, J. T. *In* Chartularies of St Mary's Abbey, Dublin. Vol. ii. pp. 303–98. *See above,* ii b (i). [The most complete and most accurate of the Latin annals.]

Annales Hiberniae Jacobi Grace, Kilkenniensis. Ed. with transl. Butler, R. (Irish Archaeol. Soc.) Dublin. 1842. [Mostly from same source as the Laud MS. Annals, but more corrupt.]

Annales Monasterii Beate Marie iuxta Dublin (Fragments to 1434). Ed. Gilbert, J. T. *op. cit.* Vol. ii. pp. 241–92.

Annals of Inisfallen. MS. H. 1. 7, Trin. Coll. Dublin. [A late compilation, but embodying some early sources of Munster history not to be found elsewhere.]

Caithréim Thoirdhealbhaigh [concerning the wars in Thomond, 1276–1318.] Vol. i, ed. O'Grady, S. H., with introd. by Flower, R. Vol. ii, transl. O'Grady, S. H. (Irish Texts Soc. xxvi, xxvii.) London. 1929.

Giraldus Cambrensis. Topographia et Expugnatio Hibernica. Ed. Dimock, J. *in* Opera. Vol. v. (Rolls.) 1867.

L'Histoire de Guillaume le Maréchal, comte de Striguil et de Pembroke. Ed. Meyer, P. 3 vols. (SHF.) Paris. 1891–1901.

The Song of Dermot and the Earl. An old French Poem from Carew MS. 596 Lambeth. Ed. with transl. Orpen, G. H. Oxford. 1892. [On the Conquest of Ireland.]

III. MODERN WORKS.

A. Pre-Norman Period.

Bury, J. B. Life of St Patrick and his place in history. 1905.

Green, Alice S. [Mrs J. R.]. History of the Irish State to 1014. London. 1925.

Halliday, C. The Scandinavian Kingdom of Dublin. 2nd edn. Ed. Prendergast, J. P. Dublin. 1884.

Hayden, Mary, and Moonan, G. A. Short History of the Irish People from the earliest times to 1920. London. 1921.

Hull, Eleanor. History of Ireland and her people to the close of the Tudor Period. London. 1926.

Joyce, P. W. Short History of Ireland from the earliest times to 1608. London. 1893.

Keating, G. Foras Feasa ar Éirinn. Vol. i, ed. Comyn, D. Vols. ii–iv, ed. Dineen, P. (Irish Texts Soc.) London. 1902–13.

Lanigan, J. Ecclesiastical History of Ireland. 4 vols. Dublin. 1822.

Lawlor, H. J. St Bernard of Clairvaux's Life of St Malachy of Armagh. London. 1920.

Macalister, R. A. S. The Archaeology of Ireland. London. 1928.

MacNeill, E. Phases of Irish history. Dublin. 1919.

—— The native place of St Patrick. *In* Proc. Roy. Irish Acad. xxxvii (c). pp. 118–40. Dublin. 1926.

—— Silva Focluti (for S. Uluti = Coill Ultach, *i.e.* Killultagh). *Ibid.* xxxvi (c). pp. 249–55. Dublin. 1923.

Phillips, W. Alison, *ed.* History of the Church of Ireland. By various authors. 3 vols. Oxford. In preparation.

Stokes, G. T. Ireland and the Celtic Church. 3rd edn. London. 1892.

Todd, J. H. St Patrick, apostle of Ireland. Dublin. 1864.

B. From 1169 to 1315.

Cox, Sir Richard. Hibernia Anglicana, or the History of Ireland from the Conquest by the English. 2 vols. London. 1689–90.

Curtis, E. History of Mediaeval Ireland (1110–1513). Dublin. 1923.

Davies, Sir John. A Discoverie of the true causes why Ireland was never entirely subdued…untill the beginning of his Maiesties [James I's] happie raigne. London. 1612, and later edns.

Gilbert, Sir J. T. History of the Viceroys of Ireland (to 1509). Dublin. 1865.

Green, Alice S. [Mrs J. R.] The making of Ireland and its undoing (1200–1600). London. 1909.

Lawlor, H. J. The Fasti of St Patrick's, Dublin. Dundalk. 1930.

Leland, Thomas. History of Ireland from the Invasion of Henry II. London. 1773. [The best general history before the 19th century and still valuable.]

Orpen, G. H. Ireland under the Normans (1169–1333). 4 vols. Oxford. 1911–20.

Richey, A. G. Short History of the Irish People to the Plantation of Ulster. Dublin. 1887.

Round, J. H. The Commune of London. London. 1899. [Contains two important chapters (vii and viii) relating to the Conquest of Ireland.]

Stokes, G. T. Ireland and the Anglo-Norman Church to the dawn of the Reformation. London. 1889.

Wood, H. The Office of Chief Governor of Ireland (1172–1509). *In* Proc. Roy. Irish Acad. xxxvi (c). pp. 206–38. Dublin. 1923. [Contains the best list of Chief Governors and Deputies.]

CHAPTER XIX.

SCOTLAND TO 1488.

[This bibliography also covers the author's chapter on Scotland which will appear in Vol. VIII.]

I. BIBLIOGRAPHIES.

Anderson, A. O. Early sources of Scottish history. Vol. I. pp. xxi–ci. *See below,* II.
Brown, P. Hume. History of Scotland. Vol. I. pp. 322–8. *See Gen. Bibl.* V.
Hannay, R. K. Scottish history and the national records. Edinburgh. 1919.
Livingstone, M. Guide to the public records of Scotland. Edinburgh. 1905.
Terry, C. Sanford. Catalogue of publications of Scottish historical and kindred Clubs and Societies, 1780–1908. Glasgow. 1909. Continuation, 1908–27, by Matheson, C. Aberdeen. 1928.
—— Index to papers relating to Scotland described or calendared in the Historical MSS. Commission's Reports. Glasgow. 1908.
Thomson, J. M. The public records of Scotland. Glasgow. 1922.

II. ORIGINAL AUTHORITIES.

Abbotsford Club Miscellany. Ed. Maidment, J. Edinburgh. 1837.
Accounts of the Great Chamberlains of Scotland and some other officers of the Crown, rendered at the Exchequer (1326–1453). Ed. Thomson, T. 3 vols. (Bannatyne Club.) Edinburgh. 1817, 36.
Accounts of the Lord High Treasurer of Scotland. Vol. I (1473–98). Ed. Dickson, T. (Cal.SP.) Edinburgh. 1877.
Acts of the Lords Auditors of Causes and Complaints, 1466–1494. Ed. Thomson, T. (RC.) [Edinburgh.] 1839.
Acts of the Lords of Council in Civil Causes, 1478–95. Ed. Thomson, T. (RC.) [Edinburgh.] 1839. [Vol. II (1496–1501), ed. Neilson, G. and Paton, H. (Cal. SP.) Edinburgh. 1918, contains introdn. and additions to the preceding.]
Acts of the Parliaments of Scotland. Vols. I, II (1124–1567). Ed. Thomson, T. and Innes, C. (RC.) [Edinburgh.] 1844, 14.
Adamnan. Vita S. Columbae. Ed. Fowler, J. T. Oxford. 1920.
Ancient Laws and Customs of the Burghs of Scotland. Vol. I (1124–1424). Ed. Innes, C. Vol. II (1424–1707). Ed. Renwick, R. (Scottish Burgh Records Soc.) Edinburgh. 1868, 1910.
Anderson, A. O. Early sources of Scottish history. 2 vols. Edinburgh. 1922.
—— Scottish Annals from English chroniclers, 500–1286. London. 1908.
Barbour, John. The Bruce. Ed. Skeat, W. W. (Scottish Text Soc.) Edinburgh. 1894.
Bede. Ecclesiastical History. Ed. Plummer, C. 2 vols. Oxford. 1896.
Boece, Hector. Murthlacensium et Aberdonensium episcoporum vitae. Ed. Moir, J. (New Spalding Club.) Aberdeen. 1894.
—— Scotorum Historiae (with Ferrerius' continuation to 1488). Paris. 1574. Engl. transl. Bellenden, J. Edinburgh. 1536; and 1821.
Calendar of Documents relating to Scotland preserved in H.M.'s Public Record Office, London (1108–1509). Ed. Bain, J. 4 vols. (Cal.SP.) Edinburgh. 1881–8.
Chronica de Mailros (contemporary for *c.* 1140–1270). Ed. Stevenson, J. (Bannatyne Club.) Edinburgh. 1835.
Chronicles of the Picts, Chronicles of the Scots, and other early memorials of Scottish history. Ed. Skene, W. F. (Cal.SP.) Edinburgh. 1867.
Chronicon de Lanercost, 1201–1446. Ed. Stevenson, J. (Bannatyne Club.) Edinburgh. 1839.
Collectanea de rebus Albanicis relating to the history of the Highlands and Islands. Ed. Skene, W. F. (Iona Club.) Edinburgh. 1847.

Concilia Scotiae, ecclesiae Scoticanae statuta, 1225–1559. Ed. Robertson, J. 2 vols (Bannatyne Club.) Edinburgh. 1866.

Documents and Records illustrating the history of Scotland, and the transactions between the Crowns of Scotland and England, preserved in the Treasury of H.M.'s Exchequer. Ed. Palgrave, F. (RC.) London. 1837.

Documents illustrative of Sir William Wallace, his life and times. Ed. Stevenson, J. (Maitland Club.) [Edinburgh.] 1841.

Documents illustrative of the history of Scotland, 1286–1306. Ed. Stevenson, J. 2 vols. (Cal.SP.) Edinburgh. 1870.

Fordun, John of. Chronica gentis Scotorum [to 1383]. Ed. Skene, W. F., with Engl. transl. (Historians of Scotland, Vols. i and iv.) Edinburgh. 1871–2. *As* Scotichronicon (with Bower's continuation to 1447). Ed. Hearne, T. 5 vols. Oxford. 1722. *Also* ed. Goodall, W. 2 vols. Edinburgh. 1759.

Fraser, W. The Douglas Book. 4 vols. Edinburgh. 1885.

Gough, H. Scotland in 1298. Documents relating to the campaigns of Edward I in that year. Paisley. 1888.

Gray, Sir Thomas. Scalacronica. Ed. Stevenson, J. (Maitland Club.) Edinburgh. 1836. Engl. transl. Maxwell, Sir H. Glasgow. 1907.

Hailes, Lord. Annals of Scotland, 1057–1370. 3 vols. Edinburgh. 1797.

Henry the Minstrel (Blind Harry). The actis and deidis of William Wallace. Ed. Moir, J. (Scottish Text Soc.) Edinburgh. 1889.

Lawrie, A. C. Annals of the reigns of Malcolm and William, 1153–1214. Glasgow. 1910.

—— Early Scottish Charters prior to 1153. Glasgow. 1905.

Lindsay, Robert, of Pitscottie. The historie and cronicles of Scotland, 1437–1575. Ed. Mackay, Æ. J. G. 2 vols. (Scottish Text Soc.) Edinburgh. 1899.

Maitland Club Miscellany. Vol. iv. Pt. i. Ed. Robertson, J. Glasgow. 1847.

Major, J. A history of Greater Britain [to 1509] compiled from the ancient authorities. Ed. Constable, A. (Scottish History Soc.) Edinburgh. 1892.

Marwick, J. D. Records of the Convention of the Royal Burghs of Scotland, 1295–1597. Edinburgh. 1870.

National manuscripts of Scotland (facsimiles). Pts. i and ii (1097–1488). (Cal.SP.) Southampton. 1867, 70.

Patrick, D. Statutes of the Scottish Church, 1225–1559. (Scottish History Soc.) Edinburgh. 1907.

(Ragman Rolls): Instrumenta publica sive processus super fidelitatibus et homagiis Scotorum domino regi Angliae factis 1291–1296. Ed. Thomson, T. (Bannatyne Club.) Edinburgh. 1834.

Registrum magni sigilli regum Scotorum. Vol. i (1306–1424). New edn. Thomson, J. M. (Cal.SP.) Edinburgh. 1912. Vol. ii (1424–1513). Ed. Paul, J. B. (*Ibid.*) 1882.

Rotuli scaccarii regum Scotorum. The Exchequer Rolls. Ed. Stuart, J. and Burnett, G. Vols. i–ix (1264–1487). (Cal.SP.) Edinburgh. 1878–86.

Rotuli Scotiae in turri Londinensi et in domo Westmonasteriensi asservati, 1291–1516. Ed. Macpherson, D. and others. 2 vols. (RC.) London. 1814, 19.

Rymer, T. Foedera. *See Gen. Bibl.* iv.

Scottish History Society Miscellany. Vol. ii. Edinburgh. 1904.

Stevenson, J. Illustrations of Scottish history from the twelfth to the sixteenth century; selected from unpublished manuscripts in the British Museum and the Tower of London. (Maitland Club.) Glasgow. 1834.

—— The life and death of King James the First of Scotland. (Maitland Club.) [Edinburgh.] 1837.

Tacitus. Vita Agricolae. Ed. Furneaux, H. and others. Oxford. 1923.

Teulet, A. Inventaire chronologique des documents relatifs à l'histoire d'Écosse conservés aux archives du royaume à Paris. (Abbotsford Club.) Edinburgh. 1839. [For the reigns of Alexander III—Mary Stuart.]

Turgotus. Life of St Margaret. Ed. Forbes-Leith, W. 3rd edn. Edinburgh. 1896.

Turnbull, W. B. D. D. Extracta e variis cronicis Scocie. From the ancient manuscript in the Advocates' Library. (Abbotsford Club.) Edinburgh. 1842.

Wyntoun, Andrew of, The original Chronicle of (to 1408). Ed. Amours, F. J. 6 vols. (Scottish Text Soc.) Edinburgh. 1903–14.

III. MODERN WORKS.

A. General.

Brown, P. Hume. History of Scotland. Vol. I. *See Gen. Bibl.* v.

Burton, J. H. History of Scotland, from Agricola's invasion. 8 vols. Edinburgh. 1905.

Lang, Andrew. History of Scotland, from the Roman occupation. Vol. I. Edinburgh. 1900.

Pinkerton, J. History of Scotland, 1371–1542. 2 vols. London. 1797.

Terry, C. Sanford. History of Scotland from the Roman evacuation. Cambridge. 1920.

Tytler, P. F. History of Scotland, 1242–1603. 9 vols. Edinburgh. 1828–43.

B. Special.

Agnew, A. The hereditary sheriffs of Galloway. 2 vols. Edinburgh. 1893.

Allen, J. R. and Anderson, J. The early Christian monuments of Scotland. Rhind lectures. Edinburgh. 1903.

Ancient and Historical Monuments of Scotland. Reports of Royal Commission. County of Berwick. (Edinburgh. 1915); Caithness. (*Ibid.* 1911); Dumfries. (*Ibid.* 1916); East Lothian. (*Ibid.* 1924); Kirkcudbright. (London. 1914); Sutherland. (Edinburgh. 1911); Wigtown. (London. 1912.)

Anderson, J. Scotland in early Christian times. Rhind lectures. 2 vols. Edinburgh. 1881.

—— Scotland in pagan times. Rhind lectures. 2 vols. Edinburgh. 1883, 86.

Antiquaries of Scotland, Society of. Proceedings. Edinburgh. 1851 ff., in progress.

Argyll, Duke of. Scotland as it was and is. Edinburgh. 1887.

Bain, J. The Edwards in Scotland, 1296–1377. Rhind lectures. Edinburgh. 1901.

Barron, E. M. The Scottish War of Independence. London. 1914.

Bellesheim, A. History of the Catholic Church in Scotland. 4 vols. Edinburgh. 1887–90.

Bremner, R. L. The Norsemen in Alban. Glasgow. 1923.

Brøgger, A. W. Ancient emigrants: a study of the Norse settlements of Scotland. Rhind lectures. Oxford. 1929.

Brown, P. Hume. Early travellers in Scotland. Edinburgh. 1891.

—— Scotland before 1700 from contemporary documents. Edinburgh. 1893.

—— Surveys of Scottish history. Glasgow. 1919.

Burton, J. H. The Scot abroad. Edinburgh. 1883.

Chalmers, G. Caledonia. 8 vols. (New Club.) Paisley. 1887–1902.

Christison, D. Early fortifications in Scotland. Edinburgh. 1898.

Cochran-Patrick, R. W. Early records relating to mining in Scotland, 1219–1683. Edinburgh. 1878.

—— Mediaeval Scotland. Glasgow. 1892.

—— Records of the coinage of Scotland, from 1357. Edinburgh. 1876.

Cunningham, J. The church history of Scotland from the commencement of the Christian era. 2 vols. Edinburgh. 1882.

Curle, A. O. The treasure of Traprain. Glasgow. 1923.

Curle, J. A Roman frontier post and its people: the fort of Newstead. Glasgow. 1911.

Diack, F. C. The Newton Stone and other Pictish inscriptions. Paisley. 1922.

Dowden, J. The Celtic Church in Scotland. London. 1894.

—— The mediaeval Church in Scotland. Glasgow. 1910.

Drummond, J. Sculptured monuments in Iona and the West Highlands. Edinburgh. 1881.

Dunbar, A. Scottish kings: a revised chronology of Scottish history, 1005–1625. Edinburgh. 1899.

Forbes, A. P. Kalendars of Scottish saints. Edinburgh. 1872.

Fraser, J. The question of the Picts. (Scottish Gaelic Studies. Vol. II, pt. 2.) Aberdeen. 1928.

Grant, I. F. The social and economic development of Scotland before 1603. Edinburgh. 1930.
Gray, J. Sutherland and Caithness in Saga time. Edinburgh. 1922.
Gregory, D. History of the Highlands and Islands of Scotland. London. 1881.
Henderson, G. The Norse influence on Celtic Scotland. Glasgow. 1910.
Innes, Cosmo. Lectures on Scotch legal antiquities. Edinburgh. 1872.
—— Scotland in the Middle Ages. Edinburgh. 1860.
—— Sketches of early Scotch history. Edinburgh. 1861.
Jusserand, J. J. The romance of a king's [James I] life. London. 1896.
Keith, Robert. Historical catalogue of the Scottish bishops, to 1688. Edinburgh. 1824.
Lesley, J. The history of Scotland from the death of King James I. Ed. Thomson, J. (Bannatyne Club.) Edinburgh. 1830.
Macdonald, A. History of the Clan Donald. 2 vols. Inverness. 1896, 1900.
Macdonald, G. The Roman Wall in Scotland. Glasgow. 1911.
—— and Park, A. The Roman forts on the Bar Hill. Glasgow. 1906.
MacGibbon, D. and Ross, T. The castellated and domestic architecture of Scotland. 5 vols. Edinburgh. 1887–92.
—— —— The ecclesiastical architecture of Scotland. 3 vols. Edinburgh. 1896–7.
MacKenzie, W. M. The battle of Bannockburn. Glasgow. 1913.
Mackie, J. D. and Pryde, G. S. The estate of the burgesses in the Scots Parliament and its relation to the Convention of Royal Burghs. St Andrews. 1923.
Mackinnon, J. Constitutional history of Scotland from early times to the Reformation. London. 1924.
—— Social and industrial history of Scotland from the earliest times to the Union. 2 vols. Glasgow and London. 1920–1.
Metcalfe, W. M. Legends of the Saints. 3 vols. (Scottish Text Soc.) Edinburgh. 1896.
Miller, S. N. The Roman fort at Balmuildy. Glasgow. 1922.
—— The Roman fort at Old Kilpatrick. Glasgow. 1928.
Mitchell, A. and Cash, C. G. Scottish topography. 2 vols. (Scottish History Soc.) Edinburgh. 1917.
Moore, Margaret F. The lands of the Scottish kings in England. London. 1915.
Munro, R. Ancient Scottish Lake dwellings. Edinburgh. 1882.
—— Prehistoric Scotland. Edinburgh. 1899.
Pagan, Theodora. The Convention of the Royal Burghs of Scotland. Glasgow. 1926.
Paul, J. B. The Scots Peerage. 9 vols. Edinburgh. 1904–14.
Pinkerton, J. Lives of the Scottish saints. Revised and enl. by Metcalfe, W. M. 2 vols. Paisley. 1889.
Rait, R. S. An outline of the relations between England and Scotland, 500–1707. London. 1901.
—— The Parliaments of Scotland. Glasgow. 1924.
—— The Scottish Parliament before the Union of the Crowns. Glasgow. 1901.
Reeves, W. On the Celi-de, commonly called Culdees. *In* Trans. Roy. Irish Acad. xxiv. Dublin. 1867.
Robertson, E. W. Scotland under her early kings. Edinburgh. 1862.
Scott, A. B. The Pictish nation, its people and its church. Edinburgh. 1918.
Scottish Historical Review. Ed. MacLehose, J. 25 vols. Glasgow. 1904–28.
Simpson, W. D. The historical Saint Columba. Aberdeen. 1926.
Skene, W. F. Celtic Scotland. 3 vols. Edinburgh. 1867.
Smith, G. G. Scottish literature, its character and influence. London. 1919.
Terry, C. Sanford. The Scottish Parliament, its constitution and procedure. Glasgow. 1905.
Viking Club Saga Book. London. 1892 ff.
Watson, W. J. The history of the Celtic place-names of Scotland. Rhind lectures. Edinburgh. 1926.

CHAPTER XX.

SPAIN, 1252–1410.

[Some of the books and documents listed in the Bibliography of Vol. vi, ch. xii
are also useful for this period.]

BIBLIOGRAPHIES.

See the Bibliography to Vol. vi, ch. xii, pp. 912, 916, 917, 920.

I. KINGDOMS OF LEON AND CASTILE.

A. ORIGINAL DOCUMENTS.

(i) *Published.*

(Alfonso IV, rey de Portugal.) Carta...ao Papa Clemente VI, de 12 de fevereiro de
1345. Lisbon. 1910. [On the occupation of the Canaries.]

(Cartagena, Alfonso de, Bishop of Burgos.) Alegações feitas contra os portugueses,
a favor do rei de Castela e Leão, no concilio de Basilea, sobre a conquista das
Canárias. Anno de 1435. Lisbon. 1912. [Facsimile.]

Coetlosquet, E. M. du. Chartes inédites, tirées des archives de Pampelune et de
Soria, relatives à Du Guesclin et à ses compagnons d'armes. *In* Rev. hist. de
l'Ouest. vii (1896). 205–21, 597–614.

Colección de documentos inéditos del Archivo de Simancas. Mercedes Enriqueñas.
Ed. de Castilla y Peroso, F. R. *in* Rev. Hist. Latina. iii (1876). 182–4.

Cortes de los antiguos reinos de León y de Castilla. 5 vols. (RAH.) Madrid. 1861–1903.
Also Introdn. by Colmeiro, M. 2 vols. Madrid. 1883–4. [Cortes 1020–1576.]

Daumet, G. Note sur quelques documents castillans des Archives Nationales. *In*
Bulletin hispanique. xvii (1915). 1–14. [On Alfonso XI before the Hundred
Years' War.]

Documento histórico (de 1387). Ed. Alvarez de la Braña, R. *in* Bol. de la Soc. Cast.
de Excursiones. ii (1905–6). 322–3. [On John of Gaunt's attempt to acquire
Castile.]

Documentos de la época de D. Alfonso el Sabio. *In* Mem. Hist. Españ. (RAH.)
Vol. i. pp. 1–344. Vol. ii. pp. 1–135.

Documentos de la época de D. Sancho el Bravo. *Ibid.* Vol. iii. pp. 421–68.

Innocent VI et Blanche de Bourbon. Lettres du pape. Ed. Daumet, G. Paris.
1898.

Lettre du roi Sanche IV à Alonso Pérez de Guzmán sur défense de Tarifa (2 janvier
1295). Ed. Morel-Fatio, A. *in* Bull. hisp. ii (1900). 15–24.

Libro de los Fueros de Castilla. Ed. Sanchez, G. Barcelona. 1924.

Pactos, tratados, y avenencias que mediaron entre los reyes de Aragón, Navarra, y
el bastardo Enrique de Trastamara, con motivo de la invasión del reinado de
Castilla. Ed. Casañ y Alegre, J. (Colec. de doc. inéd. del Archivo gen. del
reino de Valencia, i.) Valencia. 1894.

Paz y Melia, A. Documentos de los siglos xii–xv, correspondientes a los reinos de
España, excepto Cataluña. (Series de los...docs. del Arch. y Bibl. del...Duque
de Medinaceli, i.) Madrid. 1915.

Proyecto de matrimonio entre un príncipe de Castilla, hijo de Pedro el Cruel, y una
princesa de Aragón, hija de Pedro el Ceremonioso. *In* Rev. España Regional.
June. 1888.

Testaments d'Alphonse X le Savant. Ed. Daumet, G. BEC. lxvii (1906). 70–99.

Traité d'alliance offensive et défensive entre le roi de Castille, Pierre le Cruel, et
le comte d'Armagnac, Jean Ier (1357). *In* Rev. d. soc. sav. vii (1878). 54–61.

Tratado de alianza que otorgó...Sancho IV de Castilla a favor de...Jaime II de
Aragón...1291. Ed. Sinisterra, V. *in* Rev. de Arch., Bibl., y Mus. 1st ser
viii (1878). 316.

Cartas, etc. de Juan I de Castilla. (18th cent. copy.) Nat. Lib., Madrid. 13102.

Cartas, privilegios, etc. de Sancho IV y Fernando IV sobre asuntos de Toledo. (18th cent. copy.) *Ibid.* 13095.

Copia de los Reyes de Castilla y León, desde D. Pelayo hasta Doña Juana, madre de Carlos 5°...sacada de la descripción que está en la sala de los reyes del Alcazar... de Segovia, que...Phelipe segundo perfiziono y amplio, siguiendo a los mas atentados y verdaderos coronistas de España, como es Estevan de Garibay, y Çurita...y otros. (17th cent.) Bibl. Nat., Paris. 200 (no. 502 of the Catalogue of Morel-Fatio).

Documentos del reinado de Alfonso X. Nat. Lib., Madrid. 23, 431, 681, 700, 751, 773, 892, 6735, 6866, 9975, 13022, 13023, 13063, 13065, 13069, 13071, 13074–7, 13089, 13094, 13098, 13100, 13124.

Documentos de Alfonso XI. *Ibid.* 23, 612, 5784, 6370, 6427, 6735, 13017, 13029, 13030, 13064, 13069, 13074, 13076, 13078, 13089, 13094, 13096, 13097, 13098, 13099, 13100, 13102.

Documentos del reinado de Pedro I. *Ibid.* 628, 1354, 1419, 1496, 5784, 9428, 13096, 13098, 13099, 13106.

Documentos del tiempo de Enrique III. *Ibid.* 638.

Documentos del tiempo de Sancho IV. *Ibid.* 13023, 13063, 13078, 13089, 13095, 13119.

Fernando IV. Cartas y otros escritos. *Ibid.* 13069, 13071, 13094–6.

Juan I. Cartas y otros escritos. *Ibid.* 763, 6370, 6915, 6932, 13018, 13089, 13102, 13116.

Liber gestorum Aegidii Albornozii. (16th–17th cent.) Roy. Lib. Escurial. R. III. i.

Libro de diferentes Cuentas de...las Rentas Reales, y gasto de la Casa Real en el Reynado de D. Sancho IV, era de MCCCXXXI y MCCCXXXII...1293 y 1294. Sacado de un Tomo original...de Toledo...(por el P. Burriel). (18th cent.) Nat. Lib., Madrid. 13090.

Notas refr. a la batalla de Aljubarrota. *Ibid.* 6020, 7089, 9394, 13102.

Noticias de hijos de Enrique II de Castilla.... (1409, 17th cent. copy.) *Ibid.* 186761.

Papeles selectos de los reinados de Enrique III, Juan II, y Enrique IV. (18th cent. copy.) *Ibid.* 13236.

Testamento del Rey D. Pedro. (17th cent. copy.) *Ibid.* 10640.

B. ORIGINAL AUTHORITIES.

(i) *Published.*

Chronica del...Rey D. Alfonso el Onzeno. Valladolid. 1551. [Sometimes attributed to Núñez de Villazán. Reaches 1344.] Ed. Cerdá y Rico, F. *in* Col. de las crónicas...de Castilla. Vol. VII. Madrid. 1787 ; *and in* Bibl. de autores españoles. Vol. LXVI. Madrid. 1875. Ríos y Ríos, A. de los. Nota presentada a la RAH. sobre el autor de la Crónica y Poema de Don Alfonso XI. Madrid. [1866?]

Cronicón de Valladolid (1333–1539). Ed. Sainz de Baranda, P. *in* Col. de doc. inéd. para la hist. de España. Vol. XIII. pp. 5–228.

Diez de Games, Gutierre. Crónica de D. Pedro Niño, conde de Buelna. Ed. de Llaguno Amirola, E. *in* Col. de las crónicas...de Castilla. Vol. III. Madrid. 1782. [For the reign of Henry III after his majority.]

Dormer, D. J. Enmiendas y advertencias a las coronicas de...D. Pedro, D. Enrique el Segundo, D. Juan el Primero y D. Enrique el Tercero, que escrivió D. Pedro López de Ayala.... Saragossa. 1683.

Espinosa, F. de. Sobre las Leyes y los Fueros de España. Barcelona. 1927.

[Gracia, Pedro de?] Historia del Rey D. Pedro y su descendencia, que es el linage de las dos Castillas. *In* Semanario Erudito. XXVIII. pp. 222–88; XXIX. pp. 3–60.

López de Ayala, Pedro. La Crónica del Rey D. Enrique IIde Castilla. Toledo. 1516. First edn., with chronicles of Peter I and John I. *Also* ed. de Llaguno Amirola, E. *in* Col. de las crónicas...de Castilla. Vols. I, II. Madrid. 1779–80; *and in* Bibl. de autores españoles. Vol. LXVIII. Madrid. 1877.

[Manuel, Juan, Infante de Castilla?] Chronicon Dni Joannis Emmanuelis. *In* España Sagrada. Vol. II. pp. 215–22. *See Gen. Bibl.* IV. Complete chronicle, ed. Baist, G. *in* Romanische Forschungen. VII (1893). 551–6.

[Rodriguez de Cuenca, Juan?] Sumario de los Reyes de España, por el Despensero mayor de...Doña Leonor, mujer del Rey Don Juan el Primero de Castilla. Ed. de Llaguno Amirola, E. *in* Col. de las crónicas...de Castilla. Vol. III. Madrid. 1781. [From Pelayo to John II. Valuable for characters of the kings the author knew personally.]

[Sanchez de Tovar, Fernando?] Chronica del muy esclarecido principe y rey don Alonso; el qual fue par de Emperador, e hizo el libro de las siete partidas. *With the* Chronica del Rey D. Sancho el Bravo.... Valladolid. 1554. Puyol, J. El presunto cronista Fernán Sánchez de Valladolid. BRAH. LXXVII (1920). 507–33.

—— Chronica del...rey Don Fernando...nieto del rey don Alonso.... Valladolid. 1554. *Also in* Memorias de D. Fernando IV de Castilla. Ed. Benavides, A. Vol. I. Madrid. 1860.

(ii) *Manuscripts.*

Crónica de los Reyes de Castilla. (15th cent. copy.) Roy. Lib., Madrid. 2-I-2. Other MSS. Nat. Lib., Madrid. 14970, 8817 (French version), 1335 (*id.*), 1522 (*id.*), 8817 (*id.*); Bibl. Nat., Paris. esp. 220 (no. 139 of the Catalogue of Morel-Fatio). [Begins with Ferdinand I.]

Fernandez de Velasco, Pedro, Condestable de Castilla. Epítome de los Reies de Castilla desde D. Pelaio hasta...Henrique IV. (16th cent.) Nat. Lib., Madrid. 1233.

Floranes, R. Disertación sobre el lugar del sepulcro de la Reina Dña Blanca de Borbón. (18th cent.) *Ibid.* 1168[11].

Historia verdadera del Rey Don Pedro de Castilla...sacada de unos papeles antiguos del archivo de la casa de Estepa. (19th cent.) Bibl. de Catalunya. 522.

Memorial de las personas notables que...se nombran (en las crónicas de Alfonso X y sus sucesores hasta Enrique III). (16th cent.) Nat. Lib., Madrid. 1223.

Memorias y apuntamiento del Rey Don Pedro...extractados de varios autores por D. Rafael de Floranes. (18th cent.) *Ibid.* 11264[11].

Miranda y Paz, Francisco de. Historia...(de) Enrique el segundo. (18th cent.) *Ibid.* 5941.

Relación de las cosas notables ocurridas en tiempo de...Alfonso X e de su muerte. (16th cent.) *Ibid.* 712.

Suma de crónicas de los Reyes de Castilla y de León desde...Pelayo hasta...Juan el 2°. (16th cent.) *Ibid.* 10652.

(Sumario hecho en tiempo de Enrique III.) (15th cent.) Roy. Lib., Madrid. 2-J-5. [Largely identical with that of the steward of Doña Leonor, but stops before John I.]

C. MODERN WORKS.

(i) *General.*

Catalina García y López, J. Castilla y León durante los reinados de Pedro I, Enrique II, Juan I, y Enrique III. 2 vols. (Hist. gen. de España. RAH.) Madrid. 1892–3.

Fernández Duro, C. La Marina de Castilla. (Hist. gen. de España. RAH.) Madrid. 1893. [From 1110 to 1492.]

Ficker, J. Ueber d. nähere Verwandtschaft zwischen gotisch-spanischem und norwegisch-isländischem Recht. (MIOGF. Supplt. II.) Innsbruck. 1886.

Hinojosa, E. Das germanische Element im spanischen Rechte. Weimar. 1910.

Mayer, E. Historia de las instituciones sociales y políticas de España y Portugal durante los siglos V a XIV. Spanish edn. 2 vols. Madrid. 1925–6.

Piskorski, W. Las Cortes de Castilla en el periodo de tránsito de la edad media a la moderna, 1188–1520. Transl. Sánchez Albornoz, C. Barcelona. 1930. [Original Russian edn. Kiev. 1897.]

Salas y Rodriguez, F. J. de. Marina española de la edad media. Vol. I. Madrid. 1864. [No more publ.]

(ii) *Monographs.*

Alfonso el Sabio, como rey y conquistador de la provincia de Cádiz. Cadiz. 1892.

Alfonso the Wise, King of Castile. *In* Fraser's Magazine. xcii (1875). 627 ff.

Alvarez. Examen filosófico de los actos de D. Alfonso el XI como legislador. Madrid. 1849.

Amado de Salazar, J. M. Historia crítica del reinado de D. Pedro de Castilla y su completa vindicación. Madrid. 1852.

Amador de los Ríos, R. La Bandera del Salado. BRAH. xxi (1892). 464–71.

—— Los restos mortales del Rey Don Pedro I de Castilla y sus vicisitudes. *In* Rev. de Arch., Bibl., y Mus. 3rd ser. x (1904). 105–18.

Andrés, A. D. Pedro González de Mendoza, el de Aljubarrota, 1340–1385. BRAH. lxxviii (1921). 255–73, 353–76, 415–36, 496–505; lxxix. 29–42, 144–87.

Apuntes para la historia de D. León Lusignan VI, Rey de Armenia y primero de este nombre de Madrid, Andújar y Villareal (1380). Madrid. 1893. [John I of Castile pensioned the dethroned Leo.]

Arántegui y Sans, J. Apuntes históricos sobre la artillería española en los siglos xiv y xv. Madrid. 1887. Dictamen de la...Academia de la Historia acerca de ..."Apuntes...." Madrid. 1886.

Ayora y Somayor, F. de. El Rey D. Pedro de Castilla el Justiciero defendido. 3rd edn. Madrid. 1750.

Azevedo, P. de. Sobre a expedição ás Canárias em 1341. *In* Bol. Acad. das Sciencias de Lisboa. vi (1912). 210–17.

Ballesteros, A. Alfonso X Emperador (electo) de Alemania. Madrid. 1918. [Inaug. disc. RAH.]

—— Las cortes de 1252. *In* Anales...Junta para ampliación de estudios, etc. iii, 3. pp. 109–41.

—— Un detalle curioso de la biografía de Alfonso X el Sabio. BRAH. lxxiii (1918). 408–19.

—— Doña Leonor de Guzmán. *In* La España moderna. ccxxxii (1908). 67–76.

—— Dónde nació Alfonso X de Castilla? BRAH. lxxix (1921). 9–10.

—— Un testamento histórico. *In* La España moderna. ccli (1909). 166–77. [On D. Philip, son of Sancho IV.]

—— and P. Alfonso X de Castilla y la corona de Alemania. *In* Rev. de Arch., Bibl., y Mus. 3rd ser. xxxiv (1916). 1–23, 187–219; xxxv (1918). 223–42; xxxix (1919). 142–62; xl. 467–90.

Barrantes Maldonado, P. Crónica del Rey D. Enrique tercero deste nombre en la Casa de Castilla y de León. Madrid. 1868.

Berni y Catalá, J. Disertación en defensa del Rey Don Pedro el Justiciero. Valencia. 1777.

Blázquez y Delgado-Aguilera, A. Juicio histórico-crítico sobre el fratricidio de D. Pedro I de Castilla en...Montiel. Ciudad Real. 1889.

Busson, A. Die Doppelwahl des Jahres 1257 und das römische Königthum Alfons X von Castilien. Münster. 1866.

Carta a respeito da heroina de Aljubarrota, Brites de Almeida, por F. M. F. 2nd edn. Coimbra. 1880.

Chandos, John, Herald of. Life of the Black Prince. Ed. Pope, M. K. and Lodge, E. C. Oxford. 1910.

Cirot, G. L'espionnage en Espagne au temps de la Reconquête. *In* Bull. hisp. xix (1917). 259–64.

—— Le témoignage de López de Ayala au sujet de D. Fadrique, frère de Pierre le Cruel. *In* Hispania. v (1922). 70–6.

Coetlosquet, E. M. du. Du Guesclin et le drame du château de Montiel. *In* Rev. hist. de l'Ouest. vi (1889). 250–65.

Contrastes históricos. D. João Iº Rei de Castella, e D. João Iº Rei de Portugal. *In* Panorama. viii. Lisbon. 1844. p. 77.

Coroleu, J. Cartas en las cuales D. Pedro de Castilla y D. Pedro el Ceremonioso reciprocamente se retratan. *In* Rev. España Regional. iii (1887). 713–22.

—— Los Reyes apócrifos. Un falso D. Pedro el Cruel. *Ibid.* iii (1887). 635–40.

—— Tratado de alianza entre Pedro el Ceremonioso y varios nobles castellanos contra D. Pedro de Castilla. *Ibid.* iii (1887). 902–8.

Croce, B. Un' ambasciata del Re di Castiglia a Tamerlano...1403. ASPN. n.s. I (1915). 368–73.

Daumet, G. Étude sur l'alliance de la France et de la Castille au xiv⁰ et au xv⁰ siècles. (BHE. 118.) Paris. 1898.

—— Études sur les relations d'Innocent VI avec D. Pedro I Roi de Castille au sujet de Blanche de Bourbon. Rome. 1897.

—— Jean de Rye au siège d'Algeciras. *In* Bull. hisp. xii (1910). 265–74.

—— Mémoire sur les relations de la France et de la Castille (1255–1320). Paris. 1913.

Déprez, E. La bataille de Nájera, 3 avril 1367. Le "communiqué" du Prince Noir. RH. cxxxvi (1921). 37–59.

Dillon, J. T. History of the reign of Peter the Cruel, King of Castile and Leon. 2 vols. London. 1788. French transl. 2 vols. Paris. 1790.

Discursos leídos ante S.M. el Rey y la Real Familia el día 23 de Noviembre de 1921, en la solemnidad que las RR.AA. celebran...para conmemorar el vii centenario del nacimiento del Rey D. Alfonso el Sabio. Madrid. 1921. [Contains discourses of J. Ribera, A. Bonilla San Martín, etc.]

Dufresne, J. Henri de Trastamare à Bagnères (1367). *In* Rev. de Gascogne. xxxiv (1893). 512–18.

[Dulaurier, N.] Une conférence sur l'histoire d'Arménie ou la vérité vraie déclarée à propos de la brochure anonyme intitulée "La Vérité sur le Prince Léon d'Arménie-Lusignan." Par Irénée Guasco [pseud.]. Paris. 1879.

Escobar, F. Conquista de Lorca por Alfonso el Sabio. *In* Bol. R. Acad....Toledo. iii (1922). 35–42.

Fanta, A. Ein Bericht über die Ansprüche des Königs Alfons auf den deutschen Thron. MIOGF. vi (1885). 94–104.

Fernández Guerra, A. Discurso acerca del reinado de Pedro I, leído en la Academia de la Historia. Madrid. 1868.

Ferrer del Río, A. Examen histórico-crítico del reinado de D. Pedro de Castilla. Madrid. 1851.

Forma de las antiguas Cortes de Castilla, con algunas observaciones sobre ellas. Madrid. 1823. [Only fasc. I (Alfonso V–Alfonso X) publ.]

Freminville, Le Chevalier de. Histoire de Bertrand Du Guesclin. Brest. 1841.

Fromme, B. Die spanische Nation und das Konstanzer Konzil. Münster. 1894.

Gaibrois de Ballesteros, M. Historia del reinado de Sancho IV de Castilla. 3 vols. Madrid. 1922–8.

—— Tarifa y la política de Sancho IV de Castilla. BRAH. lxxiv (1919). 418–36, 521–9; lxxv. 349–55; lxxvi. 53–77, 123–60, 420–48; lxxvii. 192–215.

García Rámila, I. Las Cortes de Castilla. *In* Rev. de Arch., Bibl., y Mus. 3rd ser. xlvi (1925). 84–99, 262–78.

Garran, C. Episodio militar del siglo xiv. La batalla de Nájera: 3 de abril de 1367. Logroño. 1902.

Genevay, A. and Hartez, E. d'. Les grains de sable (études historiques). Un trait de Pierre le Cruel. Paris. 1884.

Golmayo, Pedro Benito. D. Pedro el Cruel y D. Enrique II. *In* Rev. de Madrid. 3rd ser. iv (1843). 313–60.

Gómez de la Serna, P. (Sobre el reinado de D. Alfonso X...el Sabio.) Madrid. 1857. [Inaug. disc. RAH.]

González Dávila, G. Historia de la vida y hechos del rey don Henrique Tercero de Castilla. Madrid. 1638.

González de Clavijo, R. Historia del Gran Tamorlan e itinerario y enarración del viaje y relación de la Embaxada que Ruy Gonçalez de Clavijo le hizo, por mandado del...Rey D. Henrique Tercero de Castilla. Seville. 1582.

González Lafuente, M. Guzmán el Bueno, dechado de regeneradores. Madrid. 1901.

Guardiola y Valero, E. D. Pedro de Castilla y D. Juan Alfonso de Albuquerque. *In* Revista contemporánea. lxvii (1887). 361–82.

Guichot, J. D. Pedro Primero de Castilla. Seville. 1878.

Guzmán el Bueno y Padilla, J. de. Conquista de Gibraltar (en 1309 por Alonso Pérez de Guzmán). *In* La España moderna. xxix (1891). 75–84.

Hay, Paul, Sieur du Chastelet. Histoire de Bertrand Du Guesclin...avec plusieurs pièces originales touchant...histoire...d'Espagne. Paris. 1666.

Hergueta, N. Apuntes para la biografía de D. Martín García o González, secretario de D. Sancho el Bravo. *In* Rev. de Arch., Bibl., y Mus. 3rd ser. IX (1903). 328–38.

Hermann, W. Alfons X von Castilien als römischer König. Berlin. 1897.

Ibañez de Segovia Peralta y Mendoza, G., Marqués de Mondéjar. Memorias históricas del Rey D. Alonso el Sabio i observaciones a su Chronica. Madrid. 1777.

Jamison, D. F. Life and times of Bertrand Du Guesclin. 2 vols. London. 1864.

Jara, A. [Cardinal Gil de] Albornoz en Castilla. Madrid. 1914.

Jiménez de Sandoval, C. Batalla de Aljubarrota. Madrid. 1872. Informe…por J. Gómez de Arteche. Madrid. 1873.

Kolditz, A. G. F. De Alphonso X, Castellae Legionisque rege, cognomine sapientis indigno. Zerbst. 1757.

Lafuente, V. Supuesto parto de una supuesta reina. BRAH. XII (1888). 112–15. [Note on document of 1304, apparently referring to the wife of D. Sancho, Fernando IV's brother.]

Ledo del Pozo, J. Apología del Rey Dn. Pedro de Castilla, conforme a la Crónica verdadera de…Ayala. Madrid. [c. 1780.]

L'Escale, M. de. La vertu resuscitée, ou la vie du cardinal Albornoz. Paris. 1629.

López, A. Cruzada contra los sarracenos en…Castilla…(1276). *In* Archivo Ibero-Americano. VIII (1918). 321–7.

López de Córdoba, L. Memorias de una dama…(de 1363 a 1412). Ed. Castro A. de, *in* La España moderna. CLXIII (1902). 120–46; CLXIV. 116–33.

Luce, S. Histoire de Bertrand Du Guesclin et de son époque. Vol. I. La jeunesse de Bertrand (1320–64). Paris. 1876. [No more publ.]

Macías, M. Dónde pasó su infancia Alfonso el Sabio? *In* Bol. Com. Mon. Orense. VI (1920). 249–55.

Margry, P. La conquête et les conquérants des iles Canaries. Paris. 1896.

Meister, J. G. S.I.S. Alphonsus sapiens. Weissenfels. [1677?]

Mély, F. de. La table d'or de Pèdre de Castille. Paris. 1889.

Méndez Bejarano, M. Alfonso X, polígrafo. *In* Bol. R. Soc. de Geog. LXIII (1922). 190–204.

Mérimée, P. Histoire de D. Pèdre Ier, roi de Castille. *In* Revue des Deux Mondes. n.s. XX, XXI. 1847–8. *Also* Paris. 1848. Engl. transl. London. 1849.

Merriman, R. B. The Cortes of the Spanish Kingdoms in the later Middle Ages. AHR. XVI (1911). 476–95.

Montoto, J. M. Historia del reinado de D. Pedro I de Castilla. 2nd edn. Seville. 1874.

Moraleda y Esteban, J. de. D. Alfonso el Sabio. *In* Bol. R. Acad.…Toledo. III (1922). 5–15.

Morel-Fatio, A. La donation du Duché de Molina à Bertrand du Guesclin. BEC. LX (1899). 145–76.

Núñez da Cunha, J. Epitome da vida e ações de Dom Pedro o primeiro deste nombre entre os reis de Castilla. Lisbon. 1666.

Núñez de la Peña, J. Conquista y antigüedades de las Islas de la Gran Canaria y su descripción. Madrid. 1676.

Otto, H. Die Verzichtleistung des Königs Alfons von Castilien [of the Holy Roman Empire]. MIOGF. XVI (1895). 128–32.

Palma, el Bachiller. Divina retribución sobre la caída de España en tiempo del noble rey D. Juan el primero. Ed. Escudero de la Peña, J. M. Madrid. 1879.

Pardo de Figueroa, M. Datos históricos relativos a la inscripción que en…1859, se colocó en una torre de Medina Sidonia, donde estuvo presa y murió D. Blanca de Borbón esposa de D. Pedro de Castilla. Cadiz. 1859.

Pérez de Castro, M. Estudios histórico-militares. La batalla del Salado. *In* Rev. de España. XXV (1872). 552–65.

Pérez de Guzmán, J. Un nuevo Guzmán el Bueno. *In* La España moderna. CCCI (1914). 5–17.

—— La princesa Cristina de Noruega y el infante D. Felipe, hermano de D. Alfonso el Sabio. BRAH. LXXIV (1919). 39–65.

Pérez Navarrete, A. Las grandezas de…Don Gil de Albornoz. Bologna. 1635.

[Picado Franco de Jaque Godinez de Paz, L. M.] Vindicación del Rey D. Pedro I de Castilla…Por Onil Pidoca Narcof de Jaque. Barcelona. 1831.

Piñal de Castilla, E. and Carnevali y de Imaz, F. Archivos de Andalucía. El Rey D. Pedro I de Castilla y su descendencia. Seville. 1919.

Pita Ezpelosin, F. El reinado de Alfonso XI bajo el punto de vista militar. *In* Rev. técnica de Infanteria y Caballeria. xix (1900). 425–32.

Porreño, B. Vida y hechos hazañosos del gran Cardenal...Albornoz. Cuenca. 1626.

Quintana, M. J. Guzmán el Bueno. *In* Vidas de Españoles célebres. Paris. 1827. pp. 211–18, 479–80.

Redlich, O. Zur Wahl des römischen Königs Alfons X von Castilien (1257). MIOGF. xvi (1895). 659–62.

Ríos y Ríos, A. de los. Cómo y porqué se llamó a D. Pedro el Cruel Pero Gil. BRAH. xxxvi (1900). 58–65.

Romances espagnoles relatives à Pierre-le-Cruel. Paris. 1841.

Ruiz de Obregon y Retortillo, J. Alfonso X el Emplazado. *In* La España moderna. cclxxvii (1912). 95, 114. *Also in* Rev. de Arch., Bibl., y Mus. 3rd ser. xxxii (1915). 420–39.

Salas y Rodriguez, F. J. de. Expediciones marítimas de D. Pedro I de Castilla y D. Pedro IV de Aragón. Madrid. 1868. [Inaug. disc. RAH.]

Salvá, A. Las Cortes de 1392 en Burgos. Burgos. 1891.

Sanchez, G. Sobre el ordenamiento de Alcalá (1348) y sus fuentes. *In* Rev. de Derecho Privado. ix, 3. Madrid. 1922.

—— Para la historia de la redacción del antiguo derecho territorial castellano. *In* An. Hist. del Derecho esp. 1930.

Sanchez, T. A. (Fernández, P.) Carta...al J. Berní y Catalá...sobre...Rey D. Pedro el Justiciero. Madrid. *n.d.*

Saralegui y Medina, M. Fernández Pérez de Andrade y el fratricidio de Montiel. *In* Cuadros de la Historia. Madrid. 1908.

—— Silueta del Almirante de Castilla, D. Alfonso Jofre de Tenorio. Introd. by Novo y Colson, P. Madrid. 1910.

Scheffer-Boichorst,P. Zur Geschichte Alfons X von Castilien. MIOGF. 1888. 226–48.

Serrano, L. Alfonso XI y el Papa Clemente VI durante el cerco de Algeciras. *In* Publ. de la Escuela Españ. de Arqueol. e Hist. en Roma. iii. pp. 1–35.

—— El ayo de Alfonso el Sabio. *In* Bol. R. Acad. Españ. vii (1920). 571–602.

Sitges, J. B. Las mujeres del Rey D. Pedro I de Castilla. Madrid. 1910.

Soldevilla, F. Matrimonios y amoríos de Alfonso XI. Madrid. 1879.

Spalding, C. A. W. Peter der Grausame. Berlin. 1797.

Storer, E. Peter the Cruel. Baltimore. 1910.

Suárez, D. D. Alfonso X. Sus ideas políticas y sociales. Madrid. 1861. [doct. diss.]

Torres Campos, R. Carácter de la conquista y colonización de las Islas Canarias. Madrid. 1901. [disc. RAH.]

Torres y Franco Romero, L. de. Las bodas del Rey D. Pedro I de Castilla. *In* Rev. de Arch., Bibl., y Mus. 3rd ser. xx (1909). 28–42, 247–62.

Tubino, F. M. A propósito de la historia del reinado de Pedro I de Castilla. *In* Bol. del Ateneo. Valencia. v (1872–3). 289–97.

—— Pedro de Castilla, la leyenda de Dña Maria Coronel y la muerte de D. Fadrique. Madrid. 1887.

Ulloa, M. de. Estudios históricos. De la esclarecida reina de Castilla Doña María de Molina. *In* Mem. lit. de la R. Acad. Sevillana de Buenas Letras. ii. pp. 94, 119.

Valls Taberner, F. Relacions familiars i politiques entre Jaume el Conqueridor i Anfos el Savi. *In* Bull. hisp. xxi (1919). 9–52.

Vargas Ponce, J. de. Elogio del Rey Alonso el Sabio. Madrid. 1782.

—— Vida de D. Pedro Niño, primer conde de Buelna. Madrid. 1807.

Vera y Figueroa, J. A. de, Conde de la Roca. El Rei D. Pedro defendido. Madrid. 1649.

Vieira Natividade, M. A batalha de Aljubarrota. Alcobaça. 1891.

V[illeneuve], M[adame] de. Anecdotes de la cour d'Alphonse, onzième...de Castille. Pt. i. Amsterdam. 1756.

Ward, M. Alfonso the Wise, King of Castile. *In* Macmillan's Magazine. xxvi (1872). 126 ff.

Zanelli, A. Il giuramento di fedeltà di Buoso da Dovara ad Alfonso X di Castiglia, 1271. ASI. 5th ser. x (1892). 122.

II. KINGDOM OF ARAGON.

A. ORIGINAL DOCUMENTS.

(i) *Published*.

Acta Aragonensia...aus dem diplomatische Korrespondenz Jaymes II (1291–1327). Ed. Finke, H. 3 vols. Berlin. 1908 ff., in progress.

Cartas de...Santa Isabel, Infanta de Aragón, Reyna de Portugal, hija del Rey Don Pedro el Tercero...y de la Reyna Doña Constanza...al Rey D. Jayme el Segundo, su hermano. Ed. Dormer, D. J. *in* Discursos varios de Historia. Saragossa. 1683. pp. 101–53.

Colección de cartas inéditas del Archivo General de la Corona de Aragón, Reinado de D. Juan I. Ed. de Bofarull y Sans, F. *in* Rev. Hist. Latina. III (1876). 17–22.

Cuentas de Roger de Lauria. Ed. Huici, A. *in* Rev. del Centro de Estudíos hist. de Granada. IV (1914). 57–66, 149–56, 261–8, 369–72 ; V (1915). 102–11.

Documenti riguardanti l' abdicazione di Giacomo II di Aragona al trono di Sicilia (1295). Ed. Starrabba, R. *in* Arch. stor. Siciliano. n.s. VII (1883). 275–93.

Documentos concernientes a la armada que en 1351 mandó aprestar...Pedro IV de Aragón en contra de Genoveses. *In* Mem. hist. Españ. (RAH.) Vol. II. pp. 249–389.

Documentos inéditos de antiguos reyes de Aragón. Ed. Miret y Sans, J. *in* Bol. R. Acad. de Buenas Letras de Barcelona. VI (1911–12). 48–56.

Documentos que contiene un volumen rotulado "Concordias entre el Rey y el Duque de Trastamara." Ed. Morón y Liminiana, J. *in* Rev. de Arch., Bibl., y Mus. 2nd ser. IX (1883). 292–305, 411–14.

Istruzioni date dal re Pietro IV d' Aragona al riformatore...di Sardegna D. Raimondo de Boyl nel 1338. Ed. Pillito, J. Cagliari. 1863.

Jaime de Aragón. Das Register nº 318 des Archivs der Aragonischen Krone in Barcelona. Ed. Zeissberg, H. von. Repr. from SKAW. 1898. [Letters from James II to his daughter Isabella and her husband.]

Jaime II de Aragón, el cardenal Mincio de Murrovalle...y Arnaldo de Vilanova, 1310. Ed. Pou y Martí, J. M. *in* Archivo Ibero-Americano. XX (1923). 110–12. [A letter from the king to the cardinal.]

La Mantia, G. Codice diplomatico dei re aragonesi di Sicilia. Vol. I (1282–1320). Palermo. 1917.

—— Documenti su le relazioni del re Alfonso III di Aragona con la Sicilia (1285–1291). *In* Anuari de l'Inst. d'Estudis Catalans. II (1908–9). 357–63.

Lettre de Philippe de Valois à Alphonse IV...d'Aragon, tirée des registres du Parlement de Paris. Ed. Michel, F. Paris. 1835.

Manescal, H. Sermo vulgarment anomenat del...Senyor Don Jaume Segon. Barcelona. 1602.

Miret y Sans, J. Lettres closes des derniers Capétiens directs. MA. 2nd ser. XIX (1915). [Fifteen letters addressed to James II of Aragon.]

Ordenanzas para la casa y corte de los reyes de Aragón (siglos XIII y XIV). *In* Cultura española. 1906. pp. 327–38.

Proceso contra Bernardo de Cabrera, mandado formar por...D. Pedro IV. *In* Col. de doc. inéd. del Arch. Gen....Aragón. Vols. XXXII–XXXIV.

Procesos de las antiguas cortes y parlamentos de Cataluña, Aragón, y Valencia. Vols. I–III. Compromiso de Caspe; IV. Unión de Barcelona y Aragón; V. Ordenaciones de la Casa Real de Aragón por Pedro IV; VI and VII. Idem por diversos monarcas; VIII. Municipalidades y cartas-pueblas. (*Ibid.* I–VIII.)

Régné, J. Catalogue des Actes de Jaime Iᵉʳ, Pedro III, et Alfonso III, rois d'Aragon, concernant les Juifs (1213–91). REJ. LX–LXX. 1910–20. *Also* publ. separately (1213–85). Paris. 1911, 14.

—— Catalogue d'Actes pour servir à l'histoire des Juifs de la couronne d'Aragon sous le règne de Jaime II (1291–1327). REJ. LXXIII–LXXVIII. 1921–4.

Solmi, A. Nuovi documenti per la storia della conquista aragonesa. *In* Archivio stor. Sardo. V (1909). 142–57.

Treguas de D. Jaime II de Aragón con el noble D. Juan Manuel, hijo del Infante D. Manuel, en 1296. Ed. Chabás. BRAH. XXIX (1896). 433–40.

Viaje de Pedro IV a Cerdeña en 1354. Documentos. Ed. Soler, A. G. *in* Bol. R. Acad. de Buenas Letras de Barcelona. V (1909–10). 88–93.

(ii) *Manuscripts.*

Pedro IV. Cartas latinas sobre varios negocios. (1383, modern copy.) Nat. Lib., Madrid. 10206.

B. Original Authorities.

(i) *Published.*

Carbonell, P. M. Chronica de Espanha fins aci no divulgada : que tracta dels...reys dels Gots : y gestes de aquells : y dels Cortes de Barcelona : e Reyes de Arago.... Barcelona. 1546. [Compilation from the *Crónica* of Peter IV, etc., very few additions.]

Coronación y consagración de reyes y ceremonias que en ella se guardan, hecha por D. Ramón Obispo, Coronación de los reyes de Aragón, ordenada por D. Pedro III. *In* Col. de doc. inéd. para la hist. de España. Vol. xiv. pp. 556–68.

Desclot, Bernat. Crónica del Rey En Pere [Peter III] e dels seus antecessors passats. Ed. Buchon, J. A. C. *in* Chroniques étrangères relatives aux expéditions françaises pendant le xiiie siècle. Paris. 1840. pp. 565–736. English transl. (1276–85). Critchlow, F. L. Princeton. 1928.

[Dezcoll, Bernat.] Crónica del Rey de Aragon, D. Pedro IV. Spanish transl. ed. de Bofarull, A. Barcelona. 1850.

Excerpta ex Chronica S. Victoris Massiliensis. *In* España Sagrada. Vol. xxviii. pp. 337–9. *See Gen. Bibl.* iv. [From 715 to the beginning of the reign of Alfonso V.]

Genealogia dels Reys Daragó e de Navarre e comptes de Barchinona. Manuscrit del segle xv. (Biblioteca de "La Veu de Monserrat," vol. i.)

Juan I, Vindicación del Rey D., hecha por él mismo. *In* Rev. Hist. Latina. iii (1876). 147–54.

Libro de los fechos et conquistas del Principado de Morea compilado por comandamiento de don Fray Johan Ferrández de Heredía...Chronique de Morée aux xiiie et xive siècles. Transl. and ed. Morel-Fatio, A. (Soc. de l'Orient latin.) Geneva. 1885.

[Peter IV, king of Aragon?] Historia de la Corona de Aragón. (Generally known as "Crónica de San Juan de la Peña.") Saragossa. 1876. [Up to Alfonso IV. In Spanish and Latin. The Catalan text is unpublished.]

Registro Merino de Zaragoza, el Caballero don Gil Tarín, 1291–1312. Ed. de Bofarull y de Sartorio, M. Saragossa. 1889.

Relación histórica de la famosa invasión del exercito y armada de Francia en Cataluña en 1285 y de la valerosa resistencia que los Catalanes, Aragoneses, y Valencianaos... hicieron por tierra y por mar. Madrid. 1793.

Tomic Cauller, P. Histories e conquestes dels Reys de Arago e Comtes de Barcelona. Barcelona. 1495; 1534; and 1886.

Vagad, Gauberto Fabricio de. Crónica de...(los...reyes...de Aragón). Saragossa. 1499.

(ii) *Manuscripts.*

Blancas, J. de. Apuntamientos históricos de Aragón. (17th cent.) Nat. Lib., Madrid. 1504.

Chronica de los Reyes y Obispos de Aragón o Manual de Pribilegios de Aragón, con notas de Urrea. (17th cent.) *Ibid.* 1605.

Crónica universal desde la creación del mundo hasta Alfonso V de Aragón, en catalán. (15th cent.) Bibl. Nat., Paris. MS. esp. 13 (no. 121 of the Catalogue of Morel-Fatio).

Domenech, Jaime. Resumen historiale o compilación abreviada de les histories quasi de tota Europa e de algunes de Assia e de Africa, fins...Pere el Quart. (Copy made 1742.) Bibl. Nat., Paris. 186 (no. 122 of the Catalogue of Morel-Fatio).

Flos mundi. Chronique universelle en catalan. (15th cent.) Bibl. Nat., Paris (no. 120 of the Catalogue of Morel-Fatio). [Ends at 1233.]

Infeudatio regni Aragonum. (14th cent.) Roy. Lib. Escurial. P. ii. 7.

Martínez de Lobera, Fr. Pedro. Anales de la Corona de Aragón con la suma de la vida de sus Reyes. (18th cent.) Nat. Lib., Madrid. 6742.

Monfar y Sors, Diego. Genealogia Comitum Barcinonae : necnon et Aragoniae Regum. (18th cent.) *Ibid.* 51.

Tarafa, Francisco. Chronica de Cavallers Cathalans. (16th cent., 18th cent. copy.) Roy. Lib., Madrid. 2-F-4; Bibl. Nat., Paris. 102 (no. 387 of the Catalogue of Morel-Fatio [Epitome of the counts of Urgell, etc., by Monfar y Sors]); Collection Moreau, 1962 (no. 500 of the Catalogue of Morel-Fatio).

C. Modern Works.

Abarca, P. Los Reyes de Aragón en anales históricos. 2 vols. Madrid and Salamanca. 1682, 84.

Aguiló, E. de K. Pretensións de Jaume II d'Aragó a la Corona de Mallorca. *In* But. Soc. arqueol. Luliana. 1904.

—— Transacció sobre la sucesió en el Regne de Mallorca, per mort sens infans del Rey En Sanxo. *Ibid.* 1902.

Amari, M. Sull' ordinamento de la Repubblica Siciliana del 1282. Palermo. 1882.

—— Trattato stipolato da Giacomo II di Aragona col sultano d' Egitto il 29 gen. 1293. *In* Atti d. R. Accad. d. Lincei. Ser. III. Mem. d. Cl. di scienze morali, etc. XI (1883). 423 44.

Baer, F. Studien zur Geschichte der Juden im Königreich Aragonien während des 13 und 14 Jahrhts. (Ebering's Hist. Studien, 106.) Berlin. 1913.

Barberá, J. M. de. Los restos de Roger de Lauria, dónde están? Tarragona. 1892.

Basmadjian, K. J. Jacques II, roi d'Aragon, et Oschin, roi de la Petite Arménie (1319–20). *In* Rev. de l'Orient latin. XI (1907). 1–6.

Berger, E. Jacques II d'Aragon, le Saint-Siège et la France. *In* Journ. des Savants. n.s. VI (1908). 281–94, 348–59.

Blancas, J. de. Ad Regum Aragonum veterumque Comitum depictas effigies, in regia Caesaraugustinensis Deputationis Aula positas, inscriptiones. Saragossa. 1587.

—— Inscripciones latinas a los retratos de los reyes de Sobrarbe, condes antiguos y reyes de Aragón....Contienen una breve noticia de cada uno....Se añaden...otras noticias...por...D. J. Dormer. Saragossa. 1680.

—— Aragonensium rerum commentarii. Saragossa. 1588. *Also in* Schottus, A., etc. Hispaniae illustratae. Vol. III. Frankfort. 1606. pp. 566–839. Spanish transl. Hernández, P. Manuel. (Bibl. de escritores aragoneses.) Saragossa. 1878.

—— Regum Aragoniae catalogus, cum succincta eorum vita. *In* Schottus, A., op. cit. Vol. II. pp. 853–60.

Bofarull y Sans, F. de. Generación de Juan I de Aragón. Apéndice doc. á Los Condes de Barcelona vindicados por P. de Bofarull y Mascaró. *In* Mem. R. Acad. de Buenas Letras de Barcelona. Barcelona. 1896.

Bonet, J. Noticia sobre algunos partidarios de Jaime II (1285). *In* But. Soc. arqueol. Luliana. March and May. 1897.

Bozzo, S. V. Una cronaca siciliana inedita del secolo XIV e il codice Q q. E. 24 della Biblioteca Comunale di Palermo. Bologna. 1884.

Cánovas del Castillo, A. Historia de la dominación española en Italia. Madrid. 1860. [Inaug. disc. RAH.]

Capmany y Montpalau, A. de. Práctica y estilo de celebrar cortes en...Aragón...Cataluña y Valencia, y una noticia de las de Castilla y Navarra. Madrid. 1821.

Carreras y Candi, F. Entences y templers en les montayes de Prados (1279 a 1300). *In* Bol. R. Acad. de Buenas Letras de Barcelona. II (1903-4). 217–57.

—— Pedrec de la Reyal Casa: Ordenaments de Pere "lo Gran" e Anfós "lo Lliberal" (segle XIII). *In* Misc. Hist. Cat. II. pp. 307–18.

—— Lo siti de Balaguer de 1280. *Ibid.* pp. 37–55.

Casaus y Torres, A. Nuevas observaciones para la historia general de Aragón, Navarra, y Cataluña. Barcelona. Vol. I. 1829.

Castellano de la Peña, G. Crónica de la Corona de Aragón. Extraida de los Anales de Zurita. Saragossa. 1918.

Castillo Solórzano, A. de. Epitome de la vida y hechos del...Rey D. Pedro de Aragón, tercero de este nombre. Saragossa. 1639.

Comenge, I. El protofísico de Pedro el Ceremonioso. *In* Bol. R. Acad. de Buenas Letras de Barcelona. I (1901-2). 151–7.

Croce, B. Primi contatti fra Spagna ed Italia. *In* Atti d. Accad. Pontif. rom. di Archeol. 1893.

Danvila y Collado, M. Las libertades de Aragón. Madrid. 1881.

Daumet, G. Semonce du pape Benoît XII à Pierre IV d'Aragon, pour ses relations trop fréquentes et intimes avec les musulmans. *In* Bull. hisp. vii (1905). 305-7.

Dormer, D. J. Los Nobles...que no se quisieron partir, ni dexar al señor Rey en la isla de Cerdeña. *In* Discursos varios de historia. Saragossa. 1683. pp. 245-59. [Peter IV in 1354.]

Féraud, L. C. Expédition du roi Pierre III d'Aragon à Collo...d'après une chronique catalane. *In* Revue Africaine. xvi (1872). 241-58.

Fernández Duro, C. El apelativo y la patria del almirante Roger de Lauria. BRAH. xxxviii (1901). 8-20.

Finke, H. Die Beziehungen der aragonesischen Könige zur Literatur, Wissenschaft, und Kunst im 13 u. 14 Jahrht. *In* Archiv für Kulturgeschichte. viii (1910). 20-42.

Fondevilla, F. La nobleza catalano-aragonesa capitaneada por Ferrán Sánchez de Castro en 1274. *In* Coleccíon Jaumel. 2nd pt. pp. 1061-1168.

Gaspar Remiro, M. Una reclamación de Jaime II de Aragón al sultán de Marruecos, Abusaid Otman ben Abdehac (1323). *In* Homenaje á M. Pidal. i (1925). 819-37.

Girbal, E. C. Nuevos datos y aclaraciones para ilustrar la genealogía de D. Juan I de Aragón y especialmente la serie de los Duques de Gerona. *In* Rev. Gerona. i (1876). 3-7.

Girona y Llagostera, D. Itinerari del rey en Marti (1396-1402 y 1403-10). *In* Anuari de l'Inst. d'Estudis Catalans. iv (1911-12). 81-184; v (1913-14). 515-655.

Haberkern, E. Der Kampf um Sizilien in den Jahren 1302-1337. Berlin. 1921.

Herquet, K. Juan Fernández de Heredia, Grossmeister des Johanniterordens, 1377-1396. Mühlhausen. 1877.

Herrera, A. de. Comentarios de los hechos de los españoles, franceses, y venecianos en Italia...desde...1281 hasta...1559. Madrid. 1624.

Ibarra y Rodriguez, E. El rey y la nobleza de Aragón en los tiempos primitivos. *In* Rev. de Aragón. ii (1901). 239-42, 267-71.

Jiménez Soler, A. La Corona de Aragón y Granada, Historia de las relaciones entre ambos reinos. *In* Bol. R. Acad. de Buenas Letras de Barcelona. iii (1905-6). 101-34, 186-224, 295-324, 333-65, 450-76, 485-96; iv (1907-8). 49-91, 146-80, 200-25, 271-98, 342-75.

—— Episodios de la Historia de las relaciones entre la Corona de Aragón y Túnez. *In* Anuari de l'Inst. d'Estudis Catalans. i (1907-8). 195-224.

—— La expedición a Granada de los infantes D. Juan y D. Pedro en 1319. *In* Rev. de Arch., Bibl., y Mus. 3rd ser. xi (1904). 353-60; xii (1905). 24-36.

—— La política española de Jaime II. Münster. 1925.

—— El sitio de Almería en 1309. Barcelona. 1904.

Jordán Asso del Río, I. Historia de la economía política de Aragón. Saragossa. 1798.

Jordán de Urries, J. La lucha por Sicilia en los años de 1291 a 1302. *In* Bol. R. Acad. de Buenas Letras de Barcelona. vii (1913-14). 73-86.

—— La política exterior de Alfonso III de Aragón. *Ibid.* vii (1913-14). 441-58, 472-85.

Jove y Hevia, P. Indagaciones acerca de los ducados de Atenas y Neopatría en las coronas de Aragón y Sicilia. *In* Rev. de España. xii (1870). 230-58.

Kern, F. Analekten zur Geschichte des 13 und 14 Jahrhts. i. Eduard I von England und Peter von Aragon. MIOGF. xxx (1909). 412-23.

Kluepfel, L. Die äussere Politik Alfonso III von Aragonien...(1285-9). Berlin. 1911.

—— Die äussere Politik...(1285-91). Berlin. 1912.

Lafuente, V. de. El Privilegio general de Aragón base de la Unión. *In* Rev. Madrid. i (1881). 115-19, 174-6, 230-2, 327-30, 431-5, 477-83, 530-6, 585-9.

—— Estudios críticos sobre la historia y el derecho de Aragón. 3 vols. Madrid. 1884-6.

—— La constitución política de Aragón en 1300. *In* Mem. R. Acad. de Ciencias Moral. y Polít. viii (1893). 167-216.

—— Las primeras cortes de Aragón. *In* Rev. Hisp.-Amer. iii (1881). 375-92, 514-30.

Lasala, M. Reseña histórico-política del antiguo reino de Aragón. Saragossa. 1865.

Lecoy de la Marche, A. L'expédition de Philippe le Hardi en Catalogne. RQH. xlix (1891). 62–127.

Llabrés y Quintana, G. La conquista de Menorca per Alfons III. *In* Jochs Florals de Barcelona. xxxviii. 1896.

López, A. Pedro IV de Aragón y los Santos Lugares de Palestina. *In* Archivo Ibero-Americano. xiv (1920). 126–8.

Martínez Martínez, F. El tercer casamiento de Pedro el Ceremonioso. Valencia. 1924.

Maupassant, J. Relations de Pierre IV…d'Aragon, avec la France, de 1340 à 1380, d'après les archives de la Couronne d'Aragon. *In* Positions des Thèses. École nationale des chartes. (1907.) pp. 117–21.

Miralles de Imperial. Relaciones diplomáticas de Mallorca y Aragón con el Africa septentrional durante la edad media. Barcelona. 1904.

Miret y Sans, J. Itinerario del Rey Alfonso III de Cataluña, IV en Aragón, el conquistador de Cerdeña. *In* Bol. R. Acad. de Buenas Letras de Barcelona. v (1909–10). 3–15, 57–71, 114–23.

—— Négociations de Pierre IV d'Aragon avec la Cour de France (1366–7). *In* Rev. hisp. xiii (1905). 76–135.

—— Negociacions diplomàtiques d'Alfons III de Catalunya-Aragó ab el rey de França per la croada contra Granada (1328–32). *In* Anuari de l'Inst. d'Estudis Catalans. ii (1908–9). 265–336.

—— Notes sobre la expedició del rey Pere lo Gran a Berbería. *In* Bol. R. Acad. de Buenas Letras de Barcelona. vii (1913–14). 354–60.

—— Ramón de Melany, embajador de Alfonso IV de Aragón en la corte de Francia. *Ibid.* ii (1903–4). 192–202.

—— Rectitut de Jaume II. *Ibid.* vi (1912). 260–7.

—— Saqueig de Sasser, Sardenya, en 1329. *Ibid.* iv (1907–8). 431–47.

—— Tres princesas griegas en la corte de Jaime II de Aragón. *In* Rev. hisp. xv (1906). 668–720. Nuevos documentos de las tres princesas griegas. *Ibid.* xix (1908). 112–34.

—— Viatges del Infant en Pere, fill de Jaume I en 1268 i 1269. Barcelona. 1908.

Miron, E. L. The Queens of Aragon. London. 1913.

Moncada, Francisco de, conde de Osuna. Expedición de los Catalanes y Aragoneses contra Turcos y Griegos. Barcelona. 1623. Ed. Foulché-Delbosc, R. New York and Paris. 1919. [Best edn.]

Nanot Renart, P. Pedro IV de Aragón juzgado por sus obras literarias. *In* Revista contemporánea. x (1877). 445–62.

Noticia de un principe desconocido en la historia de Cataluña y Aragón. *In* Rev. Hist. Latina. iii (1876). 210–11. [Peter, son of John I.]

Ortiz, J. Compendio de la vida de D. Francisco Fernández Pérez de Aranda, ayo y preceptor que fué del Infante D. Fernando, hijo del Rey D. Juan I de Aragón. Madrid. 1777.

Parpal y Marqués, C. La conquista de Menorca en 1287 por Alfonso III de Aragón. Barcelona. 1901.

—— Itinerario que siguió…Alfonso III al conquistar a Menorca. *In* Rev. de Menorca. 3rd ser. i (1898). 134–6.

Pedrell, F. Joan I compositor de música. *In* Estudis Universitaris Catalans. iii (1909). 2–30.

Pella y Forgas, J. La gran invasión francesa en Cataluña del año 1285. *In* Rev. de Ciencias hist. iv (1886). 120–45.

Ramos y Loscertales, J. M. El cautiverio de la Corona de Aragón durante los siglos xiii, xiv, y xv. Saragossa. 1915.

(Roca, J. M.) Johan I i les supersticións. *In* Bol. R. Acad. de Buenas Letras de Barcelona. x (1921). 125–69. [Unfinished.]

Rohde, H. E. Der Kampf um Sizilien in den Jahren 1291–1302. Berlin. 1913.

Romero, O. A. Historia y vicisitudes de la magistratura conocida con el nombre de Justicia de Aragón. Madrid. 1881. [disc. RAH.]

Sagarra, F. de. Noticias y documentos inéditos referentes al Infante D. Alfonso, primogénito de D. Jaime I y de Doña Leonor de Castilla. Barcelona. 1918.

Sarret y Arbós, J. Treva de Jaume II d'Aragó ab el rey de Mallorca. *In* Estudis Universitaris Catalans. IV (1910). 247–8.

Serrano Sanz, M. Notas acerca de los judíos aragoneses en los siglos XIV y XV. *In* Rev. de Arch., Bibl., y Mus. 3rd ser. XXXVII (1917). 324–46.

Silva, P. Giacomo II d' Aragona e la Toscana (1307–9). ASI. Anno LXXI, 2 (1913). 23–57.

Sitges, J. B. La muerte de D. Bernardo de Cabrera, consejero del Rey D. Pedro IV de Aragón (1364). Madrid. 1911.

Soldevila, F. Pere II el Gran, el desfiament amb Carles d'Anjou. Barcelona. 1919.

Swift, F. D. Marriage alliance of the Infante Pedro of Aragon and Edward I of England, 9 Oct. 1372. EHR. v (1890). 326–8.

Tomacelli, D. Storia de' reami di Napoli e Sicilia del 1250 al 1303. 2 vols. Naples. 1846.

Zurita y Castro, J. de. Anales de la Corona de Aragón. 6 vols. Saragossa. 1562–80.

—— Indices rerum ab Aragoniae regibus gestarum ab initiis regni ad annum MCDX. Saragossa. 1578.

III. CATALONIA.

[Many of the works under Aragon are also applicable to Catalonia.]

A. ORIGINAL DOCUMENTS.

Censo de Cataluña, ordenado en tiempo del Rey D. Pedro el Ceremonioso. *In* Col. de doc. inéd. del Arch. Gen....Aragón. XII comp.

Cortes de los antiguos reinos de Aragón y de Valencia, y Principado de Cataluña. 27 vols. (RAH.) Madrid. 1896 ff., in progress. [As yet only Catalonian Cortes, 1064–1479, published.]

Documents historichs catalans del sigle XIV. Colecció de cartas familiars correspondents als regnats de Pere del Punyalet y Johan I. [Ed. Coroleu, J.] Barcelona. 1889.

B. MODERN WORKS.

Marinesco, C. La Catalogne et l'Arménie au temps de Jacques II (1291–1327). (Repr. from Mélanges de l'École Roumaine en France.) Paris. 1923.

Miller, W. The Catalans at Athens. Rome. 1907.

Rubió y Lluch, A. Estudios sobre los historiadores griegos acerca de las expediciones catalanas a Oriente. *In* Rev. de Ciencias hist. III (1881). 57–70.

—— Els governs de Matheu de Moncada y Roger de Lluria en la Grecia Catalana. *In* Anuari de l'Inst. d'Estudis Catalans. IV (1912). 3–58.

—— La Grecia catalana des de la mort de Roger de Lluria fins a la de Frederic III de Sicilia (1370–7). *Ibid.* v (1913–14). 393–485.

—— La Grecia catalana des de la mort de Frederic III fins a la invasió navarresa (1377–9). *Ibid.* VI (1915–20). 127–200.

Sanchis y Guillén, V. Expedición de Catalanes y Aragoneses al Oriente en el siglo XIV. Madrid. 1890.

Schlumberger, G. Expéditions des "Almugavares," ou routiers catalans en Orient, de l'an 1302 à l'an 1311. 2nd edn. Paris. 1925.

Soldevila, F. Història de Catalunya. Vol. I. Barcelona. 1934.

CHAPTER XXI.

RUSSIA, 1015–1462.

I. BIBLIOGRAPHIES AND CRITICISM OF SOURCES.

Adelung, F. von. Kritisch-literarische Übersicht der Reisenden in Russland bis 1700, deren Berichte bekannt sind. Vol. I. St Petersburg (Leningrad) and Leipsic. 1846. [Very insufficient.]

Bagalêy, D. Russkaya istoriya. *See below*, III A.

Bestuzhev-Ryumin, K. Russkaya istoriya. *See below*, III A.

Hrushevs'kii, M. S. Istoriya Ukrayiny-Rusy. *See below*, III A.

Ikonnikov, V. S. Opyt russkoy istoriografii (Essay towards a Russian historiography). 2 vols. in 4 pts. Kiev. 1891–1908. [Fundamental: Vol. I contains a survey of collections of MSS.; Vol. II a systematical survey of historical evidence grouped in chronological order.]

Klyuchevski, V. O. Drevnerusskiya zhitiya svyatykh kak istoricheski istochnik (Old Russian lives of saints as an historical source). Moscow. 1871.

Milyukov, P. N. Istochniki russkoy istorii i russkaya istoriografiya (Bibliography of Russian history). *In* Brockhaus-Efron's Entsiklopedicheski Slovar' (article "Rossiya"). Vol. LV. pp. 430–46. St Petersburg (Leningrad). 1900.

Shakhmatov, A. Razyskaniya o drevnêyshikh russkikh lêtopisnykh svodakh (Researches into the earliest Russian annalistic compilations). St Petersburg (Leningrad). 1908.

II. COLLECTIONS OF SOURCES.

A. CHARTERS, ETC.

Arkheograficheskaya Kommissiya (Publications of). St Petersburg (Leningrad). 1836 ff.

    Akty istoricheskie. Vol. I (1334–1598). 1841.

    Akty otnosyashchiesya do yuridicheskago byta.

    Akty sobrannye Arkheograficheskoy Kommissiey. Vol. I (1294–1598). 1836.

    Akty yuridicheskie. 1838.

    Dopolnenie k Aktam Istoricheskim. Vol. I (10th century–1645). 1846.

    Pskovskaya Sudnaya Gramota. 1914.

Grigor'ev, V. V. O dostovêrnosti Yarlykov dannykh Khanami Zolotoy Ordy Russkomu Dukhovenstvu (On the authenticity of the Yarlyks given by the Khans of the Golden Horde to the Russian clergy). Moscow. 1842. [Contains the text of the Yarlyks.]

Turgenev, A. I. Historiae Russiae Monumenta ex antiquis exterarum gentium archivis et bibliothecis deprompta. Vol. I. St Petersburg (Leningrad). 1841. [Documents from the Vatican and other Roman archives.]

Vladimirski-Budanov, M. Khristomatiya po istorii russkago prava (Select documents illustrative of the history of Russian law). Vols. I and II. 4th edn. Kiev. 1889.

B. CHRONICLES.

Polnoe sobranie russkikh lêtopisey (Complete collection of Russian chronicles). Publ. by the Arkheograficheskaya Kommissiya. 24 vols. St Petersburg (Leningrad). 1841–1921.

[For other literary sources, *see* the works of Ikonnikov, V. S. and Klyuchevski, V. O., under sect. I, *above*.]

III. MODERN WORKS.

A. GENERAL.

Bagalêy, D. Russkaya istoriya (Russian history). Vol. I. Khar'kov. 1914. [With maps, plans, illustrations, and excellent bibliography.]

Bestuzhev-Ryumin, K. Russkaya istoriya (Russian history). Vol. I. St Petersburg (Leningrad). 1872. German transl. Schliemann, T. Mitau. 1873–6. [Important bibliographical introdn.]

Hrushevs'kii, M. S. Istoriya Ukrayiny-Rusy (History of Ukraina-Russia). Vols. ii and iii. L'vov. 1899–1900. [In Ukrainian (with maps).]

Karamzin, N. M. Istoriya gosudarstva Rossiyskago (History of the Russian State). Vols. ii–v. St Petersburg (Leningrad). 1818, and frequent reprints. French transl. St Thomas and Jauffret. Paris. 1819–26; German transl. Hauenschild, F. von. Riga. 1820–33. [The text is antiquated, but the notes are still valuable.]

Klyuchevski, V. O. Kurs russkoy istorii (Course of Russian history). Vol. i. Moscow. 1904. New edn. Petrograd (Leningrad). 1920. Engl. transl. Hogarth, C. J. Vol. i. London. 1911.

Lyubavski, M. K. Lektsii po drevney russkoy istorii (Lectures in ancient Russian history). 3rd edn. Moscow. 1918.

Pares, Sir Bernard. History of Russia. London. 1926.

Platonov, S. T. Lektsii po russkoy istorii (Lectures on Russian history). St Petersburg (Leningrad). 1901, and frequent reprints.

—— Uchebnik russkoy istorii (Textbook of Russian history). New edn. 2 vols. Prague. 1924. Engl. transl. Aronsberg, E., ed. Golder, F. A. New York. 1925.

Pokrovski, M. N. Russkaya istoriya s drevnêyshikh vremen (Russian history from the earliest times). Vol. i. Moscow. 1910, and frequent reprints. English transl. New York. 1928.

Rozhkov, N. Obzor russkoy istorii s sotsiologicheskoy tochki zrêniya (Survey of Russian history from the point of view of sociology). Pts. i and ii. St Petersburg (Leningrad). 1903, 5. Rev. edn. *as* Russkaya istoriya v sravnitel'no-istoricheskom osveshchenii (Russian history in the light of comparative history). Vols. i–iii. Petrograd (Leningrad). 1923.

Solov'ëv, S. M. Istoriya Rossii s drevnêyshikh vremen (History of Russia from the earliest times). Vols. i–iv. Moscow. 1851–4. 3rd edn. 1911. [The most complete survey of events.]

B. CHURCH HISTORY.

Goetz, L. C. Staat und Kirche in Altrussland (988–1240). Berlin. 1908.

Golubinski, E. E. Istoriya russkoy tserkvi (History of the Russian Church). Vol. i, in 2 pts. 2nd edn. Moscow. 1901. Vol. ii, pt. 1. 2nd edn. Moscow. 1904. [Fundamental.]

—— Istoriya kanonizatsii svyatykh v russkoy tserkvi (History of the canonisation of saints in the Russian Church). 2nd edn. Moscow. 1903.

Grigor'ev, V. V. *See above*, ii a.

Kazanski, P. S. Istoriya pravoslavnago russkago monashestva (History of Russian Orthodox Monasticism). Moscow. 1855.

Klyuchevski, V. O. *See above*, i.

Makariy, Bishop of Vinnitsa, afterwards Metropolitan of Moscow. Istoriya russkoy tserkvi (History of the Russian Church). Vols. i–viii. St Petersburg (Leningrad). 1857–77.

Priselkov. Ocherki po tserkovno-politicheskoy istorii Kievskoy Rusi x–xii vv. (Studies in the political history of the Church in Kievian Russia in the 10th–12th centuries). St Petersburg (Leningrad). 1913.

C. LAWS, INSTITUTIONS, AND SOCIAL HISTORY.

Bélyaev, I. D. Krest'yane na Rusi (The peasants in Russia). 2nd edn. Moscow. 1863.

Chicherin, B. N. Opyty po istorii russkago prava (Essays in the history of Russian law). Moscow. 1859.

D'yakonov, M. A. Ocherki obshchestvennago i gosudarstvennago stroya drevney Rusi (Studies of the social and political constitution of ancient Russia). St Petersburg (Leningrad). 1908.

Dyuvernua, N. L. Istochniki prava i sud na Rusi (Sources and administration of law in Russia). Moscow. 1869.

Goetz, L. C. Das russische Recht. 2 vols. Stuttgart. 1910–11. [On the Russkaya Pravda.]

934 *Russia*, 1015–1462

Kavelin, K. D. Vzglyad na yuridicheski byt drevney Rusi (A view of the juridical structure of ancient Russia). *In* Sobranie Sochineniy. Vol. i. Moscow. 1859.
—— O rodovych otnosheniyakh mezhdu knyaz'yami drevney Rusi (On the relations between the Princes of ancient Russia). *Ibid*. Vol. ii. Moscow. 1859.
Klyuchevski, V. O. Boyarskaya Duma drevney Rusi (The Council of Boyars in ancient Russia). 4th edn. Moscow. 1909.
Lappo-Danilevsky, A. S. Ocherk i istoriya obrazovaniya glavnêyshikh razryadov krest'yanskago naseleniya v Rossii (Survey and history of the formation of the principal categories of peasant population in Russia). *In* Krest'yansky stroy. Ed. Dolgorukov, P. D. and Tolstoy, S. L. Vol. i. Moscow. 1905.
Leontovich, T. I. Istoriya russkago prava (History of Russian law). Odessa. 1869.
Leshkov, V. N. Russki narod i gosudarstvo (The Russian people and the State). Moscow. 1858.
Meichik, D. M. Gramoty xiv i xv vv. (Charters of the 14th and 15th centuries). Moscow. 1883.
Mirsky, Prince D. S. Russia, a social history. London. 1931.
Mrochek-Drozdovski, P. N. Izslêdovaniya o russkoy Pravdê (Researches on the Russkaya Pravda). 2 vols. Moscow. 1881, 85.
Pavlov-Sil'vanski, N. P. Gosudarevy sluzhilÿe lyudi (History of the "serving" class, *i.e.* of the gentry). 2nd edn. St Petersburg (Leningrad). 1912.
—— Feodalizm v drevney Rusi (Feudalism in ancient Russia). St Petersburg (Leningrad). 1907.
Prêsnyakov, A. E. Knyazhoe Pravo v drevney Rusi (Princely law in ancient Russia). St Petersburg (Leningrad). 1909.
Samokvasov, D. Y. Drevnie goroda Rossii (Ancient Russian towns). St Petersburg (Leningrad). 1873.
—— Istoriya russkago prava (History of Russian law). 3rd edn. St Petersburg (Leningrad). 1906.
Ščepkin, E Die Erbfolgerecht bei den altslavischen Fürstenhausen. *In* Archiv für slavische Philologie. xxxiv. 1912.
Sergêevich, V. Drevnosti russkago prava (Antiquities of Russian law). 3rd edn. 3 vols. St Petersburg (Leningrad). 1900–11.
—— Lektsii i izslêdovaniya po istorii russkago prava (Lectures and researches in the history of Russian law). 4th edn. St Petersburg (Leningrad). 1910.
Solov'ëv, S. M. Istoriya otnosheniy mezhdu Russkimi knyaz'yami Ryurikova Doma (History of relations between the Princes of the House of Rurik). Moscow. 1847.
Vladimirski-Budanov, M. Obzor istorii russkago prava (Survey of the history of Russian law). 2nd edn. St Petersburg (Leningrad). 1888.
—— *See above*, ii a.
Zabêlin, I. E. Istoriya russkoy zhizni (History of life in Russia). Vol. ii. 2nd edn. Moscow. 1912.
Zagoskin, N. P. Ustavnÿe gramoty xiv–xvi vv. (Legislative charters of the 14th–16th centuries). Kazan. 1875.
—— Istoriya prava russkago naroda (History of Russian law). Vol. i. Kazan. 1899.

D. Economic History.

Aristov, N. Y. Promyshlennost' drevney Rusi (Industry in ancient Russia). St Petersburg (Leningrad). 1865.
Bakhrushin. Knyazheskoe khozyaystvo (Economic methods of the Princes). *In* Sbornik statey posvyashchennykh V. O. Klyuchevskomu. Moscow. 1909.
Berezhkov. O torgovlê Rusi s Ganzoy (On the Russo-Hanseatic trade). St Petersburg (Leningrad). 1879.
Dovnar-Zapol'ski, M. V. Istoriya russkago narodnago khozyaystva (Economic history of Russia). Kiev. 1911.
Goetz, L. C. Deutsch-russische Handelsgeschichte des Mittelalters. Lübeck. 1922.
Kulischer, J. Russische Wirtschaftsgeschichte. Vol. i. Jena. 1925.
Mavor, J. Economic history of Russia. 2nd edn. Vol. i. London. 1925.
Prozorovski, D. I. Moneta i vês v Rossii (Money and weights in Russia). St Petersburg (Leningrad). 1865.

Rozhkov, N. Gorod i derevnya v russkoy istorii (Town and country in Russian history). St Petersburg (Leningrad). 1904.

E. HISTORICAL GEOGRAPHY, TOPOGRAPHY, AND HISTORY OF SEPARATE DISTRICTS.

Barsov, N. P. Ocherki russkoy istoricheskoy geografii (Studies in the historical geography of Russia). Warsaw. 1885.

Bélyaev, I. D. Razskazy iz russkoy istorii (Tales from Russian history). Vols. ii–iv (Novgorod, Pskov, and Polotsk). Moscow. 1866–8.

—— Ocherk istorii sêverozapadnago Kraya Rossii (Outline of history of N.W. Russia). St Petersburg (Leningrad). 1867.

Grekov, B. D. Novgorodski Dom Sv. Sofii (The House of St Sophia in Novgorod). Vol. i. St Petersburg (Leningrad). 1914.

Kostomarov, N. I. Sêverno-Russkiya narodopravstva (The Democracies of North Russia). St Petersburg (Leningrad). 1863.

Lyubavski, M. K. Ocherk istorii litovsko-russkago gosudarstva (Outline of the history of the State of Lithuania and Russia). Moscow. 1910.

Nikitski, A. I. Ocherki iz zhizni Velikago Novgoroda (Studies in the life of Novgorod the Great). *In* Zhurnal ministerstva narodnago prosvêshcheniya. October, 1869. St Petersburg (Leningrad). 1869.

—— Ocherk vnutrenney istorii tserkvi v Velikom Novgorodê (Outline of the history of the Church in Novgorod). St Petersburg (Leningrad). 1879.

—— Ocherk vnutrenney istorii Pskova (Outline of the internal history of Pskov). St Petersburg (Leningrad). 1873.

—— Istoriya ekonomicheskago byta Velikago Novgoroda (Economic history of Novgorod). 2 vols. Moscow. 1893.

Petrov, N. I. Istoriko-topograficheskie ocherki Kieva (Historical topography of Kiev). Kiev. 1897.

Platonov, S. T. Proshloe russkago sêvera (The past of the Russian North). Berlin. 1924.

Shakhmatov, A. A. Vvedenie v kurs istorii russkago yazyka. Ch. i. Istoricheski protsess obrazovaniya russkikh plemen i narêchiy (Introduction to the history of the Russian language. Part i. Formation of the Russian peoples and dialects). Petrograd (Leningrad). 1916.

Zabêlin, I. E. Istoriya goroda Moskvy (History of the city of Moscow). Vol. i. 2nd edn. Moscow. 1905.

[For monographs on the history of separate territories see bibliography in Bagalêy, D. Russkaya istoriya. *See above,* iii A.]

Atlas.

Zamyslovski, E. E. Uchebny atlas i ob'yasneniya k uchebnomu atlasu po russkoy istorii (School atlas, with explanatory notes). St Petersburg (Leningrad). 1887.

F. SPECIAL PERIODS, BIOGRAPHY, AND MISCELLANEOUS.

Dashkevich, N. P. Knyazhenie Daniila Galitskago (The reign of Daniel of Galicia). Kiev. 1873.

Ekzemplyarski, A. V. Velikie i udêl'nye knyaz'ya Sêvernoy Rusi v tatarski period s 1238 po 1505 g. (The great and lesser Princes of Northern Russia during the Tartar period). 2 vols. St Petersburg (Leningrad). 1889, 91.

Linnichenko, I. Vzaimnyya otnosheniya Rusi i Pol'shi do poloviny 14 vêka (The relations of Russia and Poland to the middle of the 14th century). Kiev. 1884.

Prêsnyakov, A. E. Obrazovanie velikorusskago gosudarstva (The formation of the Great-Russian State). Petrograd (Leningrad). 1918.

Russki biograficheski slovar' (Dictionary of Russian biography). 23 vols. (Publ. by the Imperatorskoe russkoe istoricheskoe obshchestvo.) St Petersburg (Leningrad). 1896–1916. [No more publ.]

G. Archaeology and Art.

[See bibliography by Alpatov and Brunov *in* Zeitschr. für slavische Philologie. Neue Folge. II (1925). 474–505.]

Grabar', I. Istoriya russkago iskusstva (History of Russian art). Vols. I, II, and IV. St Petersburg (Leningrad). 1911–15.

Halle, F. W. Alt-russische Kunst. Orbis Pictus. Berlin. 1920.

Kondakov, N. P. The Russian Icon. Transl. with preface by Minns, E. H. Oxford. 1927.

Mouratov, P. P. L'ancienne peinture russe. Prague. 1925.

Réau, L. L'Art russe des origines à Pierre le Grand. Paris. 1921.

Tolstoy, Count I. I. and Kondakov, N. P. Russkiya drevnosti v pamyatnikakh iskusstva (Russian antiquities). Vols. IV–VI. St Petersburg (Leningrad). 1895–9.

Wulff, O. and Alpatov, M. Denkmäler der Ikonenmalerei in kunstgeschichtlicher Folge bearbeitet. Dresden. 1925.

H. Literature.

Hrushevs'kii, M. Istoriya ukrayins'koyi literatury (History of Ukrainian literature). Vols. II and III (Kievian and Galician period). Kiev. 1923. [In Ukrainian.]

Istrin, V. Ocherk istorii drevne-russkoy literatury (Outline of the history of Old-Russian literature). Petrograd (Leningrad). 1922.

Keltuyala, V. Kurs istorii russkoy literatury (History of Russian literature). Vo s. I and II. St Petersburg (Leningrad). 1908, 11.

Mirsky, Prince D. S. History of Russian literature. New York and London. 1927.

Peretts, V. N. Kratki ocherk metodologii istorii russkoy literatury (Short outline of methodology of Russian literary history). Petrograd (Leningrad). 1922. [Bibliography.]

Speranski, M. N. Istoriya russkoy literatury (History of Russian literature). Moscow. 1914.

Vladimirov, P. V. Drevnyaya russkaya literatura, XI–XIII vv. (Ancient Russian literature, 11th–13th centuries). Kiev. 1900.

CHAPTER XXII.

THE JEWS IN THE MIDDLE AGES.

[In this Bibliography mention is made only of works in languages accessible to the ordinary English student. Those which seem likely to remain unfinished are marked with an asterisk.]

I. SPECIAL BIBLIOGRAPHIES.

Dubnow, S. Weltgeschichte des jüdischen Volkes. *See below,* II B (i). [Bibliography to each chapter.]
Freidus, A. S. List of works relating to the history and condition of Jews in various countries. (New York Public Library publn.) New York. 1914.
Margolis, M. L. and Marx, A. History of the Jewish People. pp. 739–52. *See below,* II B (i).
Steinschneider, M. Die Geschichtsliteratur der Juden.* Pt. I. Frankfort-on-M. 1905.

II. GENERAL JEWISH HISTORY.

A. Sources.

(i) *Documents.*

Aronius, J. Regesten zur Geschichte der Juden im Fränkischen und Deutschen Reiche bis zum Jahre 1273. Berlin. 1902.
Eubel, K. Zu dem Verhalten der Päpste zu den Juden. *In* Römische Quartalschrift. XIII. Rome. 1889. [Calendar for 1379–1450.]
Fürst, J. Urkunden zur Geschichte der Juden.* Pt. I. Leipsic. 1844.
Stern, M. Urkundliche Beiträge über die Stellung der Päpste zu den Juden.* Kiel. 1893–6.

(ii) *Chronicles.*

Adler, E. N. Jewish Travellers. London. 1930.
Benjamin of Tudela. Itinerary. Ed. with Engl. transl. Adler, M. N. London. 1907; *also* by Asher, A. 2 vols. London. 1840–1.
Gans, D. Zemah David (Chronology). Latin transl. Leyden. 1634. German transl. Klemperer, G. Prague. 1890.
Höxter, J. Quellenbuch zur jüdischen Geschichte und Literatur. 5 vols. Frankfort-on-M. 1927 ff. [Elementary.]
Joseph ha-Cohen. Emek haBakha (The Valley of Tears). German transl. Wiener, M. Leipsic. 1858. French transl. Sée, J. Paris. 1881.
—— Chronicles (of France and Turkey). Transl. Bialloblotzky, C. F. H. 2 vols. London. 1835. [*Cf.* Loeb, I. Joseph ha-Cohen et les chroniqueurs juifs. (Repr. from REJ. XVI, XVII.) Paris. 1888.]
Neubauer, A. Mediaeval Jewish Chronicles. 2 vols. Oxford. 1887, 95. [Hebrew texts.]
—— and Stern, M. Hebräische Berichte über die Judenverfolgungen während der Kreuzzüge. *See below,* III E (ii).
Petahia of Regensburg. Travels. Ed. Benisch, A. London. 1856.
Spina, Alfonso de. Fortalitium Fidei. Nuremberg. 1494; Lyons. 1511; 1525. [Much historical material is embodied in this polemical work.]
Usque, S. Consolaçam ás Tribulaçoens de Ysrael. Ferrara. 1553. *Also* ed. Mendes dos Remedios *in* Sussidios para o estudo da historia da litteratura portuguesa. Coimbra. 1906–7.
Verga, Solomon ibn. Shebet Jehudah. Spanish transl. Leon, M. de. Amsterdam. 1640, 1744; Latin transl. Gentius, G. Amsterdam. 1690; German transl. Wiener, M. Hanover. 1856. 2nd edn. 1924.
[*Cf.* Loeb, I. Le Folk-lore juif dans la chronique du Schébet Jehuda d'Ibn Verga. REJ. XXIV, pp. 1–29; and Baer, F. Untersuchungen über Quellen und

Komposition des Schebet Jehuda. (Veröffentlichungen der Akad. für die Wissensch. des Judentums. Hist. Sekt. Vol. ii.) Berlin. 1923.]

Zedner, J. Auswahl historischer Stücke aus hebräischen Schriftstellern vom 2 Jahrht. bis auf die Gegenwart, mit vocalisirtem Texte, deutscher Übersetzung, und Anmerkungen. Berlin. 1840.

[Attention should perhaps be drawn to the Anthology of Jewish Historical Literature (Hebrew only) published by A. Kahana. Warsaw. 1922–3.]

B. MODERN WORKS.

(i) *General.*

Bédarride, J. Les Juifs en France, en Italie, et en Espagne. Paris. 1867.

Cassel, S. Article "Juden" *in* Ersch-Gruber. *See Gen. Bibl.* i.

Depping, G. B. Les Juifs dans le moyen âge: essai historique. Paris. 1834.

Dubnow, S. Jewish History. London. 1903. [An essay on the philosophy of Jewish history.]

—— Weltgeschichte des jüdischen Volkes. (Transl. from the Russian.) 10 vols. Berlin. 1925–8.

Finkelstein, L. Jewish self-government in the Middle Ages. New York. 1925.

Frankel, Z. Die Eidesleistung der Juden. Dresden. 1840.

Graetz, H. Geschichte der Juden von den ältesten Zeiten bis auf die Gegenwart. 11 vols. in 13. Latest edns. Leipsic. 1890–1911. English transl. ed. Löwy, B. and others. 5 vols. London. 1891–2; republ. with a 6th vol. (index, etc.). Philadelphia. 1891–8. Based on the earlier unrevised editions, is somewhat abbreviated, and lacks the footnotes and appendices. [This work is still unsuperseded.]

Jost, M. Geschichte der Israeliten seit der Zeit der Makkabäer bis auf unsere Tage. 9 vols. Berlin. 1820–9.

—— Geschichte des Judenthums und seiner Sekten. 3 vols. Leipsic. 1857–9.

Juster, J. Les Juifs dans l'Empire Romain. 2 vols. Paris. 1914. [Indispensable for the foundations of medieval Jewish history.]

Loeb, I. Article "Juifs" *in* Nouveau dictionnaire de géographie universelle. Ed. Vivien de Saint-Martin, L. Paris. 1879–1900.

Mann, J. Texts and studies in Jewish History and Literature. Vol. i. Cincinnati. 1931.

Margolis, M. L. and Marx, A. History of the Jewish People. Philadelphia. 1927.

Robert, U. Les signes d'infamie au moyen âge. Paris. 1891.

Scherer, J. E. Beiträge zur Geschichte des Judenrechtes im Mittelalter.* Vol. i. Die Rechtsverhältnisse der Juden in den deutsch-österreichischen Ländern. Mit einer Einleitung über die Principien der Judengesetzgebung in Europa während des Mittelalters. Leipsic. 1901.

Simonsohn, M. Die kirchliche Judengesetzgebung im Zeitalter der Reformationskonzilien von Konstanz und Basel. Breslau. 1912.

Singermann, F. Über Judenabzeichen. Berlin. 1915.

Zunz, L. Zur Geschichte und Literatur der Juden. Berlin. 1845.

—— The Sufferings of the Jews during the Middle Ages. (Transl. by Löwy, A. of the chapter "Leiden" *in* Die synagogale Poesie des Mittelalters. Berlin. 1885.) New York. 1907.

Encyclopaedia Judaica. Berlin. 1928 ff., in progress.

Jewish Encyclopaedia. 12 vols. New York. 1901–6.

Jewish Quarterly Review. London. 1889–1908. New series. Philadelphia. 1910 ff., in progress. (JQR.)

Monatsschrift für die Geschichte und Wissenschaft des Judenthums. Dresden, and later Breslau. 1851 ff., in progress. (MGWJ.)

Revue des études juives. Paris. 1880 ff., in progress. Index to vols. i–l. 1910. (REJ.) [The most valuable review for the study of general Jewish history.]

Loeb, I. Tables du Calendrier juif. Paris. 1886.

Mahler, E. Handbuch der jüdischen Chronologie. Leipsic. 1916. [For calculating dates.]

(ii) *Special Subjects.*

(a) *Social and Economic History.*

"Abgaben und Steuern" (by various writers). *In* Encyclopaedia Judaica. Vol. I. pp. 247–300. *See above,* B (i).

Abrahams, I. Jewish life in the Middle Ages. London. 1896. 2nd edn. by Roth, C. London. 1932.

Caro, G. Sozial- und Wirtschaftgeschichte der Juden im Mittelalter und der Neuzeit. Vol. I, 2nd edn. Frankfort-on-M. 1924. Vol. II. *Ibid.* 1920.

Guttmann, J. Die wirtschaftliche und soziale Bedeutung der Juden im Mittelalter. MGWJ. LI. 1907.

Hahn, B. Die wirtschaftliche Tätigkeit der Juden im Fränkischen und Deutschen Reich bis zum 2 Kreuzzug. Freiburg-i.-B. 1911.

Hoffmann, M. Der Geldhandel der deutschen Juden im Mittelalter. Leipsic. 1910.

Pinkus, F. Studien zur Wirtschaftsstellung der Juden. Berlin. 1905.

Roscher, W. Die Stellung der Juden im Mittelalter betrachtet vom Standpunkt der allgemeinen Handelspolitik. *In* Zeitschr. für die gesammte Staatswissenschaft. XXXI, pp. 503–26. Tübingen. 1875. Repr. in Ansichten der Volkswirtschaft. 3rd edn. II, pp. 321–54. Leipsic. 1878.

Schipper, I. Anfänge des Kapitalismus bei den abendländischen Juden im früheren Mittelalter, bis zum Ausgang des 12 Jahrhts. (Repr. from Zeitschr. für Volkswirtschaft, Sozialpolitik, und Verwaltung. XV.) Vienna and Leipsic. 1907.

(b) *Intellectual History and Influence.*

Abrahams, I., Bevan, E. R., and Singer, C. *edd.* The Legacy of Israel. Oxford. 1927.

—— and Yellin, D. Maimonides. London. 1903.

Berger, S Quam notitiam linguae hebraicae habuerint Christiani medii aevi temporibus in Gallia. Paris. 1893.

Blondhein, D. S. Les Parlers Judéo-Romans et la Vetus Latina. Paris. 1925.

Güdemann, M. Geschichte des Erziehungswesens und der Cultur der abendländischen Juden während des Mittelalters und der neueren Zeit. 3 vols. Vienna. 1880–8.

Guttmann, J. Die Scholastik des 13 Jahrhts. in ihren Beziehungen zum Judenthum und zur jüdischen Literatur. Breslau. 1902.

Jacobs, J. Jewish contributions to civilisation : an estimate. Philadelphia. 1919.

Krauss, S. Geschichte der jüdischen Ärzte vom frühesten Mittelalter bis zur Gleichberechtigung. Vienna. 1930.

Krautheimer, R. Mittelalterliche Synagogen. Berlin. 1927. [Mainly in Germany.]

Lieber, M. Rashi. *See below,* III B (iii).

Newman, L. I. Jewish influence on Christian reform movements. (Columbia Univ. Oriental Studies. XXIII.) New York. 1925.

Silver, A. H. Messianic speculation in Israel. New York. 1928.

Soury, J. Des études hébraïques et exégétiques au moyen âge chez les Chrétiens d'Occident. Paris. 1867.

Steinschneider, M. Die hebräischen Übersetzungen des Mittelalters. Berlin. 1893.

(c) *Disputations.*

Kahn, Z. Le livre de Joseph le Zélateur. REJ. II, III.

Loeb, I. La controverse religieuse entre les Chrétiens et les Juifs au moyen âge en France et en Espagne. Paris. 1888.

—— La controverse sur le Talmud sous Saint-Louis. REJ. I–III.

—— Polémistes chrétiens et juifs en France et en Espagne. REJ. XVIII.

Martin, Raymund. Pugio Fidei. Paris. 1651; Leipsic. 1667.

Poznánski, S. La Colloque de Tortose et de San Mateo. REJ. LXXIV–LXXVI.

Wagenseil, J. C. Tela Ignea Satanae. Altdorf. 1681. [Contains texts of Hebrew accounts of disputations of Paris and Barcelona, with Latin transl.]

(d) *Blood Accusation, etc.*

Cohn, F. Blut auf Speisen, Hostien. (Die Mikroskopische Welt. *In* Die Gegenwart. Vol. XI. pp. 808 ff.)

Frank, F. Der Ritualmord vor den Gerichtshöfen der Wahrheit und der Gerechtigkeit.
    2nd edn. 2 vols. Berlin. 1901–2.
Guidetti, C. Pro Judaeis: riflessioni e documenti. Turin. 1884.
Kembter, A. Acta pro veritate martyrii corporis et cultus publici B. Andreae Rin-
    nensis. Innsbruck. 1745.
Stern, M. Päpstliche Bullen gegen die Blutbeschuldigung. Berlin. 1893.
Strack, H. L. Das Blut im Glauben und Aberglauben der Menschheit, mit besonderer
    Berücksichtigung der Volksmedizin und des jüdischen Blutritus. 8th edn.
    Munich. 1900. English transl. The Jew and Human Sacrifice. London. 1909.
Zaviziano, G. A. Un raggio di luce: la persecuzione degli Ebrei nella storia: rifles-
    sioni. Corfù. 1891. [Very valuable appendix of documents.]

III. SEPARATE COUNTRIES

A. England.

(i) *Bibliography.*

Jacobs, J. and Wolf, L. Bibliotheca Anglo-Judaica. (Publications of the Anglo-Jewish
    Hist. Exhibition. III.) London. 1888.

(ii) *Sources.*

Abrahams, I., Stokes, H. P., and Loewe, H. Starrs in the British Museum. 2 vols.
    London. 1931.
Davis, M. D. *Shetaroth:* Hebrew Deeds of English Jews before 1290. (Publications
    of the Anglo-Jewish Hist. Exhibition. II.) London. 1888.
Jacobs, J. The Jews of Angevin England : documents and records. London. 1893.
Rigg, J. M. Calendar of the Plea Rolls of the Exchequer of the Jews. Vols. I, II.
    (Jewish Hist. Soc. of England.) London. 1905, 10. Vol. III, ed. Jenkinson, H.
    (*Ibid.*) 1929.
——— Select Pleas, Starrs, and other records from the Rolls of the Exchequer of the
    Jews. (Jewish Hist. Soc. of England; and Selden Soc. XV.) London. 1902.

(iii) *Modern Works.*

Abrahams, B. L. The Expulsion of the Jews from England in 1290. (Repr. from
    JQR. 1894–5.) Oxford. 1895.
Adler, E. N. London (History of the Jews in). Philadelphia. 1930.
Adler, M. The Medieval Jews of Exeter. *In* Trans. of the Devonshire Assocn. for
    the advancement of Science, Literature, and Art. LXIII, pp. 221–40. Exeter. 1931.
Anglo-Jewish Historical Exhibition, Papers read at the. (Publications. I.) London.
    1888.
Blunt, J. E. History of the establishment and residence of the Jews in England.
    London. 1830.
Davis, M. D. The Mediaeval Jews of Lincoln. *In* Archaeol. Journal. XXXVIII. London.
    1881.
Egan, C. The status of the Jews in England. London. 1848.
Henriques, H. S. A. The Jews and the English Law. Oxford. 1908.
Hyamson, A. M. History of the Jews in England. 2nd edn. London. 1929.
Jacobs, J. Une lettre française d'un Juif anglais au XIIIe siècle. REJ. XVIII (1889).
    256–61.
Jessopp, A. and James, M. R. St William of Norwich. Cambridge. 1896.
Jewish Historical Society of England. Miscellanies. Vol. I. London. 1925, in pro-
    gress. Transactions. Vols. I–XI. London. 1894–1928, in progress.
Jewish Quarterly Review. Old series. (*See above*, II B (i).) *Passim.* (Articles by
    Joseph Jacobs, M. D. Davis, A. Neubauer, etc.)
Leonard, G. H. The expulsion of the Jews by Edward I. TRHS. n.s. Vol. v. 1891.
Little, H. G. Friar Henry of Wodstone and the Jews. *In* Collectanea Franciscana.
    Vol. II, pp. 150–7. (Brit. Soc. of Franciscan Studies. X.) Manchester. 1922.
Madox, T. History of the Exchequer. 2nd edn. London. 1769.
Neubauer, A. Notes on the Jews in Oxford. *In* Collectanea, Vol. II, pp. 274–316, with
    sheet of addenda. (Oxford Hist. Soc. XVI.) Oxford. 1890.
Pike, L. O. History of Crime in England. Vol. I. London. 1873.

Prynne, W. A Short Demurrer to the Jews long-discontinued Remitter into England. 2 pts. London. 1655-6.
Rye, W. The Jews of Norwich. *In* Norfolk Antiquarian Miscellany. Vol. i. pp. 312–44. Norwich. 1877.
Schechter, F. The Rightlessness of Mediaeval English Jewry. JQR. n.s. iv (1913–14). 121–51.
Stokes, H. P. Short History of the Jews in England. London. 1921.
—— Studies in Anglo-Jewish History. London. 1913.
Tovey, d'Blossiers. Anglia Judaica. London. 1738.
[Webb, P. C.] The Question whether a Jew...was...capable...to...hold Lands..., considered by a Gentleman of Lincoln's Inn. London. 1753.

B. France.

(i) *Bibliography.*

Gross, H. Gallia Judaica. pp. 756–64. *See below* (iii).
[Periodical review of current publications in Revue des études juives. *See above*, ii b (i).]

(ii) *Sources.*

Aronius, J. Regesten zur Geschichte der Juden im Fränkischen und Deutschen Reiche bis zum Jahre 1273. Berlin. 1902.
Schwab, M. Inscriptions hébraïques de la France. (Repr. from Nouvelles Archives des Missions scientifiques. xii.) Paris. 1904.

(iii) *Modern Works.*

Arnaud, C. Essai sur la condition des Juifs en Provence au moyen âge. Forcalquier. 1879.
Azemard, E. Étude sur les Juifs de Montpellier du moyen âge. Nîmes. 1924.
Bégin, E. Histoire des Juifs dans le nord-est de France. *In* Revue Orientale. i, ii. Brussels. 1841 ff.
Bofarull y Sans, F. de. Jaime I el Conquistador y la comunidad judia de Montpellier. *In* Boletin de la R. Acad. de Buenas Letras de Barcelona. v. 1909–10.
Garnos, H. Essai historique sur la condition des Juifs dans l'ancien droit français. Paris. 1897.
Gross, H. Gallia Judaica. Paris. 1897. [A geographical dictionary, mainly important for literary history.]
Kahn, L. Les Juifs de Paris depuis le vie siècle. Paris. 1889.
Langlois, C. V. *In* Lavisse, E. Histoire de France. Vol. iii, pt. 2, pp. 221–7. *See Gen. Bibl.* v.
Lévi, I. Article "France" *in* Jewish Encyclopaedia. Vol. v. New York. 1903. [The best available general account.]
—— Histoire des Juifs de France. Vol. i. Des origines au xe siècle.* Paris. 1903.
Lieber, M. Rashi. London. 1906. [Biography of the great Franco-Jewish scholar, with good sketch of his background.]
Loeb, I. Les expulsions des Juifs de France au xive siècle. *In* Jubelschrift zum 70 Geburtstag des H. Graetz. Breslau. 1887.
Maulde, M. de. Les Juifs dans les états français du Saint-Siège. Paris. 1886.
Nordmann, A. Histoire des Juifs à Genève de 1281 à 1780. (Repr. from REJ. lxxx.) Paris. 1925.
Régné, J. Étude sur la condition des Juifs de Narbonne du ve au xive siècle. (Repr. from REJ. lv–lxiii.) Narbonne. 1912.
Renan, E. [and Neubauer, A.]. Les Rabbins français du commencement du xive siècle. (Repr. from Histoire Littéraire de la France. xxvii.) Paris. 1887.
—— Les Écrivains juifs français du xive siècle. (*Ibid.* xxxi.) Paris. 1893.
Revue des études juives. *Passim. See above*, ii b (i).
Rouet, A. Étude sur l'école juive de Lunel au moyen âge. *n.p., n.d.*
Saige, C. Les Juifs du Languedoc antérieurement au xive siècle. Paris. 1881.
Wiegand, F. Agobard von Lyon und die Judenfrage. *In* Zeitschrift zum 80 Geburtstag Prinzregent von Bayern. Munich. 1901.

C. Spain and Portugal.

(i) *Sources.*

Baer, F. Die Juden in christlichen Spanien. Pt. i. Urkunden und Regesten. Vol. i. Aragonien und Navarra. (Veröffentlichungen der Akad. für die Wissensch. des Judentums. Hist. Sekt. Vol. iv.) Berlin. 1929. [Vol. ii will give similar document sources dealing with the kingdom of Castile; in vol. iii will appear a general history on the basis of the new material. On pp. 1081–91 is an exhaustive bibliography.]

Duran i Sampone, A. Documents Aljamiats de Jueus catalans. Barcelona. 1926.

Jacobs, J. An enquiry into the sources of the history of the Jews in Spain. London. 1895.

Millas i Vallicrosa, J. Documents hebraics de Jueus catalans. (Institut d'Estudis Catalans. Secció històrico-arqueológica. Memorias. i, 3.) Barcelona. 1927.

—— Escrituras mozárabes de Hebreos toledanos. (From A. Gonzalez Palencia. Los mozárabes de Toledo en los siglos xii y xiii.) Madrid. 1930.

Régné, J. Catalogue des Actes de Jaime Ier, Pedro III, et Alfonso III, rois d'Aragon, concernant les Juifs (1213–91). REJ. lx–lxx. 1910–20. *Also* publ. separately (1213–85). Paris. 1911, 14.

—— Catalogue d'Actes pour servir à l'histoire des Juifs de la couronne d'Aragon sous le règne de Jaime II (1291–1327). REJ. lxxiii–lxxviii. 1921–4.

Remiro, D. M. Gaspar. Los Cronistas hispano-judíos; discurso...en el de su recepción pública ante la Real Academia de la Historia. Granada. [19...]

Schwab, M. Rapport sur les inscriptions hébraïques de l'Espagne. (Repr. from Nouvelles Archives des Missions scientifiques. xiv.) Paris. 1907.

Schwarz, S. Inscrições hebraicas em Portugal. (Repr. from Arqueologia e Historia.) Lisbon. 1923.

(ii) *Modern Works.*

Alonso, B. F. Los Judíos en Orense (siglos xv al xviii). Orense. 1870.

Alves, F. M. Memorias arqueológico-históricas do distrito de Bragança: os Judeus. Bragança. 1925.

Amzalak, M. B. Uma Carta de Lei inédita de D. Alfonso II onde...se trata das Judarias portuguesas. Lisbon. 1926.

Arigita y Lara, M. Los Judíos en el páis vasco. Pamplona. 1908.

Azevedo, P. d'. Culpas de David Negro. *In* Archivo Historico Portugues. i, pp. 53–7.

Baer, F. Studien zur Geschichte der Juden im Königreich Aragonien während des 13 und 14 Jahrhts. (Ebering's Hist. Studien, 106.) Berlin. 1913.

Barros Basto, A. de. Os Judeus no velho Porto. (Repr. from Revista de Estudios hebraicos em Portugal.) Lisbon. 1929.

Bofarull y Sans, F. de. Jaime I y los Judíos. *In* Congrés d'història de la Corona d'Aragó dedicat a l'alt rei En Jaume I i la seva època. Vol. ii. Barcelona. 1913.

—— Los Judíos en el territorio de Barcelona, siglos x al xii: reinado de Jaime I (1213–76). Barcelona. 1911.

Bonilla y S. Martin, A. Historia de la filosofía española. Vol. ii. Siglos viii–xii: Judíos. Madrid. 1911.

Carreras i Candi, F. L'Aljama de Jueus de Tortosa. (Mem. de la R. Acad. de Buenas Letras de Barcelona. ix, 3.) Barcelona. 1928.

—— Evolució històrica dels Jueus i Juehisants a Catalunya. *In* Butlletí dels Estudis Universitaris. Barcelona. 1909.

Castro y Rossi, A. de. Historia de los Judíos en España. Cadiz. 1847. Engl. transl. Kirwan, E. D. G. M. Cambridge. 1851.

Chone, H. Nachmanides. Nuremberg. 1930.

Corbella, R. La Aljama de Jueus de Vich. Vich. 1909.

Epstein, I. The "Responsa" of Solomon ben Adreth of Barcelona (1235–1310) as a source of the history of Spain: studies in the communal life of the Jews in Spain as reflected in the "Responsa." London. 1925.

Farinelli, A. Marrano: storia d' un vituperio. Geneva. 1925.

Fernandez y Gonzalez, D. Instituciones jurídicas de los Hebreos españoles. Vol. I.* (Bibliotheca jurídica de autores españoles, 10.) Madrid. 1881.
—— Ordenamiento formado por los procuradores de las aljamas hebreas...en... Valladolid el año 1432. Madrid. 1886.
Fidel Fita, P. España hebrea. 2 vols. Madrid. 1890, 98.
—— Estudios históricos. 8 vols. Madrid. 1882-7.
Fiter Ingles, J. Expulsión de los Judíos de Barcelona. Barcelona. 1876.
Floriano, A. C. La Aljama de Judíos de Teruel y el hallazgo de su necrópolis. (Memoria de excavaciones. I.) Teruel. 1926.
—— El Santo Oficio en Aragón: Establecimiento de la Inquisición en Teruel. BRAH. LXXXVI, LXXXVII.
—— S. Vicente Ferrer y las aljamas turolenses. BRAH. LXXXIV.
Freimann, A. Ascher ben Jehiel: sein Leben und Wirken. *In* Jahrb. der jüdisch-literarischen Gesellschaft. XII. Frankfort-on-M. 1918.
—— Die Ascheriden (1267-1391). *Ibid.* XIII. Frankfort-on-M. 1920.
[On the history of one of the most influential Spanish Rabbis and his family.]
Girbal, E. C. Los Judíos en Gerona. Gerona. 1870.
Gonzalez Simancas, M. Las Sinagogas de Toledo. Madrid. 1929.
Güdemann, M. Das jüdische Unterrichtswesen während der spanischen-arabischen Periode. Vienna. 1873.
Juster, J La condition légale des Juifs sous les rois visigoths. *In* Études...offertes... à...P. F. Girard. Paris. 1912.
Kayserling, M. Christopher Columbus and the Participation of the Jews in the Spanish and Portuguese discoveries. Transl. Gross, C. New York. 1894.
—— Geschichte der Juden in Spanien und Portugal. Vol. I. Navarra, Baskenländer, und Balearen. Berlin. 1861. Vol. II. Portugal. Leipsic. 1867.
—— Sephardim: Romanische Poesie der Juden in Spanien: ein Beitrag zur Literatur und Geschichte der spanisch-portugiesischen Juden. Leipsic. 1859.
Lea, H. C. History of the Inquisition of Spain. 4 vols. New York. 1906-7.
Lindo, E. H. History of the Jews in Spain and Portugal. London. 1848.
Loeb, I. Règlement des Juifs de Castille en 1432. REJ. XIII.
—— Le sac des Juiveries de Valence et de Madrid en 1391. *Ibid.*
Marx, A. New source for the Expulsion of the Jews from Spain. JQR. O.S. XX. 1908.
Mendez Bejarano, M. Histoire de la Juiverie de Seville. Madrid. 1922.
Menéndez y Pelayo, M. Hist. de los heterodoxos españoles. Rev. edn. Madrid. 1929.
Merchan, L. Delgado. La Judería y la Inquisición de Ciudad-Real.
Miret y Sans, J. and Schwab, M. Documents sur les Juifs catalans aux XIe, XIIe, et XIIIe siècles. REJ. LXVIII. 1914.
—— Nuevos documentos de los Judíos barceloneses de los siglos XI y XII. BRAH. LXVIII, LXIX. 1916.
Moreno de Villalba, F. De los Árabes y Hebreos españoles. Discurso. Madrid. 1851.
Perles, J. R. Salomo ben Abraham ben Adreth [Rabbi of Barcelona]: sein Leben und seine Schriften. Breslau. 1863.
Pertegas, J. R. La Judería de Valencia. (From J. Sanctis y Silvera. La iglesia parroquial de S. Tomás.) Valencia. 1913.
Rahola, C. Els Jueus a Catalunya. Barcelona. 1929.
Remedios, J. M. dos. Os Judeus em Portugal. 2 vols. Coimbra. 1895, 1928.
Rios, J. Amador de los. Estudios históricos, políticos, y literarios sobre los Judíos de España. Madrid. 1848. French transl. Magnabal, J. G. Paris. 1861.
—— Historia social, política, y religiosa de los Judíos de España y Portugal. 3 vols. Madrid. 1875-6.
Rodríguez y Fernandez, I. Segovia-Corpus. Madrid. 1902. [On the pretended Host-desecration at Segovia in 1410.]
Roth, C. History of the Marranos. Philadelphia. 1932.
Sarret y Arbos, J. Jueus a Manresa. Manresa. 1917.
Serrano y Sanz, M. Notas acerca de los Judíos aragonenses en los siglos XIV y XV. *In* Revista de Archivos, Bibliotecas, y Museos. XXXVII. 1917.
—— Origenes de la dominación española en América. Vol. I. Madrid. 1918. [Ch. I is an invaluable account of the social history of the Community of Saragossa.]

Torroella, J. B. La Jueria de Banyoles. Gerona. 1928.
Viterbo, S. Occurrencias da vida judaica. *In* Archivo Hist. Portugues. II, pp. 176–200.

D. ITALY.

(i) *Bibliographies.*

Gabrieli, G. Italia Judaica. Rome. 1924.
Morpurgo, E. Bibliografia della storia degli Ebrei nel Veneto. *In* Rivista Israelitica. VII–IX. Florence. 1910–12.

(ii) *Sources.*

Ascoli, G. Iscrizioni inedite o mal note...di antichi sepolcri giudaici nel Napolitano. (Repr. from Atti del IV Congresso Internazionale degli Orientalisti.) Florence. 1880.
Lagumina, B. and G. Codice diplomatico dei Giudei di Sicilia. Palermo. 1884 ff., in progress. [The most important collection of the sort yet published.]
Salzman, M. The Chronicle of Ahimaaz. (Columbia University Oriental Studies. XXI.) New York. 1924.

(iii) *Modern Works.*

Anfossi, M. Gli Ebrei in Piemonte: loro condizione giuridico-sociale dal 1430 al-l'emancipazione. Turin. 1914.
Balletti, A. Gli Ebrei e gli Estensi. 2nd edn. Reggio-Emilia. 1930.
Berliner, A. Geschichte der Juden in Rom. 2 vols. Berlin. 1893.
Cassuto, U. Gli Ebrei a Firenze nell' età del Rinascimento. Florence. 1918.
Ciardini, M. I banchieri ebrei in Firenze nel secolo XV. Florence. 1907.
Ciscato, A. Gli Ebrei in Padova. Padua. 1901.
Dito, O. La storia calabrese e la dimora degli Ebrei in Calabria dal secolo V alla seconda metà del secolo XVI. Rocca S. Casciano. 1916.
Ferorelli, N. Gli Ebrei nell' Italia meridionale. Turin. 1915.
Friedenwald, H. Jewish Physicians in Italy. *In* Publications of American Jewish Hist. Soc. XXVII (1922). 133–211.
Giovanni, G. de. L'Ebraismo della Sicilia. Palermo. 1748.
La Lumia, I. Gli Ebrei siciliani. *In* Studi di storia siciliana. Vol. II. Palermo. 1870.
Mifsud, A. Tracce dell' antica vitalità giudaica Maltese. *In* Archivum Melitense. IV, pp. 1–25.
Mondolfo, U. G. Gli Ebrei in una città dell' Umbria [Terni] nei secoli XV e XVI. Assisi. 1907.
Resasco, G. Segno degli Ebrei. (Repr. from Giornale Ligustico, 1888–9.) Genoa. 1889. [Comprises a general history of the Jews in Italy.]
Rodocanachi, E. Le Saint-Siège et les Juifs: le Ghetto à Rome. Paris. 1891.
Roth, C. The Jews of Malta. *In* Trans. of Jewish Hist. Soc. of England. XII. 1932.
—— Venice (History of Jews in). Philadelphia. 1930.
Spano, G. Gli Ebrei in Sardegna. *In* Rivista Sarda. I. 1875.
Straus, R. Die Juden im Königreich Sizilien unter Normannen und Staufern. Heidelberg. 1910.
Vogelstein, H. and Rieger, P. Geschichte der Juden in Rom. 2 vols. Berlin. 1896, 99.
For minor studies, *see* Gabrieli, G. Italia Judaica (*above*, i). The above list comprises only major works, and monographs omitted by Gabrieli.

E. GERMANY.

[Included in this section are also the other Teutonic provinces of the Empire: the Low Countries, Alsace, etc.]

(i) *Bibliography.*

Brann, M. and Freimann, A. Germania Judaica. Vol. I. pp. 1–3, § c. *See below*, iii.
Stern, M. Quellenkunde zur Geschichte der deutschen Juden. Vol. I. Die Zeitschriften-literatur.* (Repr. from Zeitschr. für Gesch. der Juden in Deutschland. II.) Kiel. 1892.

(ii) *Sources.*

Aronius, J. Regesten zur Geschichte der Juden im Fränkischen und Deutschen Reiche
bis zum Jahre 1273. Berlin. 1902.
Goldmann, A. Das Judenbuch der Schiffstrasse zu Wien, 1389–1420. (Quellen und
Forschungen zur Geschichte der Juden in Deutsch-Österreich. i.) Vienna and
Leipsic. 1908.
Kracauer, I. Urkundenbuch zur Geschichte der Juden in Frankfurt-am-Main von
1150–1400. Frankfort-on-M. 1914.
Lowe, W. H. The Memorbuch of Nürnberg. London. 1881.
Neubauer, A. and Stern, M. Hebräische Berichte über die Judenverfolgungen
während der Kreuzzüge. (Quellen zur Geschichte der Juden in Deutschland,
Hist. Commission für Gesch. d. Juden in Deutschland. ii.) Berlin. 1892.
Přibram, A. F. Urkunden und Akten zur Geschichte der Juden in Wien. (Quellen
und Forschungen zur Gesch. d. Juden, etc. viii.) Vienna. 1918.
Salfeld, S. Die Martyrologium des Nürnberger Memorbuches. (Quellen zur Gesch.
d. Juden in Deutschland. iii.) Berlin. 1898.
Stern, M. and Hoeniger, R. Das Judenschreinsbuch der Laurenzpfarre zu Köln.
(*Ibid.* i.) Berlin. 1888.

(iii) *Modern Works.*

(a) *General.*

Beiträge zur Geschichte der Juden in Deutschland. (Festschrift zum siebzigsten
Geburtstage Martin Philippsons.) Leipsic. 1917.
Berliner, A. Aus dem inneren Leben der deutschen Juden im Mittelalter. 2nd edn.
Berlin. 1900.
Brann, M. and Freimann, A. Germania Judaica. Frankfort-on-M. 1917, in progress.
[A geographical dictionary of German Jewish History.]
Breslau, H. Zur Geschichte der Juden in Deutschland. *In* Hebräische Bibliographie.
Vols. x, xii, xiv. Berlin. 1870–4.
Hoeniger, R. Zur Geschichte der Juden Deutschlands im frühen Mittelalter. *In*
Zeitschr. für die Geschichte der Juden in Deutschland. i. 1887.
Hoffmann, M. Der Geldhandel der deutschen Juden im Mittelalter. Leipsic. 1910.
Jahrbuch der jüdisch-literarischen Gesellschaft. Frankfort-on-M. 1906 ff.
Jahrbuch für jüdische Geschichte und Literatur. *Ibid.* 1874–93.
Kohut, A. Geschichte der deutschen Juden. Berlin. 1898.
Liebe, G. Das Judentum in der deutschen Vergangenheit. Leipsic. 1903.
Magazin für die Wissenschaft des Judenthums. Frankfort-on-M. 1874–93.
Mitteilungen des Gesamtarchivs der deutschen Juden. Berlin. 1909 ff.
Monatsschrift für die Geschichte und Wissenschaft des Judenthums. *See above,* ii b(i).
Rösel, I. Die Reichssteuern der deutschen Judengemeinden von ihren Anfängen bis
zum Mitte des 14 Jahrhts. (Schriften der Gesellschaft zur Förderung der Wissen-
schaft des Judentums.) Berlin. 1910.
Stern, M. König Ruprecht v. d. Pfalz in seinen Beziehungen zu den Juden. Kiel.
1898.
Stobbe, I. Die Juden in Deutschland während des Mittelalters. Brunswick. 1866;
anast. repr. Berlin. 1923.
Süssmann, A. Die Judenschuldentilgungen unter König Wenzel. (Schriften der
Gesellschaft zur Förderung der Wiss. des Judentums.) Berlin. 1907.
Zeitschrift für Geschichte der Juden in Deutschland. 1st series. 5 vols. Brunswick.
1887–92.
—— New series. Berlin. 1928 ff.
Zimmels, H. J. Beiträge zur Geschichte der Juden in Deutschland im 13 Jahrht.
insbesondere auf Grund der Gutachten des R. Meir Rothenburg. Vienna. 1926.

(b) *Local.*

[The amount of literature on this subject is so vast that only a small selection of
the most important works can be given here.]

Ackermann, A. Geschichte der Juden in Brandenburg. Berlin. 1906.
Altmann, A. Geschichte der Juden in Stadt und Land Salzburg. Vol. i. Berlin. 1913.

Aretin, J. C. von. Geschichte der Juden in Bayern. Landshut. 1803.
Barbeck, H. Geschichte der Juden in Nürnberg und Fürth. Nuremberg. 1878.
Brisch, C. Geschichte der Juden in Cöln und Umgebung. Mülheim. 1879–82.
Carlebach, E. Die rechtlichen und sozialen Verhältnisse der jüd. Gemeinden : Speyer, Worms, und Mainz. Leipsic. 1901.
Donath, L. Geschichte der Juden in Mecklenburg. Leipsic. 1874.
Dresemann, O. Die Juden in Aachen. Aix. 1887.
Freimann, A. and Kracauer, F. Frankfort (History of the Jews in). Philadelphia. 1929.
Geiger, L. Geschichte der Juden in Berlin. Berlin. 1871.
Glaser, A. Geschichte der Juden in Strassburg. Vol. i. Strasbourg. 1925.
Koenen, H. J. Geschiedenis der Joden in Nederland. Utrecht. 1843.
Kracauer, I. Aus der inneren Geschichte der Juden Frankfurts im 14 Jahrht. Frankfort-on-M. 1914.
—— Geschichte der Juden in Frankfurt am Main. 2 vols. Frankfort-on-M. 1925, 28.
—— Die politische Geschichte der Frankfurter Juden bis zum Jahre 1349. Frankfort-on-M. 1911.
—— Urkundenbuch zur Geschichte der Juden in Frankfurt am Main von 1150–1400. Frankfort-on-M. 1914.
Krauss, S. Die Wiener Geserah vom Jahre 1421. Vienna. 1916.
Neufeld, S. Die Hallischen Juden im Mittelalter. Berlin. 1915.
—— Die Juden im thüringischen-sächsischen Gebiet während des Mittelalters. Halle. 1926.
Nübling, E. Die Judengemeinden des Mittelalters, insbesondere die Judengemeinde der Reichsstadt Ulm. Ulm. 1896.
Rosenberg, A. Beiträge zur Geschichte der Juden in Steiermark. (Quellen und Forschungen zur Geschichte der Juden in Deutsch-Österreich. vi.) Vienna. 1914.
Rothschild, L. Die Judengemeinden in Mainz, Speyer, und Worms von 1349–1438. Berlin. 1904.
Saitschek, R. Beiträge zur Geschichte der rechtlichen Stellung der Juden in Österreich-Ungarn. Frankfort-on-M. 1890.
Schaab, A. Diplomatische Geschichte der Juden zu Mainz und dessen Umgebung. Mayence. 1855.
Scheid, E. Histoire des Juifs d'Alsace. Paris. 1887.
Scherer, J. E. Die Rechtsverhältnisse der Juden in den deutsch-österreichischen Ländern. *See above,* ii b (i).
Schwarz, I. Geschichte der Juden in Wien bis zum Jahre 1625. Vienna. 1913.
Steinberg, A. Studien zur Geschichte der Juden in der Schweiz während des Mittelalters. Zürich. 1902.
Steinthal, F. L. Geschichte der Augsburger Juden im Mittelalter. Berlin. 1911.
Stern, M. Die israelitische Bevölkerung der deutschen Städte. Pt. i, Bodensee. ii, Kiel. iii, Nürnberg. Frankfort-on-M. and Kiel. 1890–6.
Ulman, S. Studien zur Geschichte der Juden in Belgien. Antwerp. 1906.
—— Études sur l'histoire des Juifs en Belgique. Antwerp. 1927.
Ulrich, J. C. Sammlung jüdischer Geschichten...in der Schweiz. Basle. 1768; anast. repr. Berlin. 1922.
Weinberg, M. Geschichte der Juden in der Oberpfalz. Salzburg. 1909.
[Wertheimer, J.] Die Juden in Österreich. 2 vols. Leipsic. 1842.
Wolf, G. Zur Geschichte der Juden in Worms und des deutschen Städtewesens nach archival. Urkunden. Breslau. 1862.
Zwarts, J. Hoofdstukken uit de geschiedenis der Joden in Nederland. Zutphen. 1929.

F. Bohemia, etc.

Bondy, G. and Dvorský, F. Zur Geschichte der Juden in Böhmen, Mähren, und Schlesien, 906–1620. 2 vols. Prague. 1906.
Brann, M. Geschichte der Juden in Schlesien bis 1437. Breslau. 1901 ff.
Elvert, C. d'. Zur Geschichte der Juden in Mähren, etc. Brünn. 1895.
Jahrbuch für Geschichte der Juden in Cechoslav. Republik. Prague. 1929 ff.

Die Juden und Judengemeinden Mährens in Vergangenheit und Gegenwart. Brünn. 1927. [An historical dictionary.]
Stein, A. Geschichte der Juden in Böhmen. Brünn. 1904.
[Steinherz, S. *ed.*] Die Juden in Prag. Prague. 1927.

G. Hungary.

Büchler, A. Article "Hungary" *in* Jewish Encyclopaedia. Vol. vi. pp. 494–503.
Friss, A. and Weiss, M. Monumenta Hungariae Judaicae. Vol. i (1092–1539). Buda-Pest. 1903. [A source-book.]
Löw, L. Die Schicksale und Betreibungen der Juden in Ungarn. *In* Kalendar und Jahrb. für Israeliten. Ed. Busch, I. iv, v. Leipsic. 1845–6.
Zipser, M. Die Juden in Ungarn. *In* Der Orient, Litteraturblatt. vii, viii.

H. Byzantine Empire.

Andreadès, A. Les Juifs et le fisc dans l'Empire byzantin. *In* Charles Diehl. Mélanges: études sur l'histoire et l'art de Byzance. Paris. 1930.
Krauss, S. Studien zur byzantinisch-jüdischen Geschichte. (Jahresbericht der israelitisch-theologischen Lehranstalt in Wien. xxi.) Vienna. 1914.

I. Russia and Poland: the Khazars.

Balaban, M. Skizzen und Studien zur Geschichte der Juden in Polen. Berlin. 1911.
Bersohn, M. Dyplomataryusz dotyczaci Zydów w dawnej Polsce nazúrodlach archiwalnych osnuty (1388–1782). Warsaw. 1911. [A source-book.]
Dubnow, S. History of the Jews in Russia and Poland. Transl. by Friedlaender, I. 3 vols. Philadelphia. 1916–20.
Harkavy, A. Altjüdische Denkmäler aus der Krim. *In* Mém. AcadIP. Ser. vii. Vol. xxix. St Petersburg (Leningrad). 1876.
—— Regesti y Nadpisi. 3 vols. St Petersburg (Leningrad). 1876. [A source-book.]
Heppner, A. and Herzberg, J. Aus Vergangenheit und Gegenwart der jüdischen Gemeinden in den posener Ländern. Bromberg. 1909.
Kutschera, H. v. Die Chasaren. Historische Studie. Vienna. 1910.
Meisl, J. Geschichte der Juden in Polen und Russland. 3 vols. 1921–5.
Perles, J. Geschichte der Juden in Posen. Breslau. 1865.
Sternberg, H. Gesch. der Juden unter den Piasten und Jagiellonen. Leipsic. 1878.

J. The Islamic World.

Cahen, A. Les Israélites de l'Afrique septentrionale. Constantine. 1867.
Cazès, D. Essai sur l'histoire des Israélites de Tunisie. Paris. 1888.
Epstein, I. The Responsa of Rabbi Simon b. Ẓemaḥ Duran as a source of the history of the Jews in North Africa. (Jews' College publns. xii.) London. 1930.
Flad, M. Kurze Schilderung der abessinischen Juden. Basle. 1869.
Franco, M. Histoire des Israélites de l'empire ottoman. Paris. 1897.
Leszynsky, R. Die Juden in Arabien zur Zeit Mohammeds. Berlin. 1910.
Mann, J. The Jews of Palestine and Egypt under the Fatimid Caliphs. 2 vols. Oxford. 1920, 22.
Ortega, M. L. Los Hebreos en Marruecos. Madrid. 1919.
Schlouschz, N. Travels in North Africa. Philadelphia. 1927.

K. The Far East.

Loewe, H. J. M. The Jews of India. *In* Cambridge History of India. Vol. ii. Cambridge. In preparation.
Samuel, H. Sketch of the history of the Beni Israel. Bombay. 1899.
Sopher, A. Chinese Jews. Shanghai. 1927.

CHAPTER XXIII.

MEDIEVAL ESTATES.

I. ENGLAND.

A. Bibliographies.

Cooper, C. P. An account of the most important Public Records of Great Britain. London. 1832.
Giuseppi, M. S. Guide to the Manuscripts preserved in the Public Record Office. *See Gen. Bibl.* i.
Gross, C. Sources and Literature of English History from the earliest times to about 1485. *See Gen. Bibl.* i.
Hall, H. Repertory of British Archives. Pt. i. (RHS.) London. 1920.
Hardy, T. D. Descriptive catalogue of materials relating to the history of Great Britain and Ireland. *See Gen. Bibl.* i.
Royal Commission on Public Records. 1st–3rd Reports. 9 pts. London. 1912–19.
Scargill-Bird, S. R. Guide to the various classes of Documents preserved in the Public Record Office. 3rd edn. London. 1908.

B. Sources.

Bigelow, M. M. Placita Anglo-Normannica. Boston, Mass. 1879.
Book of Fees, commonly called Testa de Nevill. 3 pts. (Cal. SP.) London. 1920–31.
Bracton, Henry de. De Legibus et Consuetudinibus Angliae. Ed. Twiss, T. 6 vols. (Rolls.) 1878–83. Ed. Woodbine, G. E. Vols. i, ii. New Haven. 1915 ff., in progress.
—— Bracton's Note Book. Ed. Maitland, F. W. 3 vols. London. 1887.
Britton. Ed. Nichols, F. M. 2 vols. Oxford. 1865.
Calendar of the Charter Rolls. 6 vols. (Cal. SP.) London. 1903–27.
Calendar of the Close Rolls. (Cal. SP.) London. 1892 ff., in progress.
Calendar of the Patent Rolls. (Cal. SP.) London. 1891 ff., in progress.
Cole, H. Documents illustrative of English History. (RC.) London. 1844.
Davis, H. W. C. Regesta Regum Anglo-Normannorum, 1066–1154. Vol. i (1066–1100). Oxford. 1913.
Dugdale, W. A Perfect Copy of all Summons of the Nobility to the Great Councils and Parliaments of this Realm. London. 1685.
Fleta. 2nd edn. London. 1685.
Fortescue, Sir J. De Laudibus Legum Angliae. Ed. Amos, A. Cambridge. 1825.
—— The Governance of England. Ed. Plummer, C. Oxford. 1885.
Glanvill, Ranulf de. Tractatus de Legibus et Consuetudinibus regni Angliae. Ed. Rayner, J. London. 1780.
Haddan, A. W. and Stubbs, W. Councils and Ecclesiastical Documents relating to Great Britain and Ireland. *See Gen. Bibl.* iv.
Hall, H. The Red Book of the Exchequer. 3 vols. (Rolls.) 1896.
Hughes, A., Crump, C. G., and Johnson, C. De Necessariis Observantiis Scaccarii Dialogus. Oxford. 1902.
Liebermann, F. Die Gesetze der Angelsachsen. 3 vols. Halle-a.-S. 1903–16.
Maitland, F. W. Pleas of the Crown for the County of Gloucester. London. 1884.
—— Records of the Parliament holden at Westminster... A.D. 1305 (Memoranda de Parliamento). (Rolls.) 1893.
—— Select Pleas of the Crown. Vol. i. (Selden Soc. i.) London. 1888.
Modus Tenendi Parliamentorum. Ed. Hardy, T. D. (RC.) London. 1843.
Parliamentary History of England. [Ed. Cobbett, W. and Wright, J.] 36 vols. London. 1806–20.

Parliamentary Writs. Ed. Palgrave, Sir F. 2 vols. in 4. (RC.) London. 1827–34.
Pipe Roll Society Publications. London. 1884 ff., in progress.
Placita de Quo Warranto. [Ed. Illingworth, W.] (RC.) London. 1818.
Placitorum Abbreviatio. [Ed. Rose, G. and Illingworth, W.] (RC.) London. 1811.
Prynne, W. A brief Register. 4 pts. London. 1659–64.
Reports from the Lords' Committees...touching the Dignity of a Peer. 5 vols. London. 1820–9.
Rotuli Chartarum. Ed. Hardy, T. D. (RC.) London. 1837.
Rotuli Curiae Regis. Ed. Palgrave, Sir F. 2 vols. (RC.) London. 1835.
Rotuli Hundredorum. [Ed. Illingworth, W.] 2 vols. (RC.) London. 1812, 18.
Rotuli Litterarum Clausarum. Ed. Hardy, T. D. 2 vols. (RC.) London. 1833, 44.
Rotuli Litterarum Patentium. Ed. Hardy, T. D. (RC.) London. 1835.
Rotuli Parliamentorum. [Ed. Strachey, J. and others.] 6 vols. [London. 1767–77.] Index. (RC.) London. 1832.
Ryley, W. Placita Parliamentaria. London. 1661.
Rymer, T. Foedera. *See Gen. Bibl.* iv.
Statutes of the Realm. 11 vols. (RC.) London. 1810–28.
Stubbs, W. Select Charters and other illustrations of English Constitutional History. *See Gen. Bibl.* iv.
Wilkins, D. Concilia Magnae Britanniae et Hiberniae, a.d. 446–1718. 4 vols. London. 1737.

C. Later Writers.

Adams, G. B. Constitutional History of England. New York. 1921.
—— Council and Courts in Anglo-Norman England. New Haven. 1926.
—— The Origin of the English Constitution. 2nd edn. New York. 1920.
Atterbury, F. The Rights, Powers, and Privileges of an English Convocation stated and vindicated. London. 1700.
[Bacon, M.] An Historical Discourse of the Uniformity of the Government of England. Pt. i. London. 1647.
Baldwin, J. F. The King's Council in England during the Middle Ages. Oxford. 1913.
Barker, E. The Dominican Order and Convocation. Oxford. 1913.
Bémont, C. Chartes des libertés anglaises. Paris. 1892.
—— Simon de Montfort. Paris. 1884. New edn. in English transl. by Jacob, E. F. Oxford. 1930.
Brady, R. An historical treatise of Cities and Burghs. London. 1777.
—— An introduction to the old English History. London. 1684.
Brunner, H. Die Entstehung der Schwurgerichte. Berlin. 1872.
Clifford, F. History of Private Bill Legislation. 2 vols. London. 1885.
Coke, Sir Edward. The Fourth Part of the Institutes of the Laws of England. 7th edn. London. 1681.
—— The Second Part of the Institutes of the Laws of England. 6th edn. London. 1681.
Cox, H. Antient Parliamentary Elections. London. 1868.
Craig, Sir Thomas. Jus Feudale. Leipsic. 1716.
Davies, J. C. The Baronial opposition to Edward II. Cambridge. 1918.
Dicey, A. V. The Privy Council. London. 1887.
Dwarris, Sir F. A General Treatise on Statutes. 2nd edn. London. 1848.
Edwards, J. G. The Personnel of the Commons in Parliament under Edward I and Edward II. (Essays in Medieval History presented to T. F. Tout, no. 16.) Manchester. 1925.
Elsynge, H. The Manner of Holding Parliaments in England. London. 1768.
[Fitzherbert, Sir A.] L'Authoritie et Jurisdiction des Courts de la Maiestie de la Roygne, novelment collect et compose, per R. Crompton. London. 1594.
Franqueville, Comte de. Le système judiciaire de la Grande Bretagne. 2 vols. Paris. 1893.
Glasson, E. Histoire du droit et des institutions de l'Angleterre. 6 vols. Paris. 1882–3.

Gneist, R. History of the English Constitution. Transl. Ashworth, P. A. 2 vols. 2nd edn. London. 1889.

Hale, Sir Matthew. The Jurisdiction of the Lords' House. Ed. Hargrave, F. London. 1796.

Harcourt, L. W. V. His Grace the Steward and Trial by Peers. London. 1907.

Hatschek, J. Englisches Staatsrecht. 2 vols. Tübingen. 1905.

—— Englische Verfassungsgeschichte. Munich. 1913.

Hearne, T. A Collection of Curious Discourses. 2 vols. London. 1775.

Hody, H. A History of English Councils and Convocations. London. 1701.

Jacob, E. Studies in the period of Baronial Reform and Rebellion, 1258–1267. (Oxford Studies in Social and Legal History. Ed. Vinogradoff, P. Vol. VIII.) Oxford. 1925.

Jenkinson, C. Hilary. The first Parliament of Edward I. EHR. xxv (1910). 231–42.

Kemble, J. M. The Saxons in England. 2 vols. London. 1849.

Lambard, W. Archeion. [Ed. Lambard, T.] London. 1635.

Lapsley, G. T. Knights of the Shire in the Parliaments of Edward II. EHR. xxiv (1909). 25–42, 152–71.

Levett, A. E. The summons to a Great Council, 1213. EHR. xxxi (1916). 85–90.

Lyttelton, G. The History of the life of Henry II. 3 vols. London. 1767.

McIlwain, C. H. The High Court of Parliament. New Haven. 1910.

McKechnie, W. S. Magna Carta. 2nd edn. Glasgow. 1914.

McKisack, M. Borough representation in Richard II's reign. EHR. xxxix (1924). 511–25.

Madox, T. Baronia Anglica. London. 1741.

—— Firma Burgi. London. 1726.

—— The History and Antiquities of the Exchequer. London. 1711.

Maitland, F. W. The Constitutional History of England. Cambridge. 1908.

—— Records of the Parliament at Westminster in 1305. Introduction. London. 1893.

—— The Suitors of the County Court. *In* Collected Papers. Vol. I. Cambridge. 1911.

Makower, F. The Constitutional History...of the Church of England. (Transl. from the German.) London. 1895.

Maxwell-Lyte, H. C. Historical notes on the use of the Great Seal of England. London. 1926.

May, Sir T. E. A Treatise on the Law, Privileges, Proceedings, and Usage of Parliament. 9th edn. London. 1883.

Mitchell, S. K. Studies in Taxation under John and Henry III. New Haven. 1914.

Morris, W. A. The Constitutional History of England. New York. 1930.

—— The early English County Court. (Univ. of California publns. in hist. xiv.) Berkeley. 1926.

—— The Medieval English Sheriff to 1300. Manchester. 1927.

Palgrave, F. The Rise and Progress of the English Commonwealth. 2 pts. London. 1832.

Palmer, Sir F. B. Peerage Law in England. London. 1907.

[Parry, C. H.] The Parliaments and Councils of England. London. 1839.

Pasquet, D. Essai sur les origines de la Chambre des Communes. Paris. 1914. 2nd edn. Transl. into English by Laffan, R. G. D., preface and notes by Lapsley, G. T. Cambridge. 1925.

Pauli, R. *In* Lappenberg, J. M. and Pauli, R., Geschichte von England. 5 vols. Hamburg. 1834–58.

—— Simon de Montfort. Transl. Goodwin, U. M. London. 1876.

Petit-Dutaillis, C. Studies and notes supplementary to Stubbs' Constitutional History. *See Gen. Bibl.* v *under* Stubbs.

Petyt, W. The Ancient Right of the Commons of England asserted. London. 1680.

—— Jus Parliamentarium. London. 1739.

Pike, L. O. Constitutional History of the House of Lords. London. 1894.

Pollard, A. F. The Evolution of Parliament. 2nd edn. London. 1926.

Pollock, F. and Maitland, F. W. The history of English Law before the time of Edward I. *See Gen. Bibl.* v.

Porritt, E. The unreformed House of Commons. 2 vols. Cambridge. 1903.

Powicke, F. M. Some observations on the Baronial Council (1258–1260) and the Provisions of Westminster. (Essays in Medieval History presented to T. F. Tout, no. 9.) Manchester. 1925.

Prothero, G. W. The life of Simon de Montfort. London. 1877.

Prynne, W. Brief animadversions on the Fourth Part of the Institutes of the Lawes of England. London. 1669.

Redlich, J. The Procedure of the House of Commons. Transl. Steinthal, A. E. 3 vols. London. 1908.

Richardson, H. G. The origins of Parliament. TRHS. 4th ser. Vol. xi (1928). 137–83.

—— and Sayles, G. O. Early records of the English Parliaments. *In* Bulletin of the Inst. of Hist. Research. v (1928). 129–54; vi (1929). 71–88; 129–55.

—— —— The King's Ministers in Parliament, 1272–1377. EHR. xlvi (1931). 529–50; xlvii (1932).

—— —— The Parliaments of Edward III. *In* Bulletin of the Inst. of Hist. Research. viii (1930–1). 65–82; ix (1931–2). 1–18.

Riess, L. Geschichte des Wahlrechts zum englischen Parlament im Mittelalter. Leipsic. 1885.

—— Der Ursprung des englischen Unterhauses. HZ. xxiv. 1888.

Round, J. H. Barons and knights in the Great Charter. *In* Magna Carta Commemoration Essays. (Roy. Hist. Soc.) London. 1917. pp. 46–77.

Sayles, G. O. Representation of Cities and Boroughs in 1268. EHR. xl (1925). 580–5.

Selden, J. Titles of Honour. 3rd edn. London. 1672. *Also in* Opera omnia. Ed. Wilkins, D. Vol. iii. London. 1726.

—— Of the Judicature in Parliaments. London. [1690?] *Also in* Opera omnia. Vol. iii (*above*).

Smith, Sir Thomas. De Republica Anglorum. Ed. Alston, L. Cambridge. 1906.

Spelman, Sir Henry. English Works. Edited by Edmund [Gibson], Bishop of London. 2nd edn. London. 1727.

—— Glossarium Archaiologicum. 3rd edn. London. 1687.

Stubbs, W. Constitutional History of England. *See Gen. Bibl.* v.

—— Historical introductions to the Rolls Series. Ed. Hassall, A. London. 1902.

—— Lectures on early English History. Ed. Hassall, A. London. 1906.

Thayer, J. B. A Preliminary Treatise on Evidence at the Common Law. Boston. 1898.

Tout, T. F. Chapters in the Administrative History of Mediaeval England. 6 vols. Manchester. 1920–32.

—— The Place of Edward II in English History. Manchester. 1914.

Unwin, G. *ed.* Finance and Trade under Edward III. Manchester. 1918.

Wake, W. The State of the Church. London. 1703.

White, A. B. The Making of the English Constitution. 2nd edn. New York. 1925.

—— Some early instances of concentration of representatives in England. AHR. xix (1914). 735.

Whitelocke, B. Notes uppon the King's Writt for Choosing Members of Parlement. Publ. by Morton, C. 2 vols. London. 1766.

Wood-Legh, K. L. Sheriffs, lawyers, and belted knights in the Parliaments of Edward III. EHR. xlvi (1931). 372–88.

II. FRANCE.

A. BIBLIOGRAPHIES.

Catalogue of Books on Foreign Law founded on the collections presented by C. P. Cooper to the Society of Lincoln's Inn. Laws and Jurisprudence of France. London. 1849.

Chevalier, C. U. J. Répertoire des sources historiques du moyen âge. Bio-bibliographie. Topo-bibliographie. *See Gen. Bibl.* i.

Franklin, A. Les Sources de l'histoire de France. Paris. 1877.

Gavet, G. Sources de l'histoire des institutions et du droit français. Paris. 1899.

Langlois, C. V. Manuel de bibliographie historique. 2 pts. Paris. 1901, 4.

—— and Stein, H. Les Archives de l'histoire de France. 3 pts. (Manuels de bibliographie historique, i.) Paris. 1891–3.

Molinier, A. Les Sources de l'histoire de France (to 1494). *See Gen. Bibl.* i.
Monod, G. Bibliographie de l'histoire de France. *See Gen. Bibl.* i.
Stein, H. Manuel de bibliographie générale. (Manuels de bibliographie historique, ii.) Paris. 1897.

B. Sources.

Boutaric, E. Actes du Parlement de Paris. 2 vols. Paris. 1863, 67.
Delachenal, R. Journal des états généraux réunis à Paris au mois d'Octobre 1356. NRDF. 1900.
Dupuy, Pierre. Histoire du différend d'entre le pape Boniface VIII et Philippe le Bel, roy de France, 1296–1311, sous les pontificats de Boniface VIII, Bénédict XI, et Clément V. Paris. 1655.
Langlois, C. V. Textes relatifs à l'histoire du Parlement depuis les origines jusqu'en 1314. (Coll. textes.) Paris. 1888.
Masselin, Jean. Journal des états généraux de France tenus à Tours en 1484. Latin text and French transl. Bernier, A. Paris. 1835.
Les Olim. Ed. Beugnot, A. A. 4 vols. (Coll. doc.) Paris. 1839–48.
Ordonnances des rois de France de la troisième race. 21 vols. Paris. 1723–1849.
Philippe de Beaumanoir. Coutumes de Beauvaisis. Ed. Salmon, A. 2 vols. (Coll. textes.) Paris. 1899.
Picot, G. Documents relatifs aux états généraux et assemblées réunis sous Philippe Le Bel. (Coll. doc.) Paris. 1901.
Recueil général des anciennes lois françaises. Ed. Jourdan, A. J. L. and others. 29 vols. Paris. 1822–33.
Thierry, A. Recueil des monuments inédits de l'histoire du tiers état. Ser. i. Région du Nord. 4 vols. (Coll. doc.) Paris. 1850–70.
Vic, C. de, and Vaissete, J. J. Histoire générale de Languedoc. *See Gen. Bibl.* iv.
Viollet, P. Les établissements de Saint Louis. 4 vols. (SHF.) Paris. 1881–6.

C. Later Writers.

Boullée, M. A. Histoire complète des états généraux et autres assemblées représentatives de la France. 2 vols. Paris. 1845.
Boutaric, E. La France sous Philippe le Bel. Paris. 1861.
—— Saint Louis et Alfonse de Poitiers. Paris. 1870.
Brissaud, J. Cours d'histoire générale du droit français public et privé. 2 vols. Paris. 1904. Transl. in part *as* A History of French Public Law, by Garner, J. W. (Continental Legal History Series. Vol. ix.) Boston, Mass. 1915.
Callery, A. Histoire de l'origine, des pouvoirs, et des attributions des états généraux et provinciaux. Brussels. 1881.
de Chantérac, B. Les Assemblées de notables dans l'ancienne France. Paris. 1919.
Chénon, E. Histoire général du droit français public et privé. Vol. i. Paris. 1926.
Clerc, E. Histoire des états généraux et des libertés publiques en Franche-Comté. 2 vols. Besançon. 1882.
Coriolis. Documents relatifs à l'histoire des états généraux du royaume conservés aux archives municipales de Dijon. *In* Bulletin du comité de la langue, de l'histoire, et des arts de la France. 1853.
Coville, A. Les Cabochiens et l'ordonnance de 1413. Paris. 1888.
—— Les états de Normandie. Paris. 1894.
Declareuil, J. Histoire général du droit français. Paris. 1925.
Desjardins, A. États généraux, 1355–1614, leur influence sur le gouvernement et la législation du pays. Paris. 1871.
Dognon, P. Les Institutions politiques et administratives du pays de Languedoc. Toulouse. 1896.
Esmein, A. Cours élémentaire d'histoire du droit français. 11th edn. Paris. 1912. 13th edn. Génestal, R. Paris. 1920.
Forme générale et particulière de la convocation et de la terme des assemblées nationales ou états généraux de France, justifiée par pièces authentiques. [Ed. Lalourcé and Duval.] 2 pts. Paris. 1789.

Froidevaux, H. De regiis conciliis Philippo II Augusto regnante habitis. Paris. 1891.

Glasson, E. Histoire du droit et des institutions de la France. Vol. v. Paris. 1893.

Henrion de Pansey, P. P. N. Des Assemblées nationales en France...jusqu'en 1614. 2 vols. Paris. 1829.

Hervieu, H. E. V. Recherches sur les premiers états généraux et les assemblées représentatives pendant la première moitié du xive siècle. Paris. 1879.

Laferrière. Mémoire sur l'histoire et l'organisation comparée des états provinciaux aux diverses époques de la monarchie jusqu'en 1789. *In* Séances et travaux de l'Académie des Sciences Morales. xi.

Langlois, C. V. Article "États généraux" *in* La Grande Encyclopédie. Vol. xvi. Paris. pp. 510–23.

—— Saint Louis, Philippe le Bel, Les derniers Capétiens directs (1226–1328). *In* Lavisse, E. Histoire de France. iii, pt. 2. 1901. *See Gen. Bibl.* v.

Luchaire, A. Histoire des institutions monarchiques de la France sous les premiers Capétiens. 2 vols. Paris. 1883, 85.

—— Manuel des institutions françaises. *See Gen. Bibl.* v.

—— Les premiers Capétiens (987–1137). *In* Lavisse, E. Histoire de France. ii, pt. 2. 1901. *See Gen. Bibl.* v.

—— Louis VII, Philippe-Auguste, Louis VIII (1137–1226). *Ibid.* iii, pt. 1. 1902.

Martin, O. L'Assemblée de Vincennes de 1329 et ses conséquences. Rennes. 1908.

Mayer, C. J. Des états généraux et autres assemblées nationales. 18 vols. The Hague. 1788–9.

Picot, G. Les élections aux états généraux dans les provinces de 1302 à 1614. Paris. 1874.

—— Histoire des états généraux. 2nd edn. 4 vols. Paris. 1888.

Prentout, M. États provinciaux de Normandie. Caen. 1925.

Rathery, E. J. B. Histoire des états généraux de France. Paris. 1845.

Rowe, B. J. H. The estates of Normandy under the Duke of Bedford, 1422–35. EHR. xlvi (1931). 551–78.

Thierry, A. Essai sur l'histoire de la formation et des progrès du tiers état. Paris. 1882.

Thomas, A. Les états provinciaux de la France centrale sous Charles VII. RH. x, p. 249.

—— Le Midi et les états généraux sous Charles VII. *In* Annales du Midi. iv. Toulouse. 1892.

Tixier, O. Les théories sur la souveraineté aux états généraux de 1484. Paris. 1899.

Valois, N. Le Conseil du Roi aux xive, xve, et xvie siècles. Paris. 1888.

Viollet, P. Droit public. Histoire des institutions politiques et administratives de la France. *See Gen. Bibl.* v.

—— Recherches sur l'élection des députés aux états généraux réunis à Tours en 1468 et en 1484. Paris. 1866.

III. SPAIN.

A. Bibliographies.

Colección de Córtes de las antiguos Reinos de España, por la Real Academia de la Historia: Catálogo. Madrid. 1855.

Merriman, R. B. The Cortes of the Spanish Kingdoms in the later Middle Ages. *See below,* iii c.

Specimen of a Catalogue of the Books on Foreign Law lately presented by C. P. Cooper to the Society of Lincoln's Inn. [On the Laws of Spain.] London. 1847.

B. Sources.

Constitutions y altres Drets de Cathalunya. 3 vols. Barcelona. 1588.

Cortes de los antiguos Reinos de Aragón y de Valencia, y Principado de Cataluña. (RAH.) Madrid. 1896 ff., in progress.

Cortes de los antiguos Reinos de León y de Castilla. Vols. i–v. (RAH.) Madrid. 1861–1903.

Fuero Juzgo, en Latin y Castellano. (R. Acad. Española.) Madrid. 1815.

El Fuero Real de España. (With the gloss of Montalvo, A. Diaz de.) 2 vols. Madrid. 1781.

Fueros y observancias de las Costumbres escriptas del Reyno de Aragon. Saragossa. 1576. *Also* 2 vols. Saragossa. 1664, 78.

El Ordenamiento de Leyes, que D. Alfonso XI hizo en las Cortes de Alcalá de Henares el año de 1348. Ed. Asso y del Rio, I. J. de, and Manuel y Rodriguez, M. de. Madrid. 1774.

Ordenanças Reales de Castilla. (With the gloss of Montalvo, A. Diaz de, and of Perez, D.) 4 vols. in 2. Salamanca. 1575, 1609. *Also* 3 vols. Madrid. 1779–80.

Las Siete Partidas. 3 vols. (RAH.) Madrid. 1807.

Traducción al Castellano de los usages y demas derechos de Cataluña. Ed. Vives y Cebriá, P. N. 4 vols. Barcelona. 1832.

C. Later Writers.

Altamira, R. Historia de España y de la civilización española. *See Gen. Bibl.* v.

Antequera, J. M. de. Historia de la legislación española. 4th edn. Madrid. 1898.

Burke, U. A history of Spain. 2nd edn. Hume, M. A. S. 2 vols. London. 1900.

Capmany y Montpalau, A. de. Practica y estilo de celebrar Cortes. Madrid. 1821.

Chapman, C. E. A history of Spain founded on the Historia de España...of Rafael Altamira. New York. 1918.

Colmeiro, M. Cortes de los antiguos Reinos de León y de Castilla. Introducción. 2 vols. Madrid. 1883–4.

Coroleu, J. and Pella y Forgas, D. J. Cortes Catalanas. Barcelona. 1876.

Danvila y Collado, M. Estudios críticos acerca de los orígenes y vicisitudes de la legislación escrita del antiguo Reino de Valencia. (Sub-title) Estudios e investigaciones acerca de las Cortes y Parlamentos de Valencia. Madrid. 1905.

—— Poder civil en España. 6 vols. Madrid. 1885–6.

Fuente, V. de la. Estudios críticos sobre la historia y el derecho de Aragón. 3 vols. Madrid. 1884–6.

Hallam, H. View of the state of Europe during the Middle Ages. 11th edn. 3 vols. London. 1855.

Hinojosa, E. de. Historia general del derecho español. *See Gen. Bibl.* v.

Marichalar, A. and Manrique, C. Historia de la legislación y recitaciones del derecho civil de España. 9 vols. Madrid. 1861–76.

Marina, F. M. Teoria de las Cortes. 3 vols. Madrid. 1820. French transl. Fleury, P. L. F. 2nd edn. 2 vols. Paris. 1824.

Merriman, R. B. The Cortes of the Spanish Kingdoms in the later Middle Ages. AHR. xvi. 1911.

—— The rise of the Spanish Empire. *See Gen. Bibl.* v.

Sempere, J. Histoire des Cortes d'Espagne. (Transl. from the Spanish.) Bordeaux. 1815.

Zurita, Jerónimo. Anales de la corona de Aragon. 3rd edn. 7 vols. Saragossa. 1668–71.

IV. ITALY.

A. Bibliographies.

Potthast, A. Bibliotheca historica medii aevi. *See Gen. Bibl.* i.

Rivista storica italiana. *See Gen. Bibl.* i.

B. Sources.

Bollati, F. E. Atti e documenti delle antiche assemblee rappresentative nella monarchia di Savoia. MPH. Vols. xiv, xv. 1879.

Huillard-Bréholles, J. L. A. Historia diplomatica Friderici II. 6 vols. Paris. 1852–61.

Leicht, P. S. Parlamento Friulano. Vol. ɪ (1228–1331). (R. Accad. dei Lincei. Commissione per gli Atti delle Assemblee Costituzionali Italiane.) Bologna. 1917.
Mirbt, C. Quellen zur Geschichte des Papsttums und des römischen Katholizismus. 4th edn. Tübingen. 1924.
Theiner, A. Codex diplomaticus dominii temporalis S. Sedis. *See Gen. Bibl.* ɪv.

C. Later Writers.

Calisse, C. Storia del parlamento in Sicilia dalla fondazione alla caduta della monarchia. Turin. 1887.
Ficker, J. Forschungen zur Reichs- und Rechtsgeschichte Italiens. 4 vols. Innsbruck. 1868–70.
Giannone, P. The Civil History of the Kingdom of Naples. Transl. Ogilvie, J 2 vols. London. 1729, 31.
Leicht, P. S. Il parlamento della patria del Friuli, sua origine, costituzione, e legislazione (1231–1420). *In* Atti dell' Accad. di Udine. 3rd ser. x, xɪ. 1902, 3.
Pertile, A. Storia del diritto italiano. *See Gen. Bibl.* v.
Pozzo, F. dal. Essai sur les anciennes assemblées nationales de la Savoie, du Piémont, et des pays qui y sont ou furent annexés. Vol. ɪ. Paris and Geneva. 1829. [No more publ.]
Sclopis, F. Considerazioni storiche intorno alle assemblee rappresentative del Piemonte e della Savoia. (Appended to Atti e documenti... Ed. Bollati, F. E. *See above,* ʙ.)
—— Degli stati generali e d' altre istituzioni politiche del Piemonte e della Savoia. *In* Atti della R. Accad. di Torino. xɪɪ.

V. GERMANY.

A. Bibliographies.

Dahlmann-Waitz. Quellenkunde der deutschen Geschichte. *See Gen. Bibl.* ɪ.
Jahresberichte für deutsche Geschichte. Jahrg. 1925 ff. *See Gen. Bibl.* ɪ.
Potthast, A. Bibliotheca historica medii aevi. *See Gen. Bibl.* ɪ.

B. Sources.

Monumenta Germaniae Historica. *See Gen. Bibl.* ɪv.
Zeumer, K. Quellensammlung zur Geschichte der deutschen Reichsverfassung in Mittelalter und Neuzeit. Leipsic. 1914.

C. Later Writers.

Amira, K. v. Grundriss des germanischen Rechts. 3rd edn. Strasbourg. 1913.
Below, G. v. Der deutsche Staat des Mittelalters. Vol. ɪ. Leipsic. 1914.
Brunner, H. Grundzüge der deutschen Rechtsgeschichte. *See Gen. Bibl.* v.
Busson, A. Zur Geschichte des grossen Landfriedensbundes deutscher Städte. Innsbrück. 1874.
Gierke, O. v. Das deutsche Genossenschaftsrecht. *See Gen. Bibl.* v.
Giesebrecht, W. v. Geschichte der deutschen Kaiserzeit. 6 vols. Latest edns. Brunswick and Leipsic. 1881–95.
Heusler, A. Deutsche Verfassungsgeschichte. Leipsic. 1905.
Hintze, O. Das Königtum Wilhelms von Holland. Leipsic. 1885.
Holtzendorff-Kohler. Encyklopädie der Rechtswissenschaft. *See Gen. Bibl.* ɪ.
Quidde, L. Studien zur Geschichte des rheinischen Landfriedensbundes. Frankfort-on-Main. 1885.
Schröder, R. Lehrbuch der deutschen Rechtsgeschichte. *See Gen. Bibl.* v.
Schulte, J. F. v. Lehrbuch der deutschen Reichs- und Rechtsgeschichte. Stuttgart. 1870.
Weizsäcker, J. Der rheinische Bund. Tübingen. 1879.

VI. SCOTLAND.

A. Sources.

Acts of the Lords of Council in Civil Causes, 1478–95. Ed. Thomson, T. (RC.) [Edinburgh.] 1839. Vol. II (1496–1501). Ed. Neilson, G. and Paton, H. (Cal. SP.) Edinburgh. 1918.
The Acts of the Parliament of Scotland. Ed. Thomson, T. and Innes, C. 12 vols. (RC.) [Edinburgh.] 1844, 1814–75.
Ancient Laws and Customs of the Burghs of Scotland. Vol. I (1124–1424). Ed. Innes, C. Vol. II (1424–1707). Ed. Renwick, R. (Scottish Burgh Records Society.) Edinburgh. 1868, 1910.
Records of the Convention of the Royal Burghs of Scotland. Ed. Marwick, J. D. 6 vols. Edinburgh. 1870–90.

B. Later Writers.

Brown, P. Hume. History of Scotland. *See Gen. Bibl.* v.
Buchanan, G. Rerum Scoticarum Historia. Amsterdam. 1643.
Burton, J. H. History of Scotland. 7 vols. 1867.
Craig, Sir Thomas. Jus Feudale. Leipsic. 1716.
—— Scotland's Sovereignty asserted. London. 1695.
—— De Unione Regnorum. Ed. Terry, C. S. Edinburgh. 1909.
Hannay, R. K. Parliament and General Council. *In* Scottish Historical Review. XVIII. 1921.
—— General Council and Convention of Estates. *Ibid.* xx. 1923.
—— General Council of Estates. *Ibid.*
Innes, C. Introduction *to* The Acts of the Parliament of Scotland *in* Vol. I. *See above*, VI A.
—— Lectures on Scottish Legal Antiquities. Edinburgh. 1872.
Lang, A. History of Scotland. 4 vols. Edinburgh. 1900–7.
Mackinnon, J. The Constitutional History of Scotland. London. 1924.
Major, J. Historia Majoris Britanniae. Edinburgh. 1740.
Porritt, E. The unreformed House of Commons. Vol. II. Cambridge. 1903.
Rait, R. S. The Scottish Parliament before the Union of the Crowns. London. 1901.
—— The Parliaments of Scotland. Glasgow. 1924.
[Ridpath, G. (?)] An historical account of the Ancient Rights and Power of the Parliament of Scotland. 1703.
Ruddiman, R. An introduction to Mr James Anderson's Diplomata Scotiae. Edinburgh. 1782.
Skene, Sir J. De Verborum Significatione. Edinburgh. 1681.

CHAPTER XXIV.

PEASANT LIFE AND RURAL CONDITIONS.

The period covered by this chapter is roughly from 1200 to 1500, and the territory Western Europe (England, France, the Low Countries, Spain, Italy, and Germany). The Scandinavian kingdoms are not included, and the Slav world is only incidentally treated in connexion with the German colonisation movement. The select bibliography given below has been constructed on the same lines as the bibliography to the parallel chapter xiv of Volume vi. It contains:

1. A very few original authorities, comprising only (a) works quoted or referred to in the chapter, (b) source-books specially compiled to illustrate agrarian history, (c) some editions of original sources, in which the editorial introductions are of particular importance in throwing light upon special points. For further information as to the sources of agrarian history, reference must be made to the books in the next section, viz.

2. Important modern works, from which bibliographical information may be obtained, and a few older books which are still useful.

3. A number of articles from journals dealing with points of special importance.

I. SOURCES.

Alliot, J. M. Visites archidiaconales de Josas. Paris. 1902.

Aue, Hartmann von. Der Arme Heinrich...und Zwei jüngere Prosalegenden verwandten Inhaltes. Ed. Wackernagel, W. New edn. by Stadler, E. Basle. 1911. Transl. into English verse with introdn., etc., by Bell, C. H. *in* Peasant Life in Old German epics. Meier Helmbrecht and Der Arme Heinrich. (Columbia Univ. Records of Civilization.) New York. 1931. There is also a free version by Rossetti, D. G. *in* Works. Ed. Rossetti, W. M. Rev. edn. p. 507. London. 1911.

Bannister, A. T. Visitation Returns of the Diocese of Hereford in 1397. EHR. xliv (1929). 279, 444; xlv (1930). 92, 444.

Brownbill, J. The Ledger-Book of Vale Royal Abbey. (Lancs. and Cheshire Record Soc. lxviii.) Manchester. 1914.

Chaucer, Geoffrey. Works. Ed. Skeat, W. W. 7 vols. Oxford. 1894–7.

Crescentius, Petrus. Opus Ruralium Commodorum sive de Agricultura libri xii. Augsburg. 1471. [Crescentius lived from 1233 to 1320. His book was often translated, *e.g.* into French in 1373 and 1486, into German in 1493, and into Italian in 1478.]

Dupont, M. G. Le Registre de l'Officialité de Cerisy (1314–1457). *In* Mém. de la Soc. des Antiquaires de Normandie. xxx, p. 271. Caen and Rouen. 1880.

Grimm, Jacob (and others). Weisthümer. 7 vols. (Vols. iv–vii publ. by Hist. Commission BAW.) Göttingen. 1840–78.

Helbling, Seifried. Gedichte. Ed. Seemüller, J. Halle. 1910.

Jehan de Brie. Le Bon Berger, ou Le vray regime et gouvernement des Bergers et Bergeres....Réimprimé sur l'édition de Paris(1541) avec une notice par P. Lacroix. Paris. 1879.

Kötzschke, R. Quellen zur Geschichte der ostdeutschen Kolonisation im 12 bis 14 Jahrht. 2nd edn. Berlin. 1931.

Langland, William. The Vision of William concerning Piers the Plowman, in three parallel texts. Ed. Skeat, W. W. 2 vols. Oxford. 1886.

Maitland, F. W. Select Pleas in Manorial and other Seignorial Courts. Vol. i. Henry III and Edward I. (Selden Soc. ii.) London. 1889.

—— and Baildon, W. P. The Court Baron, being precedents for use in Seignorial and other local courts, together with Select Pleas from the Bishop of Ely's Court of Littleport. (Selden Soc. iv.) London. 1891.

Manières de Vilains, Des xxiii (xiiie siècle). [Ed. Michel, F.] Paris. 1833.

Map, Walter. De Nugis Curialium. Ed. James, M. R. (Anecdota Oxoniensia, Mediaeval ser. xiv.) Oxford. 1914. [Best edn.] Engl. transl. Tupper, F. and Ogle, M. B. London. 1924.

Montaiglon, A. de and Raynaud, G. Recueil général et complet des fabliaux des xiii et xiv siècles. 6 vols. Paris. 1872–88.

Neidhart von Reuental. Ed. Haupt, M. Leipsic. 1858. New edn. Wiessner, E. Leipsic. 1923. [For an original criticism of Neidhart's poems *see* Singer, S. Neidhartstudien. Tübingen. 1920.]

Neilson, N. The Cartulary and Terrier of the Priory of Bilsington. (British Academy.) London. 1928. [The introductions to this and the succeeding volume constitute the best survey of English Wealden and Fen-land customs in the Middle Ages.]

—— A Terrier of Fleet, Lincolnshire. (British Academy.) London. 1920.

Pierce the Ploughmans Crede (*c.* 1394). Ed. Skeat, W. W. (EETS. Original ser. No. 30.) London. 1867.

Pirenne, H. Le soulèvement de la Flandre maritime de 1323–1328. Documents inédits. Brussels. 1900. [Preceded by a long and valuable introduction.]

Stenton, F. M. Documents illustrative of the Social and Economic History of the Danelaw. (British Academy.) London. 1920. [Preceded by a very valuable introduction on village and manorial organisation and the classes of rural society, with special reference to the persistence of freedom among the peasantry.]

Walter of Henley's Husbandry, together with an Anonymous Husbandry, Seneschaucie, and Robert Grosseteste's Rules. Ed. with transl. Lamond, E. with introd. by Cunningham, W. (Roy. Hist. Soc.) London. 1890.

Wernher der Gartenaere. Meier Helmbrecht. Ed. Panzer, F. Halle. 1902. 4th edn. 1924. Transl. into English verse with introdn., etc., by Bell, C. H. *in* Peasant Life in Old German epics. Meier Helmbrecht and Der Arme Heinrich. (Columbia Univ. Records of Civilization.) New York. 1931.

Wopfner, H. Urkunden zur deutschen Agrar-Geschichte. *In* Ausgewählte Urkunden zur deutschen Verfassungs- und Wirtschaftsgeschichte. Vol. iii. Stuttgart. 1925 Repr. 1928. [A very useful collection of sources.]

II. MODERN WORKS.

A. General.

Avenel, G. d'. Histoire économique de la propriété, des salaires, des denrées, et de tous les prix en général depuis l'an 1200 jusqu'en l'an 1800. Vols. i and ii. Paris. 1894 ff.

Boissonnade, P. Le Travail dans l'Europe chrétienne au moyen âge. Paris. 1921. Engl. transl. Power, E. Life and Labour in the Middle Ages. London. 1927.

Coulton, G. G. The Medieval Village. Cambridge. 1925.

Gras, N. S. B. History of Agriculture. New York. 1923.

Handwörterbuch der Staatswissenschaften. Ed. Conrad, J., Elster, L., Lexis, W., and Loening, E. 3rd edn. 8 vols. Jena. 1909–11.

Kötzschke, R. Allgemeine Wirtschaftsgeschichte des Mittelalters. Jena. 1924.

Kovalevsky, M. Die ökonomische Entwicklung Europas bis zum Beginn der kapitalistischen Wirtschaftsform. 7 vols. Berlin. 1901–14.

Kulischer, J. Allgemeine Wirtschaftsgeschichte. Vol. i. Munich and Berlin. 1928.

Meitzen, A. Wanderungen, Anbau, und Agrarrecht der Völker Europas nördlich der Alpen. Abth. i. Siedelung und Agrarwesen der Westgermanen und Ostgermanen, der Kelten, Römer, Finnen, und Slawen. 4 vols. Berlin. 1895.

Sée, H. Geldwirtschaft, Kapitalismus, und Landwirtschaft. *In* Zeitschr. für die gesamte Staatswissenschaft. lxxxviii. p. 225. Tübingen. 1930.

Simkhovitch, V. G. Hay and History. *In* Polit. Science Quarterly. xxvii. p. 385. New York. 1913. Repr. *in* Towards the understanding of Jesus and other historical studies. p. 140. New York. 1921.

Thompson, J. Westfall. Economic and Social History of the Middle Ages (300–1300). New York and London. 1928.

—— Economic and Social History in the Later Middle Ages (1300–1530). New York and London. 1931.

Thuenen, J. H. von. Recherches sur l'influence que le prix des grains, la richesse du sol, et les impôts exercent sur les systèmes de culture. Transl. Laverrière, J. Paris. 1851.

Weber, M. Wirtschaftsgeschichte. Ed. Hellmann, S. and Palyi, M. Munich and Leipsic. 1923. Engl. transl. Knight, F. H. General Economic History. New York and London [1927].

B. ENGLAND.

Ashley, W. Introduction to Economic History and Theory. Vol. I. Pts. I and II. 3rd edn. London. 1894, 98.
—— The Bread of our Forefathers, an inquiry in Economic History. Oxford. 1928.
Ault, W. O. Some Early Village By-laws. EHR. XLV (1930). 208.
Bennett, H. S. The Reeve and the Manor in the fourteenth century. EHR. XLI (1926) 353.
Beveridge, W. The Yield and Price of Corn in the Middle Ages. *In* Economic History. (Supplt. to the Economic Journal.) Vol. I. p. 155. London. 1929.
Brodnitz, G. Englische Wirtschaftsgeschichte. Vol. I. Jena. 1918.
Cheyney, E. P. The Disappearance of English Serfdom. EHR. XV (1900). 20.
Cunningham, W. Growth of English Industry and Commerce during the Early and Middle Ages. *See Gen. Bibl.* v.
Curtler, W. H. R. The Enclosure and Redistribution of our Land. Oxford. 1920.
Davenport, F. G. The Economic Development of a Norfolk Manor, 1086–1565. Cambridge. 1906.
Denton, W. England in the fifteenth century. London. 1888.
Douglas, D. C. The Social Structure of Medieval East Anglia. (Oxford Studies in Social and Legal History. Ed. Vinogradoff, P. Vol. IX.) Oxford. 1927.
Feiling, K. An Essex Manor in the fourteenth century. EHR. XXVI (1911). 333.
Grant, I. F. Social and Economic development of Scotland before 1603. Edinburgh and London. 1930.
Gras, N. S. B. The Evolution of the English Corn Market. (Harvard Econ. Studies XIII.) Cambridge, Mass. 1915.
—— and E. C. The Economic and Social History of an English Village (Crawley Hampshire), A.D. 900–1928. (*Ibid.* XXXIV.) Cambridge, Mass. 1930.
Gray, H. L. The Commutation of Villein Services in England before the Black Death. EHR. XXIX (1914). 625.
—— English Field Systems. (Harvard Hist. Studies. XXII.) Cambridge, Mass. 1915.
Hewitt, H. J. Mediaeval Cheshire. An Economic and Social History of Cheshire in the Reigns of the three Edwards. Manchester. 1929.
Hone, N. J. The Manor and Manorial Records. 3rd edn. London. 1925.
Jolliffe, J. E. A. Northumbrian Institutions. EHR. XLI (1926). 1.
Kosminsky, E. The Hundred Rolls of 1279–80 as a source for English Agrarian History. *In* Economic History Review. III, p. 16. London. 1931.
Kriehn, G. Studies in the sources of the Social Revolt in 1381. AHR. VII (1902). 254, 458.
Levett, A. E. The Black Death on the Estates of the See of Winchester. *In* Oxford Studies in Social and Legal History. Ed. Vinogradoff, P. Vol. V. Oxford. 1916.
—— The Court and Court Rolls of St Albans Abbey. TRHS. 4th ser. Vol. VII. 1924.
—— The Financial Organisation of the Manor. *In* Economic History Review. I, p. 65. London. 1927.
Lipson, E. Introduction to the Economic History of England. Vol. I. The Middle Ages. London. 1915.
Maitland, F. W. Domesday Book and beyond. Cambridge. 1897.
—— The History of a Cambridgeshire Manor. *In* Collected Papers. Ed. Fisher, H. A. L. Vol. III. p. 366. Cambridge. 1911.
Neilson, N. Customary Rents. *In* Oxford Studies in Social and Legal History. Ed. Vinogradoff, P. Vol. II. Oxford. 1910.
—— Economic conditions on the Manors of Ramsey Abbey. Philadelphia. 1898.
—— English Manorial Forms. AHR. XXXIV (1929). 725.
Oman, C. The Great Revolt of 1381. Oxford. 1906.

Page, F. M. "Bidentes Hoylandie"; a Mediaeval Sheep-Farm. *In* Economic History. (Supplt. to the Economic Journal.) Vol. I. p. 603. London. 1929.
—— The Customary Poor-Law of three Cambridgeshire Manors. *In* Cambridge Hist. Journ. III, p. 125. Cambridge. 1930.
Page, T. W. The End of Villeinage in England. (American Econ. Assoc.) New York. 1900.
Petit-Dutaillis, C. Causes and general characteristics of the Rising of 1381. *In* Studies and Notes suppl. to Stubbs' Constitutional History. Vol. II. p. 254. *See Gen. Bibl. under* Stubbs.
Petruševski, D. M. Die Entwicklung der Grundherrschaft in England. *In* Zeitschr. für die gesamte Staatswissenschaft. LXXXVIII, p. 114. Tübingen. 1930. [The best short survey of the subject.]
—— Voztanie Yota Tailera. Ocherki iz istorii razlozheniya feodalnago stroiya v Anglii. 3rd edn. Moscow. 1927. [An important work on Wat Tyler's Rebellion of 1381, and its place in the break up of manorial organisation in England.]
Pollock, F. and Maitland, F. W. History of English Law before the Time of Edward I. Vol. I. *See Gen. Bibl.* v.
Powell, E. The Rising in East Anglia in 1381. Cambridge. 1896.
Power, E. E. The effects of the Black Death on Rural Organisation in England. *In* History. n.s. III, p. 109. London. 1918.
Prothero, R. E. (Lord Ernle). English Farming past and present. London. 1912.
Putnam, B. H. The Enforcement of the Statutes of Labourers, 1349–59. New York. 1908.
Rees, W. South Wales and the Marches, 1284–1415, a social and agrarian study. Oxford. 1924.
Réville, A. Le soulèvement des travailleurs d'Angleterre en 1381. Introd. par Petit-Dutaillis, C. Paris. 1898.
Rogers, J. E. T. History of Agriculture and Prices in England. Vols. I–III. Oxford. 1866–92.
Seebohm, F. The English Village Community. London. 1883.
—— The Tribal System in Wales. London. 1883.
Stenton, F. M. Types of Manorial Structure in the Northern Danelaw. *In* Oxford Studies in Social and Legal History. Ed. Vinogradoff, P. Vol. II. Oxford. 1910.
—— The Free Peasantry of the Northern Danelaw. *In* Arsberättelse. (Bull. de la Soc. Roy. des Lettres de Lund.) 1925–6. p. 73. Lund and London. 1926.
Tupling, G. H. The Economic History of Rossendale. Manchester. 1927.
Victoria Histories of the Counties of England, *passim. See Gen. Bibl.* I. [The chapters on Social and Economic History in this series give valuable information on rural conditions in the different counties, sometimes with reference to unpublished sources.]
Vinogradoff, P. The Growth of the Manor. London. 1905.
—— Villainage in England. Oxford. 1892.
Wretts-Smith, M. Organization of Farming at Croyland Abbey, 1257–1321. *In* Journ. of Econ. and Business Hist. IV, p. 168. Cambridge, Mass. 1931.

C. FRANCE AND THE LOW COUNTRIES.

Allard, P. Les origines du servage en France. Paris. 1913.
Allix, A. L'Oisans au moyen âge: étude de géographie historique en haute montagne. (Bibl. de l'Institut de géographie alpine; thèse de lettres.) Paris. 1929.
Barennes, F. Viticulture et vinification en Bordelais au moyen âge. Bordeaux. 1917.
Bertain, J. De la main-morte au moyen âge. Gray. 1896.
Blanchard, R. La Flandre. Paris. 1906.
Bloch, M. Les caractères originaux de l'histoire rurale française. (Inst. for sammenlignende kulturforskning. Ser. B. Skrifter. XIX.) Oslo. 1931. [The best general survey of the subject.]
—— Un problème d'histoire comparée: la ministérialité en France et en Allemagne. RDF. 4th ser. Année VII (1928). 46.
—— Rois et serfs. Un chapitre d'histoire capétienne. Paris. 1920.
Boissonnade, P. Essai sur l'organisation du travail en Poitou depuis le XIe siècle jusqu'à la Révolution. 2 vols. *In* Bull. et Mém. de la Soc. des Antiquaires de l'Ouest. XXI–XXII. Poitiers. 1899–1900.

Bonvalot, E. Le Tiers État d'après la charte de Beaumont et ses filiales. Paris. 1884.

Boucomont, A. Des mainmortes personnelle et réelle en Nivernais. Paris. 1895.

Branche, D. L'Auvergne au moyen âge. Vol. i. Clermont. 1842.

Brants, V. Histoires des classes rurales aux Pays-Bas jusqu'à la fin du xviiie siècle. Brussels. 1880.

Brutails, J. A. Étude sur la condition des populations rurales de Roussillon au moyen âge. Paris. 1891.

Cavaillès, H. Une fédération pyrénéenne sous l'ancien régime. RH. cv (1904). 1, 241.

Clouzot, É. Les marais de la Sèvre Niortaise et du Lay du xe à la fin du xvie siècle. Paris. 1904.

Combacal, A. Recherches sur le servage dans le Midi de la France. Toulouse. 1897.

Coopland, G. W. The Abbey of St Bertin and its Neighbourhood, 900–1350. *In* Oxford Studies in Social and Legal History. Ed. Vinogradoff, P. Vol. iv. Oxford. 1914.

Darmstaedter, P. Die Befreiung der Leibeigenen (Mainmortables) in Savoyen, der Schweiz, und Lothringen. Strasbourg. 1897.

Delisle, L. V. Études sur la condition de la classe agricole et l'état de l'agriculture en Normandie au moyen âge. Évreux. 1851. Repr. Paris. 1903.

Denifle, H. S. La désolation des églises, monastères, et hôpitaux en France pendant la guerre de Cent Ans. 2 vols. Paris. 1897, 99.

Des Marez, G. Les luttes sociales en Flandre au moyen âge. Brussels. 1900.

Des Méloizes, L. Le servage en Berry. Bourges. 1907.

Duvivier, C. Hospites. Défrichements en Europe et spécialement dans nos contrées aux xie, xiie, et xiiie siècles. *In* Revue d'hist. et d'archéol. i, p. 74. Brussels. 1859.

Fournier, M. Les affranchissements du ve au xiiie siècles. RH. xxi (1883). 1.

Jeanton, G. Le servage en Bourgogne. Paris. 1906.

Joubert, A. Étude sur les misères de l'Anjou aux xve et xvie siècles. Angers and Paris. 1886.

—— La vie agricole dans le Haut-Maine au xive siècle, d'après le rouleau inédit de Mme d'Olivet (1335–1342). Mamers. 1886.

Lafond, H. Étude sur le servage en Poitou d'après les cartulaires. Poitiers. 1923.

Langlois, C. V. Doléances recueillis par les enquêteurs de Saint Louis et des derniers Capétiens directs. RH. xcii (1906). 1.

Latouche, R. La vie en Bas-Quercy du xive au xviiie siècle. Toulouse. 1923.

Lodge, E. C. Gascony under English Rule. London. 1926.

—— The Estates of the Archbishop and Chapter of Saint-André of Bordeaux under English Rule. *In* Oxford Studies in Social and Legal History. Ed. Vinogradoff, P. Vol. iii. Oxford. 1912.

Luce, S. Histoire de la Jacquerie d'après des documents inédits. New edn. Paris. 1894.

Maillet, G. Les classes rurales dans la région Marnaise au moyen âge (jusqu'en 1328). (Extr. des Mém. de la Soc. des lettres, sciences, et arts de Saint-Dizier. xxi.) Saint-Dizier. 1929.

Malicorne, J. Recherches historiques sur l'agriculture dans le pays de Bray. Pt. i (912–1583). Paris. 1899.

Maulde-la-Clavière, M. A. R. de. Étude sur la condition forestière de l'Orléanais au moyen âge et à la Renaissance. Orleans. 1871.

Maury, L. F. A. Les forêts de la Gaule et de l'ancienne France, aperçu sur leur histoire, leur topographie, et la législation qui les a régies. Paris. 1867.

Musset, R. Le Bas-Maine. Étude géographique. Paris. 1917.

Pirenne, H. Histoire de Belgique. Vols. i and ii. *See Gen. Bibl.* v.

Prevost, G. A. L'Église et les campagnes au moyen âge. Paris. 1892.

Prou, M. Les coutumes de Lorris et leur propagation aux xiie et xiiie siècles. NRDF. Année viii (1884). 139, 267, 441, 523.

Regné, J. La vie économique et les classes sociales dans le Vivarais au lendemain de la guerre de Cent Ans. Aubenas. 1926.

Réville, A. Les paysans au moyen-âge, xiiie et xive siècles. Études économiques et sociales. (Extr. de la Revue Internationale de Sociologie.) Paris. 1896.

Ribbe, C. de. La société provençale à la fin du moyen âge. Paris. 1898.

Richard, J. M. Thierry d'Hireçon, agriculteur Artésien (13..–1328). BEC. LIII (1892). 383, 571.

Rivière, A. Histoire des biens communaux en France depuis leur origine jusqu'à la fin du XIIIᵉ siècle. Paris. 1856.

Robillard de Beaurepaire, C. M. de. Notes et documents concernant l'état des campagnes de la haute Normandie dans les derniers temps du moyen âge. Évreux and Rouen. 1865.

Robiou, F. Les populations rurales en France de la fin des croisades à l'avènement des Valois. RQH. XVIII (1875). 381.

Sclafert, T. Le Haut-Dauphiné au moyen âge. Paris. 1926.

Sée, H. Les classes rurales et le régime domanial en France au moyen âge. Paris. 1901.

—— Esquisse d'une histoire économique et sociale de la France depuis les origines jusqu'à la guerre mondiale. Paris. 1929. [Part II, chs. 2–6 and Part III, ch. 2 contain a good account of agrarian conditions in the Middle Ages based on the author's work on Les classes rurales, etc., but brought up to date.]

—— Étude sur les classes serviles en Champagne du XIᵉ au XIVᵉ siècle. RH. LVI (1894). 225; LVII (1895). 1.

—— Étude sur les classes rurales en Bretagne au moyen âge. In Annales de Bretagne. XI (1896). 367, 589; XII (1897). 60, 190. Also publ. separately. Paris and Rennes. 1897.

Seignobos, C. Le régime féodal en Bourgogne jusqu'en 1360. Étude sur la société et les institutions d'une province française au moyen âge; suivie de documents inédits tirés des archives des ducs de Bourgogne. Paris and Dijon. 1882.

Soulgé, l'Abbé. Le régime féodal et la propriété paysanne. Paris. 1923.

Verriest, L. Le servage dans le comté de Hainaut. Les sainteurs. Le meilleur catel. In Mém. de l'Acad. Roy. de Belgique. 2nd ser. Vol. VI. No. 3. Brussels. 1910.

Viollet, P. Droit public. Vol. II. See Gen. Bibl. v.

D. GERMANY.

Anton, K. G. Geschichte der deutschen Landwirtschaft von den ältesten Zeiten bis zum Ende des 15 Jahrhts. 3 pts. Gorlitz. 1799–1802.

Aubin, G. Der Einfluss der Rezeption des römischen Rechtes auf den deutschen Bauernstand. In Jahrbücher für Nationalökonomie und Statistik. Ser. III. Vol. XL. p. 721. Jena. 1912.

—— Zur Geschichte des gutsherrlich-bäuerlichen Verhaltnisses in Ostpreussen von der Gründung des Ordenstaates bis zur Steinschen Reform. Leipsic. 1910.

Bartels, A. Der Bauer in der deutschen Vergangenheit. Leipsic. 1900.

Bassermann-Jordan, F. Geschichte des Weinbaus unter besonderer Berücksichtigung der bayerischen Rheinpfalz. 3 vols. Frankfort-on-M. 1907.

Below, G. von. Probleme der Wirtschaftsgeschichte. Tübingen, 1920. [The second essay in this collection, entitled Die Haupttatsachen der älteren deutschen Agrargeschichte, is an indispensable introduction to the subject.]

—— Territorium und Stadt. Aufsätze zur deutschen Verfassungs-, Verwaltungs-, und Wirtschaftsgeschichte. Munich and Berlin. 1900.

—— Die Ursachen der Reformation. Mit einer Beilage: die Reformation und der Beginn der Neuzeit. Munich and Berlin. 1917.

—— Die Ursachen der Rezeption des römischen Rechts in Deutschland. Munich and Berlin. 1905.

Bretholz, B. Geschichte Böhmens und Mährens bis zum Aussterben der Přemysliden (1306). Munich. 1912. [For the German colonisation movement.]

—— Geschichte Böhmens und Mährens. Vol. I. Das Vorwalten des Deutschtums. Bis 1419. Vol. II. Hussitentum und Adelsherrschaft. Bis 1620. Reichenberg. 1921–2.

Caro, G. Grundherrschaft und Staat. In Deutsche Geschichtsblätter. IX, p. 95. Gotha. 1908.

—— Probleme der deutschen Agrargeschichte. In Viert. für Sozial- und Wirtschaftsgesch. V, p. 433. Berlin. 1907.

Curschmann, F. Hungersnöte im Mittelalter. Ein Beitrag zur deutschen Wirtschaftsgeschichte des 8 bis 13 Jahrht. Leipsic. 1900.

Danneil, F. Beitrag zur Geschichte des magdeburgischen Bauernstandes. 2 vols. Halle-a.-S. 1896, 98. [Vol. i contains a special study of the Wolmirstedt district, and vol. ii a general history of the Magdeburg peasantry up to 1680.]

Dessmann, G. Geschichte der schlesischen Agrarverfassung. Strasbourg. 1904.

Detten, G. von. Westfälisches Wirtschaftsleben im Mittelalter. Aus seinen Grundlagen und Quellen heraus entwickelt und dargestellt. Paderborn. 1912.

Deutschmann, A. Zur Entstehung des deutsch-tiroler Bauernstandes im Mittelalter. Beiträge zur Wirtschaftsgeschichte Deutsch-Tirols seit den ältesten Zeiten bis zum Eingreifen der landfürstlichen Gewalt. Innsbruck. 1913.

Dopsch, A. Die ältere Wirtschafts- und Socialgeschichte der Bauern in den Alpenländern Oesterreichs. (Inst. for sammenlignende kulturforskning. Ser. A Forelesninger. xi.) Oslo. 1930.

Egorov, D. N. Slavyano-Germanskiya Otnosheniya v Srednie Vyeka. Kolonizatsiya Meklenburga v xiii v. 2 vols. Moscow. 1915. [A study of the colonisation of Mecklenburg in the 13th century, arguing against any considerable Germanisation.]

Fuchs, C. J. Der Untergang des Bauernstandes und das Aufkommen der Gutsherrschaften. Nach archivalischen Quellen aus Neu-Vorpommern und Rügen. Strasbourg. 1888.

Goltz, T. F. von der. Geschichte der deutschen Landwirtschaft von den ersten Anfängen bis zum Ausgang des 18 Jahrhts. Vol. i. Stuttgart and Berlin. 1902.

Gothein, E. Die Hofverfassung auf dem Schwarzwald dargestellt an der Geschichte des Gebiets von St Peter. *In* Zeitschr. für die Gesch. des Oberrheins. n.s. Vol. i. p. 257. Freiburg-i.-B. 1886.

—— Die Lage des Bauernstandes am Ende des Mittelalters, vornehmlich in Südwestdeutschland. *In* Westdeutsche Zeitschr. für Gesch. und Kunst. Jahrg. 4. p. 1. Trèves. 1885.

Gradmann, R. Das ländliche Siedlungswesen des Königreichs Württemberg. (Forschungen zur deutschen Landes- und Volkskunde, im Auftrage der Zentralkommission für wissenschaftl. Landeskunde von Deutschland. Vol. xxi. Pt. i.) Stuttgart. 1913.

Hagelstange, A. Süddeutsches Bauernleben im Mittelalter. Leipsic. 1898.

Hampe, K. Der Zug nach dem Osten. Die kolonisatorische Grosstat des deutschen Volkes im Mittelalter. Leipsic and Berlin. 1921.

Hanauer, C. A. Les paysans de l'Alsace au moyen âge. Études sur les cours colongères de l'Alsace. Paris and Strasbourg. 1865.

Hanssen, G. Agrarhistorische Abhandlungen. 2 vols. Leipsic. 1880, 84.

Hertzog, A. Die bäuerlichen Verhältnisse im Elsass, durch Schilderung dreier Dörfer. Strasbourg. 1886.

Hoyer, K. Das ländliche Gastwirtsgewerbe im deutschen Mittelalter nach den Weistümern. Oldenburg i. Gr. 1910.

Hügli, H. Der deutsche Bauer im Mittelalter dargestellt nach den deutschen literarischen Quellen vom 11–15 Jahrht. Bern. 1929.

Ilgen, T. Die Grundlagen der mittelalterlichen Wirtschaftsverfassung am Niederrhein. *In* Westdeutsche Zeitschr. für Gesch. und Kunst. Jahrg. xxxii. Pt. i. p. 1. Trèves. 1913.

Inama-Sternegg, K. T. von. Deutsche Wirtschaftsgeschichte. Vols. ii, iii. Leipsic. 1891, 1901.

Kaser, K. Zur Vorgeschichte des Bauernkrieges. *In* Deutsche Geschichtsblätter. iv. p. 301. Gotha. 1903.

Kindlinger, N. Geschichte der deutschen Hörigkeit, insbesondere der sogenannten Leibeigenschaft. Mit Urkunden. Berlin. 1819. [An old book, valuable because of the useful source material which it prints.]

Knapp, G. F. Die Bauern-Befreiung und der Ursprung der Landarbeiter in den älteren Theilen Preussens. 2 vols. Leipsic. 1887.

—— Grundherrschaft und Ritterschaft. Leipsic. 1897.

Knapp, T. Gesammelte Beiträge zur Rechts- und Wirtschaftsgeschichte, vornehmlich des deutschen Bauernstandes. Tübingen. 1902.

Kötzschke, R. Die mittelalterliche ostdeutsche Kolonisation. *In* Weltgeschichte. Ed. Helmolt, H. F. Vol. vi. Ost- und Nordeuropa. iv. p. 257. Leipsic and Vienna. 1921.

Kötzschke, R. Das Unternehmertum in der ostdeutschen Kolonisation des Mittelalters. Bautzen. 1894.

Kretschmer, K. Historische Geographie von Mitteleuropa. Munich. 1904.

Kuehn, J. Das Bauerngut der alten Grundherrschaft. Eine Studie zur Geschichte des Verfalls der Grundherrschaft und der Entwicklung der Agrarverfassung in Südwestdeutschland. Leipsic. 1912.

Lamprecht, K. Deutsche Geschichte. Vol. III. *See Gen. Bibl.* v. [Contains a useful short account of the colonisation movement.]

—— Deutsches Wirtschaftsleben im Mittelalter. Untersuchungen über die Entwicklung der materiellen Kultur des platten Landes auf Grund der Quellen zunächst des Mosellandes. 3 vols. in 4. Leipsic. 1885–6.

Lappe, J. Die Wüstungen der Provinz Westfalen. Einleitung: Die Rechtsgeschichte der wüsten Marken. (Veröffentlichungen der Hist. Kommission für die Provinz Westfalen.) Münster-in-W. 1916.

Lauenstein, D. Der deutsche Garten des Mittelalters bis um dem Jahre 1400. Göttingen. 1900. [diss.]

Muggenthaler, H. Kolonisatorische und wirtschaftliche Tätigkeit eines deutschen Zisterzienserklosters im 12 und 13 Jahrht. Munich. 1924. [An account of the colonising and economic activity of the Cistercian house of Waldsassen in the north of Oberpfalz, the Fichtelgebirge, and N.W. Bohemia.]

Plehn, H. Zur Geschichte der Agrarverfassung von Ost- und Westpreussen. *In* Märkische Forschungen (Verein für Geschichte der Mark Brandenburg). n.s. Vol. XVII. p. 43. Vol. XVIII. p. 61. Leipsic. 1905.

Püschel, A. Das Anwachsen der deutschen Städte in der Zeit der mittelalterlichen Kolonialbewegung. (Abh. zur Verkehrs- und Seegeschichte. Vol. IV. Im Auftrage des hansischen Geschichtsvereins.) Berlin. 1910.

Rachfahl, F. Schleswig-Holstein in der deutschen Agrargeschichte. *In* Jahrbücher für Nationalökonomie und Statistik. Ser. III. Vol. 38. p. 433. Jena. 1909.

Reutter, H. Das Siedlungswesen der Deutschen in Mähren und Schlesien bis zum 14 Jahrht. Prague Annahof. Leipsic and Vienna. 1918.

Rietschel, S. Markt und Stadt in ihrem rechtlichen Verhältnis. Leipsic. 1897.

Rörig, F. Luft macht Eigen. *In* Festgabe Gerhard Seeliger zum 60 Geburtstage. p. 51. Leipsic. 1920.

Ropp, G. v. d. Sozialpolitische Bewegungen im Bauernstande vor dem Bauernkriege. Marburg. 1889.

Rudolph, T. Die niederländischen Kolonien der Altmark im 12 Jahrht. Berlin. 1889.

Schmidt, D. Les seigneurs, les paysans, et la propriété rurale en Alsace au moyen âge. Paris and Nancy. 1897.

Schroeder, R. Die niederländischen Kolonien in Norddeutschland zur Zeit des Mittelalters. Berlin. 1880.

Schulte, W. Die Anfänge der deutschen Kolonisation in Schlesien. *In* Silesiaca. Festschrift des Vereins für Geschichte und Alterthum Schlesiens zum siebzigsten Geburtstage seines Präses Colmar Grunhagen. p. 35. Breslau. 1898.

Schulze, E. O. Die Kolonisierung und Germanisierung der Gebiete zwischen Saale und Elbe. Leipsic. 1896.

Sebicht, R. Die Cistercienser und die niederländischen Kolonisten in der goldnen Aue. (Im 12 Jahrht.) *In* Zeitschr. der Harzvereins für Geschichte. XXI, p. 1. Wernigerode. 1888.

Sering, M. Erbrecht und Agrarverfassung in Schleswig-Holstein auf geschichtliche Grundlage, mit Beiträgen von R. Lerch, P. Petersen, und O. Büchner. *In* Zeitschr. für wissenschaftl. Landwirtschaft und Archiv des k. preuss. Landes-Oekonomie-Kollegiums. Ergänzungsband v. Pt. 2. Berlin. 1908.

Siebeck, O. Der Frondienst als Arbeitssystem. Seine Entstehung und seine Ausbreitung im Mittelalter. *In* Zeitschr. für die gesamte Staatswissenschaft. Ergänzungsheft XIII. Tübingen. 1904.

Skalweit, A. Gutsherrschaft und Landarbeiter in Ostdeutschland. *In* Jahrb. für Gesetzgebung, Verwaltung, und Volkswirtschaft im Deutschen Reich. Jahrg. 35. Pt. 3. p. 303. Leipsic. 1911.

Stolze, W. Zur Vorgeschichte des Bauernkrieges. Studien zur Verfassungs- und Wirtschaftsgeschichte vornehmlich Südwestdeutschlands in ausgehenden Mittelalter. Leipsic. 1900.

Swart, F. Zur friesischen Agrargeschichte. Leipsic. 1910.
Thoma, W. Die colonisatorische Thätigkeit des Klosters Leubus im 12 und 13 Jahrht. Leipsic. 1894.
Thompson, J. Westfall. Feudal Germany. Chicago. 1928. [Pt. ii contains the best account in English of the "new East frontier colonial Germany."]
Vogt, W. Die Vorgeschichte des Bauernkrieges. (Schriften des Vereins für Reformationsgeschichte. No. 20.) Halle. 1887.
Wandt, G. Die Germanisierung der Länder östlich der Elbe. 2 vols. (Beilage zum Programm der k. Ritter-Akad. zu Liegnitz.) Liegnitz. 1884, 89.
Winter, F. Die Cistercienser des nordöstlichen Deutschlands bis zum Auftreten der Bettelorden. Ein Beitrag zur Kirchen- und Culturgeschichte des deutschen Mittelalters. 2 vols. Gotha. 1868, 71.
—— Die Prämonstratenser des 12 Jahrhts und ihrer Bedeutung für das nordöstliche Deutschland. Ein Beitrag zur Geschichte der Christianisierung des Wendenlandes. Berlin. 1865.
Wittich, W. Epochen der deutschen Agrargeschichte. *In* Grundriss der Sozialökonomik. Vol. vii. p. 1. Tübingen. 1922. [Together with von Below's essay listed above, the best introduction to the subject.]
—— Die Grundherrschaft in Nordwestdeutschland. Leipsic. 1896.

E. Italy and Spain.

Altamira, R. Historia de España y de la civilización española. Vol. i. *See Gen. Bibl.* v.
Balaguer, V. Estado de la cultura española y especialmente Catalana en el siglo 15. Barcelona. 1893.
Bianchi, G. La proprietà fondiaria e le classi rurali nel medio evo e nella età moderna. Studio economico-sociale. Pisa. 1891.
Caggese, R. Classi e comuni rurali nel medio evo italiano. Saggio di storia economica e giuridica. 2 vols. Florence. 1907–8.
Cardénas, F. de. Ensayo sobre la historia de la propiedad territoriál en España. 2 vols. Madrid. 1873, 75.
Colmeiro, M. de. Historia de la economia politica en España. Vol. i. Madrid. 1863.
Hinojosa y Naveros, E. de. El régimen señorial y la cuestión agraria en Cataluña durante la edad media. Madrid. 1905.
Klein, J. The Mesta. A Study in Spanish Economic History, 1273–1836. (Harvard Econ. Studies. xxi.) Cambridge, Mass. 1920.
Mans Puigarnau, J. M. Las clases serviles bajo la monarquia visigoda y en los estados cristianos de la reconquista española. Barcelona. 1928.
Merriman, R. B. The Rise of the Spanish Empire in the Old World and in the New. Vol. i. *See Gen. Bibl.* v.
Salvioli, G. Storia economica d' Italia nell' alto medio evo. Naples. 1913.

CHAPTER XXV.

THE EARLY RENAISSANCE.

I. CONTEMPORARY SOURCES.

Aurispa, Giovanni. Carteggio. Ed. Sabbadini, R. (Fonti.) Rome. 1931.
Biondo, Flavio. Opera. Basle. 1559.
—— Roma instaurata. Verona. 1481.
Boccaccio, Giovanni. De casibus virorum illustrium. Strasbourg. [c. 1474–5.] French transl. Faivre, P. Bruges. 1476. English transl. Lydgate, J. London. 1494.
—— De claris mulieribus. Ulm. 1473.
—— Il Decamerone. [Naples. c. 1470.]
—— La Fiammetta. Padua. 1472.
—— Il Filocolo. Florence. 1472.
—— Il Filostrato. [Venice. c. 1481.]
—— Genealogiae deorum. Venice. 1472.
—— Das Ninfale Fiesolano. Ed. Wiese, B. Heidelberg. 1913.
—— Rime. Ed. Massèra, A. F. (Coll. di opere inedite o rare.) Bologna. 1914.
—— Teseide. Ferrara. 1475.
Bruni, Leonardo. Epistolarum libri viii. Ed. Mehus, L. Florence. 1741.
—— De studiis et literis. Cologne. [c. 1472.]
Cortesi, Paolo. De hominibus doctis dialogus. Florence. 1734.
Filelfo, Francesco. Cent-dix lettres grecques. Ed. Legrand, E. Paris. 1892.
—— Epistolarum familiarium libri xxxvii. Venice. 1502.
Frulovisi, Tito Livio dei. Opera hactenus inedita. Ed. Previté-Orton, C. W. Cambridge. 1932.
Guarino, Battista. De ordine docendi et studendi. Heidelberg. 1489. [Earliest dated edn.]
Guarino da Verona. Epistolario. Ed. Sabbadini, R. 3 vols. (R. Dep. Veneta di stor. pat. Miscellanea. Ser. iii. Vols. viii, xi, xiv.) Venice. 1915–19.
Petrarca, Francesco. Opera. Basle. 1496. Ed. Herold, J. 2 vols. Basle. 1581. (The most complete edn.) A national edition in 18 vols. is in course of publication at Florence. Vol. i. Africa. Ed. Festa, N. 1926. Vol. ii. Epp. fam. Ed. Rossi,V. 1932 ff.
—— Epistolae de rebus familiaribus et variae. Ed. Fracassetti, G. 3 vols. Florence. 1859–63.
—— Epistolae selectae. Ed. Johnson, A. F. Oxford. 1923.
—— Petrarch, the first modern scholar, etc. A selection from his correspondence. Transl. and ed. Robinson, J. H. and Rolfe, H. W. New York. 1898. New edn. 1914.
—— Le Rime. Ed. Carducci, G. and Ferrara, S. 1899. Ed. Mestica, G. Florence. 1896. Ed. Salvo-Cozzo, G. Florence. 1904.
—— Petrarch's Secret. (A transl. of the Secretum or De contemptu mundi, by W. H. Draper.) London. 1911.
—— I Trionfi. Ed. Appel, C. Halle. 1902.
Poggio Bracciolini. Epistolae. Ed. Tonelli, T. 3 vols. Florence. 1832–61.
—— Historiae de varietate fortunae libri quatuor. Paris. 1723.
—— Opera. Basle. 1538. [Best edn., but incomplete.]
Salutati, Coluccio. Epistolae. Ed. Rigaccio, J. 2 vols. Florence. 1741–2.
—— Epistolario. Ed. Novati, F. I. 4 vols. in 5 pts. (Fonti.) Rome. 1891–1911.
Traversari, Ambrogio. Latinae epistolae. Accedit eiusdem Ambrosii vita [by L. Mehus]. 2 vols. Florence. 1759.
Valla, Lorenzo. Opera. Basle. 1540.
—— Opuscula tria. Ed. Vahlen, J. Vienna. 1869.
Vegio, Maffeo. De educatione liberorum. Milan. 1491.
Vergerio, P. P. De ingenuis moribus. Venice. [1471 or 1472.]
—— Epistole. Ed. Combi, C. A. and Lucani, T. (R. Dep. Veneta di stor. pat. Monumenti. Ser. iv. Miscellanea. Vol. v.) Venice. 1887.
—— Epistolario. Ed. Smith, L. (Fonti.) Rome. 1934.
—— Epistole. Ed. Combi, C. A. and Lucani, T. (R. Dep. Veneta di stor. pat. Monumenti. Ser. iv. Miscellanea. Vol. v.) Venice. 1887.

Vespasiano da Bisticci. Vite di uomini illustri del secolo xv. Ed. Frati, L. 3 vols.
    Bologna. 1892–3. *Also* ed. Bartoli, A. Florence. 1859.
Zambeccari, Pellegrino. Epistolario. Ed. Frati, L. (Fonti.) Rome. 1929.

II. LATER WORKS.

[Adda, G. d'.] Indagini storiche sulla libreria Viscontea-Sforzesca del Castello di
    Pavia. Milan. 1875.
Boerner, C. F. De doctis hominibus graecis. Leipsic. 1750.
Burckhardt, J. Die Kultur der Renaissance in Italien. 15th edn. rev. by Geiger, L.
    and Goetz, W. Leipsic. 1926. English transl. (illustrated). Middlemore, S. G. C.
    London. 1929. Italian transl. Valbusa, D. 2 vols. Florence. 1899–1900.
Clark, J. W. Notes on Chained Libraries at Cesena, Wells, and Guildford. *In* Pro-
    ceedings...Camb. Antiq. Soc. viii. Cambridge. 1895. pp. 1–18.
—— On the Vatican Library of Sixtus IV. *Ibid.* x. 1904. pp. 11–61.
Colangelo, F. Vita del Panormita. Naples. 1820.
Eppelsheimer, H. W. Petrarca. Bonn. 1926.
Geiger, L. Renaissance und Humanismus in Italien und Deutschland. Berlin. 1882.
Giuliari, G. B. La Capitolare Biblioteca di Verona. Verona. 1888.
Gothein, E. Die Culturentwicklung Süd-Italiens. Breslau. 1886. Italian transl.
    Persico, T. Florence. 1915.
Hauvette, H. Boccace. Paris. 1914.
Hollway-Calthrop, H. C. Petrarch; his life and times. London. 1907.
Hortis, A. Studi sull' opere latine del Boccaccio. Trieste. 1879.
Hutton, E. Giovanni Boccaccio. London. [1910.]
Invernizzi, G. Il Risorgimento. Pt. i. Il secolo xv. Milan. 1878.
Janitschek, H. Die Gesellschaft der Renaissance in Italien und die Kunst. Stuttgart.
    1879.
Jerrold, M. F. Francesco Petrarca, poet and humanist. London. 1909.
Klette, T. Beiträge zur Geschichte und Litteratur der italienischen Gelehrtenrenais-
    sance. 3 vols. Greifswald. 1888–90.
Koerting, G. Boccaccio's Leben und Werke. Leipsic. 1880.
—— Petrarca's Leben und Werke. Leipsic. 1878.
Landau, M. Giovanni Boccaccio, sein Leben und seine Werke. Stuttgart. 1877.
Mancini, G. Gregorio Tifernate. ASI. 1923. pp. 65 ff.
—— Vita di Lorenzo Valla. Florence. 1891.
Martin, A. von. Coluccio Salutati und das humanistische Lebensideal. Leipsic and
    Berlin. 1916.
Masius, A. Flavio Biondo. Leipsic. 1879.
Mazzuchelli, G. M. Gli scrittori d' Italia. Brescia. 1753–63. [Does not go beyond
    the letter B.]
Michel, A. Histoire de l'Art. Vol. iii, pt. i. Paris. 1905.
Müntz, E. Les précurseurs de la Renaissance. (With appendix.) Paris. 1882, 88.
    Rev. edn. transl. into Italian by Mazzoni, G. *as* Precursori e propugnatori del
    Rinascimento. Florence. 1902.
—— and Fabre, P. La Bibliothèque du Vatican au xvᵉ siècle. EcfrAR. Paris.
    1887.
Nolhac, P. de. Pétrarque et l'humanisme. New edn. 2 vols. Paris. 1907.
Rosmini, C. de'. Vita di Francesco Filelfo. Milan. 1808.
—— Vita e disciplina di Guarino Veronese e de' suoi discepoli. 3 vols. Brescia.
    1805–6.
Sabbadini, R. Biografia documentata di Giovanni Aurispa. Noto. 1890.
—— Giovanni da Ravenna. Como. 1924.
—— Notizie sulla vita e sugli scritti di alcuni dotti umanisti del secolo xv. *In* Giornale
    stor. della letteratura italiana. v. Turin. 1885.
—— Le scoperte dei codici latini e greci ne' secoli xiv e xv. Florence. 1905. Nuove
    ricerche. Florence. 1914.
—— La scuola e gli studi di Guarino Guarini Veronese. Catania. 1896.
—— Storia del Ciceronianismo nell' età della Rinascenza. Turin. 1885.
—— Storia e critica di testi latini. Catania. 1914.
—— Vita di Guarino Veronese. Genoa. 1891.

Sandys, J. E. Harvard lectures on the Revival of Learning. Cambridge. 1905.
—— History of Classical Scholarship. Vol. I. 3rd edn. Cambridge. 1921. Vol. II.
    Ibid. 1908.
Segrè, C. Studi Petrarcheschi. Florence. 1903.
Shepherd, W. The life of Poggio Bracciolini. Liverpool. 1802. Italian transl.
    Tonelli, T. 2 vols. Florence. 1825.
Symonds, J. A. The Renaissance in Italy. 7 vols. London. 1875–86; and later reprints.
    Vols. I–III. 2nd edn. London. 1880–2.
Tatham, E. H. R. Francesco Petrarca. Vols. I, II. London. 1925 ff., in progress.
Taylor, H. O. Thought and expression in the sixteenth century. 2 vols. New York.
    1920.
Taylor, R. A. Aspects of the Italian Renaissance. 1923.
Tiraboschi, G. Storia della letteratura italiana. Venice. Vols. V and VI. *See Gen.*
    Bibl. v.
Toffanin, G. Che cosa fu l'umanesimo? Florence. [1928.]
Vahlen, I. Lorenzo Valla. Vienna. 1864.
Venturi, A. Storia dell' arte italiana. Vol. I. Milan. 1901 ff., in progress.
Voigt, G. Die Wiederbelebung des classischen Alterthums oder das erste Jahrht. der
    Humanismus. 3rd edn. by Lehnerdt, M. 2 vols. Berlin. 1893.
Walser, E. Poggius Florentinus, Leben und Werke. Leipsic and Berlin. 1914.
Wolff, M. von. Lorenzo Valla. Leipsic. 1893.
Woodward, W. H. Studies in education during the age of the Renaissance. Cambridge.
    1906.
—— Vittorino da Feltre and other humanist educators. Cambridge. 1905.
Zippel, G. Carlo Marsuppini d'Arezzo. Trent. 1897.
—— Niccolò Niccoli. Florence. 1890.

CHAPTER XXVI.

MEDIEVAL MYSTICISM.

I. BIBLIOGRAPHIES.

Chevalier, C. U. J. Répertoire des sources historiques du moyen âge. Bio-bibliographie. *See Gen. Bibl.* i.
Coulton, G. G. Five Centuries of Religion. *See Gen. Bibl.* v.
Davison, E. S. Forerunners of St Francis. London. 1928.
Peers, E. A. Ramon Lull. London. 1929.
Pourrat, P. La Spiritualité chrétienne. Vol. ii. Paris. 1925.
Underhill, E. Mysticism. 12th edn. London. 1930.
    See also the articles on individual mystics, sects, movements, etc., in Vacant and Mangenot. Dictionnaire de théologie catholique (*see Gen. Bibl.* i) and the Catholic Encyclopedia, ed. Herbermann, C. G. and others. 15 vols. New York. 1907 ; and *supra*, Vol. v, chapters xx and xxiii, for bibliographies of monastic and philosophic mysticism.

II. GENERAL SOURCES.

A. Biographical and Historical.

Acta Sanctorum Bollandiana. *See Gen. Bibl.* iv. [For early lives and legends of all canonised mystics.]
Analecta Bollandiana. Paris and Brussels. 1882 ff., in progress. (AB.)
Analecta Franciscana. Quaracchi. 1885 ff., in progress.
    [The two last for reprints of early documents.]

B. Doctrinal Background.

Augustine of Hippo, St. Opera. MPL. xxxii–xlvi.
Cassian. Dialogues. MPL. xlix, l.
Dionysius Areopagitica. Opera. MPG. iii, iv.
Gregory the Great, St. Opera. MPL. lxxv–lxxix.
Johannes Scotus (Eriugena). Opera. MPL. cxxii.
Plotinus. Enneades. Ed. Volkmann, R. 2 vols. Leipsic. 1883–4.
Proclus. Opera. Ed. Cousin, V. 6 vols. Paris. 1820–7.

C. Modern Works.

Baudot, J. Dictionnaire d'hagiographie mis à jour à l'aide des travaux les plus récents. Paris. 1925.
Besse, J. M. Les Mystiques bénédictins des origines au xviie siècle. Paris. 1922.
Buonaiuti, E. Il Misticismo medioevale. Pinerolo. 1928.
Butler, Cuthbert. Benedictine Monachism. 2nd edn. London. 1924.
—— Western Mysticism. 2nd edn. London. 1927.
Denzinger, H. J. D. and Bannwart, C. Enchiridion symbolorum et definitionum. 12th edn. Freiburg-i.-B. 1913.
Dodds, E. R. Select passages illustrating Neo-Platonism. London. 1923.
Gougaud, L. Devotional and ascetic practices in the Middle Ages. London. 1927.
—— Ermites et reclus. Ligugé. 1928.
Heiler, F. Das Gebet. Munich. 1920.
—— Der Katholizismus. Munich. 1923.
Inge, W. R. Christian Mysticism. London. 1899.
—— The Philosophy of Plotinus. 2nd edn. 2 vols. London. 1923.
Jones, Rufus. Studies in Mystical Religion. London. 1909.
Jundt, A. Histoire du panthéisme populaire au moyen âge. Paris. 1875.
Pourrat, P. La Spiritualité chrétienne. Vol. ii. Paris. 1925. [Very useful.]

Taylor, H. O. The Mediaeval Mind. 2nd edn. 2 vols. London. 1914.
Tocco, F. di. L'Eresia nel medio evo. Florence. 1884.
Underhill, E. Mysticism. 12th edn. London. 1930.
Wulf, M. de. Histoire de la philosophie médiévale. 5th edn. 2 vols. Louvain.
 1924–5. Engl. transl. Messenger, E. C. 2 vols. London. 1926.

III. ELEVENTH AND TWELFTH CENTURIES.

A. Sources.

Adam of St Victor. Opera. MPL. cxcvi.
Anselm, St. Opera. MPL. clviii, clix.
Bernard of Clairvaux, St. Opera. MPL clxxxii–clxxxv.
Die Visionen der hl. Elisabeth von Schönau. Ed. Roth, F. W. Brünn. 1884.
 [Critical text.]
Analecta S. Hildegardis. Opera Spicilegio Solesmensi parata. Ed. Pitra, J. B.
 (Analecta Sacra. viii.) Paris. 1882.
Hugh of St Victor. Opera. MPL. clxxv–clxxvii.
Joachim of Flora. L'Évangile éternel. French transl. with biography by Algerter, E.
 2 vols. Paris. 1928.
——— Expositio in Apocalipsim Psalterium decem chordarum. Venice. 1527.
——— Liber Concordie novi ac veteris Testamenti. Venice. 1519.
——— Tractatus super quatuor evangelia. Ed. Buonaiuti, E. (Fonti.) Rome. 1930.
Peter Damian, St. Opera. MPL. cxliv, cxlv.
Reginald. Libellus de vita S. Godrici. Ed. Stevenson, J. (Surtees Soc. xx.) London.
 1847.
Richard of St Victor. Opera. MPL. cxcvi.

B. Modern Works.

Bronarski, L. Die Lieder der heiligen Hildegard. Leipsic. 1922.
Buonamici. Riccardo di San Vittore. Alatri. 1898.
Coulton, G. G. Five Centuries of Religion. *See Gen. Bibl.* v.
Dahl, J. C. Die heilige Hildegardis. Mainz. 1832.
Davison, E. S. Forerunners of St Francis. London. 1928.
Fischer, H. Die heilige Hildegard von Bingen. Berlin. 1927.
Fournier, P. Études sur Joachim de Flore et ses doctrines. Paris. 1909.
Franke, W. Romuald von Camaldoli. (Ebering's Hist. Studien, 107.) Berlin. 1913.
Ghellinck, J. de. Le mouvement théologique du xiie siècle. Paris. 1914.
Grundmann, H. Studien über Joachim von Floris. Berlin. 1927.
Guignard, P. Les monuments primitifs de la Règle Cistercienne. Dijon. 1870.
Liebner, C. T. A. Richardi a S. Victore de contemplatione doctrina. 2 pts. Göt-
 tingen. 1837, 39.
May, J. Die heilige Hildegard. Munich. 1911.
Morin, G. Sant' Anselmo e la vita monastica. In *Riv. storico-critica delle scienze
 teologiche.* Vol. v. p. 11.
Riesch, H. Die heilige Hildegard von Bingen. Berlin. 1920.
Rule, M. Life and times of St Anselm. London. 1883.
Schuck, J. Das religiöse Erlebnis beim hl. Bernhard von Clairvaux. Würzburg.
 1922.
Vacandard, E. Vie de St Bernard. Paris. 1895.
Williams, Watkin. Studies in St Bernard of Clairvaux. London. 1927.
Wilmart, A. Méditations et prières de St Anselme. Maredsous. 1923.

IV. THIRTEENTH CENTURY (other than Franciscan).

A. Sources.

Aquinas, St Thomas. Opera. Rome. 1882 ff.
La Vie de Ste Douceline fondatrice des Béguines de Marseille. Ed. Albanés, J. H.
 Marseilles. 1879.
Revelationes Gertrudianae ac Mechtildianae, cura Solesmensium O.S.B. Mona-
 chorum. 2 vols. Poitiers and Paris. 1877.

Obras de Ramón Lull. 13 vols. Palma de Mallorca. 1906 ff., in progress.
Life of Ramon Lull, written about 1311. Transl. from the Catalan by Peers, E. A. London. 1927.
Offenbarungen der Schwester Mechthild von Magdeburg, oder das fliessende Licht der Gottheit, aus der einzigen Handschrift des Stiftes Einsiedeln. Ed. Morel, G. Ratisbon. 1869.
Mirror of Simple Souls.
    MSS. Vat.: Lat. 4355, Rossian 4, Chisian C. iv. 85. [These are Latin versions of the lost Franco-Flemish text.]
    B.M. Add. 37790; Bodl. 505; and St John's Coll., Camb. 71. [These are all the fifteenth-century English version. A modernised edn. of this, with some omissions, and useful introdn. by Kirchberger, C. in the "Orchard Books" series. London. 1928.]
Mosheim, J. L. von. De Beghardis et Beguinabus commentarius. Leipsic. 1790.

B. Modern Works.

Allier, R. Les Frères du Libre Esprit. *In* Religions et Sociétés. Paris. 1905.
Ancelet-Eustache, J. Mechtilde de Magdebourg. Paris. 1926.
André, M. Le B. Raymond Lulle. Paris. 1900.
Grabmann, M. Der Benediktinermystik S. von Kastl, der Verfasser des Buchleins De adhaerando Deo. *In* Theol. Quartalschrift. Tübingen. 1920.
Lueers, G. Die Sprache der deutschen Mystik des Mittelalters im Werke der Mechtilde von Magdeburg. Munich. 1926.
Mâle, E. L'art religieux du xiiie siècle en France. Paris. 1910.
Peers, E. A. Ramon Lull. London. 1929. [Full bibliography.]
Vernet, F. Articles: Bégards, Béguines, Frères du Libre Esprit, Eckhart. *In* Vacant and Mangenot. Dict. de théol. cath. *See Gen. Bibl.* i.
Zanoni, L. Gli Umiliati nei loro rapporti con l'eresia, l'industria della lana, ed i comuni nei secoli xii e xiii. (Soc. stor. Lombarda. Bibl. hist. Italica. Ser. ii. Vol. ii.) Milan. 1911.

V. FRANCISCAN MYSTICISM.

A. Sources.

B. Aegidius Assisiensis (Giles of Assisi). Aurea Dicta. Quaracchi. 1905.
De Vita B. Aegidii Assisiensis: auctore Fr. Leone. Ed. Bulletti, H. *in* Archiv. Francis. Hist. viii. 1915.
Alvarus Pelagius. De Planctu Ecclesia. Venice. 1560.
Angèle de Foligno, Ste. Le livre de l'expérience des vrais fidèles. Ed. with French transl. Ferré, M. J. Paris. 1927.
    [This supersedes the older editions of the Latin and Italian text.]
Angelo Clareno. Historia septem tribulationum. *In* Archiv f. Lit.- und Kirchengesch. d. Mittelalters. ii. 1886.
Bartholomaeus de Pisa. De conformitate vitae B. Francisci ad vitam Domini Iesu. (Analecta Franciscana. iv, v.) Quaracchi. 1906, 12.
Bonaventura, St. Opera. 10 vols. Quaracchi. 1882–1902.
Chronica xxiv Generalium O.M. (Analecta Franciscana. iii.) Quaracchi. 1897.
Documenta antiqua Franciscana. Ed. Lemmens, L. Quaracchi. 1901–2.
I Fioretti del...Santo Francesco e de' suoi frati. Ed. Passerini, G. L. Florence. [1903.] (Many edns. and translations.)
Opuscula S.P. Francisci Assisiensis. Quaracchi. 1904.
Writings of St Francis of Assisi. Transl. Robinson, P. Philadelphia. 1906.
Jacopone da Todi. Le Laude (secondo la stampa fiorentina del 1490). Ed. Ferri, G. Bari. 1915.
—— Le Satiri. Ed. Brugnoli, B. Florence. 1914.
Regula antiqua fratrum et sororum de Poenitentia seu Tertii Ord. S. Francisci. Ed. Sabatier, P. '(Opuscules de critique hist. i.) Paris. 1901.
Regula antiqua Ord. de Poenitentia. Ed. Lemmens, L. *in* Archiv. Francis. Hist. vi. 1913.

Sacrum Commercium B. Francisci cum Domina Paupertate. Ed. Minocchi, S. Florence. 1901.
Cronica Fr. Salimbene de Adam O.M. Ed. Holder-Egger, O. MGH. Script. xxxii. 1905–13.
Speculum Perfectionis. Ed. Sabatier, P. 2 vols. (British Soc. of Franciscan Studies. xiii, xvii.) Manchester. 1928, 31.
Thomas of Celano. S. Francisci Assisiensis Vita et Miracula. Ed. d'Alençon, E. Rome. 1906.
Thomas of Pavia. Dialogus de gestis S. Fratrum Minorum. Ed. Delorme, F. M. (Bibliotheca Franciscana ascetica. v.) Quaracchi. 1923.
Tres Socii. La Leggenda di S. Francesco scritta da tre suoi Compagni. Ed. Civezza, M. da, and Domenichelli, T. Rome. 1899.
Ubertino da Casale. Arbor Vitae Crucifixae Jesu. Venice. 1485.
Wadding, L. Annales Minorum. 2nd edn. 19 vols. Rome. 1731–45.

B. Modern Works.

d'Alençon, U. Leçons d'histoire franciscaine. Paris. 1918.
Callaey, F. L'idéalisme franciscain spirituel du xive siècle; Ubertin da Casale. Louvain. 1911.
—— Le Tiers Ordre de St François d'Assise. Paris. 1923.
Cuthbert, Fr. Life of St Francis of Assisi. 2nd edn. London. 1913.
—— The romanticism of St Francis. London. 1924.
Ehrle, F. Die Spiritualen, ihr Verhältniss zum Franciscaner-Orden, etc. *In* Archiv f. Lit.- und Kirchengesch. d. Mittelalters. i–iv. 1885–8.
—— Petrus Johannes Olivi. *Ibid.* iii. 1887.
Ferré, M. J. Oeuvres authentiques d'Angèle de Foligno. *In* Rev. d'hist. franciscaine. July, 1924.
—— Les oeuvres d'Angèle de Foligno. *Ibid.* Oct. 1925.
—— Principales dates de la vie d'Angèle de Foligno. *Ibid.* Jan. 1925.
Fratini, G. Vita del B. Egidio d'Assisi. Assisi. 1898.
Gebhart, E. L'Italie mystique. 6th edn. Paris. 1908.
Gilliat-Smith, E. Saint Clare of Assisi. London. 1914.
Goad, H. Franciscan Italy. London. 1926.
Goetz, U. Die Quellen zur Geschichte des hl. Franz von Assisi. Gotha. 1904.
Holzapfel, H. Handbuch der Geschichte des Franziskanerordens. Freiburg-i.-B. 1909.
Huck, J. C. Ubertin von Casale und dessen Ideenkreis. Freiburg-i.-B. 1903.
Nantes, R. de. Histoire des Spirituels. Paris. 1909.
Oliger, L. Il B. Giovanni della Verna. Arezzo. 1913.
—— Les Meditationes Vitae Christi del Pseudo-Bonaventura. (Studi Franciscani. vii, 4. viii, 1.) 1920–1.
Ozanam, A. F. Les poètes franciscains en Italie au xiiie siècle. 6th edn. Paris. 1882.
Robinson, P. A short introduction to Franciscan literature. New York. 1907.
Sabatier, P. Examen de la vie de frère Élie, etc. 1904.
—— Vie de S. François d'Assise. Paris. 1899. Édition définitive. Paris. 1931.
Seraphicae Legislationis textus originales. Quaracchi. 1897.
Seton, W. Blessed Giles of Assisi. (British Soc. of Franciscan Studies. viii.) Manchester. 1918.
Tocco, F. Studii Francescani. Naples. 1909.
Underhill, E. Jacopone da Todi. London. 1919.

VI. ENGLISH MYSTICISM.

A. Sources.

Ancren Riwle. Ed. Morton, J. (Camden Soc. lvii.) London. 1858.
The Cell of Self-Knowledge. Ed. Gardner, E. G. London. 1910. [Contains pieces by Hilton, the author of the "Cloud," etc.]
Cloud of Unknowing, The. Ed. from B.M. Harl. 674 by Underhill, E. London. 1912. French transl. Noetinger, M. (Mystiques anglaises.) Paris. 1925. [Valuable notes and introdn.]

Hilton, Walter. The Scale of Perfection. Ed. from MS. sources by Underhill, E. London. 1923. French transl. Noetinger, M. (Mystiques anglaises.) 2 vols. Paris. 1923. [Valuable notes and introdn.]
Juliana of Norwich. Revelations of Divine Love. Ed. Warrack, G. 8th edn. London. 1923.
—— The Shewings: from the Amherst MS. Transcribed by Harford, D. 3rd edn. London. 1925.
Religious pieces. Ed. from Thornton's MS. by Perry, G. G. and others. (EETS. Orig. ser. No. 26. Rev. edn.) London. 1914.
Rolle, Richard. English prose treatises. Ed. from Thornton's MS. by Perry, G. G. and others. (EETS. Orig. ser. No. 20. Rev. edn.) London. 1921.
—— The Incendium Amoris. Ed. Deanesly, M. Manchester. 1915. French transl. Noetinger, M. (Mystiques anglaises.) Paris. 1928. [Valuable notes and introdn.]
—— [Works.] Yorkshire writers: Richard Rolle...and his followers. Ed. Horstman, C. 2 vols. London. 1895-6.

B. Modern Works.

Allen, Hope E. The mystical lyrics of the Manuel des Pechiez. *In* Romanic Review. IX. 1918.
—— On the author of the Ancren Riwle. *In* Publ. of Mod. Lang. Assoc. of America. XLIV. Baltimore. 1929. pp. 635-80.
—— The origin of the Ancren Riwle. *Ibid.* XXXIII. 1918. pp. 474-546.
—— Writings ascribed to Richard Rolle, Hermit of Hampole, and materials for his biography. (Mod. Lang. Assoc. of America, Monograph series. III.) New York and London. 1927. [Most valuable.]
Clay, R. M. Hermits and Anchorites of England. London. 1914.
Inge, W. R. Studies of English Mystics. London. 1906.
Knowles, D. The English Mystics. London. 1928.

VII. GERMAN, FLEMISH, AND FRENCH MYSTICISM, FOURTEENTH AND FIFTEENTH CENTURIES.

A. Sources.

Das Buch von der Neun Felsen. Ed. Schmidt, K. Leipsic. 1859.
Busch, Johan. Chronicon Canonicorum Reg. Ord. S. Augustini Capituli Windesemensis. Antwerp. 1621. *Also* ed. Grube, K. *as* Chronicon Windeshemense *with* Liber de reformatione monasteriorum. (Geschichtsquellen d. Prov. Sachsen. XIX.) Halle. 1887.
Doctoris ecstatici D. Dionysii Cartusiani Opera omnia, cura et labore Monachorum S. O. Cartusiensis. Montreuil. 1896 ff., in progress.
Meister Eckharts lateinische Schriften, etc. Ed. Denifle, H. *in* Archiv f. Lit.- u. Kirchengesch. d. Mittelalters. II. 1886.
Meister Eckharts Schriften und Predigten. Ed. Büttner, H. 2 vols. Leipsic. 1903, 9.
Harphius, H. Theologia Mystica. Cologne. 1538.
Loer, D. Dionysii Carthusiani doctoris extatici vita. Cologne. 1532.
Gerardi Magni Epistolae XIV. Ed. Acquoy, J. G. Amsterdam. 1857.
Gerlaci Petri Ignitum cum Deo soliloquium. Cologne. 1849.
Gerson, J. Opera omnia. 5 vols. Antwerp. 1706.
Das grosse deutsche Memorial. (MS. in Universitäts- u. Landes-Bibliothek, Strasbourg.) [A collection of 16 treatises by R. Merswin or his school.]
Marcus Mastilinus. Necrologium Viridis Vallis. Brussels. 1630.
Moll, W. and Scheffer, H. Studien en bijdragen. Vols. I-III. Amsterdam. 1870-6. [For texts of Gerard Groot's works.]
Nicholas of Cusa. Opera. Basle. 1565.
Nikolaus von Basel. Bericht von der Bekehrung Taulers. Ed. Schmidt, K. Strasbourg. 1875.
Pomerius, H. De origine monasterii Viridisvallis una cum vita B. Johannis Rusbrochii. AB. IV. 1885.

Ruysbroeck, J. Werken. Ed. David, J. 6 vols. Ghent. 1858–68.
—— Oeuvres. Transl. by the Benedictines of S. Paul de Wisques. 3 vols. Brussels. 1912 ff.
Spamer, A. Texte aus der deutschen Mystik des 14 und 15 Jahrhts. Jena. 1912.
Suso, Heinrich. Opera omnia. Transl. Surius, L. Cologne. 1555.
—— Leben und Schriften. Ed. Diepenbrock, H. 4th edn. Ratisbon. 1884.
Die deutschen Schriften des seligen Heinrich Seuse. Ed. Denifle, H. S. Vol. I. Munich. 1876–80. [No more publ.] *Also* ed. Bihlmeyer, K. Stuttgart. 1907.
Tauler, Johann. Sermon...weisende auf den nähesten waren Wegk. Leipsic. 1498. Repr. Augsburg. 1508; and Basle. 1571.
Die Predigten Taulers aus der Engelberger u. d. Freiburger Handschr. sowie aus Schmidts Abschriften der ehemaligen Strassburger Handschr. Ed. Vetter, F. (Deutsche Texte d. Mittelalters, XI.) Berlin. 1911. [Critical text.]
Theologia Deutsch. Ed. Pfeiffer, F. Stuttgart. 1851.
Thomas of Cantimpré. Bonum universale de apibus. Douai. 1627.
Thomas à Kempis. Opera omnia. Paris. 1549. [Containing early lives of G. Groote and other founders of New Devotion.]

B. Modern Works.

Acquoy, J. G. Het Klooster te Windesheim. Utrecht. 1875.
Auger, A. De doctrina et meritis J. van Ruysbroeck. Louvain. 1892.
—— Études sur les Mystiques des Pays Bas au moyen âge. Brussels. 1892.
Becker, V. Les derniers travaux sur l'auteur de l'Imitation. *In* Précis historiques. Brussels. 1889.
Bonet-Maury, G. Gérard de Groote, un précurseur de la Réforme. Paris. 1878.
De Backer, A. Essai bibliographique sur le livre De Imitatione Christi. Liège. 1864.
Delacroix, H. Essai sur le mysticisme spéculatif en Allemagne au XIVe siècle. Paris. 1900.
Denifle, H. S. Akten zum Process Meister Eckharts. *In* Archiv f. Lit.- und Kirchengesch. II. 1886.
—— Das geistliche Leben. Blumenlese aus den deutschen Mystiken und Gottesfreunden. 4th edn. Graz. 1895.
De Vreese, W. L. Bijdragen tot de Kennis v. het Leven en de Werken van J. van Ruusbroec. Ghent. 1896.
—— Die Handschriften van J. van Ruusbroec's Werke. Ghent. 1900.
—— Ruysbroeck. *In* Biog. Nat. de Belgique. Vol. XX. 1910.
Engelhardt, J. G. V. Richard von St Victor und J. Ruysbroeck. Erlangen. 1838.
Grube, C. L. Gerhard Groot und seine Stiftungen. Cologne. 1883.
Hornstein, X. de. Les grands mystiques allemands du XIVe siècle. Paris. 1922.
Jundt, A. Les Amis de Dieu au XIVe siècle. Strasbourg. 1879.
—— Essai sur le mysticisme spéculatif de M. Eckhart. Strasbourg. 1871.
—— Rulman Merswin et l'ami de Dieu de l'Oberland. Paris. 1890.
Karrer, O. Meister Eckhart, das System seiner religiosen Lehre, etc. Munich. 1926.
Otto, R. Westöstliche Mystik. Klotz. 1926. [For Eckhart.]
Pfeiffer, F. Deutsche Mystiker des 14 Jahrhts. Vol. II. Leipsic. 1857. [Eckhart.]
Pryer, W. Geschichte der deutschen Mystik im Mittelalter. Leipsic. 1874.
Rieder, K. Der Gottesfreund vom Oberland. Innsbruck. 1905.
Schmidt, C. Études sur le mysticisme allemand au XIVe siècle. Paris. 1487.
—— Der Mystiker Heinrich Seuse. *In* Theol. Studien und Kritiken. Hamburg. 1843.
—— Nikolaus von Basel. Vienna. 1866. [With Friend of God treatises.]
Vansteenberghe, E. Autour de la Docte Ignorance—une controverse sur la théologie mystique au XVe siècle. Münster. 1915.
—— Le Cardinal Nicolas de Cuse. Paris. 1920.
Vetter, F. Ein Mystikerpaar des 14 Jahrhts. Basle. 1882.
Wattenbach, W. Über die Sekte der Brüder vom freien Geiste. SPAW. 1887.
Wauter d'Aygaliers, A. Ruysbroeck l'Admirable. Paris. 1923. [Valuable.]

VIII. ITALIAN MYSTICISM OF THE FOURTEENTH AND FIFTEENTH CENTURIES.

A. Sources.

Bernardino da Siena, S. Opera omnia. Paris. 1635.
—— Le Prediche volgari. Ed. Banchi, L. 3 vols. Siena. 1880–8.
Bridget, St. Revelationes. Rome. 1628.
Burlamacchi, B. G. Vita della serafica Sta Brigida. Naples. 1692.
Caterina da Genova, S. Vita e dottrina. Genoa. 1551.
Caterina da Siena, S. Opere. Ed. Gigli, G. 5 vols. Siena and Lucca. 1707–54.
—— Lettere. Ed. Misciatelli, P. 6 vols. Siena. 1922.
Columbini, Giovanni, S. Lettere. Ed. Bartoli, A. Lucca. 1856.
Dante Alighieri. Opere. Ed. Moore, E. and Toynbee, P. 4th edn. Oxford. 1924.
Razzi, S. Vite de' Santi e Beati Toscani. 2 pts. Florence. 1593, 1601.

B. Modern Works.

Alessio, F. Storia di S. Bernardino e del suo tempo. Mondovì. 1899.
Curtayne, Alice. St Catherine of Siena. London. 1929.
Fawtier, R. Sainte Catherine de Sienne. Essai de critique des sources. 2 vols. Paris. 1921, 30.
Ferrers Howell, A. G. St Bernardino of Siena. London. 1913.
Gardner, E. G. Dante and the Mystics. London. 1913
—— A Mystic of the Renaissance : Osanna Andreasi of Mantua. (Privately printed.) London. 1910.
—— Saint Catherine of Siena. London. 1907.
Hügel, F. von. The mystical element of religion as studied in Saint Catherine of Genoa and her friends. 2nd edn. 2 vols. London. 1923.
Joergensen, J. Sainte Cathérine de Sienne. (Transl. from the Danish.) Paris. 1920.
Misciatelli, P. Mistici senesi. Siena. 1911.
Studi Cateriniani. Bull. della Soc. Internaz. di Studi Cateriniani. Siena. 1923 ff., in progress.
Thureau-Dangin, P. St Bernardin de Sienne. Paris. 1896.

ADDENDA TO VOLUME II, CHAPTER X.

I. Muslim Works.

For The Biography of the Prophet by Ibn Sa'ad etc., *read* Ibn Sa'ad. Biographien Mohammeds, seiner Gefährten und der späteren Träger des Islams. Ed. Sachau, E. 9 vols. Leyden. 1905–28.

II. European Works.

For Becker, C. H. Christenthum und Islam, *read* Becker, C. H. Islamstudien. Vol. i. Leipsic. 1924.
Under Buhl, F., *add* German translation, revised and amplified by the author. Leipsic. 1930.

Add the following works:

Lammens, H. Fāṭima et les filles de Mahomet. Rome. 1912.
Moberg, H. The Book of the Himyarites. Fragments of a hitherto unknown Syriac work. Lund. 1924. [Most important for the history of Arabia shortly before Mahomet.]
Wensinck, A. J. A handbook of early Muhammadan tradition, alphabetically arranged. Leyden. 1927.

Also, numerous articles in the Encyclopaedia of Islam, now in course of publication. Leyden and Leipsic. 1913 ff.

CHRONOLOGICAL TABLE

OF

LEADING EVENTS MENTIONED IN THIS VOLUME

521–97 St Columba.
844 Kenneth MacAlpin unites the Scots and Picts.
976–1014 Brian Bórumha, King of Munster.
1018 Malcolm II adds Lothian to the Kingdom of Scotland.
1019–54 Yaroslav, Great Prince of Kiev.
1096 Treaties of Lyúbech between the princes of the house of Rurik.
  Wholesale massacres of Jews in France and Germany.
1124–53 David I, King of Scots.
1143 German colonists begin moving east of the Elbe *en masse*.
1144 Belief that William of Norwich was martyred by the Jews begins the
  "blood-accusation."
1170 Strongbow begins the Norman conquest of Ireland.
1171 Henry II of England recognised as " Lord of Ireland."
1188 The Cortes of Leon contain representatives of the cities.
1189 Pope Clement III declares the Scottish Church *filia specialis* of the
  Roman See.
1190 Massacre of the Jews at York.
1194–1240 Llywelyn the Great, Prince of Wales.
1204 Bishop Albert's crusading Order in Livonia founded.
1210–39 Herman of Salza, Grandmaster of the Teutonic Order.
1215 Badges for the Jews prescribed in the Fourth Lateran Council.
1224 The Mongols defeat the Russians at the Kalka.
1228–30 The Teutonic Order enters Prussia.
1232 Frederick II summons representatives of the towns to a general assembly
  in Sicily.
1237 Union of the Knights of the Sword with the Teutonic Order.
1240 Bātu the Mongol destroys Kiev.
1241 Battle of Liegnitz.
1242 Bātu founds the Khanate of the Golden Horde.
  Alexander Nevsky defeats the Teutonic Order on Lake Peipus.
1254 Knights of the Shire summoned to the English Parliament.
1256–63 Alfonso X the Learned of Castile draws up the *Siete Partidas*.
1258–82 Llywelyn ap Gruffydd, Prince of Wales.
1259 Treaty of Paris between France and England.
1263 Cession of the Hebrides to Scotland by Norway.
1265 Representatives of boroughs summoned to the English Parliament.
1266–85 Charles I of Anjou, King of Sicily.
1270–85 Philip III the Bold, King of France.
1271 Death of Alphonse of Poitou and Toulouse.
1271–76 Gregory X, Pope.
1272–1307 Edward I, King of England.
1273–91 Rudolf I of Habsburg, King of the Romans. Close of Interregnum.
1274 Rudolf surrenders Romagna, Ancona, and Spoleto to the Papacy.
1275 Second General Council of Lyons. Union of Latin and Greek Churches.
1276–85 Peter III the Great, King of Aragon.
1277–80 Nicholas III, Pope.
1278 Defeat and death of Ottokar II of Bohemia on the Marchfeld.
  The Statute of Gloucester (*Quo Warranto*).
1279 Rudolf renounces all imperial claims on the Papal State and Sicily.
  Statute of Mortmain.

1282 Rudolf creates his sons Albert and Rudolf Dukes of Austria and Styria.
1282-1302 The War of the Sicilian Vespers.
1282 Separation of Naples and Sicily. Peter III of Aragon, King of Sicily.
1282-83 Edward I conquers the principality of Wales.
1282 Peter III of Aragon grants the *Privilegio General.*
1283 The subjection of Prussia completed by the Teutonic Order.
1285-1309 Charles II, King of Naples.
1285-1314 Philip IV the Fair, King of France.
1285 Champagne united to the French Crown.
    Statute of Winchester.
    Second Statute of Westminster (*De Donis Conditionalibus*).
1286 Edward I issues writ *Circumspecte agatis.*
1288 Peace of Canfranc between Aragon and the Pope.
    Alfonso III of Aragon grants the *Privilegio de la Unión.*
1288-92 Nicholas IV, Pope.
1289 Battle of Campaldino.
1290 Expulsion of the Jews from England.
    Third Statute of Westminster (*Quia Emptores*).
    Death of Margaret, Queen of Scots (the Maid of Norway).
1291-1327 James II, King of Aragon.
1291 Loss of Acre. End of Latin Kingdom of Jerusalem.
    Edward I of England acknowledged as suzerain of Scotland.
    The Confederation of the Three Forest Cantons founds Switzerland.
1292-98 Adolf of Nassau, King of the Romans.
1292 John Balliol becomes King of Scots.
1293 Ordinances of Justice at Florence.
1294 Philip IV seizes Gascony.
    Celestine V, Pope.
    Treaty of Tönsberg between the Hansa and Norway.
1294-1303 Boniface VIII, Pope.
1295 The "Model" Parliament.
    Peace of Anagni between Aragon, Naples, the Pope, and France.
    Alliance of France and Scotland begins.
    Matteo Visconti becomes despot of Milan.
1296 Boniface VIII issues the bull *Clericis laicos.*
    Edward I annexes Scotland to England.
1296-1337 Frederick II, King of Sicily.
1297 Temporary reconciliation of Boniface VIII and Philip IV.
    Edward I confirms the Charters with additions.
    Closing of the Great Council at Venice.
    First Irish Parliament summoned.
1297-1305 Sir William Wallace leads Scottish War of Independence.
1298 Defeat of Venetians by Genoese at Curzola.
    Edward I defeats Wallace at Falkirk.
1298-1308 Albert I of Austria, King of the Romans.
1299 Battle of Falconaria.
1300 The Papal Jubilee.
1300-1 Expulsion of Whites from Florence. Exile of Dante.
1301 Edward I creates his eldest son Edward Prince of Wales.
1302 Renewed hostility of Boniface VIII and Philip IV.
    Battle of Courtrai. Philip IV holds "States General" at Paris.
    Matteo Visconti deposed. Guido della Torre, despot of Milan.
    Peace of Caltabellotta.
    Boniface VIII issues *Unam sanctam.*
1303 Edward I issues the *Carta Mercatoria.*
    Peace of Paris between Edward I and Philip IV.
    Capture of Boniface VIII at Anagni.
1303-4 Benedict XI, Pope.
1305 Treaty of Athis-sur-Orge between Philip IV and the Flemings.
1305-14 Clement V, Pope. Papacy transferred to France.

1306 Robert I Bruce crowned King of Scots. He continues War of Independence.
Expulsion of the Jews from France.
1307 Lyons admits French suzerainty.
Philip IV attacks the Templars.
1307–27 Edward II, King of England.
1308–10 Ferrarese War and defeat of Venice by papal army.
1308–13 Henry VII of Luxemburg, King (Emperor) of the Romans.
1309 Clement V fixes the seat of the Papacy at Avignon.
1309–43 Robert the Wise, King of Naples.
1310–18 The Lords Ordainers in England.
1310 Conspiracy of Tiepolo. Council of Ten instituted at Venice.
Henry VII conquers Bohemia for his son John.
1310–46 John of Luxemburg, King of Bohemia.
1310–13 Henry VII's Italian expedition.
1311 Clement V erases bulls against Philip IV from the papal records.
1311–22 Second tyranny of Matteo Visconti at Milan.
1311–29 Can Grande I della Scala, despot of Verona.
1311–12 General Council of Vienne.
1312 Abolition of the Order of Knights Templars.
1313 Breach of Henry VII with Papacy. His death.
Ordinance of the Staple.
1314 Double election of Lewis IV of Bavaria and Frederick the Handsome of Austria as Kings of the Romans.
Robert Bruce defeats the English at Bannockburn.
Leagues of protest formed in France against the Crown.
1314–16 Louis X Hutin, King of France.
1315 Defeat of Guelfs by Ghibellines at Montecatini in Tuscany.
The Swiss defeat Leopold of Austria at Morgarten. Renewal of Swiss Confederation.
Death of Raymond Lull.
Louis X grants charters to the Leaguers.
1316–22 Philip V the Tall, King of France.
1316–34 John XXII, Pope.
1317 Assembly at Paris declares that a woman cannot inherit the French throne.
1321 Death of Dante.
1322–28 Charles IV the Fair, King of France.
1322 Battle of Boroughbridge. Execution of Thomas Earl of Lancaster.
Parliament of York. Commons' consent necessary to fundamental Statutes.
Lewis IV defeats and captures Frederick the Handsome at Mühldorf.
1323 John XXII issues decretal *Cum inter nonnullos*.
1324 John XXII declares Lewis IV deprived of the Empire.
Lewis IV declares John XXII a heretic. The Sachsenhausen Appeal.
Publication of the *Defensor Pacis* of Marsilio of Padua and John of Jandun.
1327 Edward II of England deposed.
1327–77 Edward III, King of England.
1327 Peace of Paris between France and England.
Death of Master Eckehart.
1327–30 Lewis IV's Italian expedition.
1328–50 Philip VI of Valois, King of France. Succession through males only ("Salic Law") established.
1328 Lewis IV's lay coronation as Emperor at Rome.
Philip VI defeats the Flemings at Cassel.
Independence of Scotland recognised by the Treaty of Northampton.
Ivan I Kalitá of Moscow becomes Grand Prince
1329–71 David II, King of Scots.
1330–31 John of Bohemia in Italy.

1330 Edward III overthrows the power of Mortimer and Isabella.
1334–42 Benedict XII, Pope.
1337 Outbreak of the Hundred Years' War. Edward claims the French Crown.
1337–45 James van Artevelde rules Ghent.
1338 The Electors' Declaration of Rense. The German Diet's ordinance (at Frankfort) *Licet iuris* declares the imperial election and power to be independent of the Pope.
1339 Revolution in favour of the *popolo* in Genoa.
1340 Edward III takes title of King of France.
Edward III defeats the French in the naval battle of Sluys.
Edward III assents to Statute forbidding taxation save by consent of Parliament.
1340–41 Edward III's quarrel with Stratford, Archbishop of Canterbury.
1342 Petrarch crowned at Rome.
1342–52 Clement VI, Pope.
1342–43 Tyranny of Walter of Brienne at Florence.
1343–83 Amadeus VI ("the Green Count"), Count of Savoy.
1343–81 Joanna I, Queen of Naples.
1343 Peace of Kalisz between Casimir the Great of Poland and the Teutonic Order.
1344 Prague made an archbishopric.
1346 Renewed papal deprivation of Lewis IV.
Charles IV (of Bohemia) elected King of the Romans.
1346–78 Charles (I), King of Bohemia.
1346 Edward III defeats Philip VI at Crécy.
Defeat of the Scots at Neville's Cross.
1347 Cola di Rienzo tribune at Rome.
Edward III captures Calais.
Death of Lewis IV.
1348 Peter IV the Ceremonious of Aragon abolishes the *Privilegio de la Unión.*
Charles IV founds the University of Prague.
1348–50 The Black Death.
1348–49 Massacres of the Jews throughout Germany lead to their emigration to Poland, which becomes their headquarters.
1349–69 Peter I the Cruel, King of Castile.
1349 Charles, eldest grandson of the King of France, becomes Dauphin.
Death of Richard Rolle.
1350–64 John II the Good, King of France.
1351 Zurich joins the Swiss Confederation.
The first Statute of Provisors in England.
1352–62 Innocent VI, Pope.
1353–63 Cardinal Albornoz restores the Papal State.
1353 Berne joins the Swiss Confederation.
Boccaccio finishes the *Decameron.*
1354 Majorca finally becomes part of the Aragonese kingdom.
1354–78 St Alexis, Metropolitan of Russia.
1355 Étienne Marcel takes the lead in the States General.
Charles IV crowned Emperor at Rome.
1355–56 Charles IV promulgates the Golden Bull, fixing the number and powers of the Electors.
1356 The Black Prince defeats and captures John II at Poitiers (Maupertuis).
1356–58 The States General under Étienne Marcel attempt reforms.
1357 Cardinal Albornoz promulgates the Egidian Constitutions for the Papal State.
1358 The Jacquerie in France. Death of Marcel.
1360 Waldemar IV of Denmark sacks Wisby.
Treaties of Brétigny and Calais.
1361 Death of Tauler.

1362 First version of the *Vision of Piers the Plowman* being written.
The English Parliament opened by a speech in English.
1362–70 Urban V, Pope.
1363 Philip the Bold made Duke of Burgundy.
c. **1364** John Milič of Kroměříž begins to preach at Prague.
1364–80 Charles V the Wise, King of France.
1365 Statute of Praemunire in England.
1367 Victory of the Black Prince at Nájera.
1368–69 Charles IV's second Italian expedition.
1369 Renewal of the Hundred Years' War.
Henry II of Trastamara becomes finally King of Castile.
Treaty of Stralsund between the Hansa and Waldemar IV.
1370 The *Pfaffenbrief* adopted by the Swiss Confederation.
c. **1370** Wyclif publishes *De Benedicta Incarnatione*.
1370–78 Gregory XI, Pope.
1371 Edward III agrees to Parliament's petition for lay ministers of the
Crown.
1372 A Castilian fleet defeats the English off La Rochelle.
1372–73 Chaucer's first journey to Italy.
1373 Charles IV acquires Brandenburg.
1374 Death of Petrarch.
1375 Death of Boccaccio.
1376 The Good Parliament in England.
Death of the Black Prince.
1376–78 War of the "Eight Saints" between Florence and the Papacy.
1376–1400 Wenceslas, King of the Romans.
1377 Gregory XI returns to Rome.
Gregory XI condemns Wyclif's teaching in the *De Civili Dominio*.
Death of Edward III.
1377–99 Richard II, King of England.
1378 Revolt of the Ciompi at Florence.
Dimitri Donskoy of Moscow defeats the Tartars at Kulikovo on the Don.
1378–89 Urban VI, Pope at Rome.
1378 The Great Schism breaks out.
1378–94 Clement VII, Pope at Avignon.
1378 Death of Charles IV.
1378–1419 Wenceslas (IV), King of Bohemia.
c. **1379** Wyclif teaches his doctrine of the Eucharist.
1379 Death of Bertrand du Guesclin.
1380 Death of St Catherine of Siena.
Genoese forces surrender at Chioggia.
c. **1380** The Lollard translation of the Bible into English in progress.
1380–82 Philip van Artevelde rules Ghent.
1380–1422 Charles VI, King of France.
1381 The Peasants' Revolt in England.
1381–86 Charles III of Durazzo, King of Naples.
1381 Peace of Turin between Venice and Genoa.
1382 Archbishop Courtenay suppresses the Lollard party at Oxford.
Charles VI defeats the Flemings at Roosebeke.
1384 Philip the Bold of Burgundy becomes Count of Flanders and Franche
Comté.
Death of Wyclif.
Death of Gerard Groote.
1385 The Portuguese defeat the Castilians at Aljubarrota.
Peace of Tournai between Philip the Bold and the Flemings.
1385–1402 Gian Galeazzo Visconti, despot of Milan.
1386 The Swiss defeat Rudolf IV of Austria at Sempach.
1386–1414 Ladislas, King of Naples.
1388 The Merciless Parliament in England.
The Swiss defeat Albert III of Austria at Näfels.

1389 Richard II assumes full royal power.
1389–1404 Boniface IX, Pope at Rome.
1391 Massacres of the Jews cause the existence of crypto-Judaism in Spain.
1392 Charles VI of France becomes insane for the first time.
       Treaty of the Hansa with Novgorod (the "cross-kissing of John Niebur").
1393 Murder of John of Nepomuk.
       The *Sempacherbrief* promulgated by the Swiss Confederation.
       The "great" Statute of Praemunire in England.
1394 Death of Matthias of Janov.
       Peace between Austria and Switzerland.
1394 Benedict XIII elected Pope at Avignon.
1395 Gian Galeazzo Visconti created Duke of Milan.
1396 Truce in the Hundred Years' War.
1396–1403 Chrysoloras teaches Greek at Florence, Milan, and Pavia.
1397 The Union of Kalmar.
1398 The Parliament of Shrewsbury. Richard II banishes Norfolk and Hereford.
       France withdraws obedience from Benedict XIII.
1399 Deposition of Richard II.
1399–1413 Henry IV, King of England.
1400–8 Revolt of Owain Glyn Dŵr in Wales.
1400 Deposition of Wenceslas.
1400–10 Rupert of the Rhine, King of the Romans.
1400 Death of Chaucer.
1401 Rupert, King of the Romans, defeated by the Visconti.
1402 John Hus in charge of the Bethlehem Chapel at Prague.
1403 France returns to obedience to Benedict XIII.
1404–6 Innocent VII, Pope at Rome.
1404–19 John the Fearless, Duke of Burgundy.
1406 Pisa becomes subject to Florence.
       Gregory XII elected Pope at Rome.
1407 Murder of Louis, Duke of Orleans. The Burgundian and Armagnac factions take shape in France.
1408 France declares neutrality between the Popes. Rise of national churches.
       Revolt and union of the Cardinals of both Popes.
1409 General Council of Pisa. It deposes both Popes and elects Alexander V.
       Martin I of Aragon becomes Martin II, King of Sicily.
1410 Death of Alexander V. Election of John XXIII as Pope.
       Defeat of the Teutonic Order by the Poles at Tannenberg (Grunwald).
       Sigismund of Luxemburg, King of Hungary, elected King of the Romans.
1412 Filippo Maria Visconti becomes Duke of Milan.
1413 The Cabochian riots in Paris. The *Ordonnance Cabochienne.*
1413–22 Henry V, King of England.
1414–18 General Council of Constance.
1414–60 Guarino of Verona teaches the classics at Venice, Verona, and Ferrara.
1415 The Council of Constance deposes John XXIII. Gregory XII abdicates.
       Henry V defeats the French at Agincourt.
1415–29 Frequent discoveries of MSS of lost Latin books.
1417 The Council of Constance deposes Benedict XIII and elects Martin V Pope.
1419 Henry V captures Rouen.
       Murder of John the Fearless of Burgundy at Montereau.
1419–67 Philip the Good, Duke of Burgundy.
1420 Treaty of Troyes by which Henry V becomes Regent of France and heir to the throne.
1420–46 Vittorino da Feltre conducts his school of La Giocosa at Mantua.
1422 Deaths of Henry V and Charles VI.
1422–61 Charles VII, King of France.

1438 Bessarion settles in Italy.
1440 Lorenzo Valla proves the *Donation of Constantine* to be spurious.
1444 The Dauphin Louis invades Switzerland with the *Écorcheurs*.
1446 Peace of Constance.
1448–61 St Jonas, Metropolitan of Russia, independent of the Patriarch of Constantinople.
1453 Fall of Constantinople.
1457 Peace of Lübeck between the Duke of Burgundy and the Hansa.
1461–83 Louis XI, King of France.
1462 Ivan III becomes Grand Prince of all Russia.
1466 Peace of Thorn between Poland and the Teutonic Order.
1467–77 Charles the Bold, Duke of Burgundy.
1474 "Perpetual Peace" between Switzerland and Austria.
      Treaties of Utrecht between England and the Hansa.
1476 The Swiss defeat Charles the Bold at Grandson and Morat.
1477 The Swiss defeat Charles the Bold at Nancy.
1478 Peace of Zurich.
      Ivan III of Russia annexes Novgorod.
1480 Ivan III of Russia throws off the Tartar suzerainty.
1481 The Covenant of Stanz promulgated by the Swiss Confederation.
1492 Expulsion of the Jews from the Spanish dominions.
1496 Expulsion of the Jews from Portugal.
1499 Autonomy of Switzerland within the Empire recognised by the Peace of Basle.

INDEX

Aa, river, 249, 252

Aar, river, 78, 184 sq., 192 sq.

Aarberg-Valangin, counts of, 197

Aargau, 78, 91, 195 sq.; conquered by Swiss Confederation, 199 sq.; Austrian attempts to regain, 201 sq.; Lower, 195

Aaron of Lincoln, financier, 645

Aaron of York, 648

Aarwangen, 197

Aasle, battle of, 223

Abano, burnt, 46

Abati, Neri degli, 19

Abbeville, 348

'Abd-ar-Raḥmān III, caliph of Cordova, 637

Aber, 514 sq.

Aberconwy abbey, 514 sq.

Aberdeen, diocese of, 557

Aberdour, 550

Aberdovey, 514

Aberffraw, 514; Llywelyn the Great as prince of, *ib.*

Abergavenny, castle, massacre in, 512

Aber Glaslyn, 508

Abernethy, 550, 554

Aberystwyth, 516; taken by Glyn Dŵr, 524; recaptured, 525

Abrabanel, Isaac, 663

Abraham ibn Ezra, Jewish scholar, 660

Abruzzi, the, Abruzzo, 4, 53

Abū-Sa'īd (Bermejo), king of Granada, 577

Acciaiuoli, family of the, in Florence, 22

Acciaiuoli, Niccolò, Grand Seneschal for Joanna I of Naples, 62

Achaia, 253, 376; princes of, 59 sq., 72; see Philip I, II

Ackerman, captain of Ghent, 371

Acquasparta, cardinal, papal mediator in Florence, 12, 14

Acre, capture of, by the Mamlūks, 3, 27, 286, 316; 260

Adalbert, St, bishop of Prague, 249

Adalhausen, Dominican nunnery of, 800

Adam of Bremen, 248, 600

Adam of St Victor, poet, 784

Adam of Usk, 525

Adamnan, 549 *note*

Adda, river, 33, 45

Adelantado, administrative official in Spain, 595; *adelantamiento*, a territorial division, *ib.*

Adige, river, 47

Adolf, king of the Romans, count of Nassau, election and coronation, 85; policy, *ib.*, 104 sqq.; and Lombardy, 24; and Switzerland, 189 sq.; alliance with England against France, 85 sq., 106, 108 sq., 404; coalition against him, 86 sq.; deposed, 87; defeat and death, 11, 87 sq., 189; 89 sqq., 94, 103, 110

Adolf, count of Holstein, colonising work of, 725

Adorno, Antoniotto, doge of Genoa, submits to France, 71, 378

Adorno, Gabriele, doge of Genoa, 61

Adria, proposal for kingdom of, 377

Adriatic Sea, 28, 48, 682

Aedh, son of Cathal, king of Connaught, 543

Aedh, son of Felim, king of Connaught, 544 sq.

Aedh *Buidhe* O'Neill, king of Tirowen (Tyrone), 544; his wife, *ib.*

Aegean Sea, 15; archipelago of, 632

Aegidius Romanus, 452 *note*; *De Ecclesiastica Potestate* of, 499 *note*

Aelred, St, abbot of Rievaulx, *Meditations* of, 785; *Rule of a Recluse, ib.*; his sister, *ib.*

Aeneas Sylvius, *see* Pius II, Pope

Aeschylus, manuscript of, 759

Aethelfleda, Lady of the Mercians, 552

Aethelfrith, king of Bernicia, 549

Aethelstan, king of England, victorious at Brunanburh, 530, 552

Africa, North (Barbary), 14; Jews in, 635, 637, 650 note 1, 663; Peter III's crusade against, 584; crusade against (1390), 376; Aragonese and Castilian territories in, 572, 582 sq.; trade of, 75; Moors of, 572, 575, 581; *see also* Banū-Marīn, Morocco, Tunis

Agen, 339, 364, 430

Agenais, district of, ceded to Edward I, 306, 401, 429; subsequent vicissitudes of, 339, 357, 364, 429 sq.

Agincourt, battle of, 387, 526

Agnello, Giovanni dell', dictator in Pisa, 70

Agnes of Bohemia, daughter of Ottokar II, 92

Agnes of Habsburg, widow of Andrew III of Hungary, abbess of Königsfeld, 92, 192

Agnes, mother of Odo IV, duke of Burgundy, 335

Agobard, archbishop of Lyons, 639

Agriculture, Chap. xxiv *passim*; influence of physical features, 716 sqq.; small holdings and tenant farming, 718, 723, 729 sq., 733; influence of the towns, 718, 723 sq., 732; the work of drainage and reclamation, 724 sqq.; capitalism in agriculture, 724, 732, 734, 736 sq., 739; the large estate (*Gutsherrschaft*), 734, 736 sq.; the harvest, 736, 747; failure of harvests, 149, 233, 357; famine, 236, 723, 733; agricultural development, 729, 731; works on agriculture, 729 sq.; measures to protect, 748; exclusion of Jews from, 643 sq., 655; agriculture in France, 342; in England, 463 sq.; in Russia, 605 sq., 620; viticulture, 648, 718, 733; *see also* Cattle industry, Labour, Sheep-farming

Alfonso VIII, king of Castile, 569, 573, 581; his wife, 569

Alfonso X, the Learned, king of Castile and Leon, 23, 567, 592; his reign, 568 sqq.; and the imperial crown, 102, 568 sqq.; withdraws his claim, 79, 103, 570; and the Moors, 570 sqq.; his reconquests from, 571 sq., 593; domestic policy, 569, 572; and the Jews, 594, 652, 660 sq.; law and administration under, 569, 593, 595 sq.; *Las Partidas* of, 569, 571, 593, 595, 661; organises the *Mesta*, 749; and France, 308, 401; and Charles of Anjou, 583; and the succession, 308, 571 sq.; his death, 571; his will, 571 sq.

Alfonso XI, king of Castile, minority of, 574, 580; policy and conquests of, 567, 574, 589; death of, 574; his sons, *ib.*; 575, 581, 589

Alfonso, Don, Infante de la Cerda, exiled from Castile, 308, 320 sq., 571; attempts to secure the throne, 572 sq., 587

Alfonso, Don, son of Peter I of Castile, 579

Alfred the Great, king of Wessex, 552

Algarves, ceded to Portugal, 569; 571

Algeciras, siege of, 573; battle of (1340), 574; captured by Alfonso XI, *ib.*

Alghero, 61

Alighieri, family of, 10; *see* Dante

Aljama, Jewish quarter of town, in Spain, 650 note 1, 661

Aljubarrota, battle of, 467, 580

Allenstein, 258

Allmend, common pastures, in Switzerland, 186 sq.

Allobroges, the, 183

Almeria, siege of, 573

Almohades, 567; persecute the Jews, 638, 660

Almorávides, 567, 638

Alnwick, Malcolm Canmore slain at, 554; William the Lion captured at, 559

Alphonse, count of Poitou and Toulouse, death of, 306, 401

Alpin, dynasty of, in Scotland, 552 sqq.

Alps, mts, Roman and barbarian settlements in, 183 sq.; Henry VII crosses, 98; passes of, 187; *see* Brenner, Brünig, Furka, Lukmanier, Mont-Cenis, St Gothard, Simplon; pastures of, 190, 199, 747 sq.; Alps, Ligurian, 44; Bernese, 197; 2, 51, 54 sq., 57, 59 sq., 81 sq., 123, 183 sqq., 189, 192 sq., 199, 271, 284, 659, 716

Alsace, 85, 97, 199, 208, 377, 722; massacre of Jews in, 657; pillaged by Free Companies, 149, 361; Upper, Southern (Sundgau), 78, 202; pledged to Burgundy, 205; revolt and war in, 206

Altichiero, painter, 774

Altopascio, Guelf defeat at, 54

Altyn Ordu, *see* Golden Horde

Amadeus V, count of Savoy, supports Henry VII, 32, 98; ally of Robert of Naples, 43; policy in Savoy, 59; 39, 79

Amadeus VI, the "Green Count," count of Savoy, rise of Savoy under, 59 sq.; imperial vicar for Charles IV, 60; mediates between Venice and Genoa, 60 sq.; and allies with them, 62; supports Louis of Anjou's claim to Naples, 62 sq.; death of, 63

Amadeus VIII, count of Savoy, 72, 74, 199

Amati, faction leader in Cremona, 33

Amaury of Chartres (of Bène), doctrines of, 789; Amaurists, *ib.*

Amboise, 351

Amboten, 256, 264

Amden, 201

America, expansion westward, 725; Jews in, 663

Amiens, 341, 353, 369, 374, 382, 420, 428; treaty of (1279), 306, 401, 429; cathedral, 337

Ammianus Marcellinus, discovery of manuscript of, 762

Amory, Roger of, 424

Ampurias (Ampurdan), French successes in, 585; 587; count of, *see* Peter of Aragon

Amulo, archbishop of Lyons, 639

Anagni, 4, 12; peace of (1295), 320, 586; capture of Boniface VIII at, 15 sqq., 91, 315 sq., 752; victory of Charles of Durazzo at, 63

Anatolia, granted to the Catalan Company, 588

Ancona, submits to cardinal Albornoz, 58

Ancona, March of, 3; factions in, 43; acquisitions of the Malatesta in, 56 sq.; returns to Papacy, 58; and the Great Schism, 299; friars in, 794; rector of, *see* Oleggio

Ancren Riwle, 784 sqq.

Andalusia, 57, 644; struggle with the Moors, 567, 581; campaign in (1309), 573; massacres of Jews in, 581; trade in, 593

Andreassi, Osanna, of Mantua, 812

Andrew III, king of Hungary, 84; death of, 91

Andrew of Hungary, marries Joanna I of Naples, 62; murdered, 51, 62

Andrew, bishop of Prague, 170

Andrew, of Moray, Scottish patriot, 565

Andrey Bogolyubski, prince of Suzdal', Great Prince of Vladimir, conquers Kiev, 608 sq.; policy in Suzdal', 612; defeated by Novgorod, 618; his sons, 608 sq., 612; his brother and nephews, 612

Androin de la Roche, abbot of Cluny, cardinal, legate in the Papal States, 58 sq.; 146, 487

Andronicus II, Palaeologus, Eastern Emperor, relations with Venice and Genoa, 27 sq., 44, 48; and the Catalan Company, 588

Andronicus III, Palaeologus, Eastern Emperor, death of, 287

Andronicus IV, Palaeologus, Eastern Emperor, 61

Angarad, mother of Gerald de Barry, 513, 535

Angela of Foligno, mystic, 795 sq.

Angelico, Fra, painter, work of, 773 sq., 810

Marcel and the States General, 352 sqq.; and Charles of Navarre, 353 sqq., 360, 365 sq.; regent, 354 sqq.; enters Paris, 355; signs treaty of Brétigny, 357; accession of, 359; character, *ib.*; policy in Brittany, 360, 364 sqq.; foreign policy, 361 sqq., 366, 371; supports Don Henry in Castile, 361, 577, 579; war with England, 363 sqq., 522; recovers territory, 363 sq.; relations with the Emperor Charles IV, 146, 352, 366; imperial vicar for kingdom of Arles, 149, 366; and the Papacy, 272; and the Great Schism, 291, 366; internal policy and reforms, xi, 361 sq., 369; death of, ix, 367; 63, 368, 372, 457, 484, 730; his daughter, 367

Charles VI, king of France, as dauphin, 366; character, 368, 374 sq.; his reign, Chap. xiii; minority of, 368 sqq.; popular disturbances, 369 sq.; marriage, 374, 377; assumes the government, 372, 377; his counsellors, *ib.*; and court, 374 sq.; expedition against Brittany, 372; peace with, 374; his insanity, 372 sqq., 378, 383, 385, 388; the government during, 373, 378 sq., 384, 388, 390 sq.; internal conflicts, 381 sq.; feud between Armagnacs and Burgundians, 382 sqq., 389 sqq.; movement for reform (*L'Ordonnance Cabochienne*), 384 sq.; finances under, 369 sq., 381, 383 sq., 389; foreign policy of the reign, 376 sq.; his expeditions to Flanders, 370 sq.; wins battle of Roosebeke, 370; his expedition against Guelders, 377; Italian policy, 63, 377 sq.; acquires Genoa, 71, 378; the Empire and, 380; and the Great Schism, 294 sq., 298, 379; withdraws obedience from the Papacy, 295 sq., 379; and the intrigues of John the Fearless, 386, 388, 390 sq.; relations with England, 371, 378, 380, 468; plans to invade England, 371, 373; meeting with Richard II, 374; renewal of war, 381, 383 sq.; Henry V's claim, 386; and invasions, 386 sqq., 392; battle of Agincourt, 387; English conquer Normandy, 388 sqq.; and capture Rouen, 390; makes treaty of Troyes with Henry V, 391 sq.; disowns the dauphin, 392; alliance with Glyn Dŵr, 525; death of, 392; *Histoire de*, by Jouvenel des Ursins, 375 *note*; 331; his sons, 383 sqq., 388

Charles VII, king of France, as dauphin, 388; leads Armagnacs, 390; regent, 390 sq.; and the murder of John the Fearless, 391; disinherited by treaty of Troyes, 392; allies with Frederick III against the Swiss, 202

Charles VIII, king of France, betrothal as dauphin, 209; allies with the Swiss, 211

Charles II, the Bad, king of Navarre, count of Évreux, his claim to France, 341, 350 sqq.; allies with Edward III, 350 sq., 355, 365; and the war in Castile, 577 sqq.; heads conspiracy in Normandy, 351; allies with Marcel against the dauphin, 353 sqq.;

makes peace, 356, 360; his claim to Burgundy, 358, 360; loses French domains, 365 sq.; his wife, 350

Charles III, king of Navarre, and his father, 365; marriage, 579; and the Great Schism, 292

Charles I, king of Sicily, count of Anjou and Provence, 96, 311, 320; ally of Rudolf of Habsburg, 80, 401; position in France, 305 sq., 401; rivalry with Aragon, 582; war with Peter III, 583 sq., 590; wins Sicily, 583; loses it, 308, 584; death of, 3, 309, 402, 584

Charles II, the Lame, king of Naples (Sicily), count of Provence, a prisoner, 584; released, 3, 586; crowned by Nicholas IV, 3; his struggle for Sicily, 6 sqq., 320; ally of James of Aragon, 6 sq., 586; party to treaty of Caltabellotta, 15, 587; relations with the Papacy, 3 sqq., 17; death of, 23; 8, 52, 310; his sons, 3

Charles III of Durazzo, king of Naples and Hungary, deposes Joanna I, 63, 293; acquires Hungary, 63; murdered, 72

Charles Robert (Carobert), king of Hungary, 6, 17, 36, 62 note 1

Charles Knutson, king of Sweden, election of, 232; war with Christian I of Denmark, 241

Charles Martel of Anjou, anti-king to Andrew III of Hungary, 4, 62 *note* 1, 84; suggested king of Arles, 80; death of, 6

Charles of Blois, duke of Brittany, 347, 349, 359; killed, 360

Charles the Bold, duke of Burgundy, count of Flanders, Franche Comté, etc., ambitions of, 205; his war with the Swiss Confederation, 206 sqq.; commercial policy of, 238, 240; defeated and slain, 208; 209

Charles, duke of Calabria, son of Robert of Naples, negotiations for marriage, 32, 34 sq.; marries Catherine of Austria, 41; lord of Florence, 55, 64; death of, 55

Charles, duke of Orleans, his feud with John the Fearless of Burgundy, 382 sq., 385 sq.; prisoner at Agincourt, 387; 388

Charles, count of Valois, Anjou, and Maine, granted Aragon by Martin IV, 584 sq.; the grant revoked, 585 sq.; renounces his claim, 3, 310, 320, 586; peacemaker in Florence, 12 sqq., 320; and Boniface VIII's Sicilian plans, 8, 12; his unsuccessful invasion, 14 sq., 587; ally of Venice, 28; Clement V and, 36, 93; candidate for Empire, 31, 93, 103, 310, 324; and kingdom of Arles, 338; his Eastern plans, 310, 320; policy and influence in France, 310, 332 sq., 335, 337; and the English war, 321, 338, 405, 430; 11; his daughter, 405

Charles of Lorraine, 259

Charles, son of Philip of Taranto, slain, 40

Charles of Spain, constable of France, 350

Charlton, family of, 520

Charlton, John, lord of Powys, 520 sq.

Charolais, 379; counts of, *see* Charles the Bold, Philip the Bold

Eleonora of Aragon, wife of Ercole d'Este, 767
Eléts, destroyed by Tamerlane, 628
Elias, presbyter of the Jews in England, 654
Elizabeth of Bohemia, marriage with John of Luxemburg, 94 sq., 109, 117, 156; policy of, 157; death of, 160
Elizabeth, daughter of Edward I, 413
Elizabeth of Pomerania, wife of the Emperor Charles IV, 174
Elizabeth, St, of Schonau, mystic, 787, 801
Elna, massacre at, 309
Elsa, river, 37
Eltham, 468
Eltville, treaties of, 139 sq.
Elvira, council of, 632
Ely, bishop of, *see* Arundel
Embach, river, 252
Emicho, bishop of Spires, 120, 122
Emilia, 32, 54, 71; mercenaries in, 51; archbishop Giovanni Visconti in, 57; "Arts" in, 75
Emilian road, the, 2, 34
Emlyn, 521
Emma, handmaiden of Queen Matilda, 786 note
Empire, Eastern (Byzantine), the succession in, 61, 287; the Catalan Company in, 588 sq.; Church in, 621; civilisation of, 485, 758; art in, 528; relations with the Papacy, 287; with Russia, 599 sqq., 631; Greeks from, in Russia, 612, 621, 629; in Italy, 759 sq.; relations with Venice, 27 sq., 48; and the Jews, 634 sqq., 644, 663; conquered by the Turks, 374; fall of Constantinople, 245; 23, 644; Emperors, 27, 376, 583, 610, 631, 759; *see* Andronicus II, III, IV, Basil, Constantine VII, IX, Heraclius, John V, VI, Justinian, Theodosius; Empress, 217; *see also* Church (Eastern), Constantinople
Empire, Roman, *see* Roman Empire
Empire, Western (Holy Roman), Chaps. III, IV, V; early extent of, 184; the Interregnum in, 78 sq., 102 sq., 570; survival of the Empire, 102 sq.; the disputed election of 1314 and civil war, 114 sqq.; result of Lewis IV's reign on, 135; and the contest between Wenceslas and Rupert, 380; imperial authority, 103 sq.; edict of Henry VII, 37, 101; theorists on, 108, 124, 752; position in Italy, 54, 96 sq.; and rectorate of Burgundy, 184 sq.; and the Arelate, 103, 149; and Switzerland, 91, 186 sqq., 212; and the Teutonic Order, 261; danger from France, 108 sq., 323; Frederick III's league in Swabia, 211; Maximilian I's Imperial Chamber, *ib.*; *see also under the various countries*, relations with the Empire; relations with the Papacy, xv, 37, 54, 78, 89 sqq., 94 sqq., 100 sqq., 118 sqq., 133 sqq., 146, 187, 315, 343, 706, 752; declaration by German princes and Rudolf of Habsburg, 80; by

Henry VII, 94 sq.; doctrine of "translation of the Empire," 103, 106 sqq.; papal "approbation," 107 sq.; the Sachsenhausen Appeal, 120; "deposition" of John XXII and election of anti-pope, 124 sq.; Declaration of Rense, 130 sqq.; ordinance *Licet iuris*, 130 sq.; and papal provisions, 277 sq.; and taxation, 280; and the Great Schism, 292, 299, 380; *see also under the various Emperors and kings*, relations with the Papacy; and the Hundred Years' War, 129, 132, 344, 347, 449; constitution, 141; *see* Golden Bull of Charles IV; tolls and taxes in, 82, 88, 142 sq., 185, 211; chanceries of, 137; "men of the Empire," 217; 36, 40 sqq., 59 sq., 205, 310, 647, 732; *see also* Arles, kingdom of, College of Electors, Germany, Italy; Emperors, 51, 54, 78, 90, 141, 144 sq., 147, 151, 162, 184 sq., 186, 216, 261, 570, 601, 646 *sq.*, 787; *see* Charles the Great, Charles IV, V, Frederick I, II, III, Henry IV, VI, VII, Lewis IV, Maximilian, Otto I, Sigismund; *see also* Romans, kings of the
Engadine, the, 197, 212
Engelberg, monastery of, 186 sq., 213
Engelschalk, Albert, of Straubing, 181
Engelthal, Dominican nunnery of, 800
England, the Crown, 438, 457, 469, 478, 483 sq., 648, 653 sq., 709 sqq.; Nottingham judicial opinions (1387), 469, 471, 478; royal domain, 394; power of the magnates, ix, 484; *Curia Regis* and Great Council, 436, 438 sq., 443, 452, 458, 474, 481 sq., 672 sqq., 711 sq.; Parliament, ix sq., 237, 239, 277, 280; development, composition, and functions of, 405 sqq., 425, 439, 443, 446, 448, 451, 474, 481 sqq.; Chap. XXIII *passim*; early representation, 669 sqq., 679; the broadening of representation, 676 sqq.; the groups represented, 680 sq.; organisation and procedure, 693 sq.; and finance, 440 sq., 453 sq., 459, 468 sq., 482 sq., 673 sqq.; and administration, 453 sqq., 459, 468, 474, 476, 483; and legislation, 459, 482 sq., 678, 681; claims to sovereignty, 471; Lords, 471, 482, 693; trial by peers, 441, 471, 482, 674; impeachment, 455, 469, 471, 483; commons, x, 482, 677, 680 sq., 693, 703; Speaker, 455, 482, 693; Rolls, 479, 678, 700, 703; parliaments of Edward I, 326 sq., 394, 398, 404, 408 sqq.; the parliament of 1295, 405 sqq.; of Edward II, 415 sqq., 423 sqq., 431; of Edward III and Richard II, 345, 373, Chap. XV *passim*, 490 sq., 493, 521; of Henry IV, 523; centralisation of administration, ix, 668 sqq., 677, 683, 702, 710 sq.; basis of constitutionalism, 712 sq.; constitutional development of, compared with that of France, viii sq., 681 note 2, 683 sqq., 691 sqq., 699, 709 sqq.; and Spain, 697 sqq.; Chancery, 330, 396, 399, 405 sq., 414, 419, 423, 426, 440, 442

Philip van Artevelde in, 370; submits to Philip the Bold, 371

Gherardesca, Guido della, lord of Pisa, 41

Ghiberti, Lorenzo, sculptor, work of, 771; *Commentaries* of, *ib.*

Giani, Niccolò, 67

Gibraltar, captured from the Moors, 573; recaptured and besieged, 574

Gibraltar, Straits of, 567

Gijón, battle of, 575

Gilbert, bishop of Bangor and Hereford, 452; treasurer, 473 sqq.

Gilbert, bishop of Limerick, papal legate, 533

Gilbert, St, of Sempringham, founds Gilbertine Order, 786

Gilds, 644; of Florence, 10, 13; *Arti*, xiii, 21, 65 sq., 68 sq., 75; in Siena, 69 sq.; *see also Lana, Arte della*; in Germany, 111; of Zurich, 197; of Paris, 342; in Ireland, 544; in Spain, 593; in Flanders, xii sq.; Merchants' (Gild Merchant), 593, 620, 644, 655; *see* Hansa, Merchant adventurers

Gilgenburg, 258

Gillecomgan, husband of Gruoch of Scotland, 554 note 2

Giocondo, Fra, of Verona, scholar and architect, 762

Giornico, 209

Giotto, xix, 22; influence of, 771

Giovanni, St, da Capistrano, 659, 811

Giovanni Domenici, his *Regola del governo di cura familiare*, 766

Giovanni Gualberti, St, founds Order of Vallombrosa, 780

Giraldus Cambrensis, *see* Gerald de Barry

Gironde, river, 522

Girvan, 551

Gite, a feudal right, 717

Giustiniani, family of, 30

Giustiniani, Venetian admiral, 48

Glamorgan, conquered by the Normans, 509 sq.; 519; lordship of, 518; revolt in, 520; acquired by Hugh Despenser the younger, 422, 520; lords of, *see* FitzHamon, Gloucester, earls of

Glanville, Ranulf, 666, 675

Glappon, Charles, Prussian leader, 257

Glarus, 190; and Austria, 192 sq., 196 sq., 201; member of Swiss Confederation, 192 sq., 196 sq., 199, 203 sq., 213; alliances and policy, 197, 201, 203, 205, 210 sq., 213; possessions, 197, 201, 213

Glasgow, 565; diocese of, 557

Gleb, St, prince of Murom; murdered, 599; canonised, 600

Glendalough, 536

Glen Dochart, 550

Glendower, *see* Glyn Dŵr

Glenmama, battle of, 531

Glen-Saggart, 531

Gloucester, 431, 512, 554; Statute of, 394; parliament at (1378), 459 sq., 491; Jews

in, 653; St Peter's abbey at, 432; estates of, 447; *see also* Clare

Gloucester, Thomas of Woodstock, duke of (earl of Buckingham, Essex, and Northampton), marriage, 447, 475; his French campaign, 367, 468; policy of, 457 sq., 475, 477; leader of opposition party, 468 sqq.; decline of his power, 471 sqq., 475 sq.; arrest and death of, 477; ix, 479 sq.

Gloucester, Gilbert de Clare, the elder, earl of, lord of Glamorgan, 518; 545

Gloucester, Gilbert de Clare, the younger, earl of, 413; a Lord Ordainer, 416; slain, 421, 520; his heiresses, 421 sq., 520

Gloucester, Robert, earl of, lord of Glamorgan, 511

Gloucester, Thomas Despenser, earl of, 477

Glyn Cothi, Lewis, Welsh poet, 526

Glyn Dŵr (Glendower), Owain (Owain ap Gruffydd), lord of Glyn Dyfrdwy, 522 sq.; his revolt, 523 sq.; failure and death of, 525; 526; his daughter, 524; his family, 525

Glyn Dyfrdwy, Glyn Dŵr's revolt in, 523

Gmünd, 168

Gödersheim, 377

Godfrey, abbot of Lekno, 253

Godibert, Fleming, in Rhos, 535

Godred, king of Man, blockades Dublin, 537

Godric, St, of Finchale, 785

Golden Bull, of Frederick II, to Bohemia, 155

Golden Bull, of Charles IV, x, 54, 106, 147 sq., 154, 649; publication of, 143; its clauses, 143 sqq., 150 sq.; those relating to Bohemia, 163 sq.; its purpose and effect, 54, 145 sq., 164

Golden Horde (*Altyn Ordu*, Kipchak, *Zolotáya Ordá*), khanate of, 614; court of, 625; *see* Saray; subjection of Russia to, 615, 623, 625, 628; and the struggle for the Great Principality, 625 sqq., 630; alliance with Moscow, 625 sqq.; dissolution of, 627 sq.; conquered by Tuqtāmish, 628; khans of, 613 note, 615, 619, 621 sqq.; *see* Bātu, Mamay, Tulubugha, Tuqtāmish

Goldene Aue, reclamation of, 726

Goldingen, 264

Golin, Martin von, 258

Göllheim, battle of, 87, 189

Golub, 262

Gomera, island, 581

Gonzaga, family of, in Mantua, library of, 755; educational work of Vittorino da Feltre in, 765 sq.

Gonzaga, Cecilia, 766 sq.; Pisanello's medal of, 767, 773

Gonzaga, Elisabetta, wife of Guid' Ubaldo of Montefeltro, 767

Gonzaga, Francesco, marquess of Mantua, 767

Gonzaga, Gianfrancesco, marquess of Mantua, 766; medal of, 773

Gorizia, count of, *see* Henry

Index

Man, Isle of, 477; vikings of, 532, 537; fortresses in, 560; ceded to Scotland, *ib.*; representative institutions in, 706; king of, *see* Godred

Mande, Henry de, mystical tracts of, 803

Manetti, Antonio, 771

Manetti, Giannozzo, humanist and Hebrew scholar, 759, 761, 764 sq., 769; secretary to Nicholas V, 768; translates the Bible, *ib.*

Manfred, king of Sicily, 4, 582; death of, 583 sq.

Manfred of Sicily, duke of Athens, 589

Manfredi, Giovanni de', lord of Faenza, 56

Manilius, discovery of manuscript of, 762

Manorbier, 513, 535

Manresa, 697

Mantes, 360, 391

Mantua, 2, 25; alliance with Verona, 26 sq., 45; Henry VII and, 33, 38; alliance with Pisa and Lucca, 39; with Milan, 45; in league against the Visconti, 58; library at, 755; educational work of Vittorino da Feltre in, 765 sq., 774; court of, 767; art in, 774; lords of, *see* Bonaccolsi, Gonzaga

Manuales, faction in Murcia, 580

Manx, language, 548

Map, Walter, *De Nugis Curialium* of, 743

Mar, earldom of, 549

Marcel, Etienne, provost of the merchants of Paris, 351, 369; heads movement for reform, xi, 352 sqq.; and conspires with Charles the Bad, 353 sqq.; killed, 355

Marcellus, the tribune, 2

March, Edmund Mortimer (I), earl of, marshal, 447, 455 sq.

March, Edmund Mortimer (II), earl of, as heir to the throne, 479; 524

March, Edward, earl of, *see* Edward IV

March, Roger Mortimer (I) of Wigmore, earl of, rebels, 422; imprisoned, 424; escapes, 430; and the deposition of Edward II, 431, 434; policy of, 338, 434 sqq.; in Wales, 520; created earl of March, 430; fall and execution of, *ib.*; 439, 447, 450; his mother, 431; his daughters, 435

March, Roger Mortimer (III), earl of, as heir to the throne, 455, 458; killed, 479

March, the (in Switzerland), 192; Upper March, 197, 201

March, the Welsh, *see* Wales

Marchands de l'eau, company of, in Paris, 342

Marchfeld, victory of Rudolf of Habsburg over Ottokar II on the, 79

Mardisley, Franciscan provincial minister, 452

Mare, Sir Peter de la, Speaker of the Commons, 455 sq., 459

Maredudd ap Bleddyn, prince of Powys, 510

Maredudd ab Owain, prince of Deheubarth, 508

Maredudd ap Rhys, lord of Dinefwr, 516, 518

Maremma, the, 34

Marès, Jean des, 369, 371

Margaret, queen of Denmark, Norway, and Sweden, marriage with Hakon, 220 sq.; and the Hansa, 222 sqq.; war with Albert of Mecklenburg, 222 sqq.; secures Union of Kalmar, 224

Margaret, Maid of Norway, queen of Scotland, proposed English marriage, 562; death of, 563

Margaret of Brabant, wife of the Emperor Henry VII, 32 sq., 94; death of, 34, 99

Margaret, countess of Holland and Hainault, wife of Lewis IV, 129, 134, 146, 449; her sisters, 129, 134, 449

Margaret, daughter of Philip III of France, wife of Edward I of England, 322, 403, 407, 411

Margaret, wife of Charles of Durazzo, 72

Margaret, St, wife of Malcolm Canmore, king of Scotland, marriage of, 554; influence of, 555; 556; her daughter, 555

Margaret, daughter of Philip V of France, 337

Margaret, daughter of Charles II of Naples, marries Charles of Valois, 310, 320

Margaret of Provence, wife of Louis IX, 306

Margaret, daughter of Alexander III of Scotland, birth of, 561 sq.; marries Eric of Norway, 560

Margaret III, countess of Flanders, Artois, Franche Comté, etc., 358; marriage with Philip the Bold of Burgundy, 362, 371

Margaret Maultasch, countess of Tyrol, 128 sq., 147; marriage with John Henry of Luxemburg, 126, 133, 160 sq.; with Lewis of Brandenburg, 133, 161

Margaret of Gloucester, wife of Peter of Gaveston, 413

Maria de Molina, Doña, queen-regent in Castile, 573

Maria, Doña, of Portugal, wife of Alfonso XI of Castile, 574 sqq.

Maria de Padilla, *see* Padilla

Marie de Coucy, wife of Alexander II of Scotland, 561

Marienburg, 109, 262; capital of the Teutonic Order, 260 sq., 264; ceded to Poland, 266

Marienhausen, 268

Marienwerder (on the Niemen), castle, 259

Marienwerder (on the Vistula), founded, 254; cathedral, 261

Marignano (Melegnano), battle of, 214; 72

Marigny, Enguerrand de, 36, 310, 327; fall of, 333

Maritagium, payment exacted from serfs, 721, 727

Marjorie, illegitimate daughter of Alexander II of Scotland, 562

Markets, marketing, 718, 723 sq., 730, 734, 746

Markgenossenschaft, association of freemen, 186 sq., 740

Markyate, 785; *see* Christina of, Roger of

Marliani, archaeologist, 768

VII, 32 sqq., 44 sqq., 98; and Genoa, 44;
driven out of, 61; conflict with John XXII,
42, 45 sq., 55; crusade against, 55, 118;
policy and acquisitions under Matteo, 45
sq.; temporary decline of, 55; advance
under archbishop Giovanni, 56 sq.; and
his successors, 58 sq.; alliances against,
58, 62, 476; ally of Venice, 61; Emperor
Charles IV and, 149; policy and acquisitions of Gian Galeazzo, 71 sq.; dissolution of the State, 73; library of the, at
Pavia, 755, 764; 41, 59, 70, 74, 96, 378,
447, 452, 754, 768, 774
Visconti, Bernabò, lord of Milan, 56, 377;
warfare and negotiations in the Papal
States, 58 sq., 272; treaty of peace, 59,
66; mediates between Florence and the
Papacy, 67; death of, 71
Visconti, Catherine, 25 sq.
Visconti, Filippo Maria, duke of Milan, 74,
763, 768; medal of, 773
Visconti, Galeazzo I, lord of Milan, marriage
of, 25; exiled, *ib.*; returns under Henry VII,
33; accession of, 46; 118
Visconti, Galeazzo II, lord of Milan, 56, 71;
marries Bianca of Savoy, 59; aids Amadeus VI, 60; his library, 755, 763
Visconti, Galeazzo, 212
Visconti, Gian Galeazzo, duke of Milan,
power and policy, 63 sq., 70 sqq., 377 sq.;
supports Louis of Anjou's claim to Naples,
63; his wars and acquisitions, 71 sq.; and
the Great Schism, 293; his library, 755,
763; death of, 72 sq.; 74
Visconti, Giovanni, archbishop and lord of
Milan, power and policy, 55 sq.; and
Clement VI, 56; acquires Genoa, 57, 61;
death of, 57; 59, 71
Visconti, Giovanni Maria, duke of Milan,
74; and the Swiss Confederation, 198,
200
Visconti, Lodovico, 71
Visconti, Lodrisio, army of, 51
Visconti, Luchino, lord of Milan, 45 sq.;
policy of, 56; death of, 55
Visconti, Marco, and siege of Genoa, 44;
captures Pavia, 45
Visconti, Matteo I, lord of Milan, imperial
vicar in Lombardy, 24 sq., 33, 44 sq.,
55; negotiates peace between Venice and
Genoa, 28; captain in Milan, 24; forced
into retirement, 25; return of, under
Henry VII, 32 sq., 44 sq., 98; at Monte-
catini, 40; his acquisitions, 45 sq.; ally
of Can Grande, 45; conflict with John
XXII, 45 sq., 55; resignation and death,
46, 55; 26, 59
Visconti, Matteo II, lord of Milan, 56
Visconti, Nino, judge of Gallura, 25
Visconti, Otto, archbishop of Milan, death
of, 24; 25
Visconti, Rodolfo, 71
Visconti, Stefano, 56
Visconti, Valentine, duchess of Orleans,
375, 377, 381 sq.

Visigoths, 596; in Spain, 635, 639, 661,
696; in Gaul, 638; *Liber Iudiciorum* of,
595; king of, *see* Sisebut
Vistula, river, xvii, 248, 254 sq., 261, 267;
possessions of Teutonic Order on, 260;
colonisation on, 726
Vitalian Brethren, rise and activities of,
223 sq., 229, 233
Vitebsk, 217
Viterbo, submits to Rome, 3; Urban V at,
272; 34, 36
Vitichev, conference at (1100), 607
Vitold (Vitovt), grand duke of Lithuania,
policy of, 265 sq., 628; his daughter, *ib.*
Vitoria, 578
Vitruvius, works of, 755 sq.
Vittorino da Feltre, educationist, 762, 770;
professor of rhetoric at Padua, 758; work
of, 765 sq.; medal of, 773
Viviers, annexed by France, 109, 307, 323;
representatives of, 689; bishop of, 307,
323
Vladimir I, St, Great Prince of Kiev, and the
Church in Russia, 599 sq.; death of, 599;
descendants and house of, 599, 602 sq.,
604 sq., 610, 618; 603
Vladimir II Monomakh, Great Prince of
Kiev, prince of Pereyaslavl, defeats the
Cumans, 601; convenes conference at
Lyúbech, 602; character, 607; policy and
achievements, 605, 607, 609, 612; his
Instruction, 607; his descendants, 603,
607 sq.
Vladímir (Vladimir), prince of Polotsk,
249
Vladimir, son of Mstislav I, regent in Kiev,
608
Vladimir Yaroslavich, son of Yaroslav I,
600, 602, 605
Vladimir, town of, 609, 612, 614, 623; Great
Principality of, 612 sqq., 618; rivalry for,
623, 625 sqq.; colonists in, 612 sq.;
Tartars and "Tartar Yoke" in, 614, 621,
628; see of, 622; province of, 604, 611;
Great Prince of, 615, 618 sq., 622, 624,
626; *see* Alexander Nevsky, Andrey Bogo-
lyubski, Vsévolod, Yaroslav
Vladimir-Volynski, 604, 607, 615
Vladimiria, 615; king of, *see* Daniel, king of
Galicia and Volhynia
Vladimirko, prince of Galicia (Halicz), 610
Vladislav, king of Bohemia, 159
Vltava, river, 168, 178
Vods, tribe, 249, 254
Vogt, jurisdictional lord, 722, 729, 735,
737; administrative official in Livonia,
252, 264; vogtei, 722; *vogtbede*, a tax,
ib; *see also Gerichtsherr*
Volga, river, 248, 265, 604, 609, 611 sq.,
614, 617, 628; Niz, district on, 617 sqq.
Volhynia, principality of, 604 sq., 607, 614
sqq.; union with Galicia, 610; the Vol-
hynian Chronicle, 616; princes of, *see*
Daniel, David, Roman
Volkhov, river, 604, 619

Map 67

Germany
at the death of Charles IV

Map 67

GERMANY

AT THE DEATH OF CHARLES IV

Natural Scale 1: 6,162,500

50 40 30 20 10 0   50   100 Miles

— REFERENCE —

Luxemburg Lands............   Habsburg Lands............

Wittelsbach Lands............   Welf Lands............

Ecclesiastical Lands..........   Limits of the Swiss Confederation .—.— —

Imperial Cities underlined

Map 68

France
in 1328

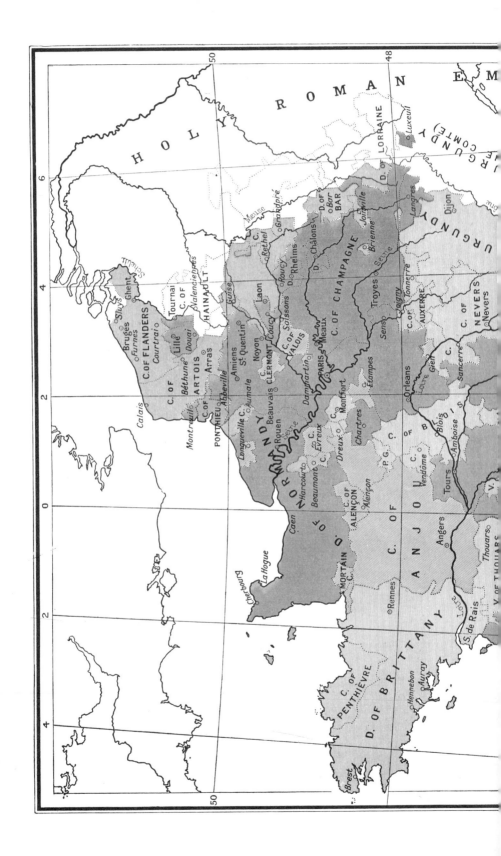

HOLY ROMAN EM

BURGUNDY (COMTÉ)

D. OF LORRAINE

Luxeuil

Meuse

C. Rethel

Grandpré

D. OF BAR
Bar

Châlons

D.

Rheims

C. OF CHAMPAGNE

Joinville

Brienne

Langres

Dijon

BURGUNDY

Troyes

Sézanne

Sens

Joigny

C. OF AUXERRE

Tonnerre

Auxerre

C. OF NEVERS
Nevers

Schelut

Ghent

Sluys

Bruges

Furnes

C. OF FLANDERS

Courtrai

Tournai

C. OF HAINAULT

Valencieppes

Lille

Douai

Béthune

ARTOIS

Arras

C. OF

Guise

St. Quentin

Laon

Coucy

Soissons

Noyon

C. OF VALOIS

CLERMONT

Meaux

PARIS

Dampmartin

Montfort

Étampes

Orleans

Loire

Gien

C.

Sancerre

Loire

Calais

Montreuil

PONTHIEU

Abbeville

Amiens

Beauvais

Longueville C.

Aumale

Rouen

Seure

Evreux

C. OF NORMANDY

C. Dreux

Chartres

C. OF

P.G.

B

Blois

Amboise

Vendôme

Tours

V.

Cherbourg

La Hogue

Caen

Harcourt

Beaumont

MORTAIN C.

C. OF ALENÇON

Alençon

C. OF ANJOU

Angers

Thouars

V. OF THOUARS

Rennes

S. de Rais

Loire

D. OF BRITTANY

C. OF PENTHIÈVRE

Hennebon

Auray

Brest

Map 68

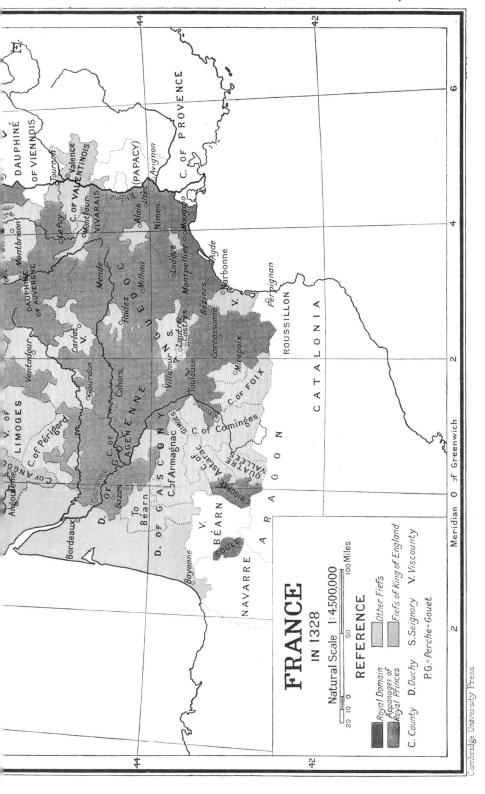

FRANCE
IN 1328

Natural Scale 1:4,500,000

20 10 0   50   100 Miles

REFERENCE

Royal Domain   Other Fiefs

Appanages of Royal Princes   Fiefs of King of England

C. County   D. Duchy   S. Seignory   V. Viscounty

P.G. = Perche-Gouet

DAUPHINÉ OF VIENNOIS

C. OF VALENCE (PAPACY) VALENTINOIS

Avignon

C. OF PROVENCE

Tournon

Valence

Montbrison

DAUPHINÉ OF AUVERGNE

Le Puy

Montlaur

Uzès

Alais

Nimes

Mende

VIVARAIS

Rhône

Milhau

Rodez

Lodève

Montpellier

Maugio

Agde

Narbonne

Béziers

V.

Perpignan

Carlat V.

Gourdon

Cahors

Castres

Carcassonne

Mirepoix

ROUSSILLON

Ventadour

V. OF LIMOGES

C. of Périgord

C. of Angoulême

Angoulême

L A N G U E D O C

A G E N E N E

Villemur S.

Laurec

Toulouse

C. OF FOIX

CATALONIA

Bordeaux

D. OF GASCONY

Bazas

To Béarn

C. of Armagnac

C. of Astarac

C. of Cominges

QUATRE VALLÉES

BIGORRE

A R A G O N

Bayonne

BÉARN

V. SOULE

NAVARRE

Meridian 0 of Greenwich

44

42

6

4

2

Map 69

France

in 1361

after the Peace of Brétigny

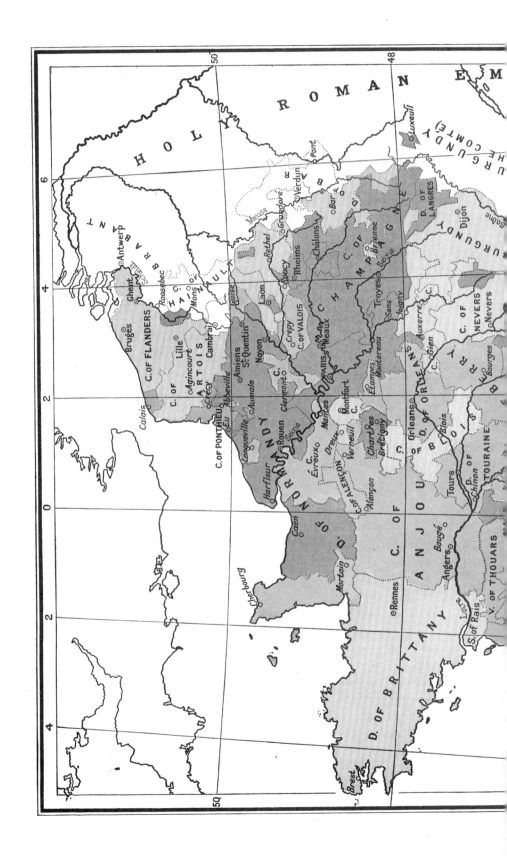

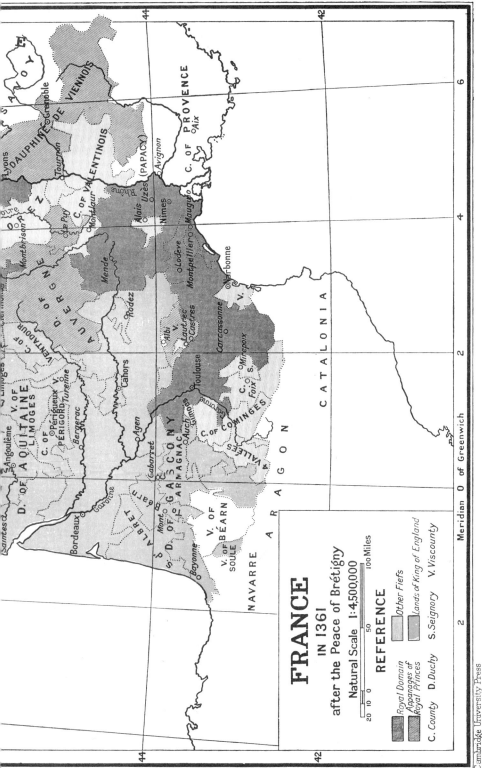

Map 69

FRANCE
IN 1361
after the Peace of Brétigny
Natural Scale 1:4,500,000

REFERENCE

Royal Domain
Appanages of
Royal Princes

Other Fiefs
Lands of King of England

C. County D. Duchy S. Seignory V. Viscounty

100 Miles

Cambridge University Press

Meridian 0 of Greenwich

CATALONIA

ARAGON

NAVARRE

V. OF
SOULE

V. OF BÉARN

V. OF
ALBRET

S. D. OF GASCONY

Bayonne

Bordeaux

Garonne

C. OF ARMAGNAC

C. OF COMINGES

VALLÉES

Auch

Limoges

Toulouse

Foix

C. OF
FOIX

Mirepoix

Carcassonne

Castres

Lautrec

V.
S.

Albi

Rodez

Mende

Cahors

Agen

Bergerac

C. OF
PÉRIGORD

Périgueux

V. of
Turenne

Angoulême

D. OF AQUITAINE

V. OF
LIMOGES

Limoges

C. OF
VENTADOUR

Saintes

Cabarret

Narbonne

Montpellier

Lodève

Nîmes

Maugio

Alais

Uzès

(PAPACY)

Avignon

C. OF PROVENCE

Aix

C. OF VALENTINOIS

Montélimar

Tournon

Le Puy

AUVERGNE

Montbrison

C. OF
FOREZ

Lyons

DAUPHINÉ OF VIENNOIS

Grenoble

SAVOY

Rhône

42

44

Map 70

Italy

circa 1340

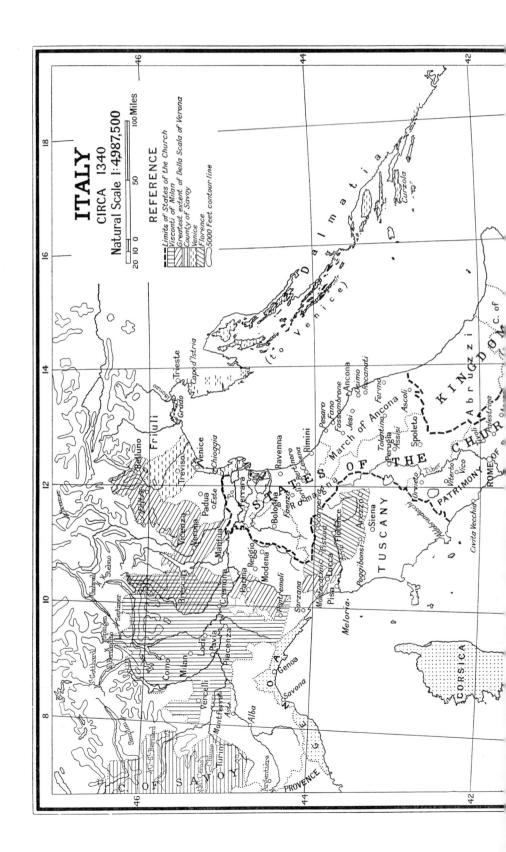

ITALY

CIRCA 1340

Natural Scale 1:4,987,500

REFERENCE

Limits of States of the Church
Visconti of Milan
Greatest extent of Della Scala of Verona
County of Savoy
Venice
Florence
5000 Feet contour line

20 10 0   50   100 Miles

Map 70

40 38 18

16

pato

SARDINIA
(to Aragon)
Arborea

KINGDOM OF SICILY
(TRINACRIA)

CALABRIA

ata

Reggio
Messina
Milazzo
Lipari

Palermo
Falconaria
Trapani
Caltabellotta
Sciacca
Catania
Syracuse
Cape Passero

40 38 36

8 10 12 14 16 18

12 Longitude East of Greenwich

W.&A.K.Johnston Ltd

Map 71

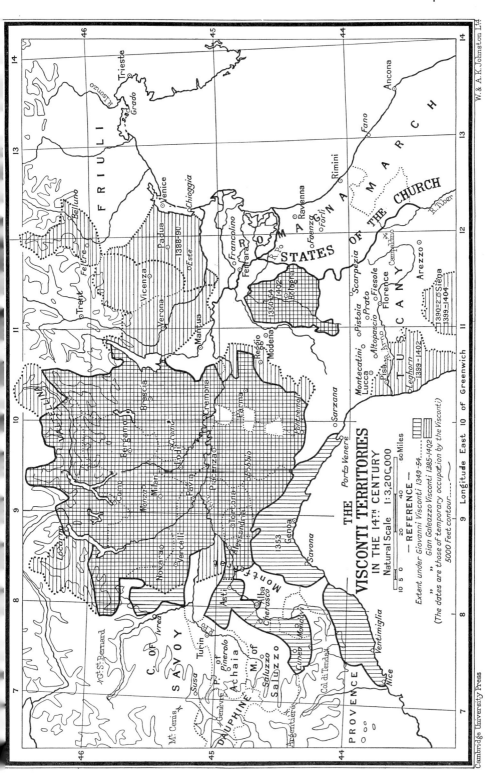

THE
VISCONTI TERRITORIES
IN THE 14TH CENTURY
Natural Scale 1:3,200,000

10 5 0   20   40   60 Miles

— REFERENCE —

Extent under Giovanni Visconti 1349–54 ....
   "   "   Gian Galeazzo Visconti (1385–1402)
(The dates are those of temporary occupation by the Visconti)
5000 Feet contour ....

Longitude East 10 of Greenwich

W. & A.K. Johnston Ltd

Map 72

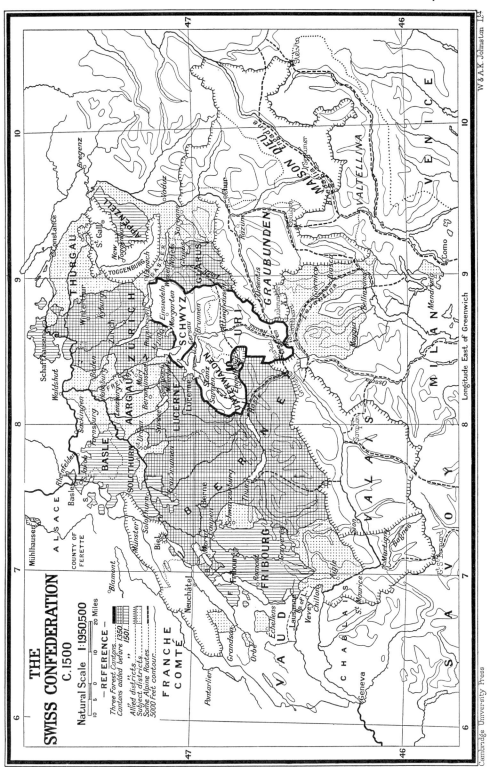

THE
SWISS CONFEDERATION
C.1500

Natural Scale 1:1950500

— REFERENCE —

Three Forest Cantons........
Cantons added before 1350..
     „   „   „   1501...
Allied districts.............
Subject districts...........
Some Alpine Routes.........
5000 Feet contour..........

Map 73
East Central Europe
in the 14th century

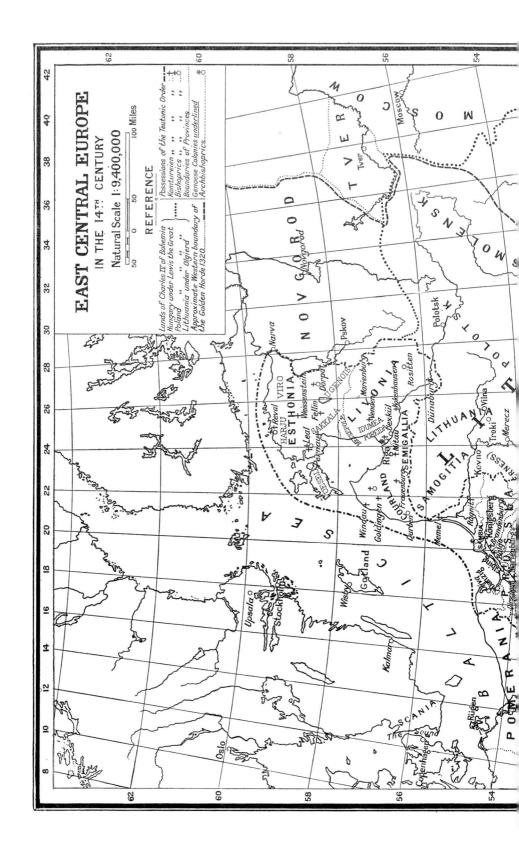

EAST CENTRAL EUROPE
IN THE 14TH CENTURY
Natural Scale 1:9,400,000

50 0 50 100 Miles

REFERENCE

Lands of Charles IV of Bohemia . . . .
Hungary under Lewis the Great . . . .
Poland ,, ,, ,, ,, ...
Lithuania under Olgierd . . . .
Approximate Western boundary of
the Golden Horde 1320 . . . .

Possessions of the Teutonic Order
Komtureien ,, ,, ,, ,,
Bishoprics ,, ,, ,, ,,
Boundaries of Provinces
Genoese Colonies underlined
Archbishoprics . . . .

Map 73

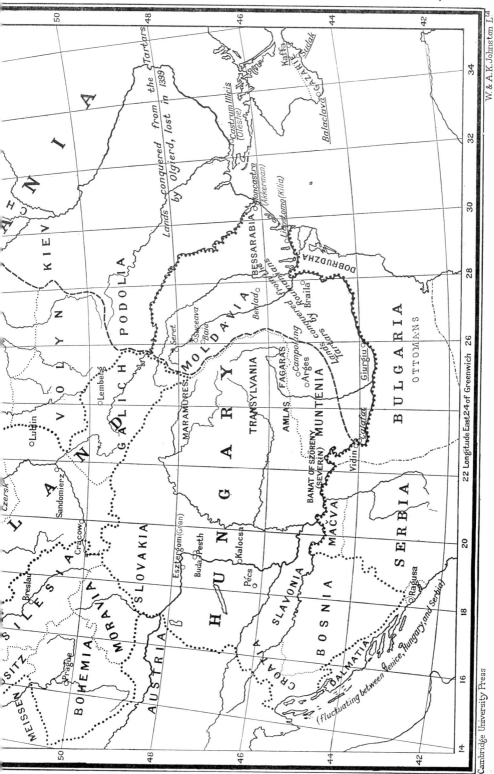

Cambridge University Press

W. & A. K. Johnston Ltd

Map 74

SCOTLAND

C. 1300

Natural Scale 1:3,000,000

10 5 0   10   20   30   40   50 Miles

— REFERENCE —

Sheriffdoms...........................ELGIN
Names of older divisions....CUMBRIA
Some routes..............................
(Edward I. itinerary in 1295)........
Land over 1500 Feet.....................

ORKNEY
(TO NORWAY)

CAITHNESS

Sutherland

ROSS

Hebrides

Rosemarkie
Applecross
Inverness
INVER NAIRN
Elgin
Forres
ELGIN
Mortlach
Forglen
Turriff
Aberdour
Buchan
Deer

MORAY

Ross

Eigg

Tiree

Iona

Atholl

ABERDEEN
Aberdeen
KINCARDINE
Mearns
Brechin
Montrose

DALRIADA

PERTH
Dunkeld
FORFAR
Angus
Dundee
Strathearn
Perth
Scone
Fortevíot
Abernethy
St Andrews
FIFE

Menteith
Dunblane
Stirling
Bannockburn
STIRLING
Lennox
Falkirk
Dunfermline
Dunbar

Dumbarton
Renfrew
Glasgow
Ellerslie
Edinburgh
Berwick
LOTHIAN
BERWICK

Islay

Kintyre

LANARK
PEEBLES
Carham
Kelso
Melrose
SELKIRK
Jedburgh
ROXBURGH

Ayr
AYR
Carrick
Girvan
DUMFRIES
Brunanburgh
by Solway Kirk Sands
Hexham
by Soleh King's Sands

GALLOWAY
WIGTON
Carlisle
CUMBRIA
Candida Casa
(Whithern)

Cambridge University Press   W. & A.K. Johnston Ltd

Map 75

IRELAND
after the
NORMAN INVASION
Natural Scale 1:2,890,000

10 5 0   10   20   30   40   50 Miles

— REFERENCE —

Seven sub-Kingdoms at Norman landing........... TARA
Towns held by Danes ,, ,, ,, ...Dublin
Early Norman families....................COURCY
Metropolitan sees. ●Armagh. Land over 500 Feet........

Map 76

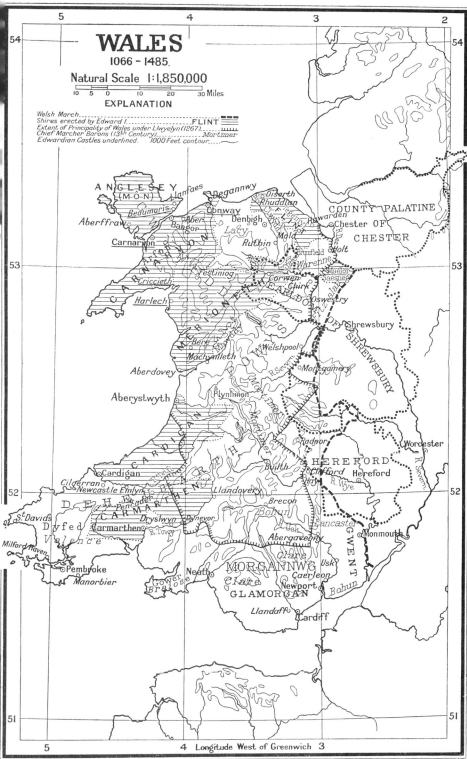

WALES

1066 - 1485

Natural Scale 1:1,850,000

10 5 0   10   20   30 Miles

EXPLANATION

Welsh March..........
Shires erected by Edward I...................FLINT
Extent of Principality of Wales under Llwyelyn (1267)......
Chief Marcher Barons (13ᵗʰ Century)..............Mortimer
Edwardian Castles underlined.   1000 Feet contour.....

ANGLESEY (MÔN)

Llanfaes
Beaumaris
Aberffraw
Aber
Bangor
Carnarvon

Deganwwy
Conway
Denbigh
Laty
Ruthin

Diserth
Rhuddlan
Howarden
Mold

COUNTY PALATINE
Chester OF
CHESTER

Criccieth
Harlech
Festiniog
Corwen
Chirk
Oswestry

Maelor
Saesneg

Bere
Machynlleth
Welshpool
Montgomery
Shrewsbury
OF SHREWSBURY
R.Severn

Aberdovey

Aberystwyth
Plynlimon

Radnor
Worcester

Cardigan
Cilgerran
Newcastle Emlyn
Pentcader
Llandovery
Builth
Clifford
Hay
R.Wye
Hereford
HEREFORD
R.Severn

D E H
CARMARTHEN
Dryslwyn
Dynevor
Brecon
Bohun
Lancaster

St.Davids
Dyfed
Valence
Carmarthen
R.Towy
Usk
Abergavenny
Monmouth

Milford Haven

Pembroke
Manorbier
Gower
Bre
Neath
MORGANNWG
Clare
Clare
Caerleon
Newport
Bohun

GLAMORGAN
Llandaff
Cardiff

51

5   4 Longitude West of Greenwich 3

Cambridge University Press

W & A.K. Johnston Lᵗᵈ

Map 77

Ponte Molle

R. Tiber

Monte
•Mario

Ponte del Popolo

Porta Salaria

Porta Pinciana

Porta Pia

NERONIAN
MEADOWS

La Gesta
(M. of Augustus)

(Vineyards and Waste)

Porta
Viridaria

Porta S. Pietro

Castello
S. Angelo

QUIRINAL

ESQUILINE

S. LORENZO

LEONINE CITY

Vatican
ST PETER'S

ORSINI

Torre della Scimmia

Monte Citorio

Maria in Via Lata

S. MARIA
MAGGIORE

Porta S. Lorenzo

Torre di Nona

MILLINI
SANGUINI
SINIBALDI
CRESCENZI

Pantheon

S. Andrea

Monte
Giordano

Piazza Navona

Camillano

Porta
Maggiore

ORSINI

MASSIMI

S. Maria
sopra Minerva

S. Apostoli

GAETANI
PANDULFI

S. Pietro in Vincoli

Regola

Arpacata
Campo dei Fiore

S. Marco

CONTI

Torre delle Milizie

Suburra

MARGANI

Torre dei Conti

S. Maria
in Aracoeli

STATI
Palace of the Senators

CAPOCCI

PIERLEONI

CAPI
TOL

FORUM

B. of
Constantine

ANIBALDI

Porta Pancrazio

S. Maria

S. Giorgio
in Velabro

Torre degli
Anguillara

Ponte Cesio

S. Maria
Cosmedin

STEFANESCHI
NORMANNI

TRASTEVERE

PALATINE

Vineyards &
Ruins

COLOSSEUM

S. Clemente

SS. Quattro Coronati

S. CROCE

LATERAN

Porta Laterana

SS. Giovanni e Paolo

CELIAN

Caput Africae?

R. Tiber

Marmora

S. Sabina

SAVELLI

CIPANI

Clivus Scauri

Settizonium

S. Gregorio

S. Stefano

AVENTINE

(Marshy)

Porta Metrobia

Porta Latina

Monte
Testaccio

Porta S. Paolo

Porta S. Sebastiano

Tor Marancia•

S. PAOLO

S. SEBASTIANO

Capo di Bove•

ROME
CIRCA 1310
Natural Scale 1:48,400

0   ¼   ½   ¾   1 Mile

REFERENCE
Aurelian and Leonine Wall........
Noble families.....................CAPOCCI
Basilicas............................⊞ S. MARIA
Medieval Towers..........• Torre dei Conti